Eleventh Edition

INTERNATIONAL BUSINESS

Environments and Operations

John D. Daniels
University of Miami

Lee H. Radebaugh
Brigham Young University

Daniel P. Sullivan
University of Delaware

PEARSON
Prentice Hall

Pearson Prentice Hall
Upper Saddle River, NJ 07458

Library of Congress Cataloging-in-Publication Data

Daniels, John D.
International business : environments and operations / John D. Daniels, Lee H. Radebaugh,
Daniel P. Sullivan.— 11th ed.
   p. cm.
Includes bibliographical references and index.
ISBN 0-13-186942-6 (casebound)
   1. International business enterprises.   2. International economic relations.   3. Investments,
Foreign.   I. Radebaugh, Lee H.   II. Sullivan, Daniel P.   III. Title.
HD2755.5.D35 2006
658.1'8—dc22   2005028569

Senior Acquisitions Editor: Michael Ablassmeir
VP/Editorial Director: Jeff Shelstad
Product Development Manager: Ashley Santora
Project Manager: Melissa Pellerano
Editorial Assistant: Stephanie Kamens
Media Product Development Manager: Nancy Welcher
Marketing Manager: Anke Braun
Associate Director Production Editorial: Judy Leale
Managing Editor: Renata Butera
Senior Production Editor: Theresa Festa
Permissions Supervisor: Charles Morris
Production Manager: Arnold Vila
Design Manager: Christy Mahon
Designer: Kevin Kall
Interior Design: Kevin Kall
Cover Design: Kevin Kall
Illustrator (Interior): Thistle Hill Publishing Services, LLC
Director, Image Resource Center: Melinda Reo
Manager, Rights and Permissions: Zina Arabia
Manager: Visual Research: Beth Brenzel
Manager, Cover Visual Research & Permissions: Karen Sanatar
Image Permission Coordinator: Craig A. Jones
Photo Researcher: Rachel Lucas
Composition/Full-Service Project Management: Integra/Thistle Hill Publishing Services, LLC
Printer/Binder: Courier—Kendallville/Phoenix
Typeface: 10/12 Palatino

Credits and acknowledgments borrowed from other sources and reproduced, with permission, in this textbook appear on appropriate page within text.

Pearson Education LTD.
Pearson Education Singapore, Pte. Ltd
Pearson Education, Canada, Ltd
Pearson Education—Japan

Pearson Education Australia PTY, Limited
Pearson Education North Asia Ltd
Pearson Educación de Mexico, S.A. de C.V.
Pearson Education Malaysia, Pte. Ltd

10 9 8 7 6 5 4 3 2 1
ISBN 0-13-186942-6

BRIEF CONTENTS

CONTENTS

12   Country Evaluation and Selection   410

CHAPTER OPENING AND CLOSING CASES

MAPS

Designed to help improve students' geographic literacy, the book's many maps add interest and illustrate facts and topics discussed in the text. Many case maps zero in on the case company's home country to give students a close-up look at foreign locales.

A complete atlas with index is available following Chapter 1.

PREFACE

This textbook is one of the best-selling international business textbooks in the United States and the world. Widely used in both undergraduate and MBA level courses, this text has been translated into Spanish, Thai, and Russian, and adopted by professors in many countries. This textbook set the global standard for studying the environments and operations of international business. The elements of success that have driven this performance anchor our efforts to make this edition the best version yet. We believe these efforts result in a textbook that provides you and your students the best possible understanding of what is happening and will likely happen in the world of business.

AUTHORITATIVE, RELEVANT, CURRENT

Students, faculty, and managers praise this book for its compelling balance between rigorous, authoritative theory and meaningful practice. Indeed, this book not only describes the ideas of international business but also uses powerful explanatory examples, scenarios, and cases to make sense of what managers do and should do. Multiple insights and real world examples are pulled from our research, talking to managers, listening to students and professors, and traveling the world. We believe no other textbook comes close to successfully blending a comprehensive review of international business theory with exhaustive attention to what happens in the many parts of the global market. We're confident that this new edition, by making international business ideas and practices more meaningful than ever before, will give your students a comprehensive, current view of international business in the twenty-first century.

RELEVANT MATERIALS THAT ENGAGE STUDENTS

Author Written Cases

An enduring strength of this text is its in-depth case profiles of cutting-edge issues in international business. This edition introduces 18 new cases and updates and revises the remaining 22. (Please see pages xxi–xxiv for a complete list of cases.) All cases are unique, written by the authors, and set the standard for integration of theory and practice in an international business textbook on the following 3 levels:

1. *Level of Analysis*: Cases engage in an extensive range of topics from environmental, institutional, country, industry, company, or individual perspectives. No one perspective dominates; all are represented and,

hence, create a meaningful representation of the world of international business.

2. *Scope of Geographic Coverage*: Cases cover topics in settings that span the globe; no region is left unaddressed, no major market is ignored.

3. *Scope of Company Coverage*: Cases look at a range of issues from a range of company perspectives, notably, large MNEs to small exporters, from old-line manufacturers to emergent cyber businesses, from companies that make products to those that deliver a service.

Opening Business Case   Each chapter starts with a provocative case written to set the stage for the major issues covered in the chapter. Designed to grab the student's attention, these cases look at fascinating issues in a way that makes students want to understand the ideas and concepts of international business. These cases, by variously taking the point of view of individuals, companies, and institutions, give a great sense of the richness of the ensuing chapter.

Closing Business Case   Each chapter closes with a rich, elaborate case that integrates the ideas and tools presented in the chapter. The closing cases are geared toward putting the student into a situation that asks, given these circumstances, what should be done? Called upon to analyze issues and decisions for which the chapter prepares them, students can then grapple with the reality of a broad range of the opportunities and challenges of international business.

New Cases in This Edition

- Globalization of Professional Sports
- Carnival Cruise Lines
- The Java Lounge—Adjusting to Saudi Arabian Culture
- Charles Martin in Uganda
- China's Business Environment
- Meet the BRICs
- Anglo American in South Africa
- Costa Rican Trade, Foreign Investment, and Economic Transformation
- Textile and Clothing Trade
- Toyota in Europe
- Western Union
- El Salvador and the U.S. Dollar
- Zara—Value Creation in the Global Apparel Industry
- The Globalization of eBay
- Alibaba.com
- NeoPets
- Parmalat—Europe's Enron
- A Career in International Business

New Chapters

This text has two completely new chapters that will give your students a comprehensive, current view of globalization and emphasize the importance of critical thinking about strategic issues.

Chapter 5: Globalization and Society   This chapter starts off by discussing the impact of MNEs on host countries and how we measure that impact from the standpoint of both the home and host countries. Then we establish a framework for making ethical decisions, focusing especially on cultural and legal differences that influence ethical behavior. We discuss several issues that managers must face as they operate abroad, such as bribery, global warming, and other environmental issues, the sale of pharmaceutical products in countries where people cannot afford to pay for them at high prices and where they suffer from serious diseases such as HIV/AIDS, and labor issues, especially the use of child labor. Finally, we discuss corporate responses to globalization in the form of codes of conduct and disclosures to the public.

Chapter 11: Strategy in International Business   Being able to think critically about strategic issues is important for managers and their companies. Chapter 11 provides a state-of-the-art explanation about strategy in international business that covers important fundamentals as well as emerging drivers of performance. New exciting cases about Zara and eBay make this chapter a great transition between the environments and operations of international business.

Looking to the Future

Each chapter offers a future scenario or scenarios that are important to managers, companies, or the world. The topic of each *Looking to the Future* feature alludes to ideas discussed in the chapter but in a way that prompts student to engage their imagination about the world they live in.

LOOKING TO THE FUTURE: Is Globalization Inevitable?

At this juncture, there is much doubt about the future growth of international business. There are three viewpoints: (1) that globalization is inevitable, (2) that international business will grow primarily along regional rather than global lines, and (3) that forces against globalization will greatly slow its growth.

The view of the inevitability of globalization is based largely on the premise that technical advances in transportation and communications are pervasive, so much so that consumers will demand the best products for the best prices regardless of their origins. Further, because MNEs have so many international production and distribution networks in place, they will pressure their home governments to place fewer rather than more restrictions on the international movement of goods and the means to produce them. If we accept this view, then we still must

companies may first promote international business in nearby countries, but expand from there once they've reached their regional goals.

The third view is that the growth of globalization will slow or may already be in the midst of collapse. Although most governments are embracing openness to international trade and investment, we have discussed some of the antiglobalization sentiments that are strong and vocal. Many people are demonstrating at meetings of international organizations, such as the World Bank and the World Trade Organization (WTO).[38] Further, affected groups in many countries are pressuring their governments to promote nationalism by raising barriers to trade and forgoing participation in international organizations and treaties. Looking historically, we see that pressure groups have often been successful (at least temporarily) in obstructing either technology or international trade that threatened their own well-being. For example, British factory workers rioted in the early nineteenth century over the mechanization of factory jobs, and the United States imposed high barriers to trade in the 1930s in efforts

NEW Point—Counterpoint

To reinforce our strong applications orientation, we have added a new, boxed theme in every chapter that brings to life a major debate in contemporary international business. We use a point-counterpoint style to highlight the diversity of perspective that managers use to make sense of vital issues. The give and take between two sides reinforces this textbook's effort to link theory and practice in ways that will undoubtedly energize class discussion.

POINT–COUNTERPOINT: IS OFFSHORING GOOD OR BAD?

POINT

Offshoring is good because it reduces costs. I'll mention just two examples. IBM must pay programmers $56 an hour including salary and benefits in the United States, but the cost in China for people with three to five years' experience is only about $12.50. IBM will save about $168 million a year by shifting this work abroad.[17] Take Claimpower, a small U.S. medical insurance billing company. By transferring work to India, it reduced costs and reduced prices to doctors. The company quadrupled its business in two years.[18]

Almost everyone accepts the employment shifts caused by labor-saving technologies, and there is nothing fundamentally different about offshoring and introducing labor-saving technologies. In both situations, companies save costs. In both situations, companies may temporarily need fewer workers in their home countries and can use the cost savings to

COUNTERPOINT

Offshoring may be good for a few people, but not for most. I keep hearing about the cost savings, but I don't find anything cheaper today. For instance, companies like Ralph Lauren and Tommy Hilfiger are making almost all their clothes where labor rates are very cheap, but they still charge upscale prices. You mentioned that Claimpower reduced its prices to doctors, but you haven't given me any examples of doctors reducing any of their fees as a result. Further, Claimpower grew fast as a result of lowering its prices, but this growth must be at the expense of other companies rather than growth in the economy; there are simply just so many insurance claims to file.

When jobs are replaced by offshoring, we're exchanging good jobs for bad ones. Displaced workers struggled for decades to work reasonable hours and gain health benefits and a retirement plan. Most important, their incomes allowed them to send their children to

NEW Geography and International Business

In appropriate chapters, we have added "Does Geography Matter?" sections. Some of the geographic variables we include to help explain the chapters' content are country location, location of population and population segments within countries, size of countries, natural resources and barriers, climate, and country size.

DOES GEOGRAPHY MATTER?

Don't Fool with Mother Nature

A major tsunami hit southern Asia in late 2004. Soon after, there was an outbreak of the deadly Marburg virus in Angola. These events publicized global vulnerability to natural disasters and communicable diseases. Each year about 130 million people are exposed to earthquake risk, 119 million to tropical cyclone hazards, 196 million to catastrophic flooding, and 220 million to drought. On average, there are 184 deaths per day from natural disasters.[41] These natural disasters are not spread uniformly around the world. For instance, Iran, Afghanistan, and India are heavily exposed to earthquakes, and some African states have the highest vulnerability to drought. At this writing, the United Nations Development Programme is developing a disaster risk index (DRI) that will show the relative level of physical exposure to natural disaster hazards. We already know that although only 11 percent of

What does this have to do with the location of operations by international companies? In addition to the possibility of damaging a company's property and injuring its personnel, these events upset markets, infrastructure, and production. Although they are most devastating in the world's poorer areas, events in high-income areas can play havoc with global supplies as well. For instance, the Kobe earthquake in Japan upset the world computer industry's production because it created semiconductor shortages.[43] Thus, natural events create additional operating risks and additional costs to insure against them. In turn, insurance companies are challenged to estimate the likelihood and cost of these events, such as through the development of models based on the statistical theory of extreme values.

The World Health Organization is developing a global atlas of infectious diseases.[44] Many of these diseases are associated with poverty. They are also associated with natural disasters. For instance, cholera and malaria outbreaks are most apt to occur after flooding. Thus, they tend to follow geographic patterns. For example, malaria kills about

New Topics and Chapter Changes

The text has been thoroughly updated to reflect the latest knowledge of international business. Most notably, this edition includes the following changes:

- Country differences in degree of globalization (Chapter 1)
- Debate on off-shoring (Chapter 1)
- Nobel economists' views on future challenges (Chapter 1)
- Integration of work from the World Values Survey (Chapter 2)
- Effect of religion on economic growth (Chapter 2)
- Growth of multilingual and transnational individuals (Chapter 2)
- Distribution of political freedom (Chapter 3)
- Evolution and diffusion of legal systems (Chapter 3)
- Operational legal concerns (Chapter 3)
- Expanded coverage of international economic analysis (Chapter 4)
- Income distribution and poverty (Chapter 4)
- Trade balances and deficits (Chapter 4)
- Major ethical issues like global warming and child labor (Chapter 5)
- Relationship between interventionist and free trade theories (Chapter 6)
- Relationship between trade and factor mobility (Chapter 6)
- Pros and cons of strategic trade policy (Chapter 6)
- Recent trade wars and retaliation (Chapter 7)
- Pros and cons of trade sanctions (Chapter 7)
- Strategy of Japanese car makers in Europe (Chapter 8)
- Combining foreign exchange markets, foreign debt markets, and foreign equity markets into single chapter (Chapter 9)
- Factors influencing the value of a currency (Chapter 10)
- Play of domestic and international factors on exchange rate values (Chapter 10)
- National disasters and health problems as locational risk problems (Chapter 12)
- Qualitative factors that impact location decisions (Chapter 12)
- Effect of location on innovation (Chapter 12)
- Resources offered by the government to international traders (Chapter 13)
- Importing and the Internet (Chapter 13)
- Debate on foreign control of key industries (Chapter 14)
- Greenfield versus acquisitions decisions (Chapter 14)
- Workplace trends and organizational forms (Chapter 15)
- Network and virtual forms of organization (Chapter 15)
- Forms of coordination (Chapter 15)
- Strategy and organizational culture (Chapter 15)
- Marketing regulation to third world countries (Chapter 16)
- Targeting market segments rather than mass markets (Chapter 16)
- Different product placements in movies and television internationally (Chapter 16)
- Pros and cons of outsourcing innovation (Chapter 17)
- Adoption of International Financial Accounting Reporting Standards by the EU (Chapter 18)
- Cooperation between the IASB and the U.S. FASB (Chapter 18)
- Accounting performance evaluation practices by MNEs (Chapter 18)

- The impact of transfer pricing on performance evaluation (Chapter 18)
- Focus on key finance decisions in MNEs (Chapter 19)
- Strategy and global staffing policies (Chapter 20)
- Value of a foreign language competency (Chapter 20)
- Success and struggles of labor movements (Chapter 20)

ENGAGING IN-TEXT LEARNING AIDS

We believe a good textbook must teach as well as present ideas. To that end, we use several in-text aids to make this book an effective learning tool. Most notably, each chapter uses all of the following:

Chapter Objectives and Summary

Each chapter begins with learning objectives and ends with a summary that ties directly to the chapter material. This linkage helps students prepare for the major issues within each chapter, appreciate their general relationships, and reinforce the important lessons of the chapter material.

Key Terms and Points

Every chapter highlights several key terms; first, each term is put in bold print when it first appears. Key points are also highlighted in the adjoining margin. These terms are then assembled in a comprehensive glossary at the end of the book.

Case Questions

The closing case of each chapter stipulates several questions to guide how you apply what you have learned in the chapter to the reality of international business. We have found in our classes that the questions at the end of the case go a long way to putting the case into perspective for students.

FACULTY AND STUDENT RESOURCES

The eleventh edition's resource package is designed to provide faculty with the tools that, by integrating the media, technology, and test questions for your particular classroom needs, greatly improve the quality of the class. These presentation and classroom resources are available on the Instructor's Resource Center on CD-ROM and online at www.prenhall.com/daniels. Specific resources include:

Instructor's Manual

This Instructor's Manual is a complete instructor's toolkit. Designed to guide the educator through the text, each chapter in the manual includes chapter objectives, a chapter overview, a detailed chapter outline that includes teaching tips and additional tips regarding the boxed features, answers to case questions and discussion questions in the text, and one to two new additional exercises. Available in print and electronically on the Instructor's Resource Center.

Test Item File

This state-of-the-art test bank contains approximately 90 multiple-choice, true/false, and essay questions per chapter. Because the test item file is a critical component of the resource package, every question was written and reviewed by the textbook authors. Many of the questions have been battle-tested in their classrooms and are based on a list of study questions generated by the authors, to ensure that the test item file covers all of the important topics in the text. Available in print and electronically on the Instructor's Resource Center.

Test Gen EQ Test Generating Software

This computerized package allows instructors to custom design, save, and generate classroom tests. The test program permits instructors to edit, add, or delete questions from the test banks; edit existing graphics and create new graphics; analyze test results; and organize a database of tests and student results. This new software allows for greater flexibility and ease of use. It provides many options for organizing and displaying tests, along with a search and sort feature. Available electronically on the Instructor's Resource Center.

PowerPoints

A comprehensive package, these PowerPoint transparencies are designed to aid the educator and supplement in-class lectures. They are available on the Instructor's Resource Center.

Companion Website

The format of our website has been updated, and it includes the same great features in a more user-friendly format. This website features an online study guide with true/false, multiple choice, and essay questions. Students can prepare for class and exams using the chapter quizzes and student PowerPoints, which are available for review or can be conveniently printed three-to-a-page for in-class note taking.

NEW Video Package

The authors, in collaboration with Prentice Hall, are committed to providing you with the most up-to-date, exciting, new video library. Not only are these videos tied to the most pertinent topics in international business, they also include footage from ABC News as well as film customized to ideas discussed in the text. The length of each video is designed to enhance, not overwhelm classroom discussion. The following segments comprise a *partial* list of the videos in the package:

1. *NIGHTLINE: Inside the Kingdom: Life in Saudi Arabia*—Saudi Arabia is a land of contradictions where Western ideas and Islamic law rub shoulders and often clash. This story gains entrance to this powerful and mysterious kingdom to examine the politics, religion, and culture of one of America's key Muslim allies. The country's rampant unemployment, declining oil revenues, and the ongoing drama in the Middle East are all on the agenda.

2. *WORLD NEWS TONIGHT: Counterfeiting in China*—The global counterfeit industry is a multibillion-dollar industry including everything from software to soap. And China, a member of the World Trade Organization, is one of the worst offenders. Fake goods produced in China cost foreign firms about $20 billion a year in lost profits. Although the government in Beijing has taken some steps to crack down, the United States says the problem is as bad as ever.

3. *WORLD NEWS TONIGHT: China Inc., IBM Sells PC Division*—China is quickly transforming itself from being simply a contract supplier of inexpensive manufactured products to being a producer of high-technology products by its own companies. This segment highlights the sale of IBM's computer division to a Chinese company and also features moves abroad by China's Haier appliance maker. There are also comments by Paul Saffo, Institute for the Future, and by Michael Dell, chairman of Dell Computer.

4. *WORLD NEWS TONIGHT: Exporting Jobs*—The United States has long wrestled with the issue of jobs leaving for other countries. Lower wages, fewer benefits, worse working conditions . . . most of which make moving jobs overseas attractive to companies. But a whole new job sector has been moving to India. If you call a major company like Dell or Delta or American Express, or if you need your X-rays read overnight, or if you need your taxes done . . . all of that may connect you to India.

5. *WORLD NEWS TONIGHT: The Money Trail: Tax Evasion*—With footage largely from the Cayman Islands, this video shows the IRS/Justice Department of the United States in its investigation into tax evasion by Americans using offshore bank accounts. It also lists on screen the countries offering secret accounts. It interviews the IRS deputy commissioner, Dale Hart, Senator Charles Grassley, and criminal tax attorney, Elliott Kajan.

ACKNOWLEDGMENTS

Every author relies on the comments, critiques, and insights of reviewers. It is a tough task that few choose to support. Therefore, we want to thank the following people for their insightful and helpful comments for the eleventh edition of *International Business: Environments and Operations.*

YUSAF AKBAR, Southern New Hampshire University
TED AZARMI, CSU–Long Beach
ROBERT M. BALLINGER, Learning Empire State College, Emeritus, Siena College
DON BEEMAN, University of Toledo
JEAN BODDEWYN, City University of New York

MARY YOKO BRANNEN, San Jose State University
ANNETTE CITZLER, Texas Lutheran University
FRANK DUBOIS, American University
WILLIAM FRECH, Ramapo College of New Jersey
P. ROBERTO GARCIA, Indiana University, Kelley School of Business
JOHN GRANT, Colorado State University
ANDREW GROSS, Cleveland State University
GEORGE HALEY, University of New Haven
CHRISTINA HEISS, UMKC
CAROL A. HOWARD, Oklahoma City University
BANG JEON, Drexel University
SEUNG H. KIM, Saint Louis University
JEFFREY KRUG, Appalachian State University
ALLEN H. KUPETZ, Rollins College
BIJOU YANG LESTER, Drexel University
BEN LEVER, College of Charleston
DAVID LYDICK, Paul D. Camp Community College
PAUL MARER, Central European University
ANDREW MARKLEY, Grove City College
RAMAN MURALIDHARAN, Indiana University–South Bend
BILL NEWBURRY, Rutgers University
LIZZIE NGWENYA-SCOBURGH, University of Northwestern Ohio
FRANK PIANKI, Anderson University
BILL RAPP, NJ Institute of Technology
KATHLEEN REHBEIN, Marquette University
JOHN RUHNKA, University of Colorado at Denver
MASSOOD V. SAMII, Southern New Hampshire University
KRISTIE SEAWRIGHT, Brigham Young University
JOHN STANBURY, GMU
WILLIAM STOEVER, Seton Hall University
LEN TREVINO, Washington State University
ROBERT WOOD, San Jose State University

In addition, we have been fortunate since the first edition to have colleagues who have been willing to make the effort to critique draft materials, react to coverage already in print, advise on suggested changes, and send items to be corrected. Because this is the culmination of several previous editions, we would like to acknowledge everyone's efforts. However, many more individuals than we can possibly list have helped us. To those who must remain anonymous, we offer our sincere thanks. In any event, special thanks go to the following faculty members who made detailed comments on previous editions.

- ERVIN BLACK, Brigham Young University
- ROBERT BUZZELL, George Mason University
- STANLEY E. FAWCETT, Brigham Young University
- STANLEY FLAX, St. Thomas University
- ELDRIDGE T. FREEMAN, Jr., Chicago State University
- RALPH GAEDEKE, California State University at Sacramento
- PHILLLIP D. GRUB, George Washington University
- URNESH C. GULATI, East Carolina College
- MICHAEL J. HAND, United States Department of Commerce

- RALPH F. JAGODKA, Mt. San Antonio Community College
- R. BOYD JOHNSON, Indiana Wesleyan University
- TUNGA KIYAK, Michigan State University
- SUMIT K. KUNDU, Florida International University
- CHARLES MAHONE, Howard University
- BEHNAM NAKHAI, Millersville University
- MOONSONG DAVID OH, California State University at Los Angeles
- NAMGYOO K. PARK, Korean Advanced Institute of Science and Technology
- ANN PERRY, American University
- DOUGLAS K. PETERSON, Indiana State University
- LUCIE PFAFF, College of Mt. St. Vincent
- ASEEM PRAKASH, University of Washington
- FERNANDO ROBLES, George Washington University
- RON SCHILL, Brigham Young University
- GEORGIA WHITE, Brigham Young University
- CRAIG WOODRUFF, American Graduate School of International Management

We would also like to acknowledge people whom we interviewed in writing cases. These are Omar Aljindi (Java Lounge—Adjusting to Saudi Arabian Culture) and Brenda Yester (Carnival Cruise Lines). Thank you to Joseph Ganitsky of Loyola University of New Orleans, for his case suggestions. Additionally, others who helped with administrative matters are Melanie Hunter, Blake Copeland, Hongbin Hu, Catherine Frost, Melissa Okimoto, Julie Hales, and Exequiel Hernandez.

It takes a dedicated group of individuals to take a textbook from first draft to final manuscript. We would like to thank our partners at Pearson Prentice Hall for their tireless efforts in bringing the eleventh edition of this book to fruition. Our thanks go to Editor, Michael Ablassmeir; Project Manager, Melissa Pellerano; Associate Director for Production, Judy Leale; Managing Editor for Production, Renata Butera; Director of Development, Stephen Deitmer; Development Editor, Elisa Adams; Senior Production Editor, Theresa Festa; Editorial Director, Jeff Shelstad; Marketing Manager, Anke Braun; Senior Marketing Manager International, Patrick Leow Sai Hsiong; Editorial Assistant, Stephanie Kames; and Designer, Kevin Kall.

ABOUT THE AUTHORS

From left to right: Daniel Sullivan, Lee Radebaugh, John Daniels.

Three respected and renowned scholars show your students how dynamic, how real, how interesting, and how important the study of international business can be.

John D. Daniels, the Samuel N. Friedland Chair of Executive Management at the University of Miami, received his Ph.D. at the University of Michigan. His dissertation won first place in the award competition of the Academy of International Business. Since then, he has been an active researcher. His articles have appeared in such leading journals as *Academy of Management Journal, California Management Review, Columbia Journal of World Business, Journal of Business Research, Journal of International Business Studies, Strategic Management Journal,* and *Weltwirtschaftliches Archiv.* On its thirtieth anniversary, *Management International Review* referred to him as "one of the most prolific American IB scholars." He has also served as president of the Academy of International Business and dean of its Fellows. He also served as chairperson of the international division of the Academy of Management. He has worked and lived a year or longer in seven different countries, worked shorter stints in approximately thirty other countries on six continents, and has traveled in many more. His foreign work has been a combination of private sector, governmental, teaching, and research assignments. He was formerly director of the Center for International Business Education and Research (CIBER) at Indiana University and holder of the E. Claiborne Robins Distinguished Chair at the University of Richmond.

Lee H. Radebaugh is the KPMG Professor and Associate Director of the MBA Program at Brigham Young University. He received his MBA and doctorate from Indiana University. He taught at Pennsylvania State University from 1972 to 1980. He also has been a visiting professor at Escuela de Administracion de Negocios para Graduados (ESAN), a graduate business school in Lima, Peru. In 1985, Professor Radebaugh was the James Cusator Wards visiting professor at Glasgow University, Scotland. His other books include *International Accounting and Multinational Enterprises* (John Wiley and Sons, 4th Edition) with S.J. Gray; *Introduction to Business: International Dimensions* (South-Western Publishing Company) with John D. Daniels; and seven books on Canada-U.S. trade and investment relations, with Earl Fry as co-editor. He has also published several other monographs and articles on international business and international accounting in journals such as the *Journal of Accounting Research*, the *Journal of International Financial Management and Accounting*, the *Journal of International Business Studies*, and the *International Journal of Accounting*. He is currently serving as editor of the *Journal of International Accounting Research*. His primary teaching interests are international business and international accounting. He is an active member of the American Accounting Association, the European Accounting Association, and the Academy of International Business, having served on several committees as the president of the International Section of the AAA and as the secretary treasurer of the AIB. He is a member of the Fellows of the Academy of International Business. He is also active with the local business community as past president of the World Trade Association of Utah and member of the District Export Council. In 1998, he was named International Person of the Year in the state of Utah and Outstanding International Educator of the International Section of the American Accounting Association.

Daniel P. Sullivan, an Associate Professor of Management at the Alfred Lerner College of Business of the University of Delaware, received his Ph.D. from the University of South Carolina. He researches a range of topics, including Globalization and Business, International Management, Global Strategy, Competitive Analysis, and Corporate Governance. His work on these topics has been published in leading scholarly journals, including the *Journal of International Business Studies, Management International Review, Law and Society Review,* and *Academy of Management Journal.* In addition, he has served on the editorial boards of *Journal of International Business Studies* and *Management International Review.* He has been honored for both his research and teaching, receiving grants and winning awards for both activities while at the University of Delaware and, his former affiliation, the A.B. Freeman School of Business of Tulane University. He has been awarded numerous teaching honors at the undergraduate, MBA, and EMBA levels—most notably, he was voted Outstanding Teacher by the students of seven consecutive Executive MBA classes at the University of Delaware and Tulane University. He has taught, designed, and administered a range of graduate, undergraduate, and non-degree courses on topics spanning Globalization and Business, International Business Operations, International Management, Strategic Perspectives, Executive Leadership, and Corporate Strategy. In the United States, he has delivered lectures and courses at several university sites and company facilities. In addition, he has led courses in several foreign countries, including China, Bulgaria, the Czech Republic, France, Switzerland, and the United Kingdom. Finally, he has worked with many managers and consulted with several multinational enterprises on issues of international business.

INTERNATIONAL BUSINESS

The world is a chain, one link in another.

—MALTESE PROVERB

chapter one

Globalization and International Business

OBJECTIVES

- To define globalization and international business and how they affect each other

- To understand why companies engage in international business and why international business growth has accelerated

- To comprehend criticisms of globalization

- To become familiar with different modes a company can use to accomplish its global objectives

- To grasp the role social science disciplines play in understanding why international business is different from domestic business

CASE: THE GLOBALIZATION OF PROFESSIONAL SPORTS[1]

Which professional sports do you follow? Baseball? Basketball? Boxing? (American) football? Figure skating? Golf? Hockey? NASCAR? Rugby? (Soccer) football? Tennis? Although you may be an avid fan of one or more of these sports, you may not realize how international these and other sports have become in terms of countries from which the players hail, where the teams earn revenue, how many people in different countries follow and watch the same players, teams, and games, and where sports may develop in the next decade. In fact, the political historian Walter LaFeber said "The most globalized business in the world, and the most lucrative, is the drug trade, but for legitimate businesses, sports is probably number 1."

Historically, professional players and their teams in most sports competed in their own countries. There were exceptions, such as the World Cup in soccer or the Grand Slams of tennis. However, few players joined foreign teams, and few teams ventured abroad to compete. Home-based fans were content to see and support local talent. But now you, like most other fans, want to see the best, and you use global standards to determine what the best is.

The development of satellite television enables you to watch live events from almost anywhere in the world. Team owners, league representatives, and sports associations have recognized the profit potential in this technology. By transmitting live sporting events abroad, they have exposed audiences to sports, teams, and players that were not very familiar to them before. This exposure helped build a bigger fan base, which, in turn, enabled sporting groups to earn more income, especially through advertising. You can now see the preeminent players and teams from all over the world simply by staying home or going to a sports bar to watch them on television. Since more fans will watch games featuring the best teams and players, professional teams now scour the world to find and develop the most talented players. For example, teams from both the National Basketball Association (NBA) and European professional basketball leagues go to remote rural areas of Nigeria to find tall youngsters, whom they sign to contracts to attend basketball camps and subsequently play professionally if they become good enough in the camps.

At the same time, players have declining allegiance to their home-town or home-country fans; rather they are willing to go wherever they can earn the most, presuming that their teams are willing to trade them or release them from their contracts and their governments permit them to work abroad. Take soccer, the world's most popular sport, whose organization, the Fédération Internationale de Football Association (FIFA), boasts more member countries than the United Nations. Although Brazil is the premier producer of soccer talent, the best Brazilian players now compete by playing for European soccer teams that can pay them more than Brazilian teams. In every sport, we find top players on the rosters of teams outside their home countries, such as the British soccer star David Beckham with Real Madrid (Spain) and Japanese baseball star Ichiro Suzuki with the Seattle Mariners (U.S.A.). Nevertheless, many fans still follow their national sport's heroes even when they're playing abroad. For instance, when Chinese basketball star Yao Ming played his first game for the Houston Rockets (U.S.A.), about 300 million people in China (more than the U.S. population) watched on television. Likewise, athletes don't completely forgo their home-country allegiances. They play for national teams when countries compete, such as in the Olympics and the World Cup for soccer.

If you're a fan of individual sports, you've probably noticed that your favorite players move from one tournament to another as they traverse the globe. Frequent, fast, and low-cost airline connections help make this possible. Take tennis. No single country has enough interested fans to keep players busy year-round in tournaments. At the same time, top-ten ranked players in recent years have come from every continent except Antarctica. Fans everywhere want to see the top players compete with each other. Thus, the Association of Tennis Professionals (ATP) sanctions 65 tournaments in 32 countries around the world. Although no tennis pro can possibly play in all these, tournament organizers in, say, Qatar or Chile must attract a good number of top players if they are to sell sufficient seats and sign a well-paid television coverage contract. Thus the tournaments compete with each other to attract players. They also compete with players' commitments to participate in the Davis Cup (a national team competition), the Olympics, and exhibition matches. To help ensure the success of sanctioned tournaments, the ATP requires tennis pros to participate in sufficient international events if they are to maintain their rankings. As a further attraction for these players, the tournaments offer much more lucrative prizes (more than $3 million in prize

countries. If you could watch multiple television channels simultaneously, you could see 9,173 hours of NBA games per year in Tunisia, even though a year has only 8,760 hours. Sports organizations are also using other means to build a fan base and source of future players abroad. For instance, the National Football League (NFL) has an auxiliary league in Europe and is sponsoring flag football programs in Chinese schools. As national and regional leagues have developed, there has been a resurgence of interest in watching national and regional competition in addition to watching the best teams and leagues from around the world. With the growth of broadband, the era of thousand-channel television may arrive soon, thus you may be able to watch sports worldwide that now appeal only to small niches, such as field hockey, squash, and Thai-boxing.

Given the growing global audience for professional sports, top players and teams have effectively become global brands. Athletes such as Tiger Woods in golf, Venus and Serena Williams in tennis, Michael Jordan in basketball, and David Beckham in soccer have been so well known and watched that companies pay millions of dollars to get them to endorse their products. Not only do companies such as Nike, Reebok, and Adidas pay them to endorse sportswear and equipment, nonsports companies pay them to endorse their products. For instance, you may have seen Tiger Woods in ads for Buick, Michael Jordan for McDonald's, the Williams sisters for Avon cosmetics, and David Beckham for Pepsi. In addition, well-known players earn money by contracting the sale of their photos and signing their names to memorabilia, such as posters, that become collectibles for the buyers.

Many teams, such as the New York Yankees in baseball and the New Zealand All Blacks in rugby, are also so well known and followed that fans from all over the world will pay for clothing or other items bearing their names and logos. Well-known sports teams sell rights to use their logos both domestically and internationally, and they have opened shops to sell souvenirs. For instance, the soccer team Manchester United (Man U), the world's most valuable sports franchise, has established its Red Café theme restaurants as far away as China and Singapore. The Glasgow (Scotland) soccer club owns shops in Ireland, has granted use of its logo on products such as sausages, and makes more money on merchandise sales than from TV rights and sponsorship combined. Similarly, companies sponsor and seek endorsements from well-known sports teams. For instance, the U.S. company Nike fought hard to become the top sportswear and sports equipment supplier to European soccer teams. The success influenced Nike's international sales growth, and it now earns more money abroad than in the United States. Other companies, such as Canon, Sharp, and Carlsberg, sponsor teams so that their logos are emblazoned on players' shirts. Still others, such as United Airlines in Chicago, pay to have arenas named after them.

Not only are teams looking for income opportunities outside their own countries, investors are looking to acquire ownership in teams abroad. One of the first investors to do this was Hiroshi Yamauchi, the CEO of Nintendo, who bought the Seattle Mariners baseball team. Malcolm Glazer, owner of the NFL's Tampa Bay Buccaneers, and two Irish horse-racing tycoons became large shareholders in Man U, and Glazer later gained a controlling interest.

Now that we've briefly outlined the growth of international professional sports, think back to when you first became a sports fan. Chances are, especially if you are male, that at one time you fantasized about being a professional sports star. Also, chances are that you've given up that fantasy. But don't despair. Because of the globalization of professional sports, you can now enjoy a greater variety and a higher level of sports competition than could any previous generation in history. Nevertheless, not everyone agrees that the unbridled globalization of sports is all for the good. For instance, Brazilian soccer fans lament the loss of their best players, and U.S. fans and public officials protested the sale of a Major League Baseball team (Seattle Mariners) to a foreigner.

WHY ARE GLOBALIZATION AND INTERNATIONAL BUSINESS IMPORTANT?

Globalization means different things to different people.[2] In this book we will use **globalization** to mean the deepening relationship and broadening interdependence among people from different parts of the world, and especially among different countries. Throughout

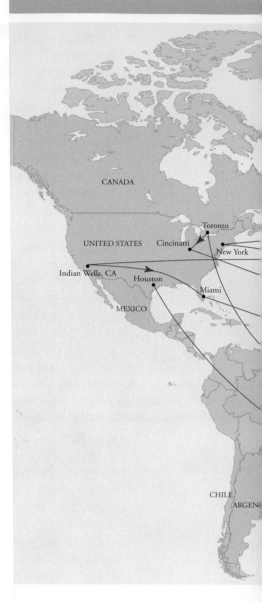

peted. (Map 1.1 shows the countries with competed during 2004.) The tournaments sales, sponsorship agreements with companies around the tennis courts. The more people sion, the more that sponsors and advertiscountries, they have more opportunity to tisers. For example, the Australian Open is Korean auto company (Kia), a Dutch beer cial institution (American Express).
ted by baseball. During most of its history, evision revenues for baseball in the United broadcast baseball games internationally.

recorded history, as people have established contacts over a wider geographic area, they have expanded the variety of resources, products, services, and markets available to them. They have altered the way they want and expect to live, and they have become more deeply affected (positively and negatively) by conditions outside their immediate domains.

The opening case illustrates how more extensive and far-flung global contact allows the best sports talent in the world to compete regardless of nationality, and fans to watch almost regardless of where they are. The changes that have led firms to consider ever more distant places as sources of supplies and markets affect almost every industry, which in turn affects us as consumers. Though we may not know it, we commonly buy products from all over the world. When they have a "Made in" label, we know their origin, but many products have so many different components or ingredients that we are challenged to say where they are made. For instance, if we order a main course of roasted veal tenderloin at Los Angeles's Bastide restaurant, its ingredients include spices from Malaysia, India, and China; wine from France; sherry vinegar from Spain; herbs from Turkey and Australia; shallots from Canada; coconut from Mexico; and veal, dates, lemon, and onions from elsewhere in the United States, all of which have traveled a combined 66,584 miles before the meal reaches our table.[3] This is a distance well over two and a half trips around the world at the equator. Although we may think of the Kia Sorento as a Korean car, is it really? The CD player is made by Matsushita, a Japanese firm. The optical pickup units, which read the CDs, are made in China and shipped to Thailand, where Matsushita adds the mechanical structure and electronic components before transporting them to Mexico for the audio systems assembly. The company then trucks the CD players to a port in the United States, from which it ships them to Kia in South Korea for fitting into the Sorento, which Kia then sends to markets abroad, such as the United States.[4]

In these and other cases, we get more variety, better quality, or lower prices because of globalization. For instance, we can buy spices we cannot grow ourselves, we can buy fresh fruits and vegetables year-round that are out of season where we live, and we can buy a car that has a less expensive CD player than if all the parts and labor had come from a single country. However, these connections between supplies and markets would not happen without international business. **International business** is all commercial transactions—private and governmental; sales, investments, and transportation—that take place between two or more countries. Private companies undertake such transactions for profit; governments undertake them for profit and for political reasons.

Why should you study international business? A simple answer is that international business comprises a large and growing portion of the world's total business. Today, global events and competition affect almost all companies—large and small—because most sell output to and secure supplies from foreign countries. Many companies also compete against products and services that come from abroad. Thus, most managers, regardless of industry, need to approach their operating strategies from an international standpoint. Recall the NBA teams in the opening case. They are looking globally for talent, and they are expanding their markets well beyond the confines of their home market. As a manager in almost any industry, you will need to consider where in the world you can obtain the quality of inputs you need at the best possible price and where you can best increase your sales.

At the same time, you will need to understand that the best way of doing business abroad may not be the same as the best way in your own country. First, when your company operates internationally, it will engage in modes of business, such as exporting and importing, that differ from those it uses domestically. To operate effectively, you must understand these different *modes*, which we'll discuss shortly. Second, the conditions within foreign countries affect the best way to conduct business there, such as how best to market your product. These conditions are physical, societal, and competitive. Thus, because these conditions vary among countries and over time, companies operating internationally have a more diverse and complex operating environment than those operating only at home. Figure 1.1 shows the relationships among these conditions and firms' operations.

Even if you never have direct international business responsibilities, understanding some international business complexities may be useful to you. Companies' international

International business is all commercial transactions between two or more countries.

- The goal of private business is to make profits.
- Government business may or may not be motivated by profit.

Studying international business is important because

- Most companies either are international or compete with international companies.
- Modes of operations may differ from those used domestically.
- The best way of conducting business may differ by country.
- An understanding helps you make better career decisions.
- An understanding helps you decide what governmental policies to support.

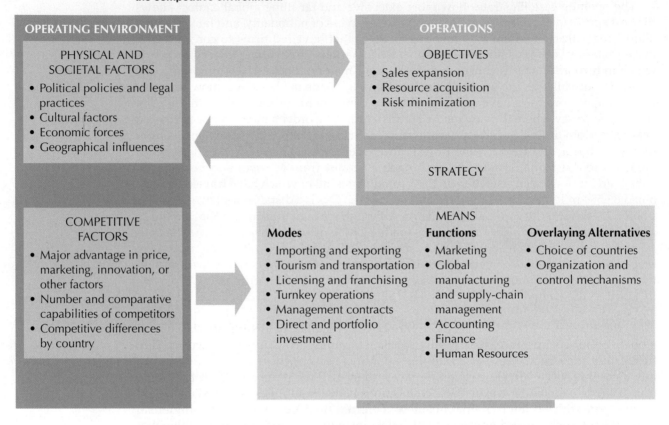

FIGURE 1.1   INTERNATIONAL BUSINESS: OPERATIONS AND INFLUENCES

The conduct of international operations depends on companies' objectives and the means with which they carry them out. The operations affect and are affected by the physical and societal factors and the competitive environment.

OPERATING ENVIRONMENT

PHYSICAL AND SOCIETAL FACTORS
- Political policies and legal practices
- Cultural factors
- Economic forces
- Geographical influences

COMPETITIVE FACTORS
- Major advantage in price, marketing, innovation, or other factors
- Number and comparative capabilities of competitors
- Competitive differences by country

OPERATIONS

OBJECTIVES
- Sales expansion
- Resource acquisition
- Risk minimization

STRATEGY

MEANS

Modes	Functions	Overlaying Alternatives
• Importing and exporting • Tourism and transportation • Licensing and franchising • Turnkey operations • Management contracts • Direct and portfolio investment	• Marketing • Global manufacturing and supply-chain management • Accounting • Finance • Human Resources	• Choice of countries • Organization and control mechanisms

operations and governmental regulation of international business affect company profits, employment security and wages, consumer prices, and national security. A better understanding of international business may help you to make more informed decisions, such as about where you want to work and what governmental policies you want to support.

THE FORCES BEHIND GLOBALIZATION

There is no firm agreement about how to measure globalization.[5] One reason is that it is a difficult concept to measure at all. Further, shifting boundaries obsolesce figures on what is international. For example, when the former Soviet Union broke apart, business transactions between Russia and Ukraine changed from domestic to international. Nevertheless, by various indicators globalization has been increasing since the middle of the twentieth century. Currently about 25 percent of world production is sold outside its country of origin, as opposed to about 7 percent in 1950. Restrictions on imports have been decreasing, and foreign ownership of assets as a percentage of world production has been increasing. In almost every year since World War II, world trade has grown more rapidly than world production.

At the same time, globalization is not as pervasive as it might appear on the surface. Only a few countries, mainly very small ones, either sell over half their production abroad or depend on foreign output for over half their consumption. Thus, most of the world's goods and services are still sold in the countries where they are produced. Further, the principal source of capital in almost all countries is domestic rather than international.[6] Finally, some countries are more globalized than others. The A.T. Kearney/Foreign Policy Globalization Index ranks 62 countries across four dimensions: economic (international trade and investment), technological (Internet connectivity), personal contact (international travel and tourism, international telephone traffic, and personal transfers of funds internationally), and political (participation in international organizations and government monetary transfers). In recent years, Ireland, Singapore, Switzerland, and the Netherlands have ranked as the most globalized countries, and Indonesia, Egypt, India, and Iran have been the least globalized. Further, a country may rank high on one dimension of globalization, but low on another. For instance, the 2004 report ranked the United States first on technology, but only 56 on economic.[7]

What has happened in recent decades to bring about the increased growth in globalization? The answer lies in the following seven factors:

1. Increase in and expansion of technology
2. Liberalization of cross-border trade and resource movements
3. Development of services that support international business
4. Growing consumer pressures
5. Increased global competition
6. Changing political situations
7. Expanded cross-national cooperation

Often these factors are interrelated. Each deserves a closer look.

Increase in and Expansion of Technology

It was only about a century and a quarter ago that Jules Verne fantasized about people traveling around the world in just 80 days. Much of what we take for granted today results from recent advances that have been accelerating at a dizzying rate. More than half the scientists who have ever lived are alive today—one reason is population growth and another is that economic and productivity growth have allowed a larger portion of the population to be involved in developing new products rather than in producing them. Much of what we buy today simply didn't exist a decade or two ago, and the development of new products is bound to accelerate. Simply, as the base of technological development increases, there are more potential applications on which scientists and engineers can work. For instance, you've undoubtedly heard of the importance of the wheel but today's scientists and engineers use modern technology to improve wheels, such as by using smart tires containing sensors that measure magnetic fields and cause vehicles to respond automatically. Further, they work on specialized wheels for new models of automobiles, carts, tractors, airplanes, and earthmoving equipment.

Tremendous strides in communications and transportation technology enable you very quickly to know about and demand products and services developed in another part of the world. Many people can remember when there was no Internet as we know it today, no commercial transatlantic jet travel, no faxing or e-mailing, no teleconferencing or overseas direct-dial telephone service, and no sales over the Internet (e-commerce sales). Moreover, the cost of improved communications and transportation has risen more slowly than costs in general. A three-minute phone call from New York to London cost $10.80 in 1970 but less than $.20 today. Because of innovations in transportation, more countries can compete for sales to a given market. For example, the sale of foreign-grown flowers in the United States used to be impractical; however, flowers from as far away as Ecuador, Israel, the Netherlands, and New Zealand now compete in the United States because the flowers can reach U.S. stores economically as early as the next day after being picked. In contrast, imagine trying to export flowers or any other perishable product by the 13-mile-a-day caravan along the Silk Road between China and Europe, which for centuries accounted for an important share of world trade.

Conducting business on an international level usually involves greater distances than does conducting domestic business, and greater distances increase operating costs and make control of a company's foreign operations more difficult. But improved communications and transportation speed up interactions and improve a manager's ability to control foreign operations. Recall in our opening case that satellite television permits sports

Business is becoming more global because

- Technology is expanding, especially in transportation and communications.
- Governments are removing international restrictions.
- Institutions provide services to ease the conduct of international business.
- Consumers know about and want foreign goods and services.
- Competition has become more global.
- Political relationships have improved among some major economic powers.
- Countries cooperate more on transnational issues.

organizers to reach worldwide consumers immediately and at very little additional cost. Improved transportation allows players and teams to compete all over the world. Further, the NFL can quickly send managers to oversee its European teams, thus improving control of its international operations. Even small companies can reach global customers and suppliers through their Web pages on the Internet. For example, Atlanta's Randy Allgaier has a Taiwanese partner whom he has never met personally, and he has contracted with a Chinese factory that he has never visited to make lighting fixtures for him—all because of modern communications, especially those over the Internet.[8]

Liberalization of Cross-Border Trade and Resource Movements

To protect its own industries, every country restricts the movement across its borders of goods and services and the resources, such as workers and capital, to produce both. Such restrictions make international business more expensive to undertake. Because the regulations may change at any time, international business is also riskier. However, over time most governments have lowered some restrictions on trade for the following reasons:

1. Their citizens have expressed the desire for easier access to a greater variety of goods and services at lower prices.
2. They reason that their domestic producers will become more efficient as a result of foreign competition.
3. They hope to induce other countries to lower their barriers in turn.

Fewer restrictions enable companies and individuals to take better advantage of international opportunities. However, with more competition, people have to work harder. Figure 1.2 shows this humorously.

FIGURE 1.2

A DOWNSIDE OF COMPETITION CAUSED BY GLOBALIZATION

Although global competition brings more efficiency, it also requires companies and workers to expend more effort.

Development of Services That Support International Business

Companies and governments have developed services that ease the conduct of international business. For example, banks have developed efficient means for companies to receive payment in their home-country currencies. When Nike sells sportswear to a French soccer team, as soon as the shipment arrives in French customs (most likely from somewhere in Asia), a bank in Paris can collect in euros and pay Nike in U.S. dollars at a bank in the United States. In contrast, if business were still being conducted as in the era of early caravan traders, Nike probably would have to accept payment in the form of French merchandise, such as perfume or wine, which it would have to ship back to the United States and sell before receiving U.S. dollars.

Although companies do barter internationally, it can be cumbersome, time-consuming, risky, and expensive.[9] Today, most producers can be paid relatively easily for goods and services sold abroad because of bank credit agreements, clearing arrangements that convert one country's currency into another's, and insurance that covers risks like damage en route and nonpayment by the buyer.

The supporting services encompass much more than finance and are far too numerous to discuss exhaustively, but we'll mention one. International postal agreements allow you to send letters and packages any place in the world by conveniently paying postage only in the country and only in the currency from which you mail them, regardless of whether they pass through other countries or fly on their airlines. Or you can send them via any of the international package service companies, such as UPS or DHL, by simply paying transportation in your own currency.

Growing Consumer Pressures

Because of innovations in transportation and communications, you and other consumers know about products and services available in other countries. Further, global discretionary income has risen to the point that there is now widespread demand for products and services that would have been considered luxuries in the past. Thus, consumers want more, new, better, and differentiated products. In the last half of the twentieth century, global consumption grew sixfold. However, this greater affluence has not been evenly spread, either among or within countries, thus companies have recently responded more to those markets, such as China, where incomes and consumption are growing most rapidly. This greater demand has also spurred companies to spend heavily on research and development and to search worldwide—via the Internet, industry journals, trade fairs, and trips to foreign countries—for innovations and differentiated products that they can sell to ever-more-demanding consumers. In addition, consumers have become more proficient at scouring the globe for better prices, such as U.S. consumers' searching the Internet to buy lower-priced prescription drugs from abroad.

Increased Global Competition

As incomes have grown globally, more consumers have satisfied their needs, thus companies develop consumer wants that they hope will become new needs. In other words, consumers have had more discretionary income, which means that dissimilar products and services compete for the same consumer expenditures. If you're selling needs, say cars, then your competition is with other car or transportation suppliers. But if you're selling wants to discretionary spenders, your competition is more widespread. For example, a family outing to see international stars in a tennis tournament may compete with any other discretionary expenditures, such as the purchase of sporting equipment or an added accessory for the family car. This expansion of competition forces most companies to seek any means to gain competitive advantages, including a global search for quality improvement or cost reduction advantages. Recall, for instance, how sports teams are now seeking talent and markets worldwide. This enhances not only their ability to gain more revenue than opposing teams, but also competitive advantages over teams in other sports and competitive advantages over any companies whose products and services compete for consumers' discretionary purchases.

The pressures or potential pressures of increased foreign competition can persuade companies to expand their business into international markets. For instance, they may market where their competitors are selling or seek supplies where their competitors are getting cheaper or differentiated products. Or, as we have especially seen in recent years, they merge with or acquire foreign companies in order to gain operating efficiencies and larger global market shares. Whereas a company such as Procter & Gamble took almost 100 years to undertake operations internationally, we now find many companies (often called **born-global companies**) starting out with a global focus because of the international experience and education of their founders.[10] Technological advancements, especially in communications and the Internet, give these start-up companies a better idea of where their markets are globally and how they may gain resources from different countries.[11]

Today, companies can respond rapidly to many foreign sales opportunities. They can shift production quickly among countries if they're experienced in foreign markets. Further, they observe and emulate competitors' management and production methods. Once a few companies respond to foreign market and production opportunities, other companies may see the foreign opportunities as well. For instance, the early success of foreign baseball players on U.S. teams undoubtedly influenced basketball and (American) football teams to look for and develop talent abroad. Firms have to become more global to maintain competitiveness; failure to do so could be catastrophic for them.

Changing Political Situations

A major reason for growth in international business has been the end of the schism between most Communist and non-Communist countries. For nearly half a century after World War II, business between these two groups was minimal. Further, even within the Communist bloc, countries strove to be as self-sufficient as possible. With the transformation of political and economic policies in the former Soviet Union, most of Eastern Europe, China, and Vietnam, trade now flourishes between those countries and the rest of the world.

A further political factor relates to governments' abilities to respond to pressures to enhance world trade. As incomes have grown, so has tax revenue. Much of the revenue has gone to programs and projects that enhance the potential of international business. For example, by spending to improve airport and seaport facilities and by building efficient highways that connect with those in neighboring countries, governments have created travel efficiencies that speed and reduce the cost of delivering goods internationally. Further, governments now provide an array of services that help their companies sell more abroad, such as information about foreign markets, contacts with potential buyers abroad, and insurance against nonpayment in the home country currency.

Expanded Cross-National Cooperation

Governments increasingly realize that their own countries' interests can be enhanced by cooperating with other countries through treaties, agreements, and consultation. They do so primarily for the following reasons:

1. To gain reciprocal advantages
2. To attack problems jointly that one country acting alone cannot solve
3. To deal with areas of concern that lie outside the territory of all countries

Countries want to ensure that companies headquartered within their borders are not disadvantaged by foreign-country policies. Thus, such countries join international organizations and enter into treaties and agreements with other countries on a variety of commercial activities, such as transportation and trade. Treaties and agreements may be bilateral (involving only two countries) or multilateral (involving a few or many). Countries commonly enter into treaties in which each allows the other's commercial ships and planes to use certain seaports and airports in exchange for reciprocal port use. They enact treaties that cover commercial aircraft safety standards and flyover rights or treaties that protect property, such as foreign-owned investments, patents, trademarks, and copyrights in each other's territory. They also enact treaties for reciprocal reductions of import restrictions (and then retaliate when others interfere with trade flows by, for example, raising barriers of their own or cutting diplomatic ties).

Countries enact treaties or agreements to coordinate activities along their shared borders, such as building connecting highways and railroads or hydroelectric dams that serve all parties. They also enact treaties to solve problems they either cannot or will not solve alone because

1. the problem is too big or will benefit from joint inputs, and/or
2. the problem results from conditions that spill over from another country.

In the first case, the resources needed to solve the problem may be too large, or one country does not want to pay all the costs for a project that also will benefit another country. For example, countries may enact a treaty whereby they share the costs of joint technology development, such as the cooperation between Japan and the United States on ballistic missile defense technology.[12] Further, many problems are truly global and cannot easily be contained within a single country, thus we've seen recent cooperation to fight the spread of diseases, such as avian flu, and to develop warning systems against natural disasters, such as a tsunami.

In the second case, one country's economic and environmental policies may affect another country or countries. For example, high real-interest rates in one country can attract funds from countries in which interest rates are lower, which can disrupt economic conditions in the latter countries because there will be a shortage of funds available for investment. This is why eight economically important countries (known as the G8 countries)—Canada, France, Germany, Italy, Japan, Russia, the United Kingdom, and the United States—meet regularly to coordinate economic policies.[13] In fact, because information can flow rapidly, particularly over the Internet, an event in one country can have almost instantaneous effects in another. Further, competitive locations may more easily shift, because companies have knowledge networks that enable them to change suppliers in response to slight cost differences among countries.[14] In addition, most environmental experts agree that there must be cooperation among countries to institute global environmental policies. So far, most countries have made agreements with at least some other countries on such issues as restricting harmful emissions, keeping waterways unpolluted, preserving endangered species, and banning the use of certain pesticides.

Three areas remain outside the territories of countries—the noncoastal areas of the oceans, outer space, and Antarctica. Until their commercial viability was demonstrated, these areas excited little interest in multinational cooperation. The oceans contain food and mineral resources. They also are the surface over which much international commerce passes. Today, treaties on the use of oceans specify the amounts and methods of fishing allowed, international discussion attempts to resolve who owns oceanic minerals, and agreements detail how to deal with pirates (yes, even today, pirates are a problem).[15] Much disagreement exists on who should reap commercial benefits from space. For example, commercial satellites pass over countries that receive no direct benefit from them but that believe they should. Antarctica, with minerals and abundant sea life along its coast, attracts thousands of tourists each year. Consequently, a series of recent agreements limit its commercial exploitation.

In general, countries whose companies are technologically able to exploit ocean, space, and Antarctic resources believe that their companies should reap all the benefits from exploitation. However, other countries (generally the poorer ones) feel that commercial benefits from such exploitation should be shared among all countries. Until this debate is settled, companies will face uncertainty as to whether and how they can commercialize these new frontiers.

Much of the cooperation we have just described has been through international organizations, such as the United Nations, the International Monetary Fund, the World Trade Organization, and the World Bank. We discuss these organizations extensively in future chapters, especially in Chapter 8. However, in the following section, we'll survey the major criticisms of globalization and its affect on of international organizations.

CRITICISMS OF GLOBALIZATION

Critics of globalization claim

- Countries lose sovereignty.
- The resultant growth hurts the environment.
- Some people lose, both relatively and absolutely.

Although we have discussed seven broad reasons for the increase in international business and globalization, the results have not been without controversy. In fact, antiglobalization forces have protested meetings of international organizations and conferences, both peacefully and violently in recent years, as they press for legislation and other means to stop or slow the globalization process. Although the critics have presented many different issues, we can place them into three broad categories: threats to national sovereignty, growth, and growing income inequality. We shall briefly explain these three issues in the following section, describe them in more depth in subsequent chapters, and discuss related issues in the Point–Counterpoint sections of this and upcoming chapters.

Threats to National Sovereignty

You have probably heard the slogan, "Think globally, but act locally," which, in essence, means that countries should do what is best for them rather than what is best for the world as a whole. Many people fear that the existence of international agreements, particularly those that lead to fewer restrictions on how goods are bought and sold, will diminish countries' **sovereignty** or freedom from external control and curtail their ability to act in their own best interests. They will not be able to "act locally," in other words.

In essence, countries compete with each other to fulfill their economic, political, and social objectives. Keep in mind that competition among countries is the means to an end—the end being the well-being of a country's citizens. However, there is no consensus on how to measure well-being, and even accepted indicators of current economic prosperity may actually foretell longer-term problems. For example, high current consumption may occur at the expense of investment for future production and consumption, and excessive use of the earth's resources may lead to long-term environmental despoliation and resource shortages in the future. Further, citizens are concerned not only with economic well-being, but also with a number of other issues that cannot be quantified, such as political independence to follow one's own set of priorities. For instance, critics of globalization argue that nations impose rules on worker protection and environmental practices that reflect a collective national priority. If the adherence to these rules is costly to companies, companies may locate where rules are less stringent. Thus critics of globalization say it is unfair to allow imports that are produced more cheaply simply because other nations require a different set of standards.

People in small countries are particularly concerned that their dependence on a larger country for supplies and sales will make them vulnerable to demands of that country which they might oppose, such as voting a certain way in the United Nations, supporting military or economic actions against a third country, or signing a treaty. They worry further that large international companies may be so powerful that they can either dictate the terms of their operations through threats to create unemployment by moving elsewhere, or avoid the control of most national political bodies by finding and using legal loopholes, such as to avoid tax payments. Finally, they worry that globalization brings homogenization of products, companies, work methods, social structures, and even language. As international differences diminish, countries can no longer maintain the traditional ways of life that help unify generations and people within their community. Thus, critics argue that they lose their ability to act according to their local best interests.

Economic Growth

Many of the criticisms against globalization are really criticisms against economic growth. The assumption is that globalization brings more production or growth, which, in turn, brings both immediate and long-term negative consequences. Certainly, as economic growth takes place, the world uses more nonrenewable natural resources. At the same time, increased production adds environmental despoliation through toxic and pesticide runoffs into rivers and oceans, air pollution from factory and vehicle emissions, and deforestation that can negatively affect weather and climate. Further, although we count production as economic output, we do not discount the future costs created from that production, which we may have to incur to sustain acceptable living standards.

Against this criticism, we need to consider that globalization brings some positive consequences to both the sustenance of natural resources and the maintenance of an environmentally sound planet. Global cooperation brings more uniform standards for combating environmental problems. The openness to products and services from abroad allows production to occur in the cheapest locations, which usually involves using the fewest resources. Finally, technologies that save on resources and that produce more cleanly, such as automobile engines that use less gas and automobile emission systems that lower air pollution, are disseminated around the world more rapidly because of companies' producing for global markets. Nevertheless, unless these positive consequences of globalization keep up with the negative costs from growth, critics will argue that the sustainability of economic improvement will be problematic in the future.

Growing Income Inequality

People look not only at absolute achievement or improvement, but also at how well they do compared to other people, especially those in other countries. Thus, improvement in global well-being is of little solace to most people unless they, themselves, are doing better *and* at least keeping up with others. For example, the Nobel economist Paul Samuelson has argued that when U.S. companies have shifted high tech work abroad, say computer programming to India, the cost saving in the United States does not necessarily make up for the lost wages in the United States. Further, this **offshoring**—the process of shifting production to a foreign country— speeds up the process by which India narrows its competitive gap with the United States, thus altering the two countries' relative economic situation.[16]

By various measurements, there has been a growing income disparity both within and among countries. Thus, even if the overall global gains from globalization are positive, there are bound to be some losers in both an absolute and a relative sense. The losers will inevitably be critics of globalization, thus a challenge is in how to bring about the positive gains from globalization while simultaneously minimizing the costs to the losers. For instance, the global community pressured Brazil to curtail logging in the Amazon region for environmental reasons. This curtailment is generally viewed as beneficial for the planet as a whole. Nevertheless, Brazil's president allowed the resumption of logging in 2005 because of large protests within Brazil by unemployed workers who saw job opportunities in logging. Further, there are consequences of globalization that we can't measure in purely economic terms. For instance, we saw in the opening case that the globalization of sports has caused Brazil's top soccer players to join European teams. Although this has increased these players' incomes and has allowed fans from all over the world to watch these players on television, it is difficult to evaluate the cost to Brazilian fans of no longer watching their best Brazilian players in person. Thus, whenever people lose, absolutely or relatively, because of globalization, they are apt to be critics of globalization.

WHY COMPANIES ENGAGE IN INTERNATIONAL BUSINESS

In our opening case and previous discussion, we have alluded to the reasons why companies engage in international business; nevertheless, it is useful to categorize these reasons. When operating internationally, a company should consider its mission (what it will seek to do and become over the long term), its objectives (specific performance targets to fulfill its mission), and strategy (the means to fulfill its objectives). Referring back to Figure 1.1, you will see that there are three major operating objectives that may induce companies to engage in international business. They are:

- To expand sales
- To acquire resources
- To minimize risk

These three objectives should guide any company's decisions of whether, where, and how to engage in international business. We'll now overview each of them.

To Expand Sales

Pursuing international sales usually increases the potential market and potential profits.

Companies' sales are dependent on two factors: the consumers' interest in their products or services and the consumers' willingness and ability to buy them. There are obviously a great many more people in the world than in any single country, so companies may increase the potential market for their goods and services by pursuing international markets.

Ordinarily, higher sales mean higher profits, assuming that costs to make the additional sales do not increase disproportionately. For example, the televising of sports competitions to viewers in multiple countries increases costs only marginally, compared to the additional revenue that sponsors of the broadcasts are willing to pay to reach more people who may be potential buyers of their products.

So increased sales are a major motive for a company's expansion into international business. Many of the world's largest companies derive more than half their sales from outside

International business encompasses many combinations of nationalities, such as those shown in this professional game played in 2005 between River Plate (Argentina) and Sao Paulo (Brazil). On the left is Uruguayan Carlos Diogo, now playing for Real Madrid (Spain) and wearing a logo from the U.S. company, Anheuser Busch. On the right is Brazilian Danilo who is wearing a logo from the Korean company, LG Electronics.

POINT–COUNTERPOINT: IS OFFSHORING GOOD OR BAD?

POINT

Offshoring is good because it reduces costs. I'll mention just two examples. IBM must pay programmers $56 an hour including salary and benefits in the United States, but the cost in China for people with three to five years' experience is only about $12.50. IBM will save about $168 million a year by shifting this work abroad.[17] Take Claimpower, a small U.S. medical insurance billing company. By transferring work to India, it reduced costs and reduced prices to doctors. The company quadrupled its business in two years.[18]

Almost everyone accepts the employment shifts caused by labor-saving technologies, and there is nothing fundamentally different about offshoring and introducing labor-saving technologies. In both situations, companies save costs. In both situations, companies may temporarily need fewer workers in their home countries and can use the cost savings to reduce prices or spend more on product developments. In either case, they can eventually increase employment because of their growth. Further, this process allows the companies to increase the number of high-value jobs (work done by high-salaried employees, such as managers) in their home countries. In fact, there is evidence that the demand for and income of higher-paid employees in the United States has increased as a result of U.S. companies' offshoring to low-labor-cost countries.[19]

Offshoring has also been good for poor countries. Using the World Bank benchmark of poverty-level income of $2 a day or less, adjusted for purchasing power, the percentage of the world's population living in poverty fell from 56 percent to 23 percent between 1980 and 2000. Further, the countries that globalized the most during that period, particularly through the offshoring that enabled them to produce for export, were the ones whose incomes grew the most.[20] The economic growth of poor countries is also increasing their ability to buy abroad, thus the growth is good for rich countries as well. For instance, the World Tourism Organization predicts that by 2020, China will be sending 100 million tourists abroad per year.[21]

COUNTERPOINT

Offshoring may be good for a few people, but not for most. I keep hearing about the cost savings, but I don't find anything cheaper today. For instance, companies like Ralph Lauren and Tommy Hilfiger are making almost all their clothes where labor rates are very cheap, but they still charge upscale prices. You mentioned that Claimpower reduced its prices to doctors, but you haven't given me any examples of doctors reducing any of their fees as a result. Further, Claimpower grew fast as a result of lowering its prices, but this growth must be at the expense of other companies rather than growth in the economy; there are simply just so many insurance claims to file.

When jobs are replaced by offshoring, we're exchanging good jobs for bad ones. Displaced workers struggled for decades to work reasonable hours and gain health benefits and a retirement plan. Most important, their incomes allowed them to send their children to universities, thus making the next generation upwardly mobile. Many of the displaced have worked loyally for their companies for 20 or 30 years. At this point, they have no other usable skills and, given their ages, scant ability for retraining. The increase in so-called high-value jobs is little solace for these people. Further, what kind of jobs are being created in poor countries? Certainly multinational enterprises (MNEs) give workers in low-wage countries more than they otherwise would have earned, and a few of the jobs are good ones. But for the most part, the hours are very long, the working conditions frightful, and the pay barely enough to survive. These MNEs are also constantly looking for new places to operate. For instance, much clothing production went to Mauritius because of cheap labor, but as soon as Mauritians began to expect their better way of life to continue, MNEs began buying more of their clothing elsewhere and laying off the Mauritian workers.[22]

Offshoring proponents paint a rosy picture about the percentage of people living in poverty, but they don't take into consideration increases in population. The Nobel economist Joseph Stiglitz points out that during the last decade of the twentieth century the number of people living in poverty increased by about 100 million.[23] Further, the movement out of poverty has been concentrated in a few countries, mainly China and India. For nearly all of Africa, central Asia, and much of Latin America, few people have benefited from the offshoring that accompanies globalization.

their home countries. You've heard of many of these companies—Volkswagen (headquartered in Germany), Ericsson (Sweden), IBM (the United States), Michelin (France), Nestlé (Switzerland), Seagram (Canada), and Sony (Japan).[24] However, smaller companies also may depend on foreign sales. Small companies (those with fewer than 20 employees) make up nearly 70 percent of U.S. exporters.[25] For example, one of these, Artcrete, a manufacturer of a concrete finishing system, sells in Australia, Belgium, Canada, France, Hong Kong, Japan, Mexico, and Saudi Arabia.[26] Many small companies also depend on sales of components to large companies, which in turn put them in finished products that they sell abroad.

Acquire Resources

Foreign sources may give companies

- Lower costs
- New or better products
- Additional operating knowledge

Manufacturers and distributors seek out products, services, and components produced in foreign countries. They also look for foreign capital, technologies, and information that they can use at home. Sometimes they do this to reduce their costs. For example, sporting goods companies rely largely on production of baseballs in Haiti, a country that doesn't even play baseball. Acquiring resources may also enable a company to improve its product quality and differentiate itself from competitors—in both cases, potentially increasing market share and profits. Although a company may initially use domestic resources to expand abroad, once the foreign operations are in place, the foreign resources, such as capital or expertise, may then serve to improve domestic operations. For example, Avon used know-how from its Latin American marketing experience to help penetrate the U.S. Hispanic market.[27]

Minimize Risk

International operations may reduce operating risk by

- Smoothing sales and profits
- Preventing competitors from gaining advantages

To minimize swings in sales and profits, companies may seek out foreign markets to take advantage of business cycle differences among countries. Sales decrease or grow more slowly in a country that is in a recession and increase or grow more rapidly in one that is expanding economically. For example, in the early twenty-first century, Nestlé experienced slower growth in Western Europe and the United States, but this slower growth was offset by higher growth in Asia, Eastern Europe, and Latin America.[28] Further, by obtaining supplies of the same product or component from different countries, companies may be able to avoid the full impact of price swings or shortages in any one country.

Many companies enter into international business for defensive reasons. They want to counter advantages competitors might gain in foreign markets that, in turn, could hurt them domestically. For example, let's say Company A fears that Company B will generate large profits from a foreign market if left alone to serve that market. Company B could use those profits in various ways (such as additional advertising or development of better products) to improve its competitive position in Company A's domestic market. Company A may then enter foreign markets primarily to prevent Company B from gaining these advantages.

MODES OF INTERNATIONAL BUSINESS

When pursuing international business, private enterprises and governments have to decide how to carry out the business, such as what mode of operation to use. Figure 1.3 shows that a company can choose from a number of operating modes. Broadly, these include exports and imports of both merchandise and service and foreign investments that are both controlled and noncontrolled. Within these categories are subcategories, such as joint ventures and management contracts, that we'll also define.

Merchandise Exports and Imports

Merchandise exports and imports usually are a country's most common international economic transaction.

More companies are engaged in exporting and importing than in any other international mode. This is especially true of smaller companies, even though they are less likely than large companies to engage in exporting. (Large companies are also more apt to engage in

FIGURE 1.3 **MEANS OF CARRYING OUT INTERNATIONAL OPERATIONS**

Companies may choose from a number of modes for conducting international business.

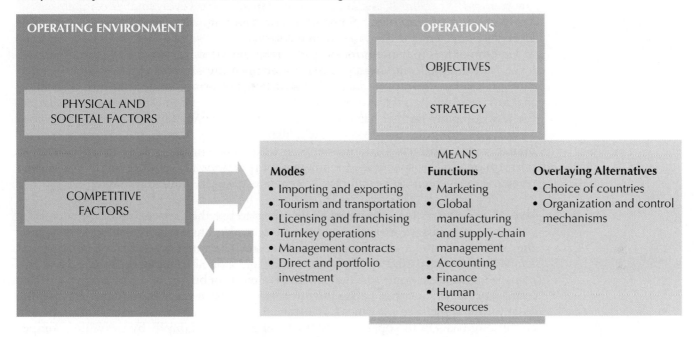

other forms of foreign operations in addition to exporting and importing.) **Merchandise exports** are tangible products—goods—sent out of a country; **merchandise imports** are goods brought into a country. Because these goods can be seen leaving and entering a country, they are sometimes called *visible exports* and *imports*. The terms *exports* and *imports* frequently apply to merchandise, not to a service. When an Indonesian plant sends athletic shoes to the United States, the shoes are exports for Indonesia and imports for the United States. For most countries, exporting and importing of goods are the major sources of international revenue and expenditures.

Service Exports and Imports

Service exports and **imports** generate nonproduct international earnings. The company or individual receiving payment is making a **service export**. The company or individual paying is making a **service import**. Service exports and imports take many forms. In this section, we discuss the following sources of such earnings:

- Tourism and transportation
- Performance of services
- Use of assets

Services have recently been the fastest growth sector for international trade.

Tourism and Transportation Let's say that the Williams sisters fly from the United States to Paris on Air France to play in the French Open tennis tournament. Their payments to Air France and their expenses in France are service exports for France and service imports for the United States. International tourism and transportation are important sources of revenue for airlines, shipping companies, travel agencies, and hotels. Some countries' economies depend heavily on revenue from these economic sectors. For example, in Greece and Norway, a significant amount of employment, profits, and foreign-exchange earnings comes from foreign cargo that is carried on ships owned by citizens of those countries. Earnings from foreign tourism are more important for the Bahamian economy than are

Service exports and imports are international nonproduct sales and purchases.

- Examples of services are travel, transportation, banking, insurance, and the use of assets such as trademarks, patents, and copyrights.
- They are very important for some countries.
- They include many specialized international business operating modes.

earnings from the export of merchandise. Similarly, in recent years, the United States has earned more from foreign tourism than from its exports of agricultural goods.

Performance of Services   Some services—banking, insurance, rentals (such as of Disney's films), engineering, management services, and so on—net companies earnings in the form of fees (payments for the performance of those services). On an international level, for example, companies pay fees for engineering services that are often handled through **turnkey operations** such as construction, performed under contract, of facilities that are transferred to the owner when they are ready to begin operating. For example, the U.S. company Bechtel has turnkey contracts in Afghanistan for rebuilding facilities destroyed during the war to oust the Taliban leadership. Companies also pay fees for **management contracts**—arrangements in which one company provides personnel to perform general or specialized management functions for another company. Disney receives management fees from managing theme parks in France and Japan.

Use of Assets   When companies allow others to use their assets, such as trademarks, patents, copyrights, or expertise under contracts, also known as **licensing agreements**, they receive earnings called royalties. On an international level, for example, sports teams license companies abroad to use their logos on shirts and caps. **Royalties** also come from franchise contracts. **Franchising** is a mode of business in which one party (the franchisor) allows another party (the franchisee) to use a trademark that is an essential asset for the franchisee's business. The franchisor, such as McDonald's, also assists on a continuing basis in the operation of the business—for example, by providing components, management services, and technology.

Dividends and interest paid on foreign investments are also treated as service exports and imports because they represent the use of assets (capital). However, countries treat the investments themselves separately in the international economic statistics they report.

Investments

Foreign investment means ownership of foreign property in exchange for a financial return, such as interest and dividends. Foreign investment takes two forms: direct and portfolio.

A direct investment involves control of a foreign company.

Direct Investment   A **direct investment** is one that gives the investor a controlling interest in a foreign company. Such a direct investment is also a **foreign direct investment (FDI)**, a term common to this text. For example, Yamauchi's ownership of the Seattle Mariners baseball team is a Japanese foreign direct investment in the United States. Control need not be a 100 percent or even a 50 percent interest. If a company holds a minority stake and the remaining ownership is widely dispersed, no other owner may be able to counter the company effectively. When two or more companies share ownership of an FDI, the operation is a **joint venture**. For instance, Disney has a joint venture for a theme park in Hong Kong with the Hong Kong government.

Companies may choose FDI as a way to access certain resources or reach a market. Today, at least 61,000 companies worldwide have over 900,000 FDIs that encompass every type of business function—extracting raw materials from the earth, growing crops, manufacturing products or components, selling output, providing various services, and so on.[29] FDI is not the domain of large companies only. For example, many small firms maintain sales offices abroad to complement their export efforts, which are FDIs along with the real estate they own abroad. Small firms are also acquiring foreign companies.[30] However, because large companies tend to have larger foreign facilities and operate in more countries, the value of their FDI is higher.

Key components of portfolio investment are

- Noncontrol of a foreign operation
- Financial benefit (for example, loans)

Portfolio Investment   A **portfolio investment** is a noncontrolling interest in a company or ownership of a loan to another party. A portfolio investment usually takes one of two forms: stock in a company or loans to a company or country in the form of bonds, bills, or notes that the investor purchases. Malcolm Glazer had a noncontrolling (portfolio) invest-ment in Manchester United, which later became a direct investment when he bought addi-tional ownership. In both situations, these were U.S. investments in the United Kingdom.

Foreign portfolio investments are important for most companies that have extensive international operations. Companies use them primarily for short-term financial gain—that is, as a means that allows a company to earn more money on its money with relative safety. Company treasurers routinely move funds among countries to earn higher yields on short-term investments.

International Companies and Terms to Describe Them

Many of the terms in international business are confusing because writers, both in the popular media and in government and academic reports, use them to define different things. Although an international company is any company operating internationally, there are many terms that differentiate their types of operations.

There are numerous ways that companies may work together in international opera-tions, such as through joint ventures, licensing agreements, management contracts, minority ownership in each other's company, or long-term contractual arrangements. An all-encompassing term to describe these operations is **collaborative arrangements**. Another term, **strategic alliance**, can sometimes mean the same thing, but more nar-rowly—to indicate an agreement that is of critical importance to the competitive viability of one or more partners. We shall use *strategic alliance* only in its narrower meaning.

The **multinational enterprise (MNE)** is a company that takes a global approach to foreign markets and production. It is willing to consider market and production loca-tions anywhere in the world. The true MNE usually uses most of the modes discussed thus far. However, it can be difficult to determine whether a company takes this global approach, so narrower definitions of the term *multinational enterprise* have emerged. For example, some say a company, to qualify as an MNE, must have direct investments in some minimum number of countries or be of a certain size. Under this definition, an MNE usually would have to be a giant company. However, a small company also can take a global approach within its resource capabilities and might use most of the operat-ing forms we have discussed; therefore, most writers today use the term to include any company that has operations in more than one country—the way that we use the term in this text.

The term **multinational corporation (MNC)** is also commonly used in the international business arena and often is a synonym for *MNE*. We prefer the MNE designation because there are many internationally involved companies, such as accounting partnerships, that are not organized as corporations. Another term sometimes used interchangeably with MNE, especially by the United Nations, is **transnational company (TNC)**.

> An MNE (sometimes called MNC or TCN) is a company that has a worldwide approach to markets and production *or* one with operations in more than one country.

WHY INTERNATIONAL BUSINESS DIFFERS FROM DOMESTIC BUSINESS

Now that we've explained the modes by which companies may operate internationally, some of which are different from those used domestically, we'll introduce country condi-tions (the companies' external environments) that may affect the way companies may operate internationally, and why. Companies should not form their strategies—or the means to implement them—without examining these external environments.

Figure 1.4 shows that the external environments include physical factors, such as a country's geography, and societal factors, such as a country's politics, law, culture, and economy. They also include competitive factors, such as the number and strength of sup-pliers, customers, and rival firms. Although companies may face regional differences within their home countries, these are usually minimal in comparison with what they face in going from one country to another.

> Managers in international business must understand social science disciplines and how they affect all functional business fields.

FIGURE 1.4

PHYSICAL AND SOCIETAL INFLUENCES ON INTERNATIONAL BUSINESS

Companies affect and are affected by their operating environment.

FIGURE 1.4

PHYSICAL AND SOCIETAL INFLUENCES ON INTERNATIONAL BUSINESS

Companies affect and are affected by their operating environment.

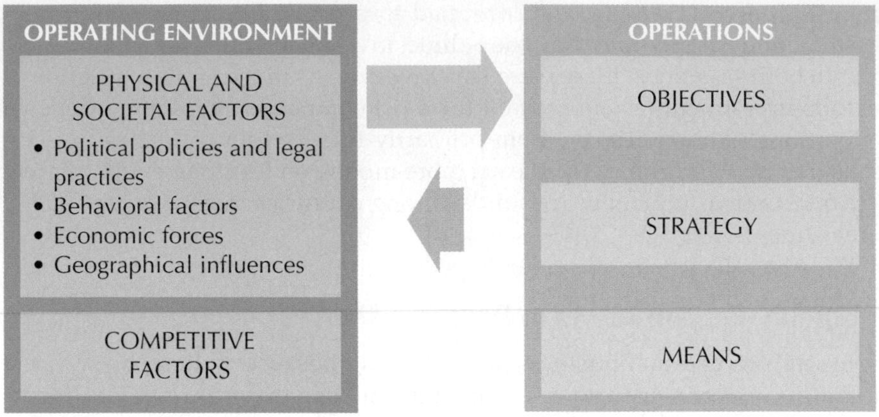

Physical and Societal Factors

The basic social science fields help explain why conditions vary around the world and cause optimal business practices to vary from place to place. To operate abroad, managers should thus have, in addition to knowledge of business operations, a working knowledge of the basic social sciences that help explain what these differences are: political science, law, anthropology, sociology, psychology, economics, and geography. We'll now introduce some physical and societal factors that demonstrate the importance of companies' external operating environments.

Political Policies   Politics helps shape business worldwide because political leaders control whether and how international business takes place. For example, the former Washington Senators of the American League had a minor league baseball franchise in Cuba, which ended when Cuba and the United States severed diplomatic relations. There are now a number of Cuban baseball players on major league teams in the United States, but most of these players had to escape from Cuba in order to play professionally abroad. China has permitted Yao Ming to play basketball in the United States for an NBA team, but it has placed restrictions on his salary and endorsements. For many years, most countries disallowed South African athletes and teams from competing internationally in protest over South Africa's racial policies. Political disputes, particularly those that result in military conflicts, can disrupt trade and investment. Even small conflicts can have far-reaching effects. For instance, the bombing of a hotel in Indonesia led international tourists to divert their trips elsewhere and international investors to consider Indonesia to be a riskier place to put funds.

Politics often determines where and how international business can take place.

Legal Policies   Domestic and international laws determine largely what the managers of a company operating internationally can do. Domestic law includes regulations in both the home and host countries on such matters as taxation, employment, and foreign-exchange transactions. For example, Disney built a theme park in Hong Kong. Hong Kong law determines how Disney's revenues from Hong Kong are taxed, how they can be exchanged from Hong Kong dollars to U.S. dollars, and the nationality and payment of workers in the park. U.S. law, in turn, determines how and when Disney's losses or earnings from Hong Kong will be treated for tax purposes in the United States. International law in the form of legal agreements between two countries governs how the earnings are taxed by both.

Each country has its own laws regulating business. Agreements among countries set international law.

International law may also determine how and whether companies can operate in certain locales. For example, companies from most countries suspended sales to Iraq because of U.N. trade sanctions over Iraq's failure to allow access to weapons inspectors.[31] How laws are enforced also affects operations. For example, most countries have laws against copying trademarks and copyrights without the authorization of the companies owning them; however, many countries do little to enforce their copyright laws. Companies should understand the treaties among countries and the laws of each country in which they want to operate, as well as how laws are enforced, to operate profitably abroad.

Behavioral Factors   The related social science disciplines of anthropology, psychology, and sociology describe, in part, people's social and mental development, behavior, and interpersonal activities. By studying these sciences, managers can better understand societal values, attitudes, and beliefs concerning themselves and others. This understanding can help them determine how and why they may need to alter operations in different countries. For example, although our opening case deals with the globalization of professional sports, there remain huge differences among countries in the popularity of different sports and how they are played. The U.S. film industry makes movies with the anticipation that a substantial portion of the revenue will come from abroad, and it makes changes so that the movies will have international acceptance. However, it has learned that sports movies do disastrously internationally because the world usually doesn't care to see movies about other people's sports.[32] Thus, the film studios adjust sports movies' budgets so that they don't depend much on foreign revenues. Japan does care about U.S. baseball, a sport that became popular in Japan during the U.S. occupation after World War II. However, Japan is a society that values harmony much more than the United States, whereas the United States values competitiveness much more than Japan. This difference influences how baseball rules differ between the two countries. In Japan, the best possible outcome of a baseball game is a tie; in the United States, a game continues until there is a winner.

The interpersonal norms of a country may necessitate a company's alteration of operations.

Economic Forces   Economics explains, among other concepts, why countries exchange goods and services with each other, why capital and people travel among countries in the course of business, and why one country's currency has a certain value compared to another's. For example, although baseball is very popular in the Dominican Republic, the placement of a major league baseball team there is not feasible because too few people can afford the high ticket prices necessary to support a team. Higher incomes in the United States than in the Dominican Republic also influence Dominican baseball players, such as Sammy Sosa, to join teams in the United States. Further, economics helps explain why, where, and when one country can produce goods or services less expensively than another can. In addition, it provides the analytical tools to determine the impact of an international company on the economies of the host and home countries and the effect of a country's economic policies and conditions on the company.

Economics explains country differences in costs, currency values, and market size.

Geographical Influences   Managers who know geography can better determine the location, quantity, quality, and availability of the world's resources, as well as the best way to exploit them. The uneven distribution of resources results in different products and services being produced or offered in different parts of the world. Take sports. Norway fares better in the Winter Olympics than in the Summer Olympics because of its climate, and except for the well-publicized Jamaican bobsled team whose members lived in Canada, tropical countries don't even compete in the winter Olympics. East Africans have dominated distance races, at least partially because they can train at higher altitudes than most other racers can. Geographical barriers such as high mountains, vast deserts, and inhospitable jungles affect communications and distribution channels for companies in many countries. The probability of natural disasters and adverse climatic conditions such as hurricanes, floods, earthquakes, tsunamis, or freezing weather make it riskier to invest in some areas than in others. These factors also affect the availability of supplies and the prices of products. For example, early twenty-first century droughts in New Zealand caused farmers there to reduce their stocks of sheep, which led to global shortages and rising prices of lamb and wool.[33] In addition, population distribution around the world and the impact of human activity on the environment exert a strong influence on international business. For example, concern about destruction of the world's rain forests may lead to regulations or to other pressures on companies, forcing them to change the place or method of their business activities.

Natural conditions affect what can be produced where.

The political, legal, social, economic, and geographic environments affect the way a company operates and the amount of adjustment it must make to its operations in a particular country, such as how it produces and markets its products, staffs its operations, and maintains its accounts. In fact, the external environment may affect each function of the company. The amount of adjustment is influenced by how much the environments of home and host countries resemble each other.

The Competitive Environment

A company's situation may differ among countries by

- Its competitive ranking
- The competitors it faces

In addition to its physical and societal environments, each company operates within its competitive environment. Figure 1.5 shows some of the most common competitive factors in international business. The competitive environment varies by industry, company, and country—and so, accordingly, do international strategies. For example, companies in industries with homogeneous products, such as copper tubing, compete more on price than do companies in industries that compete more on differentiated and innovative products, such as branded toothpaste or state-of-the-art computer chips. Strategies for the former are usually more influenced than the latter by cost savings, such as developing better equipment and operating methods, producing on a large scale to spread fixed costs over more units, and locating to secure cheap labor and materials.

Companies within the same industry also differ in their competitive strategies. Honda's being more concerned about reducing automobile costs than BMW helps explain why the former has recently moved much of its automobile production to China to take advantage of lower labor costs while the latter has not. Still another competitive factor is the size of the company and the resources it has compared to its competitors. For example, a market leader, such as Coca-Cola, has resources for many more international options than does a smaller competitor, such as Royal Crown. But being a leader in one market does not guarantee leadership in all. In most markets, Coca-Cola is the leader, with Pepsi-Cola in a strong second position; however, Coca-Cola is number three in the Indian market, after Pepsi-Cola and Thums Up, a locally owned soft drink.[34]

The competitive environment also varies among countries in other ways. For example, the domestic market in the United States is much larger than in Sweden. To spread fixed costs of product development and production, Swedish producers have had to become more highly dependent on foreign sales than U.S. producers are. The Swedish company Electrolux, for instance, had to promote exports very early in its history and depends much more on foreign sales of household appliances than do its main U.S. competitors, GE and Whirlpool. Another result of the larger U.S. market is that foreign companies have to invest much more money to gain national distribution in the United States than they do in Sweden, because there are more places to sell their products. Finally, the

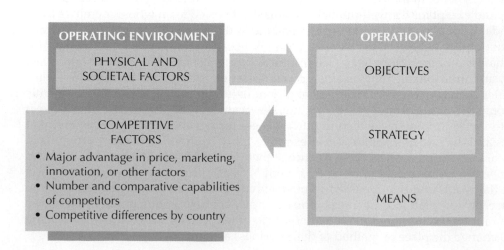

number of significant competitors in a European country, especially in retailing, is usually three or four as opposed to ten to twenty in the United States.[35]

Still another competitive factor is whether companies face international or local competitors at home and in foreign markets. Boeing and Airbus compete with each other everywhere they try to sell commercial aircraft. Therefore, what they learn about each other in one country is useful in predicting the other's strategies and actions in other countries. However, Tesco, a British grocery chain, faces different retailers as competitors in each of the foreign countries where it operates.

LOOKING TO THE FUTURE: Is Globalization Inevitable?

At this juncture, there is much doubt about the future growth of international business. There are three viewpoints: (1) that globalization is inevitable, (2) that international business will grow primarily along regional rather than global lines, and (3) that forces against globalization will greatly slow its growth.

The view of the inevitability of globalization is based largely on the premise that technical advances in transportation and communications are pervasive, so much so that consumers will demand the best products for the best prices regardless of their origins. Further, because MNEs have so many international production and distribution networks in place, they will pressure their home governments to place fewer rather than more restrictions on the international movement of goods and the means to produce them. If we accept this view, then we still must acknowledge that a challenge for the future is what we make of globalization, such as how to spread the benefits equitably and minimize the hardships on those people and companies affected negatively by increased international competition. In 2004, *The Wall Street Journal* surveyed all 32 living Nobel Prize winners in economics. One of the questions the newspaper asked them was, "What is the greatest economic challenge for the future?" Robert Fogel mentioned the problem of getting available technology and food to people who are needlessly dying. Milton Friedman cited "holding down the size and scope of government." George Akerlof named global warming. William Sharpe suggested financing health care and retirement. Both Vernon Smith and Harry Markowitz specified the need to bring down barriers to global trade. John Nash referred to the problem of increas-ing the standard of living with a shrinking amount of the Earth's surface per person. Lawrence Klein said it is "the reduction of poverty and disease in a peaceful political environment."[36]

The second view, that growth will be largely regional rather than global, is premised on studies showing that almost all the companies we think of as global conduct a dominant portion of their business in their home and neighboring countries.[37] Further, most world trade is regional, and many treaties to remove trade barriers are enacted on a regional basis. However, regionalization of either companies' or countries' international business may be a transition stage. In other words, companies may first promote international business in nearby countries, but expand from there once they've reached their regional goals.

The third view is that the growth of globalization will slow or may already be in the midst of collapse. Although most governments are embracing openness to international trade and investment, we have discussed some of the antiglobalization sentiments that are strong and vocal. Many people are demonstrating at meetings of international organizations, such as the World Bank and the World Trade Organization (WTO).[38] Further, affected groups in many countries are pressuring their governments to promote nationalism by raising barriers to trade and forgoing participation in international organizations and treaties. Looking historically, we see that pressure groups have often been successful (at least temporarily) in obstructing either technology or international trade that threatened their own well-being. For example, British factory workers rioted in the early nineteenth century over the mechanization of factory jobs, and the United States imposed high barriers to trade in the 1930s in efforts to protect American jobs.[39] At best, we can say that the globalization process has progressed in fits and starts. Recently antiglobalization interests have been successful in electing anti-immigration parties in such countries as Australia and Austria, in refusing to prevent their own companies from copying pharmaceuticals that supposedly had global patent protection in such countries as Brazil and South Africa, and in preventing ratification by the United States of such international treaties as the International Criminal Court and the Kyoto accord against global warming.[40] Finally, there is a view that for globalization to succeed, efficient institutions with clear-cut mandates are necessary; however, there is concern that neither the institutions nor the people working therein can adequately handle the complexities of an interconnected world.[41]

Only time will tell, but a company wanting to capitalize on international opportunities can't wait too long to see what happens on political and economic fronts. Investments in research, equipment, plants, and personnel training can take many years to complete.

Forecasting foreign opportunities and risks correctly is persistently challenging. However, by envisioning different ways in which the future may evolve, a company's management may better avoid unpleasant surprises. Each chapter of this text contains a section that discusses foreseeable ways in which topics covered in the chapter may develop in the future.

SUMMARY

- Globalization is the ongoing process that deepens and broadens the relationships and interdependence among countries. International business is a mechanism to bring about globalization.

- International business has been growing rapidly in recent decades because of technological expansion, the liberalization of government policies on cross-border movements (goods, services, and the resources to produce them), the development of institutions needed to support and facilitate international transactions, consumer pressures to buy foreign products and services, increased global competition, changing political situations, and cooperation in dealing with transnational problems and issues. Because of these factors, foreign countries increasingly are a source of both production and sales for domestic companies.

- Globalization has many critics, who feel it weakens national sovereignty, promotes growth that is detrimental to the earth's environment, and skews income distributions.

- Offshoring—the transferring of production abroad—is controversial in terms of who benefits when costs are reduced and whether the process exchanges good jobs for bad ones.

- Companies engage in international business to expand sales, to acquire resources, and to diversify or reduce their risks.

- A company can engage in international business through various operating modes, including exporting and importing merchandise and services, direct and portfolio investments, and collaborative arrangements with other companies.

- Multinational enterprises (MNEs) take a global approach to markets and production. Sometimes they are referred to as multinational corporations (MNCs) or transnational corporations (TNCs).

- When operating abroad, companies may have to adjust their usual methods of carrying on business. This is because foreign conditions often dictate a more suitable method and because the operating modes used for international business differ somewhat from those used on a domestic level.

- To operate within a company's external environment, its managers must have not only knowledge of business operations but also a working knowledge of the basic social sciences: political science, law, anthropology, sociology, psychology, economics, and geography.

- A company's competitive strategy influences how and where it can best operate. Likewise, from one country to another, a company's competitive situation may differ in terms of its relative strength and in terms of which competitors it faces.

- There is disagreement about the future of globalization—that it is inevitable, that it will be primarily regional, and that the growth will slow.

Carnival Cruise Lines[42]

I must go down to the seas again, for the call of the running tide

Is a wild call and a clear call that may not be denied

—John Masefield, *The Seekers*

This call of the sea has recently put cruise lines within one of the world's fastest growing industries. Although sea voyages have held an aura of mystique for centuries, only in recent decades have the general masses been able to experience open seas and exotic ports of call as a purely recreational activity. Historically, a recreational sea voyage was essentially an elitist endeavor that included gradations of luxury, prestige, and comfort on board. For instance, the modern word "posh" is an acronym for "portside out, starboard home," which referred to the cooler and more expensive cabins on trips from England to India before the advent of air conditioning. Certainly, the nonelite traveled by sea as well, but this was either to immigrate to other lands, take assignments abroad for their governments or companies, or work as crew aboard ships. However, in recent years the cruise line industry has transformed its customer demographics by targeting an economic middle class in addition to the rich. For instance, a 2004 survey of North American passengers indicated that almost half had family income between $20,000 and $60,000 per year, a group that has disposable income, but is not thought of as a rich customer segment.

What are cruises? Cruises are sea voyages for pleasure, usually ones in which passengers maintain their cabins for a fixed itinerary that brings them back to their original point of sea embarkation. In contrast to cruises, people used to use ships (passenger liners) as the major means to cross oceans and seas for business or pleasure, such as to travel between the United States and Europe. But the inauguration of transocean air service gave potential travelers a speedier and less expensive alternative, and airlines took passenger business from the liners. The competitive change was particularly marked with the advent of jet travel in the 1960s, which appealed to a growing mass market for budget-minded international travelers. The shipping lines countered with ads claiming that "getting there is half the fun" and by converting more shipboard space to low-priced accommodations. But one by one, they retired the giant luxury liners that had plied the oceans for many years.

By far, the largest cruise company is Carnival Corporation, which has more than 40 percent of the world cruise market and owns a number of cruise lines—Carnival Cruise Lines, Holland America, Princess, Cunard, Costa, Windstar, The Yachts of Seabourn, P&O, Ocean Village, Swan Hellenic, Aida, and Arosa. Through Carnival Corporation's network of cruise lines, it has cruises to every continent including Antarctica.

Carnival Corporation began because Israeli-born Ted Arison, a former partner in Norwegian Cruise Lines, saw an opportunity to develop sea travel for the masses by offering a "fun ship" concept on cruises that were less formal and luxurious than ocean liners had been. The timing was right. The aura of sea travel still prevailed, even though airlines were taking the passenger business. Because liners were being retired, there was opportunity to buy used ships at good prices. Further, growing affluence meant that more people could afford a vacation. And many of these newly vacationing people gravitated to holidays that were compatible with the "fun ship" concept, such as taking group tours and visiting theme parks and Las Vegas. Arison bought a secondhand ship, *Empress of Canada*, renamed it *Mardi Gras*, and refurbished the ship in bright colors, bright lights, discos, and casinos. On its maiden cruise from Miami in 1972, the *Mardi Gras* ran aground with 300 journalists on board, but fortunately it was undamaged. The *Mardi Gras* became successful with cruises from Miami to Jamaica, Puerto Rico, and the U.S. Virgin Islands. Carnival added ships and bought other cruise lines. Each of the different cruise lines, which Carnival calls brands, operates in different areas of the world and differs in terms of themes (for instance, Costa is based in Italy and has a very Italian flavor) and in terms of cost per cruise (for instance, the cost per night on the Cunard and Seabourne cruises is much higher than on the Carnival cruises).

Almost everything about Carnival and the entire cruise line industry is international. Take the nationality of the companies. About 30 countries offer shipping companies what are called flags

FIGURE 1.6

CRUISE PASSENGER DESTINATIONS, 2004

Source: Cruise Line International Association, *The Overview: Spring 2004*, p. 35: msworld/reports/overviews/spring04ov.doc.

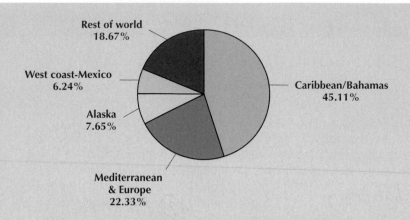

Rest of world
18.67%

West coast-Mexico
6.24%

Alaska
7.65%

Caribbean/Bahamas
45.11%

Mediterranean
& Europe
22.33%

Less subjective to countries' taxes but pay port fee wherever its ships dock

of convenience. By registering as, say, a Liberian or Mongolian legal entity, a shipping company can take advantage of the lower taxes and less stringent rules on its employment practices that those countries offer. Carnival is a Panamanian company, even though it is listed on the New York Stock Exchange, has its operating headquarters in Miami, and depends mainly on passengers who are from and originate their cruises in the United States. Its cruise line revenue is subject neither to Panamanian nor to U.S. income taxes. Nevertheless, Carnival pays substantial port fees wherever its ships dock, and the company and its passengers spend heavily in port cities.

Within the cruise line industry, only a few cruises are purely domestic, such as trips along the Mississippi River, around the Hawaiian Islands, and between the coast of Ecuador and the Galapagos Islands. Even trips from the U.S. west coast to Alaska are international because they stop in Canada in route. Because cruises are of different lengths, the industry maintains records of bed days (number of passengers times number of days on cruises). Figure 1.6 shows that the Caribbean/Bahamas comprise by far the largest destination for cruise passengers, followed by Europe and the Mediterranean, Alaska, and the west coast of Mexico. The Caribbean/Bahamas are particularly popular because the weather is warm year-round. During summer months, Carnival shifts some of its ships from Caribbean/Bahamas routes to Alaskan and Mediterranean routes. Of course, cruise ships go only where there are ports; however, Carnival works with tour operators who offer shore excursions for passengers (for additional fees). For instance, Carnival estimates that half its passengers to the Caribbean take shore excursions, such as to see Mayan ruins from Belize. Its Princess Lines' Alaskan cruises offer passengers the opportunity to take helicopters to a glacier where they can dog sled.

The biggest investment for cruise lines is in ships, and Carnival secures bids from all over the world for the ships it buys. Shipyards in several countries—such as Finland, France, Germany, Italy, Japan, and South Korea—are capable of building ships that meet the cruise industry's needs. Because shipbuilding employs many people and also uses tons of locally produced steel, governments often subsidize shipbuilding, which helps the cruise line companies. For instance, the Italian government gave its shipyard Fincantieri about $50 million in subsidies to build five ships worth $2.5 billion for Carnival. In 2004, Carnival's Cunard Line took delivery of the French-built *Queen Mary II*, the world's longest, widest, tallest, and most expensive ($800 million) cruise ship.

Shipping companies, including container vessels and other cargo ships, scour the world to find able seamen to do quality work at a reasonable cost. (By international agreement, registered seamen can enter virtually any port in the world.) However, cruise lines have some different staffing needs than cargo lines because many of the crew must be able to interact with passengers. Thus overall, about a third of seamen worldwide are from the Philippines, not only because of cost, but also because Philippine workers are generally fluent in English. Eastern Europe is the next largest source of seamen, with China and Vietnam growing in importance as a source of supply. A typical Carnival Cruise Lines ship will have crew members from over 100 different countries. Carnival has created a range of training programs for employees, including safety training, specialized departmental training, safety, and English as a foreign language.

Although Carnival pioneered the concept of cruising for the masses, this does not imply a complete lack of formality. Carnival has one or two formal nights per week, theme dinners based on national cuisines, a variety of musical entertainment, games and contests, spas, athletic facilities, and specialty performers. Because cruises occur outside the confines of any country, cruise lines avoid any national laws restricting gambling, thus Carnival ships have casinos. Passengers also have the opportunity to shop on board for merchandise from all over the world. For instance, art dealers hold auctions and seminars for cruise passengers. One such dealer, Park West Gallery, sells about 300,000 pieces of art per year on cruise ships. As one may expect, the average price per piece sold is higher on the more expensive cruises.

Because Carnival operates all over the world, it has the advantage of treating the whole world as a source of both customers and supplies. Nevertheless, its widespread operations make it vulnerable to global occurrences in politics, health, economics, and natural disasters. At the same time, the fact that ships are mobile gives Carnival the flexibility of moving its capital assets where they can best serve its needs.

In 1985, terrorists seized a cruise ship, the *Achille Lauro*, in the Mediterranean, after which cruise lines, including Carnival, instituted strict security checks for boarding passengers. Thus, they had in place before 9/11 what the airline industry had to put in place afterward. Nevertheless, 9/11 affected Carnival. Although for only one week after 9/11 cancellations exceeded bookings, Carnival had to make other adjustments. The primary one was in response to passengers' fear of flying. Carnival increased the number of U.S. ports of embarkation so that passengers could more conveniently reach their cruises by land. In addition, Carnival re-deploys cruises to avoid areas where its passengers might be in danger from revolutions and insurrections. In 2002, it even cancelled sailing to St. Croix in the U.S. Virgin Islands because of the island's high crime rate. Further, Carnival does not stop in Cuba, a popular tourist destination for Europeans and Canadians, because of U.S. government travel restrictions on U.S. citizens.

In 2002, hundreds of passengers on cruise ships based in Miami were stricken with a serious virus that caused diarrhea and vomiting. Carnival had to take one of its ships, the *Fascination*, out of service to erase all traces of the virus. This involved sanitizing everything on board, even poker chips. The following year when the SARS epidemic hit, Carnival took several precautions. Because SARS was first noted in Asia, Carnival banned passengers who had been in China, Hong Kong, Singapore, or Vietnam within the past 14 days. Because Toronto had an outbreak, Carnival personnel took temperatures of all boarding passengers from Toronto, sending home those with temperatures above 100.4 Fahrenheit.

Economic conditions can affect both demand and costs. The cruise line industry is part of the larger global tourist industry, which accounts for about 10 percent of global spending. Tourism expenditures are generally considered discretionary rather than priority, thus most consumers will spend on a cruise only if they've already satisfied their needs for daily maintenance, housing, transportation, health care, and education. Thus, it is not surprising that most of the market for taking cruises is from people in high-income countries, especially from the United States. However, the cruise line industry has been surprisingly immune from economic recessions in recent years, although during recessions, people have been more prone to take shorter cruises rather than longer ones and to depart from nearby ports rather than flying to faraway ports to commence their cruises. Nevertheless, the cruise line industry has fared well in relationship to other segments of the tourist industry during economic recessions because the all-inclusive prices per day are sometimes a bargain compared with travel to big cities or resorts. In terms of cost, the 2004 oil price increases caused Carnival to spend about $43 million more in fuel than in 2003.

The cruise line business can be adversely affected by weather conditions. During 2004, an unprecedented four hurricanes hit Florida, which is Carnival Cruise Lines' main embarkation point. Two hurricanes caused major disruptions. For example, Hurricane Francis closed ports, caused cancellation of three voyages, and shortened six others. Guests on cancelled voyages received full refunds and those on shortened voyages received partial refunds.

Overall, the future outlook for the cruise line industry and Carnival Cruise Lines is bright. With growing incomes in many countries, such as China, more people will have income to spend as tourists. At the same time, a majority of people in the targeted customer income segment have yet to take a cruise, thus they need only be convinced of the enjoyment a cruise will give them.

QUESTIONS

1. What global forces have contributed to the growth of the cruise line industry?
2. What specific steps has Carnival Cruise Lines taken to benefit from global societal changes?
3. What are some of the differences by country that affect the operations of cruise lines?
4. Although most cruise line passengers are from the United States, the average number of vacation days taken by U.S. residents is lower than in most other high-income countries. For instance, the number is 13 days per year in the United States as compared with 42 days in Italy, 37 in France, 35 in Germany, and 25 in Japan. How might the cruise lines increase sales to people outside the United States?
5. What threats exist for the future performance of the cruise line industry and specifically Carnival Cruise Lines? If you were in charge of Carnival Cruise Lines, how would you (a) try to prevent these threats from becoming a reality, and (b) deal with them if they did become a reality?
6. Discuss the ethics of cruise lines regarding the avoidance of almost all taxes while simultaneously buying ships built with governmental subsidies.

CHAPTER NOTES

1 Information for the case was taken from Matthew Graham, "Nike Overtakes Adidas in Football Field," *Financial Times* (August 19, 2004): 19; L. Jon Wertheim, "The Whole World Is Watching," *Sports Illustrated* (June 14, 2004): 73–86; L. Jon Wertheim, "Hot Prospects in Cold Places," *Sports Illustrated* (June 21, 2004): 63–66; Grant Wahl, "Football vs. Fútbol," *Sports Illustrated* (July 5, 2004): 69–72; Grant Wahl, "On Safari for 7-Footers," *Sports Illustrated* (June 28, 2004): 70–73; André Richelieu, "Building the Brand Equity of Professional Sports Teams," paper presented at the annual meeting of the Academy of International Business, Stockholm, Sweden (July 10–13, 2004); Brian K. White, "Seattle Mariners Justify Losing Streak as 'Cunning'" GlossyNews.com, July 15, 2004 (accessed November 6, 2004); "Japanese Owners Don't Want MLB in Control of World Cup," SportsLine.com wire reports, July 8, 2004 (accessed November 6, 2004); and Harald Dolles and Sten Söderman, "Globalization of Sports—The Case of Professional Football and its International Challenges," (Tokyo: German Institute for Japanese Studies, working paper, May 1, 2005).

2 For a good discussion of different ways the term is used, see Joyce S. Osland, "Broadening the Debate: The Pros and Cons of Globalization," *Journal of Management Inquiry* 10, no. 2 (June 2003): 137–54.

3 Sara Dickerman, "Air Supply: How Many Frequent-Flier Miles Did Your Dinner Earn?" *New York Times Style Magazine* (Fall, 2004): 30.

4 Sarah McBride, "Kia's Audacious Sorento Plan," *Wall Street Journal* (April 8, 2003): A12.

5 Günther G. Schulze and Heinrich W. Ursprung, "Globalisation of the Economy and the Nation State," *The World Economy* 22, no. 3 (May 1999): 295–352.

6 Martin Wolf, "Economic Globalisation," *Financial Times* (January 23, 2003): The World: 2003 section, iii.

7 "Measuring Globalization," *Foreign Policy* (March/April 2004): 54–70.

8 Betty Liu, "Cross-Border Partnerships," *Financial Times* (March 14, 2003): 9.

9 See Alister Foye, "Money Is Sunny, Barter's Smarter," *Daily Telegraph* (London) (January 24, 2002): 67; "Romania Offset Laws to Change," *Jane's Defence Weekly* (July 3, 2002): Section 1, 18; Loretta Leung, "Barter Trade Tackles Inventory Surplus," *South China Morning Post* (June 21, 2002): 4; and Nancy Dunne, "Barter Grows as Trade Deals Hit Problems," *Financial Times* (September 17, 1998): 7.

10 See Rodney C. Shrader, Benjamin M. Oviatt, and Patricia Phillips McDougall, "How New Ventures Exploit Trade-offs Among International Risk Factors: Lessons for the Accelerated Internationalization of the 21st Century," *Academy of Management Journal* 43, no. 6 (December 2000): 1227–247; and Ian Fillis, "The Internationalization Process of the Craft Microenterprise," *Journal of Developmental Entrepreneurship* 7, no. 1 (April 2002): 25–43.

11 S. Tamer Cavusgil, "Extending the Reach of E-Business," *Marketing Management* 11, no. 2 (March–April 2002): 24–29.

12 Kerry Gildea, "U.S., Japan Review Options for Future Sea-Based Missile Defense Work," *Defense Daily International* 2, no. 36 (July 12, 2002): 1–2.

13 Traditionally, there have been seven countries, the G7 countries; however, Russia now attends meetings, making the group the G8 countries.

14 Thomas L. Friedman, "Moving with the Herd," *Computerworld* 35, no. 3 (January 15, 2001): 41–43; and Daniele Archiburgi and Bengt-Ake Lundvall, eds., *The Globalizing Learning Economy* (Oxford: Oxford University Press, 2001).

15 Keith Bradsher, "Problems with Pirates Continue in Sea Lanes of South Asia," *New York Times* (August 15, 2003): W7.

16 Steve Lohr, "An Elder Challenges Outsourcing's Orthodoxy," *New York Times* (September 9, 2004): C1+; and Paul A. Samuelson, "Where Ricardo and Mill Rebut and Confirm Arguments of Mainstream Economists Supporting Globalization," *The Journal of Economic Perspectives* 18, no. 3 (Summer 2004): 135–47.

17 William M. Bulkeley, "IBM Documents Give Rare Look at 'Offshoring,'" *Wall Street Journal* (January 19, 2004): A1+.

18 Craig Karmin, "Offshoring Can Generate Jobs in the U.S.," *Wall Street Journal* (March 16, 2004): B1.

19 Robert C. Feenstra and Gordon H. Hanson, "The Impact of Outsourcing and High-Technology Capital on Wages: Estimates for the United States, 1979–1990," *Quarterly Journal of Economics* 114, no. 3 (August 1999): 907–940.

20 "Liberty's Great Advance," *The Economist* (June 28, 2003): 5.

21 Alexandra Harney, "Travel Industry," *Financial Times* (September 2, 2004): 11.

22 Carlos Tejada, "Paradise Lost," *Wall Street Journal* (August 14, 2003): A1+.

23 Joseph Stiglitz, *Globalization and Its Discontents* (New York: W.W. Norton, 2002).

24 United Nations Conference on Trade and Development, *World Investment Report 2001: Promoting Linkages* (New York and Geneva: United Nations, 2001), 90–92.

25 Office of Trade and Economic Analysis, "Small and Medium-Sized Enterprises Play an Important Role," *Export America* 2, no. 11 (September 2001): 26–29.

26 Erin Butler, "Building Products Supplier Shares Exporting Secrets," *Export America* 3, no. 3 (March 2002): 6–7.

27 Nery Ynclan, "Avon Is Opening the Door to Spanglish," *Miami Herald* (July 23, 2002): E1.

28 Suzanne Kapner, "Nestlé Says Emerging Markets Help It Show Rise in Profits," *New York Times* (August 23, 2001): W1.

29 United Nations Conference on Trade and Development, *World Investment Report 2004: The Shift Towards Services* (New York and Geneva: United Nations, 2004).

30 Carol Matlock, "The Rise of 'Small Multinationals,'" *Business Week*, February 1, 2005.

31 Mariam Shahin, "When Will Iraq Take Its Place in the 21st Century?" *Middle East* 309 (February 2001): 16–18.

32 Linn Hirschberg, "Is the Face of America That of a Green Ogre?" *New York Times Magazine* (November 14, 2004): 90–94.

33 Terry Hall, "New Zealand Seeks Lost Sheep," *Financial Times* (March 28, 2002): 36.

34 Edward Luce, "Hard Sell to a Billion Consumers," *Financial Times* (April 25, 2002): 14.

35 John Willman, "Multinationals," *Financial Times* (February 25, 2003): Comment & Analysis section, ii.

36 David Wessel and Marcus Walker, "Good News for the Globe," *Wall Street Journal* (September 3, 2004): A7+.

37 Alan M. Rugman and Cecelia Brain, "Multinational Enterprises Are Regional, Not Global," *Multinational Business Review* 11, no. 1 (Spring), 3.

38 James Harding, "Globalisation's Children Strike Back," *Financial Times* (September 11, 2001): 4.

39 The protesting British workers are known as Luddites. See Bob Davis, "Wealth of Nations," *Wall Street Journal* (March 29, 2004): A1.

40 John Ralston Saul, "The Collapse of Globalism," *Harpers* (March 2004): 33–43.

41 Harold James, *The End of Globalisation: Lessons from the Great Depression* (Cambridge, MA: Harvard University Press, 2001).

42 We appreciate the help from Brenda Yester, Vice President, Carnival Cruise Lines, who met with us. We also received information from Margot Cohen, "A New Source of Cheap Ocean Treasure," *Wall Street Journal* (September 22, 2004): A17; "Carnival Cruise Line Profile," http://www.cruise2.com/Profiles/Carnival.html (accessed November 17, 2004); Martin Gerretsen, "Travel Tips in a Post 9/11 World," *Medical Post* 38, no. 38 (October 22, 2002): 50; David F. Carr, "Royal Treatment," *Baseline* (August 1, 2004): 58; Rowland Stiteler, "QM2 Headlines an Extensive Nautical Cast," *Meeting News.com* (March 15, 2004): n.p.; "Who's Who in Cruising," *Caterer and Hotelkeeper* (February 26, 2004): 77; Donald Urquhart, "Greed and Corruption Rooted in Flag of Convenience System," *The Business Times Singapore* (March 9, 2001): n.p.; "Fall 2003: Shipbuilding Back on Course?" http://www.CruiseIndustryNews.com-Cruise (accessed November 19, 2004); Daniel Grant, "Onboard Art," *American Artist* (March 2003): 18; Nicole Harris, "Ditching the Cruise Director," *Wall Street Journal* (April 22, 2004): D1+; Douglas Frantz, "Sovereign Islands," *Miami Herald* (February 19, 1999): A1+; Adrian Sainz, "Cruise Lines Testing Passengers' Temperatures in Midst of SARS Scare," *Associated Press State & Local Wire* (April 25, 2003); Amy Yee, "Cost-cutting Liners Plumb New Depths," *Financial Times* (August 30, 2004): 24; Rana Foroohar, Liz Krieger, Sonia Kolesnikov-Jessop, Joe Cochran, and Colum Murphy, "The Road Less Traveled," *Newsweek* (May 26, 2003): 40; Jonathan Adams, "Vacations: Cruising Nowhere," *Newsweek* (July 14, 2003): 64; Cruise Lines International Association, *The Overview Spring 2004*, msword/reports/overviews/spring04OV.doc.

An Atlas

Satellite television transmission now makes it commonplace for us to watch events as they unfold in other countries. Transportation and communication advances and government-to-government accords have contributed to our increasing dependence on foreign goods and markets. As this dependence grows, updated maps are a valuable tool. They can show the locations of population, economic wealth, production and markets; portray certain commonalities and differences among areas; and illustrate barriers that might inhibit trade. In spite of the usefulness of maps, a substantial number of people worldwide have a poor knowledge of how to interpret information on maps and even of how to find the location of events that affect their lives.

We urge you to use the following maps to build your awareness of geography.

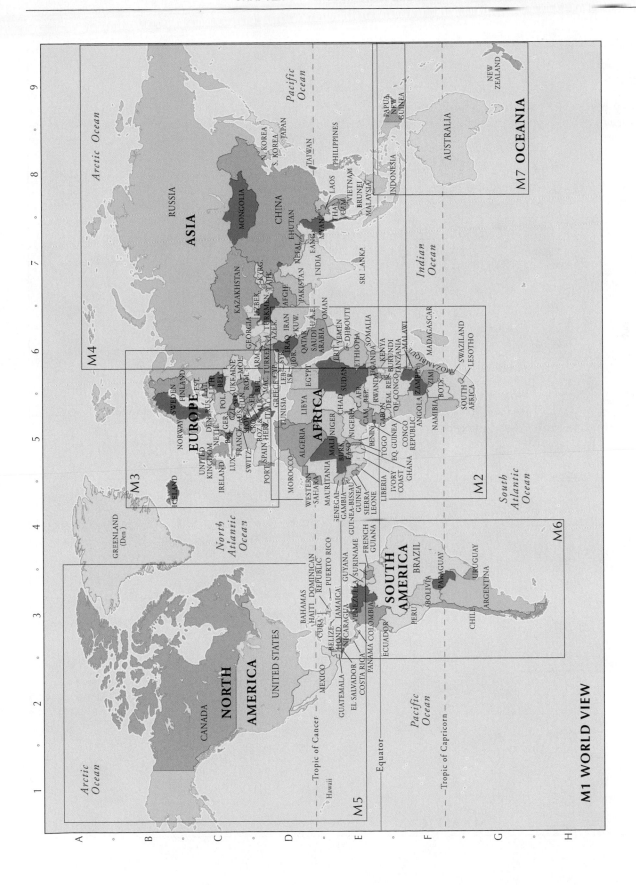

M1 WORLD VIEW

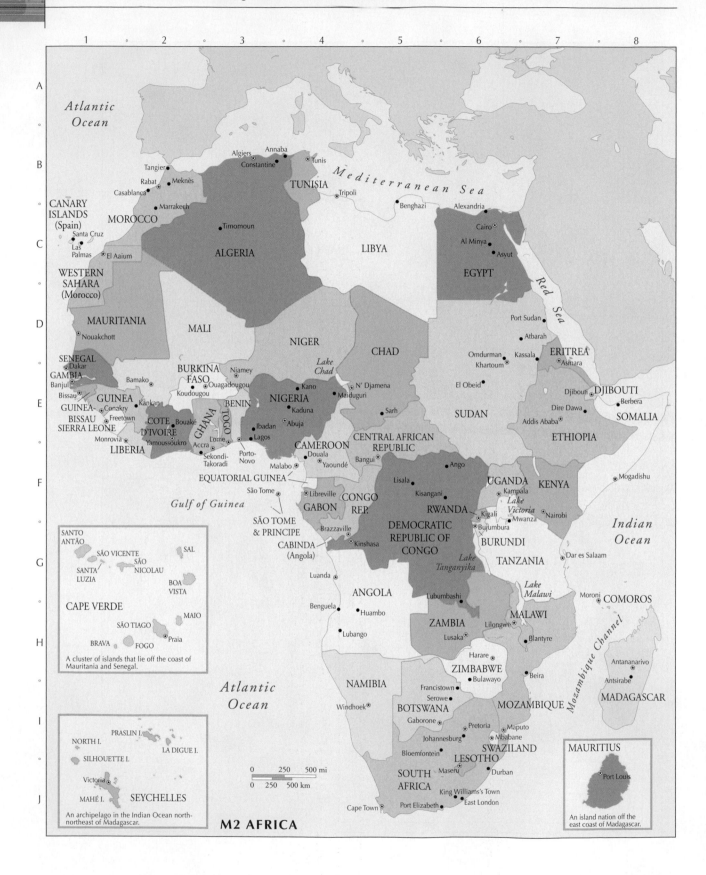

Atlantic
Ocean

Mediterranean Sea

Tangier
Algiers Annaba
Rabat Constantine • Tunis
Casablanca • Meknès
TUNISIA • Tripoli
CANARY Marrakech
ISLANDS MOROCCO
(Spain) Benghazi Alexandria
Santa Cruz • Timomoun Cairo
Las Al Minya
Palmas • El Aaium ALGERIA LIBYA Asyut
WESTERN EGYPT
SAHARA
(Morocco) *Red Sea*

MAURITANIA MALI Port Sudan
Nouakchott NIGER CHAD Atbarah
SENEGAL Omdurman Kassala ERITREA
Dakar BURKINA Niamey *Lake* Khartoum • Asmara
GAMBIA Bamako FASO *Chad* N' Djamena El Obeid Djibouti DJIBOUTI
Banjul Koudougou Ouagadougou Kano Maiduguri Dire Dawa Berbera
Bissau Kankan NIGERIA SUDAN Addis Ababa SOMALIA
GUINEA Conakry Kaduna Sarh ETHIOPIA
GUINEA- Freetown COTE Bouaké GHANA BENIN Ibadan Abuja
BISSAU D'IVOIRE TOGO Lagos CENTRAL AFRICAN
SIERRA LEONE Monrovia Lomé CAMEROON REPUBLIC
LIBERIA Yamoussoukro Accra Douala Bangui Ango Mogadishu
Sekondi- Porto- Yaoundé Lisala UGANDA KENYA
Takoradi Novo Kisangani Kampala
EQUATORIAL GUINEA Malabo Libreville RWANDA *Lake* Nairobi
São Tomé CONGO DEMOCRATIC Kigali *Victoria*
Gulf of Guinea GABON REP. REPUBLIC OF Bujumbura Mwanza *Indian*
SÃO TOMÉ Brazzaville CONGO BURUNDI Dar es Salaam *Ocean*
& PRINCIPE Kinshasa TANZANIA
CABINDA *Lake*
(Angola) *Tanganyika* *Lake*
Luanda Lubumbashi *Malawi* Moroni COMOROS
ANGOLA ZAMBIA MALAWI
Benguela Huambo Lilongwe
Lusaka Blantyre
Lubango Harare Beira
NAMIBIA ZIMBABWE
Francistown Bulawayo Antananarivo
Serowe Antsirabe
Windhoek BOTSWANA MOZAMBIQUE MADAGASCAR
Gaborone Pretoria Maputo
Johannesburg Mbabane
Bloemfontein SWAZILAND
LESOTHO
SOUTH Maseru Durban
AFRICA King Williams's Town
Cape Town Port Elizabeth East London

SANTO
ANTÃO
SÃO VICENTE SAL
SANTA SÃO
LUZIA NICOLAU
BOA
VISTA
CAPE VERDE
SÃO TIAGO MAIO
BRAVA FOGO Praia
A cluster of islands that lie off the coast of
Mauritania and Senegal.

Atlantic
Ocean

PRASLIN I.
NORTH I. LA DIGUE I.
SILHOUETTE I.
Victoria
MAHÉ I. SEYCHELLES
An archipelago in the Indian Ocean north-
northeast of Madagascar.

0   250   500 mi
0   250   500 km

MAURITIUS
Port Louis
An island nation off the
east coast of Madagascar.

M2 AFRICA

M3 EUROPE

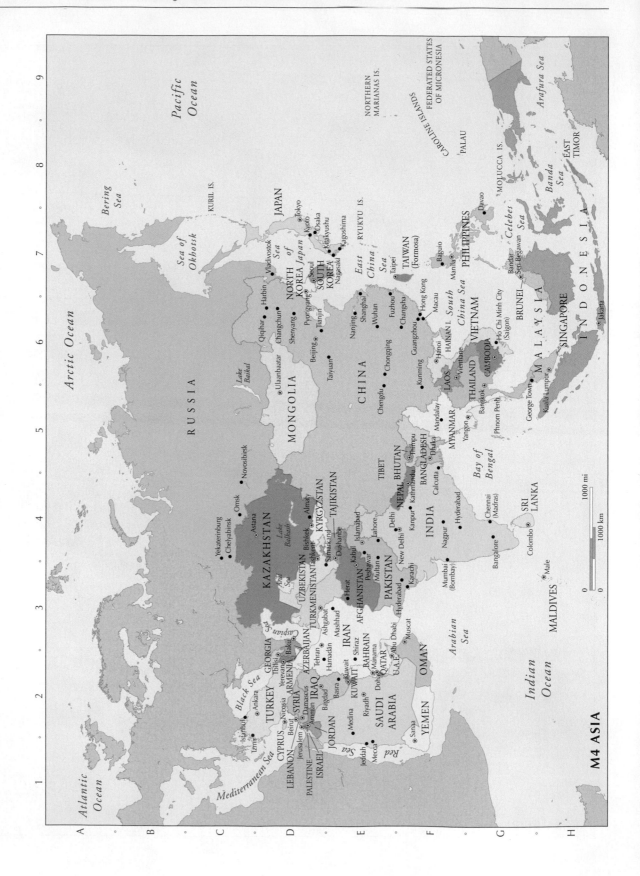

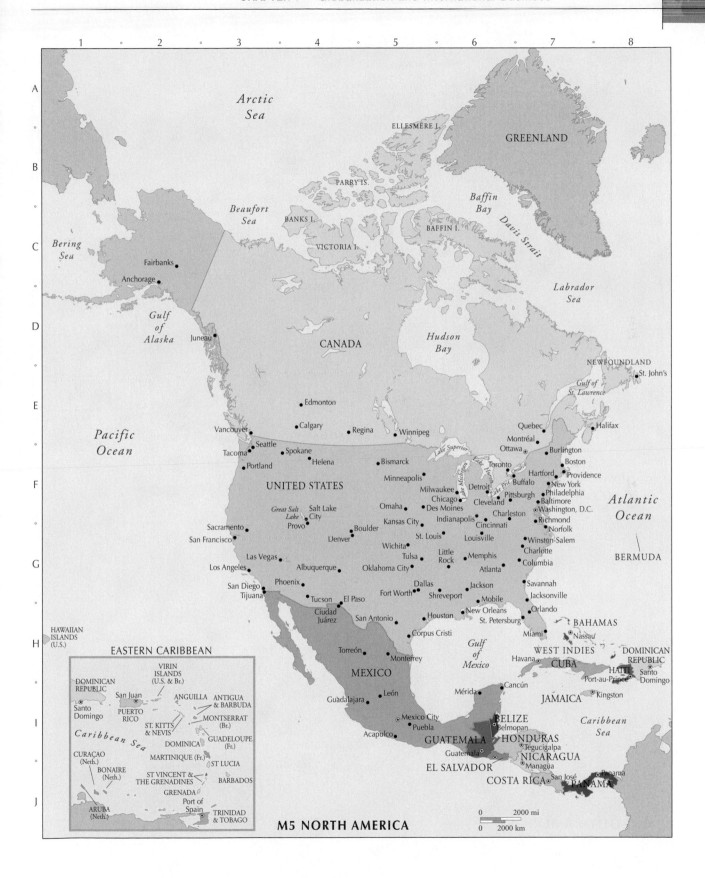

M5 NORTH AMERICA

Arctic Sea

ELLESMERE I.

GREENLAND

PARRY IS.

Baffin Bay

Beaufort Sea

BANKS I.

BAFFIN I.

Davis Strait

VICTORIA I.

Bering Sea

Fairbanks

Anchorage

Labrador Sea

Gulf of Alaska

Juneau

CANADA

Hudson Bay

NEWFOUNDLAND

St. John's

Gulf of St. Lawrence

Pacific Ocean

Edmonton

Calgary

Regina

Winnipeg

Quebec

Halifax

Vancouver

Montréal

Seattle

Ottawa

Burlington

Tacoma

Spokane

Lake Superior

Toronto

Boston

Portland

Helena

Bismarck

Lake Michigan

Lake Huron

Buffalo

Hartford

Providence

Lake Erie

Detroit

New York

Minneapolis

UNITED STATES

Milwaukee

Lake Ontario

Pittsburgh

Philadelphia

Chicago

Cleveland

Baltimore

Great Salt Lake

Salt Lake City

Omaha

Des Moines

Washington, D.C.

Atlantic Ocean

Sacramento

Provo

Kansas City

Indianapolis

Charleston

Richmond

San Francisco

Boulder

Denver

St. Louis

Cincinnati

Norfolk

Louisville

Winston-Salem

Las Vegas

Wichita

Tulsa

Little Rock

Memphis

Charlotte

BERMUDA

Los Angeles

Albuquerque

Oklahoma City

Atlanta

Columbia

San Diego

Phoenix

Dallas

Jackson

Savannah

Tijuana

Tucson

El Paso

Fort Worth

Shreveport

Jacksonville

Mobile

HAWAIIAN ISLANDS (U.S.)

Ciudad Juárez

San Antonio

Houston

New Orleans

Orlando

Corpus Cristi

St. Petersburg

BAHAMAS

Gulf of Mexico

Miami

Nassau

WEST INDIES

DOMINICAN REPUBLIC

EASTERN CARIBBEAN

Torreón

Havana

CUBA

HAITI

Monterrey

Santo Domingo

VIRIN ISLANDS (U.S. & Br.)

Port-au-Prince

DOMINICAN REPUBLIC

San Juan

ANGUILLA

ANTIGUA & BARBUDA

MEXICO

Cancún

JAMAICA

Kingston

Santo Domingo

PUERTO RICO

León

Mérida

MONTSERRAT (Br.)

ST. KITTS & NEVIS

Guadalajara

Caribbean Sea

Caribbean Sea

DOMINICA

GUADELOUPE (Fr.)

Mexico City

CURAÇAO (Neth.)

MARTINIQUE (Fr.)

Puebla

BELIZE

Belmopan

ST LUCIA

Acapulco

Guatemala

HONDURAS

BONAIRE (Neth.)

ST VINCENT & THE GRENADINES

BARBADOS

GUATEMALA

Tegucigalpa

NICARAGUA

GRENADA

EL SALVADOR

Managua

ARUBA (Neth.)

Port of Spain

TRINIDAD & TOBAGO

COSTA RICA

San José

Panama

PANAMA

0   2000 mi

0   2000 km

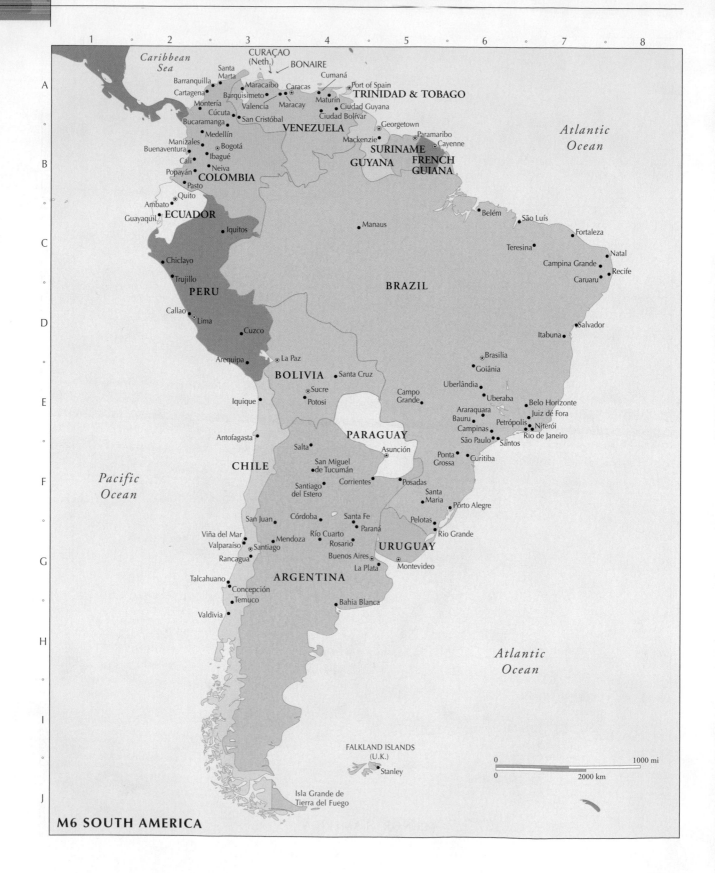

M6 SOUTH AMERICA

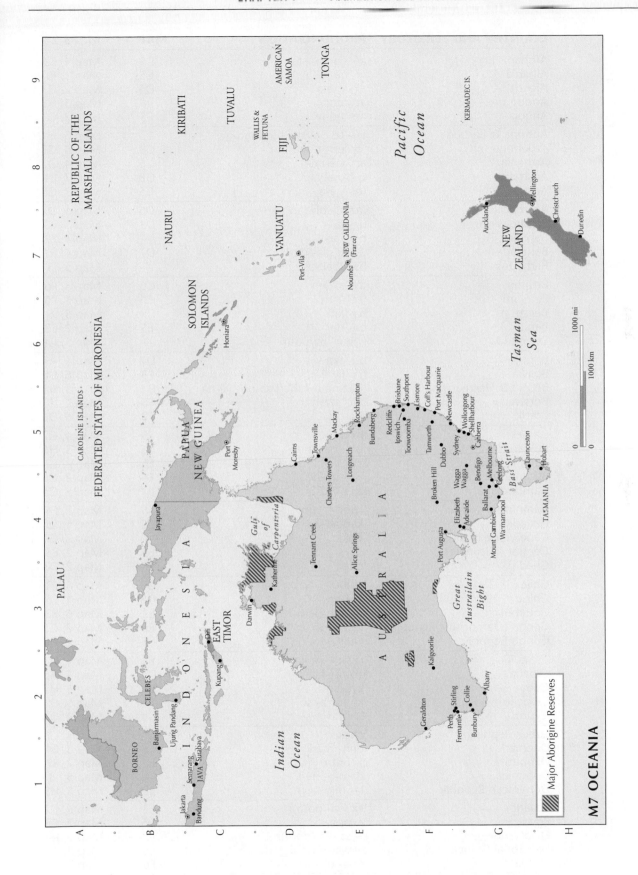

M7 OCEANIA

COUNTRY AND TERRITORY	PRONUNCIATION	MAP 1	MAPS 2-7
Afghanistan	af-'gan-ə-,stan	D7	Map 4, E3
Albania	al-'bā-nē-ə	C5	Map 3, I5
Algeria	al-'jir-ē-ə	D5	Map 2, C3
Andorra	an-'dȯr-ə	—	Map 3, H2
Angola	an-'gō-lə	E5	Map 2, G4
Antigua & Barbuda	an-'tē-g(w)ə / bär-'büd-ə	—	Map 5, I3
Argentina	,är-jen-'tē-nə	G3	Map 6, G3
Armenia	är-'mē-ne-ə	C6	Map 4, D2
Australia	ȯ-'strāl-yə	G8	Map 7, E4
Austria	'ȯs-trē-ə	C5	Map 3, G4
Azerbaijan	,az-ər-,bī-'jän	D6	Map 4, D2
Bahamas	bə-hä'-məz	D3	Map 5, H7
Bahrain	bä-'rān	—	Map 4, E2
Bangladesh	,bänJ-glə-'desh	D7	Map 4, F5
Barbados	bär-'bād-əs	—	Map 5, J3
Belarus	,bē-lə-'rüs	C5	Map 3, F6
Belgium	'bel-jəm	C5	Map 3, F3
Belize	bə-'lēz	D2	Map 5, I6
Benin	bə-'nin	E5	Map 2, E3
Bermuda	(,)bər-'myüd-ə	—	Map 5, G8
Bhutan	bü-'tan	D7	Map 4, F5
Bolivia	bə-'liv-ē-ə	F3	Map 6, E4
Bosnia & Herzegovina	'bäz-nē-ə / ,hert-sə-gō-'vē-nə	D5	Map 3, H5
Botswana	bät-'swän-ə	F5	Map 2, I5
Brazil	brə-'zil	F3	Map 6, D6
Brunei	brōo-nī'	E8	Map 4, G7
Bulgaria	,bəl-'gar-ē-ə	D5	Map 3, H6
Burkina Faso	bùr-'kē-nə-'fȧ-sō	E5	Map 2, E2
Burundi	bù-'rün-dē	E6	Map 2, G6
Cambodia	kam-'bd-ē-ə	E7	Map 4, G5
Cameroon	'kam-ə-'rün	E5	Map 2, F4
Canada	'kan-əd-ə	C2	Map 5, E5
Cape Verde Islands	'vard	—	Map 2, G1
Central African Rep.		E5	Map 2, E5
Chad	'chad	E5	Map 2, D5
Chile	'chil-ē	G3	Map 6, F3
China	'chī-nə	D8	Map 4, E5
Colombia	kə-'ləm-bē-ə	E3	Map 6, B3
Congo (Democratic Republic)	'känJ(,)gō	E5	Map 2, G5
Congo Republic	'känJ(,)gō	E5	Map 2, F4
Costa Rica	,käs-tə-'rē-kə	E2	Map 5, J7
Croatia	krō-'ā-sh(ē)ə	D5	Map 3, H5
Cuba	'kyü-bə	E3	Map 5, H7
Curaçao	'k(y)ür-ə-'sō	—	Map 5, J1
Cyprus	'sī-prəs	D6	Map 4, D2
Czech Republic	'chek	C5	Map 3, G5
Denmark	'den-,märk	C5	Map 3, E4
Djibouti	jə-'büt-ē	E6	Map 2, E7
Dominica	,däm-ə-'nē-kə	—	Map 5, I3
Dominican Republic	də-,min-i-kən	E3	Map 5, H8
Ecuador	'ek-wə-,dȯ(ə)r	E3	Map 6, C2
Egypt	'ē-jəpt	D5	Map 2, C6
El Salvador	el-'sal-və-'dȯ(ə)r	E2	Map 5, I6
Equatorial Guinea	ē-kwa'-tōr-ēal ği-nē	E5	Map 2, F4
Eritrea	,er-ə-'trē-ə	E6	Map 2, E6
Estonia	e-'stō-nē-ə	C5	Map 3, E6
Ethiopia	,ē-thē-'ō-pē-ə	E6	Map 2, E7

COUNTRY AND TERRITORY	PRONUNCIATION	MAP 1	MAPS 2-7
Falkland Islands	'fȯ(l)-klənd	—	Map 6, J4
Fiji	'fē-jē	—	Map 7, D8
Finland	'fin-lənd	B5	Map 3, C6
France	'fran(t)s	C5	Map 3, G3
French Guiana	gē-'an-ə	E3	Map 6, B5
Gabon	ga-'bōⁿ	E5	Map 2, F4
Gambia	'gam-bē-ə	E4	Map 2, E1
Georgia	'jȯr-jə	C6	Map 4, D2
Germany	'jerm-(ə-)nē	C5	Map 3, F4
Ghana	'gän-ə	E5	Map 2, E2
Greece	'grēs	D5	Map 3, I6
Greenland	'grēn-lənd	A4	Map 5, E7
Grenada	grə-nā'də	—	Map 5, J3
Guatemala	ˌgwät-ə-'mäl-ə	E2	Map 5, I6
Guinea	'gin-ē	E4	Map 2, E1
Guinea-Bissau	ˌgin-ē-bis-'aù	E4	Map 2, E1
Guyana	gī-'an-ə	E3	Map 6, B4
Haiti	'hāt-ē	E3	Map 5, H8
Honduras	hän-'d(y)ùr-əs	E2	Map 5, I7
Hong Kong	'häŋ-ˌkäŋ	—	Map 4, F6
Hungary	'həŋ-g(ə)rē	C5	Map 3, G5
Iceland	'ī-slənd	B4	Map 3, B1
India	'in-dē-ə	D7	Map 4, F4
Indonesia	ˌin-də-'nē-zhə	E8	Map 4, H7; Map 7, B3
Iran	i-'rän	D6	Map 4, E3
Iraq	i-'räk	D6	Map 4, D2
Ireland	'ī(ə)r-lənd	C5	Map 3, F1
Israel	'iz-rē-əl	D6	Map 4, D2
Italy	'it-ᵊl-ē	D6	Map 3, H4
Ivory Coast	ī'və-rē	E5	Map 2, E2
Jamaica	jə-'mā-kə	E3	Map 5, I7
Japan	jə-'pan	D8	Map 4, D7
Jordan	'jȯrd-ᵊn	D6	Map 4, D2
Kazakhstan	kə-'zak-'stan	D7	Map 4, D4
Kenya	'ken-yə	E6	Map 7, F7
Kiribati	kîr-ĭ-băs'	—	Map 7, B8
Korea, North	kə-'rē-ə	D8	Map 4, D7
Korea, South	kə-'rē-ə	D8	Map 4, D7
Kuwait	kə-'wāt	D6	Map 4, E2
Kyrgyzstan	kîr-gē-stän'	D7	Map 4, D4
Laos	'laùs	D7	Map 4, F5
Latvia	'lat-vē-ə	C5	Map 3, E6
Lebanon	'leb-ə-nən	D6	Map 4, D2
Lesotho	lə-'sō-(ˌ)tō	F6	Map 2, J6
Liberia	lī-'bir-ē-ə	E5	Map 2, F2
Libya	'lib-ē-ə	D5	Map 2, C4
Liechtenstein	lĭk'tən-stīn'	—	Map 3, G4
Lithuania	ˌlith-(y)ə-'wā-nē-ə	C5	Map 3, E6
Luxembourg	'lək-səm-'bərg	C5	Map 3, G3
Macedonia	'mas-ə-'dō-nyə	D6	Map 3, I6
Madagascar	'mad-ə-'gas-kər	F6	Map 2, I8
Malawi	mə-'lä-wē	F6	Map 2, H6
Malaysia	mə-'lā-zh(ē-)ə	E8	Map 4, G6
Maldives	môl'dīvz	—	Map 4, H3
Mali	'mäl-ē	D5	Map 2, D2
Malta	'mȯl-tə	—	Map 3, J5

COUNTRY AND TERRITORY	PRONUNCIATION	MAP 1	MAPS 2-7
Marshall Islands	mär'shəl	—	Map 7, A8
Mauritania	ˌmȯr-ə-'tā-nē-ə	D5	Map 2, D1
Mauritius	mô-'rĭsh'əs	—	Map 2, J8
Mexico	'mek-si-ˌkō	D2	Map 5, I5
Micronesia	mī'krō-nē'zhə	—	Map 7, A5
Moldova	mäl-'dō-və	D6	Map 3, G7
Mongolia	män-'gōl-yə	D8	Map 4, D5
Morocco	mə-'räk-(ˌ)ō	D5	Map 2, B2
Mozambique	ˌmō-zəm-'bēk	F6	Map 2, H6
Myanmar	'myän-ˌmär	E7	Map 4, F5
Namibia	nə-'mib-ē-ə	F5	Map 2, I4
Naura	nä'-ü-rü	—	Map 7, B7
Nepal	nə-'pȯl	D7	Map 4, E4
Netherlands	'neth-ər-lən(d)z	C5	Map 3, F3
New Caledonia	'kal-ə-'dō-nyə	—	Map 7, E7
New Zealand	'zē-lənd	G9	Map 7, H7
Nicaragua	ˌnik-ə-'räg-wə	E3	Map 5, I7
Niger	'nī-jər	E5	Map 2, D4
Nigeria	nī-'jir-ē-ə	E5	Map 2, E4
Norway	'nȯ(ə)r-ˌwā	C5	Map 3, D3
Oman	ō-'män	E6	Map 4, F2
Pakistan	ˌpak-i-'stan	D7	Map 4, E3
Palau	pä-lou'	—	Map 7, A3
Palestine	pa-lə-'stīn	—	Map 4, D1
Panama	'pan-ə-ˌmä	E3	Map 5, J8
Papua New Guinea	'pap-yə-wə	F9	Map 7, C5
Paraguay	'par-ə-ˌgwī	F3	Map 6, E4
Peru	pə-'rü	F3	Map 6, D2
Philippines	'fil-ə-'pēnz	E8	Map 4, F7
Poland	'pō-lənd	D5	Map 3, F5
Portugal	'pōr-chi-gəl	D5	Map 3, I1
Puerto Rico	'pōrt-ə-'rē(ˌ)kō	E3	Map 5, I2
Qatar	'kät-ər	D6	Map 4, E2
Romania	rō-'mā-nē-ə	D5	Map 3, H6
Russia	'rəsh-ə	C7	Map 3, D7; Map 4, C5
Rwanda	rü-'än-də	E6	Map 2, F6
St. Kitts & Nevis	'kits / 'nē-vəs	—	Map 5, I3
St. Lucia	sānt-'lü-shə	—	Map 5, I3
St. Vincent and the Grenadines	grĕn'ə-dēnz'	—	Map 5, J3
San Marino	săn mə-rē'nō	—	Map 3, H4
São Tomé and Príncipe	soun tōō̄-mĕ'prēn'-sēpə	—	Map 2, F3
Saudi Arabia	'saṷd-ē	E6	Map 4, E2
Senegal	'sen-i-'gȯl	E4	Map 2, D1
Serbia & Montenegro	'sər-bē-ə / ˌmän-tə-'nē-grō	D5	Map 3, H2
Seychelles	sā-shĕlz'	—	Map 2, J1
Sierra Leone	sē-ˌer-ə-lē-'ōn	E4	Map 2, E1
Singapore	'sinJ-(g)ə-'pō(ə)r	—	Map 4, H6
Slovakia	slō-'väk-ē-ə	C5	Map 3, G5
Slovenia	slō-'vēn-ē-ə	C5	Map 3, H5
Solomon Islands	'säl-ə-mən	—	Map 7, C6
Somalia	sō-'mäl-ē-ə	E6	Map 2, F8
South Africa	'a-fri-kə	F6	Map 2, J5
Spain	'spān	C5	Map 3, I1
Sri Lanka	(')srē-'länJ-kə	E7	Map 4, G4
Sudan	sü-'dan	E6	Map 2, E6

COUNTRY AND TERRITORY	PRONUNCIATION	MAP 1	MAPS 2-7
Suriname	sùr-ə-'näm-ə	E3	Map 6, B5
Swaziland	'swäz-ē-,land	F6	Map 2, I6
Sweden	'swēd-ᵊn	B5	Map 3, C5
Switzerland	'swit-sər-lənd	C5	Map 3, G4
Syria	'sir-ē-ə	D6	Map 4, D2
Taiwan	'tī-'wän	D8	Map 4, E7
Tajikistan	tä-,ji-ki-'stan	D7	Map 4, E4
Tanzania	,tan-zə-'nē-ə	F6	Map 2, G6
Thailand	'tī-land	E8	Map 4, F5
Togo	'tō(,)gō	E5	Map 2, E3
Tonga	'tän-gə	—	Map 7, D9
Trinidad & Tobago	'trin-ə-,dad / tə-'bā-(,)gō	—	Map 5, J3
Tunisia	t(y)ü-'nē-zh(ē-)ə	D5	Map 2, B4
Turkey	'tər-kē	D6	Map 4, D2
Turkmenistan	tûrk'-men-i-stăn'	D6	Map 4, D3
Tuvalu	tü'-vä-lü	—	Map 7, C9
Uganda	(y)ü-'gan-də	E6	Map 2, F6
Ukraine	yü-'krān	C6	Map 3, F7
United Arab Emirates	yoo-nī'tid ăr'əb i-mîr'its	D6	Map 4, E2
United Kingdom	king'dəm	C5	Map 3, F2
United States	yù-'nīt-əd-'stāts	D2	Map 5, F5
Uruguay	'(y)ùr-ə-gwī	G3	Map 6, G5
Uzbekistan	(,)ùz-,bek-i-'stan	C6	Map 4, D3
Vanuatu	van-ə-'wät-(,)ü	—	Map 7, D7
Vatican City	văt'ĭ-kən	—	Map 3, H4
Venezuela	,ven-əz(-ə)-'wā-lə	E3	Map 6, A4
Vietnam	vē-'et-'näm	E8	Map 4, G6
Western Sahara	sə-hâr'ə	D4	Map 2, C1
Yemen	'yem-ən	E6	Map 4, F2
Zambia	'zam-bē-ə	F5	Map 2, H5
Zimbabwe	zim-'bäb-wē	F6	Map 2, H6

* in thousands
+ in millions of U.S. dollars
** in U.S. dollars　　　[NA = Not Available]

To change customs is a difficult thing.

—LEBANESE PROVERB

chapter two

The Cultural Environments Facing Business

OBJECTIVES

- To be able to discuss the problems and methods of learning about cultural environments

- To understand the major causes of cultural difference and change

- To grasp behavioral factors influencing countries' business practices

- To become familiar with cultural guidelines for companies that operate internationally

CASE: THE JAVA LOUNGE—ADJUSTING TO SAUDI ARABIAN CULTURE[1]

Saudi Arabia is a land of contrasts and paradoxes. (Map 2.1 shows its location.) It has supermodern cities, but its strict Islamic religious convictions and ancient social customs, on which its laws and customs depend, often clash with modern economic and technical realities. Saudi Arabian authorities sometimes employ latitude in legal formation and enforcement to ease these clashes. Further, some of the ancient social customs have become more lax. Nevertheless, because the latitude and laxness have varied substantially, such as by industry and area of the country, both Saudis and foreigners have sometimes been perplexed about what is accepted personal and business behavior. Foreigners have, in addition, sometimes found Saudi laws and customs contrary to their own value systems.

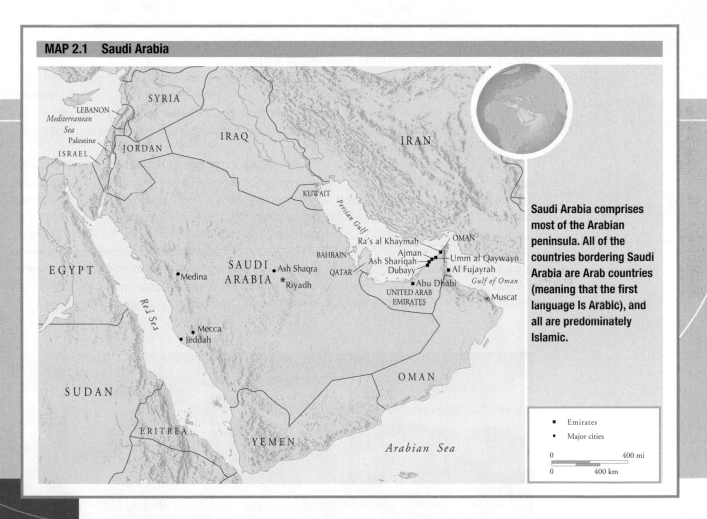

MAP 2.1 Saudi Arabia

Saudi Arabia comprises most of the Arabian peninsula. All of the countries bordering Saudi Arabia are Arab countries (meaning that the first language is Arabic), and all are predominately Islamic.

- ■ Emirates
- • Major cities

Against this backdrop, four young Saudis concluded that the time might be ripe to open a restaurant/lounge that would cater to an affluent clientele. These four young Saudis had all lived and studied abroad, and three of them had one or both parents from Arab countries (Egypt, Lebanon, and Yemen) whose customs were less conservative than those in Saudi Arabia. They had not only experienced foreign restaurants and nightlife, they had enjoyed them. They reasoned there were enough Saudis like themselves to support a foreign-type restaurant/lounge. However, because they harbored sufficient doubts, they hired Lebanese consultants to research the situation for them. Ordinarily, market research groups in Saudi Arabia have not been able to rely on family-focused interviews because of customs limiting male-female interactions except among family members and because Saudis view the home as private and even consider questions about their families as rude and an invasion of privacy. Nevertheless, these consultants successfully interviewed Saudi families by approaching them in restaurants after asking

45

permission to do so from the restaurants' managers. They reasoned that people who were affluent and who had traveled abroad would talk to them. How did they identify the people to approach? Given that women must wear robes (*abayas*) and men customarily wear robes (*thobes*), only people very familiar with Saudi society would be able to discern the economic status of the wearers. Foremost, the researchers noted people's demeanor, such as their manners and confidence in the way they comported themselves. In addition, the researchers distinguished between custom-made and off-the-rack robes, the expensiveness of wristwatches showing at the lower edge of sleeves, and the neatness of men's beards. After completing their interviews, the researchers concluded that there was sufficient market potential.

The four partners opened a very upscale 250-seat restaurant/lounge, the Java Lounge, in 2003. They chose to open in Jeddah because, as a port city, it had more contact with foreigners and was less conservative. For instance, in Saudi Arabia's interior, such as in Riyadh, women traditionally wear *garhas* that cover their faces, but in Jeddah, they do not. Further, the country has religious patrols that may hit women if they are clothed inappropriately, such as if they show any hair in public. However, these patrols are more relaxed about women's dress codes in and around Jeddah.

The appearance of the Java Lounge is no different from what one might find among modern first-class restaurants in any of the world's major cities. Further, Java Lounge's French chef, who had previously worked in Kuwait, prepares dishes that one might find on menus of upscale restaurants in Europe or North America. However, beneath this façade, operations of the Java Lounge have to deviate considerably from what one finds in restaurants outside Saudi Arabia.

To begin with, all Java's employees are male. Despite Saudi Arabia's ratification of an international agreement in 2000 to eliminate discrimination against women, rules on what women can do remain quite rigid and seem paradoxical to outsiders. On the one hand, women now outnumber men in Saudi Arabian universities. (There are separate male and female universities.) Women also own about 20 percent of all Saudi businesses, and a woman is CEO of one of Saudi Arabia's largest companies, the Olayan Financing Company. (However, most female-owned businesses can sell only to women.) Women also comprise a large portion of Saudi teachers and doctors. On the other hand, women account for only about 7 percent of the workforce. They cannot have private law or architectural firms, nor can they be engineers. They are not permitted to drive, because this may lead to evil behavior. They can work alongside men only in a few

The Java Lounge, except for the male-only upstairs section and the hubbly-bubbly apparatuses (common smoking devices found throughout the Middle East), looks very similar to upscale restaurants/lounges one sees in other parts of the world.

professions; they have traditionally worked alongside men in medicine, and they are beginning to do so in hotels and banks as well. If they are employed where men work, they must have separate work entrances and be separated from males by partitions. Usually, an adult male relative must accompany females when they deal with male clerks.

Because of the need to separate the sexes, males coming to the Java Lounge during the day without female accompaniment must use a separate entrance and sit upstairs out of sight of the families and groups of females on the ground floor. In the evening, both floors are only for families. This type of separation occurs in all retail establishments. For instance, Harvey Nichols from the United Kingdom and Saks Fifth Avenue from the United States (both are upper-end department stores) have created women-only floors. On lower levels, there is mixed shopping, all male salespeople (even for products like cosmetics and bras), and no changing rooms or places to try cosmetics. On upper floors, women can check their *abayas* and shop in jeans, spandex, or whatever. The stores have also created drivers' lounges for their chauffeurs. A downside is that male store managers can visit upper floors only when the stores are closed, which limits their observation of situations that might improve service and performance.

People from countries with strict separation between the state and religion or where few people actively engage in religion find Saudi Arabia's pervasiveness of religion daunting. Religious prohibitions prevent Java Lounge from serving any pork products or alcohol, nor can it present live music to the customers. Because there is a large black market for alcohol, Java Lounge's employees must ensure that no customers bring in alcohol to consume on the premises. If authorities were to note such consumption, they would rescind Java's operating license. During the holy period of Ramadan, people fast during the day, thus Java Lounge serves customers only in the evening.

Other companies are also affected by the pervasiveness of religion in Saudi Arabia. For example, an importer halted sales of the children's game Pokémon because the game might encourage the un-Islamic practice of gambling, and a franchisor was forced to remove the face under the crown in Starbucks' logo because Saudi authorities felt the public display of a woman's face was religiously immoral. Coty Beauty omits models' faces on point-of-purchase displays that it depicts in other countries. Companies know that they must remove the heads and hands from mannequins and must not display them scantily clad. Companies also adjust voluntarily to gain the goodwill of customers—for example, by converting revenue-generating space to prayer areas. (Saudi Arabian Airlines does this in the rear of its planes, and Harvey Nichols does this in its department store.) McDonald's dims its lights, closes its doors, and stops attending to customers during the five times per day that men are called to pray. For the period of Ramadan, when people are less active during the day, many stores shift some operating hours to the evenings when people prefer to shop.

Of course, not all operating adjustments in Saudi Arabia are due to religion. Personal interactions between cultures are tricky, and those between Saudis and non-Saudis are no exception. For example, Parris-Rogers International (PRI), a British publishing house, sent two salesmen to Saudi Arabia who failed and had to be recalled. PRI paid them on a commission basis. They expected that by moving aggressively, the two men could make the same number of calls as they could in the United Kingdom. They were used to working eight-hour days, to having the undivided attention of potential clients, and to restricting conversation to the business transaction. To them, time was money. However, they found that appointments seldom began at the scheduled time and most took place while sipping coffee at cafés. To the salesmen, the Saudis spent too much time on idle chitchat and preferred talking to acquaintances rather than discussing business matters. The salesmen began showing so much irritation at "irrelevant" conversations, delays, and interruptions from friends that they caused irrevocable damage to the company's objectives. The Saudi counterparts considered them rude and impatient.

Foreigners working in Saudi Arabia are sometimes traumatized by the country's harsh legal sanctions. Not only are there religious patrols, there are also governmental beheadings and hand-severances in public. The government expects passers-by to observe the punishments, some of which are for crimes that would not be offenses in other countries. For example, the government publicly beheaded three men in 2002 for being homosexuals.

Rules of behavior are also difficult to comprehend because religious and legal rules may sometimes be flexible to fit the situation. For instance, the charging of interest and the purchase of accident insurance are both disallowed under strict Islamic interpretations of the Koran. In the case of interest, the Saudi government gives interest-free loans for mortgages. This worked well when Saudi Arabia was awash with oil money, but borrowers must now wait about 10 years for a loan. In the case of accident insurance (by strict Islamic doctrine, there are no accidents, only preordained acts of God), the government eliminated prohibitions because businesses needed the insurance.

This flexibility is particularly prevalent for foreigners and foreign companies. For instance, Saudis are more lenient toward the visiting female executives of MNEs than toward Saudi women. Whereas they don't allow Saudi women to be flight attendants on Saudi Arabian Airlines, because they would have to work alongside men, they permit women from other Arab countries to do so. Further, in foreign investment compounds, where almost everyone is a foreigner, religious patrols make exceptions to most of the strict religious prescriptions.

But, let's return to the Java Lounge. It has been successful from the start. Its owners understood that there is an affluent niche of consumers in Saudi Arabia who want to emulate the luxury of the West. In fact, the rich people of Saudi Arabia are said to keep Paris couture alive. Even though Saudi Arabia prohibits fashion magazines and movies, this clientele knows what is in fashion. (The government also prohibits satellite dishes, but some estimates say that two-thirds of Saudi homes have them.) Women buy items from designers' collections, which they wear abroad or in Saudi Arabia only in front of their husbands and other women. Underneath their *abayas*, they often wear very expensive jewelry, makeup, and clothing. Men also want the latest high-end fashions when traveling abroad. At the same time, the Java Lounge's owners realized that as more Saudis have interacted with foreigners and as Saudi Arabia has sought to grow economically, changes have been occurring in Saudi Arabian values and social systems. For instance, a female Saudi gave the keynote address at the 2004 Jeddah Economic Forum, something that was unthinkable a few years earlier. (However, Saudi Arabia's highest religious authority later condemned the forum's use of a female speaker.) Nevertheless, these changes have occurred irregularly, more so in some parts of the country than in others and differently among people by income and educational level. Thus, Java Lounge must adhere to many traditional norms that are still deeply embedded in Saudi society.

INTRODUCTION

The opening case shows how important it is for companies to understand and adjust to ever-changing operating environments. Both the Java Lounge, a Saudi Arabian company, and Harvey Nichols, a U.K. company, are successfully operating in Saudi Arabia because of their sensitivity to the Saudi operating environment. Figure 2.1 illustrates that culture

FIGURE 2.1 **CULTURAL INFLUENCES ON INTERNATIONAL BUSINESS**

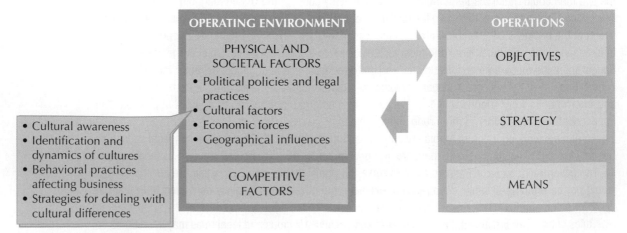

is an integral part of the operating environment. **Culture** refers to the learned norms based on attitudes, values, and beliefs of a group of people. Because people simultaneously belong to different groups that have different cultures—for example, based on their nationality, ethnicity, religion, gender, work organization, profession, age, political party membership, and income level—culture is elusive to study. Our emphasis in this chapter will be on national cultures; however, we'll also explore how the importance of these other cultural memberships may differ by country. The major problems of cultural collision in international business are when

- A company implements practices that work less well than intended.
- A company's employees encounter distress because of an inability to accept or adjust to foreign behaviors.

Business employs, sells to, buys from, is regulated by, and is owned by people. Because international business includes people from different cultures, every business function—managing a workforce, marketing output, purchasing supplies, dealing with regulators, securing funds—is subject to potential cultural problems. An international company must be sensitive to these cultural differences in order to predict and control its relationships and operations. Further, it should realize that its accustomed way of doing business might not be the only or best way. When doing business abroad, a company should first determine what business practices in a foreign country differ from those it's used to. Management then must decide what, if any, adjustments are necessary to operate efficiently in the foreign country.

This chapter will first examine cultural awareness, especially the need for building it. Second, the chapter will discuss the causes of cultural differences, rigidities, and changes. Third, the chapter will describe behavioral factors that affect the conduct of business internationally. Finally, the chapter will explore why businesses and individuals adjust—or don't adjust—to another culture.

CULTURAL AWARENESS

Building cultural awareness of national cultures is not an easy task, and no foolproof method exists for doing so.[2] Visitors to foreign countries remark on cultural differences, experts write about them, and international businesspeople find that they affect operations. Yet controversy surrounds these differences because people disagree on what they are, whether they are widespread or exceptional differences, and whether the differences are deep-seated or superficial. Further, culture cannot easily be isolated from such factors as economic and political conditions. For example, an opinion survey of a country's citizens that measures, say, attitudes toward buying a new product may reflect a response to temporary economic conditions rather than basic values and beliefs that will have lasting effects on the product's acceptance.

Some differences, such as those regarding acceptable attire, are discerned easily; others may be more difficult to perceive. All people have culturally ingrained responses to given situations and sometimes expect that people from other cultures will respond the same way as people in their own culture do. For example, in the opening case, the British salesmen for PRI budgeted their time and so regarded drinking coffee and chatting about nonbusiness activities in a café as "doing nothing," especially if there was "work to be done." In fact, their compensation system did not give them the privilege of spending much time on each business transaction. The Arab businessmen had no compulsion to finish at a given time, viewed time spent in a café as "doing something," and considered "small talk" an indication of whether they could get along with potential business partners. Because the Englishmen believed "you shouldn't mix business and pleasure," they

Almost everyone agrees that national cultures differ, but they disagree on what the differences are.

Problem areas that can hinder managers' cultural awareness are

- Subconscious reactions to circumstances
- The assumption that all societal subgroups are similar

became irritated when friends of the Arab businessmen joined their conversations. In contrast, the Arabs felt "people are more important than business" and saw nothing private about business transactions.

Some people seem to have an innate ability to do and say the right thing at the right time, and others offend unintentionally or misrepresent what they want to convey. Nevertheless, there is general agreement that businesspeople can improve their awareness and sensitivity and that training about other cultures will enhance the likelihood of succeeding in those cultures.

Researching descriptions of a specific culture can be instructive. But managers must carefully assess the information they gather because it sometimes presents unwarranted stereotypes, offers an assessment of only a segment of the particular country, or reports outdated information. In a given society, managers can also observe the behavior of those people who have the respect they would like themselves. Of course, it helps to study the overseas culture directly.

There are so many cultural variations that businesspeople cannot expect to memorize all of them for every country. Wide variations exist even in addressing people. For example, it may be difficult to know whether to use a given name or surname, which of several surnames to use, and whether a wife takes her husband's name. Making a mistake may be construed by foreign businesspeople as merely humorous, or they may perceive their counterpart as ignorant or rude, which may jeopardize a business arrangement. Fortunately, there are guidebooks for particular geographical areas, based on the experiences of many successful international managers. A manager may also consult with knowledgeable people at home and abroad—from governmental offices or in the private sector.

Unfortunately, too often when we can't explain something, such as why the Irish like cold cereal more than the Spanish, we tend simply to attribute the difference to culture without gaining a real understanding. Fortunately, researchers have fairly recently concluded milestone studies involving large numbers of respondents from a large number of countries to determine their attitudes and preferences on a large number of issues that concern business managers.[3] Although we shall report major findings from these studies throughout the chapter, we nevertheless wish to emphasize some of their shortcomings for understanding the conduct of business internationally. First, these studies have covered less than half the world's countries. Second, comparisons among countries must be interpreted cautiously because responses concerning attitudes, such as how satisfied one is with one's work situation, may themselves be affected by culture; for example, some groups of people may be happiest when complaining. Third, although national differences exist in *averages,* the variation within countries is often overlooked when looking only at averages. One writer expressed this latter point colorfully by saying, "Drivers are more likely to stop at a pedestrian crossing in the United Kingdom than in France, but it would be a grave mistake to step out into a British road in the expectation that every motorist will stop."[4] Fourth, cultures evolve, thus what we see as a current attitude may well change in the future. For instance, the opening case gave examples of how attitudes toward women are changing their roles in Saudi Arabia.

IDENTIFICATION AND DYNAMICS OF CULTURES

In the following discussion, we will first explain why nations are a useful, but not perfect, cultural reference for international business. Next, we'll discuss why cultures develop and change. Finally, we'll show the role of language and religion as stabilizing influences on culture.

The Nation as a Point of Reference

Because international business includes all commercial transactions between two or more nations, our discussion in this chapter focuses on national cultures. The nation

Although there are different norms of national cultures, there is a good deal of variation among individuals making up a norm.

provides a workable definition of a culture because the basic similarity among people is both a cause and an effect of national boundaries. The laws governing business operations also apply primarily along national lines. Within the bounds of a nation are people who share essential attributes, such as values, language, and race. There is a feeling of "we," whereas foreigners are "they." National identity is perpetuated through rites and symbols of the country—flags, parades, rallies—and a common perception of history results from the preservation of national sites, documents, monuments, and museums. These shared attributes do not mean that everyone in a country is alike. Nor do they suggest that each country is unique in all respects. In fact, nations usually include various subcultures, ethnic groups, races, and classes, some of which transcend national boundaries (for example, the ethnic Chinese in various Asian countries are hybrids of Chinese and local cultures).[5] Further, individuals' cultural makeup involves a melding of their different cultural memberships (such as gender, profession, etc.) into a national culture that is flexible enough to accommodate this diversity of memberships. In fact, the nation legitimizes itself by being the mediator of the different interests.[6] Failure to serve adequately in this mediating role may cause the nation to dissolve. Nevertheless, each nation possesses certain human, demographic, and behavioral characteristics that constitute its national identity and that may affect a company's methods of conducting business effectively in that country.

Some of the non-national cultures can link groups from different nations more closely than groups within a nation. For instance, regardless of the nation examined, people in urban areas differ in certain attitudes from people in rural areas, and managers have different work attitudes than production workers do. Thus, managers in countries A and B may hold more similar values than they hold with production workers in their own country. When international businesspeople compare nations, they must be careful to examine relevant groups—for example, by differentiating between people in rural and urban areas of a country when predicting what will be accepted. Nevertheless, these groups may differ because of organizational cultures. For example, scientists at Cambridge and MIT set up a well-funded joint institute to enhance the impact of teaching and research on economic success. However, the institute worked poorly, not because of different national or professional cultures, but because of different organizational attitudes toward links with businesses.[7]

The nation is a useful definition of society because

- Similarity among people is a cause and an effect of national boundaries.
- Laws apply primarily along national lines.

Managers find country-by-country analysis difficult because

- Subcultures exist within nations.
- Variations within some countries are great.
- Similarities link groups from different countries.

Globalization brings the traditional in contact with the modernity of other countries. Here we see Bangladeshi women in uniforms conforming to traditional custom. They are making jeans and preparing them strictly for export markets.

Cultural Formation and Dynamics

Cultural value systems are set early in life but may change through

- Choice or imposition
- Contact with other cultures

Culture is transmitted in various ways—from parent to child, teacher to pupil, social leader to follower, and one peer to another. The parent-to-child route is especially important in the transmission of religious and political affiliations. Developmental psychologists believe that by age 10, most children have their basic value systems firmly in place, after which they do not make changes easily. These basic values include such concepts as evil versus good, dirty versus clean, ugly versus beautiful, unnatural versus natural, abnormal versus normal, paradoxical versus logical, and irrational versus rational.[8]

However, individual and societal values and customs may evolve over time. Examining this evolution and its causes may reveal something about the process by which the new practices are accepted, thus aiding international companies that would like to introduce changes into the culture. Change may come about through choice or imposition. Change by choice may take place as a reaction to social and economic changes that present new alternatives. For example, when rural people choose to accept factory jobs, they change their customs by working regular hours that don't allow the social interaction with their families during work hours that farm work allowed. Change by imposition, sometimes called

MAP 2.2   Major Languages of the World

Thousands of languages are spoken globally, but a few dominate. This map shows 12 major ones. Note that English, French, or Spanish is the primary language in a significant portion of the world's countries. Some other languages, such as Mandarin and Hindi, are prevalent in only one country but are important to international business because of the number of speakers.

Source: http://www.udon.de/sprachk.htm. The number of native speakers is taken from *World Almanac and Book of Facts* (Mahwah, NJ: Primedia Reference, 2002).

cultural imperialism, has occurred, for example, when countries introduced their legal systems into their colonies by prohibiting established practices and defining them as criminal. The introduction of some, but not all, elements of an outside culture often is called *creolization, indigenization*, or *cultural diffusion.* In fact, when a company enters a different national culture, its organizational culture there will likely evolve to include elements of the national culture that it enters, elements of its own national and organizational culture, and some hybrids or new approaches that have come from interpersonal negotiations around organizational issues.[9] International business increases interactions among countries, and greater interaction induces cultural change. Thus, governments have often limited such business to protect their national cultures. However, such protection is less successful as people access foreign information through better international communications.[10]

Language as a Cultural Stabilizer

In addition to national boundaries and geographical obstacles, language is a factor that greatly affects cultural stability. Map 2.2 approximates the world's major language

A common language within countries is a unifying force.

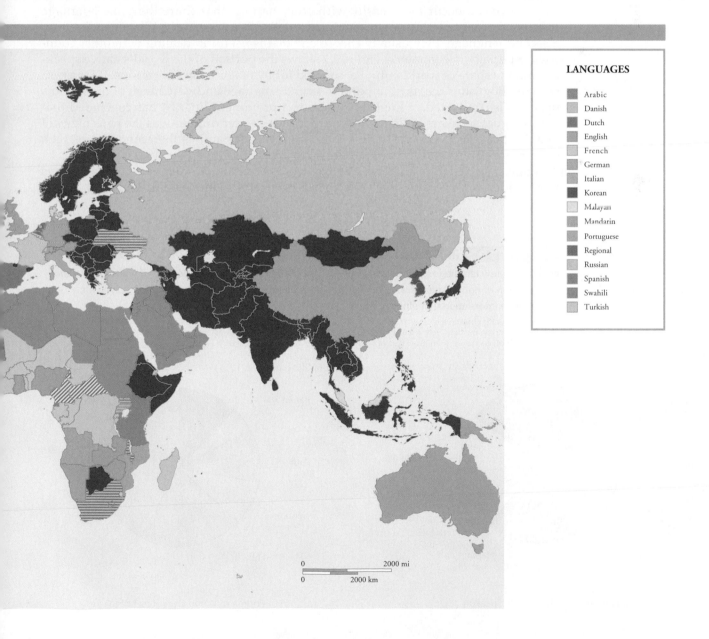

LANGUAGES

- Arabic
- Danish
- Dutch
- English
- French
- German
- Italian
- Korean
- Malayan
- Mandarin
- Portuguese
- Regional
- Russian
- Spanish
- Swahili
- Turkish

| 0 | 2000 mi |
| 0 | 2000 km |

groups. When people from different areas speak the same language, culture spreads more easily. That helps explain why more cultural similarity exists among English-speaking countries or among Spanish-speaking ones than between English-speaking and Spanish-speaking countries. Map 2.2 does not include most of the world's approximately 6,000 languages spoken in small areas by few people. When people speak only a language that has few speakers, especially if those speakers are concentrated in a small geographic area, they tend to adhere to their culture because meaningful contact with others is difficult. For example, in Guatemala, the official language is Spanish. However, there are 22 ethnic groups, three main ethnic languages, and derivations of those three.[11] The ethnic differences in Guatemala (and in some other countries) have led to political strife that undermines a company's ability to conduct business. The language diversity has also made it difficult for companies to integrate their workforces and to market their products on a truly national level.

The English, French, and Spanish languages have such widespread acceptance (they are spoken prevalently in 44, 27, and 20 countries, respectively) that native speakers of these languages haven't generally tried to learn other languages as much as do speakers of languages that are official in only one country, such as Finnish and Greek. Commerce can occur more easily with other nations that share the same language because expensive and time-consuming translation is unnecessary. When people study a second language, they usually choose one that is useful in dealing with other countries, especially in commerce. Figure 2.2 shows the portion of the world's native speakers and the share of world output accounted for by major language groups. It is easy to see why English is the most important second language and why much of the world's business is conducted in English. However, a prominent linguist has concluded that monolingual speakers of English will experience greater difficulty as the percentage of people speaking English as a first language decreases and as the economies of such countries as China and India continue to grow very rapidly.[12]

English, especially American English, words are making their way into languages worldwide, partly because the United States originates so much new technology as well

FIGURE 2.2   IMPORTANCE OF MAJOR LANGUAGE GROUPS: TWO VIEWS

Note that a few languages, especially English, account for a much larger portion of world output than for a portion of native speakers in the world. This influences the extensive use of English as a second language in international business.

Sources: Data for the chart on the left were taken from CIA. *The World Factbook* (**www.cia.gov/cia/publications/factbook/fields/2098**). Data for the chart on the right were calculated by using GDP figures from World Development Indicators database, World Bank (September 2004) and country language figures from Wikipedia (en.wikipedia.org/wiki/List_of_official languages).

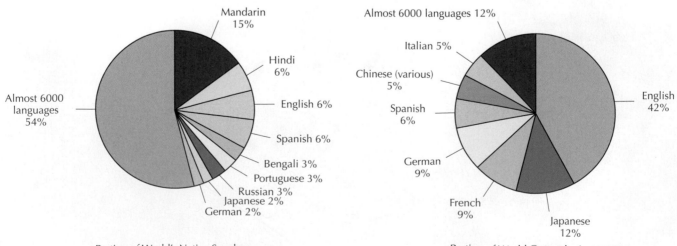

Portion of World's Native Speakers   Portion of World Output by Language

as so many products and services. When a new product or service enters another language area, it may take on an Anglicized name. For example, Russians call tight denim pants *dzhinsi* (pronounced "jeansy"), and the French call a self-service restaurant *le self*. An estimated 20,000 English words have entered the Japanese language. The intrusion of a foreign word is sometimes humorous to speakers of both languages, such as a sign in Spanish, *"Vendemos blue jeans en varios colores,"* which translates into English as "We sell various colors of blue jeans." As English has entered other languages, we see the development of hybrids, such as Spanglish (Spanish and English) and Chinglish (Mandarin Chinese and English), that may ultimately become separate languages.[13] However, some countries, such as Finland, have largely developed their own new words rather than use Anglicized versions. Because countries see language as an integral part of their cultures, they sometimes regulate their languages—for example, by requiring that all business transactions be conducted and all "Made in " labels be printed in their languages.

Religion as a Cultural Stabilizer

Religion is a strong shaper of values. Map 2.3 shows the approximate distribution of the world's major religions. In many countries, direct religious influence has been declining, so much so, for example, that northern European countries are sometimes called post-Christian societies. Nevertheless, because of centuries of direct religious influence, many of the strong values within these societies have come from the historical domination of a particular religion.[14] Within these religions—Buddhism, Christianity, Hinduism, Islam, and Judaism—are many factions whose specific beliefs may affect business, such as prohibiting the sale of certain products or work at certain times. For example, McDonald's serves neither beef nor pork in India so as not to offend its Hindu and Muslim populations,[15] and El Al, the Israeli national airline, does not fly on Saturday, the holy day in Judaism. But not all nations that practice the same religion have the same constraints on business. For example, Friday is normally not a workday in predominantly Muslim countries because it is a day of worship; however, Turkey is a secular Muslim country that adheres to the Christian work calendar in order to be more productive in business dealings with Europe. In areas in which rival religions vie for political control, the resulting strife can cause so much unrest that business is disrupted through property damage, difficulty in getting supplies, and the inability to reach customers. In recent years, violence among religious groups has erupted in such countries as India, Iraq, Nigeria, and Northern Ireland.

Many strong values are the result of a dominant religion.

DOES GEOGRAPHY MATTER?

Birds of a Feather Flock Together

Culture and geography are related in several ways as they affect each other. In this section, we'll discuss the effects of isolation versus openness, natural conditions, proximity, and clustering.

Some groups of people are more isolated from the rest of the world than others by virtue of their natural barriers (e.g., terrain and remoteness from other areas) and human processes (for example, unique language, transportation and communications connections to the outside, and xenophobia). The more isolated people are, the less likely they will influence and be influenced by other cultures. Historically, the natural barriers were very important, causing the growth of many big cities where waterways allowed the interchange of people and goods. Although airplanes and communications systems have rendered many of the natural barriers less formidable, these natural barriers still play a role. Thus, at an extreme, the isolation of tribes from each other in Papua New Guinea has resulted in about 800 different languages and little cultural diffusion either among them or with the rest of the world. Apart from the extreme, some locations have much more outside contact than others. For instance, in the opening case Jeddah, a coastal port of Saudi Arabia, has more contact externally than the Saudi Arabian interior and therefore, it has adopted more from outside cultures.

Natural conditions obviously differ globally, and these conditions affect people's preferred physical culture; that is, the Inuits of the Arctic are not likely to be influenced to accept the beachwear seen on *Baywatch*, regardless of how enamored they are with the TV show. Further, differences in natural conditions affect language, such as the Inuits having many more words than any other language to describe types of snow.

Proximity also affects cultural diffusion. People generally have more contact with groups nearby than far away. For instance, if you look at maps 2.2 and 2.3, you'll see

MAP 2.3   Major Religions of the World

Almost all regions have people of various religious beliefs, but a region's culture is most influenced by its dominant religion. Some religions' areas of dominance transcend national boundaries. The dominant religion usually influences legal and customary business practices, such as required days off for religious observance.

Source: The numbers for adherents are taken from *World Almanac and Book of Facts,* Center for the Study of Global Christianity, Gordon-Conwell Theological Seminary. World Christian Database, www.worldchristiandatabase.org, accessed September 2005. Reprinted with permission

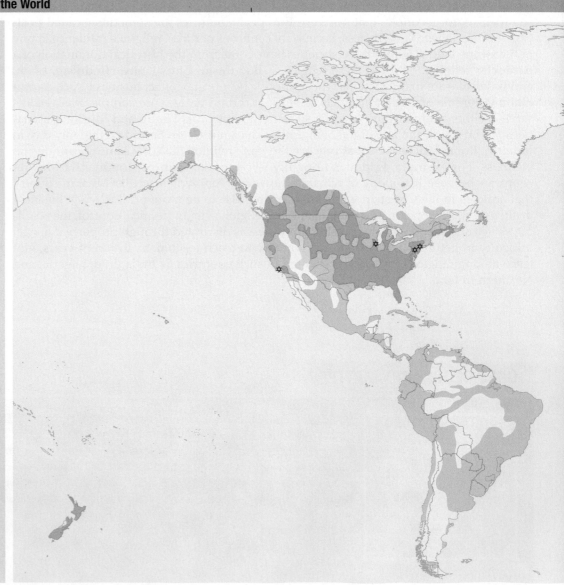

how languages and religions have tended to spread incrementally across the globe. The German-speaking countries are adjacent to each other, as are the Arabic- and most of the Spanish-speaking countries. There are similar clusters of Christianity, Islam, and Buddhism. However, although this incremental movement of culture generally holds, there are some notable exceptions created by colonization and immigration. For instance, the English and Spanish languages spread to distant parts of the world during the era of colonization.

The adage, "Birds of a feather flock together," is apropos in helping to explain the existence of clusters of people who form a subculture within national cultures. Thus, familiarity and support groups influence immigration patterns. For instance, within the United States, there is a heavy concentration of Central Americans in the Los Angeles area. New immigrants from Central America feel comfortable going there because, even if they don't have friends and family already there, they will find affinity in maintaining their language, eating habits, and general customs. Globally, we find many such patterns, such as the Hong Kong Chinese in British Columbia, Canada, and Algerians in Marseilles, France.

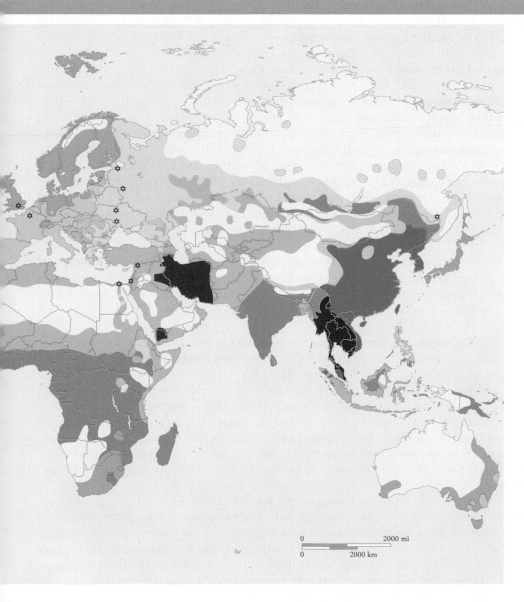

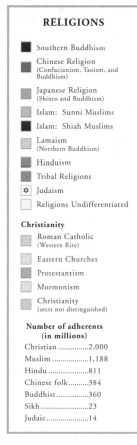

RELIGIONS

■ Southern Buddhism

■ Chinese Religion
(Confucianism, Taoism, and Buddhism)

■ Japanese Religion
(Shinto and Buddhism)

□ Islam: Sunni Muslims

■ Islam: Shiah Muslims

□ Lamaism
(Northern Buddhism)

■ Hinduism

■ Tribal Religions

✡ Judaism

□ Religions Undifferentiated

Christianity

□ Roman Catholic
(Western Rite)

□ Eastern Churches

■ Protestantism

□ Mormonism

□ Christianity
(sects not distinguished)

**Number of adherents
(in millions)**

Christian 2,000
Muslim 1,188
Hindu 811
Chinese folk..........384
Buddhist...............360
Sikh 23
Judaic....................14

0   2000 mi

0   2000 km

BEHAVIORAL PRACTICES AFFECTING BUSINESS

Attitudes and values affect business behavior, from what products to sell to how to organize, finance, manage, and control operations. Researchers define cultural variables differently, attaching different names to slightly different and sometimes overlapping attitudes and values. Similarly, businesspeople define business functions differently. The result is that there are thousands of possible ways of relating culture to business—too many to discuss exhaustively in one chapter. The following discussion merely highlights those that international managers and academic researchers have most noted as influencing different business practices from one country to another. We shall further discuss the effect of these and other cultural variables in later chapters.

Social Stratification Systems

Every culture values some people more highly than others, and such distinctions dictate a person's class or status within that culture. In business, this might mean valuing members of managerial groups more highly than members of production groups. However, what determines the ranking—or social stratification—varies substantially from country to country. A person's ranking is partly determined by individual factors and partly by the person's affiliation or membership in given groups. Affiliations determined by birth—known as **ascribed group memberships**—include those based on gender, family, age, caste, and ethnic, racial, or national origin. Affiliations not determined by birth are called **acquired group memberships** and include those based on religion, political affiliation, and professional and other associations. Social stratification affects such business functions as marketing. For example, companies choose to use people in their advertisements that their target market admires or with whom they associate.

Further, stratification affects employment practices. A study comparing banks' hiring, promotion, compensation, and staff reduction functions showed that they differed by nationality on all four functions. For example, when the banks needed to make staff reductions, British banks were most prone to discharge on the basis of performance-to-salary to save costs (for example, a middle-age manager with high salary and average performance) and German banks to discharge on the basis of minimizing personal hardship (for example, young managers, regardless of performance, who could find jobs more easily.[16]

The following discussion centers on some of the characteristics and group memberships that influence a person's ranking from country to country. In addition, two other factors are often very important—education (especially how much and where it was received) and social connections (having friends in the right places).[17]

Performance Orientation   Some nations, such as the United States, base a person's eligibility for jobs and promotions primarily on competence, creating a work environment driven more by competition than by cooperation. The United States values competence so highly that legislative and judicial actions aim to prevent discrimination on the basis of sex, race, age, and religion, even though such legislation is not fully effective. But in some other cultures, individual competence is of secondary importance. Whatever factor has primary importance—whether seniority, as in Japan (where the workplace is characterized more by cooperation than by competition), or humaneness (kindness and tolerance of mistakes)—will largely influence a person's eligibility for certain positions and compensation.[18]

The more egalitarian, or open, a society, the less difference ascribed group membership makes for receiving rewards. However, in less open societies, laws sometimes are a way to enforce or are a means to overcome distinctions on the basis of ascribed group memberships. Laws requiring racial or ethnic quotas usually aim to counter discrimination. For example, Malaysia has long had employment quotas for three ethnic groups—Malays, Chinese, and Indians—to protect employment opportunities for Malays.

Group affiliations can be

- Ascribed or acquired
- A reflection of class and status

Businesses reward competence highly in some societies.

Egalitarian societies place less importance on ascribed group memberships.

Brazil, which has more than 300 terms to designate skin color, has proposed racial quotas in universities, government jobs, and television soap operas.[19] (It plans no such quotas for the national football team, where only competence counts.) However, critics argue that quotas favor less competent over more competent people and are, therefore, discriminatory. In other cases, group memberships prevent large numbers of people from getting the preparation that would equally qualify them for jobs. For example, in much of sub-Saharan Africa, the literacy rate for women is much lower than for men, for example, 42 percent and 52 percent of men's literacy rate in Niger and Mali, respectively.[20] Companies face very different workforces from one country to another in terms of who is qualified and who among the qualified they can and do hire. In some places, such as Malaysia, they must also maintain expensive record-keeping systems.

Even when individuals qualify for certain positions and there are no legal barriers to hiring them, social obstacles, such as public opinion in a company's home country against the use of child labor, may make companies wary of employing them abroad. Further, other workers, customers, local stockholders, or government officials may oppose certain groups, making it even more difficult for companies to hire them.

Gender-Based Groups   There are strong country-specific differences in attitudes toward males and females. In China and India, there has been an extreme degree of male preference. Because of their governmental and economic pressures on family size along with personal preferences to have a son to carry on the family name and to avoid the payment of dowries by brides' families, the practices of aborting female fetuses and killing female babies are widespread despite government opposition. In fact if present trends continue, 40 million Chinese men will be unable to find women to marry by 2020.[21] However, many Chinese and Indian females have been successful in business and government positions. In some countries, such as Egypt and Qatar, there is a strong preference against gender equality.[22]

Differences among countries toward women in the workforce are particularly pronounced. The opening case indicated that women account for only 7 percent of the Saudi Arabian workforce or more than 13 men employed for every woman employed. In contrast, there are 1.2 men employed for every woman employed in the United States.[23] Even more telling are some differences in attitudes toward employing males and females. For example, more than 50 percent of both males and females in Lithuania agreed with the statement, "When jobs are scarce, men have more of a right to a job than women," but less than 10 percent of both males and females agreed with the statement in Sweden and Iceland.[24]

Barriers to employment based on gender are easing substantially in many parts of the world. Statistical and attitudinal studies from even a few years ago may be considered unreliable. One change has been the growing numbers of women and men in the United States employed in occupations previously dominated by the other gender. For instance, nursing was once a strictly female endeavor, but now about two-fifths of U.S. students in nursing school are men.[25] Another change throughout the industrial world has been the change in composition of jobs, with a decrease in production jobs requiring brawn and an increase in jobs for people who still use their hands, but who need to acquire knowledge through formal education, such as X-ray technicians and psychiatric case workers. As these shifts have occurred, the relative demand for female employees has increased.

Age-Based Groups   Many cultures assume that age and wisdom are correlated. These cultures usually have a seniority-based system of advancement. But in the United States, retirement at age 60 or 65 was mandatory in most companies until the 1980s, revealing that youth has the professional advantage. For example, U.S. television scriptwriters complain of an inability to find jobs after age 30. The emphasis on youth also explains the big U.S. market for products that are designed to make people look younger. However, this esteem for youth has not carried over into the U.S. political realm, where there is no mandatory retirement age. This difference in attitude toward age between business and government illustrates the issue's complexity. Further, there are substantial national

Country-by-country attitudes vary toward

• Male and female roles
• Respect for age
• Family ties

differences in response to the statement, "When jobs are scarce, people should be forced to retire early." For instance, almost three-quarters of respondents agree in Bulgaria, but only 10 percent in Japan.[26] Clearly, companies need to examine reference groups when considering whom they may hire and how best to promote their products.

Family-Based Groups   In some societies, the family is the most important group membership. An individual's acceptance in society largely depends on the family's social status or respectability rather than on the individual's achievement. Because family ties are so strong, there also may be a compulsion to cooperate closely within the family unit while distrusting relationships with others. In societies in which there is low trust outside the family, such as in China and southern Italy, small family-run companies are quite successful, but these companies have difficulty in growing successfully because of their reluctance to share responsibility with professional managers. The difficulty of growing and sustaining family-run companies also retards the development of indigenously owned large-scale operations, which are often necessary for many products and may be important for long-term economic development.[27]

Occupation   In every society, people perceive certain occupations as having greater economic and social prestige than others. This perception usually determines the numbers and qualifications of people who will seek employment in a given occupation. Most of these perceptions are fairly universal; for example, professionals outrank street cleaners. Generally, the higher prestige occupations are also better paid. Jobs with low prestige usually go to people whose skills are in low demand. In the United States, occupations such as babysitting, delivering newspapers, and carrying groceries traditionally go to teenagers, who leave these jobs as they age and gain additional training. In most poor countries, these are not transient occupations but are filled by adults who have very little opportunity to move on to more rewarding positions.

There are some national differences in terms of whether people prefer to be self-employed versus working for an organization. For example, in comparing the United States with the European Union, Americans have a higher preference for being self-employed and worry less about the risk of failure than the Europeans. Within the European Union, there are also differences such as the Irish having a higher preference for self-employment and a higher tolerance for risk than the Germans.[28]

Work Motivation

Employees who are motivated to work long and hard are normally more productive than those who are not. On an aggregate basis, this influences economic development positively. For example, a study on why some areas of Latin America, such as Antioquia in Colombia, developed a higher economic level than others attributed differences to an early development of a strong work ethic.[29] International companies are concerned about economic development because markets for their products grow as economies grow. They are also interested in motivation because higher productivity normally reduces production costs. Studies show substantial country-to-country differences in how much people are motivated to work and why. The following discussion summarizes the major differences.

The desire for material wealth is

- A prime motivation to work
- Positive for economic development

Materialism and Leisure   Max Weber, an early twentieth-century German sociologist, observed that the predominantly Protestant countries were the most economically developed. Weber attributed this fact to an attitude he labeled "the Protestant ethic." According to Weber, the Protestant ethic—an outgrowth of the Reformation—reflected the view that work is a way to gain salvation. Adhering to this view, people preferred to transform productivity into material gains rather than into leisure time. While this difference between Protestant and non-Protestant attitudes may no longer reflect differences in economic achievement among countries, we do find evidence that there is a positive correlation between intensity of religious belief per se (regardless of whether one is

Protestant, Catholic, Jewish, Buddhist, Hindu, or Muslim) and belief in attributes that lead to economic growth, such as belief in obeying laws and engaging in thriftiness.[30] Although this view of work as a means of salvation is weak across countries, some of the work ethic that came from this philosophy has become embedded in cultures. Further, there is strong evidence that the desire for material wealth is a prime incentive for the work that leads to economic development.[31]

Some societies take less leisure time than others, which means they work longer hours, take fewer days for holidays and vacation, and spend less time and money on leisure. For example, on average, the Japanese take less leisure time than do people in any other wealthy country. In the United States, another country where incomes probably allow for considerably more leisure time than most people use, there is still much disdain, on the one hand, for the millionaire socialite who contributes nothing to society and, on the other hand, for the person who receives unemployment benefits. People who are forced to give up work, such as retirees, complain of their inability to do anything useful. This view contrasts with views in some other societies. In much of Europe, people have been more prone than in the United States to take added productivity in the form of leisure rather than income.[32] In parts of some poor countries, such as in rural India, living a simple life with minimum material achievements is a desirable end in itself. When there are productivity gains, people are prone to work less rather than earn and buy more.[33]

However, most people today consider personal economic achievement to be commendable regardless of whether they live in wealthy or poor countries. Most people believe they would be happy with just "a little bit more," until they have that "little bit more," which then turns out to be "not quite enough." Nevertheless, countries differ in their degree of materialism. For example, some leaders in poor countries are rejecting the labels of *traditional* for themselves and *progressive* for the higher-income countries, as they stress the need for a culture that combines material comforts with spirituality.[34]

Expectation of Success and Reward One factor that motivates a person's behavior toward working is the perceived likelihood of success and reward. Generally, people have little enthusiasm for efforts that seem too easy or too difficult, where the probability of either success or failure seems almost certain. For instance, few of us would be eager to run a foot race against either a snail or a racehorse because the outcome in either case is too certain. Our highest enthusiasm occurs when the uncertainty is high—in this example, when racing another human of roughly equal ability. The reward for successfully completing an effort, such as winning a race, may be high or low as well. People usually will work harder at any task when the reward for success is high compared with that of failure.

The same tasks performed in different countries will have different probabilities of success, different rewards for success, and different consequences for failure. In cultures in which the probability of economic failure is almost certain and the perceived rewards of success are low, there is a tendency to view work as necessary but unsatisfying. Because people see little self-benefit from their efforts, this attitude may exist in harsh climates, in very poor areas, or in subcultures that are the objects of discrimination. In areas such as Cuba, where public policies distribute output from productive to unproductive workers, enthusiasm for work is low. The greatest enthusiasm for work exists when high uncertainty of success is combined with the likelihood of a very positive reward for success and little or none for failure.[35]

Assertiveness The average interest in career success varies substantially among countries. For example, one study compared the attitudes of employees from 50 countries on what it called a *masculinity-femininity index*. Employees with a high masculinity score were those who admired the successful achiever, had little sympathy for the unfortunate, and preferred to be the best rather than on a par with others. They had a money-and-things orientation rather than a people orientation, a belief that it is better "to live to work" than "to work to live," and a preference for performance and growth over quality of life and the environment. The countries with the highest masculinity scores

National norms differ in preference for performance and growth versus quality of life and the environment.

The motives for working vary in different countries.

Employees' work attitudes may change as they achieve economic gains.

People are more eager to work if

- Rewards for success are high.
- There is some uncertainty of success.

were Japan, Austria, Venezuela, and Switzerland. Those with the lowest scores were Sweden, Norway, the Netherlands, and Denmark.[36] Similarly, countries differ in the degree that individuals are assertive, confrontational, and aggressive in their relationships with others. These attitudinal differences help explain why local managers typically are motivated to react in different ways from country to country, sometimes in ways that an international manager may neither expect nor wish. For instance, a typical purchasing manager from a low masculinity country has a high need for smooth social relationships that transforms into more concern with developing an amiable and continuing relationship with suppliers than with, say, reducing costs or speeding delivery. Or local managers in some countries may place such organizational goals as employee and social welfare ahead of the foreign company's priorities for growth and efficiency.

Need Hierarchy   The hierarchy of needs is a well-known motivation theory. According to the theory, people try to fulfill lower-order needs sufficiently before moving on to higher ones.[37] People will work to satisfy a need, but once it is fulfilled, it is no longer a motivator. The Calvin and Hobbes cartoon in Figure 2.3 ties the hierarchy of needs theory to materialism theory humorously. Because lower-order needs are more important than higher-order ones, they must be nearly fulfilled before any higher-order need becomes an effective motivator. For instance, the most basic needs are physiological, including the needs for food, water, and sex. One needs to satisfy or nearly satisfy a physiological need before a security need becomes a powerful motivator. Then one must satisfy the security need, centering around a safe physical and emotional environment, before triggering the need for affiliation, or social belonging (peer acceptance). After filling the affiliation need, a person may seek an esteem need—the need to bolster one's self-image through recognition, attention, and appreciation. The highest-order need is that for self-actualization, which means self-fulfillment, or becoming all that it is possible for one to become.

The hierarchy of needs theory is helpful for differentiating the reward preferences of employees in different countries. In very poor countries, a company can motivate workers simply by providing enough compensation for food and shelter. Elsewhere, other needs will motivate workers. Researchers have noted that people from different countries attach different degrees of importance to needs and even rank some of the higher-order needs differently. Figure 2.4 illustrates these differences.

> The ranking of needs differs among countries.

FIGURE 2.3

A fulfilled need is no longer a motivator. Materialism motivates work, which leads to productivity and economic growth.

Source: CALVIN AND HOBBES © Watterson, Reprinted with permission of UNIVERSAL PRESS SYNDICATE. All rights reserved.

Calvin and Hobbes   by Bill Watterson

FIGURE 2.4 | **THE HIERARCHY OF NEEDS AND NEED-HIERARCHY COMPARISONS**

The lower hierarchy on the right has a wider affiliation bar (3) and a narrower self-actualization bar (5) than the upper one. People represented by the lower hierarchy require more affiliation needs to be fulfilled before a self-esteem need (4) will be triggered as a motivator. These people would be less motivated by self-actualization than would those represented by the upper hierarchy.

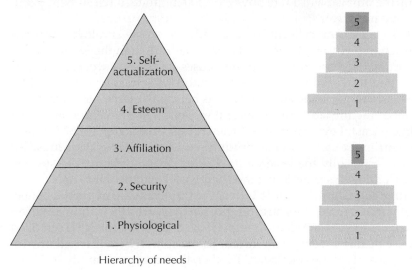

Hierarchy of needs

Relationship Preferences

We have discussed two categories of behavioral practices affecting business—social stratification systems and work motivation. Within social stratification systems, not everyone within a reference group is necessarily an equal. Further, there may be strong or weak pressures for conformity within one's group. In both cases, there are national differences in norms that influence management styles and marketing behavior. The following section discusses the values underlying these differences.

Power Distance   Employee preferences in how to interact with their bosses, subordinates, and peers varies substantially internationally. There is considerable anecdotal evidence that they perform better when their interactions fit their preferences. Therefore, companies may need to align their management styles to those preferences.

Power distance is a term describing the relationship between superiors and subordinates. Where power distance is high, people prefer little consultation between superiors and subordinates—usually wanting and having an autocratic or paternalistic management style in their organizations. Where power distance is low, people prefer and usually have consultative styles.[38]

If an international company transferred typical Dutch managers (typically low-power distance) to Morocco (typically high-power distance), these managers might consult with their subordinates in an attempt to improve their work. However, these efforts might make subordinates feel so uncomfortable that their performance deteriorates rather than improves.

It is interesting that those employees preferring an autocratic style of superior-subordinate relationship are also willing to accept decision making by a majority of subordinates. What they don't accept is the interaction between superiors and subordinates in decision making. Clearly, it may be easier for organizations to initiate certain types of worker-participation methods in some countries than in others.

There are national variations in preference for autocratic or consultative management.

Individualism Versus Collectivism   Studies have compared employees' inclinations toward *individualism* or *collectivism*. Attributes of individualism are low dependence on the organization and a desire for personal time, freedom, and challenge. Attributes of collectivism are dependence on the organization and a desire for training, good physical conditions, and benefits. In those countries with high individualism, self-actualization will be a prime motivator because employees want challenges. However, in countries with high collectivism, the provision of a safe physical and emotional environment (security need) will be a prime motivator.[39]

The degree of individualism and collectivism also influences how employees interact with their colleagues. Japan has a much more collectivist culture than the United States does, especially concerning the work group, and this causes contrasts at work. For example, a U.S. scientist invited to work in a Japanese laboratory was treated as an outsider until he demonstrated his willingness to subordinate his personal interests to those of the group. He did so by mopping the lab floor for several weeks, after which he was invited to join the group.[40] In contrast, Levi's introduced team-based production for U.S. plants because its management had observed high productivity from that system in Asian plants. U.S. employees—especially the faster, more skilled ones—detested the system, productivity decreased, and Levi's abandoned the team-based production system.[41]

However, measuring country differences in terms of individualism versus collectivism is complex and controversial.[42] As a result, people may vary their individualism depending on circumstances. For example, although China and Mexico are characterized as collectivist cultures, they differ from Japan insofar as the collectivism is based on kinship and does not carry over to the workplace.[43] Further, the concept of family in China and Mexico includes not only a nuclear family (a husband, wife, and minor children) but also a vertically extended family (several generations) and perhaps a horizontally extended one (aunts, uncles, and cousins). This difference affects business in several ways. First, material rewards from an individual's work may be less motivating because these rewards are divided among more people. Second, geographical mobility is reduced because relocation means other members of a family also have to find new jobs. Even in cases in which extended families do not live together, mobility may be reduced because people prefer to remain near relatives. Third, purchasing decisions may be more complicated because of the interrelated roles of family members. Fourth, security and social needs may be met more extensively at home than in the workplace.

Where collectivism is high, companies find their best marketing successes when emphasizing advertising themes that express group (rather than individual) values. For example, Marlboro cigarettes have had better success in Asian markets than Camel cigarettes, partially because their marketing campaigns have used group themes more.[44]

This is a good time to re-emphasize that, although there are differences in norms among countries, not everyone within any country fits the attitudinal norms. In one study, the researchers compared individual supervisors from both Hong Kong and the United States to differentiate between those who were more individualistic from those who were more collectivist. They found in both societies that the collectivists were more prone to promote people whose personalities were more like their own. In this example, the individual preferences for individualism versus collectivism were more important than the national norm related to the same preferences.[45]

Risk-Taking Behavior

Nationalities differ in how happy people are to accept things the way they are and how they feel about controlling their destinies. The following discussion examines four aspects of risk-taking behavior—uncertainty avoidance, trust, future orientation, and fatalism—across nations.

Uncertainty Avoidance   Studies on *uncertainty avoidance* show that in countries with the highest scores on uncertainty avoidance, employees prefer set rules that are not to be broken even if breaking them is sometimes in the company's best interest. Further, these employees plan to work for the company a long time, preferring the certainty of their present positions over the uncertainty of better advancement opportunities elsewhere.[46] When uncertainty avoidance is high, superiors may need to be more precise and assured in the directions they give to subordinates because the subordinates are not motivated to figure out what they need to do to advance the company's interests.

In countries characterized by high uncertainty avoidance, few consumers are prepared to take the social risk of trying a new product first. This is very important when it comes time for firms to choose where to introduce new products. For example, 40 percent of Gillette's sales come from products it has introduced in the last five years. It may be advantageous for Gillette to enter markets such as Denmark and the United Kingdom (countries with low uncertainty avoidance) before entering those in Belgium and Portugal (countries with high uncertainty avoidance).[47]

Trust Surveys that measure trust among countries by having respondents evaluate such statements as "Most people can be trusted" and "You can't be too careful in dealing with people" indicate substantial international differences. For example, a much higher percentage of Norwegians than Brazilians think most people are trustworthy.[48] Where trust is high, there tends to be a lower cost of doing business because managers do not have to spend time foreseeing every possible contingency and then monitoring every action for compliance in business relationships. Instead, they can spend time investing and innovating.[49] Norwegians and Brazilians may actually be responding to the conditions existing in their respective countries. A Norwegian businessperson going to Brazil may act too naively, whereas a Brazilian going to Norway may act too cautiously.

Future Orientation Countries also differ in the extent to which individuals live for the present rather than the future because they see risks in delaying gratification and investing for the future. For example, the future orientation is higher in Switzerland, the Netherlands, and Canada than in Russia, Poland, and Italy.[50] Where future orientation is higher, companies may be able to better motivate workers through delayed compensation, such as retirement programs.

Fatalism If people believe strongly in self-determination, they may be willing to work hard to achieve goals and take responsibility for performance. But a belief in fatalism, that every event is inevitable, may prevent people from accepting this basic cause-and-effect relationship. The effect on business in countries with a high degree of fatalism is that people plan less for contingencies. For example, they may be reluctant to buy insurance. In this regard, religious differences play a part. Conservative or fundamentalist Christian, Buddhist, Hindu, and Muslim groups tend to view occurrences as "the will of God." At the same time, highly fatalistic people are less swayed by bosses' persuasive logic than by relationships, such as personal appeals and offering something in exchange for compliance with a request.[51]

Information and Task Processing

The nineteenth-century author Margaret Hungerford wrote, "Beauty is altogether in the eye of the beholder." People do perceive and reach conclusions differently. So do cultures. Further, once people have what they perceive as accurate information, they handle this information in different ways. The following discussion examines how people from different cultures perceive, obtain, and process information.

Perception of Cues We perceive cues selectively. We may identify what things are by means of any of our senses (sight, smell, touch, sound, or taste) and in various ways within each sense. For example, through vision, we can sense color, depth, and shape. The cues people use to perceive things differ among societies. The reason is partly physiological. For example, genetic differences in eye pigmentation enable some groups to differentiate colors more finely than others can. It also is partly cultural. For example, a richness of descriptive vocabulary can allow people to express very subtle differences in color. Further, this difference in richness allows each culture to perceive some subjects more precisely than other cultures. For example, Arabic has more than 6,000 different words for camels, their body parts, and the equipment associated with them.[52] Arabic speakers can note things about camels that are most likely overlooked by other speakers.

Obtaining Information   In spite of vast differences within countries, some, such as the United States and those in northern Europe, are categorized as being **low-context cultures**—that is, most people consider to be relevant only firsthand information that bears directly on the decision they need to make. In business, they spend little time on small talk and say things directly. However, other countries—for example, those in southern Europe—are **high-context cultures** (i.e., most people believe that peripheral information is valuable to decision making and infer meanings from things said indirectly). When managers from the two types of cultures deal with each other, the low-context individuals may believe the high-context ones are inefficient and time wasters. The high-context individuals may believe the low-context ones are too aggressive to be trusted. (Recall the opening case in which the English salesmen had problems dealing with their Saudi counterparts.)

It helps managers to know whether cultures favor

- Focused or broad information
- Sequential or simultaneous handling of situations
- Handling principles or small issues first

Information Processing   Information processing is universal insofar as all cultures categorize, plan, and quantify. All cultures also have ordering and classifying systems. However, sometimes cultures do this differently from one another. In U.S. telephone directories, the entries appear in alphabetical order by last (family) name. In Iceland, entries are organized by first (given) names. Icelandic last names are derived from the father's first name: Jon, the son of Thor, is Jon Thorsson, and his sister's last name is Thorsdottir (daughter of Thor). One needs to understand the different ordering and classifying systems to perform efficiently in a foreign environment. Further, the different ordering and classifying systems create challenges that make it difficult for companies to use global data effectively. Even the use of global personnel directories is problematic because of different alphabetizing systems. Information processing also includes ordering tasks. Cultures such as those in northern Europe are called **monochronic;** in such cultures, people prefer to work sequentially (people will finish with one customer before dealing with another). Conversely, **polychronic** southern Europeans are more comfortable when working simultaneously on all the tasks they face. For example, they feel uncomfortable when not dealing immediately with all customers who need service.[53] Imagine the potential misconceptions that can occur. Northern European businesspeople might erroneously believe their southern European counterparts are uninterested in doing business with them if they fail to give them their undivided attention.

Some cultures tend to focus first on the whole and then on the parts, whereas others do the opposite. For example, when asked to describe an underwater scene in which one large fish swam among smaller fish and other aquatic life, most Japanese first described the overall picture and most Americans first described the large fish.[54] Similarly, some cultures will determine principles before they try to resolve small issues (**idealism**), whereas other cultures will focus more on details rather than principles (**pragmatism**). From a business standpoint, the differences manifest information processing in a number of ways. For example, in a society of pragmatists such as the United States, labor disputes tend to focus on specific issues—for example, increase pay by a dollar per hour. In a society of idealists such as Argentina, labor disputes tend to lead to less precise demands and workers depend instead on mass action, such as general strikes or support of a particular political party, to publicize their principles.

Communications

Thus far, we've seen how language affects culture—and international business. We now look at problems of communications—translating spoken and written language. These problems occur not only in moving from one language to another but also in communicating from one country to another that has the same official language. Second, we discuss communications outside the spoken and written language, the so-called "silent language."

Spoken and Written Language Translating one language directly into another can be difficult, making international business communication difficult. First, some words do not have a direct translation. For example, there is no one word in Spanish for everyone who works in a business (i.e., employees). Instead, there is a word, *empleados*, which means "white-collar workers," and another, *obreros*, which means "laborers." This distinction shows the substantial class difference that exists between the groups, and it affects international business because there may be miscommunication when managers in Spanish-speaking and English-speaking countries come together. Second, languages and the common meaning of words are constantly evolving. For example, Microsoft purchased a thesaurus code for its Spanish version of Word 6, but the meaning of many synonyms had changed and become insulting. The company corrected the software after newspapers and radio reports denounced the program, but by then, Microsoft had alienated many potential customers.[55] Third, words mean different things in different contexts. One company described itself as an "old friend" of China. However, it used the word for *old* that meant "former" instead of "long-term."[56] Finally, grammar is complex, and a slight misuse of vocabulary or word placement may change meanings substantially. Consider the following examples of signs in English observed in hotels around the world.

France: "Please leave your values at the desk."

Mexico (to assure guests about the safety of drinking water): "The manager has personally passed all the water served here."

Japan: "You are invited to take advantage of the chambermaid."

Norway: "Ladies are requested not to have children in the bar."

Switzerland: "Because of the impropriety of entertaining guests of the opposite sex in the bedroom, it is suggested that the lobby be used for this purpose."

Greece (at check-in line): "We will execute customers in strict rotation."

The above examples offer a humorous look at language barriers, and, in fact, the wrong choice of words usually is just a source of brief embarrassment. However, a poor translation may have tragic consequences. For example, inaccurate translations have caused structural collapses and airplane crashes, such as the collision between aircraft from Air Kazakhstan and Saudia Air over India.[57] In contracts, correspondence, negotiations, advertisements, and conversations, words must be chosen carefully. There is no foolproof way of handling translations. However, good international business managers use rules such as the following:

- Get references for the people who will do the translation for you.
- Make sure your translator knows the technical vocabulary of your business.
- Do a back translation for written work by having one person go, say, from English to French and a second person translate the French version back into English. If it comes back the same way it started, it is probably satisfactory.
- Use simple words whenever possible, such as *ban* instead of *interdiction*.
- Avoid slang. Such U.S. phrases as *blue chip stocks* and *ballpark figures* are likely to be meaningless to most businesspeople outside the United States.
- When you or your counterpart are dealing in a second language, clarify communications in several ways (such as by repeating in different words and asking questions) to ensure that all parties have the same interpretation.
- Recognize the need for and budget from the start for the extra time needed for translation and clarification.

Cross-border communications do not always translate as intended.

TABLE 2.1	BUSINESS LANGUAGE DIFFERENCES

Below are a few of the approximately 4,000 words whose common U.S. and U.K. meanings differ. Although we usually expect comprehension problems when people from two different languages communicate, we may erroneously not expect miscommunication between people from two countries that share the same language.

UNITED STATES	UNITED KINGDON
turnover	redundancy
sales	turnover
inventory	stock
stock	shares
president	managing director
paperback	limp cover

You also need to be careful with humor. Although many jokes have universal appeal, some humor does not. For instance, a Microsoft executive gave a speech to executives in India in which he quipped that he did not have the qualifications to speak because he didn't complete his MBA. However, it was very badly received because Indians put a high importance on education and in persevering rather than dropping out.[58]

When dealing among countries that share the same official language, don't assume that communication will go smoothly. For example, Hershey's launched its Elegancita candy bar with an expensive advertising campaign throughout Latin America. The ad boasted about its *cajeta*, which meant goat's milk caramel in Mexico but a vulgar word for a part of the female anatomy in much of South America.[59] Between the United States and the United Kingdom, approximately 4,000 words have different meanings. Table 2.1 shows some common business terms that differ in the two countries.

Silent Language   Of course, spoken and written language is not our only means of communicating. We all exchange messages through a host of nonverbal cues that form a silent language.[60] Colors, for example, conjure up meanings that come from cultural experience. In most Western countries, black is associated with death. White has the same connotation in parts of Asia and purple in Latin America. For products to succeed, their colors must match the consumers' frame of reference. For example, United Airlines promoted a new passenger service in Hong Kong by giving white carnations to its best customers there. The promotion backfired because people in Hong Kong give white carnations only in sympathy for a family death. Motorola had difficulty assigning certain cellular telephone numbers in China because of their sound in Mandarin. The worst is one ending in 54–7424 because it sounds like "I die, my wife dies, my child dies."[61]

Another aspect of silent language is the distance between people during conversations. People's sense of appropriate distance is learned and differs among societies. In the United States, for example, the customary distance for a business discussion is 5 to 8 feet. For personal business, it is 18 inches to 3 feet.[62] When the distance is closer or farther than is customary, people tend to feel uneasy. For example, a U.S. manager conducting business discussions in Latin America may be constantly moving backward to avoid the closer conversational distance to which the Latin American official is accustomed. Consequently, at the end of the discussion, each party may feel uneasy about the other.

Perception of time and punctuality is another unspoken cue that differs by context and may differ across cultures and create confusion. In terms of context in the United States, participants usually arrive early for a business appointment, a few minutes late for a dinner at someone's home, and a bit later for a cocktail party. In another country, the concept of punctuality in these situations may be different. A U.S. businessperson in Latin America may consider it discourteous if a Latin American manager does not keep

Silent language includes color associations, sense of appropriate distance, time and status cues, and body language.

FIGURE 2.5   KINESICS ARE NOT UNIVERSAL

Few gestures are universal. This figure shows that a common and similar gesture has different connotations internationally. The meaning in Germany also prevails in most Latin American countries.

Source: The meanings have been taken from descriptions in Roger E. Axtell, *Gestures* (New York: John Wiley, 1998). Reprinted by permission of John Wiley & Sons, Inc.

United States	**Germany**	**Greece**	**France**	**Japan**
It's fine	You lunatic	An obscene symbol for a body orifice	Zero or worthless	Money, especially change

to the appointed time. Latin Americans may find it equally discourteous if a U.S. businessperson arrives for dinner at the exact time given in the invitation.

In terms of culture, there are different ways of looking at time. People in English-speaking, Germanic, and Scandinavian countries view time as a scarce commodity. If it is lost, it cannot be recouped.[63] Thus there is a tendency to keep to schedules and emphasize short-term results, even if taking longer will yield better results. In contrast, people who view time as an event prefer to take whatever time is necessary to complete the event. In one case, a U.S. company made a presentation in Mexico in competition with a French company. Managers in the U.S. company were confident they would win the contract because they had the better technology. They scheduled a one-day meeting in Mexico City very tightly, allowing what they thought was plenty of time for the presentation and questions. However, the Mexican team arrived one hour late. One Mexican team member was called out of the room for an urgent phone call, and the whole Mexican team became upset when the U.S. team tried to proceed without the missing member. The French team allocated two weeks for discussions and won the contract even though its technology was widely known to be less sophisticated.[64]

Another silent language barrier concerns a person's position in a company. A U.S. businessperson who tends to place a great reliance on objects as prestige cues may underestimate the importance of foreign counterparts who do not have large, plush, private offices. A foreigner may underestimate U.S. counterparts who open their own doors and prepare their own drinks.

Body language, or kinesics (the way in which people walk, touch, and move their bodies), also differs among countries. Few gestures are universal in meaning. For example, the "yes" of a Greek, Turk, or Bulgarian is indicated by a sideways movement of the head that resembles the negative head shake used in the United States and elsewhere in Europe. In some cases, one gesture may have several meanings, as Figure 2.5 shows.

Managers should know that perceptual cues—especially those concerning time and status—differ among societies.

DEALING WITH CULTURAL DIFFERENCES

After a company identifies cultural differences in the foreign country where it intends to do business, must it alter its customary practices to succeed there? Can individuals overcome adjustment problems when working abroad? There are no easy answers to these questions. The following discussion highlights some of the variables that affect the degree of adjustment. These include a society's degree of willingness to accept the introduction of anything foreign, whether cultural differences are small or great, the ability of individuals to adjust to what they find in foreign cultures, and the general management orientation of the company doing business abroad.

Accommodation to Foreigners

Host cultures do not always expect foreigners to adjust to them.

Although the opening case illustrates the advantages of adjusting to the host country culture, international companies sometimes have succeeded in introducing new products, technologies, and operating procedures to foreign countries with little adjustment. That's because some of these introductions have not run counter to deep-seated attitudes or because the host society is willing to accept foreign customs as a trade-off for other advantages. Bahrain has permitted the sale of pork products (otherwise outlawed by religious law) as long as they are sold in separate rooms of grocery stores where Muslims can neither work nor shop.

Often the local society looks on foreigners and its own citizens differently. For example, Western female flight attendants are permitted to wear jeans and T-shirts in public when staying overnight in Jeddah, Saudi Arabia, even though local women cannot.[65] Members of the host society may even feel they are being stereotyped in an uncomplimentary way when foreigners adjust too much.[66] Moreover, Western female managers in Hong Kong say local people see them primarily as foreigners, not as women. There and elsewhere, foreign women are accepted as managers more readily than local women are.[67]

MAP 2.4   A Synthesis of Country Clusters

This map, based on the GLOBE study, shows that middle managers in certain countries share similar cultural attitudes and values concerning leadership that may affect business practices. Not all countries have been studied sufficiently to determine how similar they are to other countries. Note that the names for clusters are based on the majority of countries in each cluster; for example, Turkey is in the Arab group, although its language is not Arabic. Costa Rica and Guatemala are in the Latin American group although their attitudes are more similar to the Latin European group.

Source: Reprinted form *Journal of World Business,* 37, Vipin Gupta, Paul J. Hanges, and Peter Dorfman, "Cultural Clusters: Methodology and Findings," p. 13, Spring 2002. Reprinted with permission from Elsevier.

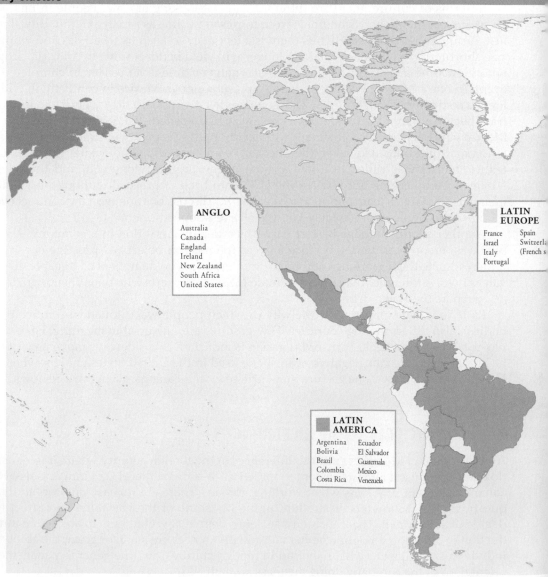

ANGLO
Australia
Canada
England
Ireland
New Zealand
South Africa
United States

LATIN EUROPE
France   Spain
Israel   Switzerl
Italy   (French s
Portugal

LATIN AMERICA
Argentina   Ecuador
Bolivia   El Salvador
Brazil   Guatemala
Colombia   Mexico
Costa Rica   Venezuela

Cultural Distance: Usefulness and Limitations

Some countries are relatively similar to one another, usually because they share many attributes that help mold their cultures, such as language, religion, geographical location, ethnicity, and level of economic development. The Human Values study included the comparison of 43 societies on 405 dimensions.[68] By averaging the distance countries are apart on each dimension, say the number of countries apart for Sweden and Spain on each dimension, one can see that some countries are close together culturally and others are far apart. By this method, Canada is culturally close to the United States and China is distant. Map 2.4 shows groups of countries from the Globe study of 58 countries by middle managers' attitudes and values about leadership. This map clusters countries by the similarity of these values and attitudes. A company should expect fewer differences (and have to consider fewer adjustments) when moving to culturally close than to culturally distant countries or within a cluster of similar countries. For instance, an Ecuadorian company doing business in Colombia should expect to have to make fewer adjustments than when doing business in Thailand.

When doing business in a similar culture, companies

- Usually have to make fewer adjustments
- May overlook subtle differences

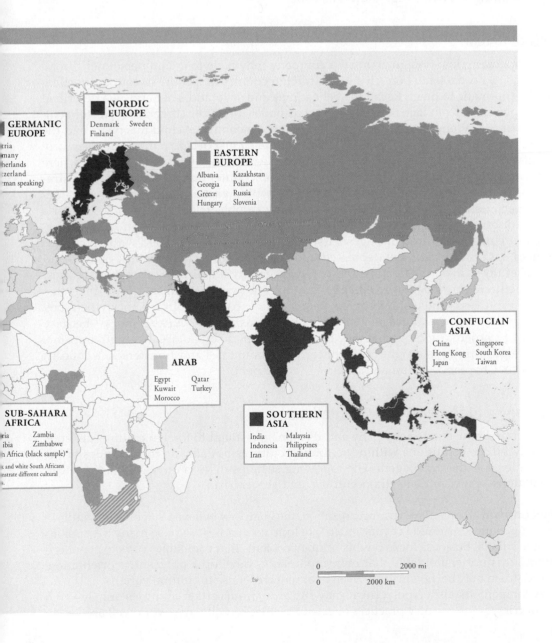

GERMANIC EUROPE
[A]ria
[Ger]many
[Net]herlands
[Swit]zerland
(German speaking)

NORDIC EUROPE
Denmark   Sweden
Finland

EASTERN EUROPE
Albania   Kazakhstan
Georgia   Poland
Greece   Russia
Hungary   Slovenia

CONFUCIAN ASIA
China   Singapore
Hong Kong   South Korea
Japan   Taiwan

ARAB
Egypt   Qatar
Kuwait   Turkey
Morocco

SUB-SAHARA AFRICA
[Nige]ria   Zambia
[Nam]ibia   Zimbabwe
[Sout]h Africa (black sample)*

[Blac]k and white South Africans
[demo]nstrate different cultural

SOUTHERN ASIA
India   Malaysia
Indonesia   Philippines
Iran   Thailand

0   2000 mi
0   2000 km

However, there still may be significant differences within similar countries that could affect business dealings. Managers may expect that seemingly similar countries (those within clusters) are more alike than they really are; a company may be lulled into a complacency that overlooks important subtleties. For example, women's roles and behaviors differ substantially from one Arab country to another. The company also needs to consider how people in the host country perceive the foreign company's entry and what it plans to do. For instance, Disney has had much more success in Japan with its theme park than in France, even though France is culturally closer to the United States than Japan. On the one hand Japan was more receptive because both children and adults viewed Mickey Mouse as a wholesome and nonthreatening figure from the Mickey Mouse Club on television, because there was a tradition of buying souvenirs on family excursions, and because Disney's requirement for super-clean imagery and smiling faces fit well with Japanese cultural norms of harmony, cleanliness, and order. On the other hand, the French knew a conniving Mickey from comic books that had been adjusted to increase sales in the French market. They thought the Disney souvenirs were tacky and that the Disney personal requirements to smile and dress a certain way were neither natural nor fitting with their high individualism.[69]

Culture Shock

When operating in a foreign country, a company may have to assign personnel abroad or at least send personnel on trips to the foreign country. Exposure to certain practices may be traumatic to them. Recall the beheadings and severances of hands we described in the opening case. In fact, there are many customary practices abroad that Western culture considers wrong, such as slavery, polygamy, concubinage, child marriage, and the burning of widows. Both companies and individuals must decide if they can effectively operate in such locales. In addition, even when people move to another country where differences are not traumatic to them, they often encounter **culture shock**—the frustration that results when having to learn and cope with a vast array of new cultural cues and expectations. Even such simple tasks as using a public telephone, getting a driver's license, or buying stamps may be lengthy tasks at first. People working in a very different culture may pass through stages. First, like tourists, they are elated with quaint differences. Later, they may feel depressed and confused—the culture shock phase—and their usefulness in a foreign assignment may be greatly impaired. Fortunately for most people, culture shock begins to ebb after a month or two as optimism grows and satisfaction improves.[70] Interestingly, some people also encounter culture shock when they return to their home countries—a situation known as **reverse culture shock**—because they have learned to accept what they have encountered abroad. Dealing with transfers to a foreign country is a significant concern for companies and transferees, a concern covered in Chapter 20, "Human Resource Management."

Company and Management Orientations

Whether and how much a company and its managers adapt to foreign cultures depends not only on the conditions within the foreign cultures but also on the attitudes of the companies and their managers. The following sections discuss three such attitudes or orientations—polycentrism, ethnocentrism, and geocentrism.

Polycentrism   In a polycentric organization, the company believes that business units in different countries should act very much like local companies. Because many discussions of international business focus on the unique problems that companies have experienced abroad, it is understandable that many companies develop a polycentric orientation. Polycentrism may be, however, an overly cautious response to cultural variety.

A company that is too polycentric may shy away from certain countries or may avoid transferring home-country practices or resources that actually may work well abroad. In

POINT–COUNTERPOINT: DOES INTERNATIONAL BUSINESS LEAD TO CULTURAL IMPERIALISM?

POINT

That international business influences globalization and that, in turn, globalization influences culture is well accepted. I certainly object neither to all international business, nor to all globalization. I do object to modern cultural imperialism. This has come about because of the technical, political, military, and economic supremacy of the Center (Western countries, primarily the United States) in relation to the Periphery (smaller, poorer countries).[71] For the last half century, and especially since the end of the Cold War, the United States has been such a superpower that its culture is being exported in ways that are detrimental to the best interests of the Periphery. In effect, U.S. companies control the international entertainment media, thus people from all over the world watch television on CNN, MTV, and the Disney Channel, and they see movies made by U.S. studios. On top of this, the world audience is barraged with advertisements for the goods from U.S. companies that they associate with the TV shows and movies, everything from Levi's to McDonald's to Coca-Cola. Naturally, these companies make their wares available to consumers worldwide. Add to this the legions of U.S. tourists, who sometimes spend more for a night's hotel lodging in the Periphery than the people serving them make in a year. This exposure to the combination of imported entertainment, extensive and subliminal advertising, mass distribution, and firsthand observation of U.S. tourists causes people, especially in the Periphery, to believe the U.S. lifestyle is as it is portrayed-both glamorous and exciting. As it is often portrayed, it is a lifestyle filled with violence and sexual freedom, one with either alienation or simplistic relations among family members. It is a seductive, although unrealistic, view, but this view causes emulation by buying products that seem American, adding American English words to their speech, and adapting behaviors they think are norms in the United States. As this emulation takes place, the nation loses some of its uniqueness that creates its self-identity and cohesiveness.

Further, as international companies come in to take advantage of the demand that has been created, they further upset the local culture and the self-identity that helps stabilize the nation state. For

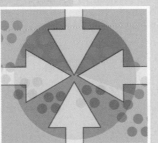

instance, they have little respect for local culture and traditions, such as when Wal-Mart builds a store in view of the ancient ruins of Teotihuacan in Mexico, which by the way, also destroys the nearby street market and the cultural heritage associated with it.[72]

The international companies tend to cluster in ways that attract workers to move from rural areas. This movement disrupts family unity by separating nuclear family members from each other or the nuclear family from its extended family for long periods of time. These same companies introduce work hours that prevent employees from going home for lunch. They use English as the language among their managers.

Rich countries can sometimes afford to take measures to offset the cultural intrusion. For instance, Canada prohibits foreign investment in culturally sensitive industries and also requires Canadian content in the entertainment media. Finland has at times prohibited architecture that runs counter to its traditional heritage. France puts restrictions on the use of languages other than French, and it subsidizes its motion picture industry. Japan limits the screening of foreign films. Even the United States limits foreign ownership of radio and television broadcasting. But poor countries in the Periphery cannot as easily take these preventive measures. They lack funds to produce sufficient quality entertainment to compete with that from abroad. Further, their electorates are often too uninformed and their political leaders often too corrupt to deal with these issues effectively.

COUNTERPOINT

I think you're wrong about there being a modern cultural imperialism. You imply that people in poor countries passively accept anything they see in either the entertainment or the advertising media. They are more sophisticated than this. Although they have certainly taken to wearing jeans and consuming soft drinks, they have rejected many of the products introduced by international companies. In other words, they pick and choose what to accept and reject based on personal interpretations of their needs in relation to the realities of the cultures in which they live.[73] These interpretations vary by culture, as indicated by a study of four cultures' different inter-pretations of the motivations of characters in the TV series *Dallas*.[74]

You also imply that cultural diffusion is a one-way process, from the Center to the Periphery. With contact, culture, such as language, diffuses in both directions and has always evolved. For instance, between 100 BC and 400 AD, about 50 Mediterranean languages disappeared as people took up Latin and Greek.[75] But then, Latin evolved into several distinct Romance languages. Currently many languages are dying, and it is important both for history and for understanding the human mind to study these. But we should keep in mind that some of the dying languages are giving way for reasons other than the growth of international business. In other words, they are giving way to languages other than English, such as to Spanish, Mandarin, and Arabic. Of course, American English is entering many other languages, but foreign words are becoming commonplace within American English as well, such as the current common inclusion of such Spanish terms as *macho*, the whole *enchilada*, and head *honcho*. While McDonald's has certainly spread its sales throughout most of the world, it is hard to find anything that it has displaced. In essence, globalization and international business, by diffusing culture two ways, have created the availability of greater food diversity within almost all countries. Thus American hamburgers, Japanese sushi, Italian pizza, Mexican tacos, and Middle Eastern pita bread are now commonly available along with local cuisine in most countries. What we see is the development of hybrid cultures rather than cultural imperialism.

However, even if we assume that the movement of media, ads, and products is one way, it does not imply that there is a change in anything other than the acceptance of the material part of culture. We cannot establish that people change their values when they view the foreign materials or buy the foreign products. Without establishing this linkage, we cannot assume that cultures are being homogenized.[76] Further, there is evidence that young people are most apt to adopt the foreign/global culture, but they revert to their traditions as they get older, thus negating the premise that their adoption causes a permanent change in a country's culture.[77]

Certainly, knowledge and availability of foreign things create wants that heretofore did not exist. To fulfill these wants may necessitate some trade-offs. Thus, are people and societies worse off because they give up, for example, lunch with the family in order to afford goods that the whole family may enjoy together? Only the individuals affected can make this decision, and globalization gives them options that otherwise would not exist. Likewise, tourism is a two-edged sword. Although you have argued about its negative effect on culture, it also has contributed to the maintenance of traditional aspects of culture. For example, Balinese dancing was resurrected because tourists wanted to see it.

Finally, international companies are often maligned for neglecting the local culture. I admit that this sometimes happens, but as we showed in the opening case, companies must adhere sufficiently to local culture lest they fail, and I can't think of any company that wants to fail. However, companies, whether foreign or local, cannot always anticipate the reactions to their practices. Take your Wal-Mart example in Mexico. Before finalizing construction plans, Wal-Mart sought advice from anthropologists and agreed to make the store lower and with a stone façade in a subdued color so that it could be seen along with other existing buildings only from atop the pyramids. The so-called traditional market that Wal-Mart might put out of business sells no traditional merchandise, rather it sells plastic items and imported Chinese goods.

---

fact, to compete effectively with local companies, an international company usually must perform some functions in a distinct way, such as by introducing new products or ways to produce and sell them. Thus, excessive polycentrism may lead to such extensive imitation of proven host-country practices that the company loses its innovative superiority.

Ethnocentrist management
overlooks national differences
and
- Ignores important factors
- Believes home-country objectives should prevail
- Thinks change is easy

Ethnocentrism   Ethnocentrism is the belief that one's own culture is superior to others. In international business, it describes a company or individual so imbued with the belief that what worked at home should work abroad that it ignores societal differences. Ethnocentrism takes three general forms.

1. Managers overlook important cultural factors abroad because they have become accustomed to certain cause-and-effect relationships in the home country. To combat this

type of ethnocentrism, managers can refer to checklists of cultural variables, such as those discussed in this chapter, to assure themselves that they are considering all the major factors.

2. Management recognizes the environmental differences but still focuses on achieving home-country rather than foreign or worldwide objectives. The result may be diminished long-term competitiveness because the company does not perform as well as its competitors and because opposition to its practices develops abroad.

3. Management recognizes differences but assumes that the introduction of its new products or ways to produce and sell them is both necessary and easy to achieve when it is really a complex process. Ethnocentrism is not entirely bad. Much of what works at home will work abroad. However, excessive ethnocentrism may cause costly business failures.

Geocentrism   Between the extremes of polycentrism and ethnocentrism are negotiated business practices that are a hybrid of the host country practices, the company's accustomed practices, and some entirely new practices.[78] For example, Toyota has purposely blended Japanese and French cultures in its French plant.[79] Geocentrism exists when a company bases its operations on an informed knowledge of its organization culture along with home- and host-country needs, capabilities, and constraints. This is the preferred approach to business dealings with another culture because it increases the introduction of innovations and decreases the likelihood of their failures.

> Geocentric management often uses business practices that are hybrids of home and foreign norms.

Strategies for Instituting Change

As we have indicated, companies may need to transfer new products or operating methods from one country to another if they are to have competitive advantages. How they make such introductions is important for assuring success. Fortunately, substantial change-agent literature exists that deals with overcoming resistance in the international arena. Further, we can gain insights from the international experiences of businesses and not-for-profit organizations. We discuss these approaches and experiences in the following sections and conclude with a discussion on the importance of learning as a two-way process, one in which companies transfer knowledge abroad from their home countries and to their home countries from abroad.

Value System   The more something counters our value system, the more difficulty we have accepting it. For example, Eritreans ate only 175 grams of fish per capita per year (compared with 20,000 grams in the United States and 70,000 grams in Japan) despite having a long coastline rich in seafood and having had endured past famines. The Eritrean government and the United Nations World Food Program faced formidable opposition in persuading Eritrean adults to eat more seafood because their value system was too set. Many had religious taboos about eating insect-like sea creatures (such as shrimp and crayfish) and fish without scales, and most grew up believing that seafood tasted putrid. But they faced little opposition among Eritrean schoolchildren because their value system and habits were not yet set.[80]

> The more a change upsets important values, the more resistance it will engender.

Cost Benefit of Change   Some adjustments to foreign cultures are costly to undertake, whereas others are inexpensive. Some adjustments result in greatly improved performance, such as higher productivity or sales. Other changes may improve performance only marginally. A company must consider the expected cost-benefit relationship of any adjustments it makes abroad. For example, Cummins Engine shuts down its plant in Mexico each December 12 so workers may honor the Virgin of Guadalupe. The company throws a celebration in its cafeteria for employees and their families that includes a priest

> The cost of change may exceed its benefit.

who offers prayers to the Virgin at an altar.[81] The cost is worth the resultant employee commitment to the company.

Resistance to Too Much Change   When German company Gruner + Jahr bought the U.S. magazine *McCall's*, it quickly began to overhaul the format. Gruner + Jahr changed the magazine's editor, eliminated long stories and advice columns, increased coverage of celebrities, made the layouts more dense, started using sidebars and boxes in articles, and refused discounts for big advertisers. But employee turnover began to increase because of low morale, and revenues fell because the new format seemed too different to advertisers.[82] Employee and advertiser acceptance might have been easier to obtain had Gruner + Jahr made fewer demands at one time and phased in other policies more slowly.

Resistance to change may be lower if the number of changes is not too great.

Participation   One way to avoid problems that could result from change is to discuss a proposed change with stakeholders in advance. By doing so, the company may learn how strong resistance to the change will be, stimulate stakeholders to recognize the need for change, and ease their fears of adverse consequences resulting from the change. Such discussion may satisfy employees that management has listened to their viewpoints, even though management makes decisions contrary to what the employees suggest.[83] Managers sometimes think that stakeholder participation is unique to countries where people have educational backgrounds that enable them to make substantial contributions and where they want to participate. Experience with government-to-government economic development and population-control programs, however, indicates that participation may be extremely important to companies even in countries where education levels are low and power distance and uncertainty avoidance are high. However, stakeholder participation is limited to the extent that proposed actions do not violate conditions in the prevailing value system and to the extent that participants are not so fatalistic that they believe they can have no control over the outcomes.

Employees are more willing to implement change when they take part in the decision to change.

Reward Sharing   Sometimes a proposed change may have no foreseeable benefit for the people who must support it. For example, production workers may have little incentive to shift to new work practices unless they see some benefits for themselves. A company's solution may be to develop a bonus system for productivity and quality based on using the new approach and to share gains with everyone affected. In one case, a U.S.-Peruvian gold-mining venture donated sheep to the Andean villagers who initially opposed the operation because they saw no benefit for themselves but later supported it.[84]

Employees are more apt to support change when they expect personal or group rewards.

Opinion Leaders   By discovering the local channels of influence, an international company may locate opinion leaders who can help speed up the acceptance of change. Opinion leaders may emerge in unexpected places. Ford sends Mexican operatives, rather than supervisors, from its plants in Mexico to one in the United States to observe operating methods. Their Mexican peers are more prone to listen to them than to their supervisors.[85] Characteristics of opinion leaders may vary by country—for example, they are generally older people in India and Korea, but not in Australia.[86]

Managers seeking to introduce change should first convince those who can influence others.

Timing   Many good business changes fall flat because they are ill-timed. For example, a labor-saving production method might make employees fear that they will lose their jobs regardless of management's reassurances. However, less employee fear and resistance will occur if management introduces the labor-saving method when there is a labor shortage. A culture's attitudes and needs may change slowly or rapidly, so keeping abreast of these changes helps in determining timing. Yet a crisis may stimulate acceptance of change. For example, family members dominate business organizations in Turkey. In some cases, poor company profits have stimulated a rapid change from "a family running the business" to a "family only on the board." But in other cases, family members continue to exert substantial influence on companies' practices even after they have no official responsibilities.[87]

Companies should time change to occur when resistance is likely to be low.

Learning Abroad The discussion so far has centered on cultural differences among countries. As companies operate abroad, they affect the host society and are affected by it. The company may learn things that will be useful in its home country or in other operations. For example, companies such as Fuji and Kodak created technology for while-you-wait photo development in Saudi Arabia because customers wanted to retrieve photos without anyone else seeing them. They transferred this technology to other countries later. Basically, natural intelligence exists in just about the same proportion throughout the world, thus innovations and good ideas may come from anywhere.

International companies should learn things abroad that they can apply at home.

LOOKING TO THE FUTURE: What Will Happen to National Cultures?

One scenario is that new hybrid cultures will develop. Contact across countries is becoming more widespread than ever. This should lead to a leveling of national cultures, which, on the surface, is occurring. People around the world wear similar clothes and listen to the same recording stars. Competitors from all over the world often buy the same production equipment, the use of which imposes more uniform operating methods on workers. These same competitors also quickly adopt each other's successful operating practices, thus creating a competitive work environment that is more global than national. As they operate in a multicultural world, they can use the experience from diversity to unleash operating potentials.[88] This globalization of culture is illustrated by Japanese tourists listening to a Philippine group sing a U.S. song in a British hotel chain in Indonesia. It is also illustrated by the emergence of combination languages, such as Spanglish.

We also see the greater mobility of people, who, whether they have dual citizenship or not, have effectively become flexible citizens.[89] Historically, when most people immigrated, they returned perhaps once in their lifetimes to their countries of birth. Thus, they were compelled to become part of a melting pot in their adopted countries, which caused them to lose most of their original cultural identity. However, increasingly they maintain residences in more than one country. They work abroad while keeping close contact with people back home through frequent visits, phone calls, and remittances. At any rate, they transfer culture in both directions and cause each nation state to be a mediator of a greater cultural diversity than heretofore existed. Similarly, we see the development of a cadre

of international managers whose national culture defies description. For instance, Carlos Ghosn, CEO of Nissan in Japan, is a Brazilian of Lebanese extraction, who was educated in France.[90]

A second scenario is that national cultures will homogenize more in visible expressions of culture, such as those mentioned above, but not in basic values. Below the surface of visible expressions of culture, people continue to hold fast to their national differences. In other words, although some tangibles have become more universal, how people cooperate, attempt to solve problems, and are motivated have tended to remain the same. Religious differences are as strong as ever. Language differences continue to bolster separate ethnic identities. These differences fragment the globe into regions and stymie the global standardization of products and operating methods.

A third scenario is that national cultures will become stronger because of nationalism. Without perceived cultural differences, people would not see themselves so apart from other nationalities. Thus, cultural identities are used to mobilize national identity and separateness. This is done by regulating and encouraging the so-called national culture through subsidies to support it, along with prescriptions on language, religion, and propaganda against foreign things.

A fourth scenario is that national borders as we see them today will change to accommodate ethnic groups. On the one hand, there is evidence of more powerful subcultures within some countries because of immigration, the global rise in religious fundamentalism, and the growing belief among ethnic groups that they should be independent from dominant groups. In recent years, for example, we've seen the breakups of Yugoslavia and Czechoslovakia for such accommodation and a civil war in Sudan that pits ethnic groups against each other. On the other hand, subcultures that transcend national boundaries, such as the Inuits in the Arctic and the Kurds in the Middle East, have less in common with people of their nationality than with their ethnic brethren in other countries, thus defying their being pigeonholed into a national reference group.

Regardless of the scenario that unfolds in the future, international business managers will need to examine cultural differences in order to know how to operate effectively. This examination should be not only on a national basis, but also on any other basis, such as profession and religion, that separates group values and attitudes.

Four scenarios for future international cultures are

- More homogeneous cultures that are hybrids of today's cultures will develop.
- Cultures will become more homogeneous in visible aspects, but not interpersonal aspects.
- National cultures will become stronger.
- National borders will change to accommodate cultures.

SUMMARY

- Culture includes norms based on learned attitudes, values, and beliefs. Almost everyone agrees that there are cross-country differences, but they disagree as to what they are.

- International companies must evaluate their business practices to ensure that they take into account national norms in their behavioral characteristics.

- In addition to being part of a national culture, people are simultaneously part of other cultures, such as a professional culture or organizational culture.

- A given country may encompass very distinct societies. People also may have more in common with similar groups in foreign countries than with groups in their own country.

- Cultural change may take place as a result of choice or imposition. Isolation from other groups, especially because of language, tends to stabilize cultures.

- People fall into social stratification systems according to their ascribed and acquired group memberships. These memberships determine a person's degree of access to economic resources, prestige, social relations, and power. An individual's affiliations may determine his or her qualifications and availability for given jobs.

- Some people work far more than is necessary to satisfy their basic needs for food, clothing, and shelter. People are motivated to work for various reasons, including their preference for material items over leisure, the belief that work will bring success and reward, and the desire for achievement.

- There are national differences in norms as to whether people prefer an autocratic or a consultative working relationship, whether they want set rules, and how much they compete or cooperate with fellow workers.

- There are national differences in norms in the degree to which people trust one another, believe in fate, and plan for the future.

- Information processing is greatly affected by cultural background. The failure to perceive subtle distinctions in behavior can result in misunderstandings in international dealings.

- People communicate through spoken, written, and silent language, based on culturally determined cues.

- Host cultures do not always expect companies and individuals to conform to their norms. They sometimes accommodate foreign companies and have different standards for foreigners.

- The company usually needs to make fewer adjustments when entering a culture that is similar to its own, but it must be very cautious not to overlook subtleties and how the host country may perceive the entry of foreigners.

- People working in a foreign environment should be sensitive to the dangers of excessive polycentrism and excessive ethnocentrism. They should try to become geocentric.

- In deciding whether to try to bring change to home- or host-country operations, an international company should consider how important the change is to each party, the cost and benefit to the company of each alternative, the use of opinion leaders, and the timing of change.

Charles Martin in Uganda[91]

James Green, vice president of U.S.-based Hydro Generation (HG), pondered about whether to continue employing Charles Martin in Uganda for the construction phase of a large dam project after he completed his assignment in the project's preliminary stage. (Map 2.5 shows Uganda and the location of the dam project.) Although Green felt that Martin's results had been quite satisfactory (every task had been completed on time and within the total budget), he worried about the means Martin had used to gain his results. In essence, Green worried that Martin was too focused on current Ugandan ways of doing business and that these practices were counter both to HG's company culture and to HG's methods of operating elsewhere. Further, he was apprehensive that some of Martin's practices could have longer-term negative repercussions for HG, even within Uganda. At the same time, he knew that Martin wanted to remain in Uganda and that HG would be hard pressed to find anyone who had a combination of U.S. business training, experience with HG, and a depth of knowledge about Uganda. Further, although Martin was only 29, he had been effective at disarming some critics of the power plant because he was quite knowledgeable about development issues.

Martin's specific assignment was only for the preconstruction phase of the power plant project, having been transferred there a year and a half earlier as project liaison specialist. His duties were three-pronged: (1) working with Ugandan governmental authorities in the capital, Kampala, and with villagers in the area where the dam was to be built to gain support and necessary permissions for the construction; (2) establishing an office and hiring people for that office who would be responsible for local purchases (including hiring), clearance of incoming goods through customs, immigration permissions for foreigners coming in to work on the project, logistics of materials going from the airport in Kampala to the dam site, and keeping records of supplies and expenditures; and (3) helping foreign visitors (mainly engineers) become accommodated and oriented when visiting Uganda.

MAP 2.5   Uganda

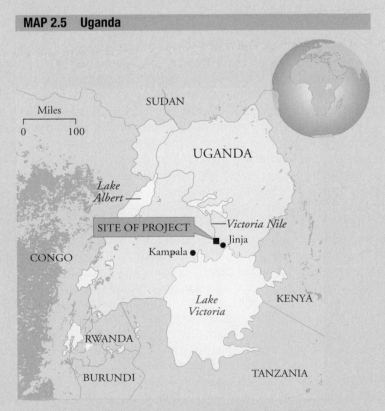

Uganda is a land-locked country in central Africa. The site of the project is near one of the two sources of the Nile River.

HG was a specialist in power plants. It had built plants in 16 countries and maintained an ownership in about half of them. The Uganda project was its first anywhere in Africa. Because dam construction involves huge amounts of capital and because many groups oppose their construction on the grounds that they typically displace large groups of people, HG wanted to build as many local allies as possible for its Ugandan project in order to prevent adverse publicity that could lead to demonstrations and costly work stoppages. Having Martin take charge in setting up the operation before construction was a new routine for HG. The objective of having him assigned there was to get an operating structure and facility in place so that incoming operating managers would not have to contend with mundane startup activities, such as obtaining licenses, installing telephones and utilities, and securing the initial staff that would hire the full range of local personnel later.

The philosophy and values of HG's founder and current CEO, Lawrence Lovell, were very influential in shaping the company's management culture. He was a devout Christian and regular attendee of the National Prayer Breakfast. He believed strongly that business activities, although secular, should embody strong Christian values. He also believed that subordinates should be given full responsibility in making and implementing decisions, but that they should be held accountable for their results.

Charles Martin, although still young by business standards, had a background that seemed well suited to the Ugandan project. After high school, he entered the University of Wisconsin–Madison where he became fascinated with Africa while taking a course about its precolonial history. After graduating with a major in African studies, he joined the Peace Corps and served in Kenya. His duties involved working with the startup of small businesses. While in the Peace Corps, he travelled as well to Ethiopia and Tanzania. Although he loved working in Kenya, he had disdain for many of the Westerners he encountered there. He felt that they thrived in expatriate ghettos by congregating mainly in Nairobi's first-class hotels and socializing almost entirely with each other. In fact, he developed a creed of "Don't draw attention to yourself, and above all, learn and respect the culture." When he finished his Peace Corps stint, he knew he wanted to return to work somewhere in Africa. Because he wanted to use his knowledge of Africa as a means rather than an end in itself, he earned an MBA at the University of Maryland. Afterward, he took a job with HG, where he worked for two years on project bidding and budgeting. He made it known both at the time of hiring and when HG became involved in negotiating for the Ugandan power plant that he wanted to be assigned to Africa.

HG saw the wisdom of having someone with both a home-country corporate perspective and a knowledge of Uganda because of Uganda's economic, political, and cultural complexity. Uganda, a country of about 25 million people, has English as its official language, but many people speak only another language, mainly Bantu or Nilotic languages of the Bugandas, Langos, Acholi, Teso, and Karamojong tribes. There has been a strong separatist movement among the Bugandas. Although about two-thirds of Ugandans are Christians (about evenly split between Roman Catholics and Anglicans), there are large numbers of Muslims and people following animistic religions. Uganda gained independence from British colonial rule in 1962 and has since had a series of misfortunes. The dictatorship of Idi Amin was ruthless and included mass murder. Uganda has had to absorb huge numbers of refugees from Rwanda, Zaire, and the Sudan. Nepotism is a norm, and the country is considered one of the most corrupt in the world. On the positive side, the entry of foreign companies is not heavily regulated, and the Ugandan government strongly favored the HG power plant because less than 5 percent of its population had access to electricity.

Now that Martin was completing his liaison tasks for the preconstuction phase of the project, Green was reviewing Martin's performance over the past year and a half. He was specifically concerned about Martin's lifestyle, some of his business practices, and his participation in tribal rituals.

Although HG had no formal guidelines on how their expatriate managers should live while abroad, the company culture was one in which these managers' lifestyles usually reflected a prosperous international company. HG paid Martin enough so that he could certainly afford to live in one of the up-scale neighborhoods where most managers of international companies resided. However, Martin preferred to live in a middle-class Ugandan neighborhood. Further, he did not frequent the places, such as churches and clubs, where expatriates typically gathered. Not only did this lifestyle not reflect the image Green thought the company should have, Martin's distance from the expatriate community might create problems for future HG expatriates; that is, Martin could not easily help them enter a social circle of their liking.

Business in Uganda typically moves slowly. For instance, one may wait months to get a phone installed, supplies delivered, or operating licenses issued. Martin quickly learned that by paying tips in advance to the responsible people, he could speed completion of HG's requirements. These were not exorbitant payments. In a country where incomes were extremely low (per capita gross domestic product of about $1,300 per year), recipients welcomed any extra income they could get. Given that Ugandan unemployment was high and that hiring was generally done through word-of-mouth rather than through formal searches, Martin mentioned to people he met that he would need to hire staff. They usually recommended relatives, whom he interviewed and hired. He reasoned that in a country like Uganda, these family connections would be useful. For instance, he hired the niece of a high-ranking custom's officer to handle import clearances.

Green felt that these practices, although legal and within the normal context of doing business in Uganda, bordered on being unethical. Further, he worried about the long-term consequences. For instance, if word got out in Uganda that HG was paying extra for its services, which would inevitably occur, might everyone come to expect extra payments for their services? In fact, if word reached high echelons of the Ugandan government, officials in these echelons might ask for large payments in lieu of finding excuses to delay the project. These payments would not only be costly, but they might also be illegal under U.S. law. Further, adverse international publicity could negatively affect HG's operations in other countries. Finally, Green disagreed with Martin's hiring practices. Although he did not doubt the employees' competence, he felt that their employment bordered on nepotism, which created two additional risks. First, their close connection with government officials might encourage participation in corruption, such as the import clearance person working with her uncle to charge extra for import approval. Second, given Uganda's history of political instability, the current "friends" in the government might be removed from their positions in the future.

Green was also concerned about tribal rituals. The dam's location would displace about 700 villagers. During early negotiations with the Ugandan government and before Martin's transfer to Uganda, HG offered a resettlement package to displaced people, and it renovated schools and health centers in their new location. HG's executives understood that its package, which cost millions of dollars, was acceptable. However, after Martin's arrival, two tribes living close to the Bujagali Falls' site of the proposed dam claimed that the river was sacred with spirits residing therein. One of the tribe's leaders said that this site was as sacred to them as Mecca is to Muslims. Their claims were publicized in the international press, and there was much international support for the tribes' claim. Martin, with permission from HG's headquarters, hired a specialist in African religions, who advised HG that it should work with the religious caretakers of the falls to find a solution. They contacted the official caretaker, who stated that spirits cannot be moved, but can be appeased. For a fee of about $7,500, he sacrificed a sheep, two cows, four goats, and many chickens by holding them down on hot coals while 40 spiritual diviners prayed and danced. Afterward, these diviners sprinkled blood on sacred trees. However, the official caretaker announced afterward that the spirits had not been appeased because Martin had not participated in the ceremony. Martin then paid another fee of about $10,000 to repeat the ceremony, in which he participated. This evidently appeased the spirits.

Green's concern was that Martin participated in the second ceremony, which he considered to be pagan and probably a sham. Although Martin's participation allowed work to progress on the project, Green felt that this participation hurt HG's image and was an affront to Uganda's majority Christian population and the many Christian missionaries there. Further, his participation might be construed in the future as a mockery of tribal customs, thereby creating a hostile environment for HG.

Having reviewed his thoughts about Martin, Green needed to make decisions about staffing the Uganda operation for its next phase. He needed to transfer a number of technical personnel to Uganda. He had already begun interviewing several senior HG people for the position of project director. But he pondered whether the new director would benefit by having on his staff an American, such as Martin, who could advise him about Ugandan norms. If so, he wondered if Martin would be the right choice for the post.

QUESTIONS

1. Describe Ugandan cultural attributes that might affect operations of a foreign company operating there.

2. Would you describe Green's and Martin's attitudes as being ethnocentric, polycentric, or geocentric? What factors do you think have influenced their attitudes?

3. Who was right, Green or Martin, about the controversial actions Martin took in the Ugandan operations? What might have been the results if he had not taken those actions?

4. In HG's next phase, the dam construction, should it employ someone whose main function is to be a liaison between HG's corporate culture and the culture of Uganda? If so, should Martin be the person for the job?

CHAPTER NOTES

1   We appreciate the help that one of Java Lounge's owners, Omar Aljindi, gave us in providing information about the company's operations. Other data were taken from Rachel Miller, "How to Exploit Pop Around the Globe," *Marketing* (August 8, 2002): point-of-purchase section, 27; Neil MacFarquhar, "Leisure Class to Working Class in Saudi Arabia," *New York Times* (August 26, 2001): A1+; Roula Khalaf, "Saudi Women Carve a Place in the Future of Their Country," *Financial Times* (January 25, 2002): 3; Steve Jarvis, "Western-Style Research in the Middle East," *Marketing News* (April 29, 2002): International section, 37; Nadim Kawach, "Job Nationalisation to Gain Peace," *Financial Times Global News Wire* (July 12, 2002); John A. Quelch, "Does Globalization Have Staying Power?" *Marketing Management* 11, no. 2 (March–April 2002): 18–27; Andy Fry, "Pushing into Pan Arabia," *Haymarket Publishing Services* (June 8, 2001): worldwide advertising section, 21; Ali Kanso, Abdul Karim Sinno, and William Adams, "Cross-Cultural Public Relations," *Competitiveness Review* 11, no. 1 (2001): 65; "Culture Shock," *Design Week* (August 25, 2000): 17; "Saudi Consumers Face Changing Environment," *Financial Times Global News Wire* (March 1, 2000): n.p.; Edward Pilkington, "Like Dallas Policed by the Taliban," *The Guardian* [London] (July 2, 2002): sec. G2, 2; James Sherwood, "Fashion: Your Highness, Is That Gucci or Dior Under Your Veil?" *The Independent* [London], (May 17, 2000): Features section, 9; Barbara Slavin, "U.S. Firms' Saudi Offices Face Manpower Issues," *USA Today* (May 13, 2002): 5A; Susan Taylor Martin, "Inside Saudi Arabia," *St. Petersburg Times* (July 21, 2002): 1A; Susan Taylor Martin, "Hanging Out at the Mall, Saudi Style," *St. Petersburg Times* (July 24, 2002): 8A; Colbert I. King, "When in Saudi Arabia . . . Do as Americans Do," *Washington Post* (February 2, 2002): A25; Donna Abu-Nasr, "Saudis Begin to Show Wear and Tear of Life Under Feared Religious Police," *AP Worldstream* (April 28, 2002): n.p.; Cecile Rohwedder, "The Chic of Arabia," *Wall Street Journal* (January 23, 2004): A11+; Roula Khalaf, "Saudi's Grand Mufti Condemns Mixed Sexes at Economic Forum," *Financial Times* (January 22, 2004): 6; Joseph A. Kéchichian, "Jeddah Forum: A Step Towards Reforms," *Gulf News* (January 22, 2004): n.p., and Parris-Rogers International (PRI) case in John D. Daniels and Lee H. Radebaugh, *International Business: Environments and Operations,* 9th ed. (Upper Saddle River, NJ: Prentice-Hall, 2001), 45–46.

2   Tomasz Lenartowicz and Kendall Roth, "Cultural Assessment Revisited: The Selection of Key Informants in 1B Cross-Cultural Studies," paper presented at the annual meeting of the Academy of International Business, Sydney, Australia (November 2001).

3   Three of the most significant are Geert Hofstede, *Cultures and Organizations: Software of the Mind* (New York: McGraw-Hill, 1997), which covered 50 countries on attitudes primarily toward relationships among people in the work environment; Ronald Inglehart, Miguel Basañez, and Alejandro Moreno, *Human Values and Beliefs: A Cross-Cultural Sourcebook* (Ann Arbor: The University of Michigan Press, 1998) included political, religious, sexual, and economic norms on 43 countries; Robert J. House, Paul J. Hanges, Mansour Javidan, Peter W. Dorfman, and Vipin Gupta, eds., *Culture, Leadership, and Organizations* (Thousand Oaks, CA: Sage Publications, 2004) examined leadership preferences in 59 countries.

4   Michael Skapinker, "The Myth of National Stereotypes," *Financial Times* (March 8–9, 2003): 6.

5 See Aihwa Ong, *Flexible Citizenship: The Cultural Logics of the Transnationality* (Durham, NC: Duke University Press, 1999); and Leo Paul Dana, *Entrepreneurship in Pacific Asia* (Singapore: World Scientific, 1999).

6 Robert J. Foster, "Making National Cultures in the National Ecumene," *Annual Review of Anthropology* 20 (1991): 235–60, discusses the concept and ingredients of a national culture.

7 "The Lively Chemistry of Transatlantic Enterprise," *Financial Times* (November 1, 2001): 13.

8 Harry C. Triandis, "Dimensions of Cultural Variation as Parameters of Organizational Theories," *International Studies of Management and Organization* (Winter 1982–1983): 143–44.

9 Mary Yoko Brannen and Jane E. Salk, "Partnering Across Borders: Negotiating Organizational Culture in a German-Japanese Joint Venture," *Human Relations* 53, no. 4 (June 2000): 451–87.

10 Philip H. Gordon and Sophie Meunier, *The French Challenge: Adapting to Globalization* (Washington, DC: The Brookings Institute, 2002); and Robert Graham, "Air France Drops English Ruling," *Financial Times* (April 7, 2000): 14.

11 A 1999 referendum required the use of Spanish in schools. See "Guatemalan Indians Lament Recognition Measure's Defeat," *New York Times* (May 18, 1999): A5.

12 "Global Culture," *Miami Herald* (February 27, 2004): 3A, quoting David Graddol.

13 "Experts: English Language Faces Increasing Corruption," *Miami Herald* (March 25, 2001): 21A.

14 Inglehart et al., 21.

15 Paul Taylor, "McDonald's Learns the Ropes of Being an American Icon Abroad," *Financial Times* (April 18, 2002): 22.

16 Michael Segalla, "National Cultures, International Business," *Financial Times* (March 6, 1998): mastering global business section, 8–10.

17 Fons Trompenaars, *Riding the Waves of Culture* (Burr Ridge, IL: Richard D. Irwin, 1994), 100–16.

18 "When Culture Masks Communication: Japanese Corporate Practice," *Financial Times* (October 23, 2000): 10; and Robert House et al., "Understanding Cultures and Implicit Leadership Theories Across the Globe: An Introduction to Project GLOBE," *Journal of World Business* 37 (2002): 3–10.

19 Larry Rohter, "Multiracial Brazil Planning Quotas for Blacks," *New York Times* (October 2, 2001): A3; and "Out of Eden," *The Economist* (July 5, 2003): 31+.

20 *Women of the World 2005* (Washington: Population Reference Bureau, 2005), 8.

21 "China to Outlaw Aborting Female Fetuses," CBC News, **www.cbc.ca/story/world/national/2005/01/07/china-abortions050107** (accessed 3/11/05); and Ranjit Devraj, "A Murderous Arithmetic," Indiantogether.org (accessed 3/11/05).

22 Hayat Kabasakal and Muzaffer Bodur, "Arabic Cluster: A Bridge Between East and West," *Journal of World Business* 37 (2002): 40–54.

23 "Labor Force Participation Trends for Women and Men," *Monthly Labor Review,* **www.bls.gov/opub/ted/2001/doc/wk3/art02.htm**.

24 Inglehart et al., op. cit., question V128.

25 "The New Workforce," Economist.com (November 1, 2001, accessed March 12, 2005).

26 Inglehart et al., op. cit., V129.

27 Francis Fukuyama, *Trust: The Social Virtues and the Creation of Prosperity* (New York: Free Press, 1995).

28 Tobias Buck, "Europeans Balk at Starting Their Own Businesses," *Financial Times* (March 3, 2004): 4.

29 Everett E. Hagen, *The Theory of Social Change: How Economic Growth Begins* (Homewood, IL: Richard D. Irwin, 1962), 378.

30 Luigi Guiso, Paola Sapienza, and Luigi Zingales, "People's Opium? Religion and Economic Attitudes," CRSP Working Paper No. 542, August 2002, accessed through Social Science Research Network Electronic Library (**papers.ssrn.com/sol13/papers.cfm?abstract_id331280**).

31 See, for example, David S. Landes, *The Wealth and Poverty of Nations* (New York: W. W. Norton, 1998).

32 Martin Wolf, "Hard Work Versus Joie de Vivre," *Financial Times* (February 20, 2002): 15.

33 David Gardner, "Indians Face 10m Rupee Question: Do You Sincerely Want to Be Rich?" *Financial Times* (July 15–16, 2000): 24.

34 See R. Inden, "Tradition Against Itself," *American Ethnologist* 13, no. 4 (1986): 762–75; and P. Chatterjee, *Nationalist Thoughts and the Colonial World: A Derivative Discourse* (London: Zed Books, 1986).

35 Triandis, op. cit., 159–60.

36 Geert Hofstede, *Cultures and Organizations: Software of the Mind* (New York: McGraw-Hill, 1997), 79–108.

37 Abraham Maslow, *Motivation and Personality* (New York: Harper & Row, 1954).

38 Hofstede, op. cit., 26; and House et al., loc cit.

39 Hofstede, op. cit., 49–78; and House et al., loc cit.

40 Book review of Patricia Gercik, *On the Track with the Japanese* (Kodansha, 1992), by James B. Treece, *Business Week* (December 28, 1992): 20.

41 Ralph T. King, "Jeans Therapy," *Wall Street Journal* (May 20, 1998): A1.

42 Maxim Voronov and Jefferson A. Singer, "The Myth of Individualism-Collectivism: A Critical Review," *The Journal of Social Psychology* 142, no. 4 (August 2002): 461–81.

43 See John J. Lawrence and Reh-song Yeh, "The Influence of Mexican Culture on the Use of Japanese Manufacturing Techniques in Mexico," *Management International Review* 34, no. 1 (1994): 49–66;

P. Christopher Earley, "East Meets West Meets Mideast: Further Explorations of Collectivistic and Individualistic Work Groups," *Academy of Management Journal* 36, no. 2 (1993): 319–46.

44 Marieke De Mooij, *Global Marketing and Advertising* (Thousand Oaks, CA: Sage, 1998).

45 John Schaubroeck and Simon S. K. Lam, "How Similarity to Peers and Supervisor Influences Organizational Advancement in Different Cultures," *Academy of Management Journal* 45, no. 6 (2002): 1120–36.

46 Hofstede, op. cit., 113.

47 See Jan-Benedict E. M. Steenkamp, Frenkel ter Hofstede, and Michel Wedel, "A Cross-National Investigation into the Individual and National Cultural Antecedents of Consumer Innovativeness," *Journal of Marketing* 63 (April 1999): 55–69; and Hellmut Schütte, "Asian Culture and the Global Consumer," *Financial Times* (September 21, 1998): mastering marketing section, 2–3.

48 Inglehart et al., op. cit., V94.

49 See Stephen Knack, "Low Trust, Slow Growth," *Financial Times* (June 26, 1996): 12; and Francis Fukuyama, *Trust: The Social Virtues and the Creation of Prosperity* (London: Hamish Hamilton, 1995).

50 The examples are taken from the GLOBE project. See Bakacsi et al., "The Germanic Europe Cluster: Where Employees Have a Voice," *Journal of World Business* 37 (2002): 55–68; and Jorge Correia Jesino, "Latin Europe Cluster: From South to North," *Journal of World Business* 37 (2002): 81–89.

51 Ping Ping Fu, Jeff Kennedy, Jasmine Tata, Gary Yuki, Michael Harris Bond, Tai-Kuang Peng, Ekkirala S. Srinivas, Jon P.Howell, Leonel Prieto, Paul Koopman, Jaap J. Boonstra, Selda Pasa, Marie-François Lacassagne, Hiro Higashide, and Adith Cheosakul, "The Impact of Societal Cultural Values and Individual Social Beliefs on the Perceived Effectiveness of Managerial Influence Strategies: A Meso Approach." *Journal of International Business Studies* 35, no. 4 (2004): 284–304.

52 Benjamin Lee Whorf, *Language, Thought and Reality* (New York: Wiley, 1956), 13.

53 For an examination of subtle differences within northern Europe, see Malene Djursaa, "North Europe Business Culture: Britain vs. Denmark and Germany," *European Management Journal* 12, no. 2 (June 1994): 138–46.

54 Richard E. Nisbett et al., "Culture and Systems of Thought: Holistic Versus Analytic Cognition," *Psychological Review* 108, no. 2 (April 2001): 291–310.

55 Don Clark, "Hey, #@*% Amigo, Can You Translate the Word 'Gaffe'?" *Wall Street Journal* (July 8, 1996): B6.

56 Rene White, "Beyond Berlitz: How to Penetrate Foreign Markets Through Effective Communications," *Public Relations Quarterly* 31, no. 2 (Summer 1986): 15.

57 Mark Nicholson, "Language Error 'Was Cause of Indian Air Disaster,'" *Financial Times* (November 14, 1996): 1.

58 Manjeet Kripalani and Jay Greene, "Culture Clash," *Business Week* (February 14, 2005): 9.

59 Christina Hoag, "Slogan Could Offend Spanish Speakers," *Miami Herald* (March 8, 2005): C1+.

60 Much of the discussion on silent language is from Edward T. Hall, "The Silent Language in Overseas Business," *Harvard Business Review* (May–June 1960). He included five variables—time, space, things, friendships, and agreements—and was the first to use the term "silent language."

61 Benjamin Fulford, "The China Factor," *Forbes* (November 13, 2000): 116–22.

62 Ibid.

63 Carol Saunders, Craig Van Slyke, and Douglas Vogel, "My Time or Yours? Managing Time Visions in Global Virtual Teams," *Academy of Management Executive* 18, no. 1 (2004): 19–31 gives an excellent explanation of four ways to view time. See also Lawrence A. Beer, "The Gas Pedal and the Brake: Toward a Global Balance of Diverging Cultural Determinants in Managerial Mindsets," *Thunderbird International Business Review* 45, no. 3 (May–June 2003): 255-27.

64 Trompenaars, op. cit., 130–31.

65 Daniel Pearl, "Tour Saudi Arabia: Enjoy Sand, Surf, His-and-Her Pools," *Wall Street Journal* (January 22, 1998): A1.

66 June N. P. Francis, "When in Rome? The Effects of Cultural Adaptation on Intercultural Business Negotiations," *Journal of International Business Studies* 22, no. 3 (1991): 421–22.

67 R. I. Westwood and S. M. Leung, "The Female Expatriate Manager Experience," *International Studies of Management and Organization* 24, no. 3 (1994): 64–85.

68 Inglehart et al., op. cit., 16.

69 Mary Yoko Brannen, "When Mickey Loses Face: Recontextualization, Semantic Fit, and the Semiotics of Foreignness," *Academy of Management Review* 29, no. 4 (2004): 593–616.

70 "Business Must Come Before Family," *Euromoney* (February 1999): 92–96.

71 John Tomlinson, *Globalization and Culture* (Chicago: University of Chicago Press, 1999).

72 "In Mexico, Ancient Life vs. Wal-Mart," *Miami Herald* (September 6, 2004): 6A.

73 Nader Asgary and Alf H. Walle, "The Cultural Impact of Globalisation: Economic Activity and Social Change," *Cross Cultural Management* 9, no. 3 (2000): 58–76.

74 Tamar Liebes and Elihu Katz, *The Export of Meaning: Cross-cultural Readings of Dallas* (New York: Oxford University Press, 1990).

75 Clive Cookson, "Linguists Speak Out for the Dying Languages," *Financial Times* (March 26, 2004): 9.

76 Jonathan Xavier Inda and Renato Rosaldo, "A World in Motion," in Jonathan Xavier Inda and Renato Rosaldo, eds., *The Anthropology of Globalization* (Malden, MA: Blackwell Publishing, 2002): 1–34.

77 Adrian Furnham and Stephen Bochner, *Culture Shock* (London: Methuen, 1986), 234.

78 Brannen and Salk, loc. cit.

79 John Tagliabue, "At a French Factory, Culture Is a Two-Way Street," *New York Times* (February 25, 2001): BU4.

80 Geraldine Brooks, "Eritrea's Leaders Angle for Sea Change in Nation's Diet to Prove Fish Isn't Foul," *Wall Street Journal* (June 2, 1994): A10.

81 Marjorie Miller, "A Clash of Corporate Cultures," *Los Angeles Times* (August 15, 1992): A1.

82 Patrick M. Reilly, "Pitfalls of Exporting Magazine Formulas," *Wall Street Journal* (July 24, 1995): B1; James Bandler and Matthew Karnitschnig, "Lost in Translation," *Wall Street Journal* (August 19, 2004): A1+.

83 Mzamo P. Mangaliso, "Building Competitive Advantage from Ubuntu: Management Lessons from South Africa," *Academy of Management Executive* 15, no. 3 (August 2001): 23–34.

84 Sally Bowen, "People Power Keeps Peru's Investors in Check," *Financial Times* (February 6, 1998): 6.

85 Roberto P. Garcia, "Learning and Competitiveness in Mexico's Automotive Industry: The Relationship Between Traditional and World-Class Plants in Multination Firm Subsidiaries," unpublished Ph.D. dissertation (Ann Arbor, MI: University of Michigan, 1996).

86 Roger Marshall and Indriyo Gitosudarmo, "Variation in the Characteristics of Opinion Leaders Across Cultural Borders," *Journal of International Consumer Marketing* 8, no. 1 (1995): 5–21.

87 Alf H. Walle, "George Davis: The Singing Miners," *Southern Folklore* 1, no. 52 (1995): 53–67.

88 Philippe Rosinski, *Coaching Across Cultures: New Tools for Leveraging National, Corporate & Professional Differences* (London: Nicholas Brealey Publishing, 2003).

89 For a good discussion of this point, see Aihwa Ong, *Flexible Citizenship: The Cultural Logics of Transnationality* (Durham, NC: Duke University Press, 1999).

90 James Mackintosh, "A Superstar Leader in an Industry of Icons," *Financial Times* (December 16, 2004): 10.

91 The people in the case are fictitious; however, some of the incidents are based on AES's experiences with a power project for Uganda. Information for that was taken from "AES Begins Compensation for the Bujagali Project Affected Residents," *The Bujagali Power Project Update* 1, no. 3 (October 2001): 1+; Deepak Gopinath, "The Divine Power of Profit," *Institutional Investor* 35, no. 3 (March 2001): 39–45; Probe International home page, "World Bank Campaign" (http://www.probeinternational.org, accessed 11/3/04); Taimur Ahmad, "We Are Devo," *Project Finance*, no. 216 (April 2001): 39–44; "Give Us Freedom and Kampala; The Baganda on the March," *The Economist* 366, no. 8310 (February 8, 2003): 64; "Uganda: Harnessing the Power of the Nile," IrinNews.org (March 21, 2003); Stephen Linaweaver, "A Case Study of the Bujagali Falls Hydropower Project, Uganda," Occasional Paper No. 42 (London: London School of Economics and Political Science, July 2002); "AAGM: Bujagali: A Dream That Ugandans Love to Hate," *Financial Times Information* (June 23, 2002); Charlotte Denny, "Nile Power Row Splits Uganda," *The Guardian* [London] (August 15, 2001, www.guardian.co.uk); Marc Lacey, "Traditional Spirits Block a $500 Million Dam Plan in Uganda," *New York Times* (September 13, 2001): B1+; Mark Turner, "Uganda's Dam-Builders Search for Consensus," *Financial Times* (October 1, 2001): 15; "Appeasing the Spirits," *The Irish Times* (January 5, 2002): 62. Information on Uganda was taken from "Face Music—History of Uganda," www.music.ch/face/inform/history_uganda (accessed 3/7/05); and "Uganda," Lonely Planet World Guide, www.lonelyplanet.com/destinations/africa/uganda/culture.htm (accessed 3/7/05).

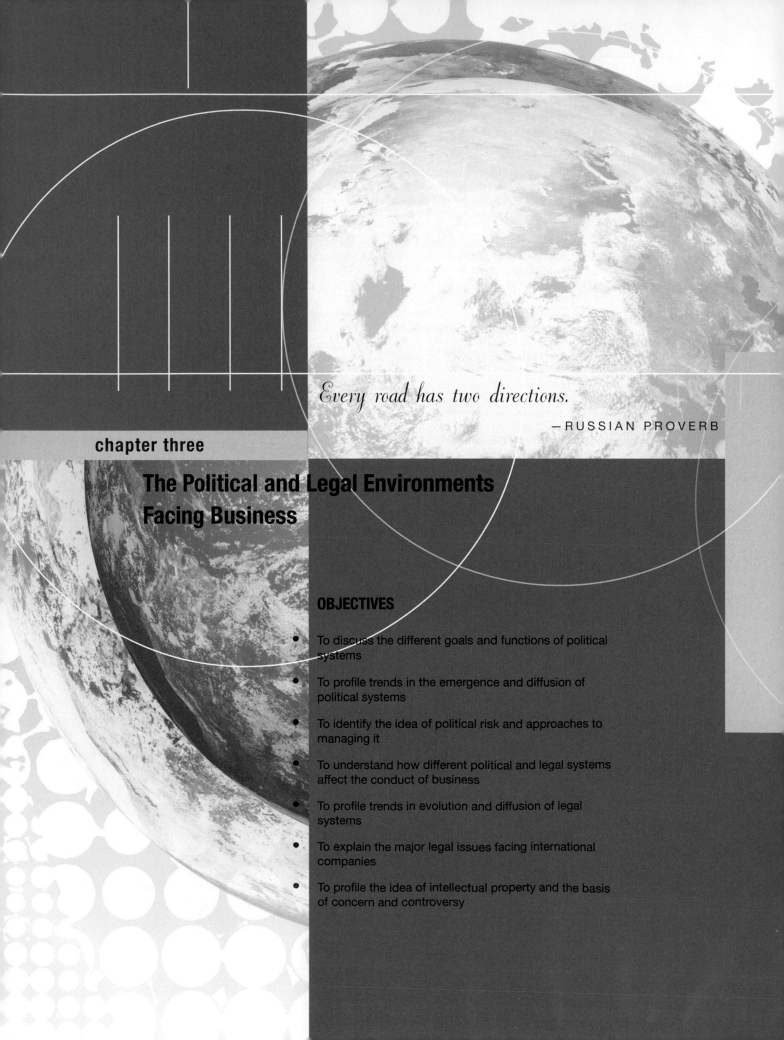

Every road has two directions.

—RUSSIAN PROVERB

chapter three

The Political and Legal Environments Facing Business

OBJECTIVES

- To discuss the different goals and functions of political systems

- To profile trends in the emergence and diffusion of political systems

- To identify the idea of political risk and approaches to managing it

- To understand how different political and legal systems affect the conduct of business

- To profile trends in evolution and diffusion of legal systems

- To explain the major legal issues facing international companies

- To profile the idea of intellectual property and the basis of concern and controversy

CASE: CHINA'S BUSINESS ENVIRONMENT[1]

From 1949 to 1979, China had a nearly autarkic economy. During these 30 years of communist rule, China prohibited foreign investment and restricted foreign trade. Although its view of communism stressed isolationism, China's policy also reflected its historical belief that contact with foreigners tended to corrupt its politics and pollute its culture. However, fearing that it was falling further behind other countries economically, China enacted the Law on Joint Ventures Using Chinese and Foreign Investment in 1978.

The period since 1979 has been one of step-by-step economic liberalization, including the gradual opening up to foreign trade and investment. Although the Communist Party still maintains a monopoly on political power, the economy today is primarily market driven and state ownership of productive assets is less than one-third of the total. The GDP has been growing since 1979 at more than 8 percent a year, making China the world's second largest economy. Should growth continue at this pace, China will become the world's largest economy in a few decades, although in per capita terms it would lag behind many Western countries. China's impressive growth has lifted hundreds of millions of Chinese from poverty, although hundreds of millions more remain poor.

MAP 3.1 China and Its Provinces

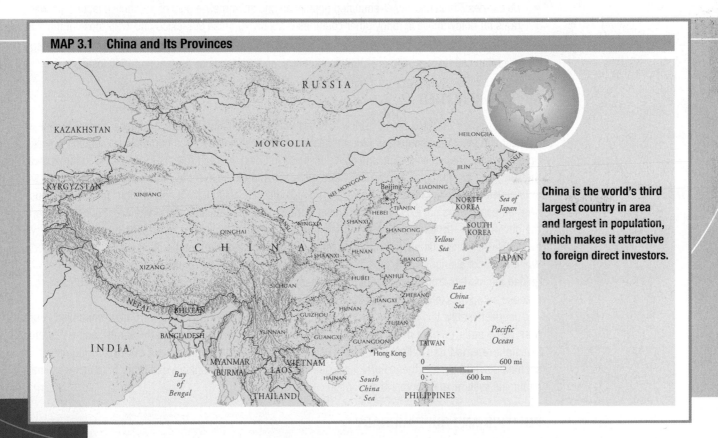

China is the world's third largest country in area and largest in population, which makes it attractive to foreign direct investors.

Fueling China's transformation since the 1980s has been a tsunami of investments by foreign companies, ranging from manufacturing ventures to export processing, licensing agreements, and a variety of service relationships (see Map 3.1). Whatever the form, these activities fall under the broad label of foreign direct investment (FDI). By the end of 2004, total FDI in China exceeded $560 billion, which was invested in over 500,000 ventures that have been set up by companies from all over the world. In 2003 China overtook the United States as the nation receiving the largest amount of FDI. Contracted FDI, an indicator of future investment, grew by 33.4 percent in 2004, to $153 billion. Finally, fully Chinese-owned enterprises are themselves becoming global players, as illustrated by China's Lenovo Group acquiring of IBM's personal- and laptop-computer business along with Haier, China's leading white goods maker, opening a manufacturing plant in South Carolina.

LAND OF OPPORTUNITY

The rush to invest in China has highlighted foreign companies' response to its compelling opportunities, namely:

- *Market potential.* China has about 1.3 billion people. A Monsanto spokesperson summed up this allure: "You just can't look at a market that size and not believe that eventually a lot of goods are going to be sold there. One aspirin tablet a day to each of those guys, and that is a lot of aspirin."

- *Market performance.* China's rapid economic growth has increased purchasing power, which has translated into rising consumer spending. Many markets in China are in the early- or mid-growth stage of their product life cycle. To be sure, in certain fields, such as telecommunications, China has leapfrogged technologically, so that today more people use mobile phones than landlines.

- *Infrastructure.* Rapid economic growth spurs government investment in market infrastructure. China is spending more than a trillion dollars on highways, airports, seaports, dams, power plants, and communication networks.

- *Resources.* China has a well-educated population and an immense pool of productive labor, with wage rates far below those in many other countries—about 1/3 those of Mexico and 1/25 those of the U.S.

- *Strategic positioning.* Companies see investment in China as a crucial part of their global strategy, given the country's growth potential, market size, and attraction as a manufacturing location.

MARKET REALITIES

Seemingly proportional to China's attractiveness was the difficulty of doing business there. The unique political and legal environment of China made local business operations a complex, demanding process. Some believed that when it comes to doing business in China, the first rule for managers is to throw away the rulebook. In particular, foreign investors were advised to forsake the notion that Western ideas will automatically work. For instance, the Western notion that one could form a corporation "for any valid business purpose" does not exist in China. Those wanting to open a business in China are required to inform the government—in excruciating detail—who they are, what they want to do, and how much they will invest. These plans must then be officially approved before the government authorizes a company to open. While many challenges were recent developments, all reflected the political and legal forces that had guided the modern transformation of the Chinese economy and, more fundamentally, the historical role of Chinese authorities in determining the path and pace of development.

Unquestionably, this situation was not unique to China. Many formerly government-controlled countries were undergoing similar transitions. However, China was a particularly tough case as foreign investors reported its political and legal business environment created a time-consuming process that seemed stacked against them. Foreigners pointed to the politics of China's elaborate bureaucracy, emergent legal system, and pervasive corruption.

POLITICS AND BUREAUCRACY

Foreign investors blamed a bureaucratic system that seems to rely on politics, not statute, to regulate their activity. Rather than the "rule of law" common in the West, China has long relied on the "rule of man" and the belief that legal rights derived from the power of an individual. This belief, highlighted in the broad authority of political officials, resulted in sweeping bureaucracy that touched virtually every aspect of life. Quipped Donald Lewis, "if the great invention of European civilization was a legal system, then China's was bureaucracy." In the 1940s, with the ascendancy of Mao Zedong and the Communist Party, the new leaders took over the imperial civil service and added a further layer of complexity by superimposing a party organization. The resulting bureaucracy created an enduring Byzantine regulatory system.

For example, foreign investors looking to open a wholly owned foreign enterprise (a WOFE, pronounced "woofie") in China had to jump through many hoops. They began by filing an application with various government ministries describing their investment and business plan, a list of the products to be produced, materials used, infrastructure required, and staff to hire and train, and technology, business methods, and skills they planned to transfer to China. Determining the proper authority depended on the priority for the type of investment. Provincial officials, for example, could approve proposals that planned to export all output. Further, the Ministry of Foreign Trade and Economic Cooperation (MOFTEC) prioritized industries—those that it encouraged, restricted, or for which it prohibited foreign involvement. Then, MOFTEC or provincial-level authorities reviewed each foreign investment application to determine whether the proposal was in the best interests of China—that is, if it would help capital formation, promote exports, create jobs, or transfer technology. Chinese officials typically subjected each application to stringent criteria applied through a cumbersome review process that reflected prevailing political goals and legal conditions. And, as a rule, foreign investors endured long negotiations (often spanning several years) with various officials before submitting their application to MOFTEC. Even then, success was difficult as MOFTEC rejected proposals that it judged offered too few benefits to China.

Greatly complicating this already complicated process was the long-running conflict between central and local Chinese authorities. The vastness of the country meant that local officials often held sway in the smallest village to the largest cities. Noted one observer, "The centre [often] has no control over the provinces. When it sends people to investigate illegal pirating of CDs, local governors block access to the factories." Similarly, the central government has tried to lower trade barriers and increase competition by allowing foreign firms to control local operations. Local officials thwarted these efforts out of fear of resulting unemployment and instability in their hometowns. The power struggle between the center and the provinces is a tradition in China, illustrated by a sixteenth-century Chinese saying: "The mightiest dragon cannot crush the local snake." So while the central government in Beijing may appear all-powerful to foreign investors, its practical reach is limited by the politics of its bureaucracy.

DEVELOPING LEGAL SYSTEM

China has come a long way since 1978 when, after decades of erratic postwar communist rule, it had no formal legal system. Since then China has launched one of the greatest floods of legislation in history. While great progress has been made, there are still problems, such as legislative gaps, haziness of interpretation, and lax enforcement. "Chinese legislation is chock full of ambiguities," says Lester Ross, a Beijing-based lawyer. He thinks this will take 10–15 years to fix. Donald Clarke, a law professor, is more pessimistic: "Look at the United States' legal system in the 1920s. It took us over 80 years to modernize it."

The growing pains in the legal system show in many ways. There is no comprehensive bankruptcy law to protect businesses. Recent draft legislation focused more on closing down certain enterprises that are deep in debt rather than protecting creditors. Nor is there an effective way to resolve contract disputes. Some foreigners, such as Sumitomo Chemical, sued their local partner in a Chinese court, only to ruin many local business relationships because taking your adversary to court violates Chinese tradition. Others, such as Newbridge Capital, used international arbitration, which is slowly gaining acceptance.

Big problems persist in how China protects intellectual property—the general term for intangible property rights that are a result of intellectual effort and include such things as patents, trademarks, designs, and copyrights. Western companies in China routinely complain that China's swift industrial rise is being powered by brazen and sophisticated theft of intellectual property. Many reasons contributed to this problem, including the developing legal system. Explained one observer, "Until recently, when China began putting intellectual property laws in place, for the past 40 years all patents were owned by the government, and could be shared by any company that was willing to use them. The Chinese government actually encouraged this, and that has left a deep impression on companies that intellectual property is there for anyone to use it."

Collectively, political biases, legal shortcomings, and puzzling legacies have contributed to the weak enforcement of existing laws. Observed Tim Clissold, who had a long career in China: "I was dealing with a society that had no rules; or more accurately, plenty of rules, but they were seldom enforced. China appeared to be run by masterful showmen: appearances mattered more than substance, rules were there to be distorted, and success came through outfacing an opponent."

CORRUPTION

The pervasive role of government in business decisions, the underdeveloped legal system and weak enforcement, and the material temptations of an emerging capitalist society inspire extensive corruption. Slowing progress was China's transition from a system of rule by man to one of systematic and objective laws. Consequently, investors faced many new questions about property and procedures with far too few solutions and guidelines. Many foreign companies regularly dealt with attempts to obtain bribes and steal property. A number of companies struggled to establish clear title to land and physical equipment. Embezzlement is a serious issue. "Tunneling," in which the relatives and friends of managers of state-owned enterprises do business, but not at arm's length, with the state firm or its subsidiaries, is a common method of embezzling that has spilled over to joint ventures with foreigners. For instance, PepsiCo spent more than a year trying to undo its tie-up with a joint-venture bottler in Sichuan after its manager secretly sold the venture to a local government bureau. James Bryant, director of Subway's Beijing sandwich operation, describes how his Chinese joint-venture partner cheated the company of $200,000. "People leave their heads at home when they come here," Mr. Bryant says. "They forget all about due diligence. They meet a guy on the street, give him a ton of money to run something and six months later he absconds with it."

THE FUTURE

The opportunities in China have attracted thousands of foreign firms. Still, many have run into a slew of problems that challenge opening and running their business in China. In this competition between opportunities and challenges, what trends signal the likely future business environment of China?

Many observers believe the key to the future of China's business environment is politics: Will China's national leadership appointments continue to be largely merit-based and pragmatic or might politics revert to ideological extremism? At this point, the country's impressive economic accomplishments make the first scenario likely. If so, China's business environment will become more consistent, transparent, and fair. Of crucial importance in this respect is that in November 2002, China joined the World Trade Organization (WTO), a global institution that sets the rules for trade between countries. WTO membership obligates China to continue to reform its business environment, moving toward transparent, rules-based, enforcement-oriented standards. For example, WTO protocols require China to clarify and expand its legal system by formally publishing its "internal rules" concerning trade and investment-related regulations. China's government has amended its legal code to conform to the WTO's stipulations on a broad range of issues, including trade, investment, and intellectual property protection. Essentially, China has to accept a system of global trading rules—everything from lower tariffs to antidumping regulations to removal of rules restricting distribution and retailing and penalties for violating trademarks and copyrights. China also has an obligation to the WTO to greatly reduce the differentiated trade and investment rules and practices among the provinces.

China's WTO membership gives foreign firms the legal right to set up wholesale, retail, distribution, and after-sale networks in China. Similarly, foreign firms no longer need to comply with local content requirements, accept previously high tariffs on imports, or submit investment proposals to China's Ministry of Commerce (MOC) that involve technology transfers. Now, such import contracts only require registration rather than government approval. Importantly, new opportunities are opening in areas that political circumstances in the past had closed or considerably limited to foreign investors. These include telecommunications, finance, insurance, transportation, tourism, advertising, accounting, education, and consulting. China has also agreed that its many state-owned enterprises may not discriminate against foreigners by giving local rivals preferential treatment. Instead, commercial considerations must apply when purchasing goods or services.

China has been criticized for the sluggish implementation of many of its WTO obligations. Still, in the short time since beginning its membership, China has further liberalized its economy and is tackling the problems that plague domestic and foreign businesses. The fact that foreign investors continue to pour money into China in the face of these challenges suggests that they optimistically view China's future business environment.

INTRODUCTION

Chapter 2 showed that the cultural issues that face international businesses are different from those that face domestic firms. This chapter carries this analysis forward, showing that once a company leaves its home country, it operates in markets with different political and legal conditions. Certainly, some countries may have business environments that are similar to its home country (say, the United States for Canadian companies). Other countries, though, may be quite different (such as China for Turkish companies). No matter the particular scenario, political and legal factors are part of the external environment that influences managerial decisions. Figure 3.1 expresses this perspective by building on the idea that relationships between government and business vary around the world.

The political and legal systems define vital parts of a country's business environment. As managers and firms navigate markets, they must understand how countries differ and converge. Determining where, when, and how to adjust their business practices, operating procedures, and strategic plan to meet these challenges, as we saw with China in our opening case, greatly boosts their chances for success. We concede that this is easier said than done. Therefore, successful companies accept the idea that countries differ on their ideas of politics and law. Understanding, rather than ignoring or worse, condemning, these intrinsic differences then positions their companies to prosper. As this chapter speaks to this issue, it is helpful to keep in mind that managers looking to operate in foreign countries (1) must discard the hope that they can straightforwardly transfer the principles and practices of the domestic business environment to foreign markets, (2) must accept the notion that political and legal systems of different countries vary, and (3) must realize that these differences affect how companies gain opportunities and deflect threats. The first part of the chapter will take a look at the political aspects of these issues, while the latter half profiles the legal aspects.

THE POLITICAL ENVIRONMENT

A country's political environment has enormous implications to managers and companies. Our look at China showed that its political system creates the freedom for foreign investors to enter the market, design operations, manage activity, and ultimately earn profits. For our purposes, a political system is the complete set of institutions, political

> The role of the political system is to integrate society.

FIGURE 3.1   **POLITICAL AND LEGAL INFLUENCES ON INTERNATIONAL BUSINESS**

EXTERNAL INFLUENCES

PHYSICAL AND SOCIETAL FACTORS
- Political policies and legal practices
- Cultural factors
- Economic forces
- Geographical influences

- Role of government in society
- Political ideologies
- Political risk
- The legal environment
- Operational and strategic legal issues

COMPETITIVE ENVIRONMENT

OPERATIONS

OBJECTIVES

STRATEGY

MEANS

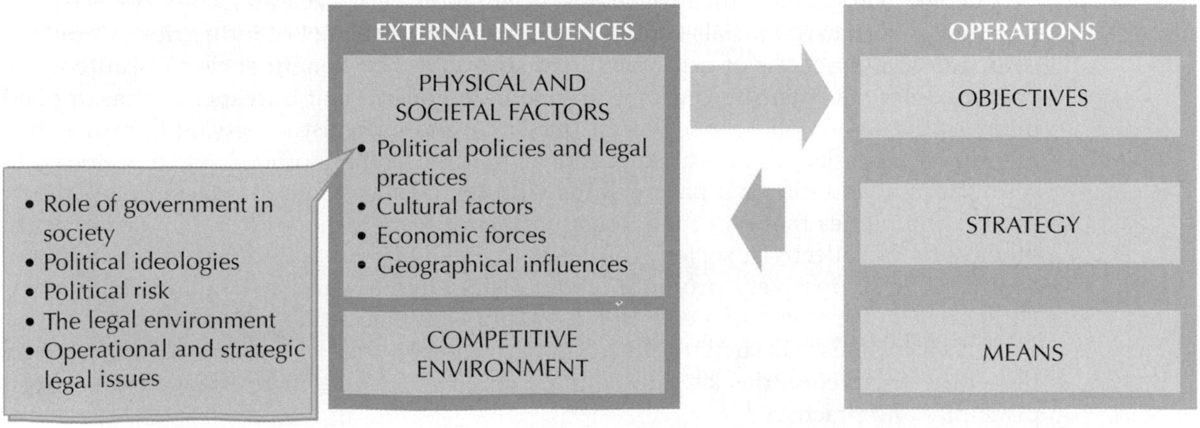

organizations, interest groups, the relationships between those institutions, and the political norms and rules that govern their functions.

The general purpose of the political system has been debated since Plato's *Republic* and Aristotle's *Politics*.[2] While different views of the specific purposes of a political system still persist, most agree that it integrates different groups into a functioning, self-sustaining, and self-governing society. Creating a legitimate consensus among people in a society can create many powerful, positive benefits that attract foreign investors and spur international trade. As such, the ultimate test of a political system is its ability to unite a society in the face of the divisive pressures of competing ideas and outlooks. Differing views of the role of government within a society, such as happened in the former Soviet Union, can effectively break a country apart. The resulting political instability can penalize companies currently operating in that market as well as discourage potential foreign investors.

Individualism and Collectivism

There are several ways to profile the similarities and differences between political systems. For example, one might ask: Should the government prioritize social equality or hierarchy? Should it emphasize individual liberty or collective security? Should it have jurisdiction in some or all areas? And what rights should citizens have in response? These and similar questions fundamentally touch on the ideas of individualism and collectivism within a political system—or, simply put, the general orientation within a society about the primacy of the rights and role of the individual versus that of the larger community. Philosophically, this debate has spanned centuries, beginning with Plato and moving on to Adam Smith, John Stuart Mill, and Milton Friedman. Basically, this debate revolves around the issue of whether society is better served by guaranteeing individual freedom and self-expression in the pursuit of economic self-interest or by developing political means and methods to subordinate the individual to the good of the collective.

The political system with an individualistic orientation is perhaps best exemplified by the United States. Its position that political officials and agencies have a limited role in society is a central tenet of individualism. In the context of its economy, this position has stark implications. Individualistic countries typically apply commercial regulations to correct market inefficiencies, such as insufficient consumer knowledge or excessive producer power. Hence, individualistic countries encourage businesses to support the good of the greater community by promoting fair and just competition. In those situations where competition is constrained or absent, government can then pass laws to regulate the market to ensure there is fair competition. Ultimately, though, government is detached from and independent of the day-to-day practice of business in an individualistic society. As such, the relationship between government and business tends to be adversarial.

The political system with a collectivist orientation, such as China, advocates the position that government officials should intervene in the structure of industries, conduct of companies, and actions of managers to ensure that they benefit society. Granted, our opening look at China showed that its elaborate government bureaucracy has applied many of the same policies one would find in an individualist society. Still, rather than relying on arm's length transactions and regulation, Chinese officials have preferred to set up formal and informal partnerships with the business community to develop successful companies that will then boost national prestige and power. Governments in other sorts of collectivist societies, such as Sweden, are more inclined to take forceful actions that aggressively promote labor, social equality, and workplace democracy. Ultimately, government in a collectivist society is highly connected to and interdependent with business; as such, the relationship between the two sectors is cooperative.[3] Presently, Asian countries keen to emulate Japan and China have engaged collectivist principles and practices.[4]

Political process functions include

- Interest articulation
- Interest aggregation
- Policy making
- Policy implementation and adjudication

Individualism refers to the primacy of the rights and role of the individual.

Collectivism refers to the primacy of the rights and role of the community.

Political officials and agencies have a limited role in an individualistic society.

Political officials and agencies have an extensive role in a collectivist society.

Political Ideology

A **political ideology** is the collection of ideas that expresses the goals, theories, and aims that constitute a sociopolitical program. The liberal principles of the Democratic Party and the conservative doctrine of the Republican Party in the United States are examples of political ideologies. Most modern societies are **pluralistic** politically—that is, different groups champion competing ideologies. Pluralism arises because groups within countries can differ from each other in language (e.g., Belgium), class structure (e.g., United Kingdom), ethnic background (e.g., South Africa), tribal groups (e.g., Afghanistan), or religion (e.g., India). These and similar dimensions influence the conduct of the political system. Managers from the United States, where there are two primary political parties, may question the political environment in those countries where there are several competing ideologies. Often, the main challenge is determining how to best articulate their interests to which political leaders.

Figure 3.2 outlines a political spectrum of the various forms of political ideologies; it thereby provides a way to profile their similarities and differences. The key issue for any sort of spectrum analysis is specifying the ideas that anchor the ends. For example, a political spectrum in a modern Islamic country might be divided in terms of the role of the clergy in a secular government. Or, in the specific case of Taiwan, one could define the political spectrum in terms of Chinese reunification versus Taiwanese independence. In both cases, moderates fall at various points between the two anchors. In Western countries, the political spectrum usually is defined along an axis with democracy anchoring one end and totalitarianism the other.

Democracy

Former British Prime Minister Winston Churchill called democracy the worst form of government—except for all the others.[5] The principles of democracy derive from the ancient Greeks, who believed that all citizens are politically and legally equal, and hence were entitled to freedom of thought, opinion, belief, speech, and association. More practically, a democracy is a political system that grants the voting citizenry the power to alter the laws and structures of government, the power to make all decisions (either by themselves or by their direct representatives), and the power of elections and the rule of law to enforce their vote. Table 3.1 lists the defining features of contemporary democratic systems.

> Political ideology—a body of constructs (complex ideas), theories, and aims that constitute a sociopolitical program.

> Pluralism—the coexistence of different ideologies.

> The ultimate test of any political system is its ability to hold a society together despite pressures from different ideologies.

> The two extremes on the political spectrum are democracy and totalitarianism.

> Democratic systems involve wide participation by citizens in the decision-making process.

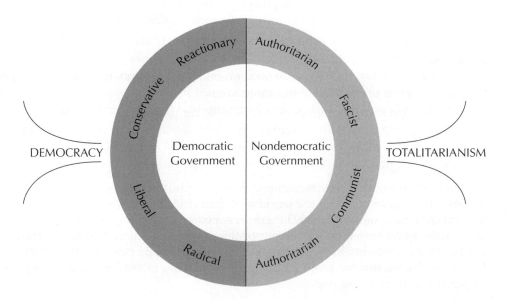

FIGURE 3.2

THE POLITICAL SPECTRUM

Although purely democratic and totalitarian governments are extremes, there are variations to each approach. For example, democratic governments range from radical on one side (advocates of political reform) to reactionary (advocates of a return to past conditions). The majority of democratic governments, however, lie somewhere in between.

TABLE 3.1   FEATURES OF CONTEMPORARY DEMOCRATIC POLITICAL SYSTEMS

- Freedom of opinion, expression, press, and freedom to organize
- Elections in which voters decide who is to represent them
- Limited terms for elected officials
- An independent and fair court system, with high regard for individual rights and property
- A nonpolitical bureaucracy and defense infrastructure
- Citizen accessibility to the decision-making process

Representative democracy—
majority rule is achieved
through periodic elections.

The defining feature of
democracy is freedom.

Factors for evaluating freedom

- Political rights
- Civil liberties

In terms of political freedom,
a country is rated as either

- Free in that it has a high
  degree of political rights
  and civil liberties
- Partly free in that it has
  tolerable degrees of political
  rights and civil liberties
- Not free in that it has low
  degrees of political rights
  and civil liberties

Presently, the population size of most countries makes full participation by all voting citizens in the democratic process impossible. Consequently, democratic countries practice various forms of representative democracy whereby citizens elect representatives to make decisions on their behalf. In some democracies, such as that in the United States, citizens directly elect a president and a legislature. In other democracies, such as in the United Kingdom, citizens vote for representatives—or ruling party—and the ruling party selects the prime minister, who is effectively the chief executive of the country. There are also hybrids of each form. Israel has a parliamentary government like that of the United Kingdom, but citizens cast votes for the prime minister. Many democracies have a few principal parties, so it is a reasonable task to form a government. Finally, democracies differ in the degree of centralized control. Canada, for example, vests political authority to the provinces at the expense of its federal government. Similarly the United States considers states' rights as a counterweight to the policy reach of the federal branch. The sixteenth-century Chinese saying, "The mightiest dragon cannot crush the local snake," as we saw in the opening case, captures this sentiment more poetically.

The fundamental element of democracy is freedom—whether it is freedom of speech, freedom of association, freedom of belief, etc. Since 1972, Freedom House has annually published an assessment of the state of political and civil freedom in all countries and select territories.[6] Procedurally, Freedom House derives measures of political rights and civil liberties from the elements of the United Nations' Universal Declaration of Human Rights.[7] It then applies these measures to each country to come up with an aggregate ranking (see Figure 3.3). Based on its score, a country is rated as:

- "Free" in that it exhibits elected rule, competitive parties in which the opposition plays an important role and has actual power. There is widespread consensus on the intrinsic and inalienable freedoms of expression, assembly, association, education, and religion.

- "Partly free" in that it exhibits limited political rights and civil liberties, exhibits unfair elections, political corruption, violence, political discrimination against minorities, military influence on politics, one-party dominance, censorship, political terror, and the prevention of free association.

- "Not free" in that it represses or denies basic rights and civil liberties within a political system ruled by military juntas, one-party dictatorships, religious hierarchies, or autocrats that allow only a minimal manifestation of political rights, severely constrained religious and social freedoms, and highly regulated private business activity.

Map 3.2 shows the distribution and range of political freedom worldwide in 2004. Notably, the citizens of 86 of the world's 192 countries lived in countries rated as "free." In terms of demographics, in 2003 there were nearly 2.8 billion people living in free societies, accounting for about 44 percent of the world's population. There were just over 1.3 billion people living in partly free societies—roughly 21 percent of the world's population. Finally, there were about 2.2 billion people living in not free societies, representing 35 percent of the world's population.

FIGURE 3.3 **COMPARATIVE MEASURES OF FREEDOM**

Free countries include Australia, Bahamas, Belgium, Canada, Chile, Czech Republic, Estonia, Japan, Mexico, South Africa, and South Korea.

Partly free countries include Albania, Brazil, Burkina Faso, Ethiopia, Malaysia, Nigeria, and Russia.

Not free countries include Algeria, Cambodia, China, Egypt, Iraq, Kenya, North Korea, Saudi Arabia, and Zimbabwe.

Source: Original art based on Freedom House survey. Adrian Karainycky, *Freedom in the World* (New York: Freedom House 1995).

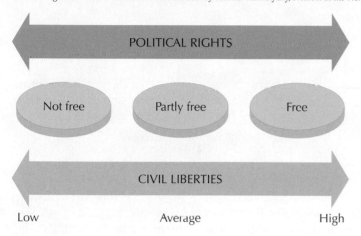

Totalitarianism

A totalitarian system is one in which a single agent, whether an individual, group, or party, monopolizes all political power. In contrast to the democratic ideal of freedom, a totalitarian system aims to subordinate all aspects of the day-to-day life of people—including occupation, income, and religion—to the power of the state. In extreme situations, personal survival is linked to the regime's survival, thereby forcibly merging the concepts of "the state" and "the people." Totalitarian states fall under the "not free" classification noted above.

Technically, totalitarianism is not a dictatorship or police state; rather it is a political ideology that involves constant indoctrination by agents of the government to eliminate any dissent, by anyone, anywhere within the system. The state relies on violence, persecution, propaganda, and censorship to forcibly suppress opposition. Political systems exhibiting totalitarian behaviors include:

- **Authoritarianism.** An authoritarian system, such as Chile under Pinochet and South Africa prior to the end of apartheid, aims to rule completely all affairs of all citizens.

- **Fascism.** The goal of a fascist state is control of people's minds and souls; more pointedly, Benito Mussolini (Italy's dictator from 1924 to 1943 and advocate of fascism) reasoned that the "Fascist conception of the state is all-embracing; outside of it no human or spiritual value may exist, much less have any value. Thus understood Fascism is totalitarian and the Fascist State, as a synthesis and a unit which includes all values, interprets, develops, and lends additional power to the whole life of a people."[8] Italy under Mussolini or Germany under Hitler exemplify fascist totalitarianism.

- **Secular totalitarianism.** Leaders in the political system use the power of the state to merge and forcibly control all aspects of the business environment. Communism is the leading example of secular totalitarianism. Theoretically, communists call for the equal distribution of wealth, a goal that they believe requires total government ownership and control of the factors of production (like land, labor, and capital). Examples of communism include the Soviet Union, Cuba, and to a lesser and lesser degree, China.

In a totalitarian system, decision making is restricted to a few individuals.

Authoritarianism—one person or a small group has absolute control over all others.

Fascism—extreme form of nationalism that calls for the supremacy of the state.

Secular totalitarianism—control is enforced through military power.

MAP 3.2   Political Freedom 2004: Global Trends in Freedom

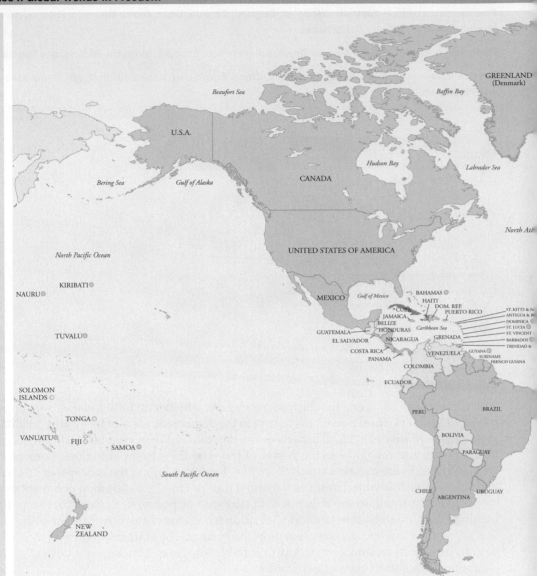

Countries classified as "free" have a high degree of political rights and civil liberties. Countries classified as "partly free" tend to be average to just below average in political rights and civil liberties. Countries classified as "not free" tend to be quite low in both political rights and civil liberties.

Source: www.freedomhouse.org. accessed June 2005.

Theocratic totalitarianism—religious leaders are the political leaders.

- **Theocratic totalitarianism.** Religious leaders are the political leaders, as exemplified by the Taliban Party in Afghanistan, and their literal interpretation of life can lead to extreme political, legal, economic, and social regimentation. The leaders of such systems usually claim to represent the Divine on earth. In the contemporary world, Iran and Afghanistan are considered theocracies.

Trends in Political Systems

The trend toward democracy is increasing. Key drivers include

- Breakdown of totalitarian regimes
- Improved communication technology
- Higher standards of living

The number of democratic states in the world has grown from 22 democratic states out of 154 total countries (14.3 percent) in 1950 to 121 democratic states out of 192 total countries (63 percent) in 2002. As a result, more people live in countries with elected democratic governments than at any other time in history. The movement toward electoral democracies has been accompanied with progress toward freer civic institutions, an active media, a strengthened judiciary, and stronger property rights.[9] The transition from state-controlled economies to market-based approaches has also stabilized operating

POLITICAL FREEDOM

- Partly Free
- Not Free
- Free

conditions for companies worldwide and supported common rules for international competition. Several factors have powered the democratization of the world.

First, many totalitarian regimes failed to deliver economic progress to the vast majority of their populations. In recourse citizens challenged the right of the state to govern, perhaps most dramatically highlighted by the fall of the Berlin Wall and the disintegration of the Soviet bloc in 1989. Since then, Eastern European countries, the former Soviet Union, and China have moved toward democracy. As formerly communist countries continue adopting democratic principles and practices, they have had to weaken the link between their political and economic systems. Similar trends appear to be unfolding in many Islamic countries. The United Nations Development Programme assessment of development in the Arab world identified many failures, including poor health systems, scant or nonexistent social safety nets, low levels of Internet penetration, and correspondingly high levels of illiteracy. Some 65 million Arabs are illiterate, two-thirds of them women. Significantly, the report put the lack of effective participatory government, as was the case in communist countries, at the root of these problems.[10]

Here we see a worker setting buoys for an undersea fiber-optic cable, a technology that has expanded an individual country's links with the world. The tremendous voice, image, and data transfer capabilities of fiber-optic cables free the movement of information about political events, economic conditions, and social standards around the world.

The Internet, by liberating communication, constrained governments' capability to regulate information flows within and across countries.

Second, improved communication technology, largely via the Internet, weakened the ability of totalitarian states to control citizens' access to information. Democracy benefits from an informed public that has access to media unfettered by restrictions on free speech. Hence, people with Internet access can more easily gather information about their own country as well as the outside world—information that totalitarian governments historically prohibited. The tendency of information freedom to increase citizens' calls for greater political freedoms worries some countries. For example, China has struggled to control access to the Internet and has blocked certain Web sites. Still, the number of Internet users in China quadrupled to 38.5 million between 2000 and 2002, spurring the government to identify inappropriate Web sites and to monitor the activities of cybercafés.[11]

Third, many people who championed democracy did so in the belief that greater political freedom would lead to economic freedom that, in turn, would then lead to higher standards of living and greater wealth accumulation. The data confirm this effect. The median per capita gross domestic product (GDP) is almost seven times higher for the most free countries than for the lowest category of not free countries. Almost all countries with a per capita GDP higher than US$15,000 are free, and most are free where per capita GDP is between US$5,000 and US$15,000. Countries that are freer grow more quickly as well. The growth rates of free, partly free, and not free countries in 1990–1998 were 3.23 percent, 1.47 percent, and 1.41 percent, respectively. Countries with high economic growth rates and a not free classification, such as China, are exceptions. Chapter 4 looks at these relationships more closely.

While there are general movements toward democracy and open economies, this does not necessarily indicate increasing homogenization of political systems. Presently, we see a further definition and development of Islamic states that do not endorse many democratic ideals. Too, many of the democracies that have recently emerged are experiencing growing pains, notably many of the former republics of the Soviet Union. Their instability stems from internal division, corruption, militaries and oligarchies (ruling power in the hands of a few), and destabilization from abroad. Some question whether these democracies will continue on the path to greater freedom in political rights and civil liberties. More provocatively, some foresee the "clash of civilizations" in which immutable cultural differences trigger a worldwide backlash against Western ideas about political rights and civil liberties. Also known as "differentialism," this argument particularly centers on the apparently innate and largely irreconcilable differences between Western and Islamic perspectives on several elements of politics and freedom.[12]

LOOKING TO THE FUTURE: Will Democracy Survive?

What will the world's political makeup look like in the next decade? Will democracy continue to spread from country to country? Will its opponents erode democracy's fundamentals? Will totalitarianism return? The emergent democracies of the 1990s, especially those in the former Soviet bloc countries, still wrestle with domestic unrest and security threats. If left unattended, some fear, they could easily escalate into turmoil, conflict, and the reappearance of state controls. Hence, the next decade will test whether many of the fledgling democracies that have emerged in the past two decades will continue their quest toward liberation or fall back into state control and political repression. Challenges to democracy are many. One stands out above all, namely, terrorism. Although the grave images of the terrorist attacks of September 11, 2001, in New York City have receded, their message is still very much in play: will the principles of freedom and personal choice that underpin democracy around the world be corrupted? Continuing tensions and attacks since 9/11 confirm that terrorism is an enduring threat to the function and permanence of democratic systems. As President George Bush commented, "Terror, unanswered, can not only bring down buildings, it can threaten the stability of legitimate governments." [13]

What forces, then, gird democracy to withstand the challenge of terrorism? Some people reason that fundamental correlates of democracy, most notably economic development and prosperity, will sustain it. Face evidence suggests as much; most wealthy countries are democratic, while most poor nations are not. The spread of prosperity to more parts of the world, from Brazil, to China, to Russia, to India, suggests more people will have greater economic incentive to protect the democratic systems that encourage economic freedoms.

Others contend that democracy depends on the vision and willpower of political leaders to liberate their societies—no matter what stands in their way. [14] A popular case in point is the steady democratization of Russia. The torch of freedom was lit in 1991 by Mikhail Gorbachev, and then fanned by the energy and goals of Boris Yeltsin and Vladimir Putin. Gorbachev took the Russian nation as far as he could; Yeltsin was there for the next steps, and when he tired of the fight, passed the duty onto Putin. The emergence of leaders around the world is a promising sign that the same transition can happen elsewhere.

Finally, indirect support for democracy may flow from Asia's alternative conception of democracy. With the exception of Japan—and, to a lesser extent, India and South Korea—most Asian countries are not democracies in the conventional Western way that see political and economic freedom as flip sides of the same coin. Most notably, their leaders are not eager to transfer power from the state to the people. In addition, many people in this region see links between the elimination of strong state controls, in the context of democracy, with the dilution of individual moral constraints, antisocial behaviors, and extreme individualism. Instead, these countries, such as China, Singapore, and Vietnam, appeared to have decided to first democratize their economies and then their politics. While the latter progression is presently conjecture, it takes support from the strong link between economic freedom and political liberty.

No matter what forces sustain and spread democracy, whether prosperity, leadership, or some combination, the political world has changed for managers. Vigilance is the order of the decade as democracy faces tests from forces it knows and from forces it has yet to confront. If democracy proves resilient and resourceful, then managers likely face the task of adjusting their operations during periodic crises. If democracy falters, then managers face the challenge of rethinking operations in a world with growing state control, repression, and threat.

Political Risk

Investing overseas exposes a company to the risk that arises from the quirks of national politics or, as commonly called, **political risk.** Generally, political risk is the chance that political decisions, events, or conditions in a country will affect the business environment in ways that lead investors to lose some or all of the value of their investment or be forced to accept a lower than projected rate of return. A variety of actions, events, and situations

Political risk—the risk that political decisions or events in a country negatively affect the profitability or sustainability of an investment.

| TABLE 3.2 | PROFILE OF LEADING SOURCES OF POLITICAL RISK |

TYPE	OUTCOME
Expropriation or nationalization	A government or political faction unilaterally takes ownership of the company's local assets. Compensation to the company, if at all forthcoming, is generally a trivial percent of the assets' value. This event was common in the 1960s and 1970s (e.g., Cuba, Chile, Venezuela, Uganda, Zambia, Ethiopia, Iran) but is rare today. However, in any event, the losses are immense.
International war or civil strife	Damages or destroys the company's local assets
Unilateral breach of contract	Decision of a government to repudiate the original contract that it had negotiated with the foreign company. The revision penalizes the firm and rewards the nation by reallocating the profits of the local operations. In addition, this extends to government approval of a local company's choice to breach its contracts with its foreign partner.
Destructive government actions	Actions such as the unilateral imposition of nontariff barriers in the form of greater local content requirement, which interferes with the transfer of goods between supply links or the distribution of goods to local consumers.
Harmful actions against people	Injurious actions that target the local staff of the company; often involves kidnapping, extortion, and terrorism.
Restrictions on repatriation of profit	Arbitrarily set limits on the gross amount of profits a foreign company can remit from its local operation.
Differing points of view	Differing interpretation of labor rights and environmental obligations that create backlash problems in the foreign company's home market.
Discriminatory taxation policies	A foreign company bears a higher tax burden than the local firm, or in some cases, the more favored foreign company, due to its nationality.

create political risks (see Table 3.2). There are several types of political risks. This section looks at the most common types, going from the least to the most disruptive.

Types of political risk, from least to most disruptive
- Systemic
- Procedural
- Distributive
- Catastrophic

Systemic Political Risks   Political processes within a country do not routinely subject foreign operations to unfair treatment. If they did, few companies would accept the hazard of investing in such countries. More commonly, domestic and international companies face political risks created by shifts in public policy. For instance, new political leadership may adopt a different approach than its predecessor, say, rejecting individualism in favor of collectivism. These regulations alter the business system for all companies. Then again, a government may target its public policy initiatives toward a specific economic sector that it believes foreign companies unduly dominate. In both situations, political change creates systemic risks that affect all firms. Systemic changes do not necessarily create political risks that reduce potential profits. Elections and policy shifts can create opportunities for foreign investors. In the 1990s, for example, a newly elected Argentina government began a radical program of deregulation and privatization of the state-centered economy. Investors who accepted the risk of these opportunities prospered as Argentina became more democratic. Our opening case shows similar patterns emerging in China.

Procedural Political Risk   Each day, people, products, and funds move from point to point in the global market. Each move creates a procedural transaction between units, whether within a company or country. Political actions sometimes create frictions that interfere with these transactions. Government corruption, labor disputes, and a partisan judicial system, for example, can significantly raise the costs of getting things done. More

POINT–COUNTERPOINT: POLITICAL RISK MANAGEMENT

The actions of host governments directly shape the success or failure of overseas operations. MNEs, under the broad label of political risk management, do their best to effectively deal with this threat either through active or passive approaches. Naturally, those who advocate active management believe that it is the best approach, while those who endorse the passive approach think their method makes more sense given the nature of politics, risk, and the environment. As we will now see, both cases have strong points.

POINT: ACTIVE POLITICAL RISK MANAGEMENT

Managers who take an active approach either (1) rely on statistical modeling to quantify the precise degree of political risk or (2) rely on the judgment of experts to estimate the general degree of political risk in a country. In the case of the former, managers believe that positive and negative political events in any country are neither independent nor random events but actually unfold in observable patterns. Hence, rigorous quantitative analysis and modeling can detect, measure, and predict future instances of political risk. Essentially, active political risk management reasons that if one measures the right set of discrete events, then one should be able to calculate the degree of political risk in a country and estimate the odds that politically risky disruptions—that is, civil strife, contract repudiation, financial controls, terrorism, regime change, ethnic tensions—will happen. This sort of approach depends on identifying indicators that best measure political risk. Often these indicators include such things as the number of generals in political power, pace of urbanization, timing of government crises, ethnolinguistic fractionalization, and degree of literacy. Upon collecting the needed data, managers objectively look at and compare the level of political risk within and across countries.

Some companies opt to assess political risks with qualitative indicators rather than quantitative measures. They do so by polling the presumably more insightful judgments of country experts. Certainly, country experts consider quantitative measures to assess political conditions in a country. However, they add their expert sense of the situation to include subjective elements of political risk. Managers applying this method often run standardized interviews with experts to identify and assess key events in a country

over a specified period. They then develop likely scenarios and assign probabilities for a finite period.

COUNTERPOINT: PASSIVE POLITICAL RISK MANAGEMENT

Many companies refrain from directly managing their political risk exposure. Instead, they treat political risk as an unpredictable hazard of international business. Often, they reason, the increasing range of conditions that vary within countries makes it foolhardy to presume that one can develop a model, no matter how methodical and systematic it may happen to be, to predict political risk. And, given that one can not accurately predict political risk, the strategically responsible thing to do is to find a cost-effective way to hedge the company's exposure to political risk. Typically, these companies shield themselves from political risks by buying insurance that protects their operations from any number of sources of political risk, including but not limited to government expropriation, involuntary abandonment, or damage to assets due to political violence. Presently, government agencies, international organizations, and private companies provide political risk insurance. Specifically,

- *Overseas Private Investment Corporation* (OPIC). OPIC encourages United States investment projects overseas by offering political risk insurance, all-risk guarantees, and direct loans. OPIC's political risk insurance protects U.S. investment ventures abroad against civil strife and other violence, expropriation, and inconvertibility of currency.

- *Multilateral development banks (MDB).* These are international financial institutions that are funded and owned by the member governments, such as African Development Bank, Asian Development Bank, and the World Bank Group. MDBs aim to promote progress in their developing member countries by providing financial incentives that encourage companies to expand into politically risky environments.

- *Private insurance.* Several companies underwrite political risk—for a price. Many insurers cover "routine" political risks that involve property and income, such as contract repudiation or currency inconvertibility. However, private suppliers of political risk coverage are especially risk averse of possible catastrophic events.

specifically, corruption among customs officials can push a foreign firm to agree to pay for "special assistance" if it wants to clear goods through customs.

Distributive Political Risks   Many countries see foreign investors as agents of prosperity. As foreign investors achieve greater success, some countries question the distributive justice of the rewards, wondering whether they are getting their "fair" share. Often, political officials decide they are not and begin a game of creeping intervention that aims to claim a greater share of rewards but in ways that do not provoke the company to leave. Generally, countries do so by revising their tax codes, regulatory structure, and monetary policy to capture greater benefits from foreign companies. This form of political risk can be quite subtle. For instance, few think of the United States as a nation with high levels of distributive political risk. However, the United States has perhaps the highest degree of political risk in the world for cigarette companies. The U.S. government has fought domestic and international cigarette companies on matters of taxation, regulation, business practice, and liability. Its successes have imposed direct costs of hundreds of billions of dollars and indirect costs that some in the industry claim are incalculable.

Catastrophic Political Risks   This type of political risk includes those random political developments that adversely affect the operations of all companies in a country. Catastrophic political risks arise from flashpoints like ethnic discord, civil disorder, or war. While uncommon, their impact disrupts the business environment for all firms. If they spiral out of control, these risks can devastate companies and countries.

THE LEGAL ENVIRONMENT

> A legal system is the mechanism for creating, interpreting, and enforcing the laws in a specified jurisdiction.

The globe may be shrinking as a place to do business, but standards of law can still be worlds apart from country to country. Consequently, national laws and regulations have a great effect on managers' plans and companies' activities in a country. All countries have, do, and will legislate a broad range of laws to regulate crucial activities, such as the investment of capital, customs duties applied to imports, or transfer of hazardous waste, as well as routine activities, like the payment of dividends to foreign investors or the type of seal to notarize a document. Generally, legal systems differ from country to country in terms of their treatment of any number of variables, including tradition, precedent, usage, custom, or religious precepts. Our opening case, in highlighting foreign investors' concerns about China's legal system, shows the importance of legal traditions, practices, and outlooks upon their activities. Perhaps most significantly, the situation in China confirms that a key aspect of a country's business environment is the legal system by which it develops, interprets, and enforces its laws.

> Legal systems differ from country to country.

For our purposes, a country's legal system is the means and methods that it uses to regulate business practices, define how companies conduct business transactions, specify the rights and obligations of those engaged in business transactions, and spell out the methods of legal redress to those who believed they have been wronged. Generally, differences in the structure of law influence the attractiveness of a country as an investment site. Still, as we saw with China, companies sometimes trade legal ambiguity for high growth potential.

Map 3.3 shows the various legal systems in the world today. Generally, legal systems fall into one of the following categories:

> Government action isn't always consistent—different agencies may have different attitudes toward business issues.

> A common law system is based on tradition, precedent, custom and usage, and interpretation by the courts.

- **A common law system** is based on tradition, judge-made precedent, and usage in which the courts assign a preeminent position to existing case law to guide dispute resolution. Countries engaging in this legal system use statutory codes and legislation but only after first looking to the rules of the court, custom, judicial reasoning, prior court decisions, and principles of equity. Canada, the United States, England, New Zealand, and Australia are common law system countries.

- **A civil law system** is based on a systematic and extensive codification of laws. Countries that engage in this legal system charge political officials, not state-employed judges, with the duty to specify an accessible and written collection of laws that apply to all citizens. Judges, rather than create law, apply existing legal and procedural codes to resolve disputes. More than 70 countries, including Germany, France, and Japan, are civil law system countries.

  A civil law system is also called a codified legal system.

- **A theocratic law system** relies on religious and spiritual principles to define the legal environment. This sort of legal system confers ultimate legal authority on religious leaders who use religious law to govern society. Islamic law, or Shari'a, is the most prevalent theocratic system at present; it is based on the Koran, the sacred text; the Sunnah, or decisions and sayings of the Prophet Muhammad; the writings of Islamic scholars, who derive rules by analogy from the principles established in the Koran and the Sunnah; and the consensus of Muslim countries' legal communities.

  A theocratic legal system is based on religious precepts.

- **A customary law system** anchors itself in the wisdom of daily experience or, more intellectually, great spiritual or philosophical traditions. Few countries in the world today operate under a legal system that is wholly customary.[15] Still, customary law sometimes plays a significant role, namely, in matters of personal conduct, in many countries with mixed legal systems.[16]

  A customary legal system follows the wisdom of daily experience.

- **A mixed legal system** emerges when two or more of the preceding legal systems function in a country. Map 3.3 shows that the majority of countries with mixed legal systems are in Africa and Asia. Even the United States has a mixed system. Unlike its 49 counterparts' use of common law, the state of Louisiana is governed by civil law. Similarly, theocratic law partly shapes the civil law system of Indonesia.

  A mixed legal system combines elements of other systems.

Diffusion of Legal Systems

Earlier, we noted that more countries are adopting democratic principles of government. The question then arises, are there similar trends in the adoption of particular legal systems across countries? Certainly, there have been many successful efforts to standardize laws among various countries. For example, European Union member-nations operate under Articles 81 and 82 of the Treaty of Rome; these are very similar to antitrust laws in the United States. More specifically, the United States and Germany officially coordinate antitrust matters concerning companies that operate in both countries. Other efforts are ongoing; the Securities and Exchange Commission of the United States changed its rules to encourage foreign companies, particularly European ones, to adopt international accounting standards by 2005, and made clear at the same time that it would consider only financial reports that fully followed such rules.[17] Compliance, however, is not automatic. Some European financial companies have asked the European Commission, the European Union's executive agency, to modify two international rules that deal with accounting for derivatives. There are similar efforts underway in setting worldwide standards in accounting, disclosure, and bankruptcy. Businesspeople champion greater harmonization of laws because they reason that specifying a uniform set of rules for all companies means they can more effectively plan and operate in other countries. Still, many efforts to standardize laws struggle worldwide, most notably in the protection of intellectual property and tax conventions. Hence, the reality of international business is that managers face differing legal systems across the world.

The evolution and diffusion of the civil and common laws systems gives managers a sense of the degree of current and likely convergence of laws across countries. The evolution of common law systems sets England as the starting point. Over a span of centuries, this legal system has diffused to the United States, Canada (except for Quebec), Australia, New Zealand, East Africa, large parts of Asia (including India), and most of the Caribbean. The primary means of diffusion was colonization. Figure 3.4 profiles the comparatively more exotic diffusion of the civil law system. France, Germany, and the Nordic countries all followed the original lead of Roman law in developing their own civil law traditions. France exported its

Trends are apparent in the adoption of legal systems across countries.

MAP 3.3   Legal Systems in the World Today

Despite the power of globalization, various legal systems still prevail in the world. Certainly, there are points of overlap and convergence. Yet, for all intent and purpose, significant differences persist between the principal forms of legal systems.

Source: http://www.droitcivil.uottawa.ca/world-legal-systems/eng-monde.html, accessed June 2005.

NORTH AMERICA

CENTRAL AMERICA

SOUTH AMERICA

legal system to Spain, Portugal, and Holland following their conquest by Napoleon. France, through Napoleon and subsequent colonial conquests, transferred its legal system to Latin America, Quebec, large parts of Europe, North and West Africa, parts of the Caribbean, and parts of Asia. The German legal system influenced Switzerland and Austria, and the Austro-Hungarian Empire transferred German commercial laws to much of today's central and Eastern Europe. Japan, interestingly, voluntarily adopted Germany's legal system and has steadily influenced the legal systems of the Republic of Korea, Taiwan, and China.

LEGAL ISSUES IN INTERNATIONAL BUSINESS

Impact of laws on international business

- National laws affect all local business activities.
- National laws affect cross-border activities.
- International treaties and conventions may govern some cross-border transactions.

A country's legal system affects many aspects of the local business activity of both domestic and foreign companies. Often, managers are concerned with a host of issues, such as: Which countries regulate the most? Do characteristics of the country influence the choice of regulation? Does regulation in a particular country create too many obstacles to getting business done? Managers generally look at these issues from two perspectives: (1) How do legal regulations impact day-to-day operations, such as the laws that govern starting a business, hiring and firing workers, enforcing contracts, and closing a business? and

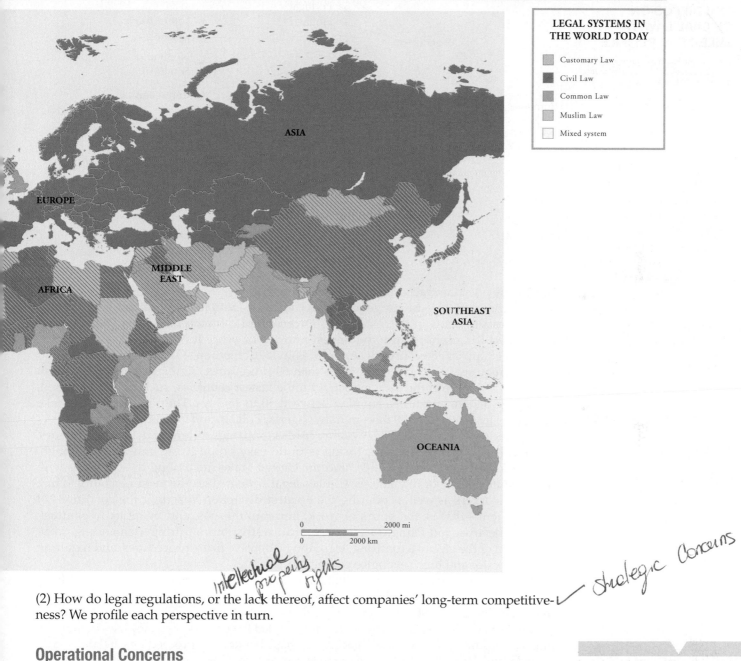

LEGAL SYSTEMS IN THE WORLD TODAY

- Customary Law
- Civil Law
- Common Law
- Muslim Law
- Mixed system

[handwritten: intellectual property rights]   *[handwritten: strategic concerns]*

(2) How do legal regulations, or the lack thereof, affect companies' long-term competitive-ness? We profile each perspective in turn.

Operational Concerns

Table 3.3 shows the range across the world in how a few countries regulate companies' day-to-day operations. Consider first the effort to start up a business; it is relatively easy in Australia, Canada, Ireland, New Zealand, and Sweden, which require that you comply with less than three registration procedures—usually, a tax, labor, and administrative registration. In contrast, Belarus, Chad, and Colombia require that you comply with about 20 or so procedures, including regulations pertaining to bank deposits, court registration, company seal, and health benefits. Consequently, it takes about two business days to start a business in Australia versus more than 70 days in Chad.

Once up and running, companies worry about entering and enforcing contracts with buyers and sellers. In general terms, the United Nations Convention on Contracts for the International Sale of Goods sets guidelines for the formulation and enforcement of contracts among its signatories. Still, there is variation across types of legal systems and specific countries. Regarding the former, countries with a common law system encourage

> Legal regulations either impact day-to-day operations or affect companies' long-term competitiveness.

> Operational concerns include
> - Starting a business
> - Entering and enforcing contracts
> - Hiring and firing local workers
> - Closing down the business

FIGURE 3.4

THE DIFFUSION OF CIVIL LAW: A SELECTIVE PROFILE

Source: Compiled from data reported in "Doing Business in 2004: Understanding Regulation," The World Bank.

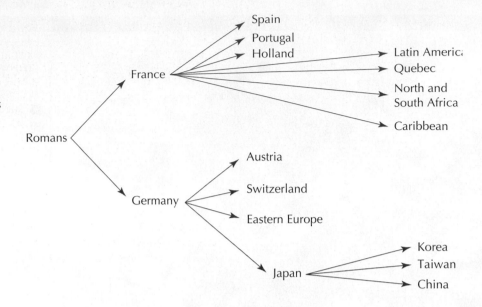

precise, detailed contracts. Countries with a civil law system encourage shorter and less specific contracts because the general civil code deals with many pertinent issues. These tendencies also show in the resulting enforcement of contracts. Australia, Norway, and the United Kingdom require the fewest number of procedures to enforce a contract, whereas countries like Burundi, Angola, Bolivia, Cameroon, El Salvador, Mexico, and Panama require compliance with more than 60 procedures. Similarly, countries vary in the span of time to enforce a contract, with the fastest countries, such as New Zealand, Singapore, Japan, and Korea running between 50 to 75 days. The same action can take anywhere from 600 to 1,500 days in Italy, Nigeria, Poland, and Guatemala.

Operating internationally inevitably leads companies to hire and, when necessary, fire local workers. In practice, hiring is quite easy while firing can be very tough. Denmark, New Zealand, Sweden, and the United States are among the countries with the most flexible labor regulations. China's legal system gives the most flexibility to hire and fire workers as well as offering the greatest discretion in setting the conditions of employment—that is, the hours of work, minimum wages, and benefits. In contrast, Angola, Belarus, and Paraguay place the most restrictions on firing, demanding documentation of the grounds for firing, legislating extensive firing procedures, and requiring lengthy notice and high severance payments.

Finally, many companies fail. At that time, closing down the business can prove difficult in some countries. The English bankruptcy law of 1732 was the first modern law to address this issue. The United States introduced its first bankruptcy law in 1800, essentially copying the English law. France, Germany, and Spain adopted their first bankruptcy laws in the early nineteenth century. Today, these legacies still shape bankruptcy proceedings. Ireland, Japan, Canada, and Hong Kong are some of the fastest and cheapest countries in which to close a business. India, the Philippines, Serbia, Chad, and Panama are some of the slowest and most expensive.

General tendencies of certain types of countries to regulate companies' operations clarify the preceding profiles. Reports suggest an inverse relationship between the per capita income of a country and its tendency to regulate business activity—that is, richer countries tend to regulate business less whereas poorer countries tend to regulate business more. For example, the average number of procedures to start a new business is 7 in high-income countries (like the U.S., Italy, and Japan), 10 in upper-middle-income countries (like Mexico, Poland, and Malaysia), 12 in lower-middle-income countries (like Brazil, Jamaica, and China) and 11 in low-income countries (like Angola, Ghana, and Vietnam). Furthermore, the legal systems of rich countries tend to regulate the major operational features of business activity more consistently than do those in poorer countries. For example, those countries

TABLE 3.3   THE REGULATION OF DAY-TO-DAY OPERATIONS IN VARIOUS COUNTRIES

COUNTRY	LEGAL ORIGIN	STARTING A BUSINESS			ENFORCING CONTRACTS			CLOSING A BUSINESS	
		NUMBER OF PROCEDURES[1]	TIME (DAYS)	COST[2] ($US)	NUMBER OF PROCEDURES[3]	TIME[4] (DAYS)	COST[5] ($US)	TIME TO INSOLVENCY (NUMBER OF DAYS)	COST[6] (% OF ESTATE, US$)
Australia	Common (English)	2	2	402	11	320	1,623	365	18
Canada	Common (English)	2	3	127	17	425	6,065	292	4
Chad	Civil (French)	19	73	870	50	604	121	3,650	38
China	Civil (German)	11	46	135	20	180	268	946	18
Germany	Civil (German)	9	45	1,341	22	154	1,483	437	8
Guatemala	Civil (French)	13	39	1,167	19	1,460	171	1,460	18
France	Civil (French)	10	53	663	21	210	896	876	18
India	Common (English)	10	88	239	22	365	444	4,123	8
Japan	Civil (German)	11	31	3,518	16	60	2,223	216	4
Korea	Civil (German)	12	33	1,776	23	75	402	534	4
Ukraine	Socialist	14	40	210	20	224	80	1,084	18
United Kingdom	Common (English)	6	18	264	12	101	120	365	8
United States	Common (English)	5	4	210	17	365	120	1,095	4

Source: Compiled from "Doing Business in 2004: Understanding Regulation," The International Bank for Reconstruction and Development/The World Bank.

[1] Number of procedures that the entrepreneur must deal with.

[2] The official costs associated with each procedure; the higher the number, the more costly the registration process.

[3] Number of procedures mandated by law or court rules that demand interaction between the parties to the dispute or between them and the judge or court officer.

[4] The number of days from the moment the plaintiff files the lawsuit in court until the moment of settlement or actual payment.

[5] Cost incurred during dispute resolution, comprising court fees, attorney fees, and payments to other professionals

[6] Cost of entire bankruptcy process, including court costs, insolvency practitioners' costs, and the costs of independent assessors, lawyers, and accountants.

that make it easy to start a business also impose fewer and simpler regulations to hire and fire workers as well as impose less regulation in their courts and bankruptcy systems.

Strategic Concerns

Successful companies develop strategic plans that describe their business goals and objectives in the effort to create long-term value. Many legal issues affect the process of value creation, ranging from where a company makes a product to how it tries to market it. Specifically, the following legal contingencies often shape an international company's strategic plans.

Product Safety and Liability   International companies often must customize products to comply with local standards if they are to do business in a particular country. Sometimes these legal standards are higher than in their home market, sometime they are just different. Product liability laws are particularly stringent in the United States, the EU, and many other wealthy countries. They are spotty, absent, or arbitrary in many poorer countries. Product safety and liability cases brought to court in the United States can include high punitive damages as part of restitution; this practice is far less common in other countries.

Marketplace Behavior   National laws determine permissible practices in pricing, distribution, advertising, and promotion of products and services. For instance, TV cigarette advertising is prohibited in many countries. In France, a manufacturer cannot offer a product it does not manufacture as an inducement to buy one of its products. Germany prohibits comparative advertising, while China prohibits comparisons if they reflect negatively on the other product.

Product Origin   National laws shape the flow of products across borders. Countries devise laws that use the origin of the product to determine the charge to the provider for the right to bring it into the local market. Also, countries measure product origin to determine the proportion of the product that is made in the local market (the idea of local content) versus made outside the local market. Local content is important to all nations, and most use this sort of law to push foreign companies to make a greater share of the product in the local market.

Legal Jurisdiction   Each country specifies which law should apply and where litigation should occur when it involves agents—whether they are legal residents of the same or of different countries. A nation's courts have the final decision on jurisdiction. Usually, a company will push the court in its home country to claim jurisdiction, believing it will then receive more favorable treatment. As such, companies must make sure that contracts include a choice of law clause and a choice of forum clause that specifies which law will govern in the event of a dispute.

Arbitration   Often, companies will resort to arbitration to resolve disputes. A small number of complaints against governments are heard through the International Centre for Settlement of Investment Disputes. This body is closely linked to the World Bank; a noncompliant government risks getting cut off from bank funds if it decides not to honor its legal debts. Generally, though, most arbitration is governed by the New York Convention, a protocol specified in 1958 that allows parties to choose their own mediators and resolve disputes on neutral ground. The international accord limits appeal options to narrow circumstances in order to make the decision more enforceable.

Intellectual Property Rights

The growing economic power of ideas in the global economy has made the theft of intellectual property a rising legal concern. In Adam Smith's time, countries drew power

---

Strategic concerns include
- Product safety and liability
- Marketplace behavior
- Product origin
- Legal jurisdiction
- Arbitration

Intellectual property—The general term for intangible property rights that are a result of intellectual effort.

A growing risk of international business is the violation of intellectual property rights. For popular products, like music, software, and movies, there are often more counterfeit products than genuine ones in the market. These images spotlight the quandary of enforcing intellectual property rights. One photo shows street vendors, in flagrant disregard of the law, selling pirated products. In the second photo, we see Chinese officials trying to enforce intellectual property rights with the high-profile destruction of confiscated products.

from agriculture prowess. Later, smokestack industries defined a nation's prosperity and power. Now, countries are competing on the strength of their brainpower to create might, prestige, and wealth. The output of this brainpower is generally called intellectual property—essentially the creative ideas, innovative expertise, or intangible insights that give an individual, company, or country a competitive advantage.

Problems arise because intellectual property, whether in the form of books, music, designs, brand names, or software, is tough to conceive but easy to copy. Indeed, the range of copied products is mind-boggling, including but by no means limited to books, music CDs, videotapes, aircraft parts, cigarettes, wristwatches, razor blades, batteries, motorcycles, shampoo, pens, toys, wine, shoes, clothing, luggage, medicines, foods, beer, perfume, cleaning supplies, and on and on and on. The costs of intellectual property theft—whether in terms of lost sales, ruined brand reputation, dangerous products, policing, or legal proceedings—are high. The International Anti-Counterfeiting Coalition

IPRs

Intellectual property rights refer to the right to control and derive the benefits from writing (copyright), inventions (patents), processes (trade secrets), and identifiers (trademarks).

Legal problems and conditions complicate specifying, regulating, and enforcing intellectual property rights.

estimates that international trade in counterfeit products runs more than $US 500 billion a year—or about 9 percent of the value of total world trade.[18]

Countries have pushed for better protection of intellectual property, generally in the form of so-called intellectual property rights (IPRs) that give the registered owners of the particular invention, literary and artistic works, and symbols, names, images, or designs the right to determine the use of their ideas. That is, the registered owner of a copyright has the legal right to say who gets to copy it or who gets to use it for what purpose. Technically, IPRs are a legally enforceable but limited monopoly, granted by a country to an innovator. An IPR specifies the period during which others may not copy the innovator's idea, thereby allowing him or her to commercialize it in order to recoup initial investments and capture potential profits. Naturally, companies seek protection of their intangible assets through enforceable patents, trademarks, and copyrights so that they may gain potential sales and profits.

Widespread piracy shows that these protections are tough to enforce. Breakdown is commonly linked to poor compliance and enforcement within a country. Legal problems arise because not all countries formally support the various conventions that protect IPRs. The Paris Convention for the Protection of Industrial Property and the Berne Convention for the Protection of Literary and Artistic Works, created in the 1880s and updated many times, are the primary regulatory codes for intellectual property.[19] More recently, the Trade Related Aspects of Intellectual Property Rights (TRIPS) code of the World Trade Organization has anchored stricter protection of intellectual property.

Many governments claim they abide by these agreements and aggressively enforce intellectual property rights. Still, as widespread theft shows, there is tremendous risk for international companies. Most directly, risk follows from the fact that an IPR granted by, say, a United States patent, trademark registration, copyright, or design registration extends only through the United States and its territories and possessions. It confers no protection in a foreign country. Furthermore, there is no shortcut to worldwide protection—one cannot register a "global" patent, trademark, or copyright, say with TRIPS. Complicating matters is the fact that countries interpret and enforce these agreements arbitrarily. For example, Indian patent law regarding pharmaceuticals protects only the processes by which drugs are made, not the drugs themselves. Therefore, Indian companies can make drugs that are under patent in other countries, provided they use a process that is different from the original.

By and large, these sorts of legal issues pose reasonable challenges that can be met with more sophisticated versions of international laws.[20] Worrisomely, the same cannot be said for piracy that is rooted in far more fundamental economic and cultural factors. Put simply, some countries are less inclined to protect intellectual property and, in fact, national attitudes can encourage violations.

Generally, poorer countries provide weaker legal protection of intellectual property than do richer countries.

Level of Economic Development   The vigor of IPR protection is highly related to a country's stage of economic development—that is, poorer countries provide weaker legal protection than do richer countries.[21] Generally, rich countries contend that protecting ideas is the only way to energize the incentive to innovate; as one analyst explained, "If stuff you create can be misappropriated, your incentive for continuing to create valuable intellectual property diminishes significantly."[22] Poorer countries counter that strict protection of intellectual property restricts the diffusion of new technologies, inflates the prices they pay for products only available from wealthier nations, and inhibits economic development by controlling the use of existing knowledge. Furthermore, few companies in poorer countries have created or registered intellectual properties. Consequently, they see little to gain by strongly protecting intellectual property. The WTO, with the vehicle of TRIPS, tries to balance this tension. It advised wealthy countries they had one year to comply with the latest rules on intellectual property but gave the poorest countries a five- to ten-year grace period.

National Cultural Attitudes   Cultural attitudes also explain differences among countries in the protection and violation of IPRs. Countries with an individualist orientation see the notion of individual ownership of an idea as intrinsically legitimate; it makes complete sense that a copyright means that if you create it, then you have the right to say who gets to copy it or who gets to use it for what purpose. In contrast, countries with a collectivist orientation extol the virtue of sharing versus individual ownership; hence they see little reason to adopt the notion of individual ownership. For instance, asked about software piracy in his country, the South Korean ambassador to the United States explained "historically, Koreans have not viewed intellectual discoveries or scientific inventions as the private property of the discoverers or inventors. New ideas or technologies were 'public goods' for everybody to share freely. Cultural esteem rather than material gain was the incentive for creativity."[23] Naturally, the attitudes of the particular players can often make or break an IPR enforcement case. For instance, one of the judges presiding over a patent litigation case in Beijing said during a seminar that he was giving on the case, still pending at the time, "Chinese intellectual property laws exist to protect Chinese intellectual property from foreign intellectual property."[24]

International businesses deal with these challenges in several ways. Our closing case discusses some of these within the context of intellectual property protection and theft in the global software industry.

Cultural attitudes influence the protection of intellectual property rights. Individualist societies are more vigilant than collectivist societies.

SUMMARY

- Political and legal systems across countries both converge and vary. The cultural (profiled in Chapter 2), political and legal, and economic (profiled in Chapter 4) systems create the potential benefits, costs, and challenges of the business environment in a country.

- Political systems can be assessed according to two dimensions: the degree to which they emphasize individualism as opposed to collectivism, and the degree to which they are democratic as opposed to totalitarian.

- Collectivism reasons that the needs of society take precedence over the needs of the individual. Collectivism encourages state intervention in society in the belief that government's role is to define the needs and priorities of a country.

- Individualism sees the primacy of the individual's freedoms in the political, economic, and cultural realms. Individualism endorses minimal intervention in the economy by the government.

- Democracy and totalitarianism are at opposite ends of the political spectrum. In a representative democracy, there is wide participation in the decision-making process. In totalitarian regimes, few citizens participate.

- The measure of political freedom looks at the degree to which fair and competitive elections occur, the extent to which individual and group freedoms are guaranteed, and the existence of freedom of the press.

- Many countries are in a state of political transition. Presently, there is a shift away from totalitarian governments and command or mixed economic systems and toward democratic political ideals and free market principles.

- Political risk is the chance that political decisions, events, or conditions affect the business environment such that investors lose some or all of the value of their investment or are forced to accept a lower than projected rate of return.

- Political risk occurs because political decisions or events in a country unexpectedly change the rules of the game under which businesses in that country operate.

- The type of legal system used in a country determines many elements of the business environment.

- Common law systems are based on tradition, precedent, and custom and usage. Civil law systems are based on a detailed set of laws organized into a code. Theocratic legal systems are based on religious precepts, as exemplified by Islamic law. Customary law systems are based on the wisdom extrapolated from daily experiences or a profound philosophical tradition. Mixed legal systems emerge from the combination of two or more of the preceding systems.

- International business is affected by laws and regulations issued by countries and international organizations. Some laws are at cross-purposes, and some diminish the ability of firms to compete with foreign companies.

- Primary legal issues in international business include product safety and liability, marketing practice, rule of origin, jurisdiction, and intellectual property protection.

- Patents, trademarks, trade names, copyrights, and trade secrets are referred to as intellectual properties. Widespread worldwide piracy of these properties is increasingly expensive for registered owners.

C A S E   Global Software Piracy[25]

I prowl the aisles of the software piracy mother lode, the Golden Shopping Arcade in Hong Kong's Sham Shui Po district. All around me in the basement of this dingy, block-long urban warehouse, eager shoppers paw through the bins and tables of the densely packed stalls. Inside a stall called the Everything CD shop, I buy the first of my installer discs, Volume 2. This tribute to pirate technology costs the same as all the other CD-ROMs at Golden Arcade, about 9 bucks or three for US$25. Incredibly, this disc has 86 programs on it, each compressed with a self-extracting installation utility. Volume 2 has a beta copy of Windows 95 as well as OS/2 Warp, CorelDraw! 5, Quicken 4.0, Atari Action Pack for Windows, Norton Commander, KeyCad, Adobe Premier, Microsoft Office, and dozens of other applications, including a handful written in Chinese. Connoisseurs of the genre compare the different versions of the installer discs like fine wines. Someone from Microsoft later tells me that the retail value of the disc is between US$20,000 and US$35,000.[26]

As this account dramatizes, software technology is dogged by the problem of digital piracy—the illegal distribution and/or copying of software for personal or business use. An explosive issue, it increasingly cuts to the perception, protection, and enforcement of intellectual property rights. Presently, software piracy ranges from an individual making an unauthorized copy of a software product for use, sale, or free distribution to a company's mismanagement of its software licenses. Table 3.4 lists the principal types of software piracy.

Technically, the standards of software piracy are unequivocal. The United States, for example, stipulates that software is automatically protected by federal copyright law from the moment of its creation. Officially, Title 17 of the United States Copyright Act grants the owner of the copyright "the exclusive rights" to "reproduce the copyrighted work" and "to distribute copies . . . of the copyrighted work" (Section 106). It also states that "anyone who violates any of the exclusive rights of the copyright owner . . . is an infringer of the copyright" (Section 501), and

TABLE 3.4   TYPES OF SOFTWARE PIRACY

End-user piracy	Users copy software without appropriate licensing for each copy, including both casual copying and distribution between individuals, and companies that do not strictly monitor the number of software licenses they install and do not acquire enough licenses to cover their software installations.
Pre-installed software	A computer manufacturer takes one copy of software and illegally installs it on more than one computer.
Internet piracy	Unauthorized copies are downloaded over the Internet. If downloads are made available on the Internet, make sure that the publisher has authorized this distribution.
Counterfeiting	Illegal copies of software are made and distributed in packaging that reproduces the manufacturer's packaging. Counterfeit registration cards with unauthorized serial numbers are often included in these packages.
Online auction piracy	Software resold in violation of the original terms of sale, NFR (not for resale), or OEM software that is never authorized for resale by a third party.
	Online distributors offering special deals with the software publisher, liquidated inventories, or acquisition through bankruptcy sales. These types of phrases are used to fool consumers into believing that they are getting genuine product that wouldn't otherwise be discounted.

Source: Microsoft Corporation, http://www.microsoft.com/piracy/how_types.mspx. Reprinted with permission from Microsoft Corporation.

the statute sets forth several penalties for violations. Ignorance of the law is no excuse for piracy; copiers are liable for the resulting copyright infringement whether or not they knew their conduct violated federal law. Thus, a software user who has purchased a license has the right to load the product onto a single computer and to make another copy for "archival purposes only."

The predicament of software is that, like any "digital" product, it is extraordinarily easy to duplicate into a copy that is usually as good as the original. Consequently, piracy and counterfeiting plague the global software industry. In 2004, industry groups reported that global software piracy, at the national, regional, and worldwide levels, was a rampant problem that showed few signs of stopping. For many nations, piracy rates exceeded 75 percent. The same situation existed for regions; notably, 70 percent of software on computers was pirated in Eastern Europe, 63 percent in Latin America, 56 percent in the Middle East and Africa, and 53 percent in the Asia-Pacific region (see Table 3.5). The cost of piracy was huge. The Business Software Alliance (BSA) estimated that software makers worldwide lost $29 billion to piracy in 2003—effectively, about $80 billion in software was installed on computers worldwide, but only $51 billion had been legally purchased.

Search for Solutions

Companies, industry associations, and governments have tried to develop political arrangements and legal codes to deal with this problem. Until recently, combating piracy was normally done by first relying on software companies to develop technical and business measures to thwart counterfeiters. For example, in the 1980s and 1990s, many software companies incorporated anticopying mechanisms into their products. Although these aggressive mechanisms were mostly effective, consumers complained that they made the software unduly difficult to use. Consumer objections led the software industry to discontinue these sorts of anticopying technologies. In response, software companies developed other means to protect against piracy, such as distribution business models (i.e., site licenses and shrink-wrap licenses) and technological protections (i.e., passwords, registration numbers, encryption, and dongles). Although somewhat annoyed, customers generally accepted these methods, and for a while it seemed that they might be sufficient to control software piracy.

In addition, software companies lobbied governments to pass and enforce laws supporting their intellectual property rights. For example, the United States elevated software piracy from a misdemeanor to a felony if 10 or more illegal copies of software were made within a six-month period and if the copies were worth a total value of over $2,500. The United States also got more vigorous in its enforcement efforts, notably threatening China with trade sanctions based on findings of especially "onerous and egregious" intellectual property violations in China.

Industry associations, notably the BSA, Software and Information Industry Association (SIIA), and the International Anti-Counterfeiting Coalition (IACC), spearheaded efforts to spur governments to toughen their laws. Generally, these multinational organizations provided global services in public policy, business development, corporate education, and intellectual property protection. The BSA, for example has members in more than 70 nations. Each national unit works to promote a legal online world by negotiating with governments and

TABLE 3.5   SOFTWARE PIRACY RANKINGS BY REGION

U.S./Canada	23%
Western Europe	36%
Asia/Pacific	53%
Middle East/Africa	56%
Latin America	63%
Eastern Europe	71%
Worldwide	36%

Source: Global Software Piracy Study 2004, Business Software Alliance, www.bsa.org/globalstudy/.

consumers in the international software and Internet markets. BSA members include companies like Microsoft, Adobe, Dell, IBM, Intel, Apple Computer, Intuit, and Macromedia.

Finally, software makers, governments, and associations, singly and jointly, successfully lobbied transnational institutions to help police piracy. The 170 member nations of the World Intellectual Property Organization (WIPO) pledged to protect intellectual property worldwide and administer several intellectual property treaties. WIPO continued to lobby members to ratify antipiracy treaties—the World Copyright Treaty (WCT) and the WIPO Performances and Phonograms Treaty (WPPT). Similarly, the World Trade Organization enacted the trade-related aspects of intellectual property rights (TRIPS) agreement to better regulate end copyright violations and counterfeiting. TRIPS requires all member nations to protect and enforce intellectual property rights according to global, not local, standards. Enacted in 1995, TRIPS was at the time the most comprehensive agreement on intellectual property.

Collectively, these actions by companies, associations, governments, and institutions gave hope that global software piracy would decline in the future. Moreover, by the late 1990s, software makers were encouraged by the fact that it looked as if piracy rates were directly related to a country's rate of market growth. The large and mature United States and Canadian software market had the lowest rate of piracy, thereby implying that as software markets in other regions matured, piracy rates would decline. Also, concerted political and company action seem to make a bigger difference. Lastly, some credited a host of other promising antipiracy initiatives, most notably the growing global reach of software companies, high-profile legal proceedings against companies using illegal software, increased government cooperation in providing legal protection for intellectual property and in criminalizing software piracy, a narrowing gap between the price of legal and illegal versions as the legal prices of software declined significantly, and efforts of the leading software associations to negotiate trade agreements that were tougher on piracy.

Piracy Persists

In 2004, global software piracy seemed on the verge of going out of control (see Table 3.6.). It did not matter which countries or regions were involved; piracy rates, if not increasing, were simply not falling. Escalating software piracy alarmed many, given the earlier expectation that tougher laws and treaties and aggressive protection and enforcement would thwart piracy. Whatever the cause, many thought piracy was poised to worsen. High-tech and law enforcement experts warned of growing piracy as people around the world, eager to join the digital age but constrained by low income, hunted for low-priced software.

In response, software companies intensified their antipiracy efforts. Many, like Adobe and Symantec, ramped up their long-running global campaigns warning consumers that copying software is illegal. Some, like Microsoft, hired former federal and police investigators, staged software stings, relayed information to prosecutors on hundreds of criminal cases, and took legal action against thousands of law-breaking Web sites. Most firms added security features, such as holograms and registration codes, to document the authenticity of the software. Some companies used search engines to prowl the Internet, seeking sites that distributed or sold pirated software.

Governments also increased their legal efforts. In the United States, the Departments of Justice and Treasury and their primary investigative agencies, the Customs Service and the FBI, carried out a series of raids worldwide against "warez" groups that reproduced, modified, and distributed counterfeit software over the Internet. The United States Senate approved the Trade Promotion Authority, thereby giving the executive branch more authority to negotiate trade agreements that protected technology companies. Too, a U.S. Department of Justice task force recommended taking a more aggressive strategy to combat piracy, counterfeiting, and other violations of intellectual property rights both domestically and overseas.

Industry associations reinforced these programs. They worked with the governments of many countries to help develop and implement the necessary legal framework to promote a safe and legal online world. For example, the BSA persisted in trying to persuade officials in Mexico, Italy, Hong Kong, and Singapore, among others, to get tougher on piracy. In addition, several software associations recommended that the United States place several countries on a high-profile offenders list because of their lack of rules protecting intellectual property rights,

TABLE 3.6	SOFTWARE PIRACY RANKINGS BY COUNTRY

TOP 20 PIRATING COUNTRIES		BOTTOM 20 PIRATING COUNTRIES	
China	92%	United States	22%
Vietnam	92%	New Zealand	23%
Ukraine	91%	Denmark	26%
Indonesia	88%	Austria	27%
Russia	87%	Sweden	27%
Zimbabwe	87%	Belgium	29%
Algeria	84%	Japan	29%
Nigeria	84%	United Kingdom	29%
Pakistan	83%	Germany	30%
Paraguay	83%	Australia	31%
Tunisia	82%	Finland	31%
Kenya	80%	Switzerland	31%
Thailand	80%	Norway	32%
El Salvador	79%	Netherlands	33%
Nicaragua	79%	UAE	34%
Bolivia	78%	Canada	35%
Guatemala	77%	Israel	35%
Dominican Republic	76%	South Africa	36%
Lebanon	74%	Reunion	39%
India	73%	Czech Republic	40%

Source: Global Software Piracy Study 2004, Business Software Alliance, http://www.bsa.org/globalstudy/.

their failure to follow vigorous enforcement actions against software theft, and their noncompliance with TRIPS. These harder-hitting programs did show elements of success. For example, China, in connection with its accession to the WTO, amended its patent law in 2000 and its trademark and copyright laws in 2001 and 2004 to make them more compliant with TRIPS. Officials in other countries, such as Costa Rica, Korea, Oman, and the Philippines, initiated or expanded antipiracy programs.

Despite these renewed efforts, some saw that the global cat-and-mouse contest between software companies and pirates slowly but surely was spiraling out of control. Sure, said skeptics, countries like China had vowed to protect intellectual property rights, while other countries, such as Hong Kong, Malaysia, and Korea, had signed major copyright treaties. However, the president of the IACC observed, "On paper, the laws and penalties are stiffer in many countries. The question now: Will those governments actually enforce those laws? I'm not optimistic." China was a particular tough case in point; software piracy had never fallen below 90 percent, despite external pressure and internal policies. China, along with other emerging markets like Russia and India, were seen as the frontline in the fight to stop piracy. Explained one analyst, "If the piracy rate in emerging markets—where people are rapidly integrating computers into their lives and businesses—does not drop, the worldwide piracy rate will continue to increase."

Compounding problems was the fact that software pirates easily cracked the latest licensing codes, duplicated holograms, falsified e-mail headers, and used anonymous post office boxes to evade capture. Noted an observer, "Like drug trafficking, the counterfeiting problem is so massive [that] you don't know how to get a handle on it. The bandits are everywhere." Worse still, counterfeiters were exhibiting more managerial sophistication. "When you are dealing with high-end counterfeits, you are talking about organizations that have a full supply chain, a full distribution chain, full manufacturing tools all in place, and it is all based on profits," explained Katharine Bostick, Microsoft's senior corporate attorney. Similarly, the increasing availability of pirated software via various Internet methods, such as spam, P2P file-sharing sites and mail-order or auction sites, many believed, would drive piracy higher in the future.

WTO

The pervasiveness and tenacity of software piracy in the face of an ever-expanding set of IPR laws, policies, and treaties raised profound questions for the software industry in particular and intellectual property rights in general. Some worried that the variety of legal traditions among the many countries stood in the way of agreement on even the definition of the problem. Certainly, TRIPS was supposed to help do so. However, TRIPs had many limitations; most notably, its failure to address the impact of the Internet made it, from the point of view of Microsoft, "woefully outdated."

Others feared that the antipiracy war might already have been lost; consumers and businesses around the world had been snapping up pirated software for so long that they might not see anything wrong with it. Similarly, in many collectivist cultures, some reasoned that software companies should openly share their software code with consumers, thereby allowing everyone to benefit from their knowledge. Finally, others thought that millions of software users saw piracy as simply their only way to deal with Western corporations that charged, in their view, exorbitant prices for an instrumental means of economic development. Microsoft, in response, proposed supplying Asian countries with a simpler, cheaper version of its Windows operating system in an effort to curb piracy. However, at the time, a pirated version of Windows XP sold in most markets in Asia for 3 to 5 percent of the price of the legitimate version. Analysts were skeptical that the offer of a cheaper and simpler version of Windows could curb piracy because illegal full-scale software copies were so readily available at a fraction of the cost, with no guarantee that the starter version of Windows might fall prey to software pirates as well. All in all, software makers found it increasingly difficult to control current software piracy and, if pushed, struggled to see how they could contain or control future abuse.

QUESTIONS

1. What is the relationship among the various governments, institutions, organizations, and companies in developing legal codes to combat software piracy?

2. In your opinion, should software companies, industry associations, home governments, or transnational institutions take the lead in aggressively negotiating with the governments of countries with high piracy rates? Why?

3. Can the software industry expect to contain and control software piracy without eventually relying on governments to take a more active role? Why would the software industry dislike greater government regulation?

4. In your opinion, what rationale do you think consumers in high theft countries (see Table 3.6) use to justify software piracy? Similarly, what ideas or conditions lead consumers in low theft countries to respect IPRs

5. What sorts of political or legal solutions should the software industry lobby governments to apply to the piracy problem?

CHAPTER NOTES

1 This case greatly benefited from comments and suggestions by Professor Paul Marer and Nao Muhan, Associate Professor of International Business at Soochow University, Taipei, Taiwan. The specific Monsanto quotation is from Jonathan Kwitny, "United States Concerns Export Mainland-Bound Goods as Embargo Loosens," *Wall Street Journal* (March 11, 1971): 1. Michael Sylvester, "Flaming Hoops," *Corporate Counsel: Market Report China* 11, no. 10 (October, 2004): 171; Mure Dickie, "A Call for More Chinese Walls, Foreign Companies Are Angered by Beijing's Inability to Tackle Piracy," *The Financial Times* (September 21, 2004): 9; Kevin Honglin Zhang, "What Attracts Foreign Multinational Corporations to China?" *Contemporary Economic Policy* (July, 2001): 336; Ping Deng, "WOFEs: The Most Popular Entry Mode into China," *Business Horizons* (July 2001): 63; Jiang Xueqin, "Letter from China," *The Nation* (March 4, 2002): 23; Chien Kirby, "Taiwan Firms Speed Up Move into China," *New York Times* (August 4, 2002); "A Disorderly Heaven," *The Economist* 370, no. 8367 (March 20, 2004): 12, US; "Bulls in a China Shop," *The Economist* 370, no. 8367 (March 20, 2004): 10, US; Joseph Kahn, "China Worries About Economic Surge That Skips the Poor," *The New York Times* (March 4, 2005); Howard French, "Whose Patent Is It, Anyway?" *The New York Times* (March 5, 2005).

Note: The frenetic pace of change in China's business environment makes any reports about its business environment hazardous. These statements should be interpreted as generalizations about the kinds of problems that investors have faced during the 1990s and in the first half of the current decade.

2 See http://plato.stanford.edu/entries/aristotle-politics/ and http://plato.stanford.edu/entries/plato-ethics-politics/.

3 Samuel Huntington, "Democracy for the Long Haul," *The Strait Times* (September 10, 1995): 1. Available: Nexis Library: News Curnws.

4 Audrey T. Sproat and Bruce R. Scott, "Japan: A Strategy for Economic Growth," Harvard Business School Case 9–378–106: 1–35.

5 "Politics Brief: Is There a Crisis?" *The Economist* (July 17, 1999): 49.

6 Adrian Karatnycky, *Freedom in the World 2001–2002: The Democracy Gap* (New York: Freedom House, 2002), http://www.freedomhouse.org.

7 On December 10, 1948, the General Assembly of the United Nations adopted and proclaimed the Universal Declaration of Human Rights and has since called upon all member countries to publicize the text of the Declaration and "to cause it to be disseminated, displayed, read and expounded principally in schools and other educational institutions, without distinction based on the political status of countries or territories." The full text of the Declaration is reported at http://www.un.org/Overview/rights.html.

8 Jaroslaw Piekalkiewicz and Alfred Wayne Penn, *Politics of Ideocracy* (Albany: State University of New York Press, 1995): 4.

9 Francis Fukuyama in *The End of History and the Last Man* (London; New. York; Melbourne; Toronto; Auckland: Penguin, 1992).

10 Christopher Patten, "Democracy Doesn't Flow from the Barrel of a Gun," *Foreign Policy*, no.138 (Sept.–Oct. 2003): 40–45.

11 Hannah Beech, "China Unplugged," *Time Asia online* 160, no. 1 (July 15, 2002).

12 Samuel Huntington, *The Clash of Civilizations and the Remaking of World Order* (New York: Simon & Schuster, 1996); and *Who Are We: The Challenges to America's National Identity* (New York: Simon & Schuster, 2004).

13 "Declaring War On Terrorism" (Text of President George W. Bush's Address to Congress and the American People), The Associated Press (September 20, 2001).

14 Huntington, op. cit.

15 Presently, only Andorra, Guernsey Island (UK), and Jersey Island (UK) apply only customary law.

16 For instance, the codification of civil law developed out of the customs of law that developed in particular communities and were slowly collected and written down by local jurists.

17 Floyd Norris, "Companies Pushed to Adopt International Audit Standards," *New York Times* (March 12, 2004): D5.

18 Nejdet Delener, "International Counterfeit Marketing: Success Without Risk," *Review of Business* 21 (Spring 2000): 16; "Countering Counterfeiting," *Business Europe* (July 28, 1999): 5–6.

19 Specifically, the Paris Convention for the Protection of Industrial Property of 1883 has been revised at Brussels (1900), Washington (1911), The Hague (1925), London (1934), Lisbon (1958), and Stockholm (1967) and amended in 1979.

20 "India: Cipra Launches 3-in-1 AIDS Pill," *Clinical Infectious Diseases* 33 (Sept. 15, 2001): ii.

21 Robert L. Ostergard, Jr., "The Measurement of Intellectual Property Rights Protection," *Journal of International Business Studies* 31 (Summer 2000): 349.

22 Stephanie Sanborn, "Protecting Intellectual Property on the Web—The Internet Age Is Making Digital Rights Management Even More Important," *InfoWorld,* 22 (June 19, 2000): 40.

23 "A High Cost to Developing Countries," *New York Times* (October 5, 1986): D2.

24 Veronica Weinstein and Dennis Fernandez, "Recent Developments in China's Intellectual Property Laws," *Chinese Journal of International Law* 3, no.1 (Spring 2004): 227.

25 Data for the case were taken from Business Software Alliance (November 25, 2002): http://bsa.org/; International Anti-Counterfeiting Coalition Recording Industry (November 25, 2002): http://www.iacc.org/; Association of America (November 25, 2002): http://www.riaa.com/; Motion Picture Association of America (November 25, 2002): http://www.mpaa.org/home.htm; Bryan W. Husted, "The Impact of National Culture on Software Piracy," *Journal of Business Ethics* 26 (August 2000): 197–211; Carol Noonan and Jeffery Raskin, "Intellectual Property Crimes," *Criminal Law Review* 38 (Summer 2001): 971; Trevor Moores and Gurpreet Dhillon, "Software Piracy: A View from Hong Kong." *Communications of the ACM* 43 (December 2000): 88; Edward Iwata, "Software Piracy Takes Toll on Global Scale," *USA Today* (August 1, 2001): C1; Jennifer Lee, "Pirates on the Web, Spoils on the Street; Cracking Codes of Popular Software, a Small Group Can Wreak Havoc," *New York Times* (July 11, 2002): E1; Suzanne Wagner and G. Lawrence Sanders, "Considerations in Ethical Decision-Making and Software Piracy," *Journal of Business Ethics* (January 2001): 161; Donald B. Marron and David G. Steel, "Which Countries Protect Intellectual Property? The Case of Software Piracy," *Economic Inquiry* 38 (April, 2000): 159; Wong Choon Mei, "Microsoft Cites Software Piracy Hotspots," *Reuters Technology* (October 23, 2002); and John Burton, "Microsoft Plans Cheaper Software to Combat Piracy Computers," *Financial Times* (June 30, 2004): 18.

26 A. Lin Neumann, "Information Wants to Be Free—But This Is Ridiculous," *Wired* (November 22, 2002), www.wired.com/wired/archive/.

The experiences of McDonald's in Russia exemplify how changes in a country's economic environment require that companies understand how business is done in the local market. First, the effort to enter Russia, then named the Union of Soviet Socialist Republics (USSR), began during the 1976 Olympics in Montreal, when George A. Cohon, then president of the Canadian subsidiary of McDonald's, contacted Soviet government officials. At that time, the entire economy of the USSR was under the control and ownership of the government. That is, the Soviet system of central planning set up in the late 1920s meant that the government made all economic decisions. Political officials determined how much got made, by whom, for whom, and at what price. No decision, even one as innocent as opening a hamburger stand, could go forward unless the state authorized it. This particular economic situation meant that the Moscow City Council, a government agency, was McDonald's official joint venture partner.

Political conditions greatly influenced the many economic decisions that went into opening the first McDonald's in Russia. Cohon initially contacted government officials in 1976; negotiations dragged on until 1988, when a formal agreement was signed. "I thought we would sign the deal in '79, before the 1980 Moscow Olympics," Cohon said. But a chill in Cold War politics, triggered by the West's boycott of the Moscow Games because of the Soviets' invasion of Afghanistan, delayed the signing of a deal with City Hall for nearly a decade. In the meantime, McDonald's opened restaurants in Hungary and Yugoslavia. The company's experiences in these centrally planned and controlled economies gave the company valuable know-how about operating in state-run economic environments.

McDonald's joint venture with the Moscow City Council, unusual in a market economy like the United States but routine in command economies like the USSR, resulted in the company running into regulatory roadblocks from various Soviet ministries. For example, managers at McDonald's would run into mysterious situations when, as Cohon explained, "When we need more sand or gravel for building and go to the department in charge, they say, 'Sorry, you're not in my five-year plan.'" Consequently, the company had to negotiate with state officials for the right to be allocated, in the then-Soviet Union central plan, sufficient shares of ordinary goods, such as sugar, flour, and meat, which were in chronically short supply across the country. While seemingly down-to-earth requests, the general scarcity for Muscovites at the time meant that many primary goods were simply unavailable. "Back then, there was no meat in stores," remembered Vladimir Malyshkov, a former official who now heads the consumer market and services department at City Hall. At the time, he diverted a shipment of beef from a state center to McDonald's. "There was a protest from the government because it was a criminal offense to take meat away from the people. The prosecutor general put me under investigation for six months. But I told them that this meat was destined for the people."

Even for some products in sufficient supply, such as mustard, government regulations prevented Soviet manufacturers from deviating from centrally set standard recipes in order to comply with the particular preferences of McDonald's. In other cases, strict government allocation regulations dictated that

MAP 4.1   Russia

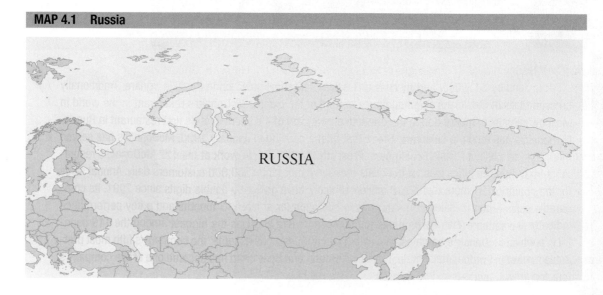

RUSSIA

Soviet plants sell all output to existing Soviet companies, thus leaving them no opportunity to provide products to McDonald's. Finally, another problem was that some supplies simply were not produced or consumed in the Soviet Union, including iceberg lettuce, pickling cucumbers, and the Russet Burbank potatoes that are the key ingredient in the company's renowned french fries.

McDonald's had to resolve these challenges within the particular context of the USSR's economic environment. McDonald's began by scouring the country for supplies, contracting for such items as milk, cheddar cheese, and beef. To help ensure ample supplies of the quality products it needed, it began to fund and educate Soviet farmers and cattle ranchers on how to grow and raise those products. Over time, the strictly controlled quality standards in the McDonald's food processing operations has helped improve Russia's food service and processing industries along with local agriculture and business practices. "McComplex," the company's unique $40 million food processing and distribution center, located in the Moscow suburb of Solntsevo about 45 minutes from its flagship Moscow restaurant, employs more than 500 people to supply local foods to both the McDonald's Russian restaurants and, over time, its restaurants in 21 other countries including Belarus, Ukraine, Moldova, Czech Republic, Hungary, Germany, and Austria. Still, since opening in 1990, when the majority of raw materials had to be imported, McDonald's has continued to expand its local supplier base. Currently, over 75 percent of the raw ingredients needed for the McDonald's Russian restaurants are purchased from more than 130 independent Russian suppliers who have created more than 80,000 jobs.

One problem McDonald's did not encounter was attracting attention or customers. McDonald's did no paid advertising prior to its Moscow opening. However, besides being the first Western-style restaurant chain to open in the former Soviet Union, it launched its first eatery in Moscow's high-profile Pushkin Square. The opening was reported by local, national, and world media. Some believe the power of the McDonald's Moscow opening reflected more than its hamburgers and fries. It was full of political symbolism, largely identified with then Soviet President Mikhail Gorbachev's efforts to move from a state-controlled to a market economy. Reflected deputy Moscow Mayor Vladimir Malyshkov, "McDonald's was the precursor of a free life in Russia."

Finding workers was a snap. High levels of local underemployment meant that the company's single help-wanted ad generated about 27,000 Russian applicants for its 605 positions. Today, McDonald's in Russia employs more than 17,000 people in its restaurants, at McComplex, and in the central office. Most company executives are Russian, and more than 1,000 of these folks began as crew members on the wait counter or fry deck of a local McDonald's. Today, every new McDonald's restaurant creates approximately 100 new job opportunities for local citizens.

When McDonald's opened its doors in January 1990, it was almost impossible to accommodate the crowd, even though it was the largest McDonald's in the world. An estimated 30,000 people, many of whom began lining up at dawn in the bitter cold, were served the first day, eclipsing the previous daily record of 9,100 set in Budapest. The crowds continued to arrive, even though the price of a Big Mac, french fries, and soft drink equaled a Russian worker's average pay for four hours of work. In contrast, lunch at a state-run or private sector cafe cost just 15 to 25 percent as much as a meal at McDonald's.

Along the way, besides the particular challenges of working within a different type of economic environment, McDonald's has also been hit by various transition crises in the Russian economy. In December 1991, the collapse of the Soviet Union left the Russian economy in dire shape. Foreign reserves, the country's holding of other countries' currencies, were exhausted, impeding the country's ability to import goods, and economic output had been declining since the 1970s, resulting in low incomes. Then President Boris Yeltsin took two vital steps to stabilize the collapsing economy. The first introduced radical economic reforms that led to a completely new system of money, banking, and finance. The second launched a so-called shock therapy program to free prices from state control in order to lure goods back into the shops as well as permit local companies to sell foreign-made goods in order to break the power of local monopolies. Immediately, the country suffered high levels of inflation and the near bankruptcy of many companies. In 1994, the government began a program of privatization in which the state began to sell its various assets and resources to private investors. Too, around this time, the government introduced major changes in the Russian currency and set up several exchange rate reforms.

These dramatic reforms had the collective effect of replacing the inefficient system of centralized state planning with a budding capitalist economy. This move meant that companies like McDonald's could now look to leverage emerging market mechanisms to better plan and control their operations. Still, these benefits were somewhat offset by enduring economic problems, notably high inflation, which continued to erode the value of personal savings, and the growing problems of massive unemployment, caused by huge layoffs at previously state-owned, now privatized companies. The economic environment became even more unstable in 1998, when the Russian government's decision to devalue the ruble (the Russian national currency) and place a moratorium on repaying the foreign debt triggered an economic meltdown. Making matters worse, Russia's central bank announced that hundreds of millions of rubles had been printed to stimulate the economy and prevent the collapse of Russia's commercial banks. Inflation quickly began increasing.

Russia, to McDonald's good fortune, has pulled through these rough patches. Growing oil revenues have filled state coffers and should expand dramatically in the next few years. The relative macroeconomic stability brought by President Vladimir Putin has attracted foreign investment and reduced capital flight. In 2002, Russia got a big psychological boost when the United States officially recognized it as a market economy and a normal part of the world trading system, rather than as a peculiar postcommunist place whose centrally planned economy imposed special rules at home and abroad. Moreover, inflation is under control, interest rates are falling, and employment and investment are growing; hence domestic demand has been expanding by nearly 10 percent a year. Cuts in tax rates and bureaucracy have increased tax revenues and made it a bit easier to start and run a business.

Finding ways to adapt to, understand, and interpret the changing economic environment of Russia, even in the face of peculiar regulations or business shocks, has led to great success for McDonald's. Presently, its 83 percent share of the Russian fast-food market dwarfs all other Russian-based fast-food outlets. An average fast-food outlet in Moscow serves 300 customers a day; the average McDonald's serves more than 3,000 customers per day. Expectedly, managers at McDonald's see great promise, stating that Russia is one of its four top growth markets in the world. Concluded McDonald's Corporation President Michael Roberts, "Our business in Russia is thriving and . . . we will continue to grow." McDonald's plans to open 25 new restaurants in 2005, predominantly in Moscow and St. Petersburg, followed by 35 in 2006 and 45 in 2007. Mr. Cohon expects to see growth continue for a long time. "Canada is a country of 30 million people and we have close to 1,400 McDonald's. Russia is a country of 150 million people and we have 128 McDonald's in Russia," he said. "So this is the tip of the iceberg. We will continue to expand."

INTRODUCTION

Earlier chapters looked at how cultural, political, and legal systems influence a company's decisions on where and how to do business internationally. This chapter completes this profile by presenting the perspectives and tools that managers use to evaluate economic environments—like those used by McDonald's in Russia. The importance of this chapter follows from the simple fact that different countries have different levels of economic development, performance, and potential. For instance, in absolute terms, world economic output more than doubled between 1975 and 2000, reaching nearly US$35 trillion. In relative terms, many countries prospered, but some more than others, and in a few cases, some not at all. Hence, estimating the attractiveness of a country as a place to do business and then, once there, making prudent investment and operational decisions depends on how well managers understand the impact of economic changes.

Managers need to understand economic environments to predict trends that might affect their company's performance.

When a company wants to do business in another country, such as McDonald's in Russia, it has to answer questions about wealth, income, stability, poverty, and the like. It also must prepare, given the dynamic nature of political and economic events, for new questions. Besides assessing the foreign markets in which they operate, managers also need to monitor those in which they do not. Globalization connects countries in many ways; change in one country likely has economic consequences in other countries.

Too, companies must keep watch on the economic changes in those countries where they may not operate but where their competitors do. Improving economic performance or revised economic policies in a particular country may unexpectedly strengthen their rivals' competitiveness.

While the pace varies from country to country, national economic environments around the world are continually changing—as highlighted in our opening case. We have seen over the past decade tremendous change in economic opportunities as more and more countries have adopted the principles and practices of free markets. Indeed, a country's economic policies give a clear indication of the government's goals and the economic tools and market reforms it must adopt. Therefore, understanding the processes of economic development and market transition prepares managers to spot those small economic changes in a particular country's environment that promise to have big market impact.

Finally, economic development is a vital topic to citizens, managers, policymakers, and institutions. The growing triumph of free markets over controlled economies has prompted many countries to unleash ambitious economic programs. To some degree, economic development efforts have helped many countries improve their standard of living. Then again, the bold development programs of many countries have fallen short of their goals. A fuller understanding of the process of economic transition and development helps managers make better decisions that benefit their companies, their countries, and the world.

The impact of economic change has a variety of characteristics. Some are direct and easily linked to environments, companies, or competitors. Others exert a more subtle influence on a firm's activities and its ultimate performance. The CEO of Hewlett-Packard, in her Annual Letter to Shareholders, gives a good sense of the range of economic factors and relationships that bear upon the international company. Specifically, she explained:

> *In terms of economic growth and stability, 2001 was one of the toughest years on record, particularly for the IT [information technology] industry. Triggered in part by the collapse of the hyper-inflated dot-com sector, in Q3 of calendar 2001, the U.S. economy softened considerably. A dramatic slowdown in business investment, compounded by the events of September 11, tipped the United States into its first recession in a decade. During 2001, the world's three leading economies slowed simultaneously for the first time since 1974. The European economy stalled, and Japan struggled to fight deflation and recession. Information technology spending plummeted. The telecommunications and manufacturing industries—two of HP's largest customer sectors—were hit especially hard by the global economic slowdown. These factors had a significant impact on HP's fiscal 2001 results.[2]*

In summary, understanding the economic environments of a country helps managers better apprise how trends and events in those markets will likely affect their companies' performance.

INTERNATIONAL ECONOMIC ANALYSIS

The World Bank reports there are 208 discrete economic environments in the world today—nearly 200 countries and a balance of territories and the like.[3] Inevitably, managers must ask which of those countries justify their attention and investment. Unfortunately, there is no universal scheme to assess the performance and potential of a country's economic environment. Granted, there are many useful approaches. Still, two conditions hamper specifying a universal method. First, it is difficult to specify the definitive set of economic indicators that precisely estimates the performance and predicts the potential of a country's economy. Second, upon specifying a set of estimators, new

A country's economic policies are a leading indicator of the government's goals and its planned use of economic tools and market reforms.

The matter of economic development is important to citizens, managers, policymakers, and institutions.

FIGURE 4.1   PHYSICAL AND SOCIETAL INFLUENCES ON INTERNATIONAL
BUSINESS

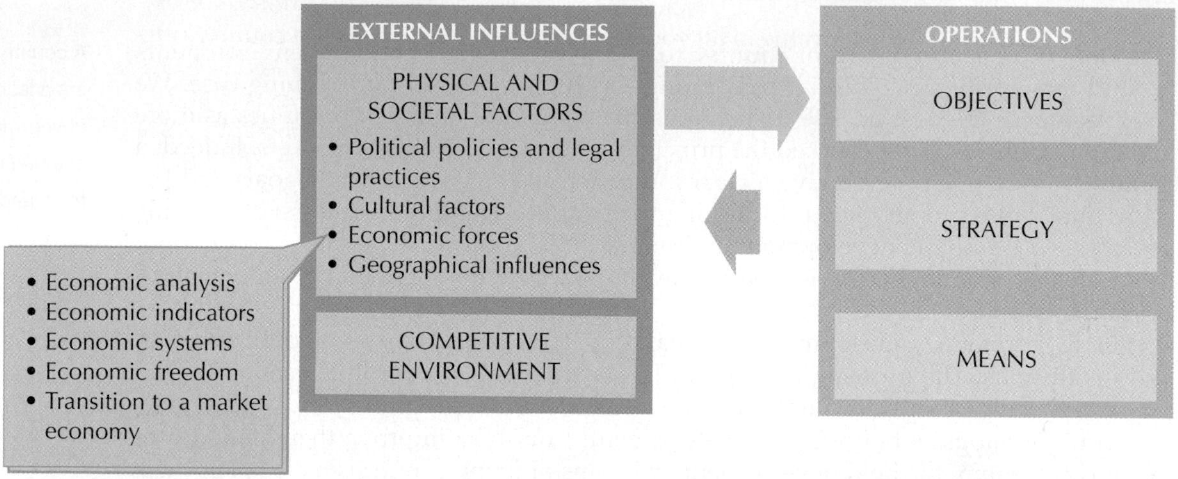

EXTERNAL INFLUENCES

PHYSICAL AND
SOCIETAL FACTORS
• Political policies and legal
  practices
• Cultural factors
• Economic forces
• Geographical influences

COMPETITIVE
ENVIRONMENT

• Economic analysis
• Economic indicators
• Economic systems
• Economic freedom
• Transition to a market
  economy

OPERATIONS

OBJECTIVES

STRATEGY

MEANS

challenges emerge when trying to understand their relationship to other elements of the economic environment.

Figure 4.1 gives a sense of the challenge. Importantly, it also suggests a way to solve it. Figure 4.1 shows some of the economic conditions that create unique market, physical, and societal factors in a country. Research has isolated many important elements of an economic environment. These include such factors as income, purchasing power, market size, income distribution, and economic infrastructure. This chapter will show that, by reducing the idea of an economic environment to its fundamental components, we can begin to determine how they shape the market. In addition, Figure 4.1 highlights the importance of applying a systems perspective to our analyses. That is, the configuration and connection of various elements underscores the fact that a change in one element in the economy can fundamentally affect other parts of the environment. The key to understanding how an economic environment works is also a function of making sense of the interactions of the parts with one another.

In summary, Figure 4.1 suggests managers can begin to assess an economic environment of a country by first looking at crucial dimensions of its economy. Then, once satisfied that these elements make sense, managers can assess their systemic relationship and estimate the likely path of transition and potential performance for that country's economy. In all cases, managers can adjust their interpretation for possible risks that might alter current activity or future performance. This chapter follows this scheme, beginning with a profile of important features of an economic environment, moving on to types of economic systems, and closing with a look at theories of economic transition and development.

Key economic forces include

• The general economic framework of a country
• Economic stability
• The existence and influence of capital markets
• Factor endowments
• Market size
• Availability of an economic infrastructure

Factor conditions—inputs to the production process, such as human, physical, knowledge, and capital resources and infrastructure— shape economic activity.

ELEMENTS OF THE ECONOMIC ENVIRONMENT

Managers use many different measures to assess a country's level of economic performance and potential. Some may be informal or idiosyncratic indicators—like the number of wireless phones or circulation patterns of newspapers—in a country. For the most part, though, managers use conventional measures to assess the economic environment. Most notably, managers usually begin their analyses by looking at the monetary value of the total flow of goods and services in the economy of a nation—the so-called gross national income. They then refine their analyses by considering related measures, particularly growth rates, income distribution, inflation, unemployment, debt, the balance of payments, and the like, that elaborate their analyses. The next two sections profile these factors.

Gross National Income

The estimator **gross national income** (GNI) measures the income generated both by total domestic production as well as the international production activities of national companies. By definition, GNI is the value of all goods and services produced by a country during a one-year period. Specifically, GNI is the market value of final goods and services newly produced by domestically owned factors of production.[4] So, for example, the value of a Ford SUV that is built in the United States and the portion of the value of a Ford SUV made in Mexico using U.S. capital and management get counted in the GNI of the United States. However, the portion of the value of a Japanese Toyota SUV that is built in the United States using Japanese capital and management would count in the GNI of Japan, not the United States. Table 4.1 identifies the 20 largest economies in the world in terms of GNI.

GNI is the broadest measure of economic activity for a country.[5] An important part of GNI is the so-called **gross domestic product** (GDP). GDP is the total value of all goods and services produced within a nation's borders over one year, no matter whether domestic or foreign-owned companies make the product.[6] Technically, GDP plus the income generated from exports, imports, and the international operations of a nation's companies equals GNI. So both a Ford and a Toyota truck manufactured in the United States would be counted in U.S. GDP, but the truck made in Mexico by Ford would not.

The absolute size of GNI reveals a lot about the market opportunity in a country. For example, Uruguay and Brazil are neighbors in South America, but Uruguay had a GNI of about $44 billion in 2003, whereas Brazil's GNI was $1.4 trillion. For this reason, many foreign companies have invested in Brazil and then exported to Uruguay instead of also investing in Uruguay.

Gross national income is the value of all final goods and services produced within a nation in a given year.

✳ Important

Gross domestic product (GDP)—the value of production that takes place within a nation's borders.

TABLE 4.1   TWENTY LARGEST ECONOMIES BY GNI, 2003

	COUNTRY	MILLIONS OF US DOLLARS
1	United States	11,012,597
2	Japan	4,360,824
3	Germany	2,085,464
4	United Kingdom	1,680,069
5	France	1,521,613
6	China	1,416,751
7	Italy	1,243,168
8	Canada	773,943
9	Spain	700,475
10	Mexico	637,159
11	Korea, Rep.	576,426
12	India	570,760
13	Brazil	479,515
14	Australia	436,470
15	Netherlands	425,556
16	Russian Federation	374,810
17	Switzerland	298,975
18	Belgium	267,250
19	Sweden	258,882
20	Austria	216,903

Source: The World Bank, http://www.worldbank.org/data/quickreference/quickref.html. WORLD BANK DEVELOPMENT INDICATORS 2003 by WORLD BANK. Copyright 2003 by the WORLD BANK. Reproduced with permission of the WORLD BANK in the format textbook via Copyright Clearance Center.

Improving the Power of GNI

Managers improve the usefulness of GNI by adjusting it for the number of people in a country, growth rate, and the local cost of living.

GNI is a robust estimator of an economy's absolute performance. However, GNI can give managers the wrong impression when they are comparing one country to another. For example, major economic powers, like the United States, Japan, and Germany, consistently claim the top spots on rankings of countries by GNI. As such, a quick look at these rankings might give the impression that these top-ranked countries are richer in a range of ways than countries like Bermuda or Luxembourg. Managers, therefore, can improve the usefulness of GNI by adjusting it for the number of people in a country, growth rate, and the local cost of living.

GNI per capita is the value of all goods and services produced in the economy divided by the population.

Per Capita Conversion   Managers transform GNI, as well as many other economic indicators, by the number of people who live in a country. This conversion leads to a per capita estimator that measures the relative performance of a country's economy. Technically, we compute the per capita GNI by taking the GNI of a country and

MAP 4.2   The World's Wealth Measured in Per Capita GNI

High-income countries are clustered in a few geographic areas of the world, whereas the developing countries are scattered throughout.

Note: No data available for Western Sahara.

Source: From *The World Bank Atlas 2001,* p. 41. WORLD BANK ATLAS '03 by THE WORLD BANK. Copyright 2003 by the WORLD BANK. Reproduced with permission of the WORLD BANK in the format textbook via Copyright Clearance Center.

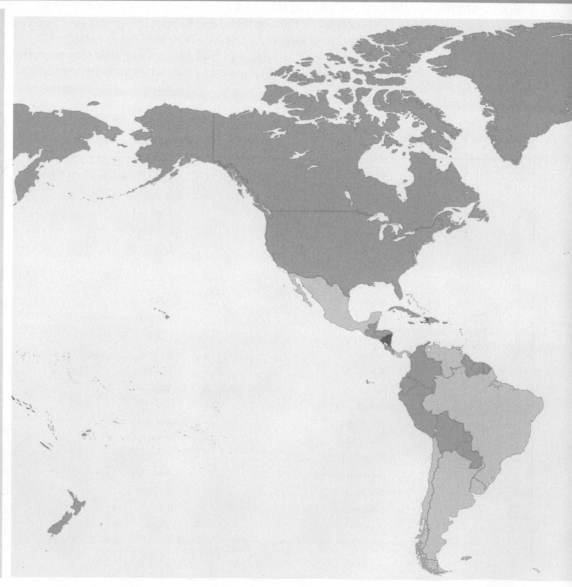

converting it into a standard currency, say the US dollar, at prevailing market rates, and then dividing the total by its population. This and other per capita indicators help explain an economy's performance in terms of the number of people who live in that country. For example, GNI may be low in absolute terms, such as is the case for Bermuda, which ranks among the smaller economies of the world. But Bermuda ranks first in the world by GNI per capita.[7] Map 4.2 classifies countries according to GNI per capita.

Officially, the World Bank reports that worldwide GNI per capita is US $5,500.[8] Table 4.2 reports the World Bank's classification scheme; it effectively orders the countries of the world into one of four categories on the basis of their per capita GNI. Officially, the World Bank refers to the low- and middle-income countries as developing countries (some refer to these as emerging countries or economies). They comprise the largest number of economies and population in the world. High-income countries are often called developed countries or industrial countries.[9]

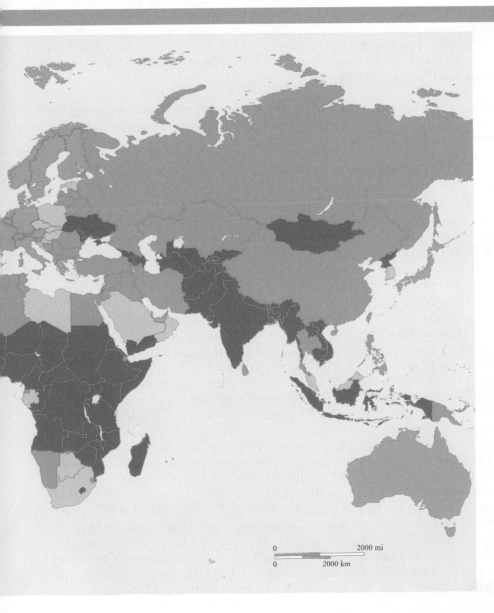

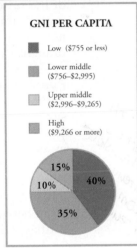

GNI PER CAPITA

- Low ($755 or less)
- Lower middle ($756–$2,995)
- Upper middle ($2,996–$9,265)
- High ($9,266 or more)

15% / 10% / 40% / 35%

GNI PER CAPITA 2003

Ranking	Economy	Atlas methodology (US dollars)
1	Luxembourg	45,740
2	Bermuda	..a
3	Norway	43,400
4	Switzerland	40,680
5	United States	37,870
6	Liechtenstein	..a
7	Japan	34,180
8	Denmark	33,570
9	Channel Islands	..a
10	Iceland	30,910
11	Sweden	28,910
12	United Kingdom	28,320
13	Finland	27,060
14	Ireland	27,010
15	San Marino	..a
16	Austria	26,810
17	Cayman Islands	..a
18	Netherlands	26,230
19	Hong Kong, China	25,860
20	Belgium	25,760

..a Not available. GNI is gross national income (gross national product). Note: Rankings include all 208 World Bank Atlas economies, but only those with confirmed Atlas GNI per capita estimates or those that rank among the top twenty are shown in rank order.

0   2000 mi
0   2000 km

Map 4.2 classifies countries according to GNI per capita. It shows that the high-income countries are clustered in a few regions and include primarily North America, Western Europe, Japan, Australia, and New Zealand. High-income countries accounted for less than 15 percent of the world's population in 2004 but nearly 80 percent of the world's GNP. Lower income countries are spread throughout the world, from Asia to Africa to South America to the Pacific Region. They account for a trivial share of the world's GNI and report GNI per capita figures from the low hundreds to low thousands (US$).

Rate of Change   Gross figures are a snapshot of one year of activity. Consequently, they do not measure the rate of change in an indicator. Understanding present and predicting future economic performance requires pinpointing the rate of change. So, for example, looking at the countries in terms of their growth rate for GNI per capita, we find a wide range in growth. For example, between 1998 and 2002, Ireland was the fastest growing economy in the world, expanding more than 8 percent. Japan, on the other hand, grew only 0.2 percent over that period. Generally, the GNI growth rate is also a broad indicator of economic potential—if GNI grows at a higher (lower) rate than the population, standards of living are said to be rising (falling). Also, the GNI growth rate highlights likely business opportunities. For example, China has been one of the fastest growing economies over the past 25 years, averaging high single-digit growth for the past several years. This growth, in turn, has resulted in the swiftest, most extensive rise out of poverty any nation has seen, a rise that has attracted immense amounts of foreign investment.

Purchasing Power Parity   Managers, when comparing markets, often convert the GNI figure in one nation in terms of the currency of their home market. This simple conversion greatly refines economic analysis. For example, the 2003 GNI per capita for India is 23,139 rupees while that in the United States is 37,160 dollars. Comparing these countries in terms of GNI per capita requires translating each currency into a common currency unit at the then prevailing rate to trade one currency for another (the so-called exchange rate). So, converting Indian rupees to U.S. dollars at official exchange rates, we estimate Indian GNI per capita at $530. This gap would suggest that there are tremendous differences between the two countries. Some managers then might wrongly decide to look no further at the Indian market.

This simple conversion can create a systematic distortion. Exchange rates tell us how many units of one currency it takes to buy one unit of another—e.g., how many Indian rupees one needs to buy one U.S. dollar. However, exchange rates do not tell us what that unit of local currency can buy in its home country. More directly, the calculation of GNI per capita does not consider the differences in costs of living from one country to another. Instead, it presumes that a dollar of income in Chicago has the same "purchasing power" of a dollar of income in Calcutta even though there is an immense gap in the cost of living between the United States and India. Consequently, GNI per capita is unable to tell us much about how many goods and services someone can buy with a unit of income in one country relative to how much someone can buy with a unit of income in another country.

Agencies, like the Central Intelligence Agency (CIA), and institutions, like the World Bank, adjust GNI per capita for a particular country in terms of its local **purchasing power parity (PPP).** Technically, the PPP is the number of units of a country's currency required to buy the same amounts of goods and services in the domestic market that one unit of income would buy in the other country. Specifically, one calculates PPP by estimating the value of a universal "basket" of goods (like soap, bread, and clothing) and services (like telephone, electricity, and energy) that can be purchased with one unit of a country's currency.[10] The resulting estimate of the GNI per capita in terms of its local purchasing power in a particular country then lets us see what a consumer in that country can actually buy with one unit of income. The most common PPP exchange rate

Purchasing power parity is an adjustment in gross domestic product per capita to reflect differences in the cost of living.

comes from comparing a basket of goods and services in a country with an equivalent basket in the United States.

So, let's return to the comparison of the United States and India. Whereas India's GNI per capita in 2003 is $530 it is, in terms of its local purchasing power parity, nearly $2,880.[11] Effectively then, GNI per capita in terms of relative PPP is higher in India because of its lower cost of living. This means that it costs far less to buy the same basket of goods in India than it does in the United States. The opposite effect occurs in the case of Switzerland. Because the cost of living is higher in Switzerland than in the United States, Switzerland's GNI per capita goes from $39,880 to $32,030 when expressed in terms of PPP. Chapter 10 takes a closer look at PPP.

Map 4.3 profiles the countries of the world in terms of their PPP. The gaps between the developed and the emerging countries of the world are apparent in a map showing average purchasing power by region. The average person in the richest region, North America, has an annual purchasing power of $33,410 in United States dollars, compared with only $1,770 for the average person in sub-Saharan Africa.

Degree of Human Development   GNI, and its expression in terms of per capita, growth rate, and PPP, give a good view of the state of growth and development in an economy. Some argue that these indicators, by focusing on monetary growth, can partially misrepresent the scale and scope of a country's level of development. Managers deal with these concerns by looking at a country's degree of human development—in terms of both economic and social factors—to estimate its current and future economic activity. Jointly considering economic and social indicators applies a richer approach to measuring development in terms of the capabilities and opportunities that people enjoy. These conditions might not immediately but ultimately will show up in income or growth figures. More specifically, the reasoning goes:

> The basic purpose of development is to enlarge people's choices. In principle, these choices can be infinite and can change over time. People often value achievements that do not show up at all, or not immediately, in income or growth figures: greater access to knowledge, better nutrition and health services, more secure livelihoods, security against crime and physical violence, satisfying leisure hours, political and cultural freedoms and sense of participation in community activities. The objective of development is to create an enabling environment for people to enjoy long, healthy, and creative lives.[12]

Hence, economic indicators certainly identify the potential consumption in a country. Still, their precise monetary focus risks missing the underlying effects of human development and capabilities that are ultimately instrumental in increasing GNI. To that end, managers can complement economic indicators by also analyzing the economic environment in terms of the overall quality of life in a country by measuring how well a country does in terms of social liberties, life expectancy, access to clean water, and literacy rates.

Beginning in 1990, the United Nations has translated this view into its Human Development Report and its principal indicator, Human Development Index (HDI).[13] Specifically, the HDI measures the average achievements in a country on three dimensions:

The Human Development Index combines indicators of real purchasing power, education, and health to give a more comprehensive measure of economic development.

- *Longevity*, as measured by life expectancy at birth
- *Knowledge*, as measured by the adult literacy rate and the combined primary, secondary, and tertiary gross enrollment ratio
- *Standard of living*, as measured by GNI per capita expressed in PPP for US dollars

By design, the HDI aims to capture long-term progress in human development, rather than short-term changes.[14]

MAP 4.3   The World's Wealth Measured in Terms of Purchasing Power Parity

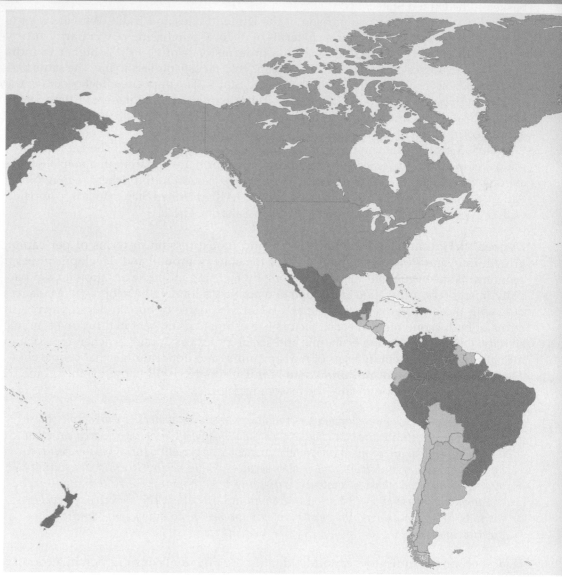

PPP adjusts income levels in a country in terms of the power consumers command to buy a universal basket of goods and services. Arraying countries in terms of PPP, versus that of GNI per capita, contracts the span between high and low income countries.

Source: www.worldbank.org, accessed June 2005. WORLD BANK ATLAS '03 by the WORLD BANK. Copyright 2003 by the WORLD BANK. Reproduced with permission of the WORLD BANK in the format textbook via Copyright Clearance Center.

How to calculate HDI Human Development index

Map 4.4 profiles the countries of the world in terms of their performance on the HDI. Operationally, the HDI is scaled from 0 to 1; countries scoring less than 0.5 are classified as having low human development (the quality of life is poor); those scoring from 0.5 to 0.8 are classified as having medium human development; while those countries that score above 0.8 are classified as having high human development.

Lastly, the United Nations refines the HDI to take into account gender and poverty. Specifically, it reports a gender-related development index that adjusts for gender inequalities, a gender empowerment measure that adjusts for gender inequality, and a measure of poverty to adjust for human deprivations and the denial of choices and opportunities for living a life one has reason to value.[15] Collectively, these indicators improve managers' sense of a country's achievements in longevity, knowledge, and a decent standard of living, all integral elements of an economic environment.

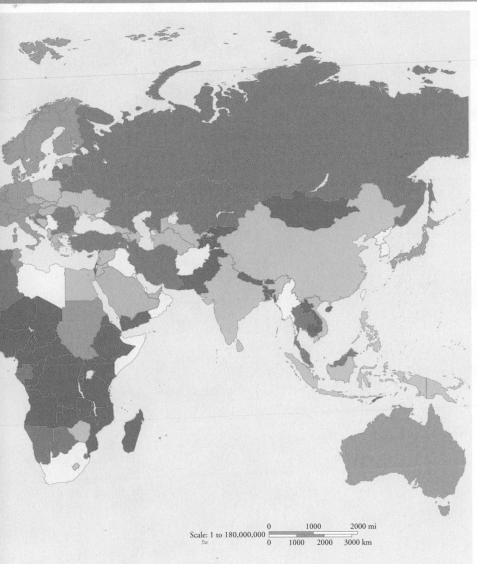

PURCHASING POWER PARITY

■	Low Income: $1990 or less
	Lower Middle Income: $1,991-$4,580
■	Upper Middle Income: $4,581-$9170
	Lower High Income: $9,170-$20,000
	Upper High Income: $20,001 or more
	No Data

PPP GDP 2003

Ranking	Economy	(millions of international dollars)
1	United States	10,923,376
2	China	6,446,033 a
3	Japan	3,567,804
4	India	3,078,024 b
5	Germany	2,291,007
6	France	1,654,018
7	United Kingdom	1,610,579
8	Italy	1,563,332
9	Brazil	1,375,756
10	Russian Federation	1,323,839

a. Estimate is based on a bilateral comparison between China and the United States (Ruoen and Kai, 1995). b. Estimate is based on regression; other PPP figures are extrapolated from the latest International Comparison Programme benchmark estimates.

Scale: 1 to 180,000,000

0   1000   2000 mi
0   1000   2000   3000 km

FEATURES OF AN ECONOMY

GNI and its variations estimate the absolute and relative income of a country. As such, these data create powerful, first-order indicators of a country's economic performance and potential. Managers also study other features of an economy, often considering measures of inflation, unemployment, debt, income distribution, poverty, and the balance of payments.

Inflation

Inflation is the pervasive and sustained rise in the aggregate level of prices measured by an index of the cost of various goods and services.[16] Inflation results when aggregate demand grows faster than aggregate supply—essentially, too many people are trying to buy too few goods, thereby creating demand that pushes prices up faster than incomes grow.[17] Managers watch the rate of inflation, given its influence on many parts of the economic environment such as interest rates, exchange rates, the cost of living, general economic confidence, and the stability of the current political system.

Inflation is a measure of the increase in the cost of living.

MAP 4.4   The Human Development Index

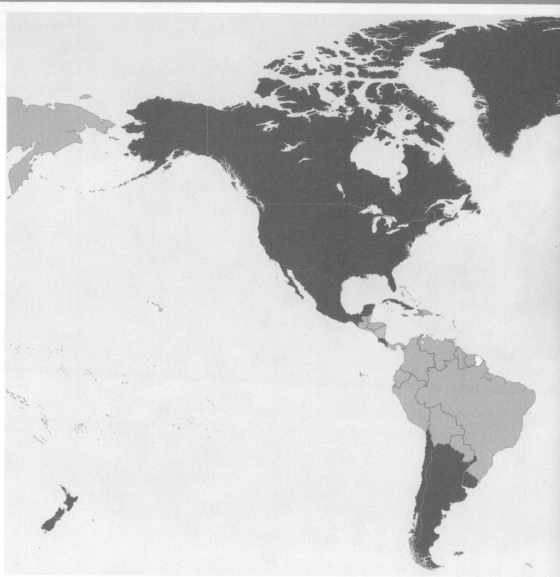

The HDI calls for understanding a country's economic performance and potential in terms of its expansion of human capability, not simply the increase in GNI per capita.

Source: http://www.nationmaster.com/red/graph-T/eco_hum_dev_ind, accessed June 2005.

The consumer price index measures the average change in consumer prices over time in a fixed market basket of goods and services.

High inflation results in higher interest rates because

- Banks need to offer high interest rates to attract money.
- Governments raise interest rates to slow down economic growth.

Consider the impact of inflation on the cost of living. Rising prices make it more difficult for consumers to buy products unless their incomes rise at the same or faster pace. Sometimes this is practically impossible. For example, during periods of rapid or "hyper-inflation" (e.g., in Brazil and the former Yugoslavia in the early 1990s or Turkmenistan in the mid-1990s) prices were rising 1 to 20 percent per day. Consequently, consumers had to spend their money as fast as they got it, or else watch it quickly turn worthless. Certainly, these are extreme cases. Still, history shows that chronic inflation, essentially annual inflation rates of 10 to 30 percent, erodes confidence in a country's currency and spurs people to search for better ways to store value.

The implications of chronic or hyper-inflation to companies are dismal. Neither they nor their customers can effectively plan long-term investments, they have no incentive to save, and ordinary investment instruments like insurance policies, pensions, and long-term bonds become speculative. Inflation also puts great pressure on governments to control it. Often, governments try to reduce inflation by raising interest rates, installing wage and price controls, and imposing protectionist trade policies and currency controls. Either alone or together, these measures slow or stop economic growth. While global

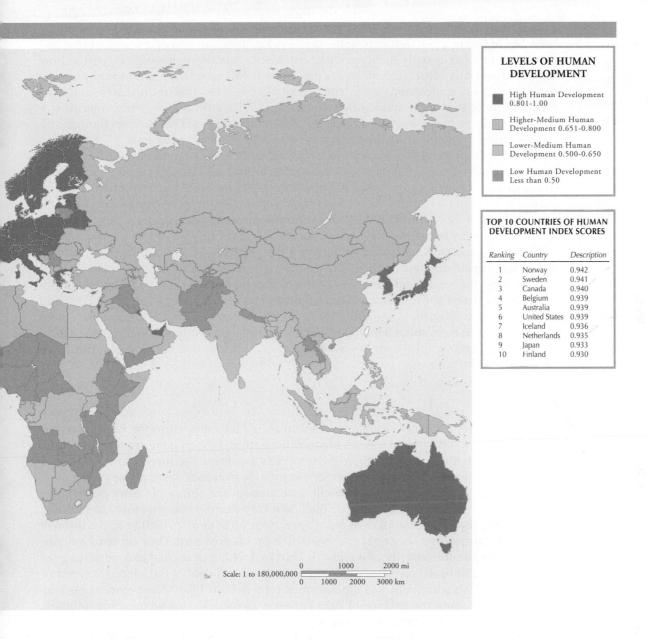

LEVELS OF HUMAN DEVELOPMENT

■ High Human Development 0.801–1.00

☐ Higher-Medium Human Development 0.651–0.800

☐ Lower-Medium Human Development 0.500–0.650

☐ Low Human Development Less than 0.50

TOP 10 COUNTRIES OF HUMAN DEVELOPMENT INDEX SCORES

Ranking	Country	Description
1	Norway	0.942
2	Sweden	0.941
3	Canada	0.940
4	Belgium	0.939
5	Australia	0.939
6	United States	0.939
7	Iceland	0.936
8	Netherlands	0.935
9	Japan	0.933
10	Finland	0.930

Scale: 1 to 180,000,000

```
0          1000        2000 mi
0   1000   2000   3000 km
```

consumer price inflation has fallen dramatically since the early 1990s, rising oil and materials prices in 2005 possibly foreshadowed the return of significant inflation.[18]

Unemployment

The unemployment rate is the number of unemployed workers divided by the total civilian labor force, which includes both the unemployed and those with jobs (all those willing and able to work for pay). In practice, measuring the number of unemployed workers actually seeking work in various countries is difficult given the lack of a standard measurement method.[19] Generally, each method has its own biases that complicate comparing unemployment statistics between countries. For example, in mid-2005, the unemployment rate in France was approximately 9.7 percent, significantly higher than the 5.2 percent rate in the United States. However, the meaning of the unemployment rate for those affected means different things in France than in the United States given their different social policies and institutional frameworks.[20]

Unemployment is a measure of the number of workers that want to work but do not have jobs.

Unemployment insurance provides temporary income to unemployed workers who actively seek employment and who meet other qualifications.

Misery index—the sum of a country's inflation and unemployment rates.

In industrialized countries, like Germany, unemployment insurance has reduced the hardship of losing a job. Certainly, some workers face long periods of unemployment and the return to work usually involves a pay cut. Hence, managers must be careful in how they interpret this contrast. Finally, unemployment estimates throughout many poorer nations routinely underestimate the true degree of joblessness and, more significantly, the productivity of those who work. Many countries in Asia, Africa, and South America face more difficult problems due to widespread underemployment. That is, even though officially employed, people work only part time, which results in low incomes.

Countries that are unable to create jobs for their citizens create a risky business environment. Generally, people out of work and unable to find jobs depress economic growth, create social pressures, and provoke political uncertainty. As such, the proportion of unemployed workers in a country shows how well a nation's human resources are used and serves as a measure of economic activity. Some economists suggest managers can get a sense of this situation by estimating the "misery index," which is the sum of a country's inflation and unemployment rates. The higher the score, the greater is the economic misery, and the more likely consumers and companies will curtail spending and investment.

Presently, the wealthier countries of the world are watching their working-age population shrink from approximately 740 million to 690 million people between 2000 and 2025. However, over the same time, the working-age population will increase across poorer countries from about 3 billion to 4 billion people. Presently, the youth of the world suffer the most unemployment in most countries, with rates twice that of adult (ages 25–65) unemployment.

Debt

Debt, the sum total of a government's financial obligations, measures the state's borrowing from its population, from foreign organizations, from foreign governments, and from international institutions. The larger the total debt becomes, the more unstable a country's economy becomes, both in the present as interest expenses direct money from more productive uses, and the future, as people worry about the ability of future generations to pay back the debt. Presently, the national debt for virtually every country is growing. For example, the U.S. national debt has grown from $1 trillion in 1980 to $5.7 trillion in 2004. Some caution that we overly emphasize the problem of debt. They contend that one can best measure the severity of a nation's debt by looking at its size as a percentage of the nation's GDP. Based on this measurement, the national debt of the United States during the mid-1990s was about half the size of its total debt in 1950. Other economists contend that comparing the balance of debt between years does not account for inflation, which makes balances from later years appear larger.

A country has two types of debt
- Internal—portion of the government debt that is denominated in the country's own currency and held by domestic residents
- External—debt owed to foreign creditors that is denominated in a foreign currency

A country's debt has two parts: internal and external. Internal debt results when the government spends more than it collects in revenues. Internal deficits occur for any number of reasons, including when an imperfect tax system prevents the government from collecting revenue, when the cost of security and social programs exceed available tax revenues, and when state-owned enterprises run deficits. Consequently, every government struggles with setting spending priorities, better controlling expenses, improving budget management, and improving tax policy. The resulting pressure to revise government policies, in the face of growing internal debt, can create economic uncertainties for investors and companies.

HIPC—those poor countries with large debts that are the target of initiatives to forgive that debt as a means of assisting their development.

External debt results when a government borrows money from foreign lenders. Presently, much of the debt burden in low-income countries dates back to the 1970s and 1980s when suddenly high oil prices pushed countries to borrow a great deal of monies to fund either domestic projects (in the belief that high prices and export earnings would be sustained) or domestic programs (in the necessity of offsetting the costs of oil price shocks, high interest rates, and low commodity prices). Some countries recovered, but many did not. Current programs, such as the Heavily Indebted Poor Countries (HIPC) initiative, alleviate these countries' severe external debt burdens. Growing understanding of the hardship of extreme debt has led creditors, mostly the world's wealthiest countries, to cancel more than $50 billion of debt owed to international agencies by many of the world's poorest countries in 2005.[21]

More recently, many countries have borrowed from international lenders to finance their movement to freer markets, a process of economic transition we look at later in the chapter. Many countries that began with this ambition but that eventually failed then increasingly had to rely on foreign debt. Governments in countries with high debt burdens, like Liberia and Zambia, must often slow the rate of economic growth or else try to borrow more money. Foreign investors monitor debt levels to gauge debt pressure on the government to revise its economic policies.

Income Distribution

GNI or PPP, even when weighted by the size of the population, can misestimate the relative wealth of a nation's citizens. That is, GNI or PPP per capita tell, on average, how much income the average person earns. Neither indicator tells us what share of income goes to what segments of the population. For example, Brazil's GNI is $1.4 trillion, a performance that ranks well in the world. Similarly, its GNI per capita is nearly $2,710, a strong regional accomplishment (its neighbors, like Guyana and Bolivia, report GNI per capita under $1,000). However, Brazil's economic performance looks questionable when one considers that the richest fifth of Brazilians (about 35 million people) receive more than 60 percent of total income, while the poorest fifth of Brazilians receive only 3 percent. The situation is worse in countries such as India where over 80 percent (more than 800 million people) of the population lives on less than $2 per day and over 40 percent live on less than $1 per day.

Uneven income distribution is not a problem of poorer nations. The poorest fifth of the United States, for instance, receive 5 percent of the national income while the richest 20 percent of the population receive about 46 percent of GNI. Finally, this distribution pattern spans the world: 20 percent of the world population claims roughly 86 percent of the world's income, whereas the bottom 20 percent has about 1 percent.[22] Therefore, managers can hone their sense of the economic potential of a country by adjusting their analyses to reflect the actual distribution of income.

Similarly, there is a strong relationship between skewed income distributions and the split between those who live in urban settings versus those who live in rural areas. For example, the urban centers of China—such as Beijing, Shanghai, Hong Kong, Shenzhen, and Guangzhou—saw their per capita income grow to US$1,135 in 2004, about 3.21 times as

Income distribution is a description of the fractions of a population that are at various levels of income.

A global concern is the growing gap between the poor and rich, especially in many developing countries. This photo gives a sense of the gap in the contrast between urban slums and upper-income housing in Sao Paulo.

much as that of the typical rural dweller. Furthermore, China projects urban income will be seven times as much as rural income in 2020.[23] So, while one sees Lexus, Porsche, and Mercedes-Benz dealerships in Beijing, many in rural China still rely on bicycles and animals for transportation. Similar situations unfold elsewhere. The median years of schooling in Vietnam is 8.1 for urban residents versus 5.4 for rural residents. And 73 percent of urban households in India have access to adequate sanitation versus 14 percent of rural households.

Poverty

A related but separate issue concerns poverty—the state of having little or no money, few or no material possessions, and little or no resources to enjoy a reasonable standard of life. So, while looking at the distribution of income is important, it presumes there actually is a wide spread of income within a country; the latter applies to many but not all countries. Many countries report average per capita yearly incomes of $20,000 and higher. At the other extreme, the poorest countries often report per capita yearly incomes well below $1,000. Specifically, in 2003, more than a third of the world's countries fell below this threshold. In some of the world's poorest countries, GNI per capita is less than $500, with the poorest country, Ethiopia, reporting $90 in 2003. Globally, the world is about 78 percent poor (average purchasing power parity income less than US$3,470 annually), 11 percent middle income, and 11 percent rich (average purchasing power parity income more than US$8,000 annually. More pointedly, the richest 1 percent of the population of the world gets as much income as the bottom 57 percent—in other words, the 50 million richest people received as much income as did the 2.7 billion poorest people. An estimated 1.3 billion people, or about one-sixth of the world's population, have incomes of less than a dollar a day.[24] Poverty appears to be growing worse worldwide. More than 80 countries had lower per capita GNI at the end of the 1990s than they had at the end of the 1980s. Income distribution is increasingly skewed. In 1960 the wealthiest 20 percent of the world's population had 30 times the income of the poorest 20 percent. This grew to 32 times in 1970, 45 times in 1980, 60 times in 1990, and 75 times in 2000.

> A global concern is the growing gap between rich and poor.

Poverty of this scale and scope impacts economic environments and analysis. In many parts of the world, workers and consumers struggle for food, shelter, clothing, clean water, health services, to say nothing of safety, security, and education. Failure results in suffering, malnutrition, mental illness, death, epidemics, famine, and war. For example, 100 percent of Canadians have access to clear water whereas 13 percent of people in Afghanistan do; per capita dietary protein supply in the United States is 121 grams, but 32 grams in Mozambique; the average life expectancy in Japan is 81 years, yet just 31 years in Botswana.[25] International companies facing such situations must deal with their implications to virtually every feature of the economic environment. Customary market systems may not exist, national infrastructures may not work, criminal behavior may be pervasive, and governments may not be able

---

TABLE 4.2	KEY COMPONENTS OF THE BALANCE OF PAYMENTS

Current Account
- Value of exports and imports of physical goods, such as oil, grain or computers (also referred to as visible trade)
- Receipts and payments for services, such as banking or advertising, and other intangible goods, such as copyrights and cross-border dividend and interest payments (also referred to as invisible trade)
- Private transfers, such as money sent home by expatriate workers
- Official transfers, such as international aid, on which the government expects no returns

Capital Account
- Long-term capital flows (i.e., money invested in foreign firms as well as profits made by selling those investments and returning the money home)
- Short-term capital flows (i.e., money invested in foreign currencies by international speculators as well as funds moved around the world for business purposes by companies with international operations)

to consistently regulate society or adopt prudent economic policies. Enduring worldwide business activity and economic progress ultimately depend on alleviating poverty.

The Balance of Payments

The **balance of payments** (BOP), officially known as the Statement of International Transactions, records a country's international transactions that take place between companies, governments, or individuals. In doing so, the BOP reports the total of all the money that comes into a country from abroad less all the money going out of the country to any other country during the same period. The BOP has two main accounts: (1) the **current account,** which tracks all trade activity in merchandise, and (2) the **capital account,** which tracks both loans given to foreigners and loans received by citizens. Table 4.2 profiles the components of each account while Table 4.3 represents an example of both accounts for the United States.

Balance of payments— a record of a country's international transactions

Current account—trade in goods and services and income from assets abroad

Capital account— transactions in real or financial assets between countries, such as the sale of real estate to a foreign investor

Merchandise trade balance—the net balance of exports minus imports of merchandise

Deficit—imports exceed exports; **surplus**—exports exceed imports

TABLE 4.3	U.S. INTERNATIONAL TRANSACTIONS, 2004 (ABRIDGED VERSION)

For updated information, click on www.bea.doc.gov and select "Balance of payments and related data" from the Bureau of Economic Analysis economic accounts. Then select "Interactive Access" for a list of tables. Table 1 is "U.S. International Transactions" the table which we selected. You can then choose annual or quarterly data for any time period of interest.

[IN MILLIONS OF DOLLARS]	
(CREDITS + DEBITS −)	2004
Current Account	
Exports of goods and services and income receipts	1,516,169
Exports of goods and services	1,147,181
Goods, balance of payments basis	807,610
Services	339,571
Income receipts	368,988
Income receipts on U.S. -owned assets abroad	365,886
Compensation of employees	3,102
Imports of goods and services and income payments	2,109,181
Imports of goods and services	1,764,256
Goods, balance of payments basis	1,473,087
Services	291,169
Income payments	344,925
Income payments on foreign-owned assets in the United States	336,064
Compensation of employees	8,861
Unilateral current transfers net	72,928
Capital and Financial Account	
Capital Account	
Capital account transactions, net	1,477
Financial Account	
U.S.-owned assets abroad, net (increase/financial outflow (−)	817,676
U.S. official reserve assets, net	2,805
U.S. government assets, other than official reserve assets, net	1,269
U.S. private assets, net	821,750
Foreign-owned assets in the United States, net (increased/financial inflow (+)	1,433,171
Foreign official assets in the United States, net	355,252
Other foreign assets in the United States, net	1,077,919
Statistical discrepancy (sum of above items with sign reversed)	51,922

Source: Bureau of Economic Analysis, "U.S. International Accounts Data" (June 1, 2005) www.bea.doc.gov

Companies monitor the balance of payments to watch for factors that could lead to currency instability or government actions to correct an imbalance.

The fundamental notion of balance means that all BOP transactions have an offsetting receipt. For instance, a country might have a surplus in **merchandise trade** (indicating that it is exporting more than it is importing), but may then report a deficit in another area, such as its investment income. Managers use the BOP as a comprehensive indicator of a country's economic stability. By measuring a country's transactions with the rest of the world, the BOP estimates a country's financial stability in the world market. For example, a deficit in merchandise trade means that the supply of that country's currency is increasing throughout the world, given that its consumers are using it to buy the imports that cause a trade deficit. Unless the government revises its economic policies, the market will do so by proxy and depreciate the value of its currency. However, as our Point–Counterpoint feature illustrates, there are others who reason differently.

For managers, the macro-level debate profiled in the Point-Counterpoint feature has key micro-level implications. In the least, monitoring trends in the BOP gives managers one more piece of data in deciding whether or not to do business in a country. More generally, it confirms the importance of the connection between a company's strategy and the implications of BOP data to economic activities and government policy. For example, some say the solution to the U.S. deficit would come from faster growth overseas, decline in the value of the U.S. dollar and slower growth in consumer spending, and a higher U.S. savings rate. Each and all of these factors, if they came to pass, would change important elements of the economic environment of the United States as well as change economic policies in countries around the world.

POINT–COUNTERPOINT: TRADE DEFICITS—ADVANTAGE OR CRISIS

POINT

The balance of trade has an innocent sound to it. Operationally, it is straightforward—simply, the amount of exports sent by Country A to other countries less the amount of imports brought into Country A from other countries. This statistic is widely reported as a leading indicator of the state of a country's economy. However, adding the term "deficit" to the balance of trade turns it into a politically charged phrase that prompts different interpretations. Some people reason that a trade deficit is a sign of a strong economy, while others counter that it is a leading indicator of crisis. Events in the United States help put this debate into perspective.

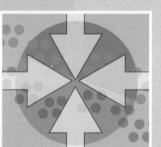

In the first week or so of each month, the U.S. Department of Commerce announces the country's trade balance. Through 2004 and 2005, the monthly announcement of the U.S.'s balance of trade gained greater prominence in light of its dramatic growth. Specifically, in January 2005, the Commerce Department reported that the U.S. trade deficit, on a monthly basis, hit an all-time high of $60.3 billion for November 2004 as Americans' appetite for foreign goods reached record levels. March 2005 saw the Commerce Department report that the current-account

deficit hit an annual record of $665.9 billion for 2004. Then, in June 2005, the United States hit a record deficit of $195.1 billion in the first quarter in trade and capital flows with the rest of the world. If this pace continued, the United States' current account deficit could reach $780 billion by the end of 2005. Each report, worse then its predecessor, reignited the debate about the implication of the United States' growing level of global debt.

One perspective saw the U.S.'s trade deficit as an indicator of the strength of the United States' economy. The Bush administration, for example, said these trade figures should be seen as testimony to the strength of the American economy and its role as an engine of global growth. Specifically, U.S. Treasury Secretary John W. Snow reported that the deficit was a sign that the U.S. economy "is growing faster than those of our trading partners in the Eurozone and in Japan. The economy is growing, expanding, creating jobs and disposable income and that shows up in the demand for imports."[26] Rob Nichols, spokesperson for the Treasury Department, added similar sentiments, noting, "We view these figures as an affirmation that we're growing faster than our trading partners by as much as 2 percent and we need them to take steps so they can grow and buy our products."[27] Effectively then, the U.S.'s trade deficit showed the strength of American consumers, and due to their inability to buy enough U.S.-made goods and services, the weakness of the United States' trading partners. According to this analysis, the responsibility for altering the trade imbalance lies not with the United States, but its trade partners. Once America's trade partners got their act together, their economies would grow and they would then have the resources to buy American products and consume more of what they produce domestically. At that time, the U.S.'s trade deficit would shrink as fast as the economies of its trade partners grew. Others echoed these thoughts, noting the trade deficit was an unimportant bookkeeping record because trade actually benefits all—successful foreign firms would invest more capital in the United States (such as by buying U.S. Treasury Bills) and we need only return the favor by buying more of their exports.

COUNTERPOINT

In counterpoint, some saw the U.S.'s growing trade deficit as an immense crisis waiting to happen. As one observer noted, "We now have the Grand Canyon of trade deficits. Actually, deficit is really a misnomer. Chasm, gorge, black hole, infinitely deep well all fit the description better."[28] While extreme, this view fit historic interpretations—technically, the trade deficit is a negative in the Commerce Department's estimates of GDP because of the assumption that imports replace U.S. products and thus, when they are growing, signal a weakening domestic economy. Senator Byron L. Dorgan, Democrat of North Dakota, said the deficit figure was reaching "dangerous levels that are hurting this country's future. This deficit manifests itself in the lives of American families every day with the loss of jobs overseas, lower wages, and a feeling of less security."[29] He and others called on President Bush to convene an emergency meeting of key government

policymakers to avert disaster. Similarly, the president of the Federal Reserve Bank of Boston noted that "Unavoidable economic logic suggests that eventually this situation will prove unsustainable."[30]

Who's right, who's wrong? In theory, a country can sustain a trade deficit for many years without its economy suffering—as long as the trade deficit is trivial compared with the country's gross national income and wealth. So, said some, a wealthy nation like the United States can endure a trade deficit for many years. However, they conceded that no nation could endure a trade deficit forever simply because it could not borrow endlessly from others without sooner or later eroding the foundations of its economy. Furthermore, theory suggested that a trade deficit is a positive economic indicator, provided the deficit is due to firms importing technology and other capital goods from abroad that they then use to improve their productivity and international competitiveness.

In the early years of the twenty-first century, many began worrying that the United States was rushing toward a balance of payments crisis. First, the United States' trade deficit was no longer trivial; at $665.9 billion for 2004, the deficit was equal to 5.7 percent of the GNI for the United States. That was a record for the United States both in absolute dollars and as a relative share of the GNI. Most economists argued that this level was unsustainable. In addition, the growing trade deficit pushed the United States to rely increasingly on foreign credit to finance its investment and consumption. Foreign governments bought $355 billion worth of American securities in 2004, slightly more than half of all the foreign money that flowed into the United States. Finally, said some, these investment and trade flows highlighted the fact that people in the United States were collectively undersaving and overconsuming. They were living beyond their means by buying too many goods and services because foreign money helped keep long-term interest rates at surprisingly low levels in America.

INTEGRATING ECONOMIC ANALYSIS

This preceding overview of economic development, in highlighting wide-scale divergence among countries, spotlights the dilemma for international companies. The high-income countries are the logical place to do business because of the quality and quantity of consumer demand. However, developing countries exhibit tremendous market potential because of the sheer size of the population—about 80 percent of all countries and 85 percent of the world's population. If and when these countries grow rapidly, they will offer enormous business opportunities. Dealing with this dilemma leads international companies to estimate a country's growth potential by gauging its current economic policies and

FIGURE 4.2

SPECTRUM OF ECONOMIC SYSTEMS

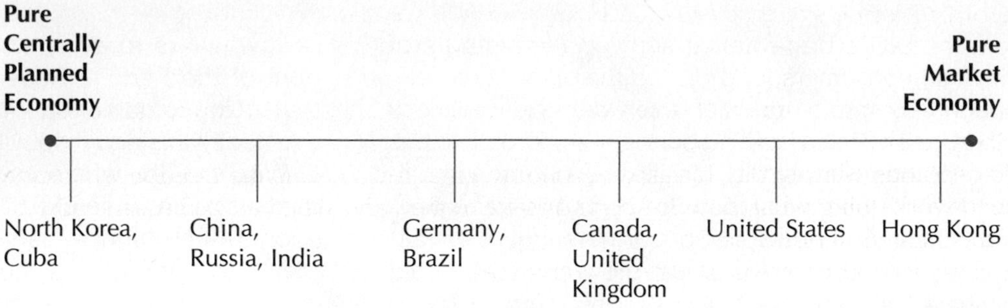

Pure Centrally Planned Economy						Pure Market Economy
North Korea, Cuba	China, Russia, India		Germany, Brazil	Canada, United Kingdom	United States	Hong Kong

practices. This estimation requires managers to go from examining individual elements of the economic environment to analyzing how a country's economic environment actually works. Managers typically handle this task from two perspectives. The first looks at the type of the current economic system in the country. The second looks at the transition process by which a country may be moving from one type of economic system to another.

Types of Economic Systems

An economic system is a mechanism that deals with the production, distribution, and consumption of goods and services in a particular society.

An **economic system** is the set of structures and processes that guides the allocation of resources and shapes the conduct of business activities. Spectrum analysis, as applied in Chapter 3, gives a sense of the range of economic systems in the world today. One end of the spectrum is anchored by the idea of capitalism, the other with that of communism (see Figure 4.2). Major differences between these ideas exist in terms of their implications to key economic matters like the ownership and control of factors of production, and the freedom of price to balance supply and demand (see Figure 4.3).

Capitalism is a free-market system built on private ownership and control. This philosophy holds that owners of capital have inalienable property rights that give them the right to earn a profit in return for their effort, investment, and risk. In contrast, communism champions a centrally planned system built on state ownership of all economic factors of production and control of all economic activity. Expectedly, as shown in Figure 4.2, there are few instances of pure expression of either capitalism or communism. Instead, managers use the principles of capitalism and communism to analyze prevailing

FIGURE 4.3   **RELATIONSHIPS BETWEEN CONTROL OF ECONOMIC ACTIVITY AND OWNERSHIP OF PRODUCTION FACTORS**

Although the most logical combinations of ownership and control are sectors A and I, most countries in the world have mixed economies with a variety of combinations of ownership and control.

		OWNERSHIP OF PRODUCTION		
		Private	Mixed	Public
CONTROL OF ECONOMIC ACTIVITY	Market	A	B	C
	Mixed	D	E	F
	Command	G	H	I

Control/Ownership	Control/Ownership	Control/Ownership
A. Market/Private	D. Mixed/Private	G. Command/Private
B. Market/Mixed	E. Mixed/Mixed	H. Command/Mixed
C. Market/Public	F. Mixed/Public	I. Command/Public

types of economic systems—a market economy, a command economy, and a mixed economy—that define economic environments across the world.

Market Economy   A **market economy,** the leading example of a capitalist economy, describes the system where individuals, rather than government, make the majority of economic decisions. Simply put, a market economy gives individuals the freedom to decide where to work doing what, how to spend or save money, and whether to consume now or later. The theoretical principles that define free-market economies are based on the principle of laissez-faire (nonintervention by government in economic matters). This principle is credited to Adam Smith and his proposition that a market economy has two general features: producers, spurred by the profit motive, efficiently make products that consumers want; and, consumers, by virtue of what they do and do not buy, determine the relationships among price, quantity, supply, and demand so that capital and labor are allocated productively.

Because individuals, not the government, make most of the economic decisions, this type of economic system depends on individuals and companies, rather than political officials and government, owning and controlling resources. Then the market economy is free to allocate goods and services as if, Adam Smith wrote, an "invisible hand" were guiding the efficient actions of self-interested individuals to combine for the common good. Hence, consumer sovereignty, whereby consumers influence the allocation of resources through their demand for products, is the cornerstone of a market economy.

A market economy depends on as few as possible government restrictions—the less invisible the "hand" becomes due to government intervention, the less efficiently will the market work. Nonetheless, the invisible hand is not infallible, given the need for some public goods (like traffic lights or national defense) and precautions that preempt those inclined to maximize personal gain in unfair ways. Therefore, a free market still needs government action to enforce contracts, protect property rights, ensure fair and free competition, regulate certain sorts of economic activities, and provide general security.

Hong Kong, Great Britain, Canada, and the United States are often cited as examples of contemporary market economies. Strictly speaking, none of them are "pure" market economies because their governments do intervene in the marketplace. However, these economies are much closer to the pure market economy model than those in most other countries.[31]

> A market economy permits an open exchange of goods and services between producers and consumers.

Command Economy   A **command economy,** also known as a centrally planned economy, describes the economic system whereby the government owns and controls all resources. Hence the government commands all authority to decide what goods and services a country will produce, the quantity in which they are produced, and the price at which they are sold to consumers.[32] For example, in a market economy, if the government wants more cars, it collects taxes and then buys cars at market prices. In a centrally planned economy, the explicitly visible hand of the government orders state-owned and state-controlled car makers to make more cars.[33] The economy of the former Union of Soviet Socialist Republics was an example of a planned economy: All decisions regarding production and distribution were made by the government.[34]

Centrally planned economies have a range of telltale features. The government owns the means of production—land, farms, factories, banks, stores, hospitals, and so forth— that are then managed by employees of the state. Consequently, the prices of goods and services do not often change in a command economy because government officials, not consumers, determine them. Quality, on the other hand, tends to vary dramatically, often getting worse over time because (1) whatever product is made is usually in short supply, (2) consumers typically have few to no other choices, and (3) there is not much incentive for companies to innovate and little profits to invest.

Centrally planned economies historically were found in communist countries. The totalitarian aims of communism spurred state economic planners to give highest priority to industrial investments and military spending. Consumer goods and food products bore the opportunity costs of these decisions, getting little to no priority. Communist

> Command economy—all dimensions of economic activity are determined by a central government plan

societies' goal of a utopian collectivist society championed national self-reliance at the expense of international trade (except that done with other communist states) and foreign investment. The option to forsake goods that were made more efficiently in noncommunist countries usually increased the inefficiencies of centrally planned economies. Finally, we must note that centrally planned economies sometimes allowed free market forces to play, such as the private household plots of collective farm members, mom and pop retail stores, or the informal "gray" markets where scarce consumer goods could be exchanged at market-determined prices. Still, these were minor exceptions that existed at the discretion of government authorities.

Command economies can appear to perform well, especially in terms of growth rates, for short periods of time, perhaps even up to a generation, because by controlling everything and everybody, the state has a tremendous ability to mobilize unemployed or underemployed resources to generate growth. Impressive growth rates can be achieved as long as the main source of growth is putting unemployed resources (principally labor) to work. Similarly, command economies typically developed large-scale, capital-intensive production that, while not competitive with global standards, often achieved marginal rates of efficiency while making acceptable products. So, for example, the Lada, a car commissioned by the central government of the former USSR in 1966, won no prizes for price, quality, or style. Still, even today, the maker of the Lada is the largest producer of family cars in Russia and Eastern Europe and provides basic transportation for many people. Finally, command economies would bolster short-term economic performance by increasing investment through "forced savings" (that is, the government allocates disproportionate shares of GNI toward state programs at the expense of consumption), and importing and copying technology and production methods from more advanced economies (thereby reducing research and development outlays).

Once a prevalent type of economic system, increasingly fewer countries have centrally planned economies. Presently, North Korea and Cuba stand out and both economies consistently perform poorly.[35] The importance of understanding the features and functions of an increasingly uncommon economic system follows from the fact that several prominent countries, namely Russia, China, Vietnam, and the countries of Central and Eastern Europe (CEE), have begun the complex task of transitioning from a command to a market economy. This transition process, discussed later in the chapter, has created business opportunities and, by the same token, market challenges that are best understood with a sense of where these countries are coming from.

Mixed Economy   As with political systems, so too for economic systems, there is no "pure" version of a market economy or a command economy. Instead, most economies, broadly labeled **mixed economies,** fall in the wide middle of the capitalism–communism spectrum (see Figure 4.2). A mixed economy is a system where economic decisions are largely market driven and ownership is largely private, but the government intervenes in many private economic decisions. Hence, the mixed economic system has elements of both market and central planning economies—the government owns key factors of production, yet consumers and private producers still influence price and quantity.[36] For example, the government may own companies that manufacture cars. But rather than telling managers how much to sell each car for, the government permits the market forces of supply and demand to set prices. A range of countries are commonly classified as mixed economies, including South Africa, Japan, South Korea, France, Brazil, Germany, and India.[37]

Inevitably, the question emerges: Why would a country not opt for one of the pure economic types, betting on either free markets or state control to maximize economic performance? In response, the proponents of mixed economies concede that an economic system should aspire to achieve the efficiencies endemic to free markets. But an economic system must also, at the least, protect society from the excesses of unchecked individualism and greed, and ideally, apply policies needed to achieve low unemployment, low poverty, steady economic growth, and an equitable distribution of wealth. Consequently, the fact that the pure forms of market and command economies are

Mixed economy—different degrees of ownership and control best describe most countries

theoretically unable to achieve both of these goals without violating their basis principles motivates a country to mix the best parts of each type.

Operationally, government intervention in the economy takes various forms. One, central, regional, or local governments may actually own some means of production, for example, the Tennessee Valley Authority in the United States that generates electricity for several states, or Airbus Industries, jointly owned by several European governments. Two, the government can influence private production or consumption decisions, for example, by buying goods and services or by subsidizing or taxing certain activities. Third, it can redistribute income and wealth in pursuit of some equity objective, for example, socialized medicine and other welfare programs. The extent and nature of government intervention, beside differing from country to country, changes over time, based on a country's political, social, cultural, and institutional traditions and trends.

Government intervention in the economy takes various forms.

Freedom, Markets, and Transition

Chapter 3 reported that since the late 1980s, two trends—the movement toward democratic political systems and the adoption of free market principles—have reshaped political and economic environments in many countries. The move toward democracy has been powered by several factors, including the failure of totalitarian regimes using centrally planned economies to deliver progress and prosperity, improved access to richer sources of information, and the quest for higher living standards. Similar factors, which we discuss below, motivate the emergence of freer markets. Most notably, though, is the realization that economic growth is vital to improving the standard of living and that economic growth is a function of economic freedom.[38] This realization, while most pronounced in the centrally planned economies like China and Russia, has also taken hold in many mixed economies, like Ireland, Brazil, and India.

Economic Freedom: Idea, Performance, and Trends

Since 1995, the Heritage Foundation and the *Wall Street Journal* have annually reported the **Economic Freedom Index.** Officially, *economic freedom* is defined as the "absence of government coercion or constraint on the production, distribution, or consumption of goods and services beyond the extent necessary for citizens to protect and maintain liberty itself. In other words, people are free to work, produce, consume, and invest in the ways they feel are most productive."[39] Operationally, this index is the most comprehensive approximation of the extent to which the government of a country intervenes with the principles of free choice, free enterprise, and free prices for reasons that go beyond the basic need to protect property, liberty, citizen safety, and market efficiency. Practically, this survey rates countries in terms of 50 independent indicators that are organized into 10 categories: trade policy, fiscal burden of government, government intervention in the economy, monetary policy, capital flows and investment, banking and finance, wages and prices, property rights, regulation, and informal market activity (such as black or shadow markets).[40]

Map 4.5 reports the classification of 161 countries in terms of their degree of economic freedom in 2005. The survey reports that 17 countries have free economies, and 56 more are rated mostly free, 70 are mostly unfree, and 12 are repressed. The 10 freest economies, in descending order, are Hong Kong, Singapore, Luxembourg, Estonia, Ireland and New Zealand (tied for fifth), the United Kingdom, Denmark and Iceland (tied for eighth) and Australia. The most repressed economies, starting with the worst offender, are North Korea, Burma (Myanmar), Libya, Zimbabwe, Turkmenistan, Laos, Cuba, Iran, Uzbekistan and Venezuela. The results of the survey confirm that market economies exhibit high economic freedom, mixed economies exhibit some economic freedom, and command economies exhibit little to no economic freedom.

For the first time in the history of the index, the United States was not one of the 10 freest economies; it ranked number 12. Technically, America's score on the index stayed the same from the preceding survey. However, several other countries had taken steps to

Factors that determine economic freedom
- Trade policy
- Fiscal burden of government
- Government intervention in the economy
- Monetary policy
- Capital flows and investment
- Banking and finance
- Wages and prices
- Property rights
- Regulation
- Black market activity

MAP 4.5   Countries Ranked According to Economic Freedom

Economic freedom captures the idea that all citizens in all counties have the right to work, produce, consume, and invest in the ways they feel are most productive. Presently, countries are classified as free, mostly free, mostly unfree, and repressed, according to the degree to which governments influence people's economic choices.

Source: The 2002 Index of Economic Freedom (The Heritage Foundation and *Wall Street Journal*, 2002), http://www.heritage.org/index/2002/world.html. Reprinted by permission of the Heritage Foundation.

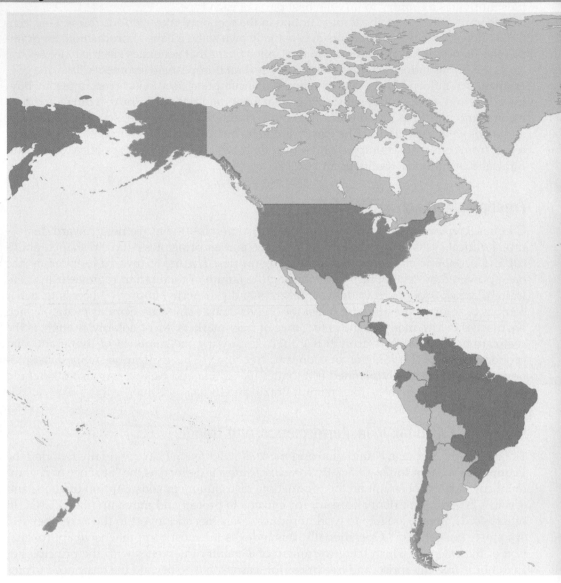

Countries with the freest economies have the highest annual growth in GNI.

reduce government regulation in their economies, thereby moving ahead of the United States. Iceland, for instance, cut taxes and reduced regulation of its banks to move to eighth place, while Chile reduced tariffs on imports to rank number 11.

The survey qualifies 73 countries as free or mostly free versus the 82 classified as mostly not free or repressed. The distribution of countries, profiled by some of the economic indicators discussed earlier in the chapter, reveals interesting patterns. Most notably, the freest economies have a per capita income of $29,219, more than twice that of the mostly free at $12,839, and more than four times that of the mostly unfree economies. Similar patterns exist regarding income, growth rates, human development, price stability, and employment. Collectively, these indicators confirm the long running trend that countries that are freer of high taxes, regulations, and other government controls achieve the highest standards of living.

The survey shows that the distribution of countries, in raw numbers, is skewed toward countries with little to no economic freedom—82 nations were rated as mostly not free and 12 nations as repressed. Looking not at the raw number of countries but the number of people in those countries highlights a significant trend. The number of people who live in repressed economies has dropped 38 percent, from 391 million to 242 million over the past decade. Meanwhile, the number of people living in free economies has

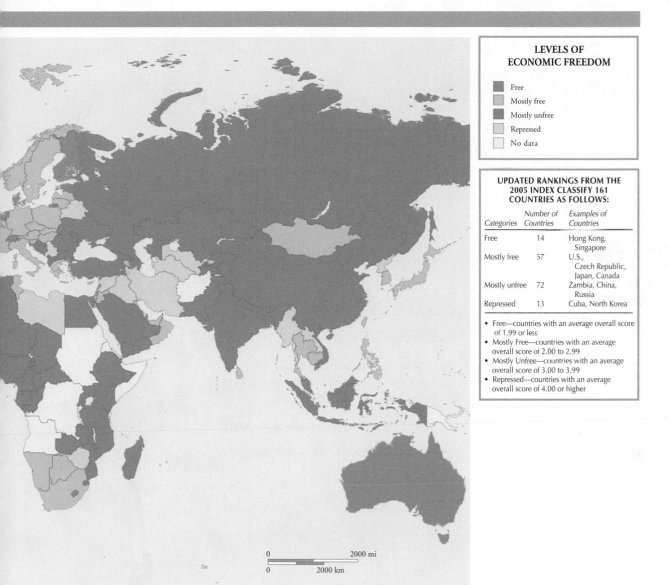

LEVELS OF ECONOMIC FREEDOM

- Free
- Mostly free
- Mostly unfree
- Repressed
- No data

UPDATED RANKINGS FROM THE 2005 INDEX CLASSIFY 161 COUNTRIES AS FOLLOWS:

Categories	Number of Countries	Examples of Countries
Free	14	Hong Kong, Singapore
Mostly free	57	U.S., Czech Republic, Japan, Canada
Mostly unfree	72	Zambia, China, Russia
Repressed	13	Cuba, North Korea

- Free—countries with an average overall score of 1.99 or less
- Mostly Free—countries with an average overall score of 2.00 to 2.99
- Mostly Unfree—countries with an average overall score of 3.00 to 3.99
- Repressed—countries with an average overall score of 4.00 or higher

0   2000 mi
0   2000 km

risen 32 percent, from 361 million to 478 million. Most of the world's population falls between these two endpoints.

The economic freedom index, looked at in longitudinal terms, identifies significant trends in the prevalence of the types of economic systems around the world. That is, over time the survey data estimate the degree to which countries are adopting elements of market, mixed, or command economies. Over the past quarter century, more and more countries have moved toward greater economic freedom. From 2004 to 2005, of the 155 countries studied, 86 countries adopted more economic freedoms, compared with 57 countries that imposed more state controls. More significantly, from 1995 to 2005, there has been a widespread move toward freer markets, not only in the former centrally planned communist states but also in Western Europe, South America, and Southeast Asia. Finally, the data show that neither geography nor country size influenced the adoption of economic freedoms. Big and small countries, from Honduras to China, located throughout the world are in the process of transitioning to market economies with more economic freedom.

> Over the past few decades, more countries have moved toward greater economic freedom.

There are many theories about the origins and causes of economic development.[41] The economic freedom index, however, has straightforward implications: Countries with the most economic freedom have higher rates of long-term economic growth and are more prosperous than are those with less economic freedom. Most significantly, those countries

MAP 4.6   GDP Per Capita Growth Rate

This map shows the average annual percentage change in a country's real GDP per capita. The widespread movement toward free markets has led to faster growth rates in many countries worldwide.

Source: From *The World Bank Atlas 2001,* p. 41. Reprinted by permission of the World Bank.

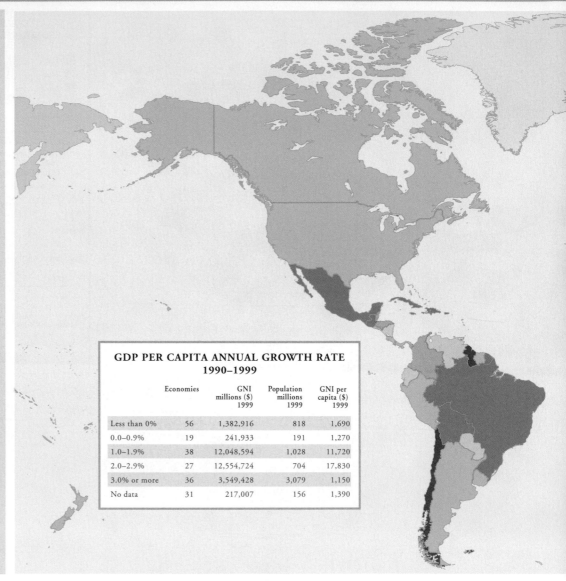

GDP PER CAPITA ANNUAL GROWTH RATE
1990–1999

	Economies	GNI millions ($) 1999	Population millions 1999	GNI per capita ($) 1999
Less than 0%	56	1,382,916	818	1,690
0.0–0.9%	19	241,933	191	1,270
1.0–1.9%	38	12,048,594	1,028	11,720
2.0–2.9%	27	12,554,724	704	17,830
3.0% or more	36	3,549,428	3,079	1,150
No data	31	217,007	156	1,390

ranking highest on economic freedom—such as Singapore and the United Kingdom—tend to have the fastest economic growth and highest living standards. In addition, there is a strong positive relationship between political freedom and economic freedom. Countries with high economic freedom show high degrees of political freedom, whereas people in countries at the bottom of the index, such as Cuba and Zambia, have little to no political freedom. Still, notwithstanding the steady increase in the number of free and mostly free countries, a significant proportion of the world's people (nearly three-quarters) live in countries that are mostly unfree.[42] Map 4.6 spotlights these relationships. Between 1990 and 2001, countries that had or were aggressively developing greater market freedoms had growing economies, while those countries that had none or were slowly doing so had sluggish to shrinking economies.[43]

Transition to a Market Economy

Most command economies are going through the process of transition to market economies.

Although mixed and command economies differ on many dimensions, they share one common feature—the government has anywhere from extensive to complete ownership of resources and exerts control over some to all parts of the economy. Over time, as market economies outperformed their mixed and command counterparts, it became apparent that

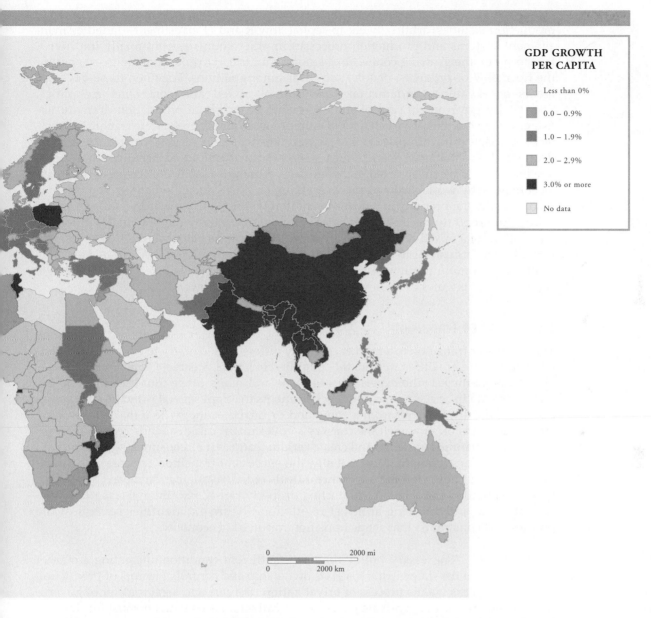

GDP GROWTH
PER CAPITA

- Less than 0%
- 0.0 – 0.9%
- 1.0 – 1.9%
- 2.0 – 2.9%
- 3.0% or more
- No data

government ownership and control of the factors of production constrained growth and prosperity. Certainly, government ownership and control had some benefits, such as lower unemployment and far-reaching social programs. Still, government control and ownership created operational inefficiency and strategic ineffectiveness.

Regarding operational inefficiency, there was a relationship between the degree of government ownership and a host of bad economics—that is, government-controlled companies cost more to run, made lower quality products at higher costs, missed or ignored changes in consumer tastes, practiced poor corporate governance, and suffered slow to no growth. Moreover, industry-level problems appeared. Governments, over time, tended toward overregulation of the economic environment and greater day-to-day intervention in market activities. In absolute terms, these limitations translated into poorly performing economies. In relative terms, these limitations meant that mixed and command economies were increasingly falling farther behind their market economy counterparts in the race for global competitiveness.

Regarding strategic ineffectiveness, many mixed and command economies, besides dealing with tough challenges here and now, were facing even more dismal futures. Granted, we noted earlier that government-directed economies often can perform well.

Over time, however, the power of their typical advantages—cheap labor, large-scale production facilities, artificially cheap capital, low R and D investment—faded as management systems and production processes in other countries continually improved. Furthermore, the growing connections among countries, as globalization grows, permit the freer flow of products, people, and ideas among nations. Together, these developments aggravate a fundamental limitation of mixed and command economies. Specifically, government control and ownership of factors of production dramatically decreases the risk-affinitive behavior of entrepreneurs and companies to pursue the sorts of knowledge innovations that increasingly are the basis of growth and prosperity. Research shows that market economies create powerful individual incentives that stimulate innovation, whereas mixed and command economies seemed to create weak or no incentives. Why work hard and risk everything on a new idea if whatever you create is automatically the property of a government that will not fairly reward you for your sacrifice? Until recently, the cost of low rates of innovative activity did not quickly erode the foundations of a mixed or command economy. However, as global markets progressively moved from industrial to intellectual enterprises, innovation in sectors as varied as health care, communications, software, and entertainment have taken greater strategic significance as engines of a country's long-run economic growth.[44]

The Means of Transition

The process of transition to a market economy differs from country to country. The steps taken in Ireland are different from those applied in China, Iceland, Chile, Brazil, Russia, or Italy. Nonetheless, the experiences of these and many other countries indicate the quest to create freer economies spurs governments to adopt several principles and practices. Specifically, the shift from a command or mixed economy to a market economy largely depends on how well the country's government can dismantle certain features (i.e., central planning systems) and create certain features (i.e., consumer sovereignty) in its economic environment. Most notably, the success of transition appears to be intricately linked to how well the government deals with privatizing the means of production, deregulating the economy, protecting property rights, reforming fiscal and monetary policies, and applying antitrust regulation. Figure 4.4 identifies several of the policies and constraints that shape transition to a market economy.

Transition includes liberalizing economic activity, reforming business activity, and establishing legal and institutional frameworks.

Privatization   A necessary, but by no means sufficient condition of creating a market economy is that the state must transfer its ownership and control of factors of production to private owners via the process of **privatization** (the sale and legal transfer of government-owned resources to private interests). Privatization is essential not just for the sake of improving general market efficiency but also because only a robust private sector can shape the relationship between supply and demand so that it leads to better production and consumption decisions. Hence, the ambition to move toward a market economy requires that government disengage from the economy by privatizing state-owned enterprises. Most immediately, privatization reduces government debt by eliminating the need to subsidize typically inefficient, money-losing, state-owned enterprises. Longer term, privatization increases market efficiency in light of the expectation that private owners will more aggressively upgrade technologies, improve business practices, and create innovations than had or would state-appointed administrators. Perhaps the key motivator is the fact that privatized companies must compete in open markets for material, labor, and capital. Hence, private enterprises succeed or fail on their own merits.[45]

Privatization—the sale of state-owned enterprises to the domestic or foreign private sector; this process helps governments reduce internal debt.

Deregulation is the removal of rules that control or restrict the operations of an industry or company.

Deregulation   Deregulation involves relaxing or removing restrictions on the free operation of markets and business practices. Doing so then allows businesses to be more productive by saving the time and money previously spent complying with regulations. Also, the reasoning goes, the resulting freedom and savings encourage managers to make the investments into the innovations that then lead to economic growth.

FIGURE 4.4   REFORMS AND ECONOMIC PROGRESS

There are several reforms that are necessary to achieve economic progress, but there are also factors that retard economic progress.

Source: Finance & Development, June 1999, Volume 36, Number 2. FINANCE AND DEVELOPMENT by IMF. Copyright 1999 by INTERNATIONAL MONETARY FUND. Reproduced with permission of INTERNATIONAL MONETARY FUND in the format textbook via Copyright Clearance Center.

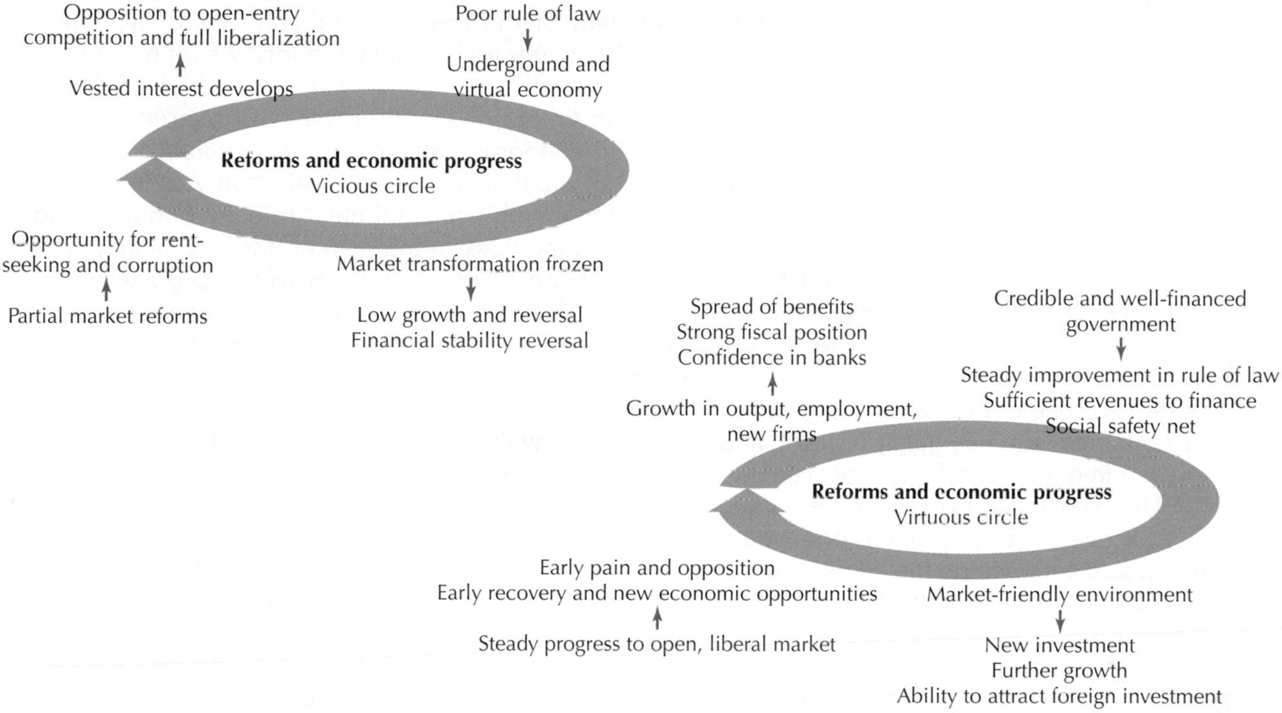

Opposition to open-entry competition and full liberalization

↑

Vested interest develops

Poor rule of law

↓

Underground and virtual economy

Reforms and economic progress
Vicious circle

Opportunity for rent-seeking and corruption

↑

Partial market reforms

Market transformation frozen

↓

Low growth and reversal
Financial stability reversal

Spread of benefits
Strong fiscal position
Confidence in banks

↑

Growth in output, employment, new firms

Credible and well-financed government

↓

Steady improvement in rule of law
Sufficient revenues to finance
Social safety net

Reforms and economic progress
Virtuous circle

Early pain and opposition
Early recovery and new economic opportunities

↑

Steady progress to open, liberal market

Market-friendly environment

↓

New investment
Further growth
Ability to attract foreign investment

Property Rights   Protection of property rights means that entrepreneurs who come up with an innovation can legally claim the present and future rewards of their idea, effort, and risk. This protection also supports a competitive economic environment by assuring investors and entrepreneurs that they, not the state, will prosper from their hard work. If this protection is lacking, as we saw in our case on the legal environment of China, companies bear a tremendous degree of risk of contract or property rights violations.

> Property rights permit an individual to own property and keep the income earned from it.

Fiscal and Monetary Reform   Economic decision making by political officials often leads governments to adopt tax or spending polices that slow growth and increase interest rates, inflation, and unemployment. Adopting free market principles requires a government to rely on market-oriented instruments for macroeconomic stabilization, set strict budget limits, and use market-based policies to manage the money supply. Inevitably, these measures create temporary economic hardships. For instance, using the market to enforce fiscal and monetary discipline leads to stable economic environments that, in turn, attract the investors, companies, and capital needed to start and finance growth.

Antitrust Laws   Markets, left to their own devices, can create situations in which a single seller or producer supplies a good or service. When one company is able to control a product's supply and, therefore, its price, it is considered a monopoly. The anticompetitive practices of monopolies are antithetical to a free market. Consequently, the government intent on liberalizing its economic system must legislate antitrust laws that encourage the development of industries with as many competing businesses as the market will sustain. In such industries, prices are kept low by the forces of competition. By enforcing antitrust laws, governments can prevent monopolies from exploiting consumers and restraining market growth.

> Antitrust laws aim to maintain and promote market competition.

Training at Moscow McDonald's," *European Management Journal* (March 1993): 102–7; Aviva Freudmann, "Supplying Big Mac's: A Lesson in Logistics," *Journal of Commerce* (May 19, 1999): 1A; Bloomberg News, "McDonald's Is Slowing Its Expansion in Russia," *New York Times* (February 20, 1999): C3; Natalia Olynec, "Big Mac Blues in Russia," *Chicago Sun Times* (February 28, 1999): 58; "Fast Food and Organized Catering in China: A Market Analysis," *Access Asia* (August 2001): 1; McDonald's Corporation 2001 Summary Report (March 12, 2002): **http://www.mcdonalds.com**; Dmitry Babich and Yulia Ignatyeva, "Big Mac Does Not Give Up," *Moscow News* (February 26, 2003); Cliff Vanderlinden, "Marking Russia's Golden Milestone," *National Post's Financial Post & FP Investing* (January 28, 2005): FP4; "McDonald's Celebrates Its 15th Anniversary in Russia," PR Newswire Europe Limited (January 31, 2005); Maria Levitov, "McDonald's Plans 105 New Outlets," *Moscow Times* (February 1, 2005); "McDonald's Russian '05 Sales Slower" (January 31, 2005), retrieved from **http://chicagobusiness.com/cgi-bin/news.pl?post_date= 2005–01–31&id=15342.**

2 Hewlett-Packard Annual Report 2001 (2002): **http://www.hp.com/hpinfo/investor/financials/annual/ 2001/text_only_10k.pdf, 2001.**

3 The World Bank Group, **www.worldbank.org/data/databytopic/class.htm**. Also, see "How Many Countries Are in the World?" at **http://geography.about.com/cs/countries/a/numbercountries.htm.**

4 Andrew B. Abel and Ben S. Bernanke, *Macroeconomics* (Reading, MA: Addison-Wesley, 1992), 30.

5 Historically, GNI was commonly referred to as gross national product. The definition and measurement of GNI and GNP are identical, but institutions such as the World Bank, the International Monetary Fund, and the Central Intelligence Agency now use the term GNI.

6 Ibid., pp. 32–33.

7 World Bank, 2003 Survey.

8 The World Bank, using its Atlas method, divides national economies according to 2003 GNI per capita. The groups are: low income, $765 or less; lower middle income, $766–$3,035; upper middle income, $3,036–$9,385; and high income, $9,386 or more. For the record, the World Bank explains the Atlas method as: "In calculating gross national income (GNI—formerly referred to as GNP) and GNI per capita in U.S. dollars for certain operational purposes, the World Bank uses the Atlas conversion factor. The purpose of the Atlas conversion factor is to reduce the impact of exchange rate fluctuations in the cross-country comparison of national incomes. The Atlas conversion factor for any year is the average of a country's exchange rate (or alternative conversion factor) for that year and its exchange rates for the two preceding years, adjusted for the difference between the rate of inflation in the country, and through 2000, that in the G-5 countries (France, Germany, Japan, the United Kingdom, and the United States). For 2001 onwards, these countries include the Euro Zone, Japan, the United Kingdom, and the United States. A country's inflation rate is measured by the change in its GDP deflator." (See **http://www.worldbank.org/data/ aboutdata/working-meth.html**).

9 The World Bank refers to the low- and middle-income countries as developing countries, even though it recognizes that not all "developing" countries are alike nor are they all "developing." **Developing countries** are also known as **emerging countries**, a term also used in describing the capital markets (debt and equity markets) in those countries as different from capital markets in the more advanced countries. In addition, the World Bank's terminology does not imply that the high-income countries have reached some preferred or final stage of development. High-income countries are also sometimes called **developed countries** or **industrial countries.** Initially this was because those countries derived a relatively high percentage of their GNP and employment from industry rather than agriculture. Now, however, these countries have a larger percentage of their GNP and employment tied up in services rather than industry. But the term *industrial country* is still popular. The developing countries include different types of countries— some with large populations, such as China (1.2 billion people) and India (997 million people), and others with small populations, such as Guyana (697,181 people). They also include countries in economic transition to a market economy, such as China, Poland, Russia, and Vietnam. Some developing countries, especially those in Asia and Latin America, are generally moving forward, while others, especially some in Africa, are not making much progress.

10 Typically, the prices of many goods will be considered and weighted according to their importance in the economy of the particular country.

11 World Bank, 2003 Survey (Atlas methodology for GNI per capita).

12 Statement by Dr. Mahbub ul Haq, Pakistani economist and a key founder, along with Dr. Amartya Sen, of the theory of human development.

13 The index was developed in 1990 by the Pakistani economist Mahbub ul Haq, and has been used since 1993 by the United Nations Development Programme in its annual report. **http://en.wikipedia.org/wiki/ Human_Development_Index.**

14 The HDI is comparable over time when it is calculated based on the same methodology and comparable trend data. HDR 2003 presents a time series in HDI for 1975, 1980, 1985, 1990, 1995, and 2001. This time series uses the latest HDI methodology and the most up-to-date trend data for each component of the index.

15 The gender-related development index (GDI) is a composite indicator that measures the average achievement of a population in the same dimensions as the HDI while adjusting for gender inequalities in the

level of achievement in the three basic aspects of human development. It uses the same variables as the HDI, disaggregated by gender. The gender empowerment measure (GEM) is a composite indicator that captures gender inequality in three key areas:

- Political participation and decision making, as measured by women's and men's percentage shares of parliamentary seats
- Economic participation and decision-making power, as measured by two indicators: women's and men's percentage shares of positions as legislators, senior officials, and managers; and women's and men's percentage shares of professional and technical positions
- Power over economic resources, as measured by women's and men's estimated earned income (PPP US$)

16 Inflation is the average rate of increase in prices of goods and services or, alternatively, a decrease in purchasing power of the national currency. When economists speak of inflation as an economic problem, they generally mean a persistent increase in the general price level over a period of time, resulting in a decline in a currency's purchasing power. Inflation is usually measured as a percentage increase in the consumer price index.

17 Technically, the inflation rate is the percentage increase in the change in prices from one period to the next, usually a year. Economists use different types of indices to measure inflation, but the one they use the most is the consumer price index (CPI). The CPI measures a fixed basket of goods and compares its price from one period to the next. A rise in the index indicates inflation.

18 For instance, as of 2003, only three countries had annual inflation rates in excess of 40 percent, the level above which it is generally considered to be acutely damaging. All major industrial countries had inflation under 3 percent (and in Japan, deflation persisted). Moreover, inflation in many middle- and lower-income countries, once stuck with extreme inflation pressure, had fallen well into single digits in the early twenty-first century. Many credited the fall in inflation to a combination of the price pressures of globalization along with more vigilant central bankers and economic policymakers. See Kenneth Rogoff, "The IMF Strikes Back," *Foreign Policy* 134 (January/February 2003).

19 The most common method of measuring unemployment was developed in the United States in the 1930s; it is followed by many other countries on the recommendation of the International Labor Organization. Technically, the U.S. government takes a monthly survey of a sample of households representing the entire civilian population, asking about the activity of each person of working age. Some countries forsake this survey method, instead deriving unemployment estimates from data on the number of people who are looking for work through the public employment offices or the number receiving unemployment compensation payments.

20 See Constance Sorrentino, "International Unemployment Rates: How Comparable Are They?" *Monthly Labor Review* (June 2000), http://www.bls.gov/opub/mlr/2000/06/art1exc.htm.

21 Alan Cowell, "Finance Chiefs Cancel Debt of 18 Nations," *New York Times* (June 12, 2005).

22 The income gap is even apparent in cyberspace. The top fifth in income make up 93 percent of the world's Internet users and the poorest fifth only 0.2 percent.

23 Zhao Huanxin, "Closing Farm-Urban Income Gap 'Top' Goal," *China Daily* (February 1, 2005):1.

24 United Nations Development Programme, 2004, http://www.undp.org

25 The Food and Agriculture Organization (FAO) of the United Nations (UN) (www.fao.org) translates the food commodities available for human consumption in a country into their protein equivalent. This measure compensates for differences in protein supplied by different foods across countries.

26 Reported in Elizabeth Becker, "U.S. Trade Deficit Hit Highest Figure Ever in November," *New York Times* (January 12, 2005).

27 Elizabeth Becker, "U.S. Trade Deficit Hits $58.3 Billion as Chinese Imports Surge," *New York Times* (March 11, 2005).

28 Quote from Joel Naroff, reported in "U.S. Trade Deficit Soars to All-Time High," *Forbes* (January 12, 2005).

29 Reported in "US Trade Deficit Soars," *Australian Times* (January 13, 2005).

30 Quote from Cathy Minehan, reported in "U.S. Trade Gap Widened to Record $60.3 Billion in Nov," *Bloomberg* (January 12, 2005).

31 Some suggest characterizing the United States and a number of other similar countries as established market economies (EMEs), the term referring both to their high levels of per capita income and to the well-developed and relatively stable nature of those institutions that support the efficient operation of sophisticated markets. Such institutions include the legal-regulatory system (both the laws themselves and their routine enforcement); financial institutions, such as the banks and the stock and bond markets; accounting systems (such as the generally accepted accounting principles, or GAP); and government supervision of market transactions (such as the Food and Drug Administration and the Federal Trade Commission in the U.S.).

32 North Korea remains perhaps the most closed economy in the world. For the most part, the policy of *juche* (self-reliance) is causing extreme hardship for its people. After floods in 1995 and 1996 wiped out or badly damaged 20 percent of the nation's crops, the government was forced to cut rice rations to about half

a bowl per day. Shortages were so severe because government policy had systematically eliminated incentives to create wealth and develop effective production techniques.

33 Companies in centrally planned economies exhibited a particular quirk. The absence of competition and bankruptcy in this sort of economic system meant that once an enterprise was up and running, it survived indefinitely, irrespective of performance. This is so because in the absence of meaningful (that is, competitive market-determined) factor and product prices, and with continuous interference by the authorities into economic decisions, an enterprise's true economic performance cannot be judged. Also, while there is little or no open unemployment, there is plenty of hidden unemployment because enterprises typically employ more people than would be needed if production were organized efficiently.

34 The command economy, which in the past has typically been associated with a communist political system, was introduced in the Soviet Union in the late 1920s and then in China and the countries of Eastern Europe after WWII. At about the same time or later on, several other countries in Asia and Cuba in Central America also became command economies.

35 To be sure, in the case of Cuba, the embargo by the United States has also been a factor.

36 Michael P. Todaro, *Economic Development,* 6th ed. (Reading, MA: Addison Wesley, 1996), 705.

37 This situation is not without precedent. After World War II, the Japanese government intervened in the economy in a significant way, even though it was not involved in the ownership of companies. For example, government agencies such as the Ministry of Finance, the Bank of Japan, and the Ministry of International Trade and Industry (MITI) helped establish a broad vision of Japan's future that rejected individualism and open markets. The government protected industry from outside competition, supported funding of preferred industries, told private banks which companies to lend to, and controlled access to technology, foreign exchange, and raw materials imports.

38 Bryan T. Johnson, Kim R. Holmes, and Melanie Kirkpatrick, "Freedom Is the Surest Path to Prosperity," *Wall Street Journal* (December 1, 1998): A22; also see www.heritage.org/index.

39 William W. Beach and Marc A. Miles, "Explaining the Factors of the Index of Economic Freedom" *2005 Index of Economic Freedom,* http://www.heritage.org/research/features/index/

40 Black and shadow markets are where goods and services are illegally traded against government regulations.

41 Notably, there are classical liberal theories in which development is understood as economic growth and capital formation and the key to economic growth is capital formation; there are social theories of development that stress the importance of "human capital" in development and the importance of education, health, fertility, etc. to growth; and neoclassical theories that emphasize the negative role that government often played in development and believe the keys to economic growth are free markets and the functions of private investment and market efficiency.

42 Over half of those people live in just two countries, India and China.

43 Source: The World Bank (http://www.worldbank.org/data/maps/images/gdp-growth.gif).

44 Ikujiro Nonaka and Hirotaka Takeuchi, *"The Knowledge-Creating Company: How Japanese Companies Create the Dynamics of Innovation"* (Oxford: Oxford University Press, 1995).

45 Four alternatives are available, alone or in some combination, to privatize state assets on a large scale. Each approach has advantages and problems, so there is no perfect way of accomplishing this difficult task. Voucher privatization distributes shares in state enterprises to all citizens. While this is politically popular, economically it is not efficient because the masses of citizens will not know how to exercise the key functions of ownership, such as deciding the firm's strategy and how to finance the business, and appointing and holding managers responsible for enhancing the long-term value of the firm. Ultimately, control will have to be passed on, in some way, to those who can effectively exercise the ownership functions. Restitution to former owners is morally right, but trying to put it into practice is a practical nightmare. Employee-management buyout (or giveaway) might seem like a good choice. But this approach rewards those who happen to be working for (potentially) profitable firms and imposes a burden on all others. Even the strong companies are not likely to be managed efficiently because the workers and managers will want job security and current income rather than maximizing the long-term value of the firm. Selling to the highest bidder makes the most economic sense. But who are the most likely to have the required kind of money? Party and government officials, their cronies, and foreign investors do. "Selling the country" to them is likely to encounter strong political resistance.

46 Frank Vanden Broucke, "The EU and Social Protection: What Should the European Convention Propose?" The Foreign Policy Centre, http://fpc.org.uk/articles/175

47 International Finance Corporation, *Privatization Principles and Practice* (Washington, DC: IFC, 1995).

48 Juan Forero, "Latin America Fails to Deliver on Basic Needs," *New York Times* (February 22, 2005).

49 The G8 Information Center at www.G-7.utoronto.ca/; Dominic Wilson and Roopa Purushothaman, "Global Economics Paper No. 99: Dreaming with BRICs: The Path to 2050," Goldman Sachs, www.gs.com/insight/research/reports/report6.html; "Bric by bric—How the world will change," at www.rediff.com/money/2003/oct/16guest1.htm; "The BRICs Are Coming—Fast. A Goldman Economist Talks About Rapid Growth in Brazil, Russia, India, and China," *Business Week,* October 27, 2003; Pratap Ravindran, "'Global Economy Will Be Built by BRICs," The Hindu Business Line (January 12, 2005), www.thehindubusinessline.com/bline/2005/01/12/stories/2005011200310900.htm; Cho Hyung-Kwon, "Will Korea Join G-10?" *The Korea Times,* times.hankooki.com/lpage/special/200311/kt2003110416353439750.htm; James F. Hoge, Jr., "A Global Power Shift in the Making—Is the United States Ready?" *Foreign Affairs* 83, no. 4 (July-August 2004): 2; Nirmala George, "India, China to Form Strategic Partnership," Associated Press (April 11,2004).

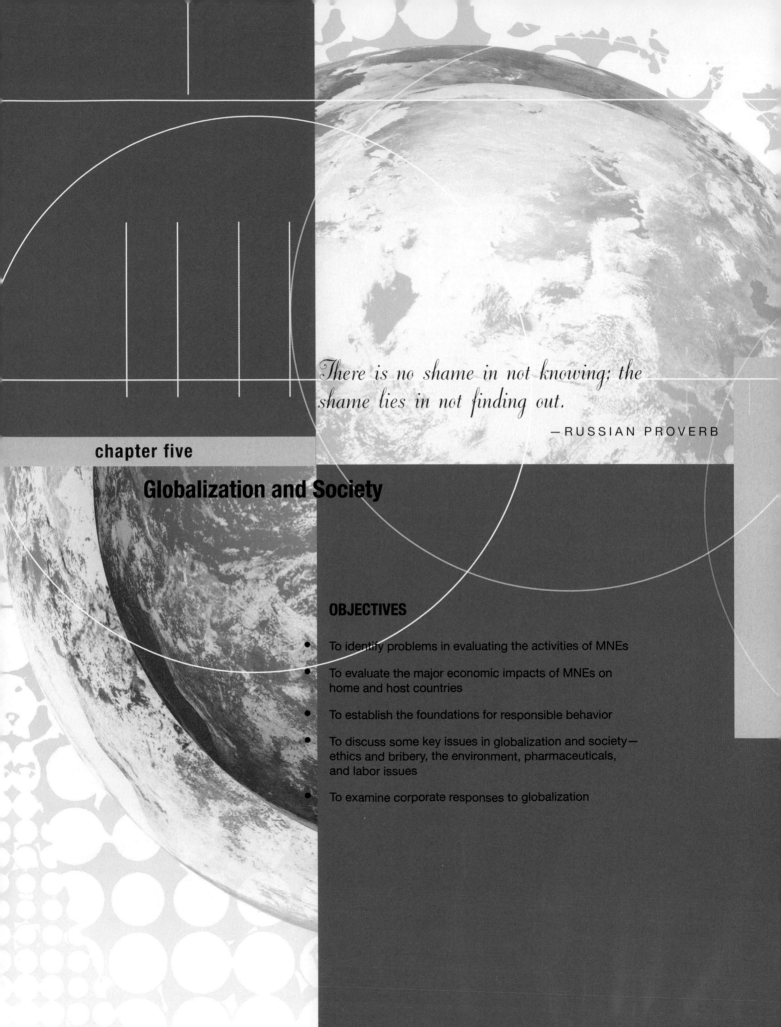

There is no shame in not knowing; the shame lies in not finding out.

—RUSSIAN PROVERB

chapter five

Globalization and Society

OBJECTIVES

- To identify problems in evaluating the activities of MNEs

- To evaluate the major economic impacts of MNEs on home and host countries

- To establish the foundations for responsible behavior

- To discuss some key issues in globalization and society—ethics and bribery, the environment, pharmaceuticals, and labor issues

- To examine corporate responses to globalization

CASE: ENVIRONMENTAL CHALLENGES FOR NEWMONT MINING IN INDONESIA[1]

Paul Lahti, the director of the Minahasa Raya mine for Newmont Mining Corp. in Indonesia, was both disappointed and relieved about Newmont's latest decision. Faced with a changing political and legal landscape, illegal miners, environmental protests, and decreasing gold reserves, Newmont had decided to close the Minahasa Raya mine.

Newmont Mining, headquartered in Denver, Colorado, is the second biggest gold producer worldwide. It began Indonesian operations in 1996 and has two mines—Batu Hijau on the island of Sumbawa and Minahasa Raya on the island of Sulawesi, as shown in Map 5.1. Newmont's involvement in Indonesia has been one of frustrations and struggles yet also great success. To understand its situation in Indonesia, it is necessary to first understand the political history of the country.

POLITICAL HISTORY OF INDONESIA

Indonesia is the fourth largest country in the world in population, with 214.5 million people, and 87 percent of the population is Muslim, making it the largest Muslim country in the world. Indonesia is an archipelago

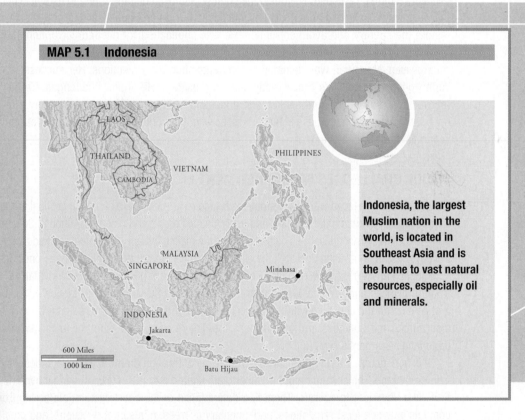

MAP 5.1   Indonesia

Indonesia, the largest Muslim nation in the world, is located in Southeast Asia and is the home to vast natural resources, especially oil and minerals.

stretching more than 3,000 miles and comprising 17,000 islands, 6,000 of which are inhabited. Sixty percent of the population resides on the island of Java, where the capital city of Jakarta is located. Indonesians fight extreme poverty, with per capita income at $570 and a 15 to 20 percent unemployment rate.

For many years prior to World War II, Indonesia, known as the Dutch East Indies, was governed under autocratic rule by the Netherlands. During World War II, the Japanese invaded the country and took control for the next three years. During this time and prior to the Japanese invasion, an independence movement by many Indonesian nationalists began forming. Although suppressed by the ruling government, the main party—the Indonesian Nationalist Party—was run by Ahmed Sukarno. The Japanese withdrew from the country upon their surrender to the Allies, and Indonesia claimed independence on August 17, 1945.

Ahmed Sukarno emerged as the country's first president and quickly established his authoritarian regime, labeled "Guided Democracy." In the mid-1960s, an attempted coup begun by the Indonesian

Communist Party (PKI) was stamped out by the national military led by the army chief of staff, General Suharto. In an effort to rid the country of a communist presence, Suharto's forces killed hundreds of thousands of suspected communists.

Never able to regain support, Sukarno passed political and military powers to Suharto. Suharto established his political "New Order" by massing power in the central government and military. The economy improved dramatically under Suharto's rule, although corruption filtered through the military, government, and legal system. He is known for using an iron fist to impose his will on the country's vast array of religious and ethnic groups.

When the Asian financial crisis of 1997 hit, Indonesia's flawed economic structure and corruption sent the country spiraling downward. Inflation hit 80 percent at one point, and the economy contracted by 14 percent. Demonstrators turned against the country's minority population of ethnic Chinese, and conflicts arose between Christians and Muslims. Companies owned by ethnic Chinese and by foreign companies employing ethnic Chinese in management positions were the targets of demonstrators and incurred serious property damage. Protesters and rioters demanded Suharto's resignation, and he eventually gave in after 32 years of rule.

On October 20, 1999, the Indonesian legislature elected Abdurrahman Wahid president, and Megawati Sukarnoputri, the daughter of Sukarno, became vice president. Both leaders were faced with the daunting tasks of restoring the economy, ridding the country of corruption, and trying to establish policies to govern the vast array of religions and ethnicities. Although known for his political acumen, Wahid was not able to restore the country and avoid corruption. He was impeached for alleged corruption in April 2001, and Megawati became Indonesia's president.

However, Megawati was defeated in the September 2004 elections. Her successor, Susilo Bangang Yudhoyono, is Indonesia's first directly elected president. His major challenges are helping Indonesia recover from two major earthquakes and a tsunami in 2004–2005, combating corruption, dealing with unpopularity due to an increase in fuel prices, solving the problem of terrorism, and dealing with the armed separatist Free Aceh Movement.

MAJOR CHALLENGES FACING NEWMONT MINING

Newmont Mining is faced with many problems in Indonesia, including a changing political and legal landscape, illegal mining, environmental protests, and declining gold prices and reserves. Although Suharto caused many problems in Indonesia, his policies helped stabilize the mining industry. Newmont worked directly with the central government rather than deal with the different local governments. All this changed once Suharto resigned.

Indonesia's current leaders have been struggling to grant power and decision-making responsibilities to the provinces and regions. Wahid was unwilling to use Suharto's tough tactics on local governments, and as a result the central government has lost much of its power to the regions. This has caused confusion among the business and industry sectors. They don't know whether to follow the central or the regional government's laws and policies.

It is not enough that the political spectrum is going through dramatic change; Indonesia's legal system is in turmoil too. The corruption of the Suharto era filtered into the courts, making it even riskier for foreign firms like Newmont to operate. There is a deterioration of the court system, stemming from the political conflicts between local regulations, parliamentary decrees, ministerial decisions, and presidential orders. Local authorities engage in political and legal battles with many western MNEs, like Newmont, because they feel the contracts drafted in the Suharto era are corrupt and benefit only the MNE. The abject poverty in most of these regions only fans the flames of conflict.

Newmont was hit head-on by the defective court system and local aggression in September 1999, when the local Minahasa district demanded $8.2 million in back pay of taxes for waste material. Newmont's contract, established with the central government of Suharto, exempted Newmont from paying any tax on mining waste materials, including topsoil and rock. However, Minahasa's local parliament passed a law allowing it to collect levies from local companies.

After forcing the mine to shut down a number of times, Minahasa's local courts, under pressure from Indonesia's Supreme Court, agreed to settle with Newmont for $500,000, and the company paid another $2.5 million to be added into employee programs and community development projects.

President Wahid passed new autonomy laws in hopes of alleviating some of the political and legal conflict. Some people fear that these laws, which took effect at the beginning of 2001, will just escalate the problems. The laws are intended to hand more of the central government's power to the regions, but neither Wahid nor subsequent presidents have passed any regulations to implement them.

With the government's move toward democracy and decentralization, local groups have found it the perfect time to demand more from companies operating in their regions. Labor activists, environmental protesters, and local social groups are demanding that corporations improve their social responsibility programs if they are to receive popular local acceptance. Under Suharto's regime, corporations could turn to the central government to brush aside any uprisings from local groups. These companies are now finding it necessary to implement social programs, engage in better labor relations, and meet local environmental regulations.

Local problems have caused Newmont to close down its Minahasa Raya mine several times for short periods since its opening. In the last quarter of 2000, former landowners blockaded the entrance to the mine at least three times, demanding more money for the land Newmont now mines. Newmont argues that it compensated the landowners fairly when it initially purchased the land.

Another major difficulty for Newmont is the fact that illegal miners are stealing gold from the mine. The number of illegal miners has tripled since 1997 because of the large number of unemployed that the recession has created.

ENVIRONMENTAL ISSUES

Ever since the opening of the Minahasa mine, Newmont has been under environmental scrutiny, with mounting evidence of pollution problems. Environmental groups claim that the tailings, or waste material, that Newmont disposes of in the ocean contains toxic levels of mercury and arsenic. Studies have found that the number of fish has drastically decreased in the area and the health of the local people has been affected. Because of these studies, the environment minister required Newmont to conduct an environmental risk assessment and to detoxify its tailings before dumping them into the ocean.

Some, however, believe the environmental problems are mainly the result of the illegal miners, who use antiquated mining practices to extract the gold. They also use mercury to separate the gold from the ore and then dump the waste into rivers. Local officials don't want to upset the local miners, though. Sam Kindangen, who heads the environmental control office of the North Sulawesi government, worries about the dangers of illegal mining. But he says, "Under the reform era, we have to consider the people. We don't want the people to demonstrate against us."

Newmont uses a waste disposal method called submarine tailing, which is banned in the U.S. under the Clean Water Act. In this method, the company pumps treated mine waste into the ocean. Newmont claims that the method is better than disposing of tailings in land facilities due to the high risk of earthquakes in Indonesia. However, many companies, such as Australian mining firm BHP Billiton, will not use submarine tailing any more, even though it is cheaper than land-based waste storage systems. After villagers began to develop strange rashes and bumps, children were born with birth defects, and various other illnesses surfaced, a local legal aid group filed suit on behalf of three villagers. Health workers felt local villagers were exhibiting symptoms of poisoning by mercury and arsenic, two by-products of the mining operations. However, Newmont disclosed the following on its Web site:

> Buyat Bay is the focus of a campaign that looks at the impact on the people's health, the fish and waters of the bay, by a nearby gold mine and its submarine tailings placement.

The campaign, initiated by local non-governmental organizations (NGOs), triggered multiple scientific studies, a $550 million dollar lawsuit, a police investigation, the detention of Newmont company officials, extensive international media coverage, and business concern over the future of foreign investment in Indonesia.

The facts are clear. The people and the fish in Buyat Bay have been extensively tested. All tests show metals levels safer than Indonesian and international safety standards for the water, the fish and the human population.

These conclusions were reached separately by the independent, government and research teams who came to Buyat Bay. More than 1700 samples were tested by 6 laboratories.

The World Health Organization (WHO), Japan's National Institute for Minamata Disease, and the Faculty of Medical Sciences from the local university (UNSRAT) also examined the people of Buyat Bay, particularly those who complained of sickness. Their findings are consistent, and conclusive. Their health pattern is typical of poor nutrition and poor sanitation.

An Indonesian court has ruled the police investigation and detention of Newmont employees was "illegal." The civil lawsuit was withdrawn as "baseless."

On top of all these problems, the price of gold and gold reserves in the mine had been declining. From February 2000 to March 2001, the price of gold declined 13 percent and has devalued a third since 1997. Since the decision to close the mine, the price of gold began to climb and was trading at $420 a ounce in mid-2005, whereas it was only $254 per ounce at its low in 1999. In addition, only about one-fifth of the reserves of gold are left in the Minahasa Raya mine. Once they are gone, the mine will be forced to shut down.

Managers of foreign firms in Indonesia like Mr. Lahti wonder whether all the risk involved with operating in the country is worth it. They have been working with local and national authorities to change some of the laws and policies governing business in the country, yet there is still much that needs to be done to reduce the political and legal uncertainty. Mr. Lahti wonders what he could have done differently to continue operations in Minahasa Raya. He wonders whether Newmont's other mine will suffer the same fate as Minahasa Raya, or whether things will change for businesses in Indonesia. In addition, Newmont is coming under increasing scrutiny for its environmental practices in Indonesia, Australia, New Zealand, Central Asia, Peru, and Bolivia, which affects its managers and its operations in all those countries.

INTRODUCTION

Criticisms to Globalization

As discussed in Chapter 1, there are three major criticisms of globalization: threats to sovereignty, growth, and increasing inequality. MNEs, which have their greatest impact on countries when they engage in foreign direct investment (FDI), are constantly confronted with these criticisms and must answer for the effect they have, both at home and in host countries. Government policies both encourage and restrict FDI. Figure 5.1 shows the major relationships between companies and both home and host countries. A major concern about FDI is that the global orientation of MNEs might make them insensitive to national interests and concerns. Although not all MNEs are huge, the sheer size of many of them troubles countries. For example, the revenues of Wal-Mart, BP, or ExxonMobil exceed the GNI of all but 18 countries in the world and are about the same size as the GNI of Sweden and Belgium. In addition, the combined revenues of the top five companies in the world—Wal-Mart, BP, ExxonMobil, Royal Dutch/Shell Group, and General Motors—exceed the combined GNI of all 61 low-income countries in the world.[2] Large MNEs have considerable power when negotiating business arrangements with governments, and executives of MNEs often deal directly with heads of state when negotiating the terms under which their companies may operate. Pressure groups in both home and host countries push their governments to devise policies that restrict or liberalize MNEs' movements. Growth in FDI suggests that these groups will more closely monitor MNEs in the future.

In spite of the size of MNEs, their power is still limited. Governments, even small ones, have significantly more power than do corporations. In addition, it is difficult to compare the revenues of companies with the GDP of countries. GDP measures only value added, whereas revenues include everything. If corporations were measured by their value added, their size would shrink between 70 and 80 percent. Thus General Motors, one of the largest corporations in the world, would have a value added less than the GDP of Bangladesh.[3]

However, FDI, whether through a wholly owned subsidiary or a joint venture, is not the only form of business that can generate problems in host countries. In this chapter,

The sheer size of MNEs is an issue.

- Some have sales larger than many countries' GNI.
- Some MNE executives deal directly with heads of state.

Pressure groups push to restrict MNEs' activities at home and abroad.

OPERATIONS

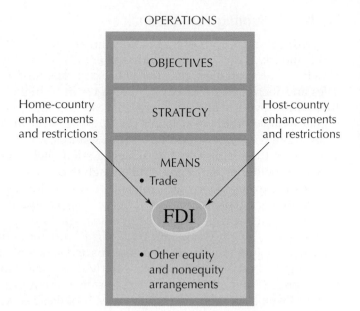

Home-country enhancements and restrictions

Host-country enhancements and restrictions

FIGURE 5.1

HOME-AND HOST-COUNTRY INFLUENCES ON COMPANIES' USE OF FDI

FDI is a major means for companies to conduct their international operations. Stakeholders influence how and whether companies operate through FDI.

we will look at the impact of FDI on home and host countries and then examine a series of issues that relate to the social responsibility of MNEs as they strive to penetrate foreign markets or source merchandise from abroad.

EVALUATING THE IMPACT OF FDI

The opening case illustrates the changing attitude of the Indonesian government toward FDI—from cooperation, to suspicion, to opposition. Other countries, such as China, have replaced obstacles with incentives for FDI.[4] Developing and industrial countries have deregulated their markets, privatized national enterprises, liberalized private ownership, and encouraged regional integration in an effort to create more favorable settings for foreign investments. Total worldwide FDI inflows rose from $202 billion in 1990 to a record $1.3 trillion in 2000. However, inflows fell 41 percent in 2001, 17 percent in 2002, and 18 percent in 2003 to only $560 billion due to the slowdown in the global economy. Most of the drop in FDI inflows in 2003 was confined to the developed countries and Central and Eastern Europe. Inflows to developing countries rose by 9 percent, with China leading the way as the world's largest host country for FDI inflows, excluding Luxembourg. As FDI policies toward services were liberalized, the structure of FDI began to shift more to services from traditional manufacturing and extractive industries.[5]

FDI has come to be seen as a major contributor to growth and development, bringing capital, technology, management expertise, jobs, and wealth. However, FDI is not without controversy.[6] Many countries that opened their markets to FDI experienced economic and social disruptions; they also watched investments by MNEs constrain existing or potential domestic companies. MNEs have also run into problems; many made big foreign investments that have performed poorly.

In their quest to optimize performance, companies allocate resources among various countries. However, this allocation is influenced by governments' interpretation of the relative costs and benefits of FDI. As managers, we must be aware of these interpretations and, at times, try to clarify them. As citizens, we need to argue for government policies that will enhance national interests. Both responsibilities require understanding why countries would react to FDI, like Indonesia in our opening case, with opposition, with suspicion, or with cooperation.

The effort to create favorable investment environments has led many countries to replace obstacles to FDI with incentives for FDI.

The growing prevalence of FDI requires a better understanding of the views of home and host countries.

Companies must satisfy

- Shareholders
- Employees
- Customers
- Society

Trade-offs Among Constituencies

To prosper and survive, a company must satisfy different groups, which we call **stakeholders.** Stakeholders include shareholders, employees, customers, suppliers, and society. In the short term, the aims of these groups conflict. Stockholders want additional sales and increased productivity, which result in higher profits and higher returns for them. Employees want safer workplaces and higher compensation. Customers want higher quality products at lower prices. Society would like to see increased corporate taxes, more corporate support for social services, and trustworthy behavior. In the long term, all of these aims must be achieved adequately or none will be attained, because each stakeholder group is powerful enough to cause a company's demise.

Management decisions made in one country have repercussions elsewhere.

Pressure groups lobby governments to restrict MNEs' activities at home and abroad. Although management must be aware of these competing interests, it has to serve them unevenly at any given period. At one time, gains may go to consumers; at another, to shareholders. Making necessary trade-offs is difficult in the home environment. Abroad, managers' poorer familiarity with customs and stakeholders complicates the challenge of choosing the best alternative—particularly if dominant interests differ among countries. Newmont Mining, for example, has to satisfy the needs of stakeholders in the United States as well as in Indonesia, and the needs of those stakeholders differ from each other.

The effects of an MNE's activities may be simultaneously positive for one national objective and negative for another.

Some critics believe that as companies try to balance the demands of constituencies in different countries, one wins and the other loses. However, that is not always the case. FDI can result in a win-win, a win-lose, or a lose-lose situation. The final result may depend on the objectives of the different constituencies, but it is not necessary for one constituent to lose in order for another to win.

FDI may result in a win-win, win-lose, or lose-lose situation for both countries involved.

As noted by the *Economist,* the advocates of **corporate social responsibility (CSR)** work from the premise that capitalism fails to serve the public interest and thus managers of companies must be pressured to act differently. On the other hand, it can be argued that managers of MNEs are best equipped to serve the interests of their shareholders, which is to increase the value of their investment. Governments are best equipped to deal with social issues and externalities or the side effects of business transactions, such as pollution, where private sector costs and benefits diverge from public sector costs and benefits.[7] This dilemma complicates the role of MNE management.

Companies are best at serving the interests of shareholders, whereas governments are best equipped to deal with social issues and externalities.

Cause-Effect Relationships

Just because two factors move in relationship to each other does not necessarily mean they are related and interdependent. For example, an increase in overall unemployment in a country and an increase in FDI doesn't mean that FDI caused unemployment. Still, opponents of FDI try to link the actions of MNEs to problems like inequitable income distribution, political corruption, environmental debasement, and societal deprivation.[8] On the other hand, proponents of MNEs link their actions positively to higher tax revenues, employment, innovation, and exports, particularly when governments consider either restricting or encouraging FDI. Although the data presented by opponents or proponents of MNEs often are accurate and convincing, there is always the problem that we don't know what would have happened had MNEs gone elsewhere or followed different practices. Technological developments, competitors' actions, and government policies are just three of the variables that distort the analysis of cause and effect.

It is hard to determine whether MNEs' actions cause societal conditions.

Individual and Aggregate Effects

One astute observer noted, "Like animals in a zoo, multinationals (and their affiliates) come in various shapes and sizes, perform distinctive functions, behave differently, and make their individual impacts on the environment."[9] Essentially then, it is ill advised to make general statements about the effects of MNEs. Much of the literature on the subject, from the viewpoints of both critics and defenders, takes isolated situations and presents

The philosophy, actions, and goals of each MNE are unique.

FIGURE 5.2   RESOURCES AND POSSIBLE CONTRIBUTIONS OF MNES

MNEs can contribute directly to investment, human resources, technology, trade, and the environment, thus contributing to host-country objectives.

Source: Adapted from *World Investment Report 1992: Transnational Corporations: Engines of Growth: An Executive Summary* by Transnational Corporations and Management Division © 1992. United Nations. Reprinted with permission of the publisher.

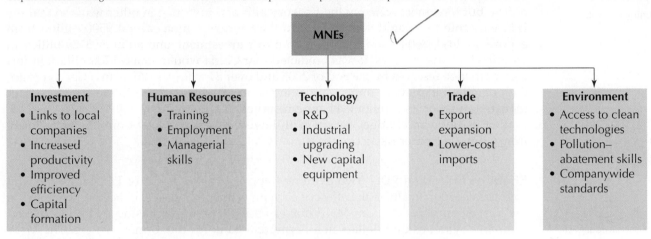

MNEs

Investment	Human Resources	Technology	Trade	Environment
• Links to local companies • Increased productivity • Improved efficiency • Capital formation	• Training • Employment • Managerial skills	• R&D • Industrial upgrading • New capital equipment	• Export expansion • Lower-cost imports	• Access to clean technologies • Pollution–abatement skills • Companywide standards

them as exemplars. The anecdotes chosen usually make interesting reading because of their spectacular or extreme nature. Still, it is dangerous for governments to make policies based on exceptions rather than the routine.

Some countries have tried to evaluate MNEs and their activities individually. Although this process might lead to greater fairness and better control, it is time-consuming and costly. Therefore, many countries apply the same policies and control mechanisms to all MNEs even though this approach risks throwing out some "good apples" along with the bad. Further, whether examining foreign investments on an individual or an aggregate basis, governments have been far from perfect in predicting future impacts.

Potential Contributions of MNEs

The sheer scale of many MNEs makes them suspect to stakeholders. However, their scale also means they have assets that can contribute to a range of national objectives. MNEs control a large portion of the world's capital, a factor that increases production. They account for most of the world's exports of goods and services, thereby creating access to foreign exchange for a country's purchase of imports. They are the major producers and organizers of technology, which is crucial to improving national competitiveness and solving environmental problems.[10] Figure 5.2 shows the major assets of MNEs that can satisfy stakeholders' objectives. Nevertheless, critics argue that MNEs use their assets inadequately when trying to satisfy these objectives.

ECONOMIC IMPACT OF THE MNE

MNEs may affect countries' balance-of-payments, growth, and employment objectives. Under different conditions, these effects may be positive or negative for the host or home country.

Balance-of-Payments Effects

Countries want capital inflows because such inflows give them the foreign exchange they need to import goods and services and pay off foreign debt. However, because FDI brings both capital inflows and capital outflows, countries fear that the net balance-of-payments effect may be negative.

Place in the Economic System   If a country runs a trade deficit, it must compensate for that deficit either by reducing its capital reserves or by attracting an influx of capital. The influx of capital may be from unilateral transfers (such as foreign aid), from the purchase by foreign governments or individuals of public or private debt, or from the receipt of foreign investment. For example, in the mid-2000s, the U.S. was running a huge trade deficit, but foreigners were buying treasury bills and investing in other ways so that the U.S. was able to bring dollars back into the country. China earned $500 billion from exports in 2004, $60 billion from foreign direct investment, and another $129 billion in additional capital inflows. It was predicted that China would amass $800 billion in foreign exchange reserves by the end of 2005 and over $1 trillion in 2006. In order to reduce the potential inflationary impact of having so much currency, the Chinese government invested most of its foreign exchange reserves in U.S. treasury bills.[11] Thus the U.S. funded its trade and budget deficits with huge inflows of money from abroad, namely from China and other Asian countries.

Effect of Individual FDI   Two extreme hypothetical scenarios of FDI highlight why countries need to evaluate the effect of each investment on their balance of payments. In the first example, a Mexican MNE makes an FDI when purchasing a Haitian-owned company by depositing dollars in a Bermudan bank for the former owners. The MNE makes no changes in management, capitalization, or operations, so profitability remains the same. However, dividends now go to the foreign owners rather than remaining in Haiti, so there is a drain on foreign exchange for Haiti and a corresponding inflow to Mexico. In the second example, a foreign MNE purchases idle resources (land, labor, materials, or equipment) in Haiti and converts them to the production of formerly imported goods. Rising consumer demand leads the MNE to reinvest its profits in Haiti. This import substitution increases Haiti's foreign exchange reserves.

Most investments or nonequity arrangements (such as licensing or management contracts) fall somewhere between these two extreme examples. Consequently, they are hard to evaluate, particularly when policymakers try to apply regulations to aggregate investment movements. A basic equation for making an analysis is:

$$B = (m - m_1) + (x - x_1) + (c - c_1)$$

Where

B = balance-of-payments effect
m = import displacement
m_1 = import stimulus
x = export stimulus
x_1 = export reduction
c = capital inflow for other than import and export payment
c_1 = capital outflow for other than import and export payment

Although the equation is straightforward, determining the value for each variable is difficult. For instance, let's evaluate the effect of a Honda automobile plant in the United States, which would be an FDI by a Japanese MNE. To calculate the net import change $(m - m_1)$, we need to know how much the United States would import in the absence of the Honda plant. The amount that Honda makes and sells in the United States is only an indication of what the United States would import, because the selling price and product characteristics of those U.S.-made cars may differ from what otherwise would be imported from Japan. Moreover, some of the sales may have been at the expense of other automobile plants in the United States or at the expense of the import of foreign autos other than Honda. By definition, the value of m_1 should include the equipment, components, and materials brought into the United States. For example, Honda buys many parts from suppliers that import them.

The value of m_1 also should include estimates of the increase in U.S. imports due to increases in national income caused by the capital inflow from Japan. For instance, assume that U.S. national income rises $50 million because of Honda's investment; the marginal propensity to import principle (which defines the fraction of a change in imports due to a change in income) says that the recipients of that income will spend some portion on imports. If this proportion is calculated to be 10 percent, imports should rise by $5 million, or 10 percent of $50 million. This has been a major problem in the United States. The large size of the GNI in the U.S., along with strong growth, mean that imports have been rising as income rises.

The net export effect is the export stimulus minus the export reduction $(x - x_1)$. It is particularly controversial because conclusions vary widely depending on evaluators' assumptions. For the Honda example, we can argue that a U.S. plant merely substitutes for imports from and production in Japan. By this assumption, there is no net export effect for the United States. For Japan, there is a negative net export effect because of Honda's export reduction. However, Honda would contend that its moves abroad are (largely) defensive. Under this assumption, Honda captures sales that would otherwise go to rival carmakers in the United States. Thus, Honda's export reduction from Japan is only its export replacement (loss) caused by moving a production plant to the United States. MNEs have argued further that their investments stimulate home-country exports of complementary products, such as auto parts in the Honda example, that can be sold in host countries through their foreign-owned facilities. Again, we must make assumptions about the amount of these exports that could have materialized had the subsidiaries not been established.

On the export side, the BOP effect is positive if the FDI results in generating exports in the host country and negative if it produces only for the local market and stops exports.

The net capital flow $(c - c_1)$ is the easiest figure to calculate because of controls at most central banks. However, the problem with using a given year for evaluation is the time lag between an MNE's outward flow of investment funds and the inward flow of remitted earnings from the investment. What appears at a given time to be a favorable or unfavorable capital flow may prove over a longer period to be the opposite because companies plan eventually to take out more capital than they originally invested abroad. For example, the time it takes Honda to recoup the capital outflow is affected by things such as its need to reinvest funds in the United States, its ability to borrow locally, and its estimation of the future dollar-to-yen exchange rate. Given the number of variables, the capital flows will vary widely among companies and projects. Another complication arises because MNEs may try to manipulate the real returns on their investments by transferring funds in disguised forms, such as through transactions between the parent and a subsidiary at arbitrary rather than market prices.[12]

Initial capital flows are positive to the host country, but the flows may be negative over time as the FDI remits dividends or other capital flows back to the home country.

The equation presented above is useful in evaluating the broad balance-of-payments effects of MNEs' investments. Still, stakeholders should use it with caution. For example, there are measurement problems. In addition, an investment movement might have some indirect effects on a country's balance of payments that are neither readily nor reliably quantifiable. An investor might bring new technological or managerial efficiencies that other companies may copy. What these other companies do may affect the economic efficiency of the host country and the export ability of those companies.

Aggregate Assumptions and Responses   Generally, MNEs' investments are initially favorable to the host country and unfavorable to the home country. However, the situation reverses after some time.[13] This occurs because nearly all foreign investors plan eventually to have their subsidiaries remit dividends back to the parent company in excess of what they sent abroad. If the net value of the FDI continues to grow through retained earnings, dividend payments for a given year ultimately may exceed the total capital transfers that comprised the initial investment. The time before reversal can vary substantially, and there is disagreement as to the aggregate time span required.

From the standpoint of home countries, restrictions on capital outflow improve the availability of short-term capital. Host country restrictions may erode confidence in the economy because companies fear they cannot move their funds where they want them.

The balance of payments effects of FDI are usually
- Positive for the host country initially and negative for the home country
- Positive for the home country and negative to the host country later

This fear reduces capital inflows and spurs capital flight. Consequently, capital outflow restrictions are useful only in buying the time needed to institute other means for solving balance-of-payments difficulties.

Governments also have sought to attract inflows of long-term capital as a means to develop production that will displace imports or generate exports. Countries, then, must determine how to benefit from FDI while minimizing the long-term adverse effects on their balance of payments.

Growth and Employment Effects

In contrast to balance-of-payments effects, the effects of MNEs on growth and employment are not necessarily a zero-sum game (gains must equal losses) among countries. Classical economists assumed that production factors were at full employment; consequently, a movement of any of these factors abroad would result in an increase in output abroad and a decrease at home. Even if this assumption were realistic, the gains in the host country might be greater or less than the losses in the home country.

> Growth and employment effects are not a zero-sum game because MNEs may use resources that were unemployed or underemployed.

The argument that both the home and the host countries may gain from FDI rests on two assumptions: (1) Resources are not necessarily fully employed, and (2) capital and technology cannot be easily transferred from one industry to another. For example, a soft-drink maker may be producing at maximum capacity for its domestic market but is limited in developing export sales due to high transportation costs. Further, the company may not simply move into other product lines or easily use its financial resources to increase domestic productivity. Establishing a foreign production facility, however, positions the company to develop foreign sales without reducing resource employment in its home market. In fact, it may wind up hiring additional domestic managers to oversee the international operations and receive dividends and royalties from the foreign use of its capital, brand, and technology.

Although stakeholders in both home and host countries may gain from FDI, some stakeholders argue that they are economic losers. Let's examine their arguments.

> Home-country labor claims that jobs are exported through FDI.

Home-Country Losses   Many U.S. and European garment manufacturers moved production to low-wage countries to gain some cost advantages and had to shut down or at least not expand their home-country plants. Thus FDI in that industry resulted in a loss of jobs in the home country while creating jobs abroad. However, one could argue that this move was inevitable. In the absence of serious protection, the home-country industry would have gone out of business due to competition from abroad, and jobs would have been lost anyway.

> Host countries may gain from FDI through
> - More optimal use of production factors
> - The use of unemployed resources
> - The upgrading of resource quality

Host-Country Gains   Host countries gain through the transfer of capital and technology. If the capital is used to acquire existing companies that are going out of business, the foreign investor can save jobs and, through the application of technology and managerial ability, create new jobs. This happened when GM purchased an interest in Daewoo Motor in 2002 for $400 million. Without the infusion of capital and expertise, Daewoo might have gone bankrupt. In other cases, FDI can provide enhanced capacity or increased capabilities of existing companies, such as in the auto industry in China. Foreign investors have partnered with Chinese auto manufacturers and helped to increase the capabilities of Chinese companies to the point that they are beginning to export autos.

Host-Country Losses   Critics argue that MNEs make investments that domestic companies otherwise would have made, thereby displacing potential local entrepreneurs. Similarly, foreign investors may bid up prices by competing with local companies for labor and other resources—such as when local companies in northern Indiana in the United States complained about Toyota's hiring the area's best workers by paying them higher wages (of course, the workers did not object).[14] Such critics argue, for example, that MNEs can raise lower-cost funds in different countries because they have operations in those countries and are known in those financial markets. Evidence for these arguments is inconclusive.

"*Great. You move to Mexico, and we all end up working at McDonald's.*"

MNEs frequently pay higher salaries and spend more on promotion than local companies do. It is uncertain, however, whether these differences result from external advantages or represent the added costs of attracting workers and customers upon entering new markets.

Critics contend that FDI destroys local entrepreneurship, an outcome that affects national development. Because the reasonable expectation of success is necessary to inspire entrepreneurship, the collapse of small cottage industries in the face of MNEs' consolidation efforts may make the local population feel incapable of competing. An example will be found in the case on Wal-Mart de Mexico in Chapter 8. However, some evidence questions this contention.[15] The presence of MNEs may increase the number of local companies in host-country markets because the MNEs serve as role models that local talent can then emulate. This is true of Wal-Mart, which cultivates strong supplier relationships and may help local suppliers get stronger. Finally, some maintain that true entrepreneurs will see large MNEs not as obstacles but as challenges.

Another argument is that investors learn better ways of doing things abroad. By observing foreign competitive conditions, they may gain access to new technology that they can transfer to their home countries. Such early access, however, may prevent the original developers from fully exploiting their technologies. It may also prevent the originating country from fully capturing the economic benefits of the innovations developed by its residents. For example, foreign investment, especially from Japan and India, has grown rapidly in high-tech industries in California's Silicon Valley. This FDI may allow non-U.S. companies to develop competitive capacities in their home countries that are based on U.S. scientific and technical investments.[16] However, Japanese companies in Silicon Valley also spend heavily on R&D, and their results spill over to nearby U.S. companies.[17]

Host countries may lose if investments by MNEs

- Replace local companies
- Take the best resources
- Destroy local entrepreneurship
- Decrease local R&D undertakings

FOUNDATIONS OF ETHICAL BEHAVIOR

In addition to balance of payments flows and growth and employment, MNEs have to worry about acting responsibly wherever they operate, whether through trade or investment. We will first concentrate on the cultural and legal foundations for ethical behavior and then look at some specific examples of ethical dilemmas the companies face as the result of globalization.

Cultural Foundations for Ethical Behavior

During the early part of the twenty-first century, several U.S. companies faced severe financial problems and even dissolution because of their managers' unethical or illegal actions. Some of these companies hid their illicit actions for a number of years through their international operations. The exposés caused public outrage, investor anxiety, and a heightened interest in companies' ethical and socially responsible behavior.

Some actions elicit almost universal agreement on what is right or wrong.[18] However, managers face many situations that are less clear. As discussed in Chapter 2, we all have beliefs about what is right and wrong based on family and religious teachings, the laws and social pressures of our societies, our observations and experiences, and our own economic circumstances. Our ethical beliefs tend to be deep-seated, so our debates with people who hold opposing viewpoints tend to be emotional. Even within a country, vastly opposing viewpoints frequently exist. To further complicate matters, our own values on given issues may differ from our employers' policies, and any of these values may differ from the prevalent societal norms or laws. As managers, we face domestic dilemmas on what we should do to be ethical and socially responsible. Internationally, the dilemmas are even greater.

On the one hand, **relativism** affirms that ethical truths depend on the groups holding them, making intervention by outsiders unethical. Adherence to or adoption of other cultures is itself a Western cultural phenomenon, one that goes back at least as far as St. Ambrose's fourth-century advice: "When in Rome, do as the Romans do." On the other hand, **normativism** holds that there are universal standards of behavior (based on people's own values) that all cultures should follow, making nonintervention unethical. Thus managers struggle with implementing what they consider to be a universal set of truths vs. adapting to local conditions on the assumption that every place is different and needs to be treated differently.

A company can face pressures to comply with a country's norms. These pressures may include laws that permit or even require certain practices, competitive advantages for rivals who adapt to local norms, or accusations of meddling if a company tries to impose its home-country practices in the foreign country. However, companies can face pressures not to comply. These pressures can come from a company's own ethical values, its home-country government, or constituencies that threaten to boycott its products or to spread adverse publicity about it or its products.

Many individuals and organizations have laid out minimum levels of business practices that they say a company (domestic or foreign) must follow regardless of the legal requirements or ethical norms prevalent where it operates.[19] One could call this behavior based on principles of honesty and fairness, or what can be called "ordinary decency."[20] Many argue that legal permission for some action may be given by uneducated or corrupt leaders who either do not understand or do not care about the consequences, such as permission to import toxic wastes. (This is one of the major criticisms levied against Newmont Mining in the opening case.) They argue further that MNEs are obligated to set good examples that may become the standard for responsible behavior.

From a business standpoint, two possible objectives are to create competitive advantages through ethical behavior and to avoid being perceived as irresponsible. In terms of the former, it is argued that responsible acts create strategic and financial success because they lead to trust, which leads to commitment.[21] In terms of the latter, nongovernmental organizations have become very active in monitoring and publicizing companies' international practices. For example, the Interfaith Center on Corporate Responsibility (ICCR) represents about 275 religious institutions. It has sponsored shareholder resolutions and has threatened to pull its $110 billion in pension funds from investments in companies whose practices it considers irresponsible.[22] It has prodded many companies to change their practices, such as encouraging ExxonMobil to deal with global warming.[23] These efforts are part of the mission of ICCR's Global Warming Working Group to educate companies about the environmental and economic threats

Many actions elicit universal agreement on what is right or wrong, but other situations are less clear.

Values differ from country to country and sometimes between employees and companies.

Relativism—ethical truths depend on the groups holding them.

Normativism—there are universal standards of behavior that all cultures should follow.

Managers need to exhibit ordinary decency—principles of honesty and fairness.

Managers need to create competitive advantages through ethical behavior and avoid being perceived as irresponsible.

NGOs are active in prodding companies to comply with certain standards of ethical behavior.

posed by the emissions of greenhouse gases from their products and operations, and to increase shareholder value by urging companies to proactively address the global warming challenge. The problem with NGOs is that they are taking the place of elected government officials in determining how best to deal with externalities. If the NGOs are simply reporting on violations of existing laws or generally accepted standards of behavior, they may be performing a useful role. If they are themselves determining what socially responsible behavior includes, and if they are generally hostile to the concept of a market economy, they may be engaging in borderline behavior of their own.

Another complicating factor is that both societies and companies often must choose between the lesser of two evils. For example, the pesticide DDT is dangerous for the environment (especially to birds), and high-income countries have banned its use. Companies from those countries subsequently have been chided for selling DDT to lower-income countries that need it to fight malaria, which is one of the world's biggest killers of humans.[24]

Social responsibility requires human judgment, which makes it subjective and ambiguous. Many multilateral agreements exist that can help companies make ethical decisions. These agreements deal primarily with employment practices, consumer protection, environmental protection, political activity, and human rights in the workplace. Despite this growing body of agreements and codes, no set of workable corporate guidelines is universally accepted and observed.

> Social responsibility requires human judgment, which is subjective and ambiguous.

Another cultural dimension of globalization concerns international business practices that do not clash with foreign values directly but that, nevertheless, may undermine the host country's long-term cultural identity. Consider the use of a company's home-country language or cultural artifacts and the introduction of products and work methods that cause changes in social relationships. Host countries have sometimes reacted negatively to such use. For example, Finns have criticized MNEs for introducing non-Finnish architecture, and France fined Bodyshop for using English in its French stores.[25]

Legal Foundations for Ethical Behavior

Ethical dilemmas entail balancing means and ends. Means are the actions we take, which may be right or wrong; ends are the results of the actions, which may also be right or wrong. Ethics teaches that "people have a responsibility to do what is right and to avoid doing what is wrong."[26] As noted above, some people argue that cultural relativism implies no method exists for deciding whether any behavior is ever appropriate. However, we contend that it is possible to measure whether behavior is appropriate. Individuals must seek justification for their behavior, and that justification is a function of cultural values (many of which are universal) and legal principles.

Some people argue that the legal justification for ethical behavior is the only important one. By this standard, a person or company can do anything that is not illegal. However, there are five reasons why the legal argument is insufficient.

> Legal justification for ethical behavior may not be sufficient since not everything that is unethical is illegal.

1. The law is not appropriate for regulating all business activity because not everything that is unethical is illegal. This would be true of many dimensions of interpersonal behavior, for example.

2. The law is slow to develop in emerging areas of concern. Laws take time to be legislated and tested in courts. Further, they cannot anticipate all future ethical dilemmas; basically, they are a reaction to issues that have already surfaced. Countries with civil law systems rely on specificity in the law, and there may not be enough laws passed that deal with ethical issues.

3. The law often is based on moral concepts that are not precisely defined and that cannot be separated from legal concepts. Moral concepts must be considered along with legal ones.

4. The law is often in need of testing by the courts. This is especially true of case law, in which the courts establish precedent.

5. The law is not very efficient. Efficiency in this case implies achieving ethical behavior at a very low cost, and it would be impossible to solve every ethical behavioral problem with a law.[27]

In spite of the pitfalls of using the law as the major basis for deciding ethical disputes, there also are good reasons for at least complying with it.

1. The law embodies many of a country's moral beliefs and is an adequate guide for proper conduct.

2. The law provides a clearly defined set of rules. Following those rules at least establishes a good precedent.

3. The law contains enforceable rules that all must follow. It puts everyone on an equal footing.

4. The law represents a consensus derived from significant experience and deliberation. It should reflect careful and wide-ranging discussions.[28]

The law is a good basis for ethical behavior since it embodies local cultural values.

The problem for companies that use a legal basis for ethical behavior is that laws vary among countries. Not all moral values are common to every culture. In addition, strong home-country governments may try to extend their legal and ethical practices to the foreign subsidiaries of domestically headquartered companies—an action known as **extraterritoriality.** For example, a subsidiary of a U.S. company operating in China might be forced to follow some U.S. laws, even though China has no comparable laws and other companies operating there are not subject to the U.S. laws. In some cases, such as with health and safety standards, extraterritoriality should not cause problems. In other cases, such as with restrictions on trade with enemies of the United States, extraterritoriality may cause tension between the foreign subsidiary and the host-country government.

As noted earlier, the law provides a clearly defined set of rules, which companies often follow strictly because of concerns about potential legal liability. However, a company may seek a loophole to accomplish an objective. Potential liability and the legality of actions varies between countries with civil law systems and those with common law ones. Civil law countries tend to have a large body of laws that specify the legality of various behaviors. Common law countries tend to rely more on cases and precedents than on statutory regulations. A company must pay attention to laws to ensure the minimum level of compliance in each country in which it operates. When faced with conflicting laws, however, management must decide which applies.

As countries tackle similar ethical issues, laws will become more similar.

In spite of the problems, the law is still a good place to start. As countries address common problems, such as in the case of bribery described below, and search for common solutions, they will enact laws that will be similar. In addition, they will tackle important issues, especially related to externalities, that must be solved in the public arena. **Externalities** are by-products of activities that affect the well-being of people or damage the environment, where those impacts are not reflected in market prices. The costs (or benefits) associated with externalities do not enter standard cost accounting schemes. That will make life much easier for companies, because then they will know the constraints under which they can operate, and they can focus on doing what they do best—maximizing shareholder value.

ETHICS AND BRIBERY

Now that we have some tools for assessing corporate behavior worldwide and have discussed the cultural and legal foundations for ethical behavior, it is time to examine some issues that companies must confront. The first of these is bribery.

FIGURE 5.4 **LIKELIHOOD OF PAYING BRIBES ABROAD BY NATIONALITY OF COMPANIES**

Transparency International asked 835 business experts in 15 countries the following: "In the business sectors with which you are most familiar, please indicate how likely companies from the following countries are to pay or offer bribes to win or retain business in this country?" The scale runs from 1 to 10, with higher scores indicating a lower propensity to pay or offer bribes.

Source: Transparency International (November 6, 2002): http://www.transparency.org.

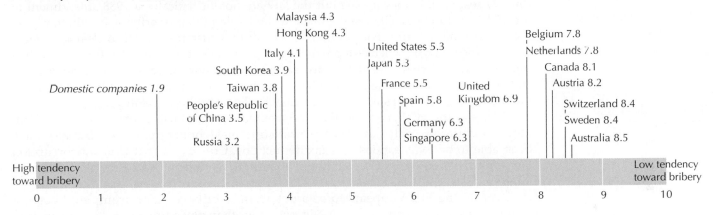

Since congressional investigations of U.S. MNEs in the 1970s, anecdotal information indicates that questionable payments to government officials by MNEs have been prevalent in both industrial and developing countries. Recent data give a sense of the proportions. The United States reported that between 1994 and 2001, it learned of instances in which foreign firms from over 50 countries offered bribes to buyers in over 100 countries, and these cases involved over 400 competitions for contracts valued at $200 billion.[29] Figure 5.4 reports the propensity of companies from various countries to offer or pay bribes.

Bribery influences the performance of countries and companies. Higher levels of corruption are strongly associated with lower growth and lower levels of per capita income.[30] Also, corruption may erode the legitimacy of a government. Bribery scandals have led to the replacement of chiefs of state in numerous countries, and officials have been jailed in a number of countries for accepting bribes. Executives in several companies have resigned, been fined, or gone to jail. Similarly, bribery inflates the costs of an MNE's operations and the prices of its products.

A common motive for bribery is to secure government contracts that otherwise might not be forthcoming or to obtain them at the expense of competitors. Another motive for bribery is to facilitate government services that companies are legally entitled to receive but that officials otherwise might delay, such as product registrations, construction permits, and import clearances. Other reported payments have been made to reduce tax liabilities, to keep a competitor from operating in a specific country, and to gain government approval for price increases. Some companies have made payments to protect the safety of their employees.

Most bribes have been in cash, but payments can include anything of value. Some payments have been made directly to government officials by the companies; most, however, have been made via intermediaries, such as local agents, and by diverse methods. For example, the relative of a person having influence over a purchasing decision sometimes has been put on the payroll as a consultant. In other cases, the person having influence has been paid as an intermediary at a fee exceeding normal commissions. Another common practice has been to overcharge a government agency and rebate the overcharge to an individual, usually in a foreign country.

In 1977, the United States passed the Foreign Corrupt Practices Act (FCPA), which outlaws the payment of bribes by U.S. firms to foreign officials, political parties, party

Bribery of public officials takes place to obtain government contracts or to get officials to do what they should be doing anyway.

Bribes are payments or promises to pay cash or anything of value.

officials, and candidates. In 1998, the overseas coverage of the FCPA was extended to include bribery by foreign firms operating in U.S. territory. The FCPA applies to companies registered in the United States and to any foreign companies that are quoted on any stock exchange in the United States.

An apparent inconsistency of the FCPA is that payments to officials to expedite their compliance with the law, officially called facilitation payments but sometimes referred to as speed money or grease money, are legal, but payments to other officials who are not directly responsible for carrying out the law are not. Specifically, a 1988 amendment to the FCPA excluded facilitation payments from its definition of bribery. Facilitation payments take many forms. For example, payment to a customs official to clear legitimate merchandise is legal, whereas a payment to a government minister to influence the customs official is illegal. The FCPA allows the former payment because government officials in many countries delay compliance with laws indefinitely until they do receive payments, even though such payments may be illegal in those countries.

Critics of the FCPA contend that U.S. companies lose business because firms from other countries not only have been permitted to make bribery payments but also have been able to take the expenses as tax deductions. Critics add that U.S. anticorruption laws might be seen as an extraterritorial attempt to meddle in other countries' domestic affairs.

Overall, the FCPA appears to be a deterrent to bribery.[31] For example, Procter & Gamble closed a Pampers plant in Nigeria rather than pay a bribe to a customs inspector.[32] The fear of penalty motivates greater compliance on the part of companies. IBM Argentina paid more than $4.5 million in bribes to officials of Banco de la Nacion Argentina in order to win a contract. The IBM parent company discovered the bribes and reported them to the U.S. government; IBM paid a civil penalty of $300,000. Similarly, Baker Hughes disclosed to U.S. officials that it had illegally authorized a $75,000 payment to an Indonesian tax official, plus illegal payments of $15,000 and $10,000 in India and Brazil. The United States did not impose any civil penalties, but it did require the company to sign a consent decree promising not to bribe foreign officials.[33] In another example of corporate efforts to eradicate bribery from the supply side, Lucent Technologies announced on April 7, 2004, that it was firing two top executives in its Chinese operations, including the president and chief operating officer, for failing to comply with the FCPA. This was significant, because Lucent generated 11 percent of its revenues from China operations in 2003.[34]

Other multilateral efforts are under way to stop bribery. Transparency International issued *Business Principles for Countering Bribery* in 2003 and noted that its principles were consistent with initiatives such as the OECD Convention on Combating Bribery of Foreign Public Officials in International Business Transactions, the International Chamber of Commerce (ICC) Rules of Combat to Combat Extortion and Bribery, and the antibribery provisions of the revised OECD Guidelines for Multinationals.

The 1997 OECD Convention was initially signed by the OECD members and five non-member nations: Argentina, Brazil, Bulgaria, Chile, and the Slovak Republic. As of January 28, 2005, 36 countries have enacted antibribery laws based upon the OECD convention, which targets the supply side of corruption in cross-border deals.[35] The implementing legislation of the U.S. is the FCPA described above, in addition to other legislation passed since the FCPA, such as Sarbanes-Oxley in 2002.[36]

The ICC Rules were issued in 1999, and the ICC has been very involved in responding to other multilateral approaches to combating bribery, such as codes of conduct issued by the OECD, the WTO, and the UN. Whereas the OECD Convention targets the supply side of bribery involving the public sector, the ICC notes that much needs to be done on the demand side, notably extortion by public officials, and in the private sector.[37]

On December 9, 2003, the United Nations held the International Anti-Corruption Day in Mexico to celebrate the signing of the UN Convention Against Corruption, which was approved by the General Assembly in October 2003. The Convention focuses on prevention as well as prosecution of corruption at both the public and private sector levels.

It is clear that many different public and private sector organizations are trying to control corruption at various levels. Transparency International, for instance, assists citizens in setting up national chapters to try to fight local corruption. It regularly compiles an international Corruption Perceptions Index (CPI) based on surveys of businesspeople, risk analysts, journalists, and the general public. Table 5.1 reports the ranking of 91 countries in terms of the perceived corruption in each. The table ranks the countries from least perceived corrupt to most perceived corrupt.

A more recent development in the efforts against bribery and corruption has been initiatives set up by industries themselves. For example, in 2005, in conjunction with the World Economic Forum, over 47 multinational construction and natural resources companies,

TABLE 5.1 **INTERNATIONAL CORRUPTION: A SURVEY OF BUSINESS PERCEPTIONS**

2004 CPI Score—relates to perceptions of the degree of corruption as seen by businesspeople, risk analysis, and the general public, and it ranges between 10 (highly clean) and 0 (highly corrupt).

RANK	COUNTRY	2004 CORRUPTION PERCEPTIONS INDEX SCORE	RANK	COUNTRY	2004 CORRUPTION PERCEPTIONS INDEX SCORE	RANK	COUNTRY	2004 CORRUPTION PERCEPTIONS INDEX SCORE
1	Finland	9.7		Trinidad & Tobago	5.3	61	Malawi	3.2
2	New Zealand	9.6					Thailand	3.2
3	Denmark	9.5		Tunisia	5.3	63	Dominican Republic	3.1
3	Iceland	9.5	34	Slovenia	5.2		Moldova	3.1
5	Singapore	9.3	35	Uruguay	5.1	65	Guatemala	2.9
6	Sweden	9.2	36	Malaysia	5.0		Philippines	2.9
7	Switzerland	9.1	37	Jordan	4.9		Senegal	2.9
8	Norway	8.9	38	Lithuania	4.8		Zimbabwe	2.9
9	Australia	8.8		South Africa	4.8	69	Romania	2.8
10	Netherlands	8.7	40	Costa Rica	4.5		Venezuela	2.8
11	United Kingdom	8.6		Mauritius	4.5	71	Honduras	2.7
12	Canada	8.5	42	Greece	4.2		India	2.7
13	Luxembourg	8.4		South Korea	4.2		Kazakhstan	2.7
13	Austria	8.4	44	Peru	4.1		Uzbekistan	2.7
15	Germany	8.2		Poland	4.1	75	Vietnam	2.6
16	Hong Kong	8.0	46	Brazil	4.0		Zambia	2.6
16	Israel	7.6	47	Bulgaria	3.9	77	Ivory Coast	2.4
	United States	7.6		Croatia	3.9		Nicaragua	2.4
18	Chile	7.5		Czech Republic	3.9	79	Ecuador	2.3
	Ireland	7.5	50	Colombia	3.8		Pakistan	2.3
21	Japan	7.1	51	Mexico	3.7		Russia	2.3
22	Spain	7.0		Panama	3.7	82	Tanzania	2.2
23	France	6.7		Slovak Republic	3.7	83	Ukraine	2.1
24	Belgium	6.6				84	Azerbaijan	2.0
25	Portugal	6.3	54	Egypt	3.6		Bolivia	2.0
26	Botswana	6.0		El Salvador	3.6		Cameroon	2.0
27	Taiwan	5.9		Turkey	3.6		Kenya	2.0
28	Estonia	5.6	57	Argentina	3.5	88	Indonesia	1.9
29	Italy	5.5		China	3.5		Uganda	1.9
30	Namibia	5.4	59	Ghana	3.4	90	Nigeria	1.0
31	Hungary	5.3		Latvia	3.4	91	Bangladesh	0.4

Source: Transparency International (April 29, 2005): http://www.transparency.org.

representing at least $300 billion in annual revenues, jointly signed a "zero-tolerance" pact against bribery in an effort to clean up the notorious corruption within their ranks. The pact represents a voluntary effort known as the Partnering Against Corruption Initiative that calls for "firms to set up extensive internal programs to educate and oversee company officials and business partners and also prohibit political contributions and charitable gifts designed to curry favor."[38]. Companies participating include Newmont Mining Corp., Rio Tinto PLC, and Bechtel Group, Inc. Participants believe that such an initiative will encourage companies within the industry to monitor each other; however, others still prefer to adhere to their own standards and antibribery objectives.

Recognizing the seriousness of bribery, the U.S. government issued the following general guidelines for establishing an effective antibribery compliance program:

- Gain full support of upper management.
- Establish and adhere to a written corporate code of conduct.
- Establish an organizational compliance structure.
- Provide anticorruption training and education seminars.
- Undertake due diligence.
- Establish auditing and internal controls.
- Set up compliance mechanisms.
- Put into place disciplinary actions for corporate offenders.[39]

It is very challenging for managers to avoid paying bribes in situations where they are expected to generate business for their companies, especially when there are demands placed on them by foreign government officials to make the payments. However, it is clear that the international community is serious about trying to eradicate bribery, and managers need to be aware of the pressures they face, company policies related to bribery, and the consequences of breaking the law, both domestically and in the foreign environment.

A zero tolerance pact against bribery was signed by companies at the 2005 World Economic Forum.

An effective antibribery compliance program for companies involves setting high standards, communicating them to relevant employees, educating employees on expected behavior, and monitoring compliance.

POINT–COUNTERPOINT: IS BRIBERY EVER JUSTIFIED?

POINT

Yes, I believe that in some instances, bribery can be justified by corporations and their employees. Although it is considered an unacceptable practice in the United States, in many countries it is either legal or considered an acceptable part of doing business. When companies pay bribes in such countries, they are simply adhering to the standards of business that are culturally acceptable in them. In fact, many argue that by making it illegal for U.S. companies to pay bribes in foreign countries, the U.S. government is essentially trying to impose its own standards on other countries and disrupting the way business is carried out within their borders. Unilever, for example, explains that it does not condone facilitation payments and tries to avoid them, but it concedes that it makes such payments when they are based on local custom.[40]

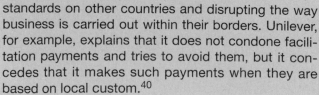

Paying bribes might also be necessary at times in order for companies to compete effectively on the international scene. Many companies are put in the situation of either paying bribes or being refused the opportunity to operate at all within certain countries. Bribes to government officials in developing countries are often required to win contracts because most of their government officials are poorly paid and are immune from prosecution when accepting bribes.[41] For example, Marathon Oil and several other U.S. oil companies have been accused of paying bribes to relatives of the ruler of Equatorial Guinea, but had they not done so, they would have been refused property rights and access to oil reserves.[42] Also, adhering to antibribery laws such as the FCPA often puts U.S. companies at a competitive disadvantage when compared to those from countries without such regulations. With regard to the situation in Equatorial Guinea, one oil executive explained that if the oil companies hadn't paid bribes, the French or the Russians or the Petronas (of Malaysia) would have.[43] So preventing U.S. companies from paying bribes doesn't preserve the "integrity" of the freemarket system, as some critics argue; it simply places an often unnecessary handicap on U.S. companies or companies from other countries with strong ethical rules and their operations abroad.

Bribery is also sometimes necessary for companies to meet desirable ends for both themselves and the host country in which they are operating. If companies were to withdraw their operations from countries in which bribery occurs, often developing nations, they would be depriving them of capital investments and jobs that could fuel their economic growth. For example, IBM and other U.S. companies claimed that the FCPA cost them a contract for air traffic control systems in Mexico. They argue that their inability to make payments to Mexican authorities led Mexico to install inferior technology.[44]

Last of all, it is unfair for the U.S. government to hold its companies to higher standards than it itself adheres to. For example, the U.S. government frequently grants foreign aid as an implicit bribe, with the understanding that the host country will grant political concessions in return. Further, governments use high-level official visits and aggressive lobbying for their home-based companies to help them win foreign business. In addition, the U.S. government has sometimes paid foreign government officials to get them to visit the United States when an American company is bidding on a contract. Similarly, it has given scholarships to family members of officials who can provide business to U.S. companies.[45]

COUNTERPOINT

Bribery is not only illegal under U.S. law, but it is also unethical, regardless of where a company is doing business. Although some countries may condone or even facilitate the payment of bribes, it is important for U.S. companies to adhere to the same principles and practices that they do in their home country. To do otherwise would result in unclear standards of behavior that could be used as justification to commit other unethical acts. For example, when Titan Corp. paid political bribes to its native consultant in Benin, it attempted to cover up its payments through accounting fraud and other false documents.[46] Monsanto, accused of paying bribes to receive permits for its genetically modified products in Indonesia, actually violated the laws of that country by failing to conduct proper audits that could have revealed its shady dealings.[47]

It may be argued that bribes are necessary to doing business in some countries, but I think otherwise. The FCPA already does allow U.S. companies to make "facilitation payments" to officials who have a direct responsibility in business transactions; going beyond such payments to make bribes to government officials and others who have no legitimate tie to the transaction upsets the concept of open and fair competition. Furthermore, holding other countries' policies toward bribery as a benchmark for our own is simply faulty logic.

People who seek to condone bribery often use the argument that the "ends" justify the "means"; however, it seems to me that more often than not the "ends" simply reinforce the fact that the "means" were unethical. In fact, companies and countries often lose more than they gain when bribery is involved. Firms whose bribery schemes have been uncovered lose credibility, jeopardize their reputations, and must face monetary penalties that often outweigh whatever they were seeking to gain through the unethical transaction. For example, Titan Corp. ended up paying over $28 million to settle the allegations levied against it by the Justice Department and the SEC; this amount far eclipsed the increased management fees it hoped to gain by bribing the Benin government. Furthermore, it was forced to close down its operations in the country—operations that could have been profitable even if they had been conducted legitimately. And even after Monsanto paid bribes to have its products approved, the Indonesian government still refused to issue it permits; the company eventually had to abandon its efforts to sell genetically modified seeds in the region anyway. It has also been pointed out in the chapter that bribery often pushes up companies' costs of operations and the prices of their goods and services.

Companies aren't the only ones that lose when they become entangled in bribery. Such practices encourage corruption in foreign countries, especially developing ones, and undermine their attempts to clean up their political and economic systems. At the time that Monsanto was engaging in bribery in Indonesia, the government there had been trying to improve its country's reputation and had even established a Corruption Eradication Commission. Monsanto's actions weakened the legitimacy of these efforts. Furthermore, by paying bribes to the Mbasogo administration in Equatorial Guinea, Marathon Oil and its counterparts were essentially supporting a regime known for torture and graft. In the end, no one really gains. Trying to justify bribery simply blurs the lines between what is ethical and what isn't. What do you think?

Although it might be easier to use the standard of cultural relativism and simply pay bribes where bribes are accepted, the rule of law is beginning to be more significant because of the efforts of the international organizations identified above. Companies need to establish policies and procedures that are consistent with their own national laws as well as the laws of the countries where they operate. As the efforts of the OECD and UN become implemented in national laws, companies will find that laws and practices from country to country will become more uniform and thus easier to implement since everyone will be operating under the same guidelines.

ETHICAL BEHAVIOR AND ENVIRONMENTAL ISSUES

As noted in the Newmont Mining case, environmental issues are extremely important, because they are a matter of life or death, either now or in the future. Companies contribute to environmental damage in different ways. Some extract natural resources, such as minerals, fossil fuels, and timber, which has a clear impact on the environment. Some resources, such as timber, may be renewable, whereas others, such as minerals, oil, and fish, may not be renewable. Some might argue that resources will never be scarce because as they become less available, their price rises, and technology or substitutes take care of the scarcity. Other companies endanger the environment because they contaminate the air, soil, or water in their manufacturing processes, or because they manufacture products, such as automobiles or electricity, that use fossil fuels and release contaminants into the environment. Thus environmental damage occurs from extracting resources and from production processes.

Sustainability means meeting the needs of the present without compromising the ability of future generations to meet their own needs; proponents of the concept of sustainability argue that sustainability takes into consideration what is best for the people and the environment.[48] Sustainability is a highly controversial term subject to interpretations by environmentalists, who are not a homogeneous group, and by industry, which also differs in its interpretations of sustainability. It is important for companies that affect the environment to establish policies for responsible behavior, which is a function of cultural and legal issues. To illustrate the challenges, we will examine the issue of global warming, the Kyoto Protocol, and the potential impact of Kyoto on corporate behavior.

Global Warming

Global warming has certainly captured the attention of the world, even in the entertainment industry. Twentieth Century Fox's hit movie, *The Day After Tomorrow*, shows the potentially devastating impact of global warming, while Michael Crichton's book, *State of Fear*, examines the dangers of politicizing science. Although there was mild criticism of *The Day After Tomorrow*, there was a vigorous debate over Crichton's book and its thesis that critics of global warming are being suppressed.

At the core of the international treaty called the Kyoto Protocol is the theory that global warming is a result of the increase of carbon dioxide and other gases that act like the roof of a greenhouse, trapping heat that would normally be radiated back into space, thus warming the planet. If the amount of carbon dioxide emitted into the atmosphere is not controlled and reduced, the rising temperature of the earth could result in catastrophic events such as melting of the polar ice cap and subsequent flooding of coastal regions, ocean disruptions, shifting storm patterns, reduced farm output, plant and animal extinctions, and droughts.[49] Even though the world is warming, however, there is no clear consensus on the scope of the problem, the cause, or the solutions.[50]

Companies that extract natural resources, generate air or water waste, or manufacture products, such as autos, that are polluters need to be concerned with their environmental impact.

Sustainability involves meeting the needs of the present without compromising the ability of future generations to meet their own needs, while taking into account what is best for the people and the environment.

Global warming results from the release of greenhouse gases that trap heat in the atmosphere rather than allowing it to escape.

But it is also clear that something can and must be done to reduce the emission of carbon dioxide, which comes from the burning of fossil fuels, methane, and other gases, hence the Kyoto Protocol. The Kyoto Protocol, which was signed in 1997, is an extension of the UN Framework Convention on Climate Change, which went into force in 1994. The Kyoto Protocol obliges the signatory countries to cut their greenhouse gas emissions to 5.2 percent below 1990 levels between 2008 and 2012. As of April 2005, 149 nations and regional economic integration organizations had signed the Kyoto Protocol,[51] but the United States, which generates 25 percent of the world's greenhouse gases, is not a party. The U.S. initially signed the agreement in 1998 but withdrew in 2001 due to concerns over domestic economic growth and exemptions for rapidly expanding developing countries like China and India.[52] China and India approved the agreement, but they are not required to reduce their emissions since they are developing countries, even though together they account for about 14 percent of the world's total greenhouse emissions. The U.S. is banking on the development of low-carbon technologies to solve the problem and would prefer to not have to meet mandatory reductions in greenhouse gas emissions for fear that economic growth would be reduced, thus creating problems with employment. The U.S. government was expected to invest $5.8 billion in 2005 alone on research on climate change and new technologies.[53]

Companies that operate in countries that have adopted the Kyoto Protocol are under pressure to reduce greenhouse gas emissions or buy credits from companies that have reduced their emissions below the target levels. That means they must invest in new technologies or change the way they do business or pay for someone else to clean up their act. In addition, MNEs are being forced to consider their global strategies, because those with operations in countries that have adopted the Kyoto Protocol are required to adhere to the same standards as local companies. The EU made the decision to set a target of 8 percent reduction below 1990 emission levels, which is more aggressive than the Kyoto Protocol targets. The Germans went even further by setting a target of 21 percent

The Kyoto Protocol was signed in 1997 to require countries to cut their greenhouse gas emissions to 5.2 percent below 1990 levels between 2008 and 2012. Some countries have adopted stricter requirements, and others, such as the U.S., China, and India, are not part of the compliance.

A man paddles a canoe past floating logs near a sawmill on the banks of Marajo Island in the Amazon River, where logging is destroying the Brazilian rain forest and reducing the world's capacity to absorb greenhouse gasses.

FIGURE 5.5

The Dilemma of Global
Warming

"Gentlemen, we have a dilemma. Pollution scientists say
it will destroy the ozone - however, Market Research
predict it will sell like hot cakes."

on the assumption that they would close down polluting, coal-fired power plants in East Germany.[54]

U.S.-based MNEs must comply
with the Kyoto Protocol in
compliance countries where
they may have operations.

U.S. companies operating in Europe are facing the pressures of operating there. Many U.S.-based MNE's, although they do not have to respond to the Kyoto Protocol in the U.S., are still preparing for what they feel is the inevitability of Kyoto. GM, for example, took part in a voluntary program to reduce greenhouse gas emissions and achieved a 10 percent reduction in North American plant emissions from 2000 to 2005. GM is now trying to determine what it needs to do for its 11 plants in Europe to comply with EU regulations.[55] DuPont has cut its greenhouse gas emissions by 65 percent since 1990, and Alcoa, Inc. has set a target to cut emissions by 25 percent by 2010.[56] Thus companies are clearly changing the way they do business, whether they are in Kyoto Protocol countries or not. MNEs are in an interesting situation since they must adapt to different standards in the different countries where they operate.

A U.S.-based MNE with manufacturing plants in the U.S., Germany, and China is confronted with different regulatory environments and must act accordingly. The legal approach to responsible behavior says it can operate according to the local laws, but the ethical approach is to go beyond the law and do whatever is necessary and economically feasible to reduce greenhouse gas emissions.

DOES GEOGRAPHY MATTER?

The Amazon

Greenhouse gas emissions are global in nature. It doesn't make any difference where you live, because you are affected by greenhouse gas emissions from around the world. So why does it matter what happens to the Amazon? The Amazon rain forest, most of which is housed in Brazil, covers an area the size of Western Europe and comprises one-third of the world's remaining tropical forests. The Brazilian rain forests cover 60 percent of Brazil's territory. In addition, it is the home of 30 percent of the world's animal and plant species. The forests themselves are one of the solutions to global warming since trees absorb carbon dioxide. That is why one of the solutions to adopting Kyoto Protocol emissions reductions is to take part in a reforestation project. However, the Amazon rain forest is threatened on two fronts—logging and burning. Logging is an important source of revenue for Brazil, a country that suffers from high unemployment and underemployment. In addition to logging operations, Brazilians are cutting down and burning large tracts of land for cattle ranching and farming. In some cases, the cattle ranchers sell their land to agricultural interests, clear additional land for pastures, and sell the lumber to the timber industry. The burning is increasing carbon dioxide emissions, and the destruction of the forests is eliminating a huge carbon dioxide sink that could benefit the rest of the world. It is estimated that the burning of the Amazon accounts for 75 percent of Brazil's greenhouse gas emissions, making Brazil one of the world's top 10 polluters.[57] In fact, Brazil pumps out 5.38 percent of the world's total greenhouse gas emissions.[58] Because of the huge logging potential, many multinational logging firms have invested heavily in the Brazilian rain forest, while critics of Brazilian policies have been clamoring for protection of the rain forest.

Thus the debate is "Who controls the rain forest?" Brazilians argue that the rain forest is theirs to control and use. Given that Brazil is a developing country with serious poverty and employment issues, the Brazilian government is hesitant to do anything that might curtail economic growth. On the other hand, environmentalists, both from within and outside of Brazil, argue that the rain forest is a global resource. Although some of the logging comes from FDI and legitimate logging operations, much of it is illegal and is conducted by Brazilian loggers and ranchers who are working on illegally occupied federal lands, a Brazilian tradition. In 2003, the first year of new President Lula da Silva's administration, Brazilian deforestation hit its second highest level ever, and it rose even more in 2004. It is estimated that during a 12-month period ending in August 2004, the Amazon was losing the equivalent of six football fields of area every minute. An average of 23,000 square kilometers (8,880 square miles) has been lost each of the last three years.[59] After the 2005 killing of an elderly U.S. nun who was trying to protect the Amazon rain forest from loggers and ranchers, the Brazilian government announced that it would crack down on illegal activities and slow the destruction of the rain forest. However, the debate on who controls the rain forest will continue for the foreseeable future.

ETHICAL DILEMMAS AND PHARMACEUTICAL SALES

Another ethical dilemma faces global pharmaceutical companies as they sell products in developing countries. GlaxoSmithKline (GSK) is one of the largest research-based pharmaceutical companies in the world, focusing on two lines of business: pharmaceuticals (prescription pharmaceuticals and vaccines) and consumer health care products. With revenues of $20 billion annually, the U.K.-headquartered company has operations in 116 countries and sales in 125 countries. It has over 100,000 employees worldwide, with 35,000 working at 82 manufacturing sites in 37 countries, over 15,000 of which are in R&D. In order to keep developing new products, GSK spends 13.9 percent of its revenues on R&D.[60] Like most research-based pharmaceutical companies, GSK undertakes the R&D, manufacturing, and sale of patented pharmaceuticals. GSK's strategy is to sell a product at a high price as long as it is covered by a patent. As soon as the patent expires, generic drug manufacturers can produce and sell the product at a fraction of the cost of the product when it was covered by the patent. Although patent laws may vary from country to country, branded pharmaceuticals are protected by patent law for 17 years from the time the Food and Drug Administration grants approval for the sale of the drug. Because of the lower cost, generic products can be sold at lower prices.

There are some exceptions to this pricing structure. Only 3 percent of GSK's revenues come from the Middle East and Africa, where GSK provides preferential prices for vaccines, also known as tiered pricing. In a tiered pricing system, consumers in industrial countries pay higher prices, and consumers in developing countries, especially the low-income developing countries, pay a lower subsidized price. In addition, GSK offers not-for-profit prices on other drugs, such as ARVs (antiretroviral) and antimalarial drugs to projects fully funded by other programs, such as the Global Fund to Fight AIDS. As we will see in the case at the end of the chapter, AIDS is a major health problem in Africa, but it is also an issue in other countries, such as Brazil where the government distributes AIDS drugs to all who need them. The issue, of course, is cost. The Brazilian government provides ARVs to its patients for only $2,000 per year, whereas the same treatment in the U.S. would cost $12,000 per year.[61]

Tiered pricing for pharmaceuticals means that companies charge a market price for products sold in industrial countries and a discounted price for products sold in developing countries.

One way to get around the high cost of patented drugs is to produce generics, which is a major industry in developing countries such as India, Brazil, and China. Generics are legitimate as long as the countries where they are produced give patent protection to the patent holders. However, many times the drugs are simply pirated versions of the real thing. The challenge is that the pirated versions, which the WHO estimates make up 10 percent of medicines sold worldwide, may lack key active ingredients.[62] That is one reason why the U.S. has hesitated to allow states to import generic drugs from countries such as Canada for fear that the drugs could be transshipped from an unauthorized factory in a developing country and either not provide the expected medical benefits or worse, cause health problems due to poor ingredients. Of course, another argument is that the industry lobbied for protection from drug imports only so that it could continue to generate high revenues from its drug patents in the U.S. before the products enter legal generic status.

Developing countries, such as Brazil, have tried to get the big pharmaceutical companies to lower the price for their drugs, because their national health care system is having a difficult time affording the drugs that it needs. Of course, the same is true for the industrial countries where health care costs are rapidly rising. Brazil is also reverse engineering key drugs, especially ARVs, so that it can produce them generically at a cheaper price. The WTO's Agreement on Trade-Related Aspects of Intellectual Property Rights (TRIPS) has also provided a mechanism for poor countries facing a health crisis, such as AIDS in Africa, allowing them to either produce generic products for local consumption or import generic products from other countries if they don't have generic capabilities themselves. This has been a major concern for pharmaceutical companies like GSK, because they are afraid the generic products could end up back in the industrial countries where they are generating the majority of their revenues. That's also where the fakes come in.

Drugs are expensive to develop. It is estimated that the price for developing a new drug is close to $1 billion in the U.S., vs. as little as $100 million in a developing country like India. India, which has a thriving unlicensed generic drug industry, used to have a lot of FDI in pharmaceuticals, but since it would not offer patents on the drugs, companies were forced to leave the country rather than give away all their secrets to their competitors. However, India's new patent protection law, which came into effect in 2005 and brings India into line with the WTO, is creating a whole new environment for pharmaceuticals. Many Indian R&D facilities have sprung up to develop new drugs that can be produced and sold by Indian companies. Foreign pharmaceuticals are now looking at different strategies for penetrating the Indian market, from FDI to licensing agreements with generic manufacturing facilities. India sells $1.15 billion worth of generic drugs in the U.S. and Europe, and it has 74 pharmaceutical manufacturing facilities approved by the FDA, more than any country outside the U.S.[63]

Another problem in global health care is that some diseases, such as malaria, which infects 300 million to 500 million people worldwide every year, don't exist in industrial countries, so pharmaceutical companies can't use tiered pricing to recoup their investments and tend to shelve projects that don't have commercial viability. This happened at GSK in its efforts to develop a vaccine against malaria. Even though the project was making progress, GSK nearly eliminated the project in 1999 until the head of the project proposed approaching outside funding agencies to get the funding necessary to continue. He and others approached the Bill and Melinda Gates Foundation, which was started by Bill Gates, the founder of Microsoft, and his wife, Melinda. The foundation provided funding to launch the Malaria Vaccine Initiative, some of which went to GSK. In conjunction with British finance experts, the foundation also came up with the idea of creating an International Finance Facility for Immunization that would allow countries to issue bonds to generate funds to purchase vaccines. In addition, the foundation backed the idea of advance-purchase contracts for the malaria vaccine. This plan would allow companies to charge a market price to the first 200 million people who receive the vaccine and a significantly

Legal generic products allow countries to purchase drugs at lower costs and comply with drug patents, whereas illegal generic products are fakes that may or may not be of high quality.

Countries with health crises, such as African countries suffering from AIDS, are allowed by TRIPS to manufacture or import generic drugs.

India is a major manufacturer of generic drugs and is now moving to R&D of new drugs.

Governments and private foundations are attempting to solve the problem of developing country access to drugs and vaccines through an International Finance Facility for Immunization and/or advance-purchase contracts.

reduced price for everyone after that.[64] The Gates Foundation is also involved in helping fund an experimental program in Zambia to provide treated mosquito nets and insecticide to spray walls of homes.[65]

The Gates Foundation is an interesting alternative to corporate social responsibility. The endowment of the foundation was funded by the Gates, not by Microsoft. If Microsoft had used its own corporate money to fund humanitarian projects, it would have seemed socially responsible, but it would also have reduced profits and thus the return to the investors. However, Bill and Melinda Gates made the decision to use their own wealth rather than Microsoft wealth to fund humanitarian projects.

Sometimes the problem is the governments, not the companies. A more effective approach to combating malaria is the use of treated mosquito nets. African governments have been pushed by a coalition of NGOs and companies to reduce or eliminate tariffs on the import of the nets. Tariffs can increase the cost of the treated nets by 30 percent or more, making the product almost prohibitively expensive for poor people. But African governments have been slow to reduce the tariffs to help their own population.

Thus the social responsibility issue is how the pharmaceutical companies can continue to generate enough revenues to create new products, their major source of competitive advantage, while at the same time being responsive to the problems of developing countries, which are long on diseases and short on funds. Should the solution come from the companies themselves, or is addressing such problems the responsibility of the individual developing countries in conjunction with the industrial countries in global forums such as the WHO? Should the companies encourage the development of generic products long before patents expire, or are they thereby running the risk of creating generics that can find their way back into the industrial markets, thus competing with their patented products? Can they afford to focus on diseases for which they can never get an adequate return to cover the development costs? Clearly companies need to establish policies such as those identified by GSK at the beginning of this section, but what is an adequate policy to pursue?

A young boy assembles filter-tipped cigarettes while sitting cross-legged on the floor in a factory in Bangladesh.

ETHICAL DIMENSIONS OF LABOR CONDITIONS

A major challenge facing MNEs is the globalization of the supply chain and the working conditions of workers. The many labor issues that companies, governments, trade unions, and nongovernmental organizations alike must deal with include fair wages, child labor, working conditions, working hours, and freedom of association. These issues are especially critical in retail, clothing, footwear, and agriculture where MNEs outsource production to independent companies abroad, usually in the developing countries of Asia, Latin America, and Africa. As noted in Figure 5.6, there are multiple pressures on companies from external stakeholders to adopt responsible employment practices in their overseas operations.

A more specific listing of worker issues is found in the Ethical Trading Initiative (ETI) Base Code in Table 5.2. The ETI is a British-based organization that focuses on ethical employment practices of MNEs; its members include representatives from Gap, Inc., Levi Strauss & Co., Marks & Spencer, The Body Shop International, and other companies, as well as from trade union organizations, NGOs, and governments. The objective of ETI is to get companies to adopt ethical employment policies and then monitor compliance with their overseas suppliers.

All the issues identified in the Base Code are important, but a few tend to get more attention than others. One is the use of child labor. According to the International Labor Organization (ILO), a UN institution, 250 million children between the ages of 5 and 17 are working worldwide. Of those, it is estimated that "180 million are young children or in work that endangers their health or well-being, involving hazards, sexual exploitation, trafficking, and debt bondage."[66] The challenge is that MNEs are working in an environment with different cultural, legal, and political rules than what they are used to in their home countries. In addition, they typically rely on local supplier companies that are responding to local pressures and situations very different from those the MNE deals with in its home market. MNEs cannot solve all the problems of child labor, especially when it is estimated that only 5 percent of child labor is employed in export industries supported by MNEs.[67] Most underage children who work do so in the informal sector of the economy, especially in agriculture, and it is difficult to protect them. According to the ILO, children who are 13 years old may be employed in light work that is not harmful to their health and that does not interfere with school. However, the ILO feels that children under the age of 18 should all be protected against the most abusive labor conditions.

Major labor issues that MNEs get involved in through FDI or purchasing from independent manufacturers in developing countries are fair wages, child labor, working conditions, working hours, and freedom of association.

An estimated 250 million children between 5 and 17 years old are working, but only about 5 percent of child labor is involved in export industries.

FIGURE 5.6

PRESSURES FOR ETHICAL BEHAVIOR OF COMPANIES ON ISSUES RELATED TO WORKERS IN THE GLOBAL SUPPLY CHAIN

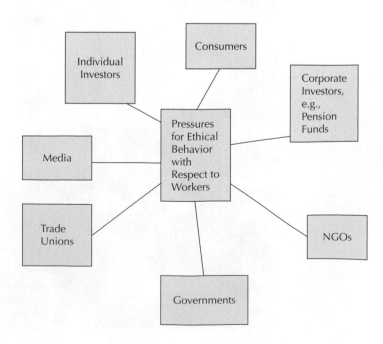

TABLE 5.2   ETHICAL TRADING INITIATIVE BASE CODE ON WORKERS

1. EMPLOYMENT IS FREELY CHOSEN

    1.1   There is no forced, bonded or involuntary prison labour.

    1.2   Workers are not required to lodge "deposits" or their identity papers with their employer and are free to leave their employer after reasonable notice.

2. FREEDOM OF ASSOCIATION AND THE RIGHT TO COLLECTIVE BARGAINING ARE RESPECTED

    2.1   Workers, without distinction, have the right to join or form trade unions of their own choosing and to bargain collectively.

    2.2   The employer adopts an open attitude towards the activities of trade unions and their organisational activities.

    2.3   Workers' representatives are not discriminated against and have access to carry out their representative functions in the workplace.

    2.4   Where the right to freedom of association and collective bargaining is restricted under law, the employer facilitates, and does not hinder, the development of parallel means for independent and free association and bargaining.

3. WORKING CONDITIONS ARE SAFE AND HYGIENIC

    3.1   A safe and hygienic working environment shall be provided, bearing in mind the prevailing knowledge of the industry and of any specific hazards. Adequate steps shall be taken to prevent accidents and injury to health arising out of, associated with, or occuring in the course of work, by minimising, so far as is reasonably practicable, the causes of hazards inherent in the working environment.

    3.2   Workers shall receive regular and recorded health and safety training, and such training shall be repeated for new or reassigned workers.

    3.3   Access to clean toilet facilities and to potable water, and, if appropriate, sanitary facilities for food storage shall be provided.

    3.4   Accommodation, where provided, shall be clean, safe, and meet the basic needs of the workers.

    3.5   The company observing the code shall assign responsibility for health and safety to a senior management representative.

4. CHILD LABOUR SHALL NOT BE USED

    4.1   There shall be no new recruitment of child labour.

    4.2   Companies shall develop or participate in and contribute to policies and programmes which provide for the transition of any child found to be performing child labour to enable her or him to attend and remain in quality education until no longer a child; "child" and "child labour" being defined in the appendices.

    4.3   Children and young persons under 18 shall not be employed at night or in hazardous conditions.

    4.4   These policies and procedures shall conform to the provisions of the relevant ILO standards.

5. LIVING WAGES ARE PAID

    5.1   Wages and benefits paid for a standard working week meet, at a minimum, national legal standards or industry benchmark standards, whichever is higher. In any event wages should always be enough to meet basic needs and to provide some discretionary income.

    5.2   All workers shall be provided with written and understandable information about their employment conditions in respect to wages before they enter employment and about the particulars of their wages for the pay period concerned each time that they are paid.

    5.3   Deductions from wages as a disciplinary measure shall not be permitted nor shall any deductions from wages not provided for by national law be permitted without the expressed permission of the worker concerned. All disciplinary measures should be recorded.

6. WORKING HOURS ARE NOT EXCESSIVE

    6.1   Working hours comply with national laws and benchmark industry standards, whichever affords greater protection.

    6.2   In any event, workers shall not on a regular basis be required to work in excess of 48 hours per week and shall be provided with at least one day off for every 7 day period on average. Overtime shall be voluntary, shall not exceed 12 hours per week, shall not be demanded on a regular basis, and shall always be compensated at a premium rate.

7. NO DISCRIMINATION IS PRACTISED

    7.1   There is no discrimination in hiring, compensation, access to training, promotion, termination or retirement based on race, caste, national origin, religion, age, disability, gender, marital status, sexual orientation, union membership or political affiliation.

8. REGULAR EMPLOYMENT IS PROVIDED

    8.1   To every extent possible work performed must be on the basis of recognised employment relationship established through national law and practice.

(Continued)

TABLE 5.2   CONTINUED

8.2   Obligations to employees under labour or social security laws and regulations arising from the regular employment relationship shall not be avoided through the use of labour-only contracting, sub-contracting, or home-working arrangements, or through apprenticeship schemes where there is no real intent to impart skills or provide regular employment, nor shall any such obligations be avoided through the excessive use of fixed-term contracts of employment.

9. NO HARSH OR INHUMANE TREATMENT IS ALLOWED

9.1   Physical abuse or discipline, the threat of physical abuse, sexual or other harassment and verbal abuse or other forms of intimidation shall be prohibited.

The provisions of this code constitute minimum and not maximum standards, and this code should not be used to prevent companies from exceeding these standards. Companies applying this code are expected to comply with national and other applicable law and, where the provisions of law and this Base Code address the same subject, to apply that provision which affords the greater protection.

Source: Ethical Trading Initiative, "Base Code," http://www.ethicaltrade.org/Z/lib/base/index.shtml. Accessed April 28, 2005.

It is difficult to know what to do. Two arguments used for hiring children in the carpet industry in India are (1) that they are better suited than adults to perform certain tasks, and (2) that if the children were not employed, they would be worse off. In many cases, children are put to work because their parents are not earning enough money to support their families or to pay off debts. Sometimes children are indentured to creditors as a way for parents to fulfill their debt obligations. An example of a well-intended policy that went wrong occurred when Bangladesh was forced to stop employing thousands of child workers in the 1990s or face U.S. trade sanctions. In this case the plight of the children worsened instead of improved.[68] In fact, it was documented that between 5,000 and 7,000 girls moved from factory work to prostitution.[69] When children lose jobs in the export industries, often they simply find work in the informal economy under even worse conditions.

Often there is pressure on MNEs operating in countries where labor policies are not the same as in their home markets to simply leave the markets. However, that is very short-sighted. It has been shown that Nike and other foreign investors, for example, have substantially improved the working conditions of workers in their plants in developing countries. They may not be able to change the entire employment practices of the countries where they operate, but they can improve working conditions for the workers at their factories and hopefully have an impact on other foreign investors. If they did not invest in developing countries, they would never be able to have any impact. There have been many criticisms of Chinese labor practices, but wages are rising and people are better off. In addition, as China implements WTO rules, it is opening up more parts of the country to FDI, and many young female workers from the interior of the country are finding work closer to home, resulting in a shortage of workers in the industrial areas and a rise in wages.

Some companies avoid operating in countries where child labor is employed, whereas others try to establish responsible policies in those same countries.

IKEA, the Swedish retailer, ran into trouble in India because it was buying carpets from companies that were using child labor extensively. Rather than just tell its suppliers to stop using child labor, the firm attacked two different problems. The first solution was to help mothers increase their earning power so that they could escape the clutches of the loan sharks that were forcing them to put their children to work as collateral for their loans. Then IKEA set up "bridge schools" to enable children to enter into mainstream education within a year.[70]

However, sometimes there is little a company can do. Nike has two age policies: 18 for the production of footwear and 16 for apparel, accessories, and equipment. Nike began some subassembly up-country from Bangkok in response to pressures from regional governments to provide more jobs outside the capital so that rural areas could retain more women. However, when Nike began operations in those areas, the prostitution trade started recruiting even younger girls because many local 16-year-olds were working in the Nike factories. The local governments wanted Nike to lower its minimum age to 14 to thwart the prostitution rings, but Nike was not able to because of its own hiring policies and the fear of reactions from corporate stakeholders concerned about the exploitation of child workers.

Another major challenge in enforcing high standards is local law. In Thailand, it is permissible for people to work 84 hours a week in seven 12-hour shifts. However, some MNEs are hesitant to allow workers that many hours for fear that they will be accused of exploitation, so they lower their maximum working hours to 60 hours as Nike does in Thailand. Although we tend to see this as a benefit to workers, it is hard for the MNEs to retain them with a 60-hour week since they want to work the maximum hours possible. Even offering higher wages doesn't seem to be a solution. In addition, since several MNEs, as well as local companies, may all subcontract to the same local manufacturers, the subcontractor may have difficulties managing its workforce when some workers can work for only 60 hours and others for 84.

MNEs may not be willing to hire local workers who want to work long hours due to concerns about exploitation.

CORPORATE CODES OF ETHICS

We have discussed many issues related to the impact of globalization on companies and the role of companies in the globalization process as well as their impact on society. How should a company behave? As noted in Figure 5.6, there are many pressures on MNEs to act responsibly. These pressures may not all be consistent, but they all must be considered and weighed.

There are four strong motivations for acting responsibly. First, unethical and irresponsible behavior could result in legal sanctions, especially in the areas of bribery and product safety. Second, such behavior could also result in consumer boycotts, although there is little evidence of the effectiveness of consumer boycotts in effecting change. Even though Nike has been subject to intense scrutiny by the media over the employment practices of its subcontractors in developing countries, its sales have never fallen because of the publicity. A U.K. study found that whereas 30 percent of consumers surveyed claimed to be ethical shoppers, fair trade products only had a 3 percent market share.[71]

Companies need to act responsibly, because unethical and irresponsible behavior
- *Could result in legal sanctions*
- *Could result in consumer boycotts*
- *Could lower employee morale*
- *Could cost sales because of bad publicity*

Third, unethical behavior can affect employee morale. Good behavior can positively influence both the workers in the developing countries as well as those in corporate headquarters back home who are proud of their company's behavior. For example, XanGo LLC, a privately held network marketing company whose product is based on the mangosteen fruit found in Asia, has actively used profits and employee time to contribute to a charity called Operation Kids, and this has been a strong rallying point for employees who are positive about the charitable work of the company. Fourth, companies never know when bad publicity is going to cost them sales. This may be one example why Nike and other apparel and clothing companies responded so quickly to criticism about allegedly unfair employment practices in developing countries.

A major component of a company's strategy for ethical and socially responsible behavior is a code of conduct. Codes of conduct in the international context can be set externally and internally. A definition of an external code of conduct is "guidelines, recommendations and rules issued by entities within society with the intent to affect the behavior of international business entities within society in order to enhance corporate responsibility."[72] For example, the ETI mentioned above has established a code of conduct for the treatment of workers. However, external codes of conduct are useful only insofar as they give companies guidance on how they should operate. The real challenge for a company is to become familiar with the codes of many different organizations, and the codes may not be consistent with each other.

A major component in a company's strategy for ethical and socially responsible behavior is a code of conduct.

Codes of conduct, involve four dimensions:

- Set a global policy that must be complied with wherever the company operates.
- Communicate the code to employees, suppliers, and subcontractors.
- Ensure that policies are carried out.
- Report results to external stakeholders.

However, armed with information about different codes of conduct as well as input from other stakeholders, companies must establish their own codes of conduct. There are four dimensions to creating such codes: (1) set a global policy that must be complied with everywhere the company operates, (2) communicate the code of conduct to all employees within the organization and to all suppliers and subcontractors, (3) ensure that its policies are carried out, and (4) report results to external stakeholders.

As an example of the first step, GlaxoSmithKline (GSK) has established a code of conduct that it discloses on its Web site. It states the following about its code:

> Our Employee Guide to Business Conduct contains the company policies that set out the standards of [behavior] we expect from employees. It requires all employees to act with integrity, comply with the law, avoid conflicts of interest and report any violations or unethical [behavior]. Detailed guidance is provided, including real-life examples, on what constitutes acceptable or unacceptable [behavior]. GSK employees have access to the guide via the company intranet. Our induction training familiarizes new employees with business conduct standards and where they can obtain support and guidance.[73]

Their code of conduct covers several different areas, including employment practices, human rights, standards of ethical conduct, and caring for the environment.[74]

In the second step, the company must communicate its code to employees, as does GSK, and to its external suppliers and subcontractors. Gap, for example, has an education program for training and helping factories to develop their own compliance programs to meet the objectives of Gap's code of conduct.[75]

Third, the company must ensure compliance with its code of conduct. GSK requires its employees to sign a statement that they have read and understand the code of conduct. Syngenta, an Anglo-Swiss agrochemicals group, found out through press reports that it was using child labor in its supply chain. The company worked with the Fair Labor Association, a nonprofit NGO, to submit its practices to external monitoring as a way of making sure that its employment practices were being followed by suppliers.[76] In addition to using NGOs, some companies have hired one of the big global audit firms, such as KPMG, to conduct compliance audits in the area of social responsibility. In other cases, the firms themselves serve as watchdogs over the behavior of subcontractors. Nike has a large staff in Thailand that visits subcontractors and works with them on issues related to the workforce. Gap was forced to revoke contracts with 136 factories in 2003 because of persistent or severe violations of its code of conduct.

The last area, reporting results to external stakeholders, is complicated. Nike used to provide a lot of information on its labor practices, but a labor activist brought suit against Nike in 1998 charging that its report was false advertising, and Nike was forced to settle the suit by paying $1.5 million to the Fair Labor Association. Since 2001 the firm has not provided as much information about its efforts to improve working conditions due to the suit. Gap, on the other hand, has begun providing a great deal of information about its corporate monitoring activities worldwide. It provides a great deal of detail about its code of conduct and practices, and it also raises questions about its challenges and failures in getting subcontractors to act responsibly.[77]

Past experience has shown companies that they need to balance the desire to provide as much information to stakeholders as they can with the risk of litigation for providing false information. But it is clear that corporate social responsibility reporting is on the rise and is an important section in the annual reports of listed companies as well as on company Web sites.

Some of the most important economic problems that countries face are global in nature—corruption, global warming, disease, and abusive labor practices. The solutions

LOOKING TO THE FUTURE: Will FDI Be Welcome and Will Foreign Investors Act More Responsibly as the Twenty-First Century Progresses?

In all likelihood, governments will continue to compete for a larger share of the benefits from the activities of MNEs. In the short term, most countries will probably work to create more favorable business environments for foreign investors. Investment inflows give developing countries ways to work around their debt burdens and capital accounts problems. Industrial countries struggling with trade-deficit problems, like the U.S., are more inclined to take a positive stance toward receiving FDI. The EU, along with other regional trade groups, will probably continue to welcome foreign investment inflows to help it attain the growth that it seeks through unification.

However, FDI may be less welcome in the longer term. Historically, attitudes toward FDI have tended to vary, leaning toward more restrictions when economies are thriving and incentives when economies are struggling. Still, it is possible that if rapid growth does not occur in some developing countries after they have attracted substantial FDI, they may adopt more regulations on FDI such as is occurring in Russia and Iran. Worse still, growing disappointment with the net benefits of foreign investment may lead some countries to fault FDI as the cause of their weaker sovereignty, their increasing poverty, and their cultural disintegration. Growing criticism from NGOs and other external stakeholders is complicating the ability of companies to operate globally.

are global in nature as well. However, what will be the future role of the MNE? Managers need to maximize the long-term value of the assets of their shareholders, but they will have to pay much closer attention to ethical behavior. It is the role of governments to deal with the externalities that result from corporate behavior, and companies will have to adjust to new regulations, especially in the area of environmental regulations.

SUMMARY

- FDI is a major source of capital and expertise, but it is also the center of a controversy over the costs and benefits to home and host countries.

- MNEs must balance the interests of different constituencies that have different objectives.

- The economic and political effects of MNEs are difficult to evaluate because of conflicting influences on different countries' objectives, intervening variables that obscure cause-effect relationships, and differences among MNEs' practices.

- MNEs may affect countries' balance-of-payments, growth, and employment objectives. Under different conditions, these effects may be positive or negative for the host or home country.

- The balance-of-payments effects of FDI involve import stimulus vs. import displacement, export stimulus vs. export displacement, and capital inflows vs. capital outflows. In the latter case, capital flows might be positive initially for the host country but negative later as the investor sends returns back to the home market.

- FDI creates jobs and economic growth in the host country. Given that resources are not fully employed, FDI may or may not have an adverse impact on jobs and economic growth in the home market.

- Relative behavior implies that we act according to the norms of the countries where we operate. Normative behavior implies that there are universal standards for ethical conduct that should be followed everywhere.

- The law is an important basis for ethical behavior, but not all unethical behavior is illegal. Thus ethical behavior must go beyond the law to include common decency.

- Bribery is a form of unethical behavior that is being addressed at the multilateral level, such as at the UN and OECD, and at the national level, such as with the Foreign Corrupt Practices Act in the U.S.

- Environmental concerns are raised with extractive industries and industries that generate air and water pollution or that produce products such as automobiles that use fossil fuels.

- The Kyoto Protocol, which requires the reduction of the emission of greenhouse gases, has not been adopted by all countries and is therefore still limited in its total global impact. However, companies must adapt to countries that have implemented the Kyoto Protocol.

- Pharmaceutical companies face challenges on how to make enough money to fund the R&D into new drugs and how to help provide critical drugs to developing countries at lower prices.

- A major challenge facing MNEs is the globalization of the supply chain and the working conditions of workers, especially in the areas of fair wages, child labor, working conditions, working hours, and freedom of association.

- Companies respond to the pressures for greater corporate social responsibility by establishing codes of conduct, distributing them to suppliers and subcontractors internationally, and ensuring compliance with the codes through effecting training and auditing programs.

C A S E   Anglo American in South Africa[78]

I n the summer of 2002, Anglo American PLC, the world's largest gold-mining organization, was on the threshold of making a very important decision concerning the health benefits it extended to its workers in South Africa. For the past two years, the company had been under the eyes of the South African government, the World Health Organization, and the Global Business Council on HIV/AIDS, as well as other nongovernment organizations and companies operating in the country, as it debated whether to provide antiretroviral therapy (ART) to the HIV-infected employees of its South African operations.

The AIDS Epidemic in South Africa

Even though sub-Saharan Africa holds just over 10 percent of the world's population, it is home to two-thirds of the world's people infected with HIV, the virus that causes AIDS. Located at the southernmost tip of the African continent, where the sub-Saharan AIDS pandemic is raging, South Africa suffers one of the highest rates of HIV infection in the world—approximately 5.3 million cases in a population of 45 million people. And according to the United Nations and the World Health Organization, the epidemic is far from reaching its peak. Each day 1,500 people are infected with the virus in South Africa, and estimates suggest that the number of cases will grow to 6 million by 2005.

The spread of this deadly disease has had a serious impact on both the population and the economy of South Africa over the past decade. In 2002, the life expectancy for a person living in the country was 50.7 years, compared to 74.16 years in Poland, a country with a similar population size and GDP per capita. It is very difficult to determine the number of deaths annually from AIDS, because many causes of death are misclassified. For example, a death certificate may say that the cause of death is tuberculosis, but the underlying problem may actually be AIDS. The Actuarial Society of South Africa separately estimated that 30 percent of deaths in 2000 were from AIDS, rising to a projected 44 percent of all deaths in 2004. The disease leaves not only families, but entire communities in ruins and vulnerable to other environmental factors, and this effect has resulted in serious implications for the South African economy.

From 1992 to 2002, the South African economy lost $7 billion annually—around 2 percent of its gross domestic product—as a result of the AIDS-related deaths of its workers. As AIDS continues to spread throughout the sub-Saharan African region, it is expected to continue to reduce per capita growth by 1 to 2 percent each year and to decrease annual GDP growth by as much as 0.6 percent by 2010 in the worst affected countries. The result will be both diminishing populations and shrinking economies with GDPs anywhere from 20 to 40 percent smaller than they would have been in the absence of AIDS.

During the 1990s, most African governments and NGOs focused on treating the problem through extensive education and condom distribution programs aimed at informing the African populace about the causes and effects of AIDS and at preventing the further spread of the disease. By the new millennium, however, it was apparent that these attempts at prevention were not enough to stem the rapid growth of the pandemic. This was partially due to a lack of financial commitment on the part of the governments. Despite a 15 percent target for health spending agreed upon at an Organization of African Unity Summit, most governments lacked both the resources and the determination to meet the goal. Additionally, due to governments' focus on the less expensive strategy of prevention as opposed to the more expensive treatment program, only about 4 percent of the people who needed treatment were receiving it.

Despite its high rate of infection and the dire threat posed by the HIV/AIDS epidemic, the South African government proved to be one of the least committed to effective intervention. Over the course of a two-year period, the government diverted only 0.6 percent of the budget to dealing with the HIV/AIDS crisis and was very resistant to widely distributing antiretroviral drugs on the basis of its being too expensive and too difficult to do effectively. The situation was not helped when the president, Thabo Mbeki, went so far as to publicly question the relationship between the HIV virus and the onset of AIDS. An additional barrier came in the form of an underfunded and inadequate health care system that lacked the necessary infrastructure and capacity to effectively deal with the sheer number of people in need of care. The country's drug-distribution networks were inefficient, and its trained health care staff was short as many as 30,000 nurses.

In addition to the government's lack of commitment, pharmaceutical companies also were exhibiting little cooperation in the fight against HIV/AIDS in South Africa. Several of these companies sued the South African government for what they claimed was poor enforcement of patent rights, making evident their concerns over the distribution of pirated versions of their drugs within the country. At the same time, the pharmaceutical industry was hesitant to provide price discounts to developing countries and was also apprehensive over the 2001 Doha Ministerial Conference's decisions concerning compulsory licensing, which would allow companies within developing countries to produce generic versions of patented drugs if the situation were serious enough. The industry feared that cheap generic drugs made available in Africa would eventually be resold by profiteers to more lucrative Western markets, cutting into profits and discouraging the development of new drugs. Despite some minor gains attained through compulsory licensing and some price reductions by the reluctant drug industry, there has been little impact on the millions of Africans inflicted with HIV/AIDS.

With the public sector and pharmaceutical companies failing so miserably to address the crisis of HIV/AIDS in South Africa, many people began looking to the private sector to make up the difference.

Anglo American's Operations in South Africa

Anglo American PLC is a mining conglomerate that operates in 61 countries through eight key businesses: gold, platinum, diamonds, coal, base metals, ferrous metals and industries, industrial metals and forest products, and financial and technical services. The company was founded in 1917 as the Anglo American Corporation of South Africa and was South Africa's first home-based public limited company. Even after becoming a multinational firm and relocating its headquarters to London, the company still dominates South Africa's domestic economy; it has interests in approximately 1,300 South African companies and manages a workforce of 90,000 employees through its main operations as well as another 44,000 through its subsidiaries in the region. Through its majority share ownership of its subsidiaries and associate companies, Anglo American controls over 25 percent of the shares traded on the South African stock market.

With such a large investment in South Africa, Anglo American was heavily affected by HIV/AIDS. Early in the 1990s, the company recognized the threat the epidemic posed to its operations in South Africa and became one of the first companies to establish a proactive and comprehensive strategy to combat the ravaging effects the epidemic was having on its workforce and production systems. The program consisted of prevention initiatives aimed at education and awareness, the distribution of condoms, financial and skill-related training to alleviate poverty, and a survey system to monitor the prevalence of the infection. The company further expanded on these policies by including both a voluntary counseling and testing program and a care and wellness program and by extending all its services to the families of employees and to surrounding communities. It also became a member of the Global Business Council on HIV/AIDS, an organization of multinational companies that focuses on alleviating the effects of AIDS throughout the world and on protecting the rights of infected workers. By doing so, it joined ranks with such corporations as DaimlerChrysler AG, Unilever PLC, AOL Time Warner, Inc., American Express Co., and the National Basketball Association in becoming involved in promoting a widespread and international response to the HIV/AIDS pandemic.

By adopting these strategies so early, Anglo American essentially became a leader in the private sector for the fight against HIV/AIDS in Africa, and many other multinational companies, including Coca-Cola, Ford Motor Corp., Colgate-Palmolive, and Chevron Texaco, soon followed its example and instigated prevention, education, and wellness programs of their own. However, the majority of companies operating in South Africa still hesitated to act. That is why Anglo American's announcement that it would be running a feasibility study to decide whether it would make antiretroviral treatments available to its vast workforce was met with so much anticipation and excitement by constituencies. Richard C. Holbrook, president of the Global Business Council on HIV/AIDS, indicated that, although the administration of the treatment to employees was not a requirement of the organization, he and other members of the council would be watching the development of the study with eagerness. It was believed that if such a program were enacted by the influential company, the bar for private-sector involvement in addressing the HIV/AIDS issue would be raised, encouraging more companies to become involved. Advocates also believed that such a bold move by the private sector would again put pressure on both the government and pharmaceutical companies to be more active as well. Anglo American's CEO, Tony Trahar, fully acknowledged these expectations, stating, "We're in the forefront here, and we're quite happy to take the lead."

The incentive for the pilot study largely came from the failure of Anglo American's policy of AIDS prevention to truly stem the growth of the disease in its workforce. By 2001, the prevalence of HIV-positive workers had risen to an average of 21 percent across all its operations, according to Brian Brink, the senior vice president of Anglo's medical division. That proportion was continuing to steadily increase by about 2 percent annually, having serious impacts on Anglo American's operations and profitability. Recent studies had indicated that the costs of AIDS could reach as much as 7.2 percent of the company's wage bill and asserted that leaving sick employees untreated would be more expensive than providing antiretroviral therapy. High absenteeism, the retraining of replacement workers, higher health and death benefits, hospitalization, and the loss of productivity and skilled labor were all expensive. Additionally, the overall effects on the economy and on the labor pool were reason for concern. Bobby Godsell, the CEO and chairman of one of Anglo American's subsidiaries, AngloGold, said that HIV/AIDS was adding as much as $6.00 to the costs of producing one ounce of gold, essentially adding around 75 million rand a year to the company's production costs.

However, only a year after the announcement was made, the word spread that Anglo American was abandoning the study, citing the risk and the expenses involved as being too great. Even though the costs of most of the necessary drugs were decreasing, the cost of distributing the drugs remained high, and most treatment regimes would still end up costing the company $750 to $2000 per year per employee—expensive when compared with the low wages and benefits Anglo American was providing to its mineworkers. At the time, average monthly wages in the mining industry in Africa were approximately 5,100 rand, or $830. It was also estimated that the providing of antiretroviral drugs could double medical aid costs by 2005, with the depreciation of the South African rand adding to expenses because drug prices are denominated in dollars. Another difficulty was the fact that the drugs cause various side effects and need to be administered under strict medical supervision. With many miners coming from neighboring countries, effectively monitoring them would be difficult. The treatments are lifelong, raising the additional question of whether Anglo American would be responsible for continuing the treatment even after the employees left the company. The fact that diet and lifestyle are also important factors and that mining requires heavy physical labor added further doubt as to how effective at providing treatment the company would be. Furthermore, the large number of unemployed Africans eager for jobs and the diversified nature of its multinational operations may have made the proposal seem all the less appealing to the company in the long run.

Anglo American's decision to discontinue the feasibility study was seen as a major setback for efforts to provide effective treatment for AIDS in Africa. Many NGOs and other stakeholders saw it as bad news for both the industry and for AIDS, lamenting that if Anglo American would not do something, no one would. The mining company tried to mediate the reaction by stating that it had not completely abandoned the idea of a pilot study and by expressing hopes that a more reasonable arrangement could be made involving the entire industry and the government. However, without effective policies by government and most companies in Africa, assistance from either of these sectors was unlikely. In contrast, by 2001, the Coca-Cola Corporation was providing free antiretroviral drug therapy to its 1,500 employees in Africa, while De Beers, in which Anglo American has a 45 percent share, was paying 90 percent of the costs of the treatment for its employees and their spouses, although their workforces were much smaller than Anglo American's. These steps raised questions about the reliability of the major mining company's reasons for not going through with the study.

QUESTIONS

1. What choices does the government of South Africa have in the face of the HIV/AIDS epidemic? What do you think it should do?

2. Why did Anglo American halt its pilot study on the feasibility of providing antiretroviral therapy to its employees? Do you agree with its decision? What recommendations would you give the company concerning its HIV/AIDS policy?

3. What role do the pharmaceutical companies play in the HIV/AIDS epidemic in South Africa? What would you recommend to a pharmaceutical company that produces HIV/AIDS drugs?

CHAPTER NOTES

1 The material for the case was taken from the following sources: "Still Living Dangerously," *The Economist* (February 10, 2000): http://www.economist.com.; Jose Manuel Tesoro, "Indonesia Courts Trouble," *Asiaweek Magazine* 26, no. 18 (May 12, 2000); "Devolve, but Do It Right," *The Economist* (July 6, 2000): http://www.economist.com; "Background Note: Indonesia," U.S. Department of State (October 2000): http://www.state.gov/r/pa/ei/bgn/2748.htm; *The World Factbook* (April 16, 2005): http://www.cia.gov/cia/publications/factbook/index.html; Jane Lee, "Newmont to Shut Indonesian Gold Mine as Illegal Mining Rises," *Bloomberg* (March 9, 2001); "Minahasa Mine Closure in Indonesia Is Scheduled for 2003," *Newmont Mining Corporation News* (March 9, 2001); Michael Schuman, "Vein of Discontent: Big Mining Loses Fortune in Indonesia: Illegal Operators Take Over Newmont and Aurora Sites, Troubles Reflect Political Breakdown," *Wall Street Journal Europe* (May 17, 2001): online edition; "Companies in Conflict Situations: Extractive Companies in Indonesia," *Changing Corporate Roles and Responsibilities* (Oxford: Oxford Analytica, January 2002): Series 2, issue 2; "Getting Ready for Statehood," *The Economist* (April 11, 2002): http://www.economist.com; "History of Indonesia," World History Information (June 2002): http://www.countryreports.org/history/indonhist.htm; "Indonesia: History and Government," WorldTravelGuide.net (June 2002): http://www.travel-guide.com/data/idn/idn580.asp; Jane Perlez and Evelyn Rusli, "Spurred by Illness, Indonesians Lash Out at U.S. Mining Giant," *The New York Times* (September 8, 2004), online edition; Newmont Mining home page: http://www.newmont.com/en/operations/indonesia/index.asp.

2 See The World Bank, *World Development Report* (2005), 256–57, and "Global 500: World's Largest Corporations," *Fortune Magazine* (July 26, 2004): F1.

3 Martin Wolf, "Countries Still Rule the World," *Financial Times* (February 6, 2002): 13.

4 Maiko Miyake and Magdolna Sass, "Recent Trends in Foreign Direct Investment," *Financial Market Trends* (June 2000): 23.

5 UNCTAD,. *World Investment Report 2004: The Shift Toward Services,* http://www.unctad.org/en/docs/wir2004_en.pdf.

6 See Gavin Boyd and John Dunning, eds., *Structural Change and Cooperation in the Global Economy* (Northampton, MA: Edward Elgar, 1999); and Joseph E. Stiglitz, *Globalization and Its Discontents* (New York: W. W. Norton, 2002).

7 "Profit and the Public Good," in "A Survey of Corporate Social Responsibility," *The Economist* (January 22, 2005): 15.

8 Mohsin Habib and Leon Zurawicki, "Corruption and Foreign Direct Investment," *Journal of International Business Studies* 33 (Summer 2002): 291–308.

9 John H. Dunning, "The Future of Multinational Enterprise," *Lloyds Bank Review* (July 1974): 16.

10 *World Investment Report 1999: Foreign Direct Investment and the Challenge of Development* (Geneva: UNCTAD, 1999).

11 Brian Bremner, Frederik Balfour, and Dexter Roberts, "China: Beware of Hot Money," *Business Week* (April 4, 2005): 52–53.

12 Peter J. Buckley and Jane Hughes, "Incentives to Transfer Profits: A Japanese Perspective," *Applied Economics* 33 (December 2001): 2009–2016.

13 Ravi Ramamurti, "The Obsolescing 'Bargaining Model'? MNE-Host Developing Country Relations Revisited," *Journal of International Business Studies* 32 (Spring 2001): 23.

14 Timothy Aeppel, "Scaling the Ladder," *Wall Street Journal* (April 6, 1999): A1.

15 For support, see William Keng and Mun Lee, "Foreign Investment, Industrial Restructuring and Dependent Development in Singapore," *Journal of Contemporary Asia* 27 (March 1997): 58–71. For a refutation, see Brian J. Aitken and Ann E. Harrison, "Do Domestic Firms Benefit from Direct Foreign Investment? Evidence from Venezuela," *American Economic Review,* 89, No. 3 (June 1995), 605.

16 David J. Teece, "Foreign Investment and Technological Development in Silicon Valley," *California Management Review* 34, no. 2 (Winter 1992): 88–106.

17 Manuel G. Serapio and Donald H. Dalton, "Globalization of Industrial R&D: An Examination of Foreign Direct Investments in R&D in the United States," *Research Policy,* no. 28 (1999): 303–16.

18 Ronald Berenbeim, "The Search for Global Ethics," *Vital Speeches of the Day* 65, no. 6 (January 1, 1999): 177–78.

19 S. Prakash Sethi, "Standards for Corporate Conduct in the International Arena: Challenges and Opportunities for Multinational Corporations," *Business and Society Review* 107, no. 1 (Spring 2002): 20–39.

20 "The Ethics of Business," in "A Survey of Corporate Social Responsibility," *The Economist* (January 22, 2005): 20.

21 David J. Vidal, *The Link Between Corporate Citizenship and Financial Performance* (New York: Conference Board, 1999).

22　Interfaith Center on Corporate Responsibility, http://www.iccr.org/.

23　Elizabeth Wine, "Ethical Crusaders Resolve to Redeem the Corporate Sinners," *Financial Times* (March 30–31, 2002): 24.

24　See "Indonesia's Plague," *Far Eastern Economic Review* 164, no. 27 (July 12, 2001): 8; and John Danley, "Balancing Risks: Mosquitos, Malaria, Morality, and DDT," *Business and Society Review* 107, no. 1 (Spring 2002): 145–70.

25　See Pirkko Lammi, "My Vision of Business in Europe," in Jack Mahoney and Elizabeth Vallance (eds.), *Business Ethics in a New Europe* (Dordrecht, Netherlands: Kluwer Academic, 1992), 11–12; and Andrew Jack, "French Prepare to Repel English Advance," *Financial Times* (January 7, 1997): 2.

26　Alfred Marcus, *Business & Society: Ethics, Government, and the World Economy* (Homewood, IL: Irwin, 1996).

27　John R. Boatright, *Ethics and the Conduct of Business* (Upper Saddle River, NJ: Prentice Hall, 1993), 13–16.

28　Ibid., 16–18.

29　"The Short Arm of the Law—Bribery and Business," *The Economist* (March 2, 2002): 78.

30　See The World Bank, *World Development Report 2002: Building Institutions for Markets*, and M. Habib and L. Zurawicki (2001), "Country-Level Investments and the Effect of Corruption—Some Empirical Evidence," *International Business Review*, 10 (6), 687–700.

31　See Jack G. Kaikati, et al., "The Price of International Business Morality: Twenty Years Under the Foreign Corrupt Practices Act," *Journal of Business Ethics* 26 (August 2000): 213–23; and Macleans A. Geo Ja-Ja and Garth L. Mangum, "The Foreign Corrupt Practices Act's Consequences for U.S. Trade: The Nigerian Example," *Journal of Business Ethics* 24 (April 2000): 245–56.

32　"The Short Arm of the Law," *The Economist*, op. cit.

33　Nelson Antosh, "Baker Hughes Offers to Settle Bribe Charge," *Houston Chronicle* (July 7, 2001): C1.

34　Ken Brown and Gee L. Lee, "Lucent Fires Top China Executives," *The Wall Street Journal Online* (April 7, 2004). Accessed on April 7, 2004.

35　OECD, "The OECD Anti-Bribery Convention: Does It Work?" (January 28, 2005), http://www.oecd.org/document/21/0,2340, en_2649_34859_2017813_1_1_1_1,00.html, accessed April 23, 2005.

36　OECD, "Steps Taken and Planned Future Actions by Participating Countries to Ratify and Implement the Convention of Combating Bribery of Foreign Public Officials in International Business Transactions" (March 10, 2005), http://www.oecd.org/topic/0,2686, en_2649_37447_1_1_1_1_37447,00.html. Accessed on April 23, 2005.

37　International Chamber of Commerce, "Extortion and Bribery in International Business Transactions," 1999 Revised Version, http://www.iccwbo.org/home/statements_rules/rules/1999/briberydoc99.asp. Accessed on April 23, 2005.

38　Glenn R. Simpson, "Multinational Companies Unite to Fight Bribery," *Wall Street Journal* (January 27, 2005): http://online.wsj.com.

39　*Fighting Global Corruption: Business Risk Management* (May 2001). U.S. Department of State, Washington, D.C., pp. 4–7. Available online at the following site: http://www.tcc.mac.doc.gov/pdf/3219.pdf. Accessed on April 23, 2005.

40　David Rudnick, "Pay Up, Pay Up and Play the Game," *Daily Telegraph*, London (July 12, 2001): 72.

41　Nancy Dunne, "Bribery Helps Win Contracts in Developing World," *Financial Times* (January 21, 2000): 6. Dunne refers to a Gallup Poll survey of almost 800 executives.

42　Michael Peel, "Spotlight on Multinationals' Africa Links: A US Senate Report Claims Oil Companies Have Contributed to the Corruption in Equatorial Guinea," *Financial Times* (September 24, 2004).

43　Peel, op. cit.

44　"Mexico Asks IBM for Proof of Alleged Bribe Request," *Wall Street Journal* (February 8, 1993). For the means-versus-end discussion, see Kent Hodgson, "Adapting Ethical Decisions to a Global Marketplace," *Management Review* (May 1992): 53–57.

45　Dana Milbank and Marcus W. Brauchli, "Greasing Wheels," *Wall Street Journal* (September 29, 1995).

46　Jonathan Karp and Any Pasztor, "Titan Agrees to Record Payment to Settle Foreign-Bribery Case," *Wall Street Journal* (March 2, 2005): A3.

47　Peter Fritsch and Timothy Mapes, "In Indonesia, a Tangle of Bribes Creates Trouble for Monsanto," *Wall Street Journal* (April 5, 2005): A1.

48　See http://www.afsc.org/trade-matters/learn-about/glossary.htm, http://en.wikipedia.org/wiki/Sustainability.

49　John Carey, "Global Warming," *Business Week* (August 16, 2004): 60–69.

50　"Hotting Up," *The Economist* (February 5, 2005): 73–74.

51　http://unfccc.int/essential_background/kyoto_protocol/status_of_ratification/items/2613.php. Accessed April 23, 2005.

52 Alison Graab, "Greenhouse Gas Market to Slow Global Warming," CNN.com. Accessed April 12, 2005.

53 Roy Spencer, "World Warms to Kyoto, but Research Will Save the Day," *USA Today* (February 17, 2005): 11A.

54 Mark Lander, "Mixed Feelings as Kyoto Pact Takes Effect," *The New York Times* (February 16, 2005).

55 Ibid.

56 John Carey, op. cit., 62.

57 "Amazon Fires Alter Climate, Rainforest," CNN.com (July 30, 2004).

58 "Greenpeace: Brazil Rainforest Destruction a National Shame," CNN.com (May 19, 2005).

59 Ibid.

60 GlaxoSmithKline 2004 Annual Report, various pages. http://www.gsk.com/index.htm.

61 Miriam Jorda, "Brazil to Stir Up AIDS-Drug Battle," *The Wall Street Journal* (September 5, 2003): A3.

62 Frederik Balfour, "Fakes!" *Business Week* (February 7, 2005): 56.

63 Manjeet Kripalani, "India: Copycats No More," *Business Week* (April 18, 2005): 51.

64 Marilyn Chase, "Malaria Trial Could Set a Model for Financing of Costly Vaccines," *The Wall Street Journal* (April 26, 2005): A1.

65 "Gates Foundation Backs Anti-Malaria Push," CNN.com, May 19, 2005. http://edition.cnn.com/2005/WORLD/africa/05/19/gates.zambia.ap/. Accessed May 20, 2005.

66 Frances Williams, "Economic Case Made for Ending Child Labour," *Financial Times* (February 4, 2004): 5.

67 Ans Kolk and Rob van Tulder, "Child Labor and Multinational Conduct: A Comparison of International Business and Stakeholder Codes," *Journal of Business Ethics* (March 2002).

68 Edward Luce, "Ikea's Grown-Up Plan to Tackle Child Labour," *Financial Times* (September 15, 2004): 7.

69 Kolk, op. cit.

70 Luce, op. cit.

71 Michael Skapinker, "Cost Cuts and False Economics," *Financial Times* (November 24, 2003): 5.

72 A. Kolk, R. van Tinder, and I. Sloekers, "International Codes of Conduct and Corporate Social Responsibility: Can Transnational Corporations Regulate Themselves?" *Transnational Corporations* 8 (2001): 11.143-180.

73 GlaxoSmithKline, http://www.gsk.com/corporate_responsibility/cr_report_2004/se_code_conduct.htm. Accessed April 28, 2005.

74 GlaxoSmithKline, http://www.gsk.com/corporate_responsibility/cr_report_2004/index.htm. Accessed April 28. 2005.

75 Amy Merrick, "Gap Offers Unusual Look at Factory Conditions," *The Wall Street Journal* (May 12, 2004): A1.

76 "Syngenta Opens Up to Independent Scrutiny," *Financial Times* (May 12, 2004): 8.

77 Sarah Murray and Alison Matiland, "The Trouble with Transparent Clothing," *Financial Times* (May 12, 2004): 8.

78 Data for this case were taken from: Mark Schoofs, "Anglo American Drops Noted Plan on AIDS Drugs," *Wall Street Journal* (April 16, 2002): A19; World Health Organization/AFRO, "Southern African Health Challenges Intensify," Press Release (September 13, 2004): 1–2; Mark Schoofs, "New Challenges in Fighting AIDS—Enlisting Multinationals in Battle," *Wall Street Journal* (November 30, 2001): B1; "AIDS in the Workplace," *Business Africa* 10, no. 13 (July 1, 2001): 1–2; "The Corporate Response," *Business Africa* 10, no. 16 (September 1, 2001): 4; Mark Schoofs, "South Africa Reverses Course on AIDS Drugs," *Wall Street Journal* (November 20, 2003): B1; "Anglo American to Provide HIV/AIDS Help for Workers," *American Metal Market* (August 7, 2002): 4; Bruce Einhorn and Catherine Arnst, "Why Business Should Make AIDS Its Business—Multinationals Are Taking Baby Steps to Control the Disease in Their Workforce," *Business Week* (August 9, 2004): 83; "Digging Deep," *The Economist* 364, no. 8285 (August 10, 2002): 55; James Lamont, "Anglo's Initiative," *Financial Times* (August 8, 2002): 10; "Anglo American to Give Mineworkers AIDS Drugs Free," *Wall Street Journal* (August 7, 2002): A13; Matthew Newmann, Scott Hensley, and Scott Miller, "U.S. Reaches Patent Compromise to Provide Drugs to Poor Nations," *Wall Street Journal* (August 28, 2003): A3; Statistics South Africa, "Labour Statistics Survey of Average Monthly Earnings," Statistical Release P0272 (February 2002): 3; UNAIDS, UNICEF, WHO, "South Africa—Epidemiological Fact Sheets," *Treat 3 Million by 2005* (2004); "Safety, Health, and Environment Report 2001," Anglo American PLC (2001): 15; "Report to Society 2002," Anglo American PLC (2002): 4–6, 33; "Annual Report 2002," Anglo American PLC (2002): 30–36; http://www2.coca-cola.com/citizenship/africa_employee_program.html; http://www.angloamerican.co.uk/about/businesses.asp; http://galenet.galegroup.com.erl.lib.byu.edu/servlet/BCRC?vrsn=137&locID=byu_main&srchtp=glbc&cc=1&c=2&mode=c&ste=74&tbst=tsCM&tab=4&ccmp=Anglo+American+PLC&mst=Anglo+American+

PLc&n=25&docNum=I2501307472&bConts=4911; Integrated Regional Information Network (IRIN), "South Africa—Antiretroviral Therapy Is Cost-Effective, Says Report," News Report (September 15, 2004); Integrated Regional Information Network (IRIN), "Africa—Greater Commitment, More Funding Urged for Treatment," News Report (September 21, 2004); http://www.cia.gov/cia/publications/factbook/geos/sf.html#people; http://www.cia.gov/cia/publications/factbook/geos/pl.html; "South Africa AIDS/HIV Statistics, http://www.avert.org/safricastats.htm, accessed May 20, 2005.

1800s–1960

In the latter part of the 1800s, most countries adopted policies whereby goods, capital, and people could move fairly freely from one country to another. At the same time, governments interfered minimally to support particular industries. The result was that individual producers determined what and where to produce. Under this regime, trade flourished and countries specialized in selling what they could produce best. Most Latin American countries specialized in the production of a single or a few commodities (raw materials or agricultural products), which they exported in exchange for other commodities and manufactured goods. Costa Rica was no exception, and it followed this regime until the early 1960s. Its farmers specialized first in coffee and later, as well, in bananas after the development of refrigerated ships. For most of the period, this regime promoted economic development for Costa Rica because commodity prices, especially coffee prices, were high. However, the accumulation of several experiences convinced Costa Rican leaders to enact government programs to diversify production and become more self-sufficient. These included its trade disruptions during two world wars, the lowering of coffee and banana prices relative to prices of manufactured products as new commodity production (especially in African countries) competed in world markets, and a realization that Latin American countries with less open international markets had insulated themselves more from adverse international conditions. As a result, Costa Rica turned to import substitution.

1960–1982

Import substitution is a policy of developing industries to make products that would otherwise be imported. Costa Rican authorities reasoned that if they limited imports, such as by taxing them heavily, both Costa Rican and foreign investors would have an incentive to produce more things within Costa Rica for Costa Rican consumers. At the same time authorities realized that Costa Rica's market was too small to support investments requiring large-scale production. To help mitigate this problem, Costa Rica joined four other countries (El Salvador, Guatemala, Honduras, and Nicaragua) in forming the Central American Common Market (CACM) to allow goods produced in any member country to enter freely into the other member countries. Thus, a company might be more willing to invest to serve a five-country market than simply a one-country market.

The results of import substitution policies were mixed. Costa Rica did diversify its economy by becoming less dependent on agriculture (25.2 percent of GDP in 1960 versus 18 percent in 1980); however, the shift was even greater in the 1950–1960 period—from 40.9 percent of GDP to 25.2 percent when the government interfered little to transform the economy. Some foreign investment did enter in the manufacturing area, but mainly just to serve the Costa Rican, rather than the entire CACM market. For example, there was considerable import substitution in the pharmaceutical industry where small-scale packaging and processing is efficient. Simply, neither local nor foreign investors were convinced that the CACM would be an enduring arrangement. Their skepticism was well founded. By the late 1970s the CACM was effectively inoperative. Civil wars in both El Salvador and Guatemala stifled those economies, Nicaragua became ideologically committed to governmental control over all aspects of its economy including trade, and El Salvador and Honduras fought a brief but consequential war.

In some cases, import substitution also led to increases in exports, like Costa Rican processing of such traditional exports as coffee and cotton seeds for both local and export markets. Nevertheless, economists grew concerned that the policies to protect local production (price controls, import prohibitions, and subsidies) were shifting Costa Rican resources away from those products that it could produce most efficiently. For example, Costa Rica became nearly self-sufficient in rice production during this period, but only because governmental policies kept lower-cost foreign-produced rice from entering the market. At the same time, Costa Rica placed controls on consumer prices of rice. Meanwhile, efficient industries could not expand fully because they had to pay more taxes to support subsidies going to inefficient producers. Further, higher consumer prices on many products gave people less disposable income. Given the concerns, Costa Rican policymakers reasoned that the country must emphasize production of goods that could be competitive in international markets. These policymakers were also influenced by the fact that some Asian countries had achieved recent rapid growth by being competitive internationally. Thus, Costa Rica shifted to an export promotion policy in 1983.

1983–EARLY 1990s

Costa Rica began removing import barriers so that only internationally competitive companies and industries would likely survive. For example, Costa Rican imports of rice increased substantially as the government decreased protection of domestic production. Policymakers also reasoned that the country would need outside capital and expertise to transform the economy. At about the same time the United States established the Caribbean Basin Initiative, whereby products originating from the Caribbean region (including Costa Rica) could enter the United States at a lower tariff (import tax) than products originating elsewhere. To capitalize on the new opportunity to export to the United States, Costa Rica formed CINDE, a private organization funded by the Costa Rican government and grants by the U.S. government. The purpose of CINDE was to develop the economy, and one of its top priorities was to attract foreign direct investment. To augment CINDE's work, Costa Rica established an Export Processing Zone (EPZ) that allowed companies (as long as they were exporting their finished output) to import all their inputs and equipment tax free, to avoid paying Costa Rican income tax for eight years, and to pay only 50 percent of the income tax rate for the next four years. By 1989, 35 companies had located in the EPZ. These were mainly textile and footwear producers that sought Costa Rica's pool of inexpensive labor. However, by this time CINDE officials worried about two factors—(1) that Costa Rica could not remain cost competitive in the type of products exported from the EPZ because other countries (mainly Mexico) were gaining even lower tariffs into the United States, and (2) that Costa Rica's highly skilled and educated workforce was not being utilized to its best advantage by being employed in the types of industries that had been attracted to the EPZ. Thus, CINDE officials decided they should work closely with the Costa Rican government to identify and attract specific types of investors that were a better match with Costa Rican resources.

EARLY 1990s–PRESENT TIME

The identification and development of target industries to be competitive internationally is a **strategic trade policy.** Among the industries that Costa Rica chose were the electronics and software industries, ones that could pay higher wages and salaries than most of those that had invested in the EPZ and ones deemed to have high future growth. Costa Rican officials also noted the characteristics of developing countries that had been attracting large amounts of electronics and software investment and concluded that Costa Rica should be able to compete. These characteristics included a highly educated workforce (especially availability of engineers and technical operators), political and social stability, relatively high levels of economic freedom, large numbers of English-speaking workers, and a quality of life that would appeal to the managers and technical personnel that foreign investors would bring in to work in the facilities.

CINDE also hired the Foreign Investment Advisory Service (FIAS) of the International Finance Corporation and World Bank to make recommendations as to the feasibility of attracting companies in this industry and on how best to attract them. FIAS concluded that attraction was feasible and suggested areas within the industry, such as power technologies, that best fit with Costa Rica's main advantage, namely, a well-educated labor force in relation to its cost. It also suggested that Costa Rica target industries that support the electronics and computer industries, such as plastics and metalworking. In addition, FIAS noted areas that Costa Rica needed to improve, such as protection of intellectual property rights and English proficiency of technicians and engineers. Costa Rica set out to make these improvements and has also changed the curriculum in its school for mid-level technicians, encouraged more airlines to use the national airport, and set up Spanish language training for foreign personnel brought in by investors.

Costa Rica has attracted such high-tech investors as Reliability, Protek, Colorplast, and Sensortronics. By far the largest foreign investment has been by Intel, which accounted for almost 40 percent of Costa Rica's exports in 1999. To help attract the Intel investment, CINDE officials anticipated all the questions and concerns Intel managers might have so that they were able to respond quickly and knowledgeably. They involved top governmental and company leaders in meetings with Intel managers; the country's president, José Figueres, even piloted the group in a helicopter to see plant sites.

After the success in attracting electronics and software investment, Costa Rica has turned to medical devices. It has attracted large investments by such companies as Abbott Laboratories, Baxter, and Procter and Gamble. Although Costa Rican exports of coffee and bananas are still important, high-tech manufactured products are now the backbone of Costa Rica's economy and export earnings.

INTRODUCTION

Trade theory helps managers and government policymakers focus on these questions

- What products should we import and export?
- How much should we trade?
- With whom should we trade?

Some trade theories prescribe that governments should influence trade patterns and others propose a laissez-faire treatment of trade.

The preceding case shows how Costa Rica has used trade and factor mobility policies to help it achieve its economic objectives. Like Costa Rica, other countries wrestle with the questions of what, how much, and with whom their country should import and export. These questions are intertwined with considerations of what they can produce efficiently and if and how they can improve their competitiveness by improving their bases of production factors. Once countries make decisions, officials enact policies to achieve the desired results. These policies have an impact on business because they affect which countries can produce given products more efficiently and whether countries will permit imports to compete against their own domestically produced goods and services. In turn, a country's policies influence which products companies might export to given countries, as well as what and where companies can produce in order to sell in the given countries. Some countries take a more laissez-faire approach, allowing market forces to determine trading relations on the premise that government policies lead to less optimum results for economies. Whether taking interventionist or laissez-faire approaches, countries rely on trade theories to guide policy development. Figure 6.1 shows that trade in goods and services and the movement of production factors are means by which countries are linked internationally.

In this chapter, we'll look first at trade theories that espouse how/whether governments should intervene directly to affect their countries' trade with other countries. In effect, these theories cover opposite ends of the spectrum. At one end are mercantilism and neomercantilism, which prescribe a great deal of government intervention to affect trade. At the other end are free-trade theories (absolute advantage and comparative advantage), which prescribe that governments should not intervene directly to affect trade. From there, we'll examine theories that help explain trade patterns (how much countries depend on trade, what products they trade, and with whom they primarily

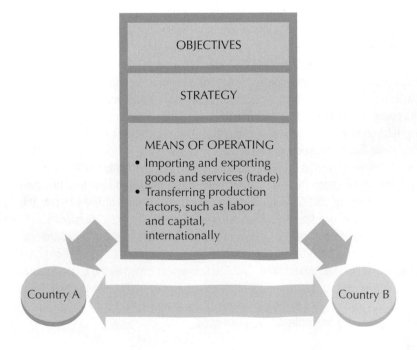

FIGURE 6.1

COMPANIES' INTERNATIONAL OPERATIONS LINK COUNTRIES ECONOMICALLY

To meet their international objectives, companies' strategies require them to trade and transfer means of production internationally, such as between countries A and B in the figure. This trading and transferring links countries economically. This chapter focuses on the linkages.

OBJECTIVES

STRATEGY

MEANS OF OPERATING
- Importing and exporting goods and services (trade)
- Transferring production factors, such as labor and capital, internationally

Country A

Country B

TABLE 6.1 **EMPHASES OF MAJOR THEORIES**

Trade theories have different emphases. Some theories are descriptive whereas others are prescriptive. A check mark indicates that a theory deals with the question for the column, and a dash indicates that it does not. In column 4, the "yes" or "no" answers the question at the head of the column, and a dash indicates that the theory does not address the question.

THEORY	DESCRIPTION OF NATURAL TRADE			PRESCRIPTION OF TRADE RELATIONSHIPS			
	HOW MUCH IS TRADED?	WHAT PRODUCTS ARE TRADED?	WITH WHOM DOES TRADE TAKE PLACE?	SHOULD GOVERNMENT CONTROL TRADE?	HOW MUCH SHOULD BE TRADED?	WHAT PRODUCTS SHOULD BE TRADED?	WITH WHOM SHOULD TRADE TAKE PLACE?
Mercantilism	—	—	—	yes	✓	✓	✓
Neomercantilism	—	—	—	yes	✓	—	—
Absolute advantage	—	✓	—	no	—	✓	—
Comparative advantage	—	✓	—	no	—	✓	—
Country size	✓	✓	—	—	—	—	—
Factor proportion	—	✓	✓	—	—	—	—
Country similarity	—	✓	✓	—	—	—	—
Product life cycle (PLC)	—	✓	✓	—	—	—	—
Porter diamond	—	✓	—	—	—	—	—

trade). These include theories of country size, factor proportions, and country similarity. Then we'll consider theories dealing with the dynamics and stability of countries' ability to be competitive in trading particular products. These theories include the product life cycle theory and the Porter diamond. Since the stability and dynamics of countries' competitive positions depend largely on the quantity and quality of their production factors (land, labor, capital, technology), we'll conclude the chapter with a discussion of factor mobility. Table 6.1 summarizes the major theories and their emphases. A check mark indicates that the theory deals with this question and a dash indicates that it does not. The "yes" and "no" apply only to the question, "Should government control trade?" because the other theories don't deal with the question.

These different theories provide insights about favorable locales for exports as well as potentially successful export products. They also help companies determine where to locate their production facilities because, in the absence of government trade restrictions, exports of given products will move from lower-cost to higher-cost production locations. However, trade restrictions may diminish export capabilities and cause companies to locate some production in the restricting countries. The theories also increase understanding about government trade policies and predict how those policies might affect companies' competitiveness.

INTERVENTIONIST THEORIES

We'll begin our discussion with theories prescribing government intervention because one of these, mercantilism, is the oldest trade theory out of which neomercantilism has more recently emerged. These are not the only reasons for governmental intervention. In fact, the subject is so large, especially protectionism and methods to bring it about, that this is the subject of the next chapter.

Mercantilism

Mercantilism is a trade theory that formed the foundation of economic thought from about 1500 to 1800.[2] Mercantilism held that a country's wealth was measured by its holdings of treasure, which usually meant its gold. According to the theory, countries should

According to mercantilism, countries should export more than they import.

export more than they import and, if successful, receive gold from countries that run deficits. Nation-states were emerging during the period from 1500 to 1800, and gold empowered central governments that invested it in armies and national institutions. These nation-states sought to solidify the people's primary allegiances to the new nation and lessen their bonds to such traditional units as city-states, religions, and guilds. One can see why mercantilism flourished.

To export more than they imported, governments imposed restrictions on most imports, and they subsidized production of many products that could otherwise not compete in domestic or export markets. Some countries used their colonial possessions to support this trade objective. Colonies supplied many commodities that the colonizing country might otherwise have had to purchase from a nonassociated country. Second, the colonial powers sought to run trade surpluses with their own colonies as an additional way to obtain revenue. They did this not only by monopolizing colonial trade but also by preventing the colonies from engaging in manufacturing. The colonies had to export less highly valued raw materials and import more highly valued manufactured products. Mercantilist theory was intended to benefit the colonial powers. The imposition of regulations based on this theory caused much discontent in colonies and was one cause of the American Revolution.

As the influence of the mercantilist philosophy weakened after 1800, the governments of colonial powers seldom aimed directly to limit the development of industrial capabilities within their colonies. However, their home-based companies had technological leadership, ownership of raw material production abroad, and usually some degree of protection from foreign competition. This combination continued to make colonies dependent on raw material production and to tie their trade to their industrialized mother countries. In fact, we still see vestiges of these relationships.

Some terminology of the mercantilist era has endured. A **favorable balance of trade,** for example, still indicates that a country is exporting more than it is importing. An **unfavorable balance of trade** indicates the opposite, which is known as a deficit. Many of these terms are misnomers. For example, the word *favorable* implies "benefit," and the word *unfavorable* suggests "disadvantage." In fact, it is not necessarily beneficial to run a trade surplus nor is it necessarily disadvantageous to run a trade deficit. A country that is running a surplus, or a favorable balance of trade, is, for the time being, importing goods and services of less value than those it is exporting.[3] In the mercantilist period, the difference was made up by a transfer of gold, but today it is made up by holding the deficit country's currency or investments denominated in that currency. In effect, the surplus country is granting credit to the deficit country. If that credit cannot eventually buy sufficient goods and services, the so-called favorable trade balance actually may turn out to be disadvantageous for the country with the surplus.

Running a favorable balance of trade is not necessarily beneficial.

Neomercantilism

Recently, the term **neomercantilism** has emerged to describe the approach of countries that try to run favorable balances of trade in an attempt to achieve some social or political objective. For instance, a country may try to achieve full employment by setting economic policies that encourage its companies to produce in excess of the demand at home and to send the surplus abroad. Or a country may attempt to maintain political influence in an area by sending more merchandise to the area than it receives from it, such as a government granting aid or loans to a foreign government to use for the purchase of the granting country's excess production.

A country that practices neomercantilism attempts to run an export surplus to achieve a social or political objective.

FREE TRADE THEORIES

Thus far, we have intentionally ignored the question of why countries need to trade at all. Why can't Costa Rica (or any other country) be content with the goods and services produced within its own territory? In fact, many countries, following mercantilist policy, did try to become as self-sufficient as possible through local production of goods and services. In this section, we'll discuss two theories supporting *free trade* (absolute advantage and comparative advantage), which hold that nations should neither artificially limit imports nor promote exports.[4] The so-called *invisible hand* will determine which producers survive as consumers buy those products that best serve their needs. Both free trade theories imply specialization. Just as individuals and families produce some things that they exchange for things that others produce, national specialization means producing some things for domestic consumption and export, while using the export earnings to buy imports of products and services produced abroad.

Theory of Absolute Advantage

In 1776, Adam Smith questioned the mercantilists' assumption that a country's wealth depends on its holdings of treasure.[5] Rather, he said, the real wealth of a country consists of the goods and services available to its citizens. Smith developed the theory of **absolute advantage,** which holds that different countries produce some goods more efficiently than other countries; thus, global efficiency can increase through free trade. Based on this theory, he questioned why the citizens of any country should have to buy domestically produced goods when they could buy those goods more cheaply from abroad.

Smith reasoned that if trade were unrestricted, each country would specialize in those products that gave it a competitive advantage. Each country's resources would shift to the efficient industries because the country could not compete in the inefficient ones. Through specialization, countries could increase their efficiency because of three reasons:

- Labor could become more skilled by repeating the same tasks.
- Labor would not lose time in switching from the production of one kind of product to another.
- Long production runs would provide incentives for the development of more effective working methods.

A country could then use its excess specialized production to buy more imports than it could have otherwise produced. But in what products should a country specialize? Although Smith believed the marketplace would make the determination, he thought that a country's advantage would be either *natural* or *acquired.*

Natural Advantage   A country may have a **natural advantage** in producing a product because of climatic conditions, access to certain natural resources, or availability of certain labor forces. The country's climate may dictate, for example, which agricultural products it can produce efficiently. Costa Rica's climate supports the production of coffee, bananas, and pineapples. Climate also is a factor in Costa Rica's export of services because of its eco-tourism industry that attracts foreign tourists to visit its extensive tropical national parks. Costa Rica imports wheat. If it were to increase its production of wheat, for which its climate and terrain are less suited, it would have to use land now devoted to the cultivation of coffee, bananas, or pineapples or to convert some of its national park areas to agricultural production, thus reducing the earnings from these products or services. Conversely, the United States could produce coffee (perhaps in climate-controlled buildings), but at the cost of diverting resources away from products such as wheat, for which its climate and terrain are naturally suited. Trading coffee for wheat and vice versa is a goal more easily achieved than if these two countries were to try to become self-sufficient in the production of both. The more the two countries' climates differ, the more likely they will favor trade with one another.

Most countries must import ores, metals, and fuels from other countries. No one country is large enough or sufficiently rich in natural resources to be independent of the rest of the world except for short periods. Costa Rica, for example, has very few minerals. The United States is self-sufficient in coal, but not in petroleum. Another natural resource

According to Adam Smith, a country's wealth is based on its available goods and services rather than on gold.

✱ Important

Natural advantage considers climate, natural resources, and labor force availability.

is soil, which, when coupled with topography, is an important determinant of the types of products a country can produce most efficiently.

Variations among countries in natural advantages also help to explain in which countries certain manufactured or processed products might be best produced, particularly if by processing an agricultural commodity or natural resource prior to exporting, companies can reduce transportation costs. Processing coffee beans into instant coffee reduces bulk and is likely to reduce transport costs on coffee exports. Producing canned latte could add weight, lessening the industry's internationally competitive edge.

Acquired Advantage   Most of the world's trade today is of services and manufactured goods rather than agricultural goods and natural resources. Countries that produce manufactured goods and services competitively have an **acquired advantage,** usually in either product or process technology. An advantage of product technology is that it enables a country to produce a unique product or one that is easily distinguished from those of competitors. For example, Denmark exports silver tableware, not because there are rich Danish silver mines but because Danish companies have developed distinctive products. An advantage in process technology is a country's ability to produce a homogeneous product (one not easily distinguished from that of competitors) efficiently. For example, Japan has exported steel in spite of having to import iron and coal, the two main ingredients for steel production. A primary reason for Japan's success is that its steel mills encompass new labor-saving and material-saving processes. Thus countries that develop distinctive or less expensive products have acquired advantages, at least until producers in another country emulate them successfully.

Acquired advantage through technology has created new products, displaced old ones, and altered trading-partner relationships. The most obvious examples of change are new products and services, such as computers and software, which make up a large portion of international business. Products that existed in earlier periods have increased their share of world trade because of technological changes in the production process. For example, early hand-tooled automobiles reached only elite markets, but a succession of manufacturing innovations—from assembly lines to robotics—have enabled automobiles to reach an ever-widening mass market. In other cases, companies have developed new uses for old products, such as the use of aloe in sunscreen. Other products have been at least partially displaced by substitutes, such as cotton, wool, and silk by artificial fibers, and hydrogen fuel cell technology may displace much of the world's petroleum trade in the future.

Resource Efficiency Example   We'll demonstrate absolute trade advantage by examining two countries (Costa Rica and the United States) and two commodities (coffee and wheat). Because we are not yet considering the concepts of money and exchange rates, we shall define the cost of production in terms of the resources needed to produce either coffee or wheat. This example is realistic because real income depends on the output of goods compared to the resources used to produce them.

Start with the assumption that Costa Rica and the United States are the only existing countries and that each has the same amount of resources (land, labor, and capital) to produce either coffee or wheat. Using Figure 6.2, let's say that 100 units of resources are available in each country. In Costa Rica, assume that it takes 4 units to produce a ton of coffee and 10 units per ton of wheat. This is shown with the Costa Rican production possibility line, whereby Costa Rica can produce 25 tons of coffee and no wheat, 10 tons of wheat and no coffee, or some combination of the two. In the United States, it takes 20 units per ton of coffee and 5 units per ton of wheat. This is shown in the U.S. production possibility line, whereby the United States can produce 5 tons of coffee and no wheat, 20 tons of wheat and no coffee, or some combination of the two. Costa Rica is more efficient (that is, takes fewer resources to produce a ton) than the

Acquired advantage consists of either product or process technology.

Free trade will bring
- Specialization
- Greater efficiency
- Higher global output

ASSUMPTIONS
for Costa Rica
1. 100 units of resources available
2. 10 units to produce a ton of wheat
3. 4 units to produce a ton of coffee
4. Uses half of total resources per product
   when there is no foreign trade

ASSUMPTIONS
for United States
1. 100 units of resources available
2. 5 units to produce a ton of wheat
3. 20 units to produce a ton of coffee
4. Uses half of total resources per product
   when there is no foreign trade

PRODUCTION	Coffee (tons)	Wheat (tons)
Without Trade:		
Costa Rica (point A)	12½	5
United States (point B)	2½	10
Total	15	15
With Trade:		
Costa Rica (point C)	25	0
United States (point D)	0	20
Total	25	20

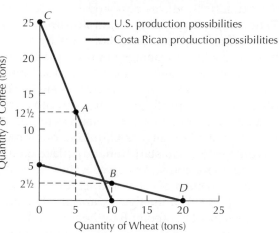

United States in coffee production, and the United States is more efficient than Costa Rica in wheat production.

To demonstrate how production can be increased through specialization and trade, we need first to consider a situation in which the two countries have no foreign trade. We could start from any place on each production possibility line; for convenience, however, we assume that if Costa Rica and the United States each devotes half of its 100 resources or 50 to producing coffee and half or 50 to producing wheat, Costa Rica can produce 12.5 tons of coffee (divide 4 into 50) and 5 tons of wheat (divide 10 into 50). These values are shown as point A in Figure 6.2. The United States can produce 2.5 tons of coffee (divide 20 into 50) and 10 tons of wheat (divide 5 into 50). These are shown as point B in Figure 6.2. Because each country has only 100 units of resources, neither one can increase wheat production without decreasing coffee production, or vice versa. Without trade, the combined production is 15 tons of coffee (12.5 + 2.5) and 15 tons of wheat (5 + 10). If each country specialized in the commodity for which it had an absolute advantage, Costa Rica then could produce 25 tons of coffee and the United States 20 tons of wheat (points C and D in the figure). You can see that specialization increases the production of both products (from 15 to 25 tons of coffee and from 15 to 20 tons of wheat). By trading, global efficiency is optimized, and the two countries can have more coffee and more wheat than they would without trade.

Comparative Advantage

We have just described absolute advantage, which is often confused with and called *comparative advantage*. In 1817, David Ricardo examined the question, "What happens when one country can produce all products at an absolute advantage?" and developed the theory of **comparative advantage**. This theory says that global efficiency gains may still result from trade if a country specializes in those products that it can produce more efficiently than other products—regardless of whether other countries can produce those same products even more efficiently.[6]

An Analogous Explanation   Although this theory may seem initially incongruous, an analogy should clarify its logic. Imagine that the best physician in town also happens to be the best medical secretary. Would it make economic sense for the physician to handle

Gains from trade will occur even in a country that has absolute advantage in all products because the country must give up less efficient output to produce more efficient output.

all the administrative duties of the office? Definitely not. The physician can earn more money by working as a physician, even though that means having to employ a less skilled medical secretary to manage the office. In the same manner, a country will gain if it concentrates its resources on producing the commodities it can produce most efficiently. It will then trade some of those commodities for those commodities it has relinquished. The following discussion clarifies why this theory is true.

Production Possibility Example In this example, assume that the United States is more efficient in producing both coffee and wheat than Costa Rica is. The United States has an absolute advantage in the production of both products. As in the earlier example of absolute advantage, again assume that there are only two countries and each country has a total of 100 units of resources available. In this example, it takes Costa Rica 10 units of resources to produce either a ton of coffee or a ton of wheat, whereas it takes the United States only 5 units of resources to produce a ton of coffee and 4 units to produce a ton of wheat (see Figure 6.3). Like our production possibility example for absolute advantage, we can start from any place on each production possibility line. However, once again for convenience, we assume that if each country uses half (50) of its resources in the production of each product, Costa Rica can produce 5 tons of coffee and 5 tons of wheat (point A in the figure), and the United States can produce 10 tons of coffee and 12.5 tons of wheat (point B in the figure). Without trade, neither country can increase its production of coffee without sacrificing some production of wheat, or vice versa.

Although the United States has an absolute advantage in the production of both coffee and wheat, it has a comparative advantage only in the production of wheat. This is because its advantage in wheat production is comparatively greater than its advantage in coffee production. Thus, by using the same amounts of resources, the United States can produce 2.5 times as much wheat as Costa Rica but only twice as much coffee. Although Costa Rica has an absolute disadvantage in the production of both products, it has a comparative advantage (or less of a comparative disadvantage) in the production of coffee. This is because Costa Rica is half as efficient as the United States in coffee production and only 40 percent as efficient in wheat production.

Without trade, the combined production is 15 tons of coffee (5 in Costa Rica plus 10 in the United States) and 17.5 tons of wheat (5 in Costa Rica plus 12.5 in the United States).

FIGURE 6.3

PRODUCTION POSSIBILITIES WITH COMPARATIVE ADVANTAGE

There are advantages to trade even though one country may have an absolute advantage in the production of all products.

ASSUMPTIONS
for Costa Rica
1. 100 units of resources available
2. 10 units to produce a ton of wheat
3. 10 units to produce a ton of coffee
4. Uses half of total resources per product when there is no foreign trade

ASSUMPTIONS
for United States
1. 100 units of resources available
2. 4 units to produce a ton of wheat
3. 5 units to produce a ton of coffee
4. Uses half of total resources per product when there is no foreign trade

PRODUCTION	Coffee (tons)	Wheat (tons)
Without Trade:		
Costa Rica (point A)	5	5
United States (point B)	10	12½
Total	15	17½
With Trade (increasing coffee production):		
Costa Rica (point C)	10	0
United States (point D)	6	17½
Total	16	17½
With Trade (increasing wheat production):		
Costa Rica (point C)	10	0
United States (point E)	5	18¾
Total	15	18¾

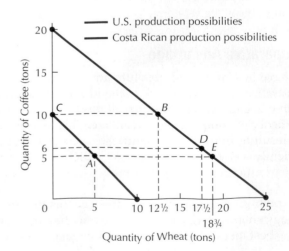

Through trading, the combined production of coffee and wheat within the two countries can be increased. For example, if the combined production of wheat is unchanged from when there was no trade, the United States could produce all 17.5 tons of wheat by using 70 units of resources (17.5 tons times 4 units per ton). The remaining 30 U.S. resource units could be used for producing 6 tons of coffee (30 units divided by 5 units per ton). This production possibility is point D in Figure 6.3. Costa Rica would use all its resources to produce 10 tons of coffee (point C in the figure). The combined wheat production has stayed at 17.5 tons, but the coffee production has increased from 15 tons to 16 tons.

If the combined coffee production is unchanged from the time before trade, Costa Rica could use all its resources to produce coffee, yielding 10 tons (point C in Fig. 6.3). The United States could produce the remaining 5 tons of coffee by using 25 units of resources. The remaining 75 U.S. units could be used to produce 18.75 tons of wheat (75 divided by 4). This production possibility is point E in the figure. Without sacrificing any of the coffee available before trade, wheat production has increased from 17.5 tons to 18.75 tons.

If the United States were to produce somewhere between points D and E in Figure 6.3, both coffee and wheat production would increase over what was possible before trade took place. Whether the production target is an increase of coffee or wheat or a combination of the two, both countries can gain by having Costa Rica trade some of its coffee production to the United States for some of that country's wheat output.

The comparative advantage theory is accepted by most economists and is influential in promoting policies for freer trade. Nevertheless, many government policymakers, journalists, managers, and workers confuse comparative advantage with absolute advantage and do not understand how a country can simultaneously have a comparative *advantage* and absolute *disadvantage* in the production of a given product. This misunderstanding helps to explain why managers face uncertain government trade policies that affect where they choose to locate their production.

Some Assumptions and Limitations of the Theories of Specialization

Both absolute and comparative advantage theories are based on specialization. They hold that output will increase through specialization and that countries will be best off by trading the output from their own specialization for the output from other countries' specialization. However, these theories make assumptions, some of which are not always valid.

Absolute + Comparative theories are based on SPECIALIZATION

Full Employment   The physician–secretary analogy we used earlier assumed that the physician could stay busy full time practicing medicine. If we relax this assumption, then the advantages of specialization are less compelling. The physician might, if unable to stay busy full time with medical duties, perform secretarial work without having to forgo a physician's higher income. The theories of absolute and comparative advantage both assume that resources are fully employed. When countries have many unemployed or unused resources, they may seek to restrict imports to employ or use idle resources.

Full employment is not a valid assumption of absolute and comparative advantage.

Economic Efficiency Objective   The physician–secretary analogy also assumed that the physician who can do both medical and office work is interested primarily in maximization of profit, or maximum economic efficiency. Yet there are a number of reasons why physicians might choose not to work full time at medical tasks. They might find administrative work relaxing and self-fulfilling. They might fear that a hired secretary would be unreliable. They might wish to maintain secretarial skills in the somewhat unlikely event that administration, rather than medicine, commands higher wages in the future. Countries also often pursue objectives other than output efficiency. They may avoid overspecialization because of the vulnerability created by changes in technology and by price fluctuations.

Countries' goals may not be limited to economic efficiency.

Division of Gains   Although specialization brings potential benefits to all countries that trade, the earlier discussion did not indicate how countries will divide increased output. In the case of our wheat and coffee example, if both the United States and Costa Rica receive some share of the increased output, both will be better off economically through specialization and trade. However, many people, including government policymakers, are concerned with relative as well as absolute economic growth, relative meaning in comparison to trading partners. If they perceive that a trading partner is gaining too large a share of benefits, they may forgo absolute gains for themselves so as to prevent relative losses.[7]

Two Countries, Two Commodities   For simplicity's sake, Smith and Ricardo originally assumed a simple world composed of only two countries and two commodities. Our example made the same assumption. Although unrealistic, this assumption does not diminish the theories' usefulness. Economists have applied the same reasoning to demonstrate efficiency advantages in multiproduct and multicountry trade relationships.

Transport Costs   If it costs more to transport the goods than is saved through specialization, then the advantages of trade are negated. In other words, in our example of Costa Rica and the United States, the countries would need to divert workers from coffee or wheat production to ship coffee and wheat between them. However, as long as the diversion reduces output by less than what the two countries gain from specialization, there are still gains from trade.

Statics and Dynamics   The theories of absolute and comparative advantage address countries' advantages by looking at them at one point in time. Thus, the theories view the advantages statically. However, the relative conditions that give countries advantages or disadvantages in the production of given products are dynamic (constantly changing). For example, the resources needed to produce coffee or wheat in either Costa Rica or the United States could change substantially because of advancements in genetically modified crops.[8] Further, our opening case showed how Costa Rica's competitive advantage has improved in the production of high tech. Thus, one should not assume that future absolute or comparative advantages will remain as they are today. We shall return to this theme later in the chapter as we examine theories to explain the dynamics of the location of production and export sources.

Services   The theories of absolute and comparative advantage deal with commodities rather than services. However, an increasing portion of world trade is in services. This fact does not render the theories obsolete, because resources must go into producing services, too. For instance, some services that the United States sells extensively to foreign countries are education (many foreign students attend U.S. universities) as well as credit card systems and collections. However, the United States buys more foreign shipping services than foreigners buy U.S. shipping services. To become more self-sufficient in international shipping, the United States might have to divert resources from its more efficient use in higher education or in the production of competitive products.

Resources are neither as mobile nor as immobile as the theories of absolute and comparative advantage assume.

Mobility   The theories of absolute and comparative advantage assume that resources can move domestically from the production of one good to another—and at no cost. But this assumption is not completely valid. For example, a steelworker in the eastern part of the United States might not move easily into a software development job on the West Coast. That worker probably would have difficulty working in such a different industry and might have trouble moving to a new area. The theories also assume that resources cannot move internationally. Increasingly, however, they do. For example, as many as 300,000 Nicaraguans are now living in Costa Rica, and U.S. companies have transferred both personnel and capital to employ in their Costa Rican investments. The movement of resources such as labor and capital is clearly an alternative to trade, a topic that we'll discuss later in the chapter. However, it is safe to say that resources are more mobile domestically than they are internationally.

THEORIES EXPLAINING TRADE PATTERNS

The free trade theories of absolute and comparative advantage demonstrate how economic growth will occur through specialization and trade; however, they do not deal with issues such as how much a country will depend on trade if it follows a free trade policy, what types of products countries will export and import, and with which partners countries will primarily trade. In this section, we'll discuss the theories that help explain these patterns.

How Much Does a Country Trade?

Although free trade theories deal with specialization, they do not imply that only one country should or will produce a given product or service. To begin with, there are **nontradable goods,** which are products and services that are seldom practical to export, primarily because of high transportation costs, regardless of production cost and efficiency differences among countries. For instance, many services fall into this category, such as haircuts and retail distribution of groceries. Apart from nontradable goods, we find that country size is a factor helping to explain why some countries depend more on trade than others and why some countries account for larger portions of world trade than others.

Theory of Country Size The **theory of country size** holds that large countries usually depend less on trade than small countries. Countries with large land areas are apt to have varied climates and an assortment of natural resources, making them more self-sufficient than smaller countries. Most large countries, such as Brazil, China, India, the United States, and Russia, import much less of their consumption needs and export much less of their production output than do small countries, such as Uruguay, the Netherlands, and Iceland.

Further, transport costs in trade affect large and small countries differently. Normally, the farther the distance, the higher the transport costs. Among countries that border each other, the smaller country tends to depend more on trade than the larger country because of transportation costs. Assume, for example, that the normal maximum distance for transporting a given product is 100 miles because, beyond that distance, prices increase too much. Almost any place in Belgium is within 100 miles of a foreign country; however, this is not true for two of its neighbors, France and Germany. Thus, Belgium's trade involves a higher percentage of its production and consumption than the comparable figures in either France or Germany.

Size of Economy Although land area is the most obvious way of measuring a country's size, countries also can be compared on the basis of economic size. Although percentage of output and consumption are ways of comparing countries, so is the absolute amount of their trade. Table 6.2 shows that of the world's top 10 exporters and importers, all are high-income countries except for China. China, although not a high-income country, has a very large economy by virtue of its large population. In fact, these 10 countries account for over half the world's exports and imports. We'll return momentarily to why these countries are so dominant in world trade, but one reason is that these countries produce so much that there is more to sell—both domestically and internationally. In addition, because these countries produce so much, incomes are high and people buy more—from both domestic and foreign sources. At the same time, little of the trade of low-income countries is with other low-income countries.

What Types of Products Does a Country Trade?

In our discussion of absolute advantage, we indicated that this advantage might be either natural or acquired. In this section, we'll discuss theories that help explain what types of products will result from these natural and acquired advantages. We won't delve again on those factors we've already discussed (climate and natural resources) that give a country a natural advantage; however, we will examine the factor endowment theory of trade. For acquired advantage, we'll discuss the importance of production and product technology.

Bigger countries differ in several ways from smaller countries. They

- Tend to export a smaller portion of output and import a smaller part of consumption
- Have higher transport costs for foreign trade

TABLE 6.2   **LEADING EXPORTERS AND IMPORTERS IN WORLD MERCHANDISE TRADE, 2003 (BILLION DOLLARS AND PERCENTAGE)**

With the exception of China, all top 10 exporters and importers are classified as high-income countries.

RANK	EXPORTERS	VALUE	SHARE OF WORLD TRADE	RANK	IMPORTERS	VALUE	SHARE OF WORLD TRADE
1	Germany	748.3	10.0	1	United States	1303.1	16.8
2	United States	723.8	9.6	2	Germany	601.7	7.7
3	Japan	471.8	6.3	3	China	413.1	5.3
4	China	437.9	5.8	4	United Kingdom	390.8	5.0
5	France	386.7	5.2	5	France	390.5	5.0
6	United Kingdom	304.6	4.1	6	Japan	382.9	4.9
7	Netherlands	294.1	3.9	7	Italy	290.8	3.7
8	Italy	292.1	3.9	8	Netherlands	262.8	3.4
9	Canada	272.7	3.6	9	Canada	245.0	3.2
10	Belgium	255.3	3.4	10	Belgium	235.4	3.0
	Total		55.8		Total		53.0

Source: World Trade Organization, *International Trade Statistics,* 2004 (Geneva: World Trade Organization, 2004), 19.

According to the factor-proportions theory, factors in relative abundance are cheaper than factors in relative scarcity.

Factor-Proportions Theory Eli Heckscher and Bertil Ohlin developed the **factor-proportions theory,** which is based on countries' production factors—land, labor, and capital (funds for investment in plant and equipment). This theory said that differences in countries' endowments of labor compared to their endowments of land or capital explained differences in the cost of production factors. These economists proposed that if labor were abundant in comparison to land and capital, labor costs would be low relative to land and capital costs. If labor were scarce, labor costs would be high in relation to land and capital costs. These relative factor costs would lead countries to excel in the production and export of products that used their abundant—and, therefore, cheaper—production factors.[9]

The factor-proportions theory appears logical. In countries in which there are many people relative to the amount of land—for example, Hong Kong and the Netherlands—land price is very high because it's in demand. Regardless of climate and soil conditions, neither Hong Kong nor the Netherlands excels in the production of goods requiring large amounts of land, such as wool or wheat. Businesses in countries such as Australia and Canada produce these goods because land is abundant compared to the number of people.

Casual observation of manufacturing locations also seems to substantiate the theory. For example, the most successful industries in Hong Kong are those in which technology permits the use of a minimum amount of land relative to the number of people employed: Clothing production occurs in multistory factories where workers share minimal space. Hong Kong does not compete in the production of automobiles, however, which requires much more space per worker.

In countries where there is little capital available for investment and where the amount of investment per worker is low, managers might expect to find cheap labor rates and export competitiveness in products that require large amounts of labor relative to capital. These managers can anticipate the opposite when labor is scarce. For example, Iran (where labor is abundant in comparison to capital) excels in the production of handmade carpets that differ in appearance as well as in production method from the carpets produced in industrial countries by machines purchased with cheap capital.

However, because the factor-proportions theory assumes production factors to be homogeneous, tests to substantiate the theory have been mixed.[10] Labor skills in fact, vary within and among countries because people have different training and education.

Production factors are not homogeneous, especially labor.

Training and education require capital expenditures that do not show up in traditional capital measurements, which include only plant and equipment values. When the factor-proportions theory accounts for different labor groups and the capital invested to train these groups, it seems to explain many trade patterns.[11] For example, because exports from high-income countries embody a higher proportion of professionals such as scientists and engineers than in low-income economies' exports, those countries are using their abundant production factors to maintain their lead in exports. Exports of low-income economies, though, show a high intensity of less skilled labor.[12] This variation in labor skills among countries has led to more international specialization by task to produce a given product. For example, a company may locate its research activities and management functions primarily in countries with a highly educated population, and it may locate its production work in countries where less skilled—and less expensive—workers can be employed.

In the top photo, wheat production is labor intensive in India because of low labor costs in relation to capital costs. The opposite is true for production in Canada, which is shown in the bottom photo.

Production Technology   The factor-proportions analysis becomes more complicated when the same product can be produced by different methods, such as with labor or capital. Thus, production technology helps to explain where products are made. For instance, Canada produces wheat with a capital-intensive method (high expenditure on machinery per worker) because of its abundance of low-cost capital relative to labor. In contrast, India produces wheat by using a much smaller number of machines in comparison to its abundant and cheap labor. In the final analysis, the optimum location of production will depend on comparing the cost in each locale based on the type of production that will minimize costs there.

Large economies are more likely to produce goods that use technologies requiring long production runs. This is because these countries develop industries to serve their large domestic markets, which, in turn, tend to be competitive in export markets.[13] However, companies may locate long production runs in small countries if they expect few barriers in other countries to the export of their output.[14] In industries where long production runs are important for gaining competitive advantages, companies tend to locate their production in few countries, using these locations as sources of exports to other countries. Where long production runs are less important, we find a greater prevalence of multiple production units scattered around the world in different countries so as to minimize the cost of transportation through exporting. In addition, high expenditures on research and development create high fixed costs for companies. Therefore, the technologically intensive company from a small nation may have a more compelling need to sell abroad than would a company with a large domestic market. In turn, this pulls resources from other industries and companies within the company's domestic market, causing more national specialization than in a larger nation.[15]

Product Technology   Figure 6.4 shows the changing composition of world trade. Manufacturing is by far the largest sector, with commercial services the fastest growing sector. Manufacturing is a sector that depends on acquired advantage, largely technology, which depends, in turn, on a large number of highly educated people (especially scientists and engineers) and a large amount of capital to invest in research and development. The high-income countries have an abundance of these features, therefore they are the originators of most new products and most manufacturing output and trade. Lower income countries depend much more on the production of primary products, thus they depend more on natural advantage. Although these primary products may encompass large amounts of process technology, the products themselves involve little change from year to year.

Companies may substitute capital for labor depending on the cost of each.

Bigger countries depend more on products requiring longer production runs.

Most new products originate in high-income countries.

FIGURE 6.4

WORLD TRADE BY MAJOR PRODUCT CATEGORY AS PERCENTAGE OF TOTAL WORLD TRADE FOR SELECTED YEARS

Manufactured products continue to be the largest product category traded (as a percentage of total world trade), but services are the fastest growing category.

Source: From World Trade Organization, *Annual Report,* various years, (Geneva: World Trade Organization).

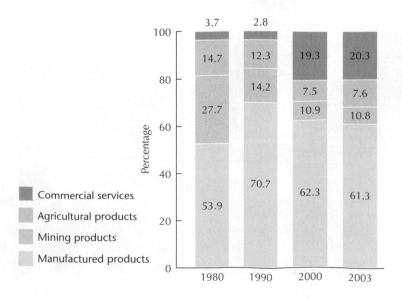

With Whom Do Countries Trade?

We have already discussed the fact that high-income countries account for the bulk of world trade. They also primarily trade with each other, whereas emerging economies mainly export primary products and labor-intensive products to high-income countries in exchange for new and technologically advanced products. In this section we'll discuss the roles of similarity among countries in terms of economic, cultural, and political levels and interests. Then, we'll examine the role that distance plays in the determination of trading partners.

Country-Similarity Theory   Thus far in this chapter, the theories explaining why trade takes place have focused on the differences among countries in terms of natural conditions and factor endowment proportions. At the same time, we showed that most trade takes place among high-income countries, a pattern that can be further explained by the **country-similarity theory.** This theory says that once a company has developed a new product in response to observed market conditions in its home market, it will turn to markets it sees as most similar to those at home.[16]

Markets in high-income countries can support the development and sale both of new products and variations of existing ones. Trade in new products occurs because countries specialize to gain acquired advantage—for example, by apportioning their research efforts more strongly to some sectors than to others. Germany is traditionally strong in machinery and equipment, Switzerland in pharmaceutical products, and Denmark in food products.[17] Trade in differentiated products occurs because companies in different countries differentiate existing products; they may gain some markets abroad, thus creating two-way trade in similar products. For example, the United States is both a major exporter and a major importer of tourist services, vehicles, and passenger aircraft because different companies from different countries have developed product variations that appeal to different consumers. For instance, both Boeing from the United States and Airbus Industrie from Europe produce aircraft that will fly people from point A to point B, but U.S. and European airlines buy both Boeing's and Airbus Industrie's aircraft because their models differ in such features as capacity, flying range, fuel consumption, and perceived reliability. Without trade, some airlines in both the United States and Europe would have to forego buying the aircraft they most want for particular routes.[18] The two companies sell them primarily within their own and each other's markets because these markets have higher economic purchasing power.

Cultural similarity also helps explain much of the direction of trade. Importers and exporters find it easier to do business in a country they perceive as being culturally similar to their home countries, such as because they speak a common language. Likewise, historic colonial relationships explain much of the trade between specific high-income and low-income economies. For instance, the colonial history of France in Africa has given an edge to Air France in serving those former colonies' international air passenger markets.[19] Likewise, much of the lack of extensive trade among nations in the Southern Hemisphere is due to the absence of historic ties. Importers and exporters find it easier to continue business ties than to develop new distribution arrangements in countries in which they are less experienced.

Political relationships and economic agreements among countries may discourage or encourage trade between them or their companies. An example of trade discouragement is the political animosity between the United States and Cuba that has caused mutual trade to be almost nonexistent for the last four decades. The United States replaced Cuban sugar imports with imports from such countries as Mexico and the Dominican Republic. An example of trade encouragement is the agreement among many European countries to remove all trade barriers with each other. This agreement has caused a greater share of the countries' total trade to be conducted within the group.

Distance Among Countries   Although the theories regarding country differences and similarities help to explain broad world trade patterns, such as those that link high-income countries and emerging economies, they are incomplete in explaining specific pairs of trading relationships. Aside from the degree of cultural and political affinity among countries, why will a country buy more from one country than from another?

High-income countries primarily trade with each other because they
- Produce and consume more
- Emphasize technical breakthroughs in different industrial sectors
- Produce differentiated products and services

Trading partners are affected by
- Distance
- Cultural similarity
- Relations between countries

Although there is no single answer to explain all product flows, the geographic distance between two countries accounts for many of these world trade relationships. In essence, greater distances usually mean higher transportation costs, thus Intel's cost to ship semiconductors from Costa Rica to the United States is lower than if it had to bring them from, say, Argentina. For example, Finland is a major exporter to Russia because its transport costs are cheap and fast compared to transport costs to major Russian markets from other countries. Acer, a Taiwanese computer maker, built a plant in Finland to serve Russia because it realized savings by shipping from Finland rather than from Asia and because a Finnish plant provided more secure storage and ease of operations than a Russian one.[20]

But transport cost is not the only factor in trade partner choice. For example, New Zealand competes with Chile, Argentina, and South Africa for out-of-season sales of apples to the Northern Hemisphere—but with a disadvantage in freight costs to the United States and Europe. It has countered this disadvantage by increasing yields, developing new premium varieties, bypassing intermediaries to sell directly to supermarkets abroad, and consolidating efforts through a national marketing board. However, such methods to overcome distance disadvantages are difficult to maintain. For example, both Chinese and Chilean orchardists have smuggled new strains of apple tree cuttings out of New Zealand.[21]

DOES GEOGRAPHY MATTER?

Variety Is the Spice of Life

As you study this chapter, you'll see that geography plays a role in many of the theories and questions concerning trade. We'll pull them together in this discussion.

Part of a country's trading advantage is explained by its natural advantage—climate, terrain, arable land, and natural resources. Thus, Saudi Arabia trades oil, a natural resource, for U.S. rice, which needs huge wet areas for production. However, remember that technology may often negate natural advantage, such as the development of substitutes (synthetic nitrate for natural nitrate) and development of different methods of production (Iceland grows and competes with hothouse-grown tomatoes).

Factor-proportions theory helps to explain where certain goods may be more efficiently produced, such as labor-intensive goods where labor is plentiful in relation to capital and land. Thus Bangladesh excels in the production of clothing requiring lots of labor in relation to either capital or land. However, these factors can change in both quantity and quality. Hong Kong has a very high population density, and it used to excel in production of labor-intensive goods. But as Hong Kong has accumulated capital and upgraded the education of its workforce, its competitive production and exports encompass more capital intensity and more skilled labor.

Usually small countries need to trade more than large countries, primarily because they are apt to have less variety of natural advantages, but there are exceptions. Small countries that also have low incomes tend to depend little on trade because they produce and consume so little. Distance from foreign markets also plays a role. For instance, geographically isolated countries, such as Fiji, trade less than would be expected from their sizes because transportation costs increase the price of traded goods substantially.[22] Conversely, Canada is a large high-income country, whose dependence on and trade per capita are not only among the world's highest, but also much higher than we would expect from the theory of country size. This may be explained largely by Canada's population dispersion. Ninety percent of its population is within a hundred miles of the U.S. border, thus shipping goods between, say, Vancouver and Seattle or Toronto and Cleveland is often more feasible than between Vancouver and Toronto.

Although distance helps us to understand the importance of pairs of trading partners, political relationships and cultural similarity are important factors as well. For example, there is a large amount of trade within regional trading organizations (to be discussed in Chapter 8) and between former colonizers and their former colonies. Of most importance, though, is the preponderance of world trade among high-income countries. These countries produce and consume more. Further, they engage in technological specialization and product differentiations to fit market niches.

THE DYNAMICS OF TRADE

Although we've alluded to the fact that trading patterns change, such as because of political and economic relations among countries and the development of new product capabilities, we'll now discuss two theories, the product life cycle theory and Porter's diamond, that help to explain how countries develop, maintain, and lose their competitive advantages.

Product Life Cycle (PLC) Theory

The international **product life cycle (PLC) theory** of trade states that the location of production of certain kinds of products shifts as they go through their life cycles, which consist of four stages—introduction, growth, maturity, and decline.[23] Table 6.3 highlights the stages.

Changes Through the Cycle Companies develop new products because there is an observed need and market for them nearby. This means that a U.S. company is most apt to develop a new product for the U.S. market, a French company for the French market, and so on. At the same time, almost all new technology that results in new products and production methods originates in high-income countries.[24] They have most of the resources to develop new products and most of the income to buy them.

Once a company has created a new product, theoretically it can manufacture that product anywhere in the world. In practice, however, the early production (*introductory stage*) generally occurs in a domestic location so that the company can obtain rapid market feedback as well as save on transport costs. At this stage, companies may sell a small part of their production to customers in foreign markets, mainly in other high-income countries, because those customers have incomes to spend on newer products.

According to the PLC theory of trade, the production location for many products moves from one country to another depending on the stage in the product's life cycle.

The introduction stage is marked by

- Innovation in response to observed need
- Exporting by the innovative country
- Evolving product characteristics

TABLE 6.3 **INTERNATIONAL CHANGES DURING A PRODUCT'S LIFE CYCLE**

Overall, production and sales shift from industrial countries to emerging economies during a product's life cycle.

	LIFE CYCLE STAGE			
	1: INTRODUCTION	**2: GROWTH**	**3: MATURITY**	**4: DECLINE**
Production location	• In innovating (usually industrial) country	• In innovating and other industrial countries	• Multiple countries	• Mainly in developing countries
Market location	• Mainly in innovating country, with some exports	• Mainly in industrial countries • Shift in export markets as foreign production replaces exports in some markets	• Growth in developing countries • Some decrease in industrial countries	• Mainly in developing countries • Some developing country exports
Competitive factors	• Near-monopoly position • Sales based on uniqueness rather than price • Evolving product characteristics	• Fast-growing demand • Number of competitors increases • Some competitors begin price-cutting • Product becoming more standardized	• Overall stabilized demand • Number of competitors decreases • Price is very important, especially in developing countries	• Overall declining demand • Price is key weapon • Number of producers continues to decline
Production technology	• Short production runs • Evolving methods to coincide with product evolution • High labor input and labor skills relative to capital input	• Capital input increases • Methods more standardized	• Long production runs using high capital inputs • Highly standardized • Less labor skill needed	• Unskilled labor on mechanized long production runs

The production process is apt to be more labor-intensive in the introductory stage than in later stages. Because the product is not yet standardized, its production process must permit rapid changes in product characteristics, as market feedback dictates. This implies high labor input as opposed to more capital-intensive automated production. Further, the capital machinery necessary to produce a product on a large scale usually develops later than product technology, only when sales begin to expand rapidly enough to warrant the high development costs of the machines for the new process. Although the early production is most apt to occur in high-income countries, which have high labor rates, this labor tends to be highly educated and skilled so that it is adept and efficient when production is not yet standardized. Even if production costs are high because of expensive labor, companies can often pass costs onto consumers who are unwilling to wait for possible price reductions later.

As sales of the new product grow (*Stage 2, growth*), competitors enter the market and demand grows substantially in foreign markets, particularly in other high-income countries. In fact, this demand may justify producing in some foreign countries to reduce or eliminate transport charges, but the sales at this stage are likely to stay almost entirely in the countries producing the product. Let's say, for example, that the innovator is in the United States and the additional manufacturing unit is in Japan. The producers in Japan will sell mainly in Japan for several reasons:

1. There is increased demand in the Japanese market for the product.
2. Producers need to introduce unique product variations for Japanese consumers.
3. Japanese costs may still be high because of production start-up problems.

Because sales are growing rapidly at home and abroad, there are incentives for companies to develop process technology. However, product technology may not yet be well developed because of the number of product variations introduced by competitors that are also trying to gain market share. So the production process may still be labor intensive during this stage, although it is becoming less so. The original producing country will increase its exports in this stage but lose certain key export markets in which local production commences.

In Stage 3, *maturity*, worldwide demand begins to level off, although it may be growing in some countries and declining in others. There often is a shakeout of producers such that product models become highly standardized, making cost an important competitive weapon. Longer production runs become possible for foreign plants, which, in turn, reduce per unit cost, thus creating more demand in emerging economies. Because markets and technologies are widespread, the innovating country no longer commands a production advantage. Producers have incentives to shift production to emerging economies where they can employ unskilled, inexpensive labor efficiently for standardized (capital-intensive) production. Exports decrease from the innovating country as foreign production displaces it.

As a product moves to Stage 4, *decline*, those factors occurring during the mature stage continue to evolve. The markets in high-income countries decline more rapidly than those in low-income economies as affluent customers demand ever-newer products. By this time, market and cost factors have dictated that almost all production is in emerging economies, which export to the declining or small-niche markets in high-income countries. In other words, the country in which the innovation first emerged—and exported from—then becomes the importer.

Verification and Limitations of PLC Theory   The PLC theory holds that the location of production facilities that serve world markets shifts as products move through their life cycle. Such products as ballpoint pens and hand calculators have followed this pattern. They were first produced in a single industrial country and sold at a high price. Then production shifted to multiple industrial country locations to serve those local markets. Finally, most production is located in low-income countries, and prices have declined.

Growth is characterized by

- Increases in exports by the innovating country
- More competition
- Increased capital intensity
- Some foreign production

Maturity is characterized by

- A decline in exports from the innovating country
- More product standardization
- More capital intensity
- Increased competitiveness of price
- Production start-ups in emerging economies

Decline is characterized by

- A concentration of production in developing countries
- An innovating country becoming a net importer

However, if transportation costs are very high, there is little opportunity for export sales, regardless of the stage in the life cycle. Additionally, there are many types of products for which shifts in production location do not usually take place. In these cases, the innovating country maintains its export ability throughout the product's life cycle. These exceptions include:

1. Products that, because of very rapid innovation, have extremely short life cycles, a factor that makes it impossible to achieve cost reductions by moving production from one country to another. For example, product obsolescence occurs so rapidly for many electronic products that there is little international diffusion of production.

2. Luxury products for which cost is of little concern to the consumer.

3. Products for which a company can use a differentiation strategy, perhaps through advertising, to maintain consumer demand without competing on the basis of price.

4. Products that require specialized technical labor to evolve into their next generation. This seems to explain the long-term U.S. dominance of medical equipment production and German dominance in rotary printing presses.[25]

Regardless of the product type, there has been an increased tendency on the part of MNEs to introduce new products at home and abroad almost simultaneously. In other words, instead of merely observing needs within their domestic markets, companies develop products and services for observable market segments that transcend national borders. In so doing, they eliminate delays as a product is diffused from one country to another, and they choose a production location that will minimize costs for serving markets in multiple countries. This production location may or may not be in the innovating company's home market.

> Not all products conform to the dynamics of the PLC.

The Porter Diamond

Why do specialized competitive advantages differ among countries—for example, why do Italian companies have an advantage in the ceramic tile industry and Swiss companies have one in the watch industry? The **Porter diamond** is a theory showing four conditions as important for competitive superiority: demand conditions; factor conditions; related and supporting industries; and firm strategy, structure, and rivalry. We have already discussed all four of these conditions in the context of other trade theories, but how they combine affects the development and continued existence of competitive advantages. The framework of the theory is, therefore, a useful tool for understanding how and where globally competitive companies develop and sustain themselves. Usually, but not always, all four conditions need to be favorable for an industry within a country to attain global supremacy.

> According to the Porter diamond theory, companies' development of internationally competitive products depends on their domestic
>
> • Demand conditions
> • Factor conditions
> • Related and supporting industries
> • Firm strategy, structure, and rivalry

Explanation of the Porter Diamond   Both PLC theory and country-similarity theory show that new products (or industries) usually arise from companies' observation of need or demand, which is usually in their home country. *Demand conditions* are the first condition in the theory. Companies then start up production near the observed market. This was the case for the Italian ceramic tile industry after World War II: There was a postwar housing boom, and consumers wanted cool floors because of the hot Italian climate. The second condition of the Porter diamond—*factor conditions* (recall natural advantage within absolute advantage theory and the factor-proportions theory)—influenced both the choice of tile to meet consumer demand and the choice of Italy as the production location. Wood was less available and more expensive than tile, and most production factors (skilled labor, capital, technology, and equipment) were available within Italy on favorable terms. The third condition—the existence of nearby *related and supporting industries* (enamels and glazes)—was also favorable. (Recall discussions of the importance of transport costs in the theory of country size, in assumptions of specialization, and in the limitation factors of PLC theory.)

The combination of three conditions—demand, factor conditions, and related and supporting industries—influenced companies' decisions to initiate production of ceramic tiles in postwar Italy. The ability of these companies to develop and sustain a competitive advantage required favorable circumstances for the fourth condition— *firm strategy, structure,* and *rivalry.* Barriers to market entry were low in the tile industry (some companies started up with as few as three employees), and hundreds of companies initiated production. Rivalry became intense as companies tried to serve increasingly sophisticated Italian consumers. These circumstances forced breakthroughs in both product and process technologies, which gave the Italian producers advantages over foreign producers and enabled them to gain the largest global share of tile exports.

Limitations of the Porter Diamond   The existence of the four favorable conditions does not guarantee that an industry will develop in a given locale. Entrepreneurs may face favorable conditions for many different lines of business. In fact, comparative advantage theory holds that resource limitations may cause companies in a country to avoid competing in some industries even though an absolute advantage may exist. For example, conditions in Switzerland would seem to have favored success if companies in that country had become players in the personal computer industry. However, Swiss companies preferred to protect their global positions in such product lines as watches and scientific instruments rather than to downsize those industries by moving their highly skilled people into a new industry.

A second limitation of the diamond concerns the increased ability of companies to attain market information, production factors, and supplies from abroad. At the same time, they face more competition from foreign production and foreign companies. The absence of any of the four conditions from the diamond domestically, therefore, may not inhibit companies and industries from becoming globally competitive. First, take the existence of demand conditions. Observations of foreign, rather than domestic, demand conditions have spurred much of the recent growth in Asian exports. In fact, such Japanese companies as Uniden and Fujitech target their sales almost entirely to foreign markets.[26] Second, domestic factor conditions can change. For example, capital and managers are now internationally mobile. Third, if related and supporting industries are not available locally, materials and components are now more easily brought in from abroad because of advancements in transportation and the relaxation of import restrictions. In fact, many MNEs now assemble products with parts supplied from a variety of countries. Finally, companies react not only to domestic rivals but also to foreign-based rivals with which they compete at home and abroad.

Using the Diamond for Transformation   In our opening case, Costa Rica transformed its economy from primary dependence on tropical agricultural products to high tech products by heeding the four conditions of the diamond. This transformation could not have occurred had Costa Rica looked only at what was available within its boundaries. Instead, it looked globally. There was and still is very little demand within Costa Rica for the high tech products, such as microchips, that it is now producing, but good transportation allows their distribution through exportation. Costa Rica initially lacked fulfillment of the factor conditions, especially the trained personnel, but it altered its educational system to tailor human resource development to the production needs and it allowed companies to bring in foreign technicians to fill human resource gaps. Likewise, it developed local supplies, such as additional power and metalworking supplies, and it attracted sufficient numbers of high tech companies so that their combined presence assured a vibrant competitive environment. Thus, understanding and having the necessary conditions to be globally competitive is important, but these conditions are neither static nor purely domestic.

POINT–COUNTERPOINT: SHOULD COUNTRIES FOLLOW STRATEGIC TRADE POLICIES?

POINT

Given the importance of acquired advantage in world trade, I think a country must develop and maintain industries that will not only be competitive but also grow and earn sufficient revenues so that its domestic economy will perform as well as the economies in other countries. At the same time, government influence is seldom neutral, so even though government decisions and policies may not seek to affect specific industries in world trade, they nevertheless have that effect. For example, U.S. government efforts to improve agricultural productivity and defense capabilities have undoubtedly helped make U.S. exports of farm and aerospace products very competitive. Further, a government's decision to help certain industries may hurt others. For example, European airlines have argued that their governments' support for high-speed rail traffic in Europe has hurt their ability to be competitive on international routes with U.S. air carriers, which profit from not having to compete much with railroads for passenger traffic in the United States. Thus, since governments will always affect industries diversely, why not concentrate on helping those that will give them the best competitive and economic advantage?

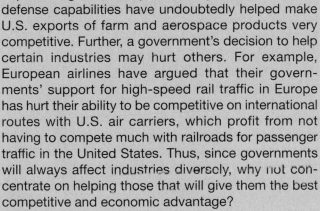

Targeting growth industries is particularly important for emerging economies. Take the Costa Rican example in the opening case. Had it not been for the country's decision to emphasize electronics and software, much more of the economy would still be depending more on coffee and bananas, for which earnings are not likely to increase as much. To make this transformation, the Costa Rican government was active rather than passive. It actively sought investments in that area, changed its educational curriculum, and agreed to build an electrical substation for Intel's use. The plan worked. Costa Rica is now dependent on skill-intensive manufactured goods that earn much more than either agriculture or manufacturing that uses unskilled labor-intensive production methods.

There are other success stories as well. For instance, Singapore successfully attracted companies that were involved in mature consumer electronics production and was able to compete globally because of its low wages in comparison to its productivity. As Singapore has become more economically developed, it has targeted and is now attracting more research and development facilities for new products with higher profit margins.[27] The Indian Ocean country of Mauritius successfully targeted textile manufacturing and a variety of service exports (such as tourism, banking, and phone betting). To achieve its aims, it increased its adult literacy rate from 60 percent to 100 percent within three years and was able to transform its dependence on sugar production. The growth rate in the 1990s was one of the world's highest.[28]

At the same time, we see examples of failures of laissez faire trade policies, such as in sub-Saharan African countries. Simply, the laissez faire policies are against government intervention, whereas government institutions are very imbedded in sub-Saharan countries.[29] Further, these institutions have few resources and operate within economies that attract little foreign private capital because the markets are so small.[30] Unless these institutions aggregate their efforts to specific industries with potential, the efforts will be too dispersed to be effective. These countries have inadequate education and infrastructure and insufficient funds to develop either to the fullest. Thus, they should ration their expenditures to support those industries that will give them the best payback.

It's not only emerging economies that have achieved success. European governments assisted Airbus Industrie's start-up, and the company has now surpassed Boeing to become the world's largest producer of passenger aircraft. Shouldn't a government like the United States shift some of its subsidies? It's now subsidizing agricultural production, even though few U.S. citizens are farmers, even though it could import sufficient agricultural products from countries such as Brazil at no higher price than U.S. consumers are paying, and even though revenue from agriculture is not likely to grow very fast in the future. I say, let's put that subsidy money into areas that are bound to be growth industries of the future, such as development of hydrogen fuel cells and cryogenics.

COUNTERPOINT

I agree that countries should try to become competitive in industries that will yield more returns. Of particular importance are emerging growth industries, because they offer the possibility of adding value (from high profits and wages) within the country where the industry operates. Further, by being first, there are marketing and production cost advantages that impede competition from other countries. However, I disagree that a strategic trade policy is the way to do it.

At the same time, I also concede that there are limited circumstances when targeting will work, particularly for small countries. In a small country, such as Costa Rica, its 2003 GNP of $35.3 billion was only about 15 percent of the value of Wal-Mart's sales for the year, thus a small economy is in a situation where the scale of decision-making is manageable and where most of the people affected know each other and can reach a mutual agreement. In a large economy, this is impossible. However, even in the Costa Rican situation, I question how much of the success has been due to a strategic trade policy and how much has been due to conditions that existed prior to targeting the entry of high tech companies. Costa Rica already had a highly educated workforce, political and social stability, relatively high levels of economic freedom, large numbers of English-speaking workers, and a quality of life that would appeal to the managers and technical personnel that foreign investors would bring in to work in the facilities.

Based on what I've just said, there is another approach for government policy, which is to alter conditions that will affect the attractiveness to companies in general, rather than to specific targeted industries. For instance, a government may alter conditions that affect factor proportions, efficiency, and innovation. It may upgrade production factors by improving human skills through education, provide infrastructure (transportation, communications, capital markets, utilities), promote a highly competitive environment, and induce consumers to demand an ever higher quality of products and services.

Let me return to your sub-Saharan African example. I agree that institutions in that area are a way of life that will not go away. However, these institutions, rather than targeting industries, might be more effective by developing means to protect the law, stabilize the population, support entrepreneurial activity in the informal sector of the economies, and deal with economic and gender inequities.[31] These actions will improve the investment environment for all industries without the need for government officials to pick industries to support.

Strategic trade policies have usually resulted in no more than small payoffs, largely because governments find difficulty in identifying and targeting the right ones.[32] For example, a country may target an industry for which global demand never reaches expectations, such as British and French joint support for supersonic passenger aircraft. Or the companies in the targeted industry do not become competitive: Consider, for example, Thailand's support of the steel companies, which have had high costs because of poorly trained managers and rising labor costs in relation to other nearby countries.[33] Moreover, there has been a tendency for too many countries to identify the same industries, so excessive competition has led to inadequate returns.[34] Or, countries compete in supporting their own production. This has happened, for example, in Brazilian and Canadian support for production of regional jets.[35] Finally, even if a country successfully targets an industry, conditions change. Once many people are employed in a distressed industry, there are pressures to continue to support it, which is costly to the supporting economy.[36]

Even if governments can identify future growth industries in which their countries can likely succeed (I think these are very big "ifs"), it does not follow that companies in those industries should receive government assistance. Let entrepreneurs take risks. The successful ones will survive, be competitive internationally, and reap the benefits for having chosen industries correctly.

FACTOR MOBILITY

In the preceding discussions, we indicated that factor conditions change in both quantity and quality. As they do, the relative capabilities of countries also change. The change may come about because of internal circumstances. For instance, if savings rates increase, countries will have more capital relative to their factors of land and labor. If they spend relatively more on education, they improve the quality of the labor factor. Currently, one of the biggest changes underway concerns relative population change. At present rates, 33 countries are projected to have smaller populations in 2050 than today primarily because of low fertility rates, such as a projected decrease of 14 percent and 22 percent in Japan and Italy respectively.

Concomitantly, eight countries are expected to account for half of the world's population increase, with India, Pakistan, and Nigeria leading the pack.[37] These changes are, of course, important in understanding and predicting changes in export production and import market locations. At the same time, the mobility of capital, technology, and people affect trade and relative competitive positions. In this section, we'll discuss why production factors move, what effects the movements have in transforming factor endowments, and the effect of international factor mobility on world trade.

Why Production Factors Move

Capital, especially short-term capital, is the most internationally mobile production factor. Companies and private individuals primarily transfer capital because of differences in expected return (accounting for risk). They find information on interest rate differences readily available, and they can transfer capital by wire almost immediately at a low cost. Short-term capital is more mobile than long-term capital, especially direct investment, because there is more likely to be an active market through which investors can quickly buy foreign holdings and sell them if they want to transfer capital back home or to another country. Further, investors feel more certain about short-term political and economic conditions in a foreign country than about long-term ones. These political and economic conditions affect investors' perceptions of risk and where they prefer to put their capital. Nevertheless, they invest long-term abroad to tap markets and lower operating costs, as illustrated in Figure 6.5. However, not all capital movements occur because of risk to and expected returns on capital. Governments give foreign aid and loans. Not-for-profit organizations donate money abroad to relieve worrisome economic and social conditions. Individuals remit funds to help their families and friends in foreign countries.

People are also internationally mobile. Of course, some people travel to another country as tourists, students, and retirees; however, this travel does not constitute labor mobility unless they work there. Unlike funds that can be cheaply transferred by wire, people

Capital and labor move internationally to

- Gain more income
- Flee adverse political situations

FIGURE 6.5

Will companies keep finding new sources of cheap labor?
Source: 1997 Joel Pett, Lexington Herald-Leader. Reprinted by permission.

must usually incur high transportation costs to work in another country. If they move legally, they must get immigration papers, and most countries give these documents sparingly. Finally, such people may have to learn another language and adjust to a different culture away from their families and friends who serve as their customary support groups. Yet about 2 percent of the world's population has migrated to another country.[38] Since this 2 percent is spread unevenly, the impact is much greater on some countries than on others.

Of the people who go abroad to work, some move permanently and some move temporarily. For example, on the one hand, some people emigrate to another country, become citizens, and plan to reside there for the rest of their lives. On the other hand, MNEs assign managers to work abroad for periods ranging from a few days to several years (usually to a place where they also transfer capital), and some countries allow workers to enter for only short periods. The United States does this by giving 10-month permits for workers from Mexico.[39] In many cases, workers leave their families behind in the hope of returning home after saving enough money while working in a foreign country. Some move legally and others move illegally (that is to say they are undocumented). People, whether professionals or unskilled workers, largely work in another country for economic reasons. For example, Indonesian laborers work in Malaysia because they can make almost 10 times as much per day as they can at home.[40] State-enterprise hotels in China entice Western executives to work for them in China to improve the hotels' economic performance.[41] People also move for political reasons—for example, because of persecution or war dangers, in which case they are known as refugees. However, once they are refugees, they usually become part of the labor pool where they live. Sometimes it is difficult to distinguish between economic and political motives for international mobility because poor economic conditions often parallel poor political conditions. For example, in the early twenty-first century hundreds of thousands of Colombians left the country, fleeing both a civil war and unemployment.[42]

Effects of Factor Movements

Factor movements alter factor endowments.

Neither international capital nor population mobility is a new occurrence. For example, had it not been for historical masses of immigration, Australia, Canada, and the United States would have a greatly reduced population today. Further, many immigrants brought human capital with them, thus adding to the base of skills that enabled those countries to be newly competitive in an array of products they might otherwise have imported. Finally, these same countries received foreign capital to develop infrastructure and natural resources, which further altered their competitive structures and international trade.

However, what about the more recent past? Evidence is largely anecdotal. Nevertheless, factor movements are substantial for many countries and insignificant for others. For example, in 2002, the foreign-born population as a percentage of total population was 38, 23, 20, 20 and 18 in Luxembourg, Australia, Switzerland, New Zealand, and Canada respectively, whereas it was no more than 2 percent in South Korea, the Slovak Republic, Hungary, and Japan.[43] Singapore has transformed itself from a labor-intensive and low-wage country to a capital-intensive and high-wage country largely because of capital accumulation that has come from abroad.[44] Although labor and capital are different production factors, they are intertwined. For example, much of Singapore's capital accumulation has been in human capital, that is, import of skilled foreigners and the education of its own workforce. Further, countries lose potentially productive resources when educated people leave, a situation known as a *brain drain*, but they may gain from the foreign earnings on those factors. For example, Ecuador lost almost 5 percent of its population between 1999 and 2001, including 10,000 teachers and many other people with substantial work skills. However, many of these people are now sending remittances back to Ecuador. El Salvador and the Dominican Republic receive much more income from remittances that their citizens working abroad send home than they receive from their exports. Overall, Latin American and Caribbean countries are receiving more from remittances than from foreign aid and foreign investment combined.[45]

The Relationship of Trade and Factor Mobility

Factor movement is an alternative to trade that may or may not be a more efficient alloca-tion of resources.[46] We'll now discuss how free trade when coupled with freedom of factor mobility internationally will usually result in the most efficient allocation of resources.

Substitution When the factor proportions vary widely among countries, pressures exist for the most abundant factors to move to countries with greater scarcity—where they can command a better return. In countries where labor is abundant compared to capital, labor-ers tend to be unemployed or poorly paid. If permitted, these workers will go to countries that have full employment and higher wages. Similarly, capital will tend to move away from countries in which it is abundant to those in which it is scarce. For example, Mexico gets capital from the United States, and the United States gets labor from Mexico.[47] If fin-ished goods and production factors were both free to move internationally, the compara-tive costs of transferring goods and factors would determine the location of production. However, as is true of trade, there are restrictions on factor movements that make them only partially mobile internationally, such as both U.S. immigration restrictions that limit the legal and illegal influx of Mexican workers and Mexican ownership restrictions in the petroleum industry that limit U.S. capital investments in that industry.

> There are pressures for the most abundant factors to move to an area of scarcity.

A hypothetical example, shown in Figure 6.6, should illustrate the substitutability of trade and factor movements under different scenarios. Assume the following:

- The United States and Mexico have equally productive land available at the same cost for growing tomatoes.

FIGURE 6.6 **COMPARATIVE COSTS OF TOMATOES BASED ON TRADE AND FACTOR MOBILITY BETWEEN THE UNITED STATES AND MEXICO**

The lowest costs occur when trade and production factors are both mobile.

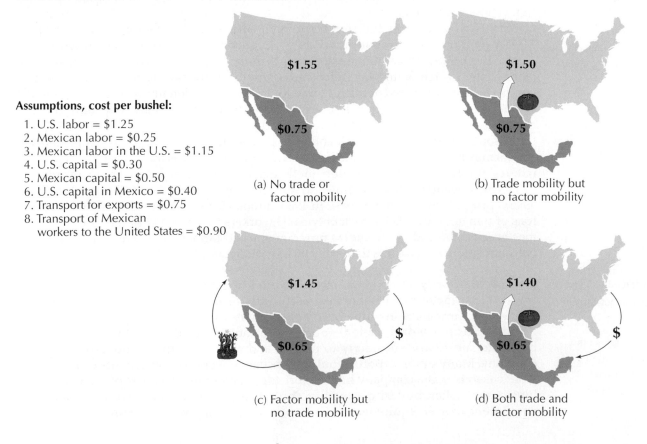

Assumptions, cost per bushel:
1. U.S. labor = $1.25
2. Mexican labor = $0.25
3. Mexican labor in the U.S. = $1.15
4. U.S. capital = $0.30
5. Mexican capital = $0.50
6. U.S. capital in Mexico = $0.40
7. Transport for exports = $0.75
8. Transport of Mexican workers to the United States = $0.90

$1.55 / $0.75
(a) No trade or factor mobility

$1.50 / $0.75
(b) Trade mobility but no factor mobility

$1.45 / $0.65
(c) Factor mobility but no trade mobility

$1.40 / $0.65
(d) Both trade and factor mobility

- The cost of transporting tomatoes between the United States and Mexico is $0.75 per bushel.
- Workers from either country pick an average of two bushels per hour during a 30-day picking season.

The only differences in price between the two countries are due to variations in labor and capital cost. The labor rate is $20.00 per day, or $1.25 per bushel, in the United States and $4.00 per day, or $0.25 per bushel, in Mexico. The capital needed to buy seeds, fertilizers, and equipment costs the equivalent of $0.30 per bushel in the United States and $0.50 per bushel in Mexico.

If neither tomatoes nor production factors can move between the two countries (see Figure 6.6[a]), the cost of tomatoes produced in Mexico for the Mexican market is $0.75 per bushel ($0.25 of labor plus $0.50 of capital), while those produced in the United States for the U.S. market cost $1.55 per bushel ($1.25 of labor plus $0.30 of capital). If the two countries eliminate trade restrictions on tomatoes between them (Figure 6.6[b]), the United States will import from Mexico because the Mexican cost of $0.75 per bushel plus $0.75 for transporting the tomatoes to the United States will be $0.05 less than the $1.55 per bushel cost of growing them in the United States.

Consider another scenario in which neither country allows the importation of tomatoes but both allow certain movements of labor and capital (Figure 6.6[c]). Mexican workers can enter the United States on temporary work permits for an incremental travel and living expense of $14.40 per day per worker, or $0.90 per bushel. At the same time, U.S. companies will invest capital in Mexican tomato production, provided the capital earns more than it would earn in the United States—say, $0.40 per bushel, which is less than the Mexican going rate. In this scenario, Mexican production costs per bushel will be $0.65 ($0.25 of Mexican labor plus $0.40 of U.S. capital) and U.S. production costs will be $1.45 ($0.25 of Mexican labor plus $0.90 of travel and incremental costs plus $0.30 of U.S. capital). Each country would reduce its production costs—from $0.75 to $0.65 in Mexico and from $1.55 to $1.45 in the United States—by bringing in abundant production factors from abroad.

With free trade and the free movement of production factors (Figure 6.6[d]), Mexico will produce for both markets by importing capital from the United States. According to the above three assumptions, doing this will be cheaper than sending labor to the United States. In reality, since neither production factors nor the finished goods they produce are completely free to move internationally, slight changes in the extent of restrictions can greatly alter how and where goods may be produced most cheaply.

In some cases, however, the inability to gain sufficient access to foreign production factors may stimulate efficient methods of substitution, such as the development of alternatives for traditional production methods. For example, U.S. tomato farmers in California depended almost entirely on Mexican temporary workers (*braceros*) until the *bracero* program terminated in 1964. In 1960, it took 45,000 workers to harvest 2.2 million tons of tomatoes. By 1999, it took only 5,000 workers to harvest 12 million tons of tomatoes because the end of the *bracero* program spurred farmers to gain efficiency through mechanization. At the same time, the real cost of tomatoes fell 54 percent.[48]

Complementarity   In our tomato example for the United States and Mexico, we showed that factor movements may substitute for or stimulate trade. When companies invest abroad, the investments often stimulate exports from their home countries. About a third of world trade (exports) is among controlled entities, such as from parent to subsidiary, subsidiary to parent, and subsidiary to subsidiary of the same company. Many of the exports would not occur if overseas investments did not exist. One reason is that a company may export capital equipment as part of the value of its investment when building a facility abroad. It may have more confidence in this equipment than in equipment built locally, and it may want maximum worldwide

---

The lowest costs occur when trade and production factors are both mobile.

Both finished goods and production factors are partially mobile internationally.

Factor mobility through foreign investment often stimulates trade because of

- The need for components
- The parent's ability to sell complementary products
- The need for equipment for subsidiaries

LOOKING TO THE FUTURE: Will Conditions for Trade Change?

When countries have few restrictions on foreign trade and factor mobility, companies have greater latitude in reducing operating costs. For example, fewer trade restrictions give them opportunities to gain economies of scale by servicing markets in more than one country from a single base of production. Fewer restrictions on factor movements give them opportunities to combine factors for more efficient production. But government trade and immigration restrictions vary from one country to another, from one point in time to another, and under different circumstances. Nevertheless, it is probably safe to say that trade restrictions have been diminishing, primarily because of the economic gains that countries foresee through freer trade. Further, restrictions on the movement of capital and technology have become freer, but whether restrictions on the movement of people are freer is questionable.

However, there are uncertainties as to whether the trend toward the freer movement of trade and production factors will endure. Groups worldwide question whether the economic benefits of more open economies outweigh some of the costs, both economic and noneconomic. Although the next chapter will discuss import restrictions (protectionism) in detail, it is useful at this point to understand the overall evolution of protectionist sentiment.

One key issue is the trade between high-income and emerging economies. At the same time that trade barriers are being lowered, many emerging economies, in which wage rates are very low, are growing economically more rapidly than are industrial countries. Concomitantly, shifts in production to emerging economies may cause the displacement of many jobs within high-income countries. There is uncertainty as to how fast new jobs will replace old ones in high-income countries and how much tolerance these countries will have for employment shifts that would be less likely to occur within protected markets. Regardless of whether freer trade or protectionism will prevail in the future, companies must try to predict what will happen to those industries in which they operate.

If present trends continue, relationships among factor endowments (land, labor, and capital) will continue to evolve. For example, the population growth rate is much higher in emerging economies than in high-income countries. Three possible consequences of this growth are continued shifts of labor-intensive production to emerging economies, shifts of agricultural production away from densely populated areas, and pressures on the high-income countries to accept more immigrants. At the same time, the finite supply of natural resources may lead to price increases for these resources, even though oversupplies have often depressed prices. The limited supply may work to the advantage of emerging economies because supplies in industrial countries have been more fully exploited.

Four factors are worth monitoring, because they could cause product trade to become relatively less significant in the future.

1. There are some indications that protectionist sentiment is growing. For example, major trading countries have recently squabbled over trade for a number of products, including genetically altered agricultural products, bananas, steel, and passenger aircraft. These sorts of disputes could prevent competitively produced goods from entering foreign countries.

2. As economies grow, efficiencies of multiple production locations also grow, which may allow country-by-country production to replace trade in many cases. For example, most automobile producers have moved into China and Thailand or plan to do so as a result of China's and Thailand's growing market size.

3. Flexible, small-scale production methods, especially those using robotics, may enable even small countries to produce many goods efficiently for their own consumption, thus eliminating the need to import those goods. For example, steel production used to take larger capital outlays that needed enormous markets before the development of efficient minimills that can produce on a small scale.

4. Services are growing more rapidly than products as a portion of production and consumption within high-income countries. Consequently, product trade may become a less important part of countries' total trade. Further, many of the rapid-growth service areas, such as home building and dining out, are not easily traded, so trade in goods plus services could become a smaller part of total output and consumption.

uniformity. Still another reason is that domestic operating units may export materials and components to their foreign facilities for use in a finished product. For example, Coca-Cola exports concentrate to its bottling facilities abroad. A foreign facility may produce part of the product line while serving as sales agent for exports of its parent's complementary products.

SUMMARY

- Some trade theories examine what will happen to international trade in the absence of government interference. Other theories prescribe how governments should interfere with trade flows to achieve certain national objectives.

- Trade theory is useful because it helps explain what might be produced competitively in a given locale, where a company might go to produce a given product efficiently, and whether government practices might interfere with the free flow of trade among countries. Other theories address the explanation of trade patterns.

- Mercantilist theory proposed that a country should try to achieve a favorable balance of trade (export more than it imports) to receive an influx of gold. Neomercantilist policy also seeks a favorable balance of trade, but its purpose is to achieve some social or political objective.

- The theory of absolute advantage proposes specialization through free trade because consumers will be better off if they can buy foreign-made products that are priced more cheaply than domestic ones.

- According to the theory of absolute advantage, a country may produce goods more efficiently because of a natural advantage (e.g., raw materials or climate) or because of an acquired advantage (e.g., technology or skill for a product or process advantage).

- Comparative advantage theory also proposes specialization through free trade because it says that total global output can increase even if one country has an absolute advantage in the production of all products.

- Policymakers have questioned some of the assumptions of the absolute and comparative advantage theories. These assumptions are that full employment exists, that output efficiency is always a country's major objective, that countries are satisfied with their relative gains, that there are no transport costs among countries, that advantages appear to be static, and that resources move freely within countries but are immobile internationally. Although the theories use a two-country analysis of products, the theories hold for multicountry trade and for services as well.

- The theory of country size holds that because countries with large land areas are apt to have varied climates and natural resources, they are generally more self-sufficient than smaller countries are. A second reason for this greater self-sufficiency is that large countries' production and market centers are more likely to be located at a greater distance from other countries, raising the transport costs of foreign trade.

- The factor-proportions theory holds that a country's relative endowments of land, labor, and capital will determine the relative costs of these factors. These factor costs, in turn, will determine which goods the country can produce most efficiently.

- According to the country-similarity theory, most trade today occurs among high-income countries because they share similar market segments and because they produce and consume so much more than emerging economies.

- Much of the pattern of two-way trading partners may be explained by cultural similarity between the countries, political and economic agreements, and by the distance between them.

- Manufactured products comprise the bulk of trade among high-income countries. This trade occurs because countries apportion their research and development differently among industrial sectors. It also occurs because consumers from high-income countries want and can afford to buy products with a greater variety of characteristics than are produced in their domestic markets.

- The international product life cycle (PLC) theory states that companies will manufacture products first in the countries in which they were researched and developed. These are almost always high-income countries. Over the product's life cycle, production will shift to foreign locations, especially to emerging economies as the product reaches the stages of maturity and decline.

- The Porter diamond shows that four conditions are important for competitive superiority: demand conditions; factor conditions; related and supporting industries; and firm strategy, structure, and rivalry.

- Production factors and finished goods are only partially mobile internationally. The cost and feasibility of transferring production factors rather than exporting finished goods internationally will determine which alternative is better.

- Although international mobility of production factors may be a substitute for trade, the mobility may stimulate trade through sales of components, equipment, and complementary products.

LUKoil[49]

CASE

Russia's GDP grew by 7 percent in 2004, which marked five straight years of growth. The growth was also higher than that of any other G8 country. Russia's oil and gas sector has fuelled the growth, accounting for about 25 percent of GDP and 40 percent of Russian exports. Russia consumes about 30 percent of its oil production and exports the other 70 percent. This dependence on petroleum exports makes Russia quite vulnerable to what happens in global petroleum markets. When the price per barrel of oil changes by $1, Russian revenues change by about $1.4 billion in the same direction.

In recent years, so much oil has been discovered in Russia that the country now has 15 percent more proven reserves than Saudi Arabia. In addition, diplomatic negotiations to solicit Russian support for the war against the Taliban and al Qaeda in Afghanistan gained Russia's control over oil exports from oil-rich Azerbaijan and Kazakhstan in Central Asia. Russian supplies are so large that the Moscow bureau chief of a New York– and London-based energy intelligence group said, "The country is choking on the crude it produces." However, because of fierce rivalry in the global oil industry, Russian control of so much oil is no guarantee it can sell at an acceptable margin. Thus, Russia depends on its oil companies to export sufficient oil to pay for imports, primarily machinery, to spur its economic development needs. The economic development is essential, both because Russian GDP per capita in 2004 at purchasing price parity of $8,900 was well below that of any other G8 country and because Russia's oil sector (a capital- rather than labor-intensive industry) employs less than 1 percent of its population.

LUKoil is Russia's largest oil company and is either the world's largest or second largest private owner of proven reserves. (Analysts disagree as to whether LUKoil or ExxonMobil is larger. Some of the world's largest oil companies, such as Saudi Aramco from Saudi Arabia and Petroven from Venezuela, and their reserves are government owned, rather than privately owned.) It controls 19 percent of Russian oil production and refining. In addition to its large investments within Russia, it has been making extensive investments abroad. Map 6.2 shows the location and types of LUKoil's foreign operations. For instance, in 2001 it acquired 100 percent of Getty Petroleum in the United States, which gave it a retail network in the mid-Atlantic and northeastern states of about 1,300 gasoline stations. In 2004, it acquired another 800 U.S. stations from ConocoPhillips. These are being rebranded as LUKoil stations. Given that Russia desperately needs capital and that both Russia and LUKoil need to export, many analysts have wondered, "Why does a Russian company see advantages in investing abroad?" Before answering this question, we'll examine LUKoil's competitive situation and strategy.

LUKoil must sell in foreign markets if it is to use its capacity adequately and earn sufficient profits. Since the beginning of the twenty-first century, Russia's export situation

MAP 6.2   Location of LUKoil's Operations

LUKoil has moved internationally, not only by exporting, but also through investments. Note that the preponderance of foreign expansion has been to nearby countries.

Source: Information was taken from *LUKoil Annual Report 2004.*

has been generally favorable. Between January 1999 and September 2000, oil prices tripled because of production cutbacks by the Organization of Petroleum Exporting Countries (OPEC), which Russia never joined; bad weather; and strong demand. Oil prices lost about half this gain because of economic uncertainty after 9/11, but they have since increased to all-time highs as a result of such factors as unrest in Venezuela, the war in Iraq, Chinese economic expansion, and production curtailment by OPEC. The result is that LUKoil has been able to sell more oil outside Russia and at a higher price than it could a few years earlier. This favorable market situation enabled LUKoil to have enough capital to invest abroad if its management reasoned that such investment would help its strategic position.

LUKoil was one of several companies created in 1991 out of the Russian state-owned petroleum monopoly. Since then, the Russian government has gradually reduced its LUKoil holdings. It sold three-quarters of its remaining 10 percent holding to ConocoPhillips in

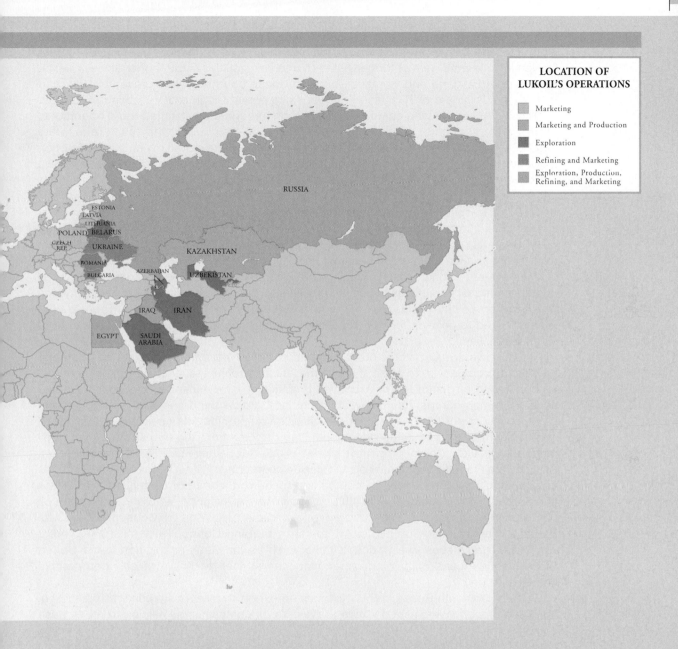

LOCATION OF LUKOIL'S OPERATIONS

- Marketing
- Marketing and Production
- Exploration
- Refining and Marketing
- Exploration, Production, Refining, and Marketing

2004. Yet LUKoil remains close to the Russian government. Russian President Vladimir Putin even cut the ribbon to open a new LUKoil filling station in New York City during his state visit to the United States. LUKoil became the first Russian oil company to integrate "from oil well to filling station." It has over 120,000 employees and about 1,100 Russian filling stations.

In addition to exporting to use its capacity, LUKoil's management has wanted foreign expansion to get bigger margins and more assurance of full on-time payment than it can get within Russia. However, why doesn't LUKoil simply export rather than make foreign investments? The answer lies in a combination of factors.

First, oil prices have fluctuated widely in the past in spite of their general upward trend since the beginning of the twenty-first century; so has the ability to market Russian oil abroad. On several occasions, oil prices have jumped over 100 percent in one year and then have plummeted to lower levels than when the jump in prices began. In fact, in the late 1990s, a global oil glut and depressed world oil prices hampered

LUKoil's ability to be profitable. So LUKoil emulated its larger Western competitors and embraced the idea of forward integration into ownership of foreign distribution. Its first foreign investments were of formerly state-owned oil facilities in the former Soviet satellite countries of Bulgaria and Romania, because these countries were close, familiar, and long-time customers of Russian oil. It has since expanded into other countries, almost entirely by buying existing companies rather than through greenfield (start-up) operations. Simply stated, when producing companies invest in distribution, they capture markets that better enable them to sell their crude oil when there are global oversupplies. Further, this integration could potentially reduce LUKoil's operating costs because LUKoil will not have to negotiate and enforce agreements by selling oil to other companies in these countries.

Second, despite having huge reserves in Russia and being a successful exporter, political relations could impair LUKoil's future export sales. For instance, an importing country could lower its purchases of Russian oil to protest some Russian political policy or simply to diversify its own sources of supplies. Further, within Russia the government owns the pipeline system through which virtually all Russian oil exports pass. Because it allocates quotas among oil companies to use the pipeline system, a competitor might gain influence with Russian political decision makers to preempt part of LUKoil's quota. Thus, LUKoil sees the need to develop foreign oil supplies and aims to make them about 20 percent of its total supplies.

Third, to be a major global competitor, LUKoil must become as efficient as the major Western oil companies. To do so, it needs the latest petroleum technology, marketing skills, and operating efficiencies. For example, its administrative expenses and cost of capital have been high compared with Western competitors. Within Russia, these needs have created only minor problems because LUKoil's competition has been other Russian oil companies that also inherited operational inefficiencies from the former state-owned oil monopoly. However, new competitive threats within Russia have been gaining momentum. BP and TotalFinaElf bought interests in Russian companies. Thus, LUKoil sees advantages in acquiring skills from foreign companies to help it compete better, both at home and abroad. With this outcome in mind, it has put independent directors from Western oil companies on its board. The 7.6 percent purchase of LUKoil by ConocoPhillips was partially brought about by LUKoil's interest in tapping ConocoPhillips's management expertise. It also sees foreign acquisitions, such as the Getty acquisition in the United States, as a means of gaining experienced personnel, technology, and competitive know-how.

In summary, both Russia and LUKoil need to export to meet their economic objectives. They see foreign investment and ties to Western oil companies as helping to meet these objectives.

QUESTIONS

1. What theories of trade help to explain Russia's position as an oil exporter? Which ones do not, and why?
2. How do global political and economic conditions affect world markets and prices of oil?
3. Discuss the following statement as it applies to Russia and LUKoil. "Regardless of the advantages a country may gain by trading, international trade will begin only if companies within that country have competitive advantages that enable them to be viable traders—and they must foresee profits in exporting and importing."
4. In LUKoil's situation, what is the relationship between factor mobility and exports?
5. Compare the role of the Costa Rican government in the chapter's opening case with the role of the Russian government in their use of trade to meet national economic objectives.

CHAPTER NOTES

1   Data for the case were taken from Debora Spar, *Attracting High Technology Investment: Intel's Costa Rican Plant* (Washington: The World Bank, Foreign Investment Advisory Service Occasional Paper 11, 1998); http://CIA.GOV/CIA/publications/factbook/geos/cs.html accessed May 25, 2004; Gail D. Triner, "Recent Latin American History and Its Historiography," *Latin American Research Review* 38, no. 1 (2003): 219–238; John Weeks, "Trade Liberalisation, Market Deregulation and Agricultural Performance in Central America," *The Journal of Development Studies* 35, no. 5 (June 1999): 48–76; Niels W. Ketelhöhn and Michael E. Porter, "Building a Cluster: Electronics and Information Technology in Costa Rica," *Harvard Business School Case 9–703–422* (November 7, 2002); John Schellhas, "Peasants Against Globalization: Rural Social Movements in Costa Rica," *American Anthropologist* 103, no. 3 (September 2001): 862–863; Jose Itzigsohn, *Developing Poverty: The State, Labor Market Deregulation, and the Informal Economy in Costa Rica and the Dominican Republic* (University Park, PA: The Pennsylvania University Press, 2000); Roy Nelson, "Intel's Site Selection Decision in Latin America," *Thunderbird, The American Graduate School of International Management Case A06-99-0016*; and Andrés Rodríguez-Clare, "Costa Rica's Development Strategy Based on Human Capital and Technology: How It Got There, The Impact of Intel, and Lessons for Other Countries," *United Nations Human Development Report 2001* (New York: United Nations Development Programme, 2001).

2   The mercantilist period is not associated with any single writer. A good coverage is in Gianni Vaggi, *A Concise History of Economic Thought: From Mercantilism to Monetarism* (New York: Palgrave Macmillan, 2002).

3   For reviews of the literature, see Jordan Shan and Fiona Sun, "On the Export-Led Growth Hypothesis for the Little Dragons: An Empirical Reinvestigation," *Atlantic Economic Review* 26, no. 4 (December 1998): 353–71; and George K. Zestos and Xiangnan Tao, "Trade and GDP Growth: Causal Relations in the United States and Canada," *Southern Economic Journal* 68, no. 4 (April 2002): 859–74.

4   For a good discussion of the history of free trade thought, see Leonard Gomes, *The Economics and Ideology of Free Trade: A Historial Review* (Cheltenham, UK: Edward Elgar, 2003).

5   Many publishers have subsequently printed his 1776 book. See, for example, Adam Smith, *An Inquiry into the Nature and Causes of the Wealth of Nations* (Washington: Regnery Publishing, 1998).

6   *On the Principles of Political Economy and Taxation*, originally published in London in 1817, has since been reprinted by a number of publishers. See, for example, David Ricardo, *On the Principles of Political Economy and Taxation* (Amherst, NY: Prometheus Books, 1996.)

7   For a good discussion of this paradoxical thinking, see Paul R. Krugman, "What Do Undergraduates Need to Know About Trade?" *American Economic Review Papers and Proceedings* (May 1993): 23–26. For a discussion of some developing countries' views th . monopolistic conditions keep them from gaining a fair share of gains from international trade, see A. P. Thirlwell, *Growth and Development*, 6th ed. (London: Macmillan, 1999).

8   See David Adams, "UN Attempts to Boost Biosafety in Developing World," *Nature* 415, no. 6870 (January 24, 2002): 353; and Hemel Hempstead, "Worldwide Project to Assess Safety of GM Crops," *Appropriate Technology* 29, no. 1 (January–March 2002): 37–38.

9   Eli J. Heckscher, *Heckscher-Ohlin Trade Theory* (Cambridge, MA: MIT Press, 1991).

10 For a discussion of how the theory does not fit the reality of trade, see Antoni Estevadeordal and Alan M. Taylor, "A Century of Missing Trade?" *The American Economic Review* 92, no. 1 (March 2002): 383–93. For a study supporting the theory, see Yong-Seok Choi and Pravin Krishna, "The Factor Content of Bilateral Trade: An Empirical Test," *The Journal of Political Economy* 112, no. 4 (August 2004): 887–915.

11 See, for example, Donald R. Davis and David E. Weinstein, "An Account of Global Factor Trade," *The American Economic Review* 91, no. 5 (December 2001): 1423–53; and Oner Guncavdi and Suat Kucukcifi, "Foreign Trade and Factor Intensity in an Open Developing Country: An Input-Output Analysis for Turkey," *Russian & East European Finance and Trade* 37, no. 1 (January–February 2001): 75–88.

12 See, for example, P. Krugman and A. J. Venables, "Globalization and the Inequality of Nations," *Quarterly Journal of Economics* 110 (1995): 857–80.

13 See Paul Krugman, "Scale Economies, Product Differentiation, and the Patterns of Trade," *The American Economic Review* 70 (December 1980): 950–59; and James Harrigan, "Estimation of Cross-Country Differences in Industry Production Functions," *Journal of International Economics* 47, no. 2 (April 1999): 267–93.

14 Drusilla K. Brown and Robert M. Stern, "Measurement and Modeling of the Economic Effect of Trade and Investment Barriers in Services," *Title Review of International Economics* 9, no. 2 (May 2001): 262–86, discuss the role of economies of scale and trade barriers.

15 See Gianmarco I. P. Ottaviano and Diego Puga, "Agglomeration in the Global Economy: A Survey of the 'New Economic Geography,' " *The World Economy* 21, no. 6 (August 1998): 707–31; and Gianmarco Ottaviano, Takatoshi Tabuchi, and Jacques-François Thisse, "Agglomeration and Trade Revisited," *International Economic Review* 43, no. 2 (May 2002): 409–35.

16 Stefan B. Linder, *An Essay on Trade Transformation* (New York: Wiley, 1961).

17 Dirk Pilat, "The Economic Impact of Technology," *The OECD Observer,* no. 213 (August–September 1998): 5–8.

18 Two discussions of intra-industry trade are Don P. Clark, "Determinants of Intraindustry Trade Between the United States and Industrial Nations," *The International Trade Journal* XII, no. 3 (Fall 1998): 345–62; and H. Peter Gray, "Free International Economic Policy in a World of Schumpeter Goods," *The International Trade Journal* XII, no. 3 (Fall 1998): 323–44.

19 Daniel Michaels, "Landing Rights," *Wall Street Journal* (April 30, 2002): A1+.

20 "That's Snow-biz," *The Economist* (April 13, 1996): 58.

21 Terry Hall, "NZ Finds Pirated Varieties in Chile," *Financial Times* (January 21, 1999): 24.

22 Jeffrey A. Frankel and David Romer, "Does Trade Cause Growth?" *The American Economic Review* 89, no. 3 (June 1999): 379–99.

23 See Raymond Vernon, "International Investment and International Trade in the Product Life Cycle," *Quarterly Journal of Economics* (May 1996): 190–207; and David Dollar, "Technological Innovation, Capital Mobility, and the Product Cycle in North–South Trade," *American Economic Review* 76, no. 1, (March 1986): 177–90.

24 This is true by various indicators. See, for example, International Bank for Reconstruction and Development, "Science and Technology," *The World Development Indicators* (Washington, DC: 2000): 300.

25 David Dollar and Edward N. Wolff, *Competitiveness, Convergence, and International Specialization* (Cambridge, MA: MIT Press, 1993).

26 Kiyohiko Ito and Vladimir Pucik, "R&D Spending, Domestic Competition, and Export Performance of Japanese Manufacturing Firms," *Strategic Management Journal* 14 (1993): 61–75.

27 James Kynge and Elisabeth Robinson, "Singapore to Revise Trade Priorities," *Financial Times* (January 21, 1997): 6.

28 Helene Cooper, "Trade Wins," *Wall Street Journal* (July 14, 1998): A1.

29 Sonny Nwankwo and Darlington Richards, "Institutional Paradigm and the Management of Transitions: A Sub-Saharan African Perspective," *International Journal of Social Economics* 31, no. 1/2 (2004): 111.

30 Jeffrey Sachs, Institutions Matter, But Not Everything," *Finance and Development* (June 2003): 38–41.

31 Nwankwo and Richards, loc. cit.

32 Paul Krugman and Alasdair M. Smith, eds., *Empirical Studies of Strategic Trade Policies* (Chicago: University of Chicago Press, 1993).

33 Paul M. Sherer, "Thailand Trips in Reach for New Exports," *Wall Street Journal* (August 27, 1996): A8.

34 Richard Brahm, "National Targeting Policies, High-Technology Industries, and Excessive Competition," *Strategic Management Journal* 16 (1995): 71–91.

35 Andrea E. Goldstein and Steven M. McGuire, "The Political Economy of Strategic Trade Policy and the Brazil-Canada Export Subsidies Saga," *The World Economy* 27, no. 4 (April 2004): 541.

36 Theresa M. Greaney, "Strategic Trade and Competition Policies to Assist Distressed Industries," *The Canadian Journal of Economics* 32, no. 3 (May 1999): 767.

37 UN Population Division (www.un.org/esa/population/unpop).

38 International Organization for Migration, *World Migration Report 2000,* www.iom.int.

39 Barry Newman, "Men at Work," *Wall Street Journal* (April 14, 2004): A+.

40 John Salt, "The Future of International Labor Migration," *Migration Review* 26, no. 4 (Winter 2002): 1077.

41 Ben Dolven, "China Recruits Foreign Talent," *Wall Street Journal* (April 15, 2004): A13.

42 "Making the Most of an Exodus," *Economist* (February 23, 2002): 41–42.

43 *Trends in International Migration* (oecd.org/dataoecd/7/49/24994376), accessed March 18, 2005.

44 See C. Chris Rodrigo, "East Asia's Growth: Technology or Accumulation?" *Contemporary Economic Policy* 18, no. 2 (April 2000): 215–27; and Paul Krugman, "The Myth of Asia's Miracle," *Foreign Affairs* 73, no. 6 (1994): 62–78.

45 Richard Lapper, "Latin Americans Scale Summit of the Remittance League," *Financial Times* (March 26, 2004): 2, using data from the Inter-American Development Bank.

46 Keith Head and John Ries, "Exporting and FDI as Alternative Strategies," *Oxford Review of Economic Policy* 20, no. 3 (Autumn 2004): 409–429.

47 See Frank D. Bean et al., "Circular, Invisible, and Ambiguous Migrants: Components of Differences in Estimates of the Number of Unauthorized Mexican Migrants in the United States," *Demography* 38, no. 3 (August 2001): 411–22; and United Nations Conference on Trade and Development, *World Investment Report 2000: Cross-border Mergers and Acquisitions and Development* (New York and Geneva: United Nations, 2000): 312.

48 Philip L. Martin and Michael S. Teitelbaum, "The Mirage of Mexican Guest Workers," *Foreign Affairs* 80, no. 6 (November–December 2001): 117–31.

49 The information from this case is from the following sources: Sabrina Tavernise and Peter S. Green, "Oil Concerns in Russia Branch Out," *New York Times* (April 2, 2002): W1; Bhushan Bahree, "Western Oil Flirts with Russia Firms, Insider Says," *Wall Street Journal* (April 29, 2002): A13; Reuters, "Mobius and Chevron Exec Nominated for LUKoil Board" (January 17, 2002): http://biz.yahoo.com/rf/020117/117507998_ 1.html; Paul Starobin, "LUKoil Is Lonesome," *Business Week Online* (April 24, 2000): http://www.business week.com:2000/00_17/b3678229.htm?scriptFramed; "LUKoil Oil Company," http://www.lukoil.com/; "LUKoil Expands at Home and Abroad," *Hart's European Fuels News* 5, no. 5 (March 7, 2001); "Focus, the Russians Are Coming," *Petroleum Economist* (December 31, 2000); Andrew Jack and Arkady Ostrovsky, "LUKoil in U.S. Petro Deal," *Financial Times* (November 4, 2000): 8; David Ignatius, "The Russians Are Pumping," *Pittsburgh Post-Gazette* (December 28, 2001): A-21; Tina Obut, "Perspective on Russia's Oil Sector," *Oil & Gas Journal* (February 1, 1999): 20; *LUKoil Annual Report,* various years; "Event Brief of September 30: ConocoPhillips and LUKoil," CCBN Wire Service, September 30, 2004; "LUKoil Leading Peers in Adding to Production Outside Russia," *Platts Oilgram News* 82, no. 69 (April 13, 2004): 1; "World Oil Price Chronology" (March 2005) (www.eia.doe.gov/emeu/cabs/chron), accessed 3/8/05; and "Russia" (www.eia.doe.gov/cabs/russia).

FIGURE 7.1   IMPORT MARKET SHARES OF CLOTHING IN THE UNITED STATES BEFORE AND AFTER THE MFA

China and India are projected to be the only two countries gaining import market share in the United States with the elimination of the Multifiber Arrangement.

Source: Data were taken from WTO Secretariat, Discussion Paper No. 5, Hildegunn Kyvik Nordås, "The Global Textile and Clothing Industry Post the Agreement on Textiles and Clothing," 2004.

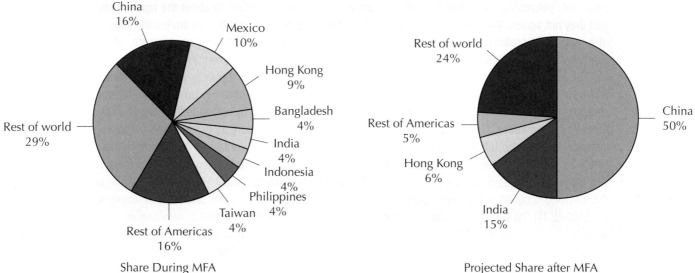

Share During MFA   Projected Share after MFA

the U.S. government to impose temporary import restrictions in case certain clothing sectors (man-made fiber trousers, cotton shirts, man-made fiber shirts, nonknit shirts, and underwear) would be too severely injured by imports. The NCTO has planned petitions for other clothing sectors as well.

Surprisingly, the NCTO has built its biggest allies among emerging economies that had quotas to sell in the United States during the MFA era. Many of these had already seen their markets decline during the 10-year phase-out period of the MFA. For instance, El Salvador lost nearly 6,000 clothing jobs in 2004. Thus, these countries' main concern was that they would be unable to compete against China and India. For instance, the Mauritian ambassador to the United States said, "African countries, south Saharan and other countries currently enjoying trade preferences will be the biggest losers, with a contraction of their market share by almost 70 percent." More than 50 nations lobbied for U.S. and EU restrictions to prevent the market takeover by Chinese and Indian producers. This lobbying was taken seriously because both the United States and EU often need the political support of these countries and use economic measures to gain such support. For instance, the United States offered Turkey more access to the U.S. textile market in an attempt to get Turkey to cooperate in the invasion of Iraq.

Publicity over the possible United States and European job loss was duly noted by China, which feared stringent restrictions if it did not voluntarily cut its exports. As a result, China announced it would place export tariffs on several clothing categories; however, critics claimed that these taxes of between 2 and 4 cents per item were too low to stem their export sales. At the same time, there was some concern in the United States that it could not push China too far without China retaliating. Retaliation could be economic, such as buying passenger aircraft from Airbus Industrie rather than from Boeing or selling much of its holdings of U.S. Treasury bonds, which the United States needed to sell to foreigners because of its budget deficit. Retaliation could also be political, such as threatening an invasion of the U.S. ally, Taiwan.

When the MFA ended in 2005, Chinese textile and clothing exports surged. During the first month, the United States lost 12,200 jobs in those industries, and the U.S. trade deficit was the largest ever recorded with a single country. During the first two months, 18 apparel factories closed down in Costa Rica, the Dominican Republic, Guatemala, and Honduras. These events created great uncertainty within the industry and for companies buying textiles and clothing products. For instance, the president of J.C. Penney's purchasing unit worried that he might buy Chinese products, only to have them barred from entering the United States because of imposition of new restrictions.

INTRODUCTION

At some point, you may work for or own stock in a company whose performance, or even survival, depends on governmental policies that affect the competitive moves of foreign producers. Likewise, governmental measures may limit your ability to sell abroad, such as by prohibiting the export of certain products to certain countries, or by making it difficult for you to buy what you need from foreign suppliers. Collectively, these governmental restrictions and incentives to trade are known as **protectionism.** In the opening case, the 30-year protectionism under the MFA not only helped many textile and clothing companies compete by manufacturing in the United States, it also helped producers in such countries as Bangladesh and Indonesia. At the same time, it harmed the competitive position of China and India and it raised the price of clothing in the United States. Similarly, governmental expenses rose in many countries due to the need to negotiate and administer the complex system of quotas that gave them access to the U.S. market.

In Chapter 6, we showed that the trade of goods and services is a major means of linking countries economically and that more linkages improve global efficiency. However, the restrictions illustrated in the opening case are not atypical. In principle, no country allows an unregulated flow of goods and services across its borders. (Figure 7.2 illustrates the effect of governmental regulations on companies' competitive positions.) Rather, governments routinely influence the flow of imports and exports. Also, governments directly or indirectly subsidize domestic industries to help them engage foreign producers at home or challenge them abroad. This chapter begins by reviewing the economic and noneconomic rationales for trade protectionism, followed by an explanation of the major forms of trade controls and their effects on companies' operating decisions.

All countries seek to influence trade, and each has economic, social, and political objectives
- Conflicting objectives
- Interest groups

CONFLICTING RESULTS OF TRADE POLICIES

Discussion of trade theory in Chapter 6 explained the gains from free trade. Despite these benefits, all nations interfere with international trade to varying degrees. Governments intervene in trade to attain economic, social, or political objectives. It is important to note,

FIGURE 7.2 **PHYSICAL AND SOCIETAL INFLUENCES ON PROTECTIONISM AND COMPANIES' COMPETITIVE ENVIRONMENT**

In response to physical and societal influences, governments enact measures that enhance or restrict companies' international trade. These measures affect competition because they improve or hinder companies' abilities and needs to compete internationally. Companies likewise influence governments to adopt trade policies that benefit them.

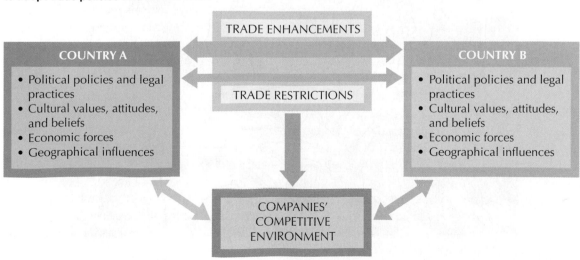

though, that governments pursue political rationality when trying to regulate trade. Governmental officials apply trade policies that they reason have the best chance to benefit the nation and its citizens—and, in some cases, their personal political longevity. Determining the best way to influence trade is complicated by frequent conflicts in the effects of policies. For example, two of the purposes of the MFA were to help workers in emerging economies and to maintain employment in a sensitive industry at home; in actuality, it helped the workers in some emerging economies while disadvantaging those in others, and it helped home-country manufacturing workers while raising prices. Governments would also like to help struggling companies and industries without penalizing those who are doing well. This goal is often impossible—especially if other countries retaliate against their protectionist actions. For example, the United States gave tax breaks to aid its exporters, but the 25-nation EU retaliated with import taxes that hurt such U.S. companies' export sales as All-Edmonds for shoes and Northland Forest Products for specialty lumber.[2]

Proposals for trade regulation reform often spark fierce debate among people and groups that believe they will be affected. Of course, those that are most directly affected (so-called stakeholders) are most apt to speak out. For example, U.S. stakeholders whose livelihood depends on a U.S. base of clothing production (workers, owners, suppliers, and local politicians) are fighting the elimination of import-restricting quotas. Displaced workers see themselves as being forced to take new jobs in new industries, perhaps even in new towns. They fear prolonged unemployment, reduced incomes, uncertain work conditions, and unstable social surroundings. People threatened in this way tend to object often and loudly.

In contrast, consumers typically buy the best product they can find for the price, often without knowing or caring about the product's origin. (See the cartoon in Figure 7.3.) Further, individual consumers often misinterpret how much retail prices rise because of import restrictions. Typically, the economic costs are spread out. For example, EU restrictions on banana imports cost EU consumers about $2 billion a year because of higher banana costs, a significant amount in total but trivial for each banana or for each consumer.

FIGURE 7.3

Organizing groups of affected workers to work toward a trade policy is easier than getting the support of consumers.

Source: Mike Thompson, *The Detroit Free Press.*

Similarly, current U.S. tariffs on peanut products from Mexico range from 140 percent to 160 percent. By 2008, peanut products can be imported from Mexico without paying a tariff. Until then, though, the cost of this tariff protection adds about 33 cents to a typical jar of peanut butter in the United States.[3] Even if consumers knew about this surcharge, they would likely not see enough incentive to band together and push their governmental leaders to rectify the situation.

ECONOMIC RATIONALES FOR GOVERNMENTAL INTERVENTION

Governmental intervention in trade may be classified as either economic or non-economic, as shown in Table 7.1. Let's begin by profiling leading economic rationales.

Unemployment

Pressure groups, whether workers, consumers, or some mix of stakeholders, often question government policymakers and businesspeople. Policymakers must decide which conflicting pressure groups to heed. Businesspeople must lobby policymakers to counter groups whose proposals might penalize them. There is probably no more effective pressure group than the unemployed; no other group has the time and incentive to picket companies, contact governmental representatives, and confront organizations. For example, unemployed U.S. steelworkers pressured U.S. lawmakers to apply tariffs and quotas to restrict steel imports in order to preserve their jobs and pensions.[4]

> The unemployed can form an effective pressure group for import restrictions.

One difficulty with restricting imports to create jobs is that other countries normally retaliate with their own restrictions. That is, trade restrictions designed to support domestic industries typically trigger a drop in production in some foreign country. For example, one country's plan to "export unemployment" to a trade partner has usually triggered quick retaliation from the latter. When the United States restricted steel imports, the EU, Brazil, and Japan threatened to restrict purchases of U.S. products, such as oranges. The United States then rescinded its steel protection.[5]

Two factors can ease the effects of retaliation. First, small trading countries are less important in the retaliation process. For example, if the United States were to further limit clothing imports, China would have more power to retaliate than Mauritius. Further, the United States is less apt to retaliate against Mauritian trade restrictions than against Chinese ones because the latter affects the U.S. economy more. Second, retaliation that decreases employment in a capital-intensive industry may not affect employment as much as the value of the trade loss would imply. For example, if the United States restricts imports of apparel from China, a labor-intensive good, any resultant Chinese retaliation against U.S. exports of the same value in a capital-intensive industry, say U.S.-produced semiconductors, would threaten fewer U.S. jobs than would be gained from maintaining apparel production. Even if no country retaliates, the restricting country may gain jobs in one sector only to lose jobs elsewhere. For example, lower imports of a product means fewer import-handling jobs.

> Import restrictions to create domestic employment
> - May lead to retaliation by other countries
> - Are less likely retaliated effectively by small economies
> - Are less likely to be met with retaliation if implemented by small economies
> - May decrease export jobs because of price increases for components
> - May decrease export jobs because of lower incomes abroad

TABLE 7.1   RATIONALES FOR GOVERNMENT INTERVENTION IN TRADE

ECONOMIC RATIONALES	NONECONOMIC RATIONALES
Prevent unemployment	Maintain essential industries
Protect infant industries	Deal with unfriendly countries
Promote industrialization	Maintain or extend spheres of influence
Improve position compared to other countries	Preserve national identity

Government policymakers must consider the conflicting effects of protectionism on different industries and companies. In other words, imports may also help create jobs in other industries, and these industries may champion free trade. For example, when the United States imposed import restrictions on steel, the U.S. company Delphi, the world's largest auto parts manufacturer, had trouble competing because steel prices increased so much.[6] Imports also stimulate exports, although less directly, by increasing foreign income and foreign-exchange earnings, which are then spent on new imports by foreign consumers. If import restrictions do increase domestic employment, fellow citizens will have to bear the costs of higher prices or higher taxes. In addition, if managers believe trade protection is a long-term policy, they may see no competitive urgency to invest in technological innovation, thus further depriving consumers of higher quality products at lower prices.

Government officials should compare the costs of higher prices with the costs of unemployment and displaced production that would result from freer trade. In addition, they must consider the costs of policies to ease the plight of displaced employees, such as for unemployment benefits or retraining. These are challenging tasks that involve difficult economic and social questions. For example, it is hard to put a price on the distress suffered by people who lose their jobs due to increasing imports. It is also difficult for working people to understand that they may be better off financially (because of lower prices) even if they must then pay higher taxes to support unemployment or welfare benefits for people who lost their jobs to rising imports.

The employment issue can slow trade liberalization because displaced workers are often the ones who are least able to find alternative work at a comparable salary. On average, trade-displaced workers in the United States earned about 13 percent less in their new job than they did on their old job—more than a third suffered a 30 percent drop in wages.[7] Similar effects have been found in Germany, Canada, and France.[8] In addition, displaced workers often spend their unemployment benefits on living expenses rather than on retraining in the hope that they will be recalled to their old jobs. When they do seek retraining, many workers, especially older ones, lack the educational background necessary to gain required skills. Worse still, some train for jobs that do not materialize.

In summary, persistent unemployment pushes many groups to call for protectionism. However, evidence suggests that efforts to reduce unemployment through import restrictions are usually ineffective.[9] Unemployment, in and of itself, is better dealt with through fiscal and monetary policies. Furthermore, as the rest of the chapter shows, governments can use other rationales to justify trade protectionism.

Infant-Industry Argument

In 1792, Alexander Hamilton presented what has become one of the oldest arguments for protectionism. The **infant-industry argument** holds that a government should shield an emerging industry from foreign competition by guaranteeing it a large share of the domestic market until it is able to compete on its own. Many emerging economies use this argument to validate their protectionist policies. The infant-industry argument presumes that the initial output costs for a small-scale industry in a given country may be so high as to make its output noncompetitive in world markets. Eventual competitiveness is not the reward for endurance but the result of the efficiency gains from achieving the economies of large-scale production and of learning from experience. Therefore, the host government needs to protect an infant industry long enough for its fledgling companies to gain economies of scale and their employees to translate experience into higher productivity. These achievements will enable a company to manufacture efficiently, thereby positioning it to compete internationally. At this point, the government can then recoup the costs of trade protection through benefits like higher domestic employment, lower social costs, and higher tax revenues.

Although it is reasonable to expect production costs to decrease over time, they may never fall enough to create internationally competitive products. This risk poses two

Possible costs of import restrictions include

- Higher prices
- Higher taxes
- Such costs should be compared with those of unemployment.

The infant-industry argument says that production becomes more competitive over time because of

- Increased economies of scale
- Greater worker efficiency

When faced with possible job loss, affected workers seek to influence trade policy to get protection. Here we see workers (fishermen) in the Philippines protesting the importation of fish from Norway.

problems for protecting an infant industry. First, governments must identify those industries that have a high probability of success. Some industries grow to be competitive because of governmental protection; automobile production in Brazil and South Korea are good examples. However, in many other cases—such as automobile production in Malaysia and Australia—the protected industries remain inefficient even after years of government aid. If infant-industry protection goes to an industry that fails to reduce costs enough to compete against imports, chances are its owners, workers, and suppliers will constitute a formidable pressure group that may prevent the importation of competing, lower priced products. Also, the security of government protection against import competition may deter managers from adopting the innovations needed to compete globally.

Second, even if policymakers can determine those infant industries likely to succeed, it does not necessarily follow that companies in those industries should receive governmental assistance. There are many examples of entrepreneurs who endured early losses to achieve future benefits without any public help. Still, policymakers regularly contend that governments should assist new companies facing high entry barriers and efficient foreign rivals because local entrepreneurs may lack the means to become competitive without assistance.

Infant-industry protection requires some segment of the economy to incur the higher cost of inefficient local production. Typically, consumers end up paying higher prices for the protected companies' products. A government can subsidize companies so that consumer prices do not increase, in which case taxpayers pay this subsidy. Too, production subsidies reduce the amount that governments can spend elsewhere, such as on education and infrastructure, a serious consideration in emerging economies. Ultimately, the validity of the infant-industry argument rests on the expectation that the future benefits of an internationally competitive industry will exceed the costs of the associated protectionism.

Industrialization Argument

Countries seek protection
to promote industrialization
because that type of
production

- Brings faster growth than
agriculture
- Brings in investment funds
- Diversifies the economy
- Brings more income than
primary products do
- Reduces imports and
promotes exports
- Helps the nation-building
process

Countries with a large manufacturing base generally have higher per capita incomes than those that do not. Moreover, a number of countries, such as the U.S. and Japan, developed an industrial base while largely regulating imports from foreign producers. Many emerging economies try to emulate this strategy, using trade protection to spur local industrialization. Specifically, they believe:

1. Surplus workers can more easily increase manufacturing output than agricultural output.
2. Inflows of foreign investment in the industrial area promote sustainable growth.
3. Prices and sales of agricultural products and raw materials fluctuate very much, which is a detriment to economies that depend on few of them.
4. Markets for industrial products grow faster than markets for agricultural products.
5. Local industry reduces imports and promotes exports.
6. Industrial activity helps the nation-building process.

We now review each of these notions.

Use of Surplus Workers   A large portion of the population in many emerging markets live and farm in rural areas. Usually, agricultural output per person is low. Consequently, many people can migrate from the agricultural to industrial sector without significantly reducing total agricultural output. Like the infant-industry argument, the **industrialization argument** presumes that the unregulated importation of lower-priced products prevents the development of a domestic industry. However, unlike the infant-industry argument, the industrialization rationale asserts that industrial output will increase, even if domestic prices do not become globally competitive, because local consumers must buy goods from local producers.[10]

Shifting people out of agriculture, however, can create problems:

When a country shifts from
agriculture to industry

- Demands on social and
political services in cities
may increase
- Output increases if the
marginal productivity of
agricultural workers is
very low
- Development possibilities
in the agricultural sector
may be overlooked

1. Workers' high expectations of industrial jobs may be unfulfilled, leading to increasing demand for social services. A major problem facing emerging economies is the migration to urban areas of people who then cannot find suitable jobs, housing, and social services. For example, China's move toward industrialization has spurred millions of people to move to cities; most have prospered but many have not. Some estimate China's urban unemployment rate runs 3 to 5 times the officially reported rate.[11] Many struggle to find work because the industrialization process has proceeded slowly, few jobs are created in traditional industries, or they lack the skills and work habits required for manufacturing jobs.

2. Improved agriculture practices, not a drastic shift to industry, may be a better means of achieving economic success. Typically, few emerging economies farm their land efficiently—doing so can create great benefits at low cost.[12] Equally, industrialization is not the only means of growth. The U.S., Canada, and Argentina grew during the nineteenth century, largely through their comparative advantage in agricultural exports. They continue to profit from exports of food products. Similarly, Australia, New Zealand, and Denmark maintain high per capita income with a mix of industry and agricultural specialization.

3. Rapid migration from rural to urban areas may abruptly reduce agricultural output, further jeopardizing a country's self-sufficiency. Interestingly, most of the world's agricultural production and exports come from high-income countries because their efficient and capital-intensive agricultural sectors enable the transfer of resources into the manufacturing sector without decreasing agricultural output.

Promoting Investment Inflows   Import restrictions, applied to spur industrialization, also may increase foreign direct investment. Barred from an attractive foreign market by trade restrictions, foreign companies may transfer manufacturing to that country to avoid the loss of a lucrative or potential market. The resulting influx of foreign companies may speed a country's industrialization. For example, Thailand's automobile import restrictions prompted foreign automakers, like GM, Ford, and BMW, to invest there. Foreign investment inflows may also add to local employment, which is attractive to policymakers.

If import restrictions keep out foreign-made goods, foreign companies may invest to produce in the restricted area.

Diversification   Export prices of many primary products fluctuate markedly.[13] For instance, coffee prices fell about two-thirds between 2000 and 2002 and then regained half the loss the next year.[14] Price variations due to uncontrollable factors—such as weather affecting supply or business cycles abroad affecting demand—can wreak havoc on economies that depend on the export of primary products. This is especially true when an economy must rely on a few commodities for job creation and export earnings. Moreover, many emerging economies depend on just one primary commodity for over a quarter of their export earnings. Frequently, they are caught in a "feast or famine" cycle, able to afford foreign luxuries one year but unable to find the funds for replacement parts for essential equipment the next. Contrary to expectation, a greater dependence on manufacturing does not guarantee diversification of export earnings. The GDPs of many emerging economies are small; a move to manufacturing may shift dependence from one or two agricultural commodities to one or two manufactured products.

Greater Growth for Manufactured Products   The **terms of trade** is the quantity of imports that a given quantity of a country's exports can buy—that is, how many bananas Country A must sell to Country B to purchase one refrigerator from Country B. Historically, the prices of raw materials and agricultural commodities do not rise as fast as the prices of finished products. Hence, over time it takes more low-priced primary products to buy the same amount of high-priced manufactured goods. Further, the quantity of primary products demanded does not rise as rapidly, so emerging nations that depend on primary products have become increasingly poorer relative to industrial countries. The declining terms of trade for emerging economies is partly explained by slowing consumer demand for agricultural products and by changes in technology that have reduced the need for many raw materials. A further explanation is that competitive rivalry transfers many of the benefits of lower production costs of primary products to consumers. In contrast, cost savings for manufactured products go mainly to higher profits and wages.

Terms of trade for emerging economies may deteriorate because

- *Demand for primary products grows more slowly*
- *Production cost savings for primary products will be passed on to consumers*

Import Substitution versus Export Promotion   Traditionally, emerging economies promoted industrialization by restricting imports in order to boost local production for local consumption. Recall the case in Chapter 6 on Costa Rica's import substitution policies from about 1960 to 1980. In recent years, many countries like Costa Rica have come to believe that import substitution is not the best approach to develop new industries. If the protected industries do not become efficient, an all too frequent outcome, local consumers may have to support them by paying higher prices or higher taxes. In addition, the reality that most industries must usually import capital equipment and other supplies reduces foreign-exchange savings. In contrast, some countries, such as Taiwan and South Korea, have achieved rapid economic growth by promoting the development of industries that export their output. This approach is known as **export-led development.** In reality, it is not easy to distinguish between import substitution versus export promotion. Industrialization may result initially in import substitution, yet export development of the same products may be feasible later. For example, India restricts the importation of automobiles and their parts, thereby letting local production capture those sales. In all likelihood, India will eventually promote the export of cars. Finally, the fact that a country concentrates its industrialization activities on products for which it would seem

Industrialization emphasizes either

- *Products to sell domestically or*
- *Products to export*

to have a comparative advantage does not guarantee that those products will necessarily become competitive exports. There are various trade barriers, discussed later in this chapter, that interfere with the export of manufacturing goods from emerging economies.

Nation Building   The performance of free markets suggests a strong relationship between industrialization and aspects of the nation-building process. Industrialization helps countries to build infrastructure, advance rural development, enhance rural people's' social life, and boost the skills of the workforce. For example, Ecuador and Vietnam maintain that industrialization has helped them move from feudal economies suffering chronic food shortages to nations with improved food security and budding export competitiveness.[15]

Economic Relationships with Other Countries

Countries monitor their absolute economic welfare as well as track how their performance compares to other countries. Governments will impose trade restrictions to improve their relative trade positions. They might buy less from other countries than those countries buy from them. They might try to charge higher export prices while keeping import prices low—though not so low as to penalize their domestic producers. Among the many motivations, four stand out.

Balance-of-Payments Adjustments   Chapter 4 showed that the trade account is a major part of the balance of payments for most countries. A trade deficit creates problems for nations with low foreign exchange reserves—the funds that help a nation to finance the purchase of foreign goods and to maintain their export trade. Governments can improve their balance of payments by improving their balance of trade. So, if balance-of-payments difficulties arise and persist, a government may restrict imports or encourage exports to balance its trade account. One way to do this is for a country to devalue its currency, which makes all of its products cheaper in relation to foreign products. However, a country may use protection more effectively so as to affect only certain products. For example, since the 1970s the U.S. has imported more from Japan than it has exported there. Trade in automobiles makes up most of the imbalance. At times, the U.S. government has tried to correct the imbalance by regulating the value and number of Japanese vehicles imported into the U.S., persuading Japanese automotive companies to locate more production within the U.S., and negotiating with the Japanese government to ease the entry of U.S.-made cars into Japan.

Comparable Access or "Fairness"   Companies and industries often argue that they are entitled to the same access to foreign markets as foreign industries and companies have to their markets. Economic theory supports this idea, reasoning that producers operating in industries where increased production leads to steep cost decreases (that is to say there are substantial cost decreases through economies of scale) but which lack equal access to a competitor's market will struggle to gain enough sales to be cost-competitive. The **comparable access argument** has been used in the semiconductor, chemicals, aircraft, softwood lumber, energy, and telecommunications industries.[16]

The argument for equal access also is presented as one of fairness. For example, the U.S. government permits foreign financial service companies to operate in the U.S., but only if their home governments allow U.S. financial service companies equivalent market access. However, some reject using the idea of fairness to justify comparable market access. First, tit-for-tat market access can lead to restrictions that may deny one's own consumers lower prices. Second, governments would find it impractical to negotiate and monitor separate agreements for each of the many thousands of different products and services that might be traded.

Domestic producers may be disadvantaged if their access to foreign markets is less than foreign producers' access to their market.

Restrictions as a Bargaining Tool   We have already discussed how countries retaliate to other countries' trade restrictions. Thus the imposition of import restrictions may be used as a means to persuade other countries to lower their import barriers. The danger in this is that each country escalates its restrictions so that, in effect, we have a trade war that impacts all the countries' economies negatively. Nevertheless, to successfully use restrictions as a bargaining tool requires careful consideration of what products to target. Basically, they need to be believable and important to the influential parties in the other country. *Believable* implies that there are either alternative sources to buy the same product or that consumers are willing to do without it. For instance, in trade retaliations between the United States and the EU, the EU has threatened to impose trade restrictions on U.S.-grown soybeans when Brazil had surplus production. Picking products important to influential parties was emphasized after the United States had placed restrictions on the importation of steel. The EU threatened to place restrictions on the importation of apples from the state of Washington and oranges from Florida. Given the importance of these two states in a close presidential election, the decision to remove the steel import restrictions was hastened by this threat.

Price-Control Objectives   Countries sometimes withhold goods from international markets in an effort to raise prices abroad. This action is most feasible when a few countries hold monopoly or near-monopoly control of certain resources. They can then limit supply so consumers must pay a higher price. This policy often encourages smuggling, such as of emeralds and diamonds. This policy may also encourage other countries to develop technology that will provide either substitute products, such as synthetic rubber in place of natural rubber, or different ways of producing the same product, such as the cultivation of sturgeons to produce caviar in the United States in response to high Russian prices for caviar from wild sturgeon.[17] Export controls are especially ineffective if a product can be digitized—such as music, video, and texts. In addition, if prices are too high or supplies too limited, people will seek substitutes.

Related to the above, at this writing, South Africa is discussing legislation to require companies to add value to its precious minerals, such as gold and diamonds, before exporting them, such as polishing diamonds and making gold jewelry. This would add employment in South Africa and increase the value of its exports. However, some companies, such as AngloGold Ashanti and De Beers, worry that doing so will raise costs too much. For instance, the cost of polishing and cutting each rough carat of diamonds may cost up to $40 in South Africa and only $10 to $15 dollars in India.[18]

A country may limit exports of a product that is in short supply worldwide in order to favor domestic consumers. Typically, greater supply drops local prices beneath those in the intentionally undersupplied world market. Argentina, for instance, has done this with natural gas, and Canada has considered doing it with patented prescription drugs.[19] Favoring consumers usually disfavors producers. Lower prices at home often prompt companies to reduce local production.

Countries also fear that foreign producers will price their exports so artificially low that they drive domestic producers out of business. High entry barriers, the reasoning goes, let the surviving foreign producers charge exorbitant prices abroad. However, competition among foreign producers limits their ability to charge exorbitant prices. It also encourages them to sell abroad. For example, low import prices have eliminated most U.S. production of consumer electronics. Still, the U.S. has some of the lowest prices in the world for consumer electronics, and there seems to be little prospect that these prices will become exorbitant in the future.

Companies sometimes export below cost or below their home-country price, a practice called **dumping.** Most countries prohibit imports of dumped products but enforcement usually occurs only if the imported product disrupts domestic production. If there is no domestic production, then host country consumers get the benefit of lower prices. Companies may dump products because they cannot otherwise build a market abroad— essentially, a low price encourages consumers to sample the foreign brand.

Export restrictions may

- Keep up world prices
- Require more controls to prevent smuggling
- Lead to substitution
- Keep domestic prices down by increasing domestic supply
- Give producers less incentive to increase output
- Shift foreign production and sales

Import restrictions may

- Prevent dumping from being used to put domestic producers out of business
- Get foreign producers to lower their prices

Companies can afford to dump products if they can charge high prices in their home market or if their home-country government subsidizes them. They may also opt to incur short-term losses abroad, presuming that they can recoup those losses when, after they eliminate their rivals or gain brand loyalty, they can then raise their prices. Ironically, home-country consumers or taxpayers seldom realize that paying high prices locally results in lower prices for foreign consumers.

An industry that believes it is competing against dumped products may appeal to its government to restrict the imports. U.S. companies in such industries as shrimp, candles, and furniture have done so in recent years.[20] However, determining a foreign company's cost or domestic price is difficult because of limited access to the foreign producers' accounting statements, fluctuations in exchange rates, and the passage of products through layers of distribution before reaching the end-consumer. The result is that governments allegedly restrict imports arbitrarily through antidumping provisions of their trade legislation and are slow to dispose of the restrictions if pricing situations change. Companies caught in this situation often lose the export market they labored to build.

Another price argument for governmental influence on trade is the **optimum-tariff theory.** This theory states that a foreign producer will lower its prices if the importing country places a tax on its products. If this occurs, benefits shift to the importing country because the foreign producer lowers its profits on the export sales. Assume that an exporter has costs of $500 per unit and is selling to a foreign market for $700 per unit. With the imposition of a 10 percent tax on the imported price, the exporter may choose to lower its price to $636.36 per unit, which, with a 10 percent tax of $63.64, would keep the price at $700 for the importer. The exporter may feel that a price higher than $700 would result in lost sales and that a profit of $136.36 per unit instead of the previous $200 per unit is better than no profit at all. Consequently, an amount of $63.64 per unit has thus shifted to the importing country. As long as the foreign producer lowers its price by any amount, some shift in revenue goes to the importing country and the tariff is deemed an optimum one. There are many examples of products whose prices did not rise as much as the amount of the imposed tariff; however, it is difficult to predict when, where, and which exporters will voluntarily reduce their profit margins.

NONECONOMIC RATIONALES FOR GOVERNMENT INTERVENTION

Economic rationales help explain many government actions on trade. However, governments sometimes use noneconomic rationales, such as the following:

- Maintenance of essential industries (especially defense)
- Prevention of shipments to unfriendly countries
- Maintenance or extension of spheres of influence
- Protecting activities that help preserve the national identity

Let's look at each rationale.

Maintenance of Essential Industries

In protecting essential industries, countries must

- Determine which ones are essential
- Consider costs and alternatives
- Consider political consequences

Governments apply trade restrictions to protect essential domestic industries during peacetime so that a country is not dependent on foreign sources of supply during war. This is called the **essential-industry argument.** For example, the U.S. government subsidizes the domestic production of silicon so that domestic computer chip producers will not need to depend on foreign suppliers. This argument for protection has much appeal in rallying support for import barriers. However, in times of real crisis or military emergency, almost any product could be deemed essential. Because of the high cost of protecting an inefficient industry or a higher-cost domestic substitute, the essential-industry argument should not be (but frequently is) accepted without a careful evaluation of costs, real needs, and alternatives. Once an industry receives protection, it is difficult to remove it because the protected companies and their employees support politicians who support their continued protection—even when the rationale for the subsidies long ago disappeared. This is why the United States, for example, continues to subsidize its mohair producers more than 20 years since mohair was deemed no longer essential for military uniforms.[21]

Prevention of Shipments to "Unfriendly" Countries

Groups concerned about security often use national defense arguments to prevent the export, even to friendly countries, of strategic goods that might fall into the hands of potential enemies or that might be in short supply domestically. For example, the United States prevented exports of data-encryption technology (data-scrambling hardware and software) until a group of U.S. high-tech companies allied themselves with privacy advocacy groups to convince the U.S. government to relax the export curbs. Now, U.S. companies can export any encryption product to the members of the European Union and other European and Pacific Rim allies without first getting permission.[22] Export constraints may be valid if the exporting country assumes there will be no retaliation that prevents it from securing even more essential goods from the potential importing country. Even then, the importing country may find alternative supply sources or develop a production capability of its own. In this situation, the country limiting exports is the economic loser. Thus, the use of trade sanctions has been controversial, as indicated in the Point–Counterpoint box.

Countries levy trade restrictions to coerce other countries to change their policies.

POINT–COUNTERPOINT: SHOULD COUNTRIES ELIMINATE THE USE OF TRADE SANCTIONS?

POINT

Yes, they should. Every time I turn around, I see my government imposing a new sanction. While some don't affect my business, others do. When they do, I lose business that took me years to develop. For instance, a few years back, my company had worked hard to develop a market for office machinery in Iraq. Then, suddenly, we could not export to Iraq and were left holding inventory that we had on the loading dock ready to ship. Thus, the trade sanctions were aimed at hurting the government of Iraq, but we were the ones who were hurt even though we had never engaged in any objectionable behavior.

Besides, I really question whether these sanctions even work. For example, the U.S. maintained a 20-year trade embargo on Vietnam. Still, Vietnamese consumers were able to buy U.S. consumer products, such as Coca-Cola, Kodak film, and Apple computers, through other countries that did not

enforce the sanctions.[23] The United States' trade embargo with Panama only made Panama's Noriega government more adamant in its opposition to the United States. Trade sanctions against Cuba were supposed to topple the Castro regime, but four decades later, he was still in power.

Further, even if trade sanctions are successful at weakening the targeted countries' economy, who really suffers in that economy? You can bet that the political leaders still get whatever they need, so that the costs of sanctions are borne by innocent people. This occurred in Iraq, where there were widespread reports of children's deaths because of inadequate supplies of food and medicine from the sanctions.

Finally, governments sometimes seem to impose trade sanctions based on one issue rather than on a country's overall record. For instance, some critics have suggested using trade policies to press Brazil to restrict the cutting of Amazon forests, even though its overall environmental record, particularly its limiting of adverse exhaust emissions by converting automobile engines to use methanol instead of gasoline, is quite good.

COUNTERPOINT

Let's face it. We're now living in a global society where actions in one country can spill over and affect people all over the world. For instance, the development of a nuclear arsenal in one country can escalate the damage that terrorists can do elsewhere. The failure of a country to protect endangered species can have long-term effects on the whole world's environment. We simply can't sit back and let things happen elsewhere that will come back to haunt us.

At the same time, some pretty dastardly things occur in some countries, and most of the world community would like to see them stopped. These include human rights violations in Myanmar, the use of child slaves to harvest cocoa in the Ivory Coast, and the use of diamond production in Sierra Leone to finance revolutions. Even if we can't stop these occurrences, we have a moral responsibility not to participate even if it costs us. If I can draw an analogy, I may get some economic benefits by buying from a criminal, and I may not stop that criminal's activity by withholding my business. However, I refuse to deal with the criminal because, in effect, that makes me a criminal's associate.

Although not all trade sanctions have been successful, many have at least been influential in achieving their objectives. These included UN sanctions against Rhodesia (now Zimbabwe), United Kingdom and United States sanctions against the Amin government of Uganda, and Indian sanctions against Nepal.[24] At the same time, it is difficult to assess the full result of a trade sanction. For instance, although there were multiple factors opposing the Duvalier regime in Haiti and apartheid in South Africa, few doubt that trade sanctions on Haiti and South Africa significantly damaged their political regimes.[25] Further, although the sanctions against Cuba have not removed Castro from office, they may have slowed his ability to create revolutions elsewhere.

Finally, when a nation breaks international agreements or acts in unpopular ways, what courses of action can other nations take? Between 1827 and World War I, nations mounted 21 blockades, but these are now considered to be too dangerous. Military force has also been used, such as for the overthrow of the Saddam regime in Iraq, but such measures have little global support. Thus, nations may take such punitive actions as withholding diplomatic recognition, boycotting athletic and cultural events, seizing the other country's foreign property, and eliminating foreign aid and loans. These may be ineffective in and of themselves without the addition of trade sanctions. In addition, countries may give incentives rather than taking punitive actions. This has occurred, for example, with North Korea to curb its nuclear program and has been suggested for Iran for the same purpose.[26]

Trade controls on nondefense goods also may be used as a weapon of foreign policy to try to prevent another country from meeting its political objectives. For example, the U.S. imposed trade sanctions on nine Chinese companies and an Indian businessman that it found had sold technology to Iran that was then put to use by that country's chemical and conventional weapons programs. The sanctions barred these firms from doing business with the U.S. government, forbade them to export goods into the U.S., and prevented U.S. companies from exporting certain items to them.[27] Still, there is potential for gains from trade as countries become friendlier. For example, the United States lifted trade sanctions against Libya in 2004, and three U.S. oil companies (Occidental Petroleum, Amerada Hess, and ChevronTexaco) received licenses to explore for Libyan oil in 2005.[28]

Maintenance or Extension of Spheres of Influence

There are many examples of governmental actions on trade designed to support their spheres of influence. Governments give aid and credits to, and encourage imports from, countries that join a political alliance or vote a preferred way within international bodies. For example, the EU has given preferential treatment of bananas from certain former colonies. Similarly, the EU and the 77 members of the African, Caribbean, and Pacific Group of States signed the Cotonou Agreement to formalize preferential trade relationships by offering members of the latter group privileged access to European markets.[29]

A country's trade restrictions may coerce governments to follow certain political actions or punish companies whose governments do not. For example, China delayed permission for Allianz, a German insurance group, to operate in China after Germany gave a reception for the Dalai Lama, the exiled Tibetan spiritual leader.[30] Many interest groups in the U.S. have called for trade restrictions on Chinese products because of China's controversial human rights record.[31]

Protecting Activities that Help Preserve the National Identity

Countries are held together partially through a unifying sense of identity that sets their citizens apart from those in other nations. To sustain this collective identity, countries limit foreign products and services in certain sectors. For many years, Japan, South Korea, and China maintained an almost total ban on rice imports, largely because rice farming has been a historically cohesive force in each nation. Recent pressures from the WTO have led them to relent.[32] Canada relies on a "cultural sovereignty" argument to prohibit foreign ownership or control of publishing, cable TV, and bookselling.[33] Similarly, France protects its cinema industry out of fear that, if unregulated, the resulting invasion of English language and Anglo-Saxon culture will weaken its cultural identity. The French government subsidizes activities in the filmmaking and dubbing industries and limits the percentage of foreign films shown on French television.[34] Korea requires theaters to show Korean films at least 146 days per year.[35]

INSTRUMENTS OF TRADE CONTROL

Governments use many rationales and seek a range of outcomes when they try to influence exports or imports. We now profile the instruments that governments use to try to do so. Because a country's trade policy has repercussions abroad, retaliation from foreign governments looms as a potential obstacle to achieve the desired objectives. Therefore, the choice of the instrument of trade control is crucial because each type may incite different responses from domestic and foreign groups. One way to understand the types of instruments is to distinguish between those that indirectly affect the amount traded by directly influencing the prices of exports or imports versus those that directly limit the amount that can be traded.

Tariffs

A common distinction is between tariff barriers and nontariff barriers. Tariff barriers affect prices; nontariff barriers may affect either price or quantity directly. A **tariff** (also called a **duty**) is the most common type of trade control and is a tax that governments levy on a good shipped internationally. That is, governments charge a tariff on a good when it crosses an official boundary—whether it be that of a nation, say Mexico, or a group of nations, like the EU, that have agreed to impose a common tariff on goods entering their bloc. Tariffs collected by the exporting country are called an **export tariff;** if collected by a country through which the goods have passed, it is a **transit tariff;** if collected by the importing country, it is an **import tariff.** The import tariff is by far the most common.

Figure 7.4 illustrates how tariff and nontariff barriers affect both the price and the quantity sold, although in a different order and with a different impact on producers. Parts (a) and (b) both have downward-sloping demand curves (D) and upward-sloping supply curves (S). In other words, the lower the price, the higher the quantity that consumers demand; the higher the price, the more that suppliers make available for sale. The intersection of the S and D curves illustrates the price (P_1) and quantity sold (Q_1) without governmental interference. When a tax (tariff) raises the price from P_1 to P_2 in part (a), the amount consumers are willing to buy will fall from Q_1 to Q_2. Producers do

> **Tariffs may be levied**
>
> - On goods entering, leaving, or passing through a country
> - For protection or revenue
> - On a per unit or a value basis

FIGURE 7.4

COMPARISON OF TRADE RESTRICTIONS

In (a), the tax on imports ($P_2 - P_1$) raises the price, which reduces the quantity demanded from Q_1 to Q_2. In (b), the quantity limit on imports ($Q_1 - Q_2$) reduces the supply available and raises prices from P_1 to P_2. The price rise in (b) is charged by producers.

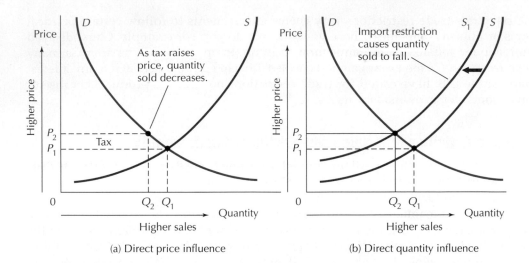

(a) Direct price influence

(b) Direct quantity influence

not benefit because the price increase goes to the government as taxes rather than to them as profits. Part (b) shows a restriction in available supply; therefore a new supply curve (S_1) is imposed. The quantity sold now falls from Q_1 to Q_2. At the lower supply, sellers raise the price from P_1 to P_2, which is shown in the intersection of the D and S_1 curves. The major difference in the two forms of trade control is that sellers raise the price in (b), which helps compensate them for the decrease in quantity sold. In (a), producers sell less and are unable to raise their price because the tax has already done this.

Import tariffs raise the price of imported goods, thereby giving domestically produced goods a relative price advantage. A tariff may be protective even though there is no domestic production in direct competition. For example, a country that wants its residents to spend less on foreign goods and services may raise the price of some foreign products, even though there are no close domestic substitutes, in order to curtail demand for imports.

Tariffs also serve as a source of governmental revenue. Import tariffs are of little importance to industrial countries, usually costing more to collect than they yield.[36] Tariffs, however, are a major source of revenue in many emerging economies. This is because government authorities in emerging economies may have more control over determining the amounts and types of goods crossing their borders and collecting a tax on them than they do over determining and collecting individual and corporate income taxes. Although revenue tariffs are most commonly collected on imports, many countries that export raw materials charge export tariffs.[37] Transit tariffs were once a major source of revenue for countries, but governmental treaties have nearly abolished them.

A government may assess a tariff on a per unit basis, in which case it is applying a **specific duty.** It may assess a tariff as a percentage of the value of the item, in which case it is an **ad valorem duty.** If it assesses both a specific duty and an ad valorem duty on the same product, the combination is a **compound duty.** A specific duty is straightforward for customs officials who collect duties to assess because they do not need to determine a good's value on which to calculate a percentage tax.

A tariff controversy concerns industrial countries' treatment of manufactured exports from emerging economies that seek to add manufactured value to their exports of raw materials (like instant coffee instead of coffee beans). Raw materials frequently enter industrial countries free of duty; however, if processed, industrial countries then assign an import tariff. Because an ad valorem tariff is based on the total value of the product, meaning the raw materials and the processing combined, emerging countries argue that the **effective tariff** on the manufactured portion turns out to be higher than the published tariff rate. For example, a country may charge no duty on coffee beans but may assess a 10 percent ad valorem tariff on instant coffee. If $5 for a jar of instant coffee covers $2.50 in coffee beans and $2.50 in processing costs, the $0.50 duty is effectively 20 percent on the manufactured portion, because the coffee beans could have entered free of duty. This anomaly further challenges emerging economies to find markets for their manufactured products. At the same time, the governments of industrial countries cannot easily remove barriers to imports of emerging economies' manufactured products, largely because these imports affect unskilled or unemployed workers who are least equipped to move to new jobs.

Nontariff Barriers: Direct Price Influences

We have shown how tariffs raise prices and limit trade. We now turn to how governments alter the price of products to limit their trade.

Subsidies   Countries sometimes make direct payments to domestic companies to compensate them for losses incurred from selling abroad, such as U.S. subsidies to cotton exporters.[38] However, they provide other types of assistance to make it cheaper or more profitable to sell overseas. For example, most countries offer potential exporters many business development services, such as market information, trade expositions, and foreign contacts. From the standpoint of market efficiency, these sorts of subsidies are more justifiable than tariffs because they seek to overcome, rather than create, market imperfections. There are also benefits to disseminating information widely because governments can spread the costs of collecting information among many users. Finally, other countries are less likely to complain about business development assistance than direct subsidies.

Trade frictions result from disagreement on the definition of a subsidy. For instance, did Canada subsidize exports of fish because it gave grants to fishermen to buy trawlers? Similarly, did India subsidize insurance when the government-owned insurance carrier incurred severe losses? Questions also surround governments' support of R&D, as well as tax programs that directly or indirectly affect export profitability. One interesting subsidy case involves commercial aircraft. Airbus Industrie and the EU claim that the U.S. government subsidizes Boeing through research and development contracts for military aircraft that also have commercial applications. Boeing and the United States government claim the EU subsidizes Airbus Industrie through low-interest government loans.[39]

Aid and Loans   Governments also give aid and loans to other countries. If the recipient is required to spend the funds in the donor country, which is known as *tied aid* or *tied loans,* some products can compete abroad that might otherwise be noncompetitive. Tied aid helps win large contracts for infrastructure, such as telecommunications, railways, and electric power projects. However, there is growing skepticism about the value of tied aid. Tied aid can slow the development of local suppliers in developing countries and shield suppliers in the donor countries from competition. These concerns led the members of the OECD to untie financial aid to developing countries, no longer obliging aid recipient countries to purchase equipment from suppliers in the donor country.[40]

Customs Valuation   The temptation exists for exporters and importers to declare a low price on invoices in order to pay a lower ad valorem tariff. Generally, most countries have agreed on preventive procedures for assessing values when their customs agents levy tariffs. First, customs officials must use the declared invoice price. If there is none, or if they doubt its authenticity, agents must then assess on the basis of the value of identical goods. If not possible, agents must assess on the basis of similar goods arriving in or about the same time. For example, there is no sales invoice when imported goods enter for lease rather than purchase. Customs officials must then base the tariff on the value of identical or similar goods. If this basis cannot be used, officials may compute a value based on final sales value or on reasonable cost. Similarly, sometimes agents use their discretionary power to assess the value too high, thereby preventing the importation of foreign-made products.[41]

Governmental subsidies may help companies be competitive.

- Subsidies to overcome market imperfections are least controversial.
- There is little agreement on what a subsidy is.
- There has been a recent increase in export-credit assistance.

Because it is difficult for customs officials to determine the honesty of import invoices

- They may arbitrarily increase value.
- Valuation procedures have been developed.
- They may question the origin of imports.

The fact that so many different products are traded creates valuation problems. It is easy (by accident or intention) to misclassify a product and its corresponding tariff. Administering more than 13,000 categories of products means a customs agent must use professional discretion to determine if, say, silicon chips should be considered "integrated circuits for computers" or "a form of chemical silicon." Marvel fought a six-year court battle to win a verdict that its X-Men Wolverines were toys (at a 6.8 percent duty) and not dolls (at a 12 percent duty). While the difference in duty may seem trivial, the difference amounted to millions of dollars. Similarly, the U.S. Customs Service had to determine whether sport utility vehicles, such as the Suzuki Samurai and the Land Rover, were cars or trucks. It assessed the 25 percent duty on trucks instead of the 2.5 percent duty on cars. Later, a federal trade court ruled them to be cars.

Because countries assess different duties and have different import controls for different countries, customs must also determine a product's origin. Otherwise, exporters and importers could misstate the origin to pay a lower duty.

Other Direct Price Influences   Countries use other means to affect prices, including special fees (such as for consular and customs clearance and documentation), requirements that customs deposits be placed in advance of shipment, and minimum price levels at which goods can be sold after they have customs clearance.

Nontariff Barriers: Quantity Controls

Governments use other nontariff regulations and practices to affect directly the quantity of imports and exports. Principal forms of quantity controls include the following:

A quota may

• Set the total amount to be traded

• Allocate amounts by country

Quotas   The quota is the most common type of quantitative import or export restriction. An import quota prohibits or limits the quantity of a product that can be imported in a given year. Quotas raise prices just as tariffs do but, being defined in physical terms, directly affect the amount of imports by putting an absolute ceiling on supply—say, for example, 1 million DVD players from a particular country in a given year. Therefore, quotas usually increase the consumer price because there is little incentive to use price competition to increase sales. A notable difference between tariffs and quotas is their effect on revenues. Tariffs generate revenue for the government. Quotas generate revenues for those companies that are able to obtain a portion of the intentionally limited supply of the product that they can then sell to local customers.

Sometimes governments allocate quotas among countries based on political or market conditions. (Recall the opening case concerning the quotas by country under the Multifiber Arrangement.) This choice can create problems because goods from one country might be transshipped, or deflected, to another country to take advantage of the latter's quota.[42] Similarly, the product may be converted into one for which there is no quota. For instance, the United States maintains sugar import quotas that result in U.S. sugar prices averaging about double the world market price for sugar. As a result, many U.S. candy producers (e.g., Fanny May, Brach's, Mars, Tootsie Roll, Hershey) have moved plants to Mexico where they can buy lower cost sugar and import the candy duty free to the United States.[43] Import quotas are not necessarily imposed to protect domestic producers. Japan has maintained quotas on many agricultural products that are not produced within the country. It has then allocated import rights to competing suppliers as a means of bargaining for sales of Japanese exports as well as to prevent excess dependence on any one country for essential foods in the event that adverse climatic or political conditions abruptly cut off supply.

A variation of an import quota is the so-called **voluntary export restraint (VER)**. Essentially, the government of Country A asks the government of Country B to reduce its companies' exports to Country A voluntarily. The term "voluntarily" is somewhat misleading; typically either Country B volunteers to reduce its exports or else Country A may impose tougher trade regulations. For example, we illustrated examples of VERs in the opening case on the textile and clothing trade. Procedurally, VERs have unique advantages. A VER is much easier to switch off than an import quota. In addition, the appearance of a "voluntary" choice by a particular country to constrain its shipments to another country tends not to damage political relations between those countries as much as an import quota does.

A country may establish export quotas to assure domestic consumers of a sufficient supply of goods at a low price, to prevent depletion of natural resources, or to attempt to raise export prices by restricting supply in foreign markets. To restrict supply, some countries band together in various commodity agreements, such as those for coffee and petroleum, which then restrict and regulate exports from the member countries. The typical goal of an export quota is to raise prices to importing countries. We'll discuss these agreements in Chapter 8.

A specific type of quota that prohibits all forms of trade is an **embargo.** Like quotas, countries—or groups of countries—may place embargoes on either imports or exports, on whole categories of products regardless of origin or destination, on specific products with specific countries, or on all products with given countries. Governments impose embargoes in the effort to use economic means to achieve political goals.

"Buy Local" Legislation   Another form of quantitative trade control is "buy local" legislation. Government purchases are a large part of total expenditures in many countries; typically, governments favor domestic producers. In the U.S., for example, "buy American" legislation requires government procurement agencies to favor domestic goods. Sometimes governments specify a domestic content restriction—that is, a certain percentage of the product must be of local origin. Sometimes they favor domestic producers through price mechanisms. For example, a government agency may buy a foreign-made product only if the price is at some predetermined margin below that of a domestic competitor. Many nations prescribe a minimum percentage of domestic content that a given product must have for it to be sold legally in their country. Also, they may prod foreign producers to add local content with the threat of import restrictions. Such programs have proven successful. For example, U.S. trade pressures against Japan-based parts exporters spurred Japanese automakers in the United States to purchase more parts from U.S.-based suppliers.

> Through "buy local" laws
> - Government purchases give preference to domestically made goods.
> - Governments sometimes legislate a percentage of domestic content.

Standards and Labels   Countries can devise classification, labeling, and testing standards to allow the sale of domestic products but obstruct that of foreign-made ones. Take product labels, for instance. The requirement that companies indicate on a product where it is made provides information to consumers who may prefer to buy products from certain nations. This technicality adds to a firm's production costs, particularly if the label must be translated for each export market. Further, raw materials, components, design, and labor increasingly come from many countries, so most products today are of mixed origin. For example, the U.S. stipulated that any cloth "substantially altered" (woven, for instance) in another country must identify that country on its label. Consequently, designers like Ferragamo, Gucci, and Versace must declare "Made in China" on the label of garments that contain silk from China.[44]

The professed purpose of standards is to protect the safety or health of the domestic population. However, some foreign companies argue that standards are just another means to protect domestic producers. For example, EU standards keep some U.S. and Canadian products out of the European market completely; this is the case with genetically engineered corn and canola oil, even though the worldwide scientific community reports that the genetic engineering poses no human health risk. Further, France grows and sells a small amount of genetically engineered corn itself.[45] At this writing, there is pending U.S. legislation to require missile defense systems aboard any aircraft landing in the United States that can carry more than 800 passengers. It just happens that no U.S. companies plan to make aircraft that large, but Airbus from Europe plans to build the A380 with that capacity.[46]

> Other types of trade barriers include
> - Arbitrary standards
> - Licensing arrangements
> - Administrative delays
> - Reciprocal requirements
> - Service restrictions

Specific Permission Requirements   Some countries require that potential importers or exporters secure permission from governmental authorities before conducting trade transactions. This requirement is known as an **import license.** A company may have to submit samples to government authorities to obtain an import license. This procedure can restrict imports or exports directly by denying permission or indirectly because of the cost, time, and uncertainty involved in the process. A **foreign-exchange control** is a similar type of control. It requires an importer of a given product to apply to a governmental agency to secure the foreign currency to pay for the product. As with an import license, failure to grant the exchange, not to mention the time and expense of completing forms and awaiting replies, obstructs foreign trade.

Administrative Delays   Closely akin to specific permission requirements are intentional administrative delays, which create uncertainty and raise the cost of carrying inventory. For example, United Parcel Service provisionally suspended its ground service between the U.S. and Mexico because of burdensome Mexican customs delays. Competitive pressure, however, moves countries to improve their administrative systems. Chinese trade authorities, for example, cut the time taken for goods manufactured by Hong Kong firms in Guangdong to pass through internal customs checks from one week to one day. Improved processes, such as electronic submission of cargo manifests, affected 68,000 nonmainland firms and reduced administration costs more than US$70 million.[47]

Reciprocal Requirements   Governments sometimes require that exporters take merchandise in lieu of money or that they promise to buy merchandise or services, in place of cash payment, in the country to which they export. This requirement is common in the aerospace and defense industries—sometimes because the importer does not have enough foreign currency. For instance, Indonesia bought Russian jets in exchange for commodities such as rubber.[48] More frequently, however, reciprocal requirements are made between countries with ample access to foreign currency that want to secure jobs or technology as part of the transaction.[49] For example, McDonnell Douglas sold helicopters to the British government but had to equip them with Rolls-Royce engines (made in the United Kingdom) as well as transfer much of the technology and production work to the United Kingdom.[50] These sorts of barter transactions are called **countertrade** or **offsets.** They often require exporters to find markets for goods outside their lines of expertise or to engage in complicated organizational arrangements that require they relinquish some operating control. All things being equal, companies avoid countertrade.[51] However, some companies have developed competencies in these types of arrangements.

Restrictions on Services   We discussed in Chapter 6 that countries depend on revenue from the foreign sale of such services as transportation, insurance, consulting, and banking, and we indicated that services are the fastest growing sector in international trade. Countries restrict trade in services for three reasons:

Three main reasons for restricting trade in services are

• Essentiality
• Standards
• Immigration

1. *Essentiality.* Countries judge certain service industries to be essential because they serve strategic purposes or because they provide social assistance to their citizens. They sometimes prohibit private companies, foreign or domestic, in some sectors because they feel the services should not be sold for profit. In other cases, they set price controls for private competitors or subsidize government-owned service organizations, creating disincentives for foreign private participation. Mail, education, and hospital health services are often not-for-profit sectors in which few foreign firms compete. When a government privatizes these industries, its customary preference for local ownership and control of essential services may preclude foreign firms from competing. For example, most countries, including the United States, restrict foreign companies from transporting cargo and passengers over their domestic routes. Other essential services in which foreign firms are sometimes excluded are media, communications, banking, and utilities.

2. *Standards.* Governments limit foreign entry into many service professions to ensure practice by qualified personnel. The licensing standards of these personnel vary by country and include such professionals as accountants, actuaries, architects, electricians, engineers, gemologists, hairstylists, lawyers, physicians, real estate brokers, and teachers. At present, there is little reciprocal recognition in licensing from one country to another because occupational standards and requirements differ substantially. This means, for example, that an accounting or legal firm from one country cannot easily do business in another country, even to service its domestic client's needs. The company must hire professionals within each foreign country or else try to earn certification abroad. The latter option can be difficult because examinations will be in a foreign language and likely emphasize materials different from those in the home country. Furthermore, there may be lengthy prerequisites for taking an examination, such as internships and course work at a local university.

3. *Immigration.* Satisfying the standards of a particular country is no guarantee that a foreigner can then work there. Earlier discussion noted that countries protect the job opportunities and security of their citizens. Too, governmental regulations often require that an organization—domestic or foreign—search extensively for qualified personnel locally before it can even apply for work permits for personnel it would like to bring in from abroad. Even if no one is available, hiring a foreigner is still difficult.[52]

DEALING WITH GOVERNMENTAL TRADE INFLUENCES

Governments' intervention in trade affects the flow of imports and exports of goods between countries. When companies face possible losses because of import competition, they have several options to deal with this situation. Four stand out: (1) Move operations to a lower-cost country. (2) Concentrate on market niches that attract less international competition. (3) Adopt internal innovations, namely greater efficiency or superior products. (4) Try to get governmental protection.

There are costs and risks with each option. Nevertheless, the record of many companies shows that success is possible. For example, competition from Japanese imports spurred the U.S. automobile industry to move some production abroad (such as to subcontract with foreign companies to supply cheaper parts), develop the ideas of the minivan and sport utility vehicle (SUV) that initially had less international competition, and adopt innovations such as lean-production techniques to improve efficiency and product quality. Granted, these methods are not realistic for every industry. Companies may lack the managerial, capital, or technological resources to shift production abroad. They may not be able to identify more profitable product niches. In addition, even if they manage to improve efficiency, their innovation may be quickly copied by foreign competitors. In such situations, companies often ask their governments to restrict imports or open export markets. In the case of automobiles, the U.S. industry sought and received protection from Japanese imports in the form of quotas. Our opening case showed that textile and clothing producers are lobbying to restrict imports into the United States.

It is impossible for governments to try to help every company that faces tough international competition. Likewise, helping one industry may hurt another. Thus, as a manager, you may propose or oppose a particular protectionist measure. Inevitably, the burden falls upon companies to convince governmental officials that their situation warrants particular governmental policies. They must identify the key decision makers, whether they are an official of the executive branch, a member of parliament, or a career civil servant. Trade policies in the U.S., for example, are often championed by members of Congress who are especially sensitive to employment and company conditions in their home districts.[53] In any situation, companies must convey to public officials that voters and stakeholders support their position. Managers can and do use the economic and noneconomic arguments presented in this chapter.

When facing import competition, companies can

- Move abroad
- Seek other market niches
- Make domestic output competitive
- Try to get protection

Companies improve the odds of success if they can ally most, if not all, companies in their industry. Otherwise, officials may feel that a particular company's problems are due to its specific inefficiencies rather than the general challenge of imports. Similarly, it helps to involve many stakeholders. When the U.S. auto industry sought relief from Japanese auto competition, for example, company managers and union representatives worked together. Managers may also identify other groups that may have a common objective, even though for different reasons. For example, the International Brotherhood of Teamsters worried about U.S. job losses because of citrus imports from Brazil. It then allied with activist groups concerned about the use of child labor in Brazil to get support for citrus import restrictions.[54] Companies often build public support by advertising their position to stakeholders. Finally, companies can lobby decision makers and endorse the political candidates who understand their situation.

Companies can take different approaches to deal with changes in the international competitive environment. Frequently, companies' attitudes toward protectionism are a function of the investments they have made to develop their international strategy. Companies that depend on freer trade and those that have integrated their production and supply chains among countries tend to oppose protectionism. In contrast, companies with single or multidomestic production facilities, such as a plant in Japan to serve the Japanese market and a plant in Taiwan to serve the Taiwanese market, tend to support protectionism. Companies also differ in their perceived abilities to compete against imports. In nearly half the cases over the last 60 years in which U.S. firms proposed protecting a U.S. industry, one or more companies in that industry opposed it. The latter typically commanded competitive advantages in terms of scale economies, supplier relationships, or differentiated products. Hence, they reasoned that not only could they successfully battle international rivals, but they also stood to gain even more as their weaker domestic competitors failed to do so.[55]

LOOKING TO THE FUTURE: The Battle of Different Interests

While some groups and companies are pushing for freer trade, others are clamoring for greater protectionism. It is probably safe to say that we will see mixtures of the two as barriers come down for some products in some countries but go up for some products in other countries. The opening case on the textile and clothing trade is indicative of the complexity of trade protection and promotion, which also exists for an array of other products as well. With the end of the Multifiber Arrangement, there are winners and losers among countries and among companies and workers within them. Further, gains to consumers may be at the expense of some workers. People who see themselves as losers are not apt to take the change without a struggle, that is, they will garner as much support for their positions as they can, and they may win. This support may well come from alliances that cross national borders, such as the alliances among clothing companies in various nations that are uniting to push their governments to enact new quota agreements. Thus, if you are a manager in an industry that may be affected by changes in governmental protection, you must watch closely to predict how the politics may affect your own economic situation.

Further, the international regulatory situation is becoming more, rather than less, complex, which challenges companies to find the best locations to produce. The next chapter will discuss the trade agreements that countries are reaching; nevertheless, it is useful to introduce the impact that these have on decision making. Every time countries negotiate a trading agreement (and these agreements are proliferating), new optimum production locations emerge. For instance, the United States and Mexico negotiated a free trade pact, which caused some U.S. imports to shift from Taiwan to Mexico. However, with an additional free trade agreement between the United States and Central America, some of the production that developed in Mexico might now shift to a Central American country. Another future free trade agreement might cause another shift in the future. All of this creates uncertainties for companies' operations.

SUMMARY

- Despite the documented benefits of free trade, no country permits an unregulated flow of goods and services across its borders.

- It is difficult to determine the effect on employment from protecting an industry due to the likelihood of retaliation and the fact that imports as well as exports create jobs.

- Policy makers continue to struggle with the problem of income redistribution due to changes in trade policy.

- The infant-industry argument for protection holds that governmental prevention of import competition is necessary to help certain industries move from high-cost to low-cost production.

- Governmental interference is often argued to be beneficial if it promotes industrialization, given the positive relationship between industrial activity and economic development.

- Trade controls are used to improve economic relations with other countries. Their objectives include improving the balance of payments, raising prices to foreign consumers, gaining fair access to foreign markets, preventing foreign monopoly prices, assuring that domestic consumers get low prices, and lowering profit margins for foreign producers.

- Considerable governmental interference in international trade is motivated by political rather than economic concerns, including maintaining domestic supplies of essential goods and preventing potential enemies from gaining goods that would help them achieve their objectives.

- Trade controls that directly affect price and indirectly affect quantity include tariffs, subsidies, arbitrary customs-valuation methods, and special fees.

- Trade controls that directly affect quantity and indirectly affect price include quotas, VERs, "buy local" legislation, arbitrary standards, licensing arrangements, foreign-exchange controls, administrative delays, and requirements to take goods in exchange.

- A company's development of an international strategy will greatly determine whether it will benefit more from protectionism or from some other means for countering international competition.

U.S.–Cuban Trade[56]

C A S E

The U.S. embargo of Cuba has been a resilient foreign policy, able to weather a variety of political leaders, economic events, and historical eras. In 2005, U.S. President Bush ruled that any sales to Cuba from the United States would have to be paid in cash in advance of shipment. A year before, he reduced the maximum remittances that people in the United States could send to family in Cuba and restricted visits to Cuba by Cuban-Americans to once in three years instead of once a year "to help the freedom-starved people of Cuba live lives free from Castro's oppression and tyranny." The reasoning was straightforward and similar to one that had prevailed over the last four decades—the Cuban economy was so weak that a demoralized population would overthrow Castro if economic conditions deteriorated just a little more. Many observers agreed and many disagreed, but let's first look at the history of the situation.

In the 1950s, more than two-thirds of Cuban foreign trade took place with the United States. After Castro overthrew the Batista government in 1959, he threatened to incite revolutions elsewhere in Latin America. The United States countered by canceling its agreements to buy Cuban sugar and Cuba retaliated by seizing U.S. oil refineries. The oil companies refused to supply Cuba with crude oil. Cuba then turned to the Soviet Union for replacement supplies. This conflict occurred at the height of the cold war tension between the United States and the Soviet Union. In 1962, the U.S. severed diplomatic relations and initiated the full trade embargo of Cuba through a presidential directive issued under the Trading with the Enemy Act. In 1963, the Treasury Department set forth the Cuban Asset Control Regulations, which prohibited all unlicensed financial transactions, forbade direct or indirect imports from

Cuba, and imposed a total freeze on Cuban government assets held in the United States. Trade between the United States and Cuba stopped.

The incidents that strained relations during the next three decades are too numerous to detail. Some threatened peace; others bordered on the absurd. They included the U.S. sponsorship of an invasion by Cuban exiles at the Bay of Pigs, the placement and removal of Soviet missiles in Cuba, the deployment of Cuban forces to overthrow regimes that the U.S. supported (such as in Nicaragua and Angola), and exposés that the CIA had tried to airlift someone to assassinate Castro and had tried to develop a powder to make his beard fall out. Figure 7.5 gives a time line of major events in U.S.-Cuban relations.

During this period, the U.S.' trade embargo endured as originally set. However, spurred by the collapse of communism in the early 1990s, the U.S. Congress passed the Cuban Democracy Act in 1992. This policy codified the ban on American travel to Cuba and extended the embargo to the foreign subsidiaries of U.S. companies operating abroad—there would be no trade, direct or otherwise, between the United States and Cuba. The act also required Cuba to hold democratic elections before the U.S. executive branch could repeal the embargo.

The Helms-Burton Act in 1996 reinforced many of these provisions as well as added stipulations for penalizing foreign companies that did business in Cuba. This act provided for legal action (to seize U.S. assets) against non-U.S. companies using expropriated property in Cuba that U.S. citizens (including Cuban exiles) had owned. It prohibited executives of these companies and their families from visiting the U.S and forbade normal U.S. relations with any future Cuban government that included Castro.

Over time, the U.S. role in the Cuban drama has played to a less sympathetic audience worldwide. Initially, many countries supported the U.S. embargo. All members of the Organization of American States except Mexico agreed in 1964 to endorse it. Gradually, countries began trading with Cuba anyway. In 1995 the United Nations voted 117 to 3 against the U.S. embargo. Only Israel and Uzbekistan voted with the U.S., and both of these countries traded with Cuba. In 1999, the Cuban National Assembly declared that the U.S. had violated the 1948 United Nations convention against genocide because of the cumulative suffering imposed by the embargo. By 2001, some 150 nations had normal trade relations with Cuba.

Events increasingly created questions about the rationale for continuing the embargo. The fall of the Berlin Wall and the end of the cold war in the early 1990s triggered many changes. The attendant collapse of the Soviet Union deprived Cuba of the estimated $3.5 to $4.5 billion in annual subsidies that sustained its feeble economy, thus the export of revolution from Cuba seemed less of a threat. In fact, Cuba's staggering economy seemed on the brink of collapse. On the one hand, in 2000 U.S. Secretary of State Colin Powell ruled out the possibility of completely lifting the Cuban embargo until Castro departed. On the other hand, in the same year, Congress passed the Trade Sanctions Reform and Export Enhancement Act, which allowed certain exports of U.S. agricultural, food, and medical products. After the passage of this act, Cuba quickly became the twenty-first largest agricultural market for the United States with

FIGURE 7.5   MAJOR EVENTS IN U.S.–CUBAN RELATIONS

There have been many significant events affecting U.S.-Cuban relations during the last hundred years.

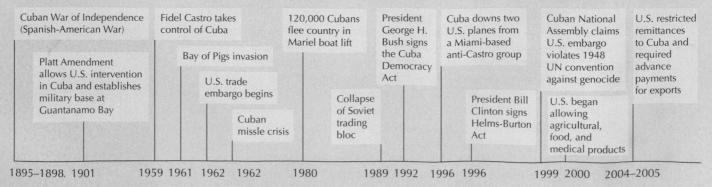

sales exceeding $400 million in 2004. U.S. agricultural interests were particularly opposed to the new cash in advance payment policies, especially since 2005 promised to see the first U.S. agricultural trade deficit in half a century.

The rest of the U.S. public seemed increasingly divided on the usefulness of the embargo on Cuba. Hardliner policies had failed for more than 40 years to dislodge Castro from power while causing adversity for some 11 million Cubans. Advocates of normal relations with Cuba argued that tighter restrictions on U.S. firms and reprisals on foreign companies would not weaken Castro's political power. In fact, they pointed to Castro's retaliation against the Cuban people in reprisal against new U.S. economic policies. These included the raising of prices in Cuba for foreign-produced goods and the elimination of the U.S. dollar as an official currency. Further, they warned that Cuban economic downturns would likely invite retaliation and aggravate U.S. immigration tensions with Cuba. A growing number of leaders in the U.S. (including heads of major firms, Democratic and Republican members of Congress, and labor leaders) publicly favored normalization of U.S.-Cuban trade rather than tightening the economic noose. For example, former U.S. Secretary of State Lawrence Eagleburger reasoned that U.S. trade actions gave Castro something, other than his inept policies, to blame for his economic blunders; he added, "The worst thing that could happen would be for the U.S. to open the gates of trade and travel." Increasing exposure to the U.S., not embargo, seemed to be a more promising force of change.

Repealing the embargo would help many U.S. industries and companies. Cuba had already attracted investments from many businesses from other countries, largely drawn by its highly qualified workforce, near-perfect literacy rate, and demand for foreign products and services. Groups in the U.S. noted the market potential of Cuba; a Texas A&M study projected that lifting the trade embargo would increase U.S. agricultural exports to Cuba to about $1.24 billion a year. Others cited the potential gains for U.S. tourism and transportation companies.

At the same time, many argued that the potential for business with Cuba was highly limited. Cuba's per capita GDP in 2003 was less than $3,000, which when coupled with its small population did not amount to much purchasing power. This was evident by the prevalence of 1950s cars in Cuba even though European and Japanese auto companies faced no embargos on their sales. Further, Cuba had to export enough to pay for imports. Sugar accounted for about 37 percent of export earnings, and the U.S. was not only awash with excess sugar, it had a sugar quota system with a number of countries that would surely balk at the diversion of their sugar sales. Certainly, there is the possibility of tourism, but the hotels in Cuba are already booked fairly full with tourists from Europe and Canada.

Finally, there was debate over the basis for the pro-embargo position. Some argued that, in an age when China is a member of the WTO and nations like Vietnam are trading with the United States, the Cuban embargo looked like a cold war relic. Moreover, besides being far tougher than the U.S. economic blockades of Iran, Iraq, and North Korea, the Cuban embargo is the longest and harshest embargo by one state against another in modern history. In addition, some questioned the politics of U.S. policy. But there seemed to be a strong personal dimension; Vice President Cheney observed that "As soon as Castro [born in 1926] is gone from the scene, there is no reason in the world why we can't have a really first-class normalized set of relationships with Cuba."

QUESTIONS

1. Should the U.S. seek to tighten the economic grip on Cuba? If so, why?
2. Should the U.S. normalize business relations with Cuba? If so, should the U.S. stipulate any conditions?
3. Assume you are Fidel Castro. What kind of trade relationship with the U.S. would be in your best interest? What type would you be willing to accept?
4. How does the structure and relationships of the American political system influence the existence and specification of the trade embargo?

CHAPTER NOTES

1 Data for the case were taken from Hildegunn Kyvik Nordås, "The Global Textile and Clothing Industry Post the Agreement on Textiles and Clothing," (Geneva: WTO Secretariat Discussion Paper No. 5, 2004); Scott Miller and Charles Hutzler, "Poor Nations Seek WTO Textile Aid," *Wall Street Journal* (October 1, 2004): A2+; Christopher Swann, "US Textile Makers to Sue Over Imports," *Financial Times* (September 2, 2004): 6; Frances Williams, "Textile Producers Weave a Web to Restrict China," *Financial Times* (October 22, 2004): 7; "U.S. Government Accepts Five More Special Textile Safeguard Petitions for Consideration," (November 3, 2004), (www.ncto.org/newsroom/pr200413.asp); United States International Trade Commission (http://dataweb.usitc.gov/scripts/tariff2005.asp); Mei Fong and Dan Morse, "Backlash Is Likely as Chinese Exports Surge," *Wall Street Journal* (March 28, 2005): A3+; Ginger Thompson, "Fraying of a Latin Textile Industry," *New York Times* (March 25, 2005): 1; and Rebecca Buckman, "Navigating China's Textile Trade," *Wall Street Journal* (September 10, 2004): A10.

2 James Cox, "Months of European Trade Sanctions Have Divergent Impact," *USA Today* (October 28, 2004): 3B.

3 Hans S. Nichols, "Taking the Fix out of Farm Subsidies," *Insight on the New* 17 (August 13, 2001): 20.

4 David E. Sanger and Joseph Kahn, "Bush's Plan to Raise Steel Tariffs Would Exempt Most Poor Nations," *New York Times* (March 4, 2002): A1+.

5 Alan M. Field, "WTO Approves Sanctions Against U.S." *Journal of Commerce—Online* (August 31, 2004): WP.

6 James Mackintosh, "Delphi Warning Raises Stakes in Battle Against Steel Tariffs," *Financial Times* (October 17, 2002): 1.

7 Lori Kletzer, "*Job Loss from Imports: Measuring the Costs*" (Washington, D.C.: Institute for International Economics, 2001).

8 Kenneth A. Couch, "Earnings Losses and Unemployment of Displaced Workers in Germany," *Industrial and Labor Relations Review* 54 (April 2001): 559; Margolis, David, "Worker Displacement in France," Mimeograph, Universite de Paris, Pantheon-Sorbonne, 90, Rue de Tolbiac, Paris (1999).

9 Fuat Sener, "Schumpeterian Unemployment, Trade and Wages," *Journal of International Economics* 54 (June 2001): 119.

10 This argument is most associated with the writings of Raul Prebisch, Hans Singer, and Gunnar Myrdal in the 1950s and 1960s. For a recent discussion, see John Toye and Richard Toye, "The Origins and Interpretation of the Prebisch-Singer Thesis," *History of Political Economy* 35, no. 3 (Fall 2003): 437–57.

11 Jiang Xueqin, "Letter from China," *The Nation* (March 4, 2002).

12 Steve Padgittm, Peggy Petrzelka, Wendy Wintersteen, and Eric Imerman, "Integrated Crop Management: The Other Precision Agriculture," *American Journal of Alternative Agriculture* 16 (January 2001): 16.

13 Sergio Lence and Dermot Hayes, "U.S. Farm Policy and the Volatility of Commodity Prices and Farm Revenues," *American Journal of Agricultural Economics* 84 (May 2002): 335–52.

14 Kevin Morrison and Deborah Hargreaves, "Commodities Are Big New Theme," *Financial Times* (September 18, 2003): 15.

15 Hou Hexiang, "Vietnam to Accelerate Industrialization and Modernization of Rural Areas" *Xinhua News Agency* (June 2, 2002): 1008; "Pushing Ecuador into the 21st Century," *LatinFinance* (March 2002): 30, retrieved from http://web.lexis-nexis.com/universe/ (July 17, 2002); "Is Inequality Decreasing? Debating the Wealth and Poverty of Nations," *Foreign Affairs* (August 2002): 178.

16 Gerald K. Helleiner, "Markets, Politics, and Globalization: Can the Global Economy Be Civilized?" *Global Governance* (July–Sept. 2001): 243; Marina Murphy, "EU Chemicals Need Flexibility: A Level Playing Field Should Be Established between the EU and US Chemicals Industries," *Chemistry and Industry* (July 1, 2002): 9; Lisa Schmidt, "How U.S. Sees Trade Rows," *Calgary Herald* (June 25, 2002): A2.

17 Annie Gowen, "U.S. Caviar with a Russian Accent," *Washington Post* (December 31, 2004): Metro, p. B1.

18 Rebecca Bream and John Reed, "S. Africa Seeks to Extract More Value from Its Natural Treasures," *Financial Times* (February 9, 2005): 6.

19 Adam Thomson, "Argentina Cuts Gas Exports to Avert a Crisis," *Financial Times* (March 27–28, 2004): 5; and Randall Palmer, "Canada Mulls Nonprescription-Drug Tactic," *Seattle Times* (February 19, 2005): A13.

20 Edward Alden and Raphael Minder, "EU and Canada Impose Retaliatory Duties on U.S. Imports," *Financial Times* (April 1, 2005): 6.

21 Stephen Moore, "Tax Cut and Spend: The Profligate Ways of Congressional Republicans," *National Review* 53 (Oct. 1, 2001): 19.

22 George Leopold, "U.S. Eases Regulations on Cryptography Exports," *Electronic Engineering Times* (July 24, 2000): 43.

23 Philip Shenon, "In Hanoi, U.S. Goods Sold But Not by U.S.," *New York Times* (October 3, 1993): A1.

24 Lance Davis and Stanley Engerman, "Sanctions: Neither War Nor Peace," *Journal of Economic Perspectives* 17, no. 2 (Spring 2003): 187–97.

25 G. Scott Erickson, "Low-Level Trade Sanctions," *Global Competitiveness* 7 (Annual, 1999): 375.

26 "Leaders: A Grand Bargain with the Great Satan? Testing Iran's Nuclear Intentions," *Economist* 374, no. 8417 (March 12, 2005): 10.

27 James Dao, "U.S. to Punish 10 Businesses for Iran Sales," *New York Times* (July 20, 2002): D-1.

28 Doug Cameron and Kevin Morrison, "U.S. Groups Win Libyan Oil Exploration Permits License Auction," *Financial Times* (January 31, 2005): 9.

29 "EU/Latin America/Caribbean: Leaders Aim to Revive Ties," *European Report* (May 15, 2002): 501.

30 Tony Walker, "China Warns Australia over Dalai Lama Visit," *Financial Times* (September 18, 1996): 1; Ying Ma, "China's America Problem," *Policy Review* (February 2002): 43–57.

31 Ann Kent, "States Monitoring States: The United States, Australia, and China's Human Rights, 1990–2001," *Human Rights Quarterly* 23 (August 2001): 583–625.

32 Gail L. Cramer, James M. Hansen and Eric J. Wailes, "Impact of Rice Tariffication on Japan and the World Rice Market," *American Journal of Agricultural Economics* 81 (December 1999): 1149.

33 Matthew Fraser, "Foreign Ownership Rules Indefensible: And There Appears to Be Appetite for Change," *Financial Post* (May 28, 2001): C2.

34 C. Christopher Baughn and Mark A. Buchanan, "Cultural Protectionism," *Business Horizons* 44 (Nov.–Dec. 2001): 5–16.

35 John Larkin, "Now Playing: Korea's Movie Industry Prevents Investment Pact with the U.S.," *Wall Street Journal* (March 20, 2002): A19.

36 "Futile Fortress," *Financial Times* (August 26, 2003): 16.

37 Bernard Hoekman and Kym Anderson, "Developing-Country Agriculture and the New Trade Agenda," *Economic Development & Cultural Change* 49 (Oct. 2000): 171.

38 Nicholas Elliot, "U.S. Farm Subsidies under Fire: Benefits Will Spread," *Barron's* (January 28, 2002): 10.

39 Neil King, Jr., Scott Miller, Daniel Michaels, and J. Lynn Lunsford, "U.S., Europe Sue Each Other at WTO over Aircraft Subsidies," *Wall Street Journal* (October 7, 2004): A2+.

40 Chi-Chur Chao and Eden S. H. Yu, "Import Quotas, Tied Aid, Capital Accumulation, and Welfare," *Canadian Journal of Economics* 34 (August 2001): 661; Mark Rice, "Australia Must Join Other Countries in Untying Overseas Aid," *Australian Financial Review* (April 4, 2002): 59.

41 Mohsin Habib and Leon Zurawicki, "Corruption and Foreign Direct Investment," *Journal of International Business Studies* 33 (Summer 2002): 291–308.

42 Peter J. Buckley, Jeremy Clegg, Nicolas Forsans, and Kevin T. Reilly, "Increasing the Size of the 'Country'": Regional Economic Integration and Foreign Direct Investment in a Globalised World Economy," *Management International Review* 41 (July 2001): 251–75.

43 Joel Millman, "Visions of Sugar Plums South of the Border," *Wall Street Journal* (February 13, 2002): A17+; and Jeremy Grant, "Signs of Decay as Companies Desert the U.S. Candy Capital," *Financial Times* (January 21, 2004): 14.

44 Blaise J. Bergiel and Erich B. Bergiel, "Country-of-Origin as a Surrogate Indicator: Implications/Strategies," *Global Competitiveness* 7 (1999): 187.

45 Judy Steed, "Caution the Law with GMOs in Europe," *Toronto Star* (June 10, 2002): D02.

46 Dennis Sevastopulo, "U.S. Bill Would Force Airbus to Install Missile Defence on A380," *Financial Times* (June 20, 2005): 2.

47 Peggy Sito, "Guangdong to Slash Internal Customs Delays," *South China Morning Post* (May 16, 2002): 1.

48 Devi Asmarani, "MPs Criticise Jakarta for Buying Pricey Russian Jets," *The Straits Time* [Singapore] (June 19, 2003).

49 Chong Ju Choi, Soo Hee Lee, and Jai Boem Kim, "A Note on Countertrade: Contractual Uncertainty and Transaction Governance in Emerging Economies," *Journal of International Business Studies* 30 (Spring 1999): 189.

50 "McDonnell and Partner Win $4 Billion British Copter Deal," *New York Times* (July 14, 1995): C5.

51 Chong Ju Choi, Soo Lee, and Jai Kim, "A Note on Countertrade: Contractual Uncertainty and Transaction Governance in Emerging Economies," *Journal of International Business Studies* 30 (Spring 1999): 189.

52 Sara Robinson, "Workers Are Trapped in Limbo by I.N.S.," *New York Times* (February 29, 2000): A12.

53 Ralph G. Carter and Lorraine Eden, "Who Makes U.S. Trade Policy?" *The International Trade Journal* XIII, no. 1 (Spring 1999): 53–100.

54 Matt Moffett, "Citrus Squeeze," *Wall Street Journal* (September 6, 1998): A1.

55 Eugene Salorio, "Trade Barriers and Corporate Strategies: Why Some Firms Oppose Import Protection for Their Own Industry," unpublished DBA dissertation, Harvard University, 1991.

56 Data for the case were adapted from Pascal Fletcher, "US Anti-Cuba Law Feeds Businessmen's Paranoia," *Financial Times* (July 2, 1996): 5; William M. Leo Grande, "From Havana to Miami: U.S. Cuba Policy as a Two-Level Game," *Journal of Interamerican Studies and World Affairs* 40, no. 1 (Spring 1998): 67–86; Albert R. Hunt, "End the Anachronistic Embargo Against Cuba," *Wall Street Journal* (April 22, 1999): A23; Pascal Fletcher, "Cuba Brands US Sanctions 'Genocide,' " *Financial Times* (September 14, 1999): 6; Daniel P. Erikson, "The New Cuba Divide," *The National Interest* (Spring 2002); Kathleen Parker, "Exposure, not Embargoes, Will Free Fidel's Cuba," *The Seattle Times* (March 14, 2001): B6; Stephen Handelman, "Will Bush Try to Refreeze Cuban Thaw?" *The Toronto Star* (January 30, 2001); "Carter's Cuba Trip Stirs Storm of Debate," *Deutsche Presse-Agentur* (May 12, 2002); Albor Ruiz, "Shifts Start in U.S.-Cuban Relations," *Daily News* (January 14, 2002): 3; Keith Suter, "U.S. Should Lift Failed Sanctions on Cuba," *Canberra Times* (May 23, 2002); Michael Doyle, "State Eyeing Cuban Trade: Lawmakers Are Seeking to Lift the Longtime Embargo," *The Sacramento Bee* (July 30, 2002); Timothy Ashby, "Who's Really Being Hurt?" *Journal of Commerce* (January 31, 2005); "The Web Site of Cuban Industry" (**www.cubaindustria.cu/English**); Theresa Borden, "Cubans Feel Pinch from Dollar Ban," *Atlanta Journal-Constitution*" (November 10, 2004): 6F.

Japanese from being able to transfer their excess imports from countries where their quotas weren't being met to ones where they were unable to meet demand due to their having already reached the maximum limits. It was primarily for this reason that they actually never met their quota for the EC, and during the seven years the quota system was in effect, Toyota was held to a 2–3 percent market share in most EU countries.

While the system seemed to be having the desired effect, even some French auto officials admitted that the eventual opening of the market was inevitable. One noted, "Can we put off change for years? Officially, yes. But honestly, I don't think so." That statement proved prophetic when the EU lifted the import quota in 1999 and additionally made it easier for the Japanese auto manufacturers to expand distribution and to sign up dealers. Although this move did not necessarily cause the Japanese to flood the European market with their products, it did open the way for them to invest more heavily in design and manufacturing facilities in the EU, to broaden the range of products they marketed there, and to customize their offerings to better appeal to European tastes.

Toyota responded to the drop in barriers by introducing a new strategy of designing vehicles targeted specifically at European customers. The new strategy involved setting up a European Design and Development center in southern France and allowing design teams across the globe to compete for projects. The Yaris, Toyota's best-selling vehicle in the EU, was designed by a Greek and was the first to be developed within the region. It subsequently was named Car of the Year 2000 in both Europe and Japan.

As another key element of its European strategy, Toyota has also set up additional production centers in the region and now manufactures all of its best European-selling vehicles in Europe. The new-generation Toyota Corolla, voted 2002 European Car of the Year, and the Avensis, the first Toyota vehicle to be exported from Europe to Japan, were both designed and built in Europe. Manufacturing facilities in Eastern Europe allow the Japanese automaker to lower production costs due to lower wages. For example, workers in Toyota's plant in Turkey earn only $3.60 an hour, giving Toyota a distinct cost advantage over European competitors, such as Volkswagen, which pays as much as $40.68 per hour to the workers in its plants in Germany.

The difference in wages, in addition to its efficient operations, has allowed Toyota to remain profitable while others are undergoing layoffs and industry-wide restructuring. Volkswagen is threatening to dismiss 30,000 workers unless it can reduce labor costs by a third in Germany. GM's European unit, having lost money in the region for the sixth year in a row, is planning to eliminate thousands of jobs and to close down at least one plant unless employees agree to work longer hours for no additional pay, and Ford's European operation cut 5,000 jobs in Western Europe. Additionally, Ford, Fiat SpA, and Volkswagen have undergone substantial management changes as they've sought to rein in operations to keep costs from running over in the new competitive market in which they are slowly losing market share. The situation seems even bleaker for them as Japanese competitors continue to open up facilities in the Eastern bloc countries recently admitted to the EU as well as other low-wage areas, such as China. Toyota is already in the process of setting up new state-of-the-art production plants in the Czech Republic and Poland—the one in the Czech Republic being established in cooperation with France's PSA Peugeot-Citroen in hopes that the joint venture will help it develop good relationships with PSA's local suppliers. Because of the elimination of internal tariffs in the EU, Toyota can manufacture automobiles anywhere within the EU and ship them to all markets duty free. Before the reduction in tariff barriers, this would not have been possible.

Other recent trends in the EU have also favored Toyota since the quotas were eliminated. In light of a sluggish European economy facing high unemployment and low growth, Europeans are becoming less loyal to European brands in their search for more economical, higher quality vehicles. In recent J. D. Power customer surveys in the U.K. and Germany, Toyota ranked first overall and scored the highest in three of seven categories, while Ford, Renault, and Volkswagen all ranked below average. Additionally, Toyota's environmentally friendly hybrid vehicle, the Prius, was voted the 2005 European Car of the Year.

Riding on its success in Europe and its growth internationally, Toyota has ambitious goals for the future. With confidence in its profitability, even in the competitive European market, and in its financial flexibility, it is driving to capture a 15 percent share of the global market by 2010 and to overtake GM as the top auto producer in volume. Considering that its European operations account for approximately 13.5 percent of its worldwide sales, coming in third only to its North American and domestic operations, would Toyota ever have been able to achieve its worldwide goals if the EU had not loosened its restrictions on imported Japanese cars?

INTRODUCTION

In some respects, the United States is the perfect example of economic integration—the largest economy in the world comprised of 50 states in the continental United States, Alaska, and Hawaii, a common currency, and labor and capital mobility. However, it is just one country. What about the rest of the world? Economic integration is the political and economic agreements among countries that give preference to member countries to the agreement. There are three ways to approach **economic integration:** global integration through the World Trade Organization; **bilateral integration,** where two countries decide to cooperate closer together, usually in the form of tariff reductions; and **regional integration,** where a group of countries located in the same geographic proximity decide to cooperate, such as is the case with the European Union.

In the mid- to late-1940s, countries decided that if they were going to emerge from the wreckage of World War II and promote economic growth and stability within their borders, they would have to assist—and get assistance from—nearby countries. This chapter discusses some of the important forms of economic cooperation.

Why do you need to understand the nature of these agreements? Trading groups, whether bilateral or regional, are an important influence on MNEs' strategies. Such groups can define the size of the regional market and the rules under which companies must operate. Companies in the initial stages of foreign expansion must be aware of the regional economic groups that encompass countries with good manufacturing locations or market opportunities. As companies expand internationally, they must change their organizational structure and operating strategies to take advantage of regional trading groups. As noted in the opening case, Toyota has been able to find success in Europe by taking advantage of changes in EU policy that allow it to adjust its design and production strategies to meet the unique needs of European consumers. In this chapter, we focus on the European Union and the North American Free Trade Agreement as regional groups because of the high level of integration in both groups—and especially the size and degree of integration in the EU. That is not to minimize the importance of other regional groups to their member countries, but we will use the EU and NAFTA to illustrate different types of regional integration. The most important thing is to understand how these and similar organizations and agreements affect company strategy.

> Economic integration—political and economic agreements among countries that give preference to member countries in the agreement
> * Bilateral
> * Regional
> * Global

THE WORLD TRADE ORGANIZATION (WTO)

Governments often actively cooperate with each other to remove trade barriers. The following discussion looks at the **World Trade Organization (WTO),** which is the major multilateral forum through which governments can come to agreements and can settle disputes regarding trade. Before doing so, we look at GATT, the philosophical and organizational predecessor of the WTO.

> The World Trade Organization is the major body for
> * Reciprocal trade negotiations
> * Enforcement of trade agreements

GATT: The Predecessor

In 1947, 23 countries formed the General Agreement on Tariffs and Trade (GATT) under the auspices of the United Nations to abolish quotas and reduce tariffs. By the time the WTO replaced GATT in 1995, 125 nations were members. Many believe that GATT's contribution to trade liberalization made possible the expansion of world trade in the second half of the twentieth century.

The fundamental principle of GATT was that each member nation must open its markets equally to every other member nation—any sort of discrimination was prohibited. The principle of "trade without discrimination" was embodied in GATT's **most-favored-nation (MFN)** clause—once a country and its trading partners had agreed to reduce a tariff, that

> GATT—the predecessor of the WTO organized by the UN after World War II to reduce trade barriers worldwide

TABLE 8.1 **GATT/WTO MILESTONES**

DATE	SITE/ROUND	NUMBER OF MEMBER NATIONS	OUTCOME
1946	London, England	—	Fifty countries met to discuss creating an international trade organization as a third world economic pillar alongside the World Bank and IMF. These discussions failed.
1947	Havana, Cuba	—	Twenty-three countries reconvened and negotiated more than 45,000 reductions in their customs duties that affected $10 billion of trade, then about one-fifth of the world's total. These agreements were codified into the General Agreement on Tariffs and Trade (GATT).
1947	Geneva, Switzerland	23	First official meeting of founding members of GATT.
1949	Annecy, France	13	Negotiated more than 5,000 tariff concessions.
1951	Torquay, England	38	Additional tariff reductions and concessions.
1956	Geneva, Switzerland	26	Additional tariff reductions and concessions.
1960–1961	The Dillon Round	26	Additional tariff reductions and concessions. GATT now formally named each Geneva, Switzerland session.
1964–1967	The Kennedy Round, Geneva, Switzerland	62	Expanded discussion to review new trade rules and passed an anti-dumping agreement.
1973–1979	The Tokyo Round	102	Reduced customs duties. Reached series of agreements on various nontariff barriers. However, these agreements were only signed by some participants. Failed to reform agricultural trade and stopped short of new agreement on emergency import measures.
1986–1994	The Uruguay Round	123	Session began in Uruguay to reflect the fact that developing countries had become the majority in GATT. Expanded discussion to review tariffs, nontariff measures, trade rules, services, intellectual property, dispute settlement, textiles, and agriculture. Created the World Trade Organization (WTO) and its mandate to cover new areas of trade.
1995	—	—	Formation of WTO
2001	Doha Development Agenda	148	Very contentious; still in process

Most-favored-nation status—once a tariff level was agreed upon, all member countries get the same tariff.

tariff cut was automatically extended to every other member country irrespective of whether they were a signatory to the agreement. GATT held several major conferences (eventually referred to as rounds) from 1947 to 1993 to address trade issues. These sessions led to many multilateral reductions in tariffs and nontariff barriers. Table 8.1 identifies these sessions.

Over time, GATT grappled with the issue of nontariff barriers in terms of industrial standards, government procurement, subsidies and countervailing duties (duties in response to another country's protectionist measures), licensing, and customs valuation. In each area, GATT members agreed to apply the same product standards for imports as for domestically produced goods, treat bids by foreign companies on a nondiscriminatory basis for most large contracts, prohibit export subsidies except on agricultural products, simplify licensing procedures that permit the importation of foreign-made goods, and use a uniform procedure to value imports when assessing duties on them.

GATT slowly ran into problems. Its success led some governments to devise craftier methods of trade protection. Some countries began to negotiate bilateral trade deals while others gave subsidies to local companies. Similarly, world trade grew more complex, and trade in services—not covered by GATT rules—grew more important. Procedurally, GATT's institutional structure and its dispute settlement system seemed increasingly overextended. Some countries objected that nonmembers, under the umbrella of the most-favored-nation clause, gained freer foreign entry for their products without making any concessions—the so-called free-rider problem. In addition, GATT could not enforce compliance with agreements; it depended on its members' commitment to cooperate with each other. These market trends and organizational challenges made trade agreements harder to work out. The Uruguay Round, the final GATT session, spanned more than seven years and accomplished less than envisioned. Restoring an effective means for trade liberalization led officials to create the WTO in 1995.

The WTO

The WTO adopted the principles and trade agreements reached under the auspices of GATT but expanded its mission to include trade in services, investment, intellectual property, sanitary measures, plant health, agriculture, and textiles, as well as technical barriers to trade. Currently, the WTO has nearly 150 members that collectively account for more than 97 percent of world trade. Around 30 other countries, including the Russian Federation, are currently in negotiations to become members. The entire membership makes significant decisions by consensus. However, there are provisions for a majority vote in the event of a nondecision by member countries. Agreements then must be ratified by the governments of the member nations.

The highest-level decision-making body in the WTO's structure is the Ministerial Conference; it meets at least once every two years. The next level is the General Council (usually ambassadors and the director of a country delegation) that meets several times a year. The General Council also meets as the Trade Policy Review Body and the Dispute Settlement Body. At the next level are the Council for Trade in Goods, the Council for Trade in Services, and the Council for Trade-Related Intellectual Property Rights (TRIPS). Specialized committees, working groups, and working parties deal with the individual agreements and other areas, such as the environment, development, membership applications, and regional trade agreements. WTO members deal with these areas separately and on an ongoing basis.

Major decision-making units of the WTO include

- Ministerial Conference
- General Council
- Goods Council
- Services Council
- Council on Trade-Related Aspects of Intellectual Property (TRIPS)

Normal Trade Relations   The WTO replaced the most-favored-nation clause of GATT with the concept of **normal trade relations** (NTR). The WTO restricts this privilege to official members in order to eliminate earlier objections to free-rider countries. Still, governments have made the following exceptions:

1. Developing countries' manufactured products have been given preferential treatment over those from industrial countries.

2. Concessions granted to members within a regional trading alliance, such as the EU, have not been extended to countries outside the alliance.

Exceptions are made in times of war or international tension.

Normal Trade Relations—same as MFN under GATT

Settlement of Disputes   Countries may bring charges of unfair trade practices to a WTO panel, and accused countries may appeal. There are time limits on all stages of deliberations, and the WTO's rulings are binding. If an offending country fails to comply with the panel's judgment, its trading partners have the right to compensation. If this penalty is ineffective, then the offending country's trading partners have the right to impose countervailing sanctions. For example, in 2002, the WTO ruled that U.S. steel tariffs were illegal and enforced its decision by rejecting a U.S. appeal that argued the tariffs were a safeguard to allow U.S. companies, 31 of which had filed for bankruptcy resulting in the loss of 45,000 jobs, to become more competitive against foreign imports.[2] The WTO determined that the woes facing the U.S. steel companies resulted from industry inefficiencies, rather than an influx of foreign steel, making protectionist measures unconscionable. The ruling effectively allowed other member nations to impose retaliatory tariffs should the U.S. refuse to lower its own on steel. Following the WTO's decision, the EU, Japan, Norway, Switzerland, China, and Brazil all compiled lists of U.S. products they would potentially take action against. The EU alone threatened to exact duties of up to 30 percent on U.S. exports valued at over $2 billion.[3] However, U.S. President George W. Bush repealed the steel duties rather than risk a major trade war.

Doha Round   Perhaps the most complex set of issues the WTO is currently faced with, however, are those it is trying to address through the Doha Round, which commenced in Doha, Qatar, in 2001. The largest of the disputes has essentially resulted in a split between developed members, such as the U.S., Japan, and the EU, and developing nations, led by Brazil and India, over the large agricultural subsidies maintained by the richer nations. At subsequent trade talks held in Cancun, Mexico, Brazil and its alliance of developing nations—known as the "Group of 22"—walked out of negotiations when the EU and Japan turned the focus of the talks to international investment rules and antitrust policies without first addressing the issue of farm-subsidy programs.

A year following Cancun, the WTO pronounced U.S. cotton subsidies to be illegal, and the U.S., in subsequent negotiations, agreed to cut farm subsidies for such crops as cotton, corn, rice, wheat, and soybeans by 20 percent in order to appease demands made by Brazil and its allies.[4] Despite these advances, the Doha Round's effectiveness and the WTO's ability to handle the large number of interests and issues presented in it are still not certain.

THE RISE OF BILATERAL AGREEMENTS

As the negotiations in Cancun broke down, Robert Zoellick, the United States' trade representative at the time, made a telling statement: "We will do our best at Cancun to keep the Doha negotiations on track. But if others falter, the Bush administration will keep negotiating for free trade—to create jobs, keep America competitive, and create opportunities for modernizing reformers around the world."[5] This declaration highlights the increasing willingness of individual countries to circumvent the multilateral system and engage in bilateral agreements, also known as *Preferential Trade Agreements* (PTAs) or *Free Trade Agreements* (FTAs), with each other to meet their global trade objectives.

The U.S. is clearly at the forefront in the recent proliferation of such agreements, with several bilateral deals either completed recently or in the works with Australia, Morocco, Chile, as well as other countries in Central and South America, sub-Saharan Africa, and Asia. Some of the deals, like the FTA with Australia, involve only the two countries. Others, such as the Central American Free Trade Agreement, bring together the U.S. with a group of countries.[6] Bilateral agreements are relatively easy for countries to pursue than are agreements in the WTO, because it is easier to resolve issues in a smaller setting.

REGIONAL ECONOMIC INTEGRATION

Going beyond the bilateral approach is the regional approach, called *Regional Trade Agreements* or RTAs. Not all are in force, but 150 of 254 registered RTAs are currently in operation, with another 70 expected to become so in the near future. It is further estimated that there could be as many as 300 operational RTAs, or "spaghetti bowl" deals involving mixtures of countries from different areas, by the end of 2007.[7]

It's logical that most trade groups contain countries in the same area of the world. Neighboring countries tend to ally for several reasons:

• The distances that goods need to travel between such countries are short.

• Consumers' tastes are likely to be similar, and distribution channels can be easily established in adjacent countries.

• Neighboring countries may have a common history and interests, and they may be more willing to coordinate their policies.[8]

There are two basic types of regional economic integration from the standpoint of tariff policies:

1. **Free Trade Agreement (FTA).** The goal of an FTA is to abolish all tariffs between member countries. Free trade agreements usually begin modestly by eliminating tariffs on

goods that already have low tariffs, and there is usually an implementation period during which all tariffs are eliminated on all products. In addition, each member country maintains its own external tariff against non-FTA countries.

2. **Customs Union.** In addition to eliminating internal tariffs, member countries levy a common external tariff on goods being imported from nonmembers. For example, the European Union established a common external tariff in 1967. It had begun to remove internal tariffs in 1959, and that process was completed in 1967 at the same time the common external tariff was established. Now the EU negotiates as one region in the WTO rather than as separate countries.

Beyond the reduction of tariffs and nontariff barriers, countries can enhance their cooperation in a variety of other ways. The EU, for example, also allows free mobility of production factors such as labor and capital. This means that labor, for example, is free to work in any country in the common market without restriction. This type of cooperation where free mobility of factors of product are added to a customs union results in a **common market.** In the absence of the common market arrangement, workers would have to apply to immigration for a visa, and that might be difficult to come by. In addition, the EU has harmonized its monetary policies through the creation of a common currency complete with a Central Bank. This level of cooperation creates a degree of political integration among member countries, which means they lose a bit of their sovereignty. Thus PTAs and RTAs generally start as free trade agreements and progress to customs unions, then move to common market status as they add free trade in services and investment.

The Effects of Integration

Regional economic integration can affect member countries in social, cultural, political, and economic ways. As we noted in Chapter 7, the imposition of tariff and nontariff barriers disrupts the free flow of goods, affecting resource allocation. Regional economic integration reduces or eliminates those barriers for member countries. It produces both **static effects** and **dynamic effects.** Static effects are the shifting of resources from inefficient to efficient companies as trade barriers fall. Dynamic effects are the overall growth in the market and the impact on a company caused by expanding production and by the company's ability to achieve greater economies of scale.

Static effects may develop when either of two conditions occurs.

1. **Trade creation**—production shifts to more efficient producers for reasons of comparative advantage, allowing consumers access to more goods at a lower price than would have been possible without integration. Companies that are protected in their domestic markets face real problems when the barriers are eliminated and they attempt to compete with more efficient producers. The strategic implication is that companies that might not have been able to export to another country—even though they might be more efficient than producers in that country—are now able to export when the barriers come down. Thus, there will be more demand for their products, and the demand for the protected, less efficient products will fall.

2. **Trade diversion**—trade shifts to countries in the group at the expense of trade with countries not in the group, even though the nonmember companies might be more efficient in the absence of trade barriers.

For example, assume that U.S. companies are importing the same product from Mexico and Taiwan. If the United States enters into an FTA with Mexico but not with Taiwan, these companies might be more likely to import goods from Mexico than from Taiwan due to lower tariffs. This does not mean, however, that Mexican products are any better or cheaper (in the absence of integration) than the Taiwanese goods, but the lower tariff gives them a competitive edge in the market.

Major types of economic integration

- Free trade area—no internal tariffs
- Customs union—no internal tariffs plus common external tariffs
- Common market—customs union plus factor mobility

Regional integration has social, cultural, political, and economic effects.

Static effects of integration— the shifting of resources from inefficient to efficient companies as trade barriers fall

Dynamic effects of integration— the overall growth in the market and the impact on a company caused by expanding production and by the company's ability to achieve greater economies of scale

Trade creation—production shifts to more efficient producers for reasons of comparative advantage

Trade diversion—trade shifts to countries in the group at the expense of trade with countries not in the group

Economies of scale—the average cost per unit falls as the number of units produced rises; occurs in regional integration because of the growth in the market size

Dynamic effects of integration occur when trade barriers come down and the size of the market increases. For example, Argentina, a country of 39.5 million people, is a member of MERCOSUR, a customs union that would eventually like to be a common market, encompassing Argentina, Brazil, Paraguay, and Uruguay. The size of that market is 221 million people. Argentine companies could export to the country's neighbors in the absence of a trade agreement, but high tariffs would probably limit their ability to compete. When the trade barriers come down, however, the market size confronting the Argentine company increases dramatically. Because of the larger size of the market, Argentine companies can increase their production, which will result in lower costs per unit, a phenomenon we call **economies of scale.** Companies can produce more cheaply, which is good because they must become more efficient to survive.

Another important dynamic effect is the increase in efficiency due to increased competition. Many MNEs in Europe have attempted to grow through mergers and acquisitions to achieve the size necessary to compete in the larger market. Companies in Mexico were forced to become more competitive with the passage of NAFTA due to competition from Canadian and U.S. companies.

Major Regional Trading Groups

There are two ways to look at different trading groups: by location and by type. There are major trading groups in every region of the world. It is impossible to cover every group in every region, so we will cover a few of the major groups. Each regional group is either a free trade agreement or a customs union, but several, such as the EU, are also common markets.

Companies are interested in regional trading groups for their markets, sources of raw materials, and production locations. The larger and richer the new market, the more likely it is to attract the attention of the major investor countries and companies.

THE EUROPEAN UNION

The largest and most comprehensive of the regional economic groups is the European Union. It began as a free trade agreement with the goal to become a customs union and to integrate in other ways. The formation of the **European Parliament** and the establishment of a common currency, the euro, make the EU the most ambitious of all the regional trade groups.[9] The key milestones for the **European Union** are summarized in Table 8.2, and Map 8.1 identifies the members of the European Union and other key European groups.

Because of the economic and human destruction left by World War II, European political leaders realized that greater cooperation among their countries would help speed Europe's recovery. Many organizations were formed, including the **European Economic Community (EEC),** which eventually emerged as the organization that would bring together the countries of Europe into the most powerful trading bloc in the world. Several other countries, including the United Kingdom, formed the **European Free Trade Association** (EFTA) with the limited goal of eliminating internal tariffs, but most of those countries eventually became part of the EU, and those that have decided not to leave EFTA (Iceland, Liechtenstein, Norway, and Switzerland) are linked together with the EU as a customs union. The EEC, later called the **European Community (EC)** and finally the **European Union** (EU), set about to abolish internal tariffs in order to more closely integrate European markets and hopefully allow economic cooperation to help avoid further political conflict.

The EU's Organizational Structure

The European Union encompasses many governing bodies, among which are the **European Commission, European Council, European Parliament,** and the **European Court of Justice.** In Chapter 3, we noted how important it is for MNE management to

European Union

- Changed from the European Economic Community to the European Community to the European Union
- The largest and most successful regional trade group
- Free trade of goods, services, capital, people
- Common external tariff
- Common currency

European Free Trade
Association—FTA involving Iceland, Liechtenstein, Norway, and Switzerland with close ties to the EU

TABLE 8.2   EUROPEAN UNION MILESTONES

From its inception in 1957, the EU has been moving toward complete economic integration. However, it is doubtful that its initial adherents ever dreamed that European cooperation would have achieved such integration as to move to a common currency.

1946	Winston Churchill calls for a United States of Europe.
1948	The Organization for European Economic Cooperation (OEEC) is created to coordinate the Marshall Plan.
1951	The Six (Belgium, France, Germany, Italy, Luxembourg, the Netherlands) sign the Treaty of Paris establishing the European Coal and Steel Community (ECSC) to begin in 1952.
1957	The Six sign the Treaties of Rome establishing the European Economic Community (EEC) and the European Atomic Energy Community (Euratom or EAEC). They become effective on January 1, 1958.
1959	The first steps are taken in the progressive abolition of customs duties and quotas within the EEC.
1960	The Stockholm Convention establishes the European Free Trade Association (EFTA) among seven European countries (Austria, Denmark, Norway, Portugal, Sweden, Switzerland, the United Kingdom). The OEEC becomes the Organization for Economic Cooperation and Development (OECD).
1961	The first regulation on free movement of workers within the EEC comes into force.
1962	The Common Agricultural Policy is adopted.
1965	A treaty merging the ECSC, EEC, and Euratom is signed. The treaty enters into force on July 1, 1967.
1966	Agreement is reached on a value-added tax (VAT) system; a treaty merging the Executives of the European Communities comes into force; and the EEC changes its name to European Community (EC).
1967	All remaining internal tariffs are eliminated, and a common external tariff is imposed.
1972	The currency "snake" is established in which the Six agree to limit currency fluctuations between their currencies to 2.25 percent.
1973	Denmark, Ireland, and the United Kingdom become members of the EC.
1979	European Monetary System comes into effect; European Parliament is elected by universal suffrage for the first time.
1980	Greece becomes tenth member of the EC.
1985	Commission sends the Council a White Paper on completion of internal market by 1992.
1986	Spain and Portugal become the eleventh and twelfth members of the EC. Single European Act (SEA) is signed, improving decision-making procedures and increasing the role of the European Parliament; comes into effect on July 1, 1987.
1989	Collapse of the Berlin Wall; German Democratic Republic opens its borders.
1990	The first phase of European Monetary Union (EMU) comes into effect. Unification of Germany.
1992	European Union signed in Maastricht; adopted by member countries on November 1, 1993.
1993	The Single European Market comes into force (January 1, 1993).
	Council concludes agreement creating European Economic Area, effective January 1, 1994.
1995	Austria, Finland, Sweden become the thirteenth, fourteenth, and fifteenth members of the EU.
1996	An EU summit names the 11 countries that will join the European single currency with all EU countries joining but Britain, Sweden, Denmark (by their choice), and Greece (not ready).
1999	The euro, the single European currency, comes into effect (January 1, 1999).
2001	Greece becomes the twelfth country to adopt the euro (January 1, 2001).
2002	The euro coins and notes enter circulation (January 1, 2002).
	The EU announces 10 new countries to join the EU in May 2004 (October 2002).
	All IS member states ratify the Kyoto Protocol
2004	Admission of Cyprus, the Czech Republic, Estonia, Hungary, Latvia, Lithuania, Malta, Poland, Slovakia, Slovenia.
2005	Membership talks with Turkey begin.
2007	Bulgaria and Romania will join.

Source: Found on the Web site for the European Union, The History of the European Union, November 2002. © European Communities, 1995–2005. Reprinted with permission. http://europe.eu.int/abc/history/index_en.htm.

understand the political environment of every country where it operates. The same is true for the EU. To be successful in Europe, MNEs need to understand the governance of the EU, just as they need to understand the governance process of each of the individual European countries in which they are investing or doing business. These institutions set parameters under which companies must operate, so management needs to understand the institutions and how they make decisions that could affect corporate strategy.

MAP 8.1   European Trade and Economic Integration

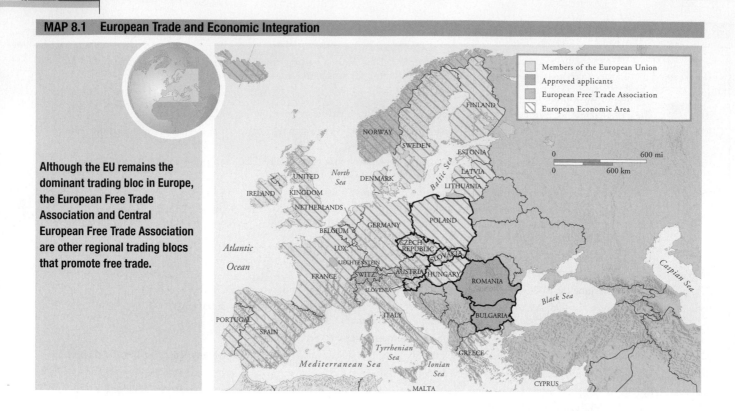

Although the EU remains the dominant trading bloc in Europe, the European Free Trade Association and Central European Free Trade Association are other regional trading blocs that promote free trade.

Members of the European Union
Approved applicants
European Free Trade Association
European Economic Area

The Commission initiates proposals for legislation, is the guardian of the treaties, and is the manager and executor of EU policies and of international trade relationships.

European Commission   The Commission provides the EU's political leadership and direction. The original intent was for the Commission to act as a supranational government for Europe. There are three distinct functions of the Commission:

1. Initiator of proposals for legislation
2. Guardian of the treaties
3. Manager and executor of Union policies and of international trade relationships[10]

The Commission manages the annual budget of the EU, manages the EU, and negotiates trade agreements.

The Council of Ministers is a collection of 25 different councils representing the different ministers in each country. The Council has the final say over legislation in conjunction with the Parliament.

European Council   The Council is also known as the Council of Ministers, which is composed of different ministers of the member countries. Each EU country has a single minister that represents it at the Council's meetings; however, participation in the Council is not limited to this one representative for each nation. There are currently nine different council configurations, such as General Affairs and External Relations, Economic and Financial Affairs, and Agriculture, and these institutions are attended by whatever State Secretary or minister each government deems appropriate.[11] For example, the Agriculture Council of Ministers is comprised of the Ministers of Agriculture of all member countries. This specific council, whose members represent their member governments, decides issues dealing with agriculture. In many respects, the Council is much more democratic than the Commission because its members are elected officials in their home countries. The Council of Ministers is presided over by a presidency, which rotates among the member states every six months.

The European Council or European Summit is comprised of the heads of state/government of each member country.

The Council has a tremendous amount of authority because it can adopt Commission-proposed legislation, amend it, or ignore it—it is the EU's ultimate decision-making body. The Council has the final say in legislative matters in cooperation with Parliament. The European Council is important because it sets priorities, gives political direction, and resolves issues that the Council of Ministers cannot resolve. The ascendancy of the European Council, or Council of Ministers, means that the efforts of the EU will have more influence and support by the individual countries, and this could hasten the integration process.

The European Parliament   The Parliament is composed of 624 members who are elected every five years, and its membership is based on country population. The three major responsibilities of the Parliament are legislative power, control over the budget, and supervision of executive decisions. The Commission presents community legislation to the Parliament. Parliament must approve the legislation before submitting it to the Council for adoption.[12]

> The three major responsibilities of the European Parliament are legislative power, control over the budget, and supervision of executive decisions.

The European Court of Justice   The Court of Justice ensures consistent interpretation and application of EU treaties. Member states, EC institutions, or individuals and companies may bring cases to the Court. The Court of Justice is an appeals court for individuals, firms, and organizations fined by the Commission for infringing treaty law.[13] The Court of Justice is relevant to MNEs because it deals mostly with economic matters. The Court is required to hear every case referred to it, even minor disputes over trade regulation and export issues.

> The European Court of Justice ensures consistent interpretation and application of EU treaties.

The Single European Act

The European Union has been moving toward a single market since the passage of the Single European Act of 1987. Among other things, the act included the elimination of the remaining barriers to a free market, such as customs posts, different certification procedures, rates of value-added tax, and excise duties.

> The Single European Act was designed to eliminate the remaining nontariff barriers to trade in Europe.

Common Trade and Foreign Policy   The EU Web site states, "The European Union is today the leading player in international trade, ahead of the United States and Japan. At a time of strong growth in international trade, it accounts for a fifth of world trade. The Union's influence on the international stage hinges on its ability to negotiate with its trade partners as a single entity."[14] As Table 8.3 shows, with the recent addition of 10 new members in 2004, the EU membership now has a population (but not GNI) greater than that of NAFTA (Canada, the United States, and Mexico), making it a formidable economic bloc.

During the formation of the European Union, the organizing countries focused mainly on economic integration and left foreign policy to the individual countries. Realizing how beneficial a common foreign policy would be to the EU, member countries began formalizing objectives in 1993 on armed conflicts, human rights, and other international foreign policy issues. Progress in this area has been slow, and the desire to incorporate an EU rapid-reaction force is constantly stalled due to differences in member opinion. National attitudes are currently the driving force behind European policy. Most European countries initially supported the United States in the war on terror. However, countries are splintered in their views on the Middle East, especially in response to the U.S.-led invasion of Iraq. Many original members of the EU, such as France and Germany, strongly opposed the invasion, whereas Britain and some of the new members of the EU, such as Poland, supported the invasion. The EU will continue to push toward a common foreign policy that will help align national differences and bring the member nations one step closer to complete integration.[15]

The Euro   Not content with the economic integration envisaged in the Single European Act, the EU nations signed the Treaty of Maastricht in 1992, which set steps to accomplish two goals: political union and monetary union. The decision to move to a common currency in Europe has eliminated currency as a barrier to trade. Although all member states are a part of the European Monetary Union, not all have adopted the euro. In fact, as of August 2005, only 12 of the 25 members of the EU had adopted the euro. The countries that adopted the euro at its launch (as a virtual currency) on January 1, 1999, were

> The Treaty of Maastricht sought to foster political union and monetary union.

TABLE 8.3 COMPARATIVE STATISTICS BY TRADE GROUP

EU MEMBER COUNTRIES	POPULATION IN MILLIONS (2003)	GNI BILLIONS OF $(2003)	PER CAPITA GNI IN $(2003)
Austria	8.1	215	26,720
Belgium	10.3	267	25,820
Denmark	5.4	182	33,750
Finland	5.2	141	27,020
France	59.7	1,523	24,770
Germany	82.6	2,085	25,250
Greece	10.7	147	13,720
Ireland	3.9	106	26,960
Italy	57.6	1,243	21,560
Luxembourg	0.4	20	43,940
Netherlands	16.2	427	26,310
Portugal	10.2	124	12,130
Spain	41.1	698	16,990
Sweden	9.0	258	28,840
United Kingdom	59.3	2,680	28,350
Cyprus	0.8	9	12,320
Czech Republic	10.2	69	6,740
Estonia	1.4	7	4,960
Hungary	10.1	64	6,330
Latvia	2.3	9	4,070
Lithuania	3.5	16	4,490
Malta	0.4	4	9,260
Poland	38.2	201	5,270
Slovakia	5.4	26	4,920
Slovenia	2.0	23	11,830
Bulgaria	7.8	17	2,710
Romania	22.2	51	2,310
Turkey	70.7	197	2,790
E-15	379.7	10,116	26,641
E-10 2004 Admits	74.3	428	5,762
E-25 (E-15 plus E-10)	454.0	10,544	23,224
E-28	554.7	10,809	19,486
NAFTA Member Countries			
Canada	31.6	757	23,930
Mexico	102.3	637	6,230
United States	291.0	10,946	37,610
Total	424.9	12,340	29,042
MERCOSUR Member Countries			
Argentina	38.4	140	3,650
Brazil	176.6	479	2,710
Paraguay	5.6	6	1,100
Uruguay	3.4	13	3,790
Total	224.0	638	2,848

Austria, Belgium, Germany, Finland, France, Ireland, Italy, Luxembourg, the Netherlands, Portugal, and Spain. Greece adopted the euro on January 1, 2001. All these countries introduced the euro in cash form at the beginning of 2002.[16] Of the 15 members of the EU prior to the expansion in 2004, only the U.K., Denmark, and Sweden elected not to adopt the euro. None of the new members that joined in 2004 have qualified to join the euro, but they can after meeting certain criteria.

The introduction of the euro has had significant consequences in Europe and elsewhere. As will be shown in Chapter 9, the euro is now one of the most widely traded currencies in the world. It is much easier for consumers inside of Europe to compare prices of goods among countries since they don't have to factor in exchange rates anymore. It is easier for companies to establish pricing policies and keep their accounting records for operations in different member countries due to the common currency. In Chapter 10, we will discuss the role of the European Central Bank in controlling the value of the euro and the criteria that each country had to implement in order to join the euro.

EU Expansion

One of the EU's major challenges is that of expansion. The latest expansion of the EU was also its largest; occurring in May 2004, it included Cyprus, the Czech Republic, Estonia, Hungary, Latvia, Lithuania, Malta, Poland, the Slovak Republic, and Slovenia. Bulgaria and Romania have been given a date of 2007 for possible admission into the EU, and Turkey has been put on hold while it continues to improve its human rights record.[17] Map 8.1 shows the current countries of the EU and the expansion countries.

The acquisition of the 10 new countries will increase the EU's population by 74.3 million and add $428 billion to its economic output. But the admission will bring many difficult problems to the zone. Most countries in Central and Eastern Europe are poor, have fledgling democracies, and depend greatly on agriculture—as much as 20 percent of GNI, compared with only 6 percent on average in the EU. They will thus strain the EU's financial resources. As noted in Table 8.3, in 2003, these 10 had a significantly lower per capita GNI ($5,762) than the existing 15 members of the EU ($26,641). The four most powerful members of the EU—France, Germany, Italy, and the United Kingdom—have 57 percent of the population and generate 71.4 percent of the GNI. However, the new countries already rely heavily on the EU for trade. For example, 69.8 percent of the Czech Republic's exports and 68.4 percent of Poland's exports go to EU countries. This compares with 54.2 percent for Germany, 53.4 percent for the United Kingdom, 62.8 percent for France, and 72 percent for the Netherlands. Another problem of expansion is governance. Both geographically and economically large members of the EU, such as France and Germany, fear that the addition of so many new countries will weaken their control and influence. On the other hand, the addition of 10 new countries moved the EU ahead of NAFTA in total population and increased the EU's power as an international trading bloc, although the expanded EU is still smaller than NAFTA in terms of total GNI and GNI per capita.

However, the EU has signed numerous free trade agreements with other countries around the world. This means that companies doing business in one EU country have access to a much larger market than anywhere else in the world. An agreement was signed in June 2002 between Chile and the EU to improve political, economic, and trade relations. The EU engaged in negotiating rounds with MERCOSUR from 2002 to 2004 and has still more rounds planned for 2005, but things are moving slowly because of the economic crisis in Argentina and because of the political and economic problems in Brazil—the two largest players in MERCOSUR.[18]

As mentioned earlier, the EFTA came into being at about the same time as the EEC but with more limited goals. However, EFTA only comprises four countries, and all but Switzerland are part of the European Economic Area (EEA), which comprises the EU and the other three EFTA countries. According to the EEA, the three EFTA countries participate in the basic four freedoms with the EU: freedom of movement of goods (excluding

The euro

- Is a common currency in Europe
- Is administered by the European Central Bank
- Was established on January 1, 1999
- Resulted in new bank notes in 2002
- Does not include the U.K., Denmark, Sweden, or the 10 new entrants to the EU as of 2005

The EU expanded from 15 to 25 countries in 2004 with countries from mostly central and eastern Europe. It has approved two more countries to enter in 2007 and is negotiating with Turkey.

agriculture and fisheries, which are included in the Agreement only to a very limited extent), persons, services and capital.[19] The difference between the EEA and the expansion of the EU is that the members of the EFTA are not interested in complete membership in the EU but just want to take advantage of the free flow of food, labor, services, and capital.

Trade Disputes Between the EU and the U.S.

The United States is the EU's largest trading partner. Relations between the two trading powerhouses worsened in early 2001 when the United States passed heavy steel tariffs and farm subsidies. As noted above, tensions eased as the United States finally dropped its tariffs after pressure from the WTO.

However, another stumbling block to EU-U.S. trade relations has come in the form of long-standing disputes over aircraft subsidies. The U.S. has accused the EU of providing as much as $15 billion in launch aid in the form of soft loans to the French aircraft manufacturer, Airbus. The U.S. claims that the loans, which don't have to be completely repaid unless the aircraft they are subsidizing perform successfully in the market, are illegal according to WTO rules. The EU has countered that the U.S. government has supported Boeing illegally through tax breaks and infrastructure improvements worth $7.4 billion, as well as through $23 billion in R&D grants funneled to the company through NASA and the Pentagon.[20] In 2004, both sides filed complaints with the WTO against the other's actions. The basis for the complaints lay in each side's perception that the other was in violation of a 1992 deal that limited the EU launch aid—in the form of soft loans—and capped Boeing's indirect aid at 4 percent of its revenue.[21] However, given that the WTO would probably come down hard on both sides should the dispute be referred to it, the EU and U.S. agreed to attempt to work out the issue through a series of bilateral negotiations. Should the talks fail, however, the case could be subjected to WTO arbitration, which would likely cool the relationship between the two sides again—a relationship already strained due to the previously mentioned disputes.

Implications of the EU for Corporate Strategy

The EU is a tremendous market in terms of both population and income, and so it is one that companies cannot ignore. There are three ways that doing business in the EU can influence corporate strategy, especially for non-EU MNEs. First, companies need to determine where to produce products. One strategy is to produce products in a central location in Europe to minimize transportation costs and the time it takes to move products from one country to another. However, the highest costs are in central Europe. As noted in the opening case in the chapter, manufacturing wages in the auto industry in Germany top $40 per hour, compared with much smaller wages in the Eastern European members of the EU. The move to a common market has certainly simplified the movement of goods from country to country, but location is also a function of total costs, not just transportation costs.

Second, companies need to determine if they will grow by new investments, as Toyota is doing with its new plant in Poland, by expanding existing investments, or by joint ventures and mergers. Toyota is entering into a joint venture with PSA Peugeot-Citroen for its new factory in the Czech Republic to take advantage of PSA's supplier network. However, mergers and acquisitions have really picked up in Europe. The market in Europe is still considered fragmented and inefficient compared with the United States, so most experts feel that mergers, takeovers, and spinoffs will continue in Europe for years to come. U.S. companies are buying European companies to gain a market presence and to get rid of competition. An example was Staples' acquisition of the mail-order business of French retailer Pinault Printemps Redoute (PPR) SA in 2002. Staples was finding it difficult to expand its operations in Europe, but with the purchase of PPR, it will

Implications of the EU for corporate strategy

- Companies need to determine where to produce products.
- Companies need to determine what their entry strategy will be.
- Companies need to balance the commonness of the EU with national differences.

acquire stores in France, Belgium, Italy, Spain, and the United Kingdom and will increase sales by $600 million.[22] European firms are also acquiring other European firms to improve their competitive advantage against U.S. companies and to expand their market presence. A good example is the purchase of Promodes Group, a French retailer, by Carrefour, another French retailer. That merger resulted in the creation of the number-one retailer in Europe.[23]

Third, companies need to balance the "commonness" of the EU with national differences. There are wider national differences in the EU than in the different states in the United States, mostly due to language and history. But there are also widely different growth rates in the EU. In 2005, for example, business was booming in Ireland and Spain, whereas it was stagnant in Germany, Europe's largest economy and historically the engine for economic growth in Europe. However, that could turn around. U.S. workers are far more mobile and flexible than European workers to take advantage of regional economic differences. That is why there has been a strong migration in recent years to the sunbelt of the United States where economies are growing rather fast. Germans, however, will not move to Spain to take advantage of faster growth rates.[24] In terms of products, Toyota is busy designing a European car, but for which Europe? Tastes and preferences and climatic differences between northern and southern Europe are huge. But they are attempting to develop a pan-European strategy through strategic production locations and design. Companies will always struggle with the degree to which they develop a European strategy vs. different national strategies inside Europe. As can be seen in Table 8.3, however, it doesn't make sense to reinvent the wheel for every small country inside Europe. Given that tariff barriers have come down and the euro has made it easier to monitor price differences throughout Europe, it is becoming easier to develop more of a pan-European strategy.

Main Challenges Facing the EU

The EU is clearly the largest (in terms of population and number of countries) and most ambitious of the RTAs. It has made remarkable progress since the signing of the Treaty of Rome in 1957 and is the model for broader integration in other parts of the world. However, there are a number of issues that the EU must resolve as it moves forward. These issues go far beyond the trade liberalization initiatives of the WTO or other free trade agreements or customs unions. However, the challenges of the EU are important for other RTAs to understand as they consider the degree of integration that they want to achieve.

First is the transition of the new entrants to the EU as well as the expansion to include Bulgaria and Romania in 2007 and possibly Turkey in the future. The new member states are coming in with lower wages, lower taxes, but with two to four times the growth rates of the original 15 members, creating some real challenges. As it is, people in the new member countries are denied unlimited freedom to work anywhere they want in the EU until 2010. The U.K., Ireland, and Sweden are the only EU countries that have given guest workers from the 10 new countries permission to work inside their national boundaries. The new entrants must work hard to prepare to enter the euro zone where they can adopt the euro as their currency. There is also the struggle to know what to do with Turkey. Beginning in October 2005, Turkey will start negotiations over its entry into the EU. Concerns over Turkey's human rights record, the fact that it would be the only Islamic state in the EU, and its political disagreements with the Greek Cypriote government are all issues that will complicate Turkey's admission into the EU.

Second is the adoption of the new constitution. On June 18, 2004, the heads of state of the 25 member nations adopted a treaty leading to a new constitution that must now be voted on in national referendums in each of the 25 countries. All the countries have to vote in favor of the treaty in order for it to be adopted. The constitution is designed to replace existing agreements and sets the rules for how the institutions of the EU will work, how power is distributed, and what types of activities the EU will cover. The constitution does not replace

Major challenges facing the EU

- The transition of new entrants
- The adoption of a new constitution
- Agricultural subsidies
- Dealing with vastly different economies in the EU

individual national constitutions, but it is designed to work with them. The forces against the adoption of the constitution include the French on one hand and the British on the other. The French are concerned about their loss of power in the expanded EU and the pressures of globalization from new entrants that have cheaper wages and lower taxes, as noted above. Given that French unemployment consistently exceeds 10 percent, the pressures of globalization are significant. The British, on the other hand, are more concerned about giving up national sovereignty. The Dutch, who fall in the British camp, are concerned about becoming a province of the EU rather than maintaining independent national sovereignty. These debates over the degree to which national sovereignty will be surrendered will be an important part of the discussion of the future of the EU. In 2005, several countries, including France, rejected the constitution, so a major challenge in the EU is to figure out what to do next. Even though the constitution was voted down, the issues that forced the negative vote must be resolved for the EU to move forward.

Third is the problem of agriculture. Given that such a small percentage of the workforce in the EU is employed in agriculture, except in some of the newer entrants such as Poland, why is agriculture a problem? The **Common Agricultural Policy** (CAP) was established in 1962 as an important element of the overall economic policy of the EU. CAP's objectives are to provide farmers with a reasonable standard of living and consumers with quality food at fair prices. The way these aims are met has changed over the years. Food safety, preservation of the rural environment, and value for money are now all key concepts.[25] A great deal has been invested in agriculture in the EU over the years, but the new 10 entrants are increasing the number of farmers in the EU by 70 percent. It will be a major challenge and financially expensive to get the new farmers up to the level of existing farmers. In addition, agricultural subsidies in the EU are a major sticking point in international trade talks as noted earlier in the chapter.

Fourth is dealing with the vastly different economies in the EU. As noted in Table 8.3, the big four economies of the EU dwarf the others in population and GNI. However, economic growth rates and levels of unemployment are very different. In early 2005, for example, unemployment in Germany was 12.6 percent of the working-age population, the highest in Germany since the 1930s, due partly to relatively slow economic growth and inflexible labor practices.[26] France's unemployment rate is close to 10 percent, whereas unemployment in Britain is around 5 percent and in Ireland it is between 4 and 5 percent. On the other hand, there are high unemployment levels in some of the new entrants, including close to 20 percent in Poland. The challenge is how to manage slow growth and high unemployment in some countries, which argues for low interest rates, with faster growth, inflation, and lower unemployment in other countries, which argues for higher interest rates. Most governments use a mixture of fiscal and monetary policy to manage their economies. EU member countries, however, don't have as much control as nonmember countries. This is because the European Central Bank controls interest rates, with controlling inflation being the major policy objective. But with economic growth strong in some countries and weak in others, it is difficult to establish a monetary policy that fits all countries in the EU. Fiscal policy refers to taxation and spending, and EU countries don't have complete control in these areas either. The EU is trying to harmonize taxation policy and tax rates, especially for value-added taxes, so that countries can't use taxes as a way to unfairly entice investment. Also, there are limits as to how much governments can spend to stimulate their economies, because they are supposed to keep budget deficits under control. EU nations are finding it difficult to meet the criteria of the stability and growth pact, partially because of the recent downturn in the European economy. Countries such as Britain that are not members of the euro zone don't have the same restrictions as euro zone members, because they control their own fiscal and monetary policy.

Clearly there are many more issues confronting the EU besides the ones listed above, but these are key ones that will determine the degree of success that the EU will have. In spite of the challenges, there are many opportunities for companies to expand their markets and sources of supply as the EU grows and encompasses more of Europe.

NORTH AMERICAN FREE TRADE AGREEMENT (NAFTA)

NAFTA, which includes Canada, Mexico, and the United States, went into effect in 1994. The United States and Canada historically have had various forms of mutual economic cooperation. They signed the **Canada-U.S. Free Trade Agreement** effective January 1, 1989, which eliminated all tariffs on bilateral trade by January 1, 1998. In February 1991, Mexico approached the United States to establish a free trade agreement. The formal negotiations that began in June 1991 included Canada. The resulting North American Free Trade Agreement became effective on January 1, 1994.

NAFTA has a logical rationale, in terms of both geographic location and trading importance. Although Canadian-Mexican trade was not significant when the agreement was signed, U.S.-Mexican and U.S.-Canadian trade were. The two-way trading relationship between the United States and Canada is the largest in the world. As noted in Table 8.3, NAFTA is a powerful trading bloc with a combined population greater than the 15-member EU and GNI greater than the 25-member EU. What is significant, especially when compared with the EU, is the tremendous size of the U.S. economy in comparison to those of Canada and Mexico. In addition, Canada has a much richer economy than that of Mexico, even though its population is about one-third that of Mexico.

Even though NAFTA is a free trade agreement instead of a customs union or a common market, its cooperation extends far beyond tariff reductions. In fact, the WTO classifies NAFTA as a services agreement rather than just a free trade agreement. NAFTA covers the following areas:

- Market access—tariff and nontariff barriers, rules of origin, and government procurement
- Trade rules—safeguards, subsidies, countervailing and antidumping duties, health and safety standards
- Services—provides for the same safeguards for trade in services (consulting, engineering, software, etc.) that exist for trade in goods
- Investment—establishes investment rules governing minority interests, portfolio investment, real property, and majority-owned or controlled investments from the NAFTA countries; in addition, NAFTA coverage extends to investments made by any company incorporated in a NAFTA country, regardless of country of origin
- Intellectual property—all three countries pledge to provide adequate and effective protection and enforcement of intellectual property rights, while ensuring that enforcement measures do not themselves become barriers to legitimate trade
- Dispute settlement—provides a dispute-settlement process that will be followed; desired to keep countries from taking unilateral action against an offending party[27]

Mexico made significant strides in tariff reduction after joining GATT in 1986. At that time, its tariffs averaged 100 percent. Since then, it has reduced tariffs dramatically. As a result of NAFTA, most tariffs on originating goods traded between Mexico and Canada were eliminated immediately or phased in over a 10-year period that ended on December 31, 2003. In a few exceptions, the phase-out period will be completed by the end of 2008. Tariffs between the United States and Mexico were, in general, either eliminated immediately or over a 5- or 10-year period that ended on December 31, 2003. Although most tariffs will be eliminated in 5 or 10 equal annual stages, there are some exceptions. In the first five years of NAFTA, Mexico trimmed its average tariff on U.S. goods from 10 percent to 2 percent, while U.S. tariffs on Mexican products dropped to less than 1 percent.[28]

NAFTA provides the static and dynamic effects of economic integration discussed earlier in this chapter. For example, Canadian and U.S. consumers benefit from lower-cost agricultural products from Mexico, a static effect of economic liberalization. U.S. producers also benefit from the large and growing Mexican market, which has a huge appetite for U.S. products—a dynamic effect.

The North American Free Trade Agreement

- Includes Canada, the United States, and Mexico
- Went into effect on January 1, 1994
- Involves free trade in goods, services, and investment
- Is a large trading bloc but includes countries of different sizes and wealth

NAFTA rationale

- U.S.-Canadian trade is the largest bilateral trade in the world.
- The U.S. is Mexico's and Canada's largest trading partner.

NAFTA calls for the elimination of tariff and nontariff barriers, the harmonization of trade rules, the liberalization of restrictions on services and foreign investment, the enforcement of intellectual property, and a dispute settlement process.

NAFTA is a good example of trade diversion; some U.S. trade with and investment in Asia has been diverted to Mexico.

In addition, NAFTA is a good example of trade diversion. Many U.S. and Canadian companies have established manufacturing facilities in Asia to take advantage of cheap labor. Now, U.S. and Canadian companies can establish manufacturing facilities in Mexico rather than in Asian countries to take advantage of relatively cheap labor. For example, IBM is making computer parts in Mexico that were formerly made in Singapore. In five years, IBM boosted exports from Mexico to the United States from $350 million to $2 billion. Had the subassemblies not been made in and exported from Mexico, they would have been made in Singapore and other Asian locations and exported to the United States. Gap Inc. and Liz Claiborne are increasingly buying garments from Mexican contractors, who can offer faster delivery than can Asian contractors.[29]

Rules of Origin and Regional Content

Rules of origin—goods and services must originate in North America to get access to lower tariffs

An important component of NAFTA is the concept of rules of origin and regional content. Because NAFTA is a free trade agreement and not a customs union, each country sets its own tariffs to the rest of the world. That is why a product entering the United States from Canada must have a commercial or customs invoice that identifies the product's ultimate origin. Otherwise, an exporter from a third country would always ship the product to the NAFTA country with the lowest tariff and then re-export it to the other two countries duty-free. "Rules of origin ensure that only goods that have been the subject of substantial economic activity within the free trade area are eligible for the more liberal tariff conditions created by NAFTA."[30]

Regional content
- The percentage of value that must be from North America for the product to be considered North American in terms of country of origin
- 50 percent for most products; 62.5 percent for autos

According to regional content rules, at least 50 percent of the net cost of most products must come from the NAFTA region. The exceptions are 55 percent for footwear, 62.5 percent for passenger automobiles and light trucks and the engines and transmissions for such vehicles, and 60 percent for other vehicles and automotive parts.[31] For example, a Ford car assembled in Mexico could use parts from Canada, the United States, and Mexico, as well as labor and other factors from Mexico. For the car to enter Canada and the United States according to the preferential NAFTA duty, at least 62.5 percent of its value must come from North America.

Special Provisions of NAFTA

Additional NAFTA provisions
- Workers' rights
- The environment
- Dispute resolution mechanism

Most free trade agreements in the world are based solely on one goal: to reduce tariffs. However, NAFTA is a very different free trade agreement. Due to strong objections to the agreement by labor unions and environmentalists, two side agreements covering those issues were included in NAFTA. When first debating NAFTA, opponents worried about the potential loss of jobs in Canada and the United States to Mexico as a result of Mexico's cheaper wages, poor working conditions, and lax environmental enforcement. NAFTA opponents, particularly U.S. union organizers, thought companies would close down factories in the north and set them up in Mexico. As a result, the labor lobby in the United States forced the inclusion of labor standards, such as the right to unionize, and the environmental lobby pushed for an upgrade of environmental standards in Mexico and the strengthening of compliance.[32]

From a labor standpoint, the NAFTA side agreement "sets forth the following general objectives: improving working conditions and living standards, promoting compliance with and effective enforcement of labor laws, promoting the Agreement's principles through cooperation and coordination, and promoting publication and exchange of information to enhance mutual understanding of Parties' laws, institutions and legal systems."[33]

From an environmental standpoint, the NAFTA side agreement "include[s] the promotion of sustainable development, cooperation on the conservation, protection and enhancement of the environment, and the effective enforcement of and compliance with domestic environmental laws. The Agreement promotes transparency and public participation in the development and improvement of environmental laws and policies."[34]

Pollution levels in Mexico have increased since the signing of NAFTA partly because there is a strong positive correlation between pollution and economic growth. However, Mexican environmental standards are getting tougher, and enforcement of those standards is improving.

Labor and environmental activists were emboldened with their success at disrupting the WTO meetings in Seattle, Washington, in November 1999, so they are expected to continue to press for improvements in labor rights and the environment in NAFTA countries. The unions are disappointed with the results of the side agreement and recognize that enforcement to punish those who break labor and environmental standards is weak. President Bush agrees that he would like to improve such standards.

Impact of NAFTA

There are pros and cons to any trade agreement, and NAFTA is no exception. It is obvious that trade and investment in NAFTA have increased significantly since the agreement was signed in 2004. The trading relationship between the U.S. and Canada is the largest bilateral flow of goods, services, and income in the world, reaching nearly $450 billion. Canada is the largest export market for U.S. goods, and Mexico is number 2, although the EU as a whole is the second largest destination of U.S. goods after Canada. Canada and Mexico are also number 2 and number 4 as exporters to the U.S. market. However, it is important to note the importance of the U.S. to both Canada and Mexico. Canada exports 85.8 percent of its merchandise to the U.S., and Mexico exports 88.9 percent of its merchandise to the U.S. Although trade between Canada and Mexico has increased since the implementation of NAFTA, the importance of NAFTA is the U.S. market to Canada and Mexico. The U.S. relies on its NAFTA partners for about 30 percent of its trade.

As a result of NAFTA, trade and investment among the member countries has increased significantly.

Due to low wages in Mexico, U.S. companies invested significantly in Mexico. It is complicated to determine wage rates, however. The Bureau of Labor Statistics reported that the hourly compensation costs in U.S. dollars for production workers in manufacturing in 2003 was $2.48 for Mexican workers, compared with $21.97 for U.S. workers and $19.28 for Canadian workers. However, a report by McKinsey and Co. stated that an assembly line worker in Mexico earns $1.47 per hour, whereas his or her counterpart in China makes $0.59 per hour. Delphi Corp., the U.S. auto parts company, employs 70,000 Mexican workers along the border, and it pays $1.90 per hour for an assembly line worker with two years of experience. Exact wage rates are difficult to measure, but it is clear that Mexican wages are lower than American and Canadian wages and higher than Chinese wages. Over the 10 years since NAFTA was implemented, U.S. companies invested an average of $12 billion per year in Mexico. Mexico's per capita income rose to $6,230 in 2003, compared with only $1,100 in China, and was higher than in any other country in Latin America, including Brazil. Mexico's economy is now the ninth largest in the world, up from number 15 when NAFTA was signed.[35]

The investment and employment pictures are complicated. One concern for U.S. workers when the agreement was being debated was that investment would move to Mexico due to that country's lower wages and lax environmental standards. As noted above, wages are significantly lower in Mexico than they are in the United States and Canada, and in fact, they are lower than wages in many of the industrialized countries of Asia. When NAFTA was signed, companies like IBM and Canon began investing in Mexico instead of Asia for certain types of manufacturing. They could enjoy many tax and tariff exemptions, labor was plentiful and cheap, and high U.S. demand was just miles away. Foreign investment in Mexico rose from $4 billion per year in 1993 to $11.8 billion per year in 1999.[36] However, when NAFTA required Mexico to strip the *maquiladoras* (companies on the Mexican border) of their duty-free status in 2001, foreign companies started looking elsewhere. This was also compounded by the weakening U.S. economy and the stronger peso. Companies like Sanyo, Canon, and French battery producer Saft left Mexico and relocated to China, Vietnam, and Guatemala, where labor is cheaper.[37] Also, now that China has opened up its market to more foreign investment as it becomes a part of the WTO, Mexicans are concerned that foreign investment is being diverted to China to take advantage of even lower manufacturing wages, estimated at between $0.56 and $1.09 per hour, and generous incentives. Even though employment in the *maquiladora* factories has dropped by more than 20 percent since 2000, Mexico is still an attractive market for investment. Although U.S. FDI to Mexico dropped after 1999 and 2000, Mexico still had the largest stock of FDI of any country in Latin America or Asia, except for Japan. As noted in the case at the end of the chapter, Wal-Mart is investing significantly in Mexico and is now the largest employer in Mexico.

A major challenge to NAFTA is immigration. As trade in agriculture increased with the advent of NAFTA, it is estimated that 1.3 million farm jobs disappeared in Mexico due to competition from the U.S. Many of these farmers ended up as illegal immigrants in the U.S. working in the agricultural and other sectors, sending home more money in wire transfers (see the opening case in Chapter 9) than Mexico received in foreign direct investment in 2003.

> A major challenge to NAFTA is illegal immigration.

NAFTA Expansion

When the United States began its discussions with Mexico and Canada, it perceived a future effort to pull together North, Central, and South America into an "Enterprise of the Americas." Since the 1994 meeting in Miami, representatives from countries in the Americas except for Cuba have been working on a Free Trade Agreement of the Americas (FTAA), which encompasses much more than just free trade but is not as comprehensive as the EU. The war on terror has slowed progress on the FTAA, and rising trade tensions between the U.S. and Brazil in the WTO have also created difficulties. However, the countries are still working together to see if they can forge an agreement. In the meantime, most countries have worked on different bilateral agreements to keep the impetus for free trade moving forward. Free trade in the Americas will benefit companies greatly. An example is U.S.-based Caterpillar. When Caterpillar exports its motor graders to Chile, it must pay $15,000 in tariffs. If it manufactures the motor graders in Brazil and ships them to Chile, it only pays $3,700 in tariffs. However, Caterpillar's Canadian competitors can ship to Chile free of tariffs because of the Canada-Chile FTA.[38]

> Representatives from 34 democracies in the Americas are in negotiations to form the Free Trade Area of the Americas.

Mexico also entered into a free trade agreement with the European Union on July 1, 2001, that will end all tariffs on bilateral trade by 2007. EU officials feel that the FTA is important for them, because their share of trade with Mexico fell from 9 percent in 1993 to 6 percent in 2000 due to the passage of the NAFTA agreement.[39]

Implications of NAFTA for Corporate Strategy

Several predictions were made when NAFTA was signed. One prediction was that companies would look at NAFTA as one big regional market, allowing companies to rationalize production, products, financing, and the like. That has largely happened in a number of industries—especially in automotive products and in electronics (e.g., in computers). Each country in NAFTA ships more automotive products, based on specialized production, to the other two countries than any other manufactured goods. Employment has increased in the auto industry in the United States since NAFTA was established, even as it has declined in Mexico because of productivity.[40] Rationalization of automotive production has taken place for years in the United States and Canada, but Mexico is a recent entrant. Auto manufacturing has moved into Mexico from all over the world. Over 500,000 Mexicans make parts and assemble vehicles for all of the world's major auto producers. NAFTA's rules of origin requiring 62.5 percent regional content have forced European and Asian automakers to bring in parts suppliers and set up assembly operations in Mexico. In one case, a Canadian entrepreneur established a metal-stamping plant in Puebla, Mexico, to supply Volkswagen, the German auto manufacturer. The VW plant assembles the revitalized Beetle that is being supplied to the U.S. market.[41] DaimlerChrysler is producing 45,000 cars and 200,000 trucks in Mexico, between 80 and 90 percent of which are being exported to the United States and Canada. DaimlerChrysler began producing a new model, the PT Cruiser, in Toluca, Mexico, for export to Canada, the United States, and Europe. It is using that one plant to manufacture one model for the entire world. The story of DaimlerChrysler's production in the United States is similar. In 1993, Chrysler exported only 5,300 vehicles to Mexico. The following year, after the signing of NAFTA, it exported 17,500, and in 2000 it exported 60,000.[42] Because barriers to trade are next to zero in the NAFTA zone, companies can set up operations wherever it makes the most sense for them to do so and then easily ship their goods to any of the three countries.

The examples here describe how production is intertwined among the member countries. However, some companies are simply leaving the United States and Canada and moving to Mexico. This is happening in the apparel and furniture industries. Initially, NAFTA rules on apparel caused the Mexican textile industry to bring jobs back from Asia, and U.S. textile companies are setting up operations in Mexico to supply both the Mexican and U.S. apparel markets. This is a good example of the concept of diversion being applied to investment—investment being diverted from Asia to NAFTA countries, especially Mexico. However, the labor cycle is turning again. Just as some companies left Asian countries like Malaysia and Singapore as labor rates increased, so too will they leave Mexico as wages increase. This is especially true since the apparel industry is moving to China to take advantage of the elimination of textile quotas by the WTO. Mexico hopes that the benefits of a closer U.S. market due to NAFTA will keep companies interested in investing, but the competition for investment will be fierce.

A second prediction was that sophisticated U.S. companies would run Canadian and Mexican companies out of business once the markets opened up. That has not happened. In fact, U.S. companies along the border of Canada are finding that Canadian companies are generating more competition for them than low-wage Mexican companies. Also, many Mexican companies have restructured to compete with U.S. and Canadian companies. The lack of protection has resulted in much more competitive Mexican firms. NAFTA has forced companies from all three countries to reexamine their strategies and determine how best to operate in the market. However, as was discussed in the context of agriculture, some industries have been hard-hit by U.S. competitors. And as will be illustrated in the Wal-Mart case at the end of the chapter, Mexican retailers have had a difficult time adjusting to giants like Wal-Mart, Target, Costco, and Carrefour.

A final prediction had to do with looking at Mexico as a consumer market rather than just a production location. Initially, the excitement over Mexico for U.S. and Canadian companies was the low-wage environment. However, as Mexican income continues to rise—which it must do as more investment enters Mexico and more Mexican companies export production—demand is rising for foreign products. But U.S. and Canadian companies need to make the transition to Mexico as a significant final consumer market.

> Mexico is being looked at more as a market for U.S. and Canadian exports than just a location for low-cost production.

REGIONAL ECONOMIC INTEGRATION IN THE AMERICAS

There are six major regional economic groups in the Americas as illustrated in Maps 8.2 and 8.3. They can be divided into Central America and South America. In Central America (not including NAFTA, which is considered North America) are the Caribbean Community and Common Market (CARICOM) and the Central American Common Market (CACM). The two major groups in South America are the Andean Community (CAN) and the Southern Common Market (MERCOSUR). In addition, the Latin American Integration Association (LAIA) encompasses 10 countries in South America plus Mexico and Cuba. The major reason for these different groups entering into collaboration was market size. The post–World War II strategy of import substitution to resolve balance-of-payments problems in many of the markets in Latin America was doomed because of

> Regional integration in Latin America has not been very successful, and countries rely more on the U.S. for trade than members of their own groups.

Latin America's small national markets. Therefore, some form of economic cooperation was needed to enlarge the potential market size so that Latin American companies could achieve economies of scale and be more competitive worldwide.

The problem is that Latin countries rely heavily on the United States as their major export market. For example, Costa Rica, a member of the Central American Common Market, exports 47.1 percent of its merchandise to the United States, 18.2 percent to the European Union, and only 4.4 percent and 3.2 percent to Guatemala and Nicaragua, two other members of CACM. Colombia, a member of the Andean Community, exports 47.1 percent of its goods to the United States, 14.4 percent to the EU, and only 19.2 percent to Ecuador, Venezuela, and Peru, three other members of CAN. Brazil, a member of MERCOSUR, exports 24.8 percent of its goods to the EU, 23.1 percent to the U.S., and only 6.2 percent to MERCOSUR member Argentina. This is very different from intrazonal trade in the EU, which constitutes more than 50 percent of the exports of each country. Each group in the Americas has slightly different objectives, but most are attempting to move beyond a simple free trade agreement and engage in other activities to help link their economies closer together. None, however, have taken the extra steps found in the EU to link together people, capital (especially currency), and politics.

The major trade group in South America is **MERCOSUR.** In 1991, Brazil, Argentina, Paraguay, and Uruguay established MERCOSUR. MERCOSUR is significant because of its size: The four original members generate 80 percent of South America's GNP. In addition, MERCOSUR has signed free trade agreements with Bolivia and Chile and is negotiating with the EU and other countries to do the same. MERCOSUR is also trying to become a customs union, but that has still not happened. In addition, the countries have not yet been able to eliminate the barriers to trade among the member nations. One could argue that MERCOSUR is a partial customs union since its goal is to also establish common external tariffs, but economic and political instability in the region and poor political relations among the countries have complicated the process of achieving free trade and customs union status. Argentina's economic crisis in 2002 spilled over into Brazil and Uruguay and threatened the stability of the entire region. The dramatic fall in the value of

MERCOSUR is a partial customs union among Argentina, Brazil, Paraguay, and Uruguay.

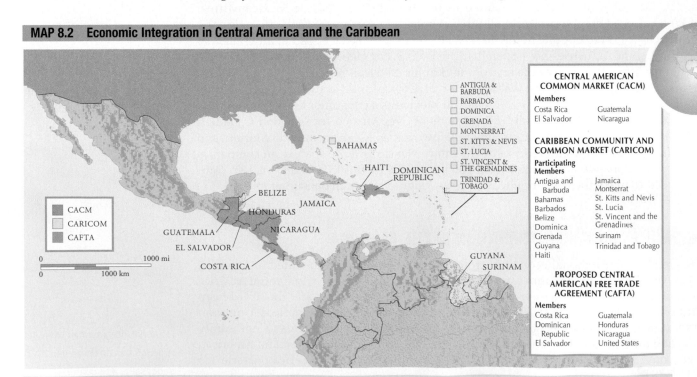

MAP 8.2   Economic Integration in Central America and the Caribbean

CACM
CARICOM
CAFTA

ANTIGUA & BARBUDA
BARBADOS
DOMINICA
GRENADA
MONTSERRAT
ST. KITTS & NEVIS
ST. LUCIA
ST. VINCENT & THE GRENADINES
TRINIDAD & TOBAGO

CENTRAL AMERICAN COMMON MARKET (CACM)

Members
Costa Rica   Guatemala
El Salvador   Nicaragua

CARIBBEAN COMMUNITY AND COMMON MARKET (CARICOM)

Participating Members
Antigua and   Jamaica
  Barbuda   Montserrat
Bahamas   St. Kitts and Nevis
Barbados   St. Lucia
Belize   St. Vincent and the
Dominica   Grenadines
Grenada   Surinam
Guyana   Trinidad and Tobago
Haiti

PROPOSED CENTRAL AMERICAN FREE TRADE AGREEMENT (CAFTA)

Members
Costa Rica   Guatemala
Dominican   Honduras
  Republic   Nicaragua
El Salvador   United States

Countries in Central America and the Caribbean have shifted their forms of integration from free trade areas to common markets: the Central American Common Market (CACM) and the Caribbean Community and Common Market (CARICOM).

the Argentine peso changed the trading structure in MERCOSUR, making Argentine products cheaper but making it more difficult for Argentine tourists to travel to the resort areas in Brazil or purchase Brazilian products. In addition, Brazilian President Lula da Silva has been increasingly visible on the world stage, trying to become the leader of the developing countries, and this has created strong resentment in Argentina.

Although the Andean Community (CAN) is not as significant economically as MERCOSUR, it is the second most important regional group in South America. As Map 8.3 shows, **CAN** has been around since 1969. However, its focus has shifted from one of isolationism and statism (placing economic control in the hands of the state—the central government) to being open to foreign trade and investment.

In 2004, the members of CAN and MERCOSUR got together with other countries in South America to launch the 12-nation South American Community of Nations (CSN), whose goals are to liberalize trade and eventually have a common currency, parliament, and passport. CSN will begin by phasing out tariffs between the member countries (CAN and MERCOSUR plus Chile, Suriname, and Guyana) on nonsensitive areas by 2004 and sensitive areas by 2019 and then moving to other areas of cooperation.[43] Besides opening up more trade opportunities and linking the two major trade groups in South America, it is hoped that CSN will give the South American countries a larger voice in global trade talks. However, the heads of state of several countries, including Argentina, didn't even attend the meetings, and most observers are not very optimistic about the success of CSN given that no other trade agreement in South America has been that successful to this point. It is important to note that Mexico, one of the major countries in Latin America, is not a part of CSN. This is largely because of Mexico's membership in NAFTA, which aligns it more closely with Canada and the U.S., whereas CSN is trying to distance itself from the U.S. Also, it would not be in Mexico's best interests to sour its relationship with the U.S. in order to align itself with CSN.

The Andean Community is one of the original regional economic groups but has not been successful in achieving its original goals.

The South American Community of Nations was organized in 2004 in an attempt to bring together CAN, MERCOSUR, Chile, Surinam, and Guyana.

MAP 8.3 Latin American Economic Integration

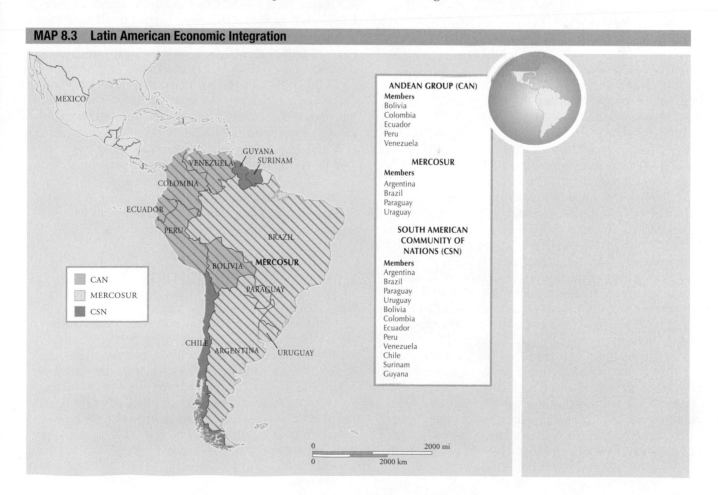

ANDEAN GROUP (CAN)
Members
Bolivia
Colombia
Ecuador
Peru
Venezuela

MERCOSUR
Members
Argentina
Brazil
Paraguay
Uraguay

SOUTH AMERICAN COMMUNITY OF NATIONS (CSN)
Members
Argentina
Brazil
Paraguay
Uruguay
Bolivia
Colombia
Ecuador
Peru
Venezuela
Chile
Surinam
Guyana

CAN
MERCOSUR
CSN

POINT–COUNTERPOINT: IS CAFTA A GOOD IDEA?

POINT

CAFTA is a *great* idea. The Central American Free Trade Agreement will link together the United States with the four countries in the Central American Common Market plus the Dominican Republic in a free trade agreement. CAFTA is an agreement that holds enormous benefits for both the United States and the six Central American nations that have signed it. It will open the door for increased trade between the U.S. and the region and will stimulate economic growth in Central America by encouraging foreign direct investment, offering shorter international supply chains that Central America would be able to more easily participate in. Furthermore, it will encourage not only economic reform but also political reform in an area historically plagued by Marxism, dictatorships, and civil wars.

One of the biggest benefits the U.S. has to gain is reciprocal tariff treatment from the participating Central American nations. Due to temporary trade-preference programs and other regional agreements, such as the Caribbean Basin Initiative (CBI), that are currently in place, 80 percent of the products from at least five Central American nations already enter the U.S. duty free. U.S. manufactured exports are subject to tariffs that average 30 to 100 percent higher than the tariffs Central American exports face when entering the U.S.[44] The one-way CBI has allowed its participating nations to increase their exports to $17 billion in 2004, as compared to $3 billion in 1987. CAFTA will allow the Central American nations to maintain these favorable gains but will level the playing field for the United States to benefit in a similar way by reducing restrictions on 80 percent of U.S. industrial exports and on more than 50 percent of its agricultural exports.[45]

There is fear that the freer inflow of Central American agricultural products will undercut U.S. agricultural prices. However, as mentioned before, the U.S. is already largely open to these products, and although the heavily subsidized U.S. sugar industry adamantly opposed CAFTA, the sugar deal will set a quota that will amount to only 1.7 percent of U.S. production in 15 years.

Many critics argue that the benefits certain CAFTA countries gain will come at the expense of other participating countries, but in truth the gains will be mutual. For example, the growth that CAFTA will foster in Central American industries, particularly its apparel industry, will also benefit exporters in the United States whose products are used in their manufacturing processes. Fifty-six percent of the apparel exports from the Central American region are produced from textiles exported from the U.S.; 40 percent of yarn exports and about 25 percent of fabric exports from the U.S. are purchased by these nations. By working together through CAFTA, the U.S. and Central America will prevent the loss of Central American apparel jobs to China, whose products contain little or no input from the U.S. The National Council of Textile Organizations, which represents more than 75 textile companies, strongly supports CAFTA.

Another argument that critics make is that CAFTA will create shifts in the job market that will lead to thousands of job losses in the manufacturing and agricultural sectors. However, predictions from the U.S. Chamber of Commerce don't bear out this claim. For example, it predicts that in North Carolina alone, CAFTA will increase industrial output by $3.9 billion and create 28,913 jobs over nine years. Other sources have stated that 250,000 jobs in Central America depend upon CAFTA being approved. And although labor organizations have decried the lack of worker-protection clauses in the agreement, a report from the International Labor Organization actually praises Central American labor laws and standards.[46]

If the U.S. would have decided to opt out of CAFTA, it would have seriously hurt its position as the leading champion of global free trade and open competition, possibly damaging its position in the WTO and its relationships with other nations with which it wishes to establish bilateral agreements.

COUNTERPOINT

No, CAFTA is *not* a good idea at all—not for the U.S. nor for the impoverished nations it is allegedly supposed to help. Recently, much has been said about how the accord will boost trade between the two regions, support constructive economic and political reforms in Central America, create thousands of jobs, and demonstrate the benefits of free trade and open competition. However, there is in fact neither evidence to bear out these claims nor consideration for the consequences of the results.

The agreement will open the participating Central American countries to more duty-free exportation on behalf of U.S. manufacturers and farmers, but will this really translate into benefits for either side? The U.S. agricultural industry already can sell pretty much all the products it wants on the worldwide market; what it really needs is an increase in the worldwide market prices, but Central America's economies are too small to even affect world prices. Plus, the increased flow of U.S. corn and rice into Central America will devastate the region's own farm economies. The idea that it will benefit the region by allowing increased imports to the United States is also faulty. Due to its giant deficit, the U.S. really cannot afford to tolerate many more imports, and the value of these imports to the U.S. is also expected to decrease in value, which means Central America will gain little economic advantage from them anyhow, especially given the concessions it must make in return. Additionally, CAFTA will actually be increasing some barriers to free trade. For example, the accord may make it harder for countries such as Guatemala to obtain access to affordable life-saving medicines because of stringent intellectual property clauses included in the agreement.

CAFTA is also a bad move for labor and workers' rights. It will most likely trigger the loss of manufacturing jobs in the U.S. and agricultural jobs in Central America. While proponents of the deal assert that it will stem illegal immigration from these poorer nations, the shift in jobs will most likely increase immigration, as it did it with NAFTA. Furthermore, it will trigger a "race to the bottom" when it comes to wages. The accord will open up U.S. labor markets to competition against a low-wage area, which will drive down the current wage level. NAFTA and other trade agreements currently in place have already stymied wage growth, which has grown a meager 9 percent over the last 30 years compared to an increase of 80 percent in worker productivity. And this depression of wages and shift of jobs created by current agreements has done little to improve the economic conditions of the developing Central American nations, where wages have grown only 12 percent since 1980, compared to 80 percent during the period between 1960 and 1979. Furthermore, there are no clauses in the agreement that address the protection of workers or the banning of child labor.[47]

Since the accord involves developing countries with vastly different interests than the U.S., it will be hard to please all parties. Although it signed CAFTA, Costa Rica is currently showing hesitance in ratifying it. The country is faced with opposition from trade unions, farm groups, and even businesses and fears the accord's stringent intellectual-property clauses and the chance that it might force the country to privatize its free universal health care system. Costa Rica's hesitancy undermines the argument posed by Washington that CAFTA is something earnestly sought after by struggling Central American countries.[48]

REGIONAL ECONOMIC INTEGRATION IN ASIA

There are seven different RTAs in Asia that are recognized by the WTO. As is the case in Latin America, regional integration in Asia has not been as successful as the EU or NAFTA because most of the countries in the region have relied on U.S. and EU markets for as much as 20–30 percent of their exports, which is not as extensive as in Latin America but still significant. However, the Asian financial crisis of 1997 and 1998 demonstrated that weakness in one country resulted in contagion throughout the region. The **Association of South East Asian Nations (ASEAN),** organized in 1967, comprises Brunei, Cambodia, Indonesia, Laos, Malaysia, Myanmar, the Philippines, Singapore, Thailand, and Vietnam (see Map 8.4). It possesses a combined gross domestic product of $737 billion and a total trade of $720 billion and promotes cooperation in many areas, including industry and trade. Member countries are protected in terms of tariff and nontariff barriers. Yet they hold promise for market and investment opportunities because of their large market size (500 million people). On January 1, 1993, ASEAN officially formed the **ASEAN Free Trade Area (AFTA).** AFTA's goal is to cut tariffs on all intrazonal trade to a maximum of 5 percent by January 1, 2008. The weaker ASEAN countries would be allowed to phase in their tariff reductions over a longer period. By 2005, most products traded among the AFTA

The ASEAN Free Trade Area is a successful trade agreement among countries in Southeast Asia.

MAP 8.4   The Association of South East Asian Nations

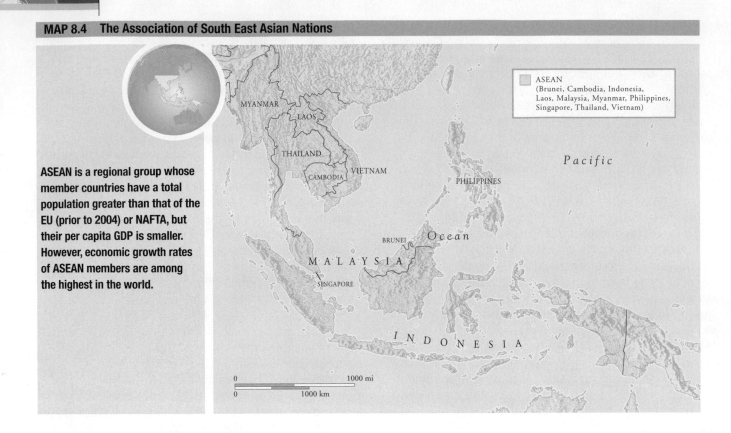

ASEAN is a regional group whose member countries have a total population greater than that of the EU (prior to 2004) or NAFTA, but their per capita GDP is smaller. However, economic growth rates of ASEAN members are among the highest in the world.

ASEAN
(Brunei, Cambodia, Indonesia, Laos, Malaysia, Myanmar, Philippines, Singapore, Thailand, Vietnam)

MYANMAR

LAOS

THAILAND

VIETNAM

CAMBODIA

PHILIPPINES

Pacific

BRUNEI   Ocean

MALAYSIA

SINGAPORE

INDONESIA

0   1000 mi
0   1000 km

countries were subject to duties from 0 to 5 percent, so AFTA has been successful in its free trade objectives.

Many MNEs are hoping that ASEAN countries will work harder to loosen their borders. Companies such as BMW, Matsushita Electrical Industrial, Honda Motor, and Procter & Gamble have operations in the ASEAN countries but aren't able to expand to their full potential because ASEAN countries aren't cooperating with each other. Malaysia, Singapore, Thailand, and the Philippines are still passing protectionist measures, which downgrade the effectiveness of AFTA and shrink trade. General Motors expanded heavily into Thailand in 1996, but in 2001 it built only 52,000 cars in a plant designed to build 130,000. Most of these cars were sent to the European market because barriers within ASEAN are too large. Unless ASEAN nations start cooperating, MNEs will move their operations to China. GM's sales doubled in China in 2001, and as GM's ASEAN chief put it, "It is growth like that, that makes it imperative for ASEAN nations to put aside their differences and embrace free trade."[49]

On the other hand, other companies have been able to take advantage of AFTA. Dell Computer, for example, established computer assembly operations in Malaysia to take advantage of Malaysia's location-specific advantages, such as incentives that Malaysia has to offer, the Multimedia Supercorridor that is like a little Silicon Valley linking Dell with its suppliers, favorable tax rates, and a good workforce. In addition, Malaysia's membership in AFTA gives Dell duty-free access to the other ASEAN countries.

APEC, the **Asia Pacific Economic Cooperation,** was formed in November 1989 to promote multilateral economic cooperation in trade and investment in the Pacific Rim.[50] It is composed of 21 countries that border the Pacific Rim—both in Asia as well as the Americas. To accomplish its objectives, APEC leaders committed themselves to achieving free and open trade in the region by 2010 for the industrial nations (which generate 85 percent of the

APEC is comprised of 21 countries that border the Pacific Rim; progress toward free trade is hampered by size and geographic distance between member countries and the lack of a treaty.

regional trade) and by 2020 for the rest of the members.[51] The difference between APEC and other regional trade groups is that there are no binding treaties. Although the group is huge, accounting for more than a third of the world's population (2.6 billion people), approximately 60 percent of world GDP (US$19,254 billion), and about 47 percent of world trade, it operates by consensus and does not have the same teeth as do other RTAs. In addition, it is not an official RTA from the perspective of the WTO, so it doesn't appear as an official group on the WTO Web site (**http://www.wto.org/english/tratop_e/region_e/ type_e.xls**). It also includes countries that border the Pacific, such as NAFTA countries, Chile, Russia, China, Hong Kong, Taiwan, many members of AFTA, and Australia and New Zealand. It is more than an Asian trade bloc, but it is not a very solid bloc.

APEC has the potential to become a significant economic bloc, especially because it generates such a large percentage of the world's output and merchandise trade. APEC is trying to establish "open regionalism," whereby individual member countries can determine whether to apply trade liberalization to non-APEC countries on an unconditional, most-favored-nation basis or on a reciprocal, free trade agreement basis. The United States prefers the latter approach. The key will be whether or not the liberalization process continues at a good pace.[52] The problem with APEC is its size. A major reason why regional integration like the EU and NAFTA work is because of close geographic proximity and a unity of purpose. APEC has too many countries with diverse interests, and it was established as a counterforce to NAFTA. It is hard to maintain serious progress for something born of a defensive rather than an offensive strategy.

REGIONAL ECONOMIC INTEGRATION IN AFRICA

As noted in Map 8.5, there are several major regional trade groups in Africa registered with the WTO. The problem is that African countries have been struggling to establish

MAP 8.5   Regional Integration in Africa

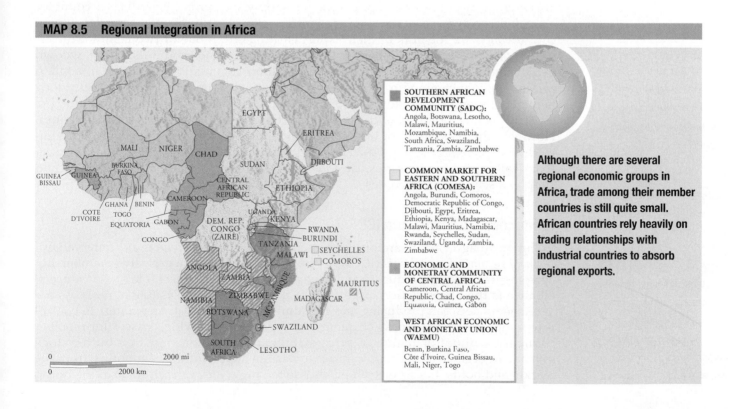

SOUTHERN AFRICAN DEVELOPMENT COMMUNITY (SADC): Angola, Botswana, Lesotho, Malawi, Mauritius, Mozambique, Namibia, South Africa, Swaziland, Tanzania, Zambia, Zimbabwe

COMMON MARKET FOR EASTERN AND SOUTHERN AFRICA (COMESA): Angola, Burundi, Comoros, Democratic Republic of Congo, Djibouti, Egypt, Eritrea, Ethiopia, Kenya, Madagascar, Malawi, Mauritius, Namibia, Rwanda, Seychelles, Sudan, Swaziland, Uganda, Zambia, Zimbabwe

ECONOMIC AND MONETRAY COMMUNITY OF CENTRAL AFRICA: Cameroon, Central African Republic, Chad, Congo, Equatoria, Guinea, Gabon

WEST AFRICAN ECONOMIC AND MONETARY UNION (WAEMU)
Benin, Burkina Faso, Côte d'Ivoire, Guinea Bissau, Mali, Niger, Togo

Although there are several regional economic groups in Africa, trade among their member countries is still quite small. African countries rely heavily on trading relationships with industrial countries to absorb regional exports.

a political identity, and the different trade groups have political as well as economic underpinnings. One group not shown on Map 8.5 is the African Union, created by 53 African countries in 2002 to take the place of the Organization of African Unity (OAU). The OAU was established in 1963 to focus on political issues in Africa, notably colonialism and racism. However, the new AU is modeled loosely on the European Union, although that type of integration will be extremely difficult in Africa. Civil war, corruption, diseases such as AIDS, and poor government infrastructures have hampered African countries and their ability to progress economically. Most African countries rely more on trade links with former colonial powers than with each other, so intrazonal trade is not significant. African markets, with the notable exception of South Africa, are relatively small and undeveloped, making trade liberalization a relatively minor contributor to economic growth in the region. However, any type of market expansion through regional integration will help these small countries.

COMMODITY AGREEMENTS

Thus far, this chapter has focused on how countries cooperate to reduce trade barriers among themselves. However, producer and consumer countries of primary commodities have also come together in an effort to stabilize commodity prices and supply. Commodities refer to raw materials or primary products that enter into trade, such as metals or agricultural products. Primary commodity exports, such as crude petroleum, natural gas, copper, tobacco, coffee, cocoa, tea, and sugar, have become much less important to developing countries over the last decades except for Africa, which depends on these commodities for 80 percent of its exports.[53] Primary commodities account for about 25 percent of world merchandise trade. Both long-term trends and short-term fluctuations in their prices have important consequences for the world economy. On the demand side, commodity markets play an important role in industrial countries, transmitting business cycle disturbances to the rest of the economy and affecting the rate of growth of prices. On the supply side, primary products account for about half, on average, of developing countries' export earnings, and many developing countries derive the bulk of their export earnings from one or two commodities.[54] Primary commodities are important to both consumers and producers. The slowdown in global growth in 2001 caused demand to fall for commodities, resulting in a fall in prices. The low commodity prices were a boon to consumer countries, because they helped companies keep down costs and, therefore, prices. But producer countries, especially developing countries, suffered because of low commodity revenues. However, the resurgence of the economy of China and its strong demand for commodities, including oil, in 2004–2005 raised the prices for commodities again. This section deals with how countries use commodity agreements to stabilize the price and supply of selected commodities.

Producers' Alliances and ICCAs

Commodity agreements are of two basic types: *producers' alliances* and *international commodity control agreements* (ICCAs). Producers' alliances are exclusive membership agreements between producing and exporting countries. An example of a producers' alliance is the Organization of Petroleum Exporting Countries (OPEC). ICCAs are agreements between producing and consuming countries. ICCAs attempt to control prices through **buffer stocks** or quotas, or they simply provide services for member countries without engaging in price stabilization mechanisms. In a buffer stock system, an organization or a country purchases a supply of the commodity from the market and holds it as security. If prices rise too high, they can sell some of the buffer

A cocoa worker spreads seeds to dry in the sun after harvest in the town of Waslala, some 208 miles north of the capital, Managua. The production of cocoa has become an alternative for the subsistent farmers in northern Nicaragua, who prefer its profitability to the fluctuations of international coffee prices.

stock. If prices get too low, they can purchase more of the commodity and add to the buffer stock. The International Cocoa Organization (ICCO) was originally both a quota and a buffer stock system. Quotas were implemented to limit the supply of cocoa on the market in order to maintain a more stable price. However, the quota system was abolished in 1980, and the ICCO tried to control prices through a buffer stock system. Member countries authorized a total of 250,000 tons of cocoa as the buffer stock, but disagreements among countries finally resulted in the demise of the buffer stock system. Now the ICCO is more of an informational organization and does not attempt to control market prices. Buffer stock systems in tin, cocoa, coffee, and sugar were once popular but have all been eliminated. The U.N. Conference on Trade and Development (UNCTAD) works very closely with and oversees all commodity agreements because of the impact of commodity prices on poverty and development.

Some commodity agreements, such as the ICCO until 1980, use or attempt to use a **quota system,** in which producing countries divide total output and sales to stabilize the price. For a quota system to work, participating countries must cooperate among themselves to prevent sharp fluctuations in supply. The quota system is most effective when a single country has a large share of world production or consumption because it is able to control supply much more easily. Three of the best examples of a quota system are oil, controlled by the OPEC countries; wool, controlled by Australia; and diamonds, controlled by the DeBeers Company in South Africa. Because DeBeers controls most of the diamond mining in the world, it can control price by determining how many diamonds to release on the world market. Not all commodity agreements work well. Countries in producers' alliances tend to disagree on the quotas allotted to them.

The type of commodity also influences a commodity agreement's effectiveness. For some commodities, especially food, beverages, and agricultural raw materials, there are differences in substitutability. For example, tea can substitute for coffee, and sugar beets might substitute for cane sugar. This limits the ability of coffee and cane sugar producers

Quota system—determines how producing and consuming countries divide total output and sales; used by OPEC to control price. However, not all commodities have a ready substitute, so those producers have more control over price.

The Organization of Petroleum Exporting Countries (OPEC)

OPEC is an example of a producer cartel that relies on quotas to influence prices. It is a group of commodity-producing countries that have significant control over supply and that band together to control output and price. OPEC is part of a larger category of energy commodities, which also includes coal and natural gas. OPEC is not confined to the Middle East. The members are Algeria, Indonesia, Iran, Iraq, Kuwait, Libya, Nigeria, Qatar, Saudi Arabia, the United Arab Emirates, and Venezuela. OPEC controls prices by establishing production quotas on member countries. Saudi Arabia has historically performed the role of the dominant supplier in OPEC that can influence supply and price. Periodically—at least annually—OPEC oil ministers gather together to determine the quota for each country based on estimates of supply and demand.

Politics are also an important dimension to OPEC deliberations. OPEC member countries with large populations need large oil revenues to fund government programs. As a result, they are tempted to exceed their export quotas to generate more revenues. A major reason for the invasion of Kuwait by Iraq in 1990 was because Kuwait was producing more than its quota, which depressed world oil prices. Iraqi President Saddam Hussein blamed Kuwait for low world oil prices, which reduced the amount of revenue Iraq could earn with its oil exports. Thus, he felt justified in invading Kuwait to gain control of its oil supplies so that he could increase his own oil revenues.

OPEC member countries produce about 40.1 percent of the world's crude oil and 16.1 percent of its natural gas. However, OPEC's oil exports represent about 48.7 percent of the oil traded internationally.[55] Therefore, OPEC can have a strong influence on the oil market, especially if it decides to reduce or increase its level of production.[56] Sometimes OPEC policies work; sometimes they don't. In 1999, OPEC met and established strict production quotas to try to raise prices. It seemed to work so well that by the third quarter of the year, prices had nearly doubled and prices remained within OPEC's target band until the terrorist attacks of September 11, 2001.[57] Several factors seemed key: Countries actually stuck to their quotas, the Asian economies were beginning to recover, and the U.S. economy was remaining strong. The last two factors led to strong demand at the same time production was being trimmed, thus causing prices to rise.[58] In particular, strong demand by China in 2004–2005 was a leading cause of the increase in world oil prices.

Keeping oil prices high has some downside for OPEC. Competition from non-OPEC countries increases because the revenues accruing to the competitors are higher. Because some OPEC countries are putting up roadblocks to production (they want things done their own way), major producers like BP, ExxonMobil, and Shell are investing heavily in areas like the Caspian Basin, the Gulf of Mexico, and Angola and are trying to enter areas like the Russian Federation. Production in these areas is expected to grow twice as fast as in the 1990s, and this growth should continue until 2010. Another problem is that higher oil prices could depress growth worldwide and thus lower demand for oil. Also, because of OPEC's power, for the most part its countries have been able to avoid competitive pressures to improve their industries—and some are, therefore, decades out of date.[59] These problems have caused OPEC's market share to fall, and it will continue to do so unless some changes are made.

Because commodities are the raw materials used in the production process, it is important for managers of companies that use commodities to understand the factors that influence their prices. During the Asian financial crisis, when commodity prices collapsed, commodity exporters suffered but commodity importers benefited from the lower commodity costs.

LOOKING TO THE FUTURE: Will the WTO Overcome Bilateral and Regional Integration Efforts?

Will regional integration be the wave of the future, or will the WTO become the focus of global economic integration? The WTO's objective is to reduce barriers to trade in goods, services, and investment. Regional groups attempt to do that and more. Although the EU has introduced a common currency and is increasing the degree of cooperation in areas such as security and foreign policy, the WTO will never engage in those issues. Regional integration deals with the specific problems facing member countries, whereas the WTO needs to be concerned about all countries in the world. However, regional integration might actually help the WTO achieve its objectives in three major ways:

1. Regionalism can lead to liberalization of issues not covered by the WTO.
2. Regionalism, given that it typically involves fewer countries with more similar conditions and objectives, is more flexible.
3. Regional deals lock in liberalization, especially in developing countries.

NAFTA and the EU are the key regional groups in which significant integration is taking place. In the future, these groups will continue to develop stronger linkages, and then they will expand to include other countries. The key for NAFTA will be whether or not the U.S. Congress can avoid getting caught up in protectionist sentiment and allow expansion to take place. If it does not, Canada and Mexico will continue to engage in bilateral agreements with non-NAFTA countries in the region along the lines of the NAFTA agreement. The EU will continue to expand east until it meets Russia, and then its expansion will either stop or take on a whole new character.

Regional integration in Africa will continue at a slow pace due to the existing political and economic problems there, but Asian integration, primarily in AFTA, will pick up steam as the economies of East and Southeast Asia recover and open up. However, the key to their growth may be China and its rapidly growing influence in Asia and the rest of the world.

SUMMARY

- The General Agreement on Tariffs and Trade (GATT), begun in 1947, created a continuing means for countries to negotiate the reduction and elimination of trade barriers and to agree on simplified mechanisms for the conduct of international trade.

- The World Trade Organization (WTO) replaced GATT in 1995 as a continuing means of trade negotiations that aspires to foster the principle of trade without discrimination and to provide a better means of mediating trade disputes and of enforcing agreements.

- Efforts at regional economic integration began to emerge after World War II as countries saw benefits of cooperation and larger market sizes. The major types of economic integration are the free trade area and the customs union, followed by broader economic and political integration in the common market.

- The static effects of economic integration improve the efficiency of resource allocation and affect both production and consumption. The dynamic effects are internal and external efficiencies that arise because of changes in market size.

- Once protection is eliminated among member countries, trade creation allows MNEs to specialize and trade based on comparative advantage.

- Trade diversion occurs when the supply of products shifts from countries that are not members of an economic bloc to those that are.

- Regional, as opposed to global, economic integration occurs because of the greater ease of promoting cooperation on a smaller scale.

- The European Union (EU) is an effective common market that has abolished most restrictions on factor mobility and is harmonizing national political, economic, and social policies. It is comprised of 25 countries, including 10 countries from mostly Central and Eastern Europe that joined in 2004. The EU has abolished trade barriers on intrazonal trade, instituted a common external tariff, and created a common currency, the euro.

- The North American Free Trade Agreement (NAFTA) is designed to eliminate tariff barriers and liberalize investment opportunities and trade in services. Key provisions in NAFTA are labor and environmental agreements.

- There are key trade groups in other parts of the world, including Latin America, Asia, and Africa.

- Many developing countries rely on commodity exports to supply the hard currency they need for economic development. Instability in commodity prices has resulted in fluctuations in export earnings. Commodity agreements, using one of several stabilization schemes, seek to stabilize prices.

C A S E   Wal-Mart de Mexico[60]

Comercial Mexicana S.A. (Comerci), one of Mexico's largest retail chains, is faced with a serious dilemma. Since Wal-Mart's aggressive entry into the Mexican retail market, Comerci has found it increasingly difficult to remain competitive. Wal-Mart's strong operating presence and low prices since NAFTA's lifting of tariffs have put pressure on Comerci, and now management must determine if Comerci's recent participation with the purchasing consortium Sinergia will be sufficient to compete against Wal-Mart. What has caused this intense competitive pressure on Comerci, and what is likely to be its future?

Mexico's retail sector has benefited greatly from the increasing trade liberalization the government has been pushing. After decades of protectionism, Mexico joined GATT in 1986 to help open its economy to new markets. In 1990, with Mexico's economy on the upswing and additional free trade negotiations with the United States and Canada taking place, the founder of Wal-Mart, Sam Walton, met with the president of Cifra, Mexico's leading retail store. Their meeting resulted in a 50/50 joint venture in the opening of Mexico's first Sam's Club, a subsidiary of Wal-Mart, in 1991 in Mexico City. It only took a couple of months after the opening to prove the store's success—it was breaking all the U.S. records for Sam's Club. The joint venture evolved to incorporate all new stores, and by 1997, Wal-Mart purchased enough shares to have a controlling interest in Cifra. In 2000, it changed the name to Wal-Mart de Mexico, S.A. de C.V., and the ticker symbol to WALMEX.

Prior to 1990, Wal-Mart had never made moves to enter Mexico or any country other than the United States. Once Wal-Mart started growing in Mexico, management created the Wal-Mart International Division in 1993. The company has expanded internationally to nine countries through new-store construction and acquisitions. It now operates in Argentina, Brazil, Canada, China, Germany, Korea, Mexico, Puerto Rico, and the United Kingdom. It also possesses a 37.8 percent owning interest in Seiyu, Ltd., a leading Japanese retailer, and has announced plans to explore opportunities in the Russian and Indian markets. Wal-Mart's operations in Canada began in 1994 with the acquisition of 122 Woolco stores. It now has over 235 stores and 6 Sam's Clubs and has strong partnerships with Canadian suppliers.

With growth stalling in the United States, Wal-Mart is looking to international expansion for growth. Over the past five years, it has opened over 400 new stores and has added to this number through acquisitions as well, resulting in over 1,300 units operated worldwide. In fiscal 2004, the international division increased sales over the previous year by 16.6 percent—to $47.6 billion—and operating profit increased 18.6 percent—to $2.4 billion. The division accounts for 18.5 percent of sales and 16 percent of profits.

Some forecasters believe Wal-Mart's growth outside of the United States will grow by an average of 26 percent for the foreseeable future and estimate that its holdings could double in size by the end of the decade. Wal-Mart's success internationally has varied by country. Although successful in countries like Mexico and Canada, where it has become the largest retailer, it has yet to prove itself in Germany and Argentina. It is learning from its past mistakes, and it is now adapting much better to local cultures and learning from partnerships formed in each country.

Wal-Mart's Competitive Advantage

Much of Wal-Mart's international success comes from the tested practices the U.S. division bases its success on. Wal-Mart is known for the slogan "Every Day Low Prices." It has expanded that internally to "Every Day Low Costs" to inspire employees to spend company money wisely and work hard to lower costs. Because of its sheer size and volume of purchases, Wal-Mart can negotiate with suppliers to drop prices to agreeable levels. It also works closely with suppliers on inventory levels using an advanced information system that informs suppliers when purchases have been made and when Wal-Mart will be ordering more merchandise. Suppliers can then plan production runs more accurately, thus reducing production costs, which are passed on to Wal-Mart and eventually the consumer.

Wal-Mart also has a unique distribution system that reduces expenses. It builds super warehouses in central locations that receive the majority of merchandise sold in Wal-Mart stores. It then transports the merchandise to the various stores, using its company-owned fleet or a partner. The central distribution center helps Wal-Mart negotiate lower prices with its suppliers because of the large purchasing volumes.

These strategies have resulted in great success for Wal-Mart. In 2001, it passed General Electric and ExxonMobil to become the largest company in the world, with sales of $217.8 million. It has the largest private-sector workforce, with 1.3 million people in 3,300 facilities throughout the world. And it even uses the second most powerful computer in the world—behind the Pentagon's—to run its logistics.

Wal-Mart in Mexico

In Mexico, Wal-Mart operates 671 units, including Sam's Clubs, Bodegas (discount stores), Wal-Mart Supercenters, Superamas (grocery stores), Suburbias (apparel stores), and VIPS restaurants. Wal-Mart encountered some difficulties with its opening in Mexico prior to the passage of NAFTA. One of the biggest challenges it faced was import charges on many of the goods sold in its stores, thus preventing Wal-Mart from being able to offer its "Every Day Low Prices." Unsure of local demand, Wal-Mart stocked its shelves with things like ice skates, fishing tackle, and riding lawnmowers—all unpopular items in Mexico. Rather than informing headquarters that they wouldn't need those items, local managers heavily discounted the items, only to have the automatic inventory system reorder the products when the first batch sold. Wal-Mart also encountered logistics problems due to poor roads and the scarcity of delivery trucks. Yet another problem was the culture clashes between the Arkansas executives and the local Mexican managers. Some of these problems were solved by trial and error, but the emergence of the North American Free Trade Agreement in 1994 helped solve most of the problems. Among other things, NAFTA reduced tariffs on American goods sold to Mexico from 10 percent to 3 percent. Prior to NAFTA, Wal-Mart was not much of a threat to companies like Comerci, Gigante, and Soriana, Mexico's top retailers. But once the agreement was signed, the barriers fell and Wal-Mart was on a level playing field with its competitors—all it needed to become number one.

NAFTA encouraged Mexico to improve its transportation infrastructure, thus helping to solve Wal-Mart's logistical problems. The signing of NAFTA also opened the gates wider to foreign investment in Mexico. Wal-Mart was paying huge import fees on goods shipped to

Mexico from areas like Europe and Asia. Foreign companies knew that if they built manufacturing plants in Mexico, they could keep costs low with Mexican labor but ship to NAFTA's free trade zone—Mexico, the United States, or Canada. As companies began to build manufacturing plants in Mexico, Wal-Mart could buy these products without paying the high import tariffs. An example of this tactic is Sony's flat-screen television line, Wega. Sam's Clubs in Mexico imported Wega TVs from Japan with a 23 percent import tariff plus huge shipping costs, resulting in a $1,600 sales price at Sam's Club. In 1999, Sony built a manufacturing plant in Mexico, thus allowing Sam's Club to purchase the Wegas without import tariffs; this tactic also yields much lower shipping fees. Sam's Clubs passed on the savings to customers—with a sales price of only $600.

The benefits of NAFTA, like lower tariffs and improved infrastructure, helped not only Wal-Mart but also its competitors, like Comerci. But Wal-Mart used the advantages of NAFTA better than anyone else. Rather than pocketing the differences the lower tariffs made, Wal-Mart reduced its prices. In 1999, it closed one of its Supercenters for a day to discount up to 6,000 items by 14 percent. Comerci and others have combated Wal-Mart's tactics by lowering their own prices, but on many items, they can't get the prices as low. Wal-Mart's negotiating power with its suppliers is large enough that it can get the better deal. Also, most of Mexico's retailers priced goods differently. They were used to putting certain items on sale or deep discount, a strategy known as "high and low," rather than lowering all prices. They have been trying to adjust their pricing structure to match Wal-Mart's, but they are still frustrated with the continued cost cutting of Wal-Mart. Competitors and certain suppliers are so angry that they have gone to Mexico's Federal Competition Commission (known in Mexico as CoFeCo) with complaints of unfair pricing practices.

Formation of Sinergia

Unable to compete with Wal-Mart under the new conditions, Comerci has been faced with extinction. Wal-Mart is the largest retailer in Mexico and owns about 55 percent of the market share in Mexico's supermarket sector, with $11.7 billion in sales and $585 million in profit in the country during 2004. In contrast, Comerci realized only $3.1 billion in sales and $93 million in net profit and has seen its market share drop to 15 percent.

Fear over the giant retailer's predominance and over its unexplained withdrawal from the Mexican National Association of Department Stores (ANTAD) in 2004 prompted Comerci to band with two other struggling homegrown supermarket chains, Soriana and Gigante, to form a purchasing consortium that would allow them to negotiate better bulk prices from suppliers. The collaboration, known as Sinergia, was initially rejected by CoFeCo and met resistance from the Consumer Product Council of Mexico, a 46-member organization representing major consumer goods companies, which feared that Sinergia would use its purchasing power to force unreasonably low prices on suppliers. However, after its second presentation to CoFeCo, the consortium was at last approved, provided that it issue regular reports to CoFeCo outlining the nature of its purchasing agreements and that it sign confidentiality agreements with the participating chains to prevent pricefixing and monopolistic behavior. As a representative body with no assets, Sinergia's purchases are currently limited to only local suppliers, and its future is still uncertain.

Should Sinergia fail to improve the situation, Comerci could still look for possible foreign buyers, like France's Carrefour, or it could duplicate the efforts of its Sinergia partner Soriana, which is attempting, with some notable success, to differentiate itself from Wal-Mart by offering products and a store atmosphere that appeal more to Mexicans' middle-class aspirations. The government may give Comerci a break if it rules against Wal-Mart's aggressive pricing, but as one analyst put it, "We do not believe the CFC will end up penalizing Wal-Mart for exercising its purchasing power in an attempt to get the best deals available in the marketplace, which is the goal of every retailer in the world, especially when [these savings] are ultimately passed on to consumers." One thing is certain, however—Comerci cannot afford to sit still.

QUESTIONS

1. How has the implementation of NAFTA affected Wal-Mart's success in Mexico?

2. How much of Wal-Mart's success is due to NAFTA, and how much is due to Wal-Mart's inherent competitive strategy? In other words, could any other U.S. retailer have the same success in Mexico post-NAFTA, or is Wal-Mart a special case?

3. What has Comerci done in its attempt to remain competitive? What are the advantages and challenges of such a strategy, and how effective do you think it will be?

4. What else do you think Comercial Mexicana S.A. should do, given the competitive position of Wal-Mart?

CHAPTER NOTES

1   Data for this case were taken from: Stephen Power, "EU Auto Industry Faces Overhaul as Japanese Gain in Market Share," *Wall Street Journal* (Oct. 14, 2004): A.1; Jathon Sapsford, "Toyota Aims to Rival GM Production," *Wall Street Journal* (Nov. 2, 2004): A.3; Mari Koseki, "Quota on Auto Exports to EC Curbed at 1.089 Million in '93," *Japan Times* 33, no. 15 (April 12–18, 1993): 14; Nick Maling, "Japan Poised for EU Lift of Export Ceiling," *Marketing Week* 22, no. 14 (May 6, 1999): 26; Todd Zaun and Beth Demain, "Leading the News: Ambitious Toyota, Buoyed by Europe, Sets Global Goals," *Wall Street Journal* (Oct 22, 2002): A.3; Mark M. Nelson, Thomas F. O'Boyle, and E. S. Browning, "International—The Road to European Unity—1992: EC's Auto Plan Would Keep Japan at Bay—1992 Unification Effort Smacks of Protectionism," *Wall Street Journal* (Oct. 27, 1988): A.1; Jathon Sapsford, "Toyota Posts 3.5% Profit Rise, Boosts Sales Forecast for Year," *Wall Street Journal* (Feb. 4, 2005): A.3; Gail Edmondson and Chester Dawson, "Revved up for Battle," *Business Week* (Jan. 10, 2005): 30; Toyota home page, http://www.toyota.com, http://www.toyota-europe.com.

2   David Moss and Nick Bartlett, "Note on WTO Disputes: Five Major Cases," Harvard Business School (September 19, 2003).

3   Neil King, Jr., Scott Miller, and Carlo Tejada, "U.S. Steel Tariffs Ruled Illegal, Sparking Potential Trade War," *Wall Street Journal* (November 11, 2003): A.1.

4   Elizabeth Becker, "U.S. Will Cut Farm Subsidies in Trade Deal," *The New York Times* (July 31, 2004): http://www.nytimes.com/2004/07/31/business/worldbusiness/31geneva.html.

5   Robert B. Zoellick, "Our Credo: Free Trade and Competition," *Wall Street Journal* (July 10, 2003): A.10.

6   Neil King, Jr. and Scott Miller, "Cancun: Victory for Whom?" *Wall Street Journal* (September 16, 2003): A.4.

7   Peter Sutherland, "The Future of the WTO Chapter II—The Erosion of Non-Discrimination," WTO (2005): http://www.wto.org/english/thewto_e/10anniv_e/future_wto_chap2_e.pdf.

8   Bela Balassa, *The Theory of Economic Integration* (Homewood, IL: Irwin, 1961), 40; Panjak Ghemawat, "Distance Still Matters: The Hard Reality of Global Expansion," *Harvard Business Review* (September 2001): 3–11.

9   For more information on the EU, check out its Web site at http://europa.eu.int/index_en.htm.

10 "The European Commission" (2002): http://europa.eu.int/inst-en.htm.

11 "The Council of the European Union" (2005): http://europa.eu.int/institutions/council/index_en.htm.

12 "The European Parliament" (2005): http://europa.eu.int/institutions/parliament/index_en.htm.

13 "The European Court of Justice" (2002): http://europa.eu.int/inst/en/cj.htm.

14 "External Trade: Introduction," Activities of the European Union: Summaries of Legislation, European Union Web site (August 2002): http://europa.eu.int/scadplus/leg/en/lvb/r11000.htm.

15 "You Can Be Warriors or Wimps; Or So Say the Americans," *The Economist* (August 8, 2002): www.economist.com.

16 http://europa.eu.int/pol/emu/overview_en.htm. Accessed May 19, 2005.

17 "EU Sets Date for Historic Union," *The Economist* (October 9, 2002): www.economist.com.

18 "Distant Friends," *The Economist* (May 16, 2002): www.economist.com.

19 http://europa.eu.int/comm/external_relations/eea/.

20 Daniel Michaels and Scott Miller, "Hopes Dwindle for U.S.-EU Deal on Aircraft Aid," *Wall Street Journal* (April 11, 2005): A.3.

21 "USA/EU economy: Subsidy Battle Threatens Trade Talks," EIU ViewsWire (April 13, 2005).

22 Joseph Pereira, "PPR Shares Skyrocket on Plan to Sell a Mail-Order Business," *Wall Street Journal* (August 23, 2002): www.wsj.com.

23 Carol Matlack, Inka Resch, and Wendy Zellner, "En Garde, Wal-Mart," *Business Week* (September 13, 1999): 54.

24 Mark Landler, "Europe: The Unlevel Playing Field," *The New York Times* (May 20, 2005), nytimes.com, accessed May 20, 2005.

25 "Overviews of the European Activities: Agriculture," http://europa.eu.int/pol/agr/overview_en.htm.

26 "German Jobless Rate at New Record," March 1, 2005, http://news.bbc.co.uk/2/hi/business/4307303.stm.

27 See Linda M. Aguilar, "NAFTA: A Review of the Issues," *Economic Perspectives* (Federal Reserve Bank of Chicago, 1992): 14; and "OAS Overview of the North American Free Trade Agreement" (2003): http://www.sice.oas.org/summary/nafta/naftatoc.asp, also on http://www.nafta.net.

28 Richard Lawrence, "NAFTA at 5: Happy Birthday?" *Journal of Commerce* (February 1, 1999).

29 Geri Smith and Elisabeth Malkin, "Mexican Makeover: NAFTA Creates the World's Newest Industrial Power," *Business Week* (December 21, 1998): 50–52.

30 "OAS Overview of the North American Free Trade Agreement, Chapter Four: Rules of Origin" (2003): http://www.sice.oas.org/summary/nafta/nafta4.asp.

31 Ibid.

32 "OAS Overview of the North American Free Trade Agreement, Chapter Twenty: Institutional Arrangements and Dispute Settlement Procedures" (2003): http://www.sice.oas.org/summary/nafta/nafta20.asp.

33 "Summary of the North American Agreement on Labor Cooperation" (2003): http://www.mac.doc.gov/nafta/3006.htm.

34 "Summary of the Agreement on Environmental Cooperation" (2003): http://www.mac.doc.gov/nafta/3005.htm.

35 Geri Smith and Cristina Lindblad, "Mexico: Was NAFTA Worth It?" *Business Week* (December 22, 2003), BW Online version.

36 Smith and Malkin, op. cit., 51.

37 "The Decline of the Maquiladora," *Business Week* (April 29, 2002): 59.

38 Robert B. Zoellick, "Speech on NAFTA Before the Foreign Trade Council," *USTR* (July 26, 2001): http://www.ustr.gov/speech-test/zoellick/zoellick_7.PDF, 7.

39 "Bilateral Trade Relations: Mexico," Europa Web site (August 2002): http://europa.eu.int/comm/trade/bilateral/mex.htm.

40 Sydney Weintraub, "A Politically Unpopular Success Story," *Los Angeles Times* (February 7, 1999): p. 2.

41 Smith and Malkin, op. cit., 51.

42 Zoellick, "Speech on NAFTA," op. cit., 3.

43 http://en.wikipedia.org/wiki/South_American_Community_of_Nations.

44 Alan M. Field, "Showdown for CAFTA," *Journal of Commerce* (April 11, 2005): 1.

45 Harold McGraw, "Is CAFTA a Good Thing?" *Miami Herald* (April 16, 2005): 25.A.

46 Alan M. Field, "Showdown for CAFTA," *Journal of Commerce* (April 11, 2005): 1.

47 Mark Weisbrot, "Is CAFTA a Good Thing?" *Miami Herald* (April 16, 2005): 25A.

48 John Lyons, "Costa Rica Balks at Free-Trade Pact," *Wall Street Journal* (May 3, 2005): A.2.

49 Jason Booth, "Southeast Asia Moves Haltingly Toward Single Consumer Market," *Wall Street Journal* (April 1, 2002): www.wsj.com.

50 Asia-Pacific Economic Cooperation (2003): http://www.apecsec.org.sg.

51 http://www.apecsec.org.sg/apec/about_apec.html. Accessed May 23, 2005.

52 http://www.apecsec.org.sg, op. cit.

53 "Trade to Pick Up Sharply in 2002 After Sharp Drop in 2001," *World Trade Organization News* (May 2, 2002): http://www.wto.org/english/news_e/pres02_e/pr288_e.htm.

54 Paul Cashin, Hong Liang, and C. John McDermott, "Do Commodity Price Shocks Last Too Long for Stabilization Schemes to Work?" *Finance & Development* 36, no. 3 (Summer 1999).

55 OPEC Annual Statistical Bulletin (2003).

56 "Frequently Asked Questions About OPEC" (2003): http://www.opec.org.

57 International Monetary Fund, "World Economic Outlook: The Information Technology Revolution" (October 2001): 52. http://www.imf.org/external/pubs/ft/weo/2001/02/index.htm.

58 "Oil: The Latest Shock," *The Economist* (September 18, 1999): 70.

59 "Does OPEC Have Sand in Its Eyes?" *Business Week* (July 1, 2002): 60.

60 The information in this case is from the following sources: Gabriela Lopez, "Mexico Probes Retail Competition as Walmex Dominates," *Reuters Company News* (May 29, 2002); Gabriela Lopez, "Mexico's Retailers Launch Price War," *Forbes* (June 24, 2002): **http://www.forbes.com/newswire/ 2002/06/24/rtr641092.html**; "Wal-Mart Around the World," *The Economist* (December 6, 2001): **http://www.economist.com/displayStory.cfm?Story_ID=895888**; David Luhnow, "Crossover Success: How NAFTA Helped Wal-Mart Reshape the Mexican Market," *Wall Street Journal* (August 31, 2001): A1; Alexander Hanrath, "Mexican Stores Wilt in the Face of US Group's Onslaught," *The Financial Times* (August 14, 2002): **www.ft.com**; Richard C. Morais, "One Hot Tamale," *Forbes Magazine* 174, no. 13 (Dec. 27, 2004): 134–147; Mike Troy, "Wal-Mart International," *DSN Retailing Today* 43, no. 23 (Dec. 13, 2004): 20–22; Ricardo Castillo Mireles, "Taking It to the Competition, Mexican Style," *Logistics Today* 45, no. 12 (Dec. 2004): 10.

All things are obedient to money.

—ENGLISH PROVERB

chapter nine

Global Foreign Exchange and Capital Markets

OBJECTIVES

- To learn the fundamentals of foreign exchange

- To identify the major characteristics of the foreign-exchange market and how governments control the flow of currencies across national borders

- To understand why companies deal in foreign exchange

- To describe how the foreign-exchange market works

- To examine the different institutions that deal in foreign exchange

- To show how companies make payment for international transactions

CASE: WESTERN UNION[1]

U.S.-based Western Union has long been known as "The Fastest Way to Send Money." The company controls nearly 80 percent of the money transfer market and is widely acknowledged as the world leader in wire transfers. A wire transfer is an electronic transfer of funds from one financial institution to another. In this case, it is a transfer from one Western Union office to another. However, Western Union is now facing stiff competition from banks threatening to encroach on its market share of the electronic money transfer business.

Western Union was started in 1851, when a group of businessmen in Rochester, NY, formed a printing telegraph company. The name of the company was changed to Western Union in 1861, when it completed the first transcontinental telegraph line. Western Union introduced its money transfer service in 1871 and started offering this service outside North America in 1989. Today, over 170,000 Western Union agent locations are found in over 190 countries and territories around the world. Money transfers account for 80 percent of Western Union's revenues, and about $40 billion is transferred annually through Western Union.

Customers have many different options when sending money through Western Union. Money can be sent in person at an agent location, over the phone, or online, and senders may use cash, debit cards, or credit cards. For example, in order to send money to Ukraine using a Western Union agent location, the customer must fill out a Send Money form. He or she will then receive a receipt, which includes a Money Transfer Control number. This number must be given to the person receiving the funds. The receiver will fill out a Receive Money form and present the Money Transfer Control number along with valid identification at a Western Union agent location in Ukraine in order to receive the money.

The funds are usually converted into the foreign currency using a foreign exchange rate set by Western Union. The transfer fees for sending money are determined based on how much money is sent, in what form it's sent (cash or debit/credit card), and where it's going. For example, sending $500 to Mexico from California costs $15, while sending $500 to Ukraine from California costs $43. Part of Western Union's attractiveness is found in its speed and anonymity. Western Union can move cash from one location of the world to another in just minutes and requires no ID, background check, or bank account.

Each year, over 80 million emigrant workers send more than $100 billion to their native countries. Most of Western Union's wire transfer business in the United States comes from Mexican emigrants who send part of their paycheck home to support their families. In 2004, Mexico received at least $16.6 billion in remittances, and about 80 percent of these remittances were sent by migrants without legal U.S. status. Four of every 10 foreign-born Hispanic adults living in the United States send money home regularly, and nearly one in five adult Mexicans receives some sort of remittance income. Annual remittance income has passed tourism to become the second-largest source of foreign exchange income in Mexico.

A class-action lawsuit was filed against Western Union in 1997 charging that Western Union offered its customers lower exchange rates than the market exchange rates without informing them of the difference. Western Union claimed that every customer was told the exchange rate during the transaction, and it was up to them to compare Western Union's rates with the market rates. The lawsuit was settled in 2000, and Western Union is now required to state on its receipts and advertisements that it uses its own exchange rate on transactions and that any difference between the company rate and the market rate is kept by the company. For example, the market exchange rate on May 19, 2005 for Mexican pesos was 10.9305 pesos/USD (US$500 = 5,465.25 pesos), while Western Union's offered exchange rate was 10.690 pesos/USD (US$500 = 5,345 pesos).

Financial institutions, such as banks, have put pressure on Western Union to use better exchange rates. Profit margins in the money-transfer business can reach 30 percent, and many banks have started to offer their own money-transfer services in an attempt to take advantage of the continued expected growth of the foreign money-transfer industry. For example, in 2001, Wells Fargo agreed to accept a consular identification card from Mexican immigrants who want to open a bank account but lack a U.S. driver's license. This card verifies Mexicans' identities without revealing their immigration status. After Wells Fargo began accepting the consular identification card, the number of bank accounts opened with the consular ID jumped by over 500 percent within three years. Wells Fargo and other U.S. banks, including Citibank and Bank of America, have established alliances with Mexican banks to offer remittance accounts to the emigrant workers in the U.S. Workers can now open a U.S. bank account with their consular ID and ask for two ATM cards. They can then deposit remittance money in the U.S. account, and their family members at home can withdraw the money from the associated Mexican bank, all at no cost.

Even the wire transfer fees at banks are cheaper than Western Union's. For example, Wells Fargo charges a $10 fee to send $500 to Mexico compared with Western Union's $15 fee for the same transaction. Many banks are moving toward elimination of exchange rate spreads (the difference between the market rate and the rate they use for the wire transfer) and transfer fees to Mexico to provide more attractive alternatives to migrant workers. This new onslaught of competition by banks has forced Western Union to cut its fees and offer new services, including a home-delivery service, where money is delivered directly to the recipient's door. Western Union is also moving into countries such as China and India in order to increase its market share. The increased competition has driven down remittance fees around the world. In Hong Kong, Western Union was forced to drop its fee from $9 to $2.60.

Migrant workers complain about the high transfer fees and exchange rate spread associated with Western Union, but many continue to use this service instead of the lower-cost method of remitting money through banks. Mexico has a history of unstable currencies and widespread inflation, resulting in a traditional mistrust of banks. Other emigrants base their choice on word of mouth or convenience and location. Many are simply unaware of the variety of choices available for sending money and don't know how to get the best deal. Another reason why many continue to use Western Union is its worldwide availability. For thousands of tiny villages, Western Union is the main link to the outside world. For example, Coatetelco is a small Mexican village south of Mexico City with no bank. A few people grow maize, chilies, and fruit, but remittances—mostly from agricultural or construction workers in Georgia and the Carolinas—account for 90 percent of the villagers' incomes. Patricio, 49, says that at the end of each month, he gets a call from his two sons, who are working illegally in Georgia. They give him a code number, and he drives or rides his horse four miles to the nearest Western Union office, located in a government telegraph office, to pick up the $600 they spent $40 to wire to him. Less expensive remittance services are available at the nearby Banamex bank in Mazatepec, but so far, Patricio and his neighbors aren't willing to travel the eight miles to get there. Besides, he says, "we do not trust the banks, and they make everything more difficult."

INTRODUCTION

Changing money from one currency to another and moving it around to different parts of the world is serious business, both on a personal and a company level. In this chapter, we will examine how the foreign-exchange market and global debt and equity markets work in international business.

To survive, both MNEs and small import and export companies must understand foreign exchange and exchange rates. In a business setting, there is a fundamental difference between making a payment in the domestic market and making a payment abroad. In a domestic transaction, companies use only one currency. In a foreign transaction, companies can use two or more currencies. For example, a U.S. company that exports skis to a French distributor will ask the French store that buys skis to remit payment in dollars, unless the U.S. company has some specific use for euros (the currency France uses), such as paying a French supplier.

Assume you are a U.S. importer who has agreed to purchase a certain quantity of French perfume and to pay the French exporter 4,000 euros for it. Assuming you had the money, how would you go about paying? First, you would go to the international department of your local bank to buy 4,000 euros at the going market rate. Let's assume the euro/dollar exchange rate is 0.7785 euros per dollar. Your bank then would charge your account $5,138 (4,000/0.7785) plus the transaction costs and give you a special check payable in euros made out to the exporter. The exporter would deposit it in a French bank, which then would credit the exporter's account with 4,000 euros. Then the foreign-exchange transaction would be complete. **Foreign exchange** is money denominated in the currency of another nation or group of nations.[2] The market in which these transactions take place is the foreign-exchange market. Foreign exchange can be in the form of cash, funds available on credit and debit cards, traveler's checks, bank deposits, or other short-term claims.[3]

An **exchange rate** is the price of a currency. It is the number of units of one currency that buys one unit of another currency, and this number can change daily. For example, on April 28, 2005, one euro could purchase US$1.2895. Exchange rates make international price and cost comparisons possible.

The foreign-exchange market is made up of many different players. Some players buy and sell foreign exchange because they are exporters and importers of goods and services. Other players buy and sell foreign exchange because of foreign direct investments—both investing capital into and pulling dividends out of a country. Others are portfolio investors—they buy foreign stocks, bonds, and mutual funds, hoping to sell them at a more profitable exchange rate later. These players have different objectives for buying and selling foreign currencies, and in the meantime, they affect supply and demand for those currencies.

MAJOR CHARACTERISTICS OF THE FOREIGN-EXCHANGE MARKET

The foreign-exchange market has two major segments: the over-the-counter market (OTC) and the exchange-traded market. The OTC market is composed of banks, both commercial banks like Bank of America and investment banks like Merrill Lynch, and other financial institutions, and it is where most of the foreign-exchange activity takes place. The exchange-traded market is composed of securities exchanges, such as the Chicago Mercantile Exchange and the Philadelphia Stock Exchange, where certain types of foreign-exchange instruments, such as exchange-traded futures and options, are traded.

Brief Description of Foreign-Exchange Instruments   *Notes*

Several different types of foreign-exchange instruments are traded in these markets, but the traditional foreign-exchange instruments that comprise the bulk of foreign-exchange trading are spot transactions, outright forwards, and FX swaps. Spot transactions involve the exchange of currency the second day after the date on which the two foreign-exchange traders agree to the transaction. The rate at which the transaction is settled is the **spot rate.** Outright forward transactions involve the exchange of currency three or more days after the date on which the traders agree to the transaction. It is the single purchase or sale of a currency for future delivery. The rate at which the transaction is settled is the forward rate and is a contract rate between the two parties. The forward transaction will be settled at the forward rate no matter what the actual spot rate is at the time of settlement. In an FX swap, one currency is swapped for another on one date and then swapped back on a future date. Most often, the first leg of an FX swap is a spot transaction, with the second leg of the swap a future transaction. For example, assume that IBM receives a dividend in British pounds from its subsidiary in the United Kingdom but has no use for British pounds until it has to pay a British supplier in pounds in 30 days. It would rather have dollars now than hold on to the pounds for 30 days. IBM could enter into an FX swap in which it sells the pounds for dollars to a trader in the spot market at the spot rate and agrees to buy pounds for dollars from the trader in 30 days at the forward rate. Although an FX swap is both a spot and a forward transaction, it is accounted for as a single transaction.

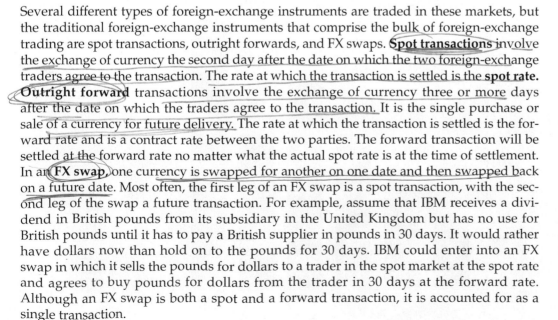

Foreign exchange—money denominated in the currency of another nation or group of nations

Exchange rate—the price of a currency

Foreign exchange market
- Over-the-counter (OTC)—commercial and investment banks
- Securities exchanges

Traditional foreign-exchange instruments
- Spot
- Outright forward   } *Notes*
- FX swap

The spot rate is the exchange rate quoted for transactions that require delivery within two days.

Outright forwards involve the exchange of currency beyond three days at a fixed exchange rate, known as the forward rate.

An FX swap is a simultaneous spot and forward transaction.

In addition to the traditional instruments, which were the only foreign-exchange instruments traded until the 1970s, there are currency swaps, options, and futures.[4] Currency swaps are OTC instruments, options are traded both OTC and on exchanges, and futures are exchange-traded instruments. Currency swaps deal more with interest-bearing financial instruments (such as a bond), and they involve the exchange of principal and interest payments. Options are the right but not the obligation to trade foreign currency in the future. A futures contract is an agreement between two parties to buy or sell a particular currency at a particular price on a particular future date, as specified in a standardized contract to all participants in that currency futures exchange.

Three other important foreign-exchange instruments

- *Currency swaps*
- *Options*
- *Futures*

Notes

The Size, Composition, and Location of the Foreign-Exchange Market

Before we examine the market instruments in more detail, let's look at the size, composition, and geographic location of the market. Every three years, the Bank for International Settlements (http://www.bis.org), a Basel, Switzerland-based central banking institution that is owned and controlled by 55 member central banks, conducts a survey of foreign-exchange activity in the world. In the 2004 survey, it estimated that $1.9 trillion in foreign exchange is traded every day.[5] Foreign-exchange activity increased substantially in 2004 by 57 percent compared to the 2001 survey. This increase more than reversed the fall in global foreign-exchange activity from 1998 to 2001. Some of the reasons for the increase are the the growing importance of foreign exchange as an alternative asset and a larger emphasis on **hedge funds** (a fund, usually used by wealthy individuals and institutions, which is allowed to use aggressive strategies that are unavailable to mutual funds). Figure 9.1 illustrates the trends in foreign-exchange trading beginning with the 1989 survey. The $1.9 trillion daily turnover includes traditional foreign-exchange market activity only—spots, outright forwards, and FX swaps. In the OTC derivatives market, daily activity increased by 74 percent to $2.4 trillion. This is also a significant escalation in activity compared with the period 1998 to 2001, when activity increased by 10 percent.

The U.S. dollar is the most important currency in the foreign-exchange market; in 2004, it comprised one side (buy or sell) of 89 percent of all foreign currency transactions worldwide, as Table 9.1 illustrates. This means that almost every foreign-exchange transaction

Size of the foreign-exchange market—$1.9 trillion daily

FIGURE 9.1

AVERAGE DAILY VOLUME IN WORLD FOREIGN-EXCHANGE MARKETS, 1989–2004

The average daily volume of foreign-exchange transactions was $1.9 trillion worldwide in 2004, up from $1.2 trillion in 2001 and $1.5 trillion in 1998.

Source: Bank for International Settlements, *Central Bank Survey of Foreign Exchange and Derivatives Market Activity 2001* (Basel, Switzerland: BIS, March 2002), 2. Reprinted by permission of the Bank of International Settlements.

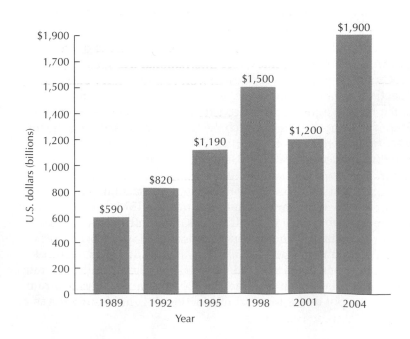

TABLE 9.1   **CURRENCY DISTRIBUTION OF GLOBAL FOREIGN EXCHANGE MARKET ACTIVITY**

CURRENCY	APRIL 1989	APRIL 1992	APRIL 1995	APRIL 1998	APRIL 2001	APRIL 2004
U.S. dollar	90	82	83	87	90	89
Euro	—	—	—	—	38	37
Japanese yen	27	23	24	21	23	20
Pound sterling	15	14	10	11	13	17
Swiss franc	10	9	7	7	6	6
All others	31	32	39	44	30	31

Source: Bank for International Settlements, *Central Bank Survey of Foreign Exchange and Derivatives Market Activity, 2004* (Basel, Switzerland: BIS, March 2004) p. 11. Reprinted by permission of the Bank of International Settlements.

Why the dollar?

conducted on a daily basis has the dollar as one leg of the transaction. There are five major reasons why the dollar is so widely traded. The dollar is:

1. An investment currency in many capital markets
2. A reserve currency held by many central banks
3. A transaction currency in many international commodity markets
4. An invoice currency in many contracts
5. An intervention currency employed by monetary authorities in market operations to influence their own exchange rates[6]

Because of the ready availability of U.S. dollars worldwide, this currency is important as a vehicle for foreign-exchange transactions between two countries other than the United States. An example of how the dollar can be used as a vehicle currency for two other countries is when a Mexican company importing products from a Japanese exporter converts Mexican pesos into dollars and sends them to the Japanese exporter, who converts the dollars into yen. Thus, the U.S. dollar is one leg on both sides of the transaction—in Mexico and in Japan. There may be a couple of reasons to go through dollars instead of directly from pesos to yen. The first reason is that the Japanese exporter might not have any need for pesos, whereas it can use dollars for a variety of reasons. The second reason is that the Mexican importer might have trouble getting yen at a good exchange rate if the Mexican banks are not carrying yen balances. However, the banks undoubtedly carry dollar balances, so the importer might have easy access to the dollars. Thus, the dollar has become an important "vehicle" for international transactions, and it greatly simplifies life for a foreign bank because the bank won't have to carry balances in many different currencies.

Another way to consider foreign-currency trades is to look at the most frequently traded currency pairs. Four of the top seven currency pairs involve the U.S. dollar, with the top two pairs being the U.S. dollar and the euro (28 percent of total) and the U.S. dollar and Japanese yen (17 percent).[7] This reinforces the idea that the dollar is a vehicle currency for trading between other currencies, which is known as *cross-trading*.

The euro is also in four of the top seven currency pairs. Although the dollar is still more popular in most emerging markets, the euro is gaining ground, particularly in eastern European countries like the Czech Republic and Hungary. The Bank for International Settlements (BIS) believes the euro resembles the German mark in the exchange market in four ways: because of "its share in global foreign exchange trading, the tightness of spreads, its volatility vis-à-vis the dollar and the yen, and its role as an anchoring currency."[8] The 2004 BIS survey showed that the euro has not yet taken market share from any of the other currencies, such as the dollar or the yen. However, this could change as the euro becomes more popular and as more countries adopt the euro.

The dollar is the most widely traded currency in the world.
- An investment currency in many capital markets
- A reserve currency held by many central banks
- A transaction currency in many international commodity markets
- An invoice currency in many contracts
- An intervention currency employed by monetary authorities in market operations to influence their own exchange rates

The dollar is part of four of the top seven currency pairs traded.
- The dollar/euro is number one.
- The dollar/yen is number two.

FIGURE 9.2

GEOGRAPHICAL DISTRIBUTION OF GLOBAL FOREIGN-EXCHANGE MARKET ACTIVITY, APRIL 2004

Source: Bank for International Settlements, *Central Bank Survey of Foreign Exchange and Derivatives Market Activity, 2004* (Basel, Switzerland: BIS, March 2004), p. 11. Reprinted by permission of the Bank of International Settlements.

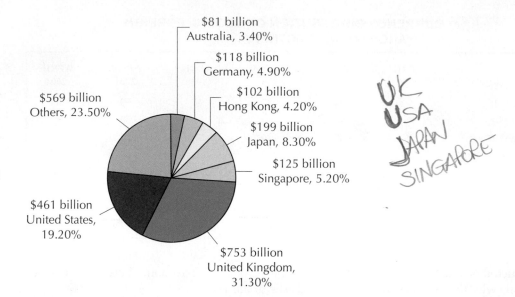

$81 billion Australia, 3.40%

$118 billion Germany, 4.90%

$102 billion Hong Kong, 4.20%

$199 billion Japan, 8.30%

$125 billion Singapore, 5.20%

$569 billion Others, 23.50%

$461 billion United States, 19.20%

$753 billion United Kingdom, 31.30%

UK
USA
JAPAN
SINGAPORE

The biggest market for foreign exchange is London, followed by New York, Tokyo, and Singapore.

Given that the dollar is clearly the most widely traded currency in the world, that would seem to indicate that the biggest market for foreign-exchange trading would be in the United States. But as Figure 9.2 illustrates, the biggest market by far is in the United Kingdom. The four largest centers for foreign-exchange trading (the United Kingdom, the United States, Japan, and Singapore) account for 64 percent of the total average daily turnover. The U.K. market is so dominant that more dollars are traded in London than in New York.[9]

DOES GEOGRAPHY MATTER?

Foreign Exchange Trades

Given that the U.S. dollar is the most widely traded currency in the world, why is London so important as a trading center? There are two major reasons for London's prominence. First, London, which is close to the major capital markets in Europe, is a strong international financial center where a large number of domestic and foreign financial institutions have operations. Thus London's geographic location relative to significant global economic activity is key. In addition, the U.K. is not part of the euro zone, even though it is a member of the EU, so euros traded in London are considered offshore euros, or Euro-euros, to be really confusing. Second, London is positioned in a unique way because of the time zone where it is located. In Map 9.1, note that at noon in London, it is 7:00 A.M. in New York and evening in Asia. The London market opens toward the end of the trading day in Asia and is going strong as the New York foreign-exchange market opens up. London thus straddles both of the other major markets in the world.

Another way to illustrate the importance of geography is to note the daily volume of market activity that takes place in different markets around the world, especially in North America and Europe. Figure 9.3 illustrates the average number of electronic conversations per hour as monitored by Reuters. It illustrates how market activity is concentrated on the time period when Asia and Europe are open or when Europe and the United States are open, even though the market is really open 24 hours a day. Since the U.S. dollar is the most widely traded currency in the world and London is the major market center for dollars traded outside of the United States, it makes sense that most market activity would take place during the hours that the U.S. and London markets are open. You can get a better price for currencies when the markets are active and liquid. As we will find in the discussion on Euroequities later in the chapter, the same is true for stock trades. Even though the market is a 24-hour market, the stocks of the largest companies in the world tend to be traded when the home markets of the companies are open. That would typically be when the United States and Europe are open.

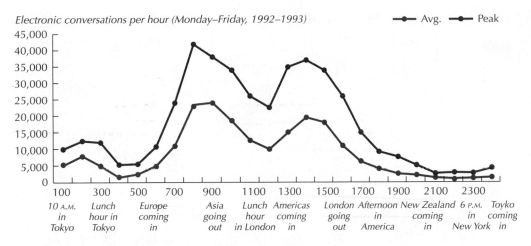

Electronic conversations per hour (Monday–Friday, 1992–1993)   — ● — Avg.   — ● — Peak

100	300	500	700	900	1100	1300	1500	1700	1900	2100	2300	

10 A.M. in Tokyo | Lunch hour in Tokyo | Europe coming in | Asia going out | Lunch hour in London | Americas coming in | London going out | Afternoon in America | New Zealand coming in | 6 P.M. in New York | Toyko coming in

Note: Time (0100–2400 hours, Greenwich Mean Time)

FIGURE 9.3

THE CIRCADIAN RHYTHMS OF THE FX MARKET

Market activity heightens when Europe and Asia are open and when Europe and the United States are open.

Note: Time (0100-2400 hours, Greenwich Mean Time)

Source: Reuters

MAJOR FOREIGN-EXCHANGE INSTRUMENTS

Now let's examine in more detail the major foreign-exchange instruments: spot, forward, options, and futures, as well as the convertibility of currencies.

The Spot Market

Most foreign-currency transactions take place between foreign-exchange traders, so the traders who work for foreign-exchange brokerage houses or commercial banks quote the rates. The traders always quote a **bid** (buy) and **offer** (sell) rate. The *bid* is the price at which the trader is willing to buy foreign currency, and the *offer* is the price at which the trader is willing to sell foreign currency. In the spot market, the **spread** is the difference between the bid and offer rates, and it is the trader's profit margin. The rate a trader quotes for the British pound might be $1.9068/59. This means the trader is willing to buy pounds at $1.9068 each and sell them for $1.9059. Obviously, a trader wants to buy low and sell high.

In this example, the trader quotes the foreign currency as the number of U.S. dollars for one unit of that currency. This method of quoting exchange rates is called the **direct quote,** also known in the foreign-exchange industry as "**American terms.**" It represents a quote from the point of view of someone in the United States. The other convention for quoting foreign exchange is "**European terms,**" which is the number of units of the foreign currency per U.S. dollar. This is also sometimes called the **indirect quote** in the United States.

When traders quote currencies to their customers, they always quote the **base currency** (the denominator) first, followed by the **terms currency** (the numerator), which seems backwards. But that is the convention that traders use. A quote for "dollar/yen" means that the dollar is the base currency and the yen is the terms currency. If you know the dollar/yen quote, you can divide that rate into 1 to get the yen-dollar quote. In other words, the exchange rate in American terms is the reciprocal or inverse of the exchange rate in European terms. For example, using the numbers in Table 9.2, 1/.009430 = 106.04.

In a dollar-yen quote, the dollar is the denominator and the yen is the numerator. By tracking changes in the exchange rate, managers can determine whether the base currency is strengthening or weakening. For example, on October 10, 2004, the dollar-yen rate was ¥110.96/$1.00, and on April 28, 2005, the rate was ¥106.04/$1.00. As the numerator falls, the base currency—the dollar—is weakening or getting less expensive. Conversely, the terms currency, or the yen in this case, is strengthening or getting more expensive. If the rate were to rise to ¥115, the base currency would be strengthening, and the terms currency would be weakening.

note

Key foreign exchange terms

- Bid—the rate at which traders buy foreign exchange
- Offer—the rate at which traders sell foreign exchange
- Spread—the difference between bid and offer rates
- American terms or direct quote—the number of dollars per unit of foreign currency
- European terms or indirect quote—the number of units of foreign currency per dollar

yen   *term currency*
dollar   *base*

MAP 9.1   International Time Zones and the Single World Market

The world's communication networks are now so good that we can talk of a single world market. It starts in a small way in New Zealand around 9:00 A.M., just in time to catch the tail end of the previous night's New York market. Two or three hours later, Tokyo opens, followed an hour later by Hong Kong and Manila, and then half an hour later by Singapore. By now, with the Far East market in full swing, the focus moves to the Near and Middle East. Bombay opens two hours after Singapore, followed after an hour and a half by Abu Dhabi and Athens. By this stage, trading in the Far and Middle East is usually thin as dealers wait to see how Europe will trade. Paris and Frankfurt open an hour ahead of London, and by this time Tokyo is starting to close down, so the European market can judge the Japanese market. By lunchtime in London, New York is starting to open up, and as Europe closes down, positions can be passed westward. Midday in New York, trading tends to be quiet because there is nowhere to pass a position to. The San Francisco market, three hours behind New York, is effectively a satellite of the New York market, although very small positions can be passed on to New Zealand banks. (Note that in the former Soviet Union, standard time zones are advanced an hour.

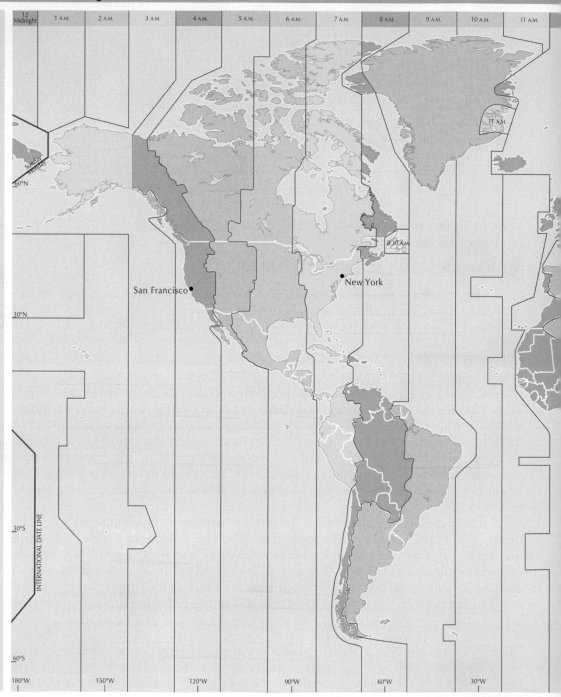

Most large newspapers, especially those devoted to business or those having business sections, quote exchange rates daily. Because most currencies constantly fluctuate in value, many managers check the values daily. For example, the *Wall Street Journal* provides quotes in American terms (US$ equivalent) and European terms (currency per US$), as shown in Table 9.2. All the quotes, except those noted as one-month, three-month, and six-month forward, are spot quotes. The spot rates are the selling rates for interbank transactions of $1 million and more. **Interbank** transactions are transactions between banks. Retail transactions, those between banks and companies or individuals, provide fewer foreign currency units

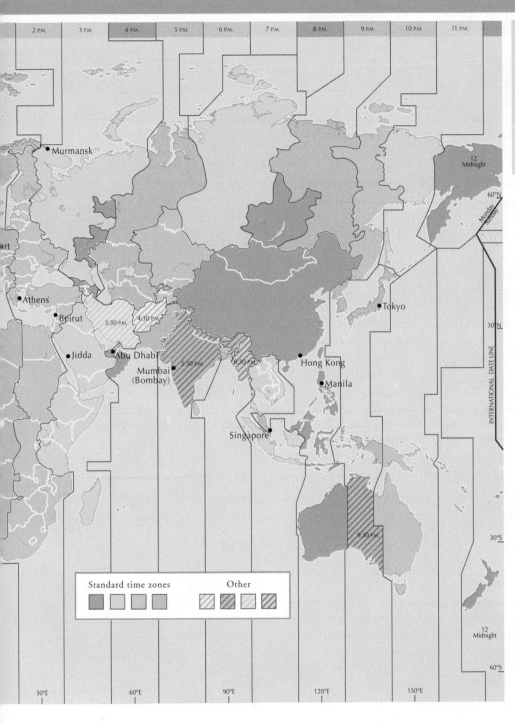

Also note that some countries and territories have adopted half-hour time zones, as shown by hatched lines.)

Source: Adapted from Julian Walmsley, *The Foreign Exchange Handbook* (New York: John Wiley, 1983), 7–8. Reprinted by permission of John Wiley & Sons, Inc. Some information taken from *The Cambridge Factfinders*, 3/e, edited by David Crystal (New York: Cambridge University Press, 1998), 440.

per dollar than interbank transactions. There are also a number of good Internet sources for exchange-rate quotes, such as CNN (**http://money.cnn.com/markets/currencies/**) and Yahoo! (**www.finance.yahoo.com/currency**).[10]

The Forward Market

As noted earlier, the spot market is for foreign-exchange transactions that occur within two business days, but in some transactions, a seller extends credit to the buyer for a period that

TABLE 9.2   FOREIGN EXCHANGE MARKETS, THURSDAY, APRIL 28, 2005

COUNTRY	US$ EQUIVALENT		CURRENCY PER US$	
	THURSDAY	WEDNESDAY	THURSDAY	WEDNESDAY
Argentina (Peso)	.3438	.3449	2.9087	2.8994
Australia (Dollar)	.7788	.7762	1.2840	1.2883
Bahrain (Dinar)	2.6525	2.6525	0.3770	0.3770
Brazil (Real)	.3917	.3972	2.5530	2.5176
Canada (Dollar)	.7991	.8004	1.2514	1.2494
1 month forward	.7995	.8007	1.2508	1.2489
3 months forward	.8002	.80115	1.2497	1.2477
6 months forward	.8020	.8032	1.2469	1.2450
Chile (Peso)	.001706	.001723	586.17	580.38
China (Renminbi)	.1208	.1208	8.2765	8.2764
Colombia (Peso)	.0004259	.0004279	2347.97	2336.99
Czech Republic (Koruna) Commercial Rate	.04213	.04275	23.736	23.392
Denmark (Krone)	.1732	.1737	5.7737	5.7571
Ecuador (US Dollar)[e]	1.0000	1.0000	1.0000	1.0000
Egypt (Pound)[y]	.1723	.1724	5.8025	5.8001
Hong Kong (Dollar)	.1282	.1282	7.8003	7.8003
Hungary (Forint)	.005109	.005174	195.73	193.27
India (Rupee)	.02291	.02288	43.649	43.706
Indonesia (Rupiah)	.0001044	.0001045	9579	9569
Israel (Shekel)	.2289	.2289	4.3687	4.3687
Japan (Yen)	.009430	.009445	106.04	105.88
1 month forward	.009455	.009469	105.76	105.61
3 months forward	.009508	.009521	105.17	105.03
6 months forward	.009594	.009607	104.23	104.09
Jordan (Dinar)	1.4117	1.4114	.7084	.7085
Kuwait (Dinar)	3.4245	3.4247	.2920	.2920
Lebanon (Pound)	.0006605	.0006609	1514.00	1513.09
Malaysia (Ringgit)[b]	.2632	.2632	3.7994	3.7994
Malta (Lira)	3.0099	3.0122	.3322	.3320
Mexico (Peso) Floating rate	.0896	.0901	11.1557	11.0951
New Zealand (Dollar)	.7285	.7206	1.3727	1.3877
Norway (Krone)	.1585	.1590	6.3091	6.2893
Pakistan (Rupee)	.01682	.01681	59.453	59.488
Peru (New Sol)	.3070	.3070	3.2573	3.2573
Phillippines (Peso)	.01839	.01839	54.377	54.377
Poland (Zloty)	.3002	.3046	3.3311	3.2830
Russia (Ruble)[a]	.03597	.03607	27.801	27.724
Saudi Arabia (Riyal)	0.2666	0.2667	3.7509	3.7495
Singapore (Dollar)	.6078	.6073	1.6453	1.6466
Slovak Republic (Koruna)	.03252	.03268	30.750	30.600
South Africa (Rand)	.1630	.1646	6.1350	6.0753
South Korea (Won)	.0009975	.0009985	1002.51	1001.50
Sweden (Krona)	.1407	.1415	7.1073	7.0671

(Continued)

TABLE 9.2	CONTINUED

	US$ EQUIVALENT		CURRENCY PER US$	
COUNTRY	THURSDAY	WEDNESDAY	THURSDAY	WEDNESDAY
Switzerland (Franc)	.8383	.8390	1.1929	1.1919
1 month forward	.8400	.8407	1.1905	1.1895
3 months forward	.8435	.8441	1.1855	1.1847
6 months forward	.8494	.8502	1.1773	1.1762
Taiwan (Dollar)	.03183	.03181	31.417	31.437
Thailand (Baht)	.02525	.02528	39.604	39.557
Turkey (New Lira)[d]	.7111	.7270	1.4063	1.3755
U.K. (Pound)	1.9068	1.9059	.5244	.5247
1 month forward	1.9040	1.9030	.5252	.5255
3 months forward	1.8989	1.8980	.5266	.5269
6 months forward	1.8929	1.8918	.5283	.5286
United Arab (Dirham)	.0723	.2723	3.6724	3.6724
Uruguay (Peso) Financial	.03990	.03990	25.063	25.063
Venezuela (Bolivar)	.000466	.000466	2145.92	2145.92
Special Drawing Rights	1.5135	1.5121	.6607	.6613
Euro	1.2895	1.2933	.7755	.7732

Special Drawing Rights (SDR) are based on exchange rates for the U.S., German, British, French, and Japanese currencies.

Source: International Monetary Fund.

[a] Russian Central Bank rate. [b] Government rate. [d] Rebased as of Jan. 1, 2005. [y] Floating rate.

Source: Wall Street Journal. Central edition [only staff-produced materials may be used] by staff. Copyright 2005 by Dow Jones & Co., Inc. Reproduced with permission of Dow Jones & Co., Inc. in the format textbook via Copyright Clearance Center.

is longer than two days. For example, a Japanese exporter of consumer electronics might sell television sets to a U.S. importer with immediate delivery but payment due in 30 days. The U.S. importer is obligated to pay in yen in 30 days and may enter into a contract with a currency trader to deliver the yen at a forward rate—the rate quoted today for future delivery.

In addition to the spot rates for each currency, Table 9.2 shows the forward rates for the British pound, Canadian dollar, Japanese yen, and Swiss franc. These are the most

The forward rate is the rate quoted for transactions that call for delivery after two business days.

A man counts his money after exchanging U.S. dollars at a money changer in Tel Aviv, Israel. The buy (NIS4.82/US$) and sell (NIS4.94/US$) spot rates are prominently displayed on the store's signage. The spread of NIS 0.12 is the trader's profit on foreign currency transactions.

A forward discount exists when the forward rate is less than the spot rate.

widely traded currencies in the forward market. Many currencies do not have a forward market due to the small size and volume of transactions in that currency.

Building on what we said earlier, we now can say that the difference between the spot and forward rates is either the **forward discount** or the **forward premium.** An easy way to understand the difference between the forward rate and the spot rate is to use currency quotes in American terms. If the forward rate for a foreign currency is less than the spot rate, then the foreign currency is selling at a forward discount. If the forward rate is greater than the spot rate, the foreign currency is selling at a forward premium.

A premium exists when the forward rate is greater than the spot rate.

Options

An option is the right but not the obligation to trade a foreign currency at a specific exchange rate.

An **option** is the right but not the obligation to buy or sell a foreign currency within a certain time period or on a specific date at a specific exchange rate. An option can be purchased OTC from a commercial or investment bank, or it can be purchased on an exchange, such as the Philadelphia Stock Exchange. For example, assume a company purchases an OTC option to buy Japanese yen at 106 yen per dollar (0.00943 dollars per yen). The writer of the option, the commercial or investment bank in this case, will charge the company a fee for writing the option. The more likely the option is to benefit the company, the higher the fee. The rate of 106 yen is called the *strike price* for the option. The fee or cost of the option is called the *premium.* On the date when the option is set to expire, the company can look at the spot rate and compare it with the strike price to see which is the better exchange rate. If the spot rate were 116 yen per dollar (0.00862 dollars per yen), it would not exercise the option because buying yen at the spot rate would cost less than buying them at the option rate. However, if the spot rate at that time were 96 yen per dollar (0.01042 dollars per yen), the company would exercise the option because buying at the option rate would cost less than buying at the spot rate. The option provides the company flexibility, because it can walk away from the option if the strike price is not a good price. In the case of a forward contract, the cost is usually cheaper than the cost for an option, but the company cannot walk away from the contract. So a forward contract is cheaper but less flexible than an option.

Futures

A futures contract specifies an exchange rate in advance of the actual exchange of currency, but it is not as flexible as a forward contract.

A foreign currency future resembles a forward contract insofar as it specifies an exchange rate some time in advance of the actual exchange of currency. However, a future is traded on an exchange, not OTC. Instead of working with a banker, companies work with exchange brokers when purchasing futures contracts. A forward contract is tailored to the amount and time frame that the company needs, whereas a futures contract is for a specific amount and specific maturity date. The futures contract is less valuable to a company than a forward contract. However, it may be useful to speculators and small companies that do not have a good enough relationship with a bank to enter into a forward contract or that need a contract for an amount that is too small for the forward market. The differences between forward contracts, which are traded OTC, and exchange-based contracts, such as futures and options, are summarized in Table 9.3.

Foreign-Exchange Convertibility

A hard currency is a currency that is usually fully convertible and strong or relatively stable in value in comparison with other currencies.

A key aspect of exchanging one currency for another is its convertibility. Fully convertible currencies are those that the government allows both residents and nonresidents to purchase in unlimited amounts. **Hard currencies,** such as the U.S. dollar, euro, British pound, and Japanese yen, are currencies that are fully convertible. They also are relatively stable in value or tend to be strong in comparison with other currencies over time. In addition, they are desirable assets. Currencies that are not fully convertible are often called **soft currencies,** or **weak currencies.** They tend to be the currencies of developing countries.

Most countries today have nonresident, or external, convertibility, meaning that foreigners can convert their currency into the local currency and can convert back into

TABLE 9.3	COMPARISON OF MARKET FEATURES FOR EXCHANGE-BASED AND OTC OPTIONS IN FOREIGN EXCHANGE MARKETS

	EXCHANGE-BASED (OPTIONS AND FUTURES)	OTC (FORWARD CONTRACTS)
Contract specifications	Standardized and customized	Customized
Regulation	Securities and Exchange Commission (SEC)	Self-regulated
Type of market	Open outcry, auction market	Dealer market
Counterparty* to every transaction	"AAA"-rated Options Clearing Corporation (OCC)	Bank on the contraside
Transparency/Visible prices	Yes	No
Margin required for short positions**	Yes	No†
Orders anonymously represented in the market	Yes	No
Required to mark positions daily	Yes	No†
Audit trail	Complete sequential and second-by-second audit trail of each transaction	No
Participants	Public customers, as well as corporate and institutional users	Corporate and institutional users

* Counterparty means the person on the other side of the transaction. For example, if IBM enters into an option on the PHLX, the counterparty to the contract would be a registered broker. If it enters into an OTC option with Citibank, the counterparty would be the bank.

** A margin is a percentage of the contract value that the company, IBM, for example, would have to pay to enter into the contract. At the end of the day, the exchange marks the value of the option to the new market price. If the value has gone up, the margin requirement also rises. That is not required in the OTC market.

† Not a requirement, but available.

Source: Reprinted by permission of the Philadelphia Stock Exchange.

their currency as well. For example, travelers to Zimbabwe can convert U.S. dollars (USD) into Zimbabwe dollars (ZWD) and convert ZWD back into USD when they leave. However, they have to show receipts of all conversions into or from ZWD inside the country to make sure that all transactions took place on the official market. Whatever the travelers converted in the official market was the maximum they would have been allowed to convert back into USD when they left. In addition, they have to declare electronics products, such as cameras and stereos, upon entering the country and then prove they had them upon leaving. The government was afraid visitors would sell the products in the black market and then try to convert the proceeds into dollars and take them out of the country. Some countries limit nonresident convertibility.

To conserve scarce foreign exchange, some governments impose exchange restrictions on companies or individuals who want to exchange money. The devices they use include import licensing, multiple exchange rates, import deposit requirements, and quantity controls. As you will read in the concluding case, Argentina's government placed exchange restrictions on individuals and companies at the beginning of 2002 to keep individuals and companies from sending money out of Argentina.

Government licenses fix the exchange rate by requiring all recipients, exporters, and others who receive foreign currency to sell it to its central bank at the official buying rate. Then the central bank rations the foreign currency it acquires by selling it at fixed rates to those needing to make payment abroad for essential goods. An importer may purchase foreign exchange only if that importer has obtained an import license for the goods in question.

Licensing occurs when a government requires that all foreign-exchange transactions be regulated and controlled by it.

Another way governments control foreign-exchange convertibility is by establishing more than one exchange rate. This restrictive measure is called a **multiple exchange-rate system.** The government determines which kinds of transactions are to be conducted at which exchange rates. Countries with multiple exchange rates often have a very high exchange rate (i.e., it takes more units of the local currency to buy dollars) for luxury goods and financial flows, such as dividends. Then they have a lower exchange rate for other trade transactions, such as imports of essential commodities and semimanufactured goods.

Another form of foreign-exchange convertibility control is the **advance import deposit.** In this case, the government tightens the issue of import licenses and requires importers to make a deposit with the central bank, often for as long as one year and interest-free, covering the full price of manufactured goods they would purchase from abroad.

Governments also may limit the amount of exchange through quantity controls, which often apply to tourism. A quantity control limits the amount of currency that a local resident can purchase from the bank for foreign travel. The government sets a policy on how much money a tourist is allowed to take overseas, and the individual is allowed to convert only that amount of money.

In the past, these currency controls have significantly added to the cost of doing business internationally, and they have resulted in the overall reduction of trade. However, the liberalization of trade in recent years has eliminated a lot of these controls to the point that they are found to be a minor impediment to trade.[11]

HOW COMPANIES USE FOREIGN EXCHANGE

Most foreign-exchange transactions stem from the international departments of commercial banks, which perform three essential financial functions: (1) They buy and sell foreign exchange; (2) they collect and pay money in transactions with foreign buyers and sellers; and (3) they lend money in foreign currency. In performing collections, the bank serves as a vehicle for payments between its domestic and foreign customers. Lending usually takes place in the currency of the bank's headquarters, but the bank might be able to provide loans in a foreign currency if it has a branch in that country.

Commercial banks buy and sell foreign currency for many purposes. For one, travelers going abroad or returning from a foreign country will want to purchase or sell back its foreign currency. Also, residents of one country wanting to invest abroad need to purchase foreign currency from a commercial bank. Further, suppose a Canadian exporter receives payment from a U.S. importer in U.S. dollars and wants to use the dollars to buy raw materials in Norway. The bank in this case simultaneously serves as a collector and acts as a dealer in a foreign-exchange transaction.

There are a number of reasons why companies use the foreign-exchange market. The most obvious is for import and export transactions. For example, a U.S. company importing products from an overseas supplier might have to convert U.S. dollars into a foreign currency to pay that supplier. In addition, company personnel traveling abroad need to deal in foreign exchange to pay for their local expenses.

Companies also use the foreign-exchange market for financial transactions, such as those in FDI. Say a U.S. company decided to establish a manufacturing plant in Mexico. It would have to convert dollars into pesos to make the investment. After the Mexican subsidiary generated a profit, it would have to convert pesos to dollars to send a dividend back to the U.S. parent.

Sometimes companies—but mostly traders and investors—deal in foreign exchange solely for profit. One type of profit-seeking activity is **arbitrage,** which is the purchase of foreign currency on one market for immediate resale on another market (in a different country) in order to profit from a price discrepancy. For example, a trader might sell U.S. dollars for Swiss francs in the United States, then Swiss francs for British pounds in Switzerland, and then the British pounds for U.S. dollars back in the United States, the goal being to end up with more dollars. Assume the trader converts 100 dollars into 150 Swiss francs when the exchange rate is 1.5 francs per dollar. The trader then converts the 150 francs into 70 British pounds at an exchange rate of .467 pounds per franc and finally converts the pounds into 125 dollars at an exchange rate of .56 pounds per dollar. In this case, arbitrage yields $125 from the initial sale of $100.

Interest arbitrage is the investing in debt instruments, such as bonds, in different countries. For example, a trader might invest $1,000 in the United States for 90 days or convert $1,000 into British pounds, invest the money in the United Kingdom for 90 days, and then convert the pounds back into dollars. The investor would try to pick the alternative that would yield the highest return at the end of 90 days.

Investors can also use foreign-exchange transactions to speculate for profit or to protect against risk. Speculation is the buying or selling of a commodity, in this case foreign currency, that has both an element of risk and the chance of great profit. For example, an investor could buy euros in anticipation that the euro will strengthen against other currencies. If it strengthens, the investor earns a profit; if it weakens, the investor incurs a loss. Speculators are important in the foreign-exchange market because they spot trends and try to take advantage of them. They can create demand for a currency by purchasing it in the market, or they can create a supply of the currency by selling it in the market. The year 2004 was a very difficult year for currency speculators. The Parker Discretionary FX Index, which measures the performance of 17 currency managers worldwide, fell in 2004, finishing with a negative return for the first time in 19 years. It continued to fall in early 2005, even though it had registered an annual return of 11.6 percent since 1986.[12]

> Interest arbitrage involves investing in interest-bearing instruments in foreign exchange in an effort to earn a profit due to interest-rate differentials.

> Speculators take positions in foreign-exchange and other capital markets to earn a profit.

THE FOREIGN-EXCHANGE TRADING PROCESS

When a company sells goods or services to a foreign customer and receives foreign currency, it needs to convert the foreign currency into the domestic currency. When importing, the company needs to convert domestic to foreign currency to pay the foreign supplier. This conversion takes place between the company and its bank, and most of these transactions take place in the OTC market. Originally, the commercial banks were the ones that provided foreign-exchange services for their customers. Eventually, some of these commercial banks in New York and other U.S. money centers such as Chicago and San Francisco began to look at foreign-exchange trading as a major business activity instead of just a service. They became intermediaries for smaller banks by establishing correspondent relationships with them. They also became major dealers in foreign exchange.

The left side of Figure 9.4 shows what happens when a U.S. company needs to sell euros for dollars. This situation could arise when a customer had to pay in euros or when

> Companies work through their local banks to settle foreign-exchange balances, but they also use investment banks and exchanges.

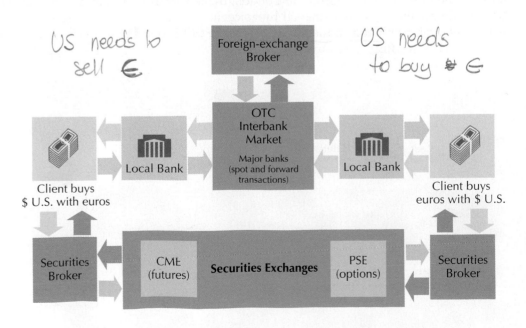

> **FIGURE 9.4**
>
> **STRUCTURE OF FOREIGN-EXCHANGE MARKETS**
>
> A company interested in exchanging currency can work with a commercial or investment bank in the OTC market or a broker on a securities exchange. Banks deal with each other in the interbank market, primarily through foreign-exchange brokers.

a German subsidiary had to send a dividend to the U.S. company in euros. The right side of the figure shows what happens when a U.S. company needs to buy euros with dollars. This situation could arise when a company had to pay euros to a German supplier. However, there are other markets and institutions in which foreign exchange is traded. Most of the foreign-exchange activity takes place in the traditional instruments of spot, outright forward, and FX swaps, and commercial banks and investment banks or other financial institutions basically trade these instruments. However, companies could also deal with an exchange, such as the Philadelphia Stock Exchange to buy or sell an option contract and the Chicago Mercantile Exchange to deal in foreign-currency futures.

[handwritten margin note: OTC exchange]

The Bank for International Settlements generates its reports on the basis of a survey of 1,200 market participants in 52 countries. However, in the 2001 survey, they mentioned that of the total institutions surveyed, between 100 to 200 are market-making banks, which means that they are willing to quote bid and offer rates to anyone in the currency or currencies in which they deal. Of this group, only a select few, such as Citigroup and HSBC, are major players.

As noted earlier, most of the foreign-exchange trades take place in the OTC market in which most of the dealers operate. These dealers operate more in the interbank market with dealers of other banks than they do with corporate clients. The BIS estimated in 2004 that 53 percent of the foreign-exchange trades took place among reporting dealers. This number is declining, compared with 64 percent in 1998. Sixty-two percent of the business between dealers takes place across national borders, whereas 38 percent of the dealers' business with nonfinancial customers takes place in the domestic market.[13]

When a company needs foreign exchange, it typically goes to its commercial bank for help. If that bank is a large market-maker, the company can get its foreign exchange fairly easily. However, if the company is located in a small market and uses a local bank, where does the bank get its foreign exchange? Figure 9.5 illustrates how foreign-exchange dealers at the banks trade foreign exchange. A bank, dealing either on its own account or for a client, can trade foreign exchange with another bank directly or through a broker. In the broker market, it can use a voice broker or an electronic brokerage system (EBS). In both the U.S. and U.K. markets, direct dealing is by far the most widely used method of trading currency; however, the use of electronic brokerages is increasing. An increase in electronic brokerage systems shows that dealers are directly trading less actively among themselves.[14] The share of electronic brokerages in interdealer trading volume was around 5 percent in 1992 but has steadily climbed to over 60 percent.[15]

A foreign-exchange broker is an intermediary who matches the best bid and offer quotes of interbank traders. There are a number of brokerage houses around the world, such as the Martin Brokers Group in London, owned by Trio Holdings. These brokers have traditionally dealt in the market by voice, linking up interbank traders. There are also retail foreign exchange traders, such as the REFCO Group Ltd., and FX CM, which is also owned by the REFCO Group.

Dealers can trade foreign exchange

- Directly with other dealers
- Through voice brokers
- Through electronic brokerage systems

FOREIGN-EXCHANGE TRANSACTIONS

Companies get access to foreign exchange through dealers or the Internet. Dealers trade directly to an interbank counterparty or through voice brokers or automated brokers.

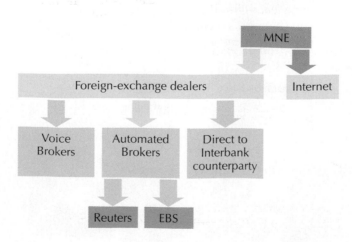

The use of brokers depends on a number of factors, such as the location of the market and the size and nature of the foreign-exchange transactions. Brokers have filled an important role because of their ability to establish networks with a wide variety of banks, thus allowing banks to buy or sell currency from other banks faster than if they had to try to contact all the different potential banks themselves. However, the voice broker market has been rapidly giving way to electronic brokerage systems.

Historically, most trades took place by telephone. A dealer in one bank would call a dealer in another bank and execute a trade. If it did not have access to enough banks to get the currency needed, it could operate through a broker. The move from voice to electronic brokerage systems was initiated by Reuters. Bloomberg is also a major player in the electronic brokerage market.

A bank gets access to the automated system by purchasing the service from Reuters or Bloomberg by paying a monthly fee and receiving a link through telephone lines to the bank's computers. Then the bank can use the automated system to trade currency. The automated system is efficient, because it lists bid and sell quotes, allowing the bank to trade immediately. For large transactions, many dealers prefer the familiarity of a trusted voice broker to find a buyer or seller. Electronic dealers are efficient but too impersonal for the large transactions. Most electronic trades average in the $1 million to $2 million range, although a trade of $10 million to $20 million will occasionally show up.[16] Electronic brokerage systems are used in one-third of all transactions for the dollar, euro, and yen.[17] Voice brokers are still widely used for derivatives and forward trades; however, spot trades are mostly electronic. EBS, a large electronic interbank system, processes an average of $100 billion in foreign exchange transactions per day.[18]

A current trend in currency trading is the establishment of Internet currency trading. During the Internet boom of the 1990s, large banks and corporations started funding Internet start-ups that were aimed at facilitating Internet exchange trading. One example is FX Connect, which is a division of State Street Corporation, a global financial services company. It provides real-time, 24-hour-a-day trading, fully interactive foreign exchange trade execution with multiple counterparties.

Internet trades of currency are becoming increasingly popular and are competing with dealers.

Commercial and Investment Banks

At one time, only the big money center banks could deal directly in foreign exchange. Regional banks had to rely on the money center banks to execute trades on behalf of their clients. The emergence of electronic trading has changed that, however. Now even the regional banks can hook up to Reuters and Bloomberg and deal directly in the interbank market or through brokers. In spite of this, the greatest volume of foreign-exchange activity takes place with the big banks.

There is more to servicing customers in the foreign-exchange market than size alone. Each year, *Euromoney* magazine surveys corporations and financial institutions to identify their customers' favorite banks and the leading traders in the interbank market. The criteria for selecting the top foreign-exchange traders include:

- Ranking of banks by corporations and other banks in specific locations, such as London, Singapore, and New York
- Capability to handle major currencies, such as the U.S. dollar and euro
- Capability to handle major cross-trades—for example, those between the euro and pound or the euro and yen
- Capability to handle specific currencies
- Capability to handle derivatives (forwards, swaps, futures, and options)
- Capability to engage in research

Other factors often mentioned are market share by size and region, advisory services, price, quote speed, credit rating, liquidity, back office/settlement, strategic advice, trade

The top banks in the interbank market in foreign exchange are so ranked because of their ability to
- *Trade in specific market locations*
- *Engage in major currencies and cross-trades*
- *Deal in specific currencies*
- *Handle derivatives (forwards, options, futures, swaps)*
- *Conduct key market research*

| TABLE 9.4 | TOP OTC AND COMMERCIAL AND INVESTMENT BANKS IN FOREIGN EXCHANGE TRADES |

TRADING BANK	ESTIMATED MARKET SHARE %	BEST IN LONDON	BEST IN NEW YORK	BEST IN TRADING EURO/DOLLAR	BEST IN $/YEN
1. Deutsche Bank	19.75	2	3	1	4
2. UBS Warburg	11.61	5	4	4	3
3. Citigroup	7.33	3	1	3	1
4. HSBC	6.64	1	5	2	2
5. Barclays	6.41	4	—	7	7
6. JPMorgan	5.38	7	2	5	5
7. ABN Amro	4.57	9	7	6	6
8. Merrill Lynch	4.45	—	—	—	—
9. Goldman Sachs	4.38	8	8	10	10
10. Morgan Stanley	4.20	—	9	—	—

Source: "2005 Euromoney Foreign Exchange Poll," *Euromoney* (May 2005): 81, 82, 84.

recommendations, out-of-hours service/night desk, systems technology, innovation, risk appraisal, and e-commerce functions.[19]

For this reason, large companies may use several banks to deal in foreign exchange, selecting those that specialize in specific geographic areas, instruments, or currencies. For example, AT&T uses Citibank for its broad geographic spread and wide coverage of different currencies, but it also uses Deutsche Bank for euros, Swiss Bank Corporation for Swiss francs, NatWest Bank for British pounds, and Goldman Sachs for derivatives.

Table 9.4 identifies the top banks in the world in terms of foreign exchange trading. They are the key players in the OTC market and include both commercial banks (such as Citigroup and JPMorgan) and investment banks (such as UBS Warburg—the London-based investment banking division of Union Bank of Switzerland and Swiss Bank Corporation—and Goldman Sachs). Whether one is looking at overall market share of foreign-exchange trading, the ranking of best banks in specific locations, the best banks in the trading of specific currency pairs, or best dealers, these top 10 banks are usually at or near the top in every category.

In addition to the OTC market, there are a number of exchanges in which foreign-exchange instruments, mostly options and futures, are traded. Two of the best-known exchanges are the **Chicago Mercantile Exchange (CME)** and the Philadelphia Stock Exchange (PHLX). The CME offers futures and futures options contracts (contracts that are options on futures contracts rather than options on foreign exchange per se) in the euro, the Japanese yen, the Mexican peso, the Australian dollar, the British pound, the Canadian dollar, the Swiss franc, the Brazilian real, the South African rand, the New Zealand dollar, the Swedish krona, the Norwegian krone, and the Russian ruble. In 2005, CME entered into an agreement with Reuters to have their futures contracts quoted, which should increase the access of trades to futures contracts.[20]

The **Philadelphia Stock Exchange** is the only exchange in the United States that trades foreign-currency options. The PHLX lists six dollar-based standardized currency option contracts: Australian dollars, British pounds, Canadian dollars, euros, Japanese yen, and Swiss francs. The PHLX has been growing faster than the CME. Much of the growth has come from MNEs. Although options cost more than futures, big companies prefer them to futures (the CME instrument) because of their greater flexibility and convenience. We will provide some examples in Chapter 19 of how companies use options to hedge against foreign-exchange risks. However, the exchange-traded instruments are still very small compared with the OTC trades.

GLOBAL CAPITAL MARKETS

There are many reasons why currencies trade hands—for import and export transactions, for foreign direct and portfolio investments, for borrowing and lending money, and for raising equity capital. Each country has its own debt and equity markets, but in this section, we will look at the role of foreign debt and equity markets in moving currency from one country to another.

Eurocurrencies

The **Eurocurrency market** is an important source of debt financing for MNEs to complement what they can find in their domestic markets. A **Eurocurrency** is any currency that is banked outside its country of origin. More specifically, a **Eurodollar** is a certificate of deposit in dollars in a bank outside of the United States. Most Eurodollar CDs are held in London, but they could be held anywhere outside of the U.S. Currencies banked inside their country of origin are known as onshore currencies, and currencies banked outside their country of origin are known as offshore currencies. In essence, the Eurocurrency market is an offshore market. A major advantage of the Eurodollar market is that it is not regulated by the Federal Reserve Board because it is offshore. The same is true for other currencies and their major regulators. The Eurocurrency market started with the deposit of U.S. dollars in London banks, and it was called the Eurodollar market. As other currencies entered the offshore market, the broader "Eurocurrency" name was adopted for market use. Given the introduction of the euro as the new currency in Europe, the term *Eurocurrency* is confusing, but the Eurocurrency market predates the euro, and the confusion will probably not go away. Eurocurrencies could be dollars or yen in London, euros in the Bahamas, or British pounds in New York City. Eurodollars constitute a fairly consistent 65 to 80 percent of the Eurocurrency market. Dollars held by foreigners on deposit in the United States are not Eurodollars, but dollars held at branches of U.S. or other banks outside the United States are.

The major sources of Eurocurrencies are:

- Foreign governments or individuals who want to hold dollars outside the United States
- Multinational enterprises that have cash in excess of current needs
- European banks with foreign currency in excess of current needs
- Countries such as Germany, Japan, and Taiwan that have large balance-of-trade surpluses held as reserves

The demand for Eurocurrencies comes from sovereign governments, supranational agencies such as the World Bank, companies, and individuals. Eurocurrencies exist partly for the convenience and security of the user and partly because of cheaper lending rates for the borrower and better yield for the lender.

The Eurocurrency market is a wholesale (companies and other institutions) rather than a retail (individuals) market, so transactions are very large. Public borrowers such as governments, central banks, and public sector corporations are the major players. Although MNEs are involved in the Eurodollar market, the Eurodollar market has historically been an interbank market. Since the late 1990s, however, there has been a shift for London banks to use nonbank customers for Eurodollar transactions. This was partly because of the introduction of the euro, the subsequent fall in foreign transactions, and consolidation in the banking sector.[21]

The Eurocurrency market is both short and medium term. Short-term borrowing is comprised of maturities of less than one year. Anything from one to five years is considered a **Eurocredit,** which may be a loan, a line of credit, or another form of medium- and long-term credit, including **syndication,** in which several banks pool resources to extend credit to a borrower and spread the risk.

A Eurocurrency is any currency banked outside of its country of origin.

Major sources of Eurocurrencies

- Foreign governments or individuals
- MNEs
- Foreign banks
- Countries with large balance-of-payments surpluses

A Eurocredit is a type of loan that matures in one to five years.

Syndication occurs when several banks pool resources to make a large loan in order to spread the risk.

A major attraction of the Eurocurrency market is the difference in interest rates compared with those in domestic markets. Because of the large transactions and the lack of controls and their attendant costs, Eurocurrency deposits tend to yield more than domestic deposits do, and loans tend to be cheaper than they are in domestic markets. Traditionally, loans are made at a certain percentage above the **London Inter-Bank Offered Rate (LIBOR),** which is the deposit rate that applies to interbank loans within London. The LIBOR rates quoted on May 11, 2005, were 3.0900 percent one month; 3.2600 percent three months; 3.4750 percent six months; 3.7750 percent one year. The British Bankers' Association average of interbank offered rates for dollar deposits in the London market was based on quotations at 16 major banks.[22] At the same time, the prime rate in the United States was 6.0 percent, based on the best rate on corporate loans posted by 75 percent of the nation's 30 largest banks. In addition, prime rates were listed as 4.25 percent for Canada, 2.0 percent for the European Central Bank, 2.64 percent for Switzerland, 4.75 percent for Britain, and 1.375 percent for Japan. However, the *Wall Street Journal* noted that it is very difficult to compare prime rates and the LIBOR rate because lending practices vary so much from country to country.

The amount of the interest rate above LIBOR that a borrower is charged all depends on the creditworthiness of the customer, and it must be large enough to cover expenses and build reserves against possible losses. The Eurocurrency market's unique characteristics mean that the borrowing rate usually is less than it would be in the domestic market. Most loans are variable rate, and the rate-fixing period is generally six months, although it may be one or three months. Another unique characteristic of the Eurocurrency market is that it is completely unregulated. No single country or agency, not even the Bank for International Settlements, regulates Eurocurrency transactions.

LIBOR is the interest rate that banks charge each other on Eurocurrency loans.

International Bonds: Foreign, Euro, and Global

Many countries have active bond markets available to domestic and foreign investors. For example, Nissan raised money through bonds issued in Japan, the United States, and Europe. The bonds issued in yen are for ¥617 billion and mature (must be paid back) in 2007 at interest rates of 0.6 to 3.6 percent. The bonds issued in euros are for ¥17 billion and mature in 2006 at interest rates of 2.5 to 5.0 percent. Even though the domestic bond market dominates total bond issues, with the U.S. market offering the best opportunities, the international bond market still fills an important niche in financing. One of the reasons why the bond (and stock) markets in the United States are so influential is because the companies of continental Europe and Japan still rely disproportionately on banks for finance—on average, banks constitute about 75 percent of corporate funding. That figure varies across Europe—from 70 percent in Germany and France to 80 percent in Spain, but it is much lower in Britain.[23] This may change, however, because banks across the world are tightening their loan outflows as a result of emerging market collapses like the ones in Asia in 1997 and Argentina in 2002. Emerging bond markets have been growing more quickly than developed markets, but they are still only 5.6 percent of the total global bond market. Investors generally focus on purchasing foreign currency from emerging markets, but the bond market is four times as large as the currency market (i.e., $1,645 billion versus $432 billion). Emerging bond markets are gradually becoming an alternative source of funding for governments, corporations, and global fixed-income investors.[24]

The international bond market can be divided into foreign bonds, Eurobonds, and global bonds. **Foreign bonds** are sold outside of the borrower's country but are denominated in the currency of the country of issue. For example, a French company floating a bond issue in Swiss francs in Switzerland would be selling a foreign bond. Foreign bonds typically make up about 18 percent of the international bond market. They also have creative names, such as Yankee bond (issued in the United States), Samurai bond (issued in Japan), and Bulldog bond (issued in England) and Panda bond (China).

Foreign bonds are sold outside of the country of the borrower but in the currency of the country of issue.

A **Eurobond** is usually underwritten (placed in the market for the borrower) by a syndicate of banks from different countries and sold in a currency other than that of the country of issue. A bond issue floated by a U.S. company in dollars in London, Luxembourg, and Switzerland is a Eurobond. Eurobonds make up approximately 75 percent of the international bond market.

The **global bond**, introduced by the World Bank in 1989, is a combination of a domestic bond and a Eurobond—that is, it must be registered in each national market according to that market's registration requirements. It is also issued simultaneously in several markets, usually those in Asia, Europe, and North America. Global bonds are a small but growing segment of the international bond market.

The international bond market is an attractive place to borrow money. For one thing, it allows a company to diversify its funding sources from the local banks and the domestic bond market and borrow in maturities that might not be available in the domestic markets. In addition, the international bond markets tend to be less expensive than local bond markets. However, not all companies are interested in global bonds or Eurobonds. Before the Asian financial crisis hit, Asian companies relied on their domestic banks more because of the ready availability of cheap loans. In addition, the companies and banks tended to develop a cozier relationship than might be the case with Western companies and banks.[25] However, the Asian financial crisis demonstrated the fundamental flaws in this strategy as banks went bankrupt and as companies were forced to face the fact that they couldn't generate enough funds to pay back the loans.

Although the Eurobond market is centered in Europe, it has no national boundaries. In contrast to most conventional bonds, Eurobonds are sold simultaneously in several financial centers through multinational underwriting syndicates and are purchased by an international investing public that extends far beyond the confines of the countries of issue.

U.S. companies first issued Eurobonds in 1963 as a means of avoiding U.S. tax and disclosure regulations. They are typically issued in denominations of $5,000 or $10,000, pay interest annually, are held in bearer form, and are traded over the counter (OTC), most frequently in London.[26] Any investor who holds a bearer bond is entitled to receive the principal and interest payments. In contrast, for a registered bond, which is more typical in the United States, the investor is required to be registered as the bond's owner in order to receive payments. An OTC bond is traded with or through an investment bank rather than on a securities exchange, such as the London Stock Exchange.

An example of a non–U.S. dollar Eurobond issue is found in the 2002 annual report of Marks & Spencer, the British retail company. In 2002, Marks & Spencer issued a £368.2 million Eurobond at 6 3/8 percent fixed rate, which was stated to mature in 2011. Marks & Spencer then entered into an interest rate swap with another company in which it agreed to exchange its fixed rate obligation with a floating rate obligation.[27] An investment bank would have facilitated the swap. Marks & Spencer probably got a reasonably good Eurobond fixed interest rate because it is a British company and was issuing the bond in Eurosterling. The counterparty (the other company in the swap agreement) might have wanted a fixed rate obligation in sterling initially but couldn't get it for whatever reason, so it had to settle for a floating rate obligation. As interest rates in Britain began to come down, it made sense for Marks & Spencer to enter into the swap to lower its overall interest charge. In a floating rate bond, the interest rate changes every six months, so as interest rates come down, the holder of the floating rate bond would end up paying lower interest to the bondholders. The holder of the floating rate bond might have wanted to trade to a fixed rate bond to eliminate the uncertainty of future interest rates and to lock in an attractive interest rate.

Another example of the use of the Eurobond market is with Gazprombank of Russia. In January 2004, Gazprombank placed a US$300 million Eurobond issue with a maturity of 2008. Seventy percent of the issue went to European investors, 18 percent to offshore structures of investors from the U.S., 5 percent to Asians, and 7 percent to other regions. This was one of many Eurobond issues made by Gazprombank, some denominated in dollars and some in euros. The deals were placed by JP Morgan Chase in London.[28]

Eurobonds are sold in countries other than the one in whose currency the bond is denominated.

A global bond is registered in different national markets according to the registration requirements of each market.

Eurobonds are typically issued in denominations of $5,000 or $10,000, pay interest annually, are held in bearer form, and are traded over the counter.

Occasionally, Eurobonds may provide currency options, which enable the creditor to demand repayment in one of several currencies, thus reducing the exchange risk inherent in single-currency foreign bonds. More frequently, however, both interest and principal on Eurobonds are payable to the creditor in U.S. dollars. It is also possible to issue a Eurobond in one currency—say, the U.S. dollar—and then swap the obligation to another currency. (The process is similar to the interest-rate swap just described.) For example, a U.S. company with a subsidiary in Britain would generate large quantities of British pounds through normal operations, and it could use the pounds to pay off a British pound bond. If the U.S. company had issued Eurobonds in dollars in London, it could enter into a swap agreement through an investment bank to exchange its future dollar obligations with a British pound obligation and use the pound revenues to pay off the swapped obligation.

Equity Securities and the Euroequity Market

Another source of financing is equity securities, where an investor takes an ownership position in return for shares of stock in the company and the promises of capital gains—an appreciation in the value of the stock—and maybe dividends. One way a company can easily and inexpensively get access to capital is through a private placement with a venture capitalist. In this case, a wealthy venture capitalist (or perhaps a venture-capital firm investing the money of one or several wealthy individuals) will invest money in a new venture in exchange for stock. Another source of demand for private placements is the corporate restructuring market in Europe. In recent years, European mergers have primarily taken place between firms in the same country, but mergers are now crossing national borders. Cross-European mergers have increased the demand for cash, and private placements have helped to fill that demand.[29]

In addition to private placements, companies can access the equity-capital market, more commonly known as the stock market. Companies can raise new capital by listing their shares on a stock exchange, and they can list on their home-country exchange or on a foreign exchange. For example, Beijing-based China Techfaith Wireless Communication Technology Limited, a designer and manufacturer of mobile handsets, offered 8.73 million shares on an IPO on NASDAQ on May 5, 2005. Its underwriters were Merrill Lynch, Lehman Brothers, and CIBC World Markets Corporation. Its shares listed at $16.27, and it raised $141.8 million. Another example of an international IPO was the listing of Sistema on the London Stock Exchange in 2004. Sistema, the largest private sector consumer services company in Russia, issued a US$1.56 billion offering in London, the largest ever Russian IPO on a public market anywhere. Sistema's offering comprised 1.8 million common shares in the form of 91.6 million Global Depositary Receipts (GDR) with 50 GDRs representing one common share. Sistema needed access to equity dollars, which it was not able to raise inside Russia, so the Euroequity market in London was an obvious site for it to list. The growth in globalization has forced companies to look at equity markets as an alternative to debt markets and banks as a source of funds.

As Map 9.2 illustrates, the 10 largest stock markets in the world in terms of **market capitalization** (the total number of shares of stock listed times the market price per share) are in the developed countries. The numbers represent all of the markets in a particular country, not just the largest market in that country. For example, the U.S. stock market is the largest in the world, and the New York Stock Exchange is the largest stock market in the U.S., but there are other markets in the U.S. as well. The five biggest individual stock exchanges in the world in terms of market capitalization are the New York Stock Exchange, NASDAQ (U.S.), Tokyo Stock Exchange, London Stock Exchange, and Euronext, closely followed by Deutsche Borse and AMEX (U.S.)[30]

It has been interesting to track the development of the emerging stock markets, as Figure 9.6 shows. The emerging markets grew steadily as a percentage of total stock

MAP 9.2   Market Capitalization, 2001 (in billions of U.S. dollars)

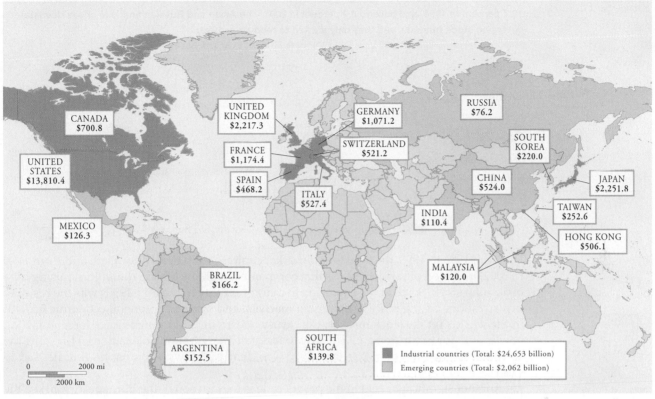

Stock markets in the developed countries far surpass those in emerging countries in terms of market capitalization (a measure of the size of a stock market: total number of shares listed times the price per share). Fifty percent of the world's market capitalization is in the U.S. market, which is comprised of the New York Stock Exchange, the American Stock Exchange, and the NASDAQ. The map illustrates the top 10 industrial markets and the top 10 emerging markets. Totals include all markets worldwide, not just the industrial and emerging countries shown on the map.

Source: Standard & Poor's, *Standard & Poor's Emerging Stock Markets Factbook 2002* (New York: McGraw-Hill, 2002).

market capitalization until the end of 1994. They dipped a little bit as a percentage of total in 1995 but recovered in 1996 to 11.1 percent of total. By 1998, however, the Asian financial crisis had clobbered the emerging stock markets, and they plunged to only 6.9 percent of total. Emerging stock markets have slowly recovered from the Asian crisis and Russian crisis of 1998. In 2000, the stock markets of developed countries, beginning with the ones in the United States, began falling. Then in 2002, the United States, in its first recession in 10 years, led the rest of the world into a global recession. At that point, investors turned their money from the United States and other major stock markets to emerging markets. However, a large supply of dollars in world markets and the recovery of the U.S. economy has brought a lot of investment capital back to the U.S. The real wild card in emerging stock markets is China. As China continues to liberalize its economy and as banks continue to have solvency problems, more and more Chinese companies are listing on Chinese exchanges, and China has the potential to become the largest emerging stock market in the world in a very short time.

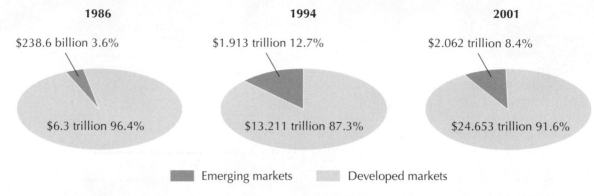

FIGURE 9.6   **GROWTH OF EMERGING STOCK MARKETS**

The market capitalization of emerging stock markets rose from 3.6 percent of the world's total in 1986 to 12.7 percent in 1994, and back to 8.4 percent in 2001. The Asian and Russian financial crises devastated emerging stock markets, and they only started to recover in 1999.

Standard & Poor's *Standard & Poor's Emerging Stock Markets Factbook 2002* (New York: McGraw-Hill, 2002).

1986   **1994**   **2001**

$238.6 billion 3.6% $1.913 trillion 12.7% $2.062 trillion 8.4%

$6.3 trillion 96.4% $13.211 trillion 87.3% $24.653 trillion 91.6%

■ Emerging markets   ■ Developed markets

From 1993 to 1998, the total world market capitalization nearly doubled, and from 1998 to 2002, it leveled off, which means that companies might be having difficulties raising cash by issuing stock. Some of the explosion in market activity in the mid-1990s was the result of privatizations taking place in emerging markets, and some was general economic growth in the world. Yet the stock market was clearly becoming a more significant force in raising new capital for expansion and as a way to facilitate mergers and acquisitions. However, the softening of the market in 2001 and 2002 was clearly a blow to companies that needed to raise cash for expansion.

Another significant event in the past decade is the creation of the **Euroequity** market, the market for shares sold outside the boundaries of the issuing company's home country. Prior to 1980, few companies thought about offering stock outside the national boundaries of their headquarters country. Since then, hundreds of companies worldwide have issued stock simultaneously in two or more countries in order to attract more capital from a wider variety of shareholders. For example, when Daimler and Chrysler merged and issued global shares around the world, it did so on 21 different markets in eight different countries: Germany, the United States, Austria, Canada, France, Britain, Japan, and Switzerland.

The Euroequity market is the market for shares sold outside the boundaries of the issuing company's home country.

The Stock Market of Buenos Aires, Argentina, an emerging market, is a flurry of activity as traders react to political and economic news in Argentina.

However, the trend of listing on more than one exchange, which was popular in the 1990s, is beginning to reverse. More and more companies are reducing the number of exchanges on which their stocks are listed. For example, in March 2005, IBM announced that it would remove its shares from the Tokyo Stock Exchange, after already removing its stock from exchanges in Vienna, Frankfurt, and Zurich. Investors are finding that the best price for their stocks is usually in their home market. Also, companies pay annual fees to list on exchanges, so if trading is light on a certain exchange, they can save money by listing on an exchange with heavier trading volume. Other reasons for delisting shares include weak market returns (fewer investors are putting their money into stocks) and increased regulation, such as the Sarbanes-Oxley Act in the United States. DaimlerChrysler still lists on 15 different stock exchanges in Germany, the United States, France, Japan, and Switzerland.

This trend toward delisting has affected even the New York Stock Exchange. Following its recent corporate governance problems, the New York Stock Exchange has decreased in popularity. However, it is still one of the most important stock exchanges in the world.[31] The U.S. market is important for U.S. and foreign companies looking for equity capital and is popular for Euroequity issues partly because of the market size and the speed with which offerings are completed. The large pension funds in the United States can buy big blocks of stock at low transaction costs. Pension fund managers regard foreign stocks as a good form of portfolio diversification.

The New York Stock Exchange identifies four major reasons why a foreign company should list on the NYSE (and these reasons could apply to U.S. companies trying to determine the benefits of listing on a foreign exchange):

1. The NYSE provides opportunities to develop a broad shareholder constituency in the United States through exposure to the widest possible range of individual and institutional investors.

2. The NYSE facilitates U.S. mergers and acquisitions through the use of an NYSE-listed security as acquisition currency.

3. The NYSE increases the visibility of a company, its products and services, and the trading of its shares in the United States.

4. The NYSE supports a company's incentive program for its U.S. employees by providing a liquid market in the United States for its shares.[32]

There are 460 foreign companies that list on the New York Stock Exchange, more than triple the number of companies that listed in 1993. The countries with the most companies listed on the NYSE are Canada (85), the United Kingdom (64), Brazil (37), Bermuda (35), the Netherlands (26) Mexico (20), and Chile (20).

The most popular way for a Euroequity to get a listing in the United States is to issue an **American Depositary Receipt (ADR).** An ADR is a negotiable certificate issued by a U.S. bank in the United States to represent the underlying shares of a foreign corporation's stock held in trust at a custodian bank in the foreign country. ADRs are traded like shares of stock, with each one representing some number of shares of the underlying stock. For example, there are 19 Japanese companies that list on the New York Stock Exchange, and all of them list ADRs. Toyota has listed ADRs on the NYSE since 1999 at a rate of two ADRs per common share of Toyota. They issue through a sponsored ADR facility operated by the Bank of New York as ADRs.

The United States is not the only market for Euroequities. There are also Global Depositary Receipts and European Depositary Receipts as illustrated in the Sistema example above, but the U.S. market dominates the depositary receipt market. However, compared to the NYSE, a much larger percentage of the total shares traded

An American Depositary Receipt (ADR) is a negotiable certificate issued by a bank that represents a share of stock of a foreign corporation.

on the London Stock Exchange belongs to foreign companies even though the total trading volume in the United States is quite large. Many foreign corporations try to raise capital in the United States, but they don't want to list on an exchange because they don't want to comply with the onerous reporting requirements of the SEC. However, those that do so get access to over 50 percent of the world's market capitalization, a fact that is a significant advantage to those that have a U.S. listing. Companies will generally list on their home country's exchange first and then venture into the international exchanges with depository receipts. Throughout the 1990s, funds raised from ADRs in developing countries averaged around $7 billion per year. Since the turn of the century, that figure has jumped to around $22 billion per year, peaking in 2000.[33]

The global share offering by DaimlerChrysler is the first of its kind in the world. Other companies with global share offerings listed on the NYSE are Celanese AG, UBS Warburg, and Deutsche Bank. It is important for MNEs to list their securities on foreign exchanges as mentioned earlier in the NYSE example. As MNEs generate more of their revenues outside of their home country, it is easier to attract investors from the countries where they are operating. As global stock markets continue to grow, especially in the emerging markets, it will be even easier for companies to raise equity capital outside of their home markets.

Some ADRs will list for the same price in the home country and foreign country exchange, but some companies list for different prices in different countries. Taiwan Semiconductor shares were worth 70 percent more in New York than they were in Taiwan in January 2000. Also, the ADRs of Infosys, an Indian software contractor, traded at nearly two-and-a-half times their value in India. At the same time, ADRs for Singapore, Japanese, and British companies were trading at the same value as in their home markets. There are a couple of reasons why that is the case. The latter countries are relatively open to the outside world, so traders spotting price differences in two markets can buy or sell securities until the price differences disappear. However, Taiwan and India have regulated markets in which foreigners are allowed to own only a certain percentage of the shares and in which currency controls make it difficult to buy and sell assets. In addition, the ADRs represent only a small percentage of the companies' shares. As the Asian markets begin to recover, the demand for high-tech stocks is pushing up the prices for ADRs. As markets open up, these price differences should eventually disappear.[34] There are a number of movements to improve stock market activity around the world. Europe's plan was to introduce a unified stock exchange once the euro was introduced. However, that remains one of the EU's unfinished projects. The beginning of this process was the creation in 2000 of Euronext N.V., which resulted from the merger of the exchanges of Amsterdam, Brussels, and Paris. In 2002, Euronext added the London International Financial Futures and Options Exchange (LIFFE), which was followed by a merger with the Portuguese exchange.

A major innovation in share trading around the world is electronic trading. U.S. electronic trading companies such as E*Trade and Charles Schwab & Company are now doing business in Europe and competing with local e-trade companies. Some of the large investment banks, such as J. P. Morgan, Morgan Stanley Dean Witter, and UBS Warburg, have joined together to strengthen Tradepoint, a British-based electronic exchange. Tradepoint Financial then began a collaboration with the SWX Swiss Exchange, resulting in a name change to virt-x. The SWX purchased the remaining shares of virt-x in 2003 and now operates as a private venture specializing in the trading of shares in Europe. More than 20 European fund managers, led by Merrill Lynch Mercury Asset Management and Barclays Global Investors, built their own electronic network, called E-Crossnet, the Investor's Crossing Network, which will help reduce the broker's role and the cost of making trades and which facilitates trading of shares in Europe. The whole world of e-trade could provide strong competition to stock exchanges in European as well as developing countries, just as it is beginning to put pressure on the major exchanges in the United States.[35]

A major source of competition to the stock exchanges will be the electronic trading of stocks through companies such as E*Trade.

POINT–COUNTERPOINT: SPECULATION IN CAPITAL MARKETS

POINT

As described above, there are a number of different reasons why people trade in foreign exchange, and one of them is speculation. Speculation per se is not illegal, nor is it necessarily bad. Just as stockbrokers invest people's money to try to earn a return that is higher than the market average, there are also foreign currency brokers who invest people's money in foreign exchange in order to make a profit for the investor. Speculation is merely taking a position in a currency in order to profit from market trends. However, speculation is not for the faint of heart. Political and economic conditions outside of the control of the speculators can quickly turn profits to losses, and probably quicker than is the case in the stock market. Currencies are inherently unstable. But currency speculation is a different way to invest money and allows investors to diversify their portfolios from traditional stocks and bonds. Just as foreign exchange can be traded for speculative purposes, trading in shares is also speculation. Even though we call such trades "investments," they are just another form of speculation hoping to gain a return that is higher than the market average and certainly higher than what a CD can yield.

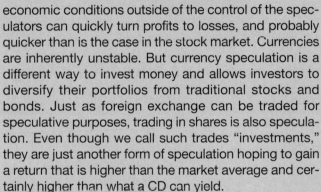

COUNTERPOINT

However, there are plenty of opportunities for a trader, whether in foreign exchange or securities, to make money illegally or contrary to company policy. One of the most publicized events in the derivatives markets in recent years involved 28-year-old Nicholas Leeson and 233-year-old British bank Barings PLC. Leeson, a trader for Barings PLC, went to Singapore in the early 1990s to help resolve some problems Barings was having. Within a year, he was promoted to chief trader. The problem was that he was responsible for trading securities and booking the settlements. This meant that there were no checks and balances on his trading actions, thus opening the door to possible fraud. When two different people are assigned to trade securities and book settlements, the person booking the settlements can confirm independently whether or not the trades were accurate and legitimate. In 1994, Leeson bought stock index futures on the Singapore International Monetary Exchange or SIMEX on the assumption that the Tokyo stock market would rise. Most traders watching Leeson's feverish trading activity assumed that Barings

had a large client that Leeson was trading for, but it turns out that he was using the bank's money to speculate. Because the Japanese economy was recovering, it made sense to assume that the market would continue to rise, thus generating more profits for Leeson and Barings. Unfortunately, something happened that nobody could predict—the January 17, 1995 earthquake that hit the port city of Kobe.

As a result of the devastation and uncertainty, the market fell, and Leeson had to come up with cash to cover the margin call on the futures contract. A margin is a deposit made as security for a financial transaction that is otherwise financed on credit. When the price of an instrument changes and the margin rises, the exchange "calls" the increased margin from the other party—in this case Leeson.[36] However, Leeson soon ran out of cash from Barings, so he had to come up with more cash. One approach he used was to write options contracts and use the premium he collected on the contracts to cover his margin call. Unfortunately, he was using Barings' funds to cover positions he was taking for himself, not for clients, and he also forged documents to cover his transactions. As the Tokyo stock market continued to plunge, Leeson fell farther and farther behind and eventually fled the country, later to be caught and returned to Singapore for trial. Barings estimated that Leeson generated losses in excess of $1 billion, which put Barings into bankruptcy. Eventually, the Dutch bank ING purchased Barings. Leeson's activities in the derivatives market were illegal and a violation of solid internal controls.

Finally, Leeson went to prison in Singapore (where he was treated for colon cancer as well). On July 3, 1999, Leeson was released from prison, and he returned to his native Britain.[37]

Since the collapse of Barings, measures have been put into place in banks to prohibit such consequences, yet negative outcomes of rogue trading continue to happen. In February 2002, Allied Irish Banks discovered that an employee, John Rusnak, at its U.S. subsidiary, Allfirst Bank, lost $750 million in foreign-exchange derivatives. At the end of 2000, Rusnak's trading showed a gain of $224 million, but the profit was not investigated by the bank because it was making a great deal of money off his trades. But because of the volatility of the U.S. market at that time, Rusnak's leveraged gains quickly turned to huge losses. AIB suspects Rusnak was involved with fictitious trades and collusion inside or outside of Allfirst Bank.[38]

LOOKING TO THE FUTURE: The Future of Foreign Exchange and Global Capital Markets

Significant strides have been made and will continue to be made in the development of foreign-exchange and capital markets. The speed at which transactions are processed and information is transmitted globally will certainly lead to greater efficiencies and more opportunities for foreign-exchange trading. The impact on companies is that costs of trading foreign exchange should come down, and companies should have faster access to more currencies.

In addition, exchange restrictions that hamper the free flow of goods and services should diminish as governments gain greater control over their economies and as they liberalize currency markets. Capital controls still impact foreign investment, but they will continue to become less of a factor for trade in goods and services.

The introduction of the euro has allowed cross-border transactions in Europe to progress more smoothly. As the euro solidifies its position in Europe, it will reduce exchange-rate volatility and should lead to the euro taking some of the pressure off the dollar so that it is no longer the only major vehicle currency in the world.

Finally, technological developments may not cause the foreign-exchange broker to disappear entirely, but they will certainly cause foreign-exchange trades to be executed more quickly and cheaply. The growth of Internet trades in currency will take away some of the market share of dealers and allow more entrants into the foreign-exchange market. Internet trade will also increase currency price transparency and increase the ease of trading, thus allowing more investors into the market.

SUMMARY

- Foreign exchange is money denominated in the currency of another nation or group of nations. The exchange rate is the price of a currency.

- The foreign-exchange market is divided into the over-the-counter market (OTC) and the exchange-traded market.

- The traditional foreign-exchange market is composed of the spot, forward, and FX swap markets. Other key foreign-exchange instruments are currency swaps, options, and futures.

- Spot transactions involve the exchange of currency on the second day after the date on which the two traders agree to the transaction.

- Outright forward transactions involve the exchange of currency three or more days after the date on which the traders agree to the transaction. An FX swap is a simultaneous spot and forward transaction.

- Approximately $1.2 trillion in foreign exchange is traded every day. The dollar is the most widely traded currency in the world (on one side of 90 percent of all transactions), and London is the main foreign-exchange market in the world.

- Foreign-exchange traders quote bid (buy) and offer (sell) rates on foreign exchange. If the quote is in American terms, the trader quotes the foreign currency as the number of dollars and cents per unit of the foreign currency. If the quote is in European terms, the trader quotes the dollar in terms of the number of units of the foreign currency. The numerator is called the "terms currency," and the denominator is called the "base currency."

- A convertible currency is one that companies can freely trade for other currencies. Some countries' currencies are partially convertible because residents are not allowed to convert them into other currencies, although nonresidents are allowed to do so.

- If the foreign currency in a forward contract is expected to strengthen in the future (the dollar equivalent of the foreign currency is higher in the forward market than in the spot market), the currency is selling at a premium. If the opposite is true, it is selling at a discount.

- An option is the right but not the obligation to trade foreign currency in the future. Options can be traded OTC or on an exchange.

- A foreign currency future is an exchange-traded instrument that guarantees a future price for the trading of foreign exchange, but the contracts are for a specific amount and specific maturity date.

- Companies use foreign exchange to settle transactions involving the imports and exports of goods and services, for foreign investments, and to earn money through arbitrage or speculation.

- Companies work with foreign exchange dealers to trade currency. Dealers also work with each other. Dealers can trade currency through voice brokers, electronic brokerage services, or directly with other bank dealers. Internet trades of foreign exchange are becoming more significant.

- The major institutions that trade foreign exchange are the large commercial and investment banks and securities exchanges. Commercial and investment banks deal in a variety of different currencies all over the world. The Chicago Mercantile Exchange specializes in futures contracts, and the Philadelphia Stock Exchange specializes in options.

- Two major sources of funds external to the MNE's normal operations are debt markets and equity markets.

- A Eurocurrency is any currency banked outside its country of origin, but it is primarily dollars banked outside the United States.

- A foreign bond is one sold outside the country of the borrower but denominated in the currency of the country of issue. A Eurobond, also called a global bond, is a bond issue sold in a currency other than that of the country of issue.

- The three largest stock markets in the world are in New York, Tokyo, and London, with the U.S. markets controlling nearly half of the world's stock market capitalization.

- Euroequities are shares listed on stock exchanges in countries other than the home country of the issuing company. Most foreign companies that list on the U.S. stock exchanges do so through American Depositary Receipts, which are financial documents that represent a share or part of a share of stock in the foreign company. ADRs are easier to trade on the U.S. exchanges than are foreign shares.

HSBC and the Peso Crisis in Argentina[39]   C A S E

HSBC Holdings plc is faced with a difficult decision regarding its Argentine subsidiary. Argentina's economy collapsed at the end of 2001, leaving both local and foreign companies suffering from a shortage of cash, a devaluing peso, and a burden of growing debt. HSBC lost $1.1 billion in 2001 because of Argentina's problems. However, the Argentine economy has recovered pretty well since the devaluation of the peso on January 8, 2002. Is the time right for HSBC to invest more in Argentina, or is it still too soon to tell?

London-based HSBC derives its name from its founding member, the Hongkong and Shanghai Banking Corporation Limited, which was established in 1865 to permit trade between China and Europe. Until the early twentieth century, Hongkong and Shanghai Banking Corporation set up offices and branches mainly in China and Southeast Asia—but also in India, Japan, Europe, and North America. As HSBC's Web site states, "In many of its branches, the bank was the pioneer of modern banking practice. From the outset, trade finance was a strong feature of the bank's business, with bullion, exchange, and merchant banking also playing an important part."

After World War II, Hongkong and Shanghai Banking Corporation expanded and diversified its business with acquisitions and alliances. Through the 1980s, it expanded into Canada, Australia, and the United States, and in the 1990s, it moved into Brazil and Argentina. In 1991, its member companies came together to form HSBC Holdings plc. HSBC pursues a balance of opportunities in developed economies and emerging markets and now has over 7,000 offices in 81 countries. It has stock market listings in London, Hong Kong, New York, and Paris.

HSBC's entry into Argentina began in 1997, when the bank acquired Roberts S.A. de Inversiones, changing its name to HSBC Argentina Holdings S.A. Along with the banking arm, HSBC bought into a general insurance agency with the purchase of Roberts. In 1994, HSBC united with New York Life to form a life and retirement insurance company, so the acquisition of Roberts was a strategic fit in both banking and insurance. HSBC Argentina has also acquired companies in pension fund management and medical care, thus creating a diversified portfolio in Argentina. HSBC is the seventh largest bank in Argentina as ranked by Tier One Capital and has 205 offices. In March 2004, it was recognized as the best bank in Argentina by *Apertura* magazine. The outlook for HSBC in Argentina looked good when it entered Argentina. In 1998, its first full year of operations, the bank had a pretax loss of $13 million but earned a profit of $67 million in 1999 and expected profits to continue growing at 100 percent.

To understand the decline of HSBC in Argentina, it is necessary to take a look at Argentina's economic history. Argentina's economy flourished in the beginning of the twentieth century, growing at an annual rate of 5 percent for three years. It attracted a flood of British and Spanish capital and was rated as one of the world's 10 richest countries—even ahead of France and Germany. However, it has been downhill since then. When Juan Perón ruled the country from 1946 to 1955, he instituted protectionist measures and printed money to finance generous benefits for workers. State intervention in all sectors led to poor productivity and structural weakness in the economy. Inflation plagued the country; there were two bouts of hyperinflation in the 1980s and two banking collapses. As a result, Argentines lost trust in the peso and invested in U.S. dollars or shipped their capital abroad.

In 1989, Carlos Menem took control of the country and set out to implement free-market reforms and to restructure monetary and economic policies. He privatized many state-run companies, tightened fiscal management, and opened up the country's borders to trade. Probably the most important policy he established was the Convertibility Law, which pegged the Argentine peso 1:1 with the U.S. dollar and restricted the money supply to its hard dollar currency reserves. This monetary arrangement was called a currency board and was established to impose discipline on the central bank. The new currency board accomplished what it set out to do: It halted inflation and attracted investment. Investors felt that there was little risk any more in investing in the peso, since it was pegged to the dollar. The sentiment that "the peso is as good as the dollar" was strong throughout the country. Because there was a stable money supply, this reduced inflation to nearly 0 percent through the rest of the 1990s and kept the exchange rate at a constant value. Real GDP grew by 6.1 percent from 1991 to 1997 compared to 0.2 percent from 1975 to 1990.

In spite of these positive developments, the currency board also had its drawbacks. It reduced the Argentine government's ability to respond to external shocks by allowing its exchange rate and monetary policy to be determined de facto by the United States. Interest rates were in reality set by the U.S. Federal Reserve; plus there was a risk margin for investing in Argentina. This arrangement was put to the test in 1995, when the Mexican peso devalued. Investors got nervous about Latin America in general and pulled investments out of Argentina. Its economy shrank by 4 percent, and many banks collapsed. The government responded by tightening bank regulation and capital requirements, and some of the larger banks took over weaker ones. Argentina increased exports and investment, and the country returned to 5.5 percent growth.

Unfortunately, the government wasn't so lucky with its results at the end of the 1990s. Commodity prices, on which Argentina heavily relied, declined; the U.S. dollar strengthened against other currencies; Argentina's main trading partner, Brazil, devalued its currency; and emerging economies' cost of capital increased. Argentina soon fell into a recession, with GDP falling to 3.4 percent in 1999 and unemployment increasing into the double digits. Argentina, because of its hard link to the dollar, was unable to compete internationally, especially in Brazil, because of its high prices. One way to correct this problem would be to devalue the currency to bring the value closer to its fundamental value. Argentina couldn't devalue unless it canceled the currency board, a move it didn't want to take because of the currency board's popularity and past success. The only way for Argentina to become more competitive was for prices to fall. As deflation set in, the government (and some private companies) found it difficult to pay its debt because it was not collecting as much revenue. Banks had been lending dollars at 25 percent interest rates even though the risk was supposed to be low.

Argentina was acquiring a burgeoning public debt. When the recession hit, tax revenue fell and spending increased to pay for such things as higher unemployment. Tax evasion is extremely high in Argentina, but the government did little to tackle the problem. The budget went from a surplus of 1.2 percent of GDP in 1993 to a deficit of 2.4 percent in 2000. Increased interest rate payments also added to the increasing budget deficit. From 1991 to 2000, the amount of interest rate payments increased from $2.5 billion to $9.5 billion annually. This drained the economy more as most of this money went to overseas investors. This currency "mismatching," meaning most of the debt is taken out in one currency but assets are held in another, was large in Argentina and would later prove disastrous.

Politicians found little they could do to help the struggling economy. They fiddled with tariffs and finally the currency board. They pegged the peso half to the dollar and half to the euro for exporters. The idea of devaluation scared investors and caused interest rates to rise even more. Unable to pay its interest payments and unwilling to declare a debt default, the government turned to the banks. The Menem government had strengthened the banking system, particularly the central bank, but his successor, Fernando de la Rua, sent a crushing blow to the sector. He strong-armed the banks into buying government bonds. This triggered a bank run, and Argentines withdrew over $15 billion between July and November 2001. In a desperate attempt to save the industry, Mr. de la Rua imposed a ceiling of $1,000 a month on bank withdrawals on December 1. Within days, the country defaulted on $155 million in public debt, the largest such default in world history. As rioters and looters took to the streets, Mr. de la Rua resigned.

Argentina struggled to find a president who was fit for the job. It went through a total of five presidents in four months, ending finally with Eduardo Duhalde. The government abandoned the currency board in January 2002 and let the peso float against the dollar. The peso began falling quickly, so the government spent around $100 million a day—to a total of $1.2 billion—to prop up the value. More money was leaking out of the banking system too (around $50 million a day), because the courts had overturned the freeze on withdrawals.

In March 2002, Mr. Duhalde imposed new restrictions on the foreign exchange market. Individuals could buy no more than $1,000 a day and companies no more than $10,000 a day. Banks and businesses had restrictions on the number of dollars they could hold and on how much money could be shipped abroad. Currency exchanges could only operate three to four hours each day—versus the typical seven hours. However, the courts kept overturning policies set by the government and had police arrest bank managers who didn't follow their rulings. Still unable to prevent the increasing flow of money out of the system, Duhalde closed all banks for a week. In the meantime, he proposed to forcibly convert billions of dollars in bank deposits into low-interest bonds. The senate refused the president's bond proposal, thus sending him back to the drawing board.

In order to repair its economy, Argentina sought help from the International Monetary Fund (IMF). However, the IMF continued to turn down Argentina's requests for help until it implemented some sweeping changes in its exchange-rate policy, fiscal policy, and banking system. In an attempt to find someone to blame, Duhalde started criticizing foreign-owned banks, such as HSBC, for not infusing more cash into the system from their headquarters. The central bank printed pesos to keep banks solvent, but this led to increased inflation. The national and provincial governments also used bond notes, quasi-currency, to pay many of their debts. This note was swapped in everyday transactions and surprisingly held its value against the peso. Almost a year after the initial freeze on bank deposits, the government lifted the remaining restrictions on withdrawing cash from banks, further easing the financial strain on the banking system.

In May 2003, Nestor Kirchner became the new president of Argentina, replacing Duhalde. Under the guidance of Kirchner and his economy minister, Roberto Lavagna, Argentina's economy has rebounded significantly. Although the country experienced hyperinflation after the abandonment of the peso's peg to the dollar, the devaluated peso is now one of the causes of the economic recovery. The peso was trading at .9920 pesos per dollar on December 31, 2001, but it fell to 3.39 pesos on December 31, 2002; 2.940 on December 31, 2003; 2.9760 on December 31, 2004; and 2.8920 on May 11, 2005. The peso is 70 percent cheaper against the dollar than it was in the 1990s, resulting in increased exports of farm products and other commodities. The devaluation has also resulted in new foreign direct investment and increased business with Brazil. The economy grew by 9 percent in 2004 and is expected to expand by 6.5 percent in 2005. Unemployment has decreased and the inflation rate has slowed.

Despite the economic growth stimulated by the devaluated peso, Argentina was still burdened by its huge debt to private creditors and the IMF. From the middle of 2002 to spring 2003, Argentina and the IMF disagreed on conditions of IMF aid. Argentina defaulted on debt payments to both the IMF and the World Bank, saying that it wouldn't make payments without a guarantee of aid from the IMF. The IMF, on the other hand, refused to grant that aid to Argentina without implementation of certain economic reforms, including spending cuts and restructuring in the banking sector. Four months after his victory, Kirchner and the IMF agreed on a deal that would allow Argentina to pay interest only on its $21 billion debt over the next three years.

In order to repay most of its debt, including overdue interest, Argentina proposed a plan to its creditors, asking them to write off 70 percent of the present net value of their government bonds. The majority of creditors reluctantly agreed, and in February 2005, Argentina closed on the biggest debt restructuring in history. However, Argentina still has debts worth nearly 75 percent of its annual economic output, and the country must agree on a new loan deal with the IMF as soon as possible.

HSBC's reaction to the crisis was similar to that of other banks in the country. It was forced to rethink loans and to decide if the political and economic instability of the country was worth the risk of continued operations. Due in part to the depreciation of the peso, HSBC lost $977 million in 2001 in Latin America, compared to a profit of $324 million in 2000. Overall, HSBC Holdings doubled its bad-debt charges to $2.4 billion, and pretax profits fell by 14 percent in 2001.

Because of the pesification instituted by the Argentine government, loan repayments to HSBC were deeply discounted. In June 2002, HSBC refused a loan payment by Perez Companc, an energy holding company, because the payment was in pesos. The original loan was for $101 million and Perez's offered payment of 104.57 pesos only equaled about $28 million at market rates. HSBC argued that debt was not covered by pesification. Despite early losses after the initial economic collapse, HSBC has remained in Argentina throughout its financial crisis and tumultuous recovery. HSBC paid on all its external obligations and has continued to capitalize its Argentine subsidiary to maintain its stability. However, after the initial crisis, HSBC refused to infuse new capital in the Argentine operations, forcing HSBC to operate on funds generated in Argentina. After suffering a $210 million loss in 2002, the Argentine subsidiary of HSBC recorded profits of $48 and $156 million in 2003 and 2004, respectively.

QUESTIONS

1. What are the major factors that caused the peso to fall in value against the dollar? What has the government done to reverse the recession?
2. What has been Argentina's experience with the IMF? Has the IMF been helpful or not?
3. How has the fall in the value of the peso affected business opportunities for companies doing business in Argentina and in exporting and importing?
4. Should HSBC invest more money in its operations in Argentina? What factors should they monitor as they make their decision?

CHAPTER NOTES

1 Sources for this case include the following: Ioan Grillo, "Wired Cash," *Business Mexico*, 12/13, no. 12/1 (Mexico City: 2003): 44; Julie Rawe, "The Fastest Way to Make Money," *Time* (June 23, 2003): A6; Rosa Salter Rodriguez, "Money Transfers to Mexico Peak as Mother's Day Nears," *The Journal Gazette* (Ft. Wayne, Ind., May 1, 2005): 1.D; Deborah Kong, "Mexicans Win Back Fee on Money They Wired," *The Grand Rapids Press* (Grand Rapids, Mich., Dec. 19, 2002): A.9; Karen Krebsbach, "Following the Money," *USBanker* 112, no. 9 (Sept. 2002): 62; Tyche Hendricks, "Wiring Cash Costly for Immigrants," *San Francisco Chronicle* (March 24, 2002): A.23; Nancy Cleeland, "Firms Are Wired into Profits," *Los Angeles Times* (Nov. 7, 1997): 1; David Fairlamb, Geri Smith, and Frederik Blafour, "Can Western Union Keep On Delivering?" *Business Week* (Dec. 29, 2003): 57; Heather Timmons, "Western Union: Where the Money Is—in Small Bills," *Business Week* (November 26, 2001): 40.

2 Sam Y. Cross, *All About the Foreign Exchange Market in the United States* (New York: Federal Reserve Bank of New York, 2002), 9.

3 Ibid.

4 Ibid., 31.

5 Bank for International Settlements, "Central Bank Survey of Foreign Exchange and Derivatives Market Activity 2004" (Basel, Switzerland: BIS, March 2005), http://www.bis.org/publ/rpfx05t.htm.

6 Cross, op. cit., 19.

7 Bank for International Settlements, op. cit., 8.

8 Gabriele Galati and Kostas Tsatsaronis, "The Impact of the Euro on Europe's Financial Markets," Bank for International Settlements (Basel, Switzerland: BIS, July 2001), http://www.bis.org/publ/work100.pdf#xml=http://search.atomz.com/search/pdfhelper.tk?sp=o=33,100000,0.

9 Cross, op. cit., 12.

10 See "Currencies" page in "Market Prices" page of the *Financial Times*, http://www.ft.com/. Also see "Currencies" page in "Markets & Investing" page in CNN Financial News, http://www.cnnfn.com/markets/currencies/; and Web links for Chapter 9 on the home page for the textbook for more links.

11 Natalia T. Tamirisa, "Exchange and Capital Controls as Barriers to Trade," IMF Staff Papers 46, no. 1 (March 1999): 69.

12 Craig Karmin, "Currency Game Is Plenty Big, Plenty Tough," *Wall Street Journal* (May 6, 2005): C1.

13 Bank for International Settlements, op. cit., 8.

14 Ibid.

15 Bank for International Settlements, Alan Chaboud, and Steven Weinberg, "Foreign Exchange Markets in the 1990s," *BIS Papers,* no. 12, part 8 (August 2002): http://www.bis.org/publ/bppdf/.

16 Stephanie Cook, "Will Brokers Go Broke?" *Euromoney* (May 1996): 90.

17 Bank for International Settlements, "A Look at Trading Volumes in the Euro" (February 2000): http://www.bis.org/publ/r_qt0002e.pdf.

18 "Free for All; Foreign-Exchange Trading," *The Economist* (Dec. 11, 2004): 79.

19 See "The Big Get Bigger—But Is It for the Best?" *Euromoney* (May 2005): 74; and "Life After Execution," *Euromoney* (May 1999): 90.

20 Deborah Kimbell, "E-FX Takes Another Step Forward," *Euromoney* (February 2005): 1.

21 Patrick McGuire, "A Shift in London's Eurodollar Market," *BIS Quarterly Review* (September 2004): 67.

22 "Money Rates," *Wall Street Journal* (May 11, 2002): www.wsj.com.

23 "Europe's American Dream," *The Economist* (November 21, 1998): 71.

24 "Global Financial Stability Report," *International Monetary Fund* (September 2002): 48.

25 "An Offer They Can Refuse," *Euromoney* (February 1995): 76.

26 Anant Sundaram, "International Financial Markets," *Handbook of Modern Finance,* ed. Dennis E. Logue (New York: Warren, Gorham, Lamont, 1994), F3–F4.

27 "Financial Review," *Marks & Spencer Annual Report and Financial Statements* (2002): http://www2.marksandspencer.com/thecompany/investorrelations/annualreport/fin_review.shtml.

28 "Gazprombanks's Eurobonds," http://www.gazprombank.ru/eng/corporate/securities/eurobonds/index.wbp (May 24, 2005).

29 "Private Equity Stirs Up the Pot," *Euroweek* (October 1999): 27–34.

30 NYSE Market Statistics. http://www.nyse.com/Frameset.html?displayPage=/marketinfo/1022221393893.html (May 25, 2005).

31 Aaron Lucchetti and Craig Karmin, "Intensity to Be a 'Global' Stock Has Waned," *Wall Street Journal* (May 10, 2005): C1.

32 "Non-U.S. Listed Companies" (2005): www.nyse.com/international/international.html.

33 "Global Financial Stability Report," International Monetary Fund (2002), www.imf.org: 56.

34 "American Depositary Receipts: Over the Odds," *The Economist* (January 15, 2000): 77.

35 Stanley Reed, "Bourse Busters," *Business Week* (August 16, 1999): 52–53.

36 More specifically, Leeson did not actually buy the contracts outright but paid a certain percentage of the value of the contract, known as the "margin." When the stock market fell, the index futures contract became riskier, and the broker who sold the contract required Leeson to increase the amount of the margin.

37 See "The Collapse of Barings: A Fallen Star," *The Economist* (March 4, 1995): 19–21; Glen Whitney, "ING Puts Itself on the Map by Acquiring Barings," *Wall Street Journal* (March 8, 1995): B4; John S. Bowdidge and Kurt E. Chaloupecky, "Nicholas Leeson and Barings Bank Have Vividly Taught Some Internal Control Issues," *American Business Review* (January 1997): 71–77; "Trader in Barings Scandal Is Released from Prison," *Wall Street Journal* (July 6, 1999): A12; Ben Dolven, "Bearing Up," *Far Eastern Economic Review* (July 15, 1999): 47; "Nick Leeson and Barings Bank," bbc.co.uk, http://www.bbc.co.uk/crime/caseclosed/nickleeson.shtml, accessed May 19, 2005.

38 "The Ogre Returns," *The Economist* (February 14, 2002): www.economist.com.

39 Information for this case found on HSBC's Web site, www.hsbc.com, and the following: Dean Baker and Mark Weisbrot, "What Happened to Argentina," *Center for Economic and Policy Research* (January 31, 2002), http://www.cepr.net/IMF/what_happened_to_argentina.htm; "A Decline Without Parallel," *The Economist* (February 28, 2002), www.economist.com; "HSBC/Argentina –2: To Work with the Argentine Govt.," *Dow Jones,* March 4, 2002, http://216.239.37.100/search?q=cache:Nmw7jFQFeREC:sg.biz.yahoo.com/020304/15/2k8tv.html+hsbc+argentina&hl=en&ie=UTF-8; "Argentina Hits HSBC Profits," *BBC News* (March 4, 2002), http://news.bbc.co.uk/1/hi/business/1853342.stm; Larry Rohter, "Peso Down Steeply, Argentines Strengthen Currency Curbs," *New York Times* (March 26, 2002), www.nytimes.com; "Sympathy, But No Cash," *The Economist* (April 22, 2002), www.economist.com; Larry Rohter, "Argentine President Unveils Crisis Legislation," *New York Times* (April 23, 2002), www.nytimes.com; "Scraping Through the Great Depression," *The Economist* (May 30, 2002), www.economist.com; "Spoilt for Choice," *The Economist* (May 31, 2002), www.economist.com; "HSBC Rejects Perez Compancu Peso Debt Payment," Reuters June 21, 2002, www.reuters.com; "Carving Up the Scraps of Power," *The Economist* (September 5, 2002), www.economist.com; "Duhalde Sifts Budget Priorities, Raising Federal Wages, Benefits," *Wall Street Journal* (September 10, 2002), www.wsj.com; Andrew B. Abel and Ben S. Bernanke, *Macroeconomics*

(Reading, MA: Addison-Wesley, 2003), 20–22; Colin Barraclough, "Reversal of Fortune,"
Business Week (May 9, 2005): 56; "Menem Pulls Out of Argentina Race," BBC News (May 15, 2003),
http://news.bbc.co.uk/1/hi/world/americas/ 3025841.stm; "Argentina Wins Vital IMF Deal,"
BBC News (September 11, 2003), http://news.bbc.co.uk/ 1/hi/business/3098590.stm;
"Argentina Takes Hard Line on IMF," BBC News (February 28, 2005),
http://news.bbc.co.uk/1/hi/business/4304317.stm.

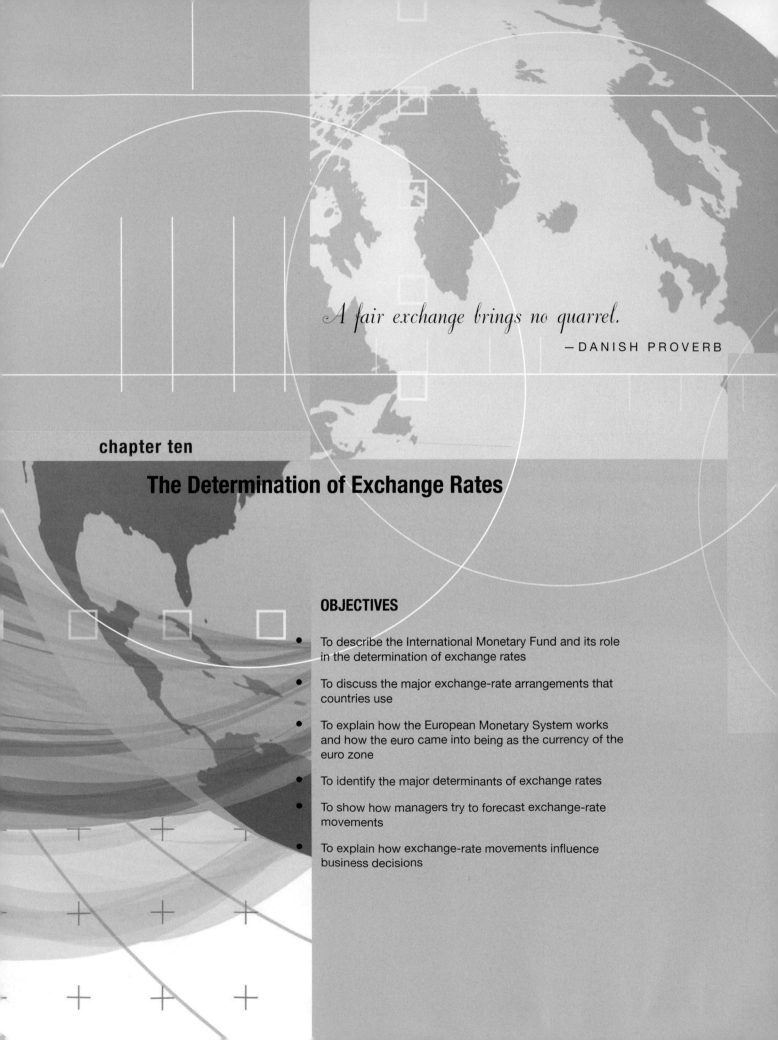

A fair exchange brings no quarrel.

—DANISH PROVERB

chapter ten

The Determination of Exchange Rates

OBJECTIVES

- To describe the International Monetary Fund and its role in the determination of exchange rates

- To discuss the major exchange-rate arrangements that countries use

- To explain how the European Monetary System works and how the euro came into being as the currency of the euro zone

- To identify the major determinants of exchange rates

- To show how managers try to forecast exchange-rate movements

- To explain how exchange-rate movements influence business decisions

CASE: EL SALVADOR AND THE U.S. DOLLAR[1]

El Salvador, a country of 6.5 million people, is the smallest and most densely populated country in Central America (see Map 10.1) and is about the size in area of the state of Massachusetts in the U.S. El Salvador is a member of the Central American Common Market (CACM), which also includes Costa Rica, Guatemala, Honduras, and Nicaragua. In 1994, the government of El Salvador decided to peg the colon, the country's currency, to the U.S. dollar (USD). After keeping the currency pegged to the dollar for seven years, the government decided to do away with the colon in 2001 and adopt the dollar as their currency. Now, El Salvador is one of 41 countries that have entered into an exchange arrangement in which they do not have their own currency. Among the other countries that do not have their own currency are the countries in the euro zone—Austria, Belgium, Finland, France, Germany, Greece, Ireland, Italy, Luxembourg, the Netherlands, Portugal, and Spain. Instead of using their own national currencies, they use the euro. Two other countries in Latin America have adopted

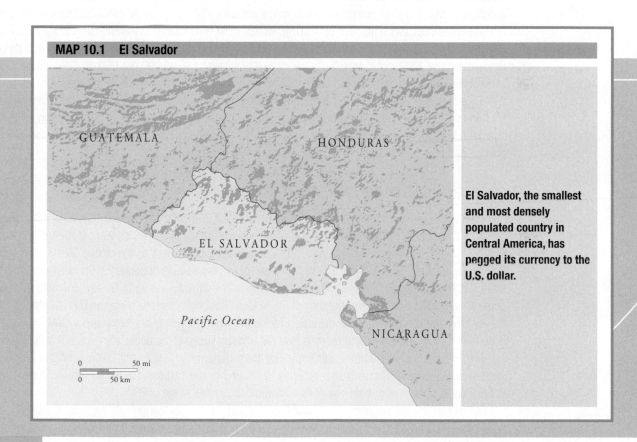

MAP 10.1   El Salvador

El Salvador, the smallest and most densely populated country in Central America, has pegged its currency to the U.S. dollar.

the dollar as their currency—Panama, which adopted the dollar when it gained independence from Colombia over a century ago, and Ecuador, which dollarized its economy in 2000 as a means of eliminating hyperinflation.

Why did El Salvador adopt the dollar? The economy of El Salvador is closely tied to the U.S. economy. At the time of the switchover to the dollar, the U.S. imported over two-thirds of El Salvador's exports. In addition, over 2 million Salvadoreans lived in the United States and wired home nearly $2 billion a year to relatives. This is over four times the total merchandise exports of El Salvador and nearly one-seventh of El Salvador's GDP. By switching to the dollar, companies and the government in El Salvador were able to get access to cheaper interest rates since dollarization eliminated, or at least reduced, the risk of devaluation, thereby infusing more confidence in foreign banks to lend to El Salvador. Corporate borrowing rates are among the lowest in Latin America and consumer credit rose as lower interest rates made it more attractive to borrow.

ECUADOR'S EXPERIENCE

Ecuador's situation was a little different from that of El Salvador, but it tied its currency to the dollar in 2000. Ecuador has a population double the size of El Salvador and a GNI a little less than twice that of El Salvador. In addition, it doesn't rely on the U.S. market as much as does El Salvador. When Ecuador decided to dollarize its economy, the president was in the midst of a political crisis, and the announcement to dollarize was totally unexpected. In 1999, Ecuador's consumer price inflation was 52.2 percent, the highest in Latin America. Until February 1999, the Central Bank had maintained a crawling peg exchange-rate system. However, pressure on the currency forced the Central Bank to leave the peg and allow the currency to float freely. It promptly devalued by 65 percent in 1999. At that time, Panama was the only country in Latin America that had dollarized, although Argentina had officially linked its currency to the dollar, so Ecuador was seen as a test case that many thought would spread to other countries in Latin America, especially El Salvador. A World Bank official, discussing the rationale for Ecuador's decision, noted that "most countries have a large amount of their debt in dollars, maintain a large percent of their reserves abroad in dollars, and write contracts indexed to the dollar." In addition, Ecuador, a member of OPEC, generates most of its foreign exchange earnings from oil, which is also priced in dollars. One difference between Ecuador and El Salvador is that Ecuador maintains its currency, the sucre (ESC), but it pegs the currency to the dollar at ESC 25,000 per USD. El Salvador no longer uses its currency but instead uses the dollar. Ecuador's experiment with dollarization has been successful, but it has not been easy. When dollarization became official in 2000, inflation rose to 96.1 percent. But it dropped back to 29.2 percent in 2001, less than 20 percent in 2002, less than 7 percent in 2003, and an estimated 2 percent in 2004. However, with 70 percent of the population living below the poverty level, Ecuador still has political and economic problems that dollarization alone will not cure.

CHALLENGES WITH DOLLARIZATION

As noted above, there are many advantages to dollarization, but what are the disadvantages? Consider El Salvador's neighbors. When El Salvador dollarized, over two-thirds of its exports went to the United States. By 2003, that had changed: 19.4 percent of El Salvador's exports went to the United States, putting the U.S. in the number two spot after Guatemala. Four of the top five destinations for Salvadorean products were CACM countries. On the import side, the U.S. was the largest supplier to El Salvador, with 34.2 percent of the market. The top five countries of origin for El Salvador's imports were the U.S., Guatemala, the EU, Mexico, and Ecuador. Of these countries, Mexico is closely linked to the dollar due to NAFTA, Ecuador is dollarized, and Guatemala's currency is also very closely linked to the dollar, although officially it is considered to have a freely floating currency. But from January 1, 2002 until December 31, 2004, the Guatemalan quetzal had actually strengthened by about 3 percent against the dollar. Thus 55.8 percent of El Salvador's imports were from countries that were closely tied to the USD.

El Salvador's other neighbors in Central America had different exchange-rate regimes. Costa Rica and Nicaragua had crawling pegs, which meant that their currencies are adjusted periodically in response to selected indicators, such as relative rates of inflation in comparison with major trading partners. However, the change is not as extreme as would be the case of an independently floating regime. Since 2002, the Costa Rican colon had fallen 32.7 percent against the dollar, and the Nicaraguan cordoba had fallen 18 percent against the dollar. The Honduran lempira was officially classified by the International Monetary Fund as an exchange rate within a crawling band, which means that the lempira maintains a value plus or minus 1 percent from a central rate, which is determined in the same way as the crawling peg described above. It gives a little more flexibility to its currency value, and the lempira has fallen about 16 percent against the dollar since 2002. The only currency that has stayed pretty close to the value of the dollar since 2002 is the Guatemalan quetzal, as mentioned above.

The problem this creates for Salvadorean companies is that they are increasingly having difficulty in export markets due to the strength of their currency against those of its Central American neighbors. How can they possibly compete against companies from Nicaragua and Honduras when those currencies have fallen by 18 percent and 16 percent against the dollar? That means that Nicaraguan and Honduran companies are reaping a huge cost advantage in export markets. El Salvador has had to move into new sources of growth, such as shipping, tourism, and communications, to avoid having its economy hollowed out due to higher costs relative to its neighbors. Many Salvadorean companies have had to change the way they do business. Fresco Group S.A., a family-owned textile company in El Salvador, has struggled to compete. Although the company was able to get low-cost loans to fund an expansion of facilities, it has had to move away from simple stitching of garments to creating designs, procuring materials, and manufacturing clothing based on a single sketch. Basically, Fresco Group has had to move upscale and leave the lower end manufacturing to other Central American companies that have benefited from weak currencies. In addition, Fresco Group is concerned about its ability to compete with textile companies from India and China since textile and garment quotas were eliminated in 2005. Management wonders if they can move upscale fast enough and convince customers that their small size and better flexibility will overcome their cost disadvantage due to the strong dollar relative to other currencies in Central America. In addition, should El Salvador continue to use the dollar as its currency? Is it possible that the other members of CACM should move to a dollar-based economy as they move to closer integration and membership in the Central American Free Trade Agreement?

INTRODUCTION

As we learned in Chapter 9, an exchange rate represents the number of units of one currency needed to acquire one unit of another currency. Although this definition seems simple, it is important that managers understand how governments set an exchange rate and what causes the rate to change. Such understanding can help them both anticipate exchange-rate changes and make decisions about business factors that are sensitive to those changes, such as the sourcing of raw materials and components, the placement of manufacturing and assembly, and the choice of final markets.

THE INTERNATIONAL MONETARY FUND

In 1944, toward the close of World War II, the major Allied governments met in Bretton Woods, New Hampshire, to determine what was needed to bring economic stability and growth to the postwar world. As a result of the meetings, the **International Monetary Fund (IMF)** came into official existence on December 27, 1945, and began financial operations on March 1, 1947.[2]

Twenty-nine countries initially signed the IMF agreement. There were 184 member countries at the beginning of 2005. The IMF's major objectives are:

- To promote international monetary cooperation
- To facilitate the expansion and balanced growth of international trade
- To promote exchange-rate stability
- To establish a multilateral system of payments
- To make its resources available to its members who are experiencing balance-of-payments difficulties[3]

The **Bretton Woods Agreement** established a system of fixed exchange rates under which each IMF member country set a **par value** for its currency based on gold and the U.S. dollar. Because the dollar was valued at $35 per ounce of gold, the par value would be the same whether gold or the dollar was used as the basis for par value. This par value became a benchmark by which each country's currency was valued against other currencies. Currencies were allowed to vary within 1 percent of their par value (extended to 2.25 percent in December 1971), depending on supply and demand. Additional moves from par value and formal changes in par value were possible with IMF approval. As we'll see later, par values were done away with when the IMF moved to greater exchange-rate flexibility.

Because of the U.S. dollar's strength during the 1940s and 1950s and its large reserves in monetary gold, currencies of IMF member countries were denominated in terms of gold and U.S. dollars. By 1947, the United States held 70 percent of the world's official gold reserves. Therefore, governments bought and sold dollars rather than gold. The understanding—though not set in stone—was that the United States would redeem dollars for gold. The dollar became the world benchmark for trading currency, and it has remained so.

When a country joins the IMF, it contributes a certain sum of money, called a quota, relating to its national income, monetary reserves, trade balance, and other economic indicators. The quota is a pool of money that the IMF can draw on to lend to countries. It is the basis of how much a country can borrow from the IMF and the amount the country can receive from the IMF as the allocation of special assets called Special Drawing Rights, which will be discussed shortly. Finally, the quota determines the voting rights of the individual members. At the beginning of 2005, the total quota held by the IMF was SDR 213 billion (US$327 billion). The United States has the largest quota, comprising 17.5 percent of the total. The next four countries are Japan (6.26 percent), Germany (6.11 percent), France (5.05 percent), and the United Kingdom (also 5.05 percent).[4] The Board of Governors, the IMF's highest authority, is composed of one representative from each member country. The number of votes a country has depends on the size of its quota. The Board of Governors is the final authority on key matters, but it leaves day-to-day authority to a 24-person Board of Executive Directors.[5]

IMF Assistance

In addition to identifying exchange-rate regimes, which we'll discuss in more depth later, the IMF provides a great deal of assistance to member countries. The IMF negotiates with a country to provide financial assistance if the country will agree to adopt certain policies to stabilize its economy. After its financial crisis in 2002, Argentina sought help from the IMF in paying back its massive debt. The IMF refused to lend to Argentina until Argentina complied with certain stringent economic criteria. In September 2003, Argentina's new president, Nestor Kirchner, announced a new economic program to restore economic growth and reduce poverty. The reforms included establishing a medium-term fiscal framework to ensure continued growth, strengthening the banking system, and facilitating corporate debt restructuring. The IMF accepted these reforms and extended a US$12.5 billion loan to help Argentina repay its debt. The loan is drawn out in stages as the country meets benchmarks and performance criteria established by the IMF.[6] However, the IMF encouraged Argentina to reach an agreement with holders of $103 billion in bonds that includes individual bondholders from all over the world. Argentina only wants to give bondholders 25 percent of their original investment in a debt-swap proposal that is not very popular among bondholders or the IMF. Argentina needs to get two-thirds of its bondholders to agree to the debt swap program in order for the IMF to improve its relationship with Argentina and give Argentina access to world debt markets.[7]

Special Drawing Rights (SDRs)

To help increase international reserves, the IMF created the **Special Drawing Right (SDR)** in 1969. The SDR is an international reserve asset created to supplement members' existing reserve assets (official holdings of gold, foreign exchange, and reserve positions in the IMF). SDRs serve as the IMF's unit of account and are used for IMF transactions and operations. By **unit of account,** we mean the unit in which the IMF keeps its records. For example, we noted earlier that the total quota the IMF holds is SDR 213 billion, which at current exchange rates (i.e., in the spring of 2005) was about $327 billion. The value of the SDR is based on the weighted average of five currencies. On January 1, 1981, the IMF began to use a simplified basket of five currencies for determining valuation. At the end of 2004, the U.S. dollar made up 39 percent of the value of the SDR; the euro, 36 percent; the Japanese yen, 13 percent; and the British pound, 12 percent.[8] These weights were chosen because they broadly reflected the importance of each particular currency in international trade and payments. The value of the SDR can be found daily in key business publications, such as the *Wall Street Journal* and the *Financial Times* of London, as well as many online currency services. Unless the Executive Board decides otherwise, the weights of each currency in the valuation basket change every five years. The Board determined this rule in 1980. A new value was established in 2000

IMF quota—the sum of the total assessment to each country, which becomes a pool of money that the IMF can draw on to lend to other countries. It forms the basis for the voting power of each country—the higher its individual quota, the more votes a country has.

The IMF lends money to countries to help ease balance-of-payments difficulties.

The SDR is
- An international reserve asset given to each country to help increase its reserves
- The unit of account in which the IMF keeps its financial records

Currencies making up the SDR basket are the U.S. dollar, the euro, the Japanese yen, and the British pound.

for the period 2001 to 2005, and the Board will decide whether or not to make a new determination in 2005 to become effective on January 1, 2006. One change to the basket in 2000 was an increase in the amount of the U.S. dollar as a move to take some of the weight off the euro, which was previously composed of the German mark and the French franc.

Although the SDR was intended to serve as a substitute for gold, it has not taken over the role of gold or the dollar as a primary reserve asset. However, several countries base the value of their currency on the value of the SDR.[9]

Evolution to Floating Exchange Rate

The IMF's system was initially one of fixed exchange rates. Because the U.S. dollar was the cornerstone of the international monetary system, its value remained constant with respect to the value of gold. Other countries could change the value of their currency against gold and the dollar, but the value of the dollar remained fixed.

On August 15, 1971, President Richard Nixon announced that the United States would no longer trade dollars for gold unless other industrial countries agreed to support a restructuring of the international monetary system. The resulting **Smithsonian Agreement** of December 1971 had several important aspects:

- An 8 percent devaluation of the dollar (an official drop in the value of the dollar against gold)
- A revaluation of some other currencies (an official increase in the value of each currency against gold)
- A widening of exchange-rate flexibility (from 1 percent to 2.25 percent on either side of par value)

This effort did not last, however. World currency markets remained unsteady during 1972, and the dollar was devalued again by 10 percent in early 1973 (the year of the Arab oil embargo and the start of fast-rising oil prices and global inflation). Major currencies began to float (i.e., each one relied on the market to determine its value) against each other instead of relying on the Smithsonian Agreement.

Because the Bretton Woods Agreement was based on a system of fixed exchange rates and par values, the IMF had to change its rules to accommodate floating exchange rates. The **Jamaica Agreement** of 1976 amended the original rules to eliminate the concept of par values in order to permit greater exchange-rate flexibility. The move toward greater flexibility can occur on an individual country basis as well as on an overall system basis. Let's see how this works.

EXCHANGE-RATE ARRANGEMENTS

The Jamaica Agreement formalized the break from fixed exchange rates. As part of this move, the IMF began to permit countries to select and maintain an exchange-rate arrangement of their choice, provided they communicate their decision to the IMF. The IMF has a surveillance program that allows it to monitor the economic policies of countries that would affect those countries' exchange rates. It also consults annually with countries to see if they are acting openly and responsibly in their exchange-rate policies. Each year, the countries notify the IMF of the exchange-rate arrangement they will use, and then the IMF uses the information provided by the country and evidence of how the country acts in the market to place each country in a specific category. There used to be three broad categories, but the IMF has now divided the countries into several categories, as Table 10.1 shows.

From Pegged to Floating Currencies

In the first three categories in Table 10.1, countries lock the value of their currency onto another currency. As illustrated in the opening case, Ecuador and El Salvador are two countries in the first category that have adopted the dollar as their currency. Fourteen countries

Exchange-rate flexibility was widened in 1971 from 1 percent to 2.25 percent from par value.

The Jamaica Agreement of 1976 resulted in greater exchange-rate flexibility and eliminated the use of par values.

The IMF surveillance and consultation programs are designed to monitor exchange-rate policies of countries and to see if they are acting openly and responsibly in exchange-rate policies.

Broad IMF categories for exchange-rate regimes

- Peg exchange rate to another currency or basket of currencies with little or no flexibility
- Peg exchange rate to another currency or basket of currencies with trading occurring within a band
- Allow the currency to float in value against other currencies, either managed or not managed

TABLE 10.1   EXCHANGE-RATE REGIMES, 2004

Exchange rates can be either fixed or pegged to another currency under very narrow fluctuations (exchange arrangements with no separate legal tender, currency board arrangements, or other conventional fixed peg arrangements), pegged to something else with a wider band of fluctuation (pegged exchange rates within horizontal bands), and floating (crawling pegs, exchange rates within crawling bands, managed floating, or independently floating).

REGIMES	NUMBER OF COUNTRIES
Exchange arrangements with no separate legal tender	41
Currency board arrangements	7
Other conventional fixed peg arrangements	41
Pegged exchange rates within horizontal bands	4
Crawling pegs	5
Exchange rates within crawling bands	5
Managed floating with no pronounced path for exchange rate	49
Independently floating	35
Total	187

Exchange arrangements with no separate legal tender: The currency of another country circulates as the sole legal tender, or the member belongs to a monetary or currency union in which the members of the union share the same legal tender. An example would be the countries in the euro area.

Currency board arrangements: A monetary regime based on an implicit legislative commitment to exchange domestic currency for a specified foreign currency at a fixed exchange rate, combined with restrictions on the issuing authority to ensure the fulfillment of its legal obligation. Two examples would be Bosnia and Hong Kong.

Other conventional peg arrangements: The country pegs its currency (formal or de facto) at a fixed rate to a major currency or a basket of currencies in which the exchange rate fluctuates within a narrow margin of at most 1/21 percent around a central rate. For example, China pegs its currency to the U.S. dollar.

Pegged exchange rates within horizontal bands: The value of the currency is maintained within margins of fluctuation around a formal or de facto fixed peg that are wider than 1/21 percent around a central rate. Many countries that used to be considered managed floating are in this category because they basically peg their currency to something else. An example would be Denmark in the new Exchange Rate Mechanism in Europe, a country that was not part of the euro group in 2002, yet was still linking itself to the euro as much as possible but at a wider degree of flexibility.

Crawling pegs: The currency is adjusted periodically in small amounts at a fixed, preannounced rate or in response to changes in selective quantitative indicators. Costa Rica and Bolivia are two examples.

Exchange rates within crawling bands: The currency is maintained within certain fluctuation margins around a central rate that is adjusted periodically at a fixed preannounced rate or in response to changes in selective quantitative indicators. Romania, Israel, and Uruguay are three examples.

Managed floating with no pronounced path for the exchange rate: The monetary authority influences the movements of the exchange rate by actively intervening in the foreign-exchange market without specifying, or precommitting to, a preannounced path for the exchange rate. India and Azerbaijan are examples.

Independent floating: The exchange rate is market determined, with any foreign-exchange intervention aimed at moderating the rate of change and preventing undue fluctuations in the exchange rate rather than at establishing a level for it. Canada, the United States, and Mexico are three examples of countries in this category.

Source: International Monetary Fund, *IMF Annual Report*, 2004, pp. 118–120.

in Africa have adopted a new currency called the CFA franc as their common currency. The value of the CFA franc is now guaranteed in euros by the French Treasury. It was guaranteed in French francs prior to the adoption of the euro. That same concept was being considered in Latin America, and it is called the *dollarization* of the economy, as illustrated in the opening case. The idea would be to take all of their currency out of circulation and replace it with dollars. Basically, the U.S. Federal Reserve System (the Fed) would have greater control over monetary decisions instead of the governments of the local countries. Prices and wages would be established in dollars instead of in the local currency, which would disappear. The concern is that this would result in a loss of sovereignty and could lead to severe economic problems if the United States decided to tighten monetary policy at the same time those countries needed to loosen policy to stimulate growth. As seen in the Argentina case in Chapter 9, this is exactly what happened in Argentina. Although Argentina's exchange-rate regime did not go to the extreme of dollarization, its currency board regime was just a step away from dollarization. The currency board tied the peso closely enough to the dollar and to the decisions the U.S. Fed made that the government's ability to use monetary policy to strengthen its stalling economy was limited. However, this is the same problem facing the member countries in the euro area.[10]

The next category, pegged exchange rates within horizontal bands, contains only a few countries, and it is a slight variation of the first three categories. The countries in this pegged category simply have a wider band but are still locked onto something else, such as the euro for Denmark, Cyprus, and Hungary, three of the countries in this category.

The last four categories have some degree of floating exchange-rate arrangements, either managed float or free float. Many countries that used to be managed floating countries have been reclassified into the fixed peg regime because they are so tightly linked to some type of anchor, like the dollar. In addition, countries are changing their regimes all the time. Chile, for example, was listed in a prior IMF survey as a country that keeps its exchange rate within a crawling band, which means that the exchange rate is adjusted periodically at a fixed pronounced rate or in response to changes in selective quantitative indicators, which, for Chile, is inflation. But in late 1999, Chile suspended the trading bands, which it had established around the peso, and moved to a floating rate regime in an effort to stimulate export-led economic growth. Likewise, in 2001, Iceland moved from a pegged regime, within a horizontal band, to a free-floating regime. Brazil did the same thing in early 1999; so did Turkey in 2001. Egypt did that in 2003, but it changed its regime again to managed floating.[11]

Map 10.2 identifies the countries that fit into each category listed in Table 10.1. Because a country's classification is subject to change constantly, it is important for managers to frequently consult the IMF for updates. In addition, it is necessary to supplement the IMF information with current events, as illustrated in the earlier examples of regime changes in Chile and Iceland. It is important for MNEs to understand the exchange-rate arrangements for the currencies of countries in which they are doing business so that those MNEs can forecast trends more accurately. It is much easier to forecast a future exchange rate for a relatively stable currency that is pegged to the U.S. dollar, such as the Hong Kong dollar, than for a currency that is freely floating, such as the Japanese yen.

Countries may change the exchange-rate regime they use, so managers need to monitor country policies carefully.

The Euro

Not content with the economic integration envisaged in the Single European Act that was discussed in Chapter 8, the EU nations signed the Treaty of Maastricht in 1992, which set steps to accomplish two goals: political union and monetary union. The decision to move to a common currency in Europe has eliminated currency as a barrier to trade. To replace each national currency with a single European currency called the euro, the countries had to converge their economic policies first. It is not possible to have different monetary policies in each member country and one currency.

The EU created the euro to replace the individual currencies of EU members.

European monetary union did not occur overnight. The roots to the system began in 1979, when the **European Monetary System** (EMS) was put into place. The EMS was set up as a means of creating exchange-rate stability within the EC at the time. A series of exchange rate relationships linked the currencies of most members through a parity grid. As the countries narrowed the fluctuations in their exchange rates, the stage was set for the replacement of the EMS with the Exchange Rate Mechanism (ERM) and full monetary union.

The Exchange Rate Mechanism was put into place to establish criteria that countries must follow to be a part of the euro zone.

According to the Treaty of Maastricht, countries had to meet certain criteria in order to comply with the ERM and be part of the **European Monetary Union (EMU).** Termed the Stability and Growth pact, the criteria outlined in the treaty and which continue for euro applicants today are the following:

- Annual government deficit must not exceed 3 percent of GDP.
- Total outstanding government debt must not exceed 60 percent of GDP.

The criteria that are part of the Growth and Stability Pact include measures of deficits, debt, inflation, and interest rates.

MAP 10.2   Exchange-Rate Arrangements, 2004

Over half of the countries in the world have a floating exchange rate, although only one-quarter of the countries' currencies are independently floating, like the U.S. dollar. Some countries have abandoned their currencies in favor of something else, such as the dollar in El Salvador.

Source: IMF Annual Report, 2004, pp. 119–120. ANNUAL REPORTS by IMF. Copyright 2004 by INTERNATIONAL MONETARY FUND. Reproduced with permission of INTERNATIONAL MONETARY FUND in the format textbook via Copyright Clearance Center.

- ANTIGUA & BARBUDA
- ARUBA
- BAHRAIN
- BARBADOS
- CAPE VERDE
- COMOROS
- DOMINICA
- FIJI
- GRENADA
- KIRIBATI
- MALDIVES
- MALTA
- MARSHALL ISLANDS
- MAURITIUS
- MICRONESIA
- NETHERLANDS ANTILLES
- PALAU
- SAMOA
- SAN MARINO
- SÃO TOMÉ & PRÍNCIPE
- SEYCHELLES
- SOLOMON ISLANDS
- ST. KITTS & NEVIS
- ST. LUCIA
- ST. VINCENT & THE GRENADINES
- THE BAHAMAS
- TONGA
- TRINIDAD & TOBAGO
- VANUATU

- Rate of inflation must remain within 1.5 percent of the three best performing EU countries.
- Average nominal long-term interest rate must be within 2 percent of the average rate in the three countries with the lowest inflation rates.
- Exchange rate stability must be maintained, meaning that for at least two years, the country concerned has kept within the "normal" fluctuation margins of the European Exchange Rate Mechanism.[12]

After a great deal of effort, 11 of the 15 countries in the EU joined the EMU on January 1, 1999. Greece joined on January 1, 2001. Those not yet participating in the euro are the United Kingdom, Sweden, and Denmark (by their choice). Sweden announced in July 2002 that it had met all the criteria for joining the EMU,[13] but voters' rejection of the euro in 2003 has placed its entry on hold for the time being.[14] The euro is being administered by the **European Central Bank (ECB),** which was established on July 1, 1998. The ECB has been responsible for setting monetary policy and for managing the exchange-rate system for all of Europe since January 1, 1999.

The U.K, Sweden, and Denmark are the only members of the original 15 EU countries that opted not to adopt the euro.

The European Central Bank sets monetary policy for the adopters of the euro.

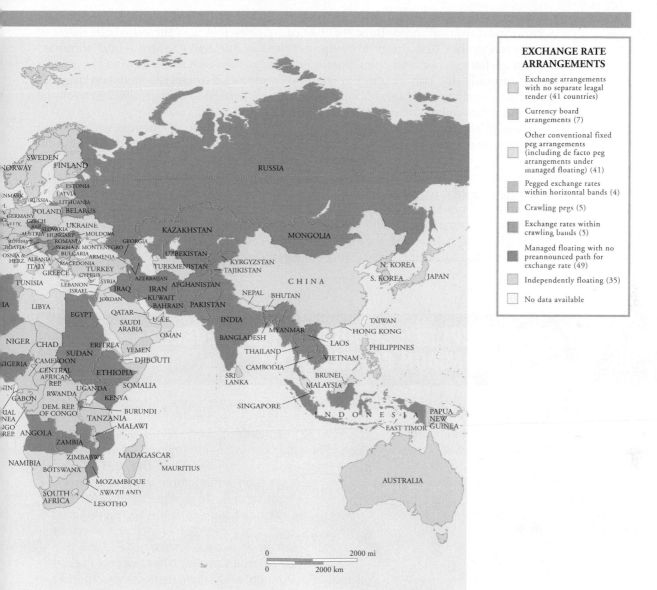

EXCHANGE RATE ARRANGEMENTS

- Exchange arrangements with no separate leagal tender (41 countries)
- Currency board arrangements (7)
- Other conventional fixed peg arrangements (including de facto peg arrangements under managed floating) (41)
- Pegged exchange rates within horizontal bands (4)
- Crawling pegs (5)
- Exchange rates within crawling bands (5)
- Managed floating with no preannounced path for exchange rate (49)
- Independently floating (35)
- No data available

The ERM is important in converging the economies of the EU. Since the ECB is an independent organization like the Fed in the United States, it can focus on its mandate of controlling inflation. Of course, different economies are growing at different rates in Europe, and it is difficult to have one monetary policy that fits all. Countries might be tempted to use an expansion fiscal policy to stimulate economic growth, but the deficit requirements of the ERM keep countries from stimulating too much.

In its first year of operation, the euro fluctuated in value between a high of $1.1827 per euro to a low of nearly $1.00 per euro. It fell in value compared to the U.S. dollar for most of 2000 and 2001 and began rising again in 2002. The euro has risen almost steadily against the dollar since then and reached a record high of $1.3625/euro on December 27, 2004.[15] By August 9, 2005, the rate was $1.2345/euro. The ECB began distributing actual banknotes, replacing individual national currencies, on January 1, 2002.

The move to the euro has been smoother than predicted. It is affecting companies in a variety of ways. Banks had to update their electronic networks to handle all aspects of money exchange, such as systems that trade global currencies, that buy and sell stocks, that transfer money between banks, that manage customer accounts, or that print out bank statements. Deutsche Bank estimated that the conversion process cost several hundred million dollars.[16] Other companies feel that the euro will increase price transparency (the ability to compare prices in different countries) and eliminate foreign-exchange costs and risks. Foreign-exchange costs are narrowing as companies operate in only one currency in Europe, and foreign-exchange risks between member states are also disappearing, although there are still foreign-exchange risks between the euro and nonmember currencies, such as the U.S. dollar.

The euro has some challenges, however. Three of the original 15 members have opted not to join, as mentioned above, and the U.K. is experiencing higher growth, lower inflation, and lower unemployment than the 12 members of the euro zone. In addition, several members of the euro zone, notably Germany, France, and Italy, have exceeded the government deficit requirement of the ERM, forcing the EU to back down on its implementation of fines for noncompliance. Finally, the 10 new members of the EU need to qualify for membership, and this will take time. Some will be able to join fairly soon, but others will delay while they attempt to meet the convergence criteria. In the meantime, they will try to narrow the fluctuation between their currencies and the euro.

POINT–COUNTERPOINT: SHOULD AFRICA DEVELOP A COMMON CURRENCY?[17]

POINT

The success of the euro and the deep economic and political problems in Africa have caused many experts to wonder if African nations should attempt to develop one common currency in Africa with a Central Bank to set monetary policy. In 2001, the 53 members of the Organization of African Unity organized the African Union, and its Association of African Central Bank Governors announced in 2003 that it would work to create a common currency by 2021.

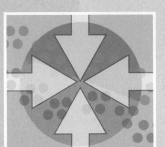

The development of a common currency would be great for Africa, because it would hasten economic integration in a continent that desperately needs to increase market size in order to achieve more trade and greater economies of scale. A common currency would lower transaction costs and make it easier to engage in trade among countries. There are several degrees of economic cooperation in Africa already, including three forms of currency cooperation. These three regional monetary unions are the Common Monetary Area (CMA), including Lesotho, Namibia, South Africa, and Swaziland, based on the South African rand; the Economic and Monetary Community for Central Africa (CAEMC), including Cameroon, Central African Republic, Chad, Republic of Congo, Equatorial Guinea, and Gabon; and the West African Economic and Monetary Union (WAEMU), including Benin, Burkina Faso, Côte d'Ivoire, Guinea-Bissau, Mali, Niger, Senegal, and Togo. The latter two monetary unions are part of the CFA franc zone, designated by the IMF as an exchange arrangement with no separate legal tender. All of the countries in the CFA franc zone are former colonies of France and maintain French as the official language except for Guinea-Bissau and Equatorial Guinea, which were ruled by Portugal and Spain, respectively. The two members of the CFA franc zone each have Central Banks that monitor the value of the CFA franc. The CFA franc zone has been successful in delivering low inflation, but it has not necessarily delivered high growth. The CMA is controlled by South Africa because of the size of its economy and the fact that the currency of the CMA is the South African rand.

In addition to the three regional monetary unions, there are five existing regional economic communities: Arab Monetary Union, Common Market for Eastern and Southern Africa, Economic Community of Central African States, Economic Community of West African States, and Southern African Development Community. These groups are working hard to reduce trade barriers and increase trade among member countries, so all these groups would have to do is combine into one large African economic union, form a Central Bank, and establish a common monetary policy as the EU does.

A major advantage of establishing a Central Bank and common currency is that institutions in each African nation will have to improve, and the Central Bank may be able to insulate the monetary policy from political pressures, which often create inflationary pressures and subsequent devaluations.

COUNTERPOINT

There is no way that the countries of Africa will ever establish a common currency, even though the African Union hopes to do so by 2021. The institutional framework in the individual African nations is not ready for a common currency. Few of the individual Central Banks are independent of the political process, so they often have to stimulate the economy in order to respond to political pressures. If the process is not managed properly and the currency is subject to frequent devaluation, there will be no pride in the region or clout on the international stage. Further, each country will have to give up monetary sovereignty and will have to rely on other measures, such as labor mobility, wage and price flexibility, and fiscal transfers, in order to weather the shocks. Even though there is good labor mobility in Africa, it is difficult to imagine that the African countries will be able to transfer tax revenues from country to country to help stimulate growth. In addition, it is difficult to transfer goods among the different countries in Africa because of transportation problems that are not an issue in the EU.

The establishment of the euro in the EU was a monumental task, but it took years to establish, following the establishment of a successful customs union and a gradual tightening of the Exchange Rate Mechanism in Europe. For Africa to establish a common currency, there needs to be closer economic integration first, so it is important to be patient and give Africa a chance to move forward. Maybe one way to move to a common currency is to strengthen the existing regional monetary unions and then gradually open up the unions to neighboring countries until there are three huge monetary unions. Then the three unions can discuss ways to link together into a common currency in Africa.

Black Markets

Of the 184 IMF member countries, 94 have currencies that are reasonably flexible, 35 of which float independently. Many of the others control their currencies fairly rigidly. In many of these countries, a black market could parallel the official market and be aligned more closely with the forces of supply and demand than is the official market. The less flexible a country's exchange-rate arrangement, the more likely there will be a thriving black market. A **black market** exists when people are willing to pay more for dollars than the official rate. In March 2005, the government of Zimbabwe arrested 10,000 people who were charged with black market activities, including selling foreign exchange. Authorities blame foreigners for a thriving foreign currency informal market where the Zimbabwe dollar is trading at up to 25,000 to the U.S. dollar against an official rate of 9000. However, many experts feel that the reason for the black market activities is poverty in Zimbabwe and that government crackdowns will simply drive the black market activities deeper. Until the government loosens controls on the currency, foreign exchange will continue to command a hefty premium in the black market.[18] In addition to buying and selling currency on the black market, people will smuggle goods into Zimbabwe and sell them at a premium, which has the same result as selling foreign currency at a premium. Zimbabwe's official currency regime is a fixed-peg arrangement and is pegged to the U.S. dollar. The movement to a floating rate would eliminate the need for a black market.

A black market closely approximates a price based on supply and demand for a currency instead of a government-controlled price.

The Role of Central Banks

Each country has a central bank that is responsible for the policies affecting the value of its currency. The central bank in the United States is the Federal Reserve System (the Fed), a system of 12 regional banks. The New York Fed, representing the Federal Reserve

System and the U.S. Treasury, is responsible for intervening in foreign-exchange markets to achieve dollar exchange-rate policy objectives and to counter disorderly conditions in foreign-exchange markets. It makes such transactions in close coordination with the U.S. Treasury and Board of Governors of the Fed, and most often it coordinates with the foreign-exchange operations of other central banks. The Fed will sell dollars for foreign currency if the goal is to counter upward pressure on the dollar. If the goal is to counter downward pressure, it will purchase dollars through the sale of foreign currency. Further, the Federal Reserve Bank of New York serves as fiscal agent in the United States for foreign central banks and official international financial organizations. It acts as the primary contact with other foreign central banks. The services it provides for these institutions include the receipt and payment of funds in U.S. dollars; the purchase and sale of foreign exchange and Treasury securities; the custody of over $900 billion in currency, securities, and gold bullion credited to over 200 foreign accounts; and the storage of over $63 billion in monetary gold for about 60 foreign central banks, governments, and official international agencies (approximately one-third of the world's known monetary gold reserves).[19] In the European Union, the European Central Bank now coordinates the activities of each member country's central bank to establish a common monetary policy in Europe, much as the Federal Reserve Bank does in the United States.

Central bank reserve assets are kept in three major forms: gold, foreign-exchange reserves, and IMF-related assets. At the end of 2003, there were SDR 2.4 trillion in reserves worldwide, of which 85.5 percent were in foreign exchange, followed by 10.8 percent in gold and 3.6 percent in IMF-related assets. The U.S. dollar was the most widely used currency as a reserve asset, with 63.8 percent of the total, up from 53.1 percent a decade earlier. It was followed by the euro at 19.7 percent and the Japanese yen at 4.8 percent.[20] However, the mix of reserve assets varies from country to country. For example, in 2002, 98.3 percent of Singapore's reserves and 96.3 percent of Japan's reserves were in foreign exchange. However, only 49.7 percent of Germany's reserves and 42.4 percent of the U.S. reserves were in foreign exchange. European countries tend to be more heavily weighted toward gold as a reserve asset than are other countries in the world, even though they have more foreign exchange than gold as reserve assets.

Central banks are concerned primarily with liquidity to ensure that they have the cash and flexibility needed to protect their countries' currencies. The mix of currencies in a country's reserves is based on its major intervention currencies—that is, the currencies in which the country trades the most. The degree to which a central bank actively manages its reserves to earn a profit varies by country.

There are several ways that a central bank can intervene in currency markets. The U.S. Fed, for example, usually uses foreign currencies to buy dollars when the dollar is weak or sells dollars for foreign currency when the dollar is strong. Depending on the market conditions, a central bank may

- Coordinate its action with other central banks or go it alone
- Enter the market aggressively to change attitudes about its views and policies
- Call for reassuring action to calm markets
- Intervene to reverse, resist, or support a market trend
- Announce or not announce its operations, be very visible or very discreet
- Operate openly or indirectly through brokers[21]

Government policies change over time, depending on economic conditions and the attitude of the prevailing administration in power. The George H. W. Bush administration, in 1989 alone, bought and sold dollars on 97 days and sold $19.5 billion. In the first two and a half years of the first Clinton administration, the U.S. Treasury intervened in the market by buying dollars on only 18 days, spending about $12.5 billion in the process.[22] During the first term of office of President George W. Bush, the U.S. Treasury rarely intervened in the market despite a decline in the value of the dollar against the euro and the yen.

From the beginning of 2003 until the end of 2004, the dollar continued to weaken against both the euro and the yen. In an attempt to strengthen the dollar, the Japanese central bank spent a record 20 trillion yen in 2003 and 10 trillion yen in the first two months of 2004. Despite the efforts of the Japanese authorities, the yen rose 11 percent against the dollar in 2003 and continued to strengthen through 2004. The Japanese finance ministry stopped its foreign exchange intervention in March 2004, but the dollar's continued weakening against both the euro and yen at the end of 2004 sparked new threats of intervention by the Japanese and Europeans. A senior Japanese finance ministry official said, "It is natural for Japan and Europe to act when the dollar alone is falling. If the (dollar's) movement affects the European economy and the Japanese economy, we should defend ourselves." If the European and Japanese decide to intervene in currency markets, it will create a situation similar to worldwide efforts to strengthen the euro in 2000.[23]

In 2005, the Central Bank of South Korea intervened heavily in currency markets to try to slow down the rise in the Korean won against the dollar by selling won and buying dollars. Since 2002, the won has appreciated 30 percent against the dollar, 17 percent of which occurred in 2004, making it one of the world's fastest rising currencies. However, the cost of intervention was high, and South Korea decided to stop when its foreign exchange reserves reached $206 billion, the fourth highest in the world.[24]

In general, the U.S. disapproves of foreign-currency intervention. The reason is that it is very difficult, if not impossible, for intervention to have a lasting impact on the value of a currency. Intervention may temporarily halt a slide, but it cannot force the market to move in a direction that it doesn't want to go, at least for the long run. For that reason, it is important for countries to focus on correcting economic fundamentals instead of spending a lot of time and money on intervention. Even when the dollar was falling in 2003–2005, the government decided not to intervene, because the dollar was simply coming back to the level it was at before the run-up of the dollar from 1995 to 2002.

Coordination of central bank intervention can take place on a bilateral or multilateral basis. The **Bank for International Settlements (BIS)** in Basel, Switzerland, links together the central banks in the world. The BIS was founded in 1930 and is owned and controlled by a group of central banks. The major objective of the BIS is to promote the cooperation of central banks to facilitate international financial stability. Although only 55 central banks or monetary authorities are shareholders in the BIS—11 of which are the founding banks and are from the major industrial countries—the BIS has dealings with some 140 central banks worldwide.[25] The BIS acts as a central banker's bank. It gets involved in swaps and other currency transactions between the central banks in other countries. It also is a gathering place where central bankers can discuss monetary cooperation.[26]

> The Bank for International Settlements in Basel, Switzerland, is owned by and promotes cooperation among a group of central banks.

THE DETERMINATION OF EXCHANGE RATES

One of the first steps in being able to forecast future values of a currency is to understand how exchange rates change in value. The exchange-rate regimes described earlier are either fixed or floating, with fixed rates varying in terms of how fixed they are and floating rates varying in terms of how much they actually float. However, currencies change in different ways depending on whether they are in floating rate or fixed rate regimes.

Floating Rate Regimes

Currencies that float freely respond to supply and demand conditions free from government intervention. This concept can be illustrated using a two-country model involving the United States and Japan. Figure 10.1 shows the equilibrium exchange rate in the market and then a movement to a new equilibrium level as the market changes. The demand for yen in this example is a function of U.S. demand for Japanese goods and services, such as automobiles, and yen-denominated financial assets, such as securities.

> Demand for a country's currency is a function of the demand for that country's goods and services and financial assets.

FIGURE 10.1

EQUILIBRIUM EXCHANGE RATE

Comparatively high inflation in the United States compared with Japan raises the demand for yen but lowers the supply of yen, increasing the value of the yen in terms of U.S. dollars. If the Japanese government wants to keep the dollar/yen exchange rate at e_0, it needs to sell yen for dollars in order to increase the supply of yen in the market and therefore decrease the exchange rate.

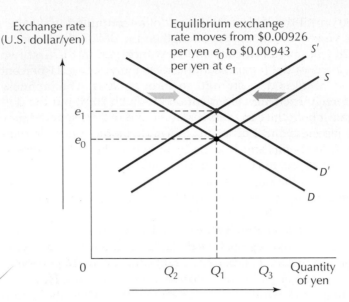

The supply of yen in this example is a function of Japanese demand for U.S. goods and services and dollar-denominated financial assets. Initially, the supply of and demand for yen in Figure 10.1 meet at the equilibrium exchange rate e_0 (for example, 0.00926 dollars per yen, or 108 yen per dollar) and the quantity of yen Q_1.

Assume demand for U.S. goods and services by Japanese consumers drops because of, say, high U.S. inflation. This lessening demand would result in a reduced supply of yen in the foreign-exchange market, causing the supply curve to shift to S'. Simultaneously, the increasing prices of U.S. goods might lead to an increase in demand for Japanese goods and services by U.S. consumers. This, in turn, would lead to an increase in demand for yen in the market, causing the demand curve to shift to D' and finally leading to an increase in the quantity of yen and an increase in the exchange rate. The new equilibrium exchange rate would be at e_1 (for example, 0.00943 dollars per yen, or 106 yen per dollar). From a dollar standpoint, the increased demand for Japanese goods would lead to an increase in supply of dollars as more consumers tried to trade their dollars for yen, and the reduced demand for U.S. goods would result in a drop in demand for dollars. This would cause a reduction in the dollar's value against the yen.

Managed Fixed Rate Regime

In the preceding example, Japanese and U.S. authorities allowed changes in the exchange rates between their two currencies to occur so that the currencies could reach a new exchange-rate equilibrium. There can be times when one or both countries might not want exchange rates to change. Assume, for example, that the United States and Japan decide to manage their exchange rates. The U.S. government might not want its currency to weaken because its companies and consumers would have to pay more for Japanese products, which would lead to more inflationary pressure in the United States. Or the Japanese government might not want the yen to strengthen because it would mean unemployment in its export industries. But how can the governments keep the values from changing when the United States is earning too few yen? Somehow the difference between yen supply and demand must be neutralized.

A government buys and sells its currency in the open market as a means of influencing the currency's price.

In a managed fixed exchange-rate system, the New York Federal Reserve Bank would hold foreign-exchange reserves, which it would have built up through the years for this type of contingency. It could sell enough of its yen reserves (make up the difference between Q_1 and Q_3 in Figure 10.1) at the fixed exchange rate to maintain that rate. Or the Japanese central bank might be willing to accept dollars so that U.S. consumers can continue to buy Japanese goods. These dollars would then become part of Japan's foreign-exchange reserves.

The fixed rate could continue as long as the United States had reserves or as long as the Japanese were willing to add dollars to their holdings. Sometimes governments use fiscal or monetary policy, for example, by raising interest rates to create a demand for their currency and to keep the value from falling. Unless something changed the basic imbalance in the currency supply and demand, however, the New York Federal Reserve Bank would run out of yen and the Japanese central bank would stop accepting dollars because it would fear amassing too many, similar to what happened to South Korea in early 2005. At this point, it would be necessary to change the exchange rate in order to lessen the demand for yen.

If a country determines that intervention will not work, it must adjust its currency's value. If the currency is freely floating, the exchange rate will seek the correct level according to the laws of supply and demand. However, a currency that is pegged to another currency or to a basket of currencies usually is changed on a formal basis—in other words, through a devaluation or revaluation, depending on the direction of the change.

> Countries may be forced to revalue or devalue their currencies if economic policies and intervention don't work.

The earlier example used two currencies, the dollar and the yen. Often, however, a number of countries intervene in currency markets, sometimes in a coordinated fashion. The G8 comprises the finance ministers of eight key industrial countries: the United States, Canada, Japan, Germany, France, Italy, the Russian Federation (for most but not all discussions due to its struggling economy), and the United Kingdom. In addition, the EU takes part in the discussions. The G8 is the most influential group of finance ministers in the world, and they meet periodically to discuss key economic issues, especially exchange rates. In past meetings of the G8 or its predecessor the G7, currency market intervention was decided, announced, and implemented, but that has not been the case in recent years, mostly due to the lack of interest by the U.S. in market intervention. However, that has not kept individual members, such as Japan, from intervening on their own.

> The G8 group of industrial countries meets often to discuss global economic issues, including exchange-rate values. The G20 is an expansion of the G8 and includes some emerging economies.

In December 1999, a new group—the G20—met for the first time. The G20 is composed of the G8 plus Argentina, Australia, Brazil, China, India, Indonesia, Mexico, Saudi Arabia, South Africa, South Korea, and Turkey. The representatives of the European Union, including the European Central Bank, bring the tally to 20. This organization is considered important because it brings some developing countries into discussions previously held only by the industrial countries. The G20 discusses a wide variety of issues, including appropriate exchange-rate policies for member countries. Among the immediate concerns are the volatility of currency markets, corporate profitability, and accounting standards, as well as the economic situations in Turkey and Argentina.[27]

Purchasing-Power Parity

Purchasing-power parity (PPP) is a well-known theory that seeks to define relationships between currencies. In essence, it claims that a change in relative inflation (meaning a comparison of the countries' rates of inflation) between two countries must cause a change in exchange rates in order to keep the prices of goods in two countries fairly similar. According to the PPP theory, if, for example, Japanese inflation were 2 percent and U.S. inflation were 3.5 percent, the dollar would be expected to fall by the difference in inflation rates. Then the dollar would be worth fewer yen than before the adjustment, and the yen would be worth more dollars than before the adjustment.

> Purchasing power parity from the standpoint of exchange rates seeks to define the relationships between currencies based on relative inflation.

An interesting illustration of the PPP theory for estimating exchange rates is the "Big Mac" index of currencies used by *The Economist* each year. Since 1986, *The Economist* has used the price of a Big Mac to estimate the exchange rate between the dollar and another currency (see Table 10.2). Because the Big Mac is sold in over 120 countries, it is easy to compare prices. PPP would suggest that the exchange should leave hamburgers costing the same in the United States as abroad. However, the Big Mac sometimes costs more and

> If the domestic inflation rate is lower than that in the foreign country, the domestic currency should be stronger than that of the foreign country.

TABLE 10.2   THE BIG MAC INDEX

	BIG MAC PRICE IN LOCAL CURRENCY*	BIG MAC PRICE IN DOLLARS**	IMPLIED PPP OF THE DOLLAR***	ACTUAL $ EXCHANGE RATE MAY 20, 2004****	UNDER (−) OVER(+) VALUATION AGAINST THE DOLLAR, % §
United States	$2.90†	2.90			
Argentina	4.35	1.48	1.50	2.9458	−49
Australia	3.25	2.27	1.12	1.4366	−22
Brazil	5.39	1.70	1.86	3.1350	−41
Britain	4.47	3.37#	1.54	1.7825	+16
Canada	3.19	2.33	1.10	1.3770	−20
Chile	1,400.70	2.18	483.00	660.3900	−25
China	10.41	1.26	3.59	8.2869	−57
Czech Rep.	56.55	2.13	19.50	26.6090	−27
Denmark	27.75	4.46	9.57	6.1959	+54
Egypt	10.01	1.62	3.45	6.2294	−44
Euro area	3.07	3.28î	1.06 ‡	1.2010	+13
Hong Kong	12.01	1.54	4.14	7.7878	−47
Hungary	530.70	2.52	183.00	210.4200	−13
Indonesia	16,100.80	1.77	5,552.00	9,051.7000	−39
Japan	261.87	2.33	90.30	113.0000	−20
Malaysia	5.05	1.33	1.74	3.8006	−54
Mexico	24.01	2.08	8.28	11.5600	−28
New Zealand	4.35	2.65	1.50	1.6477	−8
Peru	8.99	2.57	3.10	3.6015	−11
Philippines	69.02	1.23	23.80	56.1200	−57
Poland	6.29	1.63	2.17	3.8931	−44
Russia	42.05	1.45	14.50	28.9950	−50
Singapore	3.31	1.92	1.14	1.7161	−34
South Africa	12.41	1.86	4.28	6.7707	−36
South Korea	3,198.70	2.72	1,103.00	1,174.0000	−6
Sweden	29.87	3.94	10.30	7.5812	+36
Switzerland	6.29	4.90	2.17	1.2775	+69
Taiwan	75.11	2.24	25.90	33.5730	−23
Thailand	58.87	1.45	20.30	40.7750	−50
Turkey	3,950,000.10	2.58	1,362,069.00	1,565,234,0000	−11

Source: "The Big Mac Index: Food for Thought," The Economist, Map 29, 2004, pp. 71–72.

† Average of New York, Chicago, San Franciso, and Atlanta.

* The exact price is not provided in the 2004 survey. It is found by multiplying column 3 (which is provided) by the Big Mac price in dollars.

** This is found by dividing the Big Mac price in local currency by the actual exchange rate.

*** Given by The Economist. Normally, it would be found by dividing the Big Mac price in local currency by the Big Mac price in dollars.

**** At current exchange rates assumed to be on May 20, 2004; the rate is not provided by The Economist nor is the date, but using data provided in columns 2, 3, and 5 and testing using different exchange rates, it appears that May 20, 2004 is the correct date.

î Weighted average of member countries.

‡ Dollars per euro.

Dollars per pound.

§ This is found by subtracting column 4 from column 3 and dividing the results by column 4.

sometimes less, demonstrating how far currencies are under- or overvalued against the dollar. Looking at Table 10.2, a Big Mac in 2004 cost an average of $2.90 in the United States and Baht58.87 in Thailand. Dividing the baht price of the Big Mac by the dollar price of the Big Mac yields a purchasing-power parity exchange rate of Baht20.3 per dollar. However, the actual exchange rate was Baht40.8 per dollar, so the baht was undervalued against the dollar by 50 percent. Based on the actual exchange rate, a Big Mac costs only $1.45 in Thailand (Baht58.8/40.8), so Big Macs are a real bargain in Thailand compared with the United States. (Of course, transportation costs to Thailand to buy the burger will eat up the difference.) European currencies outside the euro zone were significantly overvalued against the dollar, whereas the euro zone currencies were only slightly overvalued. Most other currencies were undervalued against the dollar.[28]

There are supporters of the Big Mac index, also known as "McParity," but there also are detractors. Even though McParity may hold up in the long run, as some studies have shown, there are short-run problems that affect PPP:

- The theory of PPP falsely assumes that there are no barriers to trade and that transportation costs are zero.

- Prices of the Big Mac in different countries are distorted by taxes. European countries with high value-added taxes are more likely to have higher prices than countries with low taxes.

- The Big Mac is not just a basket of commodities; its price also includes nontraded costs, such as rent, insurance, and so on.

- Profit margins vary by the strength of competition. The higher the competition, the lower the profit margin and, therefore, the price.[29]

Despite the PPP theory flaws, most economists agree that PPP measures provide a more realistic picture of the relative size of economies than market exchange rates.

Interest Rates

Although inflation is the most important long-run influence on exchange rates, interest rates are also important. For example, a couple of articles on the foreign-exchange market in the *Wall Street Journal* note the impact of interest rates on exchange rates.

> Since 1999, Brazil has sought to achieve price stability through inflation targeting. The government decides on an acceptable range of inflation for the next year and the central bank adjusts interest rates to try to make sure the economy stays within that range. For 2005, Brazil is pursuing an inflation target of 4.5%. Given Brazil's history of hyperinflation, maintaining that goal requires stratospheric interest rates, because authorities fear heightened economic activity could fuel inflation. After six interest-rate increases in the past six months, Brazil's benchmark rate is 18.75%, one of the world's highest. Those high rates, however, have the effect of strengthening the real. With U.S. interest rates at 2.5%, international investors are selling dollars to buy Brazilian real-denominated bonds to take advantage of the higher interest rates and thus bigger returns. With the U.S. trade deficit at record highs—one cause of the weak dollar—there is little sign that the dollar will rebound anytime soon. In part, the dollar is slipping against the real because with U.S. interest rates low, investors are looking for higher rates elsewhere, especially in emerging countries such as Brazil.
>
> Noting that the U.S. Federal Reserve is likely to be the only major central bank to significantly increase interest rates this year, Stephen Jen, global head of currency research for Morgan Stanley, says higher rates "will increasingly support the dollar," in part by increasing the allure of dollar investments to international investors.[30]

To understand this interrelationship between interest rates and exchange rates, we need to understand two key finance theories: the Fisher Effect and the International Fisher

The nominal interest rate is the real interest rate plus inflation. Because the real interest rate should be the same in every country, the country with the higher interest rate should have higher inflation.

Effect. The first theory links inflation and interest rates, and the second links interest rates and exchange rates. The **Fisher Effect** is the theory that the nominal interest rate r in a country (the actual monetary interest rate earned on an investment) is determined by the real interest rate R (the nominal rate less inflation) and the inflation rate i as follows:

$$(1 + r) = (1 + R)(1 + i)$$

According to this theory, if the real interest rate is 5 percent, the U.S. inflation rate is 2.9 percent, and the Japanese inflation rate is 1.5 percent, then the nominal interest rates for the United States and Japan are computed as follows:

$$r_{US} = (1.05)(1.029) - 1 = 0.08045, \text{ or } 8.045 \text{ percent } r_j = (1.05)(1.015) - 1 = 0.06575,$$
$$\text{or } 6.575 \text{ percent}$$

The IFE implies that the currency of the country with the lower interest rate will strengthen in the future.

So the difference between U.S. and Japanese interest rates is a function of the difference between their inflation rates. If their inflation rates were the same (zero differential) but interest rates were 10 percent in the United States and 6.575 percent in Japan, investors would place their money in the United States, where they could get the higher real return.

The bridge from interest rates to exchange rates can be explained by the **International Fisher Effect (IFE),** the theory that the interest-rate differential is an unbiased predictor of future changes in the spot exchange rate. For example, the IFE predicts that if nominal interest rates in the United States are higher than those in Japan, the dollar's value should fall in the future by that interest-rate differential, which would be an indication of a weakening, or depreciation, of the dollar. That is because the interest-rate differential is based on differences in inflation rates, as we discussed earlier. The previous discussion on purchasing-power parity also demonstrated that the country with the higher inflation should have the weaker currency. Thus, the country with the higher interest rate (and the higher inflation) should have the weaker currency.

Of course, these issues cover the long run, but anything can happen in the short run. During periods of general price stability, a country (such as the U.S.) that raises its interest rates is likely to attract capital and see its currency rise in value due to the increased demand. However, if the reason for the increase in interest rates is because inflation is higher than that of its major trading partners and if the country's central bank is trying to reduce inflation, the currency will eventually weaken until inflation cools down. Although the interest-rate differential is the critical factor for a few of the most widely traded currencies, the expectation of the future spot rate also is very important. Normally, a trader will automatically estimate the future spot rate using the interest-rate differential and then adjust it for other market conditions.

Other key factors affecting exchange-rate movements are confidence and technical factors, such as the release of economic statistics.

Other Factors in Exchange-Rate Determination

Various other factors can cause exchange-rate changes. One factor not to be dismissed lightly is confidence. In times of turmoil, people prefer to hold currencies considered safe. For example, during the Kosovo crisis, money flowed into the United States because of concern over the safety of Western Europe if a true crisis were to occur in Yugoslavia and involve the Russians.

In addition to basic economic forces and confidence, exchange rates may be influenced by such technical factors as the release of national economic statistics, comments by a central bank, seasonal demands for a currency, and a slight strengthening of a currency following a prolonged weakness, or vice versa. Early in 2005, the global currency markets experienced shocks due to some misinterpreted comments by the Bank of Korea's governor. Reports that the Bank of Korea wanted to "diversify" its holdings were construed as a decision to cut dollar holdings. As a result, the dollar dropped against other currencies, rebounding only after Korean officials stated their statements had been misunderstood.[31]

Another example of how currency markets react strongly to news occurred in the spring of 2005. A reporter for the China News Service wrote an article about the impact of a possible appreciation of the Chinese yuan. Her story was translated by the *People's*

Daily online newspaper as fact and changed significantly as it moved from one news market to the other. In response to the article, currency traders and fund managers panicked, thinking that the news story reflected the intentions of the Chinese government, and the U.S. dollar plunged in value. Only after the story was revealed to be inaccurate did the dollar rise again in value.[32]

In the run-up to Brazil's presidential election of 2002, the real (Brazil's currency) hit all-time lows because of high poll ratings for a left-wing candidate whom investors feared would not be able to control the country's finances.[33] However, when the candidate, Lula da Silva of the Worker's Party, won the election and established a conservative fiscal and monetary policy, the real strengthened again.

FORECASTING EXCHANGE-RATE MOVEMENTS

The preceding section looked at the effect of the law of supply and demand on exchange rates, showed how governments intervene to manage exchange-rate movements, and explained how inflation and interest rates can be important determinants of exchange rates. This section identifies factors that managers can monitor to get an idea of what will happen to exchange rates.

Because various factors influence exchange-rate movements, managers must be able to analyze those factors to formulate a general idea of the timing, magnitude, and direction of an exchange-rate movement. However, prediction is not a precise science, and many things can cause the best of predictions to differ significantly from reality.

Managers need to be concerned with the timing, magnitude, and direction of an exchange-rate movement.

Fundamental and Technical Forecasting

Managers can forecast exchange rates by using either of two approaches: fundamental forecasting or technical forecasting. **Fundamental forecasting** uses trends in economic variables to predict future rates. The data can be plugged into an econometric model or evaluated on a more subjective basis. **Technical forecasting** uses past trends in exchange rates themselves to spot future trends in rates. Technical forecasters, or chartists, assume that if current exchange rates reflect all facts in the market, then under similar circumstances, future rates will follow the same patterns.[34] However, all forecasting is imprecise. A corporate treasurer who wants to forecast an exchange rate—say, the relationship between the British pound and the U.S. dollar—might use a variety of sources, both internal and external to the company. Many treasurers and bankers use outside forecasters to obtain input for their own forecasts. Forecasters need to provide ranges or point estimates with subjective probabilities based on available data and subjective interpretation. Biases that can skew forecasts include:

Fundamental forecasting uses trends in economic variables to predict future exchange rates. Technical forecasting uses past trends in exchange-rate movements to spot future trends.

- Overreaction to unexpected and dramatic news events
- Illusory correlation, that is, the tendency to see correlations or associations in data that are not statistically present but that are expected to occur on the basis of prior beliefs
- Focusing on a particular subset of information at the expense of the overall set of information
- Insufficient adjustment for subjective matters, such as market volatility
- The inability to learn from one's past mistakes, such as poor trading decisions
- Overconfidence in one's ability to forecast currencies accurately[35]

Good treasurers and bankers develop their own forecasts of what will happen to a particular currency and use fundamental or technical forecasts of outside forecasters to corroborate them. Doing this helps them determine whether they are considering important factors and whether they need to revise their forecasts in light of outside analysis. However, it is important to understand that no matter how carefully prepared a forecast is, it is still an educated guess. As the *Wall Street Journal* stated, "But after a benign period when global trends seemed relatively predictable, confusion now rages over many critical issues that shape trading strategies: the pace of the Federal Reserve's interest-rate increases; the direction of oil prices; the timing of a Chinese currency revaluation; uncertainty over whether the U.S. economy is slowing or merely in a soft patch—to name a few. . . . As currency managers lose conviction over the direction of global trends, they have found it harder to decide which criterion matters most when valuing currencies. '[There have been] times this year when people shift their theme within the week, and then back again.' "[36]

Forecasting includes predicting the timing, direction, and magnitude of an exchange-rate change or movement. For countries whose currencies are not freely floating, the timing is often a political decision, and it is not so easy to predict. Although the direction of a change probably can be predicted, the magnitude is difficult to forecast. Toyota Motor Corporation estimated that the yen would rise from a level of 131 yen/dollar in the beginning of 2002. For its 2002 earnings forecast, the company predicted an exchange rate of 125 yen/dollar. This was accurate in terms of the direction but not the magnitude of the strengthening of the yen. The yen rose even farther in 2002—to levels around 116 yen to the dollar. This could translate to a loss of 150 billion yen, or $1.3 billion.[37] The Bank of Japan intervened in the market to try to strengthen the dollar and to provide some respite for companies such as Toyota.

It is hard to predict what will happen to currencies and to use those predictions to forecast profits and establish operating strategies. The problem with predicting the value of a freely floating currency like the yen is that you never know what could happen to its value. You might be tempted to think that a currency linked to the dollar, like the Hong Kong dollar, would be much easier to predict. But since political control of Hong Kong was handed over to China, there have been discussions concerning Hong Kong's adoption of the Chinese yuan. Even rumors of this change spooked the region's financial markets. Hong Kong officials vowed to stick with the 19-year-old currency system, but many economists think it makes more sense for Hong Kong to change to the yuan.[38] But three years later, the Hong Kong dollar had continued to maintain its independence, while widening the trading range with the U.S. dollar. Again, experts were predicting that it was just a matter of time before Hong Kong switched to the yuan. Which prediction is correct? How should a company position itself in these two different scenarios?

Factors to Monitor

Key factors to monitor—the institutional setting, fundamental analysis, confidence factors, events, technical analysis

For freely fluctuating currencies, the law of supply and demand determines market value. However, very few currencies in the world float freely without any government intervention. Most are managed to some extent, which implies that governments need to make political decisions about the value of their currencies. Assuming governments use a rational basis for managing these values (an assumption that may not always be realistic), managers can monitor the same factors the governments follow in order to try to predict values. These factors are:

The institutional setting
- Does the currency float, or is it managed—and if so, is it pegged to another currency, to a basket, or to some other standard?
- What are the intervention practices? Are they credible? Sustainable?

Fundamental analysis
- Does the currency appear undervalued or overvalued in terms of PPP, balance of payments, foreign-exchange reserves, or other factors?
- What is the cyclical situation in terms of employment, growth, savings, investment, and inflation?
- What are the prospects for government monetary, fiscal, and debt policy?

Two tourists look at a money change board in Rome. The euro climbed to a new all-time high against the dollar after a closely watched survey showed a smaller-than-expected rise in U.S. consumer confidence.

Confidence factors

- What are market views and expectations with respect to the political environment, as well as to the credibility of the government and central bank?

Events

- Are there national or international incidents in the news; the possibility of crises or emergencies; governmental or other important meetings coming up (such as that of the G8, for example)?

Technical analysis

- What trends do the charts show? Are there signs of trend reversals?
- At what rates do there appear to be important buy and sell orders? Are they balanced? Is the market overbought? Oversold?
- What are the thinking and expectations of other market players and analysts?[39]

BUSINESS IMPLICATIONS OF EXCHANGE-RATE CHANGES

Why do we need to bother with predicting exchange-rate changes? As illustrated in the Toyota example, our operating strategies as well as translated overseas profits can be dramatically affected by exchange-rate changes. We will now look briefly at how exchange-rate changes can affect companies' marketing, production, and financial decisions.

Marketing Decisions

Marketing managers watch exchange rates because they can affect demand for a company's products at home and abroad. If Sony were selling its new 42-inch Plasma Wega TV set for 605,000 yen, it would cost $5,500 in the United States when the exchange rate was 110 yen to the dollar. At a forecast rate of 108 yen, the TV would cost $5,601. Suppose the yen rises even more—to 105—thus increasing the price of the TV to $5,762. At this point, would consumers be willing to pay $5,762 for a new TV set, or would they wait for the cost to come down? Should Sony pass on the new price to consumers or sell at the same price and absorb the difference in its profit margin? If the yen continues to strengthen beyond 105 yen, what can Sony do?

Production Decisions

Exchange-rate changes also can affect production decisions. A manufacturer in a country where wages and operating expenses are high might be tempted to relocate production to a country with a currency that is rapidly losing value. The company's currency would buy lots of the weak currency, making the company's initial investment cheap. Further, goods manufactured in that country would be relatively cheap in world markets. For example, BMW made the decision to invest in production facilities in South Carolina because of the unfavorable exchange rate between the deutsche mark (now the euro) and the dollar. However, the company announced plans to use the facilities not only to serve the U.S. market but also to export to Europe and other markets.[40] The issue worsened in 2004 when the euro rose significantly against the dollar. The devaluation of the Mexican peso came shortly after the introduction of NAFTA. Although companies had already begun to establish operations in Mexico to service North America, the cheaper peso certainly helped their manufacturing strategies.

Financial Decisions

Finally, exchange rates can affect financial decisions, primarily in the areas of sourcing of financial resources, the remittance of funds across national borders, and the reporting of financial results. In the first area, a company might be tempted to borrow money in places where interest rates are lowest. However, recall that interest-rate differentials often are compensated for in money markets through exchange-rate changes.

In deciding about cross-border financial flows, a company would want to convert local currency into its own home-country currency when exchange rates are most favorable so that it can maximize its return. However, countries with weak currencies often have currency controls, making it difficult for MNEs to do so.

Finally, exchange-rate changes can influence the reporting of financial results. A simple example illustrates the impact that exchange rates can have on income. If a U.S. company's Mexican subsidiary earns 2 million pesos when the exchange rate is 9.5 pesos per dollar, the dollar equivalent of its income is $210,526. If the peso depreciates to 10.2 pesos per dollar, the dollar equivalent of that income falls to $196,078. The opposite will occur if the local currency appreciates against that of the company's home country. This is the problem that Toyota faced in the earlier example. The yen equivalent of Toyota's dollar earnings in the United States continues to fall as the dollar falls against the yen.

It is important to learn about exchange rates and the forces that affect their change. Several years ago, a large U.S.-based telephone company was preparing a bid for a major telecommunications project in Turkey. The manager preparing the bid knew nothing about the Turkish lira, and he prepared his bid without consulting with the company's foreign-exchange specialists. He figured out the bid in dollars, then turned to the foreign-exchange table in the *Wall Street Journal* to see what rate he should use to convert the bid into lira. What he didn't realize was that the lira at that time was weakening against the dollar. By the time he received the bid, he had lost all of his profit to the change in the value of the lira against the dollar, and by the time he had finished the project, he had lost a lot of money. If he had talked to someone who knew anything about the lira, he could have forecast the future value and maybe entered into a hedging strategy to protect his receivable in lira. If managers don't understand how currency values are determined, they can make serious, costly mistakes.

LOOKING TO THE FUTURE: Changing Times Will Bring Greater Exchange-Rate Flexibility

The international monetary system has undergone considerable change since the early 1970s, when the dollar was devalued the first time. New countries have been born with the breakup of the Soviet empire, and with them have come new currencies. As those countries have gone through transition to a market economy, the currencies have adjusted as well. The countries will continue to change over to a floating rate system as they get their economies under control.

It will be interesting to see what will happen to the currencies of Latin America. Since the collapse of the Argentine peso, economists across all ideologies have stepped up to the plate to predict what will happen with Argentina's exchange-rate regime. Although the Brazilian real has strengthened against the dollar since the election of President da Silva, political and economic uncertainty argue for a long-term weakening of the real. In addition, will the members of the Central American Common Market dollarize their currencies like El Salvador, or will they maintain the policy of step-wise devaluations of their currencies?

The euro will continue to succeed as a currency and will eventually take away market share from the dollar as a prime reserve asset. In addition, its influence will spread throughout Europe as non-euro zone countries adopt the euro or at least come into harmony with it. The 10 countries who joined the EU in 2004 and the other two countries that have been approved have been pushing the EMU to allow them to switch to the euro. The EU will do this as the countries come into convergence with the ERM. Increasing trade links throughout Europe with non–euro zone countries will dictate closer alliance with the euro.

For Asia, there is no Asian currency that can compare with the dollar in the Americas and the euro in Europe. The yen is too specific to Japan, and the inability of the Japanese economy to reform and open up will keep the yen from wielding the same kind of influence as the dollar and the euro, even though the yen is one of the most widely traded currencies in the world. In fact, it is far more likely that the dollar will continue to be the benchmark in Asia insofar as Asian economies rely heavily on the U.S. market for a lot of their exports.

However, the real wild card in Asia is the Chinese yuan. The Chinese finally allowed the yuan to rise in 2005 but at a very small amount, and further changes will probably have to be made to the currency to avoid a major trade war with Europe and the U.S. The trend will continue to lead to greater flexibility in exchange-rate regimes, whether as managed floats or as freely floating currencies. Even countries that lock onto the dollar will float against every other currency in the world as the dollar floats. Capital controls will continue to fall, and currencies will move more freely from country to country.

SUMMARY

- The International Monetary Fund (IMF) was organized in 1945 to promote international monetary cooperation, to facilitate the expansion and balanced growth of international trade, to promote exchange-rate stability, to establish a multilateral system of payments, and to make its resources available to its members who are experiencing balance-of-payments difficulties.

- The Special Drawing Right (SDR) is a special asset the IMF created to increase international reserves.

- The exchange-rate arrangements of IMF countries can be either fixed or pegged to another currency or basket of currencies, pegged with different degrees of fluctuation, a managed float, or an independent float.

- The euro is a common currency in Europe that has been adopted by 12 of the first 15 members of the EU, and is slated to be adopted by the 10 countries added to the EU in 2004 as soon as they meet convergence criteria.

- African countries are committed to establishing a common currency by 2021, but there are many obstacles to accomplishing this objective.

- Many countries that strictly control and regulate the convertibility of their currency have a black market that maintains an exchange rate that is more indicative of supply and demand than is the official rate.

- Central banks are the key institutions in countries that intervene in foreign-exchange markets to influence currency values.

- The Bank for International Settlements (BIS) in Switzerland acts as a central banker's bank. It facilitates communication and transactions among the world's central banks.

- The demand for a country's currency is a function of the demand for its goods and services and the demand for financial assets denominated in its currency.

- A central bank intervenes in money markets by increasing a supply of its country's currency when it wants to push the value of the currency down and by stimulating demand for the currency when it wants the currency's value to rise.

- Some factors that determine exchange rates are purchasing-power parity (relative rates of inflation), differences in real interest rates (nominal interest rates reduced by the amount of inflation), confidence in the government's ability to manage the political and economic environment, and certain technical factors that result from trading.

- Major factors that managers should monitor when trying to predict the timing, magnitude, and direction of an exchange-rate change include the institutional setting (what kind of exchange-rate system does the country use), fundamental analysis (what is going on in terms of the trade balance, foreign-exchange reserves, inflation, etc.), confidence factors (especially political factors), events (like meetings of the G8 group of countries to discuss exchange rates), and technical analysis (trends in exchange-rate values).

- Exchange rates can affect business decisions in three major areas: marketing, production, and finance.

CASE   The Chinese Yuan—To Revalue or Not to Revalue, That Is the Question[41]

On January 7, 1994, the Chinese government, after debating what to do with its currency, decided to fix the value of the yuan (CNY) (also known as the renminbi or RMB) to the U.S. dollar at a rate of 8.690 per dollar, and over ten years later, it had settled in at 8.2765. But pressure began to build in 2005 as both the European Union and the United States faced strong competition from imports from China as well as from Chinese exports to third-country markets. As noted in the opening case in Chapter 7, a major source of tension was the elimination of textile and apparel quotas on January 1, 2005, leading to a significant rise in textile exports from China to the U.S. and EU.

Pressures for Change

When China fixed the value of its currency in 1994, it was not considered a major economic powerhouse, but by 2005, things had changed. In 1999, China was the largest country in the world in population and seventh largest in GNI. By 2003, it was the sixth largest country in the world in GNI, exceeded only by the U.S., Japan, Germany, the U.K., France, and Italy. It was also growing faster than any of the top six countries. In the decade of the 1990s, China grew by an annual average of 9.5 percent and was above 8 percent every year in the first half of the 2000s. Because of China's low manufacturing wages, it was exporting far more to the United States than it was importing. In 2004, China had a trade surplus of $155 billion with the United States, compared with a surplus of only $86 billion with the EU. However,

FIGURE 10.2   **EXCHANGE RATE OF CHINESE YUAN PER EURO AND PER U.S. DOLLAR**

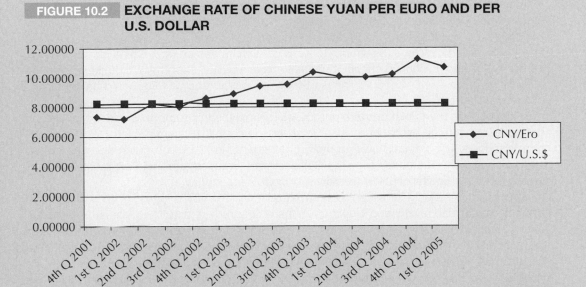

between 2002 and 2004, China's surplus with the EU doubled, whereas it grew by a little over a half with the U.S. The major problem with the EU is that during that time period, the euro had grown by 45 percent against the dollar, which meant that it had also grown by 45 percent against the yuan since the yuan was fixed against the dollar (see Figure 10.2). In effect, Chinese exports had gotten cheaper against European products both in the euro zone as well as in Europe's export markets. However, the competitive pressure of China in Asia was not the same. Since most Asian currencies were also locked onto the dollar, the yuan traded in a narrow range against those currencies. Most of the Asian countries were using China as a new market for their products, and they were not anxious to have anything upset the Chinese economy and reduce demand for their products.

Critics from the U.S. and EU argued that the yuan was undervalued by 15–40 percent and that the Chinese government needed to free the currency and allow it to seek a market level. The pressures for and against change were both political and economic. The U.S. government had been working with the Chinese for an extended period of time to get them to revalue their currency, but the Chinese government had found plenty of excuses not to do that. Finally, many members of the U.S. Congress decided to force the issue, and they announced that they would push to pass steep tariffs on Chinese exports if the Chinese didn't loosen their currency. The U.S. administration, concerned about possible protectionist threats by Congress, announced that it would give the Chinese until October 2005 to revalue its currency, or it would consider that China's exchange rate policy was, in fact, currency manipulation to improve its export position, forcing the government to negotiate sanctions against Chinese exports. The U.S. took the exchange-rate issue so seriously in 2005 that the U.S. Treasury Secretary named a special envoy to work with China on the issue.

China had its own political pressures. For one thing, a lot of people had been moving currency into China in anticipation of a revaluation of the yuan, and that was creating inflationary pressures in China. The Chinese government was forced to buy the dollars and issue yuan-denominated bonds as a way of "sterilizing" the currency—taking currency off the market to reduce inflationary pressures. The Chinese government was not very excited about revaluing the yuan and rewarding the speculators, so it kept saying that it would not announce how much, if, or when it would revalue its currency. In addition, it did not want to revalue under pressure from foreign governments, because it did not want to appear to be bowing under pressure from abroad. Finally, China has serious problems with employment. Even though China's 1.3 billion in population is growing at only 1 percent a year, it adds the equivalent of a new country the size of Ecuador or Guatemala every year. China needs to add enough jobs to keep up with its population growth and displaced workers from its agricultural sector and state-owned firms. That means that it needs to add 15–20 million new jobs per year. In comparison, the U.S. created 275,000 new jobs in April 2005, whereas China needs to create at least 1.25 million new jobs per month to keep up with its demands. If China slows down its economy to keep inflation in check, it needs to have a strong export sector to keep creating jobs. If the export sector cools because of a revalued currency, China could have political and social chaos.

The yuan is convertible for trade purposes. This means that exporters and importers can get access to foreign exchange easily. However, the capital account, which includes short-term and long-term capital flows, is more problematic. In 2005, the government loosened capital controls a little bit by allowing Chinese firms to invest abroad. But it did not completely eliminate capital controls to allow anyone to send money abroad.

What if the Chinese currency rises? What difference would it make? Critics in the U.S. assume that a yuan revaluation would solve the U.S.'s trade deficit. But Chinese exports are only 10 percent of total U.S. imports, so it would take a massive revaluation to have much impact on U.S. imports. Even a 10 percent revaluation would only reduce the trade-weighted value of the dollar by 1 percent, which is minor. One expert argued that even a 25 percent revaluation would reduce the current-account deficit by less than 5 percent. However, one could argue that the revaluation could also improve U.S. exports to other markets where exporters were facing competition from Chinese exports. Europe has a much bigger problem, because it is doubtful that the Chinese will allow their currency to revalue by 45 percent, the amount that the euro has risen against the dollar and the yuan since early 2002. European companies will still be uncompetitive, especially given China's low wages.

If the yuan rises, China's $600 billion in U.S. dollar foreign exchange reserves will fall by the amount of the revaluation. That is a major disincentive for a revaluation. In addition, the Chinese have basically invested their reserves in U.S. Treasury bills. If the Chinese decide that T-bills are a bad investment in a weaker dollar world, they might decide to invest in something else, like euros. The U.S. might be forced to raise interest rates, which could slow down the U.S. economy, which could reduce the demand for Chinese goods—which would now be more expensive anyway—which could lead to a rise in unemployment in China. Not a good idea!

Necessary Institutions

It is very easy to deal in foreign exchange in China, because the rate is fixed against the U.S. dollar. It doesn't take a lot of judgment for a trader to operate in a fixed rate world. In June 2005, the State Administration of Foreign Exchange in China (SAFE) decided to allow banks in Shanghai to trade and quote prices in eight currency pairs, including the dollar-sterling and euro-yen. Prior to that, licensed banks were only allowed to trade the yuan against four currencies—the U.S. dollar, the Hong Kong dollar, the euro, and the yen. However, all the trades were at fixed rates, and they did not involve trades in non-yuan currency pairs. SAFE also decided to open up trading to seven international banks (HSBC, Citigroup, Deutsche Bank, ABN Amro, ING, Royal Bank of Scotland, and Bank of Montreal) and two domestic banks (Bank of China and CITIC Industrial Bank).

Some argue that the steps being taken by SAFE are designed to build capability in trading before opening up the yuan to greater flexibility. Clearly, it is necessary to build capability in the banking sector as well as the regulatory sector. SAFE is responsible for establishing the new foreign exchange trading guidelines as well as for managing China's foreign exchange reserves.

Options

What can China do? There are four main options: China can maintain its fixed rate against the dollar, it can widen the trading band against the dollar, it can peg the yuan to a larger basket of currencies, or it could allow the yuan to freely float.

The first option, maintaining a fixed rate, is dangerous, because it could result in trade sanctions by the U.S. and EU against Chinese products. In that case, the EU and U.S. governments would reap the benefits of the tariffs, and China would simply lose market share, possibly leading to increased unemployment. When Chinese textile exports to the U.S. and EU jumped dramatically in early 2005, both of them began to talk about tariffs or quotas on Chinese goods. The U.S. even announced both tariffs and quotas on Chinese textiles and apparel. Then China followed up those actions by announcing duties of 400 percent against some garment exports. Will that be enough to take off the pressure for calls to revalue the yuan? What about other cheap products that China sells that will not be covered by the tariffs?

The second option, widening the trading band against the dollar, is a possibility, at least in the short run. In 2002, the yuan was trading within the 0.3 percent band of around 8.277 to the U.S. dollar, but by 2005, the band disappeared, and the yuan was trading at a fixed 8.2765. If China decides on this option, how much should it widen the band? Before permitting floating exchange rates, the International Monetary Fund allowed countries to trade their currencies within a band of 2 1/4 percent above or 2 1/4 percent below par value. If the Chinese allowed their currency to float up by 2 1/4 percent, would that take off the pressure?

The third option, pegging the yuan to a basket of currencies and possibly managing the value of the currency, would free the yuan from relying on the U.S. dollar as its main peg, and it would also result in less volatility since some currencies in the basket might be strong and others weak. If China picked the currencies of four of its major trading partners, it would pick the U.S. dollar, the euro, the yen, and the South Korean won. It might also want to include the British pound as well. The first challenge would be picking the currencies to include in the basket, the second would be to weight those currencies, and the third would be to determine how much the yuan would float against the basket. This is the policy followed by Singapore. In 1981, Singapore instituted a managed float, which is a compromise between a strong peg like the kind China has used since 1994 and a free float like the U.S. uses, where the rate is determined by market forces. Singapore uses a basket of currency reflecting the relative importance of its key trading partners. The Central Bank, the Monetary Authority of Singapore, manages the process. This has resulted in a rise in per capita income in Singapore, lower inflation, and lower interest rates.

The fourth option is to allow the yuan to freely float. That is a big risk, because there is no way of knowing how much the yuan will rise against the dollar. If it rises too far, too fast, it could choke off economic growth in China and create political and social problems. In addition, it might be difficult for an emerging foreign exchange market in China to handle the volatility. However, that is the system used for the U.S. dollar and the euro.

QUESTIONS

1. Evaluate the four choices that China faces in determining what to do with its currency value. Which choice would you choose, and why?
2. On July 23, 2005, China revalued the yuan. How much was the yuan revalued against the dollar and the euro? You can get the historical rate before and after the revaluation from http://www.oanda.com/convert/fxhistory. Which of the four options listed above was chosen, and do you think it will be successful?
3. Assume that you are a Chinese exporter. Would you prefer a Chinese export tariff on selected garment and textile exports as a way to relieve pressure against the yuan or a revaluation of the currency? Why?
4. Do you think the July 2005 revaluation will hurt you as a Chinese exporter? Why or why not?

CHAPTER NOTES

1 "El Salvador Learns to Love the Greenback," *The Economist* (September 26, 2002); John Lyons, "Squeezed by Dollarization," *Wall Street Journal* (March 8, 2005): A18; Bureau of Economic and Business Affairs, U.S. Department of State, "2001 Country Reports on Economic Policy and Trade Practices" (February 2002), http://www.state.gov/documents/organization/8202.pdf, accessed May 30, 2005; U.S. Department of State, "Background Note—El Salvador," http://www.state.gov/r/pa/ei/bgn/2033.htm, accessed May 30, 2005; U.S. Department of State, "Background Note—Ecuador," http://www.state.gov/r/pa/ei/bgn/ 35761.htm, accessed May 30, 2005; Juan Forero, "Ecuador's President Vows to Ride Out Crisis over Judges," *New York Times* (April 18, 2005).

2 "The IMF at a Glance" (May 25, 2005): http://www.imf.org/external/np/exr/facts/glance.htm.

3 Ibid.

4 "IMF Members' Quotas and Voting Power, and IMF Board of Governors" (May 19, 2005): http://www.imf.org/external/np/sec/memdir/members.htm#total.

5 "The IMF at a Glance," op. cit.

6 See IMF, "IMF Managing Director Issues Statement of Support for Argentina's New Medium-Term Program" (September 10, 2003): http://www.imf.org/external/np/sec/pr/2003/pr03154.htm.

7 Matt Moffett, "Argentina Squeezes Bondholders," *Wall Street Journal* (January 11, 2005): C1; Michael Casey, "IMF Presses Argentina on Debt Plan," *Wall Street Journal* (September 1, 2004): A10.

8 IMF, "SDR Valuation" (May 25, 2005): http://www.imf.org/external/np/fin/rates/rms_sdrv.cfm.

9 See a current issue of *International Financial Statistics* for an example of a country that uses the SDR as a basis for the value of its currency.

10 See Guillermo A. Calvo and Carmen M. Reinhart, "Capital Flow Reversals, the Exchange Rate Debate, and Dollarization," *Finance & Development* 36, no. 3 (September 1999): http://www.imf.org/external/pubs/ft/fandd/1999/09/calvo.htm; "No More Peso?" *The Economist* (January 23, 1999): 69; Steve H. Hanke, "How to Make the Dollar Argentina's Currency," *Wall Street Journal* (February 19, 1999): A19; Michael M. Phillips, "U.S. Officials Urge Cautious Approach to Dollarization by Foreign Countries," *Wall Street Journal* (April 23, 1999): A4; and "A Decline Without Parallel," *The Economist* (February 28, 2002): www.economist.com.

11 Craig Torres, "Chile Suspends Trading Band on Its Peso," *Wall Street Journal* (September 7, 1999): A21; "IMF Welcomes Flotation of Iceland's Krona," *IMF News Brief* (March 28, 2001): http://www.imf.org/external/np/sec/nb/2001/nb0129.htm.

12 "Convergence Criteria for European Monetary Union," *Bloomberg News* (August 9, 2002): www.bloomberg.com.

13 "Prime Minister Says Sweden Fulfills Criteria to Adopt Euro," *Dow Jones Newswires* (August 19, 2002): www.wsj.com.

14 Christopher Rhoads and G. Thomas Sims, "Rising Deficits in Europe Give Euro Its Toughest Challenge Yet," *Wall Street Journal* (September 15, 2003): A1.

15 "The Fall and Rise of the Euro," *BBC News* (January 5, 2004): news.bbc.co.uk; see x-rates.com (May 28, 2005).

16 Edmund L. Andrews, "On Euro Weekend, Financial Institutions in Vast Reprogramming," *New York Times* (January 2, 1999): www.nytimes.com.

17 Paul Masson and Catherine Patillo, "A Single Currency for Africa?" *Finance & Development* (December 2004): 9–15; "History of the CFA Franc," http://www.bceao.int/internet/bcweb.nsf/pages/umuse1, accessed May 30, 2005; IMF, "The Fabric of Reform—An IMF Video," http://www.imf.org/external/pubs/ft/fabric/backgrnd.htm, accessed May 30, 2005.

18 "Zimbabwe Arrests 10,000 in Black Market Crackdown," http://www.stuff.co.nz/stuff/0,2106,3292209a12,00.html, accessed May 30, 2005.

19 "Welcome to the Federal Reserve Bank: International Operations" (May 2005): http://www.ny.frb.org/aboutthefed/introtothefed.html.

20 International Monetary Fund, http://www.imf.org/external/pubs/ft/ar/2004/eng/pdf/file4.pdf; *IMF Annual Report* (2004): 101–3.

21 Sam Y. Cross, *All About the Foreign Exchange Market in the United States* (New York: Federal Bank of New York, 2002), 92–93.

22 David Wessel, "Intervention in Currency Shrinks Under Clinton," *Wall Street Journal* (September 14, 1995): C1.

23 See Jamie McGeever, "Dollar Gets Battered Across the Board," *Wall Street Journal* (December 9, 2003): C17; Sebastian Moffett, "Japan's Yen Strategy Offers Economic Relief," *Wall Street Journal* (January 12, 2004): A2; Miyako Takebe, "Japan Plans to Keep Intervening in Markets to Hold Down the Yen," *Wall Street Journal* (March 17, 2004): B4E; Alan Beattie, "Japan and ECB Consider Joint Currency Move as Dollar Falls," *The Financial Times* (December 2, 2004): 11.

24 "South Korea to Stop Currency Intervention: Report," *Yahoo! News* (May 18, 2005), http://news.yahoo.com/s/afp/20050518/bs_afp/forexusskorea_050518191953, accessed May 30, 2005.

25 "About BIS: Organisation and Governance" (May 2005): http://www.bis.org/about/orggov.htm.

26 "BIS History," Bank for International Settlements (May 2005): www.bis.org/about/history.htm.

27 "Background Information" and "Press Releases," G20 Web Site (2005): http://www.g20.org/index.htm.

28 "Food for Thought," *The Economist* (May 27, 2004): www.economist.com.

29 "The Big Mac Index: Food for Thought," *The Economist* (May 27, 2004). Quoted material contained in Federal Reserve Bank of St. Louis, Michael Pakko and Patricia Polland, "For Here or to Go? Purchasing Power Parity and the Big Mac" (St. Louis: Federal Reserve Bank of St. Louis, January 1996).

30 See "Brazil's Uncharted Terrain: Currency's Relentless Rise Gives Central Bank a New Headache," *Wall Street Journal* (March 16, 2005) www.wsj.com; and "Dollar Surprisingly Rallies, But Bears Still Growl" *Wall Street Journal* (April 1, 2005): www.wsj.com.

31 "More 'Distorted' Comments Roil Markets," *Wall Street Journal* (May 20, 2005): www.wsj.com.

32 "How a News Story, Translated Badly, Caused Trading Panic," *Wall Street Journal* (May 12, 2005): www.wsj.com.

33 "Race Against Time," *The Economist* (September 26, 2002): www.economist.com.

34 "Forecasting Currencies: Technical or Fundamental?" *Business International Money Report* (October 15, 1990): 401–2.

35 Andrew C. Pollock and Mary E. Wilkie, "Briefing," *Euromoney* (June 1991): 123–24.

36 "Currency Game Is Plenty Big, Plenty Tough," *Wall Street Journal* (May 6, 2005): www.wsj.com.

37 Because Toyota has sales in the United States, it risks losses in exchange rate translation when it records U.S. sales on its Japanese financial statements. Toyota estimated earnings for 2002 based on an exchange rate of 125 yen/dollar. If the yen strengthens to 116 against the dollar, Toyota's earnings translations will be much lower than at the 125 yen/dollar exchange rate. See Akio Hayashida and Junichi Maruyama, "Recovery Hopes Hit by Fall in U.S. Dollar," *Daily Yomiuri* (July 25, 2002): http://www.globalpolicy.org/socecon/crisis/2002/0725yomiuri.htm.

38 Dominic Lau, "Market Jitters Making HK Currency Peg Debate Taboo," *Reuters News Service* (September 24, 2002): http://asia.news.yahoo.com/.

39 Cross, op. cit., 114.

40 Oscar Suris, "BMW Expects U.S.-Made Cars to Have 80% Level of North American Content," *Wall Street Journal* (August 5, 1993): A2.

41 "China's Yuan, Softly, Softly," *The Economist* (March 31, 2005), www.economist.com/agenda/PrinterFriendly.cfm?Story_ID=3819927; Craig Karmin, "Dollar Rebound Builds on Stronger Economic Data," *Wall Street Journal* (May 16, 2005): A1; "Easing Prices Bolster Beijing's Currency Stance," *Wall Street Journal* (May 17, 2005): A10; Marcus Walker, "Euro Zone Suffers from China Syndrome," *Wall Street Journal* (May 17, 2005): A10; "Putting Things in Order," *The Economist* (March 17, 2005), http://www.economist.com/agenda/PrinterFriendly.cfm?Story_ID=3764776; "What Do Yuant From Us?" *The Economist* (May 18, 2005); Edmund L. Andrews, "Toughening Its Line, U.S. Warns China on Currency," *New York Times* (May 18, 2005); Keith Bradsher, "China's Growth Ebbs, a Deterrrent to Revaluation," *New York Times* (May 19, 2005); Andrew Browne, "U.S., China Press Yuan Row," *Wall Street Journal* (May 19, 2005): A2; Greg Hitt, "U.S. Picks Envoy to Engage China on Exchange Rates," *Wall Street Journal* (May 20, 2005): C3.

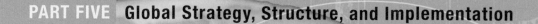

*A man must put grain in the ground
before he can cut the harvest.*

— GYPSY PROVERB

chapter eleven

The Strategy of International Business

OBJECTIVES

- To examine the idea of industry structure, firm strategy, and value creation

- To profile the features and functions of the value chain framework

- To appreciate how managers configure and coordinate a value chain

- To identify the dimensions that shape how managers develop strategy

- To profile the types of strategies firms use in international business

CASE: ZARA—VALUE CREATION IN THE GLOBAL APPAREL INDUSTRY[1]

In 2003, retail spending on clothing or apparel exceeded $1 trillion worldwide, with Europe accounting for 34 percent of the total market, the United States for 29 percent, and Asia for 23 percent. Historically, strategy in the global apparel industry was driven by a mix of production, buying, and distribution forces. Regarding production, the rule of the day was simple: Large national retailers outsourced, via global brokers, apparel production to literally tens of thousands of small apparel makers. The typical apparel manufacturing firm, almost always located in a low-wage market, employed a handful to a few dozen people who, in a highly labor-intensive process, generated specific pieces of clothing, often in a narrow range of sizes or colors. These pieces would then be integrated with the output of hundreds of other such firms spread across dozens of countries. Orchestrating the physical flows of apparel from thousands of factories in exporting countries to retailers in importing countries were multinational trading companies. Over time, as more countries generated more specialized products—one factory only made zippers, one only made linings, and so on—these trading companies became vital cross-border intermediaries.

Once assembled, global trading companies then supplied finished goods to apparel retailers, many of which had been independent, but increasingly were part of national chains. For instance, by 2005, the top five national chains accounted for more than half of apparel sales in many countries. Despite growing national concentration, retailing activities remained quite local: the top 10 retailers worldwide operated in an average of 10 countries in 2000—compared with top averages of 135 countries in pharmaceuticals, 73 in petroleum, 44 in automobiles, and 33 in electronics; they also derived less than 15 percent of their total sales from outside their home markets. No matter the home base, apparel retailers pushed trading companies to improve coordination between overseas factories and themselves in order to increase the speed and flexibility of responses to market shifts. Quicker responses to local markets helped retailers reduce forecast errors and inventory risks by planning assortments closer to the selling season, testing the market, placing smaller initial orders, and reordering more frequently.

The final link in this chain was markets and customers. Data suggested variation in local customers' preferences, even within a region or a country—that is, the British sought out stores based on social sensitivities, Germans were price-sensitive, and shoppers in the U.S. looked for a mix of variety, quality, and price. Collectively, these conditions had created a buyer-driven chain in the global apparel industry that linked fragmented factories, global brokers, national retailers, and local customers.

The growing globalization of markets seemed to change the operational choices for apparel firms—no matter what role they played. Essentially, conventional wisdom suggested that firms ought to choose a "sliver" of a particular activity—make only zippers, manage logistics, focus on store design, cater to precise customer segments—instead of trying to create value across several different activities. Essentially, many advocated the strategy: Do what you do best and outsource the rest. Now, though, reduction in tariff barriers, integration of markets, and improving economics of communications had changed the market, and in so doing, created new strategic choices. Regarding changes, nothing provided a more compelling example than the significant compression of cycle times in the apparel buyer chain (see Figure 11.1). In the 1970s, getting a garment from the factory to the customer took six months. Now it took about six weeks. And for one firm in particular, namely Zara, it took 15 days or so. Zara's emergence and success, in rejecting conventional wisdom, also set standards that called into question the relationship between industry structure, company strategy, and firm performance.

Zara, the leading division of the Spanish firm Inditex, was headquartered near La Coruña, a mid-sized city in northwest Spain (see Map 11.1). Zara opened its first store in 1975 but has since expanded to more than 400 storefronts around the world. In 2003, Zara's sales of nearly $4 billion put it behind Gap ($16 billion) and Swedish clothier H&M (about $5 billion). Since 1996 sales had increased 400 percent, profits grew 600 percent to about $400 million, and return on equity rose from 20 to 23 percent. International sales generated nearly half of total revenue.

While unknown to most, Zara used an innovative strategy to power its global expansion. Essentially, Zara redefined the idea of infotech and fashion through its integration of design, speed, production, responsiveness, information technology, and e-business methods to make and move sophisticated

FIGURE 11.1

**CHANGE IN CYCLE
TIME IN THE GLOBAL
APPAREL INDUSTRY**

Source: Zara Company documents.

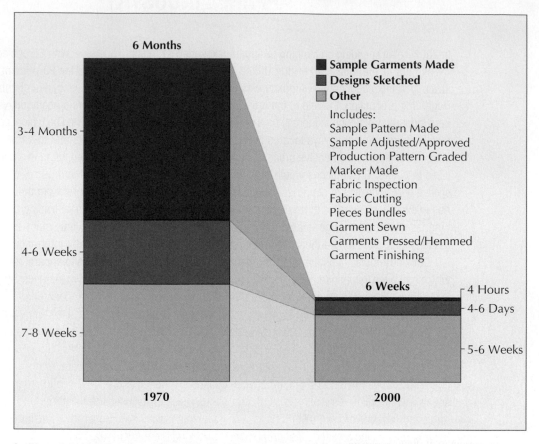

fashion at moderate prices. Operationally, Zara could translate the latest fashion trend from a catwalk in Paris to its store shelf in New York in as little as two weeks versus the industry standard of time-to-market of six months. Moreover, Zara could create new designs as the fashion season moved along to accommodate the tastes of fickle customers. In so doing, it called into question the idea of creating value in the global apparel industry. Zara's success stems from a number of competencies that spanned design, production, logistics, distribution, and retailing. We now profile key facets of each.

DESIGN

Zara rejects the conventional idea of spring and autumn clothing collections in favor of "live collections" that can be designed, manufactured, distributed, and sold almost as quickly as its customers' fleeting tastes—in fact, no style lasts more than four weeks. Zara's 300 or so designers continuously track market events, fashions trends, and customer preferences in designing about 11,000 distinct items per year—several hundred thousand SKUs, given variations in color, fabric, and sizes—compared with 2,000–4,000 items for rivals. Designers get ideas from frequent chats with store managers, industry publications, TV, Internet, film content, and trend-spotters who focus on venues such as university campuses and nightclubs. Too, Zara's so-called slaves-to-fashion staff is quick to snap digital pictures at couture shows and immediately reproduce the looks for the mass market. Always in the background, though, was the fact that Zara did not develop products to respond to a particular country's requirements. Management reasoned that the convergence of fashion and taste across national boundaries endorsed its strategic bias toward standardization. Certainly, some product designs catered to physical, cultural, or climate differences (e.g., smaller sizes in Japan, special women's clothes in Arab countries, different seasonality in South America). Still, 85 to 90 percent of the basic designs sold in Zara stores tend to be the same from country to country.

SOURCING

Zara sources from external suppliers with the help of purchasing offices in Beijing, Barcelona, and Hong Kong, as well as headquarters staff. Zara also acquires fabric, other inputs, and finished products from

MAP 11.1   Spain

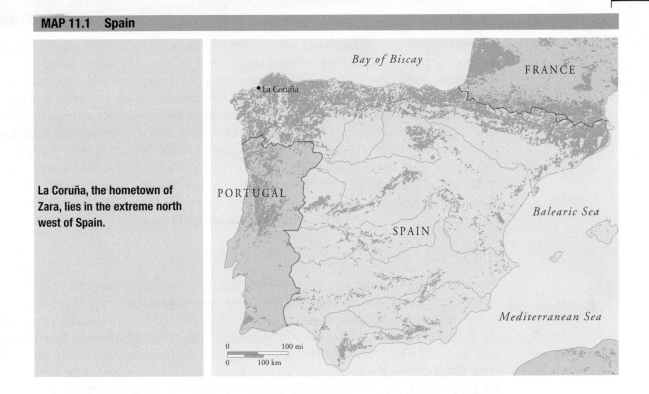

La Coruña, the hometown of Zara, lies in the extreme north west of Spain.

Bay of Biscay

• La Coruña

FRANCE

PORTUGAL

SPAIN

Balearic Sea

Mediterranean Sea

0   100 mi

0   100 km

numerous suppliers in Spain, India, Morocco, and the Far East. Linked into Zara's network, suppliers could coordinate their production with Zara's projections. About one-half of the fabric purchased is "gray" (not yet dyed) so designs can be quickly updated during a season. Explained José Maria Castellano, Inditex's chief executive, "We have the ability to scrap an entire production line if it is not selling. We can dye collections in new colors, and we can create a new fashion line in days."

PRODUCTION

Like its rivals, Zara sources finished garments from suppliers in Europe, North Africa, and Asia. Unlike its rivals, Zara employs more than 14,000 people to make about 40 percent of its finished garments in any of its 20 fully owned factories, 18 of them clustered around its headquarters in La Coruña. Essentially, Zara makes its most time- and fashion-sensitive products internally. Zara's factories are heavily automated, specialized by garment type, and focused on the capital-intensive parts of the production process—pattern design and cutting—as well as on final finishing and inspection. While it had been making garments since the 1980s, starting in 1990 Zara solicited the help of Toyota of Japan to help it install a just-in-time system. The company spent about 15 percent more to produce garments in Spain and Portugal than rivals spent in China, mainly due to labor costs. It more than compensates for this cost penalty with a lean advertising program, efficient inventory management, and quick adjustments to fashion trends.

Despite technology, many garments could not be made by machine. So Zara built a network of about 450 workshops, located primarily in Galicia and across the border in northern Portugal, which perform the labor-intensive, scale-insensitive activity of sewing the garment pieces cut at the factories. These workshops are generally small operations, averaging about 20–30 employees (although a few employ more than 100 people apiece), that specialize by product type. Zara accounts for most if not all of their business, provides them with tools, technology, logistics, and financial support, and pays them standard rates per finished garment. Basically, Zara's factories cut and color fabric into pieces of a particular garment. They then send these pieces to the workshops, which return finished garments to Zara. Upon return, the garments are inspected, ironed, folded, bagged, and electronically tagged before traveling on hanging rails along 125 miles of underground tracks that link the production sites to the logistics center.

LOGISTICS

All garments, both internally made and externally contracted, flow into Zara's massive distribution center in La Coruña or smaller satellite centers in Brazil and Mexico. Fully equipped with mobile tracking systems that dock hanging garments in the appropriate bar-coded area and carousels capable of handling 45,000 folded garments per hour, they have a simple mission: Move inventory as fast as possible from the warehouse to Zara stores around the world. Driving the process are the twice weekly deliveries to every Zara store triggered by real-time inventory data collected through a network of computer handsets feeding through the Internet. Lorena Alba, Inditex's director of logistics, regarded the warehouse as a place to move merchandise rather than to store it. According to her, "The vast majority of clothes are in here only a few hours," and none ever stayed at the distribution center for more than three days. Third-party delivery services manage the transfer of preprogrammed lots to stores. This fancy digital footwork has dropped Inditex's inventory to 7 percent of annual revenues, compared with the mid to high teens for its rivals.

MARKETING

Zara's trailblazing particularly challenges age-old retail marketing practices. Its product policy emphasizes reasonable quality goods, rapidly changing product lines, and a relatively high fashion image. The company uses virtually no advertising or promotion—it spends about 0.3 percent of its revenue on media advertising, compared with 3–4 percent for most specialty retailers. Its advertising is limited to the start of the sales period at the end of each "season." It relies extensively on word-of-mouth to market its products. Its pricing strategy is, in the words of one analyst, "Armani at moderate prices." Interestingly, management adjusts pricing for the international market, thereby making customers in foreign markets bear the costs of shipping products from Spain. For instance, prices are, on average, 40 percent higher in Northern European countries than in Spain, 10 percent higher in other European countries, 70 percent higher in the Americas, and 100 percent higher in Japan.

STORE OPERATIONS

Zara's stores have two primary purposes: present the company's face to the world and function as grassroots marketing research agents. The stores are usually in high-profile slots, most often premier shopping streets in markets such as the Champs Elysees in Paris, Regent Street in London, and Fifth Avenue in New York. Zara takes great measures to make sure it puts its best face forward. Regional teams of window dressers and interior coordinators visit each store every three weeks, making sure the window displays and interior presentations convey the right image. Back at headquarters, designers wander the mock store space and test possible themes, color schemes, and product presentation model window and store areas. The same standards apply to the staff: store employees wear Zara clothes while working, and while there is some leeway for local conditions, it is closely monitored. A store manager specifies the uniform choices twice a season from the current season's collection. It is then up to headquarters to approve.

Store managers and staff choose which merchandise to order, which to discontinue, and which to propose. Regarding the latter, Zara equipped all salespeople with wireless handheld organizers that let them punch in trends, customer comments, and orders. Networked stores continually transfer data on which merchandise is selling along with customer requests to Zara's design teams, factories, and logistics center in La Coruña. The availability of store managers capable of handling these responsibilities was, according to CEO Castellano, the single most important constraint on Zara's global expansion.

FIRM INFRASTRUCTURE

The firm infrastructure that Zara built to support these operations was a particular competency for the company. While there are many aspects, two stand out: managers' sense of customers and markets and their ability to coordinate activity worldwide. Managers believe that the allure of Zara is the freshness of its offerings, the creation of a sense of scarcity and an attractive ambience, and the positive word of mouth that results. Operationally, these ideas led to the notion of rapid product turnover, with new designs arriving in each twice-weekly shipment. Zara fans soon learned which days of the week delivery trucks came to stores and shopped accordingly. About three-quarters of the merchandise on display is changed every three to four weeks, which also corresponds to the average time between visits, given estimates that the average Zara shopper visits the chain 17 times a year, compared to an average figure of three to four times a year for competing chains and their customers. And attractive stores, outside and inside, also help. As Luis Blanc, a director at Inditex, explained, "We invest in prime locations. We place great care in the presentation of our storefronts. That is how we project our image. We want our clients to enter a beautiful store, where they are offered the latest fashions. But most important, we want our customers to understand that if they like something, they must buy it now, because it won't be in the shops the following week. It is all about creating a climate of scarcity and opportunity." Rapid turnover of stock creates a sense of "buy now because you won't see this item later," a sense amplified by small shipments, sparsely stocked display shelves, limits of one month on how long individual items can be sold in the stores, and a degree of deliberate undersupply. Finally, rapid turnover means that consumers visit Zara three or four times a season rather than just once.

Managers' adept coordination of the overlapping activities among its designers, workers, salespeople, and plants testifies to the power of this strategy. Presently, no other company can ship new fashion designs to stores as quickly as Zara. Still, the company has achieved the same profit margins with higher sales per square foot than its major rivals. Over time, Zara's strategy and business design, on the face of it, leaves rivals less and less time to integrate design, manufacturing, and distribution systems within their own global chains. Some believe that rivals have little option but to follow Zara's strategic lead; if they don't, warned a leading retail analyst, they "won't be in business in 10 years." Nonetheless, some rivals downplayed these cautions. Few big clothing retailers preferred to comment directly on Zara, instead maintaining the power of their conventional strategy to create value. "We have over 900 suppliers and we see a lot of advantages in working that way, such as flexibility, larger-volume capability, etc.," says an H&M spokeswoman. "This system has worked for us for a long time."

INTRODUCTION

The first half of this text explains that international companies operate in an environment shaped by a vast range of economic, political, legal, cultural, market, trade, monetary, governmental, and institutional forces (see Figure 11.2). In theoretical terms, these forces make up the environment of international business. In applied terms, these forces represent the system outside the international firm's boundaries that influence the actions of its managers. It is the latter dimension, what managers do to help their companies compete more effectively as international businesses, given their particular external environment, that anchors this chapter and the remainder of the text.

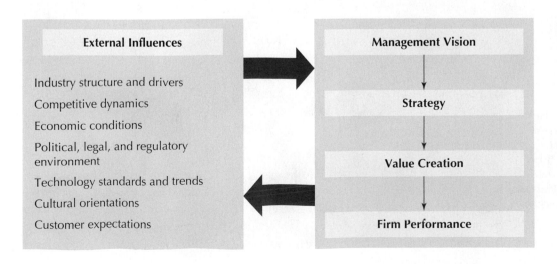

FIGURE 11.2

THE STRATEGY OF INTERNATIONAL BUSINESS

Specifically, this chapter looks at how managers, as agents of their firms, devise strategies to engage international markets in ways that sustain the company's growth and boost its profitability. The first half of the text showed that while the many commonalities that unite countries create opportunities for companies, substantial differences endure that constrain their range of actions. This chapter takes this cumulative understanding as the point of departure and moves into identifying the environmental factors that influence managers' strategic analyses, the concepts that anchor managers' evaluation of strategy, the tools that support their strategic choices, and the processes that managers use to ultimately convert their analyses into strategies that create superior value in international markets.

Ensuing chapters elaborate the framework we build in this chapter. That is, the perspective of strategy we develop in this chapter guides our analysis of several subsequent questions, including how firms choose to enter which foreign markets, which companies they opt to ally with, and how they build organizations to govern their worldwide activities. In the final section of the text, the ideas of this chapter anchor our discussions of how MNEs design and implement their marketing, manufacturing, supply, accounting, finance, and human resources strategies.

Our opening profile of Zara previews many of these issues. Specifically, when Zara began its global expansion, the conventional strategy in the apparel business was narrowly defined by the structure of the industry—a structure that was increasingly inefficient (as seen in the time needed to design and deliver clothing) and ineffective (as seen in the never-ending planning and inventory problems for apparel makers and sellers). Figure 11.1 shows how Zara rejected the strategic imperatives of the prevailing industry structure and, over the next decade, designed a strategy to create value through improved efficiency of action and effectiveness of ideas. Zara's strategy has changed the nature of the apparel industry in ways that redefine conventional ideas of global integration and national responsiveness. More specifically, Zara changed how a company in the apparel business created value in design, manufacturing, logistics, export, marketing, and service. Too, it introduced novel standards regarding how a company builds the internal systems and infrastructure to coordinate the various business functions that generate value both for the consumer and company. Most importantly, Zara's long-running series of seemingly distinct choices in production, manufacturing, staffing, logistics, and

---

Strategy is the framework that managers apply to determine the competitive moves and business approaches that run the company.

Strategy is management's idea on how to best

- Attract customers
- Stake out a market position
- Conduct operations
- Compete effectively
- Achieve goals
- Create value

While a somewhat odd mix, some say this image represents an emerging frontline of strategy in international business. The combination of low-cost locations, efficient communications, and the quest to improve living standards, whether here or at thousands of similar sites around the world, at may lead to new ideas on competition and value creation.

so on highlight the fundamental value of strategy for the international company—managing the tension between global integration and local responsiveness in a way that converts a unique strategy into superior value.

INDUSTRY, STRATEGY, AND FIRM PERFORMANCE

Before looking at the role of strategy in the MNEs, we look at some fundamental features of strategic management, specifically the ideas of and relationships among industry, strategy, and firm performance. We begin by looking at industry for the simple reason that it can significantly influence the profitability of the typical company. In general, the forces in the MNE's environment that routinely have the greatest impact on its strategy are in its immediate industry and competitive environment. Granted, BMW, for example, worries how trends in interest rates, change in political leadership, and innovations in communication technologies will affect its profitability. But BMW is far more sensitive, because it directly affects their competitive position and profit performance, to the actions of fellow industry members like Toyota, Goodyear, and Bosch.

A prominent model of strategy in a market of perfect competition, developed in the so-called *industry organization* (IO) paradigm, captures this thesis. First, the model presumes that markets are perfectly competitive; there are large numbers of fully informed buyers and sellers of a homogeneous product and there are no obstacles to entry or exit of firms into the market. In this market structure, the IO model reports that risk-adjusted rates of return should be constant across firms and industries—effectively, over time no one firm or industry should consistently outperform others.[2] Those industries in which firms do will, in the long term, attract new firms that freely enter that market, thereby creating more competition that lowers prices and lowers firms' profits. The IO model holds that the performance of a firm is a function of its market conduct, which in turn is determined by the structure of its industry.[3] Research supports this view, finding that industry effects explain up to 75 percent of the difference in average returns for companies in an industry.[4]

Beginning in the 1980s, other studies reported that over time different companies in different industries sustained different levels of profitability in ways that were moderated, but not determined, by the particular structure of their industry.[5] Certainly, these reports agreed, within the theoretical context of perfect competition, that the performance of any firm is largely determined by industry characteristics. However, the IO model's predictability was constrained by the fact that many industries exhibited imperfect competition (i.e., the presence of entry barriers that deterred new firms; the presence of a few large sellers who behaved as oligarchs; or many buyers, whether intermediate or end consumers, who were passive price takers). Moreover, studies identified many firms that were outstanding performers, year in and year out, in their industry. Some examples quickly come to mind, such as Dell in computers, General Electric in jet turbines, or Toyota in automobiles. These two anomalies—markets were not always perfectly competitive, and some firms consistently outperformed industry averages—suggest industry structure is not necessarily deterministic of firm performance. Instead, firm performance was arguably influenced by the presence of bright, motivated managers and their keen sense of developing innovative products for new and existing markets.[6] The realization that, while industry matters, so too does the quality of managers suggested that great managers who developed better strategies and built better companies outperformed their counterparts. Effectively, then, innovative strategic thinking and effort prepares managers to achieve and maintain competitive advantages despite the structure of the industry, much like the managers have done at Zara and, as we will see in our closing case, at eBay.

In summary, strategic management research reports two important relationships. First, although competition may not be necessarily perfect, industry structure directly influences a company's performance. Second, the reality that competition may not be

Perfect competition presumes

- Many buyers and sellers such that no individual affects price or quantities
- Perfect information for both producers and consumers
- Few, if any, barriers to market entry and exit
- Full mobility of resources

Bright managers find ways to create value that are not easily matched or cheaply copied by rivals.

necessarily perfect creates the potential for a company to convert an innovative strategy into superior competitiveness. Therefore, the strong relationship between industry structure, strategy, and performance means managers must understand what strategy is, the tools that they can use to make it, and the implication of their choices to the performance of their company. The first part of this chapter develops these ideas, first profiling how managers assess industry structure and then discussing how they develop strategy for international business.

The Idea of Industry Structure

Industry structure is an explanation of the functions, form, and interrelationships among

- Suppliers of inputs
- Buyers of outputs
- Substitute products
- Potential new entrants
- Rivalry among competing sellers

The idea of industry structure has many well-defined concepts that specify means to assess its character.[7] Often managers anchor analysis of industry structure by modeling the strength and importance of the so-called "five fundamental forces" of an industry. This model, shown in Figure 11.3, holds that the nature of competition in an industry is the combined outcome of the competitive pressures generated by (1) the moves of rivals battling for market share, (2) the entry of new rivals seeking market share, (3) the efforts of other companies outside the industry to convince buyers to switch to their own substitute products,[8] (4) the push by input suppliers to charge more for their inputs, and (5) the push by output buyers to pay less for products. Collectively, the five-forces model develops a picture of the structure and competition in an industry that prepares managers to figure out what fundamental forces shape strategic conduct, how strong each force is, what forces are driving changes in the industry, what strategic moves rivals are likely to make next, and what the key factors are for future competitive success. Common to each issue is the question of whether the current or future outlook suggests that firms in the industry have no, some, or great potential to make profits.

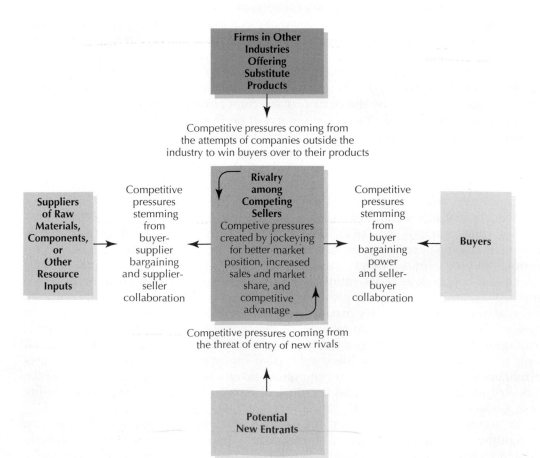

The assessment of an industry's structure provides the basis for estimating the kinds of strategic moves that companies in the industry are likely to use. For example, companies operating in an industry characterized by steep scale economies, as in the liquid screen display industry, will likely face rivals that are keenly intent on exploiting the cost-saving economies of larger-scale standardization. The fact that this objective depends on increasing sales volumes, typically at the expense of existing rivals, means that less efficient as well as small-scale companies face tremendous pressure to compete and, ultimately, survive. Conversely, those industries that are marked by a continuous stream of product innovations, as in the digital camera industry, create a different set of imperatives. In that sort of industry, creating value rests on how well a company can fund R&D, translate ideas into innovation, and get its products to market quickly with a strong brand name that has the premium image to command a high price. Product innovation, not cost control, becomes the basis for sustainable value creation.

A look at the globalization in the financial services industry demonstrates the interpretative power of the five-forces model. The opening of new markets and the advent of new technologies has spurred financial services companies to rethink how they run operations in their evolving industry. Most notably, the financial services industry is now one in which firms must compete in all world markets in order to survive. This evolution means a firm's competitive advantage depends on how well it can achieve economies of scale and economies of scope across countries. Greatly influencing these trends has been the potential for offshoring to create a truly global operating model for financial services. These developments have prompted companies to change the way they compete. Some, like Citibank, have prospered, while others, like JPMorgan Chase & Co. and Deutsche Bank, Germany's largest bank, have been scrambling. On a different front, the growing profits of the global financial services industry attract new entrants. These companies launch new strategies and products that change the nature of competition in the industry. For example, ING Direct, part of the Dutch financial giant, ING, became the fastest growing savings and loan association in the United States through a new approach to banking. The emergence of new markets in Asia and Central Europe has brought many new buyers and suppliers of all sorts of financial products. Finally, the increasing sophistication of buyers gives them incentive to sort through the growing number of options in the search for the best deal. Collectively, these forces have changed the structure of the global financial services industry, and in the process, changed the potential for profitability for industry members. We see similar scenarios in a wide cross section of industries such as textbook publishing, credit cards, mobile phones, automobiles, steel, oil, and business services.

A global industry is one in which a firm's competitive position in one country is significantly affected by its position in other countries.

Industry Change

The structure of industries is continually in flux. New products, new firms, new markets, and new managers trigger new developments in rivalry, pricing, substitutes, buyers and suppliers. Often these developments change a minor feature of the industry, such as the expansion of an existing distribution channel, thereby leaving industry members the option of continuing to operate as they had. Occasionally, though, a change redefines one or more of the five fundamental forces in an industry, such as what the merger of market leaders, like Deutsche and Dresdner or J.P. Morgan and Chase, did to intra-industry rivalry in financial services. At this time, managers must identify the force of the particular change, estimate the impact it may have on their industry and company, and determine an effective response. The types of forces that can transform an industry's structure include changes in the long-term industry growth rate, new technologies (like the Internet, modular containerization, and wireless communications), new consumer buying and usage patterns (such as buying music online or renting, receiving, and returning movie DVDs via the mail), manufacturing innovations that revise cost and efficiency frontiers (like that done with Six Sigma programs), the diffusion of business, executive, and technical expertise across countries (such as the transfer of the Western management

Industry structure changes due to events like

- *Competitors' moves*
- *Government policies*
- *Changes in industry economics*
- *Shifting buyer preferences*
- *Technological developments*
- *Rate of market growth*

approach to emerging Asian companies), change in government regulation (such as the ongoing privatization of state assets), or the entry or exit of major firms (such as the emergence of many large-scale Chinese companies).

Some industries are prone to be affected by certain forces more so than others. The ball bearings industry, for instance, is more likely to change due to rapid escalation of pricing pressures, whereas the insurance business is more likely to change to reflect the rapid emergence of more traditional and online rivals. It is worthwhile to note that while many forces of change may be in play in a given industry, generally no more than a few command the power to reset its basic structure. Managers' task is to separate major factors from minor ones and best position the firm to compete and create value in the likely new industry.

Strategy and Value

Earlier, we profiled the view that great managers make great strategies that make great companies that outperform their industry rivals. A lot of work has gone into specifying the principles and practices of each dimension of this relationship. Perhaps the most notorious one has been setting the standards of a great strategy. A quick look through any library finds literally thousands of views of the standards of a great strategy. Still, there are some common denominators. A great strategy defines the perspectives and tools managers use to appraise the company's present situation, identifies the direction the company should go, and determines how the company will get there. These issues, while straightforward, can be challenging for any firm, but especially for the international company. The latter must deal with the contingencies created by dealing with many different consumers, markets, industries, institutions, and environments.

These questions are vital aspects of strategy. Ultimately, though, each one references the fundamental principle of strategy: creating value. The idea of value can be defined in a variety of ways, including economic value, market value, pro forma value, economic value, book value, insurance value, use value, par value, and replacement **value**; and from a number of perspectives, such as those of customers, employees, stakeholders, or shareholders. For our purposes, we define **value** as the measure of a firm's capability to sell what it makes for more than the costs incurred to make it. Therefore, **strategy** is the efforts of managers to build and strengthen the company's competitive position within its industry in order to create value.

> A great strategy helps managers assess the company's present situation, identify the direction the company should go, and determine how the company will get there.

Creating Value

The nature of capitalism is fundamentally zero-sum; one party wins at the expense of the other. This relationship also anchors conventional interpretations of industry structure and firm strategy (i.e., the firm tries to maximize the price it charges consumers, whereas consumers try to minimize the price they pay to suppliers). The clarity of this relationship spurs the firm to develop a compelling value proposition that specifies its targeted customer markets, whether on a nation-by-nation or worldwide basis, and how it sees itself making and selling a product that exceeds customers' expectations. The more successfully the company does so, the greater the profits it earns. Operationally, companies create value either by making their products for a lower cost than any other firm in their industry (the strategy of low-cost leadership) or making those products that consumers are willing to pay a premium price for (the strategy of differentiation). We now profile each.

> Value is what is left over after all expenses have been deducted from the revenues of a firm.

Low-Cost Leadership   Firms that choose this strategy strive to be the low-cost producer in an industry for a given level of quality. This strategy pushes a firm to sell its products either at average industry prices to earn a profit higher than that of rivals or below the average industry prices to capture market share. Companies incur different costs because of differences in such matters as the prices they pay for raw materials and component parts, wage rates and productivity of their employees, scale of their

> Cost leadership emphasizes high production volumes, low costs, and low prices to attract customers.

production, and promotion and distribution expenses. A cost leadership strategy is a key advantage in highly competitive industries. In the event of a price war, the low-cost leader can cut its prices, thereby imposing intolerable losses on competitors, yet still earning some profits. Even without a price war, as the industry matures and prices decline, the firm that can make products more cheaply will earn profits far longer than its rivals. The cost leadership strategy usually targets a broad market. Presently, many Chinese companies are using this approach to create value. Most notably, they have combined efficient manufacturing operations; inexpensive, productive labor; and efficient distribution channels to undercut global rivals on price.[9]

Differentiation   Firms that choose this strategy aspire to develop products that offer unique attributes that they reason are highly valued by customers and which customers perceive to be better than or sufficiently different from products offered by other companies. The value added by the uniqueness of the product allows the firm to charge a higher price that more than offsets the added costs of making it. Companies like SAP, Pfizer, and Rolex, for example, create value via differentiation strategies. Each has been able to convert customer insights, skilled and creative product development, persuasive marketing programs, and premier reputations for quality into superior value creation. Companies that engage a differentiation strategy must continually find ways to develop products that have unique features that, in turn, lead buyers to prefer their goods and services versus those provided by rivals. Perhaps most importantly, differentiation strategy demands that a company develop points of uniqueness that rivals find hard if not impossible to match or copy, such as the prestige of a Rolex watch, the quality of a Lexus sedan, the superior service at a Ritz-Carlton, the fashion of a Zara suit, the wide selection of Amazon, or the one of its kind system of eBay.

> Differentiation spurs the company to provide a unique good or service that its rivals find hard, if not impossible, to match or copy.

No matter whether a firm opts for low-cost leadership or differentiation, the value creation potential of its strategy ultimately is a function of the amount of value, whether actual or perceived, that customers attribute to its products and the cost the firm incurs to make it. For both the low-cost leadership or differentiation strategies, the firm earns higher profits than its rivals when it creates more value for its customers and is able to charge them a price that rewards it. Understanding this relationship and then determining how to sustain it is the basis for superior strategy.[10]

THE FIRM AS A VALUE CHAIN

Eventually, managers move from the ambition of a low-cost or high-differentiation strategy to the reality of creating superior value. Countless questions then pop up. As we saw in the case of Zara, its executives made and continually tested decisions on issues such as: Where should we design the product? Should we make it in country a, b, or c? How can we best deliver it to customers in country x, y, and z? How do we devise marketing campaigns? Whom should we hire to staff retail operations? What role should headquarters take? And so forth. Common to each of these questions are fundamental concerns about the task of creating value, that is, how the company will design, make, move, and sell products; how it will find efficiencies in doing so; and how it will coordinate the decisions in one part of the business with those made in other parts. The challenges can and do prove treacherous.[11]

Thinking of the firm as a value chain provides a strong tool to deal with these challenges. Essentially, the **value chain** represents a framework that lets managers deconstruct the general idea of "create value" into the series of discrete activities that their company actually does to create value. So, upon specifying their company's value chain, managers can then target their insights and investments toward those activities that create value and avoid those that do not. Specifically, moving from the general idea of value creation to banking the profits from a sale requires a firm to complete a series of discrete activities. Managers must decide how the firm will handle the functions and business

> The value chain is the set of linked, value-creating activities the company performs to design, produce, market, deliver, and support a product.

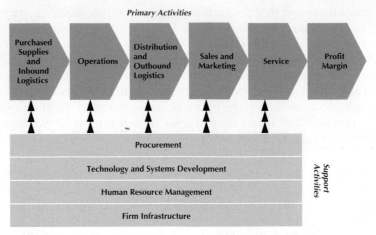

Primary Activities
Inbound logistics Receiving, warehousing, and inventory control of production inputs from company's suppliers.
Operations Processes that transform inputs into finished product.
Outbound logistics Moving the finished product into the supply chain from factory to wholesalers, retailers, or the final consumer.
Marketing & Sales Getting buyers to buy the product by using the marketing mix and advertising.
Service Customer support in terms of installation, aftersales service, complaints handling, training, and so on.

Support Activities
Procurement Purchasing the raw materials, components, and other inputs used throughout the value chain.
Technology and Systems Development Research and development, process automation, telecom and wireless systems, and other technology used to support value activities.
Human Resource Management Recruiting, development, compensating, and retaining employees as well as labor relations activities.
Firm Infrastructure Activities related to general management, accounting and finance, legal and regulatory affairs, safety and security, management information systems, and other "overhead" functions.

Value chain analysis helps managers understand the behavior of costs and the existing and potential sources of differentiation.

A value chain disaggregates a firm into its strategically relevant activities in terms of
- Primary activities that create and deliver the product
- Support activities that aid the individuals and groups engaged in primary activities

processes that move a product from its conception, through its design, its sourced raw materials and intermediate inputs, its marketing, its distribution, and its support, to the end consumer. Figure 11.4 shows how the value chain systematically organizes these elemental activities.

Technically, a value chain has four organizing dimensions:

1. *Primary activities* are those involved in the physical movement of raw materials and finished products, in the production of goods and services, and in the marketing, sales, and subsequent services of the outputs of the business. We identify primary activities with functional labels, such as in-bound logistics, operations, marketing, and so on. Hence, the five primary activities reflect classical managerial functions of the firm, where there is an organizational entity with a manager in charge of a specific task that has clear lines of functional demarcation.

2. *Support activities* make up the managerial infrastructure of the firm that supports carrying out the primary activities. The four support activities include the processes and systems installed to coordinate decisions and transactions among the various value activities.

3. *Profit margin.* The purpose of the value chain—to show how a firm creates value—is ultimately captured in the component of "profit margin." Placed at the end of the value chain, profit margin reports the difference between the total revenue generated by sales and the total cost of the activities that led to those sales.[12]

4. *Upstream and downstream.* The final element of a value chain is orientation—namely, whether the particular activity takes place upstream or downstream. Upstream refers to those activities, such as in-bound logistics, research and

development, and manufacturing, which gather and process the inputs that the company uses to make a product. Downstream refers to those activities, such as outbound logistics, marketing, and service, that deal more directly with the end customer.

Using the Value Chain

How well a company manages its value chain determines the power of its competitiveness. The value chain helps managers integrate the knowledge and skills of employees around the world in the way that lets them best leverage the company's global reach. As such, value chain analysis anchors and guides managers' effort to build expertise in those value activities that are critical to reducing costs or improving differentiation. Operationally, managers deal with the matters of configuration and coordination in setting up and running a value chain. Dispersing discrete activities of the value chain to those locations around the globe where perceived value is maximized or where the costs of value creation are minimized defines the matter of configuration. Integrating the discrete activities of the globally dispersed stages of the value chain into a cohesive, coherent whole defines the matter of coordination. Configuration and coordination are intrinsically related but each has unique features.

Value chains identify the format and interactions between different activities of the company.

Configuration

Every MNE, no matter how small or large, looks to establish elements of its value chain in the best spots in the world. The option to go anywhere in the world to do any activity gives MNEs tremendous choice in where to locate activities of their value chain. MNEs greatly improve their competitiveness and performance by configuring value activities to capture potential location economies—namely, the economies that arise from performing a value creation activity in the optimal location for that activity, wherever in the world that might be, given prevailing economic, political, and cultural conditions. Thus, if the best industrial designers are in Germany, a firm should base its design operations in Germany. If the most productive labor force for assembly operations is in China, the firm should base assembly operations in China. If the most creative advertising minds are in Italy, then the firm should create its advertising campaign in Italy. The managers' task is to find those locations, resources, and markets that best support the company's vision of creating a competitive value chain.

Configuration is the way that managers arrange the activities of the value chain.

The key caveat for location decisions is the notion that configuration should be optimized "given prevailing economic, legal, political, and cultural conditions." The complexity of this challenge has frustrated many MNEs. At one point, following yet another change in the international business environment, Jack Welch, former chairman and CEO of General Electric, thought the best location decision for GE factories was a barge, explaining that, "Ideally, you'd have every plant you own on a barge, to move with currencies and changes in the economy."[13] Earlier chapters showed that countries vary on many dimensions and that these differences directly affect business costs in a particular country. Moreover, we also saw from international trade theory that relative differences in factor costs give certain countries a comparative advantage in performing certain activities of a value chain. Therefore, several conditions shape how managers configure value chains worldwide, most notably, cost factors, business environments, cluster effects, logistics, degree of digitization, economies of scale, and buyers' needs.

Several factors influence value chain configuration

- Cost factors
- Business environments
- Cluster effects
- Logistics
- Economies of scale
- Buyers' needs

Cost Factors Differences in wage rates, worker productivity, inflation rates, and government regulations create significant variations in production costs from country to country. Consider, for example, labor costs. In 2003, the average hourly compensation (including benefits) for production workers in China was $0.80 versus $25.34 in the

Manufacturing costs vary from country to country due to wage rates, worker productivity, resource availability, and fiscal and monetary policies.

United States.[14] Consequently, footwear companies, like Nike or Reebok, locate the upstream activities (like sourcing and manufacturing) of their value chain in China and the downstream activities of their value chain (like marketing and service) in the United States. Therefore, cost factors in countries directly shape where international companies choose to locate value activities.

Business Environment   Location advantages are not the sole function of direct costs. Companies also configure their value chain to access a specific country's business environment. Governments of many countries aggressively recruit foreign investments. They often promise business-friendly business climates that offer lower corporate tax rates, more flexible operating requirements, and public policies that are responsive to industry. On the flip side, governments can create risky environments that deter local operations.

Cluster Effects   A peculiarity of value creation is the so-called *cluster effect*, in which a particular industry gradually clusters more and more related value creation effects in a specific location.[15] For example, Wall Street is a center for global finance, Baden-Wurttemberg is a center for cars and electrical engineering, Silicon Valley is a center for technology, Hollywood is a center for mass media, and Mumbai is a center for business process outsourcing. Each economic cluster creates unique location advantages that offer firms in that locale access to specialized resources that can dramatically improve the potential for innovation. Samsung, for example, became a leader in memory chip technology by establishing an R&D facility in Silicon Valley and transferring the know-how it gained back to its plants in South Korea.

Logistics is how companies obtain, produce, and exchange material and services in the proper place and in proper quantities for the proper value activity.

Logistics   At some point in every exchange along a value chain, the potential arises for a transfer of a good or service. In some situations, the value-to-weight ratio of that transaction can make a huge difference in configuration decisions. For example, the greater the value of a product to its weight, the less important storage and transportation costs matter. Therefore, the decision of where to manufacture computer chips, software, or aircraft, unlike tractor axles, carpets, or furniture, for instance, need not pay much attention to the distance between the factory and the consumer. Too, if a company builds a value chain in which just-in-time inventory practices are key parts of the in-bound and out-bound logistics activities, as we saw in the case of Zara, then it makes sense to locate key distributors, design and production centers, and logistics centers in the same area.

Degree of Digitization   The degree to which an analog product can be converted into a string of zeros and ones—the process of digitization—influences how a company configures its value chain. Increasingly, products like software, music, and books, and services like call centers, application processing, and financial consolidation, can be done virtually anywhere there is a computer and, via communication technologies, immediately be sent anywhere in the world at negligible cost and complication. Notably, for example, a host of activities that once could only be done in a few specialized places, say, the due diligence process in mergers and acquisitions that once took place largely in New York City, can now be offshored to firms in India.[16]

Scale economies refers to the decrease in the unit cost of production associated with the increase in total output.

Economies of Scale   Economies of scale refers to the reductions in unit cost achieved by producing a large volume of a product. Generally, economies of scale occur in industries with high capital costs in which those costs can be distributed across a large number of units of production, thereby resulting in lower per unit costs.

The cost of setting up a research center, production facility, and logistics hub can be substantial for some companies. For example, simply building a production site to make flat panel displays exceeds $3 billion, whereas outfitting a plant to make furniture might run a few million dollars. Therefore, steep up-front costs create high potential for scale economies, a relationship that leads managers to design value chains that exploit the potential efficiencies of a few plants centralized in one to a handful of countries, rather than operating several smaller, less efficient plants scattered across the world.

Customer Needs   Buyer-related activities, such as distribution to dealers, sales and advertising, and after sale service, usually take place close to buyers. This can press some companies to physically locate the capability to perform such activities in every country market where it has major customers. For example, the leading management consulting and accounting firms have numerous international offices to service the foreign operations of their globally dispersed clients.

DOES GEOGRAPHY MATTER?

LABOR COSTS AND LOCATION DECISIONS

Companies continually scrutinize where it makes the most sense to locate particular activities of their value chain. The location decision of many value activities is determined by cost structures—both in terms of the cost structure today as well as the likely cost structure five to ten years from now. North American footwear makers, like Nike, for example, once made shoes in the U.S., but over a 30-year span moved production from Taiwan, to the Philippines, Thailand, Korea, Vietnam, and China in the quest for the lowest possible production costs. Today, the United States imports some 70 percent of footwear. So, despite the growing uniformity of many customers, companies, and countries, cost structures can vary dramatically from country to country.

As in the footwear industry, a compelling location criterion in many industries is the cost of labor. And, within the context of labor costs, companies are looking at how they have currently configured their value chain in the face of the widening cost differentials between high-cost and low-cost countries. For example, a factory worker in the U.S. typically costs between $15 and $30 per hour. In contrast, a Chinese or Indonesian factory worker typically makes less than $1 an hour. For service employees, such as phone center employees, the savings are striking too. The labor cost savings a company realizes by outsourcing a service job to India can be as much as 60 percent. More significantly, current projections see the average wage rage in the U.S. moving to a bit over $25, to about $1.30 in China, and $0.70 in Indonesia.

Map 11.2 reports the labor costs for various countries. The extreme differentials, both current and forecasted, have tremendous implications for value creation and value chain configuration at many companies. Already, as we saw in the opening case for Chapter 3, thousands of MNEs from around the world have started operations in China in the past few years. More powerfully, the data in Map 11.2 suggest the global migration of sourcing and manufacturing operations from high-cost to rapidly developing low-cost countries such as China, India, Southeast Asia, and Central and Eastern Europe will accelerate in the next few years. Consequently, executives everywhere will need to rethink the strategic and operational implications of their idea of value creation. This process will likely lead to radical reconfiguration in the value chains of many companies in consumer electronics, chemicals, automotive components, household appliances and motors, generators, relays and industrial controls, aerospace equipment, machine shops, and architectural and structural products.

MAP 11.2   Labor Costs and Location Decisions

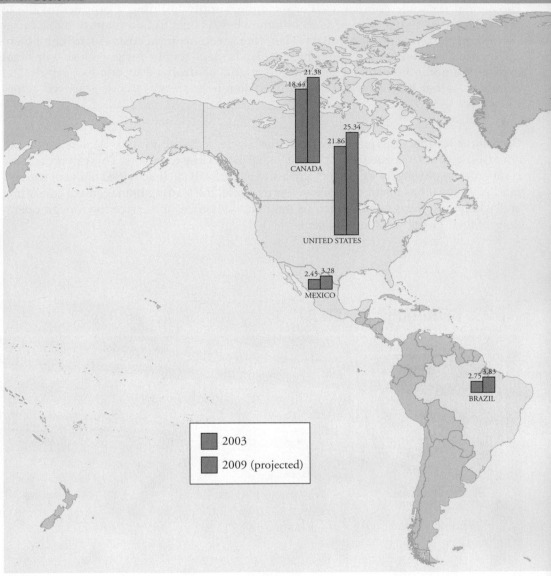

Average hourly compensation of production workers (including benefits, 2003 vs. 2009, in US $). Labor costs differ greatly from so-called high-cost to low-cost countries. These differences will likely persist for years, accelerating the ongoing migration of sourcing and manufacturing operations to low-cost locations.

Sources: "Capturing Global Advantage," by Arindam Bhattacharya, et al., Boston Consulting Group (April 9, 2004).

2003

2009 (projected)

Coordination

Coordination is the way that managers connect the discrete activities of the value chain.

The discrete activities of the value chain, as elements of a larger system, require managers to figure out how to coordinate decisions and transactions both within and across value activities. The task of coordinating the different activities that go into making and moving a product around the world, while sounding ordinary, has emerged as the basis of the superior performance that separates good from great MNEs. For example, Zara's strategy of rapid response to ever-changing fashion trends demands lots of coordination. To get started, Zara must coordinate the efforts of its many salespeople who, as wired grass-roots market researchers, punch in trends, customer comments, and orders. Each day, these data are transferred to headquarters and used to coordinate design, production, and delivery. The resulting task, for headquarters, is brutal: It must coordinate material flows from its many suppliers and ensure order transmission to its several factories and delivery status to its hundreds of storefronts.

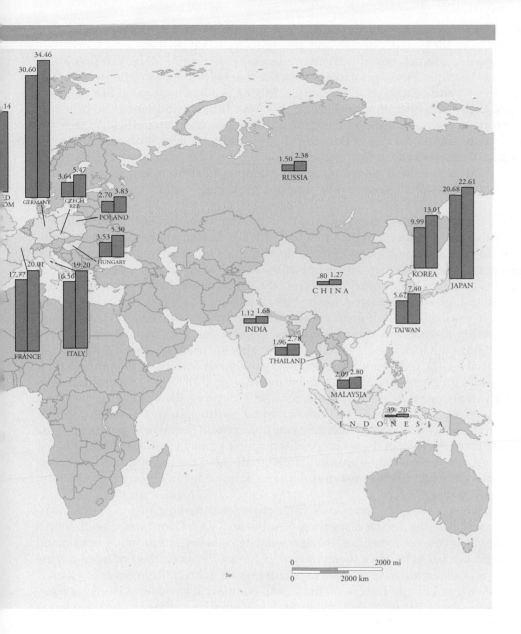

Unquestionably, coordinating value activities has been an intrinsic part of international operations since companies began venturing abroad. Managers worked hard to coordinate linkages between value activities in the belief that weaving them into a coherent whole was instrumental in achieving the synergy of international operations that are only available to MNEs.[17] This goal has assumed greater importance in the past few years, given the growing appreciation of the performance and competitive benefits of better coordinating so-called *core competencies* throughout a value chain.[18]

Technically, a **core competency** is a special outlook, skill, capability, or technology that creates unique value for the firm by creating an acknowledged thread that runs through all of the firm's value activities. Popular examples of core competencies include Wal-Mart's sophisticated information management and product distribution systems, 3M's legacy of product innovation, Intel's design of complex semiconductors, MBNA's customer orientation, Honda's expertise in engine technology management

A company's core competency is

- The unique skills and/or knowledge that is better than its competitors'
- Essential to its competitiveness

systems, Procter & Gamble's marketing-distribution skills and R&D capabilities, and Apple's eye for product design and ability to translate its ideas into innovative products. A core competency effectively gives everyone in the MNE, not just a few executives at headquarters, a principle or practice that helps them coordinate activities more coherently and cohesively. For example, MBNA is a leading United States–based credit card bank with operations in Europe and Asia. It has championed the principle that everyone in the company "think of yourself as a customer" and officially sees this idea as its core competency in everything it does and wherever it operates. Finally, the fact that rivals cannot easily match or replicate it serves as a powerful source of competitive advantage for a company. So, for example, MNBA has translated its standard of peerless customer service into superior profitability and a premier industry position.

Understanding the interactions and overlaps among the activities that make up the firm's value chain, and then linking them to the firm's core competency, is instrumental to making a value chain work. Doing so stimulates managers to see particular activities not as ends unto themselves but as the means of creating superior value for the firm. For example, the country that offers the maximum value creation for manufacturing might, given its remote location, result in higher logistics costs that reduce the value for marketing and, if great enough, for the entire value chain. Hence, managers' capability to directly associate activities, assets, costs, and revenues helps them understand how the firm creates value—both in specific activities as well as overall. More pointedly, UPS and Federal Express are slowly but forcefully expanding their operations into all parts of the world, most recently reinforcing their beachheads in China with the expansion of local hubs. Similarly General Electric, Microsoft, and Citigroup have opened research and development facilities in India, reasoning that the high productivity of the local scientific community will create new points of value creation for them. As each of these companies disperses greater portions of their value chain over greater territory, they are challenged to develop the coordination tools that enable them to transfer their extensive and unique knowledge in research, production, logistics, and service.

The global elaboration of a company's value chain leads to the question of how managers will coordinate the greater dispersion of value activities. Coordinated well, MNEs can leverage their core competencies, using them to boost sales and profits. Coordinated poorly, MNEs can fail to leverage their core competencies, let alone their more mundane capabilities and resources, from country to country—that is, breakthroughs at the John F. Welch Technology Center in Bangalore, India, will not make it to General Electric's operations in Hungary or Brazil or the United States. Therefore, managers develop value chains with an eye to how they will ultimately coordinate activities that may span anywhere from one to many nations. Several factors in particular moderate managers' analyses of how to coordinate value activities, notably, operational obstacles, national cultures, learning effects, and subsidiary networks.

Operational Obstacles   MNEs regularly run into problems when trying to get the various links of their global value chain to deal to each other. Communication challenges especially arise when trying to synchronize languages; parts flowing from the Far East to South America to their ultimate stop in the United States generate many possible points of miscommunication. In principle, companies can insist that staff rely on browser-based communications. However, this option still has a way to go. European companies, for instance, have widely adopted EDIFACT as the basis of electronic communication interface. In the United States, this interface is largely limited to large manufacturers and their first-tier suppliers, such as the relationship between Wal-Mart and Procter & Gamble. Some groups champion the language protocol of the World Wide Web, specifically hypertext markup language (HTML) or "XML," as the best global standard. So far, though, there is no agreement on the standards of business exchange. Beside communications, currencies and measurement systems (i.e., metric versus decimal) can create weak links among globally dispersed activities. In sum, well-planned coordination preempts these threats, thereby letting workers worry less about what is supposed to happen with material transfers and product delivery and worry more about creating value.

National Cultures   The globalization of a company's value chain—for example, design done in Finland, inputs sourced from Brazil, production done in China, distribution organized in the United States, and service done in Mexico—presses managers to understand how foreign cultures influence coordination. For example, the performance of even the simplest value chain depends on each link meeting a specified timetable. Companies in Western countries generally see deadlines as firm promises of delivery. Some cultures, however, see deadlines as guidelines with flexible end dates. Trying to run value chains worldwide without preparing for these sorts of operational gaps can undermine coordination. National cultures can also impose higher hurdles in coordinating a transaction from one stage of the value chain with another. Units anchored in different cultures may disagree over how much information they should share or who should take lead responsibility. Coordination can then suffer from conflict.

Learning Effects   Learning effects refer to cost savings that come from learning by doing. Managers, for example, learn by recurrence how to transfer best practices from one country to another, such as innovative ways to improve internal and external customer service. Successfully transferred, an MNE can convert higher productivity into lower costs or higher customer satisfaction into higher prices. The information about steps in the value chain that managers learn can then help them to better plan, execute, evaluate, and leverage performance. In this way, they can gain new insights into managing the value chain as a whole instead of as a collection of parts. Similarly, companies can often cut costs by 20 to 30 percent each time its cumulative output doubles, a phenomenon known as the experience curve.[19] A reduction may come about because a company covers fixed costs over more units of output, becomes more efficient as it gains operating experience, or secures quantity discounts on materials and transportation.

> Learning effects refers to the cost savings that follow from learning by doing an activity.

The matter of learning shapes how both manufacturing and service MNEs coordinate value chains. In the case of the former, MNEs' must prepare production activities for different attitudes and approaches to manufacturing across countries. For example, an MNE may have factories in different parts of the world, such as Japan and Mexico, that manufacture the same product but with different production philosophies. The Mexican factory might adopt a traditional assembly line operation given the local conditions of inexpensive labor, poor transportation infrastructure, and limited exposure to high technology. The company's Japanese factory, on the other hand, might install a lean production system to take advantage of local labor competency, manufacturing expertise, and efficient logistics. The different capital structures and productivity of each type of system complicates how managers keep both plants working in harmony with the other. If ignored, MNEs can suffer production crunches that lead to high overtime costs, reduced quality, disappointed customers, and lost sales. Service industries run into similar challenges in coordinating the sharing of specialized knowledge across their globally dispersed value chains. Management consulting firms like McKinsey & Company, Boston Consulting Group, and Bain & Company exemplify a successful approach. Their strategic asset is the consistent performance of their highly qualified people—so, for the client, no matter which professional is assigned to their case, they are confident that he or she will perform well. Crafting and sustaining such consistency across global operations has led these firms to ensure that their staff learn the client company's preferred principles and practices.

Subsidiary Networks   The current culmination of globalization trends is a world marked by real-time connectivity among the subsidiaries of an MNE. Subsidiaries around the world can exchange information freely, whether done systematically within an ERP context or tacitly via e-mails. Moreover there are an astounding number of companies, including their affiliates, which engage in international business. The United Nations reports that there are more than 200,000 MNEs that have established nearly 650,000 subsidiaries worldwide. These two trends, growing connectivity and growing populations of MNEs with dispersed subsidiary networks, results in an integrated market ecology where ideas can emerge from and easily travel to subsidiaries around the world. Skills, ideas, and technologies can be created anywhere within an MNE's global network of subsidiaries.

An increasingly vital task for managers, then, is to coordinate the company's value chain so that it can leverage the competencies developed within any subsidiary and apply them wherever they can create value within the firm's global network. For example, managers from Canada GE identified a New Zealand appliance maker, Fisher & Paykel, producing a broad range of products very efficiently in its small, low-volume plant. When the Canadians used the flexible job-shop techniques to increase productivity in their high-volume factory, the U.S. appliance business became interested. A group of managers and employees from GE's Louisville plant went to Montreal to study the accomplishments. Convinced of its potential, they systematized the program, transferred it to their operation, and soon reported that they had cut their production cycle in half and reduced inventory costs by 20 percent. Immediately, GE's Appliance Park in Louisville became a "must see" destination for other GE units, and within a year, other managers had leveraged this knowledge into the value chains for the locomotive and jet engine businesses.

Value Chains and Change

> The configuration and coordination of a value chain responds to changes in customers, competitors, industries, and environments.

Once built, a firm's value chain is not fixed in stone. Because the features and functions of products that consumers judge most critical change over time—as we see in financial services, clothing, entertainment, electronics, and so on—the basis of value creation in an industry evolves. Some firms, like Zara and eBay, anticipate market situations and begin operations with a value chain that is well configured and coordinated. Far more common, though, are firms that must rethink their value chains in the face of adverse market trends and industry situations. For example, in 1997, Sony Corporation, Japan's premier electronics company, took little notice of the Samsung Electronics Company, a South Korean television maker then snared in a life-or-death struggle to endure the Asian currency crisis. Less than a decade later, Samsung had twice the market capitalization of Sony and commands the role once claimed by Sony—the competitor with the breadth of cool products and the appeal of a premium brand. Samsung powered its rise by reconfiguring its value chain. In 1997, Samsung was a back-of-the-store brand with bulky, low-quality televisions. Since then, Samsung has upgraded its product lines to compete directly with Sony for the premium market. This task involved, in 2004, $7 billion in capital spending and, in 2005, $10 billion, the largest for any information technology company in the world. Samsung has turned this investment into huge manufacturing capacity that can build raw components for its many products, like memory chips and display panels, at some of the lowest production costs in the world. Similarly, Samsung has annually invested billions of dollars in advertising. Presently, Samsung's $12.6 billion brand value now rivals that of Sony's. Throughout it all, Samsung has dedicated almost a quarter of its worldwide staff of 88,000 to research and development. As one observer noted, "Samsung is like the old Sony . . . it has much of the spirit of Sony 10 years ago." Sony, looking to revive its operations, took the unprecedented step, for a major Japanese MNE, of naming an American as its chairman in mid-2004.[20]

POINT–COUNTERPOINT: VALUE CHAINS–REAL OR VIRTUAL?

POINT

The concept of the value chain has a strong historical basis. It was conceived in the 1960s and the 1970s by analysts charting a path of development for mineral-exporting economies.[21] It was then adopted in French planning literature in the form of the *filière* (literally, meaning "thread") to describe the perceived need for French industrial capability to span the complete thread of a value chain.[22] So, for instance, countries intent on developing world-leading capabilities in color TVs would need to set industry policies that created expertise in picture tube technology, in printed circuit board design and manufacture, in design and production of integrated circuits and other electronic components, and in metal- and plastic-forming technologies. As used in the French planning exercises, the idea of *filière* suggested that the full chain of activities should take place within national boundaries. Since then, value chain analysis has become widely used.

Presently, the value chain serves as a powerful business system concept that helps managers (1) to evaluate the company's strengths and weaknesses (2) to interpret the determinants of the internal cost structure, the basis of core competencies, and relationships with customers and (3) to link the internal features and functions of a competitor to the content of its marketplace strategy. Applying this analysis enables managers to identify how well the firm's present strategy works and the strategic issues it faces in the marketplace. Critical to this logic, ultimately, is the principle that managers applying value chain analysis follow the model's template in data collection, interpretation, and strategic decision-making. This template is defined by the real activities, functions, and business processes the firm performs in moving a product from conception, through its design, its sourced raw materials and intermediate inputs, its marketing, its distribution, and its support to the end consumer.

Some contend that dealing with the "hard realities" of international operations, no matter whether following from expanding into conventional markets or heading off to distant and different territories, is best done within the context of the "real" value chain—business is business and every firm must deal with traditional primary and support activities.[23]

Certainly, this point of view sees the striking potential of virtual value chains. However, the dazzle of virtuality may lead some companies to lose sight of the intrinsic difficulties configuring and coordinating value chains for international business operations. Therefore, the tractable ideas of real value chains better equip an MNE to deal with the enduring complications posed by geographic, to say nothing of cultural, political, and economic, distance between countries.

COUNTERPOINT

The recent emergence of the Internet has given rise to the alternative idea of the virtual value chain as the basis of superior value creation and competitive advantage.[24] This view reasons that the Internet creates a new basis for value creation via virtual means, as already successfully seen in industries as diverse as agrochemicals, biotech, and furniture.[25] Essentially, the idea of virtuality calls for managers to rethink their traditional focus on static, internally focused "chains" in order to consider the potential of virtual value networks that arrange value activities in terms of dynamic webs, both within and outside the company. These sorts of value networks, as we see at companies like eBay, Yahoo!, Alibaba, and Google, form open, interconnected environments that enable a company to configure value activities in ways that let them fully leverage their core competencies. Operationally, the idea of the virtual value chain builds on the communications technology of the Internet and its capacity to support a new business architecture that challenges the industrial-age notion of a series of sequential steps as the basis for value creation. Virtual value chains open new paths for value creation, letting managers rethink how to capture the benefits of lower search, coordination, contracting, and other transaction costs between people, agents, firms, and institutions.

Virtuality has many provocative implications as to how managers decide where and what to do. For example, Nike has very limited production facilities and Reebok owns no plants whatsoever. Both companies contract virtually all their footwear production to footwear makers in China, Vietnam, and other low-cost labor countries. Although nominally independent, their close coordination with Nike or Reebok enables these companies to create virtual production capability. This sort of virtuality helps Nike and Reebok leverage their core competencies in design and marketing, while relying on the suppliers' expertise at rapidly retooling for the manufacturing of new products to keep pace with changing tastes. We see similar situations at Dell, Corning, Li Fung, and Acer.

In the least, the relative importance of a real versus virtual value chain depends on the characteristics of a particular company's products and services. The potential of virtuality has important implications to eBay's global expansion, as we will see in our closing case, but middling for companies such as Nestle that deal with physical situations in many different geographies. Still, the combined theoretical context of "real versus virtual" opens up new paths of analysis that promises to help international companies better understand the configuration and coordination of activities and the creation of value.

GLOBAL INTEGRATION VERSUS LOCAL RESPONSIVENESS

Global and local pressures challenge how the firm configures and coordinates its value chain.

Companies that operate internationally face two asymmetric forces: Pressures for global integration and pressures for local responsiveness. The asymmetry between global and local pressures puts contradictory demands on how the firm configures and coordinates its value chain—that is, should it standardize all activities of its value chain to achieve economies of scale or should it customize all local activities to the particular demands of each country? Over time, research has reported a straightforward relationship: The higher the pressure for global integration, the greater the need to maximize efficiency and, conversely, the higher the pressure for responsiveness to local conditions, the greater the need to maximize market sensitivity. Finding a way to navigate between these two demands, however, requires the international firm face a range of macropressures that affect how its managers identify and interpret the best way to configure and coordinate a value chain. The remainder of this section looks at the source of pressures for global integration and local responsiveness. We then discuss the implications of their interaction to the types of strategies an MNE can take on and close by looking at the strategies that MNEs use to resolve the dilemma of global integration versus local responsiveness.

Pressures for Global Integration

An underlying theme of this text is the growing globalization of business. Presently, global markets now produce and consume more than 20 percent of world output and are projected to multiply twelvefold, to more than 80 percent of world output, by 2025. Similarly, more economic integration will take place in the next 30 years than occurred in the previous 10,000 or more. Managers, companies, and industries are reacting accordingly, as seen in the ongoing formation of global markets in chemicals, credit cards, financial services, accounting, food, health care, mass media, forest products, information technology, automobiles, telecommunications, and on and on. While earlier chapters have identified many contributing factors, we highlight two pressures for global integration: the globalization of markets and the efficiency gains of standardization.

The convergence of national markets and quest for production efficiency push for global integration of value activities.

Globalization of Markets

A provocative thesis, increasingly supported by global buying patterns and companies' strategies, suggests that consumers seek and accept standardized global products—whether they be Apple iPods, Samsung plasma screens, Starbuck espressos, or Zara suits.[26] Two conditions compel the globalization of markets. On one hand are the intrinsic functions of money—it is hard to acquire, difficult to save, and always in scarce supply. These functions mean that consumers, no matter which country they call home, seek to maximize their purchasing power by buying the highest quality good for the lowest possible price. Ultimately, goes this thesis, consumers do not care who provides the product, as long as it meets their needs and delivers superior value. On the flip side, communication technologies steadily elaborate the infrastructure that converges consumer preferences across countries while improving the transportation logistics that are needed to ensure the availability of standardized products worldwide. Coupled together, the quest to maximize individual purchasing power along with the growing exposure and access to higher quality goods at lower prices compels the increasing homogeneity of the global market. In so doing, this relationship spurs companies to maximize global integration and standardize activities. Our opening case provided a good example of this situation. Zara realized that offering standardized fashion styles at reasonable price points lets it achieve scale economies by leveraging its fixed costs in design, manufacturing, and retail over its global retail network. Where Zara ran into stubborn local preferences, it found it could get by with minor customization. Zara then built its value chain to reflect these imperatives and inclinations.

> A commodity is a product or resource that is traded on the basis of price, not on differences in quality or features.

There are many goods—usually called commodities—that serve the same universal need across all countries. Effectively, the tastes and preferences of consumers in different countries, if not identical, are highly similar for many sorts of products, such as petroleum, semiconductor chips, and wheat. Hence, companies can standardize their product offerings to remarkable degrees across national markets. Pressures for global integration in such markets are absolute, given that product differentiation is difficult and competition tends toward price wars.

Efficiency Gains of Standardization

Worldwide standardization of an MNE's products, purchases, methods, and policies can significantly reduce the costs of its operations. For example, if an MNE standardizes machinery in the production stage of its value chain, it can often negotiate quantity discounts on raw material purchases as well as streamline the stockpiling of inventories. The company can also realize economies in other value activities such as R&D (single product design) or advertising (universal message). Therefore, standardization, by pushing a company to mass produce a standardized product at the optimal location in the world, is a powerful means to exploit location economies.

> Standardization is the process of increasing the uniformity of a product or service by decreasing the extent of variation.

Always a factor in international business, standardization pressures have steadily increased as more countries have joined the global economy in general and the WTO in particular. As we saw in earlier chapters, virtually every country in the world is a member of or waiting to join the WTO. The liberalization of trade (accompanied by each member country's acceptance of a uniform code of international trade regulations) has spurred the emergence of many competitors who anchor their value chains in low-cost locations—for example, business process outsourcing firms in India, steel producers in China, chip designers in Taiwan, orange growers in Brazil—without forsaking access to markets worldwide. In addition, emergent companies around the world steadily add more efficient production capacity to global supply and, in the effort to capture market share, often use price as their means. These new entrants escalate cost pressure in an industry that then compels companies to minimize their costs by standardizing components of their value chain via global integration.

Pressures for Local Responsiveness

International companies face several pressures to tailor their operations to local market conditions. Thus far in the text, we have looked at the influence of the external environment, government influence on trade, and regional economic integration. Later chapters profile the implication of issues like product standards, financial regulations, distribution channels, and human resources. At this point, though, we want to emphasize two primary pressures for local responsiveness: consumer divergence and host-government policies.

Consumer Divergence   Contrary to the globalization of markets thesis, some maintain that fundamental divergences in consumer tastes and preferences across countries have and will continue to exert strong pressure for local responsiveness. Indeed, the thesis of the globalization of national markets is often painted as an extreme view that is more a random phenomenon than a consistent trend. No matter the moderating functions of money or technologies, the reasoning goes, differences in consumer tastes and preferences across countries emerge and endure due to several factors, including cultural predisposition, historical legacy, emergent nationalism (i.e., "buy local" campaigns), and economic prosperity.[27] No matter the cause, the outcome is the same: Consumers prefer goods that are sensitive to their way of life.

Cross-national divergence presses international companies to side with local responsiveness, doing such things as designing and making a product that local customers prefer (i.e., large cars in the United States, smaller cars in Europe), adopting marketing practices that speak to their situation (heavy print and media promotion in the United States, greater personal salesmanship in Brazil), and using marketing practices that address their consumption patterns (large package sizes in Australia, smaller sizes in Japan). Adapting to local consumer tastes and preferences can require a company to reconfigure its entire value chain, moving from a global to a national orientation.

In some industries, a globally oriented value chain offers minimal benefits simply because the products are unsuitable for standardization. For example, there is not much incentive for food processors, like Nestle, to integrate their value chains across countries. Food inputs are generally commodities, production has limited potential for scale economies, widespread distribution faces high costs given the low product value-to-weight ratio, and marketing is best done locally given that tastes, competitors, and retail channels differ at the local level.

Host-Government Policies   There is great variability of political, legal, and economic situations in markets around the world. The sources of many of these variations are the policies and sometimes, the lack thereof, mandated by host-country governments. We saw in earlier chapters that widespread movement toward privatization, economic freedom, legal uniformity, and deregulation reduces the variability among countries. Still, exceptions emerge as the international company moves from country to country. These exceptions typically push the firm to determine how to best configure and coordinate its value chain so that it provides the necessary degree of local responsiveness without jeopardizing its capability to create value.

A salient example of this relationship is found in health care. The pharmaceutical industry, for example has a strong need for integration. The typical pharmaceutical company sells undifferentiated products that, in turn, make the efficient scale of production vital to offset the costs of product development. Nonetheless, almost every country has installed a unique administrative system to regulate the development, practice, and delivery of health care. Consequently, pharmaceutical firms usually manufacture their product in several locations in several countries despite the fact that making pills is most economically done in a few centralized plants. Moreover, cost concerns do not dictate which production locations pharmaceutical companies choose. Rather, many plant sites are chosen in order to comply with the clinical testing, registration procedures, pricing restrictions, and marketing regulations mandated by a particular government. In theory, a pharmaceutical company could opt, as did Zara in apparel, to reject conventional industry practice. Health care, as a heavily regulated industry, largely eliminates this option. At the least, different government authorities approve each product in each country where those companies sell. Also, most governments fund huge shares of the national health care budget. They can, therefore, insist that any company that would like local support also demonstrate a high level of local responsiveness.

"Buy local" refers to the policy preference to buy locally produced goods and services.

Host governments use several forceful tools to make the MNE respond to local needs.

Host governments also have a range of aggressive tools to ensure that an MNE is locally responsive. These tools can be broad policy directives calling for economic nationalism, explicit threats or acts of trade protectionism to encourage local production, local content rules that require a specified percentage of a product be made locally, or simply national product standards that can be met only by local operations. Each policy boosts the pressure on companies to make sure that part or all of its value chain can respond to the local pressures.

Interaction

The interaction of the pressures for global integration and pressures for local responsiveness, in terms of how they bear upon an MNE, is expressed in the integration-responsiveness (IR) grid. Figure 11.5 profiles this grid, illustrating the interaction by placing particular industries in their respective quadrants. Looked at from the company level, the IR grid expresses how a company's choice of strategy is a function of the particular relationship the company sees between its idea of value creation and the corresponding pressures for global integration or local responsiveness in its industry.[28] Essentially, as we will see in a moment, one gets a sense of context and of the trade-offs that companies face by plotting their company's position in terms of the pressures for global integration and those for local responsiveness. So, for example, firms like Intel or ExxonMobil face high pressures for standardized products in a global market; there is little need or reward to respond to local market conditions with specialized chips or gas. Others, such as Nestle, see little gains from global integration but large gains from responding to the particular features of each market they operate in. Finally, most companies, from Procter & Gamble to Samsung to LVHM, do not have such clarity. Rather, they face high pressures for global integration and local responsiveness. Configuring and coordinating the value chain to deal with this dilemma is an enduring challenge for managers.

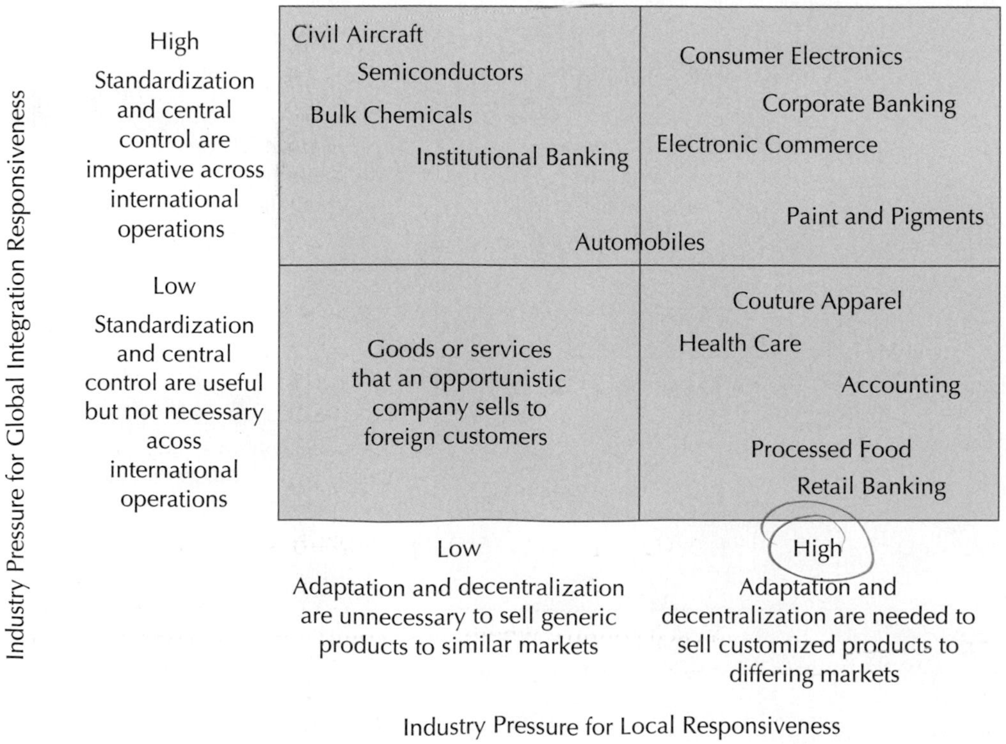

Integration is the process of combining differentiated parts into a standardized whole. Responsiveness is the process of disaggregating a standardized whole into differentiated parts.

FIGURE 11.5

THE INTEGRATION-RESPONSIVENESS GRID AND INDUSTRY TYPES

The grid:

Vertical axis label: Industry Pressure for Global Integration Responsiveness

- High — Standardization and central control are imperative across international operations
- Low — Standardization and central control are useful but not necessary acoss international operations

Horizontal axis label: Industry Pressure for Local Responsiveness

- Low — Adaptation and decentralization are unnecessary to sell generic products to similar markets
- High — Adaptation and decentralization are needed to sell customized products to differing markets

Upper-left quadrant (High integration / Low responsiveness):
Civil Aircraft
Semiconductors
Bulk Chemicals
Institutional Banking

Upper-right quadrant (High integration / High responsiveness):
Consumer Electronics
Corporate Banking
Electronic Commerce
Paint and Pigments
Automobiles

Lower-left quadrant (Low integration / Low responsiveness):
Goods or services that an opportunistic company sells to foreign customers

Lower-right quadrant (Low integration / High responsiveness):
Couture Apparel
Health Care
Accounting
Processed Food
Retail Banking

STRATEGY TYPES

When defining their strategy, MNEs looks to international markets for growth opportunities, cost reductions, and risk diversification within a context of satisfying the competing demands of global integration and local responsiveness.[29] Figure 11.6 identifies general conditions that shape the decision of when to use which type of strategy within the context of the integration-responsiveness grid. MNEs take a variety of perspectives to guide how they decide to run their operations to hit these goals and deal with this challenge. Generally, MNEs choose from four basic strategies to guide how they will enter and compete in the international environment: an international strategy, a multidomestic strategy, a global strategy, and a transnational strategy. Each of these types of strategies differs fundamentally in where managers put value activities and how they try to run them. We now define each strategy, identify its implications for configuring and coordinating a value chain, and discuss its particular advantages and liabilities.

International Strategy

Companies adopt the international strategy when they aim to leverage their core competencies by expanding opportunistically into foreign markets. International firms include the likes of McDonald's, Kellogg, Yahoo!, Wal-Mart, MBNA America, and Microsoft. The international model relies on local subsidiaries in each country to administer business as instructed by headquarters. Some subsidiaries may have latitude to adapt products to local conditions as well as to set up some light assembly operations or promotion programs. Still, ultimate and absolute control resides with managers at headquarters who reason they best know the basis and potential extension of the company's core competencies. As a rule, critical elements of the company's value chain, such as research and development or branding, are almost always centralized at headquarters. Yahoo!, for example, develops the core architecture underlying its Web products in San Jose, California. This site is also home to many of the people who develop its Web functions

FIGURE 11.6

THE INTEGRATION RESPONSIVENESS GRID AND STRATEGY TYPES

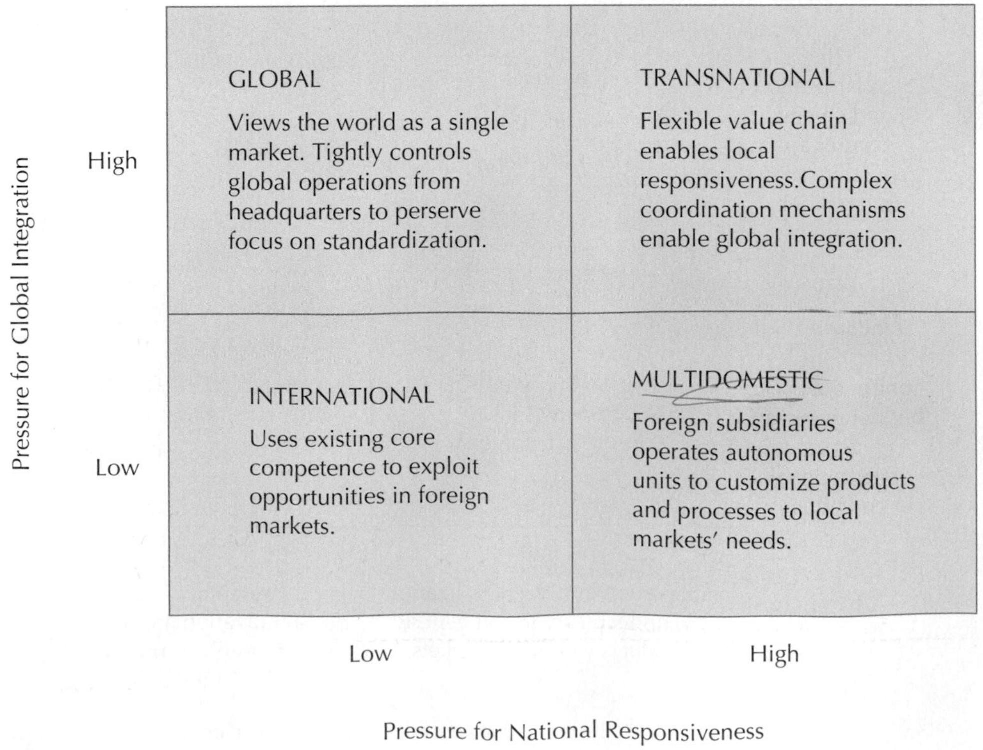

Pressure for Global Integration

High

GLOBAL

Views the world as a single market. Tightly controls global operations from headquarters to perserve focus on standardization.

TRANSNATIONAL

Flexible value chain enables local responsiveness. Complex coordination mechanisms enable global integration.

Low

INTERNATIONAL

Uses existing core competence to exploit opportunities in foreign markets.

MULTIDOMESTIC

Foreign subsidiaries operates autonomous units to customize products and processes to local markets' needs.

Low   High

Pressure for National Responsiveness

and online services. However, Yahoo! does allow national subsidiaries to customize minor aspects of its Web pages to deal with local differences in language and alphabet. Ultimately, though, headquarters is the source for new products, processes, and ideas for its overseas operations.

Firms that pursue an international strategy try to create value by transferring core competencies and unique products to those foreign markets where rivals are unable to develop, match, or sustain them. The international strategy, therefore, greatly facilitates the transfer of skills, expertise, and products from the parent company to its subsidiaries. Headquarters can translate their control over and expertise in important activities into powerful positions to command foreign operations to follow their lead. This expertise and control can take place in manufacturing processes or general management skills. The latter, for example, explains the growth of international hotel chains such as Hilton International, Starwood, and Sheraton. In summary, an international strategy makes sense if a firm has a core competence that local competitors in other markets lack and if industry conditions do not push the firm to improve its cost controls or local responsiveness. In such circumstances, an international strategy creates moderate operational costs and, often, great amounts of profits.

The liability of the international strategy is that headquarters' central role hinders identifying and responding to local conditions. Headquarters' ethnocentric orientation—a one-way view from the home office to the rest of the world—can lead to missed market opportunities and a realization among foreign operations that international activity is secondary to whatever happens in the home market. These limitations become particularly costly when other companies emphasize customizing their goods and services to local conditions. Our case study of Carrefour in Chapter 12 will show how that company ran into this problem in the United States. Carrefour tried shifting its strategy to better deal with local tastes and preferences, but this eventually proved too costly and the company closed its United States operations.

> The international strategy leverages a company's core competencies in foreign markets. It allows limited local customization.

Multidomestic Strategy

A multidomestic company, sometimes called a locally responsive company, follows a strategy that allows each of its foreign-country operations to act fairly independently. That is, the company's subsidiaries in their respective local markets have the authority to design, make, and market products that directly respond to local customers' preferences. Johnson & Johnson is an example of a company that has followed a multidomestic strategy to great success, differentiating products and services to meet different local demands and adapting organizational policies to conform to different governmental and market demands.

Firms applying a multidomestic strategy aim to build a value chain that gives each country's operations the freedom to respond to its local cultural, legal-political, and economic environments. So, for example, if the country's government is offering incentives for local manufacturing, then the local operation can build its own plant; if local consumers prefer to deal directly with people in the sales process rather than rely on mass media for information, the local company can build a sales force; if the country has a disfavorable work environment, then the local operation can opt to import products made elsewhere. Effectively, companies applying a multidomestic strategy customize their products, marketing, and service programs to local conditions. Correspondingly, these decisions require the multidomestic company to decentralize decision making from headquarters to subsidiary operations so that local executives have the authority to manage their responsibilities. Basically, managers in the multidomestic company hold the polycentric point of view that people who are close to the market (philosophically, culturally, and physically) ought to run the business. Thus, for example, the managers of the backpack factory in Singapore have the right to decide what sort of backpack they want to make—even if the size, shape, and style differs from those made in the United States, Mexico, or Germany.

> The multidomestic strategy adjusts products, services, and business practices to meet the needs of individual countries and regions.

> Management that chooses the multidomestic strategy believes in responding to the unique conditions prevailing in different markets.

A multidomestic strategy makes great sense in the face of high need for local responsiveness and low need to reduce costs via global integration. It has many other benefits, such as minimized political risk given the local standing of the company, reduced exchange rate risk given the low need to repatriate funds to the home office, greater prestige given its national prominence, higher potential for innovative products from local R&D, and higher growth potential due to entrepreneurial spirit. For example, Procter & Gamble has long followed a multidomestic strategy. The R&D unit at its Japanese subsidiary, responding to the low storage space situation in the typical Japanese home, invented technology that reduced the thickness of an infant's diaper without any loss of absorbency. This innovation created immense value for Procter & Gamble in Japan and, eventually, for Procter & Gamble worldwide.

These benefits impose high costs. The multidomestic strategy leads to widespread duplication of management, design, production, and marketing activities. Each local subsidiary must build the necessary value chain operations to meet local demands. Hence, the multidomestic strategy is often economically impossible in industries that have intense cost pressures. Too, decentralizing control of value activities to local decision makers can create unusually powerful subsidiaries that tend to behave as autonomous units. On any given matter, they may opt not to follow headquarters' policy, instead maintaining that it does not work with their situation and/or that it must be extensively adjusted to fit their local market. Whatever the explanation, the fact that the subsidiary is a virtual stand-alone operation means headquarters has to resort to persuasion in lieu of direct command to effect change. Persuasion can lead to a host of costly struggles. For example, Johnson & Johnson launched Tylenol in 1960 as an over-the-counter pain reliever in the United States. Although it was available to local operating units shortly thereafter, the Japanese unit did not begin selling it until 2000.

Global Strategy

The company adopting a global strategy chooses to respond directly to pressure to maximize integration. This decision typically spurs a company to make and market a standardized product, such as razor blades, or service, such as package delivery, for a specific global market segment. The global strategy pushes companies to think in terms of creating products for a world market, manufacturing them on a global scale in a few highly efficient plants, and marketing them through a few, focused distribution channels. Hence, companies that adopt the global strategy opt to see the world as one market and assume that there are either no differences among countries with regard to consumer tastes and preferences or, if there are, then consumers will sacrifice them if given the opportunity to buy a comparatively higher quality product for a lower price.

Operationally, MNEs that adopt a global strategy usually are or aim to become the low-cost player in their industry. Failing to do so can lead to a weak competitive position against the firm that does. The low-cost goal usually entails building global-scale production facilities in a few low-cost locations that create the platforms for efficient operations—whether it is a sneaker factory in Vietnam or a service call center in India. Firms that implement a global strategy focus on creating value by having the lowest possible cost for a particular good or service. In other words, they aim to follow the low-cost leadership strategy that converts the potential for efficient operations into cost reductions that drive profitability.

The efficiency goals of the global strategy have plain implications for configuring a value chain. R&D, production, and marketing activities are concentrated in the most favorable locations. These locations need not be in the same country; a fully optimized global value chain conceivably will locate each activity in the best possible place. The dispersed activities of the resulting value chain are then coordinated by formal linkages. Making sure the worldwide system works efficiently is the responsibility of executives at the centralized world headquarters who standardize practices and processes. Little if any strategic decision-making authority exists at the local level.

What then of pressures to respond to current or future local preferences? As a rule, the cost-sensitivity of a global strategy gives MNEs no latitude to customize their products or systems to local conditions. Customizing a product or process to particular market situations increases costs at each stage in the value chain. Different product designs require different materials, production runs become shorter, marketing programs must be adjusted, new distribution channels have to be built, and various organizational functions have to be replicated in each market. Instead, global firms strive to make, market, and service a standardized product worldwide that lets them convert global efficiency into price competitiveness and value creation.

Generally, the global strategy is best suited for those industries that put strong pressures on efficient operations and where local responsiveness needs are either non-existent or can be neutralized by offering a high-quality product for a lower price than the local substitute. Increasingly, these conditions prevail in many industries, both in the manufacturing and service sectors. The wireless industry, for example, endorses global standards that create enormous demand for standardized global products in every country.[30] Similarly, the credit card industry has specified a range of standards and rules for electronic payment protocols that supports customers using and merchants accepting this form of payment around the world. In both cases, firms act accordingly; in wireless, Qualcomm and Texas Instruments, and in credit cards, American Express, pursue a global strategy. Similarly, a global strategy can drive a one-time transaction that exploits a worldwide distribution network, standardized financial controls, and universal messages. For example, Lucasfilm released *Star Wars: Episode II—Attack of the Clones* on the same day in nine countries and a day later in another large group of countries. The movie had the third highest opening weekend of revenue in movie history. That said, there are limits to the use of a global strategy. Many consumer goods and health care markets, where demands for local responsiveness remain high, give companies little latitude to standardize operations.

> A global strategy focuses on increasing profitability by reaping cost reductions from configuring value activities to achieve available production and location economies.

Transnational Strategy

The transnational strategy type is arguably the most direct response to the growing globalization of business. It holds that today's environment of interconnected consumers, industries, and markets requires that an MNE find ways to configure a value chain that exploits location economies, coordinate value activities to effectively leverage core competencies, and throughout it all, ensure that the value chain directly deals with pressures for local responsiveness. The MNE applying a transnational strategy differentiates capabilities and contributions from country to country, finding ways to systematically learn from its various environments, and then ultimately integrating and diffusing this knowledge throughout its global operations. The transnational concept of strategy, therefore, endorses an integrated framework of technology, financial resources, creative ideas, and people that move it fundamentally beyond the ideas of the international, multidomestic, or global strategy types.

The first-order conditions of the transnational strategy—combine the market sensitivity of local responsiveness with the competitive efficiency of global integration—combines characteristics of the multinational and global strategies. However, the transnational strategy has a unique aspect that theoretically distinguishes it from the other strategy types. Specifically, the transnational strategy champions the cause of interactive "global learning" by which an MNE develops valuable skills in any of its worldwide operations, uses them to improve its core competencies, and then diffuses these innovations throughout its global operation. So, rather than the top-down (headquarters to foreign subsidiary) or bottom-up (foreign subsidiary to headquarters) flow

> A transnational strategy simultaneously exploits location economies, leverages core competencies, and pays attention to local responsiveness.

of ideas, the transnational strategy champions a flow from the idea generator to idea adopters, no matter where one or the other happens to be.

The global learning capability has many benefits. Managers find ways, for example, to develop internal capabilities that can respond in a multitude of ways to changing environments, to leverage internal resources with external networks of other companies, and to integrate subsidiaries without imposing more bureaucracy. Ultimately, these capabilities let an MNE standardize some links of the value chain to maximize efficiency as well as adapt other links to meet pressures for local responsiveness, but in a way that does not sacrifice the benefits of one for the other.

Can a firm effectively pursue a transnational strategy? Some clues can be seen in the case of General Electric. In the 1980s, growing competitive threats from emergent low-cost competitors in Asia pushed GE to look to global markets to sell products, reasoning that expanding sales volumes would lead to greater scale economies. At the time, Jack Welch declared "the idea of a company being global is nonsense. Businesses are global, not companies." In 1987, GE redefined its outlook toward globalization, elevating it to a dominant strategic theme. Since 1981, the performance standard for each business had been "be either number 1 or 2" in their domestic industry or else face divestment. 1n 1987, the standard was raised to the business's position in its global industry. Soon thereafter GE's sense of globalization moved from finding new markets to finding new worldwide sources that could provide higher quality resources for lower costs. Around this time, Jack Welch articulated his vision of the boundaryless company, explaining it was an "open, anti-parochial environment, friendly toward the seeking and sharing of new ideas, regardless of their origins." More specifically, Welch explained that the "boundaryless company we envision will remove the barriers among engineering, manufacturing, marketing, sales, and customer service; it will recognize no distinctions between domestic and foreign operations—we'll be as comfortable doing business in Budapest and Seoul as we are in Louisville and Schenectady." Soon, a score of boundarylessness success stories emerged within GE, such as our earlier example in its Appliance business, but also in the form of productivity solutions from Lighting; transaction effectiveness from GE Capital; cost-reduction techniques from Aircraft Engines; and global account management from Plastics. In addition, careers were halted if managers refused to share ideas with others. Said Welch, "We take people who aren't boundaryless out of jobs. If you're turf-oriented, self-centered, don't share with people, and aren't searching for ideas, you don't belong here." Soon thereafter, GE moved to phase three of its globalization evolution. Besides emphasizing global markets and global sources, Welch now called upon his managers to "globalize the intellect of the company," seeking best practices and compelling ideas from anyone, anywhere, and then diffusing them throughout GE. By 1999, at the end of Welch's tenure, GE was again named the most respected company in the world by the *Financial Times* and Jack Welch was judged the CEO of the twentieth century. His successor, Jeffrey Immelt, has continued these efforts, explaining that success in international business is "truly about people, not about where the buildings are. You've got to develop people so they are prepared for leadership jobs and then promote them. That's the most effective way to become more global."[31]

General Electric's performance speaks to many of the principles of the transnational strategy. General Electric made ideas, constantly renewed, enhanced, and exchanged within the expanding context of globalization, the basis of its value creation. As such, General Electric shows that the more its managers translated their knowledge, ideas, and innovations into better production methods, better designs, better marketing programs, better quality approaches, no matter where in the world the activity took place, they made more profitable decisions. As knowledge flowed from one manager in one part of the value chain to counterparts in far-flung parts of the company, integration happened more efficiently, responsiveness happened more effectively, and new ideas emerged more regularly.

Transferring capabilities and resource strengths across borders contributes to developing more powerful core competencies.

A transnational strategy aims to make the relentless renewal, enhancement, and exchange of ideas across borders the basis of value creation.

The transnational type, while appearing to offer many advantages, is difficult to build, poses serious challenges (especially in coordinating value activities), and is prone to shortfalls. For every GE, there are many Phillips, Matsushitas, Nokias, and Acers that fell short applying a transnational strategy. Which sorts of firms, then, should aspire to adopt it? Generally, a transnational strategy makes sense when a firm faces high pressures for cost reductions, high pressures for local responsiveness, and where there are opportunities to leverage core competencies extensively throughout the company's global network. In the 1990s, this mandate applied to few companies. Increasingly, competitive conditions and environmental trends spur more companies to reset their value chains to enact a transnational strategy.

LOOKING TO THE FUTURE: New Strategy Types?

The strategy gamut of "international-multidomestic-global-transnational" has prevailed for several years in international business theory. An increasingly provocative issue, given unfolding trends toward greater globalization, is: What types of international strategies might companies follow in the future?

A popular view trumpets a world where a dynamic ecology of locations and firms pushes us to go beyond the historic division of local firms versus global companies to makes sense of strategy in international business.[32] This view sees a wide scope of many different types of companies following many types of strategies. The diversity of these strategies and companies steadily creates a business world populated by a variety of local firms, regional firms, firms that operate in a few countries, firms that operate in many countries, centralized firms, and networks of firms. Against the backdrop, questions about the co-location of different places with different types of firms means strategy will emerge from the interplay among firms and places.

Some see the emergence of the so-called "metanational" as a new type of global corporation that thrives on the process of seeking out uniqueness that it might exploit elsewhere or that might complement its own existing operations. More precisely, the metanational is seen as a "company that builds a new kind of competitive advantage by discovering, accessing, mobilizing, and leveraging knowledge from many locations around the world."[33] The metanational will conquer international markets by developing value chains with three core competencies—the capability to prospect for and access untapped pockets of technology and emerging

consumer trends from around the world, to leverage knowledge scattered throughout its local subsidiaries, and to mobilize this fragmented knowledge to generate innovations that produce, market, and deliver value on a global scale. Some point to MNEs like General Electric, Samsung, Shiseido, and PolyGram as emergent metanationals, already showcasing the capacity to mobilize scattered knowledge to create world-beating innovations.

Others foresee the advent of the *cybercorp*, a company that was beyond imagination a decade ago but seeming inevitable today.[34] To this type of MNE, national boundaries are no longer a useful proxy for market segments, operational zones, or location options. The cyberspace created by evolving Internet technologies, not the physical geography of lines on a map, defines the boundaries of the cybercorp. Strategically, the cybercorp looks to develop competences that make it ready to react in real time to changes in its customers, competition, industry, and environment. The cybercorp, therefore, engages perspectives and strategies that bias its value chain toward virtuality in order to develop the flexibility to dynamically link competencies from ever-changing networks of allies and associates. Hence, the cybercorp will be built for speed, able to engage strategies that learn, evolve, and transform as required—basically, an international company optimized for cyberspace.

The new type of MNE that potentially may emerge is still more a matter of speculation than stipulation. So, no matter what specific type emerges, it is highly likely that it will blend the past with the future. Specifically, it will engage the historic markers of great strategy: superior value creation, superb core competencies, and bright management who can articulate clear visions and practical goals but also develop the organizational capability to redefine the play of ideas with real or virtual boundaries.

SUMMARY

- Managers, as agents of their firms, devise strategies to engage international markets in ways that sustain the company's growth and boost its profitability.

- Strategy is defined as the efforts of managers to build and strengthen the company's competitive position within its industry in order to create superior value.

- Value is the measure of when a firm is able to sell what it makes for more than the cost it incurred to make it.

- Firm performance is influenced by both the structure of the company's industry and the insight of managers' strategic decision making. Estimates vary on the degree of influence for both factors. Managers need to be familiar with industry- and firm-level conditions in making strategy.

- Managers typically anchor analysis of industry structure by modeling the strength and importance of the so-called "five fundamental forces."

- Firms create value either through a low-cost leadership strategy or a differentiation strategy.

- Interpreting the firm within the context of the value chain provides a strong tool to improve the accuracy of strategic analyses and decisions.

- The value chain lets managers deconstruct the general idea of "create value" into a series of discrete activities.

- The function of the value chain is shaped by how managers opt to configure and then coordinate discrete value activities.

- Firms pay close attention to location economics when configuring their value chain.

- Devising a way to coordinate value chain activities must be in ways that leverage a firm's core competencies.

- Companies that operate internationally face the asymmetric pressures of global integration versus local responsiveness.

- Change, whether in managers, competencies, industries, or environments, often spurs companies to rethink and reset their value activities.

- The firm entering and competing in foreign markets can adopt either an international, multidomestic, global, or transnational strategy.

- Often, firms use a mix of these four types due to company, industry, and environmental situations.

C A S E   **The Globalization of eBay**[35]

On Labor Day 1995, Pierre Omidyar launched the idea of eBay—an online platform that permitted efficient peer-to-peer trading in an auction format. eBay works by helping individuals, and interested big businesses, buy and sell items in thousands of categories including antiques and art, books, business and industrial, cars, clothing and accessories, coins, collectibles, crafts, dolls and bears, electronics and computers, home furnishings, jewelry and watches, movies & DVDs, music and musical instruments, pottery and glass, real estate, sporting goods and memorabilia, stamps, tickets, toys and hobbies, and travel. Net revenues grew to $225 million in 1999 and $3.2 billion in 2004; over the same span, gross margins grew from 75 percent to 81 percent.

Operationally, eBay is a Web-based forum that provides an efficient market for buyers and sellers of products that typically don't have an efficient distribution system because of information inefficiency (one does not know exactly what's available when looking for used or vintage things) and price inefficiency (one does not really know how much to pay for them). More simply, eBay is an intermediary; one could think of eBay as no more than a sophisticated software program running unattended on a bunch of networked Web servers which, once up and running, leaves all the work to sellers and buyers. Sellers pay eBay for the opportunity to design, set up, monitor, and supervise their particular auctions; buyers use eBay's software to search for products and place bids. When the auction clock runs out, the seller contacts the winning bidder and negotiates payment format and shipping terms. Throughout this process, eBay never touches the product. For this matchmaking service, for which its marginal cost is essentially nothing and its scalability essentially infinite, eBay charges between 7 percent and 18 percent of the closing auction price.

eBay linked its success to its vision of supporting interaction in the eBay Community (essentially, providing a useful online platform to value-oriented buyers and sellers), the principles of trust and safety (guaranteeing low fraud losses and high transaction protection to members of its community), and the goal of market efficiency (delivering state-of-the-art information technology that brought efficiencies to inefficient markets via its online platform). Depicted as a Venn diagram, eBay saw its competitive advantage residing in the overlapping center zone. This design resulted in three revenue streams for eBay: payment fees (21 percent of total revenue), final value fees (31 percent of total revenue), and insertion fees (48 percent of total revenue).

The straightforwardness of eBay's value proposition has stayed the same since its inception. Management confessed surprise by how extensible its strategy has been to new products, services, and markets. In 2004 eBay listed 332 million auctions involving an online community of 114 million registered members from more than 150 countries who conducted millions of trades every month. eBay's platform was the premier segment Web site in more than 18 countries and the most popular general shopping destination on the Internet in virtually every market it operated in. Few disputed eBay's self-characterization that its array of buyer and seller services made it a driving force of global e-commerce.

Increasingly, the success of eBay as an online trading platform, much like Microsoft's Windows in the PC operating systems sector, was delivering network benefits. There were a host of companies developing services to support trading on the eBay platform—such as Square Trade, a dispute-resolution service, and Auctionwatch and Andale, which automate listing of items. Too, eBay's success spurred more companies to build businesses that extended its platform. As Meg Whitman, the president and CEO, noted, the "thing is, we're not the only source of innovation. We're so well-served by letting others think about how to make this platform even more powerful." And, where they did not, eBay was ready to find solutions. For example, early on the single biggest friction point in the buyer-seller link was the lack of an easy way for the latter to pay the former. So, in 2002, eBay acquired PayPal to create a proprietary payment system that seamlessly linked buyers and sellers.

Global Expansion

The success of the U.S. operations had, by the turn of the twenty-first century, inspired eBay to define its mission as providing a global trading platform where practically anyone anywhere can trade practically anything anytime. By 2005, eBay's growing global reach meant that its members could rely on local sites that served Australia, Austria, Belgium, Canada, France, Germany, Ireland, Italy, Korea, the Netherlands, New Zealand, Singapore, Spain, Sweden, Switzerland, Taiwan, and the United Kingdom. In addition, eBay had built a presence in Latin America, China, and India.

The bulk of eBay's registered users resided in the United States. Hence, management saw overseas markets as the best opportunity to sustain growth (see Table 11.1). eBay's international markets had more than twice as many Internet users as in the U.S. (294 million in the former vs. 162 million in the latter) and a combined GDP of $12.8 trillion versus that of $10.1 trillion for the U.S. In terms of market potential, eBay estimated that it had only 1 to 5 percent penetration of the combined $27 trillion annual global merchandise markets in motors, consumer electronics, computers, clothing and accessories, books, movies, music, sports, home and garden, collectibles, toys, and jewelry and watches. International expansion seemed to

TABLE 11.1	EBAY: KEY PERFORMANCE INDICATORS	
	JUNE, 2004	5 YEAR CAGR
Registered users	114 million	126%
Active users	48 million	49%
Auction listings (daily total)	332 million	92%
Gross merchandise volume	$8 billion	96%
Gross margin	81%	—
Pro forma operating margin	35%	—
Total company revenue	$773 million	85%

make more sense as time passed. By mid-2004, eBay reported U.S. transaction revenue of $319 million, up 32 percent. International transaction revenue—which began in the second half of 1998—surged 76 percent to $273.7 million. It was not a stretch of the imagination when eBay forecasted that Europe could eventually rival the scale and scope of its U.S. operations.

Translating eBay's vision into a global strategy relied on its so-called "AAA" Program—Acquisition, Activation, and Activity. Thus far, eBay had acquired leading auction Web sites in 23 countries, had mixed the acquisition and activation component in the U.K., Korea, and Hong Kong, and applied all three elements in Canada, Germany, and India. For example, consider eBay's activity in to India. In July 2004, it acquired Baazee.com, India's top online-trading Web site, for $50 million. Explained Hani Durzy, eBay's spokesperson, "The acquisition will help us expand our global footprint. India is a nascent market. With the acquisition of Baazee.com, we can take that market to the next level." Durzy said that eBay would continue with the Baazee name for now in order to encourage more activation of potential community members. At some point, Baazee would be renamed eBay, thereby expediting Baazee users' activity by giving them access to eBay's global infrastructure. Explained Durzy, "One of the benefits of eBay is that it is a global marketplace. As Baazee becomes a part of the eBay family, its users will be able to buy and sell globally." Added Meg Whitman, "Our relationship with Baazee.com is another important step in the growth of eBay's global marketplace. Although it's early days for e-commerce in India, we believe there is great opportunity over the long term. Baazee.com's strong management team and solid focus on its community make it a natural fit with eBay." Executives at Baazee echoed these sentiments. Suvir Sujan, co-CEO of Baazee.com, said, "We built Baazee.com to change the way people buy and sell goods in India. Becoming part of eBay will allow us to provide even greater economic opportunity for our community of users."

Challenges and Solutions

Skeptics questioned eBay's outlook, calling its plan of convenient e-commerce worldwide a hard climb. Critics pointed out the many challenges awaited eBay, noting translation software, the digital divide, cultural attitudes about e-commerce, government regulations, and the pace of international expansion.

Translation Software

Early on, many people zeroed in on the challenge posed by translation software. Developing a global trading community meant that eBay had to let sellers in any country post their auction description in their native language and then rely on software to translate that post into the necessary language of potential buyers—no matter what language they preferred. Software experts noted that early editions of translation software were buggy at best, unable to handle the nuances of regional colloquialisms, informal shorthand, and slang—all of which were commonly used to describe items listed on eBay. In addition, while newer software came with memory banks that stored complex sentences in order to translate them more accurately, many programs simply translated word for word—irrespective of the structural differences between languages.

eBay dismissed these limits as valid reasons to slow its globalization strategy. It conceded that translation software was not there yet, admitting that possible nuances, idioms, and secondary meanings created problems. However, eBay noted that translation programs were steadily improving. Moreover, eBay's mindset held that the global market was ready for its idea of person-to-person auctions, with or without completely accurate translation. More precisely, Meg Whitman explained, the "great thing about eBay is that this doesn't have to be perfect. This is not diplomatic relations. This is not military secrets. This is trading $50 to $100 items. Our users have expressed a willingness to work with 'pretty good'—not perfect, but pretty good. I was with one of these vendors the other day and watched the entire eBay site translate into Italian in about 35 seconds. So, it's very cool. Our Italian staff was able to look at this and say it wasn't perfect, but it was understandable and usable. With e-mail it's a little bit more complicated because there are colloquialisms in the way people write. But we took 20 customer support e-mails and immediately translated into Italian, and our Italian users could understand them and thought that it was actually usable."

By 2004, progress was evident as eBay could apply increasingly sophisticated software that made it easier to post auctions in more and more foreign markets. Specifically, available software let companies more readily cater Web sites to international markets by automating the translation and localization of content. In eBay's case, that meant that auction pages not only read correctly in local languages, but also were worded to conform to local customs. Moreover, related software upgrades steadily introduced new features such as a vendor-management tool, improved integration with content repositories and formats, better search functionality, and more flexibility in applying security policies, all of which improved the global and national functionality of eBay's platform.

Government Regulations

Critics noted that government trade regulations would inevitably stymie eBay's global strategy. Many countries outlaw the exportation of native fossils, historical artifacts, plants, and animals. Some countries, such as Cuba, outlaw exportation of any item not sanctioned by the government. In addition, eBay could encounter legal and political hassles if it enabled sellers to export native herbs or medicines, rare currencies, anthropological relics, political memorabilia, or other sensitive goods. Complicating matters, each country presented unique cultural and legal challenges. For instance, French law makes it illegal to exhibit or sell objects with racist overtones. A few years earlier, a French judge ordered Yahoo! to "make it impossible" for Web surfers in France to gain access to sales of Nazi memorabilia because such items are "an offense to the collective memory of the country."

eBay believed it had a solution to deal with potential government regulation of e-commerce. Noting the legal challenge Yahoo! faced in France, eBay stated, "What we are going to do in France is try to help the government by putting up warning signs that say, We are a U.S.-based site that does not conform to the rules about Nazi memorabilia. We're going to bend over backward to work with the French government and French political groups to try to enable a solution that is French. . . . We've taken a 'work really closely, let's be best friends' approach with local governments and political groups."

The Digital Divide

Others contended that no matter what eBay trumpeted, the world was far from technologically ready for its vision of Web-connected buyers and sellers. Especially ominous was the digital divide—the gap between those who have and those who do not have access to technology. Many countries that eBay targeted were years, if not decades, away from convenient, affordable Internet access. Rex Bird, CEO of Body Trends, noted, "Guatemala is not going to dig the trenches for conventional lines so that villages can be wired to the Internet. It'd be a great project for the Peace Corps to come in and set up a computer with Internet access but it's going to be a very, very slow process." Then again, eBay faced more immediate problems in existing markets. India has more than 1 billion people but only 4 million Internet connections. Although many Indians who do not own computers visit cyber cafes to browse the Internet, relatively few consumers have credit cards. Many believed China was not far off from the market situation in India.

eBay pointed out that it had been aggressively moving toward letting Web-enabled cell phone users access its central Web site. Other speculated that innovations in wireless access would open up many national markets much sooner than expected. No matter what, eBay remained undaunted. Explained chief financial officer Rajiv Dutta, "Do many of the markets we've entered recently have lower per capita income and lower Internet penetration? Yes, but that will increase. . . . Our management philosophy is to build for the long term. What's a small portion of the business today may well be a very large percentage in the future."

Cultural Attitude About E-Commerce

Data suggested that many people, such as those in India, China, and greater Asia, were intrinsically distrustful of e-commerce transactions. For example, a study of cross-cultural comparison of online information usage, interpretation, and reaction revealed significant interactions between country culture, information, and uncertainty avoidance. Specifically, it appeared that online interactants—such as a buyer and seller on eBay—in high uncertainty-avoidance cultures, such as Japan, behaved differently when faced with limited information within an ambiguous decision context compared to consumers in the same situation in Germany and the United States.

Then again, the American origins of eBay posed some specific problems. Explained Nicolas Dufourcq, director of multimedia at France Telecom, "Sometimes when you are on an American portal, you feel imprisoned in a family that's clearly not yours." A European user also added that the "global scale of the site appears an arrogant claim to Europeans. . . . because of its global approach, the structure of the site is like a maze. Every time a change is made, the site becomes more complex and less self-explanatory. Any near-monopoly—and eBay has become one because of the number of visitors to its site—will eventually be shown the exit by innovative new entries to the market that cater more to local customers."

Against this backdrop, eBay ceased operations in Japan in early 2002. Reportedly, Yahoo! Japan then had 95 percent of the $2 billion online-auction Japanese market, a feat many linked to their partnership with the local company Softbank. Officially, eBay stated that they had found Japanese consumers more interested in new goods rather than used goods or collectibles.

Pace of International Expansion

Finally, some suggested eBay's ambition spurred a risky rush to globalize. Operationally, difficulties popped up for each acquisition. Moreover, eBay had paid steep premiums to acquire foreign operations; for example, eBay spent more than $200 million to buy a Korean site, Internet Auction, and a European clone, iBazar. Yet both had combined revenues of just $20 million a year after acquisition, and some analysts doubted that future results will justify the high purchase price.

eBay believed otherwise, noting the early law of Internet strategy—"Get Big Fast"—as well as predicting the world was ready for its service. More fundamentally, eBay believed the world needed its service to help transform developing nations into virtual marketplaces with a ready audience for native handicrafts, thereby infusing remote villages with cash that could improve locals' standard of living. "It's fascinating," Whitman explained. "There is a real frontier here that would truly make global trading a reality. You think about the Third World, villagers in Guatemala and Africa who have handicrafts to sell, who could list in their currency and their language and sell to the industrialized world. As that seller community makes more money for their town or village, they then have more purchasing power to buy more products and services from the more developed world. . . . Certainly it has the power to transform countries and cities and villages and empower people to make a living in ways they could not before. . . . eBay is creating new trade on a global basis that the world has never seen—that's what gets us up in the morning."

Going Forward

Some remained skeptical that eBay could transform the international business marketplace in ways that created legions of exporters and importers, helped impoverished nations, balanced the world's supply and demand, and significantly improved the efficiency of the global market. Certainly, a realistic assessment was vital. Still, in the back of everyone's mind was the staggering potential of global e-commerce and the stunning performance of eBay's global strategy thus far. Explained e-commerce analyst Steven Weinstein, "A total transformation may be slightly fanciful. But then again, look what eBay did to small business. It certainly transformed that." And, no matter what other people saw or said, Meg Whitman summed up eBay's outlook simply, saying that, "The fun thing about eBay is that we're pioneering a whole new marketplace. . . . It's going to be tremendous."

QUESTIONS

1. What is eBay's core competency? How does it relate to their chosen strategy?
2. How would you explain how eBay has decided to configure and coordinate its value chain?
3. Would you characterize eBay's value chain as virtual or real? Why?
4. Consider again your description of eBay's strategy. Is it different from what it was ten years ago? Why?
5. What implications to the challenges identified in the case have for eBay's strategy—today and in the future?

CHAPTER NOTES

1 Sources: Frank DuBois, "Globalization Risks and Information Management," *Journal of Global Information Management* 12 (April–June 2004): 3; A. Mazaira, E. Gonzalez, and R. Avendano, "The Role of Market Orientation on Company Performance Through the Development of Sustainable Competitive Advantage: The Inditex-Zara Case," *Marketing Intelligence & Planning* 2 (June 2003): 220; A. R. Bonnin "The Fashion Industry in Galicia: Understanding the 'Zara' Phenomenon," *European Planning Studies* 10 (June 1, 2002): 519; "Zara: Success on Its own Terms," **just-style.com**. (July 2004); Gary Gereffi, "International Trade and Industrial Upgrading in the Apparel Commodity Chain," *Journal of International Economics* 48 (June 1999): 37–70; "The Stars of Europe—Armancio Ortega, Chairman, Inditex," *Business Week* (June 11, 2001); John Brown, Scott Durchslag, and John Hagel, "Loosening Up: How Process Networks Unlock the Power of Specialization," *The McKinsey Quarterly* (Summer 2002): 59; "Rapid Response Retail," *Marketing* (April 3, 2003): 20; Gail Edmondson, "Has Benetton Stopped Unraveling?" *Business Week* (June 30, 2003): 76; Richard Heller, "Galician Beauty," *Forbes* (May 28, 2001): 98; William Copacino, "The True Meaning of Supply Chain Management," *Logistics Management* (June 2003); Patrick Byrne, "Closing the Gap between Strategy and Results," *Logistics Management* (March 2004).

2 In general, the higher the risk, the higher the return. Therefore, riskier projects and investments must be evaluated differently from their riskless counterparts. By discounting risky cash flows against less risky cash flows, risk-adjusted rates account for changes in the profile of the investment.

3 R. Coull, M. J. Bankes, D. J. Rossouw, P. Christmann, D. Day, and G. S. Yip, "Managing for Worldwide Competitive Advantage," *Journal of International Management* 5 (Winter 1999): 241; Jens Boyd, "Intra-Industry Structure and Performance: Strategic Groups and Strategic Blocks in the Worldwide Airline Industry," *European Management Review* 1 (2004): 132–45.

4 In particular, Schmalensee (1985) tested for evidence of business-specific differences through a single, exogenous measure of market share. His analysis also included corporate-parent effects, which he called "firm effects." Schmalensee found that industry effects accounted for about 20 percent of

variance, market-share effects accounted for less than 1 percent of variance, and corporate-parent effects did not significantly contribute to variance. He concluded that managerial influences were not important compared to differences in industry structure. R. Schmalensee, "Do Markets Differ Much?" *American Economic Review* (1985): 341–51; Richard Rumelt, "How Much Does Industry Matter?" *Strategic Management Journal* (1991): 167–86.

5   See B. Wernerfelt, "A Resource-Based View of the Firm," *Strategic Management Journal* 5 (1984): 171–80. More specficly, Rumelt (1991) found that corporate-parent effects contributed to the variance in firm performance, a finding later amplified by J. Roquebert, R. Phillips, and P. Westfall, "Markets versus Management: What 'Drives' Profitability?," *Strategic Management Journal,* 17, (1996): 653–64. It has been suggested that corporate-parent effects account for a large part (17.9 percent) of variance in the accounting profit of manufacturers. More recently, McGahan and Porter (2002) found similar evidence of corporate-parent effects. Anita McGahan and Michael Porter, "What Do We Know About Variance in Accounting Profitability?" *Management Science* 48 (2002): 834–51.

6   See, for example, Jenkins Wyn, "Competing in Times of Evolution and Revolution: An Essay on Long-Term Firm Survival," *Management Decisions* 43 (January 1, 2005): 26; Belen Villalonga, "Intangible Resources, Tobin's Q, and Sustainability of Performance Differences," *Journal of Economic Behavior & Organization* 54 (June 2004): 205.

7   Michael Porter, *Competitive Advantage* (New York: Free Press, 1985); Michael Porter, "Competition in Global Industries: A Conceptual Framework," in Michael Porter (ed.), *Competition in Global Industries* (Cambridge, MA: Harvard Business School Press, 1986): 15–60.

8   Technically, the threat of substitute comes from products outside the bounds of a particular industry. For example, the price of glass bottles, steel cans, and plastic containers influence the price of aluminum beverage cans. These substitute types of containers are not direct rivals to can makers in the aluminum can industry. Still, they influence the conduct of the aluminum can industry.

9   "Special Report: The China Price," *Business Week* (December 6, 2004).

10 Michael E. Porter, "What Is Strategy?" *Harvard Business Review* 74, no. 6 (November–December 1996): 61–79.

11 Managers may make decisions that they strongly reason support the firm's strategy, but in actuality, more often do not. Challenges emerge because often few managers understand the full demands of the company's strategy and implications to international operations. More worrisomely, managers are far more likely to make the wrong than right decision. See Dan Lovallo and Daniel Kahneman, "Delusions of Success: How Optimism Undermines Executives' Decisions," *Harvard Business Review* 81 (July 2003): 56.

12 The former follows from measuring the total revenues collected by buyers' payments for business output. The latter follows from summing the total cost the firm incurs to complete the activities that make up its value chain. Added value is created whenever the buyer's contribution exceeds the total cost.

13 Janet C. Lowe, *Welch: An American Icon* (New York: Wiley and Sons, 2002).

14 See Exhibit 7 in "Capturing Global Advantage: How Leading Industrial Companies Are Transforming Their Industries by Sourcing and Selling in China, India, and Other Low-Cost Countries," by Arindam Bhattacharya, et al., *Boston Consulting Group Publications* (April 9, 2004), www.bcg.com/publications/publications_search_results.jsp?PUBID=1101.

15 George Norman and Lynne Pepall, "Knowledge Spillovers, Mergers and Public Policy in Economic Clusters," *Review of Industrial Organization* 25 (September 2004): 155–75; James Simmie and James Sennett, "Innovative Clusters: Global or Local Linkages?" *National Institute Economic Review* 170 (October 1999): 87.

16 For example a recent report notes that "Offshoring has created a truly global operating model for financial services, unleashing a new and potent competitive dynamic that is changing the rules of the game for the entire industry. . . . There has never been an economic discontinuity of this magnitude in the history of the world," said Bain's Mark Gottfredson. "These powerful forces are allowing companies to rethink their sourcing strategies across the entire value chain." Financial firms are expanding into other areas like insurance claims processing, mortgage applications, equity research, diligence, valuation, and accounting. Deloitte forecasts that by the year 2010, the 100 largest global financial institutions will move $400 billion of their work offshore for $150 billion in annual savings. Quotes reported in "Financial Firms Hasten Their Move to Outsourcing," *New York Times* (August 18, 2004).

17 Synergy is defined as the combination of parts of a business such that the sum is worth more than the individual parts. It is often expressed in the equation $2 + 2 = 5$, with the additional unit of value the result of synergy.

18 Research reports a powerful relationship between a firm's performance and managers' sophistication in diffusing core competencies throughout the value chain. See David Collis and Cynthia Montgomery, "Competing on Resources: Strategy in the 1990s," *Harvard Business Review* (July–August 1995): 118–28; C. K. Prahalad and Gary Hamel, "The Core Competence of the Corporation," *Harvard Business Review* (May–June 1990): 79–91.

19 For instance, with a 20 percent cost reduction and an initial cost of $100 per unit, the second unit produced will cost $80, the fourth $64, and so on. In this example, the average cost per unit goes from $100 to $90 to $81.33, and so on.

20 James Brooke and Saul Hansel, "Samsung Is Now What Sony Once Was," *New York Times* (March 9, 2004).

21 N. Girvan, "Transnational Corporations and Non-Fuel Primary Commodities in Developing Countries," *World Development* 15 (1987): 713–40.

22 Raphael Kaplinsky and Mike Morris, "A Handbook for Value Chain Research" at http://www.seepnetwork.org/files/2303_file_Handbook_for_Value_Chain_Research.pdf.

23 Pankaj Ghemawat, "Distance Still Matters: The Hard Reality of Global Expansion," *Harvard Business Review* (September 2001).

24 Richard T. Pascale, "Surfing the Edge of Chaos," *Sloan Management Review* 40 (Spring 1999): 83; Eric Beinhocker, "Strategy at the Edge of Chaos," *McKinsey Quarterly* 1 (1997): 25; Mary J. Cronin, *Unchained Value: The New Logic of Digital Business* (Harvard Business School Press, 2001).

25 See Andreas Hinterhuber, "Value Chain Orchestration in Action and the Case of the Global Agrochemical Industry," *Long Range Planning* 35 (December 2002): 615; G. D. Bhatt and A. F. Emdad, "An Analysis of the Virtual Value Chain in Electronic Commerce," *Logistics Information Management* 14 (January 17, 2001): 78; S. Winter, John McIntosh, and David May, "Survival in the Korean Furniture Industry: Value-Chain Networking," *Journal of Managerial Issues* 15 (Winter 2003): 450.

26 Theodore Levitt, "The Globalization of Markets," *Harvard Business Review* 61 (1983): 92–102.

27 Regarding cultural predisposition, Japanese doctors disfavor the American-style, high-pressure sales force. Pharmaceutical sales representatives, therefore, need to adapt their marketing practices in that country. Regarding historical legacy, people drive on the left side of the road in England, thereby creating demand for right-hand-drive cars, whereas people in Ireland drive on the right side of the road, thereby creating demand for left-hand-drive cars. Similarly, consumer electrical systems are based on 110 volts in the United States, whereas many European countries use a 240-volt standard.

28 C. Prahalad and Y. Doz, *The Multinational Mission: Balancing Local Demands and Global Vision* (New York: Free Press, 1987).

29 The term *multinational corporation* (MNC) is also commonly used in the international business arena and often is a synonym for MNE. We prefer the MNE designation because there are many internationally involved companies, such as accounting partnerships, which are not organized as corporations.

30 Global System for Mobile Communications (GSM) is the name of a land mobile pan-European digital cellular radio communications system. The GSM family of wireless technology platforms includes such standards as GSM, GPRS, EDGE, and 3GSM. Collectively, the GSM is a standard that embraces all areas of technology, resulting in global, seamless wireless services for all its customers. In less than 10 years since the first GSM network was commercially launched, it became the world's leading and fastest growing mobile standard, spanning over 200 countries. At the end of January 2004 there were over 1 billion GSM subscribers. Since 1997, the number of GSM subscribers has increased tenfold. See http://www.gsmworld.com/index.shtml.

31 Direct quotes sourced from: Jack Welch and John A. Byrne *Jack: Straight from the Gut*, (New York: Warner Business Books, 2001); "GE's Two-Decade Transformation: Jack Welch's Leadership," Chris Bartlett and Meg Wozny, (Harvard Business School Case 399150, 1999); Janet C. Lowe, op. cit.

32 Joan Ricart, Michael J. Enright, Pankaj Ghemawat, Stuart L. Hart, and Tarun Khanna, "New Frontiers in International Strategy," *Journal of International Business Studies* 35 (May 2004): 175.

33 Yves Doz, Jose Santos, and Peter Williamson, *Global to Metanational: How Companies Win in the Knowledge Economy* (Cambridge, MA: Harvard Business School Press, 2001).

34 Marc Singer, "Beyond the Unbundled Corporation," *The McKinsey Quarterly* (Summer 2001): 4; Remo Hacki and Julian Lighton, "The Future of the Networked Company," *The McKinsey Quarterly* (Summer 2001): 26; James Martin, "Only the Cyber-fit Will Survive," *Datamation* 42 (November 1996): 60.

35 Sources: ebay.com/corporatehome; ebay.com/investorsrelations; "eBay's Whitman Touts International Plans," by Rachel Konrad, CNET News.com (August 15, 2000); "CEO Whitman Looks Overseas, Ponders Peer-to-Peer," by Rachel Konrad, CNET News.com (August 17, 2000); "eBay Faces International Checkpoints," by Rachel Konrad, CNET News.com (August 18, 2000); "Global Reach? eBay Isn't There Yet," *Business Week*, no. 3727 (April 9, 2001): 8; "Software Helps eBay's Global Expansion Efforts," by Tony Kontzer, *InformationWeek* (Dec. 1, 2003); "Q&A with eBay's Meg Whitman," *Business Week* (March 24, 2003): The Tech Outlook/Online Extra; "eBay Picks Up Top Indian Trading Site for $50m," Rimin Dutt, *Industrial Business Journal*—Technology (July 15, 2004); "Software Helps EBay's Global Expansion Efforts," Tony Kontzer, *InformationWeek* (Dec. 1, 2003); "eBay Lends Hand to Drop-Off Stores," Bob Tedeschi, *New York Times: E-Commerce Report* (August 30, 2004); "International Sales Boost eBay," by Rachel Konrad, *Information Week* (July 21, 2004). "Global Pains," by Katarzyna Moreno, *Forbes* 165, no. 7 (March 20, 2000): 286; "How Yahoo! Japan Beat eBay at Its Own Game," *Business Week*, no. 3735 (June 4, 2001): 58.

for exploiting temporary innovative advantages is known as the **imitation lag,** whereby a company moves first to those countries most likely to adapt and catch up to the innovative advantage, and later to other countries.[30] Those countries apt to catch up more rapidly are the ones whose companies invest a great deal in technology and whose governments offer little protection for the innovator's intellectual property rights. If the country also offers import protection, a local producer can, even if inefficient, gain a cost advantage over imported goods.

Companies also may develop strategies to avoid significant competition. For example, PriceSmart, a discount operator, has all its warehouse stores outside its home country (the United States), and has been successful by targeting locations in Central America, the Caribbean, and Asia that are considered too small to attract competitors like WalMart and Carrefour.[31] However, good locations seldom go unnoticed by competitors, as illustrated in Figure 12.6. In the opening case, we illustrated how Carrefour tries to enter growth markets before its major competitors. By being the first major competitor in a market, companies can more easily gain the best partners, best locations, and best suppliers—a strategy to gain **first mover advantage.** Similarly, companies may reduce risk by avoiding overcrowded markets. However, they may purposely crowd a market to prevent competitors from gaining advantages therein that they can use to improve their competitive positions elsewhere, a situation known as **oligopolistic reaction.**[32] For example, by 2003, 10 foreign automobile companies and about 80 Chinese companies had invested in Chinese production. Although GM estimates that by 2025, China will be

FIGURE 12.6

Avoiding competition may have some disadvantages.

Source: Copyright Martha Murphy/CartoonResource.com

"Maybe there's a good reason why no one else has broken into this market."

the world's third largest automobile market, analysts agree that the market cannot sustain so many manufacturers.[33]

At the same time, companies may gain advantages by locating where competitors are. To begin with, the competitors may have performed the costly task of evaluating locations, so a follower may get a "free ride." Moreover, there are clusters of competitors (sometimes called agglomeration) in various locations—think of all the computer firms in California's Silicon Valley. More recently, hundreds of high-tech computer companies from all over the world have located in Dubai.[34] These clusters attract multiple suppliers and personnel with specialized skills. They also attract buyers who want to compare potential suppliers but don't want to travel great distances between them. Companies operating in the cluster area may also gain better access to information about new developments because they frequently come in contact with personnel from the other companies.[35]

Monetary Risk If a company's expansion occurs through direct investment abroad, exchange rates on and access to the invested capital and earnings are key considerations. The concept of *liquidity preference* is a common theory that helps explain companies' capital budgeting decisions in general and can be applied to their international expansion decisions.

Liquidity preference, much like option theory, is the theory that investors usually want some of their holdings to be in highly liquid assets, on which they are willing to take a lower return. They need liquidity in part to make near-term payments, such as paying out dividends; in part to cover unexpected contingencies, such as stockpiling materials if a strike threatens supply; and in part to be able to shift funds to even more profitable opportunities, such as purchasing materials at a discount during a temporary price depression.[36]

> Companies may accept a lower return in order to move their financial resources more easily.

Sometimes companies want to sell all or part of their equity in a foreign facility so that the funds may be used for other types of expansion endeavors. However, the ability to find local buyers varies substantially among countries and among industries, depending largely on the existence of a local capital market and on the potential for the operation being sold. For example, the Mexican conglomerate, Grupo Carso, spun off its U.S. stake in CompUSA, a process facilitated by CompUSA's potential profits and the developed U.S. capital market.[37] However, when Nike canceled a contract with an Indonesian-Korean joint venture in Indonesia, the partners simply had to close the operation.[38]

Assuming a company does find a purchaser for its foreign facility, chances are that it intends to use the funds in another country. If the funds are not convertible, the selling company will be forced to spend them in the host country. Of more pressing concern for most investors is both the ability to convert earnings from operations abroad and the cost of doing so. It is not surprising that investors may be willing to accept a lower projected ROI for projects in countries with strong currencies than for those in countries with weak currencies.

Present capital controls and recent exchange-rate stability are useful indicators of countries' monetary situation. Additionally, companies need to predict countries' likely future exchange rate deterioration and exchange controls. Some indicators of future problems are countries' negative trade balances, declining official reserves, high inflation, and government budget deficits.

Political Risk In Chapter 3, we discussed consequences of political risk. It may occur because of changes in political leaders' opinions and policies, civil disorder, and animosity between the host and other countries—particularly with the company's home country. It may cause property takeovers as well as damage property, disrupt operations, and cause a change in the rules governing business. Further, it may create expensive operational adjustments. Recently, for example, Unilever has encountered difficulty in attracting foreign executives to work in Pakistan because of security concerns, Chiquita Brands has had to pay money to terrorists in Colombia to protect its employees there, and Coca-Cola has had interrupted services (police protection of its trucks and telephone connections) in Angola because of its policy against paying bribes.[39] Managers use three approaches to predict political risk: analyzing past patterns, using expert opinion, and examining the social and economic conditions that might lead to such risk.

> Political risk may come from wars and insurrections, takeover of property, and/or changes in rules.

Companies cannot help but be influenced by past patterns of political risk. However, predicting the risk on that basis holds many dangers. Political situations may change rapidly for better or worse as far as foreign companies are concerned. For example, foreign direct investment into the United States fell sharply after the 2001 terrorist attack in New York because foreign firms saw the United States as less safe than before. In a broader sense, expropriation of property occurred frequently in the 1970s and early 1980s, but it has been less important in recent years. Nevertheless, companies continue to worry sufficiently about takeovers so that many still seek insurance against them.

Substantial variations in political risk frequently exist within countries. With the exception of a few countries, government takeovers of companies have been highly selective, primarily affecting operations that have a visible widespread effect on the country because of their size or monopoly position. Similarly, unrest that leads to property damage and disruption of supplies or sales may not endanger the operations of all foreign companies. This may be because of the limited geographic focus of the unrest. For example, companies suffered no property damage or business disruption in Slovenia after the breakup of Yugoslavia; however, they did experience problems in other areas in the former Yugoslavia.

Asset takeover or property damage does not necessarily mean a full loss to investors. Governments have preceded most takeovers with a formal declaration of intent and have followed with legal processes to determine the foreign investor's compensation. (For example, at this writing, the government of Venezuela has announced the takeover of a majority interest in all oil company operations in the country.) Companies may examine past settlement patterns as an indicator of whether and how they may be compensated. In addition to the asset's book value, other factors may determine the adequacy of compensation. On one hand, the compensation may earn a lower return elsewhere. On the other hand, other agreements (such as purchase and management contracts) may create additional benefits for the former investor. In analyzing political risk, managers should predict the likely loss if political problems occur.

Companies may also rely on experts' opinions about a country's political situation, with the purpose of ascertaining how influential people may sway future political events affecting business. The first step is reading statements made by political leaders both in and out of office to determine their philosophies on business in general, foreign input to business, the means of effecting economic changes, and their feelings toward given foreign countries. Modern technology has improved access to press reports in foreign countries. Online services include full-text reports from newspapers and television from major parts of the world, and reports are sometimes available within hours of the original publication or broadcast. However, published statements may appear too late for a company to react. The second step is for managers to visit the country and "listen" to a cross-section of opinions. Embassy officials and foreign and local businesspeople are useful sources of opinions about the probability and direction of change. Journalists, academicians, middle-level local government authorities, and labor leaders usually reveal their own attitudes, which often reflect changing political conditions that may affect the business sector.

Companies may determine opinions more systematically by relying on analysts with experience in a country. These analysts might rate a country on specific political conditions that could lead to problems for foreign businesses, such as the fractionalization of political parties that could cause disruptive changes in government. A company also may rely on commercial risk-assessment services, such as those published by Business International, Economist Intelligence Unit, Euromoney, Political Risk Services (PRS), Bank of America World Information Services, Control Risks Information Services (CRIS), Institutional Investor, Moody's Investors Service, S. J. Rundt & Associates, Standard & Poor's Ratings Group, World Markets Research Centre, and Business Environment Risk Information (BERI). In fact, companies have been relying more on these services rather than on their internal generation of risk analyses. In essence, their reports generated internally are often too lengthy or abstract to be useful. Further, they are often not seen as credible by management decision makers.[40]

Finally, companies may examine countries' social and economic conditions that could lead to the populations' level of aspirations and the countries' level of welfare and

---

Management can make predictions based on past patterns.

Companies should

- Examine views of government decision makers
- Get a cross-section of opinions
- Use expert analysts

expectations—the higher the difference, the higher the level of frustration. If there is a great deal of frustration in a country, groups may disrupt business by calling general strikes and destroying property and supply lines. They might also replace government leaders. Moreover, frustrated groups and political leaders might try to blame problems on foreigners and make threats against foreign governments as well as expropriate foreign properties or change the rules for foreign-owned companies. However, there is no general consensus as to what constitutes dangerous instability or how such instability can be predicted. The lack of consensus is illustrated by the diverse reactions of companies to the same political situations. Rather than political stability itself, the direction of change in government seems to be very important. But even if a company accurately predicts the direction of change in government that will affect business, it will still be uncertain as to the time lag between the change and its effect.

DOES GEOGRAPHY MATTER?

Don't Fool with Mother Nature

A major tsunami hit southern Asia in late 2004. Soon after, there was an outbreak of the deadly Marburg virus in Angola. These events publicized global vulnerability to natural disasters and communicable diseases. Each year about 130 million people are exposed to earthquake risk, 119 million to tropical cyclone hazards, 196 million to catastrophic flooding, and 220 million to drought. On average, there are 184 deaths per day from natural disasters.[41] These natural disasters are not spread uniformly around the world. For instance, Iran, Afghanistan, and India are heavily exposed to earthquakes, and some African states have the highest vulnerability to drought. At this writing, the United Nations Development Programme is developing a disaster risk index (DRI) that will show the relative level of physical exposure to natural disaster hazards. We already know that although only 11 percent of the people exposed to these disasters live in the poorest countries of the world, they account for 55 percent of the deaths. In essence, they are the least prepared to deal with the catastrophes because they live in poor housing and have sub-par medical assistance. Likewise, we know that as urbanization has increased in emerging economies, people have moved to dangerous mountainsides and ravines and are ill equipped to deal with earthquakes and cyclones. For instance, when Hurricane Mitch hit Honduras in 1998, it left 10,000 dead, 20,000 missing, and 2.5 million needing emergency aid.[42] The disturbing prognosis is that the fastest urban growth is taking place in emerging economies, thus increasing the possibility of catastrophic results from natural disasters.

What does this have to do with the location of operations by international companies? In addition to the possibility of damaging a company's property and injuring its personnel, these events upset markets, infrastructure, and production. Although they are most devastating in the world's poorer areas, events in high-income areas can play havoc with global supplies as well. For instance, the Kobe earthquake in Japan upset the world computer industry's production because it created semiconductor shortages.[43] Thus, natural events create additional operating risks and additional costs to insure against them. In turn, insurance companies are challenged to estimate the likelihood and cost of these events, such as through the development of models based on the statistical theory of extreme values.

The World Health Organization is developing a global atlas of infectious diseases.[44] Many of these diseases are associated with poverty. They are also associated with natural disasters. For instance, cholera and malaria outbreaks are most apt to occur after flooding. Thus, they tend to follow geographic patterns. For example, malaria kills about 2 million people a year, mainly in Africa. The debilitating effects impact labor force participation and life expectancy. In turn, they are costly to companies. Sasol Petroleum had to set up a clinic in Mozambique to treat its workers for malaria.[45] Further, some of the areas that are most subject to disease risk are the same ones that have the poorest medical facilities. Companies also hesitate to send their personnel to epidemic areas. For example, during the Asian SARS outbreak in 2003, a number of companies (such as Wal-Mart, Gap, Liz Claiborne, Kenneth Cole) banned employee travel to affected countries, thus hindering their buying and quality-assurance programs.[46]

COLLECT AND ANALYZE DATA

Companies undertake business research to reduce uncertainties in their decision process, to expand or narrow the alternatives they consider, and to assess the merits of their existing programs. Efforts to reduce uncertainties include attempts to answer such questions as these: "Can qualified personnel be hired?" "Will the economic and political climate allow for a reasonable certainty of operations?" Alternatives may be expanded by asking, "Where are possible new sources of funds or sales?" Or they may be narrowed by querying, "Where among the alternatives would operating costs be lowest?" Evaluation and control are improved by assessing present and past performance: "Is the distributor servicing sufficient accounts?" "What is our market share?" Clearly, there are numerous details that can be useful to a company in its efforts to achieve its objectives.

A company can seldom, if ever, gain all the information its managers would like. This is because of time constraints and the cost of collecting information. Managers should estimate the costs of data collection and compare them with the probable payoff from the data in terms of revenue gains or cost savings.

Problems with Research Results and Data

The lack, obsolescence, and inaccuracy of data on many countries make much research difficult and expensive to undertake. Data discrepancies sometimes create uncertainties about location decisions. In most industrial countries, such as the United States, governments collect very detailed demographic and purchasing data, which are available cheaply to any company or individual. (But even in the United States, the Census Bureau first announced it had undercounted 3 million people and later that it had overcounted 1.3 million in the 2000 census).[47]

Using samples based on available information, a company can draw fairly accurate inferences concerning market-segment sizes and locations, at least within broad categories. In the United States, the fact that so many companies are publicly owned and are required to disclose much operating information helps a company to learn competitors' strengths and weaknesses. Further, companies may rely on a multitude of behavioral studies dealing with U.S. consumer preferences and experience. With this available information, a company can devise questionnaires or do some test marketing using a selected sample so that responses reflect the behavior of the larger target group to whom the company plans to sell. Contrast this situation to that of a country whose basic census, national income accounts, and foreign-trade figures are suspect and where no data are collected on consumer expenditures. In many countries, business is conducted under a veil of secrecy, consumers' buying behavior is a matter of speculation, market intermediaries are reluctant to answer questions, and expensive primary research may be required before meaningful samples and questions can be developed.

Many countries have agreed to standards for collecting and publishing various categories of data on the Internet. This agreement through the IMF came about because of a belief that the Mexican financial crisis of 1994 might have been averted had international financial authorities had better and more timely information about Mexico's trade, debt, and foreign-exchange reserves.[48]

Reasons for Inaccuracies   For the most part, incomplete or inaccurate published data result from the inability of many governments to collect the needed information. Poor countries may have such limited resources that other projects necessarily receive priority in the national budget. Why collect precise figures on the literacy rate, the leaders of a poor country might reason, when the same outlay can be used to build schools to improve that rate?

Education affects the competence of government officials to maintain and analyze accurate records. Economic factors also hamper record retrieval and analysis, because hand calculations may be used instead of costly electronic data-processing systems. The result may be information that is years old before it is made public. Finally, cultural factors affect responses. Mistrust of how the data will be used may lead respondents to answer incorrectly, particularly if questions probe financial details.

Of equal concern to the researcher is the publication of false or purposely misleading information designed to mislead government superiors, the country's rank and file, or companies and institutions abroad. For example, an in-house investigation in China's National Bureau of Statistics found over 60,000 cases of statistical misrepresentations that distorted such important figures as GDP, economic growth, and energy use.[49] Even if government and private organizations do not purposely publish false statements, many organizations may be so selective in the data they include that they create false impressions. Therefore, it is useful for managers to consider carefully the source of such material in light of possible motives or biases.

However, not all inaccuracies are due to government collection and dissemination procedures. Many studies by academicians describing international business practices are based on broad generalizations that may be drawn from too few observations, on nonrepresentative samples, and on poorly designed questionnaires.

People's desire and ability to cover up data on themselves—such as unreported income to avoid taxes—may distort published figures substantially. Illegal income from such activities as the drug trade, theft, bribery, and prostitution is not included in GDP figures, or it appears in other economic sectors because of money laundering. These unreported activities can be substantial. For instance, it is estimated that about $3 billion of Nigerian oil per year is stolen and shipped abroad.[50]

Comparability Problems   Countries publish censuses, output figures, trade statistics, and base-year calculations for different time periods. So companies need to compare country figures by extrapolating from those different periods.

> **Problems in information comparability arise from**
> - Differences in definitions and base years
> - Distortions in currency conversions

There also are numerous definitional differences among countries. For example, a category as seemingly basic as "family income" may include only the nuclear family—parents and children—in some countries, but it may include the extended family—the nuclear family plus grandparents, uncles, and cousins—elsewhere. Similarly, some countries define literacy as some minimum level of formal schooling, others as attainment of certain specified standards, and still others as simply the ability to read and write one's name. Further, percentages may be published in terms of either adult population (with different ages used for adulthood) or total population. The definitions of accounting rules such as depreciation also differ, resulting in noncomparable net national product figures.

Figures on national income and per capita income are particularly difficult to compare because of differences in activities taking place outside the market economy—for example, within the home, which do not, therefore, show up in income figures. The extent to which people in one country produce for their own consumption (for example, grow vegetables, bake bread, sew clothes, or cut hair) will distort comparisons with other countries where different portions of people buy these products and services.

Another comparability problem concerns exchange rates, which must be used to convert countries' financial data to some common currency. A 10 percent appreciation of the Japanese yen in relation to the U.S. dollar will result in a 10 percent increase in the per capita income of Japanese residents when figures are reported in dollars. Does this mean that the Japanese are suddenly 10 percent richer? Obviously not, because they use about 85 percent of their yen income to make purchases in yen in the Japanese economy, thus they have no additional purchasing power for 85 percent of what they buy. Even if changes in exchange rates are ignored, purchasing power and living standards are difficult to compare, because costs are so affected by climate and habit. Exchange rates, even when using PPP, are a very imperfect means of comparing national data.

External Sources of Information

Although we have indicated variables that may be useful for making locational decisions, it is impossible to include a comprehensive list of information sources. There are

> Specificity and cost of information vary by source.

simply too many. A routine search on the Internet often yields thousands of sources, and Lexis/Nexis gives full-text citations from thousands of published sources. Chances are, at least for scanning purposes, you will use the Internet to collect most of your information simply by using search engines to find information on key variables by entering words or phrases such as GDP per capita or world trade. The following discussion highlights the major types of information sources in terms of their completeness, reliability, and cost.

Individualized Reports   Market research and business consulting companies will conduct studies for a fee in most countries. Naturally, the quality and the cost of these studies vary widely. They generally are the most costly information source because the individualized nature restricts prorating among a number of companies. However, the fact that a company can specify what information it wants often makes the expense worthwhile.

Specialized Studies   Some research organizations prepare fairly specific studies that they sell to any interested company at costs much lower than those for individualized studies. These specialized studies sometimes are directories of companies that operate in a given locale, perhaps with financial or other information about the companies. They also may be about business in certain locales, forms of business, or specific products. They may combine any of these elements as well. For example, a study could deal with the market for imported auto parts in Germany.

Service Companies   Most companies that provide services to international clients—for example, banks, transportation agencies, and accounting firms—publish reports. These reports usually are geared toward either the conduct of business in a given area or some specific subject of general interest, such as tax or trademark legislation. Because the service firms intend to reach a wide market of companies, their reports usually lack the specificity a company may want for making a final decision. However, much of the data give useful background information. Some service firms also offer informal opinions about such things as the reputations of possible business associates and the names of people to contact in a company.

Government Agencies   Governments and their agencies are another source of information. Different countries' statistical reports vary in subject matter, quantity, and quality. When a government or government agency wants to stimulate foreign business activity, the amount and type of information it makes available may be substantial. For example, the U.S. Department of Commerce not only compiles such basic data as news about and regulations in individual foreign countries and product-location–specific information in the National Trade Data Bank, but it will also help set up appointments with businesspeople abroad.

International Organizations and Agencies   Numerous organizations and agencies are supported by more than one country. These include the UN, the WTO, the IMF, the OECD, and the EU. All of these organizations have large research staffs that compile basic statistics as well as prepare reports and recommendations concerning common trends and problems. Many of the international development banks even help finance investment-feasibility studies.

Trade Associations   Trade associations connected to various product lines collect, evaluate, and disseminate a wide variety of data dealing with technical and competitive factors in their industries. Many of these data are available in the trade journals published by such associations; others may or may not be available to nonmembers.

Information Service Companies   A number of companies have information-retrieval services that maintain databases from hundreds of different sources, including many of those already described. For a fee, or sometimes for free at public libraries, a company can obtain access to such computerized data and arrange for an immediate printout of studies of interest.

Internal Generation of Data

MNEs may have to conduct many studies abroad themselves. Sometimes the research process may consist of no more than observing keenly and asking many questions. Investigators can see what kind of merchandise is available, can see who is buying and where, and can uncover the hidden distribution points and competition. In some countries, for example, the competition for ready-made clothes may be from seamstresses working in private homes rather than from retailers. The competition for vacuum cleaners may be from servants who clean with mops rather than from other electrical-appliance manufacturers. Surreptitiously sold contraband may compete with locally produced goods. Traditional analysis methods would not reveal such facts. In many countries, even bankers have to rely more on clients' reputations than on their financial statements. Shrewd questioning may yield very interesting results. But such questioning is not always easy. For example, political unrest and the lack of telephones may inhibit the sampling of people.[51]

Often a company must be extremely imaginative, extremely observant, or both. For example, one soft drink manufacturer wanted to determine its Mexican market share relative to that of its competitors. Management could not make reliable estimates from the final points of distribution because sales were so widespread. So the company hit on two alternatives, both of which turned out to be feasible: The bottle cap manufacturer revealed how many caps it sold to each of its clients, and customs supplied data on each competitor's soft drink concentrate imports.

POINT–COUNTERPOINT: SHOULD COMPANIES FOREGO DIRECT INVESTMENTS IN VIOLENT AREAS?

POINT

As an executive of an MNE, I say they should. Companies have coincidently spread their operations internationally while violence has erupted against them. We're no longer concerned simply about being caught in the cross fire between opposing military groups, we're concerned about anti-globalization groups that want to inflict harm on our personnel and facilities and about groups that see us as easy marks for extortion by threatening harm or kidnapping our personnel. Still others are against foreigners, regardless of the aims of the foreigners.

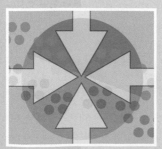

For instance, such a group in Afghanistan killed five staff members from Médecins Sans Frontières, who were there to treat sick and injured people. At the same time, getting caught in the crossfire has become a bigger risk. Arms trafficking has increased and has lowered prices, not only to revolutionaries, but also to drug and alien smugglers and to criminals involved in

money laundering.[52] As MNEs, we can't help being visible, and this visibility makes us vulnerable.

In essence, if we have direct investments where risk of violence is great, we put our personnel at risk, especially those who are foreigners in the countries. While local personnel may be at a lesser risk of say, kidnapping, experience shows that they are not immune either. Further, to operate in these risky areas, we have to send foreign personnel there. Some go as managers or technicians on long assignments. Others must go on business trips, such as to audit books, assure quality control, and offer staff advice that must involve on-site visits. The dangers are not inconsequential, for instance, about 750 Colombian kidnappings in 2004 alone.[53] Halliburton lost 42 employees in Iraq and Kuwait in the first two years after the U.S. invasion.[54]

We just find it unethical to put our employees in such situations. Of course, we don't force people to go to a danger area, and we have gotten enough people who are willing to work in these dangerous areas, partially because we have insured them heavily and paid them well. However, our experience has been that we get three types of people who want or are willing to work in these areas, and none of these types are ideal. First, we get the people who simply want the compensation, some of whom are experienced in military or undercover activities. However, these people tend to be highly independent and hard to control. Second, we get the naïve, who because of not really understanding the danger, are difficult to safeguard through training and security activities. Third, we get the thrill seekers, who find that adrenaline is like an addictive drug. These are most at risk because of the thrill of danger and the reluctance to leave when situations worsen.[55]

High risk to individuals is indicative of a political situation out of control. Thus, it is a harbinger of additional risks that may occur through governmental changes, falls in consumer confidence, and a general malaise that affects revenues and operating regulations negatively. This is not the kind of country in which to conduct operations.

COUNTERPOINT

Where there's risk, there are usually rewards. Companies should not shun areas with violence. Companies have always taken risks and employees have always migrated, as far back as the seventeenth century, when they traveled to what are now the United States, India, and Australia. They encountered such conditions as disease and hostile native populations. Had companies and immigrants not taken chances, the world would be far less developed today. Thus, you can't look at the risk from violence in isolation from other risks. Although we don't have historical data, risks are probably lower today. Disease is still a bigger risk than violence, but medical advances against a number of historical killers (such as polio, measles, smallpox, and tuberculosis) have lessened the risk from disease. Further, evacuation in case of a *real* emergency situation is much faster.

But let's assume for a moment that we decide we should avoid countries with the potential for violence against our employees. Is there any such place? The opinions we get are certainly conflicting. A vice president of a risk consulting company said, "It's an even playing field around the world. You can go to London, Caracas, Madrid, or New York, and from a terrorism standpoint, the risk is the same."[56] Another provider of intelligence placed the United States as riskier for terrorism than Iraq and placed Britain as riskier than Nepal for 2003–2004.[57] Although these analyses seem intuitively wrong, a decade after the blowing up of a government building in Oklahoma City, the deputy assistant director of the FBI said, "The threat has not gone away. We are dealing every single day with a variety of domestic terrorism threats that are alive and well and in this country [United States]."[58] About the only places that everyone agrees are low risk are Greenland and Iceland.

In addition, some industries don't have the luxury of deciding on any country in the world to put their operations. Take the petroleum industry. The companies have to go where there is a high likelihood of finding petroleum. While it would be great to find all the petroleum in places like Iceland and Switzerland, this is not the reality. Most of the realistic alternatives are in areas that have had recent bombings, kidnappings, or organized crime—the Middle East, west Africa, the Central Asian former Soviet republics, Ecuador, and Venezuela.[59] If we did not go to these places, we'd be out of business.

In effect, we'll keep operating anywhere that there are opportunities. If a place seems physically risky for our employees, we'll take whatever precautions we can. We'll share intelligence reports, put people through safety training courses (there are plenty of these available now), take security actions abroad, and perhaps not transfer spouses and children to risky areas. We do this latter practice so that we do not have to be on top of what is happening with as many people.

COUNTRY COMPARISON TOOLS

Once companies collect information on possible locations through scanning, they need to analyze the information. Two common tools for analysis are grids and matrices. In preparing either, it is useful to use a team made up of people from different functions so that production, marketing, finance, human resource, and legal factors will all be considered. However, once companies commit to locations, they need continuous updates. We shall now discuss grids and matrices.

Grids

A company may use a grid to compare countries on whatever factors it deems important. Table 12.2 is an example of a grid with information placed into three categories. The company may eliminate certain countries immediately from consideration because of characteristics it finds unacceptable. These factors are in the first category of variables, in which country I is eliminated. The company assigns values and weights to other variables so that it ranks each country according to the relative importance of attributes to it. In this hypothetical example, we've attached more weight to the size of investment needed than to the tax rate. For example, the table graphically pinpoints country II as high return–low risk, country III as low return–low risk, country IV as high return–high risk, and country V as low return–high risk.

Both the variables and the weights will differ by product and company depending on the company's internal situation and its objectives. The grid technique is useful even when a company does not compare countries because it can set the minimum score needed for either investing additional resources or committing further funds to a more detailed feasibility study. Grids do tend to get cumbersome, however, as the number of variables increases. Although they are useful in ranking countries, they often obscure interrelationships among countries.

Grids are tools that

- May depict acceptable or unacceptable conditions
- Rank countries by important variables

TABLE 12.2   SIMPLIFIED GRID TO COMPARE COUNTRIES FOR MARKET PENETRATION

Managers may choose which variables to include in the grid; this table is merely an example. Note also that managers may weight some variables as more important than others. Here, country I is immediately eliminated because the company will go only where 100 percent ownership is permitted. Countries II and IV are estimated to have the highest return; and countries II and III are estimated to have the lowest risk.

VARIABLE	WEIGHT	I	II	III	IV	V
				COUNTRY		
1. Acceptable (A), Unacceptable (U) factors						
a. Allows 100 percent ownership	—	U	A	A	A	A
b. Allows licensing to majority-owned subsidiary	—	A	A	A	A	A
2. Return (higher number = preferred rating)						
a. Size of investment needed	0–5	—	4	3	3	3
b. Direct costs	0–3	—	3	1	2	2
c. Tax rate	0–2	—	2	1	2	2
d. Market size, present	0–4	—	3	2	4	1
e. Market size, 3–10 years	0–3	—	2	1	3	1
f. Market share, immediate potential, 0–2 years	0–2	—	2	1	2	1
g. Market share, 3–10 years	0–2	—	2	1	2	0
Total			18	10	18	10
3. Risk (lower number = preferred rating)						
a. Market loss, 3–10 years (if no present penetration)	0–4	—	2	1	3	2
b. Exchange problems	0–3	—	0	0	3	3
c. Political-unrest potential	0–3	—	0	1	2	3
d. Business laws, present	0–4	—	1	0	4	3
e. Business laws, 3–10 years	0–2	—	0	1	2	2
Total			3	3	14	13

Matrices

To show more clearly the opportunity and risk relationship, managers can plot values on a matrix such as the one shown in Figure 12.7. In this particular example, Countries E and F are high-opportunity and low-risk countries in comparison with countries A, B, C, and D. Thus, countries E and F are better candidates for detailed analysis than the other countries. In reality, however, managers may sometimes have to choose between two countries, one with a high risk and high opportunity and another with a low risk and low opportunity. They are apt to make their decision based on their tolerance for risk and on the portfolio of countries where the company is already operating. Further, although A and B are less appealing than C and D, the company may nevertheless find opportunities in A and B without necessarily making a large commitment. For example, A and B may be ideal candidates for licensing or shared ownership arrangements.

But how can managers plot values on such a matrix? They must determine which factors are good indicators of their companies' risk and opportunity and weight them to reflect their importance. For instance, on the risk axis they might give 40 percent (0.4) of the weight to expropriation risk, 25 percent (0.25) to foreign-exchange controls, 20 percent (0.2) to civil disturbances and terrorism, and 15 percent (0.15) to exchange-rate change, for a total allocation of 100 percent. They would then rate each country on a scale of 1 to 10 for each variable (with 10 indicating the best score and 1 the worst) and multiply each variable by the weight they allocate to it. For instance, if they give Country A a rating of 8 on the expropriation-risk variable, the 8 would be multiplied by 0.4 (the weight they assign to expropriation) for a score of 3.2. They would then sum all of Country A's risk-variable scores to place it on the risk axis. They would plot the location of Country A on the opportunity axis similarly. Once they determine the scores for each country, they can ascertain the average scores for all countries' risks and opportunities and divide the matrix into quadrants based on the average risk and average opportunity scores.

A key element of this kind of matrix, and one that managers do not always include in practice, is the projection of where countries will be in the future. Such a projection is obviously useful. Thus, managers may rely on forecasters who are knowledgeable not only about the countries but also about forecasting methods.

Some types of information are more important to one company or for one product than another. For example, managers in a company selling a low-priced consumer product might heavily weigh population size as an indicator of market opportunity, whereas

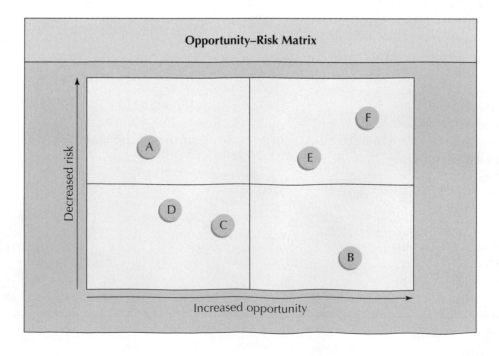

those in a company selling tire re-treading services might heavily weigh the number of vehicles registered. In terms of production location, managers in one company may be most concerned about the wage rates of low-skilled workers and managers in another with the local availability of supplies.

ALLOCATING AMONG LOCATIONS

The scanning tools we have just discussed are useful for narrowing alternatives among countries. They are also useful in allocating operational emphasis among countries, but there are other factors companies need to consider. We shall now discuss three of them: reinvestment versus harvesting, the interdependence of locations, and diversification versus concentration.

Reinvestment versus Harvesting

A company usually makes new foreign investments by transferring capital abroad. If the investment is successful, the company will earn money that it may remit back to headquarters or reinvest to increase the value of the investment. Over time, most of the value of a company's foreign investment comes from reinvestment. If the investment is unsuccessful or if its outlook is less favorable than possible investments in other countries, the company may consider harvesting the earnings to use elsewhere or even to discontinue the investment.

A company may have to make new commitments to maintain competitiveness abroad.

Reinvestment Decisions Companies treat decisions to replace depreciated assets or to add to the existing stock of capital from retained earnings in a foreign country somewhat differently from original investment decisions. Once committed to a given locale, a company may find it doesn't have the option of moving a substantial portion of the earnings elsewhere—to do so would endanger the continued successful operation of the given foreign facility. The failure to expand might result in a falling market share and a higher unit cost than that of competitors.

Aside from competitive factors, a company may need several years of almost total reinvestment and allocation of new funds in one area in order to meet its objectives. Over time, a company may use the earnings to expand the product line further, integrate production, or expand the market served from present output. Another reason a company treats reinvestment decisions differently is that once it has experienced personnel within a given country, it may believe those workers are the best judges of what is needed for that country, so headquarters managers may delegate certain investment decisions to them.

Harvesting Companies commonly reduce commitments in some countries because those countries have poorer performance prospects than do others, a process known as **harvesting** or **divesting.** For example, Marks & Spencer closed its continental European stores to concentrate its efforts on improving performance in its home U.K. market.[60] J. Sainsbury withdrew from the Egyptian market because its management did not expect a turnaround in its poorly performing operation there.[61] Dana sold its U.K. facility to use funds to concentrate on developing different automotive technologies.[62] Goodyear sold its Indonesian rubber plantation because of its decision to no longer produce rubber itself.[63] Some indications suggest that companies might benefit by planning divestments better and by developing divestment specialists. Companies have tended to wait too long before divesting, trying instead expensive means of improving performance. Local managers, who fear losing their positions if the company abandons an operation, propose additional capital expenditures. In fact, this question of who has something to gain or lose is a factor that sets decisions to invest apart from decisions to divest. Both types of decisions should be highly interrelated and geared to the company's strategic thrust. Ideas for investment projects typically originate with middle managers or with managers in foreign subsidiaries who are enthusiastic about

Companies must decide how to get out of operations if

- *They no longer fit the overall strategy.*
- *There are better alternative opportunities.*

Managers are less likely to propose divestments than investments.

collecting information to accompany a proposal as it moves upward in the organization. After all, the evaluation and employment of these people depend on growth. They have no such incentive to propose divestments. These proposals typically originate at the top of the organization after upper management has tried most remedies for saving the operation.[64]

Companies may divest by selling or closing facilities. They usually prefer selling because they receive some compensation. A company that considers divesting because of a country's political or economic situation may find few potential buyers except at very low prices. In such situations, the company may try to delay divestment, hoping the situation will improve. If it does, the firm that waits out the situation generally is in a better position to regain markets and profits than one that forsakes its operation.

A company cannot always simply abandon an investment either. Governments frequently require performance contracts, such as substantial severance packages to employees, that make a loss from divestment greater than the direct investment's net value. Further, the length of time to go through insolvency (up to 10 years) alters the percentage of value recovered from a divestment. For example, in Japan, Singapore, and Finland, investors recover on average over 90 percent of the value, whereas, in Brazil, Cambodia, and Madagascar, they typically recover nothing.[65] Finally, many large MNEs fear adverse international publicity and difficulty in reentering a market if they do not sever relations with a foreign government on amicable terms.

Interdependence of Locations

The derivation of meaningful financial figures is not easy when foreign operations are concerned. Profit figures from individual operations may obscure the real impact those operations have on overall company activities. For example, if a U.S. company were to establish an assembly operation in Australia, the operation could either increase or reduce exports from the United States, thus affecting U.S. profit figures. Alternatively, the same company might build a plant in Malaysia to produce a product using cheaper labor; however, doing that would necessitate more coordination costs at headquarters. Or perhaps by building a plant in Brazil to supply components to Volkswagen of Brazil, the company may increase the possibility of selling to Volkswagen in other countries. As a result of the Australian, Malaysian, or Brazilian projects, management would have to make assumptions about the changed profits in the United States and elsewhere.

A further interdependence occurs because much of the sales and purchases of foreign subsidiaries may be made from and to units of the same parent company. The prices the company charges on these transactions will affect the relative profitability of one unit compared to another. Further, a company may not set the net value of a foreign investment realistically, particularly if it bases part of the net value on exported capital equipment that is obsolete at home and useless except in the country where it is being shipped. By stating a high value, a government may permit the company to repatriate a larger portion of its earnings.

Geographic Diversification versus Concentration

Strategies for ultimately reaching a high level of commitment in many countries are

- Diversification—go to many fast and then build up slowly in each
- Concentration—go to one or a few and build up fast before going to others
- A hybrid of the two

Ultimately, a company may gain a sizable presence and commitment in most countries; however, there are different paths to that position. Although any move abroad means some geographic diversification, the term **diversification strategy** when used for location decisions describes a company's movement rapidly into many foreign markets, gradually increasing its commitments within each one. A company can do this, for example, through a liberal licensing policy to ensure sufficient resources for the initial widespread expansion. The company eventually will increase its involvement by taking on activities that it first contracted to other companies. At the other extreme, with a **concentration strategy,** the company will move to only one or a few foreign countries until it develops a very strong involvement and competitive position there. There are, of course, hybrids of these two strategies—for example, moving rapidly to most markets but increasing the commitment in only a few. The following subsections discuss major variables a company should consider when deciding which strategy to use.[66] (See Table 12.3.)

TABLE 12.3   PRODUCT AND MARKET FACTORS AFFECTING CHOICE BETWEEN DIVERSIFICATION AND CONCENTRATION STRATEGIES

If the conditions under "prefer diversification" exist, a company is likely to benefit by moving rapidly into many countries simultaneously; otherwise, the company might move to just one or a few foreign countries until a substantial presence is developed there.

PRODUCT OR MARKET FACTOR	PREFER DIVERSIFICATION IF:	PREFER CONCENTRATION IF:
1. Growth rate of each market	Low	High
2. Sales stability in each market	Low	High
3. Competitive lead time	Short	Long
4. Spillover effects	High	Low
5. Need for product adaptation	Low	High
6. Need for communication and distribution adaptation	Low	High
7. Program control requirements	Low	High
8. Extent of constraints	Low	High

Source: "Marketing Expansion Strategies in Multinational Marketing," from *Journal of Marketing*, Vol. 43, Spring 1979, p. 89. Reprinted by permission of the American Marketing Association © 1979.

Growth Rate in Each Market   When the growth rate in each market is high or needs to be high, a company usually should concentrate on a few markets because it will cost a great deal to expand output sufficiently in each market. Further, costs per unit are typically lower for the market-share leader. For instance, in our opening case, we saw that Carrefour needed to build sufficient distribution presence within a country in order to be cost effective. However, slower growth or need for growth in each market may result in the company's having enough resources to build and maintain a market share in several different countries.

Sales Stability in Each Market   A company may smooth its earnings and sales because of operations in various parts of the world. This smoothing results from the leads and lags in the business cycles. In addition, a company whose assets and earnings base are in a variety of countries will be less affected by occurrences within a single one; for example, a strike or expropriation will affect earnings from only a small portion of total corporate assets. Further, currency appreciation in some countries may offset depreciation in others.[67] Although diversification is usually of secondary importance as a motive for foreign expansion, it is nevertheless an added advantage of operating abroad. Further, a company may be leery of depending too much on too few foreign locations.[68]

> Fast growth favors concentration because companies must use resources to maintain market share.

The more stable that sales and profits are within a single market, the less advantage there is from a diversification strategy. Similarly, the more interrelated markets are, the less smoothing is achieved by selling in each.

Competitive Lead Time   We have discussed why Carrefour has wanted to gain first-in advantages. If a company determines that it has a long lead time before competitors are likely to be able to copy or supersede its advantages, then it may be able to follow a concentration strategy and still beat competitors into other markets. Otherwise, it may need either to forego entry into some markets or to share ownership in order to fulfill a diversification strategy.

> The longer the lead time, the more likely the company is to use a concentration strategy.

Spillover Effects   **Spillover effects** are situations in which the marketing program in one country results in awareness of the product in other countries. These effects are advantageous because additional customers may be reached with little additional cost. This can happen if the product is advertised through media sent cross-nationally, such as U.S. television ads that reach Canadians. When marketing programs reach many countries, such as by cable television or the Internet, a diversification strategy has advantages.

Need for Product, Communication, and Distribution Adaptation   Companies may have to alter products and their marketing to sell abroad, a process that, because of cost, favors a concentration strategy. The adaptation cost may limit the resources the company has for expanding in many different markets. Further, if the adaptations are unique to each country, the company cannot easily spread the costs over sales in other countries to reduce total unit costs. For example, Ben & Jerry's took a concentration strategy by moving into the British market with as rapid an increase in distribution as possible so that it could cover the high fixed costs of its local adaptations in ice cream production and advertising.[69]

Program Control Requirements   The more a company needs to control its operations in a foreign country, the more it should develop a concentration strategy. This is because the company will need to use more of its resources to maintain that control. Its need for more control could result from various reasons, including the fear that collaboration with a partner will create a competitor or the need for highly technical assistance for customers.

Extent of Constraints   If a company is constrained by the resources it needs to expand internationally compared to the resources it can muster, it will likely follow a concentration strategy. For example, Ben & Jerry's first tried to enter the United Kingdom and Russian markets almost simultaneously but quickly dissolved its Russian operation. A company manager explained the decision by saying, "We simply don't have the people and resources. We're a small company. You tie up two or three senior managers and you have a measurable effect on the company's performance."[70]

NONCOMPARATIVE DECISION MAKING

Because companies have limited resources at their disposal, it might seem that they maintain a storehouse of foreign operating proposals that they may rank by some predetermined criteria. If this were so, management could simply start allocating resources to the top-ranked proposal and continue down the list until it could make no further commitments. This is often not the case, however. They make *go-no-go* decisions by examining one opportunity at a time and pursuing it if it meets some threshold criteria.

To begin with, companies sometimes need to respond quickly to prospects they had not anticipated. For example, many companies begin exporting because potential customers approach them. Likewise, other companies may approach them with a joint venture or licensing proposal. Similarly, undertakings may be one-time possibilities because a government or another company publishes a request for proposals. For example, when the government of India announced that foreign companies could invest in Indian newspapers, foreign publishers had to react quickly.[71] Or there may be a chance to buy properties that another company divests. For instance, when Enron faced bankruptcy, it needed to sell many of its foreign facilities, thus companies such as Tractebel from Belgium and Royal Dutch/Shell bid on Korean facilities.[72]

Finally, defensive decisions may need to be made quickly. For instance, many companies' customers are other companies. They sell products, components, or services to those customers domestically, which then become embodied in a product or service that their customers sell. If an important customer makes a foreign direct investment, the supplier may have compelling reasons to make a foreign direct investment as well. First, it would like to get that customer's business. Second, if a competitor becomes the supplier in the foreign location, that competitor may improve its chances of serving the customer in the domestic market as well. Third, there may be prohibitions to serving the foreign market through exports. For example, Tredegar Industries sells plastic materials, primarily to Procter & Gamble (P&G) for use in paper diapers. When P&G decided to produce in China and needed a supplier nearby, Tredegar had little choice except to make an investment in China as well.[73]

Two major factors restricting companies from comparing investment opportunities are cost and time. Clearly, some companies cannot afford to conduct very many investigations simultaneously. If these investigations are conducted simultaneously, they are apt to be in various stages of completion at a given time. For example, suppose a company completes its investigation for a possible project in Australia but is still researching projects in New Zealand, Japan, and Indonesia. Can the company afford to wait for the results from all the surveys before deciding on a location? Probably not. The time interval between completions probably would invalidate much of the earlier results and necessitate updating, added expense, and further delays.

MAKING FINAL COUNTRY SELECTIONS

Thus far, we have examined location decisions on a very broad basis. At some point, a company must perform a much more detailed analysis of specific projects and proposals in order to make allocation decisions. For new investments, companies need to make on-site visits and detailed estimates of all costs and expenses. They will need to consider different locations within a given foreign country. They will need to evaluate whether they should enter the market alone or with a partner. For acquisitions, they will need to examine financial statements in detail. For expansion within countries where they are already operating, managers within those countries will most likely submit capital budget requests that include details of expected returns. As we indicated earlier, companies use a variety of financial criteria to evaluate foreign investments. In addition, they rely on qualitative analysis that includes such factors as expected competitive response and the fit of new activities with existing ones.

LOOKING TO THE FUTURE: Will the Prime Locations Change?

Demographers expect a slowing in the growth of global population through the year 2050. In fact, a number of high-income countries, Japan and Italy for example, should have declining populations. At the same time, population growth should remain robust in many emerging economies, particularly those in sub-Saharan Africa. The result of this is that the percentage of people living in currently high-income countries is expected to fall to 13.7 percent from a 2000 figure of 19.7 percent. The least developed countries will have the biggest increase. Further, because the world's population will continue to age, the share of the working-age population should fall for high-income countries and increase in many developing countries. Since there is a positive relationship between the changes in the size of the working-age population and per capita GDP, the growth in per capita GDP should be higher in today's emerging economies than in today's high-income countries.[74] These demographic changes, if they materialize, will have implications both for the location of markets and the location of labor forces.

An intriguing future possibility is the near officeless headquarters for international companies. Technology may permit some people to work from anywhere as they e-mail and teleconference with their colleagues, customers, and suppliers elsewhere. Thus, they could live anywhere in the world and work from their homes. The use of offices at home is already occurring within some professions.[75] However, if people can work from their homes, they may move their homes where they want to live rather than living where their employers are now headquartered. Since we're talking here about the highly creative and highly innovative self-motivated people, they can usually get permission to live in almost any country of the world. A leading researcher on urbanization and planning has shown that beginning at least as early as the Roman Empire, these types of people have been drawn to certain cities that were the centers of innovation. He said that this attraction is due to people's improvement through interchange with others like themselves, like "a very bright class in a school or a college. They all try to score off each other and do better." Thus, if he is correct, the brightest minds may work more at home, but still need the face-to-face interaction with their colleagues.[76] His arguments are provocative, particularly since we now have technology to allow people to communicate without traveling as much, yet business travel continues to increase. Hence, people need face-to-face interaction. He further suggests that these people will be drawn to the same places that attract people to visit as tourists. Concomitantly, another view is that in leading Western societies, the elite made up of intellectuals and highly educated people is increasingly using its capability to delay and block new technologies. If successful, their efforts will result in the emergence of different countries at the forefront of technological development and acceptance.[77]

SUMMARY

- Because companies seldom have sufficient resources to exploit all opportunities, two major considerations facing managers are which markets to serve and where to locate the production to serve those markets.

- Companies' decisions on market and production location are highly interdependent because companies often need to serve markets from local production and because they want to use existing production capacity.

- Scanning techniques aid managers in considering alternatives that might otherwise be overlooked. They also help limit the final detailed feasibility studies to a manageable number of those that appear most promising.

- Because each company has unique competitive capabilities and objectives, the factors affecting the choice of operating location will be slightly different for each. Nevertheless, companies take the environmental climate into consideration. Most companies are influenced by the relative size of country markets, the ease of operating in the specific countries, the availability and cost of resources, and the perceived relative risk and uncertainty of operations in one country versus another.

- Companies may reduce the risk of liability of foreignness by moving first to countries more similar to their home countries. Alternatively, they may contract with experienced companies to handle operations for them, limit the resources they commit to foreign operations, and delay entry to many countries until they are operating successfully in one or a few.

- The amount, accuracy, and timeliness of published data vary substantially among countries. Managers should be particularly aware of different definitions of terms, different collection methods, and different base years for reports, as well as misleading responses.

- Sources of published data on international business, including data found on the Internet, may be provided by consulting firms, government agencies, international agencies, trade associations, and organizations that serve international businesses. The cost and specificity of these publications vary widely.

- Companies frequently use several tools to compare opportunities in various countries, such as grids that rate country projects according to a number of separate dimensions and matrices, such as one on which companies plot opportunity on one axis and risk on another.

- When allocating resources among countries, companies need to consider how to treat reinvestments and divestments, the interdependence of operations in different countries, and whether they should follow diversification versus concentration strategies.

- Companies must develop location strategies for new investments and devise means of deemphasizing certain areas and divesting if necessary.

- Companies often evaluate entry to a country without comparing that country with other countries. This is because they may need to react quickly to proposals, to respond to competitive threats, and because multiple feasibility studies seldom are finished simultaneously.

FDI in South Africa[78]

Many businesspersons within and outside South Africa predicted that the 1994 end of apartheid (the system of minority white rule that lasted about forty years and prevented South African blacks from fairly participating in the political, economic, and social affairs of the country) would lead to political instability and an antibusiness government. They speculated that newly elected politicians would take revenge against the whites that had oppressed them and against businesses that had been their collaborators. Instead, the political changeover with the election of Nelson Mandela went smoothly, as have subsequent elections of his successor, Thabo Mbeki. Mandela, Mbeki, and their party, the African National Congress, have had a positive attitude toward business, especially toward foreign companies. So, in the postapartheid euphoria, the new political leaders awaited increasing FDI. They reasoned that the end of external sanctions and internal protests would encourage foreign businesses to develop local opportunities. They also hoped that MNEs that had left South Africa during the apartheid era would return—for example, between 1986 and 1991, 235 of the 360 U.S. MNEs in South Africa left the country.

Why would the South African government want FDI? Unquestionably, jobs are a compelling reason. For more than a decade, South Africa had had one of the highest unemployment rates in the world, officially estimated at 31 percent in 2003. Growth is another reason. South Africa's savings and investment rates have been too low to finance sufficient business expansion. A third reason is that foreign investment in state-owned companies usually improves the quality of their goods and services. Finally, competition from foreign investment can spur local companies to innovate; South Africa used this rationale to justify opening its banking and telecom sectors to foreign investors. Boosting competitive rivalry was important in South Africa because its market had been dominated by quasi-monopolistic conglomerates set up during the apartheid regime. Finally, as a leading commodity exporter South Africa is vulnerable to prolonged market downturns in industrialized countries. FDI would help diversify its economy.

No one questions the enormous opportunities within South Africa. In 2004 it had almost 43 million people, an improving logistics infrastructure, advanced financial sector, a GDP per capita at purchasing-price parity of $10,700, vast mineral wealth, and good access to more than 100 million people in southern Africa. (Map 12.2 shows South Africa's location.) At the same time, there has been a rapid influx of foreign investment in South African equity funds due largely to an appreciating currency (rand) that contributed to a dollar return of over 50 percent in 2004. The IMF described South Africa's macroeconomic framework as the best among emerging markets around the world. South Africa seemingly has built the foundation for sustainable business development within a stabilizing democracy—an ideal place for FDI.

However, since the end of apartheid, FDI results for South Africa have been mixed. Between 1995 and 2002, in South Africa the stock of FDI grew from $15.1 billion to $51 billion, a figure much higher than in any other African country. This growth of almost 240 percent seems impressive and quite similar to the growth rate in Mexico during the same period. Further, South Africa now earns more from the export of BMWs, Mercedes, and Volkswagen than from the export of gold. Nevertheless, the growth rate was much lower than in some other emerging economies, such as Brazil and India, and somewhat disappointing given the expectations of postapartheid South Africa. The problem appeared to be a mix of economic, risk, operational, incentive, image, and geographical challenges. We now look at each.

Generally, investors go where they see large markets and a history of sustainable growth. The former is evident in South Africa but the latter is not. South Africa has had a sustained economic growth rate of about 3 percent per annum, which is well below the 5 to 7 percent growth rate needed to adequately address its social problems. While South Africa has made considerable progress since 1994 in terms of households with access to clean water and use

MAP 12.2   South Africa and its Location

MILEAGE FROM JOHANNESBURG

To New York: 7,960 mi / 12,810 km
To London: 5,609 mi / 9,026 km
To Tokyo: 8,420 mi / 13,550 km

ANGOLA
Pop. 10,593,171
NAMIBIA
Pop. 1,820,916
BOTSWANA
Pop. 1,591,232
SOUTH AFRICA
Pop. 43,647,658
LESOTHO
Pop. 2,207,954

ZAMBIA
Pop. 9,959,037
MALAWI
Pop. 10,000,416
MOZAMBIQUE
Pop. 19,607,519
ZIMBABWE
Pop. 11,376,676
SWAZILAND
Pop. 1,123,605

South Africa's location is advantageous for serving the high-population market of Southern Africa. However, South Africa is far from the markets of industrial countries.

Source: CIA Yearbook, 2002. http://www.cia.gov/cia/publications/factbook/index.html

of electricity, households in formal housing, people attending schools, and development of port facilities, it still has problems. These include unemployment, rising inequality, declining life expectancy, and declining population. For instance, the high incidence of AIDS reduced life expectancy in South Africa from 63 years in 1990 to 47 years in 2004. About half the population, mostly black, live below the poverty line. Complications arise from civil unrest and slow economic growth in much of southern Africa. These countries are important export markets. Turmoil there reduces earnings for South African export industries, thereby slowing the savings and investment cycle need to fund growth.

South Africa has enjoyed political stability since the fall of apartheid. Still, other political problems have created risks. The Corruption Perception Index rated South Africa as the third-least corrupt country in Africa, the forty-fourth out of 142 countries ranked in 2004, and less corrupt than a number of EU countries. Although this ranking is not comparatively bad, the former South African president of the Associated Chambers of Commerce noted, "In the case of South Africa, the extent of perceived corruption makes for a lack of confidence which, in turn, has led to a sluggish rate of fixed investment in both the public and private sector." There have also been personal safety issues. South Africa has had one of the highest crime rates in the world, and its local police provide some of the lowest crime protection of any country. Its murder rate, the highest in the world, is more than five times the rate in Brazil, the next highest country. Protecting people and property adds a great deal of cost; firms typically had to spend between 5 to 10 percent of their budgets on additional security. Finally, instability in the region, particularly in Zimbabwe and Angola, threatened South Africa.

Foreign companies have often run into troubles in South Africa. Staffing is a recurring problem. The exodus of young, highly qualified whites has created shortages of skilled executives and labor. In response, Xerox has opened and operated a training program for technical and sales staff and has adopted a school in the predominately black township of Thembisa. All in all, some companies have reasoned that effectively running a South African operation would demand more management time than is justified by the potential returns.

The image of South Africa has created other problems. Trying to convince an executive to leave the comparatively safer haven abroad to manage a new subsidiary in unruly Johannesburg has been hard. Too, the financial emigration of some South African corporate giants—switching their home stock market listings to foreign bourses in an effort to distance themselves from the negative perceptions of corruption and crime in South Africa—has fanned suspicions. Some officials and commentators have increasingly condemned white South Africans for unduly criticizing their country and have warned that doing so jeopardizes foreign investments.

The South African government has given mixed signals to foreign companies. Although it gives lip service to the desire for FDI, the minister of public enterprises said in 2004 that the country has no plans to sell off any large state-owned companies. The minister of agriculture and land affairs said that foreigners should not be allowed to buy land because they were pushing up prices too much. The black economic empowerment program says that technology firms must sell 25–35 percent of their equity to black investors by 2009, a policy that is counter to that of some companies, such as Microsoft, that insist on 100 percent ownership.

Geography adds a final hurdle. The country is at the tip of a poor continent, making it hard to export and hard to buy imports at a low price. South Africa is so distant from industrial countries that potential investors sometimes do not evaluate opportunities impartially. Compounding physical distance are popular misinterpretations. For example, a survey of corporate executives from around the world by South African officials concluded that one U.S. executive's remark, "We still see South Africa as one big game reserve," typified its challenge to attract foreign investment. Too, people abroad often assume that mining dominates South Africa's economy; actually, it accounts for less than 10 percent of GDP. Similarly, people think that most of the world's diamonds come from South Africa; actually, it is the world's fifth largest producer.

Nevertheless, there are some factors that may bode well for future opportunities in South Africa. For example, the global geopolitical environment may be shifting in favor of Africa as governments and companies want to become less dependent on oil from OPEC, especially Arab OPEC, countries. Further, the United States and the EU have argued that aid is necessary for African countries, lest they be havens for terrorist activities. As funds flow into Africa, South Africa may find more markets elsewhere in Africa and be the natural gateway for FDI that penetrates African markets.

QUESTIONS

1. What are the costs and benefits to South Africa of having more foreign direct investment? Of having less?

2. How might a company try to weigh fairly the opportunities and risks of investing in South Africa?

3. If South Africa is to receive more foreign direct investment, how should it prioritize policies to attract it?

4. Assume you represent a non–South African company and are considering foreign expansion. What factors would you consider when comparing South Africa with other emerging markets where you might locate? What about in terms of developed markets? What about in terms of other African markets?

CHAPTER NOTES

1 Data for this case were taken from: www.carrefour.com; Eirmalasare Bani, "Carrefour Gives Priority to Locally-Made Products," *Business Times* [Malaysia] (November 9, 1998): 3; "Carrefour Globalizes Sales," *Gazeta Mercantil Online* (October 13, 1998): Business & Company News, n.p.; Michiyo Nakamoto, "Carrefour Sounds Alarm for Japan's Ailing Retail Market," *Financial Times* (December 8, 2000): 36; Jo Johnson, "Carrefour Chief Has No Regrets About Promodès Takeover," *Financial Times* (April 25, 2001): 32; Rosabeth Moss Kanter, "Global Competitiveness Revisited," *Washington Quarterly* 22, no. 2 (Spring 1999): 39–58; "Report: Carrefour Plans Expansion," *HFN* 75, no. 50 (December 10, 2001): 3; "Global Strategy—Why Tesco Will Beat Carrefour," *JRetail Week* (April 6, 2001): 14; "Carrefour Closes Hong Kong Chain After Site Pitfalls," *JRetail Week* (September 1, 2000): 3; "Carrefour Beats Wal-Mart to Global Crown," *JRetail Week* (December 15, 2000): 5; "Carrefour Aims to Win Global Retail Battle," *MMR* 17, no. 12 (June 26, 2000): 60; Lisa Vincenti, "Carrefour to Enter Wal-Mart's Turf?" *HFN* 74, no. 4 (January 24, 2000): 8; "Hypermarkets for Britain," *The Economist* (July 3, 1976): 77; "French Retailer Abandons 'Hypermarkets' in U.S." *New York Times* (September 8, 1993): D4; "Strategies for Retail Globalisation," *Financial Times* (March 13, 1998): 4; "Carrefour Opens Three Supermarkets in Chile," *Gazeta Mercantil Online* (August 29, 1997): front page section; Mark Albright, " 'This Is Just Way Too Big': European-Style Hypermarkets Not as Hot in U.S.," *St. Petersburg Times* (February 12, 1990): 7; "AEON Acquires Carrefour's Japan Unit," *Japan Economic Newswire*, March 10, 2005; Robert Guy Matthews, "Problems in Carrefour's Home Market Sank CEO," *Wall Street Journal* (February 4, 2005): A1+; Dexter Roberts, Wendy Zellner, and Carol Matlack, "Let China's Retail Wars Begin," *Business Week Online* (January 17, 2005); Adam Jones and Mariko Sanchanta, "Carrefour to Quit Japan and Mexico," *Financial Times* (March 11, 2005): 16; and Luc Vandevelde, "Carrefour N'a Besoin de Personne Pour Se DMévelopper," *Les Echos* (March 1, 2005): 32.

2 Paul Taylor, "Apple Puts Overseas Launch of iPod Mini on Pause, "*Financial Times* (March 26, 2004): 15.

3 Shige Makino, Takehiko Isobe, and Christine M. Chan, "Does Country Matter?" *Strategic Management Journal* 25 (2004): 1027–43.

4 Bob Lutz, *GUTS: The Seven Laws of Business That Made Chrysler the World's Hottest Car Company* (New York: Wiley, 1998).

5 Philip Parker, "Choosing Where to Go Global: How to Prioritise Markets," *Financial Times* (November 16, 1998): mastering marketing section, 7–8.

6 Capgemini and Merrill Lynch, *World Wealth Report 2004*, n.p.; and "LVMH Enters Indian Market," *Businessline* (July 17, 2002): 1.

7 David Gonzalez, "Fried Chicken Takes Flight, Happily Nesting in U.S.," *New York Times* (September 20, 2002): A4; and Joel Millman, "California City Fends Off Arrival of Mexican Supermarket," *Wall Street Journal* (August 7, 2002): B1+.

8 Don E. Schultz, "China May Leapfrog the West in Marketing," *Marketing News* 36, no. 17 (August 19, 2002): 8–9.

9 Mikhail V. Gratchev, "Making the Most of Cultural Differences," *Harvard Business Review* 79, no. 96 (October 2001): 28–30.

10 Khanh T. L. Tran, "Blockbuster Finds Success in Japan" *Wall Street Journal* (August 19, 1998): A14; and Cecile Rohwedder, "Blockbuster Hits Eject Button as Stores in Germany See Video-Rental Sales Sag," *Wall Street Journal* (January 16, 1998): B9A.

11 Joan Penner-Hahn and J. Myles Shaver, "Does International Research and Development Increase Patent Output? An Analysis of Japanese Pharmaceutical Firms," *Strategic Management Journal* 26 (2005): 121–40.

12 David Luchnow, "Missing Piece of the Mexican Success Story," *Wall Street Journal* (March 4, 2002): A11+.

13 See James Lamont, "South African Companies May Have to Report AIDS Rates," *Financial Times* (August 15, 2002): 1; and James Lamont, "Investors in South Africa 'Bewildered by Action on AIDS'," *Financial Times* (September 12, 2002): 9.

14 Andrew Bartmess and Keith Cerny, "Building Competitive Advantage Through a Global Network of Capabilities," *California Management Review* (Winter 1993): 78–103.

15 G. Bruce Knecht, "Going the Wrong Way Down a One-Way Street," *Wall Street Journal* (March 18, 2002): A1.

16 Michael Peel, "Bitter-Sweet Confections of Business in Nigeria," *Financial Times* (November 20, 2002): 10.

17 Alfredo J. Mauri and Arvind V. Phatak, "Global Integration as Inter-Area Product Flows: The Internationalization of Ownership and Location Factors Influencing Product Flows Across MNC Units," *Management International Review* 41, no. 3 (Third Quarter 2001): 233–49.

18 Nagesh Kumar, "Multinational Enterprises, Regional Economic Integration, and Export-Platform Production in the Host Countries: An Empirical Analysis for the U.S. and Japanese Corporations," *Weltwirtschaftliches Archive* 134, no. 3 (1998): 450–83.

19 Lisa Bannon, "As Holiday Season Approaches, Toy Shipments Are Imperiled," *Wall Street Journal* (October 4, 2002): A9.

20 "Volkswagen Switches Work to Low-Cost Unit in Slovakia," *Financial Times* (December 19, 1995): 4.

21 Matthew Karnitschnig, "Germany Inc. Spreads Its Tentacles to Escape Taxes," *Wall Street Journal* (April 30, 2003): A15; and Martin Wolf, "Europe Must Integrate Its Labour Markets and Welfare," *Financial Times* (April 6, 2005): 13.

22 World Bank, International Finance Corporation, *Doing Business in 2005* (Washington: The International Bank for Reconstruction and Development, 2005).

23 John Hongxin Zhao, Seung H. Kim, and Jianjun Du, "The Impact of Corruption and Transparency on Foreign Direct Investment: An Empirical Analysis," *Management International Review* 43, no. 1 (2003): 41–63.

24 Sheri Prasso and Paul Magnusson, "Welcome Back?" *Business Week* (August 16, 1999): 54.

25 Hoon Park, "Determinants of Corruption: A Cross-national Analysis," *Multinational Business Review* 11, no. 2 (2003): 29–48.

26 B. Kazaz, M. Dada, and H. Moskowitz, "Global Production Planning under Exchange-Rate Uncertainty," *Management Science* 51, no. 7 (2005): 1101–9.

27 Sarah Ellison and Eric Bellman, "Clean Water, No Profit," *Wall Street Journal* (February 23, 2005): B1+.

28 See Srilata Zaheer and Elaine Mosakowski, "The Dynamics of the Liability of Foreignness: A Global Study of Survival in Financial Services," *Strategic Management Journal* 18, no. 6 (June 1997): 439–64; and Stewart R. Miller and Arvind Parkhe, "Is There a Liability of Foreignness in Global Banking? An Empirical Test of Banks' X-Efficiency," *Strategic Management Journal* 23, no. 1 (January 2002): 55–75.

29 For a good discussion of differences, see Dean Xu and Oded Shenkar, "Institutional Distance and the Multinational Enterprise," *Academy of Management Review* 27, no. 4 (2002): 608–18.

30 Philip Parker, "Choosing Where to Go Global: How to Prioritise Markets," *Financial Times* (November 16, 1998): mastering marketing section, 7–8.

31 Joel Millman, "PriceSmart to Restate Results Due to an Accounting Error," *Wall Street Journal* (November 11, 2003): B9.

32 Edward B. Flowers, "Oligopolistic Reactions in European and Canadian Direct Investment in the United States," *Journal of International Business Studies* (Fall–Winter 1976): 43–55; and Frederick Knickerbocker, *Oligopolistic Reaction and Multinational Enterprise* (Cambridge, MA: Harvard University, Graduate School of Business, Division of Research, 1973).

33 David Murphy and David Lague, "As China's Car Market Takes Off, the Party Grows a Bit Crowded," *Wall Street Journal* (July 3, 2002): A8; and James Mackintosh and Richard McGregor, "Auto Industry," *Financial Times* (August 25, 2003): 13.

34 Hugh Pope, "Q: Why Are the World's IBMs Putting Down Roots in the Desert? A: Dubai," *Wall Street Journal* (January 23, 2001): A18; Lynn K. Mytelka and Lou Anne Barclay, "Using Foreign Investment Strategically for Innovation," paper presented at the Conference on Understanding FDI-Assisted Economic Development, University of Oslo, Norway (May 22–25, 2003).

35 See J. Myles Shaver and Fredrick Flyer, "Agglomeration Economies, Firm Heterogeneity, and Foreign Direct Investment in the United States," *Strategic Management Journal* 21, no. 12 (December 2000): 1175–93; Philippe Martin and Gianmarco I. P. Ottaviano, "Growth and Agglomeration," *International Economic Review* 42, no. 4 (November 2001): 947–68; and Edward E. Leamer and Michael Storper, "The Economic Geography of the Internet Age," *Journal of International Business Studies* 32, no. 4 (Fourth Quarter 2001): 641–65.

36 Liquidity preference is much like options theory, associated with the work of Robert C. Merton, Myron S. Scholes, and Fisher Black. For a good, terse coverage, see John Krainer, "The 1997 Nobel Prize in Economics," *FRBSF Economic Letter* no. 98–05 (February 13, 1998).

37 Andrea Mendel-Campbell and Robin Emmott, "Carso to Spin Off US Holding," *Financial Times* (September 15, 2001): 18.

38 Sadanand Dhume and Maureen Tkacik, "Footwear Is Fleeing Indonesia," *Wall Street Journal* (September 9, 2002): A12+.

39 See Farhan Bokhari, "Western Expatriates Give Way to Local Heroes," *Financial Times* (August 30, 2002): 8; Joseph T. Hallinan and Janet Adamy, "Chiquita Says It Paid Terrorists to Protect Workers in Colombia," *Wall Street Journal* (May 11, 2004): B10; and Henri E. Cauvin, "Braving War and Graft, Coke Goes Back to Angola," *New York Times* (April 22, 2001): Section 3, 1+.

40 Marvin Zonis and Sam Wilkin, "Driving Defensively Through a Minefield of Political Risk," *Financial Times* (May 30, 2000): Mastering Risk section, 8–10.

41 United Nations Development Programme, *Reducing Disaster Risk: A Challenge for Development* (New York: United Nations, 2004).

42 Paul L. Knox and Sallie A. Marston, *Places and Regions in Global Context,* 3rd edition (Upper Saddle River, NJ: Pearson Education, 2004): 120.

43 Robert A. Manning, "The 21st Century Will Be Asia's Century," *Pittsburgh Post-Gazette* (January 2, 2000): E1.

44 http://globalatlas.who.int/.

45 "A Threat Deadlier Than a Landmine," *Financial Times* (December 2, 2002): 10.

46 Amy Merrick and Ann Zimmerman, "Wal-Mart Bans Some Work Travel Due to SARS," *Wall Street Journal* (April 10, 2003): 36.

47 "Census Bureau Issues Data on Accuracy of 2000 Count," *New York Times* (April 16, 2003): A13.

48 Robert Chote, "Nations Rally to IMF's Statistics Standards," *Financial Times* (July 30, 1996): 4.

49 James Kynge, "Pyramid of Power Behind Numbers Game," *Financial Times* (February 28, 2002): 6.

50 Chip Cumins, "Crude Theft," *Wall Street Journal* (April 13, 2005): A1+.

51 "Market Research," *Financial Times* (March 5, 2003): 9.

52 Moisés Naím, "The Five Wars of Globalization," *Foreign Policy* (January–February, 2003): 29–36.

53 Andy Webb-Vidal, "Farc Poised for New Battle in Long War," *Financial Times* (April 11, 2005): 12.

54 "Doing Business in Dangerous Places," *Economist* 372, no. 8388 (August 14, 2004): 11.

55 Ibid.

56 Mary Kissel, "U.S. Expats Deal with Terror Threat," *Wall Street Journal* (May 12, 2004): B4a, quoting Frank Holder, of Kroll, Inc.

57 "Global Terrorism Index," *Economist* (August 30, 2003): 74, using data from the World Markets Research Centre.

58 Andrew Ward, "Terror Threat from Within Keeps America on High Alert," *Financial Times* (April 19, 2005): 3, quoting John Lewis.

59 Harry Hurt III, "Making the World Safer, One Client at a Time," *New York Times* (May 11, 2004): C12.

60 Erin White, "Marks & Spencer CEO to Step Down," *Wall Street Journal* (July 11, 2002): B8.

61 Susanna Voyle and James Drummond, "J. Sainsbury to Withdraw from Egypt," *Financial Times* (April 10, 2001): 23.

62 Nikki Tait, "Dana Set to Sell UK-Based Components Arm," *Financial Times* (November 29, 2000): 22.

63 Bernard Simon, "Goodyear Sells Its Last Plantation," *Financial Times* (December 1, 2004): 18.

64 See Jean J. Boddewyn, "Foreign and Domestic Divestment and Investment Decisions: Like or Unlike?" *Journal of International Business Studies* 14, no. 3 (Winter 1983): 28; Michelle Haynes, Steve Thompson, and Mike Wright, "The Determinants of Corporate Divestment in the U.K.," *Journal of Industrial Organization* 18, no. 8 (December 2000): 1201–22; and Jose Mata and Pedro Portugal, "Closure and Divestiture by Foreign Entrants: The Impact of Entry and Post-Entry Strategies," *Strategic Management Journal* 21, no. 5 (May 2000): 549–62.

65 World Bank and International Finance Corporation, *Doing Business in 2005* (Washington: The International Bank for Reconstruction and Development, 2005): 69.

66 Igal Ayal and Jehiel Zif, "Marketing Expansion Strategies in Multinational Marketing," *Journal of Marketing* 43 (Spring 1979): 84–94.

67 B. Kazaz, M. Dada, and H. Moskowitz, loc. cit.

68 Woo Wing Thye, "Malaysia Still Attracts FDIs as Firms Diversify," *Business Times* [Kuala Lumpur] (September 12, 2002): 6.

69 Diane Summers, "Chunky Monkey Invasion," *Financial Times* (August 11, 1994): 7.

70 See Neela Banerjee, "Ben & Jerry's Is Discovering That It's No Joke to Sell Ice Cream to Russians," *Wall Street Journal* (September 9, 1995). The quotation comes from Betsy McKay, "Ben & Jerry's Post-Cold War Venture Ends in Russia with Ice Cream Melting," *Wall Street Journal* (February 7, 1997): A12.

71 Edna Fernandes, "India to Let Foreigners Invest in Newspapers," *Financial Times* (June 26, 2002): 6.

72 "Enron Assets Outside U.S. Go Up for Sale; Activity Seen in South Korea and India," *Wall Street Journal* (January 22, 2002): A6.

73 G. George, D. Wood, and John D. Daniels, ""Tredegar Industries: From Spin-off to Success," *Journal of Applied Case Studies* 2, no. 1 (2000): 47–58.

74 International Monetary Fund, *World Economic Outlook, September 2004* (Washington: International Monetary Fund, 2004): 143–9.

75 Deborah Hargreaves, "'Virtual' Staff Make Themselves at Home in Offices of the Future," *Financial Times* (May 14, 1999): 8.

76 Peter Hall, *Cities in Civilization: Culture, Technology, and Urban Order* (London: Weidenfeld and Nicholson, 1998).

77 David Aviel, "The Causes and Consequences of Public Attitudes to Technology: A United States Analysis," *International Journal of Management* 18, no. 2 (2001): 166.

78 Jon Jeter, "South Africa's Image Problem Deters Investors," *Washington Post* (October 17, 1999): A21; Ben Laurance, "South Africa: Down but Not Out," *The Observer* (February 14, 1999): 4; Adrienne Roberts, "Overseas Interest Hard to Pin Down," *Financial Times* (September 20, 1999): survey edition, p. 4; "Business: VeldCom," *Economist* 347, no. 8068 (May 16, 1998): 64; "Corruption A Factor in Offshore Listings," *Global News Wire*, South African Press Association (July 20, 2001); "FDI Revival Begins at Home," *Global News Wire*, South African Press Association (January 31, 2001); James Lamont, "South

Africa Sees Rise in Investment," *Financial Times* (August 3, 2001): 7; "Small Mercies," *Economist* (October 11, 2003): 52; "Emigration," *Financial Times* (April 13, 2004): 5; Wyndham Hartley and Farouk Chothia, "South Africa Politics: Less Risky," *EIU Newswire* (July 13, 2004); "South Africa Economy: Empowerment Before Growth?" *EIU Viewswire* (May 19, 2004); "Business on Hold?" *South African Privatisation*" 371, no. 8381 (June 26, 2004): 78; "Foreign Interest in South Africa Takes Off," *Funds International* (January 2005): 1; F. W. de Klerk, "An African First-World Country," *Wall Street Journal* (September 23, 2004): A14; "Africa: Turnaround in FDI Inflows Last Year," *UNCTAD Press Release* (September 22, 2004); http://www.cia.gov/cia/publications/factbook/geos/sf.html; and http://lcweb2.loc.gov/frd/cs/zatoc.html.

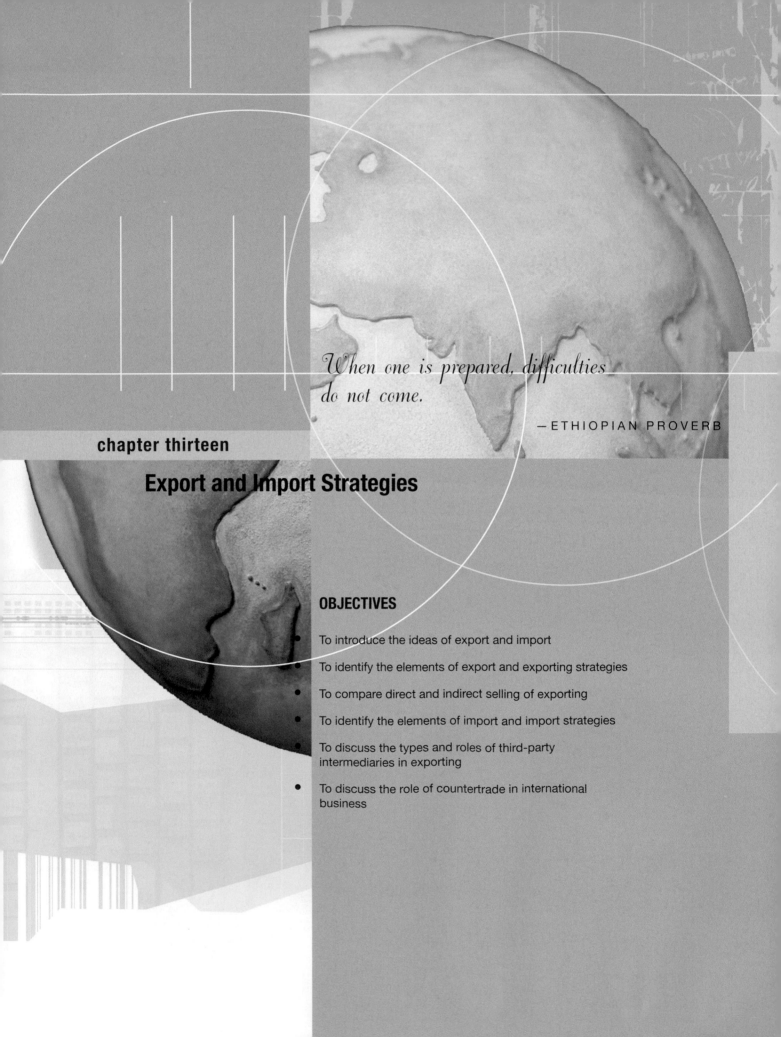

When one is prepared, difficulties do not come.

—ETHIOPIAN PROVERB

chapter thirteen

Export and Import Strategies

OBJECTIVES

- To introduce the ideas of export and import

- To identify the elements of export and exporting strategies

- To compare direct and indirect selling of exporting

- To identify the elements of import and import strategies

- To discuss the types and roles of third-party intermediaries in exporting

- To discuss the role of countertrade in international business

CASE: GRIEVE—A SMALL-BUSINESS EXPORT STRATEGY[1]

The top American exporters, like Boeing, Caterpillar, and General Electric, generate about 30 percent of the merchandise exports of the United States. Their smaller shipments are usually much larger than the largest shipments of smaller exporters. However, the U.S. Department of Commerce reports that nearly 90 percent of U.S. companies that export are small businesses, and the bulk of those have fewer than 20 employees. An exemplar of this situation is the Grieve Corporation of Round Lake, Illinois, near Chicago.

Grieve manufactures laboratory and industrial ovens, furnaces, and heat processing systems. The company began operations in 1949 with "one goal in mind . . . to create a line of industrial heat processing equipment our customers could believe in." The company has always taken great pride in offering complete custom engineering design and manufacturing services. Indeed, management believed that it built "ovens and furnaces for which there simply are no equals." Since 1949, Grieve's only business has been to design and manufacture industrial ovens and furnaces. Over time, Grieve had built core competencies in meeting any customer's particular requirements, officially aiming to be "more than manufacturers but rather problem-solving professionals who take the time to understand your needs." Presently, Grieve applies its knowledge and experience to build industrial ovens and furnaces that ranged from routine heating applications to state-of-the-art systems that met the rigid specifications of clean room, semiconductor, and pharmaceutical environments. Operationally, Grieve does so from its 100,000-square-foot facility in Round Lake, which houses corporate headquarters, sales, engineering, research, and manufacturing.

Before Grieve got involved in exporting, it occasionally experienced problems when one of its customers moved its manufacturing facilities overseas. Initially, Grieve would continue to supply that customer with ovens or furnaces, but the customers' purchases would gradually fade as it began sourcing from local providers. Despite more than a few lost sales, three reasons had dissuaded Grieve from proactively considering exports.

1. *The nature of its product.* Industrial ovens and furnaces, besides being relatively expensive, are large and bulky. Top management assumed the product's size would make shipping costs so high that Grieve would price itself out of the market. For example, shipping a fully automated furnace system from the factory in Round Lake to a customer in the Philippines cost just under $41,000.

2. *Management's nagging doubts about its chance of success abroad.* Grieve is a small business, and management assumed that it lacked the resources needed to support a successful export program. Managers were busy doing all that needed to be done to serve their customers in the domestic market. They struggled to see how they could stretch their already thin management structure to develop and direct international operations.

3. *General concern about competition.* Grieve battled many seasoned exporters from Germany, Japan, and the United Kingdom. These companies were fierce rivals that made a good product for a good price. Even within the United States, Grieve ran into strong competition from local producers in markets outside the Chicago area.

Over time, pressure built on Grieve, pushing it to the tough realization that something had to be done about international markets. Not only was the company losing customers overseas to local suppliers, but it was also beginning to experience increasing competition from foreign companies in the U.S. market. Top management realized that it needed to respond to growing competition or face the prospects of slowly but surely losing its market position. In addition, Grieve regularly shipped its products to both California and Connecticut, its number-one and number-two markets. Both of these markets have strong local competition and high transportation costs, something management figured would help give the company a start in serving international markets.

With these thoughts running through his mind, Patrick J. Calabrese, Grieve's president, attended a one-day trade seminar that featured market analysis and trade reports from the U.S. ambassadors to the ASEAN countries (specifically, Brunei Darussalam, Cambodia, Indonesia, Laos, Malaysia, Myanmar, the Philippines, Singapore, Thailand, and Vietnam). While listening to their presentation, he once again wondered whether or not it made sense to export to Asia. By the time of the final speaker, Mr. Calabrese had growing confidence that there might be rewarding market opportunities for his firm in one of the world's fastest-growing regions. However, he was largely unfamiliar with the ASEAN region, a problem compounded by the company's lack of any sort of official sales offices or representatives in any of the ASEAN countries. He was also concerned how his company would take on the British, German, and Japanese competition that had already established positions in those markets.

Grieve's marketing staff decided to sample potential interest in Asia by advertising in industry reports and trade publications that circulated in Southeast Asia, such as the *Asian Industrial Reporter*, *Asian Literature Showcase*, and *World Industrial Reporter*. To learn more about the market, Calabrese worked with a representative from the International Trade Administration of the Chicago Export Assistance Center—this center, like others in major metropolitan areas throughout the United States, are one-stop shops ready to provide small- or medium-sized businesses with export assistance. These offices provide assistance from representatives of the U.S. Small Business Administration, the U.S. Department of Commerce, the U.S. Export-Import Bank, and other public and private organizations. Various representatives of the Chicago Export Assistance Center helped Calabrese plan a trip to Asia by arranging for interpreters at each stop on his itinerary and by coordinating meetings with various personnel at several U.S. embassies.

Calabrese's trip aimed to determine market potential and begin recruiting possible sales agents. He had received inquiries from some distributors that were familiar with Grieve's product line, but had not responded to them. However, Calabrese's staff had recently begun filing correspondences and sales contacts by country, rather than their earlier system of sorting them by company name. Hence, he had a start on local potential distributors and customers. In addition, Calabrese tapped the U.S. Department of Commerce's Agent/Distributor Search to get leads on several other possible distributors. This service specifically helps small- to medium-sized exporters enlist the help of commercial specialists at U.S. embassies and consulates to search the market for qualified agents, distributors, or representatives.

The trip was a big success for Grieve. Interviews were held with 28 potential agents over 28 days, and exclusive agents were signed up in each country. During his travels and discussions, Calabrese quickly learned that he had to cut shipping costs. If not, the cost of transporting product from the U.S. to these markets would leave little for profits. Grieve immediately began trying to figure out how to streamline its packaging. In addition, the company began shopping among freight forwarders to find the best rates, which varied depending on the forwarder's experience and its relationship with a particular steamship company. In addition, Calabrese's trip confirmed his sense of the importance of visiting potential customers in Asia personally rather than relying on the local sales manager or representative. As he explained:

> The one thing that I found is that almost to an individual, [Asian customers] are very keen on a personal association. If I were to give anybody advice, I would never send a second-level individual. Never send a marketing manager or sales manager; I would send a top manager. If your company isn't too large to prohibit it, I would send the president or chairman. On the other end, you are talking to the owner of a small distributor or the president of a small manufacturing company, and you've got to meet [that person] on an equal level. My limited experience is [these people] are very cognizant of this; in other words, they are pretty much attuned to a president talking to a president. They also like to feel secure that they are dealing with someone who can make decisions. Another thing I found is that potential customers want to feel that you are financially secure and that you have sufficient funding to continue to work with them for a period of years, because it takes some time and some money on our end to get these people going. Follow-up is incredibly important. I heard all kinds of stories about American [businesspeople] who would come over and spend a day and talk to potential customers and leave [catalogs]. Then the first time the potential customers would send a fax asking for information, they didn't hear from them for two weeks, and that just turns them right off.

True to their tradition of engineering solutions, Grieve soon found ways to streamline its product into more compact forms. Still, it continually struggled with high transport costs and significant competition from local companies as it worked to penetrate foreign markets. Throughout it all, top management stayed optimistic. Management believed they had a competitive product that people would buy. As Calabrese pointed out, "Our strength is that we are selling engineered products, using our 45 years of expertise to build something for them." Through his experiences in Southeast Asia, Calabrese learned some valuable lessons about exporting successfully, specifically:

1. Know your products well. Many people who go to Asia from the United States know little about their own products. In some cases, potential agents who have studied company brochures know more about the products than the company representative.

2. Learn about the competition in the foreign market and the potential sale for your products. Keep an open mind: You may have to adjust your selling strategy, or even your product, to appeal to customers.

3. Advertise in the local market before going there to determine the interest level and to build contacts.

4. Work hard. Too many foreign visitors want to spend a lot of time playing golf or seeing the sights.

5. Build a strong response base back home. Most foreigners complain about poor factory backup, lengthy delays in getting correspondence answered, and delays in getting quotations.

6. Arrange for your own transportation, and don't rely on the potential representative to solve your problems for you. That shows a lack of understanding of the local environment.

7. Make someone at the home office the principal contact for the representative. People need someone who will answer questions and provide assistance.

8. Learn the customs and business etiquette of the countries you visit. Once again, the U.S. Department of Commerce can provide assistance in this area.

9. Have the authority to make decisions and commit the company. If you are going to meet with the top person in the representative organization, have the authority to make the same sorts of decisions.

10. Be prepared. Before hopping on a plane, determine the right market for your company and think about how you'll service overseas customers.

Calabrese's initial foray overseas led to a new appreciation of the rewards and pitfalls of exporting. On balance, though, he came to the realization that export was no longer an option: Exporting had to become part of Grieve's strategy. Once he gained experience in Asian markets, he expanded his export activity to other countries. This new way of doing business has created some challenges, but it also has helped Grieve fortify its competitive position and earn higher profits.

This photo shows one of the world's largest container ships, owned by the Danish company Maersk, approaching the harbor in Singapore.

INTRODUCTION

As our look at Grieve demonstrates, successful exporting is a challenging process. Once a company has identified the good or service it wants to sell, it must explore market opportunities, a process that entails extensive market research. Next, it must develop a production or service development strategy, prepare the goods or services for the market, determine the best means for transporting the goods or services to the market, sell the goods or services, receive payment, and respond to service calls and warranty claims. Complicating matters is that the company must manage these activities while at the same time developing policies that address the different cultures, market forces, banking systems, and legal requirements that inevitably show up when doing business in foreign markets. Granted, a firm could try to go it alone. However, the degree of planning and preparation required at each step persuades many companies, especially small and medium-sized enterprises (SMEs) that do not have export managers, to rely on specialists to move goods and services from one country to another, agents or distributors to sell the goods or services, banks to collect payment, and public agents to lend wisdom.[2]

Companies respond to many motivations when entering foreign markets. In this chapter, we will focus primarily on the issue of an export strategy (see Figure 13.1). Before beginning, though, it helps to define two fundamental terms. In the broadest sense, *exporting* refers to the sale of goods or services produced by a company based in one country to customers that reside in a different country. *Importing* is just the reverse: The purchase of goods or services by a company based in one country from sellers that reside in another. The idea of exporting manufactured goods presents a pretty clear situation. For instance, a U.S. company manufactures physical goods that are shipped to customers in India, Brazil, or Russia. Particular aspects of services present situations that can make it a bit tougher to define exporting and importing.[3] For example, engineering contractors, like Bechtel, are said to export services when they construct buildings, roads, utilities, airports, seaports, or other forms of infrastructure in a foreign country. Consultants, such as McKinsey & Company, export when they perform services for foreign clients. Investment banks, such as Goldman Sachs, export when they help a foreign company, say Haier of China, arrange

FIGURE 13.1   **EXPORTING AND IMPORTING IN INTERNATIONAL BUSINESS**

Exporting and importing are necessary functions for implementing companies' international strategies.

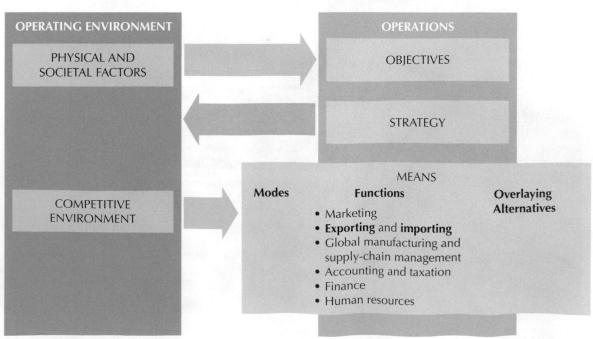

financing from global sources or when they assist customers, such as Lenovo's acquisition of IBM's personal computer business, to structure foreign business acquisitions. On the other hand, the opening of a Hyatt, McDonald's, or Starbucks in a foreign market is not considered to be exporting but a foreign direct investment. The remainder of the chapter elaborates these ideas, examining export and import strategies, the features of indirect versus direct selling in international markets, and the matter of countertrade.

EXPORT STRATEGY

As we saw in Chapter 12, a company's choice of entry mode to a foreign market depends on different factors, such as the ownership advantages of the company, the location advantages of the market, and the internalization advantages that result from integrating transactions within the company's value chain.[4] Ownership advantages are the firm's specific assets, international experience, and the ability to develop either low-cost or differentiated products within the context of its value chain. For example, Boeing capitalizes on its ownership advantage through the development of sophisticated aircraft; doing the same would be difficult for a new entrant to the market. The location advantages of a particular market are a combination of market potential and investment risk. Internalization advantages are the benefits of retaining a core competency within the company and threading it through the value chain rather than opting to license, outsource, or sell it. For example, Grieve could have explored licensing its oven and furnace technology to local manufacturers in Southeast Asia. Instead, management preferred to maintain control over its core competencies and serve Southeast Asia through exports from its U.S. plant.

In general, companies that have low levels of ownership advantages either do not enter foreign markets or, if they do, enter through low-risk modes such as exporting. Exporting requires a significantly lower level of investment than other modes of international expansion, such as FDI. Expectedly, the lower risk of export typically results in a lower rate of return on sales than other modes of international business. In other words, the usual return on export sales may not be stupendous, but neither is the risk. Exporting allows managers to exercise operational control but does not provide them the option to exercise as much marketing control. An exporter usually resides far from the final consumer and often enlists various intermediaries to manage marketing and service value activities.[5]

The choice of exporting as an entry mode is not just a function of ownership, location, and internalization advantages. It also must fit the company's strategy. Companies typically consider these questions in evaluating the export option.

- What do we want to gain from exporting?
- Is exporting consistent with our other goals?
- What demands will export place on our key resources—management and personnel, production capacity, and financing—and how will we meet these demands?
- Does export help us leverage our core competency without undue risk of diffusion?
- Does export fit into the current configuration of our value chain? Can our existing coordination methods also deal with the managerial demands created by export transactions?
- Are the projected benefits of export worth the costs, or would our resources be better used for developing new domestic business?[6]

These questions require managers to take into account issues such as global concentration, synergies, and strategic motivations. Global concentration, for instance, means that many global industries have only a few major players, and a company's strategy for penetrating a particular market might depend on the competition. If the competition is servicing markets by exporting, the company might also do well following the same strategy. However, if the competition has found ways to create superior value by servicing the local market through foreign direct investment, the company might not be as successful in the future if it only exports to the market.[7]

Entry mode depends on ownership advantages of the company, location advantages of the market, and internalization advantages that result from integrating transactions within the company.

Companies that have lower levels of ownership advantages either do not enter foreign markets or use low-risk strategies such as exporting.

Strategic considerations affect the choice of exporting as an entry mode.

Strategic Advantages of Exports

Export offers strategic benefits. Most notably, companies export to increase sales revenues. This holds for both service companies as well as manufacturers. Many of the former, such as accountants, advertisers, lawyers, and consultants, export their services to meet the needs of clients working abroad. Companies that are capital and research intensive, such as automobile or pharmaceutical companies, export to achieve economies of scale by spreading their research, product development, and capacity expenditures over a larger sales area. Similarly, many companies that are not the leaders in their domestic markets may more actively seek export sales as an indirect way to counter the volume advantage commanded by the market leader. For example, in Japan, Matsushita and Toyota are market leaders in, respectively, consumer electronics and motor vehicles. However, Sony and Sanyo, as followers of Matsushita, and Nissan and Honda, as followers of Toyota, approach exports more aggressively. Export sales can be a means of alleviating the problem of excess capacity in the domestic market. In addition, some companies export rather than invest abroad because of the perceived higher risk of operating in foreign environments. Finally, many companies export to a variety of markets as a diversification strategy. For example, Grieve developed markets in Southeast Asia to expand its sales base and to reduce its high reliance on sales in the United States. Because economic growth is not the same in every market, export diversification allows a company to use strong growth in one market to offset weak growth in another. Similarly, the company that develops more customers reduces its vulnerability to the loss of particular customers.

It is appealing to depict the export process as a proactive strategy that management meticulously designs. However, research reports the cases of accidental exporters who, responding to circumstances, enter overseas markets by chance and attain great success. Hence, we need to note the role of serendipity as a catalyst for companies to begin to export. For example, Edward Cutler, owner and founder of Pennsylvania-based Squigle, makes a unique brand of toothpaste for people who cannot tolerate the harsh foaming agents commonly found in mass-produced toothpastes. After launching his toothpaste in 1998, Mr. Cutler focused on the U.S. market. News of the product's performance spread over the Internet and Squigle began getting inquiries from people in Taiwan, Turkey, and elsewhere. One customer, a canker-sore sufferer in Britain, was so enthusiastic about the toothpaste that he began importing Squigle to England for sale there. That was good news for Mr. Cutler, because it let him expand abroad at little cost or risk. Now, he is eager to start exporting more product, explaining that "We're looking to sell overseas for the same reason the big companies do: Most of the world's population lies outside the United States."[8]

Lastly, a strategic advantage of exporting is the potential of greater profitability. For several reasons, companies can sell their products at a greater profit abroad than at home. This often happens because the competitive environment in the foreign market is different, possibly because in that market, the product is in a different stage of its life cycle. A mature mature at home often triggers extreme price competition, whereas a growth stage in foreign markets may permit charging premium prices. Greater profitability also may come about because of different government actions at home and abroad that affect profitability—for example, differences in the taxation of earnings or the regulation of prices. If, however, companies must divert efforts from domestic sales to service the greater demands of foreign markets, they may lack the resources to sustain their overall growth objectives.

Characteristics of Exporters

Research on the characteristics of exporters consistently reports the following:

1. The probability of being an exporter increases with company size, as defined by sales revenues.
2. Export intensity, the percentage of total revenues coming from export sales, is not positively correlated with company size. The greater the percentage of exports to total revenues, the greater the intensity.

Exporting

- Expands sales
- Achieves economies of scale in production
- Is less risky than FDI
- Diversifies sales locations

The first conclusion follows from the idea that small companies can grow in the domestic market without having to export, but large companies must export if they are to increase sales.[9] And, yes, the largest companies, such as Sony, Boeing, and Nokia, are routinely the biggest exporters in their countries. Still, the data show that small companies are progressively expanding their export capability. For instance, small business makes up about 88 percent of U.S. exporters, and they account for one-fifth of the value of exports from the United States.[10] As we saw earlier, Grieve is a perfect example. Technically a small company in terms of total sales, its export revenues influence its competitiveness and performance. The company's export activity supports its market share overseas as well as fortifies its competitive position in the United States. Others report similar effects; a study of Canadian companies found that the size of the firm was not the most important factor in determining a company's propensity to export, the number of countries it exported to, or its degree of export intensity. Rather, factors such as managements' outlook on risk and industry factors were as important as firm size—that is, small high-tech or highly specialized companies that operate in market niches with a global demand as well as small companies that sell expensive capital equipment were highly inclined to export. Therefore, managers who were more likely to take a risk were also more likely to engage in exporting, and companies were more likely to engage in exporting if they were operating in industries in which the leading companies were exporters.[11]

> The largest companies are the biggest exporters, but small companies are expanding their export capability.

Stages of Export Development

In a broad sense, several factors trigger exporting.[12] A company can export goods and services to related companies, such as branches and subsidiaries, or it can export to independent customers. Sometimes a company exports its products to its related companies overseas, which then sell them to local consumers. Other times, a company exports semifinished goods that are used by its related companies as inputs in their manufacturing process. In many cases, however, the sale is to a third party, and in those situations, the exporter may sell directly to the buyer or indirectly via an intermediary.

As noted earlier, many companies begin exporting by serendipity rather than by design—an unsolicited sales order arrives in the mail, a contact is made at an industry conference, in personal travels abroad a manager discovers new options, etc. The often unplanned stimulus to export, if not dealt with systematically, can create unforeseen problems. Therefore, achieving the strategic advantages of exports depends on developing a sound yet insightful export strategy. Figure 13.2 identifies the three phases of export development.[13]

These phases have less to do with company size than with degree of export development—both large and small companies can be at any particular stage. Increasingly, we see more newly formed companies begin exporting sooner in their life cycle than ever

> The probability of a company's being an exporter increases with the size of the company. Export intensity is not positively correlated with company size.

Phase 1 — **Preengagement**
- Companies selling goods and services solely in the domestic market
- Those companies considering but not currently exporting

Phase 2 — **Initial Exporting**
- Companies that do sporadic, marginal exporting
- Companies that see lots of potential in export markets
- Companies unable to cope with exporting demands

Phase 3 — **Advanced**
- Companies become regular exporters
- Companies gain extensive overseas experience
- Companies may use other strategies for entering markets

FIGURE 13.2

PHASES OF EXPORT DEVELOPMENT

As companies gain greater expertise and experience in exporting, they diversify their markets to countries that are farther away or have business environments that increasingly differ from that of their home country.

before. A new generation of entrepreneurs and managers with a keen awareness of international business is essentially "born global." That is, there is a growing trend for some firms to step straight onto the world stage, making exporting the primary goal of the firm from day one of operations.[14] In particular, the flexibility and cost efficiencies of generating international sales via the Internet make these sorts of companies, as well as their more conventional counterparts, increasingly able to engage a range of export options. A company's Web site gives Internet users around the world instant access to the company's product line and even the ability to initiate sales directly. For example, the small U.S. company Evertek Computer Corporation sells new and refurbished computers and parts. Evertek purchased an Internet-based program from the U.S. Commerce Department called BuyUSA.com, which helps it find buyers around the world. Within one year of starting to use BuyUSA.com, Evertek began selling in 10 new countries, with single purchases reaching up to $75,000.[15]

"Born global" companies make exporting a primary goal from inception.

Pitfalls of Exporting

Companies often see exporting as different—and far more difficult—from selling goods and services in their home market. As a rule, most companies prefer to concentrate on domestic rather than foreign markets because of their familiarity with their own environment along with the powerful reluctance to adjust their customary ways for trade regulations, cultural differences, and foreign exchange situations. Export veterans often recount that selling abroad comes with plenty of challenges. Exporting strains resources, staff, and attention; the scarcity of all these factors, no matter how big or small the company, restricts management. Typically, potential exporters have a sense of the likely need to adjust their operations for different languages, cultures, and market demands. Similarly, most realize that exchange-rate fluctuations and transaction processes require more sophisticated financial management. Many companies especially struggle with the fact that export transactions may require that they help foreign customers obtain financing to buy the products. That is, often exporters must help foreign customers find ways to get the needed financing—whether in the form of trade credits, government financing support, or bank guarantees—or else lose the sale. Companies used to providing financing in terms of the traditional thirty- or sixty-day trade credit cycle in their home market are naturally reluctant to begin taking on the greater risk and complications of financing export transactions.

As companies move from initial to advanced exporting, they tend to export to more countries and expect exports as a percentage of total sales to grow.

An enduring barrier to exporting is unawareness of foreign market opportunities.

Rare is the new exporter that does not stumble once or twice before hitting their stride. Too, unlike larger companies, smaller exporters lack the resources to cover many missteps. Therefore, we can get a better sense of the elements of an export strategy by identifying the major problems that face exporters. Aside from the problems that are common to international business, such as language and other cultural factors, companies new to exporting commonly run into the following sorts of problems:

First-time exporters often become discouraged or frustrated with the exporting process because they encounter problems, delays, and pitfalls.

- Failure to obtain qualified export counseling in developing a plan to guide export expansion
- Insufficient commitment by top management to overcome the initial difficulties and financial requirements of exporting
- Misestimating the complexity and costs of ocean shipping and customs clearance to export transactions
- Poor selection of overseas agents or distributors
- Chasing orders from around the world instead of establishing a base of profitable operations and manageable growth
- Neglecting export markets and customers when the domestic market booms
- Failure to treat international distributors on an equal basis with their domestic counterparts
- Unwillingness to modify products to meet other countries' regulations or cultural preferences
- Failure to print service, sales, and warranty messages in locally understood languages

- Failure to consider use of an export management company or other marketing intermediary when the company does not have the personnel to direct specialized export functions
- Failure to prepare for disputes with customers; at that point no court system can be called upon as a last resort (other than international arbitration, which is seldom a viable alternative for small and midsize exporters)[16]

Designing an Export Strategy

Designing an export strategy helps managers avoid making the mistakes mentioned above. Figure 13.3 shows an international business transaction chain. A successful export

In designing an export strategy, managers must

- Assess export potential
- Get expert counseling
- Select a market or markets
- Formulate and implement an export strategy

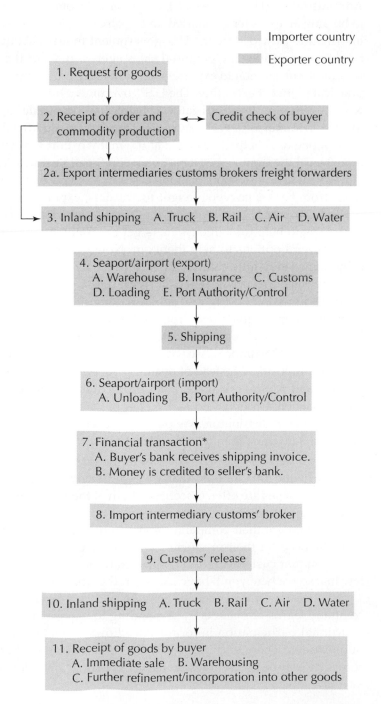

Importer country
Exporter country

1. Request for goods

2. Receipt of order and commodity production ←→ Credit check of buyer

2a. Export intermediaries customs brokers freight forwarders

3. Inland shipping   A. Truck   B. Rail   C. Air   D. Water

4. Seaport/airport (export)
   A. Warehouse   B. Insurance   C. Customs
   D. Loading   E. Port Authority/Control

5. Shipping

6. Seaport/airport (import)
   A. Unloading   B. Port Authority/Control

7. Financial transaction*
   A. Buyer's bank receives shipping invoice.
   B. Money is credited to seller's bank.

8. Import intermediary customs' broker

9. Customs' release

10. Inland shipping   A. Truck   B. Rail   C. Air   D. Water

11. Receipt of goods by buyer
    A. Immediate sale   B. Warehousing
    C. Further refinement/incorporation into other goods

FIGURE 13.3

INTERNATIONAL BUSINESS TRANSACTION CHAIN

In between negotiating a sale and delivering/receiving the goods and services, both the exporter and the importer consider a variety of shipping and financial issues.

* Financial transactions occur at every stage of this process.

Source: Export America, Vol. 1, November 1999, 17. Magazine Published by the International Trade Administration of the U.S. Dept. of Commerce.

(and import) strategy must evaluate element of the transaction chain. To establish a successful export strategy, management must:

1. *Assess the company's export potential by examining its opportunities and resources.* The company needs to determine if there is a market for its goods and services. This task requires it to identify the degree to which it can potentially leverage its core competency into overseas sales. Next, it needs to make sure it has enough production capacity, or can quickly develop it, if success comes faster than expected.

2. *Obtain expert counseling on exporting.* Most governments provide assistance for their domestic companies, although the extent of commitment varies by country. As we saw in our opening case on Grieve, the best place to start for small-and-medium-sized U.S. companies is with the nearest Export Assistance Center of the International Trade Administration (ITA) of the U.S. Department of Commerce. Such assistance is invaluable in helping an exporter get started. In the case of Grieve, for example, Mr. Calabrese used information provided by the U.S. government to learn about Asian markets, plan business trips, and identify potential sales agents. Indeed, the U.S. government offers a wealth of information to exporters, most notably providing assistance and advice on the practical points of exporting. The U.S. government offers many trade support services at **www.export.gov**, an official gateway to international trade support provided by agencies like the Commerce Department, State Department, and Small Business Administration. Finally, personal help is available at the many export assistance centers run by various branches of the Commerce Department and Small Business Administration.

As a company's export plan increases in scope, it may want to get specialized assistance from banks, lawyers, freight forwarders, export management companies, export trading companies, and others. For example, consider the challenge companies face to find ways to help foreign customers get the funds to buy their product; exporters can enlist several options to help them out. Notably, exporting versus domestic sales typically carries very little collection risk because the exporter can more easily demand the buyer provide irrevocable **letters of credit (L/Cs),** covered in detail in Chapter 18, that are confirmed by a local bank. Too, unlike in domestic sales, an exporter can also secure government payment guarantees from organizations such as the Export-Import Bank of the United States (Ex-Im Bank), or purchase government-backed insurance, such as from the Federal Credit Insurance Association. Finally, hiring an agent can make export a straightforward proposition. Instead of dealing with each individual order and making sure the product and paperwork are all lined up, a company can rely on a distributor to oversee the transaction. Observed Edward Cutler of Squigle, the toothpaste maker, "It is just easier to deal with distributors. We prefer to deal in master shippers of 144 tubes. We don't have to do anything then but slap a label on it."[17]

3. *Select a market or markets.* The part of the export strategy that trips up many companies, particular smaller ones that are experimenting with export, is selecting a market. Small companies are often discouraged when their first forays abroad fail. Often, many follow hunches about markets instead of applying the standards of sound business strategy that got their companies going in the first place. Entrepreneurs may overestimate the need for their product or service in a potential market. Likewise, it's tough to try to conquer customers from London to Lisbon in a day. "Said one analyst, "Look at a few markets where you'll have success rather than trying to sell throughout Europe."[18]

A company can passively or actively select an export market. In the latter case, the company learns of markets by responding to requests from abroad that result from its occasional participation in local trade shows or its periodic advertisements in trade publications. Then, encouraged by the apparent interest and potential demand, the company can begin to investigate its export options. For instance, Mr. Calabrese of

Grieve got much more interested in Southeast Asia as an area for export sales as a result of the trade seminar he attended featuring the U.S. ambassadors to the ASEAN countries. A company also can determine the markets to which products that are similar to it own are currently being exported. For example, the United States Census Bureau publishes extensive statistics on foreign trade activities and patterns that an exporter can use to identify markets for different types of exports. Similarly, the National Trade Data Bank (NTDB) provides specific industry reports for different countries. The NTDB is updated monthly. Other countries typically provide similar forms of assistance.

4. *Formulate and implement an export strategy.* In this step, a company considers its export objectives (immediate and long term), the specific tactics it will use, the schedule of activities and deadlines that enable it to achieve its objectives, and the allocation of resources that allows it to accomplish the different activities. Then, managers implement the strategy by getting the goods and services to foreign consumers.

A detailed export business plan is an essential element of an effective export strategy. Table 13.1 provides a sample of such a plan. Certainly, the development of the plan depends on the company, its outlook toward export markets, and the nature of its core competencies. For a small- or medium-size company, the plan usually commands top management's attention, as was the case with Grieve. Larger companies might establish a separate export department to deal with international markets. Research consistently shows that management commitment precedes a firm's success in export.[19] The creation of an export department is a powerful indicator of commitment by top management.

IMPORT STRATEGY

Thus far, we have talked mostly about exporters and exporting. In contrast, *importing* is the bringing of goods and services into a country and results in the importer paying money to the exporter in the foreign country. Traditional goods imports are fairly straightforward. When Nissan North America ships a sedan from Nissan Japan to the U.S. market, it creates an import for the United States. In addition, there are a variety of service imports. SAP software, from the German software company of the same name, is a service (even though software usually comes in a physical package, it is classified as a service product). Foreign banks, such as Royal Bank of Canada, that provide financial services to U.S. customers also create service imports.

Two basic types of imports

- Industrial and consumer goods to independent individuals and companies
- Intermediate goods and services that are part of the firm's global supply chain

Strategic Advantages of Imports

There are two types of imports: (1) those that provide industrial and consumer goods and services to individuals and companies that are not related to the foreign buyer, and (2) those that provide intermediate goods and services to companies that are part of the firm's global supply chain. Before continuing, it is useful to ask—why import in the first place? Generally, companies import because they can buy goods or services at lower prices from foreign suppliers, because the goods or services are of higher quality than similar goods produced locally, or because the goods or services needed in their production processes are unavailable from local companies. Essentially, an importer seeks lower-priced or better-quality supplies, materials, or components that help it improve its capability to create value. As we saw in earlier chapters, the specialization of labor makes export to and import from countries around the world more efficient than manufacturing every product in every country. As such, Nike buys shoes manufactured by companies located in several Asian countries, including Korea, Taiwan,

TABLE 13.1   AN EXPORT BUSINESS PLAN

A detailed export business plan is an essential element in the implementation of a sound yet insightful export strategy. The plan must consider company resources, identify specific markets, and establish specific plans for dealing with marketing, legal, manufacturing, personnel, and financial elements. Finally, it must include a schedule to implement the plan.

I. Executive summary
- A. Key elements of the plan
- B. Description of business and target markets
- C. Brief description of management team
- D. Summary of financial projections

II. Business history
- A. History of company
- B. Products-services offered and their unique advantages
- C. Domestic-market experience
- D. Foreign-market experience
- E. Production facilities
- F. Personnel—international experience and expertise
- G. Industry structure, competition

III. Market research
- A. Target countries
  1. Primary
  2. Secondary
  3. Tertiary
- B. Market conditions in target countries
  1. Existing demand
  2. Competition
  3. Strengths and weaknesses of the economy—barriers to entry, etc.

IV. Marketing decisions
- A. Distribution strategies
  1. Indirect exporting
  2. Direct exporting
  3. Documentation
  4. Direct investment, strategic alliances
- B. Pricing strategy
- C. Promotion strategy
- D. Product strategy

V. Legal decisions
- A. Agent/distributor agreements
- B. Patent, trademark, copyright protection
- C. Export/import regulations
- D. ISO 9000
- E. Dispute resolution

VI. Manufacuring and operations
- A. Location of production facilities for exports
- B. Capacity of existing facilities
- C. Plans for expansion
- D. Product modification necessary to adapt to local environment

VII. Personnel strategies
- A. Personnel needed to manage exports
- B. Experience and expertise of existing personnel
- C. Training needs of existing personnel
- D. Hiring needs in the short term and long term

VIII. Financial decisions
- A. Pro forma financial statements and projected cash flows assuming export activity
- B. Identification of key assumptions
- C. Current sources of funding—private and bank funding
- D. Financial needs and future sources of funding
- E. Tax consequences of export activity
- F. Potential risk and sources of protection

IX. Implementation schedule

China, Thailand, Indonesia, and Vietnam, because of their ability to make shoes for low prices. It would be practically impossible to manufacture the same products in countries with high labor costs, sell them at a reasonable price, and still make a profit. Similar situations exist in industries with a high degree of global competitive rivalry. Such industries, like consumer electronics and telecommunications, push the procuring company to try to combat import competition by switching to foreign suppliers whose components then enable it to lower the cost or boost the quality of its finished products. The automobile industry exemplifies this situation. Global competition in this industry spurs companies to seek out the highest quality inputs for the lowest price wherever they happen to be made and then import them into the countries that house their factories.

Companies also import products that are unavailable in the local market. For example, North America imports bananas from tropical climates because the climate of North America is not suitable for growing bananas. Simply put, North Americans would not enjoy fresh bananas were it not for imports. Similarly, a potential importer may seek new foreign products that complement its existing product lines, thereby giving it more ways to create value. Finally, an importer, like an exporter, might try to diversify its operating risks by systematically tapping international markets. In virtually every sort of industry structure, developing alternative suppliers usually makes a company less vulnerable to the dictates or fortunes of a single supplier. For example, many large customers of U.S. steel makers, such as companies in the automobile industry, have diversified their steel purchases to include European, Chinese, and Korean suppliers. This strategy has reduced the risk of supply shortages for the U.S. automobile industry in case of a strike among U.S. steelworkers.

There is less research, relative to the study of export strategies, of import strategies. However, research consistently identifies three broad types of importers.

1. Those that opportunistically look for any product around the world that they can import. They might specialize in certain types of products—such as sports equipment or household items—but they are typically scanning the globe, looking for products that will generate profits for them.
2. Those that look at foreign sourcing to get the highest quality products at the lowest possible price. For instance, a small Utah-based company called ForEveryBody started out selling a variety of bath and body products. Soon, however, it branched out into decorative products for the home, so it identified manufacturers in China that could supply it with specific products for its stores.
3. Those that use foreign sourcing as part of their global supply chain. Chapter 16 looks at how companies use this strategy.

The import process is illustrated in Figure 13.3. Expectedly, it mirrors the export process, involving both strategic and procedural issues. In fact, managers could straightforwardly adapt the export business plan in Table 13.1 to serve as the framework for an import business plan. Managers begin by studying potential markets, looking to pinpoint possible suppliers and potential policy situations. They then determine the legal ramifications of importing the products, both in terms of the products themselves and the countries from which they come. Managers also evaluate the role of third-party intermediates, such as freight forwarders and customs agents, as well as arrange financing for the purchase.

Importing requires a certain degree of expertise in dealing with institutions and documentation. Not every company may command this proficiency. Consequently, a company may opt to enlist an import broker to manage the process. The **import broker** obtains various government permissions and other clearances before forwarding the requisite paperwork to the carrier that is scheduled to deliver the goods to the importer. Import brokers in the United States are certified as such by the U.S. Customs Service to perform the functions needed to transport products into the country.

The Role of Customs Agencies

When importing goods into any country, a company must be familiar with the customs operations of the importing country because once cargo reaches a port of entry, customs officials take control of the product and process. In this context, "customs" are the

---

Margin notes:

Three broad types of importers

- Looking for any product around the world to import and sell
- Looking for foreign sourcing to get their products at the cheapest price
- Using foreign sourcing as part of their global supply chain

An import broker is an intermediary who helps an importer clear customs.

Customs agencies assess and collect duties and ensure that import regulations are adhered to.

country's import and export procedures and restrictions, not its cultural aspects. The primary duties of the U.S. Customs Service, for example, are the assessment and collection of all duties, taxes, and fees on imported merchandise, the enforcement of customs and related laws, and the administration of certain navigation laws and treaties.[20] As a major enforcement organization, it also deals with smuggling operations and is increasingly involved in antiterrorism.[21]

An importer needs to know how to clear goods, what duties to pay, and what special laws exist regarding the importation of products. On the procedural side, when merchandise reaches the port of entry, the importer must file documents with customs officials, who assign a provisional value and tariff classification to the merchandise. The U.S. government has over 10,000 tariff classifications, and approximately 60 percent of them are subject to interpretation—that is, a particular product could fit more than one classification. It is almost an art form for companies to determine the tariff classification that will result in the lowest assessment. Then customs officials examine the goods to determine whether there are any restrictions on their importation. If so, the goods may be rejected and prohibited from entering the country. If the goods are allowed to enter, the importer pays the duty and the goods are then released. The amount of the duty depends on the product's country of origin, the type of product, and other factors.

A broker or other import consultant can help an importer minimize import duties by:

- *Valuing products in such a way that they qualify for more favorable duty treatment.* Different product categories have different duties. For example, finished goods typically have a higher duty than do parts and components.
- *Qualifying for duty refunds through drawback provisions.* Some exporters use in their manufacturing process imported parts and components on which they paid a duty. In the United States, the drawback provision allows domestic exporters to apply for a 99 percent refund of the duty paid on the imported goods, as long as they become part of the exporter's product.
- *Deferring duties by using bonded warehouses and foreign trade zones.* Companies do not have to pay duties on imports stored in bonded warehouses and foreign trade zones until the goods are removed for sale or used in a manufacturing process.
- *Limiting liability by properly marking an import's country of origin.* Because governments assess duties on imports based in part on the country of origin, a mistake in marking the country of origin could result in a higher import duty. For example, in the United States, if a product or its container is not properly marked when it enters the country, the product could be assigned a marking duty equal to 10 percent of the customs value. This would be in addition to the normal tariff.[22]

Import Documentation

Generally, there is a great deal of paperwork involved in the import business. The arrival of a shipment at a port requires the importer to file specific documents with the port director in order to take title. Specifically, the importer receives the products without purchasing them—that is, it takes the title of ownership but without laying out any money. These documents are of two different types: (1) those that determine whether customs will release the shipment, and (2) those that contain information for duty assessment and statistical purposes. The specific documents that customs requires vary by country but usually include an entry manifest, a commercial invoice, and a packing list. For example, the exporter's commercial invoice contains information such as the country of origin, the port of entry to which the merchandise is destined, information on the importer and exporter, a detailed description of the merchandise, including its purchase price, and the currency used for the sale.

Ways a customs broker can help

- Value products to help them qualify for more favorable duty treatment
- Qualify for duty refunds through drawback provisions
- Defer duties by using bonded warehouses and foreign trade zones
- Limit liability by properly marking an import's country of origin

Drawback provisions allow U.S. exporters to apply for a refund of 99 percent of the duty paid on imported components, provided they are used in the manufacture of goods that are exported.

Importers must submit documents to customs that determine whether the shipment is released and what duties are assessed.

POINT–COUNTERPOINT: A DIRTY DILEMMA—EXPORTING HAZARDOUS WASTE

POINT

Many people see export as a positive sum process—the more companies and countries export, the more they improve their performance and respond to consumers and companies worldwide that wish to import their products. Increasingly, though, some spotlight the dark side of export with regard to the trade of hazardous waste. For instance, low labor costs, weak environmental regulations, and growing processing capacity have made Asia a high-tech dumping ground for everything from simple computer chips to elaborate circuit boards.[23] For example, an estimated 20 million computers become obsolete each year in the U.S. An estimated 200 tons of these computers end up in shipping containers bound for China, India, Bangladesh, or Pakistan, among other countries, where entire industries have sprung up that dismantle old computers, monitors, circuit boards, scanners, printers, routers, cell phones, network cards, and on and on and on.

Many companies see this export process as serving many goods. It gives them a way to meet growing social pressure to retain responsibility for the product they sell. More and more companies, such as LG, Matsushita/Panasonic, Mitsubishi, Motorola, NEC, Nokia, Philips, Samsung, Siemens, and Sony Ericsson, support corporate cradle-to-grave responsibility for obsolete cell phones. Honoring this obligation, in terms of strict economics, is best done via exporting obsolete products to other countries, particularly the poorer ones, who have an interest in and infrastructure to recycle. Disposal costs for hazardous waste in developing countries are fractions of the cost in wealthier countries. As far back as 1988, disposal costs in developing countries ranged from US$2.50 to US$50 per ton, compared with costs of US$100 to US$2,000 per ton in the United States, Japan, and the United Kingdom.[24] While costs have increased in poorer countries, they have increased at a far greater rate in wealthier countries. Lower disposal costs in developing countries largely follow from low or nonexistent environmental standards, less stringent laws, and an absence of public opposition due to a lack of information concerning the dangers involved. Given these considerations, the economic logic for exporting hazardous waste from wealthy to poor countries is indisputable.

COUNTERPOINT

In contrast, a range of observers and institutions contend that growth in the hazardous waste exports have created dangerous recycling industries in many countries. Electronic waste is a mixture of more than a thousand chemicals, including toxic metals (e.g., lead, barium, and mercury), acids, plastics, and chlorinated and brominated compounds. When electronic parts are burned to separate copper, solder, or other metals from plastic coatings, dioxins and other hazardous chemicals are released to the air. Shattering computer monitors to get at the components releases toxic phosphor dust. The problems, explained Madhumita Dutta of Toxics-Link Delhi, a nongovernmental organization, are far less disturbing than the problems created by the "appalling" working conditions in the typical recycling facility: "Everything from dismantling the computer to pulling out . . . parts of the circuit boards to acid washing boards to recover copper is done with bare hands without any protective gear or face protection." Moreover, the processing wastes run off into municipal drains or simply outside the perimeter of the facility. Finally, local air quality suffers as, for example, "circuit boards are burned after acid washing, spewing deadly smoke and exposing workers and people living around these facilities."[25]

In their defense, many companies that export electronic wastes to the developing world defend their environmental records. Luc Lateille of the Canadian firm BMP Recycling, for example, explained that "we don't send junk . . . we only send the materials that they are looking for."[26] Local entrepreneurs, companies maintain, create value for themselves and their countries by recovering, recycling, and reusing scarce resources. Said Atul Maheshwar, owner of a mud-brick recycling depot in India, "If your country keeps sending us the material, our business will be good."[27] Officially, many companies stop short of commenting on the working conditions of the typical local recycling facility. Whatever the case, growing concern among developing countries has prompted them to address the growing amount of electronic wastes shipped to their countries for disposal or recycling. Recently, the Asia-Pacific Regional Scoping Workshop on the Environmentally

Sound Management of Electronic Wastes proposed that manufacturers of electronic wastes be responsible for hazardous materials at the end of the products' lives.[28] The group also recommended that countries set tougher standards to monitor and control cross-boundary shipments of electronic wastes. Others, under the general rule of the Basel Convention on the Transboundary Movement of Hazardous Wastes and Their Disposal, argue for more aggressive measures, such as an international ban on the export of any and all hazardous wastes, no matter whether for recovery, recycling, reuse, or final disposal. As a final note, as of mid-2005, 148 countries had ratified the Basel Convention. The United States, which generates approximately 60 percent of the world's hazardous waste, is the only industrial country in the world that has yet to endorse the Basel Convention.[29]

Types of exporting

- Direct—goods and services are sold to an independent party outside the exporter's home country
- Indirect—goods and services are sold to an intermediary in the domestic market, which then sells the goods in the export market

THE EXPORT PROCESS

Exporting may be either indirect or direct. Indirect exports are sold to an independent intermediary in the domestic market, which then sells the product in the export market to the final consumer. Direct exports are goods and services sold to an independent intermediary outside of the exporter's home country, which then sells the product in the export market to the final consumer. Generally, services are more likely to be sold in a direct basis whereas goods are exported both directly and indirectly. We now examine each approach.

Indirect Selling

Third-party intermediaries—companies that facilitate the trade of goods but that are not related to either the exporter or the importer

There is nothing mysterious about selling and buying goods indirectly. An exporter using **indirect selling** simply sells goods to or through an independent domestic intermediary in its home country. The intermediary then exports the products to customers in foreign markets. Indirect selling permits the exporter to use the same customer solicitation methods, terms and conditions of sale, packaging, shipping protocol, and credit and collection procedures for all customers, no matter whether they are down the street or around the world. The task and responsibility of dealing with the complications created by export sales are transferred to the export intermediary.

Figure 13.3 shows that exporters and importers use a variety of third-party intermediaries—companies that facilitate the trade of goods but that are not related to either the exporter or the importer. Export intermediaries can range in size, from specialized, small one-person operations to international trading companies with a globally dispersed staff. A company that exports or is planning to export must decide whether its internal staff will handle certain essential activities or if it will contract with other companies. Regardless of the choice, the following functions must occur:

1. Stimulate sales, obtain orders, and do market research.
2. Make credit investigations and perform payment-collection activities.
3. Handle foreign traffic and shipping.
4. Act as support for the company's overall sales, distribution, and advertising staff.

Companies often use external specialists for exporting before developing internal capabilities.

A company's experience in export and import along with the sophistication of its financial and management resources largely influence its inclination for indirect selling. The challenge of preparing export documents, preparing customs documents in the importing country, and identifying the best means of transportation can quickly overwhelm the resources of any SME. In recourse, companies often turn to external specialists and intermediary organizations when they begin export operations. These companies have a range of skills, such as updated knowledge of trade laws and regulations, taxes and duties, insurance and transportation, to move shipments through customs as efficiently as possible.

Too, if and when problems arise at the entry port due to technicalities in the law or glitches in the system, brokers can expedite resolution or, in more serious situations, represent their clients at trials and tribunals and deal directly with government officials. Most companies that are starting to export find intermediaries offer an operationally easier and relatively risk-free approach.[30]

Exporters pay a price for these benefits. One, profit margins are much lower for indirect export sales versus direct sales, given that the need to let the intermediary make a profit requires the company to reduce its sales price. Two, the exporter forsakes control over important aspects of its international sales, like delivery schedules and customer service, to the intermediary. If control is a crucial concern, a company can opt to employ export intermediaries in any number of less comprehensive ways, including using them to provide short-term financing for the goods in transit or managing the conversion of national currencies. These choices efficiently deal with the matters of financing sales and extending credit. The price for these services, depending on whether the intermediary is working on salary, commissions, or retainer plus commission, can be high.

The major types of indirect intermediaries are the **export management company (EMC)**, the **export trading company (ETC)**, and export agents, merchants, or remarketers. The terms *EMC* and *ETC* are often used interchangeably, especially for the smaller intermediaries. The larger intermediaries, however, are almost always referred to as ETCs or simply trading companies, because they deal with both exports and imports. We now look at each type.

Export Management Companies

An EMC usually acts as the export arm of a manufacturer—although it can also deal in imports—and often uses the manufacturer's own letterhead in communicating with foreign sales representatives and distributors. The EMC primarily obtains orders for its clients' products through the selection of appropriate markets, distribution channels, and promotion campaigns. It collects, analyzes, and furnishes credit information and advice regarding foreign accounts and payment terms. The EMC may also take care of export documents, arrange transportation (including the consolidation of shipments among multiple clients to reduce costs), set up patent and trademark protection in foreign countries, and assist in establishing alternative forms of doing business, such as licensing or joint ventures.[31]

An EMC acts as the export arm of a manufacturer.

EMCs operate on a contractual basis, often as the agent for an exporter, and provide exclusive representation in a well-defined foreign territory. Their contract with the company specifies pricing, credit and financial policies, promotional services, and basis for payment. An EMC might operate on a commission basis for sales (unless it takes title to the merchandise) and take a retainer for other services. EMCs usually concentrate on complementary and noncompetitive products so that they can present a more complete product line to a limited number of foreign importers.

EMCs operate on a contractual basis, usually as an agent of the exporter.

In the United States, most EMCs are small, entrepreneurial ventures that tend to specialize by product, function, or market area. The Federation of International Trade Associations (FITA) estimates that there are between 600 to 1,000 EMCs in the United States and that each represents, on average, about 10 suppliers. This means that few U.S. companies use EMCs, although FITA believes that thousands more would benefit from doing so.[32]

Most EMCs are small, entrepreneurial ventures that specialize by product, function, or market area.

Although EMCs perform an important function for companies, they are not the answer for all export situations. EMCs, for the most part, are relatively small and may have limited financial resources. Thus, some may not be able to warehouse a company's product or to offer extended in-house financing to foreign customers. Inevitably, EMCs focus their efforts on those products that bring them the most profits. New lines, or those with limited potential, get overlooked or ignored. Finally, and most worrisomely, manufacturers fear that using an EMC will push it to relinquish control over crucial aspects of its foreign sales. Manufacturers sometimes have no control over whom the EMC sells to,

An EMC is not a perfect solution. Often they have too few resources, give too little attention, and take too much control.

the selling price it charges, or the quality of promotional campaigns. Some companies have discovered that if an EMC does not actively promote their products, then they may be unable to do much to generate exports. Therefore, manufacturers need to trade-off their preference for control with the cost of directly managing export operations.[33]

Export Trading Companies

ETCs are like EMCs, but they tend to operate on the basis of demand rather than of supply. They identify suppliers who can fill orders in overseas markets.

In 1982, the U.S. government enacted the Export Trading Company Act, which removed some of the antitrust obstacles to the creation of ETCs in the United States. Specifically, this legislation allowed the formation of ETCs by groups of competitors to market products jointly, without fear of antitrust action, as Dutch, Japanese, and British competitors had done for decades. It was reasoned that using ETCs, without the legal barriers that constrained companies' export mobility, would lead to greater exports of U.S. goods and services and increased international competitiveness of U.S. companies. Significantly, the legislation permitted banks to make equity investments in commercial ventures that qualified as ETCs, something that had previously not been possible. Policymakers hoped that permitting banks to engage in commercial, nonbanking transactions in the context of an ETC would encourage them to be more receptive to international trade finance requests, thereby removing additional barriers that diminished the export interest and performance of U.S. companies. Operationally, the Federal Reserve Board approves these applications before the bank can start export operations. Many of the banks concentrate on customers in their geographical market and in parts of the world in which they already have built a network. ETCs are important to banks, because banks provide the financial side of the export business, so being able to invest in an ETC gives the banks access to more of the business than just the financing side.

ETCs in the United States are exempt from antitrust provisions, thereby allowing them to collaborate with other companies to penetrate foreign markets.

ETCs resemble EMCs, and the terms are often used interchangeably. An important distinction though is that ETCs operate more on the basis of demand than of supply. ETCs are like independent distributors that match buyers with sellers and, as such, see their value creation as a function of finding out what foreign customers want and then identifying domestic suppliers. Therefore, rather than representing a single manufacturer, an ETC tries to work with as many manufacturers as it can to provide products to overseas customers. Effectively, ETCs operate as commissioned agents, charging the seller or the buyer a percentage of the value of the export while generally refusing to carry inventory in their own name or perform after-sale service activities.

Foreign Trading Companies

The only similarity between foreign trading companies and U.S. export trading companies is the designation "trading company." Exporters from Japan, Great Britain, the Netherlands, and several other traditional trading nations found long ago that wide-reaching trading companies could market and distribute products more efficiently than any single producer could. This, as we noted above, was the basis for the legislation that permitted ETCs in the United States. More recently, exporting companies from nontraditional trading countries, such as Argentina and Brazil, have applied this lesson. Notably, Japanese trading companies such as Mitsubishi, Mitsui, and Itochu are huge conglomerates with marketing, financial, and distribution arms that permit a truly global reach.[34] In 1995, these three Japanese companies were the top three companies on *Fortune*'s list of the 500 largest global companies. By 2004, though, none of these three remained anywhere near the top, and all trading companies from Japan, Korea, Germany, and the like have tumbled as a result of new accounting rules that significantly lowered their revenues. Previously foreign trading companies booked the gross value of their trades as revenue, but now they comply with U.S. Generally Accepted Accounting Principles and report transactions on a net basis.[35]

Direct Selling

Competitive pressures to better exploit core competencies and value chains ultimately push exporters to consider (1) building a network of **sales representatives,** either salaried or commissioned, that are stationed in key markets around the world and that deal with distributors, foreign retailers, or end users, or (2) developing their own international marketing capability, charging in-house sales personnel to monitor the actions and activities of foreign **distributors.** Exporters undertake **direct selling** to give them greater control over the marketing function and to earn higher profits.

In the case of building a network of sales representatives, the company may give them exclusive rights to sell in a particular geographic area or may have them compete with other sales representatives that also represent the firm. It is more common for sales representatives to have exclusive rights to a territory. For example, Grieve's sales representatives operate on an exclusive basis in their respective markets. A distributor in a foreign country is a merchant who purchases the products from the manufacturer and sells them at a profit. Distributors usually carry a stock of inventory and service the product. They also usually deal with retailers rather than end users in the market. Companies, in evaluating potential foreign sales representatives or distributors, usually look at the following issues:

- The size and capabilities of its sales force
- Its sales record
- An analysis of its territory
- Its current product mix
- Its facilities and equipment
- Its marketing policies
- Its customer profile
- The principles it represents and the importance of the inquiring company to its overall business
- Its promotional strategies

A company that has sufficient financial and managerial resources and decides to export directly rather than working through an intermediary has to build some sort of organization capabilities. These capabilities may take any number of forms, ranging from a separate international division, to a separate international company, to full integration of international and domestic activities. In addition, the company needs to fine-tune its control and coordination system to deal with the contingencies of export sales. However the company opts to design its organization, direct selling calls for an international sales force that is separate from its domestic counterpart because foreign markets demand different types of expertise.

Exporters can also sell directly to foreign retailers. Usually, these products are limited to consumer lines. The growth of global retail chains, such as Wal-Mart and Ahold, increasingly facilitates the export of an increasing range of products directly to storefronts around the world. This trend gives existing exporters greater coverage and "born global" exporters, notably those emerging in China, immediate access to a wide market.[36] Exporters can also sell directly to end users. A good way to generate such sales is by printing catalogs or attending trade shows. They can also generate sales when foreign buyers see company brochures or respond to advertisements in trade publications.

An example of a company that sells directly to buyers is Cooley Distillery, the sole Irish-owned distiller of Irish whiskey. Cooley exports more than 80 percent of its production, up from about 25 percent in 1990. Cooley has a powerful customer list and sells in over 40 countries, including the top 25 retailers in Europe. In spite of this situation, Cooley has elected to sell ex-distillery, which means that the customer takes title directly from Cooley's distillery and handles all the shipments. Cooley maintains a small

Direct selling involves sales representatives, distributors, or retailers.

A sales representative usually operates on a commission basis.

A distributor is a merchant who purchases the products from the manufacturer and sells them at a profit.

bonded warehouse in the United Kingdom to handle just-in-time shipments to super-market chains that order small quantities, but it generally lets the buyer handle ship-ping and storage in foreign markets.[37]

Direct Selling Through the Internet

Electronic commerce is an increasingly important means by which companies export. Forrester Research found that 7 percent of revenues from worldwide trade in 2002 was from e-commerce and estimated that by 2007, e-commerce will produce 20 percent of revenues in world trade.[38] E-commerce will be especially important for SMEs that can't afford to establish an elaborate sales network internationally. We already see Internet marketing growing among export companies in emerging countries, as they use it to overcome some of the capital and infrastructure barriers of international markets. For example, exporters in Chile use extranets to communicate with importers around the world, while exporters in Costa Rica found online shops to be a good way of increasing product turnover with higher margins.[39] Others report the Internet supports the emergence of companies using virtual export channels to serve international markets.[40]

E-commerce has a range of features and functions. Research reports that it is easy to engage, provides faster and cheaper delivery of information, generates quick feedback on new products, improves customer service, accesses a global audience, levels the field of competition, and supports electronic data interchange (EDI) with both suppliers and customers.[41] Through Internet exporting, companies can establish home pages in different languages to target different audiences. In the case of industrial products, they can install software to track hits to their home page and then send sales representatives to potential customers or have local distributors contact them. In the case of consumer products, companies can sell their products directly to consumers worldwide.

Export Documentation

Direct selling requires the exporter to comply with the battery of documents that regulate international trade. Duty rates, customs clearance, and entry processes differ for each country. Tariff classifications, value declaration, and duty management can create confusion and high costs. Customs and security initiatives have imposed new regulations on companies that make it more difficult than ever to trade internationally. By sovereign right, each country determines whether domestic products or products transshipped through its borders can be exported to certain countries. In the United States, an exporter needs to consult the U.S. Department of Commerce to determine if its products can be shipped under a general license or if they must be exported under an individually validated license (IVL). For example, exports of certain high-tech products might be restricted for national security reasons, so an exporter must apply for an IVL to determine whether the exportation is permitted. Of the many documents that must be completed, some of the most important are the following:

- A **pro forma invoice** is an invoice, like a letter of intent, from the exporter to the importer that outlines the selling terms, price, and delivery if the goods are actually shipped. If the importer likes the terms and conditions, it will send a purchase order and arrange for payment. At that point, the exporter can issue a commercial invoice.
- A **commercial invoice** is a bill for the goods from the buyer to the seller. It contains a description of the goods, the address of buyer and seller, and delivery and payment terms. Many governments use this form to assess duties.
- A **bill of lading** is a receipt for goods delivered to the common carrier for transportation, a contract for the services rendered by the carrier, and a document of title.

- A **consular invoice** is sometimes required by countries as a means of monitoring imports. Governments can use the consular invoice to monitor prices of imports and to generate revenue for the embassies that issue the consular invoice.

- A **certificate of origin** indicates where the products originate and usually is validated by an external source, such as the chamber of commerce. It helps countries determine the specific tariff schedule for imports.

- A **shipper's export declaration** is used by the exporter's government to monitor exports and to compile trade statistics.

- An **export packing list** itemizes the material in each individual package, indicates the type of package, and is attached to the outside of the package. The shipper or freight forwarder, and sometimes customs officials, use the packing list to determine the nature of the cargo and whether the correct cargo is being shipped.

Foreign Freight Forwarders

Preference to sell direct to foreign customers but reluctance to supervise the transport of goods from one country to another prompts companies to employ the services of a freight forwarder. Popularly known as the "travel agents of cargo," freight forwarders help exporters move shipments to foreign buyers. A freight forwarder is an agent for the exporter in moving cargo to an overseas destination.[42] The freight forwarder is used for both imports and exports, because one company's exports are another company's imports. Even export management companies and other types of trading companies often use the specialized services of foreign freight forwarders.

The **foreign freight forwarder** is the largest export intermediary in terms of value and weight of products managed. However, the services it offers are more limited than those of an EMC. Once an exporter makes a foreign sale, it hires the freight forwarder to obtain the best routing and means of transportation based on space availability, speed, and cost. The freight forwarder will get the products from the manufacturing facility to the air or ocean terminal and then overseas. The forwarder secures space on planes or ships and necessary storage prior to shipment, reviews the letter of credit, obtains export licenses, and prepares required shipping documents. It also may advise on packing and labeling, purchase transportation insurance, repack shipments damaged en route, and warehouse products, which save the exporter the capital investment of warehousing. However, the freight forwarder does not take title to the goods or act as a sales representative in a foreign market. It simply deals with the preparation and transportation of goods.

The freight forwarder usually charges the exporter a percentage of the shipment value, plus a minimum charge depending on the number of services provided. The forwarder also receives a brokerage fee from the carrier. Despite these costs, using a freight forwarder is usually less costly for an exporter than providing the service internally, because most companies, especially the SMEs, find it difficult to set up a full-time department to deal with freight issues and keep up with shipping regulations. The forwarder also can get exporters shipping space more easily (because of its close relationship with carriers) and consolidate shipments to obtain lower rates.

Freight forwarders, especially the smaller ones, sometimes specialize in the mode used—such as surface freight, ocean freight, and airfreight—and the geographical area served. Increasingly, however, the freight forwarders handle many modes—truck, rail, and airfreight, for example.[43] The movement of goods across different modes from origin to destination is known as **intermodal transportation**. Ocean freight is the cheapest way to move merchandise, but it also is the slowest. Even though it still dominates global trade, its position is eroding somewhat. Ocean freight rates are based on space first and weight second. Rate schedules also differ depending on the ports and the direction the goods travel. For example, different rates apply to shipments from the United States to Germany and to shipments from Germany to the United States. Forwarders help manufacturers get the best

A foreign freight forwarder is an export or import specialist dealing in the movement of goods from producer to consumer.

The typical freight forwarder is the largest export intermediary in terms of value and weight handled.

Different transportation modes:

- Surface freight (truck and rail), ocean freight, and airfreight
- Intermodal transportation—the movement across different modes from origin to destination

contract and help prepare the products for export. Exporters can load merchandise in a container for shipment overseas, or they can rely on a freight forwarder to consolidate their shipments with others. As mentioned in the opening case, Grieve's president shops for quotes from different freight forwarders when booking space on cargo ships. Even large companies compare rates. The person who handles the export of Shell Oil Company's non-hazardous lubricating oils and greases negotiates rates with the steamship lines himself, but if the forwarders' steamship line rates are lower, he will use the forwarders instead.

Three trends favor the airfreight business over ocean freight: More frequent shipments, lighter-weight shipments, and higher-value shipments. The trend toward global manufacturing, which we discuss in Chapter 17, along with contracting product life cycles have created a boom in airfreight traffic. Airfreight is much more effective in accomplishing these trends than is ocean freight. Higher-value shipments are more likely to use airfreight as long as they are not too bulky, because the exporter wants to get the product into the hands of the importer as soon as possible and collect on the sale. In most cases, the exporter cannot get paid for the sale until delivery is completed. Federal Express and UPS have launched ad campaigns targeted at small businesses to promote their shipping services. Indeed, both companies have translated technology into a host of services in logistics, freight forwarding, customs clearance, technology, and finance that may open up export opportunities for more companies.[44]

> Factors favoring airfreight over ocean freight: more frequent shipments, lighter-weight shipments, higher-value shipments

LOOKING TO THE FUTURE: The Technology of Trade

An irony of growing globalization is the fact that export and import is more of a procedural challenge today than ever before and likely will continue to be so for many years. Besides the heightened importance of national and international security, companies must navigate complex national, regional, and global trade agreements, all the while ensuring that they are compliant with a host of international regulation. Faced with the growing impossibility of keeping up with change, international traders are rethinking their goals and expectations. While many forces influence their analyses, the general idea and specific applications of technology is the driving force.

Advances in transportation and communications systems steadily facilitate export growth and make it easier for companies to reach international markets. One example of advances in communications is electronic data interchange, namely the electronic movement of information that enables companies to connect the flow of goods, funds, and information within an integrated system of different technologies. The resulting real-time synchronization of their export and import activities enables companies to redefine the way they connect with their foreign customers.

The growing sophistication of trade intermediaries, both in traditional terms like EMCs and ETCs, as well as emerging forms, like Federal Express and UPS, to integrate trade and technology is changing the efficiencies and effectiveness of export and import operations. These companies, particularly the latter two, increasingly rely on state of the art technology to help exporters understand their current trade practices and identify opportunities and risks. So, for example, these intermediaries command the system capabilities that enable exporters to perform more efficiently through such integration mechanisms as online shipping and tracking information that let the company and customer know when the shipments will reach customs; consolidated billing inclusive of all transportation, customs brokerage, duties, taxes, and package delivery services; and the capabilities to handle product returns, warranty claims, parts exchanges, and reverse logistics. More strategically, technology lets these intermediaries provide help in key areas, such as compliance (meeting government trade regulations, customs procedures, and administrative issues) and tariffs (helping exporters design business processes so that they can use technology to adapt quickly to changing regulations and tariffs).

Companies, especially smaller ones, increasingly respond to these solutions, confident that technology will let them better solve many of the traditional headaches of trade and open up new opportunities for export and import.

TABLE 13.2	TYPES OF TRADE INFORMATION BY SOURCE
U.S. Government Agencies	• Market demographics, product demand, and competition • Distribution channels and joint venture partners • U.S. customs, regulatory, and tax issues • Sales finance • Credit and insurance • Trade events, partners, and trade leads • Shipping documentation and requirements • Pricing, quotes, and negotiations • Help with trade problems
Trade Associations and Trade Groups	• Market demographics, product demand, and competition • Advertising and sales promotion alternatives • Distribution channels • Customs regulations and tax issues
Export Intermediaries	• Distribution channels • Host-country legal, accounting, and tax requirements • Sales finance • Credit and insurance • Logistics

Sources of Assistance

Making sense of the various forms of trade regulations and requirements is tough under the best of circumstances. Companies typically have many options from the private and public sectors to help them figure out the best option. As a case in point, our opening look at Grieve highlighted the export assistance provided by the International Trade Administration of the Chicago Export Assistance Center, as well as the U.S. Department of Commerce's Agent/Distributor Search. Potential exporters, therefore, can tap a wealth of public resources in the form of national, state, and local trade offices, to say nothing of freight forwarders, international banks, or general trade consultants. Table 13.2 profiles leading sources and the types of help they provide.

In the United States, a number of institutions, most notably the Department of Commerce and its affiliates, help firms identify and realize export opportunities.

By and large, government agencies are particularly useful resources. Federal, state, and local governments, seeing the benefits of international trade, actively aid the efforts of potential and active exporters and, to lesser degree, protect the interests of struggling importers. Japan, for instance, relies on several offices, such as the Small and Medium Enterprise Agency, Agency of Industrial Science and Technology, and Ministry of International Trade and Industry. The latter, often referred to as "MITI," plays a vital role in developing strategic policy and providing operational assistance in order to help Japanese companies profitably trade internationally. Programs in the United States give a sense of the financial help that is available to the international trader. The Ex-Im Bank and Small Business Administration (SBA), for instance, help international traders get private sector loans to fund their export transaction financing needs. These federal agencies help arrange the financing of the manufacturing costs of goods for export, purchase of goods or services, and foreign accounts receivable and standby letters of credit. Similarly, most states and several cities fund and operate export financing programs, including preshipment and postshipment working capital loans and guarantees, accounts receivable financing, and export insurance. The limited reserves of some states and cities push them to make their assistance contingent upon the exporter's proof that they do not risk losing much if the deal falls apart. An exporter need only provide proof of a letter of credit or sufficient credit insurance to satisfy this requirement. Chapter 19 examines these aspects of export financing more precisely. In some situations, some states and cities require the exporter to do part of the export deal within the jurisdiction of the funding authority. Often, meeting this call for local content can be done by using transportation facilities, such as an air or sea port, in the city or state.

COUNTERTRADE

Unquestionably, currency is the preferred payment medium for any export or import transaction—it is easy, fast, and straightforward to transact. Sometimes, though, companies must adapt to the reality that buyers in many countries cannot do so, whether due to the fact that their home country's currency is nonconvertible, the country doesn't have enough cash, or it doesn't have sufficient lines of credit. Sometimes companies and countries find it practically impossible to generate enough foreign exchange to pay for imports. In recourse, they devise creative ways to buy products. For example, Indonesia traded 40,000 tons of palm oil, worth about US$15 million, with Russia in exchange for Russian Sukhoi fighter aircraft.[45] This trade, like others that fall under the umbrella term **countertrade,** illustrates that buyers and sellers often find creative ways of settling payment for imports and exports.

Countertrade refers to any one of several different arrangements that parties negotiate so that they can trade goods and services with limited or no use of currency. Technically, countertrade can be divided into two basic types: barter, based on clearing arrangements used to avoid money-based exchange; and buybacks, offsets, and counter purchase, which are used to impose reciprocal commitments.[46]

Countertrade is an inefficient way of doing business. By default, companies prefer the straightforward efficiency of cash or credit. In the case of countertrade, rather than simply consulting current foreign exchange rates, buyers and sellers must enter complex and time-consuming negotiations to reach a fair value on the exchange—how many gallons of palm oil for how many planes, for example. In some situations, the goods that are sent as payment may be poor quality, packaged unattractively, or difficult to sell and service. Also, there is a lot of room for price and financial distortion in countertrade deals, given that nonmarket forces set the prices of these goods. Ultimately, countertrade and its variations threaten free market forces with protectionism and price fixing that can complicate trade relations with other countries.

Still, the harsh reality of international trade means that countertrade is often unavoidable for companies that want to do business in markets that have limited or no access to cash or credit. Complicating matters is the fact that as much as companies may dislike them, many emerging markets prefer forms of countertrade to preserve their limited monetary assets, generate foreign exchange, and improve the balance of trade. In addition, these methods help emerging markets reduce their need to borrow working capital as well as let them access the technology and marketing expertise of MNEs. More significantly, benefits beyond financing the immediate transaction do accrue to companies. Accepting the option to countertrade shows managers' good faith and flexibility in the face of onerous conditions. These sensitivities can position the firm to gain preferential access to emerging markets. Philosophically, the idea of countertrade fits with many countries' basic notions of business. For example, the idea of "barter and trade" is part of some African traditions that are reluctant to conform to "Euro-centric" methods of cash payment.

It is difficult to gauge the size of the countertrade market. Estimates in the past have ranged from 10 to 40 percent of total global exports. This figure has proven tough to verify due to inconsistent reporting and disclosure. Countertrade generally increases in economies that are experiencing widespread economic problems. In Argentina, countertrade among common citizens has increased due to a severe shortage of cash.[47]

Countertrade is when goods and services are traded for each other.

Countertrade is primarily used when a firm exports to a country whose currency creates barriers to an efficient buy-sell exchange.

Countertrade has several disadvantages.
- It is inefficient.
- It is risky.
- It is complicated.
- It is cumbersome.

There are several types of countertrade. The three most common are barter, buybacks, and offset.

Barter

Barter, the oldest form of countertrade, is a transaction in which goods or services are traded for goods or services of equal value without any exchange of cash or credit. Each term of the exchange is negotiated in terms of the immediate trade of goods or services. For instance, Thailand and Indonesia signed a $40 million deal in which Indonesia would supply Thailand with an agricultural aircraft, train carriages, and fertilizer in exchange for Thai rice—no monies were or would be exchanged.[48] There are barter firms that act as an intermediary between the exporter and importer, often taking title to the goods received by the exporter for a price or selling the goods for a fee and a percentage of the sales value.

Barter occurs when goods or services are traded for goods or services.

Buybacks

Buybacks are products the exporter receives as payment that are related to or originate from the original export. Buyback arrangements are quite common in the sale of technology, licenses, and even complete "turnkey" factories. Payment is made in full or in part either by products manufactured in the new facility or by production from the new license or technology. Buyback countertrade is especially popular for turnkey infrastructure projects. For example, the customer pays for the project, say a steel mill, with government-backed long-term credit. The exporting contractor first guarantees that the project will work when completed and then agrees to buy back products or services from the completed facility or to serve as a distributor for products exported from the host country. The host-country buyer uses these hard currency payments to liquidate the original long-term credit. Throughout the relationship, no cash changes hands and no credit arrangements are necessary. The buyback contract merely states that the output from the newly constructed facility is to be applied to the original price of the exports. This sort of arrangement was worked out between PepsiCo and Russia. Pepsi provided syrup to state-owned bottling plants in Russia and received Stolichnaya vodka in return, which it then marketed in the West.

Buybacks—products the exporter receives as payment that are related to or originate from the original export

Offset Trade

An increasingly important form of countertrade is **offset trade,** a transaction that takes place when an exporter sells products for cash and then helps the importer find opportunities to earn hard currency. Offsets are most often used for big-ticket items, such as military sales. The Czech government made offset the deciding factor, as opposed to technical and performance criteria and price, in its jet fighter procurement.[49] Offset arrangements are usually one of two types.

In offset trade, the exporter sells goods for cash but then undertakes to promote exports from the importing country in order to help it earn foreign exchange.

1. Direct offsets include any business that relates directly to the export. Generally, the exporter seeks contractors in the importer's country to joint-venture or coproduce certain parts if applicable. For example, an aircraft exporter could partner with a company in the importer's country to manufacture components that would be used in the manufacture of the aircraft.
2. Indirect offsets include all business unrelated to the export. Generally, the exporter is asked by the importer's government to buy a country's goods or invest in an unrelated business.[50] Some of the most common direct offset practices in military sales include coproduction, licensed production, subcontractor production, overseas investment, and technology transfer. Examples of indirect offsets might include assisting in the export of unrelated products from the host country or generating tourist revenues for the host country.

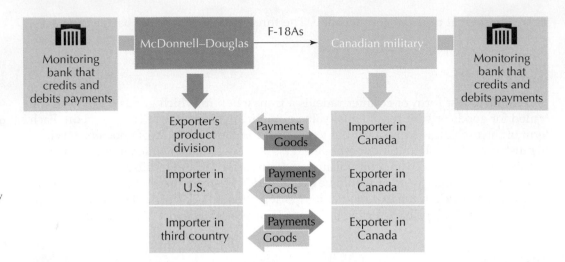

Figure 13.4 shows how one might structure an offset transaction. As specified in the figure, the transaction involves the primary exporter, the importing government, and other secondary exporters and importers. Whether companies get into the complexities of offset trade depends mainly on the demand for their products, whether they have alternative sources of supply, and the extent of foreign-exchange problems in the buying country. In any case, offset trade results primarily from foreign-exchange shortages and is a good example of how companies and governments can compensate for such a shortage through creative business transactions.

SUMMARY

- The probability of a company's becoming an exporter increases with company size, but the extent of exporting does not directly correlate with size.

- Companies export to increase sales revenues, use excess capacity, and diversify markets.

- Companies new to exporting (and also some experienced exporters) often make many mistakes. One way to avoid mistakes is to develop a comprehensive export strategy that includes an analysis of the company's resources as well as its export potential. Companies can also improve the odds of export success by working with an experienced export intermediary.

- As a company establishes its export business plan, it must assess export potential, obtain expert counseling, select a country or countries where it will focus its exports, formulate its strategy, and determine how to get its goods to market.

- Importers need to be concerned with strategic issues (why import rather than buy domestically) and procedural issues (what are the steps that need to be followed to get goods into the country).

- Customs agencies assess and collect duties, as well as ensure that import regulations are adhered to.

- Exporters may deal directly with agents or distributors in a foreign country or indirectly through third-party intermediaries, such as export management companies or other types of trading companies.

- Internet marketing is a new form of direct exporting that is allowing many small- and medium-size companies to access export markets as never before.

- Trading companies can perform many of the functions for which manufacturers lack the expertise. In addition, exporters can use the services of other specialists, such as freight forwarders, to facilitate exporting. These specialists can help an exporter with the complex documentation that accompanies exports.

- Government agencies in some countries, such as the Ex-Im Bank in the United States, provide assistance in terms of direct loans to importers, bank guarantees to fund exporters' working capital needs, and insurance against commercial and political risk.

- Countertrade is any one of several different arrangements by which goods and services are traded for each other, on either a bilateral or a multilateral basis.

- Barter means trading goods or services for goods or services. Offsets are agreements by which the exporter helps the importer earn foreign exchange or the transfer of technology or production to the importing country.

Alibaba.com [51]

lectronic commerce is changing the way companies around the world do business by making it easier and cheaper for them to buy and sell to each other. Before the Internet, tracking down a product to import or finding foreign customers to export to were daunting challenges for the typical small- and medium-sized enterprise (SME). Often these companies had to rely on the occasional trade shows, followed by expensive and time-consuming travels to foreign lands to identify possible products, check on potential suppliers, or conduct primary market research. Along the way, companies could opt to contact various Consulates or Embassies in foreign countries to help out, either by promoting the export of their products or assisting with the import of goods. While sounding straightforward, these were expensive options that commanded a lot of time from managers. Consequently, international trade was largely limited to those companies who could afford to attend expensive trade shows, publish costly brochures, travel internationally, and hire agents and export trading companies.

Now, the Internet provides a cost-effective way for SMEs, even those on a shoestring budget, to jump these hurdles. Indeed, the Internet has opened up a new era of business opportunities, making information on any conceivable product from virtually any market easily and cheaply available. Combined with falling trade barriers and more efficient logistics, courtesy of the WTO and companies like FedEx, DHL, and UPS, dramatic possibilities to import and export have fueled the growth of global trade. The U.S. Small Business Administration estimates that the number of small businesses exporting goods or services tripled from 1994 through 2004. Growing even faster is the value of what they trade; the value of export sales has tripled in the past five years. Forrester Research sees cross-border e-marketplace trade done by U.S. companies exceeding US $400 billion in 2005.

Many companies are taking advantage of online technologies and starting or expanding their international trade. They rely on the Internet as their primary channel for getting information, sourcing products or services, finding suppliers and marketing their products, and tapping into new markets; in many cases, these companies build a virtual value chain online. International traders, both potential and practicing, have nearly infinite resources to tap online. They can browse through catalog repositories, B2B exchanges, electronic trade boards, trade journals, and virtual trade shows to find a product they would like to import or a market that might buy their export. Increasingly, as more firms throughout the world access the Internet, many entrepreneurs and trading companies use this technology as their primary means to develop their import and export business.

Recently, the emergence of country-specific portals and Web exchanges has accelerated this process. As eBay has done for consumer-to-consumer e-commerce, several sites have created online bazaars for international traders, where exporters can lay out their wares and haggle with potential buyers from the far corners of the world. For instance, potential importers looking for products from Korea can access www.global.kita.net, those targeting India can check out www.trade-India.com, and those fixed on Europe need only visit www.europages.com to tap into high-quality electronic trade boards. One can track down country-specific B2B exchanges for practically every country with a quick check of the open directory project at www.dmoz.org/Business/E-Commerce/Marketplaces. While many sites exist, they share the goal of serving as a trade agency that promotes a country's or region's commercial potential with the global community. This goal leads these sites to provide a variety of direct services to big and small international traders, such as trade consulting, export training, cyber trade infrastructures, international special exhibitions, virtual trade shows, and new trade strategies.

Conceptually, there is little exceptional about these sorts of sites—they simply help move products from sellers in one place to buyers in another place. Operationally, they represent remarkable business-to-business Web sites that are changing the mechanics of import and export for everyone, but especially, for SMEs. These sites create flexible and dynamic platforms that let buyers and sellers of everything from bamboo toothpicks to farm tractors efficiently find each other and effectively work out the terms of trade. Besides introducing mom-and-pop shops from around the world to each other, these sorts of sites have opened up the vast and largely uncharted small-business hinterland in markets from Tibet to Patagonia. Long the unseen production sites of many pieces of the global economy, companies in these far away places only had the option to trade within the context of global supply chains directed by large companies. Now, within the world of these new trade Web sites, they have the option to go straight to buyers and sellers. Consequently, these Web sites have greatly reduced many of the barriers to international trade and, in the process, helped legions of small businesses become importers and exporters.

Like many parts of the global economy, this sort of e-commerce is having a big impact in China. Spearheading this effort is Alibaba.com, a Chinese Internet company that specializes in introducing manufacturers across China with buyers in China and also around the world. Founded in 1999 by Jack Ma, who has been dubbed the father of the Chinese Internet, Alibaba.com has three parts—Alibaba China is China's largest online marketplace for domestic trade, Alibaba International is its English-language site that hosts traders from more than 200 countries, and TaoBao (which means "digging treasure") is a consumer site now free to all users (and is the company's strategic response to eBay). As a side note, Ma said he chose the Arabian Nights–inspired name because it is meaningful to people around the world. He said the name stuck after a San Francisco waitress replied "Open, Sesame!" to Ma's request for her thoughts when he said "Alibaba."

Based in Hangzhou, about two hours' drive south of Shanghai, Alibaba began operations in 1999 with the goal of getting big by staying small. That is, Jack Ma has always stressed that his target customers are small businesses around the world—in his own words, "shrimps," not "whales." On a typical day, the online community trading on Alibaba.com contains around 50,000 buyers and 120,000 sellers from more than 200 countries who are looking to initiate an import or export transaction. Acting as an online global trade fair, Alibaba allows many smaller companies with export and import ambition but shoestring budgets to reach the global market. More specifically, most of Alibaba's 500,000 members are SMEs in developing countries around the world. They are located in rural areas, as well as large cities, in countries such as Kyrgyzstan, Sierra Leone, and Peru. By and large, few of these are glamorous high-tech companies but rather low-tech companies making many labor-intensive, scale-insensitive products. However, technology gives them the option to expand their market reach and grow their businesses—essentially, they can use Alibaba's infrastructure to create a global business from an apartment in a small town in nearly every country in the world.

The lure of Alibaba is compelling: Importers around the world can request bids from Chinese manufacturers for a mind-boggling array of goods, such as cookware, poker chips, washing machines, or mp3 players. Product options are ever expanding; already Alibaba had organized more than a thousand product categories, each with many sub-categories. In addition, Alibaba offered new channels to trade services. For example, the classic garage inventor in Chicago now had the option to design a product and then use Alibaba to find Chinese factories eager and able to manufacture and ship it to customers worldwide. Operationally, buyers around the world use Alibaba to find potential supplies that often have the lowest costs in the world, thereby eliminating the need to hire a representative in China to buy directly from the manufacturers on their behalf. So, for example, an enterprising Argentinian looking to buy

500 DVD players need only visit Alibaba.com, search among the dozens of potential suppliers, learn their terms of trade, contact the preferred vendor, and set the deal in motion. Said the cofounder of www.meetChina.com, a similar e-commerce site, "We want to make buying 1,000 bicycles from China as easy as buying a book from Amazon.com."

Historically, an importer often worried that the unknown supplier might defraud her—after all, she is in Buenos Aires, the supplier is in Guangzhou, and she has heard horror stories of export fraud. Increasingly, as sites like Alibaba inject more transparency into the process of imports and exports, buyers can worry less about fraud. Specifically, users of Alibaba, like those on similar e-commerce sites, can post information about their companies on the site as well as access information about the reliability of other users. Buyers also have the option to access Alibaba's basic screening and background checks on its registered users. Finally, they can access the seller's posted references, say one from his bank, to verify his status. Collectively, this data let the importer in Argentina cross-check potential trade partners in Guangzhou, quickly getting a sense of their credibility and reliability. Operationally, this is how Alibaba makes money—it offers the basic service of listing a company and its products on its Web site free of charge. It then generates revenue from the 85,000 members who pay $250 to $10,000 a year for services such as personalized Web pages and certification.

So, as it has in other parts of the business world, technology is opening new opportunities for international traders. Historically, globalization had given a disproportionate amount of power and benefits to large companies. Rather than being overtaxed by the challenge of trading internationally, large companies could rely on their well-equipped international divisions to supervise exports and imports. Now, though, Internet and telecommunications advancements were spreading trade opportunities throughout the world, both in the wealthier nations as well as deep into developing countries. Where this might go from this point was anyone's call.

QUESTIONS

1. List, in separate columns, the benefits and costs of using sites like Alibaba's to trade internationally. What does your analysis say to companies like Grieve (in our opening case) as they think about their export strategy?

2. Is it reasonable to speculate that eventually most trade between small- and medium-sized firms might take place in the context of sites like Alibaba.com? If so, does that influence your inclination to consider importing and exporting?

3. Visit www.alibaba.com, www.trade-india.com, and www.europages.com. Compare and contrast these Web sites.

4. Visit www.alibaba.com, go to "Advanced Search," and enter the product you seek in the relevant box. Select required criteria and click on "Search." Review the list of companies that qualify and find a suitable one. Analyze this process for ease, usefulness, and potential value.

5. How transparent do sites like Alibaba.com make the import-export transaction? Would you still worry about fraud?

CHAPTER NOTES

1 http://www.grievecorp.com/.

2 An SME is generally defined as a business with less than 250 employees.

3 D. D. Chadee and J. Mattsson, "Do Service and Merchandise Exporters Behave and Perform Differently? A New Zealand Investigation," *European Journal of Marketing* 32, no. 910 (Nov. 24, 1998): 830.

4 John H. Dunning, "The Eclectic Paradigm of International Production: Some Empirical Tests," *Journal of International Business Studies* 19 (Spring 1988): 1–31.

5 Sanjeev Agarwal and Sridhar N. Ramaswami, "Choice of Foreign Market Entry Mode: Impact of Ownership, Location and Internalization Factors," *Journal of International Business Studies* 23, no. 1 (First Quarter 1992): 2–5.

6   U.S. Department of Commerce, *Guide to Exporting, 1998* (Washington, DC: U.S. Department of Commerce and Unz & Co., Inc., November 1997), 3.

7   W. Chan Kim and Peter Hwang, "Global Strategy and Multinationals' Entry Mode Choice," *Journal of International Business Studies* 23, no. 1 (First Quarter 1992): 32–35.

8   Mark Stein, "Export Opportunities Aren't Just for the Big Guys", *New York Times,* March 24, 2005.

9   Andrea Bonaccorsi, "On the Relationship Between Firm Size and Export Intensity," *Journal of International Business Studies* 23, no. 4 (Fourth Quarter 1992): 606.

10 Paul Magnusson, "The Split-Up That's Slanting the Trade Deficit," *Business Week* (June 7, 1999): 38.

11 Jonathan L. Calof, "The Relationship Between Firm Size and Export Behavior Revisited," *Journal of International Business Studies* 25, no. 2 (Second Quarter 1994): 367–87; James Obben and Phumzile Magagula, "Firm and Managerial Determinants of the Export Propensity of Small- and Medium-Sized Enterprises in Swaziland," *International Small Business Journal* 21, no. 1 (Feb. 2003): 73.

12 Paul Westhead, Mike Wright, and Deniz Ucbasaran, "International Market Selection Strategies Selected by 'Micro' and 'Small' Firms," *Omega* 30, no. 1 (Feb. 2002): 51.

13 Leonidas C. Leonidou and Constantine S. Katsikeas, "The Export Development Process: An Integrative Review of Empirical Models," *Journal of International Business Studies* 27, no. 3 (Third Quarter 1996): 524–25.

14 O. Moen, "The Born Globals: A New Generation of Small European Exporters," *International Marketing Review* 19, no. 2 (April 30, 2002): 156.

15 "A San Diego Company Uses the Internet to Go Global," news on U.S. Department of Commerce Web site (August 18, 2002): http://www.usatrade. gov/website/website.nsf/WebBySubj/Main_WhatsNew081802.

16 "Most Common Mistakes of New-to-Export Ventures," *Business America* (April 16, 1984): 9.

17 Ibid, Stein.

18 Benson Smith and Tony Rutigliano, *Discover Your Sales Strengths* (Warner Business Books, 2003).

19 Paul Beamish et al., "The Relationship Between Organizational Structure and Export Performance," *Management International Review* 39 (First Quarter 1999): 51.

20 Since a practical discussion of importing procedures in every trading country of the world is impossible within this chapter, we focus on the matter of importing to the United States. We hasten to note, though, that while U.S. import requirements and procedures provide a sufficient base for judging situations in other countries, a company must assess the importing regulations applicable to those countries in which they plan to engage.

21 See the home page of U.S. Customs for an organizational chart and for specific responsibilities. See also "Mission Statement, Organizational Chart" (2002).

22 U.S. Department of the Treasury, U.S. Customs Service, *Importing into the United States* (Washington, DC: U.S. Government Printing Office, September 1991).

23 Helen Baulch, "Error: Dumping Does Not Compute," *Alternatives Journal* 28, no. 3 (Summer 2002): 2.

24 Zada Lipman, "A Dirty Dilemma: The Hazardous Waste Trade," *Harvard International Review* 23 (2002): 67.

25 Baulch, op. cit.

26 Baulch, op. cit.

27 Reported in "E-Waste Ignored in India," by Karl Schoenberger, Mercury News, at www.ban.org/ban_news/ewaste_ignored_031228.html.

28 "E-Waste Importers," *Hazardous Waste Superfund Week* 24, no. 50 (Dec. 23, 2002).

29 See "Secretariat of the Basel Convention, Competent Authorities," Membership List, April 18, 2005. By definition, a "Competent Authority" means one governmental authority designated by a Party to be responsible within such geographical area as the Party may think fit, for receiving the notification of a transboundary movement of hazardous wastes or other wastes, and any information related to it, and for responding to such a notification. Retrieved from http://www.basel.int/, April 29, 2005.

30 Lee Li, "Joint Effects of Factors Affecting Exchanges Between Exporters and Their Foreign Intermediaries: An Exploratory Study," *Journal of Business & Industrial Marketing* 18, no. 2–3 (February–March 2003): 162–178; Mike W. Peng and Anne S. York "Behind Intermediary Performance in Export Trade: Transactions, Agents, and Resources," *Journal of International Business Studies* 32, no. 2 (Summer 2001): 327.

31 See U.S. Department of Commerce, *Guide to Exporting, 1998,* op. cit., 20; and Philip MacDonald, *Practical Exporting and Importing,* 2nd ed. (New York: Ronald Press, 1959), 30–40.

32 Courtney Fingar, "ABCs of EMCs," The Federation of International Trade Associations (July 2001): http://fita.org/emc.html; Nelson T. Joyner, "How to Find and Use an Export Management Company," April 1999, http://www.fita.org/aotm/0499.html.

33 "Basic Question: To Export Yourself or to Hire Someone to Do It for You?" *Business America* (April 27, 1987): 14–17.

34 The *sogo shosha,* the Japanese equivalent word for trading company, can trace its roots back to the late nineteenth century, when Japan embarked on an aggressive modernization process. At that time, the trading companies were called *zaibatsu*—large, family-owned businesses composed of financial and manufacturing companies usually held together by a large holding company. These companies were very powerful, so U.S. General Douglas MacArthur (sent to Japan to institute New Deal reforms after WWII) broke them up and made many of their activities illegal. However, the families and relationships did not

go away, so the *zaibatsu* reformed into the *keiretsu* organizations, meeting the letter of the law even if they didn't exactly meet the spirit of the law. There was greater concern after World War II about the reconstruction of Japan than about eliminating all vestiges of the past, so the *keiretsus* linking financial, manufacturing, and trading companies started up again. When these trading companies were first organized after World War II, their primary functions became handling paperwork for import and export transactions, financing imports and exports, and providing transportation and storage services. However, their operations expanded significantly beyond exporting to include investing in production and processing facilities, establishing fully integrated sales systems for certain products, expanding marketing activities, and developing large bases for the integrated processing of raw materials.

35 Paola Hjelt, "The *Fortune* Global 500," *Fortune* (July 26, 2004): 159.

36 Jiang Jingjing, "Wal-Mart's China Inventory to Hit US$18b This Year," *China Business Weekly* (November 29, 2004). Retrieved from **http://www.chinadaily.com.cn/english/doc/2004-11/29/content_395728.htm**.

37 Author's interview of John Teeling, Executive Chairman of Cooley Distillery (2002).

38 Julie Meringer, "E-Commerce Next Wave: Productivity and Innovation," Forrester Research, in a speech to the World Trade Organization in Geneva (April 22, 2002): **http://www.wto.org/wto/english/tratop_e/devel_e/sem05_e/**.

39 Merlin Bettina, "Internet Marketing in Exports—A Useful Tool for Small Businesses," *Small Enterprise Development* 15, no. 4 (Dec. 2004): 38.

40 Anna Morgan-Thomas and Susan Bridgewater, "Internet and Exporting: Determinants of Success in Virtual Export Channels," *International Marketing Review* 21, no. 4 (April 1, 2004): 393.

41 A. J. Campbell, "Ten Reasons Why Your Business Should Use Electronic Commerce," *Business America* (May 1998): 12–14.

42 U.S. Department of Commerce, *Guide to Exporting, 1998*, op. cit., 63.

43 Helen Richardson, "Freight Forwarder Basics: Contract Negotiation," *Transportation & Distribution* (May 1996). Available in Lexis/Nexis News: CURNWS.

44 "UPS Unveils 'What Can Brown Do for You?' Ad Campaign," *Business First* (February 7, 2002).

45 "Indonesia to Increase Sukhoi Planes to 16," *Xinhua General News Service* (April 9, 2005).

46 J. F. Hennart, "Some Empirical Dimensions of Countertrade," *Journal of International Business Studies* 21 (1990): 243–70.

47 See Jonathon Bell, "Plane Trading," *Airfinance Journal* (June 1998): 34–36; and Elizabeth Love/Quilmes, "Argentina: The Post-Money Economy," *Time* (February 5, 2002): **http://www.time.com/time/world/article/0,8599,199474,00.html**.

48 "Commodities: Thai Countertrade Deal Signed," Laksamana.net (June 10, 2002): **http://www.laksamana.net/printcfm?id=2893**.

49 Ross Davies, "A Deal with Strings Attached," *Financial Times* (July 17, 2002): www.ft.com.

50 American Countertrade Association, "Forms of Countertrade" (2002): www.countertrade.org/index.html.

51 www.alibaba.com; www.trade-india.com; www.dmoz.org/Business/E-Commerce/Marketplaces; www.europages.com; www.meetchina.com; Justin Doebele, "Fast as a Rabbit, Patient as a Turtle," *Forbes*, (July 3, 2000): p. 78; Justin Doebele, "Standing Up to a Giant," *Forbes Global*, (April 25, 2005): p. 30; Daniel Roth, "The Amazing Rise of the Do-It-Yourself Economy," *Fortune*, (May 30, 2005): p. 45; "Chinese E-Commerce Sites Allow Small Firms to Reach Wider Base," *Wall Street Journal*, (February 25, 2004); Jack Ma, "From Shanghai to Davos," *Asian Wall Street Journal*, (February 20, 2001).

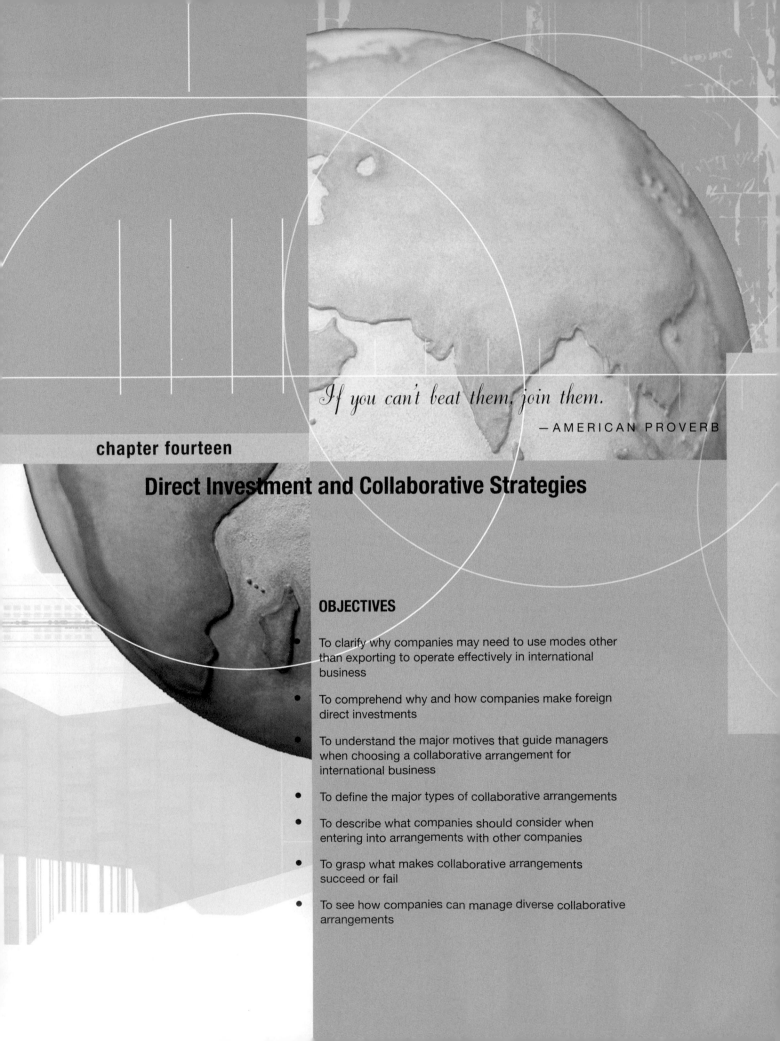

If you can't beat them, join them.

—AMERICAN PROVERB

chapter fourteen

Direct Investment and Collaborative Strategies

OBJECTIVES

- To clarify why companies may need to use modes other than exporting to operate effectively in international business

- To comprehend why and how companies make foreign direct investments

- To understand the major motives that guide managers when choosing a collaborative arrangement for international business

- To define the major types of collaborative arrangements

- To describe what companies should consider when entering into arrangements with other companies

- To grasp what makes collaborative arrangements succeed or fail

- To see how companies can manage diverse collaborative arrangements

CASE: CISCO SYSTEMS[1]

Cisco Systems was founded in 1984 and is now the world's largest supplier of data networking equipment and the leading global supplier of computer networking solutions. In 2004, Cisco's sales were over $22 billion, and it employed more than 34,000 people. About 45 percent of its sales were outside the Americas. Figure 14.1 shows the distribution of its sales globally. Interestingly, only about 12 percent of Cisco's property and equipment were outside the United States because it depended so heavily on exports for its foreign sales. Nevertheless, Cisco uses a variety of operating modes to tap foreign opportunities. It has 100 percent owned foreign direct investments, which comprise two pillars in its growth strategy, internal growth and acquisitions. Two of the latter are its purchases of Pentacom in Israel and CoCom in Denmark. Cisco sees partnerships as the third pillar in its growth strategy. Like some companies from other countries, such as Philips from the Netherlands and Samsung from Japan, Cisco sees its ability to ally effectively with other companies to be a distinctive strength. Cisco collaborates in many ways. It has joint ownership of production, distribution, and technology development facilities with other companies. It contracts with other companies to share technology, to have goods and components produced, and to distribute. One of its biggest types of partnerships is with governments of over 150 countries. These are both philanthropic and profit motivated in that they develop future resources. The partnerships are for academics to train students in skills so that they can work in information technology (IT) jobs.

The company's official Strategic Alliances Team manages crucial partnerships with industry-leading technology and integrator companies, and it also drives collaborative development to accelerate new market opportunities. Implementing this strategy led Cisco to develop a range of alliance and partnership programs with U.S. and non-U.S. companies that help Cisco better compete both domestically and internationally. Map 14.1 shows a sample of these collaborations.

Cisco's worldwide alliances help it achieve many objectives. They spur Cisco to continue learning and to refine its competences. They enable Cisco to meet customer needs that fall outside its area of core competence, while simultaneously permitting Cisco and its partners to enhance their competitiveness by focusing on their respective core competencies. For example, Cisco established a joint venture with the Singaporean company, ePic, whereby the two companies use their complementary technology for an Internet video monitoring service. Some Cisco alliances are between one of its foreign subsidiaries and a foreign subsidiary of another company, such as one between Its and IBM's Japanese subsidiaries. In this one, IBM's software sets conditions to gain network access, and Cisco's equipment denies access to people unable to meet preset conditions. Cisco's global alliances vice president observed, "If there's technology outside Cisco that works well, we acquire it. And if we feel that we don't need it internally, we'll partner with an organization to help get it to our customers."

Alliances have permitted Cisco to limit its capital outlays in potentially lucrative but risky ventures. For example, Cisco partnered with Motorola in a joint venture, Spectrapoint Wireless, by spending $300 million to acquire the wireless assets of German-based Bosch Telecom. They pledged to spend $1 billion more on the venture over the next five years to become leaders in this market. One year later, Motorola and Cisco called off the partnership because the projected market did not materialize.

Alliances, by pooling resources, have also allowed Cisco to more effectively deal with market leaders. For instance, IBM has been the supply leader in IT. In 2004, Cisco joined an alliance with Dell, EDS, EMC, Microsoft, Sun, and Xerox to counter IBM's leadership by establishing joint development activities in the United States and the United Kingdom.

Cisco believes that alliances improve its processes, reduce its costs, and expose it to the best competitive practices. Finally, collaboration provides Cisco a cost-effective means to expand into new markets. Consequently, its vice president of strategic alliances said, "The number of alliances we are doing is picking up. Given the current economic climate, partnering is more appealing than acquisitions. The investments are more affordable, and you can still speed up time to market."

Cisco relies on about 150 employees to oversee its many alliances. To manage these alliances, these employees depend on the technology that has made Cisco successful—technology that facilitates communications. Thus, they rely on the World Wide Web, e-mail, file sharing, and conferencing to provide a network that efficiently links partners across corporate and national boundaries. These linkages have

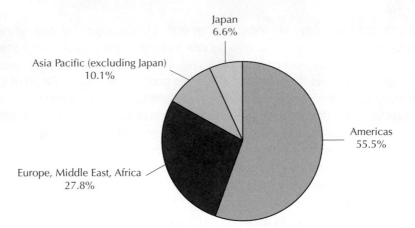

FIGURE 14.1

GEOGRAPHIC COMPOSITION OF CISCO SYSTEMS NET SALES, 2004

The figures are for the fiscal year ending July 31, 2004. Although Cisco deals globally, most of its sales are in the Americas.

Source: Cisco Systems, *Annual Report,* 2004, p. 21.

demonstrated and made available Cisco's capabilities to its partners, such as the Cisco Connection and Cisco Internet Business Roadmap. The Cisco Connection provides on-line information and interactive services worldwide, including software upgrades, technical assistance, order status, seminar registration, documentation, and training. The Cisco Internet Business Roadmap adds information on solutions, programs, tools, and sales resources. Both programs provide Cisco and its partners instant global communications, enhanced productivity, consistent business systems, lower business costs, and scalability. Essentially, "For many established companies, the Web has legitimized alliances," noted a Cisco partner in wireless communications security, the director of Accenture's global alliance practice.

Managing collaborative agreements poses challenges. Not all agreements result in companies' realizing the value or achieving the business objectives that they initially expected. Cisco has generally standardized the mechanics of partnership agreements. However, it continues working to improve the odds of collaborative success by better managing the matters of trust, commitment, and culture that shape what it calls "interwoven dependencies and relationships" with its partners.

MAP 14.1   Sample of Cisco's International Collaborations

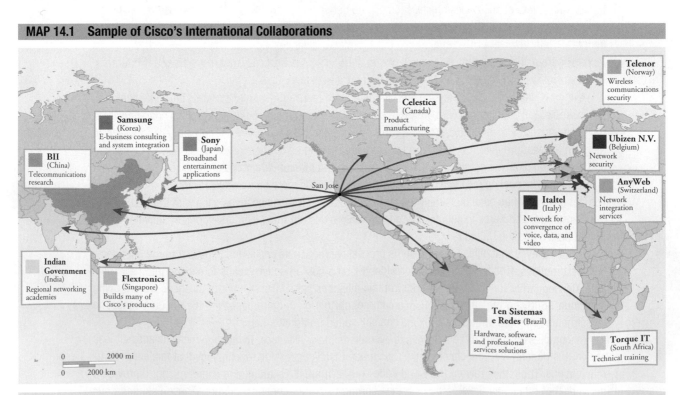

The map shows merely a small sample of Cisco's vast network of global collaborations.

Early on, Cisco sought partners with similar organizational cultures to avoid personal and strategic conflicts. This strategy also helped assure a continuation of partnership arrangements if responsible Cisco or partner employees happened to leave their positions. However, globalization has pushed Cisco to a broader range of markets, whether to follow the expansion patterns of its customers, to solicit the business of possible customers, or to study new ideas and new products. Doing so has exposed Cisco to different organizational and national cultures.

Cisco realized the full cultural impact of this international expansion when traffic to Cisco.com started pouring in from places like Barcelona, Beijing, and Berlin. Originally, Cisco published Cisco.com only in English, so it had limited usefulness to potential partners and customers who spoke Spanish, Mandarin, or German. Cisco decided that it would have to speak their languages if it wanted to win their support, cooperation, and business.

Cisco first tried to develop its own translation software; eventually it partnered with Lionbridge Technology to build a human-translation system that automated the process. (Lionbridge Technology is a U.S. company that also depends heavily on collaborative agreements worldwide.) Even though the system is automated, staff can make cultural changes and tweak the translations appropriately along the way. Cisco.com is now published in many languages. Moreover, although Cisco manages the site's back-end systems centrally, it relies on its nearly 70 local sales and support offices around the world to maintain language-specific pages and ensure that documents are relevant to partners within various countries.

Despite occasional problems, alliances are an important aspect of Cisco's international strategy. Cisco started early and has continued strongly in using partnerships to extend its ability to service customers in more markets around the world. Its philosophy of mutually beneficial partnerships (in whatever nation they happen to call home) and its efforts to improve partners' performance have boosted Cisco's competitiveness through innovative products, strong distribution, and a global service network. Concomitantly, its partners enhance their business credibility and gain greater market penetration.

INTRODUCTION

Figure 14.2 shows that companies must choose an international operating mode to fulfill their objectives and carry out their strategies. In the preceding chapter, we discussed exporting and importing, which are the most common modes of international business.

FIGURE 14.2 **COLLABORATIVE ARRANGEMENTS AS INTERNATIONAL BUSINESS OPERATING MODES**

Companies must handle international business operations on their own or collaborate with other companies. Their choice is influenced externally by physical and societal factors and by their competitive environment. Their choice is also influenced by their objectives and strategies.

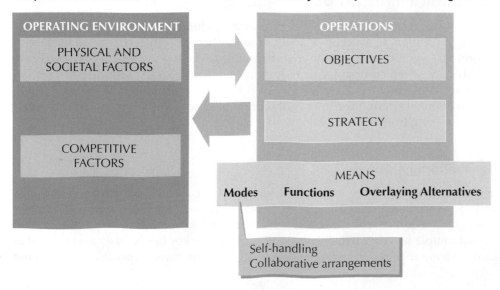

FIGURE 14.3

ALTERNATIVE OPERATING MODES FOR FOREIGN MARKET EXPANSION

A company may use more than one operating mode within the same location. Those shaded in purple are collaborative arrangements. Note that exporting is the only mode for market expansion in which production is in the home country.

PRODUCTION OWNERSHIP	PRODUCTION LOCATION	
	Home country	Foreign country
Equity arrangements	a. Exporting	a. Wholly owned operations b. Partially owned with remainder widely held c. Joint ventures d. Equity alliances
Nonequity arrangements		a. Licensing b. Franchising c. Management contracts d. Turnkey operations

In fact, most companies would prefer to sell abroad by exporting, thus enabling them to produce within the familiar environments of their home countries rather than abroad. Nevertheless, there are some compelling reasons that make exporting and importing impractical. We'll first discuss these reasons. When companies depend on foreign production, they may own that production in whole or in part, develop the foreign operation or acquire it, and use some type of collaborative agreement with another company. We'll next explain the modes associated with each of these options and discuss the advantages and problems with each. We'll conclude the chapter by discussing management of these modes, particularly as foreign operations evolve over time.

Figure 14.3 shows the types of operating modes, categorized by whether the company has foreign ownership, whether the mode involves collaboration, and whether production is located in the home country versus a foreign country. The truly experienced MNE with a fully global orientation usually uses most of the operational modes available, selecting them according to company capabilities, specific product, and foreign operating characteristics. Further, those modes may be combined. For example, Cisco owns a Japanese subsidiary, but it also exports systems into Japan. Further, its Japanese subsidiary owns another Japanese company in collaboration with IBM.

WHY EXPORTING MAY NOT BE FEASIBLE

Companies may find more advantages by producing in foreign countries than by exporting to them. The advantages occur (1) in situations where production abroad is cheaper than at home; (2) when transportation costs to move goods or services internationally are too expensive; (3) when companies lack domestic capacity; (4) when products and services need to be altered substantially to gain sufficient consumer demand abroad; (5) when governments inhibit the import of foreign products; and (6) when buyers prefer products originating from a particular country.

Cheaper to Produce Abroad

Although companies may have products or services that consumers abroad would like to buy, producing them within their home markets may be too expensive, especially if other companies can make reasonably similar substitutes at a lower cost. Hence, competition requires that companies control their costs. For example, Turkey has been a growing market for the sale of automobiles. However, it is generally less expensive to produce them within

Turkey than to export them to Turkey because producers can pay skilled labor and sophisticated engineers less than in their home countries. Further, Turks work more days per year and longer hours per day than workers in the companies' home countries, thus the companies use their equipment more fully and reduce capital costs per unit produced. Thus, United States, Japanese, and European automakers and their parts suppliers, who compete with each other worldwide, have established Turkish production to serve the Turkish market. These companies sell some output in Turkey and some of it in export markets.[2]

Transportation Costs

When companies add the cost of transportation to their production costs, they find that some products and services become impractical to export. Generally speaking, the farther the market from the home country, the higher the transportation costs. Further, the higher the transportation costs relative to production costs, the more difficult for companies to develop viable export markets. For example, the international transportation cost for a soft drink is a high percentage of the manufacturing cost, so a sales price that includes both the manufacturing and transportation costs would have to be so high by exporting that soft drink companies would sell little abroad. Thus companies, such as Coca-Cola and PepsiCo, depend on bottling plants in all the countries where they sell. (Nevertheless, such companies as Perrier and Evian have managed to find niche markets for exported bottled water that sells at high prices relative to production costs.) Some services are impossible to export. Thus companies such as BP and McDonald's must have retail establishments abroad if they are to sell to foreign consumers because people are not going to send their cars to the United Kingdom to fill up their tanks with BP's petrol, nor will people fly to the United States just to buy a Big Mac. However, products such as watches have low transportation costs relative to production costs. Because watch manufacturers lose few sales because of export transportation costs, companies such as Universal Genève and Seiko export watches from Switzerland and Japan, respectively, into the markets where they sell them. Further, tourists do travel internationally just to visit Disney's theme parks because they are sufficiently different from home-country substitutes.

> Transportation raises costs so much that it becomes impractical to export some products.

Lack of Domestic Capacity

As long as a company has excess capacity, it may compete effectively in export markets despite high transport costs. This ability might occur if domestic sales cover fixed operating expenses, enabling the company to set foreign prices on the basis of variable rather than full (variable + fixed) costs. In fact, the company's average cost of production per unit goes down as foreign sales increase, but this cost decrease continues only as long as there is unused capacity. Thus, companies typically produce in one location from which they export before they establish plants in more than one country. For example, Volkswagen placed its first plant to build the new Beetle at its facilities in Mexico, which served global markets. However, when demand pushed that plant toward capacity, Volkswagen announced it would build a second plant in Europe to serve the European market.[3] The second plant freed Mexican capacity to serve nearby markets while reducing transportation costs for serving the European market.

> Excess capacity
> - Usually leads to exporting rather than new direct investment
> - May be competitive because of variable cost pricing

Need to Alter Products and Services

Companies often need to alter products to gain sufficient sales in a foreign market. This affects their production in two ways. First, it entails an additional investment, such as an automobile company's adding an assembly line to put steering wheels on the right as well as on the left. As long as an additional investment is needed to serve the foreign market anyway, investors might consider making that investment abroad to save transport costs. Second, the company loses certain economies from large-scale production, thus its least-cost production location to serve given markets may shift from one country

> Product alterations for foreign markets may lead to foreign production of the products.

to another. The more that products must be altered for foreign markets, the more likely production will shift to those foreign markets. Whirlpool, for example, finds that U.S. demand is for top-loading washing machines with large capacities using 110 electrical voltage, but European demand is for front-loading washing machines (more efficient in using energy and water) with smaller capacity using 220 voltage.[4] Given the differences in product preferences, Whirlpool produces in both the United States and Europe.

Trade Restrictions

Although governments have been reducing import barriers through the World Trade Organization, bilateral agreements, and regional trading groups, they still restrict many imports. Thus, companies may find they must produce in a foreign country if they are to sell there. For example, Volkswagen decided to build Skoda in India because of India's 121 percent duty on the imports.[5]

Managers must view import barriers along with other factors, such as the market size of the country imposing the barriers and the scale of technology used in production. For example, import trade restrictions have been highly influential in enticing automobile producers to locate in Brazil because of its large market. Similar restrictions by Central American countries have been ineffective because of their small markets. However, Central American import barriers on products requiring lower amounts of capital investment for production and therefore smaller scale technology and markets (for example, pharmaceuticals) have been highly effective at enticing direct investment.

Removing trade restrictions among a group of countries also may attract direct investment, possibly because the expanded market may justify scale economies and possibly because the output from a new location can be feasibly exported. For example, Israel has received an influx of high-tech direct investment to produce for markets in countries with which it has signed free trade agreements.[6]

Country of Origin Effects

Government-imposed legal measures are not the only trade barriers to otherwise competitive goods. Consumer desires also may dictate limitations. Consumers may prefer to buy goods produced in their own country rather than another (perhaps because of nationalism).[7] If they feel strongly enough, they may even push for identification labels showing that goods are domestically produced (for instance, a green and gold logo for Australian made products[8]). They may require labels showing where products are made, such as U.S. labeling of agricultural products, or preferences for domestic goods when governments make purchases, such as the state of Missouri's buy-American requirements.[9] Or, they may believe that goods from a given country are superior, like German cars and French perfume, therefore preferring those countries' products. In actuality, consumers often view the quality of identical products differently on the basis of country of origin.[10] They may also fear that service and replacement parts for imported products will be difficult to obtain. Adding to this need to invest directly is the global rise in just-in-time (JIT) manufacturing systems, which decrease inventory costs by having components and parts delivered as needed. These systems favor nearby suppliers who can deliver quickly.

In any of these cases, companies may find advantages in placing production where their output will have the best acceptance.

NONCOLLABORATIVE FOREIGN EQUITY ARRANGEMENTS

A company may or may not take ownership in the foreign facilities that provide products and services for them. It may simply contract with another company to produce or provide services on its behalf, or it may take some ownership equity in foreign operations, such as in warehousing, sales offices, or production facilities. Referring again to Figure 14.3, you'll

If imports are highly restricted, companies

• Often produce locally to serve the local market
• Are more likely to produce locally if market potential is high relative to scale economies

Consumers sometimes prefer domestically produced goods because of

• Nationalism
• A belief that these products are better
• A fear that foreign-made goods may not be delivered on time

see that there are four types of equity arrangements. In this section, we'll discuss two forms of foreign direct investment (FDI) that do not involve collaboration (wholly owned operations and partially owned with the remainder widely held). We'll also discuss the resources and methods for making FDI.

Foreign Direct Investment and Control

For direct investment to take place, control must accompany the investment. Otherwise, it is a portfolio investment. If ownership is widely dispersed, then a small percentage of the holdings may be sufficient to establish control of managerial decision making. Generally, the more ownership a company has, the greater is its control over the decisions. However, governments often protect minority owners so that majority owners do not act against their interests. There are three primary reasons that spur companies to want a controlling interest—internalization theory, appropriability theory, and freedom to pursue global objectives. We'll now discuss each of these.

Internalization   Control through self-handling of operations (internal to the organization) is **internalization**.[11] This concept comes from *transactions cost theory*, which holds that companies should seek the lower cost between handling something internally and contracting another party to handle it for them. In actuality, a company may not easily find another company to handle something for it because, for example, it has a unique technology not easily understood by others. In many other cases, a company's self-handling may reduce costs because:

> Internalization theory holds that it is sometimes cheaper to handle operations oneself than to contract with another company.

1. Different operating units within the same company are likely to share a common corporate culture, which expedites communications. For example, executives participating in a Thought Leadership Summit on Digital Strategies concluded that trust, lack of a common terminology, and lack of shared knowledge are major obstacles to collaboration.[12]

2. The company can use its own managers, who understand and are committed to carrying out its objectives. For example, when GE acquired a controlling interest in the Hungarian company Tungsram, it was able to expedite control and changes because it put GE managers in key positions.[13]

3. The company can avoid protracted negotiations with another company on such matters as how income will be divided between them. For example, the U.S. brewer Anheuser-Busch made an investment in the Mexican brewer Grupo Modelo (brewer of Corona). But the companies lost valuable time as they argued over how to calculate Mexican earnings.[14]

4. The company can avoid possible problems with enforcing an agreement. For example, Vidal Sassoon engaged in a long legal battle with Procter & Gamble over its claims that Procter & Gamble ceased support so that it could boost its Pantene brand.[15]

Appropriability   The idea of denying rivals access to resources is called the **appropriability theory**.[16] Companies are reluctant to transfer vital resources—capital, patents, trademarks, and management know-how—to another organization. The company receiving these resources can use them to undermine the competitive position of the foreign company transferring them. For example, Chinese automakers such as SAIV, Dongfeng, and Changan have collaborative arrangements with major global auto competitors, such as GM, Volkswagen, Nissan, and Ford. They make no secret of their desire to learn from their partners so as to become global competitors in their own right.[17] For this reason, although Intel transfers nonvital resources to partnerships, it has strategically blocked other companies' acquisition to its vital resources by handling them within its wholly owned operations.[18]

> Companies may want to operate through FDI to lessen the chance of developing competitors.

FDI eases companies' ability to pursue global strategies.

Pursuit of Global Strategies   When a company has a wholly owned foreign operation, it may more easily have that operation participate in a global or transnational strategy. For example, if a U.S. company owned 100 percent of its Brazilian operation, it might be able to take actions that, although sub-optimizing Brazilian performance, could deal more effectively with actual or potential competitors and customers on a global basis—such as decreasing prices to an industrial customer in Brazil to gain that customer's business in Germany. But if the company shared ownership in Brazil, the lower prices might be detrimental to the other owners in Brazil. Because most countries have laws to protect minority shareholders' interests, sharing of ownership may restrict a company from implementing a global or transnational strategy.

Methods for Making FDI

Foreign direct investment is usually an international capital movement. Although most FDI requires some type of international capital movement, an investor may transfer many other types of assets. For example, Westin Hotels has transferred very little capital to foreign countries. Instead, it has transferred managers, cost control systems, and reservations capabilities in exchange for ownership in foreign hotels. There are two ways companies can invest in a foreign country. They can either acquire an interest in an existing operation or construct new facilities, the latter known as a *greenfield investment*. We'll now discuss the reasons for each.

The advantages of acquiring an existing operation include

- Adding no further capacity to the market
- Avoiding start-up problems
- Easier financing

Reasons for Buying   Whether a company makes a direct investment by acquisition or start-up depends, of course, on which companies are available for purchase. The large privatization programs occurring in many parts of the world have put hundreds of companies on the market, and MNEs have exploited this new opportunity to invest abroad. For example, foreign companies, such as Vivendi from France, bought many British utility companies when they were privatized.[19]

There are many reasons for seeking acquisitions. One is the difficulty of transferring some resource to a foreign operation or acquiring that resource locally for a new facility, especially if the company feels it needs to adapt substantially to the local environment or operate through a multidomestic strategy.[20] Personnel is a resource that foreign companies may find difficult to hire, especially if local unemployment is low. Instead of paying higher compensation than competitors do to entice employees away from their old jobs, a company can buy an existing company, which gives the buyer not only labor and management but also an existing organizational structure. This may be particularly important if the company is making an FDI to augment its capabilities, such as to acquire knowledge.[21]

Through acquisitions, a company may also gain the goodwill and brand identification important to the marketing of mass consumer products, especially if the cost and risk of breaking in a new brand are high. Further, a company that depends substantially on local financing rather than on the transfer of capital may find it easier to gain access to local capital through an acquisition. Local capital suppliers may be more familiar with an ongoing operation than with the foreign enterprise. In addition, a foreign company may acquire an existing company through an exchange of stock. In other ways, acquisitions may reduce costs and risks—and save time. A company may be able to buy facilities, particularly those of a poorly performing operation, for less than the cost of new construction. If an investor fears that a market does not justify added capacity, acquisition enables it to avoid the risk of depressed prices and lower unit sales per producer that might occur if it adds one more producer to the market. Finally, by buying a company, an investor avoids inefficiencies during the start-up period and gets an immediate cash flow rather than tying up funds during construction.

Companies may choose to build if

- No desired company is available for acquisition.
- Acquisition will lead to carry-over problems.
- Acquisition is harder to finance.

Reasons for Greenfield   Although acquisitions offer advantages, a potential investor will not necessarily be able to realize them. Companies frequently make foreign investments in sectors where there are few, if any, companies operating, so finding a company to buy may be difficult. In addition, local governments may prevent acquisitions because they want more competitors in the market and fear market dominance by foreign enterprises. Even if acquisitions are available, they often don't succeed.[22] The acquired companies might have substantial problems. Personnel and labor relations may be both poor and difficult to change, ill will may have accrued to existing brands, or facilities may be inefficient and poorly located. Further, the managers in the acquiring and acquired companies may not work well together, particularly if the two companies are accustomed to different management styles and practices or if the acquiring company tries to institute many changes.[23] Finally, a foreign company may find local financing easier to obtain if it builds facilities, particularly if it plans to tap development banks for part of its financial requirements.

MOTIVES FOR COLLABORATIVE ARRANGEMENTS

The same reasons why companies establish collaborative arrangements for domestic operations carry over to their international operations as well. For example, a company such as McDonald's that franchises most of its operations in the United States also franchises most of its operations in foreign countries—for the same reasons, which we'll discuss in the next section. Companies also establish collaborative arrangements abroad for different reasons than they collaborate domestically. For example, one of the reasons that Cisco established a joint venture in India was because Indian laws prohibited its gaining 100 percent ownership. Figure 14.4 shows both the general and internationally specific reasons for collaborative arrangements. This figure also refers back to the three objectives of international business introduced in Chapter 1.

Scale alliances aim at providing efficiency through the pooling of similar assets so that partners can carry out business activities in which they already have experience. *Link alliances* use complementary resources to expand into new business areas.[24] Keep in mind that each organization participating in a collaborative agreement has its own primary objective for operating internationally and its own motive for collaborating. For example, GM entered a joint venture with Russian Avtovaz. GM wanted production of Avtovaz's low-priced vehicle to sell in developing countries, and Avtovaz wanted GM's financial and technical resources to make sport utility vehicles in Russia.

FIGURE 14.4 **RELATIONSHIP OF STRATEGIC ALLIANCES TO COMPANIES' INTERNATIONAL OBJECTIVES**

Collaborative arrangements may serve companies' goals, regardless of whether they operate internationally. In addition, there are gains from collaborative arrangements that are specific to companies' international operations.

OBJECTIVES OF INTERNATIONAL BUSINESS
- Sales expansion
- Resource acquisition
- Risk minimization

MOTIVES FOR COLLABORATIVE ARRANGEMENTS

General
- Spread and reduce costs
- Specialize in competencies
- Avoid or counter competition
- Secure vertical and horizontal links
- Learn from other companies

MOTIVES FOR COLLABORATIVE ARRANGEMENTS

Specific to International Business
- Gain location-specific assets
- Overcome legal constraints
- Diversify geographically
- Minimize exposure in risky environments

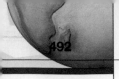
General Motives for Collaborative Arrangements

In this section, we'll explain the reasons that companies collaborate with other companies in either domestic or foreign operations: to spread and reduce costs, to allow them to specialize in their competencies, to avoid competition, to secure vertical and horizontal links, and to gain knowledge.

Spread and Reduce Costs   To produce or sell abroad, a company must incur certain fixed costs. At a small volume of business, it may be cheaper for it to contract the work to a specialist rather than handle it internally. A specialist can spread the fixed costs to more than one company. If business increases enough, the contracting company then may be able to handle the business more cheaply itself. Companies should periodically reappraise the question of internal versus external handling of their operations.

A company may have excess production or sales capacity that it can use to produce or sell for another company. The company handling the production or sales may lower its average costs by covering its fixed costs more fully. Likewise, the company contracting out its production or sales (outsourcing) will not have to incur fixed costs that may have to be charged to a small amount of production or sales. Using this capacity also may reduce start-up time for the outsourcing company, providing earlier cash flow. Further, the contracted company may have environment-specific knowledge, such as how to deal with regulations and labor, that would be expensive for the contracting company to gain on its own. Also, contracting companies may lack the resources to "go it alone." By pooling their efforts, they may be able to undertake activities that otherwise would be beyond their means. This is especially important for small and young companies.[25] But it is important for large companies when the cost of development and/or investment is very high. For example, the development cost of Disney's theme park in Hong Kong is so high it strains the capabilities of even a company as large as Disney. So the Hong Kong government will share ownership and costs.[26]

Specialize in Competencies   The **resource-based view** of the firm holds that each company has a unique combination of competencies. A company may seek to improve its performance by concentrating on those activities that best fit its competencies, depending on other firms to supply it with products, services, or support activities for which it has lesser competency. Large, diversified companies are constantly realigning their product lines to focus on their major strengths. This realigning may leave them with products, assets, or technologies that they do not wish to exploit themselves but that may be profitably transferred to other companies. For example, Caterpillar, Coca-Cola, and Philip Morris do not think their competencies lie in the clothing business, so they have licensed their logos to other companies to put them on clothing.[27] In addition, companies may be able to pool their competencies through collaboration so that they realize greater gains than they could realize by acting alone.[28] However, a collaborative arrangement has a limited time frame, which may allow a company to exploit a particular product, asset, or technology itself at a later date if its core competencies change.

Avoid or Counter Competition   Sometimes markets are not large enough to hold many competitors. Companies may then band together so as not to compete. For example, approximately 30 communications carriers including GTE, MCI, AT&T, and Cable and Wireless have teamed to form New World, a broadband fiber-optic network connecting the United States with Latin America and the Caribbean.[29] Companies may also combine resources to fight a leader in the market. Recall in the opening case that Cisco joined six other companies to counter IBM's leadership. Another example is Coca-Cola's and Danone's formation of a joint venture for marketing bottled water in the United States so that they would be large enough to challenge PepsiCo and Nestlé, the two companies with the largest market shares.[30] Or companies may simply collude to raise everyone's profits. Only a few countries, mainly the United States, Canada, and those within the European Union take substantial actions against the collusion of competitors.[31]

Secure Vertical and Horizontal Links   There are potential cost savings and supply assurances from vertical integration. However, companies may lack the competence or resources necessary to own and manage the full value chain of activities. For example, recall the LUKoil case in Chapter 6. LUKoil has abundant oil reserves but lacks final distribution skills so, in addition to making acquisitions abroad, it has established collaborative arrangements in countries that assure markets for its petroleum.

Horizontal links may provide finished products or components. For finished products, there may be economies of scope in distribution, such as by having a full line of products to sell, thereby increasing the sales per fixed cost of a visit to potential customers. For example, Duracell, the biggest maker of consumer batteries, and Gillette, the biggest maker of razor blades, combine their sales forces in many parts of the world to gain economies of scope.[32]

One of the fastest growth areas for collaborative arrangements has been in industries with projects too large for any single company to handle—for example, new aircraft and communications systems. From such an arrangement's inception, different companies (sometimes from different countries) agree to take on the high cost and high risk of developmental work for different components needed in the final product. Then a lead company buys the components from the companies that did parts of the developmental work.

Gain Knowledge   Many companies, if they are open to new ideas and have the capacity to implement innovations, pursue collaborative arrangements to learn about a partner's technology, operating methods, or home market so that their own competencies will broaden or deepen, making them more competitive in the future.[33] For example, Chinese governmental authorities allow foreign companies to tap the Chinese market in exchange for their transference of technology. Sometimes each partner can learn from the other, a motive driving joint ventures between U.S. and European wine makers, such as the Opus One Winery owned by Constellation Brands' Robert Mondavi from the United States and Baron Philippe de Rothschild from France.[34]

International Motives for Collaborative Arrangements

In this section, we'll continue discussing the reasons why companies enter into collaborative arrangements, covering those reasons that apply only to international operations. Specifically, these reasons are to gain location-specific assets, overcome legal constraints, diversify geographically, and minimize exposure in risky environments.

Gain Location-Specific Assets   Cultural, political, competitive, and economic differences among countries create barriers for companies that want to operate abroad. When they feel ill-equipped to handle these differences, they may seek collaboration with local companies who will help manage local operations. For example, Wal-Mart first tried to enter the Japanese market on its own, but gave up after having disappointing sales. It has since returned with a Japanese partner, Seiyu, who is more familiar with Japanese tastes and rules for opening new stores.[35] In fact, most foreign companies in Japan need to collaborate with Japanese companies who can help in securing distribution and a competent workforce—two assets that are difficult for foreign companies to gain on their own there. This has been especially true in pharmaceuticals. The top 10 Western pharmaceutical companies have about 45 percent of the global drugs market, but only about a quarter of the Japanese market.[36] Access to distribution was the primary reason that Merck entered a joint venture with Chugai in Japan for the development and marketing of over-the-counter drugs.[37]

Overcome Governmental Constraints   Many countries limit foreign ownership. For example, the United States limits foreign ownership in airlines serving the domestic market and in sensitive defense manufacturers. Mexico limits ownership in the oil industry. China

Legal factors may be

- Direct prohibitions against certain operating forms
- Indirect (for example, regulations affecting profitability)

and India are particularly restrictive, often requiring foreign companies either to share ownership or make numerous concessions to help them meet their economic and sovereignty goals. Thus, companies may have to collaborate if they are to serve certain foreign markets.

Government procurement, particularly military procurement, is another area that may force companies to collaborate. In effect, governments may give preference to bids that include national companies. For example, Northrop Grumman from the United States teamed with Rolls-Royce in the United Kingdom to supply marine engines for both the British and U.S. navies.[38]

Collaboration hinders
nonassociated companies
from pirating the asset.

Collaboration can be a means of protecting an asset. Many countries provide little de facto protection for intellectual property rights such as trademarks, patents, and copyrights unless authorities are prodded consistently. To prevent pirating of these proprietary assets, companies sometimes have made collaborative agreements with local companies, which then monitor that no one else uses the asset locally. Also, some countries provide protection only if the internationally registered asset is exploited locally within a specified period. If a company does not use the asset within the country during that specified period, then whatever entity first does so gains the right to it. For example, Burger King did not use its name in time within the Australian market. Another company now uses it there, and Burger King sells its fare within Hungry Jack restaurants.[39]

Collaborative arrangements
allow for greater spreading
of assets among countries.

Diversify Geographically   By operating in a variety of countries (geographic diversification), a company can smooth its sales and earnings because business cycles occur at different times within the different countries. Collaborative arrangements offer a faster initial means of entering multiple markets. Moreover, if product conditions favor a diversification rather than a concentration strategy (recall the discussion in Chapter 12), there are more compelling reasons to establish foreign collaborative arrangements. However, these arrangements will be less appealing for companies whose activities are already widely extended or those that have ample resources for such extension.

The higher the risk managers
perceive in a foreign market,
the greater their desire to form
collaborative arrangements in
that market.

Minimize Exposure in Risky Environments   Companies worry that political or economic changes will affect the safety of assets and their earnings in their foreign operations. One way to minimize loss from foreign political occurrences is to minimize the base of assets located abroad—or share them. A government may be less willing to move against a shared operation for fear of encountering opposition from more than one company, especially if they are from different countries and can potentially elicit support from their home governments. Another way to spread risk is to place operations in a number of different countries. This strategy reduces the chance that all foreign assets will encounter adversity at the same time.

TYPES OF COLLABORATIVE ARRANGEMENTS

The forms of foreign operations differ in the amount of resources a company commits to foreign operations and the proportion of the resources located at home rather than abroad. Licensing, for example, may result in a lower additional capital commitment than a foreign joint venture will.

Throughout this discussion, keep in mind that there are trade-offs. For example, a decision to take no ownership in foreign production, such as through licensing to a foreign company, may reduce exposure to political risk. However, learning about that environment will be slow, delaying (perhaps permanently) your reaping the full profits from producing and selling your product abroad.

Companies have a wider
choice of operating form when
there is less likelihood of
competition.

Keep in mind also that when a company has a desired, unique, difficult-to-duplicate resource, it is in a good position to choose the operating form it would most like to use. The preferred form may be exporting, selling from a wholly owned direct investment, or participating in a collaborative arrangement. However, when it lacks this bargaining strength, it faces the possibility of competition. It may have to settle on a form that is lower on its priority list; otherwise, a competitor may preempt the market.

A further constraint facing managers is finding a desirable collaboration partner. For example, if the collaboration includes a transfer of technology, it may be impossible to find a local company familiar enough with the technology or having sufficiently similar values and priorities as the company transferring technology.[40] In effect, there are costs associated with transferring technology to another entity. Usually it is cheaper to transfer within the existing corporate family, such as from parent to subsidiary, than to transfer to another company. The cost difference is especially important when the technology is complex because a subsidiary's personnel are more likely to be familiar with approaches the parent uses.

Some Considerations in Collaborative Arrangements

We have just discussed reasons for companies' entering collaborative arrangements. Before explaining the types of arrangements, we shall discuss two variables that influence managers' choice of one type of arrangement over another: their desire for control over foreign operations and their companies' prior foreign expansion.

Control   The more a company depends on collaborative arrangements, the more likely it is to lose control over decisions, including those regarding quality, new product directions, and where to expand output. This is because each collaborative partner has a say in these decisions, and the global performance of each may be improved differently. External arrangements also imply the sharing of revenues, a serious consideration for undertakings with high potential profits because a company may want to keep them all for itself. Such arrangements also risk allowing information to pass more rapidly to potential competitors. The loss of control over flexibility, revenues, and competition is an important variable guiding a company's selection of forms of foreign operation. Thus, government regulations against FDI, especially with wholly owned operations, is controversial and the subject of the Point–Counterpoint discussion in this chapter.

> Internal handling of foreign operations usually means more control and no sharing of profits.

POINT–COUNTERPOINT: SHOULD COUNTRIES LIMIT FOREIGN CONTROL OF KEY INDUSTRIES?

POINT

I believe they should. A *key industry* is one that might affect a very large segment of the economy by virtue of its size or influence on other sectors. Thus, I'm talking neither about foreign control of small investments, nor about noncontrolling interest in large investments. However, even without taking a controlling interest, foreign companies can find many means of profiting from foreign operations through collaborative agreements. Likewise, these collaborative agreements can bring host countries the foreign resources they need, such as technology, capital, export markets, and branded products.

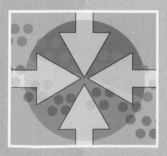

Of course, each country should determine for itself what a key industry is, and, in fact, each does. For example, Mexico limits foreign control in its oil industry because it is such a dominant part of the Mexican economy. The United States is primarily concerned about security, thus the president can halt any foreign investment that endangers national security. The United States also prohibits foreign control of television and radio stations because they could be used as instruments of foreign propaganda. It protects domestic transportation, so vital for national security, by prohibiting foreign control of domestic airlines and by preventing foreign airlines and ships from transporting passengers and cargo from one U.S. city to another.

In short, history shows that home governments have used powerful foreign companies to influence policies in the countries where they operate. During colonial periods, firms such as Levant and the British East India Company often acted as the political arm of their home governments. More recently, home governments, especially the United States, have pressured their companies to leave certain areas (e.g., Libya, Nicaragua), not to pay taxes to a regime (e.g., Angola, Panama), and not to permit their subsidiaries to do business with certain countries (e.g., Cuba, Vietnam), even though the countries where the subsidiaries were located had trading relations with those countries. At the same time, some companies are so powerful that they can influence their home country governments to intercede on their behalf. Probably the most notorious example was United Fruit Company (UFC) in so-called banana republics, which persuaded the U.S. government to overthrow governments to protect its investments. Miguel Angel Asturias, a Nobel laureate in literature, referred to UFC's head as the "Green Pope" [who] "lifts a finger and a ship starts or stops. He says a word and a republic is bought. He sneezes and a president . . . falls. . . . He rubs his behind on a chair and a revolution breaks out."[41]

Whenever a company is controlled from abroad, decisions about that company can be made abroad. Such control means that corporate management abroad can make decisions about personnel staffing, export prices, and the retention and payout of profits. These decisions might cause different rates of expansion in different countries and possible plant closings with subsequent employment disruption in some of them. Further, by withholding resources or allowing strikes, MNEs may affect other local industries adversely. In essence, the MNE looks after its global interests, which may not coincide with what is best for an operation in a given country.

COUNTERPOINT

Although people make passionate arguments against foreign control of key industries, they don't convince me that such control leads to differences in companies' decisions or that limits on foreign ownership are in the best interests of people in host countries.

Are important decisions actually made outside the host countries? If so, are these decisions different from those that would be made by local companies? Certainly, companies make strategic global decisions at headquarters, but typically they depend on a good deal of local advice before making those decisions.

Further, MNEs staff their foreign subsidiaries mainly with nationals of the countries where they operate, and these nationals make most routine decisions. Regardless of the decision makers or ownership of companies, managers make decisions based on what they think is best for their companies' business, rather than based on some local socioeconomic agenda. At the same time, their decisions have to adhere to local laws and consider the views of suppliers and customers. Of course, MNEs sometimes make locally unpopular decisions, but so do local companies. In the meantime, governments can and do enact laws that apply both to local and international companies, and these laws can assure that companies act in the so-called local interest.

Although preventing foreign control of key industries may be well intentioned, the resultant local control may lead to the protection of inefficient performance. For instance, Mexican protection of its petroleum industry has led to high prices and poor service. Further, the key industry argument appeals to emotions rather than reason. For instance the arguments in the United States for security make little sense on close examination. For instance, there were no laws against foreign ownership of security-sensitive industries until 1989, well after the threats from the Cold War had subsided. Although foreign propaganda through foreign ownership of radio and television stations is the rationale for ownership restrictions, there are no such restrictions on foreign ownership of U.S. newspapers. (Is this because people who read the news are presumed to be less swayed by propaganda?) In fact, Murdoch (Australian) and Thompson (Canadian) own many U.S. newspapers. The protection of U.S. domestic transportation for security reasons is a sham, just to protect the U.S. shipbuilding industry and U.S. maritime employees. For instance, U.S. merchant flagships must employ only U.S. citizens as crews because of the vulnerability of putting a bomb on a ship in U.S. waters, but foreign flag carriers regularly use U.S. ports and foreigners can join the U.S. Navy.

The banana republic arguments are outdated and go back to **dependencia theory,** which holds that emerging economies have practically no power in their dealings with MNEs. Although this theory was popular in the 1970s and 1980s, it is largely out of vogue today.[42] More recent **bargaining school theory** states that the terms for a foreign investor's operations depend on how much the investor and host country need the other's assets.[43] In effect, companies need countries because of their markets and resources. Countries need international companies because of their technology, capital, access to foreign markets, and expertise. Through a bargaining process, they come to an agreement or contract that stipulates what the MNE can and cannot do. Thus, this agreement limits the absolute power of the MNE, even if it has 100 percent ownership.

I completely disagree that either countries or companies can necessarily gain the same through collaborative agreements as through foreign direct investment. Although collaborative agreements are often preferable, we have discussed the advantages from a company's standpoint of having wholly owned foreign operations. With wholly owned operations, companies are, therefore, less concerned about developing competitors and are more willing to transfer essential and valuable technology abroad.

Prior Expansion of the Company   When a company already has operations (especially wholly owned ones) in place in a foreign country, some of the advantages of contracting with another company to handle production or sales are no longer as important. The company knows how to operate within the foreign country and may have excess capacity it can use for new production or sales. However, much depends on whether the existing foreign operation is in a line of business or performs a function that is closely related to the new product, service, or activity being initiated abroad. When there is similarity, as with production of a new type of office equipment when the company already produces office equipment, it is likely that the new production will be handled internally. In highly diversified companies or where operations are limited (such as when subsidiaries produce components only for the parent), the existing foreign facility may be handling goods or functions so dissimilar to what is being planned that it is easier to deal with an experienced external company.

Licensing

Under a licensing agreement, a company (the licensor) grants rights to intangible property to another company (the licensee) to use in a specified geographic area for a specified period. In exchange, the licensee ordinarily pays a royalty to the licensor. The rights may be for an *exclusive license* (the licensor can give rights to no other company for the specified geographic area for a specified period of time) or nonexclusive (it can give away rights). The U.S. Internal Revenue Service classifies intangible property into five categories.

> MNEs want returns from their intangible assets.

1. Patents, inventions, formulas, processes, designs, patterns
2. Copyrights for literary, musical, or artistic compositions
3. Trademarks, trade names, brand names
4. Franchises, licenses, contracts
5. Methods, programs, procedures, systems

> Licensing agreements may be
> - Exclusive or nonexclusive
> - Used for patents, copyrights, trademarks, and other intangible property

Usually, the licensor is obliged to furnish technical information and assistance, and the licensee is obliged to exploit the rights effectively and to pay compensation to the licensor.

Major Motives for Licensing   Frequently, a new product or process may affect only part of a company's total output and then only for a limited time. The sales volume may not be large enough to warrant establishing overseas manufacturing and sales facilities. A company that is already operating abroad may be able to produce and sell at a lower cost and with a shorter start-up time, thus preventing competitors from entering the market. For the licensor, there is less risk of operating facilities and holding inventories. The licensee may find that the cost of the arrangement is less than if it developed the new product or process on its own.

> Licensing often has an economic motive, such as the desire for faster start-up, lower costs, or access to additional resources.

For industries in which technological changes are frequent and affect many products, companies in various countries often exchange technology or other intangible property rather than compete with each other on every product in every market. Such an arrangement is known as *cross-licensing*. For example, Fujitsu from Japan, Saifun Semiconductors from Israel, and Advanced Micron Devices from the United States entered a technology-sharing, cross-licensing agreement for complementary nonvolatile memory technology.[44]

Payment   The amount and type of payment for licensing arrangements vary. Each contract tends to be negotiated on its own merits. For example, the value to the licensee will be greater if potential sales are high. Potential sales depend, in turn, on such factors as the geographic scope of the sales territory, the length of time the asset will have market value, and the market experience of using the asset elsewhere.

Some developing countries set price controls on what licensees can pay or insist that licensees be permitted to export licensed goods. Their reasoning is that selling only to the local market results in small-scale production that spreads fixed costs inadequately and raises consumer prices. Licensors have countered that if licensees export, they should pay higher royalties because the companies could not sell an exclusive license to parties in other countries. MNEs also have argued that the development of process technologies for small-scale production in countries with small markets is often too costly but is done when economically feasible.

Companies commonly negotiate a "front-end" payment to cover transfer costs when technology is involved. In addition, they usually charge fees based on actual or projected use, regardless of whether the transfer includes technology. Licensors of technology do this because it usually takes more than simply transferring *explicit* knowledge, such as through publications and reports. The move requires the transfer of *tacit* knowledge, such as through engineering, consultation, and adaptation. The licensee usually bears the transfer costs so that the licensor is motivated to assure a smooth adaptation. Of course, the license of some assets, such as copyrights, have much lower transfer costs.

Technology may be old or new, obsolete or still in use at home, when a company licenses it. Many companies transfer technology at an early or even a developmental stage so that products hit different markets simultaneously. This simultaneous market entry is important when selling to the same industrial customers in different countries and when global advertising campaigns can be effective. On the one hand, a licensee may be willing to pay more for a new technology because it may have a longer useful life. On the other hand, a licensee may be willing to pay less for a newer technology, particularly that in the development phase, because of its uncertain market value.

Sales to Controlled Entities   Although we think of licensing agreements as being collaborative arrangements among unassociated companies, most licenses are given to companies owned in whole or part by the licensor. A license may be necessary to transfer technology abroad because operations in a foreign country, even if 100 percent owned by the parent, usually are subsidiaries, which are separate companies from a legal standpoint. When a company owns less than 100 percent, a separate licensing arrangement may be a means of compensating the licensor for contributions beyond the mere investment in capital and managerial resources.

Franchising

Franchising includes providing an intangible asset (usually a trademark) and continually infusing necessary assets.

Franchising is a specialized form of licensing in which the franchisor not only sells an independent franchisee the use of the intangible property (usually a trademark) essential to the franchisee's business but also operationally assists the business on a continuing basis, such as through sales promotion and training. In many cases, the franchisor provides supplies. For example, Domino's Pizza grants to franchisees the goodwill of the Domino's name and support services to get started, such as store and equipment layout information and a manager-training program. As part of the continual relationship, it offers economies and standardization through central purchasing, such as centrally purchasing mozzarella cheese in New Zealand to use worldwide.[45] In a sense, a franchisor and a franchisee act almost like a vertically integrated company because the parties are interdependent and each produces part of the product or service that ultimately reaches the consumer.

Franchisors once depended on trade shows a few times a year and costly visits to foreign countries to promote their expansion. However, because of the Internet, they now receive e-mailed requests for information around the clock, seven days a week. Nevertheless, the acceptance of the franchising concept depends very much on the existence of high levels of income, education, mass media, and entrepreneurial spirit.[46]

Franchising is said to have originated when King John of England granted tax-collecting franchises. In the eighteenth century, German brewers franchised beer halls as distributors.[47] Today, franchising is most associated with the United States, although many international franchisors are from outside the United States. Franchising is most associated with fast food, but franchising exists in a huge array of businesses. A Danish company, Cryos International, even franchises sperm banks in about 40 countries and supplies the frozen sperm from donors in Denmark.[48] The fastest growth businesses of U.S. foreign franchising have been food and business services because the U.S. market for these businesses is fairly mature. U.S. companies can find more growth abroad than at home.

> Many types of products and many countries participate in franchising.

Organization of Franchising A franchisor may penetrate a foreign country by dealing directly with franchisees or by setting up a *master franchise* and giving that organization (usually a local one) the rights to open outlets on its own or develop subfranchisees in the country or region. In the latter case, subfranchisees pay royalties to the master franchisee, which then remits some predetermined percentage to the franchisor. McDonald's handles its Japanese operations this way. Companies are most apt to use a master franchise system when they are not confident about evaluating potential franchisees and when it would be expensive to oversee and control franchisees' operations directly.[49]

If the franchisor is not well known to many local people, it may find it difficult to convince them to make investments. People are usually willing to make investments in known franchises because the name is a guarantee of quality that can attract customers. It therefore is common for lesser-known franchisors to enter foreign markets with some company-owned outlets that serve as a showcase to attract franchisees.

Operational Modifications Securing good locations for franchises can be a major problem. Finding suppliers can add difficulties and expense. For example, McDonald's had to build a plant to make hamburger buns in the United Kingdom, and it had to help farmers develop potato production in Thailand.[50] Another concern for foreign franchise expansion has been governmental or legal restrictions that make it difficult to gain satisfactory operating permission.

> Franchisors face a dilemma.
> - The more standardization, the less acceptance in the foreign country.
> - The more adjustment to the foreign country, the less the franchisor is needed.

Many franchise failures abroad result from the franchisor's not developing enough domestic penetration first. Franchisors need to develop sufficient cash and management depth before considering foreign expansion. However, even a franchisor that is well established domestically may have difficulty in attaining foreign penetration, as evidenced by problems of Burger King in the United Kingdom, Wendy's in Australia, and Long John Silver's in Japan. A dilemma for successful domestic franchisors is that their success comes from three factors: product and service standardization, high identification through promotion, and effective cost controls. When entering many foreign countries, franchisors may encounter difficulties in transferring these success factors. At the same time, the more adjustments made to the host country's different conditions, the less a franchisor has to offer a potential franchisee. U.S. food franchisors' success in Japan is mostly due to that country's enthusiastic assimilation of Western products. Even so, food franchisors have had to make adjustments there. Wendy's sells a teriyaki burger, and Little Caesars has asparagus, potatoes, squid, and seaweed as pizza toppings.[51] McDonald's changed the pronunciation of its name in Japan to "MaKudonaldo" and substituted *Donald* for *Ronald McDonald* because of pronunciation difficulties.[52]

Management Contracts

Management contracts are used primarily when the foreign company can manage better than the owners.

One of the most important assets a company may have at its disposal is management talent, which it can transfer internationally, primarily to its own foreign investments. Management contracts are means by which a company may transfer such talent—by using part of its management personnel to assist a foreign company for a specified period for a fee. The company may gain income with little capital outlay. Contracts usually cover three to five years, and fixed fees or fees based on volume rather than profits are most common.

An organization usually pursues international management contracts when it believes that a foreign company can manage its existing or new operation more efficiently than it can. For example, the British Airport Authority (BAA) has contracts to manage airports in Indianapolis (U.S.A.), Naples (Italy), and Melbourne (Australia) because it had developed successful airport management skills, and the Dutch Schipol Group operates airport facilities in Aruba, Stockholm (Sweden), and Brisbane (Australia).[53]

With management contracts, the host country gets the assistance it wants without foreign companies' control of the operations. In turn, the management company receives income without having to make a capital outlay. This pattern has been important in Middle East hotel operations where governments have highly restricted foreign ownership. However, the operating fees and contract terms have been declining for many of the international hotel operators because of the development of more local expertise and greater competition. This has led such companies as Six Continents, Le Meridien, and Hilton to seek more properties to manage in order to maintain former income levels.[54]

Turnkey Operations

Turnkey operations are

- Most commonly performed by construction companies
- Often performed for a governmental agency

Turnkey operations are a type of collaborative arrangement in which one company contracts with another to build complete, ready-to-operate facilities. Companies building turnkey operations are frequently industrial-equipment manufacturers and construction companies. They also may be consulting firms and manufacturers that decide an investment on their own behalf in the country is infeasible.

The Hong Kong International Airport was named the world's best airport for 2005 in a worldwide passenger survey. The airport was completed in 1998 through a $20 billion turnkey contract with U.S. engineering company Bechtel.

The customer for a turnkey operation is often a governmental agency. Recently, most large projects have been in those developing countries that are moving rapidly toward infrastructure development and industrialization.

One characteristic that sets the turnkey business apart from most other international business operations is the size of the contracts. Most contracts are for hundreds of millions of dollars, and many are for billions, which means that only a few very large companies—such as Bechtel, Fluor, and Kellogg Rust—account for most of the international market. For example, Bechtel built a semiconductor plant for Motorola in China and a pipeline for BP in Algeria.[55] Smaller firms often serve as subcontractors for primary turnkey suppliers. However, large companies are vulnerable to economic downturns when governments cancel big contracts.

The nature of these contracts places importance on hiring executives with top-level contacts abroad, as well as on ceremony and building goodwill, such as opening a facility on a country's independence day or getting a head of state to inaugurate a facility. For example, the Swedish-Swiss company ABB and Brazil's Companhia Brasileira de Projectos e Obras formed a joint venture to construct a turnkey dam for the government of Malaysia. They timed the signing of the contract so that the Malaysian premier could be present for the ceremony.[56] Although public relations is important to gaining turnkey contracts, other factors—such as price, export financing, managerial and technological quality, experience, and reputation—are necessary to sell contracts of such magnitude.

Payment for a turnkey operation usually occurs in stages as a project develops. Commonly, 10 to 25 percent comprises the down payment, with another 50 to 65 percent paid as the contract progresses, and the remainder paid once the facility is operating in accordance with the contract. Because of the long time frame between conception and completion, the company performing turnkey operations can encounter currency fluctuations and should cover itself through escalation clauses or cost-plus contracts. Because the final payment is usually made only if the facility is operating satisfactorily, it is important to specify in a contract what constitutes "satisfactorily." For this reason, many companies insist on performing a feasibility study as part of the turnkey contract so they don't build something that, although desired by a local government, may be too large or inefficient. Inefficiency could create legal problems, such as determining who caused it, that hold up final payment.

Many turnkey contracts are for construction in remote areas, necessitating massive housing construction and importation of personnel. Projects may involve building an entire infrastructure under the most adverse conditions, such as Bechtel's complex for Minera Escondida, which is high in the Andes. So turnkey operators must have expertise in hiring workers willing to work in remote areas for extended periods, and in transporting and using supplies under very adverse conditions. One such area with adverse conditions has been Iraq, where large turnkey operations are being used for reconstruction.[57]

If a company holds a monopoly on certain assets or resources, such as the latest refining technology, other companies will find it difficult to compete to secure a turnkey contract. As the production process becomes known, however, the number of competitors for such contracts increases. Companies from industrial countries have moved largely toward projects involving high technology, while companies from such countries as China, India, Korea, and Turkey can compete better for conventional projects for which low labor costs are important. For example, the Chinese companies China State Construction Engineering and Shanghai Construction Group have worked on a subway system in Iran, a railway line in Nigeria, an oil pipeline in Sudan, and office buildings in the United States.[58]

Joint Ventures

A type of ownership sharing popular among international companies is the joint venture, in which more than one organization owns a company. Recall from the opening case that Cisco participates in numerous joint ventures. Although companies usually form a joint

Joint ventures may have various combinations of ownership.

venture to achieve particular objectives, it may continue to operate indefinitely as the objective is redefined. Joint ventures are sometimes thought of as 50/50 companies, but often more than two organizations participate in the ownership. Further, one organization frequently controls more than 50 percent of the venture. The type of legal organization may be a partnership, a corporation, or some other form permitted in the country of operation. When more than two organizations participate, the joint venture is sometimes called a **consortium.**

Almost every conceivable combination of partners may exist in an international joint venture as long as at least one of the partners is foreign. These include:

- Two companies from the same country joining together in a foreign market, such as NEC and Mitsubishi (Japan) in the United Kingdom
- A foreign company joining with a local company, such as Great Lakes Chemical (U.S.) and A. H. Al Zamil in Saudi Arabia
- Companies from two or more countries establishing a joint venture in a third country, such as that of Diamond Shamrock (U.S.) and Sol Petroleo (Argentina) in Bolivia
- A private company and a local government forming a joint venture (sometimes called a mixed venture), such as that of Philips (Dutch) with the Indonesian government
- A private company joining a government-owned company in a third country, such as BP Amoco (private British-U.S.) and Eni (government-owned Italian) in Egypt

The more companies in the joint venture, the more complex the management of the arrangement will be. For example, when the Australian government privatized Hazelwood Power Station, a British company (National Power), an Australian company (the Commonwealth Bank Group), and two U.S. companies (PacifiCorp and Destec Energy) bought the electric utility company. This involved four companies in the decision making.[59] Figure 14.5 shows that as a company increases the number of partners and decreases the amount of equity it owns in a foreign operation, its ability to control that operation decreases.

Certain types of companies favor joint ventures more than others do. Companies that like joint ventures are usually new at foreign operations or have decentralized domestic decision making. Because these companies are used to extending control downward in their organizations, it is easier for them to do the same thing internationally.

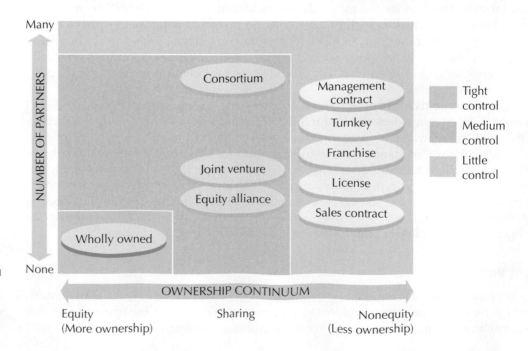

FIGURE 14.5

CONTROL COMPLEXITY RELATED TO COLLABORATIVE STRATEGY

The more equity and the fewer partners, the more easily a company can usually control its foreign operations. Note that the nonequity arrangements may take one or many partners.

Source: The figure was adapted from *European Management Journal* 12, no. 1, Shaker Zahra and Galal Elhagrasey, "Strategic Management of International Joint Ventures," March 1994, pp. 83–93. Reprinted with permission of Elsevier.

Equity Alliances

An **equity alliance** is a collaborative arrangement in which at least one of the collaborating companies takes an ownership position (almost always minority) in the other(s). In some cases, each party takes an ownership, such as by buying part of each other's shares or by swapping some shares with each other. For instance Panama-based Copa and Colombia-based AeroRepublic took equity in each other.[60] The purpose of the equity ownership is to solidify a collaborating contract, such as a supplier-buyer contract, so that it is more difficult to break—particularly if the ownership is large enough to secure a board membership for the investing company. The airline industry epitomizes the use of equity alliances. We will discuss the airline industry in the ending case of this chapter.

Equity alliances help solidify collaboration.

PROBLEMS OF COLLABORATIVE ARRANGEMENTS

Although collaborative arrangements have many advantages, some companies avoid them. Many arrangements develop problems that lead partners to renegotiate their relationships. Partners might renegotiate responsibilities, ownership, or management structure. In spite of new relationships, many agreements break down or are not renewed at the end of an initial contract period. For example, in the case of joint ventures, about half break up because one or all partners become dissatisfied with the venture. Often, one partner buys out the other's interest so that the operation continues as a wholly owned foreign subsidiary. In other breakups, companies agree to dissolve the arrangement or they restructure their alliance.

Figure 14.6 shows that joint venture divorce (and divorce from other collaborative arrangements) can be planned or unplanned, friendly or unfriendly, mutual or nonmutual. The major strains on collaborative arrangements are due to five factors: the importance to the partners, differing objectives, control problems, comparative contributions and appropriations, and differences in culture.[61] In spite of our focus on these problems, we do not mean to imply that there are no success stories. There are. For example, the joint venture between Xerox (U.S.) and Rank (U.K.) has performed well for a long period of time, and it even has a joint venture itself in Japan with Fuji Photo, which has also performed well.

About half of joint ventures break down, primarily because partners
- *View the joint ventures' importance differently*
- *Have different objectives for the joint ventures*
- *Disagree on control issues or fail to provide sufficient direction*
- *Perceive they contribute more than their counterparts do*
- *Have incompatible operating cultures*

FIGURE 14.6 ALTERNATIVE DISSOLUTION OF JOINT VENTURES

There is considerable variation in both the way that joint ventures dissolve and the outcome of the operation after the dissolution. Any of the scenarios might have any of the outcomes.

Source: Adapted from Manuel G. Serapio, Jr. and Wayne F. Cascio, "End Games in International Alliances." *Academy of Management Executive* (May 1996): 67.

DIVORCE SCENARIOS	EXAMPLES	OUTCOMES	EXAMPLES
Planned vs.	General Motors (U.S.) and Toyota (Japan)	Termination by Acquisition	Daewoo Motors (South Korea) and General Motors (U.S.)
Unplanned	AT&T (U.S.) and Olivetti (Italy)	Termination by Dissolution	Meiji Milk (Japan) and Borden (U.S.)
Friendly vs.	Vitro (Mexico) and Corning (U.S.)	Termination by Reorganization/ Restructuring of the Alliance	Matsushita Electric Industries Co. (Japan) and Solbourne Computer (U.S.)
Unfriendly	Coors Brewing Co. (U.S.) and Molson Breweries (Canada)		
Both agree vs.	Ralston Purina (U.S.) and Taiyo Fishery (Japan)		
One Partner Refuses to Agree	Sover S.P.A. (Italy) and Suzhou Spectacles No. 1 Factory (China)		

Collaboration's Importance to Partners

One partner may give more management attention to a collaborative arrangement than the other does. If things go wrong, the active partner blames the less active partner for its lack of attention, and the less active partner blames the more active partner for making poor decisions. The difference in attention may be due to the different sizes of partners. For example, if the joint venture is between a large and a small company, the venture comprises a larger portion of operations for the small company than for the large one, so the small company may take more interest in the venture. Further, if there are disagreements that necessitate legal action for settlement, the smaller firm may be disadvantaged because it lacks the resources to fight the larger company. For example, Igen, a small U.S. firm, licensed its technology to Boehringer Mannheim of Germany, a company whose sales are more than a hundred times those of Igen. When the two companies disagreed over royalty payments, Igen fought four years and spent $40 million in legal fees (about one year's sales amount) to win a settlement of over a half billion dollars.[62] However, this example is unusual because most small companies cannot or will not fight a larger company so effectively.

Differing Objectives

Although companies enter into collaborative arrangements because they have complementary capabilities, their objectives may evolve differently over time. For instance, one partner may want to reinvest earnings for growth and the other may want to receive dividends. One partner may want to expand the product line and sales territory, and the other may see this as competition with its wholly owned operations. A partner may wish to sell or buy from the venture, and the other partner may disagree with the prices. Or there may be different views about performance standards. For example, GM has a joint venture in Thailand with Fuji Heavy Industries to make and export vehicles to Opel in Germany and Subaru in Japan. Because of disagreements over quality, both companies perform inspections, which is time-consuming and expensive. They have even argued over standards for paint jobs.[63]

Control Problems

By sharing the assets with another company, one company may lose some control on the extent or quality of the assets' use. For example, the Israeli company, Remedia, partly owned by the U.S. company, H.J. Heinz, partnered with the German company, Humana Milchunion, to make baby formula. Humana Milchunion removed vitamin B_1 from the concentrate for the formula without notifying its partners. Thus the partners did not add the vitamin, thus causing the death of three infants.[64]

Some companies have well-known trademarked names that they license abroad for the production of some products that they have never produced or had expertise with. For example, Pierre Cardin has licensed its label to hundreds of licensees in scores of countries. These licensees put the label on hundreds of products, from clothing to sheets and clocks to deodorants. Monitoring and maintaining control of so much diversity was so difficult that bad-quality Pierre Cardin–labeled products hurt the image of high-quality Pierre Cardin-labeled products. Pierre Cardin had to restructure its agreements and advertise heavily to reestablish the cachet of its name.[65] In today's world, problems in one country are quickly communicated to consumers in other countries.

In collaborative arrangements, even though control is ceded to one of the partners, both may be held responsible for problems. For example, in KFC's joint venture in China, the financial reporting to Chinese authorities was the Chinese partner's responsibility. However, China held both partners liable for tax evasion as a result of underreporting income.[66] Moreover, in joint ventures and management contracts, there are gray areas as to who controls employees. Further, employees may have anxieties about who is in charge. For example, in a proposed joint venture between Merrill Lynch, from the United States, and UFJ, from Japan, a Japanese senior manager queried, "Who is going to be in charge—a Japanese or an American, or both?"[67]

When no single company has control of a collaborative arrangement, the operation may lack direction. At the same time, if one partner dominates, it must still consider the other company's interests.

Partners' Contributions and Appropriations

One partner's capability of contributing technology, capital, or some other asset may diminish compared to its partner's capability over time. For example, in P&G's joint venture with Phuong Dong Soap & Detergent in Vietnam, P&G wanted to expand, but Phuong had neither the funds to expand nor the willingness to allow P&G to gain a larger ownership.[68] The weak link may cause a drag on the collaborative arrangement, resulting in dissension between the partners. Further, one partner may be suspicious that the other is taking more from the operation (particularly knowledge-based assets) than it is. In almost all collaborative arrangements, there is a danger that one partner will use the other partner's contributed assets, enabling it to become a competitor. (Probably the only exception would be turnkey projects to build infrastructure.) In fact, there are many examples of companies "going it alone" after they no longer needed their partner, particularly if the purpose of the collaboration is to gain knowledge. It is difficult for companies that compete head-on within their core businesses in some markets to cooperate fully for the same core business in another market. In the case of joint ventures, both are apt to see substantial gains when each partner offers market expansion and technology to the other.

Differences in Culture

Companies differ by nationality in how they evaluate the success of their operations. For example, U.S. companies tend to evaluate performance on the basis of profit, market share, and specific financial benefits. Japanese companies tend to evaluate primarily on how an operation helps build its strategic position, particularly by improving its skills. European companies rely more on a balance between profitability and achieving social objectives.[69] These differences can mean that one partner is satisfied while the other is not. Anheuser-Busch attributed its joint venture breakup with Modelo (Mexican) to the fact that Modelo was run like a family business and was reluctant to share control.[70] Moreover, some companies don't like to collaborate with companies of very different cultures. In spite of these potential problems, joint ventures from culturally distant countries survive at least as well as those between partners from similar cultures.[71]

In addition to national culture, differences in corporate cultures may also create problems within joint ventures. For example, one company may be accustomed to promoting managers from within the organization, while the other opens its searches to outsiders. One may use a participatory management style, and the other an authoritarian style. One may be entrepreneurial and the other risk averse. For this reason many companies will develop joint ventures only after they have had long-term positive experiences with the other company through distributorship, licensing, or other contractual arrangements. However, as is the case with marriage, a positive prior relationship between two companies does not guarantee that partners will be well-matched in a joint venture.[72] Compatibility of corporate cultures also is important in cementing relationships.

MANAGING FOREIGN ARRANGEMENTS

If collaboration can better achieve the company's strategic objectives than "going it alone" can, the company should give little consideration to taking on duties itself. However, as the arrangement evolves, partners will need to reassess certain decisions. For example, a company's resource base may change compared to that of other companies, making collaboration either more or less advantageous. Further, the external environment changes. Perhaps a certain location becomes economically risky, or its host government forbids foreign ownership in areas where the arrangement would like to do future business. Because of these changes, a company needs continually to reexamine the fit between collaboration and its strategy. Thus, a company likely uses various modes of operations simultaneously because of its own capabilities, the specific products involved, and the characteristics of each foreign market. We shall now discuss how companies change their operating forms, how they may find and negotiate with potential partners, and how they need to assess performance of collaborative arrangements.

Dynamics of Collaborative Arrangements

The evolution to a different operating mode may
- Be the result of experience
- Necessitate costly termination fees
- Create organizational tensions

In Chapter 12, we discussed how companies typically move from external to internal handling of foreign operations and how they deepen their mode of commitment over time as they gain more experience. However, the cost of switching from one form to another—for example, from licensing to wholly owned facilities—may be very high because of having to gain expertise from and possibly pay termination fees to another company.

Collaboration with a local company provides the opportunity to learn from the local partner, enabling the company confidently to make a deeper commitment. At the same time, the learning in one market may enable a company to enter another market at a higher level of commitment.

Thus, companies' capabilities relative to specific locations, which may change over time, should influence the form of operations undertaken. These capabilities may increase or decrease. Figure 14.7 illustrates a type of matrix that relates country attractiveness with operating forms. The company should take a higher level of commitment, such as wholly owned operations, in the countries that appear in the top left

FIGURE 14.7   COUNTRY ATTRACTIVENESS–COMPANY STRENGTH MATRIX

Countries that would appear closest to the top left-hand corner of the matrix are the most desirable for operations. Ordinarily, these are the countries for which wholly owned operations are most desirable. Those in the top right-hand corner usually require collaboration of companies with complementary resources. For those in the bottom right-hand corner, companies may gain some return through nonequity arrangements. Because capabilities and country attractiveness can change, companies' modes of operation may need to be dynamic.

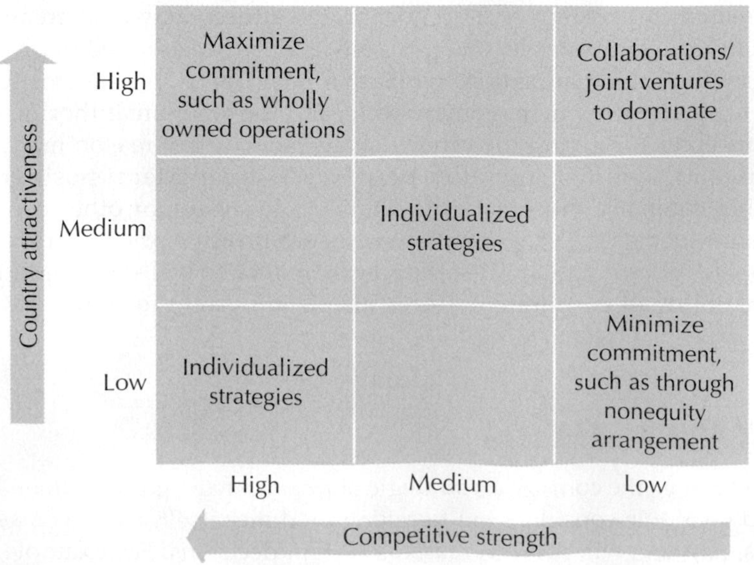

Country attractiveness	High	Maximize commitment, such as wholly owned operations		Collaborations/ joint ventures to dominate
	Medium		Individualized strategies	
	Low	Individualized strategies		Minimize commitment, such as through nonequity arrangement
		High	Medium	Low
		Competitive strength		

corner of the matrix because those countries are not only very attractive, they fit with the companies' capabilities. In the top right corner, the country attractiveness is also high, but the company has a weak competitive strength for those markets, perhaps because it lacks knowledge of how to operate therein. If the cost is not too high, the company might attempt to gain greater domination in those markets by partnering with another company whose assets are complementary. A company might divest in countries in the bottom right corner or "harvest" by pulling out all possible cash it could generate while at the same time not replacing depreciated facilities. It could also engage in nonequity arrangements, thereby generating some income without the need to make investment outlays. In other areas, the company must analyze situations individually in order to decide which approach to take. These are marginal areas that require specific judgment.

Although this type of matrix may serve to guide decision making, managers must use it with caution. First, it is often difficult to separate the attractiveness of a country from a company's position. In other words, the country may seem attractive because of the company's fit with it. Second, some of the recommended actions take a defeatist attitude to a company's competitive position. There are simply many examples of companies that built competitive strength in markets that competitors had previously dominated or that built profitable positions without being the competitive leader.

Tension may develop internally as a company's international operations change and grow because individuals may gain or lose responsibilities as control locations change. For example, moving from exporting to foreign production may reduce the size of a domestic product division. Various profit centers all may perceive they have rights to the sales in a country the company is about to penetrate. Legal, technical, and marketing personnel may have entirely different perspectives on contracts. Under these circumstances, a team approach to evaluating decisions and performance may work. A company also must develop means of evaluating performance by separating those things that are controllable and noncontrollable by personnel in different profit centers.

At the same time, there is evidence that as companies enter more collaborative arrangements, they get better performance from them.[73] However, better performance is most associated with the use of similar types of collaborations from one place to another.[74] In essence, they may choose partners better and learn how to get better synergies between their partners and their own operations.

Finding Compatible Partners

A company can seek out a partner for its foreign operations or it can react to a proposal from another company to collaborate with it. In either case, it is necessary to evaluate the potential partner not only for the resources it can supply but also for its motivation and willingness to cooperate. A company can identify potential partners by monitoring journals, attending technical conferences, and developing links with academic institutions. It can also find partners by participating in social activities. After a company makes contact and builds rapport with managers of one local firm, those managers may offer introductions to managers in other firms.[75] A company can increase its own visibility by participating in trade fairs, distributing brochures, and nurturing contacts in the locale of potential collaboration—increasing the probability that it will be considered a partner by other companies. The proven ability to handle similar types of collaboration is a key professional qualification. For example, Cisco's track record in collaborations has undoubtedly influenced other companies to consider Cisco as a partner. Because of a good track record, a partner may be able to depend more on trust rather than expensive control mechanisms to ensure that its interests will not be usurped. Once into a collaboration, partners may also be able to build partner trust through their actions in the collaborative arrangement.[76] But every company has to start somewhere. Without a proven track record, a company may have to negotiate harder with and make more concessions to a partner.

In technology agreements

• Seller does not want to give information without assurance of payment
• Buyer does not want to pay without evaluating information

Negotiating Process

The value of many technologies would diminish if they were widely used or understood. Contracts historically have included provisions that the recipient will not divulge this information. In addition, some sellers have held onto the ownership and production of specific components so that recipients will not have the full knowledge of the product or the capability to produce an exact copy of it. Many times, a company wants to sell techniques it has not yet used commercially. A buyer is reluctant to buy what it has not seen, but a seller that shows the process to the potential buyer risks divulging the process technology. It has become common to set up preagreements that protect all parties.

Another controversial area of negotiation is the secrecy surrounding arrangements' financial terms. In some countries, for example, governmental agencies must approve licensing contracts. Sometimes these authorities consult their counterparts in other countries regarding similar agreements to improve their negotiating position with MNEs. Many MNEs object to this procedure because they believe that contract terms between two companies are proprietary information with competitive importance and that market conditions usually dictate the need for very different terms in different countries.

Contractual Provisions

By transferring assets to a joint venture or intangible property rights to another company in a licensing agreement, a company undoubtedly loses some control over the asset or intangible property. A host of potential problems attend this lack of control and should be settled in the original agreement. At the same time, you need to develop sufficient rapport with partners so that common sense, rather than the contract, is used to run the collaboration.[77] Although it is impossible to anticipate all points of future disagreement and include coverage of them in a contract, provisions should outline

• Terminating the agreement if the parties do not adhere to the directives
• Methods of testing for quality
• Geographical limitations on the asset's use
• Which company will manage which parts of the operation outlined to the agreement
• What each company's future commitments will be
• How each company will buy from, sell to, or use intangible assets that come from the collaborative arrangement

Contracts should be spelled out in detail, but if courts must rule on disagreements both parties are apt to lose something in the settlement. Contract termination and formal settlement of disputes are costly and cumbersome. If possible, it is much better for parties to settle disagreements on a personal basis. The ability to develop a rapport with the management of another company is an important consideration in choosing a partner.

Performance Assessment

When collaborating with another company, managers must

• Continue to monitor performance
• Assess whether to take over operations

Management also should estimate potential sales, determine whether the arrangement is meeting quality standards, and assess servicing requirements to check whether the other company is doing an adequate job. Mutual goals should be set so that both parties understand what is expected, and the expectations should be spelled out in the contract.

In addition to the continual assessment of the partner's performance in collaborative arrangements, a company also needs to assess periodically whether the type of collaboration should change. For example, a joint venture may replace a licensing agreement. In some cases, even though a partner is doing what is expected, a company may assess that collaboration is no longer in its best interest. For instance, the company may decide that it wants a wholly owned FDI so that it has greater freedom.

LOOKING TO THE FUTURE: Why Innovation Breeds Collaboration

A half century ago, John Kenneth Galbraith wrote that the era of cheap invention was over and, "because development is costly, it follows that it can be carried out only by a firm that has the resources associated with considerable size."[78] The statement seems prophetic in terms of the estimated billions of investment dollars needed to bring a new commercial aircraft to market, eliminate death from diseases, develop defenses against unfriendly countries and terrorists, guard against cyberspace intrusions, and commercialize energy substitutes for petroleum. Moreover, markets must be truly global if high development costs are to be recouped. The sums companies need for developing and marketing these new inventions are out of reach of most companies acting alone. Of course, companies might become ever larger through internal growth or through mergers and acquisition. Although we have seen some examples of such growth, governments have nevertheless placed limits because of antitrust concern. Further, companies realize the cost of integrating a merged or acquired company can be very high. Therefore, collaborative arrangements will likely become even more important in the future. They are likely to involve both horizontal and vertical linkages among companies from many industries in many countries. However, there is evidence that collaborative arrangements slow the speed of innovation.[79] Thus, large companies that have resources to go it alone may have advantages over small companies that do not.

Although some product developments require huge sums, most are much more modest. Nevertheless, companies lack all the product- and market-specific resources to go it alone everywhere in the world, especially if national differences dictate operating changes on a country-to-country basis. These situations present opportunities for alliances that employ complementary resources from different companies.

Collaborative arrangements will bring both opportunities and problems as companies move simultaneously to new countries and to contractual arrangements with new companies. For example, collaborations must overcome differences in a number of areas:

- Country cultures that may cause partners to obtain and evaluate information differently
- National differences in governmental policies, institutions, and industry structures that constrain companies from operating as they would prefer
- Corporate cultures that influence ideologies and values underlying company practices that strain relationships among companies
- Different strategic directions resulting from partners' interests that cause companies to disagree on objectives and contributions
- Different management styles and organizational structures that cause partners to interact ineffectively[80]

The more partners there are in an alliance, the more strained the decision-making and control processes will be.

SUMMARY

- Selling abroad by exporting home country production may not be advantageous because of lower production costs abroad, high transport costs, the need to alter products substantially, protectionist barriers, lack of domestic capacity, and consumer preferences to buy from specific countries.

- Companies often prefer to operate with foreign direct investment, especially wholly owned, because such operations may lower their costs, lessen the possibility of developing competitors, and free them to follow global strategies.

- Some advantages of collaborative arrangements, whether a company is operating domestically or internationally, are to spread and reduce costs, allow a company to specialize in its primary competencies, avoid certain competition, secure vertical and horizontal links, and learn from other companies.

- Some motivations for collaborative arrangements that are specific to international operations are to gain location-specific assets, overcome legal constraints, diversify among countries, and minimize exposure in risky environments.

Analysts conclude that the problems of combining unions after PanAm's acquisition of National was a major contribution to PanAm's eventual demise.

Other things simply may not mesh well in alliances. In the now defunct USAirways–British Airways agreement, British Airways was strong in connections from London to Europe and Asia. But USAirways's strength was at New York's LaGuardia Airport, which is purely domestic—most connecting passengers had to change airports. When Northwest and KLM allied, it was expected that KLM would help Northwest improve its service; however, the organizations could not work well in that effort because of entrenched Northwest employees who would not cooperate.

QUESTIONS

1. Discuss a question raised by the manager of route strategy of American Airlines: Why should an airline not be able to establish service anywhere in the world simply by demonstrating that it can and will comply with the local labor and business laws of the host country?

2. The president of Japan Air Lines has claimed that U.S. airlines are dumping air services on routes between the United States and Europe, meaning they are selling below their costs because of the money they are losing. Should governments set prices so that carriers make money on routes?

3. What will be the consequences if a few large airlines or networks come to dominate global air service?

4. Some airlines, such as Southwest and Alaska Air, have survived as niche players without going international or developing alliances with international airlines. Can they continue this strategy?

CHAPTER NOTES

1 Data for the case were drawn from company information retrieved from www.cisco.com; http://newsroom.cisco.com/dlls/partners/success_stories/index.html; http://www.cisco.com/public/countries_languages.shtml; http://www.cisco.com/warp/public/756/partnership/; Cisco Systems, *Annual Report 2004*; Tim McCollum, "Foreign Affairs," *The Industry Standard* (August 2, 2000); Edward B. Roberts and Wenyun Kathy Liu, "Ally or Acquire? How Technology Leaders Decide," *MIT Sloan Management Review* 43, no. 1 (Fall 2001): 26; Nikhil Hutheesing, "Marital Blisters," *Forbes* (May 21, 2001): 30; Danny Ertel, "Alliance Management: A Blueprint for Success," *Financial Executive* 17, no. 9 (Dec. 2001): 36–41; Debra Rankin and Michael Parent, "Cisco Systems Inc.," *Ivey Business Journal* 65, no. 3 (Jan. 2001): 55; David Ticoll, "Learning from Cisco," *Tele.com* (April 17, 2000): 62; "Cisco to Invest $10mn to Set Up 34 Academies," *The Times of India* (January 16, 2001); and "First Speaker-Cum-MP3 Player," *The Business Times Singapore* (September 2, 2002), section ITSHELF; "Cisco Systems KK, IBM Japan Team Up," *AFX News Limited* (September 23, 2004); and Simon London, "EDS Chases IBM's Dominance in Computing," *Financial Times* (October 18, 2004): 23.

2 Hugh Pope, "Ford Forges Ahead with Turkey Plans," *Wall Street Journal* (July 24, 2000): A17+.

3 John Griffiths, "VW May Build Beetle in Europe to Meet Demand," *Financial Times* (November 11, 1998): 17.

4 Peter Marsh, "The World's Wash Day," *Financial Times* (April 29, 2002): 6.

5 "Skoda Brings New Luxury Car, Octavia," *The Statesman* (India) (November 17, 2001), FT Asia Africa Intelligence Wire.

6 Aluf Benn, "Why Peace Doesn't Pay," *Foreign Policy* 124 (May–June 2001): 64–65.

7 Jill Gabrielle Klein, "Us Versus Them, or Us Versus Everyone? Delineating Consumer Aversion to Foreign Goods," *Journal of International Business Studies* 33, no. 2 (Second Quarter, 2002): 345–63.

8 "Yes, You Can Help Our Balance of Payments," *The Daily Telegraph* (Sydney) (June 4, 2005): 5.

9 Lynda V. Mapes, "Food Fight Ensues over Labeling," *Seattle Times* (April 25, 2002): A1; and Ken Leiser, "Toyota's Inroads with State Bypass 'Buy American' Law," (March 6, 2002): A1.

10 John S. Hulland, "The Effects of Country-of-Brand and Brand Name on Product Evaluation and Consideration: A Cross-Country Comparison," *Consumer Behavior in Asia: Issues and Market Practice* (1999): 23–39.

11 Internalization theory, or holding a monopoly control over certain information or other proprietary assets, builds on earlier market-imperfections work by Ronald H. Coase, "The Nature of the Firm," *Economica* 4, (1937): 386–405. It has been noted by such writers as M. Casson, "The Theory of Foreign Direct Investment," Discussion Paper No. 50 (Reading, England: University of Reading International Investment and Business Studies, November 1980); Alan M. Rugman, *Inside the Multinationals: The Economics of Internal Markets*

(New York: Columbia University Press, 1981); David J. Teece, "Transactions Cost Economics and the Multinational Enterprise," Berkeley Business School International Business Working Paper Series, No. IB-3, 1985; B. Kogut and U. Zander, "Knowledge of the Firm and the Evolutionary Theory of the Multinational Corporation," *Journal of International Business Studies* 24, no. 4 (1993): 625–45; and Peter W. Liesch and Gary A. Knight, "Information Internalization and Hurdle Rates in Small and Medium Enterprise Internationalization," *Journal of International Business Studies* 30, no. 2 (Second Quarter 1999): 383–96.

12 Eric M. Johnson, "Harnessing the Power of Partnerships," *Financial Times* (October 8, 2004): Mastering Innovation, 4.

13 Paul Marer and Vincent Mabert, "GE Acquires and Restructures Tungsram: The First Six Years (1990–1995)," *OECD, Trends and Policies in Privatization* III, no. 1 (Paris: OECD, 1996), pp. 149–85 and their unpublished 1999 revision, "GE's Acquisition of Hungary's Tungsram."

14 Leslie Crawford, "Anheuser's Cross-Border Marriage on the Rocks," *Financial Times* (March 18, 1998): 16.

15 Gary Gentile, "Hair Products," *Miami Herald* (September 3, 2004): 4C.

16 Stephen Magee, "Information and the MNC: An Appropriability Theory of Direct Foreign Investment," in *The New International Economic Order*, Jagdish N. Bhagwati, ed. (Cambridge, Mass.: MIT Press, 1977), pp. 317–40; C.W. Hill, L. P. Hwang, and W. C. Kim, "An Eclectic Theory of the Choice on International Entry Mode," *Strategic Management Journal* 11 (1990): 117–8; and Ashish Arora and Andrea Fosfuri, "Wholly Owned Subsidiary Versus Technology Licensing in the Worldwide Chemical Industry," *Journal of International Business Studies* 31, no. 4 (Fourth Quarter 2000): 555–72.

17 Peter Wonacott, "Global Aims of China's Car Makers Put Existing Ties at Risk," *Wall Street Journal* (August 24, 2004): B1+; and Norihiko Shirouzu and Peter Wonacott, "People's Republic of Autos," *Wall Street Journal* (April 18, 2005): B1+.

18 Allan Afuah, "Strategies to Turn Adversity into Profits," *Sloan Management Review* 40, no. 2 (Winter 1999): 99–109.

19 Andrew Taylor, "Overseas Groups Get on the UK Utility Map," *Financial Times* (June 17, 2002): 4

20 Anne-Wil Harzing, "Acquisitions Versus Greenfield Investments: International Strategy and Management of Entry Modes," *Strategic Management Journal* 23, no. 3 (March 2002): 211–27.

21 Jaideep Anand and Andrew Delios, "Absolute and Relative Resources as Determinants of International Acquisitions," *Strategic Management Journal* 23, no. 2 (February 2002): 119–34.

22 One such indication is from a study by Alan Gregory, which is cited in Kate Burgess, "Acquisitions in US 'Disastrous' for British Companies," *Financial Times* (October 11, 2004): 18.

23 John Child, David Faulkner, and Robert Pitethly, *The Management of International Acquisitions* (Oxford: Oxford University Press, 2001); and Peter Martin, "A Clash of Corporate Cultures," *Financial Times* (June 2–3, 2001): weekend section, p. xxiv.

24 Pierre Dussauge, Bernard Garrette, and Will Mitchell, "Asymmetric Performance: The Market Share Impact of Scale and Link Alliances in the Global Auto Industry," *Strategic Management Journal* 25 (2004): 701–11.

25 A. L. Zacharakis, "Entrepreneurial Entry into Foreign Markets: A Transaction Cost Perspective," *Entrepreneurship Theory & Practice* 22, no. 2 (1998): 23–39; and Rodney C. Shrader, "Collaboration and Performance in Foreign Markets: The Case of Young High-Technology Manufacturing Firms," *Academy of Management Journal* 44, no. 1 (February 2001): 45–60.

26 Rahul Jacob, "Hong Kong Banks on New Disney Park for Boost," *Financial Times* (August 31, 2001): 6.

27 John Wilman, "Coca-Cola Aims to Put Fizz into Fashion," *Financial Times* (January 2, 1999): 1.

28 T. K. Das and Bing-Sheng Teng, "A Resource-Based Theory of Strategic Alliances," *Journal of Management* 26, no. 1 (2000): 31–61.

29 "New World Ready to Build Caribbean Fiber System," *Fiber-Optics News* 20, no. 26 (June 26, 2000): 1.

30 Betsy McKay and Robert Frank, "Coke, Danone Discuss Joint Venture," *Wall Street Journal* (June 17, 2002): B5.

31 John M. Connor, "Global Antitrust Prosecutions of Modern International Cartels," *Journal of Industry, Competition and Trade* 4, no. 3 (September 2004): 239.

32 Peter Marsh, "Profile Duracell," *Financial Times* (May 10, 1999): 27.

33 Destan Kandemir and G. Tomas Hult, "A Conceptualization of an Organizational Learning Culture in International Joint Ventures," *Industrial Marketing Management* 34, no. 5 (July 2005): 440.

34 Robert F. Howe, "The Fall of the House of Mondavi," *Business 2.0*, 6, no. 3 (April 2005): 98.

35 Yumiko Ono and Ann Zimmerman, "Wal-Mart Enters Japan with Seiyu Stake," *Wall Street Journal* (March 15, 2002): B5.

36 Michiyo Nakamoto, "Global Reach Through Tie-Ups," *Financial Times* (April 30, 2002): healthcare section, p. 3.

37 "Merck and Chugai Form OTC Venture," *Financial Times* (September 19, 1996): 17.

38 "Northrop Grumman, Rolls-Royce Awarded Type 45 Destroyer Engine Contract," *Defense Daily International* 2, no. 11 (March 16, 2001): 1.

39 Julie Bennett, "Road to Foreign Franchises Is Paved with New Problems," *Wall Street Journal* (May 14, 2001): B10.

40 Peter J. Lane, Jane E. Salk, and Marjorie A. Lyles, "Absorptive Capacity, Learning, and Performance in International Joint Ventures," *Strategic Management Journal* 22 (2001): 1139–61.

41 Miguel Angel Asturias, *Strong Wind*, translated by Gregory Rabassa (New York: Delacorte Press, 1968): 112.

42 For an extensive treatise on the theory, see Robert A. Packenham, *The Dependency Movement: Scholarship and Politics in Development Studies* (Cambridge, MA: Harvard University Press, 1992). For some different national views of its validity, see Ndiva Kofele-Kale, "The Political Economy of Foreign Direct Investment: A Framework for Analyzing Investment Laws and Regulations in Developing Countries," *Law & Policy in International Business* 23, no. 2–3 (1992): 619–71; and Stanley K. Sheinbaum, "Very Recent History Has Absolved Socialism," *New Perspectives Quarterly* 13, no. 1 (January, 1996).

43 Ravi Ramamurti, "The Obsolescing 'Bargaining Model'? MNC-Host Developing Country Relations Revisited," *Journal of International Business Studies* 32 (Spring 2001): 23; Yadong Luo, "Toward a Cooperative View of MNC-Host Government Relations: Building Blocks and Performance Implication," *Journal of International Business Studies* 32 (Fall 2001): 401.

44 "Advanced Micro, Fujitsu and Saifun Announce Collaboration," *JCN Newswire* (July 31, 2002).

45 Pierre Dussauge, "Domino's Pizza International, Inc.," Case #398-048-1 (Jouy-en-Josas, France: H.E.C., 1998).

46 Richard C. Hoffman and John F. Preble, "Global Diffusion of Franchising: A Country Level Examination," *Multinational Business Review* 9, no. 1 (Spring 2001): 66–76.

47 John F. Preble, "Global Expansion: The Case of U.S. Fast-Food Franchisors," *Journal of Global Marketing* 6, nos. 1–2 (1992): 186, citing D. Ayling, "Franchising in the U.K.," *The Quarterly Review of Marketing* (Summer 1988): 19–24.

48 Lizette Alvarez, "Spreading Scandinavian Genes, Without Viking Boats," *New York Times* (September 30, 2004): A4.

49 Fred Burton, Adam R. Cross, and Mark Rhodes, "Foreign Market Servicing Strategies of UK Franchisors: An Empirical Enquiry from a Transactions Cost Perspective," *Management International Review* 40, no. 4 (Fourth Quarter 2000): 373–400.

50 John K. Ryans, Jr., Sherry Lotz, and Robert Krampf, "Do Master Franchisors Drive Global Franchising?" *Marketing Management* 8, no. 2 (Summer 1999): 33–38.

51 Julie Bennett, "Product Pitfalls Proliferate in a Global Cultural Maze," *Wall Street Journal* (May 14, 2001): B11; and Jane Wooldridge, "Fast Food Universe," *Miami Herald* (November 28, 2004): J1.

52 Peng S. Chan and Robert T. Justis, "Franchise Management in East Asia," *Academy of Management Executive* 4, no. 2 (May 1990): 75–85. For other changes by McDonald's in Europe, see Heather Ogilvie, "Welcome to McEurope: An Interview with Tom Allin, President of McDonald's Development Co.," *Journal of European Business* 2, no. 67 (July–August 1991): 5–12.

53 Bertrand Benoit, "BAA Wins License to Run Chinese Airports," *Financial Times* (August 30, 1999): 13; and Jodi Richards, "Sensational Schipol," *Airport Business* 19, no. 3 (March 2005): 12–14.

54 Peter Goddard and Guy Standish-Wilkinson, "Hotel Management Contract Trends in the Middle East," *Journal of Leisure Property* 2, no. 1 (January 2002): 66–80.

55 Bechtel Web site, http://www.bechtel.com/projprof.html.

56 "Signing of ABB Deal for Malaysia's Bakun Dam on September 30," *Agence France Presse* (September 21, 1996); and "Malaysia Signs Dam Contract," *Financial Times* (October 3, 1996): 7.

57 Glenn R. Simpson and Chip Cummins, ""Fuel for the Fire," *Wall Street Journal* (April 14, 2004): A1+; and Sheila McNulty, "Haliburton Boosted by Iraq Work," (April 23–24, 2005): 8.

58 David Murphy, "Chinese Construction Companies Go Global," *Wall Street Journal* (May 12, 2004): B10.

59 Benjamin A. Holden and Nicholas Bray, "British, Australian and Two American Firms to Purchase Utility in Australia," *Wall Street Journal* (August 5, 1996): A4.

60 Luis Zalamea, "AeroRepublica, Copa Offer Details of New Alliance," *Aviation Daily* 359, no. 47 (March 11, 2005): 5.

61 There are many different ways of classifying the problems. Two useful ways are found in Manuel G. Serapio, Jr., and Wayne F. Cascio, "End Games in International Alliances," *Academy of Management Executive* 10, no. 1 (1996): 62–73; and Joel Bleeke and David Ernst, "Is Your Strategic Alliance Really a Sale?" *Harvard Business Review* (January–February 1995): 97–105.

62 Terrence Chea, "No Perfect Partnership," *Washington Post* (June 3, 2002): E1.

63 Gregory L. White, "In Asia, GM Pins Hope on a Delicate Web of Alliances," *Wall Street Journal* (October 23, 2002): A23.

64 Ramit Plushnick-Masti, "German Firm Faulted for Taking Vitamin Out of Baby Formula," *Miami Herald* (November 12, 2003): 19A.

65 William H. Meyers, "Maxim's Name Is the Game," *New York Times Magazine* (May 3, 1987): 33–35; and Keith W. Strandberg, "EganaGoldpfeil Group Moves Forward with Pierre Cardin Watches," *National Jeweler* 96, no. 19 (October 1, 2002): 36.

66 Marcus W. Brauchli, "PepsiCo's KFC Venture in China Is Fined for Allegedly False Financial Reporting," *Wall Street Journal* (July 27, 1994): A10.

67 David Ibison, "Culture Clashes Prove Biggest Hurdle to International Links," *Financial Times* (January 24, 2002): 17.

68 Samantha Marshall, "P&G Squabbles with Vietnamese Partner," *Wall Street Journal* (February 27, 1998): A14.

69 Joel Bleeke and David Ernst, "The Way to Win in Cross-Border Alliances," *Harvard Business Review* (November–December 1991): 127–35.

70 Leslie Crawford, "Anheuser's Cross-Border Marriage on the Rocks," *Financial Times* (March 18, 1998): 16.

71 Seung Ho Park and Gerardo R. Ungson, "The Effect of National Culture, Organizational Complementarity, and Economic Motivation on Joint Venture Dissolution," *Academy of Management Journal* 40, no. 2 (April 1997): 279–307; Harry G. Barkema, Oded Shenkar, Freek Vermeulen, and John H. J. Bell, "Working Abroad, Working with Others: How Firms Learn to Operate International Joint Ventures," *Academy of Management Journal* 40, no. 2 (April 1997): 426–42, found survival differences only for differences in uncertainty avoidance.

72 Mike W. Peng and Oded Shenkar, "Joint Venture Dissolution as Corporate Divorce," *Academy of Management Executive* 16, no. 2 (May 2002): 92–105.

73 Bharat Anand and Tarun Khanna, "Do Firms Learn to Create Value? The Case of Alliances," *Strategic Management Journal* 21, no. 3 (March 2000): 295–315.

74 Anthony Goerzen and Paul W. Beamish, "The Effect of Alliance Network Diversity on Multinational Enterprise Performance," *Strategic Management Journal* 26 (2005): 333–54.

75 Anne Smith and Marie-Claude Reney, "The Mating Dance: A Case Study of Local Partnering Processes in Developing Countries," *European Management Journal* 15, no. 2 (1997): 174–82.

76 Sanjiv Kumar and Anju Seth, "The Design of Coordination and Control Mechanisms for Managing Joint Venture–Parent Relationships," *Strategic Management Journal* 19, no. 6 (June 1998): 579–99; T. K. Das and Bing-Sheng Teng, "Between Trust and Control: Developing Confidence in Partner Cooperation in Alliances," *Academy of Management Journal* 23, no. 3 (July 1998): 491–512; Arvind Parkhe, "Building Trust in International Alliances," *Journal of World Business* 33, no. 4 (1998): 417–37; and Prashant Kale, Harbir Singh, and Howard Perlmutter, "Learning and Protection of Proprietary Assets in Strategic Alliances: Building Relational Capital," *Strategic Management Journal* 21, no. 3 (March 2000): 217–37.

77 Africa Ariño and Jeffrey J. Reuer, "Designing and Renegotiating Strategic Alliance Contracts," *Academy of Management Executive* 18, no. 3 (2004): 37–48.

78 John Kenneth Galbraith, *American Capitalism* (Boston: Houghton Mifflin, 1952), 91–92.

79 Eric H. Kessler, Paul E. Bierly, and Shanthi Gopalakrishnan, "Internal vs. External Learning in New Product Development: Effects of Speed, Costs and Competitive Advantage," *R & D Management*, 30, no. 3 (July 2000): 213–23.

80 These are adapted from Arvind Parkhe, "Interfirm Diversity, Organizational Learning, and Longevity in Global Strategic Alliances," *Journal of International Business Studies* 22, no. 4 (Fourth Quarter 1991): 579–601.

81 Data for the case were taken from Andrea Rothman, "U.S. to World: Airline Deals Hinge on Open Skies," *Business Week* (January 11, 1992): 46; Andrea Rothman, Seth Payne, and Paula Dwyer, "One World, One Giant Airline Market?" *Business Week* (October 5, 1992): 56; "All Aboard," *Economist* (February 29, 1992): 78; "Wings Across the Water," *Economist* (July 25, 1992): 62; Agis Salpukas, "Europe's Small Airlines Shelter Under Bigger Wings," *New York Times* (November 8, 1992): E4; "Code Breakers," *Economist* (November 21, 1992): 78–79; Bridget O'Brian and Laurie McGinley, "Mixing of U.S., Foreign Carriers Alters Market," *Wall Street Journal* (December 21, 1992): B1; Bill Poling, "United, American Spar with USAir, BA over Proposed Deal," *Travel Weekly* (November 12, 1992): 49; Joan M. Feldman, "The Dilemma of 'Open Skies,'" *The New York Times Magazine* (April 2, 1989): 31; Philippe Gugler, "Strategic Alliances in Services: Some Theoretical Issues and the Case of Air-Transport Services," paper prepared for the Danish Summer Research Institute (DSRI), Denmark, August 1992; Martin Tolchin, "Shift Urged on Foreign Stakes in Airlines," *New York Times* (January 9, 1993): 17; Agis Salpukas, "The Big Foreign Push to Buy into U.S. Airlines," *New York Times* (October 11, 1992): F11; Robert Crandell, "When Less Really Means More," *Financial Times* (September 17, 1996): 17; Emma Tucker, "Commission to Approve Lufthansa-SAS Venture," *Financial Times* (January 16, 1996): 3; Scott McCartney, Diane Brady, Susan Carey, and Asra Q. Nomani, "U.S. Airlines' Prospects Are Grim on Expanding Access to Asian Skies," *Wall Street Journal* (September 25, 1996): A1; Michael Skapinker, "Austrian Air Switches Allegiance to Star Alliance," *Financial Times* (September 22, 1999): 9; Edward Alden and Michael Skapinker, "United Airlines–Lufthansa Join Battle for Air Canada," *Financial Times* (October 20, 1999): 1; Michael Skapinker, "Continental Chairman Calls for Creation of Third Air Alliance," *Financial Times* (October 5, 1998): 20; Michael Skapinker, "Passengers Not Convinced," *Financial Times* (November 19, 1998): business of travel section, p. iii; Michael Skapinker, "Boarding Business Class Now," *Financial Times* (July 9, 1998): 13; J. A. Donoghue, "Network Is Everything," *Air Transport World* 36, no. 8 (August 1999): 9; Leonard Hill, "Global Challenger," *Air Transport World* 36, no. 12 (December 1999): 52–54; Robert Gribben, "City," *The Daily Telegraph* [London] (December 21, 1999): 29; Michael A. Taverna and John D. Morrocco, "Airlines Play Catch-Up in Partnership Game," *Aviation Week and Space Technology* 150, no. 12 (March 22, 1999): 70; Leonard Hill, "80 Years Young," *Air Transport World* 36, no. 10 (October 1999): 44–47; "Star Alliance Welcomes Asiana, Lot and Spanair to Its Roster of World Class Airlines," *PR Newswire* (June 1, 2002); Shirene Shan, "Alliances Bring Benefit to Passengers," *New Straits Times Press* [Malaysia] (May 14, 2002): Industry aviation section, p. 24; "Global Alliances Vulnerable to Shakeups in Four Areas," *Airline Financial News* 20, no. 23 (June 10, 2002); Kevin Done, "Air France–KLM Ahead on Savings," *Financial Times* (April 12, 2005): 30; and www.iccwbo.org/home/statements_rules/statements/1995/state_aid.asp.

Laws control the lesser man. Right conduct controls the greater one.

—CHINESE PROVERB

chapter fifteen

The Organization of International Business

OBJECTIVES

- Profile the evolving understanding of the organization of international business

- Describe traditional and contemporary structures

- Study the systems used to coordinate and control operations

- Profile the role of organization culture

- Examine special situations in the organization of international business

CASE: JOHNSON & JOHNSON[1]

The typical pharmaceutical company has a strong need for global integration because it depends on the sale of products that are costly to develop and are sensitive to scale economies. At the same time, pharmaceutical companies often must be highly responsive to national market conditions because different government authorities must approve each product in each country and, furthermore, because sales and distribution differ from country to country. Consequently, headquarters and its subsidiaries are involved in implementing the company's strategy. Building an organization that can meet this mission is tough. Perhaps no one else does it better than Johnson & Johnson (J&J).

Since J&J began U.S. operations in 1886, it has evolved into the most broadly based health care company in the world. International activity started in 1919 with J&J Canada. J&J now has more than 200 operating companies located throughout the world, sells products in more than 175 countries, generates annual global revenues of more than $47 billion, and employs about 111,000 people worldwide, of whom more than 60,000 work in 56 countries other than the United States. Its steady success is renowned. Through 2004, the company has increased annual sales for 72 consecutive years, has earned money every year since going public in 1944, and has 43 consecutive years of dividend. In 2004, J&J was named the most admired pharmaceutical company in the world and among the top 10 among all companies across all industries.

J&J's strategy aims for leadership in its three core areas: pharmaceuticals, medical devices, and consumer products. Although a straightforward mission, J&J carries it out by using a complex organization structure that combines responsibility between 37 product groups and 14 health care areas, known as platforms. For example, its product groups include Centocor, Neutrogena, and Ethicon Endo-Surgery. They develop, manufacture, and market products to consumers and health care professionals worldwide. The health care platforms, called "platforms for growth," include biotechnology, gastrointestinals, and wound care. These are distinct health care platforms that contain a related group of products, technologies, pathologies, modalities, and/or customers. They act as staging areas from which J&J leverages its knowledge, development skills, marketing expertise, and global reach.

Structurally, the executive committee of the company is the principal management group responsible for all of J&J's operations worldwide. In addition, certain executive committee members serve as worldwide chairmen of group operating committees, which are comprised of managers who represent key operations within the group, as well as management expertise in other specialized functions. These committees oversee and coordinate the activities of domestic and international companies related to each of the consumer, pharmaceutical, and professional segments of business. The operating management of each company is headed by a chairman, president, general manager, or managing director who reports directly to, or through a line executive to, a group operating committee.

J&J is organized on the principles of decentralized management in the belief that managers who are closest to customers and competitors should make decisions. Hence, each international subsidiary is, with a few exceptions, managed by citizens of the country where it is located. Indeed, J&J sets the structure of its organization in terms of the configuration of its individual operating units. Map 15.1 shows the worldwide distribution of these units. By design, J&J has decentralized a great deal of autonomy to each unit, giving it the freedom to act as it believes is best given local market conditions. Decentralization, explained Ralph Larsen, CEO from 1989 to 2002, "gives people a sense of ownership and control—and the freedom to act more rapidly." His successor, William Weldon, concurred, adding, "The magic around J&J is decentralization." Essentially, this policy enables J&J to behave like more than 200 innovative, entrepreneurial small firms that respond to the unique opportunities and threats in their local market yet still capture the benefits of the information, knowledge, and expertise generated by global operations.

Traditionally, J&J did not enter new markets with sweeping armies of home-office managers directed by headquarters-based generals. Rather, it added subsidiaries by investment, alliance, or acquisition of another company. J&J advised the president of the new company to call home if he or she needed help, and then it waited for superior results. Basically, headquarters believed that people who understood how the company created value, had familiarity with the company's core competency, and were culturally

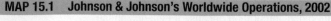

MAP 15.1   Johnson & Johnson's Worldwide Operations, 2002

Johnson & Johnson sells in virtually every part of the world. The map indicates where J&J has operations. The numbers indicate the number of operating units per country.

Source: http://www.jnj.com/ investor/annual_reports/2001/family companies.htm;jsessionid=E33P85MFZT O14CQPCCGSU0A.

familiar and physically close to the market ought to be running the local business. Thus, for example, the baby oil managers in Italy ran their own factory and got to decide how big a bottle to put the baby oil in— even if that bottle differed from the one sold in Germany, Japan, or Mexico. Historically, noted one observer, the heads of J&J's foreign subsidiaries enjoyed so much autonomy that they were called "kings of their own countries." Traditionally, headquarters had installed some system to coordinate and control activities among countries. Often, headquarters negotiated financial targets with the heads of the separate business units but then let them figure out the best way to meet them.

Expectedly, there was friction between operating units and headquarters. Competitive pressures that pushed for global integration continually tested the company's commitment to decentralization. Moreover, senior management conceded that decentralization created some costs, such as inconsistent market development and duplication of efforts. For example, J&J launched Tylenol in 1960 as an over-the-counter pain reliever in the United States. Although it was available to local operating units shortly thereafter, the Japanese unit did not begin local sales until 2000. So, while decentralization enabled J&J to respond quickly to local needs, it slowed the global diffusion of products and programs.

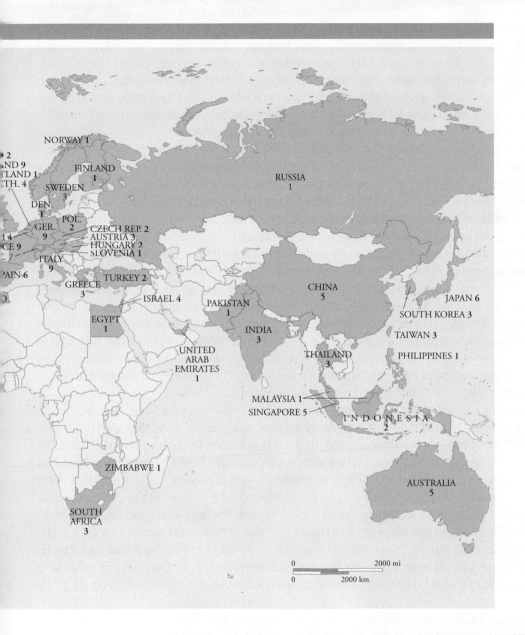

NORWAY 1

2
ND 9
LAND 1
TH. 4
FINLAND
1
SWEDEN
3
DEN.
1
POL.
GER. 2
14 9
CE 9 CZECH REP. 2
AUSTRIA 3
HUNGARY 2
SLOVENIA 1
ITALY
9
AIN 6
GREECE
3
TURKEY 2

RUSSIA
1

CHINA
5

JAPAN 6

SOUTH KOREA 3

TAIWAN 3

ISRAEL 4

PAKISTAN
1

EGYPT
1

INDIA
3

UNITED
ARAB
EMIRATES
1

THAILAND
3

PHILIPPINES 1

MALAYSIA 1
SINGAPORE 5

I N D O N E S I A
2

ZIMBABWE 1

AUSTRALIA
5

SOUTH
AFRICA
3

0   2000 mi

0   2000 km

In response, senior management has streamlined how country managers coordinate and control value activities. For instance, J&J moved responsibility for various activities from operating units to headquarters. The group operating committees at headquarters now deal with many issues that are common to many or all operating units, such as human resources, finance, science and technology, government affairs, corporate advertising, corporate communications, and quality management. Senior executives reasoned that this approach lets the company use its global perspective to develop standards that enable headquarters and local operations to better coordinate value activities. In addition, headquarters reasoned that using standardization to coordinate some activities frees operating units to concentrate on issues that most affect their day-to-day performance. In addition, headquarters took greater charge of the job of coordinating product production and marketing around the world. Granted, they still gather input from the local managers and meet with them to thrash out a unified marketing strategy; for example, they may debate whether cleanliness or beauty is the better promotion theme. Ultimately, though, when J&J rolls out a product, country managers no longer have the automatic option to reject it.

These programs have had successes. For example, implementing an updated version of Windows across all operating units at the same time saved J&J an estimated $80 million. Still, years after starting to integrate information technologies, headquarters finds it hard to get all of its business units to go along with even the most benign changes in policy. Some business units, for example, argue that they can't adopt some corporate technology standards or bear their share of the cost for infrastructure upgrades. When she first started to integrate information technology, J&J's chief information officer JoAnn Heisen had to convince business units just to answer the surveys on what type of systems they were operating. Similar sorts of problems have led headquarters to selectively use market controls systems to benchmark the performance of operating companies against competitors and each other.

To a one, J&J's senior management believed in the value of an organization that could leverage knowledge and expertise across the company. Meeting this mission shaped how they designed their organization. Early on, J&J aimed to improve the global perspective of local decision making. It opened numerous channels of communication and forums for discussion that cut across the organization and encouraged and enabled its far-flung units to share their ideas with counterparts. Self-directed councils—of research, engineering, and operations directors, among others—meet regularly to swap ideas. Successful employees are rotated among various operating units and affiliates, sharing their expertise and collaborating with their new workgroup. J&J also developed "FrameworkS," a process that rotates employees through an ongoing dialogue with senior management on strategic topics that cut across the company's business units. Plugged back into their worldwide networks, these employees then transfer information to their counterparts. Similarly, J&J elaborated its planning at the business-unit level by adding initiatives on major issues such as biotechnology, the restructuring of the health care industry, and globalization in order to challenge assumptions and to open managers to new thinking on how they can better coordinate value activities. Collectively, these efforts enable J&J to link and leverage its more than 200 pockets of resources and expertise in ways that promote learning and collaboration.

An integral element of J&J is its powerful organization culture—or what a former CEO, Mr. Larsen, referred to as the "glue that binds this company together." Specifically, since 1943, J&J has used a one-page ethical code of conduct, "Our Credo," to guide how it fulfills its business responsibilities. The Credo tells all managers, worldwide, who and what to care about and in what specific order. The Credo begins, "We believe our first responsibility is to the doctors, nurses, patients, mothers and fathers who use our products and services." Continuing on, it addresses both the communities where J&J operates and the roles and duties of J&J employees. Shareholders come last, long after suppliers and distributors. The Credo declares that shareholders will get a fair return if those other constituents get first priority. J&J has translated its Credo into 36 languages for its workforce across Africa, Asia-Pacific, Eastern Europe, Latin America, the Middle East, and North America. The company relies on its Credo to promote a clear, shared understanding of the company's mission and objectives among its global workforce.

No matter the details of its particular structure, systems, and culture, J&J's leaders believe the basis of the company's continued success rested upon building an organization that is flexible enough to exploit the knowledge and skills of each employee. Indeed, given the choice of staffing international operations with folks who would unquestionably implement top management orders or hiring local people who were entrepreneurial innovators, J&J regularly opted for the latter. Management reasoned that the costs of letting people on the front lines make their own decisions were trivial given the benefits of letting them capitalize on their initiative, develop their capabilities, and broaden their perspectives. Decentralization has been, is, and will be the foundation of J&J's continued success. More pointedly, explained the CEO, "I am here to passionately protect the values of J&J. Our credo is value-based. It comes down to people, values, and environment."

INTRODUCTION

Organizing is the process of creating the structure, systems, and culture needed to implement the company's strategy.

Artfully engineering an organization that configures globally dispersed resources to meet the mandates of multinational operations is the frontier of international business. While most international managers find it easier to decide what to do, many believe the basis of competitive advantage is devising an organization of such clarity that the intricate task of creating value while effectively mediating worldwide integration versus local differentiation becomes straightforward.[2] Therefore, this chapter examines how international companies build the organization to implement their chosen strategy.

We begin with the notion that formulating the appropriate strategy for international business is just the first step of a long process—essentially, an insightful strategy is a necessary but not sufficient condition for long-term success. Instead, MNEs invest enormous energy into finding ways to implement their strategy effectively and efficiently. This task inevitably turns managers' attention to the issue of how they should organize their international operations. J&J exemplifies this situation, showing the power of building an organization that takes a comprehensive view of integrating a structure of decentralized national units, tailoring technology, human resources, reward systems, information systems to coordinate and control value activities, and developing a meaningful organization culture through its Credo. Throughout all these tasks, managers articulate what must be done to sustain the company's competitive advantage, how employees individually and collectively can contribute, how it specifies and coordinates interdependencies among value activities, the means it would take to control situations that go awry, and the values and ideals that define its culture. As such, J&J gives a sense of the great deal of time that managers spend, arguably more than that spent on fine-tuning their strategy, to build the organization that can implement their strategy.

J&J also showcases the demanding variety of managerial activities that have to be performed both by people at headquarters and the local subsidiaries. Complicating this task is the fact that there are often numerous ways to tackle each activity, many activities must be launched and supervised simultaneously, and many people in many operations in many countries are often resistant to change. Consequently, building an organization to implement the chosen strategy, as we see in Figure 15.1, presents managers with the tough job of integrating the efforts of many different people, teams, groups, and units into a smoothly functioning whole.

> Implementing a new strategy is a tough job that requires adept management.

THE CAUSES OF CHANGE

How an MNE organizes its operations is one of the most provocative issues in international business. Perhaps no other topic in current management studies has undergone as much revision in the past few years. Indeed, it would not be overly dramatic

---

FIGURE 15.1   **THE ORGANIZATION OF INTERNATIONAL BUSINESSES**

Organization is how companies build the structures, systems, and culture to create a dynamic work environment used to implement their chosen strategy.

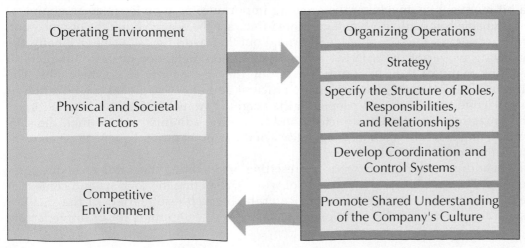

to say that our ideas of the organization of international business are undergoing the sort of changes that require fundamentally reinterpreting many principles and practices.

For generations, managers facing the task of building an organization could reasonably concern themselves with designing the system of lines and boxes that depicted its formal structure. Essentially, managers aimed to specify the formal arrangement of work within the company by specifying who did what job, who worked in which unit, who reported to whom, and who could make which decisions. The output of this effort was the company's formal structure. The company's structure basically instituted a system of control that largely relied on an arrangement of constraints and contracts to ensure compliance by all employees throughout the world. Beginning with General Motors and DuPont in the early twentieth century, this general model performed well for many MNEs. However, preceding chapters have reported that various competitive pressures, industry conditions, and market opportunities spur MNEs to configure novel value chains. These configurations, in turn, create coordination and control challenges that can overwhelm the functionality provided by the formal specification of structure. Indeed, some scholars advise that the very question of asking how an organization should be formally structured is anachronistic, given the realization of many MNEs that "reconfiguring the formal structure is a blunt and sometimes brutal instrument of change. A new structure creates new and presumably more useful managerial ties, but those can take months and often years to evolve into effective knowledge-generating and decision-making relationships."[3]

In times of rapid change, few MNEs have the luxury to await the slow emergence of crucial "knowledge-generating and decision-making relationships." As a result, managers now question their customary approaches to organizing their companies, hoping to find ways to jumpstart the development of and then sustaining these relationships. In the past few years, MNEs around the world have adopted radical programs to do so, as seen in widespread calls to downsize, delayer, restructure, reengineer, and reinvent the organization. Unquestionably, the structure of the company is a vital part of this reinterpretation. Now, though, managers elaborate their idea of organization from that of the specification of boxes and lines with the integrated development of complementary systems and organization culture that supports their chosen strategy.

Two sets of trends, one environmental, the other organizational, steadily pile pressure on managers to engage this challenge. Regarding environmental trends, the first is the growth and diffusion of international business. Globalization has changed the opportunity set and efficiency frontier for companies. As we saw in Chapter 11, MNEs respond in kind, engaging unprecedented strategies that demand more sophisticated organizations—think of, for example, the cases of Zara and eBay. The second trend is a bit more subtle, involving the growing importance of knowledge as an engine of sustainable competitive advantage. More MNEs see the need to build the organization that accelerates the spread of ideas throughout their worldwide business. Finally, the growing power of the Internet as an organization metaphor pushes managers to rethink many of their assumptions of how they get people to do their jobs. The Internet has emerged as a supremely efficient and effective global organization of knowledge, resources, and people. In the height of irony, the Internet has no formal organization, no board of directors, and no central administrator. Rather, the self-organizing and self-regulating capabilities of the Internet prompt questioning conventional notions of control.

In addition, workplace trends are resetting organization standards for many companies. The speedily evolving nature of work is changing the conduct and context of employees' jobs, whether it takes place in the biggest headquarters or the smallest subsidiary. Most notably, employees working with computers, for example, create

Revolutionary changes in the market environment and nature of work are pushing managers to question how their companies organize work.

More sophisticated strategies typically involve different key activities that create new organizational requirements.

value through work that has astonishing variability, problem solving, and intellectual content. The flexibility of computers means that, unlike earlier work environments, there are fewer jobs that senior managers can standardize in terms of the one best way to perform. Change in the nature of work has changed the nature of management. In the least, it is difficult and usually counterproductive to supervise workers charged with reasoning or problem-solving tasks. Moreover, the higher the level of manager in the hierarchy, historically, the more he or she knew about the various jobs in the company. Similarly, front-line employees at the subsidiary level presumably knew little more than their immediate responsibilities in the local marketplace. Today, employees who are closer to customers and competitors increasingly know as much, if not a bit more, about creating value than many managers back at headquarters. Hence, senior executives face growing pressure to empower employees around the world to make decisions and develop the basis of common ideas and ideals that ensure they will act in the best interests of the MNE. Finally, competitive changes and performance expectations have changed the social contract between employee and organization. Employees' traditional concerns for security, pay, and benefits have expanded to greater interest in participating in decision making, devising solutions to unique problems, and receiving challenging assignments that improve their professional mobility.

ORGANIZATION IN THE INTERNATIONAL BUSINESS

The enormity of environmental and workplace trends is redefining the principles of the organization of international business. Companies now seek the complementary mix of structure, systems, and values that can build the organization needed to create value. Some companies, like Oticon in Sweden, Cisco in the United States, and Li Fung in Hong Kong, have engaged unprecedented formats. Rather than forcing employees into a conventional organization model, they build organizations that are flexible enough to exploit the knowledge and unique skills of employees. Others, like Nestle in Switzerland, Cemex in Mexico, and Tata in India, have not abandoned their historic notions of organization. Instead, they fine-tune their organization, trying to find a better combination of how they arrange the work environment, coordinate and control value activities, and create a common framework of values that encourages workers around the world to act creatively, responsibly, and entrepreneurially. These far more prevalent sorts of companies use a range of options to supplement their traditional organization, including cross-functional task forces, dual reporting relationships, informal networking, and incentive compensation tied to group performance.

The opening profile of J&J exemplifies this situation in highlighting that organization of international business is the totality of choices a company makes in its structure, systems, and culture. As shown in Figure 15.1, this straightforward model helps us analyze the organizational capabilities a company needs to translate its ambitions into actions. Research on this general issue has applied many perspectives. While many studies use specialized terms, such as *organization context, architecture,* or *gestalt,* they share the same premise: Organization in the international company is a function of how the company defines the formal structure that specifies the framework for work, develops the systems that coordinate and control what gets done, and cultivates a set of shared values and ideals among employees around the world. This chapter, therefore, looks at the various components of organization in the international business. We begin by examining the idea of structure, move on to coordination and control systems, and culminate with a profile of how employees think, act, and behave in the context of organization culture. The chapter then closes with a discussion of special situations in international business that shape how a company designs its organization.

Organization is defined by the formal structure, coordination and control systems, and the organization culture.

ORGANIZATION STRUCTURE

Organization structure—the formal arrangement of roles, responsibilities, and relationships within an organization—is a powerful tool with which to implement strategy. Recall our profile of Zara in Chapter 11; its management believes that how they had designed their company was an instrumental aspect of its success. "Our structure," said Inditex CEO Jose Maria Castellano, "gives us tremendous advantages over our competition." International companies specify the structure that groups individuals and operational units in the ways that managers reason best support the strategy of the firm. For example, if an MNE is pursuing a multidomestic strategy but designs a structure that delegates little responsibility to local subsidiaries, it will likely fail to implement its strategy.

Ultimately, a company's choice of structure depends on many factors, including the configuration of the company's value chain in terms of the location and type of foreign facilities, as well as the impact of international operations on total corporate performance. More immediately, two issues stand out: vertical differentiation, the matter of how the company balances centralization versus decentralization in decision making, and horizontal differentiation, the matter of how the company opts to divide itself into specific units to do specific jobs. We now look at each more closely.

Vertical Differentiation: Centralization versus Decentralization

Our profile of strategy in Chapter 11 shows that every MNE faces the tough task of balancing global integration with local differentiation. This dichotomy can be expressed in many ways, such as efficiency versus effectiveness, standardization versus customization, or even science versus art. Irrespective of the terms used, the dilemma is the same: All companies must address who has what authority to make what decisions—for example, who makes factory location decisions? Where does the responsibility for product promotion decisions lie? Do senior managers or the staff of local subsidiaries decide how to market products? In addition, what are the responsibilities of foreign subsidiaries in terms of, how, when, and what they report to headquarters? For instance, J&J's efforts to implement its strategy required that headquarters decide how much authority to delegate to the directors of its subsidiaries, various primary and support departments, plants, sales offices, distribution centers, and other operating units. In broad terms, determining where in the hierarchy is the authority to make what decisions is the issue of **vertical differentiation.** In practical terms, companies determine where in the hierarchy is the authority to make what decisions by working out the issue of centralization versus decentralization.

In some MNEs, top managers make all the decisions and lower-level managers and employees simply carry out their orders. At the other extreme are MNEs that push decision making down to the managers who are closest to the action, assigning them the responsibility to provide substantive input into the decision-making process or delegating them the authority to actually make decisions. The former companies are centralized, and the latter are decentralized. For the MNE, the rule of thumb is that decisions made at the foreign-subsidiary level are considered decentralized, whereas those made above the foreign-subsidiary level are considered centralized. Table 15.1 shows that **centralization** and **decentralization** are based on different principles and beliefs, with each having its pros and cons for how a company designs its organization.

We usually associate centralized decision making with an international or global strategy, decentralized decision making with a multidomestic strategy, and a combination of the two with a transnational strategy. The reason for choosing one over the other is partly a function of companies' attitudes. For example, the ethnocentric attitude one likely finds in an international company encourages it to develop core competencies in its home country and then closely supervise their transfer and use abroad. A polycentric attitude, of the sort commonly found in the company pursuing a multidomestic strategy, encourage it to decentralize decision making to foreign subsidiaries because headquarters personnel believe that

---

Structure is the formal arrangement of jobs within a company that specifies roles and relationships.

Differentiation means that the organization is comprised of many different units that work on different kinds of tasks.

Centralization is the degree to which high-level managers, usually above the country level, make important decisions and pass them down to lower levels for implementation.

Decentralization is the degree to which lower level managers, usually at or below the country level, make and implement important decisions.

| TABLE 15.1 | **THE PRINCIPLES AND PRACTICE OF CENTRALIZATION AND DECENTRALIZATION** |

CENTRALIZATION

Premise

Decisions should be made by senior managers who have the experience, expertise, and judgment to find the best course of action for the company.

The effective configuration and coordination of the value chain depends on headquarters retaining authority over what happens.

Centralized decision making ensures that operations in different countries help achieve global objectives.

Advantages

Facilitates coordination of the value chain

Ensures that decisions are consistent with strategic objectives

Gives senior executives the authority to direct major change

Preempts duplicating activities across various subsidiaries

Reduces the risk that lower-level employees make costly, wrong decisions.

Ensures consistent dealing with stakeholders—government officials, employees, suppliers, consumers, and the general public

Disadvantages

Discourages initiative among lower-level employees

Demoralized lower-level employees simply wait to be told what to do.

Information flows from the top down, thereby preempting possible innovations from bottom-up information flow.

Factors Encouraging More Centralization

General environment and specific industry call for global integration and worldwide uniformity of products, purchases, methods, and policies

Interdependent subsidiaries that share value activities or deal with common competitors and customers

Need for company to move its resources—capital, personnel, or technology—from one value activity to another

Lower-level managers are not as capable or experienced at making decisions as upper-level managers.

Decisions are important and the risk of loss is great.

DECENTRALIZATION

Premise

Decisions should be made by the employees that are closest to and most familiar with the situation.

The effective configuration and coordination of the value chain depends on headquarters letting local managers deal with local market conditions.

Decentralized decision making ensures that operations in different countries operate toward achieving global objectives by meeting national goals.

Advantages

Decisions made by those who directly deal with customers, competitors, and markets

Encourages lower-level managers to exercise initiative

Motivates greater effort to do a better job by lower-level employees

Enables more flexible response to rapid environmental changes

Permits holding subsidiary managers more accountable for their unit's performance

Disadvantages

Puts the organization at risk if many bad decisions are made at lower levels.

Impedes cross-unit coordination and capture of strategic fits.

Subsidiary will likely favor its own projects and performance at the expense of global or overall performance.

Factors Encouraging More Decentralization

General environment and specific industry call for local responsiveness

Products, purchases, methods, and policies are suitable for local adaptation.

Economies of scale can be achieved via national production.

Lower-level managers are capable and experienced at making decisions.

Decisions are relatively minor but must be made quickly.

Company is geographically dispersed.

Low need for foreign nationals to reach senior-level headquarters positions.

people on the spot know best what to do. The company pursuing a transnational strategy would actively balance the competing needs for centralization and decentralization, aiming for a sensitivity that enables it to deal simultaneously with global and local pressures.

The idea of centralization-decentralization, often defined as an either-or proposition, is in actuality a relative phenomenon that is marked by trade-offs, compromises, and exceptions. Simply put, as we saw with J&J, the locus of decision making is a long-running contest between managers at headquarters and those at the local subsidiary. If anything, this contest highlights the idea that an MNE is never completely centralized or decentralized. Few organizations could function effectively if all decisions were made by only a select group of top managers. Nor, for that matter, could organizations function if all decisions were delegated to employees at the lowest levels.

Horizontal Differentiation: The Design of the Formal Structure

All MNEs must horizontally differentiate their international operations—that is, managers must divide the company into discrete units that are assigned responsibility for specialized tasks. More specifically, **horizontal differentiation** describes how the company designs its formal structure to (1) specify the total set of organizational tasks; (2) divide those tasks into jobs, departments, subsidiaries, and divisions so that the work gets done; and (3) assign authority and authority relationships to make sure work gets done in ways that support the company's strategy. In traditional terms, MNEs resolved these issues on the basis of function, type of business, geographical area, or some combination of the preceding. We now examine these design standards.

Functional Structure

A functional structure, as depicted in Figure 15.2 (a), is the ideal way to organize work when a company's products share a common technology and competitive pressures push for a cost-leadership strategy. A functional structure helps managers maximize scale economies by arranging work responsibilities and relationships in the most efficient format. So, for example, this structure creates specific departments that group personnel in terms of traditional business functions—i.e., production people work with other production people, marketing people work with other marketing people, finance works with other finance people, and so on.

Functional divisions are popular among companies with a narrow range of products, particularly if the production and marketing methods are undifferentiated among them, and where market change is more measured than erratic. For instance, oil and mineral extraction companies, such as ExxonMobil or British Petroleum, commonly use this structure.

A weakness of a functional structure is its inability to respond to environmental changes that require coordination between departments. Put simply, this structure does not build the knowledge-generating and decision-making relationships that facilitate marketing people coordinating their decisions with people in the production and finance departments. The extreme vertical differentiation of a functional structure—a long chain of command that spans many levels of the hierarchy—often results in deliberate decision making that grows slower as the volume of pertinent data grows quicker than the many layers of the hierarchy can process it.

Divisional Structures

Whereas executives specify roles and relationships in a functional structure in terms of inputs, they use the divisional structure format to specify them according to outputs. Each division in a company is assigned responsibility for a different set of products or markets. In theory, an MNE can opt for an international division, a global product structure, or a worldwide area structure.

FIGURE 15.2 PLACEMENT OF INTERNATIONAL ACTIVITIES WITHIN THE ORGANIZATIONAL STRUCTURES FOR INTERNATIONAL BUSINESSES

Although most companies have mixed structures, these five examples are simplified versions of the most common organizational structures for international businesses.

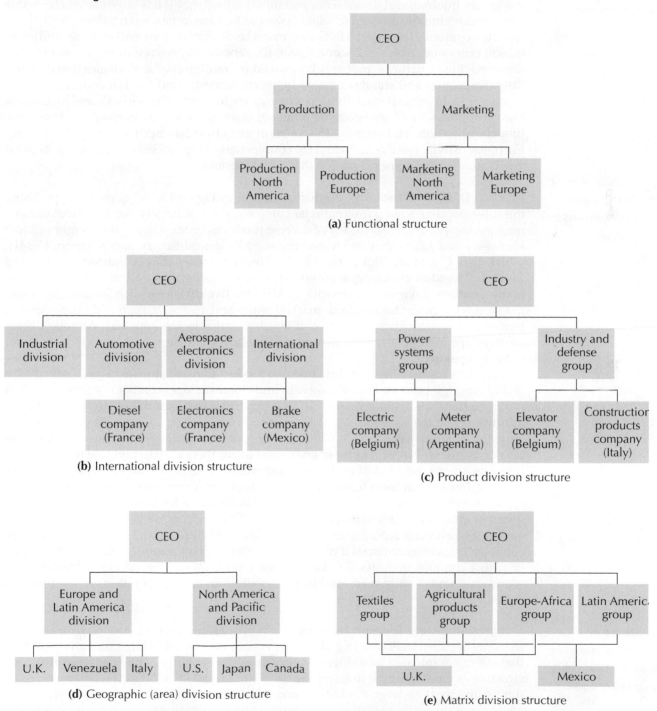

(a) Functional structure

(b) International division structure

(c) Product division structure

(d) Geographic (area) division structure

(e) Matrix division structure

International Division Structure Grouping each international business activity into its own division—as depicted in Figure 15.2 (b)—puts internationally specialized personnel together to handle such diverse matters as export documentation, foreign-exchange transactions, and relations with foreign governments. This format has several advantages. Its capacity to respond quickly to environmental changes enables the company to deal with several different markets in real time. Too, this structure prevents duplication of these activities in more than one place in the organization. Often domestic division managers are evaluated on the basis of performance within the domestic divisions for which they are responsible. As such, they may withhold their products, personnel, technology, and other resources from international operations in order to boost their performance. An international division can preempt this tendency if it is large enough to enable personnel within the division to wield power within the larger organization.

The segmentation of an MNE into discrete divisions does frustrate its ability to exploit economies of scale or scope. Given the separation between domestic and foreign divisions, this structure is probably best suited for multidomestic strategies that demand little integration and standardization between domestic and foreign operations. Still, managers in an international division structure try to use methods like shared logistics or budget routines to achieve possible points of manufacturing integration or administrative coordination. Historically, this form of structure has been less popular among European MNEs relative to their U.S. counterparts largely because the latter depend much more on the domestic market than do the former.

Product Division Structure   Product divisions, as Figure 15.2 (c) depicts, are probably the most popular among international companies today, largely because most companies' businesses involve a variety of diverse products.[4] For example, the merger of Moet Hennessy and Louis Vuitton created the world's largest luxury goods group, LVMH, which lists Christian Dior perfume, Tag Heuer watches, Louis Vuitton trunks, and Moet & Chandon champagne among its many brands. The dissimilarity among its many products led managers to split LVMH into five divisions, each focusing on a single product segment for its global market: wines and spirits; fashion and leather goods; perfumes and cosmetics; watches and jewelry; and selective retailing. Although there are overlaps in target markets, distribution channels, and supply chains, divisions tend to be independent.

As is true for the functional structure, the product division structure is well suited for a global strategy because both the foreign and domestic operations for a given product report to the same manager, who can find synergies between the two (e.g., by sharing information on the successes and failures of each one). Further, a separate product group structure enhances a company's ability to sell or spin off certain product lines because they are not as interwoven with its other lines. Most likely, there will be duplicate functions and activities among the product divisions. Moreover, there is no formal means by which one product division can learn from another's international experience. Finally, different subsidiaries from different product divisions within the same foreign country will report to different groups at headquarters. For example, Figure 15.2 (c) illustrates that the Belgian electric and elevator subsidiaries report to different headquarters divisions. So synergy could be lost within countries if different subsidiaries don't communicate with each other or with a common manager. Similarly, at one time in Westinghouse, one subsidiary was borrowing funds locally at an exorbitant rate, while another unit in the same country had excess cash.

Geographic (Area) Division Structure   Companies are prone to use geographic divisions, as depicted in Figure 15.2 (d), in the event that they have large foreign operations that are not dominated by a single country or region (including the home country). This structure is more common to European MNEs than for U.S. MNEs. The latter tend to be dominated by their large domestic market. This sort of structure is useful when managers can gain economies of scale in production on a regional rather than on a global basis because of market size or the particular sorts of production technologies for the industry. Historically, this structure has been commonly associated with companies pursuing multidomestic strategies. This structure's degree of decentralization gave country managers wide leeway to adapt everything from purchasing inputs to designing packaging to local conditions.

An international division

- Creates a critical mass of international expertise
- Often struggles to get resources from domestic divisions

Product divisions are popular among international companies with diverse products.

Geographic divisions are popular when foreign operations are large and are not dominated by a single country or region.

A drawback of this structure is the likely costly duplication of work among areas as the company locates similar value activities in several places rather than consolidating them in the most efficient place. For example, Nestle had more than 500 factories in nearly 90 countries that sold its 8,000 brands in almost every country in the world. Consequently, headquarters in Switzerland struggled to determine the costs of raw materials its subsidiaries bought from suppliers from around the world. In an extreme case, each of Nestle's more than 40 U.S. factories purchased raw materials independently. This lack of coordination, compounded by the fact that Nestle used 5 different e-mail systems, meant that its U.S. factories were paying more than 20 different prices for vanilla to the same supplier.[5]

Matrix Structure

Some MNEs pursue strategies that try to simultaneously deal with competing pressures for global integration and local responsiveness. This choice requires designing a structure that simultaneously attains the benefits of the functional and divisional structures in the form of a matrix structure, as depicted in Figure 15.2 (e). Rather than formally subordinating either integration or responsiveness, a matrix structure theoretically equips an MNE to gain the benefits of both as well as prevent prematurely excluding one.

Operationally, a matrix structure specifies that a subsidiary reports to more than one group (functional, product, or geographic). The basis premise is that making each group share responsibility over foreign operations will encourage each group to more willingly exchange information and resources.[6] For example, product-group managers must compete among themselves to ensure that R&D personnel responsible to a functional group, such as production, develop technologies for their product groups. These product-group managers also must compete to ensure that geographic-group managers paid enough attention to their product lines. Not only product groups, but also functional and geographic groups must compete among themselves to obtain resources held by others in the matrix. For example, the amount of resources needed to develop textile products in Mexico depends partly on the competition between the Europe-Africa group and the Latin America group and partly on the competition between the textiles group and the agricultural products group for resources. Consequently, the matrix structure is a useful compromise when managers face great difficulty integrating or separating foreign operations.

A matrix structure has drawbacks. It requires that groups compete, whether for scarce resources, whose preferred operating methods take precedence, who gets what share of reward, or who bears what share of risk. Likely disputes among lower-level managers require that upper management step in to decide. Besides delaying the decision, upper management may favor a specific executive or group, to the annoyance of the other group. As others in the organization see this happen, they may conclude the locus of power lies with a certain individual or group. In this case, group managers reason they are destined to lose, stop championing their group's unique needs, and thereby eliminate the multiple knowledge-generating and decision-making relationships that a matrix is supposed to engage.

Most notably, a matrix structure institutes a dual hierarchy that violates the unity-of-command principle. This principle, which holds that an unbroken chain of command and communication must be instituted from the manager to each worker. Often, the resulting blurred lines of responsibility and relationships within a matrix structure confuse the clarity of the chain of command. In this situation, a superior may not monitor his or her subordinates because he or she wrongly assumes that someone else is. For instance, managers in the Latin America group might ignore the day-to-day operations at the Mexican textile unit because they figure that their counterparts in the textile division are supposed to do so. Meanwhile, managers in the textile division may wrongly assume that the Latin America group is overseeing its Mexican operations. More specifically, the CEO of Dow Chemical, an early adopter of the matrix structure, explained that "We were an organization that was matrixed and depended on teamwork, but there was no one in

A matrix organization

- Institutes overlaps among functional and divisional forms

- Gives functional, product, and geographic groups a common focus

- Has dual reporting relationships rather than a single line of command

charge. When things went well, we didn't know whom to reward; and when things went poorly, we didn't know whom to blame."[7] The misassumption that someone else was handling the responsibility has led some companies, like Dow Chemical, ABB, and Citibank, to return to structures that clearly specify roles and relationships.[8]

Mixed Structure

Each firm's structure is idiosyncratic, reflecting

- Legacies
- Executive preferences
- Circumstances

In reality, the organizational charts of few MNEs neatly mimic a functional, divisional, or matrix structure. This circumstance leads us to the final format—the mixed structure that combines various functional, area, and product dimensions. Because of growth dynamics, companies seldom, if ever, get all of their activities to correspond to the basic organizational structures described here. Most develop a mixed structure. For example, a recent acquisition might report to headquarters until it can be consolidated efficiently within an existing product division. Or circumstances regarding a particular function, product, or country might necessitate that it be handled separately—that is, apart from the overall structure. Similarly, changes in industry conditions, firm capabilities, and institutional environments often require structures to change at an uneven pace. For example, IBM's recent European reorganization aimed to "have decision-making staff closer to customers," a goal that required reducing the scale of IBM's EMEA headquarters, a major unit since the end of World War II, and moving many of its responsibilities to two new, much smaller, hubs in Madrid and Zurich.[9] Some operations may be wholly owned, thus enabling a denser network of communications to develop than in other operations, where there is only partial or no ownership of the foreign operations. Further, the overall structure gives an incomplete picture of divisions in the organization. PepsiCo is organized by product lines (soft drinks and snacks), which would seem to imply that each line is integrated globally. However, each product line has its own international division, which separates it from domestic operations.

Contemporary Structures

Some MNEs find that the preceding types of structures, typically referred to as traditional structures, provide an inadequate format to respond to the demands of their dynamic environments and complex strategies.[10] Specifically, there is a growing sense that increasing international activities, expanding internal relationships, rising expectations of foreign customers, and growing power of knowledge-based strategies creates opportunities that exceed the range of traditional structures. Moreover, lower trade barriers and cheaper telecommunications and computing capabilities enable a globally dispersed labor force to collaborate more easily. These changes increasingly push MNEs from the classic structure of separate businesses organized in different countries to a worldwide company that can divide and parcel out work to the most efficient locations. Capitalizing on these opportunities has spurred MNEs to conceive ways to arrange roles and responsibilities so that more employees, particularly those in the front line who deal more directly with resources and markets, have greater authority. Hence, the past few years has seen many companies engage new ways to structure work in ways that make them more locally responsive without sacrificing the potential of global integration.

IBM provides a case in point. Like many MNEs operating in Europe, IBM had traditionally pursued a multidomestic strategy that was supported by a geographic area structure that provided for a subsidiary for each country. IBM relied on a large regional office in Paris to oversee its national subsidiaries and consolidate operations where possible. Integration within the European Union in the 1990s pushed IBM to move more decision making from local subsidiaries to its regional office in the effort to develop a pan-European strategy that would achieve greater cross-national integration. In 2005,

IBM announced that it would lay off up to 13,000 workers, mostly in Europe, and hire up to 14,000 workers in India as part of its ongoing evolution in its strategy of globalizing its operations by moving back-office work like accounting, compliance, call support, and procurement to low-cost locations. Technological, regulatory, and competitive pressures pushed IBM to dismantle the national and regional administrative fiefdoms it had established in each country in Europe in the postwar years, in favor of hiring Indian software engineers who could work on projects anywhere in the world, via the Internet, from their hometowns. IBM reasoned that it no longer made sense to maintain traditional types of structures when it could, as its rivals had, adopt a leaner, global style of operation that let managers send work digitally across the Internet to where it could be done most efficiently. "We're still going to have deep roots locally, but we are increasingly globalizing our operations and processes," said Robert J. Moffat, an IBM senior vice president, to deal with the new realities of organizing international operations.[11]

Examples of contemporary structures take a range of names, such as *learning organization, virtual organization,* or *modular structure.* No matter the variations in the name, they all share the same premise: A structure should not be defined by, or limited to, the horizontal, vertical, or external boundaries that block the development of knowledge-generating and decision-making relationships in the company. This idea was popularized by Jack Welch, former chairman and CEO of General Electric, who wanted to eliminate vertical and horizontal boundaries within the company as well as break down barriers between the company and its customers, suppliers, and other stakeholders. More specifically, he noted:

> *The simplest definition of what we are trying to create—what our objective is—is a bound-aryless Company—a company where the artificial barriers and walls people are forever building around themselves or each other for status—security—or to keep change away— are demolished—and everyone has access to the same information—everyone pulls in the same direction—and everyone shares in the rewards of winning—in the soul as well as in the wallet.[12]*

Contemporary structures, therefore, aim to have few to no boundaries between different vertical ranks and functions, different units in different geographic locations, and the firm and its suppliers, distributors, joint venture partners, strategic allies, and customers.

In practical terms, *boundaries* refer to the horizontal constraints that follow from having specific employees only do specific jobs in specific units and the vertical constraints that separate employees into specific levels of the hierarchy. Horizontal and vertical boundaries are characteristics of traditional structures. Effectively, each degree of specification in the hierarchy of a company in a traditional structure installs boundaries that block the movement of ideas. In response, contemporary structures call for loosely connected networks that self-organize and self-govern, where managers maximize information flows by minimizing the structure that gets in the way of people developing knowledge-generating and decision-making relationships. Contemporary structures, for example, question the purpose and largely reject the features of traditional structures, like chains of command, formal departments, and precise reporting relationships. In their place, they champion notions of limitless spans of control, ad hoc teams, and self-organizing groups. We now profile leading examples of contemporary structures: the network, virtual structure, and project structure.

Network Structure

An emergent structural option for managers is the network format, which is a small core organization that outsources value activities in which it does not command a core competency to those that do (see Figure 15.3). This approach allows organizations to focus on those activities in which they create maximum value and contract out other activities to

Boundarylessness refers to eliminating vertical, horizontal, or external boundaries that hinder information flows.

A network organization is a small core organization that outsources value activities to key partners.

FIGURE 15.3

A SIMPLE DEPICTION OF THE NETWORK STRUCTURE

Differentiated units to which headquarters delegates decision-making authority. These units, whether they are local marketing subsidiaries, international production centers, or cross-functional teams, are the front line of the network with responsibility for sensing, processing, and acting upon specialized and generalized information in an entrepreneurial fashion.

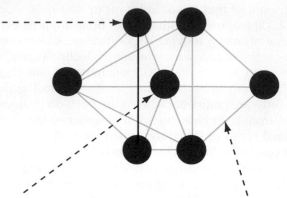

The formal center of the network, this unit coordinates strategic objectives and operational polices across the differentiated units, ensures the efficient flow of resources, supplies, components and funds throughout the network, and effectively collects, sorts and distributes the organization's accumulated wisdom, knowledge and experiences.

The channels of exchange that manage and fine-tune the volume, content, and flow of hard and soft information. These linkages animate the network by setting paths of interaction, coordination, and integration between differentiated yet interdependent functional, area, and product units.

those companies that can do those activities better than they do—as the saying goes, "do what you do best and outsource the rest." MNEs like Nike, L.L. Bean, and Cisco Systems emphasize their design skills and hire other MNEs, like Sanmina or Flextronics, to make their products. Similarly, many financial institutions, hotel chains, and credit card companies have found that they can create more value by offshoring call center functions to those companies that have a core competency in that activity.

A network structure helps MNEs outsource activities, from manufacturing to service, calls, yet still maintain a sense of organization. That is, the relationship between the MNE and the companies it networks with is not merely a matter of efficient ordering and order fulfillment processes that adhere to specific contractual parameters. Rather, the network structure promotes an extensive web of relationships between the different companies in ways that let managers keep track of the workflow even though it is being done by other companies. Essentially, then, an MNE partners with select suppliers and then develops specialized decision-making relationships that let the collectivity of companies jointly manage value activities. Cisco, for instance, is essentially a research and development company that uses many outside suppliers and independent manufacturers to assemble the products it designs. Capitalizing on its core competency in design but still retaining some say in its outsourced production led Cisco to build a global network. Operationally, Cisco has entered into joint ownership arrangements with other companies to share production, distribution, and technology-development facilities. It contracts with other companies to share technology and relies on other companies to produce and distribute goods and components. Cisco organizes its many alliances with the communication technology that made Cisco successful. The company uses the Internet, e-mail, file sharing, and conferencing to link partners across corporate and national boundaries. More formally, the company designed the Cisco Connection and Cisco Internet Business Roadmap in order to give its partners easier communication and flexible relationships.

While a novel format for many MNEs today, variations of the network structure have been in play in other countries for many years. Most notably, Japanese companies often use the so-called *keiretsu* structure, which is basically an integrated collectivity of nominally independent companies in which each company owns a small percentage of others in the network. Many German companies are similarly intertwined, but there is no formal term to describe them.[13] Keiretsus, as they work in Japan, rely on long-term strong personal relationships among high-level managers in the different companies. The same directors often serve on more than one board. Sometimes keiretsus are vertical—for example, the network between Toyota and its parts suppliers. Sometimes they are horizontal and no single company dominates, as is the case with the Mitsubishi keiretsu.[14]

Virtual Organization

A virtual organization is the antithesis of a traditional vertical hierarchy. Rather than seeking to control value chain activities through direct ownership of businesses, virtual organizations acquire resources or strategic capabilities by creating a temporary network of independent companies, suppliers, customers, and even rivals. This temporary network then relies on information technology to create the links needed to share skills, costs, and access to one another's markets.[15] The inspiration for this structural approach largely comes from the film industry in which people from around the world are essentially "free agents" who move from project to project applying their skills—directing, talent search, costuming, makeup, set design—as needed.

Operationally, a virtual organization consists of a small core of full-time employees that temporarily hires outside specialists to work on opportunities that arise. An example of a virtual organization is StrawberryFrog, an international advertising agency based in Amsterdam. The peculiar name of this company was inspired by a rare, tiny amphibian with a red body and blue legs; its CEO explains that the nimble strawberry frog is the opposite of the existing "dinosaur agencies, established in the industrial age as monoliths, which have the greatest difficulty in adapting to the new era."[16] StrawberryFrog officially employs 70 staffers, known as "frogs," from 25 nations but enlists as needed countless freelancers from around the world. Free of the overhead, constraints, and complexity of traditional structures, StrawberryFrog claims to offer advertisers agility and cost effectiveness, as well as innovative and "culturally neutral" creative work. The company has leveraged its loosely coupled network to do work in Europe, Asia, and the U.S. for Mitsubishi, Sony Ericsson, Pfizer, Sprint, IKEA, MTV, and Research in Motion. Finally, the use of temporary arrangements among members means that the virtual organization can quickly assemble and reassemble itself to meet a changing competitive environment.[17] Market mechanisms such as contracts, rather than hierarchy and authority, hold the virtual organization together; poorly performing companies are removed and replaced by better performing companies.

A virtual organization is a temporary arrangement among partners that can be easily reassembled to adapt to market change.

The flexibility of virtual structures means poorly performing firms can be quickly replaced.

Project Structure

Oticon, a Danish hearing-aid manufacturer, has no departments or employee job titles. All work is project based, and the teams that work on a particular project form, disband, and form again as the flow of work requires. Begun in the early 1990s, Oticon's famous "spaghetti organization" was a trailblazer in identifying new ways to use organizational means to foster the dynamic capabilities that many reasoned drive knowledge-generating and decision-making relationships.[18] Operationally, employees at Oticon "join" particular project teams that need their particular sets of skills and abilities. Once they complete the project—say, designing a new product or analyzing the performance of global distribution channels—the team disbands. Since there are no formal departments to return to, employees then take their skills, competencies, and experiences to other projects. Project structures are fluid and flexible and, given the absence of the customary boundaries found in a traditional structure, they can make decisions and take action quickly.

So far, this particularly radical form of structure has proven difficult to sustain. Senior managers often struggle with living by the promise not to intervene in delegated decision-making rights. In actuality, frequent managerial intervention can erode the credibility of this promise and create motivation problems for employees. In some cases, "spaghetti" sorts of project structure have given way to a more traditional matrix organization.[19]

POINT–COUNTERPOINT: HIERARCHIES OR HYPERARCHIES?

POINT

At its most elegant, organizational structure is the formal arrangement of jobs within an organization that enable the company to get stuff done. From this simple premise flows a compelling debate: Should MNEs adopt a hierarchy or hyperarchy as the structure of their organization for international operations?

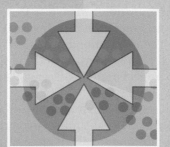

Proponents of the hierarchy argue that this format is the enduring foundation for how managers across the world determine the optimal degrees of work specialization, the best approach to departmentalization, the ideal degree of rules, regulations, policies, and procedures, an efficient chain of command, a functional span of control, and the right balance between centralization and decentralization. Indeed, many see the hierarchy as the basis of the tried-and-true professional management model. First developed in the 1920s by General Motors, DuPont, Sears, and Standard Oil, hierarchical structures, like the functional, divisional, and matrix formats, have provided a powerful framework that guided the international expansions of thousands of companies from virtually every country in the world. The absolute clarity of the hierarchy—its bias toward extreme degrees of vertical and horizontal differentiation—enables developing the sophisticated planning systems, information systems, and control systems that allow top management to command and control operations. Indeed, one of the great advocates of this hierarchy structure, Harold Geneen of ITT, said that he believed it helped him in his quest "to make people as predictable and controllable as the capital resources that they're responsible for."

Certainly, supporters of the long-proven authority of the hierarchy recognize the implication of technological, regulatory, and competitive trends to organizational standards—that is, the environments of international business are changing and so too are companies' strategies and organizations. However, rather than discarding the principles of the hierarchy, they believe it is a strong foundation for future success. Moreover, managers' continuing efforts to fortify this foundation by reengineering business functions and process, with the help of programs like total quality management, scenario and contingency planning, supply chain management, and Six Sigma, clarify the division of work and differentiation of authority.[20] On the flip side, defenders of the hierarchy point out that moving from the rhetoric of new forms of boundaryless structures to the day-to-day reality of coordinating and controlling international operations is a huge leap that calls for common sense and thoughtful adjustment.

COUNTERPOINT

In contrast, some scholars herald the dawn of the *hyperarchy*, believing this revolutionary format provides a structure that remedies the intrinsic limitation of the hierarchy as well as positions a company to better deal with the environment of globalization. Technically, a hyperarchy is "a large-scale, self-organizing community that sets free unusually high degrees of energy and engagement—despite the lack of clear or direct economic payoff for participants."[21] As such, a hyperarchy can unleash the intrinsic motivation of employees, thereby letting it get past the hierarchy's tendency to stifle workers' ability to adapt, innovate, and take calculated risks. Perhaps the best-known hyperarchy is the Linux project, the vanguard of the broader open-source software movement in which program source code is given away to volunteers who help fix bugs and design new features without any direct monetary compensation. Operationally, the hyperarchy engages a battery of simple rules to increase transparency and symmetry of information. So, for example, because Linux programmers can pretty much see what everyone else is doing, everyone has an incentive to reciprocate when others share information with them. In the course of such sharing, participants build reputations, good or bad, throughout the community. Reciprocity and reputation thus work together to establish trust as the primary transaction currency in a hyperarchy.

The contest between hierarchies and hyperarchies will likely be determined by the environment; after all, the purpose of structure is to arrange work so that a company can effectively implement its strategy. As such, some contend that the twenty-first century had ushered in a fundamental shift in our idea of organization. Now, markets reward companies that build a boundaryless organization that supports an energizing strategic purpose rather than precisely designing a structure that looked great on paper but fell apart in the stress-test of reality. Finally, some pointed to events at Intel as possibly foreshadowing how the contest between hierarchies and hyperarchies might shake out. Andy Grove, CEO of Intel for many years and *Time*'s Man of the Year in 2000, believed that organization structure had to find ways to encourage and energize constructive confrontation in ways that let people agree, disagree, but ultimately commit to the same goals. Management had to develop the structure that, as Andy Grove reasoned, enabled them to "Let chaos reign and then rein in chaos."[22]

COORDINATION AND CONTROL SYSTEMS

Thus far we have looked at the idea of structural differentiation—the vertical and the horizontal dimensions, or the lack thereof, found in a company's structure. Still, at the outset of the chapter, we noted that MNEs must also deal with the question of how to coordinate and control the activities that make up their value chains. Again, as we saw in the case of Zara and eBay in Chapter 11, MNEs are increasingly devising sophisticated strategies to create value. These strategies challenge managers to then build the coordination methods and control measures that complement the company's chosen organizational structure (and we will see, in the next section, the organization culture that shapes individual attitudes and actions). Research consistently reports that MNEs use several coordination and control tools to manage the strategic performance of their value chains. We profile each in turn.

> Systems are the framework of processes and procedures used to ensure that an organization can fulfill all tasks required to achieve its objectives.

Coordination Systems

The importance of coordination follows from the simple reality of life in the MNE. The division of value activities across countries often leads different groups of managers and employees to develop different concerns and orientations. Depending on whether they are headquarters- or subsidiary-based or working in primary or support value activities, they often tend to think and act in ways that are anchored in their immediate responsibilities. If unchecked, this tendency can lead employees in separate functions, subsidiaries, and countries to stop thinking about their counterparts, thereby making it difficult for managers to develop the knowledge-generating and decision-making relationships that coordinate worldwide activities into an integrated whole. In extreme circumstances, people may deliberately or mistakenly act in self-serving ways to the detriment of the company. Without some means to coordinate what people do, the competitiveness of a value chain, no matter how brilliantly configured, will erode.

> Coordination systems link the various activities of a company.

Managers tap several approaches to coordinate the operations of interdependent units and individuals. We look at three prevalent approaches: coordination by standardization, by plans, and by mutual adjustment.

Coordination by Standardization Companies with far-flung operations aim to establish a day-to-day infrastructure that prescribes many of the ways that employees do their jobs, work with one another, and deal with customers. A key motivation is the realization that a high degree of operational consistency helps the company leverage its core competency as well as brings the advantages of scale to its organization of activities. Therefore, MNEs specify routines that standardize many features of operations, ranging from the mundane—for example, dress and decorum that are spelled out in employee manuals—to the strategic—for example, dealing with joint venture partners or assessing potential markets. Starbucks, for example, standardizes many features of its products, processes, and procedures in order to replicate the look, operations, and feel of the elusive atmosphere of its U.S. coffee shop concept around the world. Standardization, by prescribing how managers and workers do their jobs, installs the policies to coordinate decisions among units in the company.

> Coordination by standardization
> - Sets universal rules and procedures that apply to units worldwide
> - Enforces consistency in performance of activities in geographically dispersed units

Growing pressure to leverage innovations across value activities push many MNEs to expand standardization to also specify rules and regulations about how employees interact. Technically called *formalization*, this method of coordination aims to reduce the sorts of workplace uncertainty that complicate the exchange of ideas and resources. For example, formalizing distribution lists for production or marketing updates eliminates potential oversights in how the MNE collects, processes, and disseminates information.

An important assumption underlying coordination by standardization is that the rules and procedures that the company devises apply to every situation in every unit in every country where it has operations. Regular exceptions to the rules undermine the authority of standardization and create points of uncertainty that impede coordination. Consequently, coordination by standardization is ideally suited for strategies that champion constancy and predictability in industries that are more stable than volatile. As such, companies following an international or geocentric strategy are inclined to emphasize coordination by standardization. In the case of the former, the intent to transfer, protect, and leverage core competencies spurs explicit specification of rules and regulations. In the case of the latter, the deep integration among typically consolidated value activities leaves no room for surprises—specific transfers of resources and components are needed at specific plants at specific times, otherwise production grinds to a halt. Standardizing coordination methods—such as the structures for processing information—helps eliminate delays and mistakes.

Coordination by Plan   The fact that industry conduct, competitive dynamics, host-government attitudes, and many other factors differ among countries greatly complicates coordination by standardization. Some companies are more sensitive to this pressure than others, particularly those that create value by adapting operations to local conditions. Notably, MNEs following a multidomestic strategy, versus those following a geocentric strategy, are more likely to reason that coordination by standardization is not the best approach. Although diversity may preclude universal rules and procedures, it does not excuse managers of the responsibility of coordinating value activities. In such situations, the MNE may opt to establish objectives and schedules that give interdependent units greater discretion in developing coordination systems. Relying on general objectives and detailed schedules, rather than rules and regulations, is the basis for coordination by plan. Provided they comply with the deadlines and targets of the plan, interdependent units have some latitude to adapt their operations. Effectively, a detailed planning document establishes a framework for the next quarter to year that gives managers a blueprint for coordination.

Planning under the best of circumstances is tough in the MNE. Despite advances in communications technologies, some managers prefer to deal with their counterparts through face-to-face or voice-to-voice contact. Geographic distance and cultural divergence increase the time, expense, and possibility of error in cross-national communications. More serious is the fact that no matter how carefully a project is planned, something may still go wrong with it, or more poetically, "the best-laid plans of mice and men often go awry."[23] Several conditions aggravate this situation, such as periodic disruptions, sensitivity to government regulations, and conflict with local partners. Combined, planning objectives and schedules may need to be revised, a tendency that constrains coordination.

Companies often use a range of executive development and education programs to get people familiar with their preferred planning format and preempt the preceding threats. For example, many companies have adopted Six Sigma programs, a rigorous and disciplined process that utilizes data and statistical analysis to measure and improve a company's operational performance, practices, and systems. MNEs, like General Electric, Motorola, Allied-Signal, and DuPont, use it to anchor their planning process. The ability of Six Sigma programs to improve coordination by plan makes it so important that few question its purpose and most understand its procedures. So, for example, each year

General Electric sends about 10,000 newly hired and longtime managers to its Leadership Development Center for a three-week course on the company's Six Sigma quality initiative. More than 5,000 "Master Black Belt" and "Black Belt" Six Sigma experts have graduated from the program with the goal of driving forward thousands of quality initiatives throughout the company's global operations. Other MNEs that rely on coordination by plan use related methods. They develop teams with members from different countries to build scenarios on how the future may evolve.[24] Some aim to locate international and domestic personnel in closer proximity to each other—for example, by placing the international division in the same building or complex as the product divisions. Finally, others place foreign personnel on the board of directors and top-level committees to engage foreign viewpoints in the planning processes.

Coordination by Mutual Adjustment   Unlike the explicit features of standardization and planning, some MNEs coordinate value activities through a range of informal mechanisms. Basically, these mechanisms create ways for employees to engage fellow employees more often over matters of joint importance in a process called *coordination by mutual adjustment*. For example, 3M has technology experts in more than 100 laboratories around the world that work in ways that support coordination of knowledge-generation and decision making. Specifically, 3M's management uses techniques such as a Technical Council, composed of the heads of the major labs, that meets monthly and has a three-day annual retreat to discuss ways to improve cross-unit transfer of technology. In addition, management created a broader-based Technical Forum, composed of scientists and technical experts chosen as representatives, to facilitate grassroots communication among employees throughout its labs.[25] Both methods of interaction, by enabling the flexible exchange of ideas, create the capability that lets employees coordinate by mutual adjustment.

> Coordination by mutual adjustment requires managers to interact with counterparts to enable flexible coordination mechanisms.

Certainly, MNEs that opt to encourage mutual adjustment also adopt a formal structure and install standardization and planning systems. However, they also see great value in engaging an adaptable approach to coordination that involves creating more opportunity and incentive for interdependent parties to talk to one another. This approach can lead to many coordination mechanisms, such as developing teams from different countries to work on special projects of cross-national importance so that they share viewpoints, giving divisions and subsidiaries credit for business resulting from cooperative efforts so that they are encouraged to view activities broadly, establishing liaisons among subsidiaries within the same country so that different product groups can combine action on a given issue, and rotating managers between domestic and international positions in order to encourage more engagement. For instance, General Electric frequently transfers managers across divisional, business, or functional lines for sustained tours of duty. Senior management believes that these sorts of transfers enable managers to develop relationships with colleagues in other parts of the company that, by weakening insular thinking and promoting idea sharing, make it possible to better coordinate operations. In summary, companies use coordination by mutual adjustment to give managers and workers the means to jointly figure out how to define a situation and devise a solution they see as vital to making the value chain work.

Mutual adjustment can be a very effective coordination tool when an MNE faces new problems that cannot be defined with customary rules or procedures. Too, MNEs can preempt resistance to a particular initiative before it interferes with its strategy by getting employees on board before the launch. Still, coordination via mutual adjustment creates new challenges. Operationally, decisions can get bogged down in discussion as new viewpoints reset the debate. More fundamentally, the premise of mutual adjustment resets the power of the organization. Headquarters must accept the notion that innovations, knowledge, and skills can arise anywhere within the firm's global network, not just at the center—headquarters must adjust too.[26] The role of senior managers then moves from telling people what to do to facilitating what they do if they expect to transfer valuable innovations from a particular subsidiary to other parts of the organization.

> The frequent discussion and feedback needed to make mutual adjustment work can be costly.

Control Systems

Every MNE, at some point, must decide how to regulate what people can and cannot do or else risk spinning out of control. Hence, control systems are a fundamental part of a well-designed organization. Control is necessary because once an MNE adopts a strategy, it must ensure that employees implement its various elements as planned. Operationally, this requires managers to build the control systems that make sure that people are not doing inappropriate things, and ideally, people are doing what needs to be done. Control takes precedence in the case of the former: People are not performing properly, coordination problems are emerging, and management must take steps to correct the situation. An effective control system ensures that activities are completed in ways that attain the company's strategy. Control systems regulate the allocation and utilization of resources and, in so doing, facilitate the coordination process, no matter whether anchored in standardization, planning, or mutual adjustment routines. That said, the criterion that determines the effectiveness of control systems is how well it compels actions that support strategy. Finally, experiences at several companies, like Barings Bank, Andersen Consulting, Parmalat, WorldCom, and Enron, show that the lack of controls or the wrong kinds of controls can cause irreparable damage.

There are three prevalent methods of control:

- *Market control,* whereby the MNE uses external market mechanisms, like price competition and relative market share, to establish internal performance benchmarks and standards. In this mode, headquarters evaluates each discrete unit of the organization, say one of the 200 plus units of J&J, by looking at any number of market bases measures, such as percentage of total corporate profits each contributes. Control systems start when the unit fails to meet its target.

- *Bureaucratic control,* whereby the MNE uses centralized authority to install an extensive set of rules and procedures to govern a broad range of activities. Units that fail to comply with the policies and procedures trigger alarms that attract the attention of senior managers.

- *Clan control,* whereby the MNE relies on shared values among all employees to idealize the preferred behaviors. Clan control encourages employees to identify strongly with the shared idea of what's important in their company. This identification then guides and controls how they do their job.

MNEs identify which sort of control system will work best with how they have configured and are trying to coordinate their value chain. For instance, companies following a geocentric strategy tend to favor a mix of market controls, given that they can use considerable marketplace competition to evaluate the performance of their clearly specified and distinct products—such as computer chips or automobile tires. In contrast, transnational companies tend to rely on clan control. The importance of open exchange among geographically diffuse people who are strongly encouraged to develop knowledge-generating and decision-making relationships fits well with less direct control tools. Ultimately, few MNEs rely on a single approach to control. Instead, they aim to design the control system that complements how the company has decided to coordinate its activities.

Control Mechanisms

MNEs use a range of control mechanisms to direct the activities of individuals toward the achievement of organizational goals. We now look at some of the principal mechanisms.

Reports   Reports, while sounding somewhat innocuous, are a powerful control mechanism. Headquarters needs timely reports to allocate resources, monitor performance, and reward personnel. Decisions on how to use capital, personnel, and technology continue without interruption, so reports must be frequent, accurate, and up-to-date. Headquarters uses reports to evaluate the performance of subsidiary personnel in order to reward and motivate them. These personnel adhere to reports and try to perform well on the tasks that are reported in them so that they receive more rewards. They also seek feedback so they will know how well they are performing and can alter their performance accordingly.[27]

The intricacies of international business make reports an important element of this sort of control system. For example, geographical distance often leads managers to standardize coordination methods. Similarly, headquarters often has less frequent contact with people in the foreign operations, which moves them to rely on extensive reports for control. MNEs often use reports to identify deviations from plans that could indicate problem areas. The focus of the reports may be to monitor short-term performance or longer-term indicators that match the company's strategy.

Increasingly, information technology makes reports an even more attractive control mechanism. For example, most MNEs use ERP (enterprise resource planning) to monitor value activities, including product planning, parts purchasing, maintaining inventories, interacting with suppliers, providing customer service, and tracking orders. The resulting data give managers a remarkable control tool. For instance, the Japanese retailer Ito-Yokado, which owns and operates the 7-Eleven convenience store franchise in Japan, has linked each store's automated cash registers into an ERP system that records sales and monitors inventory as well as schedules daily and weekly tasks for store managers. The ERP system tracks how often managers used the built-in analytical tools, graphs, and forecasts. Headquarters then tells those managers that have not checked in often enough to increase their activities.[28]

Finally, MNEs typically use reports for foreign operations that resemble those they use domestically. Managers reason that:

- If reports have worked well domestically, they will also work well internationally.
- There are economies from carrying over the same types of reports. Extension eliminates the need to establish new types of reporting mechanisms. Also, corporate management's familiarity with the system leverages learning.
- Reports with similar formats enable management to better compare one operation with another.

Visits to Subsidiaries   Not all information exchange occurs through formalized written reports. Within many MNEs, especially those relying on coordination by adjustment and clan control, members of the corporate staff often visit subsidiaries in order to confer and socialize with local managers. Although this attention may alleviate misunderstandings, there are some "rules" for conducting visits properly. On the one hand, if corporate personnel visit the tropical subsidiaries only when there are blizzards at home, the personnel abroad may perceive the trips as boondoggles. On the other hand, if a subsidiary's managers offer too many social activities and not enough analysis of operations, corporate personnel may consider the trip a waste of time. Further, if visitors arrive only when the corporate level is upset about foreign operations, local managers may always be overly defensive. Nevertheless, visits can serve the goal of controlling foreign operations because they enable the visitors to collect information and offer advice and directives.

Management Performance Evaluation   MNEs aim to evaluate subsidiary managers separately from their subsidiary's performance in order to avoid penalizing or rewarding them for conditions beyond their control. For example, headquarters may decide not to expand further in a country because of its slow growth and risky economic and political environment. Nonetheless, the company should still reward that country's managers for

Reports are intended first to evaluate operating units and second to evaluate management in those units.

doing a good job in the face of adversity. However, what is within a subsidiary manager's control varies from company to company (because of decision-making authority differences) and from subsidiary to subsidiary (because of local conditions). Take currency gains or losses. Who is responsible depends on whether working capital management decisions occur at headquarters or at the subsidiary level—and on whether there are instruments such as forward markets in a particular country that allow for hedging against currency value changes.

Another uncontrollable area is when headquarters managers make decisions that will optimize the entire company's performance, perhaps at the expense of a particular subsidiary. In addition, the normal profit-center records may well obscure the importance the subsidiary has within the total corporate entity.

One way to overcome the problems of evaluating performance is to look at a budget agreed upon by headquarters and subsidiary managers. Doing this can help the MNE differentiate between a subsidiary's worth and its management's performance. The budget should cover the goals for each subsidiary that will help the MNE achieve an overall objective.

Companies must evaluate results in comparison to budgets but realize that it is hard to compare countries using standard operating ratios.

A system that relies on a combination of measurements is more reliable than one that does not.

Cost and Accounting Comparability   Different costs among subsidiaries may prevent a meaningful comparison of their operating performance. For example, the ratio of labor to sales for a subsidiary in one country may be much higher than that for a subsidiary in another country, even though unit production costs may not differ substantially. So management must ensure that it is comparing relevant costs. Different accounting practices can also create reporting and accountability problems. Most MNEs keep one set of books that are consistent with home-country principles and another to meet local reporting requirements. Clearly, headquarters needs to use considerable discretion in interpreting the data it uses to evaluate subsidiary performance, especially if it is comparing performance with competitors from other countries whose accounting methods are different from its own.

Evaluative Measurements   Headquarters should evaluate subsidiaries and their managers on a number of indicators rather than emphasizing one. Financial criteria tend to dominate the evaluation of foreign operations and their managers, particularly when an MNE relies on plans to coordinate and a bureaucracy to control international operations. For instance, managers at British Petroleum's various divisions have some autonomy to run their units as they see fit provided they meet their budgets and comply with corporate guidelines. Although many different criteria are important, the most important for evaluating both the operation and its management are "budget compared with profit" and "budget compared with sales value," because these immediately affect consolidated corporate figures. Many nonfinancial criteria are also important, such as market-share increase, quality control, and managers' relationship with host governments.

Information Systems   Corporate management often requires additional data to coordinate and control operations. Examples of key needs include:

- Information generated for centralized coordination, such as subsidiary cash balances and needs, so that headquarters can move funds effectively
- Information on external conditions, such as analyses of local political and economic conditions, so that headquarters can plan where to expand and constrict operations
- Information that can be used as feedback from parent to subsidiaries, such as R&D breakthroughs, so that subsidiaries can compete more effectively
- Information that subsidiaries can share so that they can learn from each other and be motivated to perform as well as other subsidiaries
- Information for external reporting needs, such as to stakeholders and tax authorities

MNEs routinely face three problems in acquiring information: (1) the cost of information compared to its value, (2) redundant information, and (3) information that is irrelevant. For example, much of the information that is useful to a subsidiary, such as whom to contact to clear items through customs, need not be reported to headquarters. To cope, companies periodically reevaluate the information sources they use. Expanding global telecommunications, Internet links, and e-mail systems enable managers throughout the world to share information more quickly and easily than ever before. On the one hand, this technology may permit more centralization, because headquarters can more easily examine the global conditions and local performance, as we saw in the case of 7-Eleven in Japan. On the other hand, managers in foreign locations may become more autonomous because they have more information at their disposal, as we saw in our profile of J&J.

> Management should reevaluate information needs periodically to keep costs down, and it should ensure that information is being used effectively.

ORGANIZATION CULTURE

So far, we have looked at the roles that structure and systems play in defining the organization of a company. We now turn to the final element of this profile—the culture of the organization. In theory, one could look at organization culture in an applied fashion, specifying it as the way things get done in a company on a day-to-day basis. Alternatively, we could follow the suggestion of Chapter 2 and adopt a more philosophical view, defining organization culture as a deeply embedded set of shared normative principles that guide action and serve as standards to evaluate one's own and others' behaviors. We opt for a little of both, defining **organization culture** as the set of fundamental assumptions about the organization and its goals and practices that members of the company share. As such, organization culture is a system of shared values about what is important and beliefs about how the world works.

> Organization culture is the shared meaning and beliefs that shape how employees act.

Historically, companies were sensitive to the idea that culture played some sort of role in the organization. However, several reasons have led managers to take a more expansive view of organization culture, seeing it as a powerful tool that can be directly managed to encourage and support the goals and behaviors that help the company achieve its strategy. Studies confirm a significant link between organization culture and the financial performance of a firm—that is, facets of organization culture, like the values and principles of management, nature of the work climate and atmosphere, traditions and ethical standards, are directly related to a company's financial performance.[29] More generally, others report that culture is the most critical component of a company's transition from "good" to "great" status. Technology, product development, and financial stewardship play principal roles in this transition. Still, most managers link the goal of becoming a great company to developing an organization culture that champions unwavering faith and passion, rigorous discipline and focus, clearly communicated and practiced core values and timeless principles, strong work ethics, and finding and promoting people with the right outlook.[30] In summary, great companies developed organization cultures that gave employees a consistent way to organize how they relate to their job, to each other, to customers, to shareholders, and to business partners.

> Key features of a company's organization culture include
> - Values and principles of management
> - Work climate and atmosphere
> - Patterns of "how we do things around here"
> - Traditions
> - Ethical standards

The Growing Importance of Culture

The importance of organization culture will likely increase. Earlier chapters highlighted growing pressures on companies to improve their global competitiveness. Later chapters detail many of the novel approaches companies use to do so, for instance, reconfiguring their value chains to streamline manufacturing processes or maximizing supply chain efficiencies with better coordination mechanisms. Research suggests that none of these approaches has much of a chance of producing sustainable benefits and lasting competitive advantage without an organization that has a complementary culture. Indeed, it is generally unwise for a company to undertake strategic moves that conflict with the values shared by managers and employees. Certainly, companies could develop the set of

> The organization culture often shapes the strategic moves a company will consider and reject.

constraints, controls, and contracts that compel employees to do their best. However, this traditional outlook is costly and often counterproductive.

This limitation is especially glaring given reports that successful companies develop an organization culture that instills in their employees degrees of enthusiasm and job involvement above and beyond that justified by economic rewards alone—"Objectives don't get you there. Values do," said Jack Welch of General Electric. Put simply, strategy-supportive cultures stimulate people to take on the challenge of realizing the company's vision, to do their jobs competently and with enthusiasm, and to collaborate with others to execute the strategy. Moreover, a powerful organization culture lessens the need to regulate employees' behaviors with more elaborate structures and systems. Therefore, the apparent power of culture to build a high-performance organization puts the onus on managers to create the organization that inspires this sort of behavior. Or, put more directly, to build an organization that people don't want to just work for, they want to belong to, like Honda.

More practically, increasingly sophisticated value chain configurations produce more interdependence among subsidiaries. Maximizing coordination and maintaining control of value activities prompts managers to contact, both formally and informally, their peers in other subsidiaries more frequently. Often, managers set up cross-cultural teams to tackle issues common to different country operations. These teams generally are composed of people chosen because of their skills and expertise, not because of their positions, and they are made up of equals, not of a superior and subordinates. The ability of the team to reach consensus is dependent on the group members' enthusiasm as well as peer pressure within the groups, rather than on the structure of the organization or the comprehensiveness of the company's system. Moreover, in the event of poor performance, success will not follow from revising their formal structure to force changes in roles or revising systems to force change in interpersonal relationships. Rather, success will likely follow from reshaping the individual attitudes and actions of managers that then support the work ethic that triggers the individual-level behaviors of learning and collaboration.[31]

Companies use various approaches and tools to promote a shared understanding of their mission, objectives, and accomplishments among the workforce. Here we see a celebration of Honda's product leadership and production quality at its Marysville, Ohio plant. At the ceremony, American Honda President Koichi Kondo noted that "customer loyalty is recognition that our U.S. associates build products of the highest quality, reliability and value."

Finally, the shared values that make up organization culture influence what employees perceive, how they interpret, and what they do to respond to their world. At J&J, for example, the company anchors its ideas of value creation and strategic purpose in the principles embodied in "Our Credo." Our opening case reported that this manifesto unifies J&J employees worldwide by championing a set of common values that provides a constant reminder of the company's responsibilities to its stakeholders. So, when confronted with opportunities or threats, the organizational culture influences what employees can do and how they conceptualize, define, analyze, and resolve issues.

Challenges and Pitfalls

Rather than letting the organization's culture emerge naturally, companies increasingly develop and manage, just as they do with regards to their structure and systems, their set of shared values and beliefs. Our Looking to the Future segment profiles an increasingly popular way companies do so. Still, MNEs run into particular difficulty managing their organization culture. Most immediately, managers from different countries often have different values that differ from those endorsed by the company. Complicating matters is the fact that many people in an MNE have slight exposure to the values held by senior managers. The severity of this problem is directly proportional to the importance of knowledge-generating and decision-making relationships to the MNE's competitiveness.[32] That is, convergent values ease the exchange of ideas between people from different countries, whereas different values tend to create boundaries and barriers. MNEs also run into cultural conflicts that prevent cross-national teams, an increasingly popular management tool, from working well. For instance, at one company the U.S. managers complained that the U.K. managers were too bureaucratic, and the U.K. managers complained that the U.S. managers would try to reach decisions without a thorough analysis.[33] Furthermore, there is evidence that mixing national cultures on teams does not necessarily improve performance.[34]

To overcome these challenges, many companies promote closer contact among managers from different countries. The aim is to convey a shared understanding of global goals and norms along with improving the transfer of ideas and best practices from one country to another.[35] For example, General Electric's Leadership Development Center offers advanced courses for senior managers that sometimes focus on a single management topic for up to a month. All classes involve managers from different GE businesses and different parts of the world. Some of the most valuable learning comes in between the formal class sessions when managers from different businesses and stationed in spots around the world trade ideas. Besides spreading best practices throughout the organization, knowledge sharing also improves each GE manager's understanding of the company.[36] Explained Jeffrey Immelt, chairman and CEO of General Electric, the company tries "very hard to provide a company, a set of values, and a culture that employees can be proud of, whether it be in Pittsfield, Paris, Shanghai, or London."[37] Operationally, many companies frequently rotate managers among operations in different countries in order to develop increased knowledge of and commitment to a common set of values and objectives. Both approaches exemplify how companies actively develop and fine-tune the shared understanding of the company's strategy and values.

Strategy and Organization Culture

The principles and practices of organization culture vary with the type of strategy (see Figure 15.4). For example, the company pursuing a global strategy aims to develop a forceful culture that helps everyone around the world understand and accept the

Organization culture varies with the type of strategy the company pursues.

FIGURE 15.4

**ORGANIZATIONAL
CULTURE ASPECTS OF
TYPES OF STRATEGIES**

	Low — Pressure for National Responsiveness — High	
High Pressure for Global Integration **Low**	**GLOBAL** Strategic objectives: Productivity and efficiency Strategic emphasis: Integration, competitive advantage Dominant attribute: Standardized goal achievement, global competitiveness Leadership style: Production-and achievement-oriented, decisive control orientation Bonding: Goal orientation, production, competition	**TRANSNATIONAL** Strategic objectives: Integration, responsiveness, learning Strategic emphasis: Innovation, ideas and growth Dominant attribute: Innovation, creativity, dynamism flexibility Leadership style: Innovator, risk affinitive, congruence between individual values and company goals Bonding: Flexibility, risk, entrepreneurship
	INTERNATIONAL Strategic objectives: Leverage core competencies Strategic emphasis: Control, stability, predictability Dominant attribute: Formal order, rules and regulations, uniformity Leadership Style: Director, administrator, enforcer Bonding: Rules, policies and procedures, clear expectations	**MULTIDOMESTIC** Strategic objectives: Local responsiveness Strategic emphasis: Esprit de corps, commitment, consensus Dominant attributes: Cohesiveness, trust, affiliation, Leadership style: Mentor, facilitator, coach, adaptability Bonding: Loyalty and tradition

standard set of goals, priorities, and practices. Essentially, a global strategy's requirement to standardize value activities usually also requires standardizing employees' views. As such, culture in this strategic context greatly influences how people think and behave. Alternatively, companies following a multidomestic strategy require people to share fewer common values and tolerate greater variety in the local interpretation of corporate goals. Adapting value activities for local markets requires accepting more local autonomy, a requirement that rests on sensitivity to local outlooks and norms.

Despite specific differences, organization culture shares similar attributes across the different types of strategies. First, employees typically perceive an organization culture on the basis of what they see, hear, or experience within the company. Hence, senior managers must establish and exemplify the set of assumptions about the company and the shared values and ideals. Top management's actions have a powerful influence on an MNE's culture, given that the sheer volume of information sent to foreign outposts often dilutes or distorts perceptions. Second, even though individuals have different backgrounds, work at different organizational levels, or think about different ambitions, they tend to describe the organization's culture in similar terms. Getting people who are more likely to differ to share ideas and values spur MNEs to forsake manipulating employees through traditional approaches of reward and punishment and adopt those that motivate them to accept and endorse "how things are done around here." Consequently, executives must visibly develop, communicate, and practice the values and ideals that encourage and sustain individual involvement. Finally, organizational culture is a descriptive term. It's concerned with how employees perceive their company, not with whether they think that what it does or aims to do is intrinsically right. Managers must develop the flexible processes that encourage and tolerate a range of interpretations and opinions as needed.

LOOKING TO THE FUTURE: The Role and Rise of Corporate Universities

Companies' belief that instead of simply letting the organization's culture emerge naturally, managers must increasingly develop and monitor, just as they do with their structure and systems, their shared values, has led to a variety of approaches. Most notably, it has fueled a boom in corporate universities—physical and virtual institutions that lead training efforts, facilitate continuous organizational learning, and help upgrade company competencies and capabilities. Presently, corporate universities are growing by leaps and bounds in the U.S., thriving in Europe, and making serious inroads in Asia. In the past few years, there has been exponential growth and the emergence of over a thousand new corporate universities. In the U.S., the number of corporate universities grew from around 400 in 1988 to more than 1,600 in 2002 and includes nearly half of the *Fortune* 500.[38] At the current pace of growth, the number of corporate universities will exceed the number of traditional universities by 2010. In a nutshell, the boom in corporate universities symbolizes the growing appreciation of the importance of proactively managing organization culture.

Historically, corporate universities had the mandate to teach employees practical skills and workplace systems—think of McDonald's Hamburger University in Illinois, established in the 1950s with the mission to prepare people to run a franchise. Now, corporate universities plainly confess that their goal is to "inculcate everyone from the clerical assistant to the top executive in the culture and values that make the organization unique and special and to define behaviors that enable employees to 'live the values.' "[39] For example the CEO of Unipart, a British auto parts maker, noted that his company's university "is at the very heart of the business" and a "key enabler for future growth of the business."[40] Like many other CEOs, he runs his own monthly course on the philosophy and principles of Unipart's approach to business.

Senior executives' turns as teacher yield great benefits. The director of LVMH's university noted that "it gives them access to people they would never get access to. It is the role of our top senior executives to get a feel for what is going on."[41] Managers at LVMH gain similar benefits. Typically, they go though two-and-a-half-day forums that create many networking opportunities; then, when they return to their unit, if they run into a problem, they can more comfortably call someone for help. In addition, they pick up new management tools, reporting that they go back to their divisions with six or seven new ideas and with the knowledge that they have been able to benchmark their work against that of other executives from around the world. Finally, corporate universities go a long way in integrating diverse workforces. Hiring more engineers in Bombay or Beijing makes great economic sense but it also requires the company to find ways to help people learn to work effectively in global work groups. Done well, explained the vice president of Unisys University, corporate universities provide continual learning for employees in ways that align employees' learning with the strategy of the business and impact strongly the culture of the organization.[42]

Some MNEs build university sites around the world; Unisys, for example, has campuses in each of the five geographic areas where it has a large presence, namely North America, Europe, the U.K., Latin America, and Asia and the South Pacific. Increasingly, many are using e-learning tactics like live webcasts, online chat and discussion groups, videoconferences, and interactive sessions to greatly expand the role of corporate universities. Whether real or virtual, the growing power of corporate universities as agents be an agent for insight and ideas may ultimately usher in a new role—the crucible of company strategy. That is, some foresee a potential future whereby the corporate university becomes the strategic center for the company, formulating strategy rather than following it and developing the leadership that can build an organization that moves the company from where it is today to where it should be tomorrow.

ORGANIZATION IN SPECIAL SITUATIONS

Acquisitions and shared ownership pose situations that may complicate how managers run their organization. We discuss each in turn.

Acquisitions

A policy of expansion through acquisition often leads to a mix of overlapping geographic responsibilities and markets as well as new lines of business that do not fit well with the

An acquired company usually does not completely mesh with the existing organization.

acquirer's current organization. This problem especially arises when the acquiring company's culture differs from that of the acquired one. These differences can follow from company practices and national practices—for example, British managers may have trouble adjusting to U.S. companies' more short-term perspectives and to Japanese companies' decision-making processes.[43] Other complications arise when existing management in an acquired firm is accustomed to forms of coordination and control that give them considerable autonomy—say, systems of coordination by mutual adjustment coupled with methods of clan control. When managers in the acquired company resist the call to adopt, say, methods of coordination by standardization and bureaucratic control, headquarters may opt to replace them with its personnel. The latter may then perform poorly due to less familiarity with the acquired company's competitive situation.[44] Often attempts to centralize decision making or to change operating methods generate distrust, apprehension, and resistance from local government authorities. Political officials, sensing the shift in activity to other markets, may use various means to ensure that decision making remains vested within the country. Nonetheless, there are many successful acquisitions. For example, Siemens's acquisition of Westinghouse's fossil-fuel power plant operations began with Siemens planning the integration process when considering an acquisition and then putting an integration manager in charge.[45]

Shared Ownership

Shared ownership usually makes control harder than it would be with wholly owned operations, but there are mechanisms that can work.

Ownership sharing limits the flexibility of corporate decision making. For example, Nestlé shares ownership with Coca-Cola in a joint venture for the production and sale of canned coffee and tea drinks, and Nestlé has less autonomy for this operation than for those it owns wholly because Coca-Cola has an equal voice in decision making. Nevertheless, there are administrative mechanisms that enable a company to influence the arrangement of roles, responsibilities, and procedures even with a minority equity interest. These mechanisms include spreading the remaining ownership among many shareholders, contract stipulations that board decisions require more than a majority (giving veto power to minority stockholders), dividing equity into voting and nonvoting stock, and side agreements on who will control decision making. A company can also retain control over some core competency or resource the subsidiary needs, such as a patent, a brand name, or a raw material. When a joint venture is with a competitor, organization issues transcend the joint venture itself. Employees in the partner's organization may have been conditioned over the years to compete against the other. It becomes difficult to get them to cooperate for the success of the joint venture, a situation that can greatly complicate how the company builds an organization with a useful corporate culture.

Dynamic Nature of Performance

The nature of a company's organization evolves as its business evolves. When only exporting, an export department attached to a product or functional division may suffice for a company. But if international operations grow—say, the company starts overseas production in addition to exporting—an export department will likely be insufficient. At that point, the company will likely consider a more comprehensive organization for its international operations, say, replacing the international division with a product division supplementing coordination by standardization with coordination by plan, and expanding its sense of collective values.

THE ROLE OF LEGAL STRUCTURES

When operating abroad, companies may choose among legal forms that affect their decision making, taxes, maintenance of secrecy, and legal liability. Most choose a subsidiary form for which there are additional legal alternatives that vary by country.

Branch and Subsidiary Organizations

When establishing a foreign operation, a company often must decide between making that operation a branch or a subsidiary. A foreign branch is a foreign operation not legally separate from the parent company. Branch operations are possible only if the parent holds 100 percent ownership. A subsidiary, however, is an FDI that is legally a separate company, even if the parent owns all of the voting stock. The parent controls a subsidiary through its voting stock and through its preferred organization structure, systems, and culture. Because a subsidiary is legally separate from its parent, legal authorities in each country generally limit liability to the subsidiary's assets. Creditors or winners of legal suits against the subsidiary do not usually have access to the parent's other resources. This concept of limited liability is a major factor in the choice of the subsidiary form. With few exceptions, claims against a company for its actions are settled by courts either where the actions occur or where the subsidiary is legally domiciled.

Because subsidiaries are separate companies, a question arises concerning which decisions the parent may be allowed to make. Generally, this does not present a problem because there have been few limiting situations. However, court cases in several countries—for example, France and the United States—have ruled that companies were conspiring to prevent competition when the parent dictated which markets its subsidiary could serve. Public disclosures also moderate this situation. Generally, the greater the control the owner has, the greater the secrecy it can maintain. In this respect, branches are usually subject to less public disclosure because they are covered by tight corporate restrictions.

These examples show that there are organizational advantages to the branch or the subsidiary form. Each form also has different tax advantages and implications and may have different initiation and operating costs as well as abilities to raise capital. A company must consider its objectives for type of organization, its potential liability, its need for secrecy, and tax exposure when deciding whether to use a branch or subsidiary to operate abroad.

There are tax and liability differences for branches and subsidiaries.

Types of Subsidiaries and Operating Form

An MNE establishing a subsidiary in a foreign country usually chooses from various legal forms. Although there are too many forms to list here, we can report the distinctions that managers heed in designing their organization:

* The ability of the parent to sell its ownership
* The number of stockholders required to establish the subsidiary
* The percentage of foreigners who can serve on the board of directors
* The amount of required public disclosure
* Whether equity may be acquired by noncapital contributions, such as goodwill
* The types of businesses (products) that are eligible
* The minimum capital required for establishing the subsidiary

Before deciding its legal operating form, an MNE has to weigh these considerations and identify their implications to its preferred organization.

SUMMARY

* The organization of international business is challenging due to the geographic and cultural distances that separate countries, the need to operate differently among countries, the large number of uncontrollable factors, the high uncertainty resulting from rapid change in the international environment, and problems in gathering reliable data in many places.

* Organization in the MNE is an integrated function of its formal structure, coordination and control systems, and the shared values that make up its culture.

- Prevailing environmental and workplace trends pressure managers to question their customary approaches to organizing their companies.

- Vertical differentiation is the matter of how the company balances centralization versus decentralization of decision making. Horizontal differentiation is the matter of how the company opts to divide itself into specific units to do specific jobs.

- The degree of centralization in a company is influenced by the pressures for global integration versus local responsiveness, the competence of headquarters versus subsidiary personnel, and decision importance, expediency, and quality expectations.

- Traditional structures, like the functional, divisional, and matrix formats, rely on hierarchical formats to specify the arrangement of roles, responsibilities and relationships among employees.

- Contemporary structures, like the network or virtual formats, arrange work roles, responsibilities, and relationships in ways that eliminating the horizontal, vertical, or external boundaries that block the development of knowledge-generating and decision-making relationships.

- Firms engaging different strategies must develop different organizations to implement those strategies successfully. Firms engaging international, multidomestic, global, or transnational strategies need to tailor their structure, systems, and cultures to the demands of the strategy.

- No matter what sort of structure the MNE uses, it needs to develop coordination and control mechanisms to prevent duplication of efforts, to ensure that headquarters managers do not withhold the best resources from the international operations, and to include insights from anywhere in the organization.

- Coordination can take place via standardization, plans, and mutual adjustment. Standardization relies on specifying standard operating procedures, planning relies on general goals and detailed objectives, and adjustment relies on frequent interaction among related parties.

- Companies exercise control through market, bureaucratic, and clan mechanisms. Market control relies on external market mechanisms, bureaucratic control relies on extensive rules and procedures, and clan control relies on shared values among all employees.

- Organizational culture refers to the set of values and norms that is shared among employees. Values and norms express themselves as the behavior patterns or style of an organization that new employees are encouraged to follow by their fellow employees.

- MNEs opt to develop and manage, just as they do with regard to their structure and systems, their set of shared values and beliefs. The strategy that the company is pursuing moderates the approaches and tools it uses.

- Special control problems arise for acquired operations, operations that have historical autonomy, operations that are not wholly owned, and operations resulting from changes in companies' strategies. The legal structure of foreign operations may also raise control problems.

C A S E   GE Hungary[46]

General Electric is the world's largest company in terms of market capitalization (number of shares times share price). Between 1989 and 2002, GE invested $1 billion in Tungsram and, in the process, gained 100 percent of its shares. Founded in Hungary in 1896, Tungsram is one of the world's oldest lighting companies. With this and other acquisitions, GE became the world's largest lightbulb company. (The Big Three—GE, Dutch-based Philips, and German-based Siemens—collectively control about 75 percent of the world's lighting market.)

Between 1995 and 2001, GE expanded its Hungarian operations in other businesses as well. It acquired 98 percent of Budapest Bank (BB), one of Hungary's largest banks, and an interest in Medicor, a medical equipment and instrument manufacturer. In addition, GE made greenfield investments in the manufacturing of industrial equipment and electrical switches and in an operation to repair airplane engines. In 2001, all of these except BB, a subsidiary of

GE Capital, were combined into a new holding company, GE Hungary Inc. The purpose of the holding is to allow GE's manufacturing operations to negotiate with the government of Hungary with a single voice; to centralize and standardize purchasing, accounting, human resource management, and legal representation, thereby generating cost savings; and to assist in the establishment of new GE businesses in the country. Nevertheless, the five combined businesses—Lighting (employing 11,000 persons), Power Controls (1,000 employees), Engine Services (100), Medical Systems (300), and Power Systems (500)—report separately to GE's product divisions, which are headquartered in the United States. Because the lighting group, Tungsram, is by far the largest of GE's Hungarian businesses, we'll concentrate most of our discussion on that group.

From a control standpoint, GE has relied on corporate reorganization, restructuring of operations, infusion of its corporate culture, and the implementation of a standardized reporting system.

Tungsram has developed important lighting source innovations and has traditionally sold most of its production outside of Hungary. Its market position eroded during the closing era of communist rule in Hungary, and the government hired the consulting firm Arthur D. Little (ADL) to assess the situation. ADL concluded that Tungsram's cost levels were too high and its exploitation of marketing opportunities too weak. Further, it was investing less and spending less on R&D as a percentage of sales compared to its competitors. Nevertheless, Tungsram could be turned around, ADL concluded, with restructuring help from a strategic investor if the investor would provide capital, production technology, and management know-how. GE became that strategic investor.

Corporate Reorganization

During the early 1990s, GE managed its European lighting acquisitions on a multidomestic basis, meaning it allowed them to operate quite autonomously. GEL, the company's lighting division, believed this autonomy was necessary because each country's operations differed significantly in terms of R&D, production capability, product structure, and market characteristics. However, in 1992, GE decided to move rapidly toward more centralized control, believing that, regionally and globally, such a move would facilitate the transfer of experience from one subsidiary to another, especially through the standardization of operations, functions, products, and culture. In addition, GE wanted to gain a common image within and among its different product groups so that it could introduce new products more effectively into foreign markets. GEL established its European headquarters in London (GE Lighting Europe, or GELE), and Tungsram lost much of the autonomy it had enjoyed until then. Figure 15.5 shows GE-Tungsram's place in a simplified GE organization structure.

GELE-London decided (1) to introduce in Europe the GE brand lightbulbs as a high-priced "quality" product by using the yellow and blue GE logo, which was well known and carried a quality image in the United States, and (2) to continue selling under the Tungsram name, but to position it as a low-priced (value for money) brand, to be promoted less than the GE brand, even though the products were identical, except for the packaging. This has been a sensitive issue among Hungarians, who are proud of Tungsram's century-old tradition, scientific achievements, global reach, and name recognition in Europe.

To understand the rationales of the next two major reorganizations involving the company, we must get ahead of our story about the Tungsram restructuring. Throughout the 1990s, U.S. manufacturing productivity improvements in lighting sources slowed, and lighting competition intensified in the United States and in global markets, especially from low-cost Chinese firms. GEL's response was to close U.S. and west European plants and to transfer production to lower-cost locations, particularly in Mexico and Hungary. The choice of Hungary has been supported by the successful restructuring of Tungsram, by the sophisticated quality assurance systems required in lighting, and by the country's central location in Europe. In 2002, GE-Tungsram became GEL's new Center for Europe, the Middle East, and Africa. The increased concentration of GEL's production and R&D in Hungary made this a logical move.

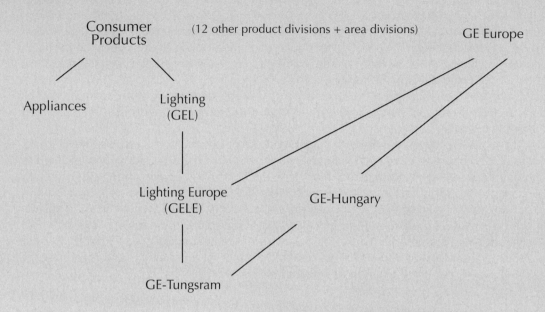

FIGURE 15.5   GE-TUNGSRAM IN GE'S ORGANIZATION STRUCTURE
This simplified drawing shows that GE operates with a matrix structure, although the product groups have traditionally had much more power than the areas groups. Therefore, GE-Tungsram reports to both an area (country) group and to a product group.

Restructuring

The Tungsram acquisition was a strategic investment for GE, made quickly to take advantage of the opportunity; however, subsequent audits showed that many costly changes were needed to make Tungsram competitive. Labor productivity was low due to overstaffing, bureaucratic administrative structures, and insufficient automation. GE reduced the labor force from nearly 20,000 in early 1990 to about 9,500 in 1993 (subsequently increased to 11,000). The acquired production facilities could not reach the quality standards demanded in Western markets, so GE bought new equipment; upgraded the telecommunications system; installed personal computers; refurbished buildings; and improved health, safety and environmental standards.

GEL consolidated its R&D, so that more than half of it now takes place in Hungary and much of the rest in the United States. A team representing all of GE's major business units makes decisions on GE's R&D priorities. Once GEL gains approval from this team for its projects, it appoints a program manager for each project. The program manager chooses team members from a large "GEL talent pool" located in different countries and made up of functional specialists, such as marketing and accounting personnel, as well as scientists and engineers. Task-oriented teams form and disband as needs change. GEL informs the entire talent pool of planned programs and projects, encouraging individuals to volunteer as team members, though the selection is up to the program manager. The company demotes individuals who, over a period of time, are not chosen as team members and convinces them to leave the company. GEL rewards not only technical competence but also initiative, business sense, and the ability and willingness to work constructively as a member of a team.

Culture as Control at Tungsram

GE's corporate culture is strong, and it helps unify behavior among company personnel. The culture is based partly on U.S. norms, such as pride and optimism, and partly on the styles and practices of GE's top managers, notably that of its former CEO, Jack Welch, who believed in the quick sale of underperforming units or massive layoffs to improve those units' performance.

Initially, GEL proceeded cautiously with changing the inherited culture at Tungsram. However, in 1992, following the appointment of a new CEO at Tungsram, GEL decided to introduce the GE corporate culture more decisively and quickly. As is customary in all GE operations worldwide, GE translated its 95-page manual, *Integrity: The Spirit and Letter of Our Commitment*, into Hungarian and required all Tungsram employees (as it does everywhere it operates) to pledge observance of its contents. The manual describes behavior to eliminate corruption, instructs that one must deal fairly with coworkers (regardless of gender, nationality, or creed), and requires absolute fairness in dealing with competitors and suppliers.

Many aspects of GE's culture ran counter to those at Tungsram. For example, the norm in the United States is to be inner-directed—believing that it is up to each individual to succeed and that outside constraints can be overcome if only one tries hard enough. However, the norm in Hungary used to be outer-directed—believing that uncontrollable outside forces, rather than the will of the individual, are decisive in determining outcomes (perhaps brought about by decades of Soviet rule, when there was little self-determination). In addition, GE's use of layoffs and selloffs to improve performance contrasted sharply with the experience at Tungsram, where there was a history of paternalism. For example, many Tungsram employees received company subsidies to buy apartments and vacationed at company resorts. Their children attended company kindergartens and their families rooted for Tungsram-sponsored sports teams. The best way to get a job at Tungsram was recommendation by a current employee; however, once employed, satisfactory work performance led to lifetime job security. Personal relationships and reciprocal favors were much more important than formal rules. Thus, GE faced the task of trying to enforce a universal code in a paternalistic national and corporate culture.

Initially, the going was not easy for GEL. Resentment, fed by early layoffs, the shedding of noncore businesses, and uncertainty about what GE had in store for Tungsram, led to lots of complaints by employees and by the labor unions representing them, resulting in a spate of unfavorable publicity in the Hungarian press. Gradually, however, GE succeeded in making its norms and practices accepted by a large majority of the workforce. The stabilization and eventual increase in employment certainly helped, as did the continuous substantial improvements in productivity and quality, and the resulting expansion of production and R&D.

Campaigns to Change Culture

One distinctive feature of GE's culture under Jack Welch was that corporate strategic initiatives were applied, with strength and fervor, in every one of GE's diverse businesses and in each of its subsidiaries, whether in the United States, Hungary, or Japan. In Welch's two decades as CEO (1981–2001), he introduced major strategic initiatives that have all been continued, becoming routine after a while.[47] These were required throughout the GE organization, Tungsram being no exception. One of these initiatives was Internet digitalization, which aims to eliminate the use of paper while generating three kinds of profit opportunities: buying inputs, marketing products, and reducing overhead. GE labels them "e-buy," "e-sell," and "e-make." For example, GE buys in excess of $50 billion in goods and services each year. Transferring some of this to online auctions has given GE access to more suppliers and lower costs, generating net savings in the 5 to 10 percent range.

The greatest hurdle to the implementation of initiatives, says Welch, was not technology but culture. For example, in Internet digitalization, salespeople worried that they might be destroying their jobs, so GE offered them bonuses to get them to help customers use GE Web sites when ordering. Separate teams, again comprised of some of the best managers, were put together to come up with potential Internet-based strategies for different businesses and products. To make sure executives would become willing agents of change in the campaign, Welch "suggested" that each of GE's top 3,000 managers should get Internet mentors, preferably under the age of 30, as he himself had done. "It is a great way to turn the organization upside down," he said.

How do such strategic initiatives play out "down in the trenches"? Miklos Csapody, former vice president and director of GE-Tungsram and director of GEL's Technology Development and R&D, said,

> The changeover [to digitalized workflows] is taking place at an amazing pace. For example, [in] the beginning, no one at Tungsram was allowed to turn on a printer or to copy anything on certain days. And the idea was not to postpone the printing or copying until later. The boss stood at the door asking, "Why do you have to print or copy?" If the explanation seemed reasonable, then an independent digitization team was called in to discover the source of the problem and to eliminate it.[48]

Control by Reports

When Hungary had central planning, the government set costs and prices. It also owned companies, which faced no domestic competition and could not go bankrupt. The purpose of companies' reporting systems was to check plan fulfillment, not to control costs or improve profits. Under GE, all units must prepare standard reports on just about all aspects of costs and operations. Everyone faces a great deal of pressure to improve performance. Benchmarking—comparing performance indicators at one plant with those achieved by other plants that manufacture similar products, or with industry standards—has become an important tool of management control.

Improvement, then, has become the key word at Tungsram. Reducing labor, inventory, and scrap costs are critical to profitability. Initially, GEL compared Tungsram's performance against its U.S. counterparts within the GE lighting division. But this was difficult because of different operating methods. GEL invested to make Tungsram technically equivalent to facilities in the United States. GEL also implemented enterprise resource planning (ERP) modules, which standardize business practices everywhere. For example, under ERP, GEL's order processing is uniform throughout the company. Standardization of equipment and business practices eases GEL's ability to compare performance through benchmarking. Apparently, the standardization, benchmarking, and reporting have been helping to improve performance, inasmuch as Tungsram has continuously reduced its scrap rate, material content, and unit labor costs.

However, making Tungsram as good as other GEL units is not GE's ultimate aim. GE compares its managers and its operations against the best in the industry.

Future Organization Challenges

Today, a growing concern of GEL and of the management and employees of Tungsram is that competition from China is getting rapidly more intense. The technology of manufacturing light sources is pretty standard, except for the newest products. As China is improving quality and as its plants are receiving subsidies from local governments, the long-term strategic concern is how long GE will be willing and able to remain in the business of manufacturing light sources. In this business, foreign companies did not have much of a chance to invest in China because scores of municipal and regional governments decided to establish and subsidize light-source factories, thus generating employment through import substitution policies. As the production capacity being built is getting to be more than sufficient to meet domestic demand, China's firms are rapidly penetrating foreign markets. Jeff Immelt, Jack Welch's successor as GE's CEO, says, "Either you'll be a big investor in China or your biggest competitors will come from China."[49]

QUESTIONS

1. Define national and corporate cultures. How did GE's and Tungsram's cultures differ? How did GE attempt to use its culture as a control mechanism in Hungary and elsewhere?

2. What were the pros and cons of changing GEL's European operations from multidomestic to regional or global? Would such a change work the same for all of GE's product divisions?

3. What factors might account for (a) GE's initial acquisition and subsequent expansion of light-source manufacturing and R&D in Hungary? and (b) GE's establishing new types of businesses in Hungary?

4. In what ways does GE attempt to gain synergy among its operations in different countries and among its different businesses?

CHAPTER NOTES

1 Case developed from information reported at www.jnj.com; various Annual Reports at http://www.investor.jnj.com/releases.cfm; Brian O'Reilly, "J&J Is on a Roll," *Fortune* (December 26, 1994): 178–85; Howard Rudnitsky, "One Hundred Sixty Companies for the Price of One," *Forbes* (February 26, 1996): 56–60; "Can J&J Keep the Magic Going?" Fortune (May 27, 2002): 117; "J&J Stops Babying Itself," *Business Week* (September 13, 1999): 95; Geoff Dyer, "Hoping for a Ride as Smooth as a Baby's Bottom: Interview with Bill Weldon, Johnson & Johnson," *Financial Times* (September 20, 2002): 15; Robert Scheier, "Central Intelligence: Johnson & Johnson," *CIO Insight* (December 1, 2001); Melody Petersen, "From the Ranks, Unassumingly," *New York Times* (February 24, 2002): Section 3, 2; "Going Beyond Band-Aids: Akira Matsumoto," *Japan Today* (September 21, 2002); Amy Barrett and John Carey, "A Prescription for Trouble at J&J?" *Business Week* (April 11, 2005): 44; Amy Barrett and Michael Arndt, "J&J: Don't Stop Dealmaking Now," *Business Week* (Dec. 20, 2004): 39; "J.&J.'s a Big Deal in Year's Mergers," *The New York Times* (Dec 17, 2004): C2.

2 "The Organization Man, Dead at 76," *Journal of Business Strategy* 18, no. 6 (Nov.–Dec. 1997): 19(5).

3 Chris Bartlett and Sumantra Ghoshal, "Matrix Management: Not a Structure, a Frame of Mind," *Harvard Business Review* 68 (July–August 1990): 138–45.

4 Julian Birkinshaw, "The Structures Behind Global Companies," *Financial Times* (December 4, 2000): Mastering Management section, 2–4.

5 "Nestle Is Starting to Slim Down at Last," *Business Week* (October 27, 2003): 56–58; "Daring, Defying, to Grow," *Economist* (August 7, 2004): 55–57.

6 John W. Hunt, "Is Matrix Management a Recipe for Chaos?" *Financial Times* (January 12, 1998): 10.

7 Richard Hodgetts, "Dow Chemical CEO Wiliam Stavropoulos on Structure," *Academy of Management Executive* (May 30, 1999): 30.

8 John Gapper and Nicholas Denton, "The Barings Report," *Financial Times* (October 18, 1995): 8.

9 "Axe to Fall Heavily at IBM, Unions Fear," *New York Times* (May 6, 2005).

10 The professional management model, the strategy-structure-systems model, was first adopted by General Motors, Du Pont, Sears, and Standard Oil in the 1920s. Not until the post–World War II era did many companies began to develop divisional structures that then led to the rapid adoption of diversification strategies. Some reason that the network structure and its variants will follow the same pattern, moving from the few in the early 2000s to the many over the ensuing decades.

11 Steve Lohr, "I.B.M. to Lay Off 10,000 to 13,000," *New York Times* (May 4, 2005).

12 Statement from Jack Welch's Letter to Shareholders, "Boundarylessness Company in a Decade of Change," reported in General Electric's 1990 Annual Report.

13 "A Tangled Web," *Financial Times* (June 12, 2001): Germany section, 7.

14 The businesses are extremely diverse, and they include mining, real estate, credit cards, and tuna canning. Typically, the core companies within a *keiretsu* buy and sell with each other only if it makes business sense. In Mitsubishi's case, it is hard to understand why a real estate company would need to do business with, or invest in, a tuna canning company. However, managers can exchange information that is useful to more than one company, can underwrite each other's financing, and can gain more clout when lobbying for government legislation. Strong, long-term personal relationships among managers in the companies build common interests that do not depend on formal controls. Nevertheless, this cushioning from stand-alone competition may retard a company's attainment of optimum efficiency and many of the relationships appear to be weakening during Japan's long recession.

15 Sonny Ariss, Nick Nykodym, and Aimee Cole-Laramore, "Trust and Technology in the Virtual Organization," *SAM Advanced Management Journal* 67 (Autumn 2002): 22–26; William M. Fitzpatrick and Donald R. Burke, "Competitive Intelligence, Corporate Security and the Virtual organization," *Advances in Competitiveness Research* 11 (2003): 20–46.

16 Scott Goodson and StrawberryFrog, "Special Report: Global Players," *Advertising Age* 75 (January 26, 2004): S4; Juliana Koranteng, "Virtual Agency Goes Global via the Web," *AdAgeGlobal* 1 (November 2000): 46.

17 Alf Crossman and Liz Lee-Kelley, "Trust, Commitment and Team Working: The Paradox of Virtual Organizations," *Global Networks: A Journal of Transnational Affairs* 4 (October 2004): 375–391; Philip J. Holt and James E. Lodge, "Merging Collaboration and Technology: The Virtual Research Organization," *Applied Clinical Trials* 12 (October 2003): 38–42.

18 Henrik Holt Larsen, "Oticon: Unorthodox Project-Based Management and Careers in a "Spaghetti" Organization," *Human Resource Planning* 25 (December 2002): 30.

19 Nicolai J. Foss. "Selective Intervention and Internal Hybrids: Interpreting and Learning from the Rise and Decline of the Oticon Spaghetti Organization," *Organization Science* 14 (May–June 2003): 331–50.

20 Darrell Rigby, "Bain & Company's 2005 Management Tools & Trends," www.bain.com/management_tools/ (Retrieved August 2, 2005).

21 Loren Cary, "The Rise of Hyperarchies," *Harvard Business Review* (March 2004).

22 More specifically, Mr. Grove reasoned: "Let chaos reign, then rein in chaos. Does that mean that you shouldn't plan? Not at all. You need to plan the way a fire department plans. It cannot anticipate fires, so it has to shape a flexible organization that is capable of responding to unpredictable events." Michael E. Rock, Case Example: Intel's Andy Grove, www.canadaone.com/magazine/mr2060198.html.

23 The saying is adapted from a line in "To a Mouse," by Robert Burns: "The best laid schemes o' mice an' men/Gang aft a-gley," http://www.bartleby.com/59/3/bestlaidplan.html. Retrieved April 18, 2005.

24 Daniel Erasmus, "A Common Language for Strategy," *Financial Times* (April 5, 1999): Mastering Information Management section, 7–8.

25 Sumantra Ghoshal and Christopher Bartlett, "Changing the Role of Top Management: Beyond Structure to Process," *Harvard Business Review* 73 (January–February 1995): 93–94.

26 Jennifer Spencer, "Firms' Knowledge-Sharing Strategies in the Global Innovation System: Empirical Evidence from the Flat Panel Display Industry," *Strategic Management Journal* 23 (March 2003): 217–33.

27 Anil K. Gupta, Vijay Govindarajan, and Ayesha Malhotra, "Feedback-Seeking Behavior Within Multinational Corporations," *Strategic Management Journal* 20 (March 1999): 205–22.

28 N. Shirouzu and J. Bigness, "7-Eleven Operators Resist System to Monitor Managers," *Wall Street Journal*, (June 16, 1997): B1.

29 Eric Flamholtz and Rangapriya Kannan-Narasimhan, "Differential Impact of Cultural Elements in Financial Performance," *European Management Journal* 23 (February 2005): 50–65; Ursula Fairbairn, "HR as a Strategic Partner: Culture Change as an American Express Case Study," *Human Resource Management* 44 (Spring 2005): 79–84.

30 Jim Collins, *Good to Great: Why Some Companies Make the Leap. . . and Others Don't*, (New York: HarperCollins, 2001). For example, on the importance of technology, Collins reports that "80% of the good-to-great executives—from more than 1400 companies over a 15 year span—we interviewed didn't even mention technology as one of the top five factors in the transition."

31 Ibid., Ghoshal and Bartlett, (1995): 138–40.

32 Tatiana Kostova, "Transnational Transfer of Strategic Organizational Practices: A Contextual Perspective," *Academy of Management Review* 24 (1999): 308–24; Nitin Nohria and Sumantra Ghoshal, "Differentiated Fit and Shared Values: Alternatives for Managing Headquarters-Subsidiary Relations," *Strategic Management Journal* 15 (July 1994): 491–502. For a discussion of how capabilities improve with experience, see Andrew Delios and Paul Beamish, "Survival and Profitability: The Roles of Experience and Intangible Assets in Foreign Subsidiary Performance," *Academy of Management Journal* 44 (2001): 1028–38.

33 Alison Maitland, "Bridging the Culture Gap," *Financial Times* (January 28, 2002): 8.

34 P. Christopher Early and Elaine Mosakowski, "Creating Hybrid Team Cultures: An Empirical Test of Transnational Team Functioning," *Academy of Management Journal* 43 (2000): 26–49.

35 Dinker Raval and Bala Subramanianm, "Effective Transfer of Best Practices Across Cultures," *Competitiveness Review*, (Summer–Fall 2000): 183.

36 John A. Byrne, "How Jack Welch Runs GE," *Business Week* (June 8, 1998): 90; Miriam Leuchter, "Management Farm Teams," *Journal of Business Strategy* (May 1998): 29–32; "The House That Jack Built," *The Economist* (September 18, 1999).

37 "In Search of Global Leaders: View of Jeffery Immelt, Chairman and CEO, General Electric," *Harvard Business Review* (1 August, 2003).

38 Corporate Universities Overview, http://www.glresources.com/ls_cu.php. Eric Morath, "In-House Corporate Universities Growing in Popularity," *Crain's Detroit Business* (June 2002): 17– 23.

39 Jeanne C Meister, *Corporate Universities: Lessons in Building a World-Class Work Force* (New York: McGraw-Hill, 1998).

40 John Griffiths, "Unipart University," *Financial Times* (March 21, 2002).

41 Della Bradshaw, "LVMI I," *Financial Times* (March 21, 2002).

42 Steve Trehern, "More Than Just Learning Process," *Financial Times* (March 21, 2002).

43 John Child, *The Management of International Acquisitions* (Oxford: Oxford University Press, 2001).

44 Peter Martin, "A Clash of Corporate Cultures," *Financial Times* (June 2–3, 2001): weekend section, xxiv.

45 Mansour Javidan, "Siemens CEO Heinrich Von Pierer on Cross-Border Acquisitions," *Academy of Management Executive* 16 (February 2002): 13–15.

46 By Paul Marer, then Professor and Academic Director, CEU Graduate School of Business, Budapest.

47 Jack Welch, *Jack: Straight from the Gut* (New York: Warner Books, 2001).

48 "Interview with Miklos Csapody," *Magyar Tudomany* [Hungarian Science] (June 2001).

49 Jeff Immelt, presentation before the American–Hungarian Chamber of Commerce (Budapest, June 20, 2002).

May both seller and buyer see the benefit.

—TURKISH PROVERB

chapter sixteen

Marketing Globally

OBJECTIVES

- To understand a range of product policies and the circumstances in which they are appropriate internationally

- To grasp the reasons for product alterations when deciding between standardized versus differentiated marketing programs among countries

- To appreciate the pricing complexities when selling in foreign markets

- To interpret country differences that may necessitate alterations in promotional practices

- To comprehend the different branding strategies companies may employ internationally

- To discern complications of international distribution and practices of effective distribution

- To perceive why and how emphasis in the marketing mix may vary among countries

CASE: AVON[1]

Avon, founded in 1886, is one of the world's largest manufacturers and marketers of beauty and related products. The company is headquartered in the United States, but over 70 percent of its sales are outside the country. It does business in more than 120 countries through direct investments, licensing, franchising, and distributor arrangements. Map 16.1 shows how Avon divides the world regionally and the portion of its business in each region.

Avon moved into the Canadian market in 1914. Its next foreign market entry was 40 years later—into Venezuela. Its big thrust into new international markets has been since 1990. It entered 23 new countries in the 1990s and another 11 between 2000 and 2005, most recently into Finland, Macedonia, Kazakhstan, Bosnia, and Vietnam. Avon's recent emphasis on foreign operations is due to a slowed U.S. growth potential. First, there is little or no usage gap (untapped market) in the United States for cosmetics, fragrances, and toiletries. Even if there were, only about 5 percent of the world's women live in the United States and Canada. Second, Avon's U.S. sales rely heavily on independent salespersons (almost always women working part time and known as "Avon ladies" or "Avon representatives"), who make direct sales to households by demonstrating products and giving beauty advice. They then place sales orders with Avon and deliver orders to the customers once they receive them. But as more U.S. women have entered the workforce full time, they have become less receptive to door-to-door salespersons, have less time to spend on makeup demonstrations, want to receive their purchases immediately, and are less willing to work as Avon ladies. Avon has recently adjusted to these problems by selling in J.C. Penney's, Sears, and Avon retail outlets. It has also begun pushing sales on university campuses.

Concomitantly, many foreign markets have been ideal for Avon's growth. For example, the lack of developed infrastructure in the rural areas of such countries as Brazil and the Philippines deters women from leaving their homes to shop for cosmetics. But in these countries, Avon ladies reach consumers in some of the most remote areas, such as by canoe in the Amazon region of Brazil. (Avon has 800,000 representatives in Brazil, up from 150,000 a decade earlier.) In transitional economies, Avon's market entry coincided with pent-up demand from the period of centrally planned economic policies. For example, Avon entered Ukraine with free makeovers at meeting halls in nine major cities, which 240,000 people attended. In rapid-growth economies, such as Chile and Malaysia, Avon taps a growing middle-class market that can afford its products. In all of the aforementioned countries, there are ample labor supplies of potential Avon ladies.

Avon gears product lines to the needs of specific markets, such as selling a skin cream, Sol & Cor, in the Brazilian market that combines a moisturizer, sunscreen, and insect repellent. The company also sells creams in parts of Asia to lighten the complexion, but the desire for skin lightening is too small elsewhere to justify marketing efforts. In essence, Avon is very willing to adapt to local preferences. For instance, within Europe, the Spanish prefer bigger bottles of personal care products, and Avon provides them. Nevertheless, Avon has been diminishing its customization for individual markets. Instead, most products are available everywhere, but the portion of consumers who buy particular products varies. The Japanese buy more technology-driven skin care products, and the Mediterranean consumers buy more long-lasting citrus fragrances.

When Avon develops new products for a given country, it disseminates the information to its facilities elsewhere. For example, Avon-Japan developed emulsion technologies to produce lotions and creams with lighter textures and higher hydration levels, and many Avon operations in other countries now use the process. After Avon successfully introduced a separate line of health and wellness products in Argentina, it next launched them in Spain, Mexico, and Brazil and then in the United States and Puerto Rico. In addition to developing products for specific markets, Avon emphasizes standardized products using global brands that appeal to women of many nationalities. One of these is a family of skin-protection products using the Anew brand. Some other global brands are Rare Gold, beComing, and Far Away fragrances. Through standardized products and brands, Avon creates a uniform global quality image while saving costs from uniform ingredients and packaging. Global branding also helps inform consumers that the company is international. This helps sales in countries such as Thailand, where consumers prefer to buy beauty products made by foreign companies.

MAP 16.1   Avon's Operating Regions and Net Sales by Regions, 2004

Avon operates in over 120 countries on every continent except Antarctica.

Source: Avon Annual Report, 2004.

GREENLAND
(Denmark)

CANADA

UNITED STATES

MEXICO

HAITI   DOMINICAN
REPUBLIC
CUBA
PUERTO RICO
BELIZE
GUATEMALA   HONDURAS JAMAICA
EL SALVADOR   NICARAGUA
COSTA RICA   VENEZUELA   GUYANA
PANAMA   COLOMBIA   SURINAME
FRENCH
GUIANA
ECUADOR

SOLOMON
ISLANDS

PERU   BRAZIL

FIJI   BOLIVIA
VANUATU   PARAGUAY
NEW
CALEDONIA

CHILE   URUGUAY
ARGENTINA

NEW
ZEALAND

Although Avon prominently displays its name on most of its products worldwide, many of its brand names differ among countries. The company prints instructions in local languages, but may or may not put the brand names in that language. It often uses English or French brand names because consumers consider the United States and France as high-quality suppliers for beauty products. For example, Avon sells skin care products called Rosa Mosqueta (in Spanish), Revival (in English), and Renaissage (in French) in Chile, Argentina, and Japan, respectively. In each case, the Avon logo appears prominently on the products' containers as well.

Each country operation sets its own prices to reflect local market conditions and strategic objectives. The prices are subject to change for each sales campaign. Avon runs a new campaign with different special offers every two weeks in the United States and every three weeks abroad. The shortness of campaigns is helpful for adjusting prices in highly inflationary economies.

Avon's promotion is primarily through brochures that Avon ladies deliver to potential customers during each campaign. The company prints about 600 million brochures in 15 languages, dwarfing the

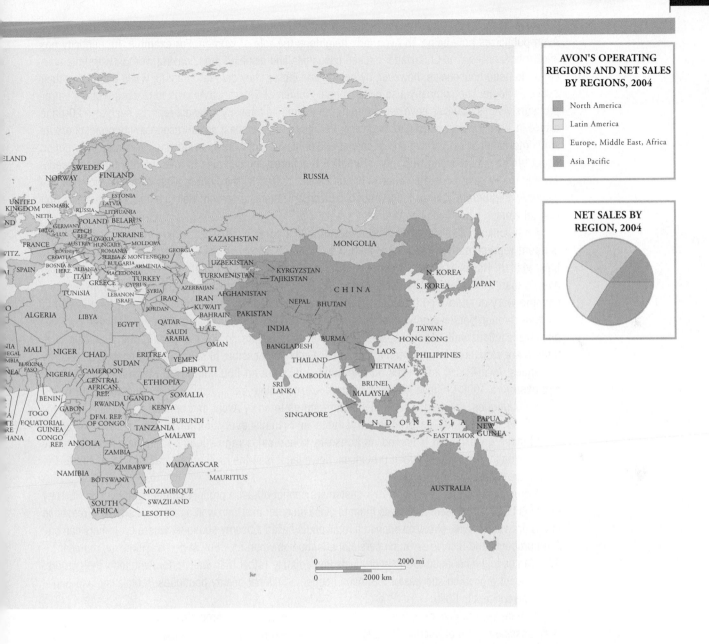

AVON'S OPERATING REGIONS AND NET SALES BY REGIONS, 2004

- North America
- Latin America
- Europe, Middle East, Africa
- Asia Pacific

NET SALES BY REGION, 2004

circulation of any magazine or commercial publication. Additionally, Avon relies on both print and television advertising. Because of the success that some competitors gained from using a celebrity to promote a brand, Avon has done likewise. Most recently the Mexican film star Salma Hayek has been the face of Avon.

The basic aim of Avon's campaign is the same throughout the world—to promote its products and image, increase the number of customers served, and recruit new representatives. However, Avon has traditionally altered the execution of promotions to meet the specific needs of different markets. For example, it used the theme "Just Another Avon Lady" in the United States and Canada to show that women in all walks of life use Avon. In Germany, the ads sought to change Avon's image of being old-fashioned. In Japan, where more than 2,000 cosmetic companies compete and Avon is not a leading competitor, the company sought consumer awareness of its name. However, in 2000, it launched its first global ad campaign, "Let's Talk," with print and television ads.

Avon seeks to develop a global image of being a company that supports women and their needs. Avon publicizes how being an Avon lady heightens the role of women. For example, its publicity has shown how civil war in El Salvador caused casualties and disabled men, leaving women with little education to head households; however, by being Avon ladies, they can earn income while continuing their duties at home. The company also gives annual Women of Enterprise Awards to leading women entrepreneurs. Avon's activities have generated further favorable publicity in media reports, such as a 20-page article in *Veja,* a weekly Brazilian magazine. Perhaps Avon's biggest social responsibility projects are its work internationally in fighting breast cancer and domestic violence. Avon ladies disseminate information about breast cancer along with their promotion brochures and sell pins to raise money for local needs. Avon is the largest corporate donor to breast cancer research. The fight against domestic violence is a newer Avon program. It is working through local organizations to prevent violence through education and to treat women who have been victims.

Avon basically duplicates its distribution method in foreign countries, which means it sells to independent representatives (about 4.9 million worldwide) who have taken orders from customers they have visited. However, it varies aspects of its distribution among countries. To begin with, not all of Avon's distribution abroad is door-to-door. In Russia, during decades of communist rule, women became wary of knocks on the door—a discomfort that persists—so representatives primarily sell at work or through personal networks. Such selling is similar in India because women associate door-to-door transactions with old-newspaper and old-clothes buyers. In parts of Brazil, many upscale customers are cloistered in apartments that are virtually inaccessible to salespeople because of security entrances. Avon-Brazil advertises on television and offers an 800 number to reach that clientele. In response to a 1998 Chinese law prohibiting house-to-house sales, Avon quickly opened about 6,000 beauty boutiques, lined up 9,000 independent stores to carry Avon, and opened 1,000 beauty counters. Thus, Avon made its products available in virtually every corner of the country. In 2005, the Chinese government loosened its house-to-house sales regulations by allowing Avon to make direct sales in three largely urban provinces; however, it is in the rural areas that direct selling has the most advantage.

A drawback of direct selling is that customers cannot obtain a product whenever they want it. They must wait until a representative visits them to place an order and then wait again to receive it. In response to this drawback, Avon-Malaysia opened a retail outlet called a beauty boutique, where customers can buy Avon products and receive as much personal attention as when they buy at home. Moreover, representatives can go to the boutique to obtain products immediately, rather than waiting for Avon to fill their orders. The concept proved so successful that Avon opened additional beauty boutiques in Malaysia and duplicated the concept in Chile.

In an interesting departure from the Malaysian experience, Avon-Argentina opened a "Beauty Center" in an upscale suburb of Buenos Aires. In addition to selling products, as in Malaysia, this center provides customers with a wide variety of services, such as hairstyling and manicures. The center also serves to build an upscale image among customers who would normally shop at retail outlets and buy imported products. Avon now follows this same approach in Mexico and Venezuela, and it has opened a spa on Fifth Avenue in New York City.

In some countries, particularly emerging economies, getting merchandise to consumers in rural areas is a major challenge. Mail systems are unreliable, and personal delivery to representatives is expensive. Because of this problem, Avon-Philippines pioneered a system of branch selling. Instead of delivering orders to the homes of district managers, who in turn would arrange delivery to representatives as in the United States, Avon-Philippines has established franchise centers that stock merchandise. Franchise managers visit the centers and pick up merchandise for the representatives in their district. This saves the representatives from making arduous treks, sometimes two hours by bus. The centers have experimented with more retail-like services such as wide aisles, shopping carts, and scanners at checkout so that the franchise managers can fill and pay for their orders quickly. Avon has since adopted the franchise center concept in other countries, such as Indonesia.

In the preceding discussion, we saw how Avon transferred successful practices in one country to other countries. To encourage the transfer of know-how, Avon brings marketing personnel from different countries together to share what it calls "best practices." It also promotes competition among countries, such as chairman's awards for country-level initiatives to improve sales, quality, and efficiency.

Avon anticipates that international operations will account for the bulk of its growth in the foreseeable future. Its products are still not available to a large portion of the world's women. Recall the closing case of Chapter 4 on the BRICs, which showed that Brazil, Russia, India, and China are expected to be the fastest growth markets in the near future. Avon seems well positioned to serve those markets. It has been in Brazil since 1963 and is the leader in that market. It is also the leader in the Russian market. In India, it has about 5 percent of the market, but it has devised a plan to launch a greater variety of products and at lower prices. It is number 2 after L'Oreal in the Chinese market. The lifting of direct sales bans should help it there.

FILLING GLOBAL NEEDS AND WANTS

The Avon case points out that similar marketing principles are at work in domestic and foreign markets. However, environmental differences often cause managers to apply these principles differently abroad.

This chapter begins our discussions of international operating functions. Figure 16.1 shows the place of functions in international business. Specifically, we will begin this chapter with a discussion of international marketing strategies. We will then examine how managers apply international product, pricing, promotion, branding, and distribution strategies—the marketing mix—to the countries where they operate. Finally, we will discuss how emphasis within the marketing mix may need to vary to fit the conditions of each country where the company is selling. Throughout each of these sections, we will discuss whether companies should follow globally integrated or locally responsive practices.

> Domestic and international marketing principles are the same, but managers often need to apply them differently because of environmental differences.

FIGURE 16.1   MARKETING IN INTERNATIONAL BUSINESS

Marketing is one of the necessary functions for implementing companies' international strategies.

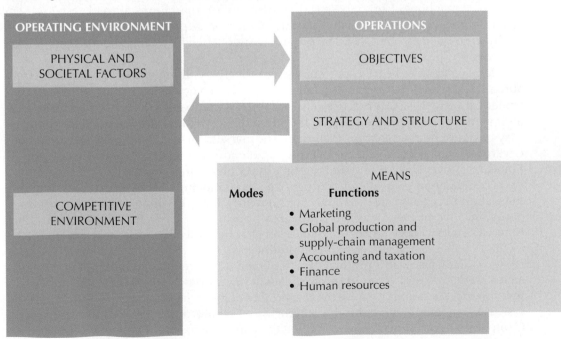

MARKETING STRATEGIES

Most marketing texts classify companies' marketing orientations, although there is some variation in the categories they use. We will begin this section with discussion of the international application of these orientations, which basically determine the degree to which companies follow either a globally integrated or locally responsive strategy. We will conclude this section by explaining the concept of market segmentation and how it relates both to the orientations and to all the elements of the marketing mix.

Overall international marketing strategies should depend on the company's

• Marketing orientation
• Target market

Marketing Orientations

This section highlights the international application of five common marketing orientations: production, sales, customer, strategic marketing, and societal marketing.

Production Orientation   With production orientation, companies focus primarily on production—either efficiency or high quality—with little emphasis on marketing. There is little analysis of consumer needs; rather, companies assume customers want lower prices or higher quality. Although this approach has largely gone out of vogue, it is used internationally for certain cases:

- Commodity sales, especially those for which there is little need or possibility of product differentiation by country
- Passive exports, particularly those that serve to reduce surpluses within the domestic market
- Foreign-market segments or niches that may resemble the market at which the product is aimed initially

Price is the most important factor in selling many commodities.

Companies sell many raw materials and agricultural commodities, such as sugar and tin, primarily on the basis of price because there is universal demand for the undifferentiated product. However, even for commodity sales, companies have realized that marketing efforts may yield positive international sales results. For example, the promotion of the Chiquita brand on bananas has helped increase global supermarket distribution in a glutted market. In addition, oil producers, such as Petroven, LUKoil, and Aramco, have bought branded gasoline-distribution operations abroad to help them sell an otherwise undifferentiated product. Commodity producers also put efforts into business-to-business marketing by providing innovative financing and assuring timely, high-quality supplies.

Passive sales occur when

• Advertising spills over.
• Foreign buyers seek new products.

Many companies begin exporting very passively by filling unsolicited requests from abroad. At this point, companies adapt their products very little, if at all, to foreign consumers' preferences. This practice suffices for many companies that view foreign sales as an appendage to domestic sales. In this situation, companies frequently export only if they have excess inventory for their domestic markets. In fact, fixed costs are sometimes covered from domestic sales so that they quote lower prices on exports as a means of liquidating inventories without disrupting the domestic market.

The unaltered domestic product may have appeal abroad.

A company may develop a product aimed at achieving a large share of its domestic market and then find there are market segments abroad willing to buy that product. Sometimes the product may have universal appeal, such as French champagne. Other times, a company may target a mass market at home as well as niche markets in foreign locations; one example is U.S. bourbon producers that sell to niche markets worldwide. A company may also use a production orientation when selling in countries with only a small market potential. For example, in small low-income countries, MNEs may make few product alterations because the market size does not justify the expense to them and because competitors are apt to be other MNEs that also make few product alterations. Companies may not even adjust the voltage requirements and plugs of electrical products to local standards, leaving the job of conversion to local purchasers instead.

ELBONIAN CALL CENTER

WE DON'T HAVE THAT SOFTWARE IN STOCK.

BUT MAY I INTEREST YOU IN A SET OF PORCELAIN UNICORN FIGURINES THAT WEAR PANTS?

REALLY? WOW. YOUR COUNTRY HAS WAY TOO MUCH MONEY.

FIGURE 16.2

Sometimes you sell when and where you least expect. However, most international sales require a well-conceived and implemented marketing program.

Source: DILBERT © Scott Adams/Dist. by United Features Syndicate, Inc.

Sales Orientation   Internationally, sales orientation means a company tries to sell abroad what it can sell domestically and in the same manner on the assumption that consumers are sufficiently similar globally. A company may make this assumption because of its ethnocentricity or because it lacks sufficient information about the foreign market it wishes to serve. This orientation differs from the production orientation because of its active rather than passive approach to promoting sales. However, there is much anecdotal evidence of foreign marketing failures because of assumptions that product acceptance will be the same as at home or that heavy sales efforts abroad can overcome negative foreign attitudes toward the product, its price, or method of distribution. Yet there also are successful examples of marketing abroad with little or no research on what foreign consumers want. Figure 16.2 illustrates this point humorously.

The greatest ability for a company with a sales orientation to sell the same product in multiple countries occurs when consumer characteristics are similar and when there is a great deal of spillover in product information, such as between the United States and Canada. A company may first develop the product for its home market. It may develop a new product to launch almost simultaneously in multiple countries, as Whirlpool did for high-capacity front-loading washing machines.[2] Or it may develop the product abroad and introduce it later to its home market, as Mars did with Whiskas, a cat food.

> A company may develop a product with an appeal in more than one country
>
> - Because of spillover in product information from its home country
> - Through a simultaneous multicountry launch
> - By developing the product abroad

Customer Orientation   In a company that operates according to sales orientation, management usually is guided by answers to questions such as: Should the company send some exports abroad? Where can the company sell more of product X? That is, the product is held constant and the sales location is varied. In contrast, a customer orientation asks: What and how can the company sell in country A? In this case, the country is held constant and the product and method of marketing it is varied.

Sometimes a company wants to penetrate markets in a given country because of the country's size, growth potential, proximity to home operations, currency or political stability, or any of a host of other reasons. In the extreme of this approach, a company would move to products completely unrelated to its existing product lines. Though an uncommon strategy, some companies have adopted it. For example, Chilena de Fosforos, a Chilean match producer, wanted to tap the Japanese market because of Japanese growth and size, competition within the Chilean market, and the promotional appeal of being able to say "We supply Japan." However, because the company was not price competitive in Japan for matches, it successfully entered the Japanese market by making chopsticks—a product that would use its poplar forest resources and wood-processing capabilities.[3] Or this orientation may lead a company to add products to its portfolio. For instance, Avon plans to sell nutritional products in India along with its line of beauty products.[4]

As with a production orientation, a company using a customer orientation may do so passively. Increasingly, purchasing agents are setting product specifications and then seeking out contracts for the foreign manufacture of components or finished products. For example, the Hong Kong company Yue Yuen Industrial Holdings produces about 14 percent of

> A customer orientation takes geographic areas as given.

the world's footwear, mainly to specification for companies such as Nike.[5] In such cases, the supplier depends on the buyer to determine what final customers want. The supplier is primarily concerned with pricing and delivering what it is selling abroad.

Strategic Marketing Orientation   Most companies committed to continual rather than sporadic foreign sales adopt a strategy that combines production, sales, and customer orientations. Companies that don't make changes to accommodate the needs of foreign markets may lose too many sales, especially if aggressive competitors are willing to make desired adaptations. Recall, for example, how Avon adapted its selling method in China in response to government regulations. Yet expertise concerning a type of product and how to sell it may be important, and companies want their foreign sales to be compatible with their expertise and with their means of dealing with competitors. Companies therefore tend to make marketing variations abroad without deviating very far from their experience. For example, breweries such as Heineken, Stroh, Bass, and Lion, when faced with restrictions against alcoholic beverages in Saudi Arabia, have turned to sales of non-alcoholic beer (marketed as malt rather than beer). Products such as computers or even coffee or tea would probably be too far from managers' areas of expertise. The U.S. home builder Pulte Homes, in entering the Argentine market, kept the same floor plans and exterior look of its U.S. homes to gain economies of standardization, but it added bidets in the bathrooms and large rear patios to fit Argentine preferences.[6]

Societal Marketing Orientation   Companies with societal marketing orientations realize that successful international marketing requires serious consideration of potential environmental, health, social, and work-related problems that may arise when selling or making their products abroad. Such groups as consumer associations, political parties, and labor unions are becoming more globally aware—and vocal. They can quell demand when they feel a product in some way violates their concept of social responsibility. Companies must increasingly consider not only how a product is purchased but also how it is made and disposed of and how it might be changed to be more socially desirable. Such considerations have led Coca-Cola to develop a vitamin-enriched beverage for Botswana and returnable glass containers for Argentina and Brazil.[7] They also led Avon to be the first cosmetic company to ban testing on animals.[8]

Targeting and Segmenting Markets

Although population may give a rough estimate of market size, there are few products that virtually the entire population consumes. Thus, based on the orientations we have just discussed, companies must determine the target market(s) for their products and services. There are three basic alternatives.[9] First, a company may segment by country, for instance, targeting the Japanese market because of its population size and purchasing power. However, this approach may overlook the heterogeneity of consumers within Japan and the existence of Japanese whose consumption behavior is similar to segments in other countries. Second, a company may identify some segments on a global basis, such as segments based on income. Thus each country will have the same segments, but the proportional size of each segment will vary by country. Third, a company can combine these by looking first at countries as segments and then identifying segments within each country. These within-country segments can then be compared with those in other countries. Once a company makes this determination, it can tailor its product offerings, promotion, branding, and distribution to be compatible with the needs of each target market. In effect, a company may hold one or more elements of these marketing functions constant while altering the others. For instance, Chanel aims its cosmetics' sales to a segment that transcends national boundaries. It uses branding, promotion, pricing, and distribution globally, but it adapts the cosmetics to local ethnic and climatic norms.[10]

The most common strategy is product changes as adaptations, done by degree.

Companies consider effects on all stakeholders when selling or making their products.

Companies must decide on their target markets, which may include segments that exist in more than one country.

At the same time, most companies have multiple products and product variations that appeal to different target groups in their home countries, thus they must decide which to introduce abroad and whether to target them to mass versus niche markets. Sales to a mass market may be necessary if a company is to gain sufficient economies in production and distribution. For example, some foreign beer companies have failed in China by concentrating on the premium sector, which is so dispersed that resultant high distribution costs made them unprofitable.[11] In contrast, General Motors, which has multiple automobile makes and models that it targets to different income groups, entered the Chinese market only with its Buick models. Although this is a niche strategy (selling to high-income Chinese consumers), this is a large enough niche to support the sales.

The most common way of identifying market segments within a country is through demographics, such as income, age, gender, ethnicity, and religion. Of course, these may be combined, such as identifying a segment that consists of females age 20 to 30 with incomes over $20,000 per year. In addition, target markets may be further segmented by psychographics (attitudes, values, and lifestyles). Because the percentage of people that fall into any segment may vary substantially from one country to another, a niche market in one country may be a mass market in another. For example, Avon positions itself as a mass market brand in the United Kingdom, but a prestige brand in Russia. A company may be content to accept a combination of mass and niche markets; however, if it wishes to appeal to mass markets in each country, even when the countries are dissimilar, it may need to change elements in its marketing program. For instance, U.S.-based Bell South successfully managed to reach a mass Venezuelan market by selling fewer minutes on phone cards. It added $4 phone cards to the $10 and $20 cards that it customarily sold.[12]

PRODUCT POLICY

Cost is a compelling reason for standardizing marketing as much as possible globally. When companies change any part of their marketing mix (product, price, promotion, brand, and distribution) to serve foreign markets, they incur additional costs of having to coordinate and control added diversity. Within the marketing mix, changes in products to fit foreign markets are the most expensive. Simply, a company must spend on additional development while perhaps losing economies of scale from long production runs. Despite the cost disadvantages, we saw that companies adopt marketing orientations that involve product adaptations to foreign markets. We shall now consider reasons for making product alterations for foreign markets, the costs of product alterations, the extent and mix of product lines, and product life cycle considerations.

Reasons for Making Product Alterations

We'll now examine the legal, cultural, and economic reasons for companies to alter their products to fit the needs of customers in different countries.

Legal Reasons   Explicit legal requirements are the most obvious reason for altering products for foreign markets. If you don't meet the requirements, you won't be allowed to sell. The exact requirements vary widely by country but are usually meant to protect consumers.[13] Pharmaceuticals and foods are particularly subject to regulations concerning purity, testing, and labeling. Automobiles sold in the United States must conform to safety and pollution standards not found in many other countries. However, Europe imposes stricter roof-strength standards than the United States.[14] In a seemingly bizarre ruling, China prohibited sales of the Cyndi Lauper song "I Drove All Night" because it sent an unsafe message to motorists.

> Legal factors are usually related to safety or health protection.

When foreign legal requirements are less stringent than domestic ones, a company may not be legally compelled to alter its products for foreign sale. However, the company will have to weigh such decisions as whether following high domestic standards abroad will raise prices and whether domestic or foreign ill will may result by lowering product standards. Some companies have met home-country criticism for selling abroad—especially in low-income economies—such products as toys, automobiles, contraceptives, and pharmaceuticals that did not meet home-country safety or quality standards. In fact, there is considerable controversy about MNEs' products and promotion in low-income countries, which we discuss in the Point–Counterpoint section of this chapter.

POINT–COUNTERPOINT: SHOULD FIRST WORLD GOVERNMENTS REGULATE THEIR COMPANIES' MARKETING IN THIRD WORLD COUNTRIES?

POINT

International companies sell products in Third World countries that their home countries ban. They also advertise and promote products in Third World countries for which there are restrictions in their home countries. If we have made a domestic decision to curtail dissemination of these products because of their dangers, we have a moral obligation to prevent the same dangers abroad. I know that my statement smacks of extraterritoriality. But let's face it, too many consumers in low-income countries have such poor education that they, like children in First World countries, cannot make intelligent decisions. Further, these consumers often have corrupt political leadership that does not look after their interests. Finally, we have some moral obligation to assure that these consumers spend on needs, rather than on wants that our MNEs have created through clever promotion programs. If First World governments don't regulate to protect consumers in Third World countries, no one will.

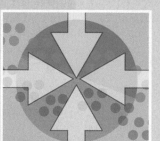

There are many examples of companies' exportation of products that do not meet quality standards at home. There are also examples of exporting dangerous products. For example, DDT is so dangerous to the environment that all First World countries have banned its use, but MNEs export it from these First World countries. First World countries have pretty much abandoned the battery recycling business because of strict antipollution requirements to prevent lead poisoning that shows up only after the slow cumulative ingestion through the years. Thus, companies export the batteries to Third World countries that have either weak or weakly enforced pollution laws.[15]

Although First World countries have not banned the use of tobacco, they have attempted to limit its use through warning labels, prohibitions on sales to minors, and limitations on smoking in certain public areas. The World Health Organization (WHO) estimates that tobacco is the leading cause of preventable death in the world, killing about five million people per year. As the First World has taken more actions against tobacco, tobacco companies have increased their promotions in Third World countries that now account for 70 percent of tobacco-related deaths.[16]

There are also examples of products that are suitable for the mass market in First World countries, but not in Third World countries. The most famous case involved infant formula sales in Third World countries, where infant mortality rates increased when bottle-feeding supplanted breast-feeding. Because of low incomes and poor education, mothers frequently overdiluted formula and gave it to their babies in unhygienic conditions. The governments of Third World countries did little to stop the sales. Global publicity about the situation led WHO to pass a voluntary code to restrict formula promotion, but not sales, in developing countries. Critics hit Nestlé hardest because it had the largest share of infant formula sales in Third World countries and because its name-identified products facilitated the organization of a boycott. The company ceased advertising that could discourage breast-feeding, limited free formula supplies at hospitals, and banned personal gifts to health officials.[17]

MNEs also pay too little attention to the needs of consumers in poor countries. Instead, they primarily develop products suitable to the needs of consumers in high-income countries who can afford them. In some cases, these are superfluous products, for consumers with low incomes, but MNEs introduce and promote them heavily in Third World countries. Thus, Third World consumers end up buying products like soft drinks rather than spending their money on nutritional and health needs. Further, MNEs spend little to develop products to fit the needs of Third World consumers. Take phamaceutical research. Only 10 percent of the global health research budget is spent on diseases that account for 90 percent of the global disease burden, mainly diseases that largely bypass the First World countries.[18] Instead of spending heavily on life-threatening Third World diseases like malaria, Chagas disease, and sleeping sickness, they spend on lifestyle treatments, such as penile erectile dysfunction and baldness. Surely we can find regulatory means to force companies to meet the real needs of Third World countries rather than concentrating on selling dangerous and superfluous products there.

COUNTERPOINT

You paint a picture of consumers in Third World countries as being incapable of making intelligent purchasing decisions. If this is true, which it may be or not, the answer is education rather than limiting people's choices by regulating international companies. In fact, there are many examples of behavior change, both by consumers and governments in Third World countries, when they learn the facts. For instance, Thailand has restricted tobacco smoking in response to statistics showing that smoking is the leading cause of death among its Buddhist monks.[19]

Your argument that products banned at home should not be sold abroad assumes that the home government knows best, which may reflect a difference in cultural values rather than a danger to consumers. For instance, some countries have banned the sale of the abortion pill RU-486 on moral grounds. To ban sales in other countries, which accept a different morality, would seem to be cultural imperialism. Further, the conditions between First and Third World countries are sometimes so different that they need different regulations. Let's take your example of DDT exports. Third World countries realize its adverse long-term effect on the environment, but in the short term, more than 25 of these countries face a crisis from malaria. DDT is simply the best way to kill the disease-carrying mosquitoes. Until there is some better solution, banning exports of DDT will do more harm than good. Certainly, if one government has found a product dangerous, it should pass on this information to other governments; in terms of DDT and toxic materials exports, this is already being done.

It is true that tobacco companies are now promoting more heavily in Third World countries. However, if, for example, the U.S. government were to limit Philip Morris's sales to or promotion of tobacco to Third World countries, citizens of those countries would still be able to buy tobacco. Many Third World countries have indigenous tobacco production, many of which are even government-owned enterprises, such as the China National Tobacco Company. If Philip Morris were to curtail its advertising there, then smokers would simply buy from a different company, especially an already established company in the particular market.

I'm glad you brought up the infant formula situation because it shows the complexity of the issue we're discussing. Although there was a correlation between infant formula promotion and infant formula sales in Third World countries, it is not clear that this promotion led to a decline in breast-feeding. Other factors also influenced the increase in bottle-feeding—specifically, more working mothers and fewer products and services being made in the home. These factors led people to feed babies "home brews," which were also often served unsanitarily. Promotion of infant formula may simply have persuaded them to give up the "home brews" in favor of the most nutritious breast milk substitute available. Nevertheless, MNEs' curtailment of promotion when coupled with campaigns for mothers to breast-feed led to increases in breast-feeding. Thus, the hard work by well-intentioned antiformula groups seemed to have worked. However, the HIV virus is transmitted through breast milk, which is a particular problem in southern Africa where many women are HIV/AIDS infected.[20] Now there are campaigns to get mothers not to breast-feed. This simply shows the futility of trying to legislate what is good for people.

In fact, how far can we go to try to protect people? For instance, in First World countries, obesity is a growing health problem. We're attacking it through education, the same way I said we should attack problems in Third World countries. I can't imagine our banning sugars, fats, and carbohydrates or rationing the purchase of them. Certainly products such as soft drinks seem superfluous when people are ill-nourished and in poor health. But there is no clear-cut means of drawing a line between people who can afford and people who cannot afford these products. Further, companies such as Coca-Cola have experimented with adding nutrition to products, but consumers have not been very receptive.

Companies do alter products to fit the needs of low-income people, everything from smaller packages to less sleek electrical appliances. Although you criticized pharmaceutical companies for not attacking their health needs, these same companies spend heavily to find solutions to health problems that occur in both First and Third World countries, such as cancer and diabetes. However, pharmaceutical companies must recoup their expenses if they are to survive, thus they must concentrate on drugs for which they can be paid. There are many governmental research centers and nonprofit foundations that are better candidates for solving the Third World health problems.

One of the more cumbersome product alterations for companies is adjusting to different laws on packaging, such as the placement of warning labels. For example, the EU requires such labeling on foods with .9 percent or more of bioengineered ingredients, but the United States has no warning-label requirements at all.[21] This difference has caused Unilever to use different types of oil (soy oil in the United States and vegetable oil in Europe) in its Hellmann's mayonnaise so as to avoid warning labels in Europe.[22] Another problem concerns laws that protect the environment. Some countries prohibit certain types of containers, such as Denmark's ban on aluminum cans. Other countries restrict the volume of packaging materials to save resources and decrease trash. There also are differences in national requirements as to whether containers must be reusable and whether companies use packaging materials that must be recycled, incinerated, or composted.

A recurring issue is the need to arrive at international product standards and eliminate some of the wasteful product requirements for alterations among countries. Although countries have reached agreement on some products (sprocket dimensions on movie film, technical standards on mobile phones, bar codes to identify products), other products (railroad gauges, power supplies, and electrical socket shapes) continue to vary. A global standard has usually resulted from companies wanting to emulate a dominant producer, such as making personal computers that are IBM compatible. In reality, there is both consumer and economic resistance to standardization, such as U.S. consumers' reluctance to adapt the metric system. Economically, a complete changeover would be more costly than simply educating people and relabeling. Containers would have to be redesigned and production retooled so that sizes would be in even numbers. (Would American football have first down with 9.144 meters to go?) Even for new products or those still under development, companies and countries are slow to reach agreement because they want to protect the investments they've already made. At best, international standards will come very slowly.

Marketing managers must also watch for the indirect legal requirements that may affect product content or demand. In some countries, companies cannot easily import certain raw materials or components, forcing them to construct an end product with local substitutes that may alter the final result substantially. Legal requirements such as high taxes on heavy automobiles also shift companies' sales to smaller models, thus indirectly altering demand for tire sizes and grades of gasoline.

Cultural Reasons   Religious differences obviously limit the standardization of product offerings on a global basis, thus food franchise companies eschew sales of pork products in Islamic countries and meat of any kind in India. However, cultural differences affecting product demand are often not so easily discerned. For example, Toyota was initially unsuccessful in selling pickup trucks in the United States until it redesigned the interior with enough headroom for drivers to wear 10-gallon cowboy hats.[23] Volkswagen and Audi have extended the wheelbase for China in order to accommodate more passengers for weekend outings.[24] International food marketers alter ingredients (especially fat, sodium, and sugar) substantially to fit local tastes and requirements. For instance, a Kellogg's All-Bran bar has three times as much salt in the United States as in Mexico.[25]

Economic Reasons   If a country's average income is low, insufficient numbers of consumers may be able to buy a product the MNE sells domestically. The company therefore may have to design a cheaper model. Whirlpool has done this with automatic washing machines to sell in Brazil, China, and India.[26] In some cases, consumers have so little extra cash that they buy personal items in small quantities as they need them. For these markets, Gillette sells razor blades and 3M sells scouring pads in smaller package sizes.[27]

Even if a market segment has sufficient income to purchase the same product the company sells at home, differences in infrastructure may require product alterations. Low-income countries generally have poorer infrastructures, and companies may gain advantages by selling products that will withstand rough terrain and utility outages.

Margin notes:

Although some standardization of products would eliminate wasteful alterations, there is resistance because

- A changeover would be costly.
- People are familiar with the "old."

Examination of cultural differences may pinpoint possible problem areas.

Personal incomes and infrastructures affect product demand.

Whirlpool sells washing machine models in remote areas of India that have rat guards to protect hoses, extra-strong parts to survive transportation on potholed roads, and heavy-duty wiring to cope with electrical ebbs and surges.[28] In Japan, the infrastructure for automobiles reflects crowded conditions and high land prices. Some U.S. automobile models are too wide to fit into elevators that carry cars to upper floors to be parked, and they cannot make narrow turns on back streets.

Finally, differences in income distribution may affect demand for certain products. In countries where people with purchasing power typically have household servants, they may forego purchasing labor-saving products. Whirlpool discovered this when trying to sell automatic washing machines in some markets. It bought "obsolete" technology from Korea so as to sell less automated, two-tub machines in those markets.[29]

Alteration Costs

Companies can usually reduce production and inventory costs substantially through product standardization. Nevertheless, as we have just demonstrated, there are some-times compelling reasons to alter products for different national markets. Some product alterations are cheap to make yet have an important influence on demand. One such area is packaging, which is a common alteration exporters make because of legal and climatic requirements. Before making a decision, marketing managers should always compare the cost of an alteration with the cost of lost sales from no alterations.

Some alterations cost less than others.

One cost-saving strategy a company can use to compromise between uniformity and diversity is to standardize a great deal while altering some end characteristics. Whirlpool puts the same basic compressor, casing, evaporator, and sealant system in its refrigerators for all countries, but changes such features as doors and shelves for different countries.[30]

Extent and Mix of the Product Line

Most companies produce multiple products. It is doubtful that all of these products could generate sufficient sales in a given foreign market to justify the cost of penetrating that market. Even if they could, a company might offer only a portion of its product line, perhaps as an entry strategy.

Narrowing the product line allows for concentration of efforts.

In reaching product line decisions, marketing managers should consider the possible effects on sales and the cost of having one product as opposed to a family of products. Sometimes a company finds it must produce and sell some less lucrative products if it is to sell the more popular ones, such as sherry glasses to match crystal wine and water glasses. Or a company may be forced into a few short production runs in order to gain the mass market on other products. A company that must set up some foreign production to sell in the foreign market may be able to produce locally those products in its line that have longer production runs and import the other products needed to help sell the local production.

If the foreign sales per customer is small compared to those in the domestic market, selling costs per unit may be higher because of the fixed costs associated with selling. In such a case, the company can broaden the product line to be handled, either by grouping sales of several manufacturers or by developing new products for the local market that the same salesperson can handle. For example, Avon sells products in some countries that it does not handle in the United States to increase the average order per household, such as Crayola products in Brazil, Disney products in Mexico, and *Reader's Digest* in Canada, Brazil, Australia, France, and New Zealand.

Broadening the product line may gain distribution economies.

Product Life-Cycle Considerations

There may be differences among countries in either the shape or the length of a product's life cycle. A product facing declining sales in one country may have growing or sustained sales in another. For example, cars are a mature product in Western Europe, the United States, and Japan. They are in the late growth stage in South Korea and in the early growth stage in India. At the mature stage, automobile companies must emphasize characteristics that encourage people to replace their still functional cars, such as by emphasizing lifestyle, speed, and accessories. In the early growth stage, they need to appeal to first-time buyers who worry about cost, thus they emphasize fuel consumption and price.[31]

PRICING

Within the marketing mix, companies place much importance on price. A price must be low enough to gain sales, but high enough to guarantee the flow of funds required to carry on other activities, such as R&D, production, and distribution. The proper price will not only assure short-term profits but also give the company the resources necessary to achieve long-term competitive viability. Pricing is more complex internationally than domestically because of the following factors:

- Different degrees of governmental intervention
- Greater diversity of markets
- Price escalation for exports
- Changing values of currencies
- Differences in fixed versus variable pricing practices
- Companies' strength with suppliers

Let's examine each of these factors.

Governmental Intervention

Governmental price controls may

- Set minimum or maximum prices
- Prohibit certain competitive pricing practices

Every country has laws that affect the prices of goods at the consumer level. A governmental price control may set either maximum or minimum prices. Controls against lowering prices usually prevent companies from eliminating competitors in order to gain monopoly positions. Many countries also set maximum prices for numerous products, which can lower companies' profits.

The WTO, under its anti-dumping regulations, permits countries to establish restrictions against any import that comes in at a price below that charged to consumers in the exporting country. Although countries may not establish restrictions, the possibility that they will makes it more difficult for companies to differentiate markets through pricing. A company might want to export at a lower price than that charged at home for several reasons. One reason might be to test sales in the foreign market. For example, a company may find it cannot export to a given country because tariffs or transportation costs make the price to foreign consumers prohibitively high. Yet its preliminary calculations show that by establishing foreign production, it may be able to reduce the price to the foreign consumer substantially. Before committing resources to produce overseas, the company may want to test the market by exporting so as to sell the product at the price it would charge if it produced locally. A company may be able to complete this test marketing before companies in the importing country can persuade their government to restrict imports. Nestlé tested the U.K. market in this way by exporting for a year from Canada to see if enough of a market would develop to justify completing a frozen-food plant to make Lean Cuisine products. Shipping such dishes as spaghetti bolognese in refrigerated ships and paying customs duties made the costs of the exported products much higher than their U.K. selling prices. However, the cost of this test was small compared to the value of the information gained and the amount of Nestlé's eventual commitment.

A company may also charge different prices in different countries because of competitive and demand factors. It may feel that prices can be kept high in the domestic market by restricting supply to that market. Excess production then can be sold abroad at a lower price, as long as that price covers variable costs and contributes to overhead.

Greater Market Diversity

Although there are numerous ways a company can segment the domestic market and charge different prices in each segment, country-to-country variations create even more natural segments. For example, companies can sell few sea urchins or tuna eyeballs in the United States at any price, but they can export them to Japan, where they are delicacies. Levi's jeans often cost twice as much in the United Kingdom than in the United States.[32] In some countries, a company may have many competitors and thus little discretion in setting its prices. In other countries, it may have a near monopoly due either to the stage in the product life cycle or to government-granted manufacturing rights not held by competitors. In near-monopoly markets, a company may exercise considerable pricing discretion, using any of the following:

- A **skimming strategy**—charging a high price for a new product by aiming first at consumers willing to pay the price, and then progressively lowering the price
- A **penetration strategy**—introducing a product at a low price to induce a maximum number of consumers to try it
- A **cost-plus strategy**—pricing at a desired margin over cost

Consumers in some countries simply like certain products more and are willing to pay more for them.

Country-of-origin stereotypes also limit pricing possibilities. For example, exporters in emerging economies often must compete primarily through low prices because of negative perceptions about their products' quality. But there are dangers in lowering prices in response to adverse stereotypes because a lower price may reduce the product image even further.

Diversity in buying on credit affects sales. Credit buying increases costs, which consumers in some countries are more willing to pay than are consumers in other countries. For example, the Japanese are more reluctant than Americans to rely on consumer credit. Thus, in Japan it is less possible than in the United States to use credit payments as a means of inducing the sale of goods. The tax treatment of interest payments also affects whether consumers will pay in cash or by credit.

Cash versus credit buying affects demand.

Price Escalation in Exporting

Another reason pricing is complex internationally is price escalation. If standard markups occur within distribution channels, lengthening the channels or adding expenses somewhere within the system will further increase the price to the consumer. For example, assume the markup is 50 percent and the product costs $1.00 to produce. The price to the consumer would be $1.50. However, if production costs were to increase to $1.20, the 50 percent markup would make the price $1.80, not $1.70 as might be expected. Figure 16.3 shows price escalation in export sales, which occurs for two reasons:

Price generally goes up by more than transport and duty costs.

1. Channels of distribution usually span greater distances and so exporters need to contract with organizations that know how to sell in foreign markets.
2. Tariffs are an additional cost that may be passed on to consumers.

There are two main implications of price escalation. Seemingly exportable products may turn out to be noncompetitive abroad if companies use cost-plus pricing—which many do.[33] To become competitive in exporting, a company may have to sell its product to intermediaries at a lower price to lessen the amount of escalation. It should determine what price will maximize profits.

FIGURE 16.3   PRICE ESCALATION IN EXPORTING IF COMPANIES USE COST-PLUS PRICING

If both the producer/exporter and the importer/distributor charge 50 percent more than their costs, the added $.40 of transport and tariff costs actually increases the price to consumers in country B to $1.35 more than in country A because of markups. This may prevent the product from selling competitively.

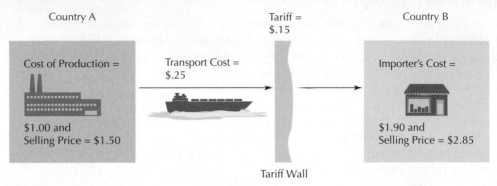

Currency Value and Price Changes

Pricing decisions must consider replacement costs.

For companies accustomed to operating with one (relatively) stable currency, pricing in highly volatile currencies can be extremely troublesome. Marketing managers should make pricing decisions to assure the company of enough funds to replenish its inventory and still make a profit. Otherwise, it may be making a "paper profit" while liquidating itself—that is, what shows on paper as a profit may result from the company's failure to adjust for inflation while the merchandise is in stock. The company must consider not only inflation's effect on prices but also the possibility its income taxes will be based on the paper profits rather than on real profits. Table 16.1 illustrates a pricing plan to make a target profit (after taxes) of 30 percent on the cost of replacing inventory when the company collects from its sale (replacement cost). The company that does not use a similar plan may soon lack sufficient funds to operate because of receiving too little to have enough merchandise to sell later. The longer the company waits to receive payment for its merchandise, the more important it becomes for it to use a graduated pricing model. For example, during high inflationary periods within various Latin American countries, companies have to raise prices very frequently.[34]

Two other pricing problems occur because of inflationary conditions:

1. The receipt of funds in a foreign currency that, when converted, buy less of the company's own currency than had been expected
2. The frequent readjustment of prices necessary to compensate for continual cost increases

In the first case, the company sometimes (depending on competitive factors and governmental regulations) can specify in sales contracts an equivalency in some hard currency. For example, a U.S. manufacturer's sale of equipment to a company in Uruguay may specify that payment be made in dollars or in pesos at an equivalent price, in terms of dollars, at the time payment is made. In the second case, frequent price increases make it more difficult for the company to quote prices in letters or catalogs. Perpetual price rises may even hamper what the company would otherwise prefer for distribution. For example, price increases in vending machine sales are frequently difficult because of the need to change machines and to come up with coins or tokens that correspond to the desired percentage increase in price.

Currency-value changes also affect pricing decisions for any product that has potential foreign competition. For example, when the U.S. dollar is strong, companies can sell non–U.S.-made goods more cheaply in the U.S. market because their price in dollars decreases. In such a situation, U.S. producers may have to accept a lower profit margin to

TABLE 16.1	**EFFECT OF TAX AND INFLATION ON PRICING**

For the sake of simplicity, this example assumes a company waits a year before it gets paid for its inventory—either because the inventory is stocked before it is sold or because purchasers take time to pay. If the payment cycle is shorter, the company would need to adjust the inflation rate.

The pricing structure for payment one year after acquiring inventory is calculated as follows: Replacement cost is cost plus inflation until collection, or $1,000 + 0.36(1,000) = 1,360$; income after taxes is profit goal times replacement cost, or $0.30(1,360) = 408$. Income after taxes is 60 percent of taxable income; thus, taxable income may be calculated as $408 \div 0.6$, or 680; tax is $0.4(680) = 272$; sales price is original cost (1,000) plus taxable income (680); markup on replacement is sales price (1,680) less replacement cost (1,360), or 320.

Assume: Cost at beginning is 1,000

36% inflation

40% tax rate

30% profit goal on replacement cost after taxes

IF SOLD AND COLLECTED AS SOON AS INVENTORY IS ACQUIRED		IF SOLD AND COLLECTED A YEAR AFTER INVENTORY IS ACQUIRED	
Cost	1,000	Replacement cost	1,360
Markup	500	Markup on replacement	320
Sales price	1,500	Sales price	1,680
Minus cost	1,000	Minus original cost	1,000
Taxable income	500	Taxable income	680
Tax @ 40%	200	Tax @ 40%	272
Income after taxes	300	Income after taxes	408

be competitive. When the dollar is weak, however, foreign producers may have to adjust their margins downward.

When companies sell similar goods in multiple countries, price differences among them must not exceed by much the cost of bringing the goods in from a lower-priced country, or spillover in buying will occur. Ice cream manufacturers can vary their prices by a large percentage from country to country because the transportation costs compared to the product's price render large-scale movements across borders impractical. However, if the transportation costs compared to the product's price are low, consumers can feasibly buy abroad and import when prices vary substantially from country to country. For example, automobile prices in Canada are typically much lower than those in the United States, so some Canadian distributors have been selling to U.S. customers where GM has not authorized them to sell. The selling and handling of goods through unofficial distributors, the **gray market,** can undermine the longer-term viability of the distributorship system, cause a company's operations in different countries to compete with each other, and prevent companies from charging what the market will bear in each country. Therefore, GM has sought to prevent this gray market activity by disallowing warranty work on these vehicles by U.S. dealers and curtailing vehicle allocations to dealers involved in the gray market.[35] Some other companies try to keep prices fairly close among countries to prevent such movements. The courts in some countries uphold the right of companies to maintain prices through distributor agreements, but companies have to monitor compliance and can find enforcement difficult.[36] At the same time, attempts to maintain price differences among countries has been controversial, such as the higher prices U.S. consumers pay for prescription drugs.

Fixed versus Variable Pricing

MNEs often negotiate export prices, particularly to foreign distributors. Small companies, especially those from low-income countries, frequently give price concessions too

---

TABLE 16.2   IMPORT-EXPORT PRICE NEGOTIATIONS

The goal is to delay a pricing commitment while discussing a whole package of other commitments.

IMPORTER'S REACTION TO PRICE OFFER	EXPORTER'S RESPONSE
1. Your offer is too expensive.	- Ask what is meant by too expensive.
	- Find out what is considered acceptable and on what basis.
	- Respond by providing justification.
	- Avoid lowering your price until you learn more about what the other party is looking for.
	- Find out if the objection is due to your price offer or if it reflects other factors.
	- Ask yourself, "If I'm too expensive, why are they negotiating with me?"
2. We don't have that kind of budget.	- Find out how large the budget is, and for what time frame.
	- Explore whether your offer can fit within the overall budget by combining several budget lines.
	- Propose deferred payment schedules.
	- Confirm the order and postpone deliveries until a new budget is allocated.
	- Split your order into smaller units or miniorders to meet current budget limitations.
3. That's not what we are looking for.	- Ask what they are looking for, and insist on specifics.
	- Keep questioning until you understand the real needs.
	- Repackage your offer in light of the new information received.
4. Your offer is not competitive.	- Ask what "not competitive" means.
	- Find out if competitors' offers are comparable to yours.
	- Find weaknesses in other offers and emphasize your strengths.
	- Reformulate your offer by avoiding direct comparison with competition. Stress the unique features of your products/services.

Source: Copyright © 2000 from "Business Negotiations: Making the First Offer" from the *International Trade Journal*, no. 2 (2000): 12–16, by Claude Cellich. Reproduced by permission of Taylor & Francis Group, LLC, http://www.taylorandfrancis.com.

quickly, limiting their ability to negotiate on a range of marketing factors that affect their costs:

- Discounts for quantity or repeat orders
- Deadlines that increase production or transportation costs
- Credit and payment terms
- Service
- Supply of promotional materials
- Training of sales personnel or customers

Table 16.2 shows ways in which an exporter (or other marketers as well) may deal more effectively in price negotiations.

Custom influences price negotiations, such as reluctance of German managers to take the time to bargain. Rather, they tend simply to say "thanks" and look for another provider.[37] The extent to which manufacturers can or must set prices at the retail level varies substantially by country. There is also substantial variation in whether, where, and for what products consumers bargain in order to settle on an agreed price. For instance, in the United States consumers commonly bargain for automobiles, real estate, and large orders of industrial supplies, but not for grocery items. However, some automobile dealerships sell only on a fixed price basis, and bargaining for smaller items is increasing because the Internet allows consumers to confront distributors with alternative prices they have obtained easily. In contrast, consumers in most low-income countries commonly bargain for both large and small items, but more likely in markets than in retail stores.[38]

There are country-to-country differences in

● Whether manufacturers set prices
● Whether prices are fixed or bargained in stores
● Where bargaining occurs

Company to Company Pricing

Dominant companies with clout can get suppliers to offer them lower prices, in turn enabling them to gain cost advantages over competitors. But if they buy locally they have this clout only where they have the dominance. Take dominant retailers. Wal-Mart, Marks & Spencer, and Carrefour have such clout in their domestic U.S., U.K., and French markets, respectively. However, they have been hard-pressed to gain the same advantage when entering the other's home market.

The Internet is also causing more companies to compete for the same business, especially when there are sales of largely undifferentiated materials. Thus many industrial buyers are claiming large price decreases through Internet buying. However, sellers can improve their positions by negotiating and by combining Internet communications with face-to-face communications.[39]

PROMOTION

Promotion is the presentation of messages intended to help sell a product or service. The types and direction of messages and the method of presentation may be extremely diverse, depending on the company, product, and country of operation.

The Push-Pull Mix

Promotion may be categorized as **push,** which uses direct selling techniques, or **pull,** which relies on mass media. An example of push is Avon's door-to-door selling of cosmetics; an example of pull is magazine advertisements for a brand of cigarettes. Most companies use combinations of both marketing strategies. For each product in each country, a company must determine its total promotional budget as well as the mix of the budget between push and pull.

Several factors help determine the mix of push and pull among countries:

● Type of distribution system
● Cost and availability of media to reach target markets
● Consumer attitudes toward sources of information
● Price of the product compared to incomes

Generally, the more tightly controlled the distribution system, the more likely a company is to emphasize a push strategy because it requires a greater effort to get distributors to handle a product. This is true, for example, in Belgium, where distributors are small and highly fragmented, forcing companies to concentrate on making their goods available. Also affecting the push-pull mix is the amount of contact between salespeople and consumers. In a self-service situation, in which there are no salespersons to whom customers can turn for opinions on products, it is more important for the company to use a pull strategy by advertising through mass media or at the point of purchase.

Push is more likely when

● Self-service is not predominant.
● Advertising is restricted.
● Product price is a high portion of income.

Because of diverse national environments, promotional problems are extremely varied. For example, about 70 percent of India's population is rural, and many in rural areas are illiterate, poor, and without access to televisions and radios. Some mass consumer merchandisers such as Colgate-Palmolive, Unilever, Coca-Cola, and Pepsi are providing samples at religious pilgrimages that millions attend in the expectation that their subsequent word-of-mouth promotions will yield sales.[40]

In many countries, government regulations pose an even greater barrier. For example, Scandinavian television has long refused to accept commercials. Other countries may put legal constraints on what a company says, thus affecting the push-pull mix. For example, in the United States, pharmaceutical companies have been using more pull promotions even for prescription drugs. They talk about the product and brand in television ads and tell viewers to ask their physicians about it. European countries are more restrictive. Thus, Pfizer is advertising in Europe about the symptoms of erectile dysfunction and telling TV viewers to talk with their physicians about it; however, Pfizer never mentions its drug, Viagra in these ads.[41]

Finally, the amount of consumer involvement in making a purchase decision varies by country because of income levels. When a product's price compared to consumer income is high, consumers usually will want more time and information before making a decision. Information is best conveyed in a personal selling situation, which fosters two-way communication. In emerging economies, MNEs usually have to use more push strategies for mass consumer products because incomes are low compared to price.

Standardization of Advertising Programs

The savings from using the same advertising programs as much as possible, such as on a global basis or among countries with shared consumer attributes, are not as great as those from product standardization. Nevertheless, they can be significant.

In addition to reducing costs, advertising standardization may improve the quality of advertising at the local level (because local agencies may lack expertise), prevent internationally mobile consumers from being confused by different images, and speed the entry of products into different countries. For example, Sony's "My first Sony" is aimed at young consumers all over the world. However, globally standardized advertising usually means a program that is *similar* from market to market rather than one that is *identical* in each. For example, Pepsi had Tina Turner sing the Pepsi-Cola theme song with local bands in different countries.[42] Some of the problems that hinder complete standardization of advertising relate to translation, legality, and message needs.

Standardization usually implies using the same advertising agency globally. However, companies may differentiate campaigns among countries even if they use the same agency everywhere. By using the same agency, companies such as IBM, Colgate, and Tambrands have found that they can take good ideas in one market and quickly introduce them into other markets because they need not worry about legal and ethical problems from having one agency copy what another has done. However, some companies, such as Procter & Gamble, prefer to use more than one agency to keep the agencies in a state of perpetual competition and to cover one agency's weak spots by drawing on the ideas of another agency.

Translation When media reach audiences in multiple countries, such as MTV programs aired throughout most of Europe, ads in those media cannot be translated because viewers watch the same transmission. However, when a company is going to sell in a country with a different language, translation is usually necessary unless the advertiser is trying to communicate an aura of foreignness. Toyota did this in ads in the United States that were completely in French and Italian with subtitles.[43] The most audible problem in commercial translation is dubbing, because words on an added sound track never quite correspond to lip movements. Marketing managers can avoid dubbing problems by creating commercials in which actors do not speak, along with a voice or print overlay in the appropriate language.

A growing type of dubbing in advertising involves product placement in movies and television shows. Because these shows are widely distributed internationally, a wide audience sees the placement. However, the product may not be available everywhere.

Advantages of standardized advertising include

- Some cost savings
- Better quality at local level
- Rapid entry into different countries

Using the same brand name globally is hampered by

- Language differences
- Acquisitions

Technology now permits the products to be removed and replaced for given markets. *Spider Man II* had Cadbury Schweppes' Dr. Pepper logo on a refrigerator for U.S. screenings, but in Europe it had PepsiCo's Mirinda logo.[44]

On the surface, translating a message would seem to be easy. However, some messages, particularly plays on words, simply don't translate—even between countries that have the same language. The number of ludicrous but costly mistakes companies have made attest to translation difficulties. Sometimes what is an acceptable word or direct translation in one place is obscene, misleading, or meaningless in another. For example, the Milk Board's ad "Got milk?" comes out as "Are you lactating?" in Spanish.[45] Another problem is in choosing the language when a country has more than one. For example, in Haiti, a company might use Creole to reach the general population but French to reach the upper class.

Legality   What is legal advertising in one country may be illegal elsewhere. The differences result mainly from varying national views on consumer protection, competitive protection, promotion of civil rights, standards of morality and behavior, and nationalism. For instance, China bans ads for feminine hygiene pads, hemorrhoid medications, and athlete's foot ointment during three daily meal times.[46] In terms of consumer protection, policies differ on the amount of deception permitted, what can be advertised to children, whether companies must list warnings on products of possible harmful effects, and the extent to which they must list ingredients. The United Kingdom and the United States allow direct comparisons with competitive brands (such as Pepsi versus Coca-Cola), while the Philippines prohibits them. Only a few countries regulate sexism in advertising.

Some governments restrict the advertising of some products (such as contraceptives) because they feel they are in bad taste. Elsewhere, governments restrict ads that might prompt children to misbehave or people to break laws (such as advertising automobile speeds that exceed the speed limit) and those that show barely clad women. New Zealand banned a Nike ad in which a rugby team tackles the coach, as well as a Chanel ad in which the model said to her male lover before kissing him, "I hate you. I hate you so much I think I'm going to die from it, darling." In both cases, the ads were deemed to threaten violence.[47]

Message Needs   An advertising theme may not be appropriate everywhere because of national differences in how well consumers know the product and how they perceive it, who will make the purchasing decision, and what appeals are most important. For example, few Japanese own dishwashers even though they own most other appliances. In addition to size constraints, which some manufacturers have overcome with new designs, many Japanese housewives feel guilty buying for the sake of convenience. Matsushita, which promotes convenience elsewhere, has shifted its Japanese ads to hot water conservation and hygiene.[48]

The reaction to how messages are presented may also vary. For example, Leo Burnett Worldwide produced a public service advertisement to promote checkups for breast cancer. It showed an attractive woman being admired in a sundress with a voice-over message, "If only women paid as much attention to their breasts as men do . . . " Japanese viewers found it a humorous way to draw attention to an important health issue, but French viewers found it offensive because there is nothing humorous about the issue.[49]

Given the increase in television transmission that reaches audiences in multiple countries, advertisers are being forced to find common themes and messages that will appeal to potential consumers in all the countries where their ads are viewed.

BRANDING

A brand is an identifying mark for products or services. When a company registers a brand legally, it is a trademark. A brand gives a product or service instant recognition and may save promotional costs. Because companies have spent heavily in the past to create brand awareness, *Business Week* magazine estimates that at least 100 global brands are worth at least a billion dollars. U.S. companies dominate the ownership of these

Companies from many countries exhibit their logos wherever they operate internationally. At this shopping mall in Bucharest, Romania, the logos for Gorenje (Slovenia), McDonald's (United States), Orion (Hungary), Samsung (Korea), and Tuborg (Denmark) are clearly displayed.

brands, garnering 54 out of the 100 most valuable brands. Of the top dozen, U.S. companies own nine. These top dozen brands in order are as follows: Coca-Cola, Microsoft, IBM, GE, Intel, Nokia (Finland), Disney, McDonald's, Toyota (Japan), Marlboro, MercedesBenz (Germany), and Citi.[50] MNEs must make four major branding decisions:

1. Brand versus no brand
2. Manufacturer's brand versus private brand
3. One brand versus multiple brands
4. Worldwide brand versus local brands

The international environment substantially affects only the last of these.

Some companies, such as Coca-Cola, have opted to use the same brand and logo globally. This helps develop a global image, especially for customers who travel internationally. Other companies, such as Nestlé, associate many of their products under the same family of brands, such as the Nestea and Nescafé brands, in order to share these brands in their goodwill. Nevertheless, there are a number of problems in trying to use uniform brands internationally.

Language Factors

One problem is that brand names may carry a different association in another language. For example, GM renamed its Buick LaCrosse in Canada after it discovered the word was slang in Quebec for masturbation.[51] Coca-Cola tries to use global branding wherever possible but discovered that the word *diet* in Diet Coke had a connotation of illness in Germany and Italy. The brand is called Coca-Cola Light outside the United States.

Unilever has successfully translated the brand name for its fabric softener, while leaving its brand symbol, a baby bear, intact on the packaging. The U.S. name *Snuggle* is *Kuschelweich* in Germany, *Cajoline* in France, *Coccolino* in Italy, and *Mimosin* in Spain. But *Snuggle* did not quite convey the same meaning in English-speaking Australia, where Unilever uses *Huggy*. However, brand symbols don't necessarily work everywhere either. Big Boy put its customary statue (a boy with checkered overalls and cowlick curl) outside its restaurant in Thailand, and many Thais placed offerings at his feet because they thought it was Buddha.[52]

Pronunciation presents other problems, because a foreign language may lack some of the sounds of a brand name or the pronunciation of the name may have a different meaning than the original. For example, Marcel Bich dropped the *H* from his name when branding Bic pens because of the fear of mispronunciation in English. Some locally popular soft drinks have unappetizing meanings when pronounced in English—Mucos (Japan), Pipi (Yugoslavia), Pshitt (France), and Zit (Greece).

Different alphabets present still other problems. For example, consumers judge English brand names by whether the name sounds appealing, while brand names in Mandarin and Cantonese need to have visual appeal as well because the Mandarin and Cantonese alphabets are pictograms. Such companies as Coca-Cola, Mercedes-Benz, and Boeing have taken great pains to assure not only that the translation of their names is pronounced roughly the same as in English but also that the brand name is meaningful. For example, Coca-Cola is pronounced *Ke-kou-ke-le* in Mandarin and means tasty and happy. Further, companies have sought names that are considered lucky in China, such as a name with eight strokes in it and displayed in red rather than blue. Similarly, the digit eight is overrepresented in product prices, such as ending a price with an eight.[53]

Brand Acquisitions

Much international expansion takes place through acquisition of companies in foreign countries that already have branded products. For example, when Avon acquired Justine in South Africa, it kept the Justine name because the brand was well known and respected. However, Sara Lee acquired various Brazilian coffee roasters and is now trying to consolidate them into a national brand because stretching the promotional budget over so many brands means that promotions are not as effective as they might be, given that less is spent on any one brand to build significant positive recognition.[54] Overall the portion of local brands to international brands is decreasing; however, there are many examples of strong local brands that companies cannot easily displace.[55]

Country-of-Origin Images

Companies should consider whether to create a local or a foreign image for their products. The products of some countries, particularly high-income countries, tend to have a higher-quality image than do those from other countries.[56] There are also image differences concerning specific products from specific countries. For example, many Japanese believe that clothing made abroad is superior to that made in Japan. Thus, Burberry has created separate labels for its products made in Japan and made in the United Kingdom (Burberry London brand). The British have a positive image of Australian wine, thus a young Australian winery sought a very Australian name, Barramundi, for its wine exports to the United Kingdom.[57]

Images of products are affected by where they are made.

But images can change. Consider that for many years various Korean companies sold abroad under private labels or under contract with well-known companies. Some of these Korean companies, such as Samsung, now emphasize their own trade names and the quality of Korean products. At the same time, the Korean LG Group, best known for its GoldStar brand, has introduced a line of high-end appliances with a European-sounding name, LG Tromm.[58]

In an innovative effort to create a British ice cream flavor along the lines of its American Cherry Garcia, Ben & Jerry's ran a contest for the best name and flavor. Cool Britannia won out over such entrants as Minty Python, Grape Expectations, Choc Ness Monster, and The Rolling Scones.[59]

One of the ongoing international legal debates concerns product names associated with location. The EU protects the names of many EU products, such as Roquefort and Gorgonzola cheeses, Parma ham, and Chianti wine. However, the EU does not protect the names associated with non-EU products, such as Florida orange juice and Idaho potatoes. At this writing, there is still a debate on whether U.S. companies can make Roquefort or whether the EU can produce Florida orange juice.[60]

Generic and Near-Generic Names

Companies want their product names to become household words, but not so much that competitors can use trademarked brand names to describe their similar products. In the United States, the brand names Xerox and Kleenex are nearly synonymous with copiers and paper tissues, but have nevertheless remained proprietary brands. Some other names that were once proprietary, such as cellophane, linoleum, and Cornish hens, have become **generic**—available for anyone to use.

In this context, companies sometimes face substantial differences among countries that may either stimulate or frustrate their sales. For example, aspirin and Swiss army knives are proprietary names in Europe but generic in the United States, a situation that impairs European export sales of those products to the United States because U.S. companies can produce aspirin and Swiss army knives.

DISTRIBUTION

A company may accurately assess market potential, design goods or services for that market, price them appropriately, and promote them to probable consumers. However, it will have little likelihood of reaching its sales potential if it doesn't make the goods or services conveniently available to customers. Companies need to place their goods where people want to buy them. For example, does a man prefer to buy shampoo in a grocery store, barbershop, drugstore, or some other type of outlet?

Distribution is the course—physical path or legal title—that goods take between production and consumption. In international marketing, a company must decide on the method of distribution among countries as well as the method within the country where final sale occurs.

Companies may limit early distribution in given foreign countries by attempting to sell regionally before moving nationally. Many products and markets lend themselves to this sort of gradual development. In many cases, geographic barriers and poor internal transportation systems divide countries into very distinct markets. In other countries, very little wealth or few potential sales may lie outside the large metropolitan areas. In still others, advertising and distribution may be handled effectively on a regional basis. See the section, "Does Geography Matter?" that expands on these points.

DOES GEOGRAPHY MATTER?

Is Necessity the Mother of Invention?

You've probably heard the saying that it is as "difficult as selling a refrigerator to Eskimos." Climate is, thus, a great influence on the demand for many products—clothes, sporting equipment, snow tires, air conditioners, and sunscreen, to name a few. Thus, climate is a variable when identifying market segments. Further, seasonal changes that occur at opposite times in the northern and southern hemispheres allow you to spread your sales more evenly during the year, such as by focusing ski sales in Switzerland during December through March and in Chile during June through September. This hemispheric difference may also cause you to make adjustments. Lucasfilm wanted to debut early *Star Wars* films during school vacation periods that corresponded to the hot months in both hemispheres, thus debuts were months apart between New York and Buenos Aires.

Natural conditions—such as mountains, waterways, and deserts—create both barriers and expediencies to distribution. For example, countries can more easily build infrastructure where there are flat areas without obstructions, thus, other things being equal, these areas provide better internal distribution possibilities.

Emigration is largely clustered because people move where others of their ethnic group have gone before, thus forming subcultures. Understanding where these groups exist can help identify target markets.[61] For instance, Guatemala's Pollo Campero, when entering the U.S. market, went first to Los Angeles, where there are more than a million Central Americans.

The distance between production and a target market first of all affects pricing. Since transportation cost roughly correlates with distance, there is usually a higher cost to serve farther locations. This extra cost must either be passed on to consumers or absorbed by the selling company. Further, if markets are close to each other, it is more difficult to maintain different price schedules between them because promotion likely reaches both markets and consumers will buy from the less expensive location. In fact, the closeness of most Canadians to the U.S. border has influenced Canadian stores to stay open longer and operate on more days, lest Canadians cross the border to buy in the United States.

Although geography does play a role in marketing, as people have more disposable income as well as knowledge about products from elsewhere this role has become less important. Thus people in tropical climates do buy winter clothes and skis because they travel to snowy areas for recreation. And there's even a market for refrigerators among the Eskimos.

We have already discussed operating forms for foreign-market penetration. In Chapters 13 and 17 we discuss distribution channels to move goods among countries and how the title to goods gets transferred. This section does not review these aspects of distribution; it discusses distributional differences and conditions within foreign countries that an international marketer should understand.

Difficulty of Standardization

Within the marketing mix, MNEs find distribution one of the most difficult functions to standardize internationally, for several reasons. Each country has its own distribution system, which an MNE finds difficult to modify because it is entwined with the country's cultural, economic, and legal environments. Nevertheless, many retailers are successfully moving internationally.

Some of the factors that influence how goods will be distributed in a given country are citizens' attitudes toward owning their own store, the cost of paying retail workers, labor legislation differentially affecting chain stores and individually owned stores, legislation restricting the operating hours and size of stores, the trust that owners have in their employees, the efficacy of the postal system, and the financial ability to carry large inventories. For example, Hong Kong supermarkets, compared to those in the United States, carry a higher proportion of fresh goods, are smaller, sell smaller quantities per customer, and are located more closely to each other. This means that companies selling canned, boxed, or frozen foods will encounter less demand per store in Hong Kong than in the United States. They would also have to make smaller deliveries because of store sizes and would have a harder time fighting for shelf space.

A few other examples should illustrate how distribution norms differ. Finland has few stores per capita because general-line retailers predominate there, while Italian distribution has a fragmented retail and wholesale structure. In the Netherlands, buyers' cooperatives deal directly with manufacturers. Japan has cash-and-carry wholesalers for retailers that do not need financing or delivery services. In Germany, mail-order sales are very important; not so in many low-income countries that have less reliable delivery systems.

How do these differences affect companies' marketing activities? One soft drink company, for example, has targeted most of its European sales through grocery stores. However, the method for getting its soft drinks to those stores varies. In the United Kingdom, one national distributor has been able to gain sufficient coverage and shelf space so that the soft drink company can concentrate on other aspects of its marketing mix. In France, a single distributor has been able to get good coverage in the larger supermarkets

Distribution reflects different country environments

- It may vary substantially among countries.
- It is difficult to change.

but not in the smaller ones; consequently, the soft drink company has been exploring how to get secondary distribution without upsetting its relationship with the primary distributor. In Norway, regional distributors predominate, so the soft drink company has found it difficult to effect national promotion campaigns. In Belgium, the company could find no acceptable distributor, so it has had to assume that function itself.

Choosing Distributors and Channels

We will now compare why companies self-handle their distribution or contract other companies to do it for them, and discuss how they should choose outside distributors.

Internal Handling   When sales volume is low, it is usually more economical for a company to handle distribution by contracting with an external distributor. By doing so, however, it may lose a certain amount of control. However, small companies may lack the resources necessary to handle their own distribution.[62] Managers should reassess periodically whether sales and resources have grown to the point that they can handle distribution internally.

Circumstances conducive to the internal handling of distribution include not only high sales volume but also the following factors:

- When a product has the characteristic of high price, high technology, or the need for complex after-sales servicing (such as aircraft), the producer probably will have to deal directly with the buyer. The producer may simultaneously use a distributor within the foreign country that will serve to identify sales leads.

- When the company deals with global customers, especially in business-to-business sales—such as an auto-parts manufacturer that sells original equipment to the same automakers in multiple countries—such sales may go directly from the producer to the global customer.

- When the company views its main competitive advantage to be its distribution methods, such as some food franchisors, it eventually may franchise abroad but maintain its own distribution outlet to serve as a "flagship." Amway, Avon, and Tupperware are examples of companies that have successfully transferred their house-to-house distribution methods from the United States to their operations abroad. Dell Computer has successfully handled its own mail-order sales in Europe.

Distributor Qualifications   A company usually can choose from a number of potential foreign distributors. Common criteria for selecting a distributor include:

- Its financial strength
- Its good connections
- Extent of its other business commitments
- Current status of its personnel, facilities, and equipment
- Its reliability as an honest performer

The distributor's financial strength is important because of the potential long-term relationship between company and distributor and because of the assurance that money will be available for such things as maintaining sufficient inventory. Good connections are particularly important if sales must be directed to certain types of buyers, such as governmental procurement agencies. They are also important in societies, such as China with its Confucianist heritage, where connections and mutual loyalty are often more important than product and price for making sales.[63] The amount of other business commitments can indicate whether the distributor has time for the company's product and whether it currently handles competitive or complementary products. The current status

Distribution may be handled internally

- When volume is high
- When companies have sufficient resources
- When there is a need to deal directly with the customer due to the nature of the product
- When the customer is global
- To gain a competitive advantage

Some evaluation criteria for distributors include their

- Financial capability
- Connections with customers
- Fit with a company's product
- Other resources
- Trustworthiness

of the distributor's personnel, facilities, and equipment indicates not only its ability to deal with the product but also how quickly start-up can occur. Finally, the enforcement of contracts largely depends on the regulations of the country where the distributor is located, making it harder for the international company to require compliance. Further, in some parts of the Middle East and Latin America, manufacturers cannot terminate agreements because of poor performance. Thus, a distributor's history of reliance and image as a responsible business entity help enable trust to be a means for enforcing performance.[64]

Spare Parts and Repair   Consumers are reluctant to buy products that may require spare parts and service in the future unless they feel assured these will be readily available in good quality and at reasonable prices. The more complex and expensive the product, the more important after-sales servicing is. When after-sales servicing is important, companies may need to invest in service centers for groups of distributors that serve as intermediaries between producers and consumers. Earnings from sales of parts and after-sales service sometimes may exceed that of the original product.

> Spare parts and service are important for sales.

Gaining Distribution   Companies must evaluate potential distributors, but distributors must choose which companies and products to represent and emphasize. Both wholesalers and retailers have limited storage facilities, display space, money to pay for inventories, and transportation and personnel to move and sell merchandise, so they try to carry only those products that have the greatest profit potential.

In many cases, distributors are tied into exclusive arrangements with manufacturers that impede new competitive entries. For example, for many years breweries in the United Kingdom owned the pubs, where they sold only their own beer. This forced Anheuser-Busch to enter the market strictly with supermarket sales. Currently, Japan is a country in which many manufacturers such as Shiseido, Toshiba, and Hitachi have arrangements with thousands of distributors to sell only their products. Further, any company that is new to a country and wants to introduce products that some competitors are already selling may meet difficulty in finding distributors to handle its brands. Even established companies sometimes find distribution difficult for their new products, although they have the dual advantage of being known and of being able to offer existing profitable lines only if distributors accept the new unproven products.

A company wanting to use existing distribution channels may need to analyze competitive conditions carefully to offer effective incentives for those distributors to handle the product. It may need to identify problems distributors have to gain their loyalty by offering assistance. Companies alternatively may offer other incentives such as higher profit margins, after-sales servicing, and promotional support—any of which may be offered on either a permanent or introductory basis. The type of incentive should also depend on the comparative costs within each market. In the final analysis, however, incentives will be of little help unless the distributors believe a company's products are viable. The company must sell the distributors on its products as well as on itself as a reliable company.

> Distributors choose what they will handle. Companies
> - May need to give incentives
> - May use successful products as bait for new ones
> - Must convince distributors that product and company are viable

Of course, a company may use a combination of self-distribution and independent distributors. For instance, Kodak has done this very successfully in Russia. It handles some direct sales to big customers, such as LUKoil, which it convinced to give cameras as gifts to employees rather than giving them books or bottles of vodka. Otherwise, it handles retail operations through distributors that it supports with extensive advertising, store decorations, rebate programs, and market research.[65]

Hidden Costs in Distribution

When companies consider launching products in foreign markets, they must determine what final consumer prices will be to estimate sales potential. Because of different national distribution systems, the cost of getting products to consumers varies widely from one country to another. Five factors that often contribute to cost differences in distribution are infrastructure conditions, the number of levels in the distribution system, retail inefficiencies, size and operating-hours restrictions, and inventory stock-outs.

In many countries, the roads and warehousing facilities are so poor that getting goods to consumers quickly, at a low cost, and with minimum damage or loss en route is problematic. For example in China, despite its market potential, companies find difficulty in transporting their products nationally because of poor roads and theft en route and from warehouses.[66]

Many countries have multitiered wholesalers that sell to each other before the product reaches the retail level. For example, national wholesalers sell to regional ones, who sell to local ones, and so on. Japan, although changing rapidly, has had many more levels of distribution than such countries as France and the United States.[67] Because each intermediary adds a markup, they drive product prices up.

In some countries, particularly low-income countries, low labor costs and a basic distrust by owners of all but family members result in retail practices that raise consumer prices. This distrust is evident in companies' preference for counter service rather than self-service. In the former, customers wait to be served and shown merchandise. A customer who decides to purchase something gets an invoice to take to a cashier's line to pay. Once the invoice is stamped as paid, the customer must go to another line to pick up the merchandise after presenting the stamped invoice. In some countries counter service is common for purchases as small as a pencil. The additional personnel add to retailing costs, and the added time people must be in the store means fewer people can be served in the given space. In contrast, most retailers in some (mainly high-income) countries have equipment that improves the efficiency of handling customers and reports, such as electronic scanners, cash registers linked to inventory control records, and machines connecting purchases to credit-card companies.

Many countries, such as France, Germany, and Japan, have laws to protect small retailers. These effectively limit the number of large retail establishments and the efficiencies they bring to sales. Most countries have historic and present patchwork systems that limit days or hours of operations for religious purposes or to protect employees from having to work late at night or on weekends.[68] At the same time, the limits keep retailers from covering the fixed cost of their space over more hours, so these costs are passed on to consumers. Where retailers are small, there is little space to store inventory. Wholesalers must incur the cost of making small deliveries to many more establishments and sometimes may have to visit each retailer more frequently because of stock outages.

The Internet and Electronic Commerce

The growth in online households creates new distributional opportunities and challenges in selling globally over the Internet.

Estimates vary widely on the current and future number of worldwide online households and the electronic commerce generated through online sales. Nevertheless, they all indicate substantial growth. Table 16.3 shows one example of estimates of present and future Internet usage by region. As electronic commerce increases, customers worldwide can quickly compare prices from different distributors, which should drive prices down.

Electronic commerce offers companies an opportunity to promote their products globally. However, it does not relieve them of the need to develop the marketing tools we have discussed throughout the chapter. For some products and services, such as airline tickets and hotel space, the Internet has largely replaced traditional methods of marketing. But even here, companies may need to adapt to country differences, such as providing access through different languages.[69] There are certainly many success stories. For example, the New Zealand company Tristyle International sells prefabricated housing. About 95 percent of its sales are export and 40 percent of its sales are through the Internet.[70]

| TABLE 16.3 | INTERNET USAGE BY REGION, 2005 |

The Internet usage and population figures were updated on March 31, 2005. Note that the regions with lower penetration rates have recently had higher usage growth. If these trends continue, the number of users by regions will change drastically in the next few years.

WORLD REGIONS	POPULATION (2005 EST.)	POPULATION % OF WORLD	INTERNET USAGE	USAGE GROWTH 2000–2005	PENETRATION (% POPULATION)	WORLD USERS %
Africa	900,465,411	14.0 %	13,468,600	198.3 %	1.5 %	1.5 %
Asia	3,612,363,165	56.3 %	302,257,003	164.4 %	8.4 %	34.0 %
Europe	730,991,138	11.4 %	259,653,144	151.9 %	35.5 %	29.2 %
Middle East	259,499,772	4.0 %	19,370,700	266.5 %	7.5 %	2.2 %
North America	328,387,059	5.1 %	221,437,647	104.9 %	67.4 %	24.9 %
Latin America/Caribbean	546,917,192	8.5 %	56,224,957	211.2 %	10.3 %	6.3 %
Oceania/Australia	33,443,448	0.5 %	16,269,080	113.5 %	48.6 %	1.8 %
WORLD TOTAL	**6,412,067,185**	**100.0 %**	**888,681,131**	**146.2 %**	**13.9 %**	**100.0 %**

Source: Miniwatts International, Ltd., www.internetworldstats.com.

The Internet also permits suppliers to deal more quickly with their customers. For example, Lee Hung Fat Garment Factory of Hong Kong supplies apparel to about 60 companies in Europe and now flashes picture samples of merchandise to them over the Web. Customers, such as Kingfisher of the United Kingdom, can tinker with the samples and transmit new versions back to Hong Kong so that Lee Hung Fat produces exactly what the distributors want.[71]

Global Internet sales are not without problems. Many households, especially in emerging economies, lack access to Internet connections. Therefore, if a company wants to reach mass global markets, it will need to supplement its Internet sales with sales using other means of promotion and distribution. A company also needs to set up and promote its Internet sales, which can be very expensive. Further, a switch to the Internet sales may upset existing distribution and, if unsuccessful, make future sales more difficult.[72]

A company cannot easily differentiate its marketing program for each country where it operates. The same Web advertisements and prices reach customers everywhere, even though different appeals and prices for different countries might yield more sales and profits. If the company makes international sales over the Internet, it must deliver what it sells expeditiously. This may necessitate placing warehouses and service facilities abroad, which the company itself may or may not own and manage.

Finally, the company's Internet ads and prices must comply with the laws of each country where the company makes sales. This is a challenge because a company's Web page reaches Internet users everywhere. Clearly, although the Internet creates new opportunities for companies to sell internationally, it also creates new challenges for them.

MANAGING THE MARKETING MIX

Although every element in the marketing mix—product, price, promotion, brand, and distribution—is important, the relative importance of one versus another may vary from place to place and over time. Thus management must monitor and adjust its marketing programs accordingly.

Once a company is operating in a country and estimates that country's market potential, it must calculate how well it is doing there. A useful tool in this respect is **gap analysis**, a method for estimating a company's potential sales by identifying market segments it is not serving adequately.[73] When sales are lower than the estimated market potential for a given type of product, the company has potential for increased

Gap analysis is a tool to help managers estimate why sales are less than the potential. The top of the bar represents total sales potential for a given period. Point A is the total of sales for all companies. The difference between A and the top of the bar is a usage gap. From the bottom of the usage gap bar to B are competitors' current sales. The company loses to competitors who distribute where the company does not, have product variations the company lacks, or are doing a better job of marketing. The bar sizes vary overall and by country because gap sizes vary.

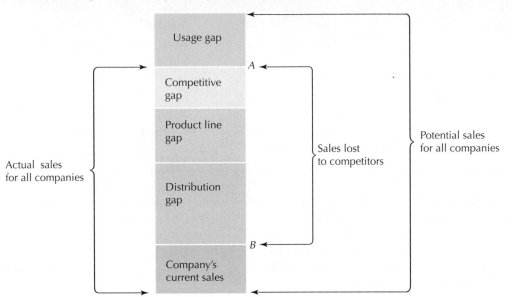

sales. Figure 16.4 is a bar showing four types of gaps: usage, competitive, product line, and distribution. To construct such a bar, a company first needs to estimate the potential demand for all competitors in the country for a relevant period, say for the next year or the next five years. This figure is the height of the bar. Second, a company needs to estimate current sales by all competitors, which is point A. The space between point A and the top of the bar is a usage gap, meaning that this is the growth potential for all competitors in the market for the relevant period. Third, a company needs to plot its own current sales of the product, point B. Finally, the company divides the difference between point A and point B into three types of gaps based on its estimate of sales lost to competitors. The distribution gap represents sales lost to competitors who distribute where the company does not. The product line gap represents sales lost to competitors who have product variations the company does not have. The competitive gap is the remaining unexplained sales lost to competitors who may have a better image or lower prices.

Companies may have different-sized gaps in different markets. The large chocolate companies have altered their marketing programs among countries because of their different gaps.[74] In some markets, they have found substantial usage gaps; that is, less chocolate is being consumed than would be expected on the basis of population and income levels. Industry specialists estimate that in many countries more than 80 percent of the population has never tasted a chocolate bar. They project that if more people in those countries could be persuaded to try chocolate bars, the companies' sales should increase with the market increase. This assumption has led companies to promote sales in those areas for chocolate in general.

The U.S. market shows another type of usage gap. Nearly everyone in this market has tried most chocolate products, but per capita consumption has fallen because of growing concern about weight. To increase chocolate consumption in general, Nestlé for a short

---

The difference between total market potential and companies' sales is due to gaps

- Usage—less product sold by all competitors than potential
- Product line—company lacks some product variations
- Distribution—company misses geographic or intensity coverage
- Competitive—competitors' sales not explained by product line and distribution gaps

time promoted chocolate as an energy source for the sports minded. Note, however, that building general consumption is most useful to the market leader. Nestlé, with U.S. chocolate sales below those of Mars and Hershey, actually benefited its competitors during the short-lived campaign.

Chocolate companies also have found that they have product line gaps in some hot climates in the market for sweetened products. By developing new products, such as chocolate products that melt less easily, they have been able to garner a larger share of that market. In some markets, such as Ferrero Rocher in the United States, its emphasis in recent years has been on gaining more distribution in mainstream outlets.

Finally, there are competitive gaps—sales by competitors that cannot be explained by differences between one's own product line and distribution and those of the competitors. That is, competitors are making additional sales because of their prices, advertising campaigns, goodwill, or any of a host of other factors. In markets where per capita chocolate consumption is high, companies exert most of their efforts in gaining sales at the expense of competitors.

While gap analysis is primarily a means of prioritizing elements in the marketing mix within given countries, it is also possible to use the tool by aggregating needs among countries. For example, let's say that the product line gap is too small in a single country to justify the expenses of developing a specific new product, such as a heat-resistant chocolate bar. Nevertheless, the combined market potential among several countries for this product may justify the product and promotional developmental costs. Thus, managers need to improve country-level performance along with enhancement of synergies among the countries where they operate.

LOOKING TO THE FUTURE: Will the "Haves" and the "Have-Nots" Meet the "Have Somes"?

Most projections are that disparities between the "haves" and "have-nots" will grow in the foreseeable future, both within and among countries. Further, because "haves" will be more educated and more connected to the Internet, they will be better able to search globally for lower prices for what they buy. Therefore, globally, the affluent segment will have even more purchasing power than their incomes indicate. Further, they will not likely forgo buying because of antimaterialistic sentiments. As these people's discretionary income increases, some luxury products will become more commonplace (partly because it will take fewer hours of work to purchase them), and seemingly dissimilar products and services (such as cars, travel, jewelry, and furniture) will compete with each other for the same discretionary spending. Because of better communications and rising educational levels of the haves, they will want more choices. However, these choices may not fall primarily along national lines. Rather, companies will identify consumer niches that cut across country lines.

At the other extreme, because of growing numbers of poor people with little disposable income, companies will have opportunities to develop low-cost standardized products to fit the needs of the have-nots. In reality, low-income households collectively have considerable purchasing power, and it is a segment that MNEs have largely ignored. For instance, there are 680 million households with incomes of less than $6,000 per year in the 18 largest low-income and transitional economies. They have roughly $1.7 trillion to spend, mainly on housing, food, health care, education, communications, finance charges, and consumer goods.[75] Thus, companies will have conflicting opportunities—to develop luxury to serve the haves and to cut costs to serve the have-nots.

Index of Japan for a mobile site for connectivity in the Asian market and with In-Fusio for mobile phone connectivity elsewhere. In the meantime, NeoPets has spawned some copies, such as PowerPets, Cyberpets, and Virtual Dog, but none of these has developed a following nearly as large as NeoPets'.

QUESTIONS

1. In the past, we've seen many types of children's products, ranging from Ninja turtles to Hula Hoops, that have turned out to be fads. How do you think NeoPets can prevent its concept from becoming a fad?

2. Although NeoPets has been successful thus far in gaining members by word of mouth, should it turn to some more proactive promotion? If so, what should it be?

3. What country-to-country differences in acceptability of NeoPets might exist? How might NeoPets deal with them?

4. Examine each of the criticisms about Neopets' practices. What should NeoPets and regulatory agencies do about each of them?

5. Neopets depends mainly on a youth market. Can it extend its concept to an adult market? If so, how?

CHAPTER NOTES

1 Information came from Avon Annual Reports from 1995 through 2004; *Outlook* (Avon's monthly in-house magazine) from 1995 through 2002; AVP–Q4 2004, Avon Products, Earning Conference Call (February 1, 2005); Miriam Jordan, "Knock Knock," *Wall Street Journal* (February 19, 2003): A1+; Ramin Setoodeh, "Calling Avon's Lady," *Newsweek* (January 3, 2005): 98–101; "Avon Products Inc.," *Wall Street Journal* (April 11, 2005): 1; "Avon Beauty Plans Greater Mass Market Penetration," *Business Line* (April 22, 2003): 1; and "Avon: Opportunity Knocks," *Brand Strategy* (April 5, 2005): 20.

2 "The World's Wash Day," *Financial Times* (April 29, 2002): 6.

3 Matt Moffett, "Learning to Adapt to a Tough Market, Chilean Firms Pry Open Door to Japan," *Wall Street Journal* (June 7, 1994): A10.

4 "Avon Beauty Plans Greater Mass Market Penetration," *Businessline* (April 22, 2003): 1.

5 Jon E. Hilsenrath, "Overseas Suppliers to U.S. Brands Thrive," *Wall Street Journal* (March 10, 2000): A13.

6 Evan Pérez, "A Bit of America Rises Near Old-World Buenos Aires," *Wall Street Journal* (January 16, 2002): B1.

7 Betsy McKay, "Drinks for Developing Countries," *Wall Street Journal* (November 27, 2001): B1+; and Betsy McKay, "Coke's Heyer Finds Test in Latin America," *Wall Street Journal* (October 15, 2002): B4.

8 "Avon: Opportunity Knocks," *Brand Strategy* (April 5, 2005): 20.

9 Manoj K. Agarwal, "Developing Global Segments and Forecasting Market Shares: A Simultaneous Approach Using Survey Data," *Journal of International Marketing* 11, no. 4 (2003): 56.

10 Rebecca Rose, "Global Diversity Gets All Cosmetic," *Financial Times* (April 10–11, 2004): W11.

11 Leslie T. Chang, "Nestlé Stumbles in China's Evolving Market," *Wall Street Journal* (December 8, 2004): A10.

12 Allen L. Hammond and C. K. Prahalad, "Selling to the Poor," *Foreign Policy* 142 (May–June 2004): 30–37.

13 "Music for the Masses," *Financial Times* (December 14, 2004): 9.

14 Milo Geyelin and Jeffrey Ball, "How Rugged Is Your Car's Roof?" *Wall Street Journal* (March 4, 2000): B1.

15 Bernardo V. Lopez, "Upshot," *BusinessWorld* (September 18, 2003): 1.

16 Garrett Mehl, Heather Wipfli, and Peter Winch, "Controlling Tobacco," *Harvard International Review* 27, no. 1 (Spring 2005): 54–58.

17 "Cause for Concern with Nestlé in the Spotlight Again over Its Advertising Tactics," *Marketing Week* (February 11, 1999): 28–31.

18 Sarah Houlton, "Drugs for Neglected Diseases," *Pharmaceutical Executive* 23, no. 8 (August 2003): 28.

19 Mehl, et al., loc. cit.

20 Michael Waldholz, "Sparks Fly at AIDS Meeting over Breast-Feeding," *Wall Street Journal* (July 12, 2000): B2; and Jolene Skordis and Nicoli Nattrass, "Paying to Waste Lives: The Affordability of Reducing Mother-to-Child Transmission of HIV in South Africa," *Journal of Health Economics* 21, no. 3 (May 2002): 405.

21 Scott Miller, "EU's New Rules Will Shake Up Market for Bioengineered Food," *Wall Street Journal* (April 16, 2004): A1.

22 Deboral Ball, Sarah Ellison, Janet Adamy, and Geoffrey A. Fowler, "Recipes Without Borders?" *Wall Street Journal* (August 18, 2004): B1+.

23 Norihiko Shirouzu, "Tailoring World's Cars to U.S. Taste," *Wall Street Journal* (January 15, 2001): B1.

24 Norihiko Shirouzu and Peter Wonacott, "People's Republic of Autos," *Wall Street Journal* (April 18, 2005): B1+.

25 Ball, et al., loc. cit.

26 Miriam Jordan and Jonathan Karp, "Machines for the Masses," *Wall Street Journal* (December 9, 2003): A19.

27 David A. Griffith, Aruna Chandra, and John K. Ryans, Jr., "Factors Influencing Advertising Message and Packaging," *Journal of International Marketing* 11, no. 3 (2003): 30.

28 Keith Bradsher, "India Gains on China among Multinationals," *International Herald Tribune* (June 12–13, 2004): 13.

29 Niraj Dawar and Amitava Chattopadhyay, "The New Language of Emerging Markets," *Financial Times* (November 11, 2000): mastering management section, p. 6.

30 "The World's Wash Day," *Financial Times* (April 29, 2002): 6.

31 Arvind Sahay, "Finding the Right International Mix," *Financial Times* (November 16, 1998): mastering marketing section, pp. 2–3.

32 Brandon Mitchener, "Inexpensive Levi's May Soon Be Easier to Find in Britain," *Wall Street Journal* (April 6, 2001): A13.

33 Matthew B. Myers, "The Pricing of Export Products: Why Aren't Managers Satisfied with the Results?" *Journal of World Business* 32, no. 3 (1997): 277–89.

34 Peter Rosenwald, "Surveying the Latin American Landscape," *Catalog Age* 18, no. 2 (February 2001): 67–69.

35 Dave Guilford, "GM Takes Hard Line on Gray Market," *Automotive News* 76, no. 5994 (July 22, 2002): 4.

36 Elin Dugan, "United States of America, Home of the Cheap and the Gray: A Comparison of Recent Court Decisions Affecting the U.S. and European Gray Markets," *The George Washington International Law Review* 33, no. 2 (2001): 397–418.

37 Ana Campoy, "Think Locally," *Wall Street Journal* (September 27, 2004): R8.

38 C. Gopinath, "Fixed Price and Bargaining," *Businessline* (July 15, 2002): 1.

39 Claude Cellich, "FAQ . . . About Business Negotiations on the Internet," *International Trade Forum* no. 1 (2001): 10–11.

40 Rasul Bailay, "A Hindu Festival Attracts the Faithful and U.S. Marketers—Target Millions of Worshippers in India, Hoping to Expand Reach," *Wall Street Journal* (February 12, 2001): A18.

41 David Pilling, "Direct Promotion of Brands Gives Power to the Patients," *Financial Times* (April 30, 2001): iii; and Sarah Ellison, "Viagra Europe Ads to Focus on Symptoms," *Financial Times* (March 22, 2000): B10.

42 Dana L. Alden, Jan-Benedict E. M. Steenkamp, and Rajeev Batra, "Brand Positioning through Advertising in Asia, North America, and Europe: The Role of Global Consumer Culture," *Journal of Marketing* 63, no. 1 (January 1999): 75–87.

43 Eleftheria Parpis, "Say What?" *Adweek* 42, no. 32 (August 6, 2001): 16.

44 Charles Goldsmith, "Dubbing in Product Plugs," *Wall Street Journal* (December 6, 2004): B1+.

45 Rick Wartzman, "Read Their Lips," *Wall Street Journal* (June 3, 1999): A1.

46 Geoffrey A. Fowler, "China Cracks Down on Commercials," *Wall Street Journal* (February 19, 2004): B7A.

47 Sally D. Goll, "New Zealand Bans Reebok, Other Ads It Deems Politically Incorrect for TV," *Wall Street Journal* (July 25, 1995): A12.

48 Yumiko Ono, "Overcoming the Stigma of Dishwashers in Japan," *Wall Street Journal* (May 19, 2000): B1+.

49 Sarah Ellison, "Sex-Themed Ads Often Don't Travel Well," *Wall Street Journal* (March 31, 2000): B7.

50 "Top 100 Brands Scoreboard, 2005" *Business Week Online* http://businessweek.com/brand/2005/index.asp?con

51 "Embarrassed GM to Rename Car with Risque Overtones," *Yahoo News Canada* (October 22, 2003).

52 Robert Frank, "Big Boy's Adventures in Thailand," *Wall Street Journal* (April 12, 2000): B1; and Julie Bennett, "Product Pitfalls Proliferate in a Global Cultural Maze," *Wall Street Journal* (May 14, 2001): B11.

53 Lee Simmons and Robert M. Schindler, "Cultural Superstitions and the Price Endings Used in Chinese Advertising," *Journal of International Marketing* 11, no. 2 (2003): 101.

54 Miriam Jordan, "Sara Lee Wants to Percolate Through All of Brazil," *Wall Street Journal* (May 8, 2002): A14+.

55 Isabelle Schuiling and Jean-Noël Kapferer, "Executive Insights: Real Differences between Local and International Brands: Strategic Implications for International Marketers" *Journal of International Marketing*, 12, no. 4 (2004): 197.

56 Philip Kotler and David Gertner, "Country as Brand, Product, and Beyond: A Place Marketing and Brand Management," *Journal of Brand Management* 9, no. 4–5 (April 2002): 249–61; and Keith Dinnie, "National Image and Competitive Advantage: The Theory and Practice of Country-of-Origin Effect," *Journal of Brand Management* 9, no. 4–5 (April 2002): 396–98.

57 Gideon Rachman, "Christmas Survey: The Brand's the Thing," *The Economist* 353, no. 8150 (December 18, 1999): 97–99.

58 Seah Park, "LG's Kitchen Makeover," *Wall Street Journal* (September 22, 2004): A19.

59 Tara Parker-Pope, "Minty Python and Cream Victoria? Ice Creams Leave Some Groaning," *Wall Street Journal* (July 3, 1996): B1.

60 Paul Meller, "WTO Said to Weigh In on Product Names," *New York Times* (November 19, 2004): W1.

61 "Opportunities in Sub-Culture," *Businessline* (February 12, 2004): 1.

62 Oliver Burgel and Gordon C. Murray, "The International Market Entry Choices of Start-Up Companies in High-Technology," *Journal of International Marketing* 8, no. 2 (2000): 33–62.

63 Gary F. Keller and Creig R. Kronstedt, "Connecting Confucianism, Communism, and the Chinese Culture of Commerce," *The Journal of Language for International Business* 16, no. 1 (2005): 60–75.

64 S. Tamer Cavusgil, Seyda Deligonul, and Chun Zhang, "Curbing Foreign Distributor Opportunism: An Examination of Trust, Contracts, and the Legal Environment in International Channel Relationships," *Journal of International Marketing* 12, no. 2 (2004).

65 Gary C. Anders and Danila A. Usachev, "Strategic Elements of Eastman Kodak's Successful Market Entry in Russia," *Thunderbird International Business Review* 45, no. 2 (March–April 2003): 171.

66 James T. Areddy, "Solving China's Logistics Riddle," *Wall Street Journal* (October 15, 2003): A18+.

67 IBPC Osaka at **www.ibpcosaka.or.jp/network/e_trade_japanesemarket/index2.html**.

68 Marko Grunhagen, Stephen J. Grove, and James W. Gentry, "The Dynamics of Store Hour Changes and Consumption Behavior: Results of a Longitudinal Study of Consumer Attitudes Toward Saturday Shopping in Germany," *European Journal of Marketing* 37, no. 11–12 (2003): 1801–19.

69 Rita Marcella and Sylvie Davies, "The Use of Customer Language in International Marketing Communication in the Scottish Food and Drink Industry," *European Journal of Marketing* 38, no. 11–12 (2004): 1382.

70 *New Zealand Business* 18, no. 11 (December 2004): 21–27.

71 Anil K. Gupta and Vijay Govindarajan, "The Rising Cost of Waiting," *CIO* 13, no. 19 (July 15, 2000): 54.

72 Moen Øystein, Iver Endresen, and Morten Gavlen, "Executive Insights: Use of the Internet in International Marketing: A Case Study of Small Computer Software Firms," *Journal of International Marketing* 11, no. 4 (2003).

73 J. A. Weber, "Comparing Growth Opportunities in the International Marketplace," *Management International Review*, no. 1 (1979): 47–54; and Van R. Wood, John R. Darling, and Mark Siders, "Consumer Desire to Buy and Use Products in International Markets: How to Capture It, How to Sustain It," *International Marketing Review* 16, no. 3 (1999): 231–42.

74 "Chocolate Makers in Switzerland Try to Melt Resistance," *Wall Street Journal* (January 5, 1981): 14; William Hall, "Swiss Chocolate Groups Aim to Keep Outlook Sweet," *Financial Times* (April 11–12, 1998): 23; William Hall, "Wraps Come Off Chocolate's Best-Kept Secret," *Financial Times* (June 5, 1998): 20; and Stephanie Thompson, "Chocolate Gets Boost," *Advertising Age* 73, no. 30 (July 29, 2002): 12.

75 Allen L. Hammond and C. K. Prahalad, "Selling to the Poor," *Foreign Policy* (May/June 2004): 30–37.

76 Information was taken from Graeme Philipson, "NeoPets: The Chosen One for a Whole Matrix of Kids," *The Age* (Melbourne, Australia) (March 16, 2004): ; www.**Neopets.com** (accessed May 16, 2005); "In-Fusio and NeoPets Team for Wireless-to-Web Entertainment Application," *Wireless News* (March 18, 2005): 1; Kharif and Stephen Baker, "Advertisers Take Aim at Gamers," *Business Week Online* (June 22, 2004); Michael Snider, "Hey Kids! Let's Play Adver-games," *Maclean's* 115, no. 51 (December 23, 2002): 36–37; Helen Ward, "'Sneaky' Cyber Ads Condemned," *Times Educational Supplement* (August 16, 2002): 3; Phil Nettleton, "Paedophiles Hack into Kids' Emails," *The People* (April 25, 2004): 29; Ho Ka Wei, "Net a Pet," *The Straits Times* (Singapore) (March 8, 2002); Thomas R. Eisenmann, *NeoPets, Inc.*, Harvard Business School Case No. 9-802-100 (revised May 12, 2002); Nancy Lees, "NeoPets Connects Kids and Brands On-Line," *Kidscreen* (August 1, 2003): 35; Brent Hopkins, "Pet Project," *Daily News of Los Angeles* (December 16, 2003): B1; John C. Beck and Mitchell Wade, "Gaming the Future," *Across the Board* 42, no. 1

(January/February 2005): 48–54; Daren Fonda, "Pitching It to the Kids," *Time* (June 28, 2004): 52–54; Will Wade, "A Market Research Machine Is Built on Cyberpets," *International Herald Tribune* (February 27, 2004): 17; Nick Wingfield, "Web's Addictive NeoPets Are Ready for a Big Career Leap," *Wall Street Journal* (February 22, 2005): B1; K. Oanh Ha, "NeoPets Site for Children Stirs Controversy," *Knight Ridder Tribune Business News* (September 14, 2004): 1; Brent Hopkins, "NeoPets Headed to the Silver Screen," *Knight Ridder Tribune Business News* (March 25, 2005): 1; and "NeoPets to Invade Games Aisle!" *BusinessWire* (October 1, 2003).

Right mixture makes good mortar.

—ENGLISH PROVERB

chapter seventeen

Global Manufacturing and Supply Chain Management

OBJECTIVES

- To describe different dimensions of global manufacturing strategy

- To examine the elements of global supply chain management

- To show how quality affects the global supply chain

- To illustrate how supplier networks function

- To explain how inventory management is a key dimension of the global supply chain

- To present different alternatives for transporting products along the supply chain from suppliers to customers

CASE: SAMSONITE'S GLOBAL SUPPLY CHAIN[1]

Samsonite Corporation is a U.S.-based company that manufactures and distributes luggage all over the world. In fiscal year 2002, Samsonite generated $736.3 billion in revenues but incurred losses equal to $3.59 per share in 2002, $2.01 in 2001, and $2.53 in 2000. Samsonite was listed on the NASDAQ stock market, but it was delisted in January 2002 for failing to meet NASDAQ standards. Samsonite began in 1910 in Denver, Colorado, and it took many years for it to become a global company. In 1963, Samsonite set up its first European operation in the Netherlands and later, in 1965, began production in Belgium. Shortly thereafter, it erected a joint-venture plant in Mexico to service the growing but highly protected Mexican market. By the end of the 1960s, Samsonite was manufacturing luggage in Spain and Japan as well. In addition to its manufacturing operations, Samsonite was selling luggage worldwide through a variety of distributors.

In the 1970s, business began to take off in Europe. In 1974, Samsonite developed its first real European product, called the Prestige Attaché, and business began to expand in Italy, causing it to rival Germany as Samsonite's biggest market in Europe. Although the U.S. market began to turn to softside luggage in the 1980s, the European market still demanded hardside luggage, so Samsonite developed a

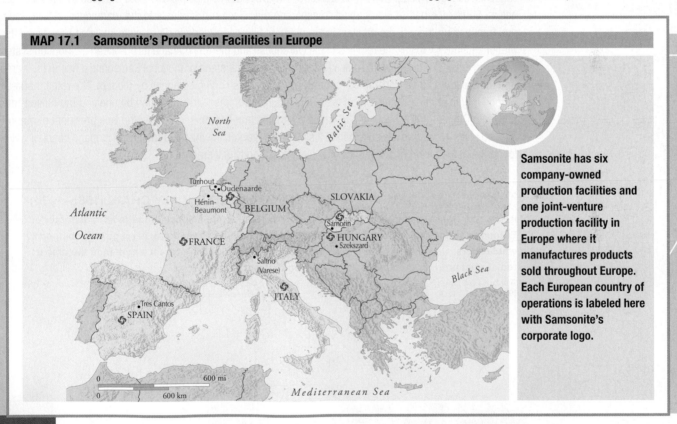

MAP 17.1 Samsonite's Production Facilities in Europe

Samsonite has six company-owned production facilities and one joint-venture production facility in Europe where it manufactures products sold throughout Europe. Each European country of operations is labeled here with Samsonite's corporate logo.

new hardside suitcase for Europe called the Oyster case. Then softside luggage began to increase in importance, although Europe was still considered a hardside market. In the 1980s, Samsonite opened a new plant in France to manufacture the Prestige Attaché and other key products.

With the fall of the Iron Curtain in the early 1990s, Samsonite purchased a Hungarian luggage manufacturer and began to expand throughout Eastern Europe. During this same time period, Samsonite established several joint-venture companies throughout Asia, including China, to extend its reach there.

To establish products of high quality, Samsonite embarked on two different programs. The first was an internal program in which Samsonite conducted a drop test, a tumble test, a wheel test, and a handle test to determine if its products were strong enough and of sufficient quality for customers. The second program was two different, independent quality-assurance tests:

1. The European-based ISO 9002 certification
2. The GS Mark, which is the number 1 government-regulated third-party product test market of Germany

The GS Mark, *Gepruefte Sicherheit* (translated "Tested for Safety"), is designed to help companies comply with European product liability laws as well as other areas of quality and safety. To enhance quality, Samsonite introduced state-of-the-art CAD-CAM machinery in its plants. Samsonite also introduced a manufacturing technique in which autonomous cells of about a dozen employees assembled a product from start to finish.

As noted in Map 17.1, Samsonite had six company-owned production facilities and one joint-venture production facility in Europe in 2002. In addition, it has subsidiaries, joint ventures, retail franchises, distributors, and agents set up to service the European market. Although Samsonite initially serviced the European markets through exports, the transportation costs were high, and the demand for luggage soared in Europe, so Samsonite decided to begin production in Belgium in 1965.

In the early years, Samsonite had a decentralized supply chain, as illustrated in Figure 17.1, whereby it operated through different wholesale layers before it finally got the product to the retailers.

As Samsonite's business grew, management decided to centralize its supply chain so that products were manufactured and shipped to a central European warehouse, which then directly supplied retailers upon request (see Figure 17.2). This centralized structure was put into place to eliminate the need to rely on wholesalers. Samsonite had to worry about transporting manufactured products to the warehouse, storing them, and transporting them to the retailers in the different European markets. Samsonite invested heavily in information technology to link the retailers to the warehouse and thereby manage its European distribution system more effectively. Retailers would place an order with a salesperson or the local Samsonite office in their area, and the order would be transmitted to the warehouse and shipping company by modem. The retail market in Europe began shifting at the turn of the new century, so Samsonite responded by opening franchised retail outlets in October 2002, beginning in Antwerp and spreading to other areas. As the vice president of marketing and sales put it, "We are anticipating a shift in the market, in which the traditional luggage channel will no longer be at the forefront and a wide new retail opportunity will emerge."

FIGURE 17.1   SAMSONITE'S DECENTRALIZED SUPPLY CHAIN (1965–1974)

In the early years of market penetration in Europe, Samsonite shipped luggage from its factories in Europe to factory warehouses, then to national warehouses. From there, luggage was shipped to wholesalers, who sold to retailers. This cumbersome distribution system lengthened the time it took to get product to retailers and increased the cost.

Source: F. De Beule and D. Van Den Bulcke, "The International Supply Chain Management of Samsonite Europe," Discussion Paper 1998/E/34, Centre for International Management and Development, University of Antwerp, p. 13.

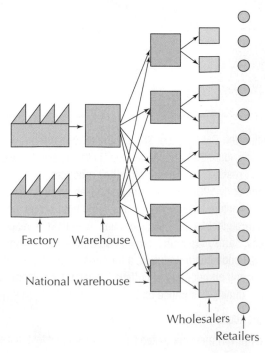

Factory   Warehouse

National warehouse →

Wholesalers

Retailers

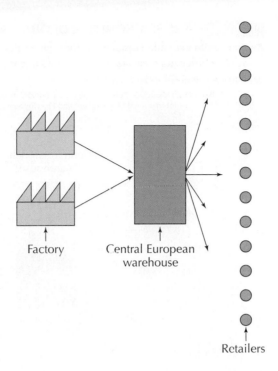

FIGURE 17.2

SAMSONITE'S CENTRALIZED SUPPLY CHAIN (1975–mid-1980s)

Samsonite decided to supply the European market by shipping products directly from the factory to a centralized European warehouse and from there to the retailers upon request.

Source: F. De Beule and D. Van Den Bulcke, "The International Supply Chain Management of Samsonite Europe." Discussion Paper No. 1998/E/34, Centre for International Management and Development, University of Antwerp, p. 14.

As noted earlier, Samsonite sold two basic types of suitcases: hardside and softside. Most of the R&D was initially done in the United States, but the need to develop products for the European market led the company to establish R&D facilities in Europe. Samsonite invested heavily in R&D and in the manufacture of specialized machinery to help keep a competitive edge. To facilitate the transportation and storage of suitcases, Samsonite located its production facilities close to the centralized warehouse. Softside luggage is less complex technologically, and Samsonite purchased Oda, the Belgium softside luggage company, to enter that market. Then it licensed its technology to other European companies. By the mid-1990s, 48 percent of Samsonite's sales came from hardside luggage, 22 percent from softside, and 30 percent from attaché cases and travel bags, some of which were hardside and some softside. However, the trend for hardside luggage in Europe is changing. By fiscal 2000, softside luggage comprised 51 percent of European sales. In 2001 and 2002, sales of softside luggage continued to increase as a percentage, and hardside luggage sales declined.

As Samsonite expanded throughout the world, it continued to manufacture its own products and license production to other manufacturers. Then Samsonite entered into subcontract arrangements in Asia and Eastern Europe. In Europe, the subcontractors provide final goods as well as the subassemblies used in Samsonite factories. Figure 17.3 illustrates Samsonite's coordination of outsourced parts and finished goods, along with its own production.

Samsonite is a good example of the challenges a firm faces in determining how best to manage the supply chain from supplier to consumer. The greater the geographic spread of the company, the more challenging the management of the supply chain becomes.

INTRODUCTION

The Samsonite case illustrates a number of dimensions of the supply chain networks that link suppliers with manufacturers and customers. The objective of this chapter is to examine these different networks and how a company can manage the links most effectively to reach customers. As Figure 17.4 shows, global manufacturing and supply chain management is important in companies' international business strategies. In a survey conducted by Deloitte Consulting, 91 percent of the respondents agreed that supply chain management holds significant importance for a company's future success. And according to the survey's results, the three primary benefits companies expect when they

As Samsonite expanded production throughout Europe, it had to deal with subcontractors as well as its own factories. Its success in Europe was due to its ability to manage the supply chain from supplier to factory to warehouse to consumer.

Source: F. De Beule and D. Van Den Bulcke. "The International Supply Chain Management of Samsonite Europe," Discussion Paper No. 1998/E/34. Centre for International Management and Development. University of Antwerp, p. 21.

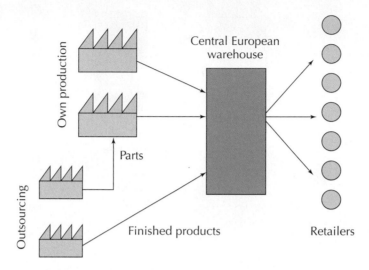

implement supply chain systems are improved customer service levels, a reduction in total inventory, and a decrease in total supply chain costs.[2]

We will start by discussing global manufacturing strategy and then move to supply chain management issues. In terms of global supply chain management, we will look at supplier networks, inventory management, and transportation networks.

A company's **supply chain** encompasses the coordination of materials, information, and funds from the initial raw material supplier to the ultimate customer.[3] It is the management of the value-added process from the suppliers' supplier to the customers' customer.[4]

Figure 17.5 illustrates the concept of a global supply chain. Suppliers can be part of the manufacturer's organizational structure, as would be the case in a vertically integrated company, or they can be independent of the company. The direct suppliers also have their networks. In a global context, the suppliers can be located in the country where the manufacturing or assembly takes place, or they can be located in one country and ship materials to the country of manufacture or assembly. The output of the suppliers can be shipped directly to the factory or to an intermediate storage point. The output of the manufacturing process can be shipped directly to the customers or to a warehouse network, as was the case with Samsonite. The output can be sold directly to the end consumer or to a distributor, wholesaler, or retailer, who then sells the output to the final consumer. As was the case in the supplier network, the output can be sold domestically or internationally.

An important dimension of the supply chain is **logistics,** also sometimes called **materials management.** According to the U.S.-based Council of Supply Chain Management Professionals, "Logistics Management is that part of Supply Chain Management that plans, implements, and controls the efficient, effective forward and reverse flow and storage of goods, services and related information between the point of origin and the point of consumption in order to meet customers' requirements."[5] Materials management is inbound logistics or the movement and management of materials and products from purchasing through production. The difference between supply chain management and logistics is one of degree. Logistics focuses much more on the transportation and storage of materials and final goods, whereas supply chain management extends beyond that to include the management of supplier and customer relations.

A recent study carried out by AMR Research produced a list of the top 25 supply-chain companies—ones that have excelled in their ability to manage their supply chain networks

Supply chain—the coordination of materials, information, and funds from the initial raw material supplier to the ultimate customer

Logistics (also called materials management)—that part of the supply chain process that plans, implements, and controls the efficient, effective flow and storage of goods, services, and related information from the point of origin to the point of consumption in order to meet customers' requirements

FIGURE 17.4 GLOBAL MANUFACTURING AND SUPPLY CHAIN MANAGEMENT IN INTERNATIONAL BUSINESS

Both global manufacturing and global supply chain management are necessary functions for implementing companies' international strategies.

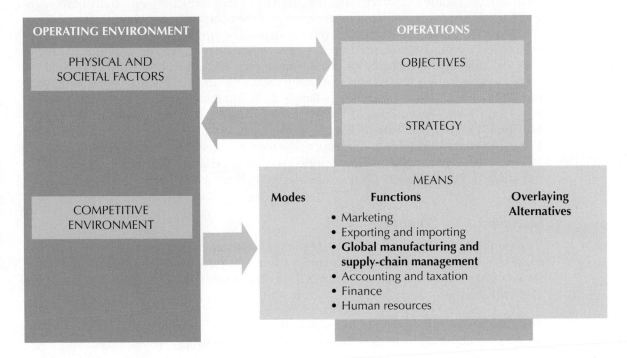

and to come up with innovative ways to solve supply-chain issues. The list consists of companies located throughout the world—including Canon in Japan, L'Oreal in France, Procter & Gamble in the United States, Tesco in the U.K., POSCO in Korea, Nokia in Finland, and Woolworths in Australia—demonstrating the international scope of the supply chain function.[6] The companies that we will study in this chapter are considered to be part of a global network that links together designers, suppliers, subcontractors, manufacturers, and customers. The supply chain network is quite broad, and the coordination of the network takes place through interactions between firms in the networks.[7]

GLOBAL MANUFACTURING STRATEGIES

In the opening case, Samsonite initially exported to Europe, but it eventually set up Samsonite-Europe and established manufacturing facilities in different countries. Samsonite invested in Europe because of the location-specific advantages of the European

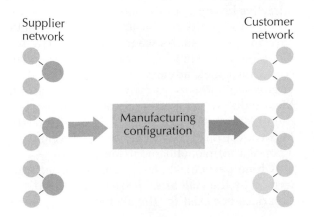

FIGURE 17.5

THE GLOBAL SUPPLY CHAIN

The global supply chain links the suppliers' supplier with the customers' customer, accounting for every step of the process between the raw material and the final consumer of the good or service.

market (big demand). It entered through foreign direct investment because it wanted to take advantage of the firm-specific assets that it possessed (an excellent product line and a solid manufacturing process) and internalize those advantages rather than sell them to an outside manufacturer.[8] Although Samsonite entered into some licensing agreements and subcontracted some manufacturing, the majority of its production, especially of its high-end hardside luggage, was kept under control of the company's network.

Although Samsonite engaged in its own manufacturing for the most part, it also subcontracted, or outsourced, manufacturing to other firms. Nike, for example, does not own any manufacturing facilities, but it subcontracts manufacturing to other companies. So Nike is basically a design and marketing company. Mattel does not own manufacturing facilities in China to manufacture Barbie dolls, but it subcontracts the manufacturing to a Hong Kong–based company that has investments in China. Some of the toys in McDonald's Happy Meals or Burger King meals are also subcontracted to a Hong Kong–based manufacturer that produces the toys in China.

The success of a global manufacturing strategy depends on four key factors: (1) compatibility, (2) configuration, (3) coordination, and (4) control.[9]

Manufacturing Compatibility

Compatibility in this context is the degree of consistency between the foreign investment decision and the company's competitive strategy. Direct manufacturing made sense in Samsonite's case but not in Nike's case. Company strategies that managers must consider are:

- *Efficiency/cost*—reduction of manufacturing costs
- *Dependability*—degree of trust in a company's products, its delivery, and price promises
- *Quality*—performance reliability, service quality, speed of delivery, and maintenance quality of the product(s)
- *Flexibility*—ability of the production process to make different kinds of products and to adjust the volume of output
- *Innovation*—ability to develop new products and ideas[10]

Cost-minimization strategies and the drive for global efficiencies force MNEs to establish economies of scale in manufacturing, often by producing in areas with low-cost labor. This is one of the major reasons why many MNEs established manufacturing facilities in Asia, Mexico, and Eastern Europe. This type of foreign direct investment is known as offshore manufacturing, but clearly any manufacturing that takes place outside of a company's home country is considered "offshore." Offshore manufacturing escalated sharply in the 1960s and 1970s in the electronics industry as one company after another set up production facilities in the Far East, mostly in Taiwan and Singapore. Those locations were attractive because of low labor costs, the availability of cheap materials and components, and the proximity to markets. Even the athletic shoe market left the United States for Taiwan and Korea. As wages rose in Korea, however, manufacturing began to shift to other low-cost countries—China, Indonesia, Malaysia, Thailand, and Vietnam. Many U.S. companies took advantage of special tariff provisions to assemble products in the *maquiladora* industry as mentioned in Chapter 8. Companies could ship components to Mexico duty-free for assembly at special plants on the border with the U.S. and then ship the finished goods back to the U.S. with duties collected only on the value added in Mexico. The tariff provisions, along with close proximity to Mexico, made the *maquiladoras* a popular form of offshore manufacturing.

China particularly has become the hot spot for manufacturing and has even been termed by the *Wall Street Journal* "the world's factory floor." Although reliable information does not exist for the average hourly wages in the country, a recent investigation

Maquiladora workers make bras in Mexico. Offshore manufacturing by U.S. companies helps reduce costs by using low-cost workers in developing countries like Mexico.

carried out by a consultant hired by the U.S. Bureau of Labor Statistics came up with a rough estimate of 64 cents an hour—a number that includes both the pay rate and employer contributions for benefits and insurance. This rate contrasts sharply with the average of $21.11 earned by U.S. factory workers and even the $2.48 earned by workers in Mexico.[11] China's output is so large and wide-ranging that it exerts deflationary pressure around the world on products such as textiles, TVs, furniture, auto parts, and mobile phones. It is now the world's fourth largest industrial base behind the United States, Japan, and Germany. Many MNEs set up operations in China in the 1980s to capitalize on China's huge population and growing demand. Companies have now found that it is more cost-effective for them to manufacture products in China, not just for the local market but also for export to the rest of the world. Foreign companies with manufacturing facilities in China, such as General Electric, Toshiba, Siemens, Samsung, and General Motors, have expanded their focus from the local market to exports. Philips Electronics produces some of its products solely in China and plans to make China its global supply base, from which it will export its products around the world.[12]

However, when employing a cost-minimization strategy, many companies overlook important elements—such as shipping distances, extra inventory, political and security risks, and the availability of skilled and educated workers—which causes them to underestimate the costs of outsourcing to low-wage countries. Some companies are recognizing the need to look beyond labor rates to the costs of employee benefits as well.[13] When it decided to build more of its cars in North America, Toyota elected to locate its plant in southern Ontario as opposed to the United States based upon the fact that Canada's nationalized health care system keeps worker medical costs at half of those in the U.S.[14]

Despite the popularity of manufacturing in one low-cost location, many other factors must also be taken into consideration. The growing customer demand for *dependability* and prompt deliveries have caused companies such as Dell to locate plants closer to customers rather than in low-wage areas. Many companies are also responding to the importance of *innovation* and *quality*. For example, the Japanese company, Kenwood, decided to shift production back to Japan after several years of outsourcing to Malaysia to take advantage of specially trained workers and low defect rates. Canon is also keeping 80 percent of its capital spending in Japan in order to maintain its "technological edge."[15] The need for responsiveness or *flexibility* because of differences in national markets may result in regional manufacturing to service local markets.

As a company's competitive strategies change, so too do its manufacturing strategies. In addition, MNEs may adopt different strategies for different product lines, depending on the competitive priorities of those products. For example, Toyota has developed a family of vehicles based on a single, low-cost platform that is targeted for emerging markets. In order to keep the prices for these vehicles low enough to compete in the developing world, Toyota has abandoned its traditional practice of sourcing key components from its Japanese plants and is instead locating factories for these parts in low-wage areas such as South America, Africa, and Southeast Asia that can also take advantage of regional free-trade zones and that are close to the targeted emerging markets. The new strategy has allowed Toyota to reduce the cost of manufacturing this family of vehicles by 20–25 percent.[16] However, there are concerns that these cost savings have come at the expense of the quality the company is known for.

Manufacturing Configuration

Next, the company's managers need to determine the configuration of manufacturing facilities. There are three basic configurations that MNEs consider as they establish a global manufacturing strategy. The first is to have centralized manufacturing and to offer a selection of standard, lower-priced products to different markets. That is basically a manufacture-and-export strategy. It is common for new-to-export companies to use this strategy, typically through their home-country manufacturing facilities. This is also important for expensive items where economies of scale in manufacturing are important and where there is little need to localize the product for consumption in different markets, such as aircraft. The second configuration is the use of regional manufacturing facilities to serve customers within a specific region. That is what Samsonite did initially in Europe with its production facilities in Belgium and what Toyota is doing in its Third World markets. Third, market expansion in individual countries, especially when the demand in those countries becomes significant, might argue for a multidomestic approach in which companies manufacture products close to their customers, using country-specific manufacturing facilities to meet local needs.[17] Although Samsonite did not manufacture in every country where it sold its products, it divided its broad European regional strategy into smaller areas, setting up seven factories to manufacture products for the European market. Unless the company has manufacturing facilities in every country where it is doing business, it must combine exporting with manufacturing. In reality, MNEs choose a combination of these approaches depending on their product strategies.

Often, countries will also specialize in the production of parts or final goods, a process known as rationalization. When Samsonite opened a new factory in Hénin-Beaumont, France, in the 1980s, it manufactured the Prestige Attaché case and the Beauty case. Doing so allowed it to stop production of those products in Oudenaarde, Belgium, so that it could focus on the new Oyster product line there. That allowed Samsonite to specialize in the manufacture of certain products in certain plants. It then exported its production to the centralized European warehouse for distribution to retailers all over Europe.

Coordination and Control

Coordination and control fit well together. *Coordinating* is the linking or integrating of activities into a unified system.[18] The activities include everything along the global supply chain from purchasing to warehousing to shipment. It is hard to coordinate supplier relations and logistics activities if those issues are not considered when the manufacturing configuration is set up. Samsonite took configuration and coordination into account when it set up its second manufacturing facility in Europe. As demand increased in Europe and as new product lines were added, Samsonite knew that it needed to open up a second plant. However, it wanted to maintain the central European warehouse concept, so it identified a location that would allow it to coordinate transportation and storage relatively easily and quickly.

Manufacturing configuration
- Centralized manufacturing in one country
- Manufacturing facilities in specific regions to service those regions
- Multidomestic—facilities in each country

Some companies specialize in manufacturing according to product or process.

Coordination—linking or integrating activities into a unified system

Control—systems, such as organizational structure and performance measurement systems, to ensure that managers implement company strategies

Once the company determines the manufacturing configuration that it will use, it must adopt a control system to ensure that company strategies are carried out. *Control* can be the measuring of performance so that companies can respond appropriately to changing conditions. Another aspect of control structure is the organizational structure, and Samsonite established a European headquarters in Oudenaarde, Belgium, to coordinate all of its activities in Europe.

INFORMATION TECHNOLOGY AND GLOBAL SUPPLY CHAIN MANAGEMENT

Earlier in the chapter, we defined global supply chain management and provided a simplified view of a global supply chain in Figure 17.5. A comprehensive supply chain strategy should include the following elements: (1) customer service requirements, (2) plant and distribution center network design, (3) inventory management, (4) outsourcing and third-party logistics relationships, (5) key customer and supplier relationships, (6) business processes, (7) information systems, (8) organizational design and training requirements, (9) performance metrics, and (10) performance goals.[19] In this section, we will discuss information systems as a key part of the global supply chain management system. In the remainder of the chapter, we will discuss total quality management, inventory management, and two key networks: supplier networks and transportation networks. Global supply chain management integrates these networks beyond the firm itself to improve customer satisfaction levels and enhance profitability.

> A key to making the global supply chain work is a good information system.

The key to making a global information system work is information. As noted earlier in the chapter, Samsonite invested heavily in information technology that allowed it to speed up the delivery time to retailers. Information could be transmitted to the warehouse directly by the retailer or through a salesperson, which triggered an order to ship immediately. Many companies use **electronic data interchange (EDI)** to link suppliers, manufacturers, customers, and intermediaries, especially in the food manufacturing and carmaking industries, in which suppliers replenish in high volumes. In a global context, EDI has been used to link exporters with customs to facilitate the quick processing of customs forms, thus speeding up the delivery of products across borders. Wal-Mart is known for its revolutionary use of EDI to connect its suppliers to its inventory ordering system.[20] Wal-Mart depends upon over 68,000 suppliers located throughout the world.[21] As noted in the Wal-Mart case in Chapter 8, Wal-Mart's information system was one of its competitive advantages in lowering costs and capturing market share in Mexico. However, EDI has some drawbacks. It is relatively limited and inflexible. It provides basic information but does not adapt easily to rapidly changing market conditions, a necessary condition in the global marketplace. It is relatively expensive to implement, so many small- and medium-size companies find it difficult to afford. Also, it is based on proprietary rather than on widely accepted standards, so systems tend only to be able to link together suppliers and their customers. In addition, it focuses more on the business-to-business value chain and does not deal effectively with end-use customers.[22]

> EDI (electronic data interchange)—the electronic linkage of suppliers, customers, and third-party intermediaries to expedite documents and financial flows

The next wave of technology affecting the global supply chain was the implementation of information technology packages known as **enterprise resource planning (ERP).** Companies such as the German software giant SAP, Oracle, Baan, and PeopleSoft introduced software to integrate everything in the back office of the firm—the part of the business that dealt with the firm itself but not with the customer (known as the front office). Around 27 percent of small companies, 57 percent of large companies, and 70 percent of enterprise-sized companies in the United States possess operational ERP systems, with another 16 percent currently looking into implementing ERP for the first time.[23] ERP is essential for bringing together the information inside the firm and from different geographic areas, but its inability to tie in to the customer and take advantage of e-commerce has been a problem.

> ERP (enterprise resource planning)—software that can link information flows from different parts of a business and from different geographic areas

The next technological wave linking together the parts of the global supply chain is **e-commerce.** As an example, Dell Computer Corporation has a factory in Ireland that

E-commerce—the use of the
Internet to join together
suppliers with companies and
companies with customers

Extranet—the use of the
Internet to link a company with
outsiders

Private technology exchange
(PTX)—an online collaboration
model that brings
manufacturers, distributors,
value-added resellers, and
customers together to execute
trading transactions

Quality—meeting or exceeding
the expectations of a customer

supplies custom-built PCs all over Europe. Customers can transmit orders to Dell via call centers or Dell's Web site. The company relays the demand for components to its suppliers. Trucks deliver the components to the factory and haul off the completed computers within a few hours. Dell has established an **extranet** for its suppliers—a linkage to Dell's information system via the Internet—so that they can organize production and delivery of parts to Dell when they need it. Dell uses the Internet to plug its suppliers into its customer database so that it can keep track of changes in demand. It also uses the Internet to plug customers into the ordering process and allows them to track the progress of their order from the factory to their doorstep.[24] Wal-Mart moved its EDI-based infrastructure from traditional but expensive value-added networks (VAN) to the Internet. This has been good news for many of its 68,000 worldwide vendors. All of their transactions with Wal-Mart are now on the Web—a substantial cost savings over VANs for Wal-Mart and its vendors.[25]

Despite the bursting of the dot-com bubble in 2000, most experts agree that the Internet will revolutionize communications across all levels of the global supply chain, but it will occur at different speeds in different areas. The number of worldwide Internet users is rising—reaching nearly 935 million in 2004, with predictions that the number will exceed 1 billion in 2005.[26] Meanwhile, Internet trade between businesses rose 73 percent in 2001, and online retail spending rose by 56 percent.[27] Since then, Internet trade has continued to rise. The real attraction of the Internet in global supply chain management is that it not only helps to automate and speed up internal processes in a company through its **intranet** but also spreads efficiency gains to the business systems of its customers and suppliers.[28] The new technology wave using the Internet is that of **private technology exchange (PTX)**, which is an online collaboration model that brings manufacturers, distributors, value-added resellers, and customers together to execute trading transactions and to share information about demand, production, availability, and more. PTXs will increase the efficiency of the supply chain and reduce costs for participants. Some of the front-running companies participating in PTXs are Ace Hardware, Cisco, and the Ford Motor Company. The technology is still new, so not many companies have adopted the model.[29]

The challenge in global supply chain management is that some networks can be managed through the Internet, but others—especially in emerging markets—cannot because of the lack of technology. Even though the Internet growth numbers are impressive, e-commerce still only accounts for 2 percent of all trade. The use of the Internet varies by location and by industry. North America is at least five years ahead of some countries in Europe, especially Eastern Europe. Industries such as computing and electronics, aerospace and defense, and motor vehicles are blasting ahead, while industrial equipment, food and agriculture, heavy industries, and consumer goods are lagging behind.[30] It is no coincidence that the leaders in e-commerce are those that have invested significant amounts of money over the years in information technology—notably in the defense and motor vehicles industries.

QUALITY

An important aspect of all levels of the global supply chain is total quality management, and this is true for service as well as manufacturing companies. **Quality** is defined as meeting or exceeding the expectations of the customer. More specifically, it is the conformance to specifications, value, fitness for use, support (provided by the company), and psychological impressions (image).[31] For example, no one wants to buy computer software that has a lot of bugs. However, the need to get software to market quickly may mean getting the product to market as soon as possible and correcting errors later. In the airline industry, service is a key. Some airlines, such as Singapore Air, have developed a worldwide reputation for excellence in service. That is a distinct competitive advantage, especially when trying to attract the business traveler.

Quality—or lack thereof—can have serious ramifications for a company. Ford Motor Company lost around $1 billion in 2001 because of faulty Firestone tires placed on its Ford

Explorers. Because of this and other quality problems, Ford, General Motors and DaimlerChrysler, are taking a hard look at the way Japanese carmakers manufacture their cars with higher efficiency and fewer defects. As DaimlerChrysler puts it, we're "raiding Toyota Motor Corporation for quality expertise." The American car companies, which have typically lagged behind the Japanese in quality, are learning to root out problems before assembly and bring each supplier into the design process earlier, hoping to spot component problems early. They are finding some success, particularly in their international plants. Ford's Brazil plant produces some of the best quality results of any of its factories.[32] Each year, J. D. Power & Associates releases two different quality rankings on automobiles: the Initial Quality Study (IQS) and the Vehicle Dependability Study (VDS), which measures quality after three years of ownership. In both cases, Toyota ranked number one in 2004, and the Japanese cars in general outpaced the U.S. and European manufacturers in terms of quality. However, quality has been increasing for all manufacturers, and Korean companies significantly increased their quality ratings in 2004.[33]

Quality can mean **zero defects,** an idea perfected by Japanese manufacturers who refuse to tolerate defects of any kind. Before the strong emphasis on zero defects, U.S. companies operated according to the premise of **acceptable quality level (AQL).** This premise allowed an acceptable level of poor quality. It held that unacceptable products would be dealt with through repair facilities and service warranties. This type of manufacturing/operating environment required buffer inventories, rework stations, and expediting. The goal was to push through products as fast as possible and then deal with the mistakes later. However, it is increasingly evident that AQL is inferior to zero defects, and global companies that take quality more seriously will beat the competition.[34]

Total Quality Management

The Japanese approach to quality is **total quality management (TQM).** TQM is a process that stresses three principles: (1) customer satisfaction, (2) employee involvement, and (3) continuous improvements in quality.[35] The goal of TQM is to eliminate all defects. TQM often focuses on benchmarking world-class standards, product and service design, process design, and purchasing.[36]

The center of the entire process, however, is customer satisfaction, which to achieve may raise production costs. The difference between AQL and TQM centers on the attitude toward quality. In AQL, quality is a characteristic of a product that meets or exceeds engineering standards. In TQM, quality means that a product is "so good that the customer wouldn't think of buying from anyone else."

TQM is a process of continuous improvement at every level of the organization—from the mailroom to the boardroom. It implies that the company is doing everything it can to achieve quality at all stages of the process, from customer demands to product design to engineering. For example, if management accounting systems are focused strictly on cost, they will preclude measures that could lead to higher quality. The key is to understand the company's overall strategy. TQM does not use any specific production philosophy or require the use of other techniques, such as a just-in-time system for inventory delivery. TQM is a proactive strategy. Although benchmarking—determining the best processes used by the best companies—is an important part of TQM, using the best practices of other companies is not intended to be a goal. TQM means that a company will try to be better than the best.

Executives who have adopted the zero-defects philosophy of TQM claim that long-run production costs decline as defects decline. The continuous improvement process is also known as *kaizen*, which means identifying problems and enlisting employees at all levels of the organization to help eliminate the problems. The key is to make continuous improvement a part of the daily work of every employee. TQM in a global setting is challenging because of cultural and environmental differences. In 1987, Samsonite entered into a cooperation agreement with a Hungarian luggage manufacturer to produce and supply low-end softside luggage for Samsonite, but it did not produce enough quality products due to

Zero defects—the refusal to tolerate defects of any kind

Acceptable quality level—there is a tolerable level of defects, and defects can be corrected through repair and service warranties

TQM (total quality management)—a process whose goal is to eliminate all defects

Kaizen—the Japanese process of continuous improvement, the cornerstone of TQM

Six Sigma—a quality control system aimed at eliminating defects, slashing product cycle times, and cutting costs across the board

the lack of advanced technology. Samsonite was forced to invest heavily in the Hungarian partner to get it up to world-class standards. Eventually, its efforts were successful.

A new management tool, Six Sigma, is starting to displace TQM as the corporate-reengineering tool of choice. **Six Sigma** is a highly focused system of quality control that scrutinizes a company's entire production system. It aims to eliminate defects, slash product cycle times, and cut costs across the board. The Six Sigma process uses data and rigorous statistical analysis to identify "defects" in a process or product, reduce variability, and achieve as close to zero defects as possible. It involves driving toward six standard deviations between the mean and the nearest specification limit in any process—from manufacturing to transactional and from product to service.[37] It was introduced by Motorola in the 1980s and has been adopted by many MNEs, including General Electric, GlaxoSmithKline, and Lockheed Martin. It is unknown whether Six Sigma will eliminate the use of TQM, but for now, it is important for companies to explore both tools to determine the one that will better improve quality in the organization.[38]

Quality Standards

Levels of quality standards

• General level—ISO 9000, Malcolm Baldrige National Quality Award

• Industry-specific level

• Company level

There are three different levels of quality standards: (1) a general level, (2) an industry-specific level, and (3) a company level. The first level is a general standard, such as the Deming Award, which is presented to firms that demonstrate excellence in quality, and the Malcolm Baldrige National Quality Award, which is presented annually to companies that demonstrate quality strategies and achievements. However, even more important than awards is certification of quality.

The **International Organization for Standardization (ISO)** in Geneva was formed in 1947 to facilitate the international coordination and unification of industrial standards. From the beginning it has partnered with the IEC (International Electrotechnical Commission), which is the originator of global technical standards. It also collaborates with the International Telecommunications Union and the World Trade Organization.

ISO 9000—a global set of quality standards intended to promote quality at every level of an organization

ISO 14000 – a quality standard concerned with environmental management

There are two main families of standards issued by ISO: ISO 9000 and ISO 14000. ISO 9000 is concerned with quality management, or "what the organization does to enhance customer satisfaction by meeting customer and applicable regulatory requirements and continually to improve its performance in this regard."[39] ISO 14000 is concerned with environmental management and what the company does to improve its environmental performance.

ISO 9000 is a set of universal standards for a Quality Assurance system that is accepted around the world. The standards apply uniformly to companies in any industry and of any size. ISO 9000 is intended to promote the idea of quality at every level of an organization. Initially, it was designed to harmonize technical norms within the EU. Now it is an important part of business operations throughout Europe. The ISO is an NGO and is a network of standard setters in 151 countries throughout the world. In 2000, the ISO revised the standards and refers to them now as the ISO 9000:2000.

Basically, under ISO 9000:2000, companies must document how workers perform every function that affects quality and install mechanisms to ensure that they follow through on the documented routine. ISO 9000:2000 certification entails a complex analysis of management systems and procedures, not just quality-control standards. Rather than judging the quality of a particular product, ISO 9000:2000 evaluates the management of the manufacturing process according to standards it has created in 20 domains—from purchasing to design to training. A company that wants to be ISO certified must fill out a report and then be certified by a team of independent auditors.[40] The process can be expensive and time-consuming. Each site of a company must be separately certified. The certification of one site cannot cover the entire company. Most MNEs claim ISO certification, but as noted in a humorous way in Figure 17.6, ISO is not the solution to all quality issues. However, ISO certification of suppliers will help companies to get more business, especially with European companies. When companies are choosing among different suppliers, it would be very beneficial for the supplier to have ISO certification.

FIGURE 17.6

ISO 9000 CERTIFICATION: AN IMPORTANT EDGE?

Source: DILBERT reprinted by permission of United Feature Syndicate, Inc.

U.S. companies that operate in Europe are becoming ISO certified to maintain access to the European market. When DuPont lost a major European contract to an ISO-certified European company, it decided to become certified. By doing so, not only was DuPont able to position itself better in the European market, but it also benefited from the experience of going through ISO certification and focusing on quality in the organization. Some European companies are so committed to ISO certification that they will not do business with a supplier that is certified if its suppliers are not also ISO certified. They want to be sure that quality flows back to every level of the supply chain.

In addition to the general standards described earlier, there are industry-specific standards for quality, especially for suppliers to follow. In addition, individual companies set their own standards for suppliers to meet if they are going to continue to supply them. Samsonite's concerns in Eastern Europe and its subsequent work with Eastern European suppliers to meet its quality requirements are an example of how companies set their own standards and work with suppliers.

> Non-European companies operating in Europe need to become ISO certified in order to maintain access to that market.

SUPPLIER NETWORKS

Global sourcing and production strategies can be better understood by looking at Figure 17.7. **Sourcing** is the firm's process of having inputs (raw materials and parts) supplied to it for the production process. Figure 17.7 illustrates the basic operating environment choices (the home country or any foreign country) by stage in the production process (sourcing of raw materials

> Sourcing—the process of a firm having inputs supplied to it from outside suppliers (both domestic and foreign) for the production process

FIGURE 17.7   **GLOBAL SOURCING AND PRODUCTION STRATEGY**

Companies confront many possibilities when sourcing raw materials, parts, and components, and assembling them into final goods to serve worldwide markets. For example, a U.S. company could source components in the United States, assemble them in Mexico, and export the final product back to the United States or to other countries. To be global, a company must choose "abroad" at least once.

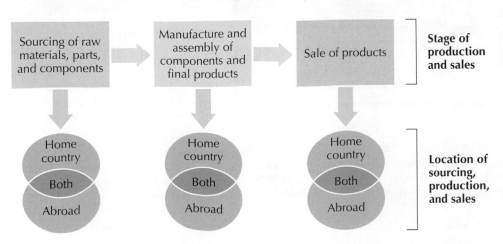

and parts and the manufacture and assembly of final products). Global sourcing is the first step in the process of materials management, which includes sourcing, inventory management, and transportation between suppliers, manufacturers, and customers.

For example, Ford assembles cars in Hermosillo, Mexico, and ships them into the United States for end-use consumers. The cars are designed by Mazda, a Japanese company, and use some Japanese parts. Ford can purchase parts manufactured in Japan and ship them to the United States for final assembly and sale in the U.S. market, or it can have Japanese- and U.S.-made parts shipped to Mexico for final assembly and sale in the United States and Mexico. For Mexican assembly, some of the parts come from the United States, some from Japan, and a small percentage from Mexico.

When Ford decided to manufacture the Escort in Europe, it used the global sourcing of parts from plants in 15 different countries for final assembly in the United Kingdom and Germany, as Figure 17.8 illustrates. Although the Escort was last manufactured in 1999, it was replaced by the Focus. Figure 17.8 is a comprehensive example of how parts from the old Escort, and probably the new Focus, come from different countries.

Another good example of global sourcing is the Kia Sorento. This popular sport utility vehicle consists of 30,000 parts and components supplied from around the world. The car is

FIGURE 17.8   **THE GLOBAL COMPONENT NETWORK FOR FORD'S EUROPEAN MANUFACTURING OF THE ESCORT**

Ford assembles Escorts in only two facilities in Europe, but parts and components used in the automobiles come from all over the world.

Source: From *World Development Report 1987* by World Bank, copyright 1984 by the World Bank. Used by permission of Oxford University Press, Inc.

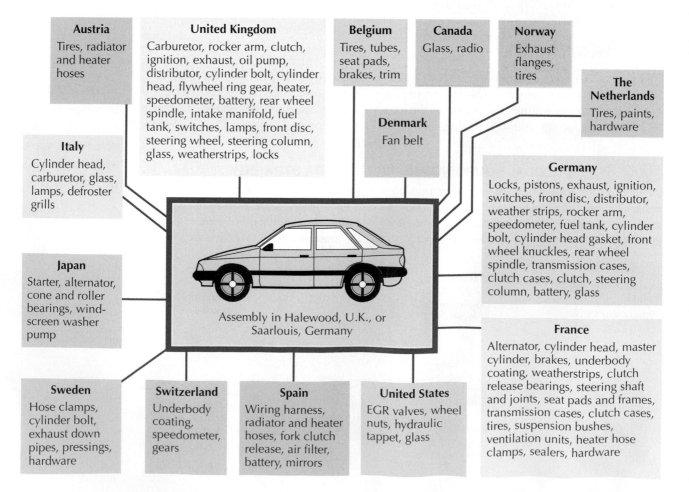

Austria
Tires, radiator and heater hoses

United Kingdom
Carburetor, rocker arm, clutch, ignition, exhaust, oil pump, distributor, cylinder bolt, cylinder head, flywheel ring gear, heater, speedometer, battery, rear wheel spindle, intake manifold, fuel tank, switches, lamps, front disc, steering wheel, steering column, glass, weatherstrips, locks

Belgium
Tires, tubes, seat pads, brakes, trim

Canada
Glass, radio

Norway
Exhaust flanges, tires

The Netherlands
Tires, paints, hardware

Italy
Cylinder head, carburetor, glass, lamps, defroster grills

Denmark
Fan belt

Germany
Locks, pistons, exhaust, ignition, switches, front disc, distributor, weather strips, rocker arm, speedometer, fuel tank, cylinder bolt, cylinder head gasket, front wheel knuckles, rear wheel spindle, transmission cases, clutch cases, clutch, steering column, battery, glass

Japan
Starter, alternator, cone and roller bearings, windscreen washer pump

Assembly in Halewood, U.K., or Saarlouis, Germany

France
Alternator, cylinder head, master cylinder, brakes, underbody coating, weatherstrips, clutch release bearings, steering shaft and joints, seat pads and frames, transmission cases, clutch cases, tires, suspension bushes, ventilation units, heater hose clamps, sealers, hardware

Sweden
Hose clamps, cylinder bolt, exhaust down pipes, pressings, hardware

Switzerland
Underbody coating, speedometer, gears

Spain
Wiring harness, radiator and heater hoses, fork clutch release, air filter, battery, mirrors

United States
EGR valves, wheel nuts, hydraulic tappet, glass

especially reliant on brand-name European and U.S. suppliers such as ZF Sachx AG, BorgWarner Inc., Autolive Inc., and Michelin Group, which help to both bolster its image and increase its appeal in foreign markets. To obtain these parts, the Korean-based company must have them shipped from as far away as Wales and Mexico. With such a far-flung supplier network, the Sorento's supply chain may seem vulnerable to disruptions caused by natural disasters and political disturbances; however, Kia's diversified parts sourcing, ability to shift supply routes and to switch factories on short notice, advanced planning and ordering, and regular communication with suppliers have actually given it the adaptability to respond to such risks.[41]

Companies can manufacture parts internally or purchase them from external (unrelated) manufacturers. Samsonite manufactured most of the parts that went into its luggage, but it sourced some of the parts from unrelated suppliers—such as wheels for suitcases from Czech suppliers. It also sourced semifinished softside parts from Eastern European subcontractors to use in its own factories. Companies can also assemble their own products internally or subcontract to external companies, as noted earlier in the examples of Nike, Mattel, and McDonald's Happy Meals toys. Manufacture of parts and final assembly may take place in the company's home country, the country in which it is trying to sell the product, or a third country.[42]

> Companies can manufacture parts internally or purchase them from external manufacturers.

Sourcing in the home country enables companies to avoid numerous problems, including those connected with language differences, long distances and lengthy supply lines, exchange-rate fluctuations, wars and insurrections, strikes, politics, tariffs, and complex transportation channels. However, for many companies, domestic sources may be unavailable or may be more expensive than foreign sources. In Japan, foreign procurement is critical, because nearly all of that country's uranium, bauxite, nickel, crude oil, iron ore, copper, coking coal, and approximately 30 percent of its agricultural products are imported. Japanese trading companies came into being expressly to acquire the raw materials needed to fuel Japan's manufacturing.

> Using domestic sources for raw materials and components allows a company to avoid problems with language differences, distance, currency, politics, and tariffs, as well as other problems.

Companies pursue global sourcing strategies for a number of reasons:

1. To reduce costs—due to less expensive labor, less restrictive work rules, and lower land and facilities costs
2. To improve quality
3. To increase exposure to worldwide technology
4. To improve the delivery-of-supplies process
5. To strengthen the reliability of supply by supplementing domestic with foreign suppliers
6. To gain access to materials that are only available abroad, possibly because of technical specifications or product capabilities
7. To establish a presence in a foreign market
8. To satisfy offset requirements
9. To react to competitors' offshore sourcing practices[43]

> Companies outsource abroad to lower costs and improve quality, among other reasons.

In some ways, global sourcing is more expensive than domestic sourcing. For example, transportation and communications are more expensive, and companies may have to pay brokers and agent fees. Given the longer length of supply lines, it often takes more time to get components from abroad, and lead times are less certain. This problem increases the inventory carrying costs and makes it more difficult to get parts to the production site in a timely manner. If imported components come in with errors and need to be reworked, the cost per unit will rise, and some components may have to be shipped back to the supplier. However, R. C. Willey, a furniture company owned by Berkshire Hathaway, imports furniture from China to its stores in the Western United States, and finds that it can get product cheaper than buying the furniture from the East Coast of the U.S. and shipping it across the country.

Three major configurations of sourcing have emerged:

1. Vertical integration
2. Outsourcing through industrial clusters
3. Other outsourcing

Vertical integration occurs when the company owns the entire supplier network or at least a significant part of it. The company may have to purchase raw materials from outside suppliers, but it produces the most expensive parts itself. By integrating vertically, the company is able to reduce transactions costs (such as finding suppliers, selling output, negotiating contracts, monitoring contracts, and settling disputes with unrelated companies) by internalizing the different levels in the value chain.[44]

Outsourcing through industrial clusters is an alternative way to reduce transportation costs and transactions costs. Under clustering, buyers and suppliers locate in close proximity in order to facilitate doing business. An example is where Dell Computer Corporation established an assembly operation in the Multimedia Supercorridor in Malaysia, where it is close to its key suppliers.

The Japanese *keiretsus* are a group of independent companies that work together to manage the flow of goods and services along the entire value-added chain.[45] Toyota's highly coordinated supplier network is among the most successful and well known of the Japanese *keiretsus* and is a good example of industrial clustering, almost bordering on vertical integration, since parts suppliers tend to set up shop close to Toyota's assembly operations, and Toyota usually has an ownership interest in the suppliers. However, recent changes in its global markets and price pressures resulting from the high cost of steel and the strong yen have caused the company to start looking beyond its closely knit supplier base in Japan. In order to meet its goal of cutting costs for buying car parts by 30 percent—an objective outlined in its "Construction of Cost Competitiveness for the 21st Century" program—Toyota is putting pressure on its *keiretsu* suppliers by benchmarking them to China's cheaper suppliers and by courting suppliers outside Japan. These outside suppliers are leaping at the chance of breaking into the supplier network of the world's second-largest automaker.[46]

Outsourcing independent of industrial clusters is a third way of dealing with sourcing. This occurs when companies don't want to be close to competitors for security reasons or where transportation costs and inventory management costs are not major issues.

Make or Buy Decision

MNE managers struggle with a dilemma: Which production activities should be performed internally and which ones could be subcontracted to independent companies? That is the *make or buy decision*. In the case of subcontracting, companies also need to decide whether the activities should be carried on in the home market or abroad. A recent survey of the use of outsourcing by businesses reveals the importance of control measures. Accenture conducted a survey of 150 executives from *Fortune* 1000 companies about the biggest barriers to expanding their use of outsourcing. Nearly one half (48 percent) reported that loss of operational control was the biggest barrier. Other barriers were cultural barriers in the organization (19 percent), costs (14 percent), and long-term dependency on an external organization (11 percent).[47]

In deciding whether to make or buy, MNEs could focus on those parts that are critical to the product and that they are distinctively good at making. They could outsource parts when suppliers have a distinct comparative advantage, such as greater scale, lower-cost structure, or stronger performance incentives. They also could use outsourcing as an implied threat to underperforming employees that if they don't improve, the companies will move their business elsewhere.[48]

In determining whether to make or buy, the MNE needs to determine the design and manufacturing capabilities of potential suppliers compared to its own capabilities. If the supplier has a clear advantage, management needs to decide what it would cost to catch up to the best suppliers and whether it would make sense to do so.

POINT–COUNTERPOINT: SHOULD FIRMS OUTSOURCE INNOVATION?

POINT

Yes, firms should outsource innovative processes if doing so will allow them to maintain their focus and to effectively position themselves in the increasingly competitive high-tech and electronics industries. Data show that more and more companies are coming to realize the advantages of doing so. Suppliers are taking on such responsibilities as designing and manufacturing prototypes, converting them into workable products, upgrading mature products, conducting quality tests, putting together user manuals, and selecting parts vendors. For example, the designs of 65 percent of PC notebooks and those of 70 percent of PDAs are outsourced. Companies such as Dell, Motorola, and Philips are buying complete designs from Asian developers, while even Boeing is collaborating with an Indian company to develop software for its 7E7 Dreamliner jet.

Companies that are willing to outsource some of the R&D and the technological designs of their products can experience enormous cost savings. Although innovation is a key to remaining competitive, more and more companies are finding that their internal R&D teams aren't producing results that justify the large amount of investments put into them. Thus, in the face of demanding customers and relentless competition that put pressure on margins, these companies must find a way to reduce their costs or to increase their R&D productivity. Outsourcing has proven to be a viable solution. Companies can save millions of dollars by simply buying designs rather than developing them in-house. For example, industry estimates indicate that using a predesigned platform for cell phones can reduce the costs of developing them from scratch—which takes approximately $10 million and 150 engineers—by 70 percent! Furthermore, demands by retailers and customers as well as the uncertainty of future market trends require that companies develop a range of product models, which is very costly. Third-party developers are better equipped to handle these costs as they can spread them over many buyers and have the expertise to develop a wide variety of models from a single basic design.

Outsourcing also allows companies to get their products on the market faster, and in the electronics and technology industries, where products become commodities in a matter of months, that speed becomes crucial to maintaining a competitive advantage. Hewlett-Packard claims that by working with partners and suppliers on designs it now takes 60 percent less time for it to get a new concept to the market. PalmOne has also reduced its product development time by months, decreased the number of defects by 50 percent, and increased its gross margins by 20 percent by outsourcing.

Critics worry that by outsourcing technology, companies are outsourcing their sources of competitive advantage, but outsourcing certain design and development processes allows these companies to better focus on their true core competencies. Few, if any, companies plan on completely eliminating their own R&D forces, and most insist that they will continue with the more proprietary R&D work. By shifting some of the less critical work to outside vendors, they will be able to focus more on the latest innovations and on the next-generation technologies that can truly serve to differentiate them. As one executive from Lucent explains, "Outsourcing [is] about the flexibility to put resources in the right places at the right time."

No one company can manage everything in-house. Even the chief technology officer of Nokia—a company that once prided itself on developing almost everything on its own—has stated, "Nobody can master it all." The companies that are going to survive in the future are those able to efficiently and effectively control a network of partners and suppliers around the world.

COUNTERPOINT

No, companies should not outsource their research, design, and development functions. Recent trends have gone beyond outsourcing larger key components to outsourcing the R&D for entire lines of complete products! Many companies insist that although they may outsource some design and development work, they still keep core R&D in-house, but how do they know where to draw the line? How do they determine what is core intellectual property and what is commodity technology? The truth is that outsourcing turns intellectual property into commodity technology that becomes available to most anyone. By working with South Korean chipmakers to develop its DRAM memory chips, Toshiba allowed the technology behind these components to become commoditized, and it is now struggling to stay ahead of competitors.[49]

A company's competitive advantage often depends on trade secrets that set it apart from its rivals. Outsourcing innovation enhances the risk that a company will pass on these trade secrets and proprietary technologies to suppliers and partners, thereby fostering new competitors. Suppliers rarely cooperate solely with one customer, thus the R&D they do for one can easily be transferred to another. Such was the case for the Japanese company Sharp, which worked closely with its suppliers to develop a "sixth generation" plant able to make much larger flat panels for televisions than "fifth generation" plants were able to make. Unfortunately, its suppliers also work closely with Sharp's rivals, many of them Taiwanese companies, and not long after the completion of the plant, these competitors were constructing their own "sixth generation" facilities. As a result, Sharp has started to take extra precautions, such as secretly rewriting software on some of the equipment it has purchased and fixing machinery in-house rather than having suppliers do it to keep vendors from knowing the problems that may exist in the equipment they have sold to competitors.[50]

There is also the risk that suppliers and partners will take what information and technology has been shared with them and become competitors themselves. After Motorola hired the Taiwanese company BenQ Corp. to design and manufacture mobile phones for it, the company began selling the phones under its own brand name in the highly competitive Chinese market, causing Motorola to terminate the contract.

Perhaps more important than giving rise to new competitors is losing competitive edge and the incentive to invest in new technology. While some assert that outsourcing certain development and design work allows companies to focus more on new innovative technologies, in actuality, this outsourcing more often prompts companies to decrease the amount they invest in internal R&D and to become lazy in their pursuit of future breakthroughs, relying too much on suppliers to do the work for them. Jim Andrew, the senior vice president of Boston Consulting Group, warns, "If the innovation starts residing in the suppliers, you could incrementalize yourself to the point where there isn't much left."

High-tech and electronics companies that outsource their innovative processes risk losing the essence of what their actual business is, becoming mere marketing fronts for other companies. It also sends a bad message to investors, who might have difficulty finding the intrinsic value in a company that owns little true intellectual property and whose profits from successful products are most likely simply being paid out in licensing fees to the companies that actually developed them.

While much has been made of the outsourcing of manufacturing the past few decades, the outsourcing of innovation poses a potentially larger threat to high-tech firms who see it as a shortcut to cost savings. Looking to immediate cost savings as justification for outsourcing technology and innovation is short-sighted, and firms that do so will ultimately damage their competitive positions and lose viability as true players in their industries.[51]

Supplier Relations

Robert W. Lane, the CEO of John Deere, once stated,

> Our supplier partners have been at the heart of [our] effort to put superior value into our products . . . around the world and throughout the enterprise. Together with our suppliers and dealers, we are enriching the word "value" to include the very best design, quality, delivery, process and the very best cost, all at the same time. We know it has not been easy for suppliers and it still isn't! Following our example, suppliers have had to make major adjustments in how they do business. We've been pretty demanding on ourselves and others, but I'm confident . . . that by working together to aggressively reduce costs, increase quality, and improve delivery time, they've become stronger businesses, as well as stronger Deere suppliers. Like us, they too need a great business in order to sustain long-term success.[52]

If MNEs outsource instead of source parts from internal production, they need to determine the degree of involvement with suppliers.

If an MNE decides it must outsource rather than integrate vertically, it must determine how to work with suppliers. Toyota pioneered the Toyota Production System in order to work with unrelated suppliers. Toyota sends a team of manufacturing experts to each of its key suppliers to observe how the supplier organizes its factory and makes its parts. Then the team advises on how to cut costs and boost quality. It is also common for Toyota to identify two suppliers for each part and have the suppliers compete aggressively with each other. The supplier that performs the best gets the most business. However, both suppliers know that they will have an ongoing relationship with Toyota and will not be dumped easily.[53]

This is a good example of the close relationships that Japanese companies develop with their suppliers. It is very different from the arm's-length relationship that U.S. companies tend to have with their suppliers. Further, Toyota has been able to reduce the number of supplier relationships it develops, which allows it to focus on a few key suppliers, promising to give them a lot of business if they perform up to Toyota standards.

The decision to work closely with suppliers requires a great deal of trust and oftentimes involves making drastic—sometimes risky—changes. However, such changes can provide large strategic advantages. Such is the case for J. C. Penney and its Hong Kong–based supplier of shirts, TAL Apparel Ltd. The retailer literally allows its supplier to take over some of its own processes. Rather than simply responding to orders sent to it from Penney, TAL tracks the retailer's sales data directly, running it through its personally designed computer program to determine the number of shirts to make, as well as their sizes, colors, and styles. These shirts are then shipped directly to individual J. C. Penney stores, completely bypassing the retailer's warehouses. This cooperation has resulted in quicker merchandise turnovers and an inventory level of virtually zero—a significant improvement over the eight months' worth of inventory the retailer used to keep. TAL has also been allowed to handle market testing and the design of new shirt styles, which has given it the ability to respond more quickly and effectively to customer demands. With the leverage given it, TAL can roll out a new style in just four months.[54]

Not all customer-supplier relationships are as collaborative as those of Toyota and J. C. Penney, however. Sometimes large customers can use their strong market presence and buying power to place additional demands on suppliers. For many years, General Motors Corp. has placed heavy pressure on its U.S. suppliers to lower costs by certain set percentages each year and to then pass those cost savings on to GM via lower prices. Now, given GM's plans to shift important resources overseas to markets such as China, South Korea, and Europe over the next few years, some suppliers and management consultants working with GM have indicated that suppliers may be pressured to set up facilities in China to accommodate GM.[55]

The relationships MNEs establish with their suppliers are largely based on their individual competitive strategies, the nature of their products, the competitive environment they are faced with, the capabilities of their suppliers, and the level of experience and trust they share with them. MNEs must consider these factors as they determine what kind of supplier relationship will best meet their needs.

The Purchasing Function

The purchasing agent is the link between the company's outsourcing decision and its supplier relationships. Just as companies go through stages of globalization, so does the purchasing agent's scope of responsibilities. Typically, purchasing goes through four phases before becoming "global":

1. Domestic purchasing only
2. Foreign buying based on need
3. Foreign buying as part of procurement strategy
4. Integration of global procurement strategy[56]

Phase 4 occurs when the company realizes the benefits that result from the integration and coordination of purchasing on a global basis and is most applicable to the MNE as opposed to, say, the exporter. When purchasing becomes this global, MNEs often face the centralization/decentralization dilemma. Should they allow each subsidiary to make all purchasing decisions, or should they centralize all or some of the purchasing decisions? The primary benefits of decentralization include increased production facility control over purchases, better responsiveness to facility needs, and more effective use of local suppliers. The primary benefits of centralization are increased leverage with suppliers, getting better prices, eliminating administrative duplication, allowing purchasers to develop specialized

Global progression in the purchasing function

- Domestic purchasing only
- Foreign buying based on need
- Foreign buying as part of a procurement strategy
- Integration of global procurement strategy

knowledge in purchasing techniques, reducing the number of orders processed, and enabling purchasing to build solid supplier relationships.[57]

Companies pursue five major sourcing strategies as they move into phases 3 and 4 in the preceding list (foreign buying as part of procurement strategy and integration of global procurement strategy):

Sourcing strategies in the global context

- Assign domestic buyers for foreign purchasing
- Use foreign subsidiaries or business agents
- Establish international purchasing offices
- Assign the responsibility for global sourcing to a specific business unit or units
- Integrate and coordinate worldwide sourcing

1. Assign domestic buyer(s) for international purchasing
2. Use foreign subsidiaries or business agents
3. Establish international purchasing offices
4. Assign the responsibility for global sourcing to a specific business unit or units
5. Integrate and coordinate worldwide sourcing[58]

These strategies move from the simple to the more complex. Companies start by using a domestic buyer and progress all the way to integrating and coordinating world-wide sourcing into the company's purchasing decisions so that there is no difference between domestic and foreign sources. Some companies are going even further than the last step and are coordinating worldwide purchasing with competitor companies. Two automakers, Nissan and Renault, have been able to save millions of dollars in production costs by entering into joint purchasing agreements with each other. Approximately 40 percent of the parts the companies use in their vehicles are the same, and the two are looking to increase this amount to 70 percent to achieve further cost reductions.[59]

Figure 17.9 summarizes some of the key concepts in the preceding discussion in terms of selecting the best supplier. The key is for managers to select the best supplier, establish a solid relationship, and continuously evaluate the supplier's performance to ensure the best price, quality, and on-time delivery possible.

The use of the Internet in purchasing (termed *e-sourcing*) is growing in popularity. A study based on the responses of U.S. and European companies found that those that use e-sourcing negotiate a 14.3 percent reduction in goods and services costs, cut sourcing cycles in half, reduce sourcing administrative costs by 60 percent, and shorten time-to-market cycles by 10 to 15 percent.[60]

INVENTORY MANAGEMENT

Distance, time, and uncertainty in foreign environments cause foreign sourcing to complicate inventory management.

Whether a company decides to source parts from inside or outside the company or from domestic or foreign sources, it needs to manage the flow and storage of inventory. This is true of raw materials and parts sourced from suppliers, work-in-process and finished-goods inventory inside the manufacturing plant, and finished goods stored at a distribution center, such as the centralized European warehouse for Samsonite. As noted in the example of the Kia Sorrento, if the company sources parts from a variety of suppliers from around the world, distance, time, and the uncertainty of the international political and economic environment can make it difficult for managers to determine correct reorder points for the manufacturing process.

Just-in-Time Systems

JIT—sourcing raw materials and parts just as they are needed in the manufacturing process

One reason why companies might hesitate when considering whether to source parts from foreign suppliers is because of just-in-time (JIT) inventory systems. "JIT systems focus on reducing inefficiency and unproductive time in the production process to improve continuously the process and the quality of the product or service."[61] The JIT system gets raw materials, parts, and components to the buyer "just in time" for use, sparing companies the cost of storing large inventories. That is what Dell hoped to accomplish in its Irish plant by having parts delivered just as they were to enter the production process and then go out the door to the consumers as soon as the computers were built. However, the use of JIT means that parts must have few defects and must arrive on time. That is why companies need to develop solid supplier relationships to

FIGURE 17.9   ASSESSING THE ORGANIZATION'S GLOBAL SOURCING NEEDS AND STRATEGY

Source: Reprinted with permission from the publisher, the Institute for Supply Management, Inc. TM, "The Globalization of the Supply Environment." *The Supply Management Environment,* by Stanley E. Fawcett, 2000, Vol. 2, p. 53.

STEPS IN GLOBAL SOURCING PROCESS	QUESTIONS ANSWERED AT EACH STEP
Evaluate operating and competitive environments.	Is global sourcing a valuable competitive option? Can global sourcing help us better meet customers' real needs?
Define scope of international purchasing effort.	How intensive and extensive does the global sourcing effort need to be? • What items should we global source? • What structure and infrastructure are needed? • What skills will our purchasers need? • Does a cost/benefit analysis support the selected scope?
Identify and evaluate potential suppliers worldwide.	Who are the best suppliers for each item? Where are they located worldwide? Can they provide world-class support to our global operations? What is their total order performance? • Total cost • Delivery • Quality • Innovation • Responsiveness
Determine appropriate nature of buyer-supplier relationship.	Given our needs, the supplier's location and capabilities, and the channel's logistical challenges, what type of buyer-supplier relationship should we establish?
Request/evaluate proposals from suppliers.	Are the proposals truly comparable at the total-ownership level? Who is the best supplier in the short term? Long term?
Select "best" supplier, establish contract terms and conditions, and build desired relationship.	Is future negotiation needed? Are roles and responsibilities clearly understood? Are performance expectations clearly stated and understood? How are resources, risks, and rewards going to be shared?
Continual reevaluation of implementation status, requirements, and capabilities.	Is the buyer-supplier relationship fully established? Effective? Is the selected supplier performing at world-class standards? Based on changes in our own operations, our competitive requirements, and our customers' needs, does this relationship still make sense?

ensure good quality and delivery times if JIT is to work and why industrial clustering is a popular way of linking closer with suppliers.

Foreign sourcing can create big risks for companies that use JIT, because interruptions in the supply line can cause havoc. Foreign companies are becoming experts at meeting the requirements of JIT—ships that take two weeks to cross the Pacific dock within an hour of scheduled arrival, and factories are able to more easily fill small orders. However, because of distances alone, the supply chain is open to more problems and delays.[62] Companies such as Toyota that have set up manufacturing and assembly facilities overseas to service local markets have practically forced their domestic parts suppliers to move overseas as well in order to allow Toyota to continue with JIT manufacturing. That is why so many Japanese parts suppliers, such as DENSO, a major Toyota supplier, have moved to the United States and Mexico to be near their major customers. (See the DENSO case at the end of the chapter.)

A company's inventory management strategy—especially in terms of stock sizes and whether or not JIT will be used—determines frequency of needed shipments. The less frequent the delivery, the more likely the need to store inventory somewhere. Because JIT requires delivery just as the inventory is to be used, some concession must be made for

It is hard to combine foreign sourcing and JIT production without having safety stocks of inventory on hand, which defeats the concept of JIT.

inventory arriving from foreign suppliers. Sometimes that means adjusting the arrival time to a few days before use rather than a few hours. Kawasaki Motors Corp., U.S.A. carries a minimum of three days' inventory on parts coming from Japan, with an average inventory of five days.[63]

Quality of inventory is important, because inventory with significant amounts of defects will create problems for JIT. If the buyer has to purchase more because of expected defects, there will be not only wasted inventory but also higher carrying costs. Nike contracts out the manufacture of shoes to China, but it also has a Nike team on hand at the factories in China to ensure high-quality manufacturing. The geographic distance between buyer and supplier, language differences, and cultural differences can increase the time it takes to educate suppliers on how to supply products of high quality.[64]

JIT typically implies sole sourcing for specific parts in order to get the supplier to commit to the stringent delivery and quality requirements inherent in JIT. However, if the only supplier is a foreign supplier, it would be too risky to permit just one supplier. That means cultivating multiple suppliers, at least one of which may be a foreign supplier. The problem is that using multiple suppliers may preclude the buyer from getting volume pricing from the supplier. One strategy is that buyers may use a sole supplier for all but critical inputs. Then it is best to cultivate solid secondary suppliers.[65]

Foreign Trade Zones

Foreign trade zones (FTZs)— special locations for storing domestic and imported inventory in order to avoid paying duties until the inventory is used in production or sold

In recent years, **foreign trade zones (FTZs)** have become more popular as an intermediate step in the process between import and final use. FTZs are areas in which domestic and imported merchandise can be stored, inspected, and manufactured free from formal customs procedures until the goods leave the zones. The zones are intended to encourage companies to locate in the country by allowing them to defer duties, pay fewer duties, or avoid certain duties completely. Sometimes inventory is stored in an FTZ until it needs to be used for domestic manufacture. As noted earlier, one of the problems with JIT is the length of the supply line when relying on global sourcing, possibly causing either the buyer or the supplier to stockpile inventory somewhere until it is needed in the manufacturing process. One place to stockpile inventory is in a warehouse in an FTZ.

FTZs can be general-purpose zones or subzones. A general-purpose zone usually is established near a port of entry, such as a shipping port, a border crossing, or an airport, and it usually consists of a distribution facility or an industrial park. A subzone usually is physically separate from a general-purpose zone but is under the same administrative structure. Since 1982, the major growth in FTZs has been in subzones rather than in general-purpose zones because companies have sought to defer duties on parts that are foreign sourced until they need to be used in the production process. There are currently 250 general-purpose zones and 450 subzones in the U.S. For example, the major growth in subzones in the United States has been in the automobile industry, especially in the Midwest. Subzone activity is spreading to other industries, especially to shipbuilding, pharmaceuticals, and home appliances, and it is becoming more heavily oriented to manufacturing and assembly than was originally envisioned. Merchandise in U.S. FTZ's may be assembled, exhibited, cleaned, manipulated, manufactured, mixed, processed, relabeled, repackaged, repaired, salvaged, sampled, stored, tested, displayed, and destroyed.[66]

FTZs are used worldwide. In Japan, they are being established for the benefit of foreign companies exporting products to that country. Japanese zones serve as warehousing and repackaging facilities at which companies can display consumer goods for demonstration to Japanese buyers.[67]

In the United States, there are FTZ projects in 50 states and Puerto Rico, $246.9 billion a year in merchandise is handled in FTZs, and $18.8 billion is exported from FTZs each year.[68] FTZs in the United States have been used primarily as a means of providing greater flexibility as to when and how customs duties are paid. However, their use in the export business has been expanding. The exports for which these FTZs are used fall into one of the following categories:

- Foreign goods transshipped through U.S. zones to third countries
- Foreign goods processed in U.S. zones and then transshipped abroad
- Foreign goods processed or assembled in U.S. zones with some domestic materials and parts, then reexported
- Goods produced wholly of foreign content in U.S. zones and then exported
- Domestic goods moved into a U.S. zone to achieve export status prior to their actual exportation[69]

Transportation Networks

For a firm, the transportation of goods in an international context is extremely complicated in terms of documentation, choice of carrier (air or ocean), and the decision on whether to establish its own transportation department or outsource to a third-party intermediary. Transportation is one of the key elements of a logistics system. The key is to link together suppliers and manufacturers on the one hand and manufacturers and final consumers on the other. Along the way, the company has to determine what its warehouse configuration will be. For example, McDonald's provides food items to its franchises around the world. It has warehouses in different countries to service different geographic areas. In the Samsonite case, there was no discussion of the issues surrounding transportation and warehousing from suppliers to Samsonite's factories, but the movement of goods from factories to retailers was an important issue.

Third-party intermediaries are an important dimension of transportation networks. Outsourcing of both manufacturing and other supply-chain functions is becoming increasingly popular. In a recent survey of *Fortune* 500 companies, 83 percent acknowledged they outsource one or more logistics functions to third-party providers.[70]

For example, Panalpina is a Swiss forwarding and logistics services provider that focuses on intercontinental airfreight and sea freight. However, it specializes in integrated forwarding, which means that instead of providing limited standardized options to its customers, Panalpina offers globally integrated, flexible, and customized solutions to their individual supply chain networks.[71] Using its main hub in Luxembourg to connect to 500 branches in 80 countries throughout the world, as well as to partners in another 60 countries, Panalpina seeks to simplify the complexity of its customers' supply chains by handling their transportation, distribution, customs brokerage, warehousing, and inventory control and also provides door-to-door transport insurance and real-time track and trace systems.[72] One company that Panalpina provides such services to is IBM and its operations in Latin America. Through its selected airfreight services provider, ASB-Air, and through the management of its local branches, Panalpina coordinates vehicles to pick up IBM products in Europe and to transport them to its cargo hub in Luxembourg. From there, the goods travel by air to its cargo center in Miami. In Miami, products destined for various locations in South America are split and reconsolidated into pallets that are then loaded directly into Panalpina space-controlled aircraft and transferred to its own company warehouses operated by its own staff. The personnel in the warehouses complete all customs details, taking advantage of the onsite offices of customs authorities, and update the company's information systems with current status messages. Once customs has been cleared, an electronic data transfer is sent to IBM while the goods are shipped to IBM warehouses. Panalpina maintains control of the goods throughout the entire process, using electronic documentation and tracking to maintain real-time data and to keep IBM informed. In this example, you can see all of the elements of the transportation networks that are so essential in international logistics.[73]

The logistics management that companies like Panalpina engage in is very detail oriented, requiring the ability to gather, track, and process large quantities of information. To be effective, logistics companies need to implement key technologies, including communications technologies, satellite tracking systems, bar-coding applications, and automated materials handling systems.[74]

Transportation links together suppliers, companies, and customers.

Third-party intermediaries, such as Panalpina, are crucial in storing and transporting goods.

LOOKING TO THE FUTURE: The Role of China in the Supply Chain

As global competition increases in virtually all major industries, especially those that rely on R&D and that are sensitive to price competition, it will be important for MNEs to strengthen their supply chain at all levels. It is clear that China will emerge as an important element in all levels of the supply chain because of low manufacturing wages and investments in capital equipment that allow it to manufacture higher level products with better quality. China will be important as a location for outsourcing to third-party suppliers, as is the case in furniture, textiles, and possibly auto parts. In addition, it will become increasingly important as a location for manufacturing as MNEs search for ways to drive down costs in order to be more competitive in the global economy.

However, two things will temper the future move to China. One is quality. Although Chinese quality is improving, it is still not at the level that the Japanese require for zero defects, TQM, and JIT. However, it would be a mistake to assume that the Chinese will not be able to improve their quality to worldwide standards as they gain more experience and as they use proprietary process technology transferred by MNEs to China. Just as Honda was able to transfer auto assembly technology to the U.S. and achieve high standards of quality, so will companies be able to transfer technology to China and achieve similar results. The second tempering factor is the future of the yuan. If the currency floats and reaches a significantly higher level against the dollar, China may lose some of its cost advantage. However, it is doubtful that the Chinese government will allow that to happen. What is certain is that China is a force to be reckoned with, and companies must develop a China strategy as part of their sourcing, purchasing, and manufacturing strategy.

SUMMARY

- A company's supply chain encompasses the coordination of materials, information, and funds from the initial raw materials supplier to the ultimate customer.
- Logistics, or materials management, is that part of the supply chain process that plans, implements, and controls the efficient, effective flow and storage of goods, services, and related information from the point of origin to the point of consumption in order to meet customers' requirements.
- The success of a global manufacturing strategy depends on compatibility, configuration, coordination, and control.
- Cost-minimization strategies and the drive for global efficiencies often force MNEs offshore to low-cost manufacturing areas, especially in Asia and Eastern Europe.
- Three broad categories of manufacturing configuration are one centralized facility, regional facilities, and multidomestic facilities.
- The key to making a global supply chain system work is information. Companies are rapidly turning to the Internet as a way to link suppliers with manufacturing and eventually with end-use customers.
- Quality is defined as meeting or exceeding the expectations of customers. Quality standards can be general (ISO 9000), industry-specific, or company-specific (AQL, zero defects, TQM, and Six Sigma).
- Total quality management (TQM) is a process that stresses customer satisfaction, employee involvement, and continuous improvements in quality.
- Global sourcing is the process of a firm having raw materials and parts supplied to it from domestic and foreign sources.

- Domestic sourcing allows the company to avoid problems related to language, culture, currency, tariffs, and so forth. Foreign sourcing allows the company to reduce costs and improve quality, among other things.

- Under the make or buy decision, companies have to decide if they will make their own parts or buy them from an independent company.

- Companies go through different purchasing phases as they become more committed to global sourcing.

- When a company sources parts from suppliers around the world, distance, time, and the uncertainty of the international political and economic environment can make it difficult for managers to manage inventory flows accurately.

- Just-in-time focuses on reducing inefficiency and unproductive time in the production process to continuously improve the process and quality of the product or service.

- The transportation system links together suppliers with manufacturers and manufacturers with customers.

Denso Corporation and Global Supplier Relations[75] C A S E

In 2005, DENSO Corporation, the Japanese auto parts supplier formerly known as NIP-PONDENSO, was struggling to determine what strategy it should pursue to succeed and move forward into the twenty-first century. Should it continue to be tightly linked to Toyota as its major parts supplier? Or, given that it makes products other than auto parts, should it become less dependent on the automotive industry in general and on Toyota in particular? Should it continue to invest so many resources in Japan even though economic growth is next to zero and signs of recovery are minimal? And because the demand for its product varies so much from customer to customer, DENSO also wondered how it could better manage its production and inventory levels. As the CEO stated, "Component suppliers are facing ever-tougher standards as automobile manufacturers fight a global battle for survival."

Background on DENSO

DENSO is the third-largest auto parts supplier in the world, just behind Robert Bosch of Germany and Delphi of the United States. Prior to 1949, it was a part of Toyota, but then it spun off into a separate company even though Toyota still retains 25 percent of DENSO's issued stock and is DENSO's major customer. Thus, DENSO is part of the Toyota *keiretsu* that includes companies in automotive parts, steel, precision machinery, automatic looms, textiles, household wares, office and housing units, and other products. As Map 17.2 shows, DENSO's world headquarters and most of its domestic manufacturing facilities are in Aichi prefecture on the east coast of Japan and close to Toyota City, the headquarters for Toyota Corporation. Toyota's domestic manufacturing plants are also located in Aichi prefecture, so there is a close proximity between DENSO and Toyota plants.

Although DENSO is a major supplier to Toyota, it supplies parts to all companies manufacturing automobiles in Japan. In addition, it is the most global of the Japanese auto parts companies. DENSO's consolidated sales in FY 2005 were $26.2 billion, and DENSO generated 55.5 percent of its revenues from customers in Japan, 20.8 percent from the Americas, 13.1 percent from Europe, and 10.3 percent from Asia and Oceania. DENSO employs 104,000 people in 31 countries and regions, including Japan.

Map 17.3 shows that DENSO has production facilities in every world region except Africa and Russia. DENSO initially expanded overseas to supply Toyota's overseas plants, but now it supplies other auto companies overseas as well.

MAP 17.2   DENSO Corporation in Japan

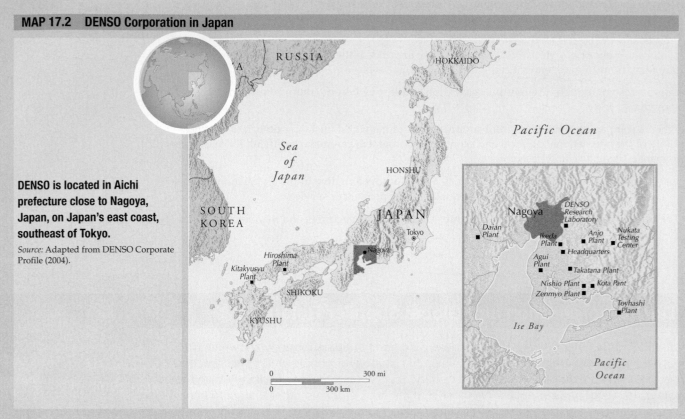

DENSO is located in Aichi prefecture close to Nagoya, Japan, on Japan's east coast, southeast of Tokyo.

Source: Adapted from DENSO Corporate Profile (2004).

MAP 17.3   DENSO'S Global Network

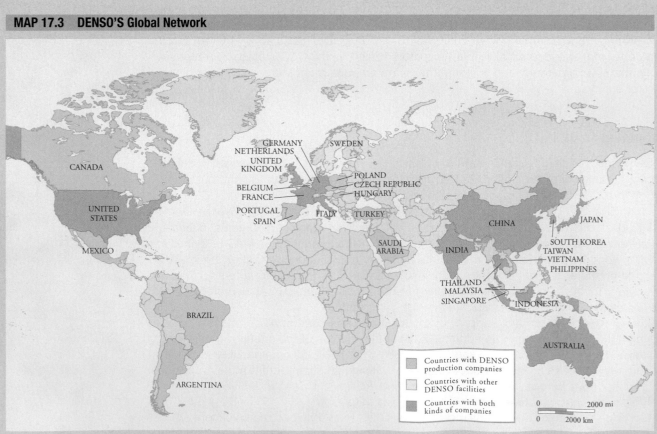

With production facilities in almost every world region, DENSO is Japan's most global auto parts company.

Source: Adapted from DENSO Corporation Profile (2004).

Quality Standards and Manufacturing Practices of DENSO

DENSO has to meet tough quality standards. First, it needs to satisfy Toyota's rigid quality standards by using TQM and by striving for zero defects. Second, it complies with both ISO 9001 and QS9000 certification so that it can qualify as a supplier for auto manufacturers in Europe and North America. QS9000 is a quality standard specifically for the auto industry. Chrysler (now DaimlerChrysler), Ford, and General Motors established QS9000 in 1994 to provide requirements and measurables (events that can be quantified and specific measures that can be used to describe those events) for the automotive industry. QS9000 is derived from ISO 9001, but it is more specific to the auto industry. Under the guidelines, suppliers must adapt their quality systems to meet the expectations of the automakers. QS9000 is required for any supplier of Ford, General Motors, and DaimlerChrysler.

DENSO separates its production facilities into a parts manufacturing area, a subassembly area, and a final assembly area. It uses a flexible and automated assembly line with significant robotics. DENSO's Takatana plant assembles instrument panels for its customers. DENSO has created a "green belt" around the plant, perhaps so workers can look at trees, not other factories. It also has invested heavily in an information system for production control, even though it traditionally has used and is currently using a *kanban* system for Toyota. The *kanban* system is a JIT system pioneered by Toyota. *Kanban* literally means "card" or "visible record" in Japanese. The *kanban* cards are used to control the flow of production through a factory. For example, Toyota uses *kanban* in the assembly of a Lexus at its Tsutsumi assembly plant just south of Toyota City, and DENSO supplies automatic air conditioners to the plant on a JIT basis. In the *kanban* system used by Toyota, DENSO ships air conditioners to the Tsutsumi plant just before they need to go into production. They are kept in a bin that has a card attached to it identifying the number of air conditioners in the bin. When the assembly process begins, a production-order card signifies that a bin of air conditioners needs to be moved to the assembly line. When the bin is emptied, it is moved to a storage area and replaced with a full bin. The *kanban* card is removed from the empty bin and is used to order a replacement from DENSO. DENSO ships parts to Toyota approximately 8 to 10 times a day, 24 hours a day. In order to service Toyota, DENSO keeps roughly a five-day inventory of some parts.

The same process used by Toyota is also used by DENSO to manufacture the air conditioner. An air conditioner requires an electronic control unit, a cabin air temperature sensor, an ambient air temperature sensor, a solar radiation sensor, a coolant temperature sensor, an evaporator sensor, a compressor with magnetic clutch, a heater core, a condenser, expansion valves, and so on. DENSO manufactures some of these parts, and outside suppliers manufacture others. DENSO's assembly plant for its instrument clusters (speedometer, etc.) used to run on one 8-hour shift, which was at about 80 percent capacity. However, its parts production was running two shifts.

DENSO has pretty good labor relations in Japan, because its labor union is a company union. However, DENSO management still maintains that salary negotiations are pretty tough. Workers are hired for life and paid a salary, which is based on a mixture of age, expertise, and performance. There is a relatively small wage gap among DENSO employees. Employee performance is evaluated every six months, with a bonus paid every six months.

DENSO's Future

In assessing DENSO's strengths and weaknesses, management feels that its production and production training are very strong. However, it needs to further improve its R&D if it is going to continue to move forward. The key is to continue to develop new products, both inside and outside the auto industry, if it is going to continue to generate revenues. DENSO still engages in lifetime employment, and it feels that this employment system helps it to improve continuously.

Domestic demand in Japan has been relatively flat since the mid-1990s, which has made it difficult for DENSO to keep generating growth in revenues. Because it is dependent on the auto industry, its fortunes rise and fall with those of Toyota and its other key customers. Fortunately for DENSO, Toyota's sales in Japan began to pick up in 2003 and 2004, and DENSO's revenue grew 24.6 percent in FY 2004, largely due to Toyota's recovery and its increased demand for DENSO parts. It is making a big push to sell to DaimlerChrysler, because it is the third-largest auto company in the world, just behind GM and Ford. Approximately 44.5 percent of DENSO's sales come from overseas customers. DENSO's plants in the United States and Mexico service the U.S. market. As a whole, DENSO is still growing, but demand varies for different divisions. The electronics division, for example, is growing, so DENSO management has been shifting employment to that division. Because of lifetime employment, DENSO does not want to lay off workers, so it finds new product lines to which it can shift workers. Then it retrains them for the job. Each of its plants has an on-site education facility. Usually, however, DENSO's employees stay in one division until they retire.

A major challenge DENSO faces is that Toyota is still based on a *kanban* system, even though the rest of the industry is moving away from *kanban.* Toyota uses forecasts, which can help DENSO plan its production, but the final production cycle is based on *kanban.* Mitsubishi and Honda, however, request products based on forecast of demand and do not use *kanban.* Their final orders are placed three days in advance, and they have much more fluctuation in demand than does Toyota. Toyota tries to schedule a relatively flat production schedule, meaning that there is not a great deal of fluctuation in its demand, whereas the demand from Mitsubishi and Honda fluctuates a great deal. Even though DENSO supplies all major auto companies in Japan, it relies on Toyota for 56 percent of its revenues.

The U.S. subsidiary of DENSO purchased supply chain management software to help it in demand planning, forecasting and scheduling, order management, and shipping control. This purchase will help DENSO International America to fulfill the needs of all its customers, not just Toyota. An alternative to *kanban* is MRP—material requirements planning. MRP is a computerized information system that addresses complex inventory situations like DENSO's (manufacturing parts for its own use as well as for several different auto companies). MRP calculates the demand for parts from the production schedules of the companies that use the parts. DENSO's dilemma is that some of its customers forecast demand, but Toyota uses *kanban* and requires delivery of parts when it empties its bins. DENSO is hoping that it can establish a good MRP or similar computer-based information system to solve the complexity of producing so many parts for so many different companies.

Global Challenges

While relying heavily on Japan and Toyota for revenues, DENSO is working hard to become an international company. It currently develops its manufacturing systems and equipment in Japan and then exports them to the rest of the world and allows local facilities to make adjustments. However, DENSO is now looking more carefully at the entire supply chain in its four major regions—Japan, North and South America, Europe, and Australia and Asia—and it is trying to design systems that will take into consideration the broader needs of the company so as to minimize the adjustments that have to be made. It has invested heavily in North America to supply Toyota and other major customers, but there are two areas of the world that will require significant expansion in the coming decade: China and Europe.

China is important for a number of reasons. First, the car market in China is growing rapidly, and most of the large auto companies, including Toyota, are investing there. For DENSO to supply its customers, it needs to be in China, or it will lose market share to local Chinese auto parts manufacturers. In addition, Toyota has made it clear that it wants DENSO and other key suppliers to benchmark prices against China's cheaper suppliers. If DENSO cannot match Chinese prices and still maintain quality, it will force Toyota to use more and more non-*keiretsu* suppliers. In 2005, DENSO increased its presence in China by investing $1 million to establish a new plant in Tianjin, China, where Toyota also has a plant, to produce car navigation systems. DENSO now has over a dozen production facilities in China and is expected to expand even more.

Europe is also important, because DENSO is such a small player in the market. The elimination of barriers against Japanese auto sales in Europe has spurred an increase in European investment by Toyota and other Japanese companies. Given DENSO's limited presence in Europe, Toyota was forced to enter into a joint venture with Peugeot in order to get access to its parts suppliers. However, DENSO is excited about its potential in Europe and has established engineering centers in Germany, the U.K., Italy, and Sweden to accompany its production centers in Europe, including the Czech Republic, Hungary, and Italy. DENSO is working hard to reduce two sales gaps in Europe—the usage gap and distribution gap. DENSO is a world leader in car air conditioners and navigation systems, two areas where installation rates in Europe are quite low and where DENSO thinks it can expand sales significantly, thus reducing the usage gap. The distribution gap represents sales lost to competitors, and DENSO feels that its relatively small market share in Europe can be expanded as it establishes more plants in Europe and designs and manufactures components that meet the specific needs of European automakers. Toyota's expansion into Europe will be a major impetus for DENSO's growth there.

QUESTIONS

1. What is driving DENSO's globalization efforts, and what do you see as the major challenges confronting the company?
2. What challenges will DENSO face in maintaining its commitment to quality in the future?
3. From the standpoint of inventory management, why is it going to be difficult for DENSO to supply companies other than Toyota?

CHAPTER NOTES

1 The information in this case is from the following sources: F. De Beule and D. Van Den Bulcke, "The International Supply Chain Management of Samsonite Europe," Discussion Paper No. 1998/E/34, Centre for International Management and Development, University of Antwerp (1998); "Samsonite History" (2002): www.samsonite.com; "Company Briefing Book," *Wall Street Journal*, www.wsj.com (January 27, 2000); "Tüv Essen," http://tuvessen.com/; *Samsonite Quarterly Report*, SEC form 10-Q (2002); and "Samsonite Introduces POINT A Franchise Concept," Samsonite Web site (October 1, 2002): www.samsonite.com.

2 "Energizing the Supply Chain—Trends and Issues in Supply Chain Management," *Deloitte Consulting LLC* (1998/99): 7.

3 Deloitte & Touche, "Energizing the Supply Chain," *The Review* (January 17, 2000): 1.

4 Stanley Fawcett, "Supply Chain Management: Competing Through Integration," in Tom L. Beauchamp and Norman E. Bowie, eds., *Ethical Theory and Business* (Upper Saddle River, NJ: Prentice Hall, 1993), 514.

5 Council of Supply Chain Management Professionals, "Supply Chain Management/Logistics Management Definitions," http://www.cscmp.org/Website/AboutCSCMP/Definitions/Definitions.asp. Accessed June 11, 2005.

6 *AMR Research* (2004). "The AMR Research Supply Chain Top 25 and the New Trillion Dollar Opportunity." http://www.i2.com/assets/pdf/resources/analyst_papers/The_AMR_Research_Supply_Chain_Top_25.pdf

7 Homin Chen and Tain-Jy Chen, "Network Linkages and Location Choice in Foreign Direct Investment," *Journal of International Business Studies* 29, no. 3 (Third Quarter 1998): 447.

8 For a discussion of firm-specific advantages, location-specific advantages, and internalization, see the following: John H. Dunning, *International Production and the Multinational Enterprise* (London: Allen & Unwin, 1981); Peter Buckley & Mark Casson, *The Future of the Multinational Enterprise* (London: Macmillan Press, 1976); and Peter Caves, "International Corporations: The Industrial Economics of Foreign Investment," *Economica* 56 (1971): 279–93.

9 Stanley E. Fawcett and Anthony S. Roath, "The Viability of Mexican Production Sharing: Assessing the Four Cs of Strategic Fit," *Urbana* 3, no. 1 (1996): 29.

10 See S. C. Wheelwright, "Reflecting Corporate Strategy in Manufacturing Decisions," *Business Horizons* 21 (February 1978); S. C. Wheelwright, "Manufacturing Strategy: Defining the Missing Link," *Strategic Management Journal* 5 (1984): 77–91; Frank DuBois, Brian Toyne, and Michael D. Oliff, "International

Manufacturing Strategies of U.S. Multinationals: A Conceptual Framework Based on a Four-Industry Study," *Journal of International Business Studies* 24, no. 2 (Second Quarter 1993): 313–14; and Robert H. Hayes, Steven C. Wheelwright, and Kim B. Clark, *Dynamic Manufacturing* (New York: Free Press, 1988), 10–11.

11 Peter Coy, "Just How Cheap Is Chinese Labor?" *Business Week* (December 13, 2004): 46.

12 Karby Leggett and Peter Wonacott, "Surge in Exports from China Gives a Jolt to Global Industry," *Wall Street Journal* (October 10, 2002): www.wsj.com.

13 "The Misery of Manufacturing," *The Economist* (September 27, 2003): 61–62.

14 Norihiko Shirouzu, "Toyota to Build More of Its Autos in North America," *Wall Street Journal* (May 10, 2005): A.2.

15 "(Still) Made in Japan," *The Economist* (April 10, 2004): 57–59.

16 Norihiko Shirouzu and Jathon Sapsford, "Heavy Load—For Toyota, a New Small Truck Carries Hopes for Topping GM," *Wall Street Journal* (May 12, 2005): A.1.

17 Michael E. McGrath and Richard W. Hoole, "Manufacturing's New Economies of Scale," *Harvard Business Review* (May–June 1992): 94.

18 Fawcett and Roath, op. cit., 29.

19 Deloitte Counseling, "Energizing the Supply Chain: Trends and Issues in Supply Chain Management" (2000): www.dc.com.

20 Richard Karpinski, "Wal-Mart Mandates Secure, Internet-Based EDI for Suppliers," Internetweek.com (September 12, 2002): http://www.internetweek.com/supplyChain/INW20020912S0011.

21 Wal-Mart, *2005 Annual Report.*

22 "You'll Never Walk Alone," in "Business and the Internet: A Survey," *The Economist* (June 26, 1999): 11–12.

23 Kevin Reilly, "Over 20% of Small Manufacturing and Services Companies Are Evaluating ERP for the First Time in the Next 12 Months," *AMR Research* (May 23, 2005): www.amrreaserch.com.

24 Check the annual report on www.dell.com (2002) and as updated in subsequent reports.

25 Karpinski, op. cit.

26 "Worldwide Internet Users Will Top 1 Billion in 2005," *Computer Industry Almanac Inc.* (September 3, 2005): http://www.c-i-a.com/pr0904.htm.

27 "How E-Biz Rose, Fell, and Will Rise Anew," *Business Week* (May 13, 2002): http://www.businessweek.com.

28 "You'll Never Walk Alone," op. cit., 17.

29 Cindy Cronin, "Five Success Factors for Private Trading Exchanges," *e-Business Advisor Magazine* (August 2001): http://businessadvisor.us/Articles.nsf/aid/CRONC01 [new link is http://e-businessadvisor.com/].

30 Ibid., 17, 20.

31 Lee J. Krajewski and Larry P. Ritzman, *Operations Management: Strategy and Analysis*, 4th ed. (Reading, MA: Addison-Wesley, 1996), 141–42.

32 See "Detroit Is Cruising for Quality," *Business Week* (September 3, 2001): www.businessweek.com; and Todd Zaun et al., "Auto Makers Get More Mileage from Low-Cost Plants Abroad," *Wall Street Journal* (July 31, 2002): www.wsj.com.

33 J. D. Power & Associates Press Releases, "2004 Vehicle Dependability Study" and "2004 Initial Quality Study," http://www.jdpower.com/cc/global/pr/search.asp. Accessed June 13, 2005.

34 Hayes, Wheelwright, and Clark, op. cit., 17.

35 Krajewski and Ritzman, op. cit., 140.

36 Ibid., 156.

37 http://www.sixsigmasurvival.com/SixSigmaDefinition.html.

38 PricewaterhouseCoopers, "Six Sigma and Internal Control" (2002): http://www.pwcglobal.com/extweb/manissue.nsf/DocID/A09497E3D72ABCD085256B92005E627D.

39 International Organization for Standardization, "What Makes ISO 9000 and ISO 14000 So Special," http://www.iso.org/iso/en/aboutiso/introduction/index.html#twentytwo.

40 See Jonathan B. Levine, "Want EC Business? You Have Two Choices," *Business Week* (October 19, 1992): 58; and The International Organization for Standardization home page (2005): http://www.iso.org/iso/en/iso9000-14000/understand/selection_use/selection_use.html.

41 Sarah McBride, "Kia's Audacious Sorento Plan—Foreign Parts—and Some Careful Planning—Go into Korean Car," *Wall Street Journal* (April 8, 2003): A.12.

42 Masaaki Kotabe and Glen S. Omura, "Sourcing Strategies of European and Japanese Multinationals: A Comparison," *Journal of International Business Studies* (Spring 1989): 120–22.

43 Robert M. Monczka and Robert J. Trent, "Global Sourcing: A Development Approach," *International Journal of Purchasing and Materials Management* (Spring 1991): 3.

44 R. D'Aveni and D. Ravenscraft, "Economies of Integration versus Bureaucracy Costs: Does Vertical Integration Improve Performance?" *The Academy of Management Journal* 37, no. 5 (1994): 1167–1206; O. Williamson, "Vertical Integration and Related Variations on a Transaction-Cost Theme," in J. Stiglitz and G. Mathewson, eds., *New Developments in the Analysis of Market Structure* (Cambridge, Mass.: MIT Press, 1986); and O. Williamson, *The Economic Institutions of Capitalism* (New York: The Free Press, 1985).

45 Russell Johnston and Paul R. Lawrence, "Beyond Vertical Integration—The Rise of the Value-Adding Partnership," *Harvard Business Review* (July–August 1988): 98.

46 Chester Dawson, "A 'China Price' for Toyota," *Business Week* (February 21, 2005): 50–51.

47 "Few Companies Use Outsourcing as Strategic Business Imperative," *Supply Chain Brain* (2002): www.supplychainbrain.com.

48 John McMillan, "Managing Suppliers: Incentive Systems in Japanese and U.S. Industry," *California Management Review* (Summer 1990): 38.

49 "Still Made in Japan," op. cit.

50 Ibid.

51 The above material was adapted from Pete Engardio and Bruce Einhorn, "Outsourcing Innovation," *Business Week* (March 21, 2005): 84–94.

52 Robert W. Lane, "Competing Globally, Winning Locally," speech to the Waterloo Chamber of Commerce (August 19, 2004): http://www.deere.com/en_US/compinfo/speeches/2004/040819_lane.html.

53 Joseph B. White, "Japanese Auto Makers Help Parts Suppliers Become More Efficient," *Wall Street Journal* (September 10, 1991): 1.

54 Gabriel Kahn, "Invisible Supplier Has Penney's Shirts All Buttoned Up," *Wall Street Journal* (September 11, 2003): A.1.

55 Lee Hawkins Jr., "GM Is Pushing Its U.S. Suppliers to Reduce Prices," *Wall Street Journal* (April 7, 2005): A.2.

56 Monczka and Trent, op. cit., 4–5.

57 Stanley E. Fawcett, "The Globalization of the Supply Environment." *The Supply Environment 2* (Tempe, AZ: NAPM, 2000).

58 Robert M. Monczka and Robert J. Trent, "Worldwide Sourcing: Assessment and Execution," *International Journal of Purchasing and Materials Management* (Fall 1992): 17–18.

59 Guy Anderson, "Nissan Gearing Up for a Partnership," *The Wall Street Journal* (December 8, 2004): 42.

60 Tim Minahan, "Making E-Sourcing Strategic," *The Aberdeen Group* (September 2002): http://www.aberdeen.com/ab_company/hottopics/esourcing2002/default.htm.

61 Krajewski and Ritzman, op. cit., 732.

62 Gabriel Kahn, Trish Saywell, and Quenna Sook Kim, "Backlog at West Coast Docks Keeps Chrismas Toys at Sea," *Wall Street Journal* (October 21, 2002): from the Wall Street Journal Online Edition.

63 Shawnee K. Vickery, "International Sourcing: Implications for Just-in-Time Manufacturing," *Production and Inventory Management Journal* (Third Quarter 1989): 67.

64 Ibid., p. 69.

65 Ibid., p. 70.

66 International Trade Administration, "What Activity Is Permitted in Zones?" (2005): http://ia.ita.doc.gov/ftzpage/info/activity.html.

67 "World Becomes Smaller as Japan, Central Europe Catch Zone Fever," *The Journal of Commerce* (October 1991): 6B.

68 "Information Summary," Foreign-Trade Zones Board (January 2005): http://ia.ita.doc.gov/ftzpage/ar-2003.pdf.

69 John J. DaPonte Jr., "Foreign-Trade Zones and Exports," *American Export Bulletin* (April 1978).

70 Thomas A. Foster, "The Trends Changing the Face of Logistics Outsourcing Worldwide," *Global Logistics & Supply Chain Strategies* (June 2004): http://www.glscs.com/archives/ 06.04.3pl.htm?adcode=90.

71 Interview with John D. Daniels. 2005. "Company Analysis: 'Panalpina in Latin America'"

72 "Company Information," Panalpina Web site (2005): http://www.panalpina.com/company/.

73 "Transporting IBM Products to Latin America," Panalpina Web site (2005): http://www.panalpina.com/press/casestudies/.

74 Fawcett, "The Globalization of the Supply Environment," op. cit., 11.

75 Information for this case taken from company reports from Toyota and DENSO; interviews with DENSO management; "DENSO International America Selects Future Three for E-Commerce Initiative," Future Three press release (August 6, 2002): http://www.future3.com/DENSO.htm.; Xinhua News Agency, "Nippon Denso Eyes China's Auto Parts Market" (May 18, 2002), http://www.china.org.cn/english/BAT/32841.htm, accessed June 14, 2005; "DENSO Establishes New Company in Tianjin, China to Produce Car Navagation Systems" (July 13, 2005): http://www.globaldenso.com/en/newsreleases/050613-01.html; "President's Message," DENSO FY 2004 Annual Report, www.globaldenso.com/en/investors/message/.

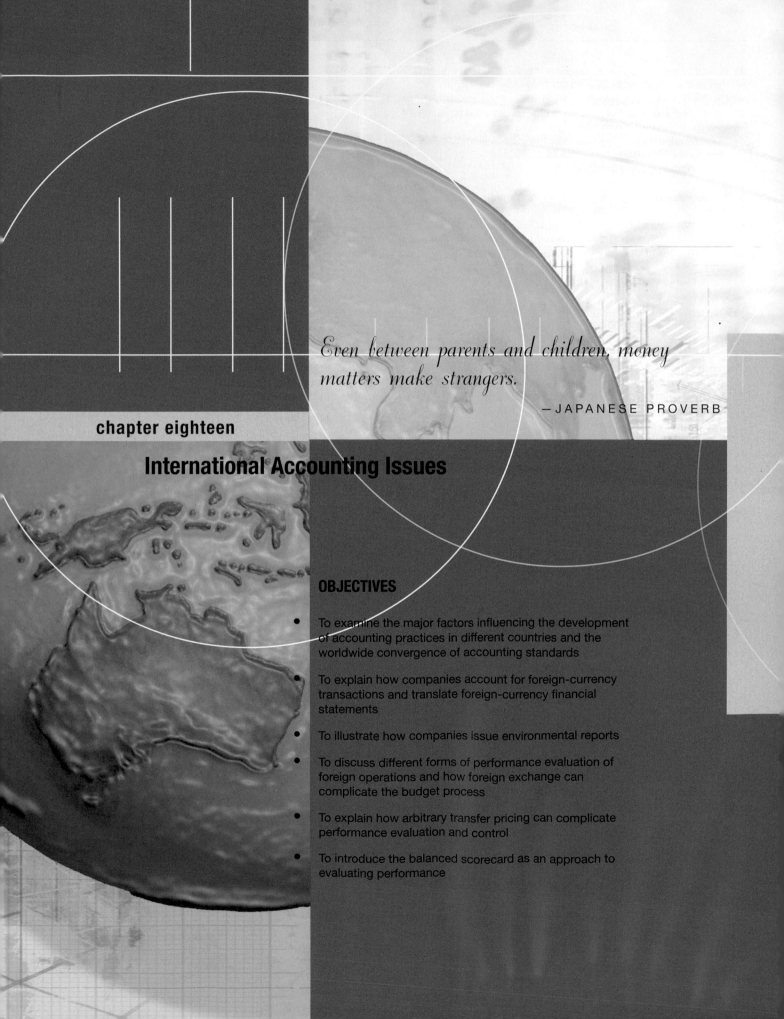

Even between parents and children, money matters make strangers.

—JAPANESE PROVERB

chapter eighteen

International Accounting Issues

OBJECTIVES

- To examine the major factors influencing the development of accounting practices in different countries and the worldwide convergence of accounting standards

- To explain how companies account for foreign-currency transactions and translate foreign-currency financial statements

- To illustrate how companies issue environmental reports

- To discuss different forms of performance evaluation of foreign operations and how foreign exchange can complicate the budget process

- To explain how arbitrary transfer pricing can complicate performance evaluation and control

- To introduce the balanced scorecard as an approach to evaluating performance

CASE: PARMALAT–EUROPE'S ENRON[1]

In January 2002, a European magazine published an article titled "Enron: Could It Happen Here?" At the time the article was published, perhaps most people outside the United States would have answered "no" to that question. In the wake of massive corporate frauds at Enron and WorldCom, there was a feeling outside the U.S. that such scandals were "an American problem" caused by the more aggressive business environment and practices in that country. However, a family-owned Italian firm was about to show the world that massive corporate scandals can happen anywhere.

After Calisto Tanzi inherited his father's company at age 22, he directed it into the production of dairy products in 1961 and created the Parmalat brand in 1963. Parmalat was the first Italian manufacturer of branded milk. In 1966, using packaging technology from Tetra Pak, Parmalat created its signature product, milk pasteurized at ultra high temperatures (UHT), giving milk a shelf life of over six months. UHT milk provided Parmalat with a technological competitiveness in the milk industry, placing Parmalat ahead of its competition. In 1970 the law permitted the sale of whole milk in grocery stores, removing the limitation of specialty milk shops. Parmalat quickly became the dominant milk supplier of Italy.

Parmalat became known as the "champion's milk" after sponsoring the Ski World Cup and world champion Formula One race car driver Nicki Lauda in the 1970s. The company moved into new markets with the production of cheese, butter, and a variety of desserts near the end of the 1970s. As it increased in popularity, Parmalat also began international expansion through acquisitions in Germany and France, which marked the beginning of a global dairy empire.

The author of such growth was Calisto Tanzi, an almost legendary figure in Italy. It was he who discovered the power of sports marketing to make Parmalat a famous brand. He had friends in important government positions who helped pass laws favoring Parmalat. A pious Catholic, Tanzi was a generous benefactor who sponsored the restoration of Parma's eleventh-century basilica and funded its professional soccer team. And he seemed modest about his achievements. He didn't smoke, drank little, and drove his own Lexus. Throughout Parmalat's expansion, Mr. Tanzi maintained a paternalistic approach to the business. "He would stand, for example, at the plant, spoon in hand, ready to taste the first sample each time a new yoghurt [flavor] was launched" (*Guardian*, 2003).

In 1989, the firm was acquired by a holding company and changed its name to Parmalat Finanziaria SpA. The milk giant showed healthy profits every year, and its balance sheet appeared strong with large amounts of cash on hand. This allowed Parmalat to go public in Italy and raise capital in the U.S. and other countries by selling shares and issuing bonds. The company used this new capital to expand into Latin America, where it dominated the dairy markets in Brazil, Argentina, Venezuela, and several other countries.

By the early 1990s, Parmalat was not only popular among grocery shoppers—investors and creditors deemed the firm a profitable business partner. Large international banks collected hefty fees by helping the company issue bonds, list stock in foreign markets, and raise capital to fund international acquisitions. As CFO Alberto Ferraris put it, "outside my office, there was always a line of bankers, asking about new business." There was only one problem—the profits reported by Parmalat were only an illusion created by a set of accounting manipulations.

ACCOUNTING ISSUES

One of the most interesting aspects of Parmalat's case is the simplicity of its fraudulent accounting. The purpose of the fraud was straightforward—to hide operating losses so as to not disappoint investors and creditors. The core of the scheme was double billing to Italian supermarkets and other retailers. By standard accounting procedures, every time product is shipped to a customer, a company records a receivable that it later expects to collect as cash. Since receivables count as sales revenue, Parmalat billed customers twice for each shipment, thus greatly enlarging its sales. The company used these inflated revenues as a means to secure loans from several international banks.

By 1995, Parmalat was losing more than $300 million annually in Latin America alone. These continued operating losses caused company executives to search for more complex ways of masking the firm's true performance. Using a trick called "off–balance sheet financing," executives set up three shell companies based in the Caribbean. These firms pretended to sell Parmalat products, and Parmalat would send them

FIGURE 18.1

Source: http://www.businesscartoons.
co.uk/4220.htm

"Benson, have you been dressing up these company accounts again?"

fake invoices and charge costs and fees to make the "sales" look legitimate. Then Parmalat would write out a credit note for the amount the subsidiaries supposedly owed it and take that to banks to raise money. Off-balance sheet financing was also used to hide debts. The company transferred over half of its liabilities to the books of small subsidiaries based in offshore tax havens such as the Cayman Islands. This allowed Parmalat to present a "healthy" balance sheet and a profitable income statement to investors and creditors by hiding large amounts of debt and overstating sales revenue. In 2002, Parmalat reported liabilities of close to $8 billion on its consolidated balance sheet. In reality, the company had roughly $14 billion in debt.

Taking advantage of its image, Parmalat issued bonds in the U.S. and Europe, which were backed up by falsified assets, especially cash. "It was a reversal of logic," said the chief investigating magistrate after the scheme was discovered. Usually, companies take on debt to grow. But in Parmalat's case, "they had to grow to hide the debt." In other words, the company would obtain loans to pay off previous loans. Investigators report that without the accounting manipulations, the company would have reported operating losses every year between 1990 and 2003.

The circle of hiding operating losses by incurring increasingly larger amounts of debt eventually became hard to sustain. To perpetuate the fraud, Parmalat needed to continue incurring debt, paying interest on old debts with no real cash of its own, and finding new ways to create false sales. Alberto Ferraris, who was appointed CFO in March 2003, mentioned that "he couldn't understand why the company was paying so much to service its debt; the interest payments seemed far higher than warranted for the €5.4 billion in debt on the books." By the late 1990s, auditors in Argentina and Brazil raised several red flags that pointed to problems with Parmalat's accounting. In early December 2003, the company failed to make a €150 million bond payment. This puzzled those familiar with the company because, according to the 2002 financial statements, Parmalat had plenty of cash on hand.

The fraud became public on December 19, 2003, when Grant Thornton, the company's auditor, made an interesting discovery. While auditing Bonlat, a fully owned subsidiary of Parmalat based in the Cayman Islands, the auditors contacted Bank of America to confirm a letter held by Bonlat in which Bank of America allegedly certified that the company had €3.95 billion in cash. Bank of America responded that such an account didn't exist. This finding led to a serious investigation into the financial position of Parmalat, which uncovered the accounting tricks described previously.

THE CONSEQUENCES

Parmalat filed for bankruptcy protection on December 24, 2003. CEO Calisto Tanzi resigned and was detained by Italian authorities three days later and sent to prison. Also accused of fraud are Fausto Tonna, CFO during most of the period under investigation; Stefano Tanzi and Lorenza Penca, son and daughter of Calisto Tanzi; and other key employees believed to have been involved in the scheme. Initially, it was thought that misstatements were created only to hide operating losses; however, more recent information has shown that the Tanzi family financially benefited from the fraud. For example, Calisto Tanzi "admitted shifting some $620 million from Parmalat to his family's travel businesses."

Enrico Bondi was appointed by the government as CEO of Parmalat to direct recovery efforts. As part of his campaign, he has brought lawsuits against Grant Thornton and Deloitte, the auditors, for not performing the audit with proper care and not bringing their suspicions to the attention of management. Additionally, Bondi is suing major international banks, such as Bank of America, Credit Suisse First Boston, Citigroup, and Deutsche Bank. The lawsuits accuse the banks of ignoring the fraud in order to obtain fees from doing business with Parmalat. As mentioned above, these banks were instrumental in helping the company raise capital to fund its international expansion. The banks and the auditors deny any wrongdoing and claim they were victims of the scheme.

Parmalat, in turn, has been sued by investors, banks, and other organizations. In the U.S., the SEC filed a complaint against Parmalat on December 29, 2003, alleging that the company fraudulently raised money through bonds in the U.S. by overstating assets and understating liabilities. On July 30, 2004, Parmalat agreed to settle with the SEC without admitting or denying the claims. Parmalat won't be fined but has agreed to make changes to strengthen its board of directors and improve governance. Other than the SEC settlement, the rest of the lawsuits remain unresolved.

Besides the legal battles that have resulted from the fraud, Bondi's restructuring campaign calls for aggressive changes in Parmalat's organization. On March 29, 2004, the company announced it would narrow its focus to markets in Italy, Canada, Australia, South Africa, Spain, Portugal, Russia, and Romania, while it would pull out of other regions. Latin American countries "with strong and profitable positions" such as Colombia, Nicaragua, and Venezuela would be retained. In addition, Parmalat would cut its work force from 32,000 to less than 17,000, slash the number of brands from 120 to 30, and concentrate on "healthy lifestyle" products.

Not only were employees and investors affected by the scandal. In the aftermath of the discovery, dairies across Europe and Latin America faced uncertainty about sales of their milk. For example, GLP of France was owed €1.25 million by Parmalat at the time of the bankruptcy announcement. A Hungarian cooperative, which sold 80 million liters of milk a year to Parmalat, was left wondering if it would be able to continue selling its milk. Brazil's dairy farmers asked their government to pressure the local unit of the Italian food company to make sure they got paid. In that country, Parmalat controlled 10 percent of the country's pasteurized milk market, a quarter of its long-life UHT milk market, and 40 percent of the market for long-life carton-packaged cream.

MAKING SENSE OF WHAT HAPPENED

In Europe, the Parmalat scandal created deep concern among authorities. The European Commission suggested that it would like to strengthen auditing standards by insisting that member countries introduce accounting-oversight boards similar to those in the United States. Many organizations have proposed reforms to prevent another scandal of such magnitude.

Although the fraud was perpetrated through a set of accounting tricks, several issues converged to allow such manipulations to happen. One of the clearest deficiencies at Parmalat was its corporate governance system. As a family-owned business, the company was tightly controlled by insiders, especially Calisto Tanzi, who held the positions of CEO and chairman of the board of directors. Most of the other board members were family members or managers of Parmalat. This prevented the company from having a strong independent voice to stop the actions taken by management. In addition, Italian law allowed Parmalat to have two auditors instead of one. Grant Thornton was the main auditor, but Deloitte audited some of the subsidiaries, including Bonlat, where the fraud was uncovered. This arrangement made it more difficult for the auditors to have one clear, coherent picture of Parmalat's financial condition. Finally, and perhaps most importantly, management integrity failed. In the end, a manager determined to commit fraud will most likely succeed even in a very good governance system.

In the aftermath of Parmalat's fraud, investigators were left wondering how a few accounting numbers could fool so many people. One thing, however, was clear—Europe now had its very own Enron.

INTRODUCTION

International business managers cannot make good decisions without relevant and reliable information about accounting and taxation (Figure 18.2). Although accounting and information systems specialists provide such information, managers must also understand which data they need and the problems specialists face in gathering it from different accounting systems around the world. The accounting and finance functions are closely related. Each relies on the other to fulfill its own responsibilities.

The chief financial officer of any company is responsible for procuring and managing the company's financial resources. This individual is usually one of the members of the top management team of a company. The CFO relies on the controller, or chief accountant, to provide the right information for making decisions.

In addition, the internal audit staff ensures that corporate policies and procedures are followed. They and the CFO and controller work closely with the external auditor to try to safeguard the assets of the business. However, as shown in the Parmalat scandal, not everything works the way it should, especially when management is responsible for the fraud.

The actual and potential flow of assets across national boundaries complicates the finance and accounting functions. The MNE must learn to cope with differing inflation rates, exchange-rate changes, currency controls, expropriation risks, customs duties, tax rates and methods of determining taxable income, levels of sophistication of local accounting personnel, and local as well as home-country reporting requirements.

A company's controller collects and analyzes data for internal and external users. The overall objective of **accounting** is to provide information that management can use to make good decisions.

> *Accounting is a service activity. Its function is to provide quantitative information, primarily financial in nature, about economic entities that is intended to be useful in making economic decisions—in making reasoned choices among alternative courses of action.*[2]

The role of the corporate controller has expanded beyond the traditional roles of management accounting. Today's controller is engaged in other activities in the international arena, such as evaluating potential acquisitions abroad, disposing of a subsidiary or a

The accountant is essential in providing information to financial decision makers.

FIGURE 18.2   **ACCOUNTING IN INTERNATIONAL BUSINESS**

Accounting is one of the necessary functions for implementing companies' international strategies.

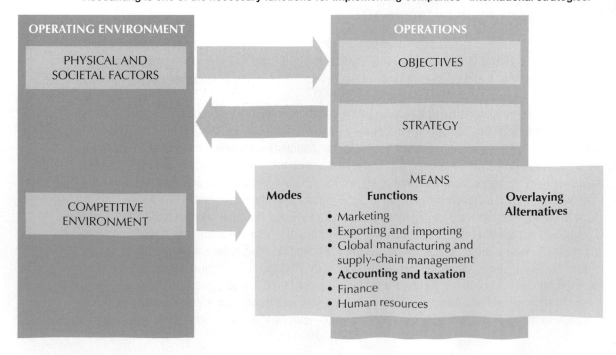

FIGURE 18.3

The role of the corporate controller has expanded beyond the traditional roles of management accounting.

Source: From the *Wall Street Journal*— Permission, Cartoon Features Syndicate.

"Remember when they used to be called 'bean counters'?"

division, managing cash flow, seeking new sources of financing, hedging currency and interest rate risks, tax planning, and helping in the planning of corporate strategy. Today's accountant must have a much broader perspective of business in general—and international business in particular for the purposes of this book—than was the case even as recently as a decade ago (see Figure 18.3).

The controller of an international company must be concerned about different currencies and accounting systems.

As noted in Chapter 15 and elaborated on in this chapter, foreign managers and subsidiaries are usually evaluated at headquarters on the basis of data generated in the company's reporting system that is set up and coordinated by the controller's office. The controller generates reports for internal consideration, local government needs, creditors, employees, suppliers, stockholders, and prospective investors. The controller handles the impact of many different currencies and inflation rates on the statements and should be familiar with different countries' accounting systems.

This chapter discusses some key accounting issues facing companies that do business abroad. Initially, we will examine how accounting differs around the world and how global capital markets are forcing countries to consider harmonizing their accounting and reporting standards. Then we will examine some unique issues facing MNEs, such as accounting for foreign-currency transactions, translating foreign-currency financial statements, reporting on foreign operations to shareholders and potential investors, and evaluating the performance of foreign operations and managers. Although the focus will be on problems of MNEs, many of these issues affect any company doing business overseas, even a small importer or exporter. Foreign-currency transactions, such as denominating a sale or purchase in a foreign currency, must be accounted for in the currency of the parent company, and this is true of both large and small firms.

FACTORS INFLUENCING THE DEVELOPMENT OF ACCOUNTING WORLDWIDE

Both the form and the content of financial statements are different in different countries.

One problem that an MNE faces is that accounting standards and practices vary around the world. Financial statements in different countries even look different in both form (or format) and content (or substance). To illustrate that substance (the content and quality of

TABLE 18.1   **VIVENDI UNIVERSAL BALANCE SHEETS**

CONSOLIDATED STATEMENT OF FINANCIAL POSITION

(In millions of euros)	2004	DECEMBER 31, 2003	2002
ASSETS			
Goodwill, net	€ 15,555	€ 17,789	€ 20,062
Other intangible assets, net	7,640	11,778	14,706
Property, plant and equipment, net	5,063	6,365	7,686
Investments in equity affiliates	880	1,083	1,903
Investment in NBC Universal	696	—	—
Other investments in equity affiliates	184	1,083	1,903
Other investments	2,449	3,549	4,138
Total long-term assets	31,587	40,564	48,495
Inventories and work-in-progress	443	744	1,310
Accounts receivable and other	6,545	8,809	9,892
Deferred tax assets	1,219	1,546	1,613
Short-term loans receivable	73	140	640
Marketable securities	263	259	88
Cash and cash equivalents	3,158	2,858	7,295
Total current assets	11,701	14,356	20,838
TOTAL ASSETS	€ 43,288	€ 54,920	€ 69,333
SHAREHOLDERS' EQUITY AND LIABILITIES			
Share capital	€ 5,899	€ 5,893	€ 5,877
Additional paid-in capital	6,109	6,030	27,687
Retained earnings and others	1,613	—	(19,544)
Total shareholders' equity	13,621	11,923	14,020
Minority interests	2,959	4,929	5,497
Other equity	1,000	1,000	1,000
Deferred income	100	560	579
Provisions	2,236	2,294	3,581
Long-term debt	4,549	9,621	10,455
Other non-current liabilities and accrued expenses	3,826	2,407	3,894
	28,291	32,734	39,026
Accounts payable	10,046	12,261	13,273
Deferred taxes liabilities	3,207	5,123	7,857
Bank overdrafts and other short-term borrowings	1,744	4,802	9,177
Total current liabilities	14,997	22,186	30,307
TOTAL SHAREHOLDERS' EQUITY AND LIABILITIES	€ 43,288	€ 54,920	€ 69,333

The accompanying notes are an integral part of these Consolidated Financial Statements.

Source: http://finance.vivendiuniversal.com/finance/download/pdf/20050401_6K_MEL_%20part2.pdf. Accessed June 1, 2005.

information in the financial statements), let's compare the balance sheets of France-based Vivendi Universal, the subject of the closing case (Table 18.1); Intel, the U.S.-based microcomputer components company (Table 18.2); and Marks & Spencer, the U.K.-based retail company (Table 18.3). The balance sheets for Vivendi Universal and Intel are in the format of

TABLE 18.2 **INTEL CORPORATION CONSOLIDATED BALANCE SHEETS**

DECEMBER 25, 2004 AND DECEMBER 27, 2003 (IN MILLIONS—EXCEPT PAR VALUE)	2004	2003
Assets		
Current assets:		
Cash and cash equivalents	$ 8,407	$ 7,971
Short-term investments	5,654	5,568
Trading assets	3,111	2,625
Accounts receivable, net of allowance for doubtful accounts of $43 ($55 in 2003)	2,999	2,960
Inventories	2,621	2,519
Deferred tax assets	979	969
Other current assets	287	270
Total current assets	24,058	22,882
Property, plant and equipment, net	15,768	16,661
Marketable strategic equity securities	656	514
Other long-term investments	2,563	1,866
Goodwill	3,719	3,705
Other assets	1,379	1,515
Total assets	$48,143	$47,143
Liabilities and stockholders' equity		
Current liabilities:		
Short-term debt	$ 201	$ 224
Accounts payable	1,943	1,660
Accrued compensation and benefits	1,858	1,559
Accrued advertising	894	716
Deferred income on shipments to distributors	592	633
Other accrued liabilities	1,355	1,302
Income taxes payable	1,163	785
Total current liabilities	8,006	6,879
Long-term debt	703	936
Deferred tax liabilities	855	1,482
Commitments and contingencies (Notes 17 and 18)		
Stockholders' equity:		
Preferred stock, $0.001 par value, 50 shares authorized; none issued	—	—
Common stock, $0.001 par value, 10,000 shares authorized; 6,253 issued and outstanding (6,487 in 2003) and capital in excess of par value	6,143	6,754
Acquisition-related unearned stock compensation	(4)	(20)
Accumulated other comprehensive income	152	96
Retained earnings	32,288	31,016
Total stockholders' equity	38,579	37,846
Total liabilities and stockholders' equity	$48,143	$47,143

Source: http://download.intel.com/intel/annualreports/AR_2004.pdf. Accessed June 1, 2005.

Assets = Liabilities + Shareholders' equity

The major difference between Vivendi Universal and Intel is the order of liquidity. Vivendi Universal starts with the least liquid assets (those that are harder to convert into cash quickly) and goes to the most liquid assets, whereas Intel starts with the most liquid assets and moves to the least liquid. The former practice is very common among

TABLE 18.3   **MARKS & SPENCER BALANCE SHEETS**

	GROUP		COMPANY	
	3 APRIL 2004 £M	29 MARCH 2003 AS RESTATED £M	3 APRIL 2004 £M	29 MARCH 2003 £M
Fixed assets				
Tangible assets:				
Land and buildings	2,151.9	2,148.4	—	—
Fit out, fixtures, fittings and equipment	1,295.3	1,248.2	—	—
Assets in the course of construction	50.4	38.5	—	—
	3,497.6	3,435.1	—	—
Investments	10.0	29.7	7,643.2	7,643.2
	3,507.6	3,464.8	7,643.2	7,643.2
Current assets				
Stocks	398.0	361.8	—	—
Debtors:				
Receivable within one year	971.6	853.1	262.7	247.8
Receivable after more than one year	1,779.3	1,559.5	—	—
Investments	325.9	304.0	—	—
Cash at bank and in hand	394.7	167.9	—	—
	3,869.5	3,246.3	262.7	247.8
Current liabilities				
Creditors: amounts falling due within one year	(1,884.7)	(1,710.9)	(2,325.9)	(2,246.8)
Net current assets/(liabilities)	1,984.8	1,535.4	(2,063.2)	(1,999.0)
Total assets less current liabilities	5,492.4	5,000.2	5,580.0	5,644.2
Creditors: amounts falling due after more than one year	(2,519.6)	(1,810.0)	—	—
Provisions for liabilities and charges	(49.3)	(186.1)	—	—
Net assets before net post-retirement liability	2,923.5	3,004.1	5,580.0	5,644.2
Net post-retirement liability	(469.5)	(895.8)	—	—
Net assets	2,454.0	2,108.3	5,580.0	5,644.2
Capital and reserves				
Called up share capital	651.2	685.7	651.2	685.7
Share premium account	45.2	23.8	45.2	23.8
Capital redemption reserve	1,924.8	1,886.9	1,924.8	1,886.9
Revaluation reserve	356.4	370.6	—	—
Other reserve	(6,542.2)	(6,542.2)	—	—
Profit and loss account	6,018.6	5,683.5	2,958.8	3,047.8
Shareholders' funds (including non-equity interests)	2,454.0	2,108.3	5,580.0	5,644.2
Equity shareholders' funds	2,369.1	1,990.1	5,495.1	5,526.0
Non-equity shareholders' funds	84.9	118.2	84.9	118.2
Total shareholders' funds	2,454.0	2,108.3	5,580.0	5,644.2

Approved by the Board

24 May 2004

Alison Reed, Chief Financial Officer

Source: http://www2.marksandspencer.com/thecompany/investorrelations/annual_report04/j/j2.shtml. Accessed June 1, 2005.

European companies, whereas the Intel approach is used by U.S.-based companies. Even foreign companies, like German auto manufacturer DaimlerChrysler, that issue financial statements according to U.S. **generally accepted accounting principles (GAAP)** use the same liquidity format as does Vivendi Universal.

The balance sheets for Marks & Spencer are prepared in a different format known as the analytical format:

$$\text{fixed assets} + \text{current assets} - \text{current liabilities} - \text{noncurrent liabilities}$$
$$= \text{capital and reserves}$$

In the case of Marks & Spencer, "creditors: amounts falling due after more than one year" is the same as long-term debt in the Intel report. Some terms are different, such as *inventories* under the current assets section of Intel's report, which means the same as *stocks* in the Marks & Spencer report, and *receivables* and *payables* or *liabilities* for Intel and Vivendi Universal and *debtors* and *creditors* for Marks & Spencer. Intel uses the term "*stockholders' equity*" whereas both Marks & Spencer and Vivendi Universal use "*shareholders' equity*." In addition, Intel presents only a set of consolidated financial statements, whereas Marks & Spencer presents both company (meaning "parent company") and group ("consolidated") financial statements. Some observers argue that differences in format are a minor matter, a problem of form rather than substance. In fact, however, the substance also differs, because companies can measure assets and determine income differently in different countries. This concept will be illustrated in the Vivendi Universal case at the end of the chapter.

Accounting Objectives

It is important for the accounting process to identify, record, and interpret economic events. Every country needs to determine the objectives of the accounting system it has put into place. According to the **Financial Accounting Standards Board** (FASB), the private sector body that establishes accounting standards in the United States, financial reporting, the external reporting of accounting information, should provide information for the purposes of

- Investment and credit decisions
- Assessment of cash flow prospects
- Evaluation of enterprise resources, claims to those resources, and changes in them[3]

To establish objectives, managers have to determine who are the major users of financial information. The **International Accounting Standards Board** (IASB) and its predecessor, the **International Accounting Standards Committee,** identify the following key users:

- Investors
- Employees
- Lenders
- Suppliers and other trade creditors
- Customers
- Governments and their agencies
- The public[4]

It is important to identify users, because a focus on different users might result in different financial information being reported. For example, Germany's major users have historically been creditors, so accounting has focused more on the balance sheet, which contains a description of the company's assets. In the United States, however, the major users are investors, so accounting has focused more on the income statement. Investors see the income statement as an indication of the future success of the company, which affects the company's stock price (or share price) and its flow of dividends. There is no

The accounting process identifies, records, and interprets economic events.

The Financial Accounting Standards Board (FASB) sets accounting standards in the United States.

The IASB is an international private sector organization that sets accounting standards.

Critical users of accounting information are investors, employees, lenders, suppliers and other trade creditors, customers, governments and their agencies, and the public.

Equity markets are an important source of influence on accounting in the United States and the United Kingdom. Banks are influential in Germany and Switzerland, and taxation is a major influence in Japan and France.

consensus on whether there should be a uniform set of accounting standards and practices for all classes of users worldwide—or even for one class of users—but the general movement toward the development of accounting standards and practices seems to be focusing on financial information for investors.

In Figure 18.4, we identify some of the forces leading to the development of accounting practices internationally. Although all of the factors shown in the figure are significant, their importance varies by country. For example, investors are an influence in the United States and the United Kingdom, but creditors—primarily banks—are more of an influence in Germany and Switzerland.

Taxation has a big influence on accounting standards and practices in Japan and France, but it is less important in the United States. Cultural issues cut across all countries and strongly influence the development of accounting. Certain international factors also have weight, such as former colonial influence and foreign investment. For example, most countries that are current or former members of the British Commonwealth have accounting systems similar to the United Kingdom's. Former French colonies use the French model, and so forth. Thus, companies from those countries use standards and practices that are similar to companies from other countries in the same group. The international public accounting firms, such as KPMG, Deloitte, PricewaterhouseCoopers, and Ernst & Young, are also important sources of influence as they transfer high levels of auditing practices worldwide.

These differences in accounting influences have resulted in differences in accounting standards and practices. However, the major development in accounting worldwide is now the issue of **convergence,** which implies that through negotiations between the FASB and IASB, we are moving closer to having one set of accounting standards that can be used in capital markets. Before understanding the issue of convergence, however, we need to understand the underlying differences among countries, and culture is a key force.

Convergence is the process of bringing different national generally accepted accounting principles (GAAP) into line with International Accounting Standards issued by the IASB.

FIGURE 18.4   **ENVIRONMENTAL INFLUENCES ON ACCOUNTING PRACTICES**

The importance of any of these environmental influences on accounting practices varies by country.

Source: Reprinted from *The International Journal of Accounting,* vol. 10, no. 3, by Lee H. Radebaugh, "Environmental Factors Influencing the Development of Accounting Objectives, Standards and Practices—The Peruvian Case", p. 41, © 1975. Reprinted by permission from Elsevier Science.

KPMG is one of the four largest public accounting firms in the world, offering auditing and tax services to multinational clients.

Cultural Differences in Accounting

A major source of influence on accounting standards and practices is culture. Of special interest to international investors are the differences in measurement and disclosure practices among countries—measurement meaning "how companies value assets, including inventory and fixed assets"; disclosure meaning "how and what information companies provide and discuss in their annual and interim reports for external users of financial data." Much of the work on culture and accounting is initially based on Geert Hofstede's pioneering research on the structural elements of culture, particularly those that most strongly affect behavior in the work situations of organizations and institutions.[5] Hofstede's work was then extended into the accounting area by Sidney Gray,[6] which resulted in classifying countries according to disclosure and measurement principles, specifically secrecy/transparency and optimism/conservatism.

Figure 18.5 depicts the accounting practices of various groupings of countries within a matrix of the cultural values of secrecy–transparency and optimism–conservatism. With respect to accounting, secrecy and transparency indicate the degree to which companies disclose information to the public. Countries such as Germany, Switzerland, and Japan tend to have less disclosure (illustrating the cultural value of secrecy) than do the United States and the United Kingdom—both are Anglo-American countries—which are more transparent or open with respect to disclosure. This is illustrated by the more extensive footnote disclosures in reports of the Anglo-American countries than is the case elsewhere. However, the Parmalat scandal illustrates that companies that list on global exchanges, borrow money from the largest banks in the world, and have their financial statements audited by the best accounting firms in the world can also be secretive. In addition, as companies from the upper right quadrant of secrecy and conservatism utilize capital markets more extensively, they move closer to the Anglo-American mode. This is especially true of companies like Deutsche Bank and DaimlerChrysler that adopted U.S. GAAP for reporting purposes. As more European companies adopt International Financial Reporting Standards issued by the IASB, they will become more transparent and optimistic.

Optimism and conservatism (in an accounting, not a political sense) are the degree of caution companies exhibit in valuing assets and recognizing income—an illustration of the measurement issues mentioned earlier. Countries more conservative from an accounting

Culture influences measurement and disclosure practices

- Measurement—how to value assets
- Disclosure—the presentation of information and discussion of results

Secrecy and transparency refer to the degree to which corporations disclose information to the public. Optimism and conservatism refer to the degree of caution companies display in valuing assets and recognizing income.

FIGURE 18.5

CULTURAL DIFFERENCES IN MEASUREMENT AND DISCLOSURE FOR ACCOUNTING SYSTEMS

Anglo-Saxon countries (such as the United Kingdom and the United States) have accounting systems that tend to be transparent and optimistic. Systems in Germanic countries, for example, tend to be secretive and conservative.

Source: International Accounting and Multinational Enterprises, 5th edition, by Lee H. Radebaugh and Sidney J. Gray, Copyright © 2002, John Wiley & Sons, Inc. Reprinted by permission of John Wiley & Sons, Inc.

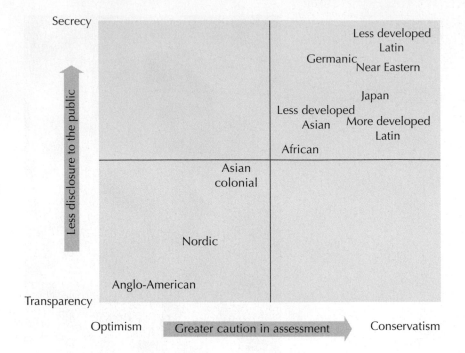

British companies are optimistic when recognizing income. U.S. companies are slightly less optimistic. Japanese and continental European companies are even less optimistic than U.S. companies.

point of view tend to understate assets and income, while optimistic countries tend to be more liberal in their recognition of income. Banks primarily fund French companies, which is true also in Germany and Japan, and banks are concerned with liquidity. So French companies tend to be very conservative both when recording profits that keep them from paying taxes and when declaring dividends in order to pile up cash reserves to service their bank debt. In contrast, U.S. companies want to show earnings power to impress and attract investors. British companies tend to be more optimistic in earnings recognition than are U.S. companies, but U.S. companies are much more optimistic than continental European and Japanese companies. The Asian financial crisis demonstrated that most Asian countries still fit squarely in the upper-right quadrant of measurement and disclosure. In particular, companies from Korea and Southeast Asia were guilty of a lack of transparency, which made it difficult for banks and investors to know where to lend and invest their money. They often put their money in Asian companies on the basis of relationships and reputation instead of good financial information.

Classification of Accounting Systems

Although accounting standards and practices differ significantly worldwide, we can still group systems used in various countries according to common characteristics. Figure 18.6 illustrates one approach to classifying accounting systems. It does not attempt to classify all countries, but it simply illustrates the concept using several developed Western countries. Although all major industrial countries are moving to an accounting model that favors investors and thus is more similar to the micro-based countries at the bottom on Figure 18.6, it is important to understand the macro tradition to understand how difficult it is to converge accounting standards from different parts of the world.

The authors of Figure 18.6 used the concept of natural science to classify countries. As you move from left to right, you move from the general to the specific. Macro-uniform systems are shaped more by government influence than are micro-based systems. The major accounting influences on countries that fit into the macro-uniform category are a strong legal system, especially a codified legal system rather than a common law system, and tax law. These systems also tend to be more conservative and secretive about disclosure. Japan and Germany are legal-based systems, and Spain and France are tax-based systems. The former Soviet-bloc countries would also fit in the macro category. However,

Macro-uniform accounting systems are shaped more by government influence, whereas micro-based systems rely on pragmatic business practice.

FIGURE 18.6   **CLASSIFICATION OF ACCOUNTING SYSTEMS OF DEVELOPED WESTERN COUNTRIES**

Accounting systems can be macro-uniform or micro-based depending on how important government influence is.

Source: From C. W. Nobes, "A Judgmental International Classification of Financial Reporting Practices," *Journal of Business Finance and Accounting* (Spring 1983): Reprinted by permission of Blackwell Publishing Ltd.

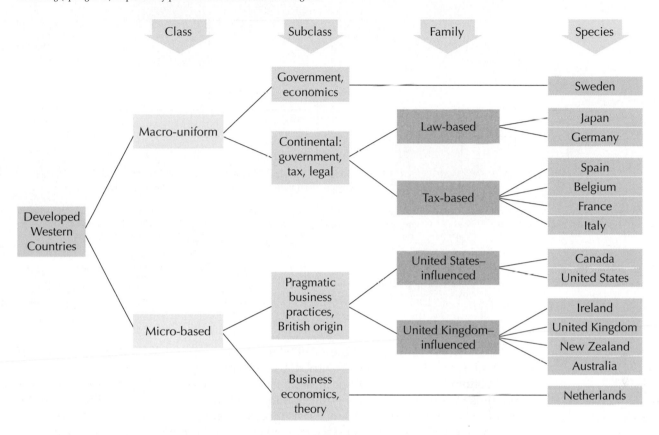

China is trying to adopt international accounting standards that are more in line with capital markets, thus being more micro than macro in orientation.

Micro-based systems include features that support pragmatic business practice and have evolved from the British system. The United States is an example of a country that fits in the micro category. It exhibits more optimism and transparency than countries in the macro category, and it also relies less on legal and tax requirements than do Germany, France, and Japan. The focus tends to be more on capital markets and less on banks and tax authorities. Other countries that closely model the United States are Mexico and Canada, two members of NAFTA. The British model is also a micro-based model, but it relies even less on legal and tax influences than does the United States. Current and former members of the British Commonwealth, such as the Bahamas, Australia, and New Zealand, also fit into this category.[7]

More recently, Nobes has updated his classification scheme to distinguish between strong and weak equity markets and shareholder orientations (see Figure 18.7). This incorporates changes that are taking place internationally where some companies in countries such as Germany and Japan are accounting on a basis consistent with U.S. GAAP or IFRS.[8] The shortcoming of both Figures 18.6 and 18.7 is that they do not include a large part of the world. However, companies from countries that have a weak equity market, which is true of most countries in Latin America, Asia, and Africa, will tend to be more tax and legal oriented and will fit in the weak equity part of Figure 18.7. Some companies from the developing countries will list on a global stock market, such as the

Countries can be distinguished between those with strong and weak equity market and shareholder orientations.

FIGURE 18.7   **PROPOSED SCHEME FOR CLASSIFICATION ACCORDING TO STRONG AND WEAK EQUITY MARKET ORIENTATION**

Source: Christopher Nobes and Robert Parker, *Comparative International Accounting*, 7th ed. (England: FT Prentice Hall, 2002), p. 67.

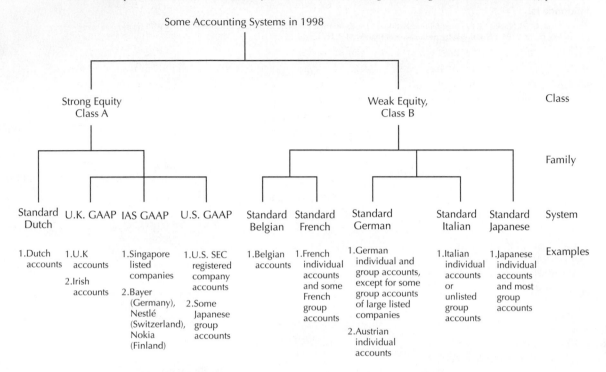

New York Stock Exchange, and they will be much more optimistic and transparent than if they had decided to stay in their local markets to raise capital.

The bottom line is that MNEs need to adjust to different accounting systems around the world, thus making the accounting function more complex and costly. The financial statements of a company include not only the statements themselves but also the accompanying footnotes. Companies that list on stock exchanges usually provide an income statement, a balance sheet, a statement of stockholder equity, and a cash flow statement. In addition, they provide extensive footnotes, depending on the country where they list. The financial statements of one country differ from those in another country in six major ways:

Major reporting issues

- Language
- Currency
- Type of statements
- Financial statement format
- Extent of footnote disclosures
- Underlying GAAP on which the financial statements are based

1. Language
2. Currency
3. Type of statements (income statement, balance sheet, etc.)
4. Financial statement format
5. Extent of footnote disclosures
6. Underlying GAAP on which the financial statements are based

A company wishing to provide financial information for investors throughout the world needs to deal with all six issues. As far as language goes, English tends to be the first choice of companies choosing to raise capital abroad. For example, in its 2004 annual report, DaimlerChrysler lists the languages available for the following publications:

Annual Report (German, English)

Form 20-F (English)

Interim Reports for the 1st, 2nd and 3rd Quarters (German, English)

Environment Report (German, English)

Social Responsibility Report (German, English)

DaimlerChrysler also points out that the financial statements of DaimlerChrysler AG are prepared in accordance with German GAAP, and the consolidated financial statements are prepared in U.S. GAAP. French company Vivendi Universal provides its annual report in French and English, and the currency of the report is the euro. The financial statements are provided in French GAAP.

Many companies also provide a significant amount of information on their home pages on the Internet in different languages. Managers can just click on the desired language button, and all the information is provided in that language. For example, Ericsson, the Swedish telecommunications company, has a home page full of information for people all over the world. The company even has a link, www.ericsson.com.br, which gives financial information, as well as general information, in Portuguese for Brazilian readers.

A second issue in classifying systems is currency. As we saw in Vivendi Universal's balance sheets in Table 18.1, the financial statements are provided in euros. Intel's financial statements are in U.S. dollars, and Marks & Spencer's reports are in British pounds. Ericsson used to provide its balance sheet and income statement in Portuguese to Brazilian readers and in the real, Brazil's currency, but that is no longer the case. The same is true for the Internet site of Finnish company Nokia, which allows investors to access the site in their own language but provides financial information in English.

Financial statement format is not a big issue, but it can be confusing for a manager to read a balance sheet prepared in an analytical format, as is the case with Marks & Spencer, when the manager is used to seeing it in the balance format, as is the case with Intel. A major area of difference is the use of footnotes. Footnote disclosures in the United States tend to be the most comprehensive in the world. For example, U.S. companies go into great detail describing the way certain information is determined as well as the detail behind the numbers. Greater transparency is synonymous with more extensive footnote disclosures.

Finally, the most problematic area is that of differences in underlying GAAP. A major hurdle in raising capital in different countries is dealing with widely varying accounting and disclosure requirements. Although this problem is decreasing as more stock exchanges allow the use of International Financial Reporting Standards, some countries care more about those differences than others. In Germany and the Netherlands, for example, the principle of **mutual recognition** applies. That means that a foreign registrant that wants to list and have its securities traded on the Frankfurt or Amsterdam stock exchange need only provide information prepared according to the GAAP of the home country (this will change by 2007 as European companies adopt International Financial Reporting Standards of the IASB and require firms that list on those exchanges to use the new standards instead of other international standards, such as U.S. GAAP). However, other exchanges, like the New York Stock Exchange and NASDAQ, require foreign registrants either to reconcile their home-country financial statements with the local GAAP or to recast their financial statements in accordance with local GAAP. In the United States, this information is provided in a document called Form 20-F, which companies must file with the SEC. That is what Vivendi Universal does for its financial statements registered in the United States.

> Major approaches to dealing with accounting and reporting differences
> - Mutual recognition
> - Reconciliation to local GAAP
> - Recast financial statements in terms of local GAAP

International Accounting Standards and Global Convergence

Despite the many differences in accounting standards and practices, a number of forces are leading to harmonization, such as:

- A movement to provide information compatible with the needs of investors
- The global integration of capital markets, which means that investors have easier and faster access to investment opportunities around the world and, therefore, need financial information that is more comparable
- The need of MNEs to raise capital outside their home-country capital markets while generating as few different financial statements as possible

> Major forces leading to convergence
> - Investor orientation
> - Global integration of capital markets
> - MNEs' need for foreign capital
> - Regional political and economic harmonization
> - MNEs' desire to reduce accounting and reporting costs

- Regional political and economic harmonization, such as the efforts of the EU, which affects accounting as well as trade and investment issues
- Pressure from MNEs for more uniform standards to allow greater ease and reduced costs in general reporting in each country

Spurred by these developments, some countries and organizations are working to harmonize accounting standards on a regional as well as an international level. Regionally, the most ambitious effort is taking place in the EU, which is interested in promoting the free flow of capital throughout Europe. The EU's initial accounting directives identified the type and format of financial statements that European companies have to use, the measurement bases on which they should prepare financial statements, and the importance of consolidated financial statements. It also required auditors to ensure that financial statements reflect a true and fair view of the operations of the company being audited instead of just adhering to the national laws of the different countries.

The EU's directives improved the comparability of financial statements, but member countries can still interpret the directives differently. Thus, EU companies listing outside their home countries must still provide two sets of financial statements—the home-country statements and reconciliation. Since most European companies provide company and group reports, as we noted with Vivendi Univeral and Marks & Spencer, companies would use local standards for company reports but not necessarily for group reports since the EU directives did not apply to group reports. Thus you can have a situation like that of German company DaimlerChrysler, which provides financial information for company reports in German GAAP and consolidated or group accounts in U.S. GAAP.

To enhance the harmonization process, the EU has decided to support the efforts of the International Accounting Standards Board. In the spring of 2002, the EU directed its member countries to adopt International Accounting Standards, as set forth by the IASB, by 2005. The reason for choosing the IASB is that the EU can influence those standards because it is represented on the IASB, and it also avoids funding and developing a competing standards-setting body.[9]

The IASC, the forerunner of the IASB, was organized in 1973 by the professional accounting bodies of Australia, Canada, France, Germany, Japan, Mexico, the Netherlands, the United Kingdom and Ireland, and the United States, and has worked toward harmonizing accounting standards. Initially, the IASC wanted to develop standards that would have rapid and broad acceptance, focusing mostly on improved disclosure. However, it became obvious that the major stock exchanges of the world would never accept such loose standards for companies that wanted to list on the exchanges. There were too few standards and too many alternatives permitted for the standards that had been issued. In addition, there was no enforcement mechanism other than the best efforts of the member organizations to ensure that the standards would be adhered to in the individual countries.

The turning point in the significance of IASC standards came in 1995 when the **International Organization of Securities Commissions** (IOSCO) announced publicly that it would endorse IASC standards if the IASC developed a set of core standards acceptable to IOSCO. IOSCO is significant because it is comprised of the stock market regulators of most of the stock markets in the world, including the SEC in the United States. Once IASC completed its work, IOSCO would permit foreign companies to list on their exchanges using IASC standards without having to reconcile to local GAAP. That official endorsement came in May 2000 when IASB completed a core set of standards acceptable to IOSCO. As the former chairman of the U.S. SEC stated, "the significance of transparent, timely and reliable financial statements and its importance to investor protection has never been more apparent. The current financial situations in Asia and Russia are stark examples of this new reality. These markets are learning a painful lesson taught many times before: investors panic as a result of unexpected or unquantifiable bad news."[10] The feeling is that these issues would be minimized by the adoption of a universal set of standards acceptable to all stock markets worldwide.

The EU is harmonizing accounting to promote the free flow of capital. Other countries in Europe, including those of Eastern Europe and the former Soviet Union, are following the lead of the EU.

The International Organization of Securities Commissions wanted the IASC (forerunner of the IASB) to develop a core set of accounting standards in which securities regulators can be confident.

Another major factor affecting the harmonization of accounting standards worldwide was the reorganization of the IASC in 2000. The international professional activities of the accountancy bodies were initially organized under the International Federation of Accountants (IFAC) in 1977. IFAC comprises 163 professional accounting organizations representing 119 countries and over 2.5 million accountants.[11] Map 18.1 identifies IFAC member countries. In 1981, IASC and IFAC agreed that IASC would have full and complete autonomy in the setting of international accounting standards and in the issue of discussion documents on international accounting issues. At the same time, all members of IFAC became members of IASC. This relationship continued until the IASC's constitution was changed in May 2000 as part of the reorganization of the IASC. IFAC would be responsible for issues that affect accountants, such as ethics, auditing standards, educational requirements, certification requirements, and so on.

Trustees for the IASC foundation searched for and appointed members of the IASB. In order to ensure a broad international basis, the trustees of the foundation came from North America (six trustees), Europe (six), Asia/Pacific (four), and at-large (three). The IASB consists of 14 members (two of which are part-time), appointed by the trustees. Although the board members are not chosen for geographical reasons, they come from industrial countries where an investor orientation is widely established. The trustees brought the new structure into effect on April 1, 2001.[12]

When the IASB was organized, all of the old International Accounting Standards were adopted, and the board then began to go through each standard to upgrade them. Then the board began to issue new standards, called **International Financial Reporting**

MAP 18.1   Membership of the International Federation of Accountants

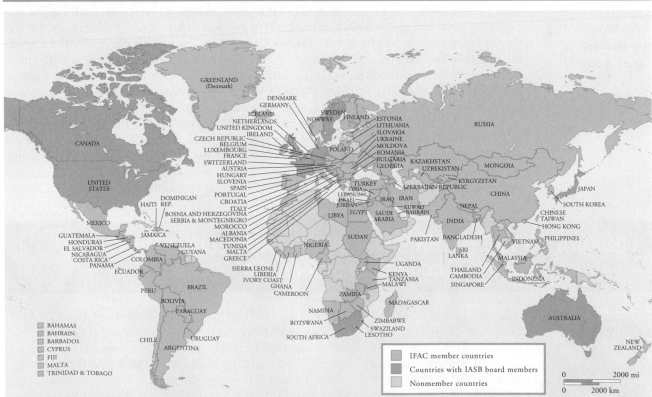

The IFAC membership consists of 163 accountancy organizations from 119 countries. The members from the United States are the American Institute of Certified Public Accountants, the Institute of Management of Accountants, and the National Association of State Boards of Accountancy. The U.S. affiliate members are the IASB's 14 board members. These board members come from 9 countries.

Source: See http://www.ifac.org/MemberBodies.html for list of member countries of IFAC.

Standards (IFRS). Thus when we use the term **IFRS,** we refer to the new standards as well as the old IAS.

> The IASB comprises professional accounting bodies and is attempting to harmonize accounting standards through issuing International Financial Reporting Standards (IFRS).

The new objectives of the IASB are:

(a) to develop, in the public interest, a single set of high quality, understandable and enforceable global accounting standards that require high quality, transparent and comparable information in financial statements and other financial reporting to help participants in the world's capital markets and other users make economic decisions; (b) to promote the use and rigorous application of those standards; and (c) to bring about convergence of national accounting standards and International Accounting Standards to high quality solutions.[13]

Two major events have greatly expanded the influence and effectiveness of the IASB. The first is the decision of the EU (and European Economic Area), Australia, and New Zealand to require all of their publicly listed companies to adopt IFRS in 2005 (2007 for New Zealand). In the case of the EU, this means that over 9,000 publicly listed companies will use IFRS for their consolidated financial statements. An exception is given to companies like DaimlerChrysler that are using U.S. GAAP for their consolidated financial statements. They have until 2007 to convert from U.S. GAAP to IASB GAAP. The acceptance of IFRS has not been an easy task for the EU due to a standard on accounting for financial derivatives that is heavily opposed by the French, especially the French banks.[14] In addition, it will take a few years to know just exactly how companies from different countries actually adopt the standards.

> The EU and other countries have agreed to require IFRS for publicly listed companies.

The second is the decision of the FASB and IASB to adopt a process of convergence of accounting standards. In the past, the FASB and IASB have not exactly competed with each other, but they have maintained a professional distance. That is no longer the case. Now the FASB and IASB have joint projects to establish new standards, such as a standard on revenue recognition; they are trying to eliminate existing differences in standards in a short-term convergence project for standards that should be easy to converge; and the FASB is explicitly considering the impact on the IASB of every standard it sets.[15] In some ways, this convergence process has been very unsettling to some Europeans, especially the French, because they feel that the close cooperation of the two boards is making the new IFRS suspiciously similar to standards issued by the FASB. The fact that there are several Americans on the IASB is further evidence to them that the board does not have a strong enough European presence and influence. The board is examining a new constitution that will broaden representation of other countries on the foundation and the board, but the Europeans would like to see the IASB have a distinctly European flavor in order to establish standards that are more "European." This is another good example of how culture and tradition come into play, even though the standards are supposed to be for investors worldwide. It will be interesting to see what happens to the future of international accounting standards.

> FASB and IASB are trying to converge their standards through a variety of different activities.

LOOKING TO THE FUTURE: Will IASB GAAP Become the Global Accounting Standard?

It is very possible. With the adoption of IFRSs by the EU, Australia, and New Zealand, nearly 100 countries in six continents will be requiring or permitting the use of IFRSs for some or all domestic listed companies.[16] From an accounting standpoint, the key question is this: "What will become the Coca-Cola of accounting standards—U.S. GAAP or IASB GAAP?" In other words, which will have the most recognized brand name in accounting standards? IASB GAAP has a lot going for it. It is being set by most of the major countries in the world, so it is the product of a great deal of negotiation, compromise, and broad-based input. It is appealing to the Europeans, because they have a lot of influence in the development of its standards. In addition, as noted above, it has the backing of the EU. Also, after 2007 the

EU will no longer allow companies to list on European exchanges in U.S. GAAP. Before, a number of companies, even European companies, prepared their consolidated financial statements in U.S. GAAP so that they could list in the U.S. as well as on European exchanges to raise capital. It was a lot easier to list in one set of standards instead of having to generate many different sets of financial statements. By 2007, companies will have to list on European exchanges using IASB GAAP, and if they want to also list in the U.S., they will have to list according to U.S. GAAP. However, at least the new IASB GAAP is modeled after the capital-markets orientation of the United Kingdom and the United States. At some point, it is possible that the U.S. will simply adopt IASB GAAP or allow it to be used for companies listing in the U.S.

The major vote in favor of U.S. GAAP is that half of the world's stock market capitalization is located in the United States, and companies that want access to U.S. capital must play by U.S. rules. There has been a movement by some MNEs and especially by the IASB and countries that have adopted IASB GAAP to have the U.S. permit the use of IASB GAAP for foreign companies that want to list in the U.S. To this point, that has not been possible. The U.S. has always felt that its standards were the best in the world and that it would be unfair for U.S. companies competing for cash in the U.S. market to allow foreign companies to list using IASB GAAP, which is perceived as more flexible and less comprehensive than U.S. GAAP. Foreign companies that want to list outside their national market will typically look to the U.S. first and thus will have to adopt U.S. reporting requirements.

However, the convergence project between the FASB and IASB may solve this problem in the long run. To its credit, the IASB has expanded coverage of key topics and has narrowed the alternatives available to companies. The IASB has sold itself as being principles-based rather than rules-based. Principles-based accounting means that the standard-setter identifies key principles in a conceptual framework that are used to set standards and then tries to establish rules that are simple but that conform to the key principles. A rules-based system is very legalistic with lots of detail and difficulty. U.S. GAAP is very rules-based and complicated. However, the FASB and IASB are narrowing the differences in existing standards and developing new standards together. Now they jointly write new standards so that the wording is even the same.

A foreign company listing on the New York Stock Exchange has to issue a Form 20-F as explained in Chapter 9. In Form 20-F, the company reconciles its income statement, balance sheet, and statement of shareholders' equity from the foreign GAAP to U.S. GAAP. Companies that list according to IASB GAAP will eventually find that the reconciliation between U.S. and IASB GAAP becomes so small as to be insignificant. At that point, there will be virtually no difference between U.S. GAAP and IASB GAAP. Maybe the future will be like a merger of Coca-Cola and Pepsi.

TRANSACTIONS IN FOREIGN CURRENCIES

When a company operates outside the domestic market, it must concern itself with the proper recording and subsequent accounting of assets, liabilities, revenues, and expenses that are measured or denominated in foreign currencies. These transactions can result from the purchase and sale of goods and services as well as the borrowing and lending of foreign currency.

Recording of Transactions

Any time an importer has to pay for equipment or merchandise in a foreign currency, it must trade its own currency for that of the exporter to make the payment. Assume Sundance Ski Lodge, a U.S. company, buys skis from a French supplier for 28,000 euros when the exchange rate is $1.1000/euro. Sundance records the following in its books:

Purchases	5,500	
Accounts payable		5,500
€ 5,000 @ 1.1000		

If Sundance pays immediately, there is no problem. But what happens if the exporter extends 30 days' credit to Sundance? The original entry would be the same as the one here, but during the next 30 days, anything could happen. If the rate changed to $1.1500/euro by the time the payment was due, Sundance would record a final settlement as:

Accounts payable	5,500	
Loss on foreign exchange	250	
Cash	5,750	

The merchandise stays at the original value of $5,500, but there is a difference between the dollar value of the account payable to the exporter ($5,500) and the actual number of dollars that the importer must come up with to purchase the euros to pay the exporter ($5,750). The difference between the two accounts ($250) is the loss on foreign exchange and is always recognized in the income statement.

The company that denominates the sale or purchase in the foreign currency (the importer in the current case) must recognize the gains and losses arising from foreign-currency transactions at the end of each accounting period, usually quarterly. In the example here, assume the end of the quarter has arrived and Sundance still has not paid the French exporter. The skis continue to be valued at $5,500, but the payable has to be updated to the new exchange rate of $1.1500/euro. The journal entry would be

Loss on foreign exchange	250	
Accounts payable	250	

The payable now would be worth $5,750. If settlement were to be made in the month following the end of the quarter and the exchange rate were to remain the same, the final entry would be:

Accounts payable	5,750	
Cash	5,750	

If the U.S. company were an exporter and anticipated receiving foreign currency, the corresponding entries (using the same information as in the example here) would be:

Accounts receivable	5,500	
Sales	5,500	
Cash	5,750	
Gain on foreign exchange	250	
Accounts receivable	5,500	

In this case, a gain results because the company received more cash than if it had collected its money immediately.

Correct Procedures for U.S. Companies

The procedures that U.S. companies must follow to account for foreign-currency transactions are found in Financial Accounting Standards Board Statement No. 52, "Foreign Currency Translation." Statement No. 52 requires companies to record the initial transaction at the spot exchange rate in effect on the transaction date and to record receivables and payables at subsequent balance sheet dates at the spot exchange rate on those dates. Any foreign-exchange gains and losses that arise from carrying receivables or payables during a period in which the exchange rate changes are taken directly to the income statement.[17]

Procedures vary in other countries, however. Some countries recognize transaction losses but not gains in their income statements. That means that a loss reduces income and a gain increases income. Other countries allow a loss that results from a major devaluation to adjust the value of the underlying asset rather than be taken directly to income. However, the IASB and FASB rules are the same, so fewer and fewer countries will account for foreign currency transactions differently from what is done in the U.S.

Foreign-currency receivables and payables give rise to gains and losses whenever the exchange rate changes. Transaction gains and losses must be included in the income statement in the accounting period in which they arise.

The FASB requires that U.S. companies report foreign-currency transactions at the original spot exchange rate and that subsequent gains and losses on foreign-currency receivables or payables be put on the income statement.

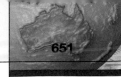

TRANSLATION OF FOREIGN CURRENCY FINANCIAL STATEMENTS

Even though U.S.-based MNEs receive reports originally developed in a variety of different currencies, they eventually must end up with one set of financial statements in U.S. dollars to help management and investors understand their worldwide activities in a common currency. The process of restating foreign-currency financial statements into U.S. dollars is **translation.** The combination of all of these translated financial statements into one is **consolidation,** as illustrated in the financial statements of Vivendi Universal, Intel, and Marks & Spencer.

> Translation—the process of restating foreign-currency financial statements.
>
> Consolidation—the process of combining the translated financial statements of a parent and its subsidiaries into one set of financial statements.

Translation in the United States is a two-step process:

1. Companies recast foreign-currency financial statements into statements consistent with U.S. GAAP. This occurs because a U.S. company with a subsidiary in Brazil, for example, must keep the books and records in Brazil according to Brazilian GAAP. For consolidation purposes, however, the resulting financial statements have to be issued according to U.S. GAAP in format as well as content. As an example of content, Brazil might require that inventories be valued a certain way. For the U.S. consolidated financial statements, however, inventories must be valued according to U.S., not Brazilian, standards.

2. Companies translate all foreign-currency amounts into U.S. dollars.

FASB Statement No. 52 describes how companies must translate their foreign-currency financial statements into dollars. All U.S. companies, as well as foreign companies that list on a U.S. exchange, must use Statement No. 52.

Translation Methods

Statement No. 52 and IAS 21, the relevant translation standards issued by the FASB and IASB, both allow companies to use either of two methods when translating foreign-currency financial statements into dollars: the **current-rate method** (called the closing rate method by the IASB) or the **temporal method.** The method the company chooses depends on the **functional currency** of the foreign operation, which is the currency of the primary economic environment in which that entity operates. For example, one of Coca-Cola's largest operations outside the United States is in Japan. The primary economic environment of the Japanese subsidiary is Japan, and the functional currency is the Japanese yen. The FASB identifies several factors that can help management determine the functional currency. Among the major factors are cash flows, sales prices, sales market data, expenses, financing, and intercompany transactions. For example, if the cash flows and expenses are primarily in the foreign operation's currency, that is the functional currency. If they are in the parent's currency, that is the functional currency.

> The functional currency is the currency of the primary economic environment in which the entity operates.

If the functional currency is that of the local operating environment, the company must use the current-rate method. The current-rate method provides that companies translate all assets and liabilities at the current exchange rate, which is the spot exchange rate on the balance sheet date. All income statement items are translated at the average exchange rate, and owners' equity is translated at the rates in effect when the company issued capital stock and accumulated retained earnings.

> The current-rate method applies when the local currency is the functional currency.

If the functional currency is the parent's currency, the MNE must use the temporal method. The temporal method provides that only monetary assets (cash, marketable securities, and receivables) and liabilities are translated at the current exchange rate. The company translates inventory and property, plant, and equipment at the historical exchange rates, the exchange rates in effect when the assets were acquired. In general, the company translates most income statement accounts at the average exchange rate, but it translates cost of goods sold and depreciation expenses at the appropriate historical exchange rates.

> The temporal method applies when the parent's reporting currency is the functional currency.

Companies can choose the translation method—current rate or temporal rate—that is most appropriate for a particular foreign subsidiary, so they don't have to use one or the other for all subsidiaries. Vivendi Universal, with manufacturing and sales offices in

FIGURE 18.8   **SELECTION OF TRANSLATION METHOD**

According to FASB Statement No. 52, management can choose either the current-rate method or the temporal method to translate the financial statements of a foreign subsidiary or branch from the foreign currency to the parent currency (the U.S. dollar for a U.S. firm). The choice of translation method depends on the choice of functional currency.

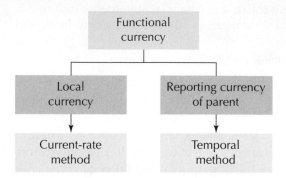

many locations all around the world, uses the current rate for some and the temporal rate for others. Historically some of its most important functional currencies were the French franc, British pound, Italian lira, Spanish peseta, and U.S. dollar. The euro has now replaced the franc, lira, and peseta and is the key functional currency for Vivendi Universal. Coca-Cola operates in over 200 countries and uses 52 different functional currencies.[18] This is typical of most MNEs.

Figure 18.8 summarizes the selection of translation method, depending on the choice of functional currency. As in the preceding explanation, if the functional currency is the currency of the country where the foreign subsidiary is located, the current-rate method applies. If the functional currency is the reporting currency of the parent company, the temporal method applies.

Tables 18.4 and 18.5 show a balance sheet and income statement developed under both approaches in order to compare the differences in translation methodologies. Some of the key exchange rates in U.S. dollars per unit of the foreign currency are:

TABLE 18.4   **BALANCE SHEET, DECEMBER 31, 2005**

	POUNDS	TEMPORAL METHOD		CURRENT-RATE METHOD	
		RATE	DOLLARS	RATE	DOLLARS
Cash	20,000	1.6980	33,960	1.6980	33,960
Accounts receivable	40,000	1.6980	67,920	1.6980	67,920
Inventories	40,000	1.5606	62,424	1.6980	67,920
Fixed Assets	100,000	1.5000	150,000	1.6980	169,800
Accumulated depreciation	(20,000)	1.5000	(30,000)	1.6980	(33,960)
Total	180,000		284,304		305,960
Accounts payable	30,000	1.6980	50,940	1.6980	50,940
Long-term debt	44,000	1.6980	74,712	1.6980	74,712
Capital stock	60,000	1.5000	90,000	1.5000	90,000
Retained earnings	46,000	*	68,652	*	77,481
Accumulated translation adjustment					12,507
Total	180,000		284,304		305,640

* Retained earnings is the sum of all income earned in prior years and translated into dollars and this year's income. There is no single exchange rate used to translate retained earnings into dollars.

TABLE 18.5 **INCOME STATEMENT, 2005**

	POUNDS	TEMPORAL METHOD		CURRENT-RATE METHOD	
		RATE	DOLLARS	RATE	DOLLARS
Sales	230,000	1.5617	359,191	1.5617	359,191
Expenses:					
Cost of goods sold	(110,000)	1.5600	(171,600)	1.5617	(171,787)
Depreciation	(10,000)	1.5000	(15,000)	1.5617	(15,617)
Other	(80,000)	1.5617	(124,936)	1.5617	(124,936)
Taxes	(6,000)	1.5617	(9,370)	1.5617	(9,370)
Translation gain (loss)	24,000		(9,633)		37,481
Net Income	24,000		28,652		37,481

$1.5000	Historical exchange rate when fixed assets were acquired and capital stock was issued
$1.6980	Current exchange rate on December 31, 2005
$1.5617	Average exchange rate during 2005
$1.5606	Exchange rate during which ending inventory was acquired
$1.5600	Historical exchange rate for cost of goods sold

Also, the beginning balance in retained earnings for both methods is assumed to be $40,000. The foreign currency was rising in value (strengthening) between the time when the capital stock was issued ($1.500) and the end of the year ($1.6980), so the balance sheet reflects a positive accumulated translation adjustment under the current-rate method. This is consistent with the idea that assets were gaining value in a strong currency.

Disclosure of Foreign-Exchange Gains and Losses

A major difference between the two translation methods is in the recognition of foreign-exchange gains and losses. Under the current-rate method, the gain or loss is called an *accumulated translation adjustment* and is taken directly to the balance sheet as a separate line item in owners' equity. Under the temporal method, the gain or loss is taken directly to the income statement and thus affects earnings per share.

With the current-rate method, the translation gain or loss is recognized in owners' equity. With the temporal method, the translation gain or loss is recognized in the income statement.

ENVIRONMENTAL REPORTS

Earlier in the chapter, we discussed the major financial statements companies must present in order to list on stock exchanges in the United States and elsewhere. One report that is not required but is often presented by companies is an environmental report. Typically, the environmental report is separate from the annual report and is not part of the financial statements or footnotes. Companies from countries in the EU tend to provide environmental reports because of the importance given to environmental issues in Europe and the fact that the EU adopted the Kyoto Protocol against global warming. However, given that there are no specific guidelines given on environmental reporting, there are wide differences in the type and extent of disclosures. BMW, the German automotive company, provides some information on the environment in a section on sustainability that is contained in a report that accompanies but is not part of the annual report. Other than commenting on its commitment to sustainability, which was discussed in more detail in Chapter 5, BMW provides little concrete information.

Environmental reports identify the impact of the company on the environment, focusing on the use of natural resources, how to reduce the emission of greenhouse gases, and efforts to recycle waste.

On the other hand, Finnish timber giant Stora Enso has a fairly comprehensive Sustainability Report that includes information on environmental and social issues. In its report, which is 60 pages long, Stora Enso states the following about its environmental disclosures:

> Stora Enso took a major step forward in bridging sustainability principles into everyday actions when Group-level environmental performance targets were formulated in 2004. The main idea has been to formulate targets that can be reliably measured, and which address the concerns expressed during our regular contacts with stakeholders.[19]

Then Stora Enso identifies four key areas where it measures impact:

1. Guaranteeing the sustainability of fibre sources
2. Measures to combat climate change
3. Improving occupational health and safety
4. Addressing sustainability challenges in emerging markets[20]

One of Stora Enso's emissions target areas is sulphur dioxide emissions to the air. The company set a group target of a 15 percent reduction from 2004 by the end of 2009. When it identifies areas in which to set targets, it uses the following rationale: (1) measurable, (2) relevant to global environmental issues, (3) clear, (4) important to stakeholders, and (5) achievable.[21] As companies, especially European companies, struggle to meet the demands of the Kyoto Protocol and national requirements to improve the environment, they will begin to improve the quantity and quality of their reporting. In the U.S., companies such as ExxonMobil are being forced by external stakeholders to improve their environmental reporting.[22]

PERFORMANCE EVALUATION AND CONTROL

In Chapter 15, we discussed the importance of using reports as a part of the control mechanism. The setting of strategic objectives usually requires managers to focus on choosing a suitable numeric target. Objectives can be quantified in terms of a particular budget number or financial ratio and seem to vary considerably from country to country. Possible targets include return on investment, sales, cost reduction, quality targets, market share, profitability, and budget to actual. As noted above, there may also be environmental targets that companies are trying to reach, especially given that many companies must meet Kyoto Protocol goals for reducing greenhouse gas emissions.

The choice of target depends on the company, the home country, the strategic intent—global vs. multidomestic, sales vs. cost minimization, and so forth. Sales or market share is particularly relevant for a unit that has no control over its input costs and whose primary purpose is to sell the goods of some other unit. Profitability, measured as a ratio or some other measure, is most appropriate for a fully fledged strategic business unit. In one study of U.S.-based MNEs, it was found that the most utilized measure of performance for all subsidiaries was return on investment (ROI).[23] In a more recent study of British MNEs, companies tended to use budget vs. actual comparisons, followed by some form of ROI.[24] In a study of Japanese MNEs, where the culture is significantly different from what is found in the U.S. and U.K., it was found that sales were the most important criterion for performance evaluation.[25] As can be seen, there are some major differences in selecting performance evaluation tools, and most MNEs use a variety of measures, not just one.

Different measures are used to evaluate performance of foreign operations, including ROI, sales, cost reduction, quality targets, market share, profitability, and budget to actual.

Foreign Exchange in the Budget Process

A complicating factor for MNEs is setting targets or budgets in different currencies. Either the budget will be set at headquarters in dollars (for a U.S.-based MNE) and then translated into local currency, or it will be set at the foreign location in the local currency

TABLE 18.6 **POSSIBLE COMBINATION OF EXCHANGE RATES IN THE CONTROL PROCESS**

RATE USED FOR RELATIVE DETERMINING BUDGET	RATE USED TO TRACK PERFORMANCE TO BUDGET	ACTUAL AT TIME OF BUDGET	PROJECTED AT TIME OF BUDGET	ACTUAL AT END OF PERIOD
Actual at time of budget		A-1	A-2	A-3
Projected at time of budget		P-1	P-2	P-3
Actual at end of period (through updating)		E-1	E-2	E-3

Source: Donald R. Lessard and Peter Lorange, "Currency Changes and Management Control: Resolving the Centralization/Decentralization Dilemma," *Accounting Review* 52 (July 1977): 630.

and then translated into dollars for use at the headquarters. Either way, the MNE must deal with currency in the budgeting process.

Lessard and Lorange identify the different ways that firms can translate the budget from the local currency into the parent currency and then monitor actual performance (see Table 18.6).[26] Three different exchange rates are used in Table 18.6. The first is the actual exchange rate in effect when the budget was established, the second is the rate that was projected at the time the budget was established in the local currency, and the third is the actual exchange rate in effect when the budgeted period actually takes place. The attractiveness of the first exchange rate is that it is an objective spot rate that actually exists on a given day. It is a reasonable rate to use in a stable environment, but it may be meaningless in an unstable foreign exchange environment. The projected rate is an attempt on the part of management to forecast what it thinks the exchange rate will be for the budgeted time period. For example, management might project in November 2005 that the exchange rate between the U.S. dollar and the British pound will be $1.8600 during the first six months of 2006, so that would be the projected exchange rate used in the budgeting process. The actual exchange rate found in cell E-3 is an update of the exchange rate that was in effect when the budget was established. It provides the actual exchange rate in effect when the time period takes place.

These three exchange rates need to be considered for both the establishment of the budget as well as the monitoring of performance. In cells A-1, P-2, and E-3, the exchange rate used to establish the budget and monitor performance is the same, so any variances will be due to price and volume, not the exchange rate. The value of P-2 over A-1 and E-3 is that it forces management to think initially of what its performance will be if the forecast is reasonably accurate. A-1 never takes into account what the exchange rate will be, and it does not attempt to reconcile the difference in the budget comparing the original rate with that of the actual rate. Given the instability in exchange rates, however, some would argue that a forecast exchange rate is no more accurate than any other exchange rate. E-3 does take into consideration what performance is at the actual exchange rate, but it does not force management to be forward thinking during the budget process.

A-3 and P-3 result in a variance that is a function of operating results and exchange rate changes. Under A-3, the budget is established at the initial exchange rate, but actual performance is translated at the actual exchange rate. Thus, there is an exchange rate variance that is the difference between the original and the actual rate. P-3 results in a variance that is the difference between what management thought the exchange rate would be and what it actually was at the end of the operating period. If management's forecast was reasonably accurate, P-3 should result in a very small foreign exchange variance. If the exchange rate between the parent and local currency is relatively stable, A-3 should also result in a relatively small foreign exchange variance. However, it is important to realize that the use of A-3 and P-3 means that someone (usually local management) will be held accountable for exchange rate variances.

When using a budget, management must select a currency to set the budget and a currency to evaluate performance.

TABLE 18.7	EXCHANGE RATES USED BY U.K. MNEs

	RATE USED FOR PERFORMANCE EVALUATION			
RATE USED TO DETERMINE BUDGET	**ACTUAL AT TIME OF BUDGET**	**PROJECTED AT TIME OF BUDGET**	**ACTUAL AT END OF PERIOD**	**TOTAL**
Actual at Time of Budget	A-1 10 Firms	A-2 0 Firms	A-3 4 Firms	14 Firms
Projected at Time of Budget	P-1 0 Firms	P-2 16 Firms	P-3 11 Firms	27 Firms
Actual at End of Period	E-1 0 Firms	E-2 0 Firms	E-3 0 Firms	0 Firms
Total	10 Firms	16 Firms	15 Firms	

Source: Adapted from Demirag & De Fuentes, "Exchange Rate Fluctuations and Management Control in UK-Based MNCs: An Examination of the Theory and Practice," *The European Journal of Finance,* 5: 3–28 (1999).

> **The most widely used approaches to translate budgets and compare with performance use forecasts of the exchange rate.**

As illustrated in Table 18.7, the most widely used approaches for taking into consideration foreign exchange when comparing budget with actual performance for a sample of British MNEs are A-1, P-2, and P-3. The use of a forecast rate for setting budgets is by far the preferred approach. A forecast is usually made by the economists in the corporate treasury or in consultation with banks. If the budget process is centralized, corporate treasury probably consults its lead international bank or a couple of banks to get a consensus forecast of exchange rates. If the process is decentralized, the local operations probably consult one or more local money-center banks for a consensus forecast of exchange rates.

Another interesting twist to using P-2 and P-3 is for companies that extensively use hedging strategies. In that case, the company may use a hedge rate instead of a forecast rate for setting budgets. Assume, for example, that a U.S.-based MNE decides to hedge its future balance sheet and income statement in Brazil by entering into forward contracts. Since management knows the forward rate, it could set its budget at the forward rate instead of a forecast rate from a bank. The variance would be the difference between the forward rate and the future spot rate.

Budgeting and Currency Practices

What do MNEs actually do? In one study, fewer than half the firms surveyed judged subsidiary performance in terms of translated dollar amounts, and only 12 percent used both standards.[27] In another study, it was found that a significant number of firms in the sample used both dollar and local currency budgets compared to actual profits and actual sales.[28]

In a study of British subsidiaries of Japanese firms, it was noted that the "companies indicated that financial statements presented in sterling (local currency) provided them with better understanding of the performance of their companies' operations and their management. . . . None of the companies translated their profit budgets into yen for performance evaluation purposes . . . [and] none of the parent companies sent a copy of the translated yen statements." The local currency financial statements were sent to Japan for translation into yen at a company fixed standard exchange rate. In essence, subsidiary managers were unaware of their performance in parent currency terms.[29]

> **Top management of a U.S.-based MNE needs to decide if foreign operations need to see results in dollars or just the local currency.**

It is interesting that the Japanese companies did not concern their foreign subsidiary management with yen results, whereas U.S. companies tend to make their foreign managers very aware of the impact of currency on results. In part, that is because U.S. companies focus heavily on earnings forecasts in dollars, and they expect foreign subsidiary management to be concerned about the impact of their operations in dollars as well.

POINT–COUNTERPOINT: SHOULD LOCAL SUBSIDIARY MANAGEMENT BE HELD RESPONSIBLE FOR EXCHANGE RATE CHANGES?

POINT

A major problem in performance evaluation is determining who should be held responsible for exchange rate changes. On the one hand, local subsidiary management must be held responsible for exchange rate changes. Since they are operating in the local environment, they are best able to determine what is going on with the local currency and can best forecast its future value. They are held responsible for competitive pressures, supplier relationships, labor relations, and a host of other operating issues. They can't always control these variables either, so why should they not be held accountable for exchange rate changes? In addition, if the MNE is a U.S.-based MNE, management must meet earnings forecasts every quarter. In order to forecast earnings, they must get the cooperation of every unit around the world. Earnings forecasts are always made in dollars, and analysts could care less what happens to the currency. They just want to make sure that the company hits its target in dollars. Thus local management must be able to accurately predict what its earnings will be in dollars, not just the local currency, because the results of its operations will be consolidated with operations from around the world. If each foreign operation is going to hit its forecast, it needs to pay attention to

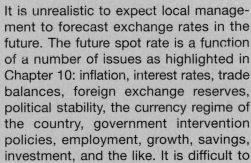

exchange rates and how a potential change in rates could affect its earnings forecast.

COUNTERPOINT

It is unrealistic to expect local management to forecast exchange rates in the future. The future spot rate is a function of a number of issues as highlighted in Chapter 10: inflation, interest rates, trade balances, foreign exchange reserves, political stability, the currency regime of the country, government intervention policies, employment, growth, savings, investment, and the like. It is difficult to accurately predict all of those factors, especially if the government actively intervenes in the market. In addition, there are other factors that could affect the value of a currency, such as war and natural disasters, like the tsunami in Southeast Asia in 2004.

If local management cannot accurately predict the future value of a currency, how can they be held accountable for results in dollars? They are much better equipped to set targets in the local currency and try to meet those targets. HQ treasury can take the local currency results and enter into hedging strategies so that the local results achieve dollar results, or it can instruct local management to enter into hedging strategies. But local management should focus on local results in order to be competitive in the local market.

TRANSFER PRICING AND PERFORMANCE EVALUATION

One of the additional elements of management of the multinational enterprise is **transfer pricing.** This refers to the pricing of goods and services that are transferred (bought and sold) between members of a corporate family—for example, parent to subsidiaries, between subsidiaries, from subsidiaries to parent, and so on. As such, internal transfers include raw materials, semifinished and finished goods, allocation of fixed costs, loans, fees, royalties for use of trademarks, copyrights, and other factors. In theory, such prices should be based on production costs, but in reality often they are not.

One of the important reasons for arbitrarily establishing transfer prices is taxation. However, taxation is only one of a number of reasons why internal transfers may be priced with little consideration for market prices or production costs. Companies may underprice goods sold to foreign affiliates so that the affiliates can then sell them at prices that their local competitors cannot match. If tough antidumping laws exist on final products in the affiliate country, a company could underprice components and semi-finished products to its affiliates. The affiliates could then assemble or finish the final product at prices that would have been classified as dumping prices had they been imported directly into the country rather than produced domestically.

Transfer pricing refers to prices on intracompany transfers of goods, services, and capital.

There are conflicting reasons for setting transfer prices that make it difficult for top management to select the correct price.

High transfer prices might be used to circumvent or significantly lessen the impact of national controls. A government prohibition on dividend remittances could restrict a firm's ability to maneuver income out of a country. However, overpricing the goods shipped to a subsidiary in such a country would make it possible for funds to be taken out. High transfer prices would also be of considerable value to a firm when it is paid a subsidy or earns a tax credit on the value of goods it exports. The higher the transfer prices on exported goods, the greater the subsidies earned or tax credit received.

High transfer prices on goods shipped to subsidiaries might be desirable when a parent wishes to lower the apparent profitability of its subsidiary. This might be desirable because of the demands of the subsidiary's workers for higher wages or greater participation in company profits; because of political pressures to expropriate high-profit, foreign-owned operations; or because of the possibility that new competitors might be lured into the industry by high profits. There might also be inducements for having high-priced transfers go to the subsidiary when a local partner is involved, the inducement being that the increase in the parent company profits will not have to be split with the local partner. High transfer prices may also be desired when increases from existing price controls in the subsidiary's country are based on product costs (including high transfer prices for purchases).

Table 18.8 identifies the conditions in a subsidiary's country inducing either a high or a low transfer price on flows between affiliates and the parent. The challenge with setting an optimal transfer price is that there could be conflicting conditions in the local country. For example, a subsidiary could be in a country with a low corporate income tax rate, which calls for low transfer prices on goods shipped from the parent to the subsidiary in order to maximize profits at the subsidiary level, and with high political instability, which calls for high transfer prices in order to get money out of the country as quickly as possible.

As with transfer pricing of goods, the allocation of overhead has national and cross-national implications. On the cross-national side, firms must determine what to do with corporate overhead. For example, IBM's world headquarters is located in New York, but its operations are located worldwide. How does IBM allocate those costs to its operations in different countries, and what are the tax implications of this issue? This becomes a real issue for performance evaluation, because the allocation of corporate overhead directly reduces operating profit, which reduces return on invested capital, potentially pushing that return below the company's cost of capital. On the purely national side, companies struggle with the general concept of allocating overhead and the ways that affects product costs.

TABLE 18.8   **CONDITIONS IN SUBSIDIARY'S COUNTRY INDUCING HIGH AND LOW TRANSFER PRICES ON FLOWS BETWEEN AFFILIATES AND PARENT**

CONDITIONS IN SUBSIDIARY'S COUNTRY INDUCING *LOW TRANSFER PRICES* ON FLOWS FROM PARENT AND *HIGH TRANSFER PRICES* ON FLOWS TO PARENT	CONDITIONS IN SUBSIDIARY'S COUNTRY INDUCING *HIGH TRANSFER PRICES* ON FLOWS FROM PARENT AND *LOW TRANSFER PRICES* ON FLOWS TO PARENT
High ad valorem tariffs	Local partners
Corporate income tax rate lower than in parent's country	Pressure from workers to obtain greater share of company profit
Significant competition	Political pressure to nationalize or expropriate high-profit foreign firms
Local loans based on financial appearance of subsidiary	Restrictions on profit or dividend remittances
Export subsidy or tax credit on value of exports	Political instability
Lower inflation rate than in parent's country	Substantial tie-in sales agreements
Restrictions (ceilings) in subsidiary's country on the *value* of products that can be imported	Price of final product controlled by government but based on production cost
	Desire to mask profitability of subsidiary operations to keep competitors out

Source: Jeffrey S. Arpan, *Intracorporate Pricing: Non-American Systems and Views* (New York: Praeger, 1972).

THE BALANCED SCORECARD

The concept of the **balanced scorecard** (BSC) is another approach to performance measurement increasingly being used by companies, especially in the United States and Europe. Approximately 50 percent of *Fortune* 1,000 companies in North America and about 40 percent in Europe use a version of the BSC, according to a recent survey by Bain & Co.[30] This approach endeavors to more closely link the strategic and financial perspectives of a business and takes a broad view of business performance.[31] The balanced scorecard provides a framework to look at the strategies giving rise to value creation from the following perspectives:

1. *Financial*—growth, profitability, and risk from the perspective of shareholders
2. *Customer*—value and differentiation from the customer perspective
3. *Internal business processes*—the priorities for various business processes that create customer and shareholder satisfaction
4. *Learning and growth*—the priorities to create a climate supporting organizational change, innovation, and growth

Although the focus is still ultimately on financial performance, the balanced scorecard approach reveals the drivers of long-term competitive performance. In simple terms, learning and growth help create more efficient business processes, which create value for customers, who reward the firm financially. The challenge is to clearly identify these drivers, to agree on relevant measures, and to implement the new system at all levels of the organization. The significant aspect about this measurement approach, however, is that it also creates a focus for the future because the measures used communicate to managers what is important.

Although a firm's BSC is a proprietary strategic tool and is generally not available to the general public, its principles are evident in the strategic decisions made by MNEs. IKEA, the Swedish firm, is a case in point. With strong roots in the Swedish culture and a centralized operating style, IKEA has grown to become the world's largest furniture retailer. The company uses a global strategy to spread a simple concept: to offer the broadest range of furniture at the lowest price possible. IKEA's success begins with internal learning and growth by ensuring that all employees are trained in the cost-saving, hands-on, customer-focused mentality. This enables employees to focus on creating efficient processes that keep costs down. For example, the design team is constantly looking for new materials and suppliers to lower the cost of furniture without sacrificing quality. Since its founding, IKEA has identified a customer base that would find value in low-cost, innovative furniture: young couples looking to furnish their first apartment. This strategic cohesiveness has rewarded the company with phenomenal growth. By the end of 2004, IKEA operated 201 stores in 35 countries, with sales of €13.6 billion. In 2005 alone, it opened 21 new stores after opening 49 new stores between 1999 and 2004.[32]

Although the BSC offers the advantages of logically connecting financial performance with its nonfinancial drivers, establishing a coherent scorecard for an MNE has its challenges. For example, as IKEA grows, it faces different customer bases in different countries. IKEA must also ensure that its streamlined product line has appeal in its several markets of operation. The cultural, geographical, and financial complexity of an MNE makes it challenging to establish a set of interrelated cause-and-effect performance measures. This task appears simpler for MNEs with global strategies like IKEA. However, multidomestic MNEs such as Philips, the Dutch electronics company, have successfully implemented the BSC concept.

Perhaps the balanced scorecard helps solve many of the control and evaluation dilemmas presented throughout this chapter. Adequate use of the BSC helps managers avoid using only one measure of performance (such as ROI or sales growth)

The balanced scorecard is an approach to performance measurement that closely links the strategic and financial perspectives of a business.

and forces them to link financial measures with the nonfinancial factors that drive them. In addition, subsidiaries are evaluated based on a coherent set of performance bases instead of just one base that may or may not be directly controlled by that subsidiary. Thus the BSC concept has been refined into a strategic management system, which replaces the traditional focus on the budget as the center for the management process.[33]

SUMMARY

- The MNE must learn to cope with differing inflation rates, exchange-rate changes, currency controls, expropriation risks, customs duties, tax rates and methods of determining taxable income, levels of sophistication of local accounting personnel, and local as well as home-country reporting requirements.

- A company's accounting or controllership function is responsible for collecting and analyzing data for internal and external users.

- Culture can have a strong influence on the accounting dimensions of measurement and disclosure. The cultural values of secrecy and transparency refer to the degree of disclosure of information. The cultural values of optimism and conservatism refer to the valuation of assets and the recognition of income. Conservatism results in the undervaluation of both assets and income.

- Financial statements differ in terms of language, currency, type of statements (income statement, balance sheet, etc.), financial statement format, extent of footnote disclosures, and the underlying GAAP on which the financial statements are based.

- Important users of financial statements that must be considered in determining accounting standards are investors, employees, lenders, suppliers and other trade creditors, customers, governments and their agencies, and the public.

- Some of the most important sources of influence on the development of accounting standards and practices are culture, capital markets, regional and global standard-setting groups, management, and accountants.

- The International Accounting Standards Board (IASB), an independent, privately funded accounting standard setter, is charged with developing a single set of high-quality, understandable, and enforceable global accounting standards. Standards developed by the IASB require transparent and comparable information in general-purpose financial statements.

- In cooperation with national accounting standard setters around the world, especially the Financial Accounting Standards Board (FASB) in the United States, the IASB hopes to achieve convergence in accounting standards.

- When transactions denominated in a foreign currency are translated into dollars, all accounts are recorded initially at the exchange rate in effect at the time of the transaction. At each subsequent balance sheet date, recorded dollar balances representing amounts owed by or to the company that are denominated in a foreign currency are adjusted to reflect the current rate.

- Companies enter foreign-exchange gains and losses arising from foreign-currency transactions on the income statement during the period in which they occur. Companies enter gains and losses arising from translating financial statements by the current-rate method as a separate component of owners' equity. Companies enter gains and losses arising from translating according to the temporal method directly on the income statement.

- Many different performance evaluation measures are used for global operations, especially return on investment and budget compared with actual performance.

- In comparing budget with actual performance, MNEs need to decide which rate to use to translate the budget into the parent currency and in which currency to monitor results. Then the MNE must decide who is responsible for exchange rate variances.

- MNEs may set arbitrary transfer prices to take advantage of tax differences between countries or to accomplish other corporate objectives, such as performance evaluation, profit manipulation, etc.

- The balanced scorecard provides a framework to look at the strategies giving rise to value creation from the following perspectives: financial, customer, internal business processes, and learning and growth.

Vivendi Universal[34]

C A S E

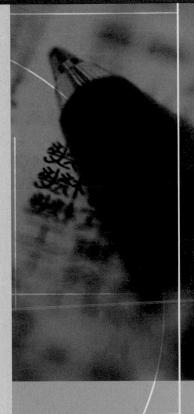

In December of 2000 French-based Vivendi's merger with France's Canal+ and Canada's Seagram Co. Ltd. created a global communications giant with diverse products in many countries throughout the world. This merger of French and Canadian companies brought together two organizations with different cultures and accounting standards. The merger was overwhelmingly approved by the shareholders of Vivendi, Seagram, and Canal+, with votes in favor of the merger of 96.6 percent, 90.4 percent, and 98.6 percent, respectively. Following the merger, Vivendi Universal (VU) began its battle with the conflicting French and U.S. generally accepted accounting principles (GAAP) and made a serious attempt to inform its millions of global shareholders of the many differences between them. (Although Seagram was based in Canada, it prepared its financial statements in accordance with U.S. GAAP because over 50 percent of its shareholders were U.S. residents.) Beginning in 2005, VU will face additional accounting challenges as France, a member of the European Union, makes the transition from French GAAP to International Financial Reporting Standards (IFRS).

Company Statistics and Information

Vivendi Universal's organization can be traced back to a French imperial decree enabling the company, then called CGE, to supply water in Lyons, France. CGE excelled in "environmental" operations and expanded its water operations with waste management, energy, and transportation operations. In 1998, CGE changed its name to Vivendi. The merger creating Vivendi Universal in 2000 put the company in the world spotlight.

In 2004, VU employed close to 38,000 people worldwide in 77 countries. The previous year, the company reported operating income of € 3,309 million on revenues of € 21,428 million. VU is listed on the New York Stock Exchange and on Eurolist. Vivendi is focused on two strategic areas: media and telecommunications.

VU's media business consists of three major companies: Canal+ Group, Universal Music Group, and Vivendi Universal Games. Canal+ is the leader in digital and pay-TV in France with the world's third largest film library. Canal+ attracts subscribers primarily through its film and sports programming, broadcasting popular events such as the French L1 professional soccer league championship, UEFA Champions League, and other major European soccer leagues, as well as horse racing, major rugby games (including the Top 16), golf tournaments, boxing championships and various U.S. sports, including the NBA. Universal Music Group is the world's largest music company with a market share of 24.7 percent in 2004. In that year, one out of every four albums sold worldwide was a Universal album. Vivendi Universal Games (VUG) is a global developer, publisher, and distributor of interactive entertainment. VUG produces such popular games as Warcraft, the fastest growing game in its category.

The telecommunications business is made up of two major companies: SFR Cegetel Group and Maroc Telecom. SFT Cegetel is the number two mobile (SFR) and fixed-line (Cegetel) telecommunications operator in France. Maroc Telecom is the leading mobile and fixed-line telecommunications operator in Morocco. Vivendi's move into the telecom industry occurred after 2002, so its holdings in that area are smaller than in media, where VU has more extensive experience. See Table 18.9 for Vivendi's business segment breakdown and Table 18.10 for a regional revenue breakdown.

lower net asset value being assigned to acquisitions, which results in higher gains on the sales of businesses as compared to U.S. GAAP. Additionally, the amortization of goodwill charged to earnings is lower under French GAAP than under U.S. GAAP.

The adjustment of a net loss of €1.135 billion under U.S. GAAP and €13.597 billion under French GAAP is a change of 1,198 percent. The difference to the millions of VU shareholders and investors throughout the world on this change in accounting loss is huge. The paragraph cited here also suggests the major differences between U.S. GAAP and French GAAP on income statements.

Reporting in Compliance with IFRS

In 2002, the European Commission approved a law requiring all members of the EU to adopt IFRS by 2005. This created a new accounting challenge for Vivendi Universal. In its 2003 20-F filed with the SEC, Vivendi noted the following:

As of January 1, 2005, Vivendi Universal's consolidated financial statements will be established in accordance with the International Financial Reporting Standards (IFRS) in effect as of December 31, 2005. . . . To ensure consistency of accounting policies and of their implementation within the group, the IFRS conversion is currently being led by a central project team for the whole group, in coordination with dedicated teams within each business unit. The first phase of the project, in progress, referred to as "diagnosis phase," aims at analyzing the main differences in accounting principles as compared with French GAAP and U.S. GAAP currently applied by the group and at evaluating the impacts of those differences. In addition, it aims at assessing the ability of the group's information system to produce IFRS-compliant financial information and to identify the required adaptations, if any.

The main differences between French GAAP and IFRS involve some of the same differences between French GAAP and U.S. GAAP noted above. First, IFRS don't require goodwill amortization, so the change will increase Vivendi Universal's net income since under French GAAP goodwill is amortized (expensed) on a straight-line basis over a period of up to 40 years. Second, financial derivative instruments that are currently reported as off-balance sheet commitments will have to be recorded on the balance sheet, so that certain financial assets will have to be recorded at market values. This could have a positive or negative effect on VU's balance sheet, depending on the market fluctuations of the assets involved. Third, the cost of repurchasing shares will have to be recorded as a reduction of shareholders' equity regardless of their future use, whereas French GAAP doesn't always require reducing equity for stock repurchases.

In April 2005, VU released a statement summarizing the main impacts of the transition to IFRS. The change affected the following areas:

Shareholders' equity of €15,798 million as of December 31, 2004, compared to €13,621 million in French GAAP

Revenues of €18,724 million, compared to €18,893 million in French GAAP

Net income of €3,821 million, compared to a profit of €754 million in French GAAP. This improvement takes into account the positive impact of the cancellation under IFRS of the foreign currency translation adjustment associated with the NBC Universal transaction as of January 1st, 2004 (approximately €2,490 million) and the elimination of goodwill amortization (€638 million).

Financial net debt of €4,724 million as of December 31, 2004, compared to €3,135 million in French GAAP. In IFRS, financial net debt represents 29.9% of shareholders' equity, to be compared with 23% in French GAAP.

Although the intricacies of IFRS compared to French GAAP are beyond the scope of this case, the impact of changes in accounting standards is obvious. The adoption of IFRS increased Vivendi's equity by 16 percent, increased net income by 407 percent, and increased net debt by 51 percent. These changes greatly affect the comparability of current financial statements based on IFRS with past financial statements based on French GAAP. In addition, the discrepancies between IFRS and U.S. GAAP will remain so long as Vivendi is listed on the NYSE, although those discrepancies will narrow as IFRS and U.S. GAAP become closer.

Accounting Issues Arise

As part of the 2000 merger VU was forced to sell its stake in British Sky Broadcasting Group PLC (BSkyB), but since it could not find a buyer, VU transferred the stake to Deutsche Bank in exchange for cash. Under French GAAP, the proportion of BSkyB debt carried by these shares should have stayed on Vivendi's books. However, VU's auditor, Arthur Andersen, argued that under U.S. securities law, this debt could be removed from the balance sheet, allowing the media group to post a profit, something it was doing with another company it audited named Enron. It seems that VU successfully disguised these accounts from the firm's liabilities, though the measures were against French GAAP according to the findings of an investigation published by *Le Monde,* a French newspaper. A COB investigation also discovered letters and e-mails that showed how VU's management, led by Chairman Jean-Marie Messier, attempted to discourage its French auditor, Salustro-Reydel, from applying French GAAP to VU's BSkyB shares. Messier resigned as chairman in July 2002.

Messier's successor, Jean-Rene Fourtou, reorganized Vivendi along two strategic business groups: media and telecommunications. The process involved selling 24.6 billion euros worth of assets and investing 24.1 billion euros to increase the Group's stake in SFR Cegetel Group and Maroc Telecom and acquire a 20 percent controlling interest in NBC Universal. By 2004, VU had reported a profit, increased cash flows, and reduced its debt levels. Most of these improvements occurred due to aggressive divestitures and acquisitions. The challenge ahead of Vivendi Universal is to produce profits through ongoing operations rather than through large-scale financial transactions.

QUESTIONS

1. Based on this short description, do you agree with Vivendi Universal's acquisition and diversification strategy?
2. Since Vivendi Universal listed its shares on the New York Stock Exchange, why didn't it just adopt U.S. GAAP as Seagrams did or as DaimlerChrysler does?
3. As Vivendi Universal began to adopt IFRS, the differences between its financial statements and U.S. GAAP financial statements narrowed significantly. Why is that the case?
4. What challenges face European companies that move from their own GAAP to IFRS? What challenges do these moves create for Vivendi Universal's investors in France and abroad?

CHAPTER NOTES

1   Judith Burns, "Parmalat to Settle SEC Charges of Fraud for U.S. Bond Offering," *Wall Street Journal (Europe)* (30 July 2004); "The Pause After Parmalat," *The Economist* (17 January 2004); Allessandra Galloni and Yaroslav Trofimov, "Tanzi's Power Games Helped Parmalat Rise, But Didn't Cushion Fall," *Wall Street Journal (Europe)* (8 March 2004); Michael Gray, Carlotta Amaduzzi, and Stephen Deane, "Corporate Governance Lessons from Europe's Enron; The Milk Sheikh Whose Dream Curdled," *The Guardian* (31 December 2003); Peter Gumbel, "How It All Went So Sour," *Time (Europe)* (November 29, 2004); Hoover's Online: "Parmalat," downloaded 19 April 2005 from **www.hoovers.com**; Michelle Perry, "Enron: Could It Happen Here?" *Accountancy Age* (25 January 2004); David Reilly and Allesandra Galloni, "Spilling Over: Banks Come Under Scrutiny for Role in Parmalat Scandal," *Wall Street Journal (Europe)* (28 September 2004); David Reilly and Matt Moffett, "Parmalat Inquiry Is Joined by Brazil," *Wall Street Journal (Europe)* (7 January 2004); Susannah Rodgers and Kenneth Maxwell, "Parmalat Fallout Hits

Farmers; Dairies Worry About Their Future as Milk Seller Misses Payments," *Wall Street Journal (Europe)* (15 January 2004); Securities and Exchange Commission (SEC): *Complaint #18527* (29 December 2003); Wall Street Journal: "Parmalat to Trim Key Operations in 10 Countries," *Wall Street Journal (Europe)* (29 March 2004); "How Parmalat Differs from U.S. Scandals," *Knowledge@Wharton* (28 January 2004), http://knowledge.wharton.upenn.edu/.

2 *Statement of the Accounting Principles Board No. 4,* "Basic Concepts and Accounting Principles Underlying Financial Statements of Business Enterprises" (New York: American Institute of Certified Public Accountants, 1970), par. 40. Quoted in Earl K. Stice, James D. Stice, and K. Fred Skousen, *Intermediate Accounting,* 15th ed. (Thomson/Southwestern, 2004), p. 1.

3 Financial Accounting Standards Board, "Objectives of Financial Reporting by Business Enterprises," *Statement of Financial Accounting Concepts No. 1* (Stamford, CT: FASB, 1979), paragraphs 34–54.

4 International Accounting Standards Committee, *International Accounting Standards 1998* (London: IASC, 1998), paragraph 9, pp. 36–37.

5 Geert Hofstede, *Culture's Consequences: International Differences in Work-Related Values* (Beverly Hills: Sage, 1980); Geert Hofstede and Michael H. Bond, "The Confucius Connection: From Cultural Roots to Economic Growth," *Organizational Dynamics* 16, no. 4 (1988); Geert Hofstede, *Cultures and Organizations* (Maidenhead, England: McGraw-Hill, 1991).

6 Sidney J. Gray, "Towards a Theory of Cultural Influence on the Development of Accounting Systems Internationally," *Abacus* (March, 1998).

7 C. W. Nobes and R. H. Parker, eds., *Comparative International Accounting,* 6th ed. (Englewood Cliffs, NJ: Prentice-Hall, 2000).

8 Christopher Nobes and Robert Parker, *Comparative International Accounting,* 7th ed. (England: FT Prentice Hall, 2002).

9 "Uniform Rules for International Accounting Standards from 2005 Onwards," *European Parliament Daily Notebook* (March 12, 2002).

10 Arthur Leavitt, "The Numbers Game," presentation at New York University Center for Law and Business, New York, September 28, 1998.

11 "About IFAC," http://www.ifac.org/About/. Accessed June 1, 2005.

12 See the Web site of the International Accounting Standards Board for more details, including the members of the Board and the organizational structure, at http://www.iasb.org/.

13 IASB Constitution, paragraph 2.

14 Andrew Peaple, "Major Economies at Loggerheads over Global Accounting Rules," *Wall Street Journal* (February 8, 2004), online edition.

15 FASB, *Convergence with the International Accounting Standards Board (IASB),* http://www.fasb.org/intl/convergence_iasb.shtml.

16 Deloitte, "Use of IFRSs for Reporting by Domestic Listed Companies, by Country, Status as of 2005," http://www.iasplus.com/country/useias.htm, accessed June 2, 2005.

17 Financial Accounting Standards Board, "Foreign Currency Translation," *Statement of Financial Accounting Standards No. 52* (Stamford, CT: FASB, December 1981), 6–7.

18 Coca-Cola Annual Report, www.cocacola.com.

19 Stora Enso, *Sustainability 2004,* p. 4.

20 Ibid.

21 Ibid., pp. 12–13.

22 See http://www.exxonmobil.com/corporate/files/corporate/CCR2002_enviro.pdf.

23 S. Robbins and R. Stobaugh, "The Bent Measuring Stick for Foreign Subsidiaries," *Harvard Business Review* (September–October 1973).

24 A. Appleyard, N. Strong, and P. Walton, "Budgetary Control of Foreign Subsidiaries," *Management Accounting (UK)* (September 1990): 44–45.

25 M. Shields, C. Chow, Y. Kato, and Y. Nakagawa, "Management Accounting Practices in the U.S. and Japan: Comparative Survey Findings and Research Implications," *Journal of International Financial Management and Accounting* 3, no. 1 (1991): 61–77.

26 Donald Lessard and Peter Lorange, "Currency Changes and Management Control: Resolving the Centralization/Decentralization Dilemma," *Accounting Review* (July 1977).

27 Robbins and Stobaugh, op. cit.

28 Helen Morsicato, *Currency Translation and Performance Evaluation in Multinationals* (Ann Arbor, MI: UMI Research Press, 1980).

29 I. S. Demirag, "Management Control Systems and Performance Evaluations in Japanese Companies: A British Perspective," *Management Accounting* (UK) (July–August 1994): 18–20, 45.

30 A. Gumbus and B. Lyons, "The Balanced Scorecard at Phillips Electronics," *Strategic Finance* 84, no. 5 (2002): 45–50.

31 R. Kaplan and D. P. Norton, "The Balanced Scorecard—Measures That Drive Performance," *Harvard Business Review* (January–February 1992): 71–79.

32 http://franchisor.ikea.com/showContent.asp?swfId=facts1.

33 R. Kaplan and D. P. Norton, *The Strategy-Focused Organization* (Cambridge, MA: Harvard Business School Press, 2001).

34 "Challenges Ahead for Vivendi's New CEO," knowledge@wharton, July 31, 2002, http://www.upenn.edu/researchatpenn/article.php?310&bus; "Q&A: Messier on the Record: Settling into the Hot Seat," *Business Week Online*, July 1, 2002, http://www.businessweek.com/magazine/content/02_26/b3789079.htm; www.vivendiuniversal.com. The following information was downloaded on 20 April 2005: Vivendi Universal 2003 Form 20-F; Vivendi Universal 2004 Operating and Financial Review and Prospects & Audited Consolidated Financial Statements as of December 31, 2004; Press Release: *Positive Impact of IFRS*, 14 April 2005; strategic plans from www.vivendiuniversal.com.

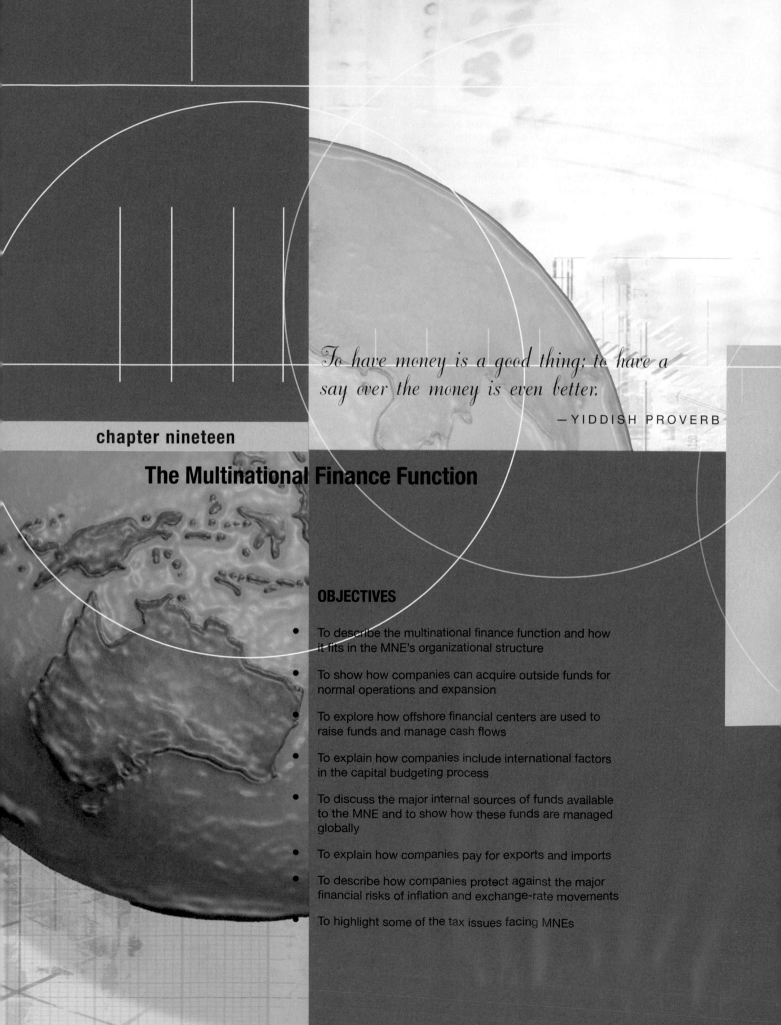

To have money is a good thing; to have a say over the money is even better.

— YIDDISH PROVERB

chapter nineteen

The Multinational Finance Function

OBJECTIVES

- To describe the multinational finance function and how it fits in the MNE's organizational structure

- To show how companies can acquire outside funds for normal operations and expansion

- To explore how offshore financial centers are used to raise funds and manage cash flows

- To explain how companies include international factors in the capital budgeting process

- To discuss the major internal sources of funds available to the MNE and to show how these funds are managed globally

- To explain how companies pay for exports and imports

- To describe how companies protect against the major financial risks of inflation and exchange-rate movements

- To highlight some of the tax issues facing MNEs

CASE: NU SKIN ENTERPRISES IN ASIA[1]

Nu Skin Enterprises, a U.S.-based network-marketing company, operates in approximately 40 countries throughout Asia, the Americas, and Europe. In 2004, Nu Skin generated 84 percent of its $1.14 billion in revenues from Asia, with Japan generating 51 percent of revenues and China generating 10 percent (greater China, including Hong Kong and Taiwan, generate a total of 20 percent). Nu Skin's other key market in Asia is South Korea, and it also has operations in other markets in Asia, South Asia, and the Pacific. Because Nu Skin operates in so many countries, exchange-rate volatility has always affected its bottom line. Rate volatility became even more important, however, once Japan displaced the United States as Nu Skin's leading market. After Nu Skin began operations in Japan in 1993 and up until mid-2002, the yen continued to weaken while fluctuating against the dollar, and this translated into millions of dollars of losses for Nu Skin in exchange-rate exposure despite huge gains in local revenues. By mid-2005, however, the dollar had weakened significantly against the yen, reversing the gains it had piled up in the early part of the decade.

BACKGROUND ON NU SKIN

Nu Skin, a leader in multilevel marketing, was founded in 1984 in Provo, Utah. Blake Roney, a young entrepreneur, envisioned the development and distribution of personal care products through direct selling similar to the strategy of Amway. His idea was to organize a sales force of independent, self-motivated entrepreneurs who would build their own organizations supported by Nu Skin products and marketing materials. As sales started increasing, Roney expanded the product line to include premium items like shampoos, lotions, makeup, skin care products, and nutritional products. A few years later, Nu Skin expanded its nutritional line with the acquisition of Pharmanex and created a technology division called Big Planet.

Nu Skin's international strategy was to open one new market per year. It opened its first international office in Canada in 1990. Its exposure to the Asian market started in Hong Kong in 1991. In 1993, Nu Skin opened an office in Japan, the world's largest direct-sales market. Nu Skin saw great opportunity in Japan because other direct-sales companies had proven successful in the Asian market. Asians, particularly the Japanese, enjoy direct selling, door-to-door selling, and the personal contacts acquired using this model of selling. As a result, network marketing companies have flourished in Japan.

Nu Skin does not outlay a large capital investment when opening a new market. It generally starts with one office, one warehouse, and up to 60 employees with one expatriate (U.S. manager). Nu Skin financed its entry into Japan the same way it financed its entry in other markets—with internal sources of funds. The U.S. corporate office allocates internal funds for the opening of new markets. Nu Skin finances its growth in each market mainly with its retained earnings. In 1996, Nu Skin management created a holding company called Nu Skin Asia Pacific (NSAP) to manage the financials of Nu Skin's Asia Pacific markets. Nu Skin then went through a public offering in order to be listed on the New York Stock Exchange, and in 2002, Nu Skin issued a second public offering, which helped it to raise money for expansion into China in 2003.

Although Chinese regulations did not allow Nu Skin to implement its direct selling model, the company opened several retail stores in an attempt to form a foundation for future growth. This new retail model was the first of its kind for Nu Skin. Once Nu Skin began operating in China, sales grew rapidly. In 2004, revenues in China grew 174 percent over the prior year, making China Nu Skin's third largest market in the world after Japan and the U.S., with the U.S. not that far ahead and growing much slower. Nu Skin envisions significant market potential in China and plans to open 80 to 100 new stores there in 2005. One major problem with China is the inability to penetrate the market using the same direct selling model that Nu Skin uses elsewhere to such great success. In 1998, China banned direct selling after riots occurred from the collapse of a pyramid scheme. Although none of the U.S. direct marketing firms like Avon, Amway, and Nu Skin were implicated, they were affected by the new laws. However, with the opening of China after entrance into the WTO, China pledged to look at direct marketing once again. In 2005, the Chinese government gave Avon permission to engage in direct marketing, but restricted its activities to cities in Beijing, Tianjin, and Guangdong province. The concern on the part of China is not only the possibility of another collapse such as the one that occurred in 1998, but also the fact that direct marketing firms thrive on mass meetings and rallies to pump up enthusiasm. With the cosmetics market expanding so rapidly in China and the fact that much of the interior of China is not being accessed by retailers, the potential for direct selling of cosmetics is huge.

FOREIGN EXCHANGE EXPOSURE

It didn't take long for Nu Skin to realize the impact of foreign exchange rates on net income. In 1993, when Nu Skin Japan (NSJ) began operations, the dollar/yen exchange rate was very volatile, fluctuating from 125 yen/dollar at the beginning of the year to the yen strengthening to 109 by the end of the year. The yen strengthened again in 1995 when it hit 80.63 to the dollar. However, the situation changed in mid-1995, and the dollar began to strengthen against the yen. From an average high of 84.33 yen in 1995, the yen weakened in value to over 110 to the dollar by the end of 1996. The Asian financial crisis hit Japan from 1997 to 1998, and the exchange rate fluctuated drastically while the economy hit rock bottom. Fortunately for Nu Skin, direct-sales businesses typically do well in depressed economies with high unemployment because such firms, like Nu Skin, provide a way for people to begin their own businesses. Sales continued to climb despite the economic woes in Japan.

Nu Skin has used hedging strategies to reduce the risk of currency fluctuations involved in its international operations. To understand how the volatility in exchange rates affects Nu Skin, it is necessary to view an example of how Nu Skin uses dollars and yen. NSJ earns profits in Japan, denominated in yen, which are translated into dollars for the financial reports; the subsequent dividends are then converted into dollars and deposited into dollar-based bank accounts. When the value of the yen was weak compared to the dollar (as it was in 1997 versus the previous years), that translated into fewer dollars. In 1998, the yen weakened even further against the dollar, translating into millions in lost dollar-based revenues for Nu Skin. The futures market showed doubt in the yen strengthening against the dollar. Because of the futures outlook and the general fluctuation of the market, Nu Skin sought to reduce its exposure to the exchange-rate market. It increased its hedging activities by entering into forward contracts, which guaranteed receivables at certain dollar/yen exchange rates. Although exchange-rate losses amounted to $5.5 million in 1997, this hedging policy helped minimize the losses on its books.

The trend changed in 2002, when the dollar weakened against the yen from a high in February 2002 of 134.77 yen/dollar to a low in July of 115.71. This helped Nu Skin's dollar-based revenues because such a large portion of its income is from Japan. Third-quarter earnings in Japan and Korea were up 7 percent from 2001 in constant currency terms, but they were up 9 percent when taking the new exchange rate into account. The yen continued to strengthen against the dollar through 2004. Although revenue in Japan decreased 3 percent in constant currency terms in 2004, revenue increased by 4 percent when taking foreign currency exchange rates into account.

Nu Skin chose another strategy to minimize exchange-rate risk—borrowing in local currencies. Exchange-rate differentials from its debt offset the differentials from its assets. Nu Skin has ¥8.3 billion in long-term debt, which is denominated in Japanese yen. When the yen strengthens against the dollar, the loan translates into a higher amount in dollars, and when the yen weakens against the dollar, the loan translates into a lower amount in dollars. This offsets the exchange-rate gains and losses from Nu Skin's revenues in Japan. Nu Skin lowers the possibility of peak profits it may make from exchange-rate translations, but it also lowers the possibility of valleys. Although Nu Skin does not eliminate the risk in foreign-exchange transactions from its international operations, it significantly lowers that risk, thus helping to stabilize its revenues in the long run.

Nu Skin's expansion into China presents new exchange-rate risks for the company. The Chinese yuan is currently pegged to the dollar, which minimizes the impact of foreign currency fluctuations on profits from China. However, if the Chinese government allows the yuan to float freely against the dollar, a strengthening of the yuan would increase Nu Skin's revenue and profits, while a weakening of the yuan would negatively impact profits.

INTRODUCTION

Why do you need to understand capital markets, cash management, and financial risk? Having a good product idea is not sufficient for success. MNEs need to get access to capital markets in different countries in order to finance expansion. Indeed, finance is integral to firms' international strategies, as Figure 19.1 shows. The small company involved only tangentially in international business may not be concerned about global capital markets, but it will probably still have to deal in foreign-exchange through its commercial bank in order to settle payments for exports and imports. However, the MNE investing and operating abroad usually is concerned about access to capital in local markets as well as in large global markets. In Chapter 9, we discussed the nature of global debt and equity markets. This chapter briefly examines external sources of funds available to companies operating abroad and focuses more on internal sources of funds that arise from intercompany links. Nu Skin's intercompany lending in Japan illustrates that point. The chapter also examines international dimensions of the capital investment decision, global cash management, including payments and receipt of payment for exports and imports, foreign exchange risk-management strategies, and international tax issues.

THE TREASURY AND FINANCE FUNCTIONS

One of the most important people on the management team is the chief financial officer. This chapter focuses on the CFO's most important global treasury responsibilities. Figure 19.2 illustrates how the CFO's responsibilities fit into the organizational structure of the firm and how global finance fits into the treasury function.

The finance function in the firm focuses on cash flows, both short-term and long-term. The role of financial management is to maintain and create economic value or wealth by maximizing shareholder wealth—the market value of existing shareholders' common stock.[2] The management activities related to cash flows can be divided into four major areas.

The corporate finance function acquires and allocates financial resources among the company's activities and projects. Four key functions are

- Capital structure
- Long-term financing
- Capital budgeting
- Working capital management

FIGURE 19.1   FINANCE IN INTERNATIONAL BUSINESS

Finance is one of the necessary functions for implementing companies' international strategies.

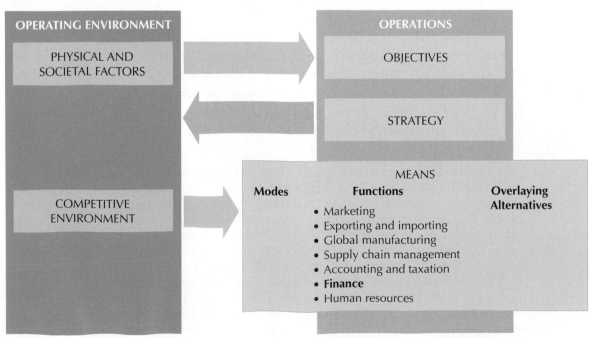

OPERATING ENVIRONMENT

PHYSICAL AND SOCIETAL FACTORS

COMPETITIVE ENVIRONMENT

OPERATIONS

OBJECTIVES

STRATEGY

MEANS

Modes   Functions   Overlaying Alternatives
- Marketing
- Exporting and importing
- Global manufacturing
- Supply chain management
- Accounting and taxation
- **Finance**
- Human resources

LOCATION OF TREASURY FUNCTION IN THE CORPORATE ORGANIZATIONAL STRUCTURE

The treasury function falls under the responsibility of the chief financial officer, and it comprises domestic and foreign responsibilities. The global finance function within treasury is a resource to all of the strategic business units of a company.

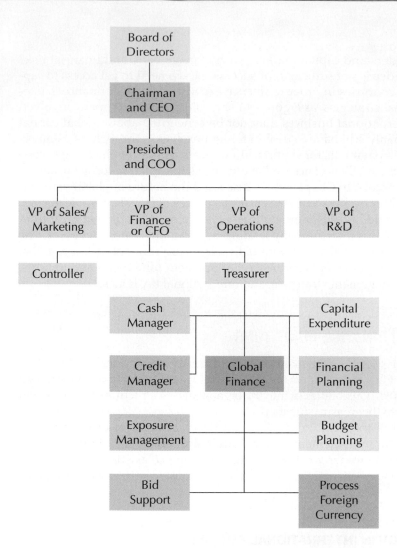

1. *Capital structure*—determining the proper mix of debt and equity
2. *Long-term financing*—selection, issuance, and management of long-term debt and equity capital, including location (in the company's home country or elsewhere) and currency (the company's home currency or a foreign currency)
3. *Capital budgeting*—analyzing investment opportunities
4. *Working capital management*—proper management of the company's currency assets and liabilities (cash, receivables, marketable securities, inventory, trade receivables and payables, short-term bank debt)

We will discuss these areas and also the impact of taxation on each of these decisions.[3]

The CFO acquires financial resources and allocates them among the company's activities and projects. Acquiring resources (financing) means generating funds either internally (within the company) or from sources external to the company at the lowest possible cost. When Nu Skin needed to expand, it used internal funds, issued stock, and borrowed money in the U.S. and in Japan. Allocating resources (investing) means increasing stockholders' wealth through the allocation of funds to different projects and investment opportunities.[4]

The CFO's job is more complex in a global environment than in the domestic setting because of forces such as foreign-exchange risk, currency flows and restrictions, political risk, different tax rates and laws pertaining to the determination of taxable income, and regulations on access to capital in different markets. In the remainder of the chapter, we will examine the following areas: (1) global debt markets, (2) offshore financial centers, (3) capital budgeting in an international context, (4) internal sources of funds, (5) methods of payment from trade, (6) foreign-exchange risk management, and (7) taxation.

CAPITAL STRUCTURE

The CFO must determine the proper capital structure of the company—the mix between long-term debt and equity. Many companies, such as Nu Skin, started off with an initial investment and then grew through internally generated funds. However, when those sources were inadequate to fund continued growth into new markets, they had to decide the proper mix of debt and equity. The degree to which a firm funds the growth of the business by debt is known as **leverage.** The weighted average cost of capital of a company is found as follows:

$$
\begin{matrix} \text{Weighted} \\ \text{average Cost} \\ \text{of Capital} \end{matrix} = \begin{bmatrix} \text{after-tax} \\ \text{cost of} \\ \text{debt} \end{bmatrix} \times \begin{matrix} \text{proportion} \\ \text{of debt} \\ \text{financing} \end{matrix} + \begin{bmatrix} \text{cost} \\ \text{of} \\ \text{equity} \end{bmatrix} \times \begin{matrix} \text{proportion} \\ \text{of equity} \\ \text{financing} \end{matrix}
$$

The degree to which companies use leverage instead of equity capital—known as stocks or shares—varies from country to country. Country-specific factors are a more important determinant of a company's capital structure than is any other factor, because companies tend to follow the financing trends in their own country and their particular industry within their country. Japanese companies, for example, are more likely to follow the capital structure of other Japanese companies than they are of U.S. or European companies. Leveraging is often perceived as the most cost-effective route to capitalization, because the interest companies pay on debt is a tax-deductible expense, whereas the dividends paid to investors are not.

However, leveraging may not be the best approach in all countries for two major reasons. First, excessive reliance on long-term debt increases financial risk and thus requires a higher return for investors. Second, foreign subsidiaries of an MNE may have limited access to local capital markets, making it difficult for the MNE to rely on debt to fund asset acquisition.[5] In a study of foreign subsidiaries of U.S. MNEs, it was found that the debt/asset of those studied averaged 0.545, which means that 54.5 percent of assets were funded by debt and 45.5 percent were funded by equity.[6] The debt/asset ratio on average for companies in a selected group of countries can be found in Table 19.1. Note the relatively higher reliance on equity capital by the U.K., U.S., and Canadian companies relative to companies from other countries in Europe and Asia.

There are many factors that influence the choice of capital structure, both within a country and by MNEs with affiliates in different countries, such as local tax rates, the

Leverage—the degree to which a firm funds the growth of business by debt

The amount of leverage used varies from country to country.

| TABLE 19.1 | CAPITAL STRUCTURES AROUND THE WORLD: CAPITAL STRUCTURE PERCENTAGES FOR SELECTED COUNTRIES RANKED BY COMMON EQUITY RATIOS, 1995 |

COUNTRY	EQUITY	TOTAL DEBT	LONG-TERM DEBT	SHORT-TERM DEBT
United Kingdom	68.3%	31.7%	N/A	N/A
United States	48.4	51.6	26.8%	24.8%
Canada	47.5	52.5	30.2	22.7
Germany	39.7	60.3	15.6	44.7
Spain	39.7	60.3	15.6	44.7
France	38.8	61.2	23.5	43.0
Japan	33.7	66.3	23.3	43.0
Italy	23.5	76.5	24.2	52.3

Source: Scott Besley and Eugene F. Brigham, *Essentials of Managerial Finance,* 13th ed. (Mason, OH: Thomson/South-Western, 2005), Chapter 9

degree of development of local equity markets, and creditor rights. One study of the capital structure of foreign affiliates of U.S.-based MNEs found the following:

> *Ten percent higher local tax rates are associated with 2.8 percent higher debt/asset ratios, with internal borrowing particularly sensitive to taxes. Multinational affiliates are financed with less external debt in countries with underdeveloped capital markets or weak creditor rights, reflecting significantly higher local borrowing costs. Instrumental variable analysis indicates that greater borrowing from parent companies substitutes for three-quarters of reduced external borrowing induced by capital market conditions. Multinational firms appear to employ internal capital markets opportunistically to overcome imperfections in external capital markets.[7]*

In addition, different tax rates, dividend remission policies, and exchange controls may cause a company to rely more on debt in some situations and more on equity in others. It is important to understand that the different debt and equity markets discussed in this chapter and in Chapter 9 have different levels of importance for companies worldwide.

One of the major causes of the Asian financial crisis in 1997 was that Asian companies relied too much on debt to fund their growth, especially bank debt. The lack of development of bond and equity markets in those countries forced companies to rely on bank debt for growth. Many of the Asian banks borrowed dollars from international banks and lent the money to local companies in local currencies, not dollars. When the Asian currencies fell against the dollar, many of the banks could not service their loans and went into bankruptcy. Some of the Asian companies that borrowed dollars directly from foreign banks couldn't generate enough local currency to pay off the debt, and they were brought close to bankruptcy. As a result, many companies were forced to exchange debt for equity, thereby losing some of their control or selling themselves outright to foreign investors who could pay off their dollar debt.[8] Argentine companies and banks also had a large amount of foreign debt, a factor that helped escalate its monetary crisis in 2002. Companies recently renegotiated contracts with their foreign lenders in an effort to restructure some of their loans.

An MNE that needs to raise capital through debt markets has a number of options. The local domestic debt market is the first source that a company will tap. This means Japan for Japanese companies, but it could also mean Japan for the Japanese subsidiary of a U.S. company. Nissan lists several types of long-term debt in its annual report. In its 2003 *Annual Report*, it listed bonds and notes in Japanese yen, U.S. dollars, and euros.[9] As mentioned in the opening case, Nu Skin funded some of its expansion in Japan through borrowing yen. Its long-term debt includes the long-term portion of Japanese yen denominated ten-year notes issued to the Prudential Insurance Company of America in 2000. The notes bear interest at an effective rate of 3.0 percent per annum and are due October 2010, with annual principal payments that began in October 2004. As of December 31, 2004, the outstanding balance on the notes was 8.3 billion Japanese yen, or $81.2 million, $1.35 million of which was included in the current portion of long-term debt.[10]

MNEs have an advantage, because they can tap local debt and equity markets, foreign debt and equity markets (such as the Eurodollar, Eurobond, and Euroequity markets), and internal funds from the corporate family. Most local companies are locked into local debt markets or possibly foreign debt markets, but they don't have the ability to raise funds as extensively as do the local affiliates of MNEs.

OFFSHORE FINANCIAL CENTERS

Companies can raise debt or equity funds in their domestic market or offshore. **Offshore financing** is the provision of financial services by banks and other agents to nonresidents. In its simplest form, this involves the borrowing of money from nonresidents and lending to nonresidents.[11] A good example of legitimate offshore financing is the use of the Eurodollar market. A U.S. company can raise Eurodollars in London by working with a bank to issue bonds or syndicate a loan.

Offshore financial centers (OFC) are cities or countries that provide large amounts of funds in currencies other than their own and are used as locations in which to raise and accumulate cash. Usually, the financial transactions are conducted in currencies other than the currency of the country and are thus the centers for the Eurocurrency market. An OFC could be defined as any financial center where offshore activity takes place, but a more practical definition of an OFC is a center where the bulk of financial center activity is offshore on both sides of the balance sheet, where the transactions are initiated elsewhere, and where the majority of the institutions involved are controlled by nonresidents.[12] OFCs are referred to as:

- Jurisdictions that have relatively large numbers of financial institutions engaged primarily in business with nonresidents
- Financial systems with external assets and liabilities out of proportion to domestic financial intermediation designed to finance domestic economies
- More popularly, centers which provide some or all of the following services: low or zero taxation [hence the term **tax haven country**]; moderate or light financial regulation; banking secrecy and anonymity[13]

Generally, the markets in these centers are regulated differently—and usually more flexibly—than domestic markets. These centers provide an alternative, (usually) cheaper source of funding for MNEs so that they don't have to rely strictly on their own national markets. Offshore financial centers have one or more of the following characteristics:

- Large foreign-currency (Eurocurrency) market for deposits and loans (in London, for example)
- Market that is a large net supplier of funds to the world financial markets (in Switzerland, for example)
- Market that is an intermediary or pass-through for international loan funds (in the Bahamas and the Cayman Islands, for example)
- Economic and political stability
- Efficient and experienced financial community

A woman walks past the Bahamas Financial Centre in Nassau, Bahamas, billed as the leading offshore financial center in the world. A growing number of wealthy Americans have begun moving their money to offshore accounts to avoid paying taxes. As a result, the Bahamas' thriving financial district contributes almost as much to the country's economy as the tourist industry.

- Good communications and supportive services
- Official regulatory climate favorable to the financial industry, in the sense that it protects investors without unduly restricting financial institutions[14]

These centers are either operational centers, with extensive banking activities involving short-term financial transactions, or booking centers, in which little actual banking activity takes place but in which transactions are recorded to take advantage of secrecy and low (or no) tax rates. In the latter case, individuals may deposit money offshore to hide it from their home-country tax authorities, either because the money is earned or to be used illegally—such as in the drug trade or to finance terrorist activities—or because the individual or company does not want to pay tax. London is an example of an operational center; the Cayman Islands are an example of a booking center. Although there are many offshore financial centers, the most important are Bahrain (for the Middle East), Brussels, the Caribbean (servicing mainly Canadian and U.S. banks), Dublin, Hong Kong, London, New York, Singapore, and Switzerland. London is a crucial center because it offers a variety of financial services in both debt and equity transactions and has a large domestic market; it also serves the offshore market. The Caribbean centers (primarily the Bahamas, the Cayman Islands, and the Netherlands Antilles) are essentially offshore locations for New York banks. Switzerland has been a primary source of funds for decades, offering stability, integrity, discretion, and low costs. Singapore has been the center for the Eurodollar market in Asia (sometimes called the Asiadollar market) since 1968, thanks to its strategic geographic location, its strong worldwide telecommunications links, and government regulations that have facilitated the flow of funds. Hong Kong is critical because of its unique status with respect to China and the United Kingdom and its geographic proximity to the rest of the Pacific Rim. Bahrain, an island country in the Persian Gulf, is the financial center of petrodollars (dollars generated from the sale of oil) in the Middle East.

The Organization for Economic Cooperation and Development has been working closely with the major OFCs to ensure that they are engaged in legal activity. While not

---

Offshore financial centers can be operational centers or booking centers.

Key offshore financial centers are in the Bahamas, Bahrain, the Caribbean, Hong Kong, Ireland, London, New York, Singapore, and Switzerland, among other locations.

FIGURE 19.3

Source: www.cartoonstock.com

"All the pins are our sales representatives - except for the one in Paraguay, that's our company treasurer."

trying to tell the sovereign countries what their tax rates should be, the OECD is trying to eliminate harmful tax practices in the following four areas:

1. The regime imposes low or no taxes on the relevant income (from geographically mobile financial and other service activities).

2. The regime is ring-fenced [i.e., separated] from the domestic economy.

3. The regime lacks transparency, for example, the details of the regime or its application are not apparent, or there is inadequate regulatory supervision or financial disclosure.

4. There is no effective exchange of information with respect to the regime.[15]

The OECD is trying to eliminate the harmful tax practices in tax-haven countries.

In 2000, the OECD identified 47 preferential tax regimes (tax haven countries) that were potentially harmful and began negotiating with them to improve their practices. Within a relatively short time, the list was whittled down to 14 countries that did not agree to improve their transparency and effective exchange of information. Negotiations are continuing with those 14. As shown in the Parmalat case, however, policing needs to be done at the corporate level, not just the OFC level.

POINT–COUNTERPOINT: OFFSHORE FINANCIAL CENTERS SHOULD BE SHUT DOWN

POINT

The problem with OFCs is that they operate in a shroud of secrecy that allows companies to establish operations there that are used for illegal and unethical behavior. In December 2001, U.S. energy giant Enron filed for bankruptcy, resulting in one of the largest bankruptcies in corporate history. One of the contributors to Enron's problems was the creation of hundreds of subsidiaries in tax havens, including 662 in the Cayman Islands, 119 in Turks and Caicos, 43 in Mauritius, and 8 in Bermuda. The subsidiaries were used to pass off corporate debts, losses, and executive compensation.[16]

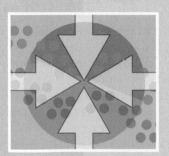

As pointed out in Chapter 18, Parmalat set up three shell companies based in the Caribbean to capture cash. The shell companies allegedly sold Parmalat products, and Parmalat sent them fake invoices and charged costs and fees to make the sales look legitimate. Then Parmalat would write out a credit note for the amount the subsidiaries supposedly owed it, and take that to banks to raise money. Given the location of the subsidiaries, you would think that the banks would have been suspicious, but Parmalat got away with these activities. Off-balance sheet financing was also used to hide debts. The company transferred over half of its liabilities to the books of small subsidiaries based in offshore tax havens such as the Cayman Islands. This allowed Parmalat to present a healthy balance sheet and a profitable income statement to investors and creditors by hiding large amounts of debt, under-

stating interest expenses (thus overstating income), and overstating revenues for false bookings. Parmalat's actual debt was nearly double the amount that was disclosed to outsiders.

Terrorists and drug dealers also use OFCs to launder money. When the U.S. government went after the money of Osama bin Laden, it went after OFCs notorious for their secrecy. When a bank in the Bahamas refused to open its books to U.S. government investigators, the U.S. cut off the bank from the world's wire transfer systems. Within two hours, the bank changed policies.[17]

COUNTERPOINT

In spite of corporate malfeasance, offshore financial centers are good locations for establishing finance subsidiaries that can raise capital for the parent company or its subsidiaries. They allow the finance subsidiaries to take advantage of lower borrowing costs and tax rates. This type of activity is not illegal, because the companies are still subject to home and host country laws and tax regulations. As more and more countries tax offshore earnings, it will not be possible for companies to avoid paying taxes. The key is to improve transparency and reporting so that OFCs are not used for illegal shifting of money from one jurisdiction to another to avoid paying taxes and to hide illegal sources and uses of funds.

CAPITAL BUDGETING IN A GLOBAL CONTEXT

Capital budgeting—the process whereby MNEs determine which projects and countries will receive capital investment funds

The next international dimension of the treasury function is the capital budgeting decision whereby the MNE determines which projects and countries will receive its capital investment funds. The parent company must compare the net present value or internal rate of return of a potential foreign project with that of its other projects around the world to determine the best place to invest its resources. The technique used to compare different projects is capital budgeting.

One approach to capital budgeting is to determine the **payback period** of a project, or the number of years required to recover the initial investment made. That is typically done by estimating the annual after-tax free cash flow from the investment, determining the present value of the future cash flow for each year, and then determining how many years it will take to recoup the initial investment.

A second approach is to determine the **net present value** (NPV) of a project, which is defined as follows:

Capital budgeting techniques

- Payback period
- Net present value of a project
- Internal rate of return

$$NPV = \sum_{t=1}^{n} \frac{FCF_t}{(1+k)^t} - IO$$

where FCF_t = the annual free cash flow in time period t

k = the appropriate discount rate; that is, the required rate of return or cost of capital

IO = the initial cash outlay

n = the project's expected life

The required rate of return is the rate that the company must get from the project in order to justify the cost of raising the initial investment or at least maintaining the value of its common stock. If the NPV is positive, the project is also considered to be positive. If the NPV is negative, the company should not enter into the project.

A third approach is to compute the internal rate of return (IRR) of the project and compare it with the required rate of return. The IRR is the rate that equates the present value of future cash flows with the present value of the initial investment. If the IRR is greater than the required rate of return, the investment is considered to be positive. However, the company then needs to compare the IRR with that of competing projects in other countries.

Several things are common about each of the methods. First, the firm needs to determine the free cash flows, which involves estimating cash flows as well as bringing into the equation different tax rates from different countries. Second, in the case of both NPV and IRR, the company needs to determine what the required rate of return is.

MNEs need to determine free cash flows based on cash flow estimates and tax rates in different countries and an appropriate required rate of return adjusted for risk

Several aspects of capital budgeting are unique to foreign project assessment.

- Parent cash flows must be distinguished from project cash flows. Parent cash flows refer to cash flows from the project back to the parent in the parent's currency. Project cash flows refer to the cash flows in local currency from the sale of goods and services. Will the decision be based on parent cash flows, project cash flows, or both?

- Remittance of funds to the parent, such as dividends, interest on loans, and payment of intracompany receivables and payables, is affected by differing tax systems, legal and political constraints on the movement of funds, local business norms, and differences in how financial markets and institutions function. In addition, tax systems affect free cash flows on the project, irrespective of the remittance issue.

- Differing rates of inflation must be anticipated by both the parent and subsidiary because of their importance in causing changes in competitive position and in cash flows over time.

- The parent must consider the possibility of unanticipated exchange-rate changes because of both their direct effects on the value of cash flows as well as their indirect effects on the foreign subsidiary's competitive position.

- The parent company must evaluate political risk in a target market because political events can drastically reduce the value or availability of expected cash flows.

- The terminal value (the value of the project at the end of the budgeting period) is difficult to estimate because potential purchasers from host, home, or third countries—or from the private or public sector—may have widely divergent perspectives on the value of the project. The terminal value is critical in determining the total cash flows from the project. The total cash outlay for the project is partially offset by the terminal value—the amount of cash the parent company can get from the subsidiary or project if it sells it eventually.[18]

Because of all the forces listed here, it is very difficult to estimate future cash flows, both to the subsidiary and to the parent company. There are two ways to deal with the variations in future cash flows. One is to determine several different scenarios and then determine the payback period, net present value, or internal rate of return (IRR) of the project. The other is to adjust the hurdle rate, which is the minimum required rate of return that the project must achieve in order for it to receive capital. The adjustment is usually made by increasing the hurdle rate above its minimal level.

> Determine different cash flow scenarios or adjust the hurdle rate (the minimum required rate of return for a project)

Once the budget is complete, the MNE must examine both the return in local currency and the return to the parent in dollars from cash flows to the parent. Examining the return in local currency will give management a chance to compare the project with other investment alternatives in the country. However, cash flows to the parent are important, because it is from these cash flows that dividends are paid to shareholders. If the MNE cannot generate a sufficient return to the parent in the parent's currency, it will eventually fall behind in its ability to pay shareholders and pay off corporate debt. Finally, the decision must be made in the strategic context of the investment, not just the financial context.

INTERNAL SOURCES OF FUNDS

Although the term *funds* usually means "cash," it is used in a much broader sense in business and generally refers to working capital—that is, the difference between current assets and current liabilities. From a general perspective, funds come from the normal operations of a business (selling merchandise or services) as well as from financing activities, such as borrowing money, issuing bonds, or issuing shares. Uses of funds are for the purchase of fixed assets, paying employees and purchasing materials and supplies, and investing in marketable securities or long-term investments.

> Funds are working capital, or current assets minus current liabilities.

Cash flows in an MNE are significantly more complex than for a company that operates in a strictly domestic environment. An MNE that wants to expand operations or needs additional capital can look not only to the domestic and international debt and equity markets but also to sources within itself. For an MNE, the complexity of internal sources is magnified because of the number of its subsidiaries and the diverse environments in which they operate. Figure 19.4 shows a parent company that has two foreign subsidiaries. The parent, as well as the two subsidiaries, may be increasing funds through normal operations. These funds may be used on a company-wide basis, perhaps through loans. The parent can loan funds directly to one subsidiary or guarantee an outside loan to the other. Equity capital from the parent is another source of funds for the subsidiary.

> Sources of internal funds are
> - Loans
> - Investments through equity capital
> - Intercompany receivables and payables
> - Dividends

INTERNAL SOURCES OF FUNDS FOR MNEs

There are many ways in which MNEs can use internal cash flow to fund worldwide operations.

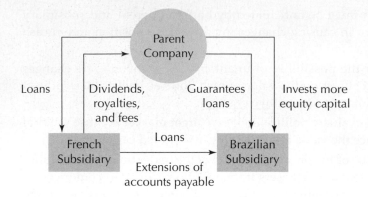

Funds also can go from subsidiary to parent. The subsidiary could declare a dividend to the parent as a return on capital, or it could loan cash directly to the parent. If the subsidiary declared a dividend to the parent, the parent could lend the funds back to the subsidiary. The dividend would not be tax deductible to the subsidiary, but it would be included as income to the parent, and the parent would have to pay tax on the dividend. If the subsidiary loaned money to the parent, the interest paid by the parent would be tax deductible to the parent and would be taxable income to the subsidiary.

Merchandise, people (in the case of MNEs involved in services), and financial flows can travel between subsidiaries, giving rise to receivables and payables. Companies can move money between and among related entities by paying quickly, or they can accumulate funds by deferring payment. They also can adjust the size of the payment by arbitrarily raising or lowering the price of intercompany transactions in comparison with the market price, a transfer pricing strategy.

Global Cash Management

Effective cash management is a chief concern of the CFO, who must answer the following three questions to ensure effective cash management:

1. What are the local and corporate system needs for cash?
2. How can the cash be withdrawn from subsidiaries and centralized?
3. Once the cash has been centralized, what should be done with it?

The cash manager, who reports to the treasurer (as illustrated in Figure 19.2), must collect and pay cash in the company's normal operational cycle and then must deal with financial

Cash budgets and forecasts are essential in assessing a company's cash needs.

MULTILATERAL CASH FLOWS

Multilateral cash flows in the absence of netting require each subsidiary to settle intercompany obligations.

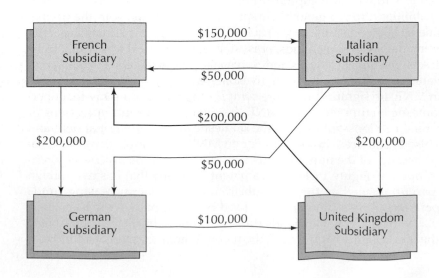

TABLE 19.2   **NET POSITIONS OF SUBSIDIARIES IN FOUR COUNTRIES (IN DOLLARS)**

Net positions show total receivables less total payables.

SUBSIDIARY	TOTAL RECEIVABLES	TOTAL PAYABLES	NET POSITION
French	250,000	350,000	(100,000)
German	250,000	100,000	150,000
Italian	150,000	300,000	(150,000)
U.K.	300,000	200,000	100,000

institutions, such as commercial and investment banks, when generating and investing cash. Before the cash manager remits any cash into the MNE's control center—whether at regional or headquarters level—he or she must first assess local cash needs through cash budgets and forecasts. Because the cash forecast projects the excess cash that will be available, the cash manager will know how much cash can be invested for short-term profits.

Once local cash needs are met, the cash manager must decide whether to allow the local manager to invest any excess cash or to have it remitted to a central cash pool. If the cash is centralized, the manager must find a way of making the transfer. A cash dividend is the easiest way to distribute cash, but government restrictions may interfere. For example, foreign-exchange controls may prevent the company from remitting as large a dividend as it would like. Cash also can be remitted through royalties, management fees, and repayment of principal and interest on loans.

Dividends are a good source of intercompany transfers, but governments often restrict their free movement.

Multilateral Netting

An important cash-management strategy is **netting** cash flows internationally. For example, an MNE with operations in four European countries could have several different intercompany cash transfers resulting from loans, the sale of goods, licensing agreements, and so forth. In Figure 19.5, for example, there are seven different transfers among the four subsidiaries.

Table 19.2 identifies the total receivables, payables, and net position for each subsidiary. Rather than have each subsidiary settle its accounts independently with subsidiaries in other countries, many MNEs are establishing cash-management centers in one city (such as Brussels) to coordinate cash flows among subsidiaries from several countries.

Figure 19.6 illustrates how each subsidiary in a net payable position transfers funds to the central clearing account. The manager of the clearing account then transfers funds

Multilateral netting—the process of coordinating cash inflows and outflows among subsidiaries so that only net cash is transferred, reducing transaction costs

FIGURE 19.6

MULTILATERAL NETTING

Multilateral netting allows subsidiaries to transfer net intercompany flows to a cash center, or clearing account, which disburses cash to net receivers.

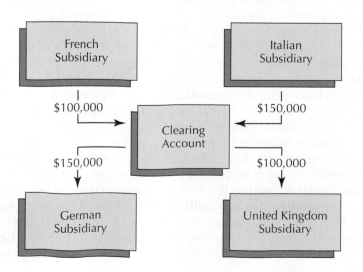

to the accounts of the net receiver subsidiaries. In this example, only four transfers need to take place. The clearing account manager receives transactions information and computes the net position of each subsidiary at least monthly. Then the manager orchestrates the settlement process. The transfers take place in the payor's currency, and the foreign-exchange conversion takes place centrally. For netting to work, the company needs to match its cash needs with software that can keep track of and transfer funds and banking relationships that allow money to be moved among corporate entities.

CASH FLOW ASPECTS OF IMPORTS AND EXPORTS

The flow of currency across national borders is complex and requires the use of special documents. To pay for imports or receive cash for exports, cash managers in treasury must deal in foreign exchange, and the transfer of funds from one bank to another across national borders can be complicated and can take time.

In descending order in terms of security to the exporter, the basic methods of payment for exports are:

- Cash in advance
- Letter of credit
- Draft or bill of exchange
- Open account

When an individual or a company pays a bill in a domestic setting, it typically uses a check. This is also known as a **draft** or a **commercial bill of exchange.** A draft is an instrument in which one party (the drawer) directs another party (the drawee) to make a payment. The drawee can either be a company like the importer or a bank. In the latter case, the draft would be considered a bank draft. Documentary drafts and documentary letters of credit are often used to protect both the buyer and the seller. They require that payment be made based on the presentation of documents conveying the title. If the exporter requests payment to be made immediately, the draft is called a **sight draft.** If the payment is to be made later—for example, 30 days after delivery—the instrument is called a **time draft.** A time draft is more flexible to the importer and more risky to the exporter because the longer the exporter has to wait for the money, the more likely something could go wrong, making it difficult or impossible for the importer to pay. In addition, if the exporter is assuming the foreign-exchange risk, the risk increases as the time increases.

With a bill of exchange, it is always possible the importer will not be able to make payment to the exporter at the agreed-upon time. A **letter of credit (L/C),** however, obligates the buyer's bank in the importing country to honor a draft presented to it, provided the draft is accompanied by the prescribed documents. However, the exporter still needs to be sure that the bank's credit is valid as well. The letter of credit could be a forgery issued by a "nonexistent bank." The exporter, even with the added security of the bank, still needs to rely on the importer's credit because of possible discrepancies that could arise in the transaction. A letter of credit does not eliminate foreign-exchange risk if the sale is denominated in a currency other than that of the exporter's country. However, a letter of credit denominated in the exporter's currency means the exporter incurs no risk of loss as a result of possible exchange-rate fluctuations. As with a draft, a letter of credit may be issued at sight or time.

When an exporter requires a letter of credit, the importer is responsible for arranging for it at the importer's bank. Figure 19.7 explains the relationships among the parties to a letter of credit. A letter of credit can be revocable or irrevocable. A **revocable letter of credit** is one that can be changed by any of the parties. However, both exporter and importer may prefer an **irrevocable letter of credit,** which is a letter that cannot be canceled or changed in any way without the consent of all parties to the transaction. With this type of L/C, the importer's bank is obligated to pay and is willing to accept any drafts (bills of exchange) at sight, meaning these drafts will be paid as soon as the correct documents are presented to

FIGURE 19.7   LETTER-OF-CREDIT RELATIONSHIPS

A letter of credit guarantees the exporter that the importer's bank will pay for the imports. The credit relationship exists between the importer and the importer's bank (the opening bank). A confirmed letter of credit has an added guarantee from the exporter's bank: If the importer's bank defaults, the exporter's bank must pay.

Source: Adapted from *Export and Import Financing Procedures* (Chicago: The First National Bank of Chicago), 22.

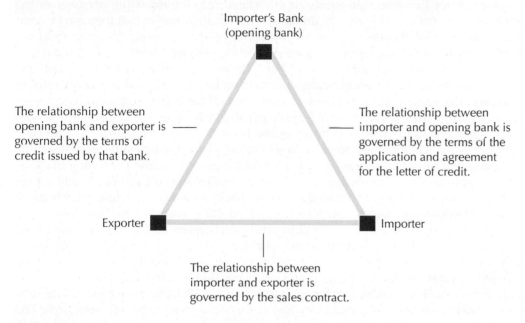

Importer's Bank
(opening bank)

The relationship between opening bank and exporter is —— governed by the terms of credit issued by that bank.

The relationship between —— importer and opening bank is governed by the terms of the application and agreement for the letter of credit.

Exporter   Importer

The relationship between importer and exporter is governed by the sales contract.

the bank. As noted earlier, an L/C can also be issued at any time. The exporter must adhere precisely to all of the conditions on the letter of credit—such as the method of transportation and the description of the merchandise—otherwise, the letter of credit will not be paid without approval of all parties to an elimination of the discrepancies.

A letter of credit transaction may include a confirming bank in addition to the parties mentioned previously. With a **confirmed letter of credit,** the exporter has the guarantee of an additional bank, sometimes in the exporter's home country, sometimes in a third country. It rarely happens that the exporter establishes the confirming relationship. Usually, the opening bank seeks the confirmation of the L/C with a bank with which it already has a credit relationship. If this letter of credit is irrevocable, none of the conditions can be changed unless all four parties to the L/C agree in advance.

An exporter occasionally may sell on **open account.** The necessary shipping documents are mailed to the importer before any payment from or definite obligation on the part of the buyer. Releasing goods in this manner is somewhat unusual because the exporter risks default by the buyer. An exporter ordinarily sells under such conditions only if it has successfully conducted business with the importer for an extended time. This is generally the arrangement when the importer and exporter are members of the same corporate group.

FOREIGN-EXCHANGE RISK MANAGEMENT

As illustrated earlier, global cash-management strategy focuses on the flow of money for specific operating objectives. Another important objective of an MNE's financial strategy is to protect against the foreign-exchange risks of investing abroad. The strategies that an MNE adopts to do this may mean the internal movement of funds as well as the use of one or more of the foreign-exchange instruments described in Chapter 9, such as options and forward contracts.

If all exchange rates were fixed in relation to one another, there would be no foreign-exchange risk. However, rates are not fixed, and currency values change frequently.

A confirmed irrevocable letter of credit is guaranteed by the exporter's bank.

Open account—the exporter bills the importer but does not require formal payment documents; usually for members of the same corporate group

Major financial risks arise from exchange-rate changes.

Instead of infrequent one-way changes, currencies fluctuate often and both up and down. A change in the exchange rate can result in three different exposures for a company: **translation exposure, transaction exposure,** and **economic or operational exposure.**

Three types of foreign-exchange exposure— translation, transaction, economic or operational

Translation Exposure

Foreign-currency financial statements are translated into the reporting currency of the parent company (assumed to be U.S. dollars for U.S. companies) so that they can be combined with financial statements of other companies in the corporate group to form the consolidated financial statements. Exposed accounts—those translated at the balance sheet rate or current exchange rate—either gain or lose value in dollars when the exchange rate changes. For example, assume a subsidiary of a U.S. company operates in Mexico and has 900,000 pesos in a bank account there. If the Mexican peso were to depreciate in relation to the dollar from 9.5 pesos per dollar to 10 pesos per dollar, the subsidiary's bank account would drop in value from $94,737 (900,000/9.5) to $90,000 (900,000/10) as a result of the depreciation. However, the subsidiary still has pesos in the bank account; it's just that the dollar equivalent of the pesos has fallen, resulting in a loss.

Translation exposure arises because the dollar value of the exposed asset or liability changes as the exchange rate changes.

The combined effect of the exchange-rate change on all assets and liabilities is either a net gain or loss. However, the gain or loss does not represent an actual cash flow effect because the cash, in the example here, is only translated into dollars, not converted into dollars. The problem is that reported earnings can either rise or fall against the dollar because of the translation effect, and this can affect earnings per share and stock prices. A good example is Nu Skin Enterprises. In 2001, when most foreign currencies were falling against the dollar, its annual report stated that earnings would have been higher if the dollar had not been so strong. When Nu Skin translated its foreign earnings into dollars, they were lower than they would have been if the dollar had remained at the same level as the previous year. The opposite happened in 2004 when the dollar was weak against the yen and euro. Earnings from Europe and Japan were higher in dollars than in local currency results.

Transaction Exposure

Denominating a transaction in a foreign currency represents foreign-exchange risk because the company has accounts receivable or payable in foreign currency that must be settled eventually. For example, assume a U.S. exporter delivers merchandise to a British importer for a total price of $500,000 when the exchange rate is 1.9000 dollars per pound, or £ 263,158 ($500,000/1.9000). If the exporter were to receive payment in dollars, there would be no immediate impact on the exporter if the dollar/pound exchange rate changed. If payment were to be received in pounds, however, the exporter might incur a foreign-exchange gain or loss. For example, with the exchange rate at 1.9000 dollars per pound, the sale would be carried on the exporter's books at $500,000, but the underlying value in which the sale is denominated would be £ 263,158. If the rate moved to 1.8800 dollars per pound by the time the receivable was collected, the exporter would receive 263,158 pounds, but that payment would be worth $494,737 (263,158*1.8800), a loss of $5,263. This would be an actual cash flow loss to the exporter.

Transaction exposure arises because the receivable or payable changes in value as the exchange rate changes.

Economic Exposure

Economic exposure, also known as operating exposure, is the potential for change in expected cash flows. Economic exposure arises from the pricing of products, the sourcing and cost of inputs, and the location of investments. Pricing strategies have both an immediate and a long-term impact on cash flows. For example, the inventory sold to the British importer probably was sold to final users before the exchange rate changed, but future sales would be affected by the rate change. Assume the exporter sold its most recent shipment of $500,000 at an exchange rate of 1.9000 dollars per pound for a cost to the importer of 263,158 pounds. At a 10 percent markup, the importer would sell the shipment for £289,474. If the dollar were to strengthen to $1.8800/£, the exporter has two choices. It can continue to sell

Economic, or operating, exposure arises from effects of exchange-rate changes on
- Future cash flows
- The sourcing of parts and components
- The location of investments
- The competitive position of the company in different markets

the merchandise at the same price, or it can lower the price. The first choice is to continue to sell the merchandise to the importer for $500,000, which would now cost the importer £265,957. At a 10 percent markup, the importer would sell the merchandise for £292,553, or £3,079 more than before the exchange rate change. At the higher price, the importer might lose market share if customers are not willing to pay the higher price. Instead of raising the price, the importer could absorb the cost increase in its profit margin and continue to sell the merchandise for £289,474. However, its profit would only be £23,517 (289,474 – 265,957) instead of £26,596 (292,553 – 265,957). Another possibility would be for the exporter to lower its price in dollars to $494,737 so that it would still cost the importer £263,158 (263,158 × 1.8800) to import the merchandise. If the exporter can't afford to lower its price and take a smaller profit margin, the importer may have to look for a new supplier.

After three years of the euro strengthening against the dollar, BMW found itself in a very difficult situation in 2005, because its costs were generated in euros (most of its manufacturing facilities were in Europe), whereas its revenues in the United States were in dollars. Thus it was generating revenues in a weak currency and costs in a strong currency, severely affecting earnings. One of its economic considerations was to expand manufacturing operations in the United States in order to balance off its revenues and expenses in the same currency.[19]

Exposure-Management Strategy

To protect assets adequately against risks from translation, transaction, and economic exposure of exchange-rate fluctuations, management must

- Define and measure exposure.
- Organize and implement a reporting system that monitors exposure and exchange-rate movements.
- Adopt a policy assigning responsibility for minimizing—or hedging—exposure.
- Formulate strategies for hedging exposure.

To protect assets from exchange-rate risk, management needs to
- *Define and measure exposure*
- *Establish a reporting system*
- *Adopt an overall policy on exposure management*
- *Formulate hedging strategies*

Defining and Measuring Exposure Most MNEs will see all three types of exposure: translation, transaction, and economic. To develop a viable hedging strategy, an MNE must forecast the degree of exposure in each major currency in which it operates. Because the types of exposure differ, the actual exposure by currency must be kept track of separately. For example, the translation exposure in Brazilian reals should be kept track of separately from the transaction exposure because the transaction exposure will result in an actual cash flow, while the translation exposure may not. Thus, the company generates one report on translation exposure and another on transaction exposure. The company may adopt different hedging strategies for the different types of exposure.

All three types of exposure must be monitored and measured separately.

A key aspect of measuring exposure is forecasting exchange rates. Estimating exchange rates is similar to fortune telling: Approaches range from gut feelings to sophisticated economic models, each having varying degrees of success. Whatever the approach, a company should estimate and use ranges within which it expects a currency to vary over the forecasting period. As noted in Chapter 10, some companies develop in-house capabilities to monitor exchange rates, using economists who also try to obtain a consensus of exchange-rate movements from the banks with whom they deal. Their concern is to forecast the direction, magnitude, and timing of an exchange-rate change. Other companies contract out this work.

Exchange-rate movements are forecast using in-house or external experts.

A Reporting System Once the company has decided how to define and measure exposure and estimate future exchange rates, it must create a reporting system that will assist in protecting it against risk. To achieve this goal, substantial participation from foreign operations must be combined with effective central control. Foreign input is important to ensure that the information the company uses in forecasting is effective. Because exchange rates move frequently, the company must obtain input from those who are attuned to the foreign country's economy. Central control of exposure protects resources

The reporting system should use both central control and input from foreign operations.

more efficiently than letting each subsidiary and branch manage its own exposure. Each organizational unit may be able to define its own exposure, but the company also has an overall exposure. AT&T, for example, requires its strategic business units (SBUs) to coordinate foreign-currency transactions with corporate treasury so that its foreign-exchange hedging unit can undertake the most cost-effective hedging strategy possible. To set hedging policies on a separate-entity basis might not take into account the fact that exposures of several entities (that is, branches, subsidiaries, affiliates, and so on) could offset one another. For example, one SBU of AT&T might have an exposed asset position in yen, and another might have an exposed liability position in yen. Without central control, both SBUs might incur hedging costs to protect their exposed positions. However, AT&T's central foreign-exchange unit in corporate treasury could offset the exposed asset position with the exposed liability position and not have to incur hedging costs.

Management of an MNE should devise a uniform reporting system for all of its subsidiaries. The report should identify the exposed accounts the company wants to monitor, the amount of exposure by currency of each account, and the different time periods under consideration. Exposure should be separated into translation, transaction, and economic components, with the transaction exposure identified by cash inflows and outflows over time.

The time periods on the report depend on the company. Companies can identify their exposure positions for different periods into the future, such as 30, 60, and 90 days; 6, 9, and 12 months; or 2, 3, and 4 years. The reason for the longer time frame is that operating commitments, such as plant construction and production runs, are fairly long term.[20]

Once each basic reporting unit has identified its exposure, the data should be sent to the next organizational level for preliminary consolidation. That level may be a regional headquarters (for Latin America or Europe, for example) or a product division, depending on the company's organizational structure. The preliminary consolidation enables the region or division to determine exposure by account and by currency for each time period. The resulting reports should be routine, periodic, and standardized to ensure comparability and timeliness in formulating strategies. Final reporting should be at the corporate level, where top management can see the amount of foreign-exchange exposure. Specific hedging strategies can be taken at any level, but each level of management must be aware of the size of the exposure and the potential impact on the company.

A Centralized Policy   It is important for management to decide at what level hedging strategies will be determined and implemented. Several hedging strategies will be discussed in the next section. To achieve maximum effectiveness in hedging, top management should determine hedging policy. Having an overview of corporate exposure and the cost and feasibility of different strategies at different levels in the company, the corporate treasurer should be able to design and implement a cost-effective program for exposure management. However, the company may have to decentralize some exposure management decisions so it can react quickly to a more rapidly changing international monetary environment. Such decentralization should stay within a well-defined policy established at the corporate level. Some companies run their hedging operations more as profit centers and nurture in-house trading desks. Those working at the trading desks actually buy and sell foreign exchange in the market rather than have the trader at a commercial bank effect the trades for the company. Most MNEs, however, are traditional and conservative in their approach, preferring to cover exposure (enter into a hedging strategy that minimizes losses due to exposed positions) rather than to extract huge profits or risk huge losses.

Formulating Hedging Strategies   Once a company has identified its level of exposure and determined which exposure is critical, it can hedge its position by adopting operational and/or financial strategies, each with cost/benefit implications as well as operational implications. The safest position is a balanced position in which exposed assets equal exposed liabilities.

Nu Skin uses operational and financial strategies to reduce exposure. Operational strategies involve adjusting the flow of money and resources in normal operations in

Hedging strategies can be operational or financial.

order to reduce foreign-exchange risk. First, management must determine the working capital needs of a subsidiary. Then it needs to adjust the flows of receivables, payables, and inventory. Although it may be wise to collect receivables as fast as possible in a country in which the local currency is expected to depreciate, the company must consider the competitive implications of doing so. If it tries to collect receivables too fast and does not give the buyer proper time to make payment, the buyer may go to another seller that is willing to offer better credit terms.

The use of debt to balance exposure is an interesting strategy. Many companies "borrow locally," especially in weak-currency countries, because that helps them to avoid foreign-exchange risk from borrowing in a foreign currency and also balances off their exposed position in assets and earnings.

Companies in Argentina that borrowed dollars found themselves in serious trouble when the peso devalued against the dollar, because they couldn't generate enough local currency revenues to pay off the higher debt. If they had borrowed in local currency, they would not have had the same problem. One problem with this strategy is that interest rates in weak-currency countries tend to be high, so there must be a trade-off between the cost of borrowing and the potential loss from exchange-rate variations. Protecting against loss from transaction exposure becomes complex. In dealing with foreign customers, it is always safest for the company to denominate the transaction in its own currency because it won't have any foreign-exchange exposure. The risk shifts to the foreign customer that has to come up with your currency. Or the company could denominate purchases in a weaker currency and sales in a stronger currency. If forced to make purchases in a strong currency and sales in a weak currency, it could resort to contractual measures such as forward contracts or options, or it could try to balance its inflows and outflows through astute sales and purchasing strategies.

Another operational strategy—leads and lags—protects cash flows among related entities, such as a parent and subsidiaries. A **lead strategy** means either collecting foreign-currency receivables before they are due when the foreign currency is expected to weaken or paying foreign-currency payables before they are due when the foreign currency is expected to strengthen. With a **lag strategy,** a company either delays collection of foreign-currency receivables if that currency is expected to strengthen or delays payables when the currency is expected to weaken. In other words, a company usually leads into and lags out of a hard currency and leads out of and lags into a weak currency.

There are two problems with a lead and lag strategy. First, it may not be useful for the movement of large blocks of funds. If there are infrequent decisions over small amounts of money, it is easy to manage the system, but as the number, frequency, and size of transactions increase, the system becomes difficult to manage. Second, leads and lags are often subject to government control, and it may be difficult to get permission to move currency.

Sometimes an operational strategy means shifting assets overseas to take advantage of currency changes. When the yen strengthened against the U.S. dollar, for example, Toyota shifted more of its manufacturing into the United States to take advantage of the cheaper dollar, something BMW is considering as mentioned above. As long as the yen was strong, it was difficult to export from Japan to the United States, so companies could service U.S. demand through production in the United States and now Canada as well.

In addition to the operational strategies just mentioned, a company may hedge exposure through financial contracts such as forward contracts and options, also known as derivatives. The most common hedge is a forward contract. For example, assume a U.S. exporter sells goods to a British manufacturer for £1 million, with payment due in 90 days. The spot exchange rate is 1.9000 dollars per pound, and the forward rate is 1.8500 dollars per pound. At the time of the sale, the transaction is recorded on the exporter's books at $1.9 million, and a corresponding receivable is set up for the same amount. However, the exporter is concerned about the exchange risk. The exporter can enter into a forward contract, which will guarantee that the receivables convert into dollars at a rate of 1.8500 dollars per pound, no matter what the actual future exchange rate is. This move will yield $1.85 million. Even though the company gets $50,000 less than it could have at the initial spot rate, it has eliminated any risk for the future. Or the exporter could wait

Operational strategies include

- *Using local debt to balance local assets*
- *Taking advantage of leads and lags for intercompany payments*

A lead strategy means collecting or paying early. A lag strategy means collecting or paying late.

Forward contracts can establish a fixed exchange rate for future transactions. Currency options can ensure access to foreign currency at a fixed exchange rate for a specific period of time.

until it collects the receivable in 90 days and gamble on a better rate in the spot market. If the actual rate at that time is 1.8700 dollars per pound, the exporter will receive $1.87 million, which is not as good as the initial receivable of $1.9 million but is better than the forward yield of $1.85 million. But if the dollar strengthens to 1.8000 dollars per pound, the exporter would be much better off with the forward contract.

A foreign-currency option is more flexible than a forward contract because it gives its purchaser the right, but not the obligation, to buy or sell a certain amount of foreign currency at a set exchange rate within a specified amount of time. For example, assume a U.S. exporter decides to sell merchandise to a British manufacturer for £1 million when the exchange rate is $1.9000 per pound. At the same time, the exporter goes to Goldman Sachs, its investment banker, and enters into an option to deliver pounds for dollars at an exchange rate of $1.9000 per pound at an option cost of $25,000. When the exporter receives the £1 million from the manufacturer, it must decide whether to exercise the option. If the exchange rate is above $1.9000, it will not exercise the option, because it can get a better yield by converting pounds at the market rate. The only thing lost is the $25,000 cost of the option, which is like insurance. However, if the exchange rate is below $1.9000—say, $1.8500—the exporter will exercise the option and trade pounds at the rate of $1.9000. The proceeds will be $1.9 million less the option cost of $25,000.

A good example of how companies use operational and financial hedging strategies is Coca-Cola. Because approximately 72 percent of Coke's operating income in 2004 came from outside of the United States, foreign-currency changes can have a major impact on reported earnings. Coke manages its foreign-currency exposures on a consolidated basis, which allows it to net certain exposures from different operations around the world and also allows it to take advantage of natural offsets—for example, cases in which British pound receivables offset British pound payables. It also uses derivative financial instruments to further reduce its net exposure to currency fluctuations. Coke enters into forward-exchange contracts and purchases currency options in several currencies, most notably the euro and Japanese yen, to hedge firm sales commitments. It also purchases currency options to hedge certain anticipated sales.[21]

TAXATION OF FOREIGN SOURCE INCOME

Tax planning influences profitability and cash flow.

Tax planning is a crucial responsibility for the CFO, because taxes can profoundly affect profitability and cash flow. This is especially true in international business. As complex as domestic taxation seems, it is simple compared to the intricacies of international taxation. The international tax specialist must be familiar with both the home country's tax policy on foreign operations and the tax laws of each country in which the international company operates.

Taxation has a strong impact on several choices:

- Location of operations
- Choice of operating form, such as export or import, licensing agreement, overseas investment
- Legal form of the new enterprise, such as branch or subsidiary
- Possible facilities in tax haven countries to raise capital and manage cash
- Method of financing, such as internal or external sourcing and debt or equity
- Capital budgeting decisions
- Method of setting transfer prices

The two major types of taxes that we will discuss are income taxes and excise taxes, such as the value-added tax (VAT) used so extensively in the EU. In the U.S., the VAT is not used, but a sales tax on consumption is used. In addition, there are other types of excise taxes, such as the taxes on cigarettes, alcohol, and gasoline. One of the big challenges in the EU is to harmonize these excise taxes. Excise taxes on beer per hectoliter divided by the degree of alcohol or sugar content range from $25.77 in Ireland to only $1.05 in Spain.

Although it might not make sense to travel from Ireland to Spain to buy beer, citizens from Britain pay a tax of $23.18, whereas the tax is only $3.37 in France. British citizens traveling to France and back can save a great deal in taxes on beer if they are so inclined.[22]

Foreign Branch

A foreign branch is an extension of the parent company rather than an enterprise incorporated in a foreign country. Any income the branch generates is taxable immediately to the parent, whether or not cash is remitted by the branch to the parent as a distribution of earnings. However, if the branch suffers a loss, the parent is allowed to deduct that loss from its taxable income, reducing its overall tax liability.

> Foreign branch income (or loss) is directly included in the parent's taxable income.

Foreign Subsidiary

While a branch is a legal extension of a parent company, a foreign corporation is an independent legal entity set up in a country (incorporated) according to the laws of incorporation of that country. When an MNE purchases a foreign corporation or sets up a new corporation in a foreign country, that corporation is called a subsidiary of the parent. Income that is earned by the subsidiary is either reinvested in the subsidiary or remitted as a dividend to the parent company. Subsidiary income is either taxable to the parent or tax deferred—that is, it is not taxed until it is remitted as a dividend to the parent. Which tax status applies depends on whether the foreign subsidiary is a controlled foreign corporation—CFC (a technical term in the U.S. tax code)—and whether the income is active or passive.

> Tax deferral means that income is not taxed until it is remitted to the parent company as a dividend.

A **controlled foreign corporation (CFC),** from the standpoint of the U.S. tax code, is any foreign corporation that meets this condition: more than 50 percent of its voting stock is held by "U.S. shareholders." A U.S. shareholder is any U.S. person or company that holds 10 percent or more of the CFC's voting stock. Any foreign subsidiary of an MNE would automatically be considered a CFC from the standpoint of the tax code. However, a joint-venture company abroad that is partly owned by the U.S.-based MNE and partly by local investors might not be a CFC if the U.S. MNE does not own more than 50 percent of the stock of the joint-venture company. Table 19.3 shows how this might work. Foreign corporation A is a CFC because it is a wholly owned subsidiary of a U.S. parent company (U.S. person V). Foreign corporation B also is a CFC because U.S. persons V, W, and X each own 10 percent or more of the voting stock, which means they qualify as U.S. shareholders and their combined voting stock is more than 50 percent of the total. This situation might exist if three U.S. companies partnered together with a foreign partner to establish a joint venture overseas. Such collaborative arrangements are not uncommon, especially in telecommunications and high-tech industries. Foreign corporation C is not a CFC because even though U.S. persons V and W qualify as U.S.

> In a CFC, U.S. shareholders hold more than 50 percent of the voting stock.

TABLE 19.3 **DETERMINATION OF CONTROLLED FOREIGN CORPORATIONS**

A controlled foreign corporation must have U.S. shareholders holding more than 50 percent of the voting shares.

SHAREHOLDER	PERCENTAGES OF THE VOTING STOCK		
	FOREIGN CORPORATION A	FOREIGN CORPORATION B	FOREIGN CORPORATION C
U.S. person V	100%	45%	30%
U.S. person W		10	10
U.S. person X		20	8
U.S. person Y			8
Foreign person Z		25	44
Total	100%	100%	100%

A TAX-HAVEN SUBSIDIARY AS A HOLDING COMPANY

A parent company can shelter income from U.S. income taxation by using a tax-haven subsidiary located in a low-tax country.

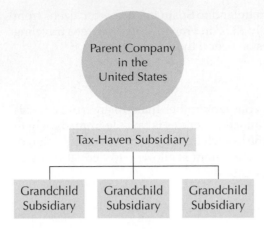

shareholders, their combined stock ownership is only 40 percent. U.S. persons X and Y do not qualify as U.S. shareholders because their individual ownership shares are only 8 percent each. When Enron set up its shell companies in tax-haven countries, it was careful to not own more than 50 percent of the stock so that it could avoid having to include the debt in those operations in its consolidated income.[23]

If a foreign subsidiary qualifies as a CFC, the U.S. tax law requires the U.S. investor to classify the foreign-source income as active income or Subpart F (or passive) income. **Active income** is derived from the direct conduct of a trade or business, such as from sales of products manufactured in the foreign country. **Subpart F income,** or passive income, which is specifically defined in Subpart F of the U.S. Internal Revenue Code, comes from sources other than those connected with the direct conduct of a trade or business, generally in tax-haven countries. Subpart F income includes:

Active income is derived from the direct conduct of a trade or business. Passive income (also called Subpart-F income) usually is derived from operations in a tax-haven country.

- *Holding company income* —primarily dividends, interest, rents, royalties, and gains on sale of stocks.

- *Sales income* —from foreign sales corporations that are separately incorporated from their manufacturing operations. The product of such entities is manufactured outside and sold for use outside the CFC's country of incorporation, and the CFC has not performed significant operations on the product.

- *Service income* —from the performance of technical, managerial, or similar services for a company in the same corporate family as the CFC and outside the country in which the CFC resides.

Subpart F income usually derives from the activities of subsidiaries in tax-haven countries such as the Bahamas, the Netherlands Antilles, Panama, and Switzerland. The U.S. government treats any country whose income tax is lower than that of the United States as a tax-haven country. The tax-haven subsidiary may act as an investment company, a sales agent or distributor, an agent for the parent in licensing agreements, or a holding company of stock in other foreign subsidiaries that are called grandchild—or second-tier—subsidiaries. This setup is illustrated in Figure 19.8. In the role of a holding company, its purpose is to concentrate cash from the parent's foreign operations into the low-tax country and to use the cash for global expansion.

Different rules regarding the tax status and deferability of income are in effect for non-CFCs, CFCs, and foreign branches.

Figure 19.9 illustrates how the tax status of a subsidiary's income is determined. All non-CFC income—active and Subpart F—earned by the foreign corporation is deferred until remitted as a dividend to the U.S. shareholder (the parent company in this example). In contrast, a CFC's active income is tax deferred to the parent, but its Subpart F income is taxable immediately to the parent as soon as the CFC earns it. If a foreign branch earns the income, it is immediately taxable to the parent company, whether it is active or Subpart F. There is an exception, however. If the foreign-source income is the lower of $1 million or 5 percent of the CFC's gross income, none of it is treated as Subpart F income. At the other

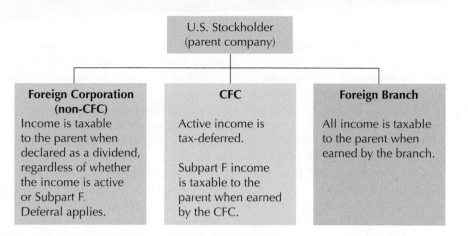

TAX STATUS OF ACTIVE AND SUBPART F INCOME FROM FOREIGN SUBSIDIARIES OF U.S. COMPANIES

Different rules regarding the tax status and deferability of income are in effect for non-CFCs, CFCs, and foreign branches.

extreme, if the foreign-source income is more than 70 percent of total gross income, all of the corporation's gross income for the tax year is treated as Subpart F income. Also, foreign-source income subject to high foreign taxes is not considered Subpart F income if the foreign tax rate is more than 90 percent of the maximum U.S. corporate income tax rate. Assuming a corporate tax rate of 35 percent in the United States, that means that a parent would not have to consider any income as Subpart F income that is earned in a country with a corporate tax rate greater than 31.5 percent (90 percent $\times$ 35 percent).[24]

Transfer Prices

As noted in Chapter 18, a major tax challenge as well as an impediment to performance evaluation is the extensive use of transfer pricing in international operations. Because the price is between related entities, it is not necessarily an **arm's-length price**—that is, a price between two companies that do not have an ownership interest in each other. The assumption is that an arm's-length price is more likely than a transfer price to reflect the market accurately.

Companies establish arbitrary transfer prices primarily because of differences in taxation between countries. For example, if the corporate tax rate is higher in the parent company's country than in the subsidiary's country, the parent could set a low transfer price on products it sells the subsidiary in order to keep taxable profits low in its country and high in the subsidiary's country. The parent also could set a high transfer price on products sold to it by the subsidiary.

The OECD is very concerned about the way companies manipulate transfer prices in order to minimize their tax liability worldwide. Their recommendation is that in order to determine the tax liability in each country, an arm's-length price should be applied, and they have issued guidelines on the matter. The OECD Center for Tax Policy and Administration meets periodically to discuss a wide range of tax issues, including the adoption of sound transfer pricing policies. The OECD issued guidelines on transfer pricing in 1979 and updated the policies in 1995 to give guidance on how to tell if a transfer between independent firms is similar to a transfer within a group and different transfer pricing methods that could be used.[25]

Companies can get into disputes with different tax jurisdictions over transfer pricing policies. Motorola, one of the world's largest mobile-phone companies, has operations that span across the world. As such, it has control over transfer prices between its operations in different countries. In August 2004, Motorola announced that the U.S. Internal Revenue Service was seeking an extra $500 million in taxes from the company. The IRS claims that Motorola set transfer prices in order to avoid paying U.S. taxes. They claim that Motorola should have shown an additional $1.4 billion in income during the period in question. As such, the IRS may force Motorola to make adjustments that would shift profit from other countries (thereby lowering its taxable income and tax paid) to the U.S.

A transfer price is a price on goods and services one member of a corporate family sells to another.

The OECD has set transfer pricing guidelines to eliminate the manipulation of prices and therefore taxes for MNEs.

Tax Credit

Every country has a sovereign right to levy taxes on all income generated within its borders. However, MNEs run into a problem when they earn income that is taxed in the country where the income is earned and where it might also be taxed in the parent country as well. This could result in double taxation.

In U.S. tax law, a U.S. MNE gets a credit for income taxes paid to a foreign government. For example, when a U.S. parent recognizes foreign-source income (such as a dividend from a foreign subsidiary) in its taxable income, it must pay U.S. tax on that income. However, the U.S. IRS allows the parent company to reduce its tax liability by the amount of foreign income tax already paid. It is limited by the amount it would have had to pay in the United States on that income. For example, assume that U.S. MNE A earns $100,000 of foreign-source income on which it paid $40,000 (40 percent tax rate) on that income in the foreign jurisdiction. If that income is considered taxable in the United States, company A would have to pay $35,000 in income taxes (35 percent tax rate). In the absence of a tax credit, company A would have paid a total of $75,000 in income tax on the $100,000 of income, a 75 percent tax rate. However, the IRS allows company A to reduce its U.S. tax liability by a maximum of $35,000—what it would have paid in the United States if the income had been earned there. If company A's subsidiary had paid $20,000 in foreign income tax (a 20 percent tax rate), it would be able to claim the entire $20,000 as a credit because it was less than the U.S. liability of $35,000. Company A will pay a total of $35,000 in corporate income tax on its foreign source income—$20,000 to the foreign government and $15,000 to the U.S. government.

Non-U.S. Tax Practices

Differences in tax practices around the world often cause problems for MNEs. Lack of familiarity with laws and customs can create confusion. In some countries, tax laws are loosely enforced. In others, taxes generally may be negotiated between the tax collector and the taxpayer—if they are ever paid at all.

Variations among countries in GAAP can lead to differences in the determination of taxable income. This, in turn, may affect the cash flow required to settle tax obligations. For example, companies in France can depreciate assets faster than would be the case in the United States, which means that they can write off their value against income, thus lowering taxable income. In Sweden, companies can reduce the value of inventories, which increases their cost of goods sold and lowers taxable income.

Corporate tax rates also vary from country to country. Table 19.4 identifies the corporate tax rates of the OECD member countries. Note that the rates range from a low of 8.5 percent in Switzerland to a high of 42.2 percent in Germany, although the Germans reduced their corporate tax burden to 25 percent. The combined corporate rate in Germany, including central government and sub-central government taxation, fell to 38.5 percent with the new legislation.[26]

Taxation of corporate income is accomplished through one of two approaches in most countries: the separate entity approach, also known as the classical approach, or the integrated system approach. In the separate entity approach, which the United States uses, each separate unit—company or individual—is taxed when it earns income. For example, a corporation is taxed on its earnings, and stockholders are taxed on the distribution of earnings (dividends). The result is double taxation.

Most other developed countries use an integrated system to eliminate double taxation. The British give a dividend credit to shareholders to shelter them from double taxation. That means that when shareholders report the dividends in their taxable income, they also get a credit for taxes paid on that income by the company that issued the dividend. That keeps the shareholders from paying tax on the dividend because the company has already paid a tax on it. Germany used to have a split-rate system with two different tax rates on corporate earnings—one on retained earnings and one on distributed earnings. However, they replaced the split rate system with an overall lower corporate tax rate on earnings.

TABLE 19.4   CORPORATE INCOME TAX RATE[1]

COUNTRY	CENTRAL GOVERNMENT CORPORATE INCOME TAX RATE[2]	ADJUSTED CENTRAL GOVERNMENT CORPORATE INCOME TAX RATE[3]	SUB-CENTRAL GOVERNMENT CORPORATE INCOME TAX RATE[4]	COMBINED CORPORATE INCOME TAX RATE[5]	TARGETED CORPORATE TAX RATES[6]
Australia[a]	34.0	34.0		34.0	Y
Austria	34.0	34.0		34.0	N
Belgium	40.2 (39.0)	40.2		40.2	Y
Canada	29.1 (28.0)	29.1	15.5	44.6	Y
Czech Republic	31.0	31.0		31.0	Y
Denmark	32.0	32.0		32.0	N
Finland	29.0	29.0		29.0	N
France[b]	37.76(33.33)	37.8		37.8	Y
Genmany[c]	42.2 (40.0)	35.0	17.0	52.0	N
Greece	40.0	40.0		40.0	n.a.
Hungary[d]	18.0	18.0		18.0	Y
Iceland	30.0	30.0		30.0	N
Ireland	24.0	24.0		24.0	Y
Italy[e]	37.0	37.0		37.0	N
Japan	30.0	27.4	13.5	40.9	Y
Korea	28.0	28.0	2.8	30.8	Y
Luxembourg	31.2 (30.0)	28.4	9.1	37.5	Y
Mexico	35.0	35.0		35.0	Y
Netherlands	35.0	35.0		35.0	Y
New Zealand[a]	33.0	33.0		33.0	N
Norway	28.0	28.0		28.0	Y
Poland[f]	30.0	30.0		30.0	n.a.
Portugal	32.0	32.0	3.2	35.2	Y
Slovak Republic	29.0	29.0		29.0	N
Spain	35.0	35.0		35.0	Y
Sweden	28.0	28.0		28.0	N
Switzerland[g]	8.5	6.38	18.54	24.9	N
Turkey	33.0 (30.0)	33.0		33.0	N
United Kingdom	30.0	30.0		30.0	Y
United States[h]	35.0	32.7	6.7	39.4	Y

Key to abbreviations:

n.a.: Data not provided

Explanatory notes:

1. This table shows "basic" (nontargeted) central, subcentral and combined (statutory) corporate income tax rates. Where a progressive (as opposed to flat) rate structure applies, the top marginal rate is shown. Further explanatory notes may be found in the Explanatory Annex.

2. This column shows the basic central government statutory (flat or top marginal) corporate income tax rate, measured gross of a deduction (if any) for subcentral tax. Where surtax applies, the statutory corporate rate exclusive of surtax is shown in round brackets ( ).

3. This column shows the basic central government statutory corporate income tax rate (inclusive of surtax (if any)), adjusted (if applicable) to show the net rate where the central government provides a deduction in respect of subcentral income tax.

4. This column shows the basic subcentral (combined state/regional and local) statutory corporate income tax rate, inclusive of subcentral surtax (if any). The rate should be the representative rate reported in Table 11.3. Where a sub-central surtax applies, the statutory subcentral corporate rate exclusive of surtax is shown in round brackets ( ).

5. This column shows the basic combined central and subcentral (statutory) corporate income tax rate given by the adjusted central government rate plus the subcentral rate.

6. This column indicates whether targeted (nonbasic) corporate tax rates exist (e.g., with targeting through a special statutory corporate tax rate applied to qualifying income, or through a special deduction determined as a percentage of qualifying income). Where a 'Y' is shown, more information can be found in Table 11.2.

(Continued)

TABLE 19.4 CONTINUED

Country-specific footnotes:

(a) For Australia, New Zealand and the UK, all with a noncalendar tax year, the rates shown are those in effect as of 1 July, 1 April and 5 April, respectively.

(b) These are the rates applying to income earned in 2000, to be paid in 2001. The rates include surcharges, but does not include the local business tax (*Taxe professionnelle*) or the turnover based solidarity tax (*Contribution de Solidarité*). More information on the surcharges is included as a comment.

(c) The rates include the regional trade tax (*Gewerbesteuer*) and the surcharge.

(d) The rates does not include the turnover based local business tax.

(e) These rates do not include the regional business tax (*Imposta Regionale sulie Attività Produttive; IRAP*). See explanatory notes for more details.

(f) Source for the information: KPMG's Corporate Tax Rate Survey.

(g) Adjusted central and sub-central tax rates are calculated by the Swiss Federal Tax Administration (see "Quels taux effectifs et nominaux d'imposition des sociétés en Suisse pour le calcul des coins fiscaux. Le procédé de la déduction fiscale en Suisse").

(h) The subcentral rate is a weighted average state corporate marginal income tax rate. See explanatory notes for more details.

Source: Organization for Economic Cooperation and Development, OECD Tax Data Base, May 30, 2005. http://www.oecd.org/document/60/0,2340, en_2649_34533_1942460_1_1_1_1,00.html.

Countries also have different systems for taxing the earnings of the foreign subsidiaries of their domestic companies. Some, such as Hong Kong, use a territorial approach and tax only domestic-source income.[27] Others, such as Germany and the United Kingdom, use a global approach, taxing the profits of foreign branches and the dividends received from foreign subsidiaries. The United States is the only country to tax unremitted earnings in the form of Subpart F income.

The EU has worked hard to eliminate tax breaks in member countries in order to level the playing field and take tax out of the equation in attracting investment. As a result, foreign companies that had set up European headquarters and financing operations in countries like Belgium and the Netherlands to take advantage of tax incentives are considering moving to Switzerland, a non-EU country, and Ireland, where corporate tax rates are only 24 percent, compared with the EU average of 30.3 percent in 2003.[28]

Value-Added Tax

A **value-added tax** has been around since 1967 in most Western European countries and is used in other countries as well. A VAT is computed by applying a VAT tax rate on total sales. However, any company that purchased materials or other inputs into its manufacturing process from companies that might have already paid a VAT on their sales needs to pay the tax only on the difference between its sales and inputs that have already been taxed. As the name implies, VAT means that each independent company is taxed only on the value it adds at each stage in the production process. For a company that is fully integrated vertically, the tax rate applies to its net sales because it owned everything from raw materials to finished product.

> With a value-added tax, each company pays a percentage of the value added to a product at each stage of the business process.

The EU has worked hard to reduce VAT rates among member countries, although there are still variations. The standard VAT rate in the EU ranges from 15 percent to 25 percent, with many countries offering reduced rates in some categories ranging from 5 to 17 percent. The VAT does not apply to exports, because the tax is rebated (or returned) to the exporter and is not included in the final price to the consumer. This practice results in an effective stimulus for exports. In addition, it is considered by U.S. tax officials and MNEs to be a subsidy to European exports, because the export price can be lower than the domestic price of goods by the amount of the VAT.

Tax Treaties: The Elimination of Double Taxation

> The purpose of tax treaties is to prevent double taxation or to provide remedies when it occurs.

The primary purpose of tax treaties is to prevent international double taxation or to provide remedies when it occurs. The United States is an active participant in 59 different tax treaties.[29] The general pattern between two treaty countries is to grant reciprocal reductions on dividend withholding and to exempt royalties and sometimes interest payments from any withholding tax.

The United States has a withholding tax of 30 percent for owners (individuals and corporations) of U.S. securities that are issued in countries with which it has no tax treaty. However, interest on portfolio obligations and on bank deposits is normally exempted from withholding. When a tax treaty is in effect, the U.S. rate on dividends generally is reduced to 15 percent, and the tax on interest and royalties is either eliminated or is reduced to a very low level.

An example is a protocol to the 1980 tax treaty between the United States and Canada. It took effect on January 1, 1996, and it

1. Reduces the withholding rate on dividends paid to a corporation owning 10 percent or more of the voting stock of the payer. The withholding rate amounted to 6 percent for payments in 1996, and 5 percent thereafter.
2. Reduces the withholding rate on interest to 10 percent.
3. Reduces the tax resulting from the imposition of both U.S. estate tax and Canadian income tax on transfers at death.[30]

Several treaties and protocols were signed between the United States and foreign countries with an effective date of January 1, 1996, and they were very similar. In those treaties involving the reduction of withholding rates on dividends, the rate was typically 5 percent, although the rate for Portugal was 15 percent in some cases, 10 percent in others.

LOOKING TO THE FUTURE: Technology and Cash Flows

As companies drive down costs to increase their profitability and market value, they will need to drive down borrowing costs. Greater emphasis will be placed on moving corporate cash worldwide to take advantage of differing rates of return. In addition, companies will need to perfect their strategies for issuing bonds at the cheapest price possible and minimizing their tax bills worldwide. However, the U.S. has been clamping down on tax minimization schemes and attacking the providers of such schemes, such as law firms and public accounting firms, as well as going after the corporate clients that are adopting such schemes. As companies establish strategies to take advantage of tax havens, they need to make sure that they are very careful to avoid strategies that will turn them into the next Enron or Parmalat. The move to drive down costs can't come at the expense of the future viability of the company.

The explosion of information and technology and the growing number and sophistication of hedging instruments (financial derivatives such as options and forwards) will significantly influence the cash-management and hedging strategies of MNEs in the future. Advances in information systems will continue to enable companies to get information more quickly and cheaply. In addition, electronic data interchange (EDI) will allow

them to transfer information and money instantaneously worldwide. Companies will significantly reduce paper flow and increase the speed of delivery of information and funds, enabling them to manage cash and to use intercompany resources much more effectively than before. Consequently, companies will reduce not only the cost of producing information but also interest and other borrowing costs.

Investment and commercial banks will continue to develop new derivative instruments that will help companies to hedge their currency and interest rate exposures in the short and long term. However, new standards in accounting for derivative financial instruments by the FASB and IASB will force companies to mark most derivatives to market and recognize gains and losses in income. In spite of the tightening of accounting standards, derivatives will be a big help to companies as they attempt to hedge their cash flows and protect against the erosion of earnings in an unstable financial environment.

The OECD, the IMF, and the EU are three institutions that will help countries narrow their tax differences and crack down on the illegal transfer of money for illegal purposes. Although illegal financial transfers have occurred for years, especially due to drug trafficking, the attacks on September 11 and subsequent moves to track down money laundering by Osama bin Laden and other terrorists have created a more urgent need to reform the global financial system. This will continue to narrow the options of companies to move funds, but that isn't a bad idea.

SUMMARY

- The corporate finance function deals with the acquisition of financial resources and their allocation among the company's present and potential activities and projects.

- CFOs need to be concerned with the international dimensions of the company's capital structure, capital budgeting decisions, long-term financing, and working capital management.

- Country-specific factors are the most important determination of a company's capital structure.

- Two major sources of funds external to the MNE's normal operations are debt markets and equity markets.

- Offshore financial centers such as Bahrain, the Caribbean, Hong Kong, London, New York, Singapore, and Switzerland deal in large amounts of foreign currency and enable companies to take advantage of favorable tax rates.

- When deciding to invest abroad, MNE management must evaluate the cash flows from the local operation as well as the cash flows from the project to the parent. The former allows management to determine how the project stacks up with other opportunities in the foreign country, and the latter allows management to compare projects from different countries.

- The major sources of internal funds for an MNE are dividends, royalties, management fees, loans from parent to subsidiaries and vice versa, purchases and sales of inventory, and equity flows from parent to subsidiaries.

- Global cash management is complicated by differing inflation rates, changes in exchange rates, and government restrictions on the flow of funds. A sound cash-management system for an MNE requires timely reports from affiliates worldwide.

- Management must protect corporate assets from losses due to exchange-rate changes. Exchange rates can influence the dollar equivalent of foreign-currency financial statements, the amount of cash that can be earned from foreign-currency transactions, and a company's production and marketing decisions.

- Foreign-exchange risk management involves defining and measuring exposure, setting up a good monitoring and reporting system, adopting a policy to assign responsibility for exposure management, and formulating strategies for hedging exposure.

- Companies can enter into operational or financial strategies for hedging exposures. Operational strategies include balancing exposed assets with exposed liabilities, using leads and lags in cash flows, and balancing revenues in one currency with expenses in the same currency. Financial strategies involve using forward contracts, options, or other financial instruments to hedge an exposed position.

- International tax planning has a strong impact on the choice of location for the initial investment, the legal form of the new enterprise, the method of financing, and the method of setting transfer prices.

- Tax deferral means that the income a foreign subsidiary earns is taxed only when it is remitted to the parent as a dividend, not when it is earned.

- A controlled foreign corporation (CFC) must declare its Subpart F income as taxable to the parent in the year it is earned, whether or not it is remitted as a dividend.

- A tax credit allows a parent company to reduce its tax liability by the direct amount its subsidiary pays a foreign government on income that must be taxed by the parent company's government.

- Countries differ in terms of the types of taxes they have (income vs. excise), the tax rates applied to income, the determination of taxable income, and the treatment of foreign source income.

- The purpose of tax treaties is to prevent international double taxation or to provide remedies when it occurs.

Dell Mercosur[31]

Todd Pickett, CFO of Dell Mercosur, was facing the end of 2002 with conflicting predictions of the value of the Brazilian currency, the real, and what to do to hedge Dell's operation in Brazil. Although Pickett was concerned about Dell's exposure in the other Mercosur countries, especially Argentina, Brazil is clearly the largest concern. The year 2002 began with the shocks resulting from the Argentine financial crisis that started at the end of 2001, and it ended with the election in October of Luiz Inácio Lula da Silva, known simply as Lula, as the president of Brazil. Lula, the leader of the Workers' Party and long-time leftist politician, had held the lead throughout the year. The markets were skeptical of Lula's potential leadership, a factor that caused the real to fall from 2.312 reais per U.S. dollar at the end of 2001 to a record 4 reais to one U.S. dollar at one point just prior to the election. After the election, the real began to strengthen somewhat, as noted in Figure 19.10, but Pickett had to base his strategies on whether the real would continue to strengthen or would weaken again.

Dell's History

Founded in 1984 by Michael Dell, the computer company operates in 34 countries with 36,000 employees, of which about 14,400 are outside the United States, and recorded $32 billion in sales for 2002. In the previous five years, Dell had expanded beyond PCs to servers, storage, and communications equipment. Most PC manufacturers have claimed poor results since the technology bubble burst in 2000—IBM left the industry in 2000 and Compaq and HP merged in 2001 in hopes of boosting their competitive position. Unlike its competitors, Dell had thrived in the previous few years, moving from a market share of 12 percent to 15 percent in 2001, the number-one spot in the industry. Fiscal 2002 was one of the toughest years to date in the PC industry. Because of the softening of the global economy and the events of September 11, demand for PCs was down sharply. Dell responded with an aggressive price strategy and reduced costs through workforce reductions and facility consolidations. Although global industry shipments fell in 2002 by 5 percent, Dell's unit shipments increased by 15 percent, thus enabling Dell to retain its number-one position.

Dell bases its success on its build-to-order, direct sales model. Dell has eliminated resellers and retailers and sells directly to the customer by phone or over the Internet. Dell customizes every computer to the customer's needs and waits to build the computer until it is ordered. As a result, Dell requires little inventory (four days on average) and is able to

---

FIGURE 19.10 **EXCHANGE RATES FOR BRAZILIAN REAL AND U.S. DOLLAR**

Source: www.x-rates.com (2002).

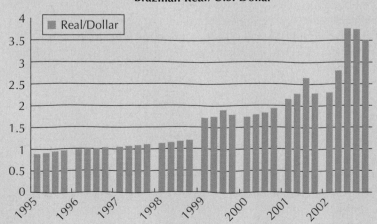

Brazilian Real/U.S. Dollar

deliver the newest technology to its customers. Costs are kept to a minimum compared to its competitors because it has no costly retail outlets and little inventory.

Dell began assembling computers in Round Rock, Texas, in 1985 and moved to global production in the following order:

1990: Opened manufacturing plant in Ireland
1996: Opened manufacturing plant in Malaysia
1998: Opened manufacturing plant in China
1999: Opened manufacturing plants in Tennessee and Brazil

Dell's 2002 Form 10K reports:

Sales outside the United States accounted for approximately 35% of the Company's revenues in fiscal year 2002. The Company's future growth rates and success are dependent on continued growth and success in international markets. As is the case with most international operations, the success and profitability of the Company's international operations are subject to numerous risks and uncertainties, including local economic and labor conditions, political instability, unexpected changes in the regulatory environment, trade protection measures, tax laws (including U.S. taxes on foreign operations), and foreign currency exchange rates.

Dell in Brazil

Dell's production facility in Brazil is in Eldorado do Sul, close to Porto Alegre, the capital of Rio Grande do Sul, the southernmost state in Brazil. In addition, its call center in Brazil, similar to Dell's call center in Bray, Ireland, services both Brazil and Argentina. Its Brazilian facility, which consists of 100,000 square feet of leased property, is the smallest of its facilities outside the United States, but the potential in Brazil and Argentina is huge, and Dell is planning further expansion. Because of the tariff-free provisions of Mercosur and the close proximity of Dell's manufacturing facilities in the south of Brazil, Dell is well positioned to service all of Mercosur with its Brazilian manufacturing operations. In FY 2002, it held a 4 1/2 percent market share in Brazil, behind HP/Compaq, IBM, and a Brazilian company. However, it was rapidly moving up to third place in the market and growing quickly.

Although Dell is divided into products and customers, it is managed generally on a geographic basis. Terry Kahler, the general manager of Dell Mercosur, reports to the head of the Americas/International Group, who in turn reports to Rosendo Parra, the vice president of the Americas/International Group in Austin, Texas. Pickett works very closely with Kahler but reports directly to the CFO staff in Austin.

Dell's revenues in Brazil are denominated in reals, and most of its operating costs are also denominated in reals. However, about 97 percent of Dell's manufacturing costs in Brazil are denominated in U.S. dollars since Dell imports parts and components from the United States. It translates its financial statements according to the current rate method, which means that assets and liabilities are translated into dollars at the current exchange rate, and revenues and expenses are translated at the average exchange rate for the period. Because of business development loans from the Brazilian government, Dell's net exposed asset position in Brazil is quite small, but it is subject to foreign-exchange gains and losses as the rate changes.

Hedging Strategy

In its Form 10K for FY 2002, Dell states its foreign currency hedging strategy as follows:

The Company's objective in managing its exposure to foreign currency exchange rate fluctuations is to reduce the impact of adverse fluctuations on earnings and cash flows associated with foreign currency exchange rate changes. Accordingly, the Company utilizes foreign currency option contracts and forward contracts to hedge its exposure on forecasted transactions and firm commitments in most of the foreign countries in which the

Company operates. The principal currencies hedged during fiscal 2002 were the British pound, Japanese yen, euro, and Canadian dollar. The Company monitors its foreign currency exchange exposures to ensure the overall effectiveness of its foreign currency hedge positions. However, there can be no assurance the Company's foreign currency hedging activities will substantially offset the impact of fluctuations in currency exchange rates on its results of operations and financial position.

The Company uses purchased option contracts and forward contracts designated as cash flow hedges to protect against the foreign currency exchange risk inherent in its forecasted transactions denominated in currencies other than [the] U.S. dollar. Hedged transactions include international sales by U.S. dollar functional currency entities, foreign currency denominated purchases of certain components, and intercompany shipments to certain international subsidiaries. The risk of loss associated with purchased options is limited to premium amounts paid for the option contracts. The risk of loss associated with forward contracts is equal to the exchange rate differential from the time the contract is entered into until the time it is settled. These contracts generally expire in 12 months or less.

The company also uses forward contracts to economically hedge monetary assets and liabilities, primarily receivables and payables that are denominated in a foreign currency. These contracts are not designated as hedging instruments under generally accepted accounting principles, and, therefore, the change in the instrument's fair value is recognized currently in earnings and is reported as a component of investment and other income (loss), net. The change in the fair value of these instruments represents a natural hedge as their gains and losses offset the changes in the underlying fair value of the monetary assets and liabilities due to movements in currency exchange rates. These contracts generally expire in three months or less.

Based on these general statements of principle, Dell's strategy is to hedge all foreign-exchange risk, which is a very aggressive hedging strategy. Since there is no options market for Brazilian reals, Pickett uses forward contracts to hedge the foreign exchange risks in Brazil.

Corporate treasury monitors currency movements worldwide and provides support to Pickett's Brazilian treasury group in terms of currency forecasts and hedging strategies. Within the broad strategy approved by corporate treasury, the Brazilian group establishes a strategy and then works with corporate on specific execution of the strategy.

There are two key parts to the strategy. One has to do with forecasting exposure, and the other has to do with designing and executing the strategy to hedge the exposure. Although the balance sheet exposure is not material, it still must be forecast and is partly a function of the cash flows generated by revenues. The revenue side is more difficult to forecast, so Pickett hedges about 80 percent of forecasted revenues. However, the Dell team in Brazil has become very adept at forecasting revenues and in executing a strategy in order to reach its target forecast. The team works hard on identifying the challenges in reaching its target and in devising policies to overcome those challenges. Its execution strategies vary widely quarter by quarter, and the management team has become very good at meeting its targets by working closely together and being flexible. Pickett and Kahler work closely together on a daily basis to execute their strategy.

The second key to the strategy is designing and executing the hedging strategy. Since revenues vary on a daily basis, Pickett does not enter into contracts all at once. Instead, he works with corporate treasury to enter into contracts in different amounts and different maturities depending on when it expects to generate the operating revenues. Revenues are generally lower at the beginning of the quarter and are always higher in the last week or two of the quarter, so he enters into contracts accordingly. Timing is a crucial issue. The gain or loss on a forward contract is the difference in exchange rates between when the contract is entered into and when it is settled. The key is to unwind (or settle) the contracts while the rate is still favorable. Pickett noted that if Dell began to unwind the contracts in the last week or two of the quarter instead of the last day or two of the quarter, it could get much more favorable foreign-exchange gains. His strategy was so successful that in some quarters, Dell was generating more financial income than operating income. Although Pickett and his treasury team have some flexibility in designing and implementing strategy, corporate treasury keeps in close touch, depending on their forecasts of the exchange rate and the strategy that Dell Brazil is following. Corporate treasury uses a consensus forecast of exchange rates that is provided by a group of banks, but banks have different scenarios. For example, in the last quarter of 2002, corporate was relying on bank forecasts that the real would revalue even more by the end of the year.

Pickett's dilemma was that his gut feeling was that the real would actually fall instead of rise. That would indicate a different hedging strategy. He was resisting entering into hedges while corporate was pressuring him to do just that. But he was closely watching the forward market, and when it began to move, he decided it was time to enter into the contracts. But who knows what will happen to Brazil if Lula, Brazil's new president, loses fiscal control of the ninth largest economy in the world, resulting in another round of inflation and a falling currency? Dell has significant market opportunities in Mercosur, but the financial risks will make for exciting times in the years to come.

QUESTIONS

1. Given how Dell translates its foreign currency financial statements into dollars, how would a falling Brazilian real affect Dell Mercosur's financial statements? What about a rising real?
2. Dell imports about 97 percent of its manufacturing costs. What type of exposure does that create for it? What are its options to reduce that exposure?
3. Describe and evaluate Dell's exposure management strategy.
4. Build a graph on the value of the real against the dollar by quarter since the third quarter of 2002. What has happened to the value of the real? Based on the change in the exchange rate, how would you evaluate Dell's hedging philosophy and strategy?

CHAPTER NOTES

1 Information for the case is taken from the Nu Skin Enterprise annual reports (1997, 1998, 2004) and personal interviews (2002); Cosmetics Design.com, "Nu Skin Looks to Chinese Expansion," February 10, 2005, http://www.cosmeticsdesign.com/news/news-ng.asp?n=57990-nu-skin-looks, accessed June 6, 2005; Laura Klepacki, "Nu Skin Celebrates 20 Years," *Women's Wear Daily* (February 20, 2004); Peter Wonacott, "China Is Letting Avon Products Do Direct Sales on a Trial Basis," *The Wall Street Journal* (April 11, 2005): A16; Leslie P. Norton, "Yuan Stays Put, Nu Skin's China Challenge," *Barron's Online* (May 9, 2005).
2 Arthur J. Keown, John D. Martin, J. William Petty, and David F. Scott, Jr., *Financial Management*, 10th ed. (Upper Saddle River, NJ: Pearson Prentice Hall, 2005), p. 5.
3 Based on David K. Eiteman, Arthur I. Stonehill, and Michael H. Moffett, *Multinational Business Finance*, 10th ed. (Reading, MA: Addison-Wesley, 2003), p. 3.
4 Keown, et al., p. 290.
5 "Theory Versus the Real World," *Finance & Treasury* (April 26, 1993): 1.
6 Mihir A. Desai, C. Fritz Foley, and James R. Hines, Jr., "A Multinational Perspective on Capital Structure Choice and Internal Capital Markets," *Journal of Economic Literature* (October 2003).
7 Ibid.
8 Henry Sender, "Financial Musical Chairs," *Far Eastern Economic Review* (July 29, 1999): 30–36.
9 "Long-Term Debt," *Nissan Annual Report* (2003), 59.
10 *Nu Skin Annual Report 2004*, p. 62.
11 IMF Monetary and Exchange Affairs Department, "IMF Background Paper: Offshore Financial Centers," June 23, 2000.
12 Ibid.
13 Ibid.
14 "How the Heavyweights Shape Up," *Euromoney* (May 1990): 56.

15 Organization for Economic Cooperation and Development, "Project on Harmful Tax Practice: The 2004 Progress Report," 22 March 2004.

16 David Cay Johnston, "How Offshore Havens Helped Enron Escape Taxes," *New York Times* (Jan. 18, 2002).

17 Lucy Komisar, "Funny Money," Metroactive News & Issues," January 24, 2002. **http://www.metroactive.com/ papers/sonoma/01.24.02/offshorebanking-0204.html**. Accessed June 7, 2005.

18 Eiteman et al., op. cit.

19 Stephen Power, "BMW's Profit Softened in Quarter," *Wall Street Journal* (May 4, 2005): A12.

20 Helmut Hagemann, "Anticipate Your Long-Term Foreign Exchange Risks," *Harvard Business Review* (March–April 1977): 82; "Foreign Currency Management," *Coca-Cola Annual Report* (2004).

21 "Foreign Currency Management," Coca-Cola Annual Report (2004).

22 John W. Miller, EU's Single Market Concept Is Challenged by Tax Battles," *Wall Street Journal* (January 26, 2005): A10; Johnston, *op. cit.*

23 Johnston, *op. cit.*

24 William H. Hoffman, et al., 2002. *West Federal Taxation: Corporations, Partnerships, Estates, and Trusts* (Cincinnati: South-Western), Section 9, p. 33.

25 OECD Center for Tax Policy and Administration, "Transfer Pricing," **http://www.oecd.org/department/ 0,2688, en_2649_33753_1_1_1_1_1,00.html**.

26 German Embassy, Washington, D.C., "German Taxation After Tax Reform 2000—In Brief," **http://www.germany-info.org/relaunch/business/taxes/german_taxes_2000b.html**. Accessed June 6, 2005.

27 The Inland Revenue Department, The Government of Hong Kong Special Administrative Region, "A Simple Guide on The Territorial Source Principle of Taxation," **http://www.ird.gov.hk/eng/paf/ bus_pft_tsp.htm**. Accessed June 6, 2005.

28 "The Cost of a Level EU Field," *Wall Street Journal* (October 9, 2003): A16.

29 U.S. Internal Revenue Service, "Income Tax Treaties," **http://www.irs.gov/businesses/corporations/ article/0,, id=96739,00.html**. Accessed June 6, 2005.

30 "U.S. Tax Treaty Developments," *Deloitte & Touche Review* (February 5, 1996): 5.

31 Interview with Todd Pickett (2002); www.dell.com (2002); Dell's 2002 10Ks (2002), **www.dell.com**; Michael Schrage, "The Dell Curve," *Wired Magazine*, no. 10.7 (July 2002): **http://www.wired.com/wired/archive/ 10.07/dell**.

Once overseas, virtually all managers eventually return home. One would think this would be a snap—pack the bags, say goodbye to colleagues, board the plane, and return to a hero's welcome. In many cases, everything but the hero's welcome happens. Observed Tom Schiro of Deloitte & Touche, "Some companies just send somebody overseas and forget about them for two years."[6] Expectedly, wise career planning can made a world of difference. For example, following a four-year assignment in Tokyo, Bryan Krueger returned to a promotion as president of Baxter Fenwal North America. When he left to start his job in Tokyo, his company had not guaranteed him a promotion upon his return. So, while away, he kept up to date with the goings-on at headquarters. Later, Mr. Krueger credited his particularly smooth return to his intensive networking. During his stint in Tokyo, he returned to the U.S. four to five times a year in order to see colleagues and friends. As he explained, "I was definitely proactive. Anyone who's not is doing himself a disservice. I made a conscious effort to stay in touch, and it paid off."[7] On the flip side, companies may be unable to entice their expatriate back home at all. While overseas, an expatriate can achieve remarkable levels of compensation, responsibility, and prestige. Coupled with a penchant for living abroad, an international career can be irresistible. For example, after stints in Singapore and London, a Morgan Stanley expatriate in India said, "I still don't want to go back to the United States. It's a big world—lots of things to see."[8] Then again, there are probably a lot of things expatriates avoid seeing. International business travel "is perhaps the most dangerous form of travel. . . . Tourists wouldn't consider flying into a Colombian war zone for a week, yet folks from oil, computer, pharmaceutical, agricultural and telecom companies do it regularly."[9] Once there, simply frequenting good hotels and restaurants with colleagues makes them prime targets.

In theory, the professional impact of an overseas assignment to one's career trajectory may be positive, neutral, or negative. Historically, the odds were on a neutral or negative outcome. Granted, companies touted the value of foreign assignments as valuable development experiences that prepared managers for greater corporate responsibilities. However, many companies were slow to reward managers' successful international experience with expanded leadership responsibilities upon their return home. This tendency often showed in the makeup of the top management ranks. For example, few CEOs at the largest U.S. companies have worked outside the United States, and few large U.S. companies have foreigners either as board members or in senior corporate positions.

The globalization of business has fundamentally changed this situation. More and more CEOs assert that international experience is an essential feature of a high-performance career. Globalization spurs MNEs, like Samsung and Dow Chemical, to see multicountry experience just as essential as multifunctional and multiproduct experience in reaching the upper echelons of the company. More pointedly, Daniel Meiland conjectures that "If you look ahead five to ten years, the people with the top jobs in large corporations, even in the United States, will be those who have lived in several cultures and who can converse in at least two languages. Most CEOs will have had true global exposure, and their companies will be all the stronger for it."[10]

INTRODUCTION

The challenge of putting the right person into the right job in the right place at the right time for the right salary takes us to the front lines of international business. From defining brave new markets to returning home, international business careers take a manager in any number of directions. At the center of it all, though, is the individual facing unprecedented challenges that often lead to amazing opportunities. The contest between challenges and opportunities, as we will now see, is the spirit of a career in international business.[11] This chapter looks at the role of the individual in international business. Specifically, this chapter discusses facets of human resource management (HRM) as they primarily apply to managers in the company with international operations. As do the series of vignettes in our opening case, we elaborate this perspective by giving our discussions a strong sensitivity to the idea of international careers.

In theory, HRM refers to the range of activities that a company, whether solely domestic or thoroughly global, takes to staff its organization. More specifically, opening and operating a business demands that companies determine their human resource needs,

Human resource management refers to activities necessary to staff the organization.

FIGURE 20.1 **HUMAN RESOURCES IN INTERNATIONAL BUSINESS**

Human resource management is a vital function for implementing a company's strategy. It takes into consideration a range of factors to put the right person into the right job in the right place at the right time for the right salary.

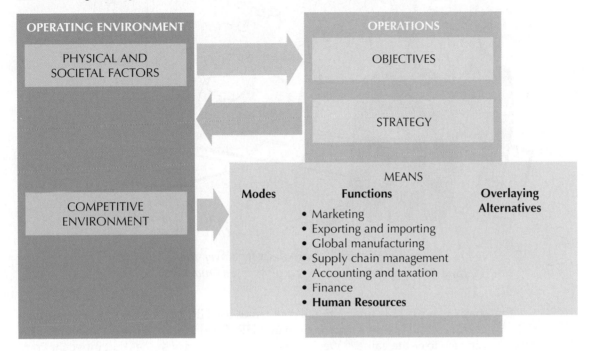

hire people to meet those needs, motivate them to perform well, upgrade their skills so that they can move onto more challenging tasks, and ultimately retain them.[12] This chapter, directly building on the themes introduced in Chapter 11 and applied since then to the various activities of the value chain, looks at HRM with the perspective that successful companies staff their operations with people that can leverage their core competencies in the face of prevailing pressures for local responsiveness and global integration. This premise emphasizes that the various HRM activities, like discrete activities in the company's value chain, perform best when managers link them to the strategy of the firm. Figure 20.1 shows the importance of human resources in international business.

Generally, HRM is more difficult for the international company than its domestic counterparts. Complications arise from enduring political, cultural, legal, and economic differences between countries—to say nothing of the struggle of simply traveling the world (see Figure 20.2). For example, leadership styles and management practices vary significantly from country to country.[13] These differences often cause difficulties between people at different units, say, headquarters and a local subsidiary. More worrisome, these differences can turn a great manager at home into an ineffective manager in foreign markets. Similarly, labor markets vary dramatically in the mix of workers, costs, and productivity. Local labor laws, as we saw in Chapter 3, often require a company to change its hiring and firing practices as well as its workplace standards. Finally, dual career and family obligations makes it tough to convince executives to leave the home office to join a foreign subsidiary. Consequently, companies must develop special recruitment, training, compensation, transfer, and retention programs to persuade executives to go abroad.

Inevitably, one wonders why companies and people put up with these aggravations. The short answer is, in the face of globalization, because they must. The long answer is that, in the face of globalization, insightfully dealing with these challenges creates competitive advantages. Both answers highlight the mandate for HRM: Develop the means and methods to build and retain the cadre of managers that will lead an international company to greater performance.

HRM is more difficult for the international company than its domestic counterpart due to

• Environmental differences
• Organizational challenges

FIGURE 20.2

The travel required to oversee international operations is stressful.

Source: From *Punch Magazine.* Reprinted by permission.

"*I've never actually met him—as soon as he's over the jet lag, it's time for another trip in search of overseas markets.*"

This chapter shows how international companies use HRM processes to meet this mandate. We begin by briefly discussing the role that HRM plays in supporting the strategy the MNE has chosen to create value.[14] We then discuss those HRM activities that move the company's personnel plans from ambition to action, namely, the selection, development, compensation, and retention of international managers.[15] The chapter concludes with a look at the relationship between the MNE and organized labor, examining the implication of the linkages among international labor relations, management action, and the firm's strategy.

THE STRATEGIC FUNCTION OF INTERNATIONAL HRM

The MNE whose HRM policies support its strategy can create superior value.

Anecdotes suggest and research confirms a powerful relationship between HRM processes, management productivity, and strategic performance in the international company.[16] We noted in Chapter 11 that Jeffrey Immelt, CEO and chairman of General Electric, believed that success is "truly about people, not about where the buildings are. You've got to develop people so they are prepared for leadership jobs and then promote them. That's the most effective way to become more global." Similarly, the then chairman of Unilever, at a roundtable discussion on how the world is changing and what management can do to respond, reasoned that "The single most important issue for us has been, and will continue to be, organization and people."[17]

Research confirms these views, showing that superior human resources can sustain high productivity, competitive advantage, and value creation for the international company. The Human Capital Index, based on a comprehensive global study of over 2,000 companies, found that superior human resource practices not only positively correlated with a firm's financial returns, but were a leading indicator of increased shareholder value.[18] Significantly, this study also found a notable pattern of causality: Superior HRM was a stronger determinant of a firm's financial performance than the thesis that superior financial outcomes lead companies to develop superior HRM practices. Or, to paraphrase Jeffrey Immelt, creating value is "truly about people, not about where the buildings are." Others report similar effects, finding that the interaction between the firm's strategy and its HRM processes accounts for more variation in firm performance than simply looking at the primary effects of HRM.[19]

The irony of this situation is that we have all heard companies trumpet "Our people are our most important asset." Still, more than a few employees can relay tales that when push came to shove, companies failed to honor this pledge. Research finds similar effects, confirming that many international companies do not match rhetoric to reality. For instance, later parts of the chapter discuss the odd fact of what happens to executives when they return home from their overseas assignment—more than half leave their company within a year. More generally, a study of the role of HRM to enhance competitiveness at more than 300 multinationals reported that effectively developing and managing human resources was one of the weakest capabilities in most firms.[20] Another study suggested that companies that significantly improved the strategic performance of their HRM practices could increase their market value by as much as 30 percent.[21] Collectively, research regularly reports that while executives acknowledge that the effectiveness of human resource practices materially affects firm performance, many firms fail to achieve their HRM goals.

The persistent gap between rhetoric and reality of the value of human resources has led to the realization that staffing people to support competitive success requires fundamentally changing how companies approach HRM. Specifically, there is growing consensus that HRM must hire, develop, reward, and retain people whose performance explicitly improves the productivity of the firm's core competencies within the context of how it has configured and coordinated its value chain. This realization compels MNEs to anchor HRM practices within the context of their strategy. In other words, HRM is not a series of discrete processes that are an agenda item—it is the agenda.

In other words, the odds that a company successfully engages its chosen strategy is significantly influenced by how well it staffs the right person in the right job in the right place at the right time for the right salary. Our earlier look at the types of strategies that international business follows provides a way to address this issue. Specifically, Chapter 11 discusses four strategies pursued by an MNE: the international strategy and its quest to leverage core competencies abroad, the multidomestic strategy and its quest to maximize the local responsiveness of its foreign operations, the global strategy and its quest to maximize global integration, and the transnational strategy and its quest to do all three tasks simultaneously.

The type of strategy that MNEs pursue has explicit HRM requirements. A company makes its strategic ambitions mere speculations if it does not build the human resources needed to achieve them. For example, General Electric is currently using a transnational strategy. Getting to this point has taken the company more than two decades. Beginning in the 1980s, General Electric focused on globalizing its markets to tighten its cost structure (the international strategy). In the late 1980s, the company moved to globalizing its material sources to get higher quality inputs for lower prices (the global strategy). Then, in the mid-1990s, it began trying to globalize its intellect, seeking, learning, and transferring ideas throughout its global operations (the transnational strategy). At each "stop" along the way to its current transnational strategy, General Electric rethought its HRM philosophy to make sure it had the human capital to achieve its strategy. Specifically, the key to its international strategy was staffing people who could optimize location economics and scale effects, the key to its global strategy was staffing people with the outlook to manage global scanning and supply chains, and the key to the transnational strategy has been staffing people around the world who can develop, transfer, and receive ideas. At each stage in General Electric's evolution, its HRM aligned the processes of employee selection, development, and compensation policies to support its strategy.

A vital part of General Electric's HRM evolution has been its use and expectations of expatriates. Explained Jeffrey Immelt, "When I first joined General Electric [in 1982] globalization meant training the Americans to be global thinkers. So Americans got the expat assignments. We still have many Americans living around the world and that's good, but we shifted our emphasis in the late 1990s to getting overseas assignments for non-Americans. Now you see non-Americans doing new jobs, big jobs, important jobs at every level and in every country." General Electric's increasingly sophisticated use of expatriates has created a cadre of international managers with the expertise to manage its

Many MNEs struggle to develop effective HRM policies.

The role and characteristics of international managers evolve over time.

core competency in developing and diffusing powerful ideas around the world. General Electric's success in international business, like that of many other companies we profile throughout this chapter, highlights the standard for HRM in an MNE: Staffing the manager with the necessary qualifications to the job that best supports and sustains the company's worldwide strategy.

STAFFING POLICIES

Talk of virtual companies operating in cyberspace, free of the bounds of national borders and the constraints of geographic conceptions of staffing policies, may eventually come to pass. Presently, though, international business takes place within in a world marked by geographical borders and populated by companies running real value chains. Indeed, there are more than 63,000 MNEs with more than 690,000 foreign affiliates spread across the 200-plus nations of the world. Staffing these thousands of home offices and foreign affiliates means that an international company ultimately must find and move managers between the various units of its operations. This task begins with how the company has defined its staffing policies to fill international jobs with those individuals who have the skills needed to perform a particular job in ways that support the company's strategy.

For the majority of MNEs, the issue of staffing policies centers on the decision of whether to run their international operations with local workers in the host nation, or expatriates sent from the home country, or a third-country national. By definition, executives in the MNE are either locals, citizens of the countries in which they are working, or expatriates, noncitizens. Expatriates are either home-country nationals, citizens of the country in which the company is headquartered or third-country nationals, citizens of neither the country in which they are working nor the headquarters country. Locals or expatriates may be employed in the company's home country or in its foreign operations. Expatriates play an important role in the international business of most companies.[22] We now discuss the reasons companies use locals and expatriates, as well as companies' human resource practices for expatriates.

Recently, staffing policies have assumed greater significance as MNEs deal with the growing importance of informal aspects of organization along with the fluid challenges posed by globalization.[23] Unquestionably, HRM aims, as it as always has, to staff people who command the skills needed to get the job done. Now, though, HRM looks for people who meet this standard but who also have professional values that are congruent with the organization culture and leadership ideals of the company. The belief is that if an MNE can staff employees whose professional values are congruent with the company's values, then it can perform more competitively—no matter what type of strategy it happens to follow.[24]

Again, let's take a quick look at General Electric for illustration of the growing importance of professional values to HRM. Recall that General Electric's transnational strategy hinged on how well the company could "globalize the intellect of the company." This goal, in turn, has required that General Electric staff its worldwide operations with people who command the technical competencies required for performing the jobs but who also share the values that support the company's transnational strategy. Explained Jack Welch, "Objectives don't get you there. Values do." His successor has continued this policy, maintaining that General Electric tries "very hard to provide a company, a set of values, and a culture that employees can be proud of, whether it be in Pittsfield, Paris, Shanghai, or London."[25]

For our purposes, the strategic values and leadership ideals of a company translate into the assumptions and generalizations that define its so-called interpretative framework. This framework, which is formed and reformed on the basis of experiences, beliefs, and prior perceptions, influences how the company understands its world and the strategy it pursues to create value. This topic, particularly how assumptions and generalizations combine to create coherent frameworks, is an enduring interest in international business studies.

Staffing policy defines the process by which the company assigns the most appropriate candidate to the foreign job.

An **expatriate** is an employee who leaves her or his native country to live and work in another.

A **third-country national** is an employee who is a citizen of neither the home nor the host country.

Companies are increasingly sensitive to the congruence between the values held by an employee and those of its organizational culture.

Three perspectives anchor an MNE's staffing policy
- Ethnocentric
- Polycentric
- Geocentric

Research spotlights three types of frameworks as they apply to an MNE's staffing policy: the ethnocentric approach, the polycentric approach, and the geocentric approach. We now turn to the fine points of each, noting how each supports and constrains staffing policies in MNEs. Before we begin though, a quick note: As you review each type, keep in mind that there is no theoretically superior approach. Each one has strengths and weaknesses that make it, depending on the company's strategy, a useful way to anchor staffing policies.

The Ethnocentric Approach

An ethnocentric staffing policy reflects the belief that the HRM principles and practices used by the home office country are intrinsically superior to those used by companies in other nations. Hence, given its success in the home market, there is no need to adapt HRM principles and practices when transferred to foreign markets.[26] As such, this staffing policy leads companies to fill management positions, no matter where in the world they are, with executives from the home office. The company believes several benefits support this decision (see Table 20.1).

An ethnocentric staffing approach fills all key management positions with home-country nationals.

MNEs that directly link firm performance to how well they transfer core competencies are keen to adopt an ethnocentric approach. Specifically, a firm earns success in its home market doing something exceptional. A legacy of success leads companies to see their business methods as the best way to do things. In such situations, companies aim to sustain their success when expanding and operating overseas by tightly controlling the transfer and regulating the use of their core competencies. A core competency, as we noted in Chapter 11, is the special outlook, skill, capability, or technology that creates unique value for the firm and which is hard for rivals to imitate. Firms that are particularly sensitive to leveraging their core competency in foreign markets see an ethnocentric staffing policy working well on two levels: the matters of transfer and protection.

Regarding transfer, staffing overseas operations with people from the home country goes a long way to ensuring that the firm's core competency makes it overseas as intended.[27] This is particularly important when the core competency is difficult to articulate, specify, or standardize—such as Apple's product design sensitivities or MBNA America's precept of "think of yourself as a customer." Posting a home-country manager to foreign operations, therefore, puts the company's core competency under the direction of the home-country manager who commands the hands-on knowledge that made the company successful in the first place. Regarding protection, companies are keen to

People transferred from headquarters are more likely to best understand the company's core competencies.

TABLE 20.1   LEADING REASONS TO STAFF FOREIGN OPERATIONS WITH EXPATRIATES

Command and control	Home-country expatriates are used to doing things the "headquarters' way" and, thus, will transfer the "correct" systems to foreign operations.
Local talent gaps	Shortage of qualified local candidates, particularly given the need to transfer specialized technologies overseas, compels sending abroad highly skilled managers.
Social integration	Transferring people to different national slots helps all parties understand the global corporate entity.
Ownership structure	Joint ventures with local partners spur foreign companies to insist on using their personnel to fill key positions in order to protect their property.
Local implementation	Transferring best practices between the home country and foreign subsidiaries usually breaks down in the details of local implementation. Expatriates can quickly resolve breakdowns or bottlenecks.
High turnover among locals	MNEs often face high turnover among local employees in foreign markets, particularly with highly trained professionals with technical skills. Each person who leaves is a risk of an intellectual property leak.
Management development	International experience and exposure to many nationalities encourage a manager's development of a global outlook.

safeguard their core competency. With it, the firm prospers; without it, the firm fails. This stark reality leads headquarters to entrust control of the company's "crown jewels" to those who they believe will unconditionally protect them—namely, fellow colleagues at headquarters. Finally, earlier chapters noted the formidable task of operating in odd, exotic places. Companies often use an ethnocentric staffing approach to reduce the degree of cognitive dissonance they face as they expand internationally. Relying on people familiar with proven workplace methods and labor procedures, even if only within the context of the home-country market, helps companies cope with the stress of foreign situations.

As the adage goes, "vices are simply virtues taken to extreme." The same is often said about an ethnocentric staffing approach. An enduring theme of international business is the differences among people, places, and processes. Force-fitting all foreign situations to a standardized staffing policy runs the risk of trying to pound circular pegs into square slots. Granted, eventually a company can make its foreign operation mirror the outward appearance of the home office. However, putting people in foreign settings doesn't automatically imbue new attitudes and, more likely, carries the price of high costs and lost opportunities. Predictably, companies have good reasons when asked why they only relied on home-country nationals to run their international operations. They often explain that there was usually no shortage of brainpower in a particular country, just a shortage of people with the right mix of technical skills, experience with their particular business methods, and trustworthiness.

In many situations, this limitation is damaging. The ethnocentric approach to staffing blinds the company to the benefit of exposure to different, possibly better, ways of doing things. Reluctance to consider this possibility can dull the firm's competitiveness. Ethnocentric staffing policies can also demotivate and demoralize local managers and workers. An implicit assumption of the ethnocentric view—namely, that all the smart, capable people were born and live within a 10-mile radius of headquarters—sends the message to subsidiary personnel that headquarters does not trust or respect them. Unless a foreign assignment is plainly intended to develop an expatriate, local employees will often resent someone coming from a foreign country who they feel is no more qualified than they are. Such resentment can lower productivity and increase turnover in local operations.

> An ethnocentric staffing can result in a narrow perspective in foreign markets.

The Polycentric Approach

A polycentric outlook accepts the legitimacy of the assumption that staffing policies ought to adapt to differences between operations in the home and host country. A polycentric staffing policy sees the effectiveness of the business practices of foreign markets as equivalent to those in the home country. Therefore, a polycentric staffing policy motivates the company to staff each operation from headquarters in the home country to each foreign subsidiary with people from the local environment—that is, Chinese run the China operations, Mexicans run the Mexico operations, Austrians run the Austria operations, and Canadians staff the corporate headquarters in Canada. Therefore, a polycentric approach is an intrinsic feature of the staffing approach in the context of the multidomestic strategy. It is inappropriate for a company whose strategies require they configure value chains to exploit location economies or coordinate value chains to leverage core competencies worldwide.

> A polycentric staffing policy uses host-country nationals to manage local subsidiaries.

Staffing foreign operations with locals has indisputable advantages (see Table 20.2). When the host country is suspicious of foreign-controlled operations, local managers may be perceived as "better citizens" because they presumably put local interests ahead of the company's global objectives. This local image may play a role in employee morale as well. Many subsidiary employees prefer to work for someone from their own country.[28] Too, there are many impediments to using expatriates, such as licensing requirements that prevent companies from using expatriate accountants and lawyers.

TABLE 20.2	LEADING REASONS TO STAFF FOREIGN OPERATIONS WITH LOCALS
Cost containment	The most compelling reason is cost. Due to tax equalization, housing allowance, cost-of-living adjustment, and other benefits, the typical expatriate compensation package is three to five times the base salary at home and several times that of a local hire.
Nationalism	Host countries that dislike foreign-controlled operations regard local managers as "better citizens" because they likely put local interests ahead of the company's global objectives. Too, host governments can restrict expatriate headcounts in order to develop indigenous talent pools.
Management development	MNEs that consistently award top jobs to expatriates often struggle to attract, motivate, and retain local employees.
Employee morale	Many subsidiary employees prefer to work for someone who is from their own country.
Expatriate failure rates	Failure rates for overseas postings can reduce performance, sidetrack careers, and corrode morale.
Product issues	The greater the need for local adaptations, the more advantageous it is for companies to use local managers, because they arguably interpret local conditions better than an expatriate.

More significantly, the stark economics of staffing international operations is a compelling motivation for a polycentric approach to staffing. Hiring local managers eliminates the exorbitant expense of sending people from the home office. On average, companies in the U.S. spend nearly $1.3 million per expatriate during the course of the typical three-year foreign assignment.[29] Many human resource managers, facing growing pressure to control the cost of expatriate assignments, respond by hiring locals. For example, FedEx, the U.S.-based express delivery company, has little more than 200 expatriates out of its 140,000 worldwide employees. It prefers to fill foreign slots with local executives because an expatriate always costs more.[30] Similarly, FedEx reasons that local managers should perform better sooner given their finer understanding of local customers, markets, and institutions. Other companies echo this view. For instance, when operating outside the U.S., Microsoft tries to hire foreign nationals rather than use expatriates. Explained its COO, Robert Herbold, "You want people who know the local situation, its value system, the way work gets done, the way people use technology in that particular country, and who the key competitors are. . . . If you send someone in fresh from a different region or country, they don't know those things."[31] More philosophically, Bill Gates, CEO and chairman of Microsoft, reasons a polycentric staffing policy is a moral obligation of international business, declaring that, when staffing an international office, "It sends the wrong message to have a foreigner come over to run things."[32]

Operationally, a polycentric staffing policy leads companies to transfer responsibility and authority to host country nationals to run the local subsidiary. Problems often arise on issues of accountability and allegiance. Accountability issues emerge when foreign subsidiaries evolve into quasi-autonomous operations that depend less and less on the home office for resources. Furthermore, host-country nationals in charge of a subsidiary tend to see their primary allegiance to their fellow local colleagues and country, rather than some distant home office. In theory, local managers ought to be able to balance the competing demands of making sense of events from a local and home office view. In practice, however, they may believe national concerns ought to take precedence over the needs of the home office.[33] Headquarters' efforts to regulate or control local activities, say by transferring a new product or streamlining logistics, are likely to run into several roadblocks.

Compounding this situation is a particularly insidious drawback of a polycentric staffing policy, namely the potential disengagement of local staff from the parent company in specific and international business in general. By definition and design, a polycentric staffing policy creates few opportunities to work outside one's own country. This outcome can severely constrain the international mobility of host-country nationals. As a result, there may be little incentive for local managers to understand foreign commercial and cultural practices. Left standing, these differences can isolate national subsidiaries

Using host-country managers helps local motivation and morale but at the possible cost of a gap with global operations due to problems with accountability and allegiance.

unto themselves. Consequently, headquarters' goal to build a global company with local operations may mutate into a loose federation of largely independent country operations with only nominal links to each other and headquarters.

The Geocentric Approach

A geocentric staffing policy seeks the best people for key jobs throughout the organization, regardless of their nationality.

Moving from a multidomestic company to a global or transnational company lessens the need to have home country or host country managers supervise local activities. So, unlike the ethnocentric and polycentric variations, a geocentric staffing policy is not tied to a particular home or host nation. Rather, a geocentric staffing policy scans the world, looking for the best people for key jobs throughout the organization, regardless of their nationality. Said Jeffrey Immelt of General Electric, explaining the company staffing policy, "It's more important to find the best people, wherever they may be, and develop them so that they can lead big businesses, wherever those may be." A geocentric policy enables the MNE to build the requisite cadre of international executives who can move between countries and cultures without forfeiting their effectiveness.[34]

A geocentric staffing policy is instrumental to companies pursing a global and, especially, a transnational strategy. Both types of strategies rely on learning opportunities around the world to generate ideas that enhance their core competencies. As the CEO of Schering-Plough explained, "Good ideas can come from anywhere. . . . The more places you are, the more ideas you will get. And the more ideas you get, the more places you can sell them and the more competitive you will be. Managing in many places requires a willingness to accept good ideas no matter where they come from—which means having a global attitude."[35] Others, seeing the power of ideas to create new core competencies, move toward a geocentric orientation. For instance, Fujio Mitarai, president of Canon, Inc., observed, "Until recently, everything we did overseas was an extension of what we were doing in Japan. From now on, we want to give birth to new value abroad. We want to make the best of the different kinds of expertise available in different countries."[36] More colorfully, some people encourage MNEs to target a new type of executive, the so-called "cosmopolitans," to staff global operations. These folks are viewed as special types of men and women who are rising to leadership positions in their companies by "finding commonalities . . . [and] spread[ing] universal ideas and juggl[ing] the requirements of diverse places."[37]

Economic factors, decision-making routines, and legal contingencies complicate a geocentric staffing policy.

A geocentric staffing policy is hard to develop and costly to maintain. Difficulty follows from the need to keep a sense of who you are and still be able to understand the views of a diverse range of people. For instance, the aggressively multinational composition of senior management that results from geocentric staffing policies arguably reduces cultural myopia and enhances local responsiveness. The gap between theory and reality, however, can be big. At, Gillette, only 15 percent of the company's expatriates are natives of the United States; 85 percent come from 27 other countries. Similarly, J. P. Morgan, the investment bank, employs more than 50 nationalities in its London office.[38] Making sense of all outlooks that potentially bear on a decision can prove overwhelming. If done poorly, geocentrism can erode the sense of common purpose. Like the Tower of Babel, the clarity of the task can get lost in a hodgepodge of differences. Similarly, the logistics of geocentrism are costly. Exposing people to different ideas in diverse places is expensive. Training and relocation costs quickly escalate when frequently transferring high-priced managers from country to country. Too, unexpected problems emerge when the higher pay and prestige enjoyed by managers placed in the company's global executive vanguard triggers resentment among those who believe they are less essential.

Finally, a geocentric staffing policy, despite MNEs' best intentions, may be practically impossible. Most host governments, keen to the importance of developing and employing local human capital, prefer that foreign subsidiaries hire locals. They often use immigration laws or workplace regulations to push the MNE to do so.

TABLE 20.3   FEATURES AND FUNCTIONS OF STAFFING APPROACHES

STAFFING APPROACH	GENERAL ASSUMPTIONS	STRATEGIC APPROPRIATENESS	ADVANTAGES	DRAWBACKS
Ethnocentric	Presumes that the leadership ideals, management values, and workplace practices of one's company are superior to those in foreign companies Headquarters makes all key decisions and foreign subsidiaries follow commands	International	Leverages a company's core competence Gives people a strong point of perspective Development of the senior management team	Can inspire belief that one's company is intrinsically better at everything Can promote cultural arrogance and illiteracy May blind people to possible innovations in other countries
Polycentric	Accepts the importance of adapting to any differences, real or imaginary, between the home and host country Headquarters makes broad strategic decision that local units adapt to their marketplace	Multidomestic	Helps people see the special virtues of a particular nation Operationally inexpensive Eases adapting to the local market's workplace norms Placates host governments and promotes local staff development	Complicates any sort of value chain coordination Isolates country operations Reduces incentive to engage international perspective Potential for quasi-autonomous country operations
Geocentric	All nations are created equal and possess inalienable characteristics that are neither superior nor inferior but simply there Headquarters and subsidiaries collaborate to identify, transfer, and diffuse best practices	Global and Transnational	Adept way to deal with different people in different counties Leverages powerful ideas worldwide Opens learning opportunities	Tough to develop, costly to run, hard to maintain Contrary to many nations' capital development plans Difficult to find qualified expatriates

Summary

The merits and drawbacks of the three approaches to staffing policy are summarized in Table 20.3. Broadly speaking, an ethnocentric approach is congruent with an international strategy, a polycentric approach is congruent with a multidomestic strategy, and a geocentric approach is congruent with the global and transnational strategies. In actuality, companies may use elements of each staffing policy, given particular opportunities and constraints, changes in configuration or coordination of their value chains, or the results of a change in leadership. Nonetheless, companies tend to champion the staffing policy that is most congruent with their current standard of value creation, such as exemplified by General Electric's aim to staff people who will "globalize the intellect of the company" and its corresponding engagement of a geocentric staffing policy.

Companies may use elements of each staffing policy but one type normally governs.

Acquisitions and joint ventures secure staff but at the price of possible conflict with existing staffing policies.

Two wild cards can unpredictably influence the declared orientation of an MNE's staffing policy. The **type of ownership** of foreign operations causes contingencies that may lead the company to unintended outcomes. For example, expatriates transferred abroad to a foreign joint venture may be in an ambiguous situation, unsure of whom they represent and uncertain of whether they should report to both partners or just the partner that transferred them. Typically, MNEs with local partners insist on using their executives for positions in which they fear local personnel will make decisions in their own, rather than in the joint venture's, best interest. For example, foreign partners commonly transfer expatriates to their Chinese joint ventures to ensure that money is spent only on business-related items.[39]

Similarly, **third-country nationals** can change how the MNE views its staffing policy.[40] Third-country nationals sometimes have more compatible technical and adaptive qualifications than do home-country expatriates. For example, a U.S. company used U.S. personnel to design and manage a Peruvian plant until it could train local managers. Years later, the company decided to manufacture in Mexico using a plant that more closely resembled the Peruvian operations than its U.S. operations in terms of size, product qualities, and factor inputs. The company used its Spanish-speaking Peruvian managers to plan and start up the Mexican facility because these managers knew the technical needs and could easily adapt to living in Mexico. When companies establish lead operations abroad, such as headquarters for a product division or a country operation that is larger than that in the home country, third-country nationals are more likely to have the competencies needed for the foreign assignments.

In summary, few MNEs question the need for expatriates to supervise, assist, and monitor local operations. Translating this belief into a cadre of high-performance expatriates compels an MNE to find those people who are prepared for an international business career, devise ways to motivate them to perform well, and capitalize on their new skills and improved outlook when they are ready for their next assignment. Therefore, we now turn to the matters of expatriate selection, development, compensation, and repatriation.

EXPATRIATE SELECTION

Expatriate selection is largely influenced by a candidate's

• Technical competence
• Adaptiveness
• Leadership ability

Some people enjoy the thrill of living and working abroad. Others, however, prefer not to work in a foreign country, particularly if they perceive an assignment as long term or permanent. Screening executives to find those with the greatest inclination and highest potential for a foreign assignment is the process of expatriate selection. This process can be quite difficult. Few MNEs have the luxury of a large cadre of mobile and experienced expatriates. Moreover, there is no specific set of technical indicators that consistently distinguish a good versus poor expatriate. This problem is especially complicated by the difficulty of judging a potential expatriate's adaptability to foreign places, people, and processes. Some companies try to deal with these constraints by selecting a team of expatriates. Nortel, for example, sends a team of three expatriates to start operations in emerging markets: an expert in international finance, an entrepreneurial sales manager, and a line manager with the softer skills needed to handle personal relationships.[41] This approach, while a solution, still depends on identifying those people in the company with the necessary capabilities. Therefore, selecting the right expatriates pushes MNEs to assess their talent pool with a range of indicators. Generally, companies look for people with skills and outlooks in the matters of technical competence, adaptiveness, and leadership ability.

Technical Competence

Technical competence often is the strongest determinant of who is selected for an international assignment.

Corporate managers, expatriates, and local staff routinely agree that technical competence, usually indicated by past job performance, is the biggest determinant of success in foreign assignments.[42] In the least, an expatriate must command the functional skills to do the job and, if necessary, understand how to fit them to foreign situations.[43] Because of the need for technical competence, managers commonly have several years' worth of work experience behind them before a company offers them a foreign assignment. This tendency also reflects the fact that expatriate selections are typically made by line managers based on the candidate's operational track record. Moreover, many companies translate a record of outstanding technical competence into the managerial attributes of self-confidence and mental toughness. These attributes support an expatriate's performance.

Adaptiveness

Experience shows that effective expatriates possess certain types of adaptive characteristics. Hence, MNEs commonly evaluate a possible expatriate in terms of the following sorts of adaptive characteristics:

Adaptiveness refers to a person's potential for
- Self-maintenance and personal resourcefulness
- Developing satisfactory relationships
- Interpreting the immediate environment

- Those needed for self-maintenance, such as personal resourcefulness, precisely because things do not always go as planned—even in ordinary occurrences such as how one travels the world. Companies go to great lengths to assess this outlook. For instance, the selection process at HSBC, like that of many MNEs, is a sophisticated process that uses a battery of tests, interviews, and exercises. However, its CEO explained, "We don't look so much at what or where people have studied but rather at their drive, initiative, cultural sensitivity, and readiness to see the world as their oyster. Whether they've studied classics, economics, history, or languages is irrelevant. What matters are the skills and qualities necessary to be good, well-rounded executives in a highly international institution operating in a diverse set of communities."[44]

- Those related to the development of satisfactory relationships with host nationals, such as flexibility and tolerance. Whether called *cultural empathy, others-orientation,* or simply *good management,* this orientation enhances an expatriate's ability to interact effectively with the many people that he or she will meet in the course of the foreign assignment. The more effectively the expatriate is prepared and predisposed to interact with different types of people, the more likely he or she will succeed in foreign

An international career has glamorous, exciting, and rewarding aspects. The price, however, can be extreme in many ways. Here we see just a small glimpse of the life of the expatriate, enduring yet another check-in routine at yet another airport.

markets. Research reports that two factors play vital roles in this process: the ability of an expatriate to develop sincere, honest friendships with foreign nationals and the expatriate's willingness to use the host-country language.

- Adaptiveness is often indicated by skills and sensitivities that help one to interpret the immediate environment in ways that reject stereotypes, preconceptions, and unrealistic expectations.[45] These outlooks motivate the expatriate to figure out how colleagues, customers, and competitors in the local market likely have made sense of what they have seen in order to respond effectively. Therefore, successful expatriates more insightfully appraise the beliefs, values, behaviors, and business practices of individuals and organizations in different countries.

Leadership Ability

Increasingly, executives see personal leadership as a key to an expatriate's success.[46] Asked why, most note that expatriates often find themselves as a senior manager at foreign subsidiaries that are usually much smaller than the parent but which require they perform top-level leadership duties. Communication skills, motivation, self-reliance, courage, risk-taking, and diplomacy become essential qualities for success. More precisely, McKinsey & Company found that successful expatriates commanded, in descending order of importance, optimism (believes future challenges can be overcome), drive (has passion to succeed), adaptability (handles ambiguity well), foresight (imagines the future), experience (has seen and done a great deal), resilience (recovers quickly from failure), sensitivity (adjusts management style to cultural differences), and organization (plans ahead, follows through).[47] We saw with Ms. Pattle of Microsoft in our opening case that working abroad requires that you wear many hats. Besides technical competency, it helps to understands cultural differences in problem solving, motivation, use of power, consensus building, as well as being able to make sense of trade rules and regulations, business practices, joint venture methodology, and similar market realities.

EXPATRIATE FAILURE

Despite the best-laid plans of mice and men, things often go astray. MNEs regularly experience this situation when they select their best and brightest managers, send them to a foreign market, pay them a huge salary, and watch them fail. Expatriate failure (narrowly defined as the manager's premature return home due to poor job performance, broadly defined as the failure of the MNEs' selection policies to find individuals who will succeed abroad) is an enduring concern. In the 1980s, research reported that between 16 and 40 percent of all American employees sent abroad to more developed countries returned from their assignments early, and almost 70 percent of employees sent to emerging markets returned home early. Recent surveys indicate that less than 10 percent of expatriates fail to complete their assignments abroad.[48]

The fall in the rate of expatriate failure testifies to the improving sophistication of the MNEs' selection process. Still, few see the fall as cause to stop and celebrate. The high financial and personal costs of expatriate failure, no matter how infrequent, are detrimental. The average cost per failure to an MNE can be as high as three times the expatriate's annual domestic salary plus the cost of relocation.[49] The direct costs of each failure can easily reach $1 million when you add the time and money spent in selection, visits to the location before the executive moves, and the expatriate's lost productivity as things gradually fall apart. Finally, an incalculable cost is the personal implications of professional failure to the formerly high-performing executive's self-confidence and leadership potential.

In extreme situations, some companies try to bypass the risk of expatriate failure by acquiring a foreign company and, therefore, its personnel. Companies may also form joint ventures with foreign firms so that the partner will contribute managers to the operation as well as take responsibility for hiring new personnel. However, relying on a partner to manage human resources creates the risk that managers may see their primary allegiance to that partner rather than to the foreign investor.

In recourse, firms try to improve the apparent causes of expatriate failure and develop preemptive training and preparation programs. Assessments of expatriate failure have concentrated on a range of factors, notably looking at the influence of issues like the expatriate's technical expertise, ability to cope with greater responsibilities overseas, challenges of the new environment, personal or emotional problems, and ability of the expatriate's spouse to adjust to the foreign environment. The growing sophistication of HRM at many MNEs has reduced the rates of expatriate failure due to insufficient technical expertise. Rare is the foreign assignment that fails because HRM did not identify the person as technically incompetent prior to his or her departure.

The other causes of expatriate failure have proven more intractable. Traditionally, attention has focused on the expatriate's adjustment to the new environment as the primary predictor of his or her failure.[50] The inability of an expatriate to adjust to the foreign assignment has consistently been linked to his or her inadequate cultural sensitivities and skills. Recently, companies have turned their attention toward the adjustment difficulties for the spouse and family.[51] Research shows that a foreign assignment is usually more stressful for the family than for the expatriate. Consequently, the leading cause of expatriate failure is the inability of a spouse to adapt to the host nation.[52] Abrupt separation from friends, family, and career isolate the spouse and children. In recourse, they often look to the working spouse or parent for more companionship and support. Almost always, the working spouse has less time because of the new job. This often fans family stress, which then affects the expatriate's work performance.

> Expatriate failure can be reduced by selection procedures that screen out inappropriate candidates.

> The leading cause of expatriate failure is the inability of a spouse to adapt to the host nation.

EXPATRIATE PREPARATION AND DEVELOPMENT

Companies recognize the need to prepare expatriates for their overseas assignment. Although easily said, many companies struggle to deal with these issues systematically. The HRM departments of most companies typically have extensive amounts of employee data. However, most of those data profile employees' technical capabilities and accomplishments. Far less data, if any at all, profile their adaptive capabilities, such as willingness to accept foreign assignments, geographic preferences, or foreign-language qualifications.[53] This data gap largely reflects the MNEs' historic preoccupation of linking expatriate selection to technical competence, a linkage that led MNEs to direct training efforts toward improving their employees' technical skills and generally leaving it up to the individual to develop his or her adaptive competencies. Achieving the latter led those managers who had an interest in international careers to travel abroad, study world events, and seek people of different ethnicities, cultures, and nationalities.[54] When eventually posted as expatriates, these executives performed well, thereby encouraging more companies, as we saw with our opening look at Honeywell, to prepare expatriates for overseas assignments with cross-cultural training.

Many MNEs prepare potential expatriates by developing their general understanding of a country, cultural sensitivity, and practical skills prior to their departure. We now look at each of these areas.

> Training and predeparture preparations can lower the probability of expatriate failure. Increasingly, preparation activities include the spouse.

> Training often includes general country orientation, cultural sensitivity, and practical advice.

General Country Understanding

The most common predeparture training is an informational briefing about the way things work in the host country. Topics typically include political structures, job design, compensation norms, housing, climate, education, health conditions, home sales, taxes, transport

example, more than half the people in the European Union claim to be reasonably conversant in English. Many envision developing their English more and more; a survey of 16,000 people living in the European Union found that more than 70 percent agreed with the statement, "Everybody should speak English." Similar attitudes are apparent in other parts of the world, most notably in China, India, and Japan. Recently, the ascendance of English has gotten a great boost; its use as the language of the Internet solidifies its status and makes it increasingly possible to conduct business all over the world using only the English interface of your preferred browser.[62] Too, the growing sophistication of translation software makes foreign language competency a moot point for those who prefer using their local language on the Internet.

Many managers respond in kind. *The Economist*, for example, reports that just under half of employers rated language skills as important—a tendency that many link to the laborious struggle to master a foreign language. Others report that language competency was ranked well behind technical competences, leadership skills, and career development but ahead of motivation for working abroad, previous success abroad, and business vision in gauging the suitability of a candidate for international assignments.[63] Finally, some say language is a misleading proxy of an expatriate's cultural sensitivity and general ability to perform in foreign markets. The CEO of Schering-Plough, for example, noted that "I've met many people who speak three or four languages yet still have a very narrow view of the world. At the same time, I've come across people who speak only English but have a real passion and curiosity about the world and who are very effective in different cultures."[64]

EXPATRIATE COMPENSATION

Compensation must neither overly reward nor unduly punish a person for accepting a foreign assignment.

If a United States MNE transfers its finance manager, who is making $150,000 per year in Seattle, to China, where the going rate is $100,000 per year, what should the manager's salary be? Or if the Chinese finance manager is transferred to the United States, what pay should the company offer? Should it compensate in dollars or yuans? Which set of fringe benefits should apply? These are a few of the many questions a company faces when it posts people to its foreign operations. MNEs managing an international workforce frequently run into problems in dealing with differing pay levels, benefits, and perquisites. On the one hand, the company must control costs. On the other, it must pay people enough to generate motivation. All things being equal, therefore, compensation can determine the success or failure of overseas work assignments. Over time, real or perceived pay inequities among home, local, and expatriate employees erodes their motivation. Therefore, MNEs must craft a well-devised compensation package that lets an expatriate maintain his or her standard of living, reflects the responsibility of the foreign assignment, and ensures that after-tax income will not fall as a result of the foreign assignment.

Types of Compensation Plans

The most common approach to expatriate pay is the balance sheet approach.

Many MNEs, especially in the United States, apply the so-called balance sheet compensation plan to manage their expatriate accounts.[65] The balance sheet approach aims to develop a salary structure that equalizes purchasing power across countries so expatriates have the same living standard in their foreign posting that they had at home—no matter which country they are transferred to for their assignment.[66] Effectively, the principle of equalization presumes that expatriates should neither profit wildly nor lose excessively simply because their companies assigned them to a foreign subsidiary. In addition, the balance sheet approach outlines how the company can provide financial incentives that offset qualitative differences between assignment locations. That is, this approach factors in guidelines for how the MNE can best provide expatriates a financial inducement for accepting an international assignment.

There are three common methods of implementing a balance sheet compensation plan.

- The *home-based method* bases the expatriate's compensation on the salary of a comparable job in his or her home city. This method, by preserving equity with home-country colleagues, treats the expatriate's compensation as if the person had never left home. This method simplifies the expatriate's eventual return. The home-based method is the most prevalent expatriate compensation plan.

- The *headquarters-based method* sets the expatriate's salary in terms of the salary of a comparable job in the city where the MNE has its headquarters. For example, if a Boston-headquartered MNE posted expatriates to its offices in London, Santiago, and Jakarta, it would give each expatriate a salary structured in terms of Boston pay rates. This plan explicitly recognizes the disruption of a foreign assignment and goes to great lengths to make sure an expatriate can live as she or he had in the home country.

- The *host-based method*, sometimes called destination pricing and localization, bases an expatriate's compensation on the prevailing pay scales in the locale of the foreign assignment. Basically, an expatriate starts with a salary equivalent to that of a local national with similar responsibilities and then adds whatever foreign-service premiums, extraordinary allowances, home-country benefits, and taxation compensation were negotiated. This method is not as personally lucrative as the home- or headquarters-based methods. Essentially, it pays an expatriate less in order to reduce tension between the expatriate and his or her colleagues in the host country due to extreme variation in pay for similar jobs.

HRM executives routinely compare the features of their compensation plans with those offered by other companies. Typically, they rely on data from consulting firms that specialize in international compensation as well as estimate cost-of-living differences from several sources.[67]

Key Aspects of Expatriate Compensation

Table 20.4 illustrates a typical expatriate compensation package. Typically, expatriates negotiate their compensation package in terms of a base salary, a foreign-service premium, allowances of various types, fringe benefits, tax differentials, and benefits. We briefly look at each.

Base Salary   An expatriate's base salary normally falls in the same range as the base salary for the comparable job in the home country. It is paid in either the home-country currency or in the local currency.

Foreign Service Premium   A foreign service premium is the extra pay the company gives to the expatriate for working outside his or her country of origin. This premium effectively rewards expatriates for undertaking the problems and complications created by moving to an unfamiliar country, living far from family and friends, dealing with the day-to-day challenges of a new culture, new language, and new workplace practices, and the reality that they will ultimately have to disrupt this life upon return to the home country. Many firms pay foreign service premiums as a percentage of base salary, ranging from 10 to 30 percent after tax.

Allowances   Expatriates receive a cost-of-living allowance (sometimes called a goods-and-services differential) to nullify the risk that they will suffer a decline in their standard of living due to the exorbitant expense of a particular city (i.e., London or Tokyo) or nation (i.e., Switzerland).[68] Some companies reduce the cost-of-living differential over time, reasoning that as expatriates adapt to their environment, they should adopt local purchasing practices—for example, buying vegetables from a neighborhood market instead of using imported packaged goods.[69]

Living is more expensive abroad because

- Habits change slowly
- People are unsure of how and where to buy

TABLE 20.4   SENDING AN EXPATRIATE ABROAD: TYPICAL EXPENSES

Situation: Global Compilers, a company based in Seattle, sends a senior executive to take charge of its Tokyo, Japan, wholly owned subsidiary. In the United States, the manager earns an annual income of US$150,000, has a working spouse and two children. Applying the balance sheet approach to determine the likely compensation generates the following scenario:

Direct Compensation Costs

Base salary	$150,000
Foreign service premium	25,000
Goods and services differential	120,000
Housing	97,000
U.S. hypothetical taxes	(38,000)

Company-Paid Costs

Education (schooling for two children)	30,000
Japanese income taxes	115,000
Transfer moving costs	47,000
Miscellaneous costs., i.e., shipping and storage; home sale or property management fees; cultural, practical, and language training; pre-assignment orientation trip, destination assistance	85,000
Working spouse allowance	75,000
Annual home leave (airfare for four, hotel, and meals)	15,000
Additional health insurance, pension supplements, evacuation coverage	20,000

A housing allowance ensures the expatriate will duplicate his or her customary quality of housing—a key concern when asked to move from mid-priced Atlanta to high-priced Shanghai. Housing costs also vary substantially because of crowded conditions that raise land prices as well as shortages of domiciles that are acceptable to expatriates.[70] Westerners pay steep premiums in some parts of Asia to rent accommodations with Western-styled bathrooms and kitchens.[71] Consequently, a housing allowance can be as much as up to a third of the expatriate's total compensation package.

A spouse allowance partly funds an expatriate's spouse's effort to find work and take cross-cultural training programs. In some cases, this allowance will offset the loss in income due to the spouse's forsaking his or her job.[72] About a quarter of MNEs provide spouses of expatriates with job-search assistance, often through networks with other companies.[73] For example, Kodak tries to find employment for spouses; when it cannot, it pays for a partial loss in income. A spouse allowance also deals with the hardship created by potential changes in total family income and status. In the home country, all members of the family may be able to work, whereas when they go abroad, only the expatriate may have the legal right to do so because generally host governments seldom grant people other than the transferred employee permission to work. Therefore, the spouse or companion of an expatriate may have to either give up well-paying and satisfying employment or be separated from the partner for long periods. Some companies increase the expatriate's compensation, and about one-third of large U.S. companies assist couples with commuter marriages.

A hardship allowance (sometimes called "combat pay") is paid to those expatriates who are assigned to a particularly difficult environment or dangerous location. Living conditions in certain settings pose severe hardships, such as harsh climatic or health conditions, or expose the expatriate family to political unrest that places everyone in danger.[74] For instance, expatriate personnel of many MNES, given their high profiles, have been targeted for kidnapping and assault. Companies have had to not only rethink their hardship allowances but also purchase ransom insurance, provide training

MNEs often provide additional compensation or more fringe benefits to employees who work in remote or dangerous areas.

programs on safety for expatriates and families, pay for home alarm systems and security guards, and assess their legal liability regarding employee safety.[75] Yet even where conditions are less severe, expatriates may encounter living conditions that are substandard to those at home, thus qualifying for a hardship allowance.

Expatriates also receive a range of miscellaneous allowances, such as a travel allowance that lets an expatriate and his or her family travel home periodically or an education allowance to finance the expatriate's children's access to a private education in the event that host-country public schools are unsuitable.

Fringe Benefits   Firms typically provide expatriates the same level of medical and retirement benefits abroad that they received at home rather than those customarily granted in the host country. However, most companies expand these benefits to deal with local contingencies—such as bearing the cost of transferring ill expatriates or family members to suitable out-of-country medical facilities or paying the premium on kidnapping insurance in high-risk countries. Many of these sorts of benefits are deducted as business expenses for the company in its home country but may not be deductible in other countries.

Tax Differentials   The ultimate objective of expatriate compensation adjustments is to ensure that expatriates' after-tax income and, presumably, their job motivation will not suffer because of the costs created by foreign assignment. Because taxes are usually assessed on the adjustments that companies make to the expatriate's base salary, companies have to adjust even further upward if the foreign tax rate is higher than the home country's. Indeed, tax equalization has become the most important, and often most costly, component of expatriate compensation. If there is no reciprocal tax treaty between the expatriate's home country and host country, then he or she may be legally obligated to pay income tax to both governments. In such situations, the MNE ordinarily pays the expatriate's tax bill in the host country.

Complications Posed by Nationality Differences

Beside over 1,700 expatriates stationed in more than 50 countries, Unilever has more than 20,000 managers spread over 90 countries.[76] Should Unilever pay executives in different countries according to the prevailing standards in each country, or should it equalize pay for each position on a global basis? Figuring out how to pay managers in different countries is complicated by many national factors, including legal, cultural, and governmental conditions. As companies employ expatriates from home and third countries, compensation issues grow more complicated.

These problems are particularly pressing for companies with a geocentric staffing policy. Both the global and transnational strategies depend on developing a cadre of international managers that most likely includes many different nationalities. The issue then emerges whether all managers who perform the same job but in different locations should be paid the same salary. For a Finnish transnational, like Nokia, this would require compensating all its foreign nationals, no matter where they worked, in terms of Finnish salary levels. If Nokia opts not to develop an equitable standard, it will likely result in the "underpaid" members of the international cadre resenting their higher paid counterparts.

Firms applying ethnocentric or polycentric staffing policies, while largely immune to these problems, also must find way to systematize their compensation programs. If not, then they may pay someone more than necessary to persuade them to go abroad, given the unequal conditions among countries. More worrisome, great disparities in pay packages for people doing the same jobs can distort the motivation of home or host country managers and impede a sense of unanimity among different parts of the global operations. Finally, even though the company with an ethnocentric or polycentric staffing policy may have few expatriates today, likely growth in its international activities will make it increasingly cumbersome to administer foreign compensation packages on a case-by-case basis.

MNEs use various cost-of-living indexes and
- Increase compensation when the foreign cost is higher
- Do not reduce compensation when the foreign cost is lower
- Remove the differential when the manager is repatriated

Companies struggle to determine the proper degree to which they should equalize pay for the same job done in different countries.

Total compensation and forms of compensation vary substantially among countries.

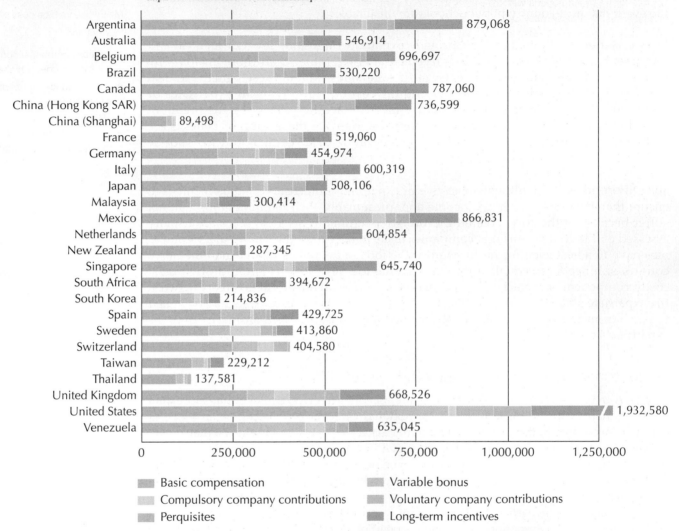

FIGURE 20.3   VARIANCE IN CEO PAY PACKAGES AMONG COUNTRIES

The average annual pay package of the chief executive of an industrial company with annual revenues of approximately US$500 million in annual sales in 26 countries. The figures from April 1, 2001, are expressed in U.S. dollars converted at then prevailing exchange rates, and are not weighted to compensate for different costs of living or levels of taxation.

Source: "Exhibit 1, Total Remuneration—Chief Executive Officer," *Worldwide Total Remuneration 2001–2002.* Towers Perrin, http://www.towers.com/towers/default.asp.

Country	Value
Argentina	879,068
Australia	546,914
Belgium	696,697
Brazil	530,220
Canada	787,060
China (Hong Kong SAR)	736,599
China (Shanghai)	89,498
France	519,060
Germany	454,974
Italy	600,319
Japan	508,106
Malaysia	300,414
Mexico	866,831
Netherlands	604,854
New Zealand	287,345
Singapore	645,740
South Africa	394,672
South Korea	214,836
Spain	429,725
Sweden	413,860
Switzerland	404,580
Taiwan	229,212
Thailand	137,581
United Kingdom	668,526
United States	1,932,580
Venezuela	635,045

Legend:
- Basic compensation
- Compulsory company contributions
- Perquisites
- Variable bonus
- Voluntary company contributions
- Long-term incentives

Stock options refer to the right to purchase a specific number of shares of stock for a specified price at specified times. They are usually granted to key employees.

Presently, there is little consensus to guide MNEs on how to deal with these issues. For example, salaries for similar jobs vary substantially among countries, as do the relationships of salaries within the corporate hierarchy. Figure 20.3 shows the disparity of annual pay packages for CEOs by company nationality as well as the great variation in the method of payment. For example, long-term incentives, such as options on restricted stock, are popular in the United States but not in Germany. However, German managers often receive compensation that U.S. managers do not, such as housing allowances and partial payment of salary outside Germany, neither of which is taxable. Similarly, countries with aggressive personal income tax rates spur employees' to ask for pay plans that reduce taxable base salaries in favor of tax-exempt fringe benefits.

Some evidence suggests that executive compensation systems around the world are adopting many of the pay practices used in the United States.[77] In 1995, the typical pay package for CEOs in 10 of the largest 26 market economies included stock-option plans; by 2000, the number had nearly doubled, to 19. Several factors suggest greater "Americanization" of executive compensation packages. The emergence of many foreign equity markets makes stock options a more attractive incentive in more countries.

FIGURE 20.4   THE DIFFERENCE IN PAY BETWEEN CEOS AND THE AVERAGE WORKER, 2000

The difference in the compensation of chief executive officers and that of the typical hourly employee varies among countries. Effectively, this simple index measures the number of times greater the compensation of the CEO is relative to that of the typical hourly employee in a particular country—i.e., a CEO in the United States, on average, was paid 531 times more than that paid to the typical hourly worker. Average employees were assumed to work in industrial companies with about $500 million in annual sales. Estimates provided by *Worldwide Total Remuneration 2001–2002.* Towers Perrin.

Source: Eric Wahlgren, "Pay and Perks," *Business Week* (April 18, 2001).

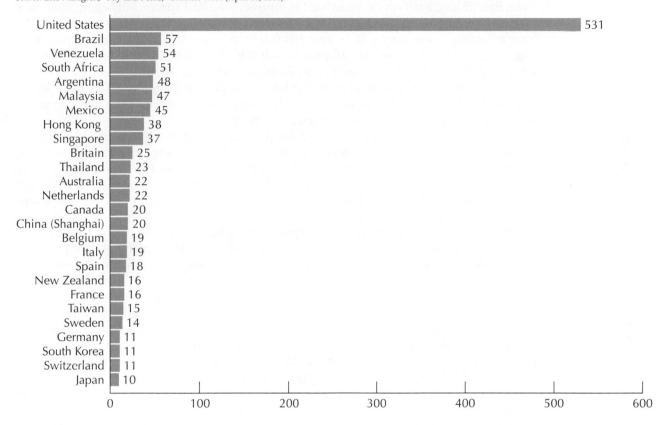

Similarly, as companies from more countries become more multinational, they have to compete globally for executive talent. Likewise, local firms often must boost compensation to retain their executives.

There is still variance among countries, however, in terms of the gap between the compensation of top executives versus that of the typical hourly employee. For example, on average, the CEOs at 365 of the largest publicly traded U.S. companies earned $13.1 million in 2002—effectively, these CEOs earned 531 times what the typical hourly employee took home (see Figure 20.4). Around the rest of the world, Brazil and Venezuela are leaders in pay disparity—though they still fall far short of the U.S. multiple. In contrast, Japan has the smallest gap between the CEO and average-worker pay. Interestingly, some debate whether U.S.-style executive pay practices can eventually set global standards when they promote wider compensation inequality between managers and workers.

EXPATRIATE REPATRIATION

In theory, HRM aims to build a staffing process that creates a cycle of events, beginning with the selection of the right expatriate, the delivery of the appropriate type of predeparture preparation, the design of a motivating compensation package, and the means to ease the ultimate reintegration of the expatriate into the home company upon completion

Returning home from a foreign assignment is fraught with difficulties.

of a successful tour of duty abroad. Success at each stage—selection, training, compensation, and repatriation—would, in a perfect world, support a self-sustaining system whereby returning expatriates would share their knowledge with colleagues and persuade other high-performing executives to also work abroad. In actuality, expatriates often face a different scenario that, to great cost in the demotivation and departure of high-performing managers, weakens the entire HRM system.[78]

Research shows that many MNEs worry more about preparing and paying workers for the foreign assignment than supporting them when they return. Consequentially, returning home can deteriorate into a dreadful part of the expatriate assignment for many executives. Specifically, a survey of repatriated executives who had successfully completed their overseas assignment found more than third held temporary assignments three months after returning home, nearly 80 percent felt that their new job was a demotion from their foreign assignment, more than 60 percent felt that they did not have opportunities to transfer their international expertise to their new job, and about 25 percent left their company within three months of returning home.[79] In general, expatriates face repatriation strains in three areas: change in personal finances, readjustment to the home-country corporate structure, and readjustment to life at home.

Changes in personal finances can be dramatic upon a manager's return home. Most expatriates enjoy abundant benefits during their foreign assignment. While abroad, many live in exclusive neighborhoods, send their children to prestigious schools, employ domestic help, socialize with elites, and still save much more money than they had before the move. Returning home to a reasonable compensation plan with far fewer perks and privileges is often demoralizing.

Readjustment to home-country corporate structure poses problems to returning executives on several levels. Returning expatriates often find that many of their previous peers have been promoted above them, they now have less autonomy as they return to being a "little fish in a big pond," and they must struggle to get back into the inner-office network. As a result, they return to a company that doesn't quite know what to do with them and, particularly in high-tech firms, sees them with knowledge and skills that aren't quite on the cutting edge. In these situations, resentment builds within repatriated executives as they typically feel they've grown professionally during their overseas post, worked hard, and sacrificed much for the company, and, hence, expect praise and promotion. More often than not, the opposite happens. One study found that some 60 to 70 percent of repatriated expatriates did not know what their position would be when they returned home, and about 60 percent said their companies were vague about the repatriation process, their pending jobs, and future career progression within the company. Compounding these tendencies is the sad fact that, for many expatriates, being out-of-sight overseas turns out to be truly out-of-mind back home. Noted Daniel Meiland, the chairman of Egon Zehender International, "Companies station people abroad and then forget about them. If anything, advancement is even more difficult for the expat when he returns to headquarters, having missed out on opportunities to network with top management."[80]

Many MNEs reply that the issue of repatriation puts them between a rock and a hard place. They note that an office does not sit vacant while the manager goes abroad for potentially a few to several years. Moreover, permitting the repatriated employee to easily bump his or her replacement upon return would likely strike many as unfair.

Readjusting to life at home, usually eagerly anticipated while abroad, can become surprisingly stressful.[81] Troubles emerge as returning expatriates and their families' experience "reverse culture shock." Upon return, managers and their families often find that they need to relearn a lot of what they once took for granted as they adapt to their "new" home. Meantime, children may struggle to fit into the local school system while spouses may feel isolated or out of touch with the career or friends they once again left behind. For example, some returning American expatriates, who spent the late 1990s abroad, regret missing the emergence of the Internet and the dot.com boom in the U.S.[82]

Repatriation tends to cause dissonance in many areas, most notably

● Financial
● Work
● Social

Managing Repatriation

Companies are not blind to the problems of expatriate repatriation. Moreover, ignoring them is not an option—the greater the difficulties that confront returning expatriates, the more difficult it becomes to convince other high-potential executives to take foreign assignments. In recourse, MNEs experiment with a range of remedies. In general, HRM executives advocate providing expatriates with advance notice of when they will return, more information about their possible new jobs, placement in jobs that leverage their foreign experiences, housing assistance, reorientation programs, periodic visits to head-quarters while working abroad, and enlisting a formal headquarters mentor to watch over their interests while they are abroad.[83]

Some companies, like Dow Chemical, make written guarantees that repatriated employees will return to jobs at least as good as those they left behind. Some companies simply explain the career risk and compensate employees so highly that they are enticed to become expatriates. Other companies integrate foreign assignments into career planning and develop mentor programs to look after the expatriates' domestic interests. Abbott Laboratories tries to keep its repatriate turnover rate less than 10 percent by focusing on career development. It also cautions workers before they leave the United States to expect the adjustment of returning home to be just as tough as going abroad and encourages them to stay in touch. Komatsu has a "return ticket policy" that pledges returning expatriates a meaningful job. Similarly, Dow Corning gives each expatriate a written guarantee of a job at the same or higher level on return. Too, Dow Corning formally assigns higher-level supervisors to serve as "godfathers" by looking after the expatriate's home-career interests. Some MNEs make the manager who originally sponsored an expatriate also responsible for finding his or her protégé a job upon return. Motorola advises its 1,500 expatriates to maintain their home network no matter how far away they travel. Finally, some companies try to resolve the less obvious hardships of repatriation. Monsanto deals with reverse culture shock by formally addressing the social expectations of returning expatriates and giving them an opportunity to showcase their new knowledge in a debriefing session. Similarly, Viacom has set up a "comprehensive expatriate administrative tracking program" that includes specific health and retirement benefits tailored to the needs of those who have undertaken more than one consecutive overseas posting.[84]

Despite these efforts, the statistics show that many expatriates are unhappy with their career when they return home. If pressed to pinpoint where repatriation begins to break down, reports suggest the principal culprit is the challenge of finding the right job for someone to return to. Personal career management, therefore, is vital to being selected for a foreign assignment as well as triumphantly returning home to greater responsibilities. As we saw with Bryan Krueger in our opening case, expatriates cannot exclusively rely on their company to safeguard their career interests. A passive approach is particularly hazardous given that expatriates often hear too late, if ever, about possible promotion opportunities back home.[85] Instead, while abroad, they must navigate the repatriation process with a clear sense of its positive and negative aspects.

Companies try to develop programs to ease repatriation frustrations.

The principal cause of repatriation frustrations is finding the right job for someone to return to.

INTERNATIONAL LABOR RELATIONS

In each country in which an MNE operates, it deals with groups of workers whose approach to the workplace reflects the local sociopolitical environment. This environment affects whether they join labor unions, how they collectively bargain, and what they want from companies. Expectedly, striking differences prevail across countries in how labor and management view each other. When there is little mobility between the two groups (generally, children of laborers become laborers, and children of managers become managers), explicit class difference exists between the managers who run the MNE and the workers they hire and fire. Labor may perceive itself in a class struggle that echoes the divisions of Marx's conception of the proletariat versus the bourgeoisie.

A labor union is an association of workers who have united to represent their collective views for wages, hours, and working conditions.

Labor-MNE relations in these countries, such as in Brazil, the United Kingdom, and France, tend to be a zero-sum game—labor wins only when the MNE loses and vice versa. In contrast, labor groups in many countries take a less confrontational approach. They are more inclined to follow the advice of their labor leaders and try to negotiate win-win solutions.[86] Often, unions in these countries rely on national legislation rather than workplace activism to check the power of the MNE. Moreover, labor's agenda may be based in a broader sensitivity of general work conditions in the country—that is, a rising tide lifts all boats—rather than specific conditions at a specific MNE.

Usually, the HRM function of an MNE deals with these situations, taking charge of the company's relations with labor both within a particular country as well as within the global context. Operationally, as we will see, HRM monitors and manages a range of workplace issues that fall under the broad umbrella of international labor relations. Importantly, HRM aims to integrate its efforts with the straightforward standard of how, why, and where might organized labor constrain how the MNE has configured or coordinates its value chain. HRM then supports the company's leadership in developing options to preempt, neutralize, or deal with these situations so that they do not interfere with its basis for creating value.

The intensity of these concerns varies with the type of strategy an MNE pursues. Companies pursuing an international or global strategy, given their heightened sensitivities to exploiting location economies, consolidating operations, and protecting the transfer and use of core competencies, are highly sensitive to labor's actions. The multidomestic and transnational companies, given their greater degrees of local responsiveness, command more flexibility to adapt operations to labor's concerns without unduly sacrificing their value creation capabilities. Still, no matter what type of strategy the firm pursues, the enduring power of labor on both a country-to-country basis as well as internationally spurs MNEs to develop beneficial relations with organized labor.

Against this backdrop, we now turn to three aspects of international labor relations. First, we discuss how labor commonly represents the motives and means of MNEs, turn to the methods and successes of labor's responses to MNEs, and close with a look at trends that moderate the relationship between MNEs and labor.

Labor's Concerns About MNEs

An ongoing debate is whether the MNE, through the power of its globally dispersed value chain, systematically weakens the rights and roles of labor. Critics argue that MNEs do so precisely because the multinationality of their product and resource flows let them manipulate markets and governments for gains that labor must ultimately bear. For example, at the time the Walt Disney Company was planning an amusement park for Europe, it began by pitting several countries against each other, before eventually narrowing it down to alternative sites in France and Spain, in the effort to get the best possible investment incentives. Ultimately, the company settled on a site just outside of Paris, France. Labor's reaction was immediate. A representative of the Confédération Générale du Travail, (General Confederation of Labour, CGT) of France, contended that the Disney Company had used the threat of locating in Spain, rather than France, in order to drive a tough bargain with government officials. Specifically, he asserted that "Disney put Barcelona and the French site in competition and, as a result of this bidding war, the French government won the contract at the expense of many laws and many hard-won social rights."[87]

In addition, once MNEs get their local operations up and running, labor contends that they can hold out longer than workers in negotiating a solution to a strike. Finally, labor argues that MNEs can easily move value activities from one country to another in the effort to exploit less restrictive labor conditions in other countries. Complicating these situations, labor adds, is the intrinsic complexity of the globally dispersed value chains of MNEs. Labor often lacks the information to determine the veracity of MNEs' claims about products and profits as well as estimate their capacity to meet workers' demands. We now review these rationales.

Collective bargaining is negotiations between labor union representatives and employers to reach agreement on a work contract.

Overall attitude in a country affects how labor and management view each other and how labor will try to negotiate better working conditions.

The degree to which organized labor can limit an MNE's operational and strategic choices is a key concern.

Labor claims it is disadvantaged in dealing with MNEs because

- It is hard to get full data on MNEs' global operations
- MNEs can manipulate investment incentives
- MNEs can easily move value activities to other countries
- Ultimate decision making can be in another country

Product and Resource Flows

Presumably, in the event of a strike in Country X, an MNE can divert output from its facilities in other countries and sell it to the consumers in Country X, thereby greatly reducing the need to settle the strike. Moreover, because each country may comprise only a small percentage of an MNE's total worldwide sales, profits, and cash flows, a strike in one country may minimally affect its global performance. Given these circumstances, an MNE faces little pressure to resolve labor tensions. Therefore, an MNE's ability to threaten dire consequences in the event of a strike and then hold out longer in the fact of actual workplace activism gives it a decisive advantage over labor in collective bargaining.

In their defense, managers point out that an MNE can supply customers in the strike-afflicted country only if it has excess capacity and produces an identical product in more than one country. Even if it meets these preconditions, an MNE would still confront the transport and tariff costs that led it to establish multiple production facilities in the first place. If the MNE partially owns the struck operation, partners or even minority stockholders may balk at financing a lengthy work stoppage. Further, if the idle facilities normally produce components needed for integrated production in other countries, then a strike may have far-reaching effects. For example, a strike at one GM facility in the United States prevented GM's Mexican plants from getting parts needed for assembly operations. Moreover, Mexican laws against layoffs meant GM had to maintain its Mexican workers on the payroll, thus adding pressure on GM to settle the strike.[88] In summary, there appear to be advantages of international diversification to enable an MNE to escape conflict with labor, but only in limited circumstances.

Value Activity Switching

MNEs often threaten to move value activities to other countries to extract wage reductions or work concessions from their employees. This tactic presses unions to accept lower compensation, fewer benefits, and less hospitable workplace conditions in favor of more job security. For example, Daimler-Benz's German workers agreed to accept lower wages after the company procured agreements from French, Czech, and British labor to work for less. This trend has gained greater visibility in the context of the offshoring of jobs. MNEs counter that this rationale only partially represents the situation. Unquestionably, production activities would seem plausible when a company has facilities in more than one country, at other times they would seem more plausible when different companies own facilities in different countries. For example, suppose a Canadian company competes with Brazilian imports. If Canadian workers demand and get substantial wage increases that result in higher product prices, the Brazilian competitor will likely seize the opportunity to build Canadian market share at the expense of the Canadian company and its workers. However, suppose the Brazilian company also owns the facility in Canada. The Brazilian management would have to weigh the cost-saving advantages of moving its production from Canada to Brazil against the losses it would incur in Canada by discarding its facilities there.

Scale and Complexity of MNEs

Observers claim it is difficult for labor unions to deal with MNEs because of the global scale of their value chains and the complexities in interpreting how they coordinate value activities. Both issues are complicated by the difficulty labor has in identifying the location of decision making and in interpreting financial data for the typical MNE. These ambiguities, critics reason, means that labor is often at the mercy of activities, decision makers, and resources that are far removed from their country. They argue that MNEs who command such positions are more likely to impose arbitrarily stringent antilabor policies in the event of workplace activism. Certainly, workers, especially with the assistance of unions, examine MNEs' financial data to determine MNEs' ability to meet their demands. Interpreting these data is a complex task because of disparities among managerial, tax, and disclosure requirements in home and host countries. Labor has been particularly leery of the possibility that MNEs might manipulate transfer prices to give the appearance that a given subsidiary cannot meet labor demands.

MNEs often reply that these concerns overemphasize their ability to increase compensation and deemphasize the seemingly more important issue of going-wage rates in both the industry and geographic area. Although MNEs may report many complex data, at least one set of financial statements must satisfy local authorities. By definition, this set should be no more difficult to interpret than that reported by a purely domestic company. In terms of transfer pricing, it is doubtful that MNEs set artificial levels to aid in collective bargaining situations since doing so eventually creates distortions and possible problems elsewhere. Specifically, if an MNE understates profits in one country, it would have to overstate them elsewhere, which would then put it at a disadvantage in collective bargaining in that country.

LABOR'S ACTIONS TOWARD MNES

Workers have responded to the power of the MNEs through several actions. First and foremost, workers have organized unions to fight, via collective bargaining with management, for higher pay, better benefits, greater job security, and improved working conditions. Unions' bargaining power is derived largely from their ability to threaten to disrupt production, either by a strike or some other form of work protest (a slowdown in the pace of work, the refusal to work overtime). This threat is credible, however, only insofar as management has no alternative but to employ workers who are not members of the union.

Labor tries to strengthen its bargaining power through cross-national cooperation.

Unions can engage in several tactics to counter MNEs' bargaining power. Internationally, unions aim to cooperate in a range of ways, sharing information, assisting bargaining units in other countries, and dealing simultaneously with MNEs.[89] The most common international cooperation among unions is exchanging information on an MNE's local policies and activities. This sort of collaboration helps determine the validity of the company's local claims as well as help it to reference precedents from other countries on bargaining issues. International confederations of unions, trade secretariats made up of related unions in a single industry or a complex of related industries, and company councils that include representatives from an MNE's plants around the world can exchange information. More specifically, European work councils (EWCs) represent a company's employees throughout the European Union. Through an EWC, a company informs and consults with workers on such issues as its current national, regional, and global performance as well as its strategies so that the employees can understand likely staffing, business, and market changes.

Labor groups in one country may support their counterparts in other countries in the view that coordinating union action across countries can effectively disrupt the coordination of a MNE's value chain. Popular measures include refusing to work overtime to supply a market normally served by striking workers' production, sending financial aid to workers in other countries, and disrupting work in their own countries. For example, French workers pledged to disrupt work at Pechiney in support of striking workers in the company's U.S. facilities.

Finally, labor can appeal to any number of transnational institutions to assist their efforts to check the power of MNEs. The International Labor Organization (ILO), for example, was founded in 1919 on the premise that the failure of any country to adopt humane labor conditions impedes other countries' efforts to improve their own conditions. Several associations of unions from different countries support similar ideals. These associations include various international trade secretariats representing workers in specific industries—for example, the International Confederation of Free Trade Unions (ICFTU), the World Federation of Trade Unions (WFTU), and the World Confederation of Labour (WCL). These organizations' activities, along with the general enhancement of worldwide communications, increasingly publicize the different labor conditions among countries. Among the newsworthy reports have been legal proscriptions against collective bargaining in Malaysia, wages below minimum standards in Indonesia, and the use of forced labor and child labor in some emerging markets. Upon publicizing such conditions, these organizations then champion economic and political sanctions to provoke change.[90] Similarly, various codes of conduct on industrial relations, such as those issued by the OECD, ILO, and EU, influence the labor practices of MNEs. Although the codes are voluntary, an MNE's compliance, or lack thereof, has symbolic significance to consumers and governments.

Labor's Success and Struggle

National unions regularly endorse calls for international cooperation with fellow organizations. Offsetting calls for unanimity is a stark reality of globalization, namely, that national unions are locked in a zero sum game, competing with each other to attract investment, and hence jobs, from MNEs. Consequently, when push comes to shove, there is little enthusiasm among workers to support their counterparts in another country. For instance, Canada and the United States have long shared a common union membership in the belief that united they stood, divided they fell. Still, there are ongoing moves among Canadian workers to form unions independent of those in the United States. One Canadian organizer summarized this attitude, explaining, "An American union is not going to fight to protect Canadian jobs at the expense of American jobs." The logic is that international unions will adopt policies favoring the bulk of their membership, which in any joint Canadian-U.S. relationship is bound to be American. Even when labor in one country helps labor in another, it likely is trying to achieve its own specific goals. For example, a union representing United States tomato pickers helped its Mexican counterpart negotiate a stronger collective agreement that limited the local workplace power of both domestic and foreign companies. This change then dissuaded the Campbell Soup Company from moving operations to Mexico. As a result of such competition between national unions, cooperation is difficult to establish.

Further impeding international unanimity among unions is the fact that unions developed independently in each country. As a result, the demography, structure, ideals, and goals of unions vary significantly from country to country. For example, the percentage of workers in unions is much higher in some countries than in others; it is much higher in Germany than in neighboring France, for example. Furthermore, many organized workers in France, Portugal, and Great Britain belong to communist unions whose view of the intrinsic class conflict of collective bargaining with MNEs clashes with the more moderate views of unions elsewhere in Germany, the Netherlands, Scandinavia, and Switzerland. Cross-national differences in unions' agendas extend to a host of comparatively more mundane matters like wage rates and workers' preferences. For example, Spanish workers are more willing to work on weekends than are German workers.

Unions in different countries prefer different methods of collective bargaining. As such, MNEs in a given country may deal with one or several unions that, depending on the situation, represent workers in many industries, in many companies within the same industry, or in only one company. If it represents only one company, the union may represent all plants or just one plant. In Sweden, bargaining tends to be highly centralized—that is, employers from numerous companies in different industries deal together with a federation of trade unions. In Germany, employers from associations of companies in the same industries bargain jointly with union federations.

Approaches to reconcile labor tension differ from country to country. The use of mediation by an impartial party is mandatory in Israel but voluntary in the United States and the United Kingdom. Among countries that have mediation practices, diverse attitudes prevail. For example, there is much less enthusiasm for it in India than in the United States. Not all differences are settled through changes either in legislation or through collective bargaining. Other means are the labor court and the government-chosen arbitrator. For example, wages in many Austrian industries are arbitrated semiannually. These sorts of ideological and operational gaps have made sustained cross-national cooperation difficult for unions.

Lastly, organized labor has met with limited success in getting national and international bodies to regulate MNEs. Certainly, national agencies have helped workers gain

---

Labor may be at a disadvantage in MNE negotiations because the

- Country bargaining unit is only a small part of MNE activities
- MNE may continue serving customers with foreign production or resources

Organized labor has, with slight success, formed international labor organizations to offset MNEs' bargaining power.

Union structure can be

- National or local
- Industry or company
- One or several for the same company

better access to the intricacies of the MNEs' decision-making process. Most notably, legislation in some countries, particularly in northern Europe, gives labor the legal right to participate in the management of companies. This idea—known as **codetermination**—emphasizes cooperative decision making within firms that benefits both the workers and the company.[91] Despite some voluntary moves toward codetermination, most examples have been mandated by the government. Labor has successfully persuaded government officials, particularly in Western Europe, to require companies to comply with worker-friendly plant closure prenotification requirements. In addition, international agencies like the ILO, EU, and OECD have adopted codes of conduct for multinational firms in

LOOKING TO THE FUTURE: Which Countries Will Have the Jobs of the Future?

As capital, technology, and information grow more mobile among countries and companies, human resource development increasingly explains competitive differences. Consequently, companies' access to and retention of more qualified personnel grows more important. Companies, however, likely will face the greater challenge of retaining highly skilled, highly valued workers in the future.

Demographers are nearly unanimous in projecting that populations will grow much faster in emerging economies (China being the notable exception) than in the wealthier countries—at least up to the year 2030. At the same time, the number of retirees as a percentage of the population in the wealthier countries will grow as people live longer and retire earlier. People will also need to be educated for more years to get the so-called better jobs. Overall, these trends indicate that there will be fewer people to do the productive work within the wealthier countries. These countries are already trying to adjust, engaging in a range of education and training programs.[92] Still, these programs have many social and economic consequences to which MNEs must adapt.

One adjustment might be for wealthier countries to encourage emigration from emerging economies, which struggle to generate enough jobs for their swelling workforce. In Canada, the United States, and parts of Western Europe, there has been a long-term migration of foreign workers, both legally and illegally, from emerging economies. This entry generates assimilation costs within wealthier countries and a brain drain from emerging economies when highly qualified people leave for other countries. Some, however, suggest that emigration benefits everyone by encouraging brain circulation among wealthier and emerging economies.[93] Specifically, an increasing number of Taiwan's, China's, Korea's, and India's biggest U.S. success stories are returning to their native homes to start companies. Nonetheless, times of economic downturns will likely see unemployed workers in the wealthier countries blame foreign workers for their plight. Under this scenario, companies will have to spend more time getting work permits and integrating different nationalities into their workforces.

Another potential adjustment in wealthier countries is the continued push toward adopting robotics and other labor-saving equipment.[94] Although this may help solve some of the shortages in workers, it will inevitably escalate companies' need for workers who command higher skill levels. Less educated members of the workforce, some reason, will likely be unemployable, forced to take lesser-paying jobs in the service sector, or to compete with immigrants for less appealing jobs. Gaps between haves and have-nots may thus widen within wealthier countries as well as between those countries and emerging economies. In this scenario, have-nots may pressure governments to push companies to shift technological development away from labor-saving priorities.

A third possible adjustment is the acceleration of business migration to emerging economies to tap rich supplies of inexpensive productive labor. At the same time, emerging economies may devise ways to support brain circulation or, if unsuccessful, to halt the process of brain drain. Either approach will shift more entry-level production jobs from wealthier countries to their emerging counterparts.[95] If successful, managers who return to their countries will likely shift many low-skilled jobs to their home market. Governments in wealthier countries will then face the tough problem of what to do with underqualified workers who face deteriorating job prospects.[96]

their relations with labor. However, these guidelines, from the view of labor, stop far short of effectively regulating MNEs. For instance, although there are some early examples of workers deterring investment outflows, acquisitions, and plant closures, the fact that these conduct codes lack any enforcement capability means they have had an inconsistent effect on companies' international business decisions and activities.

Trends in the Relationship Between MNEs and Labor

The relationship between labor and MNE is an intrinsic facet of international business. Two trends, one from the perspective of labor, the other from MNEs, promise to define the next stage of their relationship.

Union membership as a portion of the total workforce has been falling in most countries. This is illustrated in Figure 20.5. There are several reasons for this decline.

- *Increase in white-collar workers as a percentage of total workers.* White-collar workers see themselves more as managers than as laborers, and thus are less inclined to join a union.

- *Increase in service employment in relation to manufacturing employment.* There is more variation in service assignments than in manufacturing, so workers believe their situations differ from that of their coworkers.

- *Rising portion of women in the workforce.* Traditionally, women have been less apt to join unions.

- *Rising portion of part-time and temporary workers.* Workers do not see themselves in the job long enough for a union to help them much.

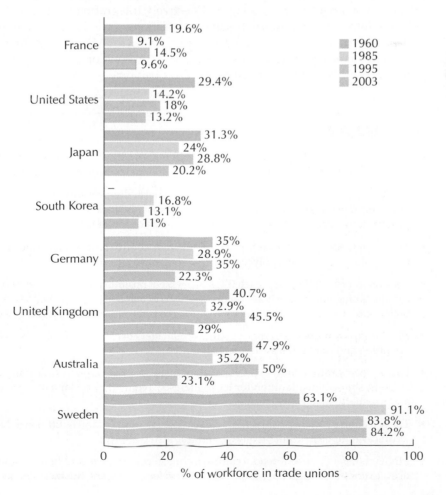

FIGURE 20.5

TRADE UNION DECLINE IN INDUSTRIALIZED COUNTRIES

For several decades, trade union membership has been consistently declining for most industrialized countries.

Compiled from various sources.

- *Trend toward smaller average plant size.* More direct interactions between workers and managers align their interests, thereby harmonizing outlooks.

- *Decline in the belief in collectivism among younger workers.* Few of today's younger workers have suffered economic deprivation; hence, they question the value of collective solutions.[97]

The overall decline in union membership is a long-running trend. Certainly, there are exceptions. Unions in Sweden, for instance, have maintained their strength because they have forged cooperative relationships with companies, like Electrolux and Volvo, to improve corporate competitiveness and to share the rewards from the success. Still, the harsh reality is that the power of unions is a function of the size of their membership rolls. Continuing decline in membership counts foreshadows unions with weaker negotiation positions and less incentive for cooperation with counterparts in other countries.

On the flip side, MNEs are developing HRM policies and practices that fortify their power. Historically, irrespective of the strategy that companies pursued, most MNEs decentralized labor relations responsibilities to the HRM manager in foreign subsidiaries. Practicality, rather than insight, motivated this policy. Country-to-country variability in labor laws, union structure, workplace attitudes, and collective bargaining processes created a complex situation that continually changed. Most MNEs reasoned that headquarters was poorly positioned and prepared to manage worldwide labor relations effectively. In recourse, they delegated the task to local managers. Presently, this outlook is giving way to a trend toward greater coordination and control of global labor policies by the senior leadership of MNEs. Coordinating globally dispersed value chains spurs headquarters to preempt the risk of disruption by sporadic workplace activism. Moreover, companies whose value creation is sensitive to labor costs no longer can delegate labor relations to a range of local managers. Effectively, integrating their global operations spurs MNEs to integrate their international labor relations. Growing attention to and integration of their labor relations creates powerful advantages for MNEs. They increasingly sharpen their understanding of how to use the threat of production switching or resource redirection to strengthen their collective bargaining positions.

Falling union membership in many countries foreshadows lower bargaining power for labor.

MNEs' efforts to develop integrated labor relations across countries increases their bargaining power.

SUMMARY

- Research and anecdotes show that the MNE whose HRM policies support its chosen strategy creates superior value. Still, many MNEs struggle to develop effective HRM policies.

- The top-level managers of foreign subsidiaries normally perform much broader duties than do domestic managers with similar cost or profit responsibilities. They must resolve communications problems, usually with less staff support, between corporate headquarters and subsidiaries.

- Three perspectives describe how companies set about staffing their international operations, namely the ethnocentric, polycentric, and geocentric approaches.

- An ethnocentric staffing approach fills management positions with home-country nationals. A polycentric staffing policy uses host-country nationals to manage local subsidiaries. A geocentric staffing policy seeks the best people for key jobs throughout the organization, regardless of their nationality.

- MNEs employ more locals than expatriate managers because the former better understand local operating and demand less compensation.

- Hiring locals rather than expatriates demonstrates that opportunities are available for local citizens, shows consideration for local interests, avoids the red tape of cross-national transfers, and is usually materially cheaper.

- The selection of an individual for an expatriate position is largely influenced by the candidate's technical competence, adaptiveness, and leadership ability.

- MNEs transfer people abroad to infuse technical competence and home-country business practices, to control foreign operations, and to develop managers' business skills.

- MNEs that transfer personnel abroad should consider their technical competencies, how well the people will be accepted, how well they will adapt to local conditions, and how to treat them when they return home from their foreign assignment.

- When transferred abroad, an expatriate's compensation usually is increased because of hardship and differences in cost of living. Transfers to remote areas typically carry higher premiums.

- The compensation of an expatriate must neither overly reward nor unduly punish a person for accepting a foreign assignment. Generally, most MNEs used the balance sheet approach to manage this dilemma.

- Training and predeparture preparations usually reduce the odds of expatriate failure. Increasingly, preparation activities include the expatriate's spouse or partner. Training often includes general country orientation, cultural sensitivity, and practical training.

- Two major international training functions are building a global awareness among managers in general and equipping managers to handle the specific challenges of a foreign assignment.

- Expatriate failure, narrowly defined, is the manager's premature return home due to poor job performance. Broadly defined, it is the failure of the MNE's selection policies to find individuals who will succeed abroad.

- Repatriation, the act of returning home from a foreign assignment, has many difficulties. The principal cause of repatriation frustrations is finding the right job for the expatriate to return to.

- A country's sociopolitical environment will largely determine the type of relationship between labor and management and affect the number, representation, and organization of unions.

- International organizations pressure companies to follow internationally accepted labor practices wherever they operate, regardless of whether the practices conflict with the norms and laws of the host countries.

- International cooperation among labor groups in a concerted effort to confront MNEs is minimal. Labor groups' initiatives include information exchanges, simultaneous negotiations or strikes, and refusals to work overtime to supply the market in a struck country.

- Labor contends that it is disadvantaged in dealing with MNEs because it is hard to get full data on MNEs' global operations, MNEs can manipulate investment incentives, MNEs can easily move value activities to other countries, and MNEs often make key decisions in another country.

Tel-Comm-Tek (TCT)[98]

C A S E

In January 2005, Steven Jones, a U.S. national and managing director of the Indian subsidiary of Tel-Comm-Tek (TCT), a U.S.-headquartered company, announced his resignation and intention to return to the United States within a month. TCT immediately began a search for his replacement.

TCT manufactures a variety of small office equipment (primarily copying machines, dictation units, laser printers, and paper shredders) in nine different countries. It distributes and sells these products worldwide, most recently reporting sales in more than 70 countries. Although it had no manufacturing facility in India, it had sold and serviced products there since the early 1980s. Originally, it hired independent importers to sell its products. It soon realized that generating higher sales required setting up its own operations. In 1992, it opened a sales office in New Delhi. Map 20.1 profiles India and some of its major cities.

By 2000, several factors spurred TCT to expand its Indian operations. TCT's Indian sales operation (with about 100 employees) had consistently reported higher sales and profitability. However, its growing success was not without some worries. Specifically, TCT feared that local trade restrictions, then under discussion by government officials, would eventually ban the import of the sorts of small office equipment that it made.

Country conditions in India made greater investment appealing. India had stable democratic institutions and corporate laws; a large English-speaking population; and productive, economical workers. Already, several foreign and Indian multinationals designed and manufactured office equipment locally.

• **Saumitra Chakraborty** At 27, Chakraborty is an assistant to the departing managing director in India. He has held that position since joining TCT upon graduating from a small, private university in Europe four years earlier. Unmarried, he consistently earns a job performance rating of competent. While he excels in employee relations, he lacks any line experience. Still, he has successfully increased TCT India's sales, largely owing to his personal connections with prominent Indian families and government officials and to his skillfulness with the ways of the Indian business environment. Besides speaking India's main languages of English and Hindi fluently, Chakraborty speaks Kannada (the local language of Bangalore).

QUESTIONS

1. Which candidate should the committee nominate for the assignment if TCT follows an ethnocentric approach to staffing? A polycentric approach to staffing? A geocentric approach to staffing? Which approach do you think makes the best sense for TCT? Why?

2. What challenges might each candidate encounter in the position?

3. How might TCT go about minimizing the challenges facing each candidate?

4. Should all candidates receive the same compensation package? If not, what factors should influence each package?

5. What recommendations can you offer to help a company facing this sort of decision that will enable it to balance professional and personal characteristics of the various candidates?

CHAPTER NOTES

1 "In Search of Global Leaders: View of Jeffrey Immelt, Chairman and CEO, General Electric," *Harvard Business Review* (1 August, 2003).

2 "In Search of Global Leaders: View of Daniel Meiland, Executive Chairman, Egon Zehnder International," *Harvard Business Review* (1 August, 2003).

3 Barbara Ettorre, "A Brave New World," *Management Review* 82, no. 4 (April, 1993): 10–16.

4 Melinda Ligos, "The Foreign Assignment: An Incubator, or Exile?" *New York Times* (October 22, 2000).

5 Jane Fraser and Jeremy Oppenheim, "What's New About Globalization?" *The McKinsey Quarterly* 2 (1997): 168–79.

6 Ligos, op. cit.

7 Sandra Jones, "Going Stateside: Once the Overseas Hitch Is Over, Homeward-Bound Expats Hit Turbulence," *Crain's Chicago Business* (July 24, 2000).

8 Barry Newman, "Expat Archipelago," *Wall Street Journal* (December 12, 1995): A1.

9 Robert Young Pelton, "The World's Most Dangerous Places," *HarperResource* (2003); Joe Sharkey, "Global Economy Is Leading to More Dangerous Places," *New York Times* (April 19, 2005).

10 "In Search of Global Leaders: View of Daniel Meiland, Executive Chairman, Egon Zehnder International," *Harvard Business Review* (1 August, 2003).

11 Paula Caligiuri and Victoria Di Santo, "Global Competence: What Is It, and Can It Be Developed Through Global Assignments?" *Human Resource Planning* 24 (September 2001): 27–36; Mark Morgan, "Career-Building Strategies: It's Time to Do a Job Assessment. Are Your Skills Helping You Up the Corporate Ladder?" *Strategic Finance* 83 (June 2002): 38–44.

12 Hoon Park, "Global Human Resource Management: A Synthetic Approach." *The Journal of International Business and Economics* (2002).

13 William Q. Judge, "Is a Leader's Character Culture-Bound or Culture-Free? An Empirical Comparison of the Character Traits of American and Taiwanese CEOs," *Journal of Leadership Studies* 8 (Fall, 2001): 63–79.

14 Montserrat Entrialgo, "The Impact of the Alignment of Strategy and Managerial Characteristics on Spanish SMEs," *Journal of Small Business Management* 40 (July 2002): 260–271; Keith D. Brouthers, "Institutional, Cultural and Transaction Cost Influences on Entry Mode Choice and Performance," *Journal of International Business Studies* 33 (Summer 2002): 203–222.

15 Ben L. Kedia, Richard Nordtvedt, and Liliana M. Perez, "International Business Strategies, Decision-Making Theories, and Leadership Styles: An Integrated Framework," *Competitiveness Review* 12 (Winter–Spring 2002): 38–53; "The New Teamwork," *Business Week* (February 18, 2002): EB12.

16 Sully Taylor, Schon Beechler, and Nancy Napier, "Toward an Integrative Model of Strategic International Resource Management," *Academy of Management Review* 21 (1996): 959–85, discusses these in the context of multidomestic and a combination of global and transnational strategies.

17 "Globesmanship," *Across the Board* 27 (January–February 1990): 26, quoting Michael Angus.

18 "Human Capital Index: Human Capital as a Lead Indicator of Shareholder Value" at Watson Wyatt Worldwide (see www.watsonwyatt.com). Retrieved March 30, 2005.

19 See, for example, N. Khatri, "Managing Human Resource for Competitive Advantage: A Study of Companies in Singapore," *International Journal of Human Resource Management* 11, no. 2 (April 1, 2000): 336.

20 R. Coleman, "HR Management Lags Behind at World Class Firms," *CMA Management* (July–August, 2002).

21 "Human Capital: A Key to Higher Market Value," *Business Finance* (December 1999): 15.

22 Some now speak of a new sort of expatriate, specifically that of the "stealth expatriate and the two prevalent types: (1) the cross-border commuter, a growing phenomenon particularly in the European Union (EU), where the relaxation of border controls and spread of low-cost airlines have made weekly commuting between cities almost commonplace and (2) the accidental expat—someone who goes on so many business trips or temporary assignments that he inadvertently incurs new fiscal liabilities or overstays his welcome as a foreign worker. See "In Search of Stealth," *The Economist* (April 21, 2005).

23 Maddy Janssens, "Developing a Culturally Synergistic Approach to International Human Resource Management," *Journal of World Business* 36 (Winter 2001): 429–51; Nicholas Athanassiou and Douglas Nigh, "Internationalization, Tacit Knowledge and the Top Management Teams of MNCs," *Journal of International Business Studies* 31 (Fall 2000): 471; Meredith Downes and Anisya Thomas, "Managing Overseas Assignments to Build Organizational Knowledge," *Human Resource Planning* 22 (December 1999): 33.

24 As we saw in Chapter 13, a company's culture can strongly affect the firm's effort to translate its strategy into value anywhere in the world it operates. Firms following international, global, and transnational strategies can boost their performance with an integrative set of values and ideals that enables better coordinating value activities.

25 "In Search of Global Leaders: View of Jeffrey Immelt, Chairman and CEO, General Electric," *Harvard Business Review* (1 August, 2003).

26 Chi-fai Chan and Neil Holbert, "Marketing Home and Away: Perceptions of Managers in Headquarters and Subsidiaries," *Journal of World Business* 36 (Summer 2001): 205.

27 Tsun-yan Hsieh, Johanne Lavoie, and Robert Samek, "Are You Taking Your Expatriate Talent Seriously?" *The McKinsey Quarterly* (Summer, 1999): 71.

28 Vijay Pothukuchi, Fariborz Damanpour, Jaepil Choi, Chao C. Chen, and Seung Ho Park, "National and Organizational Culture Differences and International Joint Venture Performance," *Journal of International Business Studies* 33 (Summer 2002): 243–66.

29 Estimate reported in the second annual study of expatriate issues, conducted from January through March 2002, sponsored by CIGNA International Expatriate Benefits, the National Foreign Trade Council, an association of multinational companies that supports open international trade and investment; and WorldatWork, http://www.prnewswire.com/micro/CI9. Retrieved September 2, 2005.

30 Valerie Frazee, "Relo Administrators Believe Expats Are Overpaid," *Business and Management Practices* 3 (July 1998): 4, quoting a survey by Runzheimer International of 103 international relocation administrators from U.S.-based companies showing that 72 percent feel pressure to cut the costs, and 52 percent are responding by hiring locals.

31 Kahn, Jeremy, "The World's Most Admired Companies," *Fortune* 140, no. 7 (October 11, 1999): 267.

32 Ibid.

33 David Ahlstrom, Garry Bruton, and Eunice S. Chan, "HRM of Foreign Firms in China: The Challenge of Managing Host Country Personnel," *Business Horizons* 44 (May 2001): 59.

34 "High-Tech Nomads: These Engineers Work as Temps on Wireless Projects All Over the World," *Time* 158 (November 26, 2001): B20; Ben L. Kedia and Ananda Mukherji, "Global Managers: Developing a Mindset for Global Competitiveness," *Journal of World Business* 34 (Fall 1999): 30.

35 "In Search of Global Leaders: View of Fred Hassan, Chairman and CEO, Schering-Plough," *Harvard Business Review* (1 August, 2003).

36 Leslie Holstrom and Simon Brady, "The Changing Face of Global Business," *Fortune* Special Section, (July 24, 2000; Retrieved from www.204.71-241-112/fortune/sections. Novermber 25, 2000).

37 R. M. Kanter, *World Class: Thriving Locally in the Global Economy* (New York: Simon & Schuster, 1995).

38 Astrid Wendlandt, "The Name Game Is a Puzzle for Expats at Work," *The Financial Times* (August 15, 2000): 3.

39 Ahlstrom, Bruton, and Chan, op. cit.

40 Calvin Reynolds, "Strategic Employment of Third Country Nationals: Keys to Sustaining the Transformation of HR Functions," *Human Resource Planning* 20 (March 1997): 33–50.

41 Hsieh, Lavoie, and Samek, op.cit.

42 Susan Schneider and Rosalie Tung, "Introduction to the International Human Resource Management Special Issue," *Journal of World Business* 36 (Winter 2001): 341–46.

43 Caligiuri and Di Santo, op. cit.; Hsieh, Lavoie, and Samek, op.cit.

44 "In Search of Global Leaders: View of Stephen Green, Group CEO, HSBC," *Harvard Business Review* (1 August, 2003).

45 Sunkyu Jun, James Gentry, and Yong Hyun, "Cultural Adaptation of Business Expatriates in the Host Marketplace," *Journal of International Business Studies* 32 (Summer 2001): 369; J. Stewart Black and Mark Mendenhall, "Cross-Cultural Training Effectiveness: A Review and a Theoretical Framework for Future Research," *Academy of Management Review* 15 (January 1990): 117.

46 "The New International Executive Business Leadership for the 21st Century," Harvard Business School and Amrop International, 1995. Reported in Andrew Crisp, "International Careers Made Easy," *The European*, no. 254 (March 24, 1995): 27.

47 Hsieh, Lavoie, and Samek, op.cit.

48 John D. Daniels and Gary Insch, "Why Are Early Departure Rates from Foreign Assignments Lower Than Historically Reported?" *Multinational Business Review* VI, no. 1 (Spring 1998): 13–23.

49 Data provided by National Foreign Trade Council. Maria L. Kraimer, Sandy Wayne, and Renata Jaworski, "Sources of Support and Expatriate Performance: The Mediating Role of Expatriate Adjustment," *Personnel Psychology* 54 (Spring 2001): 71.

50 Margaret Shaffer, David Harrison, K. Matthew Gilley, and Dora Luk, "Struggling for Balance Amid Turbulence on International Assignments: Work-Family Conflict, Support and Commitment," *Journal of Management* 27 (Jan.–Feb. 2001): 99; Chris Moss, "Expats: Thinking of Living and Working Abroad?" *The Guardian* (October 19, 2000): 4.

51 "Expat Spouses: It Takes Two," *Financial Times* (March 1, 2002); Margaret Shaffer and David Harrison, "Forgotten Partners of International Assignments: Development and Test of a Model of Spouse Adjustment," *Journal of Applied Psychology* 86 (April 2001): 238.

52 Diane E. Lewis, "Families Make, Break Overseas Moves," *Boston Globe* (October 4, 1998): 5D.

53 D. Ones and C. Viswesvaran, "Relative Importance of Personality Dimensions for Expatriate Selection: A Policy Capturing Study," *Human Performance* 12 (1999): 275–94.

54 Chris Brewster, "Making Their Own Way: International Experience Through Self-Initiated Foreign Assignments," *Journal of World Business* 35 (Winter 2000): 417; Vesa Suutari, Kerr Inkson, Judith Pringle, Michael B. Arthur, and Sean Barry, "Expatriate Assignment Versus Overseas Experience: Contrasting Models of International Human Resource Development," *Journal of World Business* 32 (1997): 351–68.

55 Valerie Frazee, "Send Your Expats Prepared for Success," *Workforce* 78 (March 1999): S6.

56 P. Christopher Earley, "Intercultural Training for Managers: A Comparison of Documentary and Interpersonal Methods," *Academy of Management Journal* 30, no. 4 (December 1987): 685–98; Sharon Leiba-O'Sullivan, "The Distinction Between Stable and Dynamic Cross-Cultural Competencies: Implications for Expatriate Trainability," *Journal of International Business Studies* 30 (Winter 1999): 709.

57 C. Panella, "Meeting the Needs of International Business: A Customer Service-Oriented Business Language Course," *The Journal of Language for International Business* 9, no. 1 (1998): 65–75; M. E. Inman, "How foreign language study can enhance career possibilities" (1987), *Eric Digest*, ED289363; C. Randlesome and A. Myers, "Cultural Fluency: Results from a UK and Irish Survey," *Business Communication Quarterly* 60, no. 3 (1997): 9–22.

58 Tanya Mohn, "All Aboard the Foreign Language Express," *New York Times* (October 11, 2000).

59 Stephen Baker, "Catching the Continental Drift: These Days, English Will Suffice for Americans Working in Europe. To Be a Player, However, the Smart Expatriate Needs the Gift of Tongues," *Business Week* (August 14, 2001).

60 Christopher Cole, "Bridging the Language Gap: Expatriates Find Learning Korean Key to Enjoying a More Satisfying Life," *The Korea Herald* (August 16, 2002).

61 Ligos, op. cit.

62 Amy Sitze, "Language of Business: Can E-Learning Help International Companies Speak a Common Language?" *Online Learning* 6 (March 2002): 19–23.

63 "International Assignments: European Policy and Practice," Man Simpson (Ed.), *Pricewaterhouse-Coopers*. Copy available at http://www.pwcglobal.com/extweb/ncsurvres.nsf/.

64 "In Search of Global Leaders: View of Fred Hassan, Chairman and CEO, Schering-Plough," *Harvard Business Review* (1 August, 2003).

65 Carolyn Gould, "What's the Latest in Global Compensation?" *Global Workforce* (July 1997).

66 Geoffrey W. Latta, "Expatriate Policy and Practice: A Ten-Year Comparison of Trends," *Compensation and Benefits Review* 31, no. 4 (July–August 1999): 35–39, quoting studies by Organization Resources Counselors.

67 For example, Towers Perrin or CIGNA specialize in international compensation. In addition, companies rely on estimates of cost-of-living differences—even if the estimates are imperfect. MNEs commonly use such sources as the U.S. State Department's cost-of-living index published yearly in *Labor Developments Abroad*, the U.N. *Monthly Bulletin of Statistics,* and surveys by the *Financial Times*, P-E International, Business International, and the International Monetary Fund's Staff Papers.

68 This practice appears to be fading, however, especially for assignments in so-called world capitals like New York, London, and Tokyo, in which companies assume there is little deprivation and many interested executives. Further, the hardships from foreign assignments are declining as advances in transportation and communications enable expatriates to keep in closer contact with people in their home countries; as

the openness of economies allows them to buy familiar goods and services; and as the general level of housing, schooling, and medical services increasingly meets their needs.

69 For example, a U.S. family based in China commonly spends more money on buying the same goods than they would back home because they often prefer to buy many Western items that must be imported and thus have been charged high tariffs. Often, expatriates obtain food and housing at higher than the local rate because they do not know the language well, where to buy, or how to bargain.

70 "Home Away from Home: Expatriate Housing in Asia," *The Korea Herald* (May 2, 2002).

71 "Tokyo Tops in H.K. Survey on Living Cost for Expatriates," *Japan Economic* Newswire (January 24, 2002).

72 Alison Maitland, "A Hard Balancing Act: Management of Dual Careers," *Financial Times* (May 10, 1999): 11.

73 Valerie Frazee, "Expert Help for Dual-Career Spouses," *Workforce* 78 (March, 1999): S18.

74 Judy Clark, "Added Global Risks Impact Security Planning for Oil, Gas Expat Workers," *The Oil and Gas Journal* 100 (April 2002): 32–37.

75 Roberto Ceniceros, "Precautions, Training Can Lessen Risk of Kidnapping," *Business Insurance* 35 (May 14, 2001): 26.

76 Gould, op. cit.

77 Towers Perrin, *2001-2002 Worldwide Total Remuneration,* http://www.towers.com/TOWERS/services_ products/TowersPerrin/wwtr01/wwtr01.htm.

78 "New Survey Suggests Ways to Maximize Expatriate Performance and Loyalty," *Internet Wire* (March 27, 2001). Estimates reported at 2001 National Foreign Trade Council's International HR Management Symposium. See also, Leslie Gross Klaff, "The Right Way to Bring Expats Home," *Workforce* 81 (July 2002): 40–44; Jeff Barbian, "Return to Sender: Companies That Fail to Effectively Manage Employees Returning from a Foreign Assignment May Find Their Investments Permanently Hitting the Road," *Training* 39 (January 2002): 40–43.

79 J. S. Black and H. B. Gregersen, "The Right Way to Manage Expats," *Harvard Business Review* (March–April, 1999): 52–62.

80 "In Search of Global Leaders: View of Daniel Meiland, Executive Chairman, Egon Zehender International," *Harvard Business Review* (1 August 2003).

81 Mila Lazarova and Paula Caligiuri, "Retaining Repatriates: The Role of Organizational Support Practices," *Journal of World Business* 36 (Winter 2001): 389–402.

82 Ligos, op. cit.

83 Linda K. Stroh, Hal B. Gregersen, and J. Stewart Black, "Closing the Gap: Expectations Versus Reality Among Repatriates," *Journal of World Business* 33 (1998): 111–124; Klaff, op. cit.

84 C. Reidy, "Corporate Synergy Leads Way in Constructing Effective Retirement and Health Benefits," *IBIS Review* (January 1996): 16–17.

85 Iris I. Varner and Teresa M. Palmer, "Successful Expatriation and Organizational Strategies," *Review of Business* 23 (Spring 2002): 8–12; Jan Selmer, "Practice Makes Perfect? International Experience and Expatriate Adjustment," *Management International Review* 42 (January 2002): 71–88.

86 Bruce E. Kaufman, "Reflections on Six Decades in Industrial Relations: An Interview with John Dunlop," *Industrial and Labor Relations Review* 55 (January 2002): 324–49.

87 Jean-Louis Chaumet, CGT Labor Representative, "*Euro-Disney News Profile,*" ABC News, (March 29, 1992).

88 Neil Templin, "GM Strike Hits Mexican Output as Talks on Settlement Resume," *Wall Street Journal* (March 20, 1996): A3.

89 Robert A. Senser, "Workers of the World: It's Time to Unite," *Commonweal* 127 (Sept. 22, 2000): 13; Julie Kosterlitz, "Unions of the World Unite: European and American Unions Working Together," *National Journal* 30 (May 16, 1998): 1134.

90 Ans Kolk and Rob van Tulder, "Child Labor and Multinational Conduct: A Comparison of International Business and Stakeholder Codes," *Journal of Business Ethics* 36 (March 15, 2002): 291–302.

91 John Addison, "Nonunion Representation in Germany," *Journal of Labor Research* 20, no. 1 (Winter 1999): 73–91.

92 The Annecy Symposium, "The Future of Work, Employment and Social Protection," *International Labour Review* 140 (Winter 2001): 453–75.

93 Anna Saxenian, "Brain Circulation: How High-Skill Immigration Makes Everyone Better Off," *Brookings Review* 20 (Winter 2002): 28–32; Moises Naim, "The New Diaspora: New Links Between Emigres and Their Home Countries Can Become a Powerful Force for Economic Development," *Foreign Policy* (July–August 2002): 96–98.

94 Mark Poster, "Workers as Cyborgs: Labor and Networked Computers," *Journal of Labor Research* 23 (Summer 2002): 339–54.

95 "We Must Halt the Brain-Drain," *Africa News Service* (December 17, 2001).

96 "The Poorest Are Again Losing Ground," *Business Week* (April 23, 2001): 130.

97 Nancy Mills, "New Strategies for Union Survival and Revival," *Journal of Labor Research* 22 (Summer 2001): 599.

98 Based on information reported in "India," *CIA World Handbook, 2004;* http://www.cia.gov/cia/publications/factbook/geos/in.html; "India: A Country Study," *Library of Congress,* http://memory.loc.gov/frd/cs/intoc.html; India, Country Profile, *BBCi,* http://news.bbc.co.uk/1/hi/world/south_asia/country_profiles/1154019.stm; and various publications of the United Nations, http://www.un.org/.

GLOSSARY

Absolute advantage: A theory first presented by Adam Smith, which holds that because certain countries can produce some goods more efficiently than other countries, they should specialize in and export those things they can produce more efficiently and trade for other things they need.

Acceptable quality level (AQL): A concept of quality control whereby managers are willing to accept a certain level of production defects, which are dealt with through repair facilities and service centers.

Accounting: The process of identifying, recording, and interpreting economic events.

Acquired advantage: A form of trade advantage due to technology rather than due to the availability of natural resources, climate, etc.

Acquired group memberships: Affiliations not determined by birth, such as religions, political affiliations, and professional and other associations.

Acquisition: The purchase of one company by another company.

Active income: Income of a CFC that is derived from the active conduct of a trade or business, as specified by the U.S. Internal Revenue Code.

Ad valorem duty: A duty (tariff) assessed as a percentage of the value of the item.

ADR: *See* American Depositary Receipt.

Advance import deposit: A deposit prior to the release of foreign exchange, required by some governments.

AFTA: *See* ASEAN Free Trade Area.

ALADI: *See* Latin American Integration Association.

American Depositary Receipt (ADR): A negotiable certificate issued by a U.S. bank in the United States to represent the underlying shares of a foreign corporation's stock held in trust at a custodian bank in the foreign country.

American terms: *See* U.S. terms.

Andean Group (ANCOM): A South American form of economic integration involving Bolivia, Colombia, Ecuador, Peru, and Venezuela.

APEC: *See* Asia Pacific Economic Cooperation.

Appropriability theory: The theory that companies will favor foreign direct investment over such nonequity operating forms as licensing arrangements so that potential competitors will be less likely to gain access to proprietary information.

Arbitrage: The process of buying and selling foreign currency at a profit that results from price discrepancies between or among markets.

Area division: *See* Geographic division.

Arm's-length price: A price between two companies that do not have an ownership interest in each other.

Ascribed group memberships: Affiliations determined by birth, such as those based on gender, family, age, caste, and ethnic, racial, or national origin.

ASEAN: *See* Association of South East Asian Nations.

ASEAN Free Trade Area (AFTA): A free-trade area formed by the ASEAN countries on January 1, 1993, with the goal of cutting tariffs on all intrazonal trade to a maximum of 5 percent by January 1, 2008.

Asia Pacific Economic Cooperation (APEC): A cooperation formed by 21 countries that border the Pacific Rim to promote multilateral economic cooperation in trade and investment in the Pacific Rim.

Association of South East Asian Nations (ASEAN): A free-trade area involving the Asian countries of Brunei, Indonesia, Malaysia, the Philippines, Singapore, and Thailand.

Back-to-back loan: A loan that involves a company in Country A with a subsidiary in Country B, and a bank in Country B with a branch in Country A.

Balance of payments: Statement that summarizes all economic transactions between a country and the rest of the world during a given period of time.

Balance-of-payments deficit: An imbalance of some specific component within the balance of payments, such as merchandise trade or current account, that implies that a country is importing more than it exports.

Balance-of-payments surplus: An imbalance in the balance of payments that exists when a country exports more than it imports.

Balance of trade: The value of a country's exports less the value of its imports ("trade" can be defined as merchandise trade, services, unilateral transfers, or some combination of these three).

Balance on goods and services: The value of a country's exports of merchandise trade and services minus imports.

Balanced scorecard: An approach to performance measurement that endeavors to more closely link the strategic and financial perspectives of a business and take a broad view of business performance.

Bank for International Settlements (BIS): A bank in Basel, Switzerland, that facilitates transactions among central banks; it is effectively the central banks' central bank.

Bargaining school theory: A theory holding that the negotiated terms for foreign investors depend on how much investors and host countries need each other's assets.

Barter: The exchange of goods for goods or services instead of for money.

Base currency: The currency whose value is implicitly 1 when a quote is made between two currencies; for example, if the cruzeiro is trading at 2,962.5 cruzeiros per dollar, the dollar is the base currency and the cruzeiro is the quoted currency.

Basic balance: The net current account plus long-term capital within a country's balance of payments.

Bid (buy): The amount a trader is willing to pay for foreign exchange.

Bilateral integration: A form of integration between two countries in which they decide to cooperate more closely together, usually in the form of tariff reductions.

Bill of exchange: *See* Commercial bill of exchange.

Bill of lading: A document that is issued to a shipper by a carrier, listing the goods received for shipment.

BIRPI: *See* International Bureau for the Protection of Industrial Property Rights.

BIS: *See* Bank for International Settlements.

Black market: The foreign-exchange market that lies outside the official market.

Body language: The way people move their bodies, gesture, position themselves, etc., to convey meaning to others.

Bonded warehouse: A building or part of a building used for the storage of imported merchandise under supervision of the U.S. Customs Service and for the purpose of deferring payment of customs duties.

Booking center: An offshore financial center whose main function is to act as an accounting center in order to minimize the payment of taxes.

Branch (foreign): A foreign operation of a company that is not a separate entity from the parent that owns it.

Brand: A particular good identified with a company by means of name, logo, or other method, usually protected with a trademark registration.

Bretton Woods Agreement: An agreement among IMF countries to promote exchange-rate stability and to facilitate the international flow of currencies.

Broker (in foreign exchange): Specialists who facilitate transactions in the interbank market.

Buffer-stock system: A partially managed system that utilizes stocks of commodities to regulate their prices.

Bundesbank: The German central bank.

Buy local legislation: Laws that are intended to favor the purchase of domestically sourced goods or services over imported ones, even though the imports may be a better buy.

Buybacks: Counterdeliveries related to, or originating from, an original export.

CACM: *See* Central American Common Market.

Canada-U.S. Free Trade Agreement: An agreement, enacted in 1989, establishing a free-trade area involving the United States and Canada.

Capital account: A measure of transactions involving previously existing rather than currently produced assets.

Capital market: The market for stocks and long-term debt instruments.

Capitalism: An economic system characterized by private ownership, pricing, production, and distribution of goods.

Caribbean Community and Common Market (CARICOM): A customs union in the Caribbean region.

Caribbean Free Trade Association (CARIFTA): *See* Caribbean Community and Common Market.

CARICOM: *See* Caribbean Community and Common Market.

Caste: A social class separated from others by heredity.

CEFTA: *See* Central European Free Trade Association.

Central American Common Market (CACM): A customs union in Central America.

Central bank: A government "bank for banks," customarily responsible for a country's monetary policy.

Central European Free Trade Association (CEFTA): An association which went into effect on July 1, 1992, with an initial membership of the Czech Republic, Slovakia, Hungary, and Poland, and whose goal was to establish a free trade area that includes the basic trade structure of the EU by the year 2000.

Centralization: The situation in which decision making is done at the home office rather than at the country level.

Centrally planned economy (CPE): *See* Command economy.

Certificate of origin: A shipping document that determines the origin of products and is usually validated by an external source, such as a chamber of commerce; it helps countries determine the specific tariff schedule for imports.

CFC: *See* Controlled foreign corporation.

Chaebol: Korean business groups that are similar to *keiretsu* and also contain a trading company as part of the group.

Chicago Mercantile Exchange (CME): The largest commodity exchange in the world, dealing primarily in agricultural products, U.S. treasury bills, coins, and some metals.

CIA: The Central Intelligence Agency, a U.S. government agency charged with gathering intelligence information abroad.

Civil law system: A legal system based on a very detailed set of laws that are organized into a code; countries with a civil law system, also called a codified legal system, include Germany, France, and Japan.

Civil liberties: The freedom to develop one's own views and attitudes.

COCOM: *See* Coordinating Committee on Multilateral Exports.

Code of conduct: A set of principles guiding the actions of MNEs in their contacts with societies.

Codetermination: A process by which both labor and management participate in the management of a company.

Codified legal system: *See* Civil law system.

Collaborative arrangement: A formal, long-term contractual agreement among companies.

COMECON: *See* Council for Mutual Economic Assistance.

Command economy: An economic system in which resources are allocated and controlled by government decision.

Commercial bill of exchange: An instrument of payment in international business that instructs the importer to forward payment to the exporter.

Commercial invoice: A bill for goods from the buyer to the seller.

Commission on Transnational Corporations: A United Nations agency that deals with multinational enterprises.

Commodities: Basic raw materials or agricultural products.

Commodity agreement: A form of economic cooperation designed to stabilize and raise the price of a commodity.

Common Agricultural Policy: A set of rules and mechanisms that regulate the production, trade, and processing of agricultural products in the European Union (EU). Its objectives are to provide farmers with a reasonable standard of living and consumers with quality food at fair prices.

Common law system: A legal system based on tradition, precedent, and custom and usage, in which the courts interpret the law based on those conventions; found in the United Kingdom and former British colonies.

Common market: A form of regional economic integration in which countries abolish internal tariffs, use a common external tariff, and abolish restrictions on factor mobility.

Communism: A form of totalitarianism initially theorized by Karl Marx in which the political and economic systems are virtually inseparable.

Communitarian paradigm: The government defines needs and priorities and partners with business in a major way.

Comparable access: A protectionist argument that companies and industries should have the same access to foreign markets as foreign industries and companies have to their markets.

Comparative advantage: The theory that there may still be global efficiency gains from trade if a country specializes in those products that it can produce more efficiently than other products.

Compound duty: A tax placed on goods traded internationally, based on value plus units.

Concentration strategy: A strategy by which an international company builds up operations quickly in one or a few countries before going to another.

Confirmed letter of credit: A letter of credit to which a bank in the exporter's country adds its guarantee of payment.

Conservatism: A characteristic of accounting systems that implies that companies are hesitant to disclose high profits or profits that are consistent with their actual operating results; more common in Germanic countries.

Consolidation: An accounting process in which financial statements of related entities, such as a parent and its subsidiaries, are combined to yield a unified set of financial statements; in the process, transactions among the related enterprises are eliminated so that the statements reflect transactions with outside parties.

Consortium: The joining together of several entities, such as companies or governments, in order to strengthen the possibility of achieving some objective.

Consular invoice: A document that covers all the usual details of the commercial invoice and packing list, prepared in the language of the foreign country for which the goods are destined, on special forms obtainable from the consulate or authorized commercial printers.

Consumer-directed market economy: An economy in which there is minimal government participation while growth is promoted through the mobility of production factors, including high labor turnover.

Consumer price index (CPI): A measure of the cost of typical wage-earner purchases of goods and services expressed as a percentage of the cost of these same goods and services in some base period.

Consumer sovereignty: The freedom of consumers to influence production through the choices they make.

Continental terms: *See* European terms.

Control: The planning, implementation, evaluation, and correction of performance to ensure that organizational objectives are achieved.

Controlled foreign corporation (CFC): A foreign corporation of which more than 50 percent of the voting stock is owned by U.S. shareholders (taxable entities that own at least 10 percent of the voting stock of the corporation).

Convergence: Efforts by the FASB and IASC to move toward a common global set of accounting standards.

Convertibility: The ability to exchange one currency for another currency without restrictions.

Coordination: Linking or integrating activities into a unified system.

Copyright: The right to reproduce, publish, and sell literary, musical, or artistic works.

Core competency: Those functions of value creation in which the firm is most competent

Corporate culture: The common values shared by employees in a corporation, which form a control mechanism that is implicit and helps enforce other explicit control mechanisms.

Corporate social responsibility: An expression used to describe what some see as a company's obligation to be sensitive to the needs of "all" of its stakeholders in its business operations and produce an overall positive impact on society.

Correspondent (bank): A bank in which funds are kept by another, usually foreign, bank to facilitate check clearing and other business relationships.

Cost-of-living adjustment: An increase in compensation given to an expatriate employee when foreign living costs are more expensive than those in the home country.

Cost-plus strategy: The strategy of pricing at a desired margin over cost.

Council for Mutual Economic Assistance (CMEA or COMECON): A regional form of economic integration that involved essentially those communist countries considered to be within the Soviet bloc; terminated in 1991.

Council of Ministers: One of the five major institutions of the EU; composed of one member from each country in the EU and entrusted with making major policy decisions.

Countertrade: A reciprocal flow of goods or services valued and settled in monetary terms.

Country analysis: A process of examining the economic strategy of a nation state, taking a holistic approach to understanding how a country, and in particular its government, has behaved, is behaving, and may behave.

Country-similarity theory: The theory that a producer, having developed a new product in response to observed market conditions in the home market, will turn to markets that are most similar to those at home.

Country size theory: The theory that larger countries are generally more self-sufficient than smaller countries.

Court of Justice: One of the five major institutions of the EU; composed of one member from each country in the EU and serves as a supreme appeals court for EU law.

CPE (centrally planned economy): *See* Command economy.

Creolization: The process by which elements of an outside culture are introduced.

Cross-licensing: The exchange of technology by different companies.

Cross rate: An exchange rate between two currencies used in the spot market and computed from the exchange rate of each currency in relation to the U.S. dollar.

Cultural imperialism: Change by imposition.

Cultural relativism: The belief that behavior has meaning and can be judged only in its specific cultural context.

Culture: The specific learned norms of a society, based on attitudes, values, and beliefs.

Culture shock: A generalized trauma one experiences in a new and different culture because of having to learn and cope with a vast array of new cues and expectations.

Currency swaps: The exchange of principal and interest payments.

Current-account balance: Exports minus imports of goods, services, and unilateral transfers.

Current-rate method: A method of translating foreign-currency financial statements that is used when the functional currency is that of the local operating environment.

Customary law system: A legal system anchored in the wisdom of daily experience or great spiritual or philosophical traditions.

Customs duties: Taxes imposed on imported goods.

Customs union: A form of regional economic integration that eliminates internal tariffs among member nations and establishes common external tariffs.

Customs valuation: The value of goods on which customs authorities charge tariffs.

Debt-service ratio: The ratio of interest payments plus principal amortization to exports.

Decentralization: The situation in which decisions tend to be made at lower levels in a company or at the country-operating level rather than at headquarters.

Deferral: The postponing of taxation of foreign-source income until it is remitted to the parent company.

Demand conditions: Includes three dimensions: the composition of home demand (or the nature of buyer needs), the size and pattern of growth of home demand, and the internationalization of demand.

Democracy: A political system that relies on citizens' participation in the decision-making process.

Dependencia theory: The theory holding that LDCs have practically no power when dealing with MNEs as host countries.

Dependency: A state in which a country is too dependent on the sale of one primary commodity and/or too dependent on one country as a customer and supplier.

Derivative: A foreign-exchange instrument such as an option or futures contract that derives its value from some underlying financial instrument.

Derivatives market: Market in which forward contracts, futures, options, and swaps are traded in order to hedge or protect foreign-exchange transactions.

Devaluation: A formal reduction in the value of a currency in relation to another currency; the foreign-currency equivalent of the devalued currency falls.

Developed country: High-income country. Also called industrial country.

Developing country: A poor country. Also known as an emerging country.

Direct foreign investment: *See* Foreign direct investment.

Direct identification drawback: A provision that allows U.S. firms to use imported components in the manufacturing process without having to include the duty paid on the imported goods in costs and sales prices.

Direct investment: *See* Foreign direct investment.

Direct quote: A quote expressed in terms of the number of units of the domestic currency given for one unit of a foreign currency.

Direct selling: A sale of goods by an exporter directly to distributors or final consumers rather than to trading companies or other intermediaries in order to achieve greater control over the marketing function and to earn higher profits.

Directive: A proposed form of legislation in the EU.

Disclosure: The presentation of information and discussion of results.

Discount (in foreign exchange): A situation in which the forward rate for a foreign currency is less than the spot rate, assuming that the domestic currency is quoted on a direct basis.

Distribution: The course—physical path or legal title—that goods take between production and consumption.

Distributor: A merchant in a foreign country that purchases products from the manufacturer and sells them at a profit.

Diversification: A process of becoming less dependent on one or a few customers or suppliers.

Diversification strategy: A strategy by which an international company produces or sells in many countries to avoid relying on one particular market.

Divestment: Reduction in the amount of investment.

Documentary draft: An instrument instructing the importer to pay the exporter if certain documents are presented.

Draft: An instrument of payment in international business that instructs the importer to forward payment to the exporter.

Drawback: A provision allowing U.S. exporters to apply for refunds of 99 percent of the duty paid on imported components, provided they are used in the manufacture of goods that are exported.

Dumping: The underpricing of exports, usually below cost or below the home-country price.

Duty: A government tax (tariff) levied on goods shipped internationally. Also called tariff.

Dynamic effects of integration: The overall growth in the market and the impact on a company of expanding production and achieving greater economies of scale.

EC: *See* European Community.

E-commerce: The use of the Internet to join together suppliers with companies and companies with customers.

Economic Community of West African States (ECOWAS): A form of economic integration among certain countries in West Africa.

Economic exposure: The foreign-exchange risk that international businesses face in the pricing of products, the source and cost of inputs, and the location of investments.

Economic Freedom Index: The Economic Freedom Index is the systematic measurement of economic freedom in countries throughout the world. The survey is sponsored by the Heritage Foundation and Wall Street Journal.

Economic integration: The abolition of economic discrimination between national economies, such as within the EU.

Economic system: The system concerned with the allocation of scarce resources.

Economics: A social science concerned chiefly with the description and analysis of the production, distribution, and consumption of goods and services.

Economies of scale: The lowering of cost per unit as output increases because of allocation of fixed costs over more units produced.

ECOWAS: *See* Economic Community of West African States.

ECU: *See* European Currency Unit.

EEC: *See* European Economic Community.

EEC Patent Convention (EPC): An important cross-national patent convention that involves the members of the EU.

Effective tariff: The real tariff on the manufactured portion of developing countries' exports, which is higher than indicated by the published rates because the ad valorem tariff is based on the total value of the products, which includes raw materials that would have had duty-free entry.

EFTA: *See* European Free Trade Association.

Elastic (product demand): A condition in which sales are likely to increase or decrease by a percentage that is more than the percentage change in income.

Electronic data interchange (EDI): The electronic movement of money and information via computers and telecommunications equipment.

Embargo: A specific type of quota that prohibits all trade.

EMC: *See* Export management company.

Emerging country: Low- and middle-income country. Also known as developing country.

EMS: *See* European Monetary System.

Enterprise resource planning (ERP): Software that can link information flows from different parts of a business and from different geographic areas.

Entrepôt: A country that is an import/export or investment intermediary; for example, Hong Kong is an entrepôt for trade between China and the rest of the world, and Luxembourg is an entrepôt for many countries' foreign direct investment.

Environmental climate: The external conditions in host countries that could significantly affect the success of a foreign business enterprise.

Environmental scanning: The systematic assessment of external conditions that might affect a company's operations.

EPC: *See* European Patent Convention.

Equity alliance: A situation in which a cooperating company takes an equity position (almost always a minority) in the company with which it has a collaborative arrangement.

ERP: *See* Enterprise resource planning.

Essential-industry argument: The argument holding that certain domestic industries need protection for national security purposes.

ETC: *See* Export trading company.

Ethnocentrism: A belief that one's own group is superior to others; also used to describe a company's belief that what worked at home should work abroad.

Eurobond: A bond sold in a country other than the one in whose currency it is denominated.

Eurocredit: A loan, line of credit, or other form of medium- or long-term credit on the Eurocurrency market that has a maturity of more than one year.

Eurocurrency: Any currency that is banked outside of its country of origin.

Eurocurrency market: An international wholesale market that deals in Eurocurrencies.

Eurodollars: Dollars banked outside of the United States.

Euroequity market: The market for shares sold outside the boundaries of the issuing company's home country.

European Central Bank (ECB): Established July 1, 1998, the ECB is responsible for setting the monetary policy and for managing the exchange-rate system for all of Europe since January 1, 1999.

European Commission: One of the five major institutions of the EU; composed of a president, six vice presidents, and 10 other members whose allegiance is to the EU and serving as an executive branch for the EU.

European Community (EC): The predecessor of the European Union.

European Council: One of the five major institutions of the European Union; made up of the heads of state of each of the EU members.

European Court of Justice: The court of the European Union. The Court is an appeals court and ensures interpretation and application of EU treaties.

European Currency Unit (ECU): A unit of account based on a currency basket composed of the currencies of the members of the EU.

European Economic Community (EEC): The predecessor of the European Community.

European Free Trade Association (EFTA): A free-trade area among a group of European countries that are not members of the EU.

European Monetary System (EMS): A cooperative foreign-exchange agreement involving most of the members of the EU and designed to promote exchange-rate stability within the EU.

European Monetary Union: An agreement by participating European Union member countries that consists of three stages coordinating economic policy and culminating with the adoption of the euro.

European Parliament: One of the five major institutions of the EU; its representatives are elected directly in each member country.

European Patent Convention (EPC): A European agreement allowing companies to make a uniform patent search and application, which is then passed on to all signatory countries.

European terms: The practice of using the indirect quote for exchange rates.

European Union (EU): A form of regional economic integration among countries in Europe that involves a free-trade area, a customs union, and the free mobility of factors of production that is working toward political and economic union.

Exchange rate: The price of one currency in terms of another currency.

Eximbank: *See* Export-Import Bank.

Exotic currencies: The currencies of developing countries. Also called exotics.

Expatriates: Noncitizens of the country in which they are working.

Experience curve: The relationship of production-cost reductions to increases in output.

Export-Import Bank (Eximbank): A U.S. federal agency specializing in foreign lending to support exports.

Export-led development: An industrialization policy emphasizing industries that will have export capabilities.

Export license: A document that grants a government permission to ship certain products to a specific country.

Export management company (EMC): A company that buys merchandise from manufacturers for international distribution or sometimes acts as an agent for manufacturers.

Export packing list: A shipping document that itemizes the material in each individual package and indicates the type of package.

Export tariff: A tax on goods leaving a country.

Export trading company (ETC): A form of trading company sanctioned by U.S. law to become involved in international commerce as independent distributors to match up foreign buyers with domestic sellers.

Exports: Goods or services leaving a country.

Exposure: A situation in which a foreign-exchange account is subject to a gain or loss if the exchange rate changes.

Exposure draft: The first draft of an accounting standard, which is open to comment by parties other than the IASC.

Expropriation: The taking over of ownership of private property by a country's government.

Externalities: External economic costs related to a business activity.

Extranet: The use of the Internet to link a company with outsiders.

Extraterritoriality: The extension by a government of the application of its laws to foreign operations of companies.

Factor conditions: Inputs to the production process, such as human, physical, knowledge, and capital resources, and also infrastructure.

Factoring: The discounting of a foreign account receivable.

Factor mobility: The free movement of factors of production, such as labor and capital, across national borders.

Factor-proportions theory: The theory that differences in a country's proportionate holdings of factors of production (land, labor, and capital) explain differences in the costs of the factors and that export advantages lie in the production of goods that use the most abundant factors.

FASB: *See* Financial Accounting Standards Board.

Fatalism: A belief that events are fixed in advance and that human beings are powerless to change them.

Favorable balance of trade: An indication that a country is exporting more than it imports.

FCPA: *See* Foreign Corrupt Practices Act.

FDI: *See* Foreign direct investment.

Fees: Payments for the performance of certain activities abroad.

Financial Accounting Standards Board (FASB): The private-sector organization that sets financial accounting standards in the United States.

FIRA: *See* Foreign Investment Review Act.

First-in advantage: Any benefit gained in terms of brand recognition and the lining up of the best suppliers, distributors, and local partners as a result of entering a market before competitors do.

First-mover advantage: A cost-reduction advantage due to economies of scale attained through moving into a foreign market ahead of competitors.

Fisher Effect: The theory about the relationship between inflation and interest rates; for example, if the nominal interest rate in one country is lower than that in another, the first country's inflation should be lower so that the real interest rates will be equal.

Fixed price: A method of pricing in which bargaining does not take place.

Floating currency: A currency whose value responds to the supply of and demand for that currency.

Floating exchange rate: An exchange rate determined by the laws of supply and demand and with minimal government interference.

Foreign bond: A bond sold outside of the borrower's country but denominated in the currency of the country of issue.

Foreign Corrupt Practices Act (FCPA): A law that criminalizes certain types of payments by U.S. companies, such as bribes to foreign government officials.

Foreign direct investment (FDI): An investment that gives the investor a controlling interest in a foreign company.

Foreign exchange: Checks and other instruments for making payments in another country's currency.

Foreign-exchange control: A requirement that an importer of a product must apply to government authorities for permission to buy foreign currency to pay for the product.

Foreign freight forwarder: A company that facilitates the movement of goods from one country to another.

Foreign investment: Direct or portfolio ownership of assets in another country.

Foreign Investment Review Act (FIRA): A Canadian law intended to limit foreign control of that country's economy.

Foreign sales corporation (FSC): A special type of corporation established by U.S. tax law that can be used by a U.S. exporter to shelter some of its income from taxation.

Foreign trade zone (FTZ): A government-designated area in which goods can be stored, inspected, or manufactured without being subject to formal customs procedures until they leave the zone.

Forfaiting: Similar to factoring but usually for longer time periods and with a guarantee from a bank in the importer's country.

Forward contract: A contract between a company or individual and a bank to deliver foreign currency at a specific exchange rate on a future date.

Forward discount: *See* Discount.

Forward premium: *See* Premium.

Forward rate: A contractually established exchange rate between a foreign-exchange trader and the trader's client for delivery of foreign currency on a specific date.

Franchising: A specialized form of licensing in which one party (the franchisor) sells to an independent party (the franchisee) the use of a trademark that is an essential asset for the franchisee's business and also gives continual assistance in the operation of the business.

Freely convertible currency: *See* Hard currency.

Free trade agreement: An agreement between countries that has the goal of abolishing all tariffs between member countries.

Free trade area (FTA): A form of regional economic integration in which internal tariffs are abolished, but member countries set their own external tariffs.

Freight forwarder: *See* Foreign freight forwarder.

Fringe benefit: Any employee benefit other than salary, wages, and cash bonuses.

FSC: *See* Foreign sales corporation.

FTZ: *See* Foreign trade zone.

Functional currency: The currency of the primary economic environment in which an entity operates.

Functional division: An organizational structure in which each function in foreign countries (e.g., marketing or production) reports separately to a counterpart functional group at head-quarters.

Fundamental forecasting: A forecasting tool that uses trends in economic vari-ables to predict future exchange rates.

Futures contract: An agreement between two parties to buy or sell a particular currency at a particular price on a par-ticular future date, as specified in a standardized contract to all partici-pants in that currency futures exchange.

FX swap: A simultaneous spot and for-ward transaction.

G7 countries: *See* Group of 7.

GAAP: *See* Generally accepted account-ing principles.

Gap analysis: A tool used to discover why a company's sales of a given product are less than the market potential in a country; the reason may be a usage, competition, product line, or distribution gap.

GATT: *See* General Agreement on Tariffs and Trade.

General Agreement on Tariffs and Trade (GATT): A multilateral arrangement aimed at reducing barriers to trade, both tariff and nontariff ones; at the signing of the Uruguay round, the GATT was designated to become the World Trade Organization (WTO).

Generalized System of Preferences (GSP): Preferential import restrictions extended by industrial countries to developing countries.

Generally accepted accounting principles (GAAP): The accounting standards accepted by the accounting profession in each country as required for the preparation of financial state-ments for external users.

Generic: Any of a class of products, rather than the brand of a particular company.

Geocentric: Operations based on an informed knowledge of both home and host country needs.

Geographic division: An organizational structure in which a company's opera-tions are separated for reporting purposes into regional areas.

Geography: A science dealing with the earth and its life, especially with the description of land, sea, air, and the distribution of plant and animal life.

Global bond: A combination of domestic bond and Eurobond that is issued simultaneously in several markets and that must be registered in each national market according to that market's registration requirements.

Global company: A company that inte-grates operations located in different countries.

Globally integrated company: *See* Global company.

Global sourcing: The acquisition on a worldwide basis of raw materials, parts, and subassemblies for the manufacturing process.

Go-no-go decision: A decision, such as on foreign investments, that is based on minimum-threshold criteria and does not compare different opportunities.

Grandchild subsidiary: An operation that is under a tax-haven subsidiary. Also called a second-tier subsidiary.

Grantback provisions: Stipulations requiring that licen*see*s provide licen-sors with the use of improvements made on the technology originally licensed.

Gray market: The handling of goods through unofficial distributors.

Gross domestic product (GDP): The total of all economic activity in a country, regardless of who owns the productive assets.

Gross national income (GNI): Formerly referred to as Gross National Product.

Gross national product (GNP): The total of incomes earned by residents of a country, regardless of where the productive assets are located.

Group of 7 (G7): A group of developed countries that periodically meets to make economic decisions; this group consists of Canada, France, Germany, Italy, Japan, the United Kingdom, and the United States.

Group of 8 (G8): The Group of 7 (G7) plus Russia.

GSP: *See* Generalized System of Preferences.

Hard currency: A currency that is freely traded without many restrictions and for which there is usually strong external demand; often called a freely convertible currency.

Hardship allowance: A supplement to compensate expatriates for working in dangerous or adverse conditions.

Harvesting: Reduction in the amount of investment. Also known as divestment.

Hedge: To attempt to protect foreign-currency holdings against an adverse movement of an exchange rate.

Heterarchy: An organizational structure in which management of an alliance of companies is shared by so-called equals rather than being set up in a superior-subordinate relationship.

Hierarchy of needs: A well-known moti-vation theory stating that there is a hierarchy of needs and that people must fulfill the lower-order needs sufficiently before they will be moti-vated by the higher-order ones.

High-context culture: A culture in which most people consider that peripheral and hearsay information is necessary for decision making because such information bears on the context of the situation.

High-need achiever: One who will work very hard to achieve material or career success, sometimes to the detriment of social relationships or spiritual achievements.

High-value activities: Activities that either produce high profits or are done by high-salaried employees such as managers.

Historically planned economy (HPE): The World Bank's term for Second-World countries in transition to market economies.

History: A branch of knowledge that records and explains past events.

Home country: The country in which an international company is headquartered.

Home-country nationals: Expatriate employees who are citizens of the country in which the company is headquartered.

Horizontal differentiation: How the company specifies, divides, and assigns the set of organizational tasks.

Horizontal expansion: Any foreign direct investment by which a company produces the same product it produces at home.

Host country: Any foreign country in which an international company operates.

HPE: *See* Historically planned economy.

Human development index: A measurement of human progress introduced by the United Nations Development Programme that combines indicators of purchasing power, education, and health.

Hyperinflation: A rapid increase (at least 1 percent per day) in general price levels for a sustained period of time.

IASC: *See* International Accounting Standards Committee.

Idealism: Trying to determine principles before settling small issues.

Ideology: The systematic and integrated body of constructs, theories, and aims that constitute a society.

IFE: *See* International Fisher Effect.

IFRS: A set of accounting standards often known by the older name of International Accounting Standards (IAS). They are issued by the International Accounting Standards Board (IASB).

ILO: *See* International Labor Organization.

IMF: *See* International Monetary Fund.

Imitation lag: A strategy for exploiting temporary monopoly advantages by moving first to those countries most likely to develop local production.

Import broker: An individual who obtains various government permissions and other clearances before forwarding necessary paperwork to the carrier that will deliver the goods from the dock to the importer.

Import deposit requirement: Government requirement of a deposit prior to the release of foreign exchange.

Import licensing: A method of government control of the exchange rate whereby all recipients, exporters, and others who receive foreign exchange are required to sell to the central bank at the official buying rate.

Import substitution: An industrialization policy whereby new industrial development emphasizes products that would otherwise be imported.

Import tariff: A tax placed on goods entering a country.

Imports: Goods or services entering a country.

In-bond industry: Any industry that is allowed to import components free of duty, provided that the components will be reexported after processing.

Independence: An extreme situation in which a country would not rely on other countries at all.

Indigenization: The process of introducing elements of an outside culture.

Indirect quote: An exchange rate given in terms of the number of units of the foreign currency for one unit of the domestic currency.

Indirect selling: A sale of goods by an exporter through another domestic company as an intermediary.

Individualistic paradigm: Minimal government intervention in the economy.

Individually validated license (IVL): A special export license under which certain restricted products need to be shipped.

Industrial country: High-income country. Also known as developed country.

Industrialization argument: A rationale for protectionism that argues that the development of industrial output should come about even though domestic prices may not become competitive on the world market.

Inelastic (product demand): A condition in which sales are likely to increase or decline by a percentage that is less than the percentage change in income.

Infant-industry argument: The position that holds that an emerging industry should be guaranteed a large share of the domestic market until it becomes efficient enough to compete against imports.

Inflation: A condition where prices are going up.

Infrastructure: The underlying foundation of a society, such as roads, schools, and so forth, that allows it to function effectively.

Input-output table: A tool used widely in national economic planning to show the resources utilized by different industries for a given output as well as the interdependence of economic sectors.

Intangible property: *See* Intellectual property rights.

Integrated system: A system for taxation of corporate income aimed at preventing double taxation through the use of split rates or tax credits.

Intellectual property rights: Ownership rights to intangible assets, such as patents, trademarks, copyrights, and know-how.

Interbank market: The market for foreign-exchange transactions among commercial banks.

Interbank transactions: Foreign-exchange transactions that take place between commercial banks.

Interdependence: The existence of mutually necessary economic relations among countries.

Interest arbitrage: Investing in debt instruments in different countries and earning a profit due to interest-rate and exchange-rate differentials.

Interest rate differential: An indicator of future changes in the spot exchange rate.

Intermodal transportation: The movement across different modes from origin to destination.

Internalization: Control through selfhandling of foreign operations, primarily because such control is less expensive to deal with in the same corporate family than to contract with an external organization.

International Accounting Standards Committee (IASC): The international private-sector organization that sets financial accounting standards for worldwide use.

International Bureau for the Protection of Industrial Property Rights (BIRPI): A multilateral agreement to protect patents, trademarks, and other property rights.

International business: All business transactions involving private companies or governments of two or more countries.

International division: An organizational structure in which virtually all foreign operations are handled within the same division.

International Fisher Effect (IFE): The theory that the relationship between interest rates and exchange rates implies that the currency of the country with the lower interest rate will strengthen in the future.

International Labor Organization (ILO): A multilateral organization promoting the adoption of humane labor conditions.

International Monetary Fund (IMF): A multigovernmental association organized in 1945 to promote exchange-rate stability and to facilitate the international flow of currencies.

International Monetary Market (IMM): A specialized market located in Chicago and dealing in select foreign-currency futures.

International Organization of Securities Commissions (IOSCO): An international organization of securities regulators that wants the IASC to establish more comprehensive accounting standards.

International standard of fair dealing: The concept that investors should receive prompt, adequate, and effective compensation in cases of expropriation.

International Trade Administration (ITA): A branch of the U.S. Department of Commerce offering a variety of services to U.S. exporting companies.

Intervention currencies: The currencies in which a particular country trades the most.

Intranet: The use of the Internet to link together the different divisions and functions inside a company.

Intrazonal trade: Trade among countries that are part of a trade agreement, such as the EU.

Investment Canada: A Canadian act whose intent is to persuade foreign companies to invest in Canada.

Invisibles: *See* Services.

IOSCO: *See* International Organization of Securities Commissions.

Irrevocable letter of credit (L/C): A letter of credit that cannot be canceled or changed without the consent of all parties involved.

Islamic law: A system of theocratic law based on the religious teachings of Islam. Also called Muslim law.

ISO 9000: A quality standard developed by the International Standards Organization in Geneva that requires companies to document their commitment to quality at all levels of the organization.

IVL: *See* Individually validated license.

Jamaica Agreement: A 1976 agreement among countries that permitted greater flexibility of exchange rates, basically formalizing the break from fixed exchange rates.

JIT: *See* Just-in-time manufacturing.

Joint venture: A direct investment of which two or more companies share the ownership.

Just-in-time (JIT) manufacturing: A system that reduces inventory costs by having components and parts delivered as they are needed in production.

Kaizen: The Japanese process of continuous improvement, the cornerstone of TQM.

Keiretsu: A corporate relationship linking certain Japanese companies, usually involving a noncontrolling interest in each other, strong high-level personal relationships among managers in the different companies, and interlocking directorships.

Key industry: Any industry that might affect a very large segment of a country's economy or population by virtue of its size or influence on other sectors.

Labor market: The mix of available workers and labor costs available to companies.

Labor union: An association of workers intended to promote and protect the welfare, interests, and rights of its members, primarily by collective bargaining.

LAFTA: *See* Latin American Free Trade Association.

Lag strategy: An operational strategy that involves either delaying collection of foreign-currency receivables if the currency is expected to strengthen or delaying payment of foreign-currency payables when the currency is expected to weaken; the opposite of a lead strategy.

Laissez-faire: The concept of minimal government intervention in a society's economic activity.

Latin American Free Trade Association (LAFTA): A free-trade area formed by Mexico and the South American countries in 1960; it was replaced by ALADI in 1980.

Latin American Integration Association (ALADI): A form of regional economic integration involving most of the Latin American countries.

Law: A binding custom or practice of a community.

Lead country strategy: A strategy of introducing a product on a test basis in a small-country market that is considered representative of a region before investing to serve larger-country markets.

Lead strategy: An operational strategy that involves either collecting foreign-currency receivables before they are due when the currency is expected to weaken or paying foreign-currency payables before they are due when the currency is expected to strengthen; the opposite of a lag strategy.

Lead subsidiary organization: A foreign subsidiary that has global responsibility (serves as corporate headquarters) for one of a company's products or functions.

Learning curve: A concept used to support the infant-industry argument for protection; it assumes that costs will decline as workers and managers gain more experience.

Letter of credit (L/C): A precise document by which the importer's bank extends credit to the importer and agrees to pay the exporter.

Leverage: The degree to which a firm funds the growth of the business debt.

Liability of foreignness: Foreign companies' lower survival rate in comparison to local companies for many years after they begin operations.

LIBOR: *See* London Inter-Bank Offered Rate.

License: Formal or legal permission to do some specified action; a government method of fixing the exchange rate by requiring all recipients, exporters, and others that receive foreign exchange to sell it to the central bank at the official buying rate.

Licensing agreement: Agreement whereby one company gives rights to another for the use, usually for a fee, of such assets as trademarks, patents, copyrights, or other know-how.

Licensing arrangement: A procedure that requires potential importers or exporters to secure permission from government authorities before they conduct trade transactions.

Lifetime employment: The Japanese custom that workers are effectively guaranteed employment with the company for their working lifetimes and that workers seldom leave for employment opportunities with other companies.

LIFFE: *See* London International Financial Futures Exchange.

Liquidity preference: A theory that helps explain capital budgeting and, when applied to international operations, means that investors are willing to take less return in order to be able to shift the resources to alternative uses.

Lobbyist: An individual who participates in advancing or otherwise securing passage of legislation by influencing public officials before and during the legislative process.

Local content: Costs incurred within a given country, usually as a percentage of total costs.

Locally responsive company: Synonym for multidomestic company.

Locals: Citizens of the country in which they are working.

Location-specific advantage: A combination of factor and demand conditions, along with other qualities, that a country has to offer domestic and foreign investors.

Logistics: That part of the supply chain process that plans, implements, and controls the efficient, effective flow and storage of goods, services, and related information from the point of origin to the point of consumption, to meet customers' requirements; sometimes called materials management.

London Inter-Bank Offered Rate (LIBOR): The interest rate for large interbank loans of Eurocurrencies.

London International Financial Futures Exchange (LIFFE): An exchange dealing in futures contracts for several major currencies.

London Stock Exchange (LSE): A stock exchange located in London and dealing in Euroequities.

Low-context culture: A culture in which most people consider relevant only information that they receive firsthand and that bears very directly on the decision they need to make.

Maastricht (Treaty of): The treaty approved in December 1991 that was designed to bring the EU to a higher level of integration and is divided into the Economic Monetary Union (EMU) and political union.

Macro political risk: Negative political actions affecting a broad spectrum of foreign investors.

Management contract: An arrangement whereby one company provides management personnel, who perform general or specialized management functions to another company for a fee.

Manufacturing interchange: A process by which various plants produce a range of components and exchange them so that all plants assemble the finished product for the local market.

Maquiladora: An industrial operation, originally developed between the United States and Mexico but now used in other geographic areas, in which components may be shipped duty free, assembled, and then re-exported.

Marginal propensity to import: The tendency to purchase imports with incremental income.

Market capitalization: A common measure of the size of a stock market, which is computed by multiplying the total number of shares of stock listed on the exchange by the market price per share.

Market economy: An economic system in which resources are allocated and controlled by consumers who "vote" by buying goods.

Market environment: The environment that involves the interactions between households (or individuals) and companies in the allocation of resources, free from government ownership or control.

Market socialism: The state owns significant resources, but allocation comes from the market price mechanism.

Materials management: *See* Logistics.

Matrix: A method of plotting data on a set of vertical and horizontal axes in order to compare countries in terms of risk and opportunity.

Matrix division structure: An organizational structure in which foreign units report (by product, function, or area) to more than one group, each of which shares responsibility over the foreign unit.

Measurement: How to value assets.

Mentor: A person at headquarters who looks after the interests of an expatriate employee.

Mercantilism: An economic philosophy based on the beliefs that a country's wealth is dependent on its holdings of treasure, usually in the form of gold, and that countries should export more than they import in order to increase wealth.

Merchandise exports: Goods sent out of a country.

Merchandise imports: Goods brought into a country.

Merchandise trade balance: The part of a country's current account that measures the trade deficit or surplus; its balance is the net of merchandise imports and exports.

MERCOSUR: A major subregional group established by Argentina, Brazil, Paraguay, and Uruguay, which spun off from ALADI in 1991 with the goal of setting up a customs union and common market.

MFA: *See* Multifibre Arrangement.

MFN: *See* Most-favored-nation.

Micro political risk: Negative political actions aimed at specific, rather than most, foreign investors.

Middle East: The countries on the Arabian peninsula plus those bordering the eastern end of the Mediterranean; sometimes also including other adjacent countries, particularly Jordan, Iraq, Iran, and Kuwait.

Ministry of International Trade and Industry (MITI): The Japanese government agency responsible for coordinating overall business direction and helping individual companies take advantage of global business opportunities.

Mission: What the company will *seek* to do and become over the long term.

Mission statement: A long-range strategic intent.

Mixed economy: An economic system characterized by some mixture of market and command economies and public and private ownership.

Mixed legal system: A legal system that emerges when two or more legal systems function in a country.

Mixed venture: A special type of joint venture in which a government is in partnership with a private company.

MNE: *See* Multinational enterprise.

Monochronic culture: A culture in which most people prefer to deal with situations sequentially (especially those involving other people), such as finishing with one customer before dealing with another.

Monopoly advantage: The perceived supremacy of foreign investors in relation to local companies, which is necessary to overcome the perceived greater risk of operating in a different environment.

Most-favored-nation (MFN): A GATT requirement that a trade concession that is given to one country must be given to all other countries.

Multidomestic company: A company with international operations that allows operations in one country to be relatively independent of those in other countries.

Multilateral agreement: An agreement involving more than two governments.

Multilateral Investment Guarantee Agency (MIGA): A member of the World Bank Group that encourages equity investment and other direct investment flows to developing countries by offering investors a variety of different services.

Multinational corporation (MNC): A synonym for multinational enterprise.

Multinational enterprise (MNE): A company that has an integrated global philosophy encompassing both domestic and overseas operations; sometimes used synonymously with multinational corporation or transnational corporation.

Multiple exchange-rate system: A means of foreign-exchange control whereby the government sets different exchange rates for different transactions.

Muslim law: *See* Islamic law.

Mutual recognition: The principle that a foreign registrant that wants to list and have its securities traded on a foreign stock exchange need only provide information prepared according to the GAAP of the home country.

National responsiveness: Readiness to implement operating adjustments in foreign countries in order to reach a satisfactory level of performance.

Nationalism: The feeling of pride and/or ethnocentrism that focuses on an individual's home country or nation.

Nationalization: The transfer of ownership to the state.

Natural advantage: Climatic conditions, access to certain natural resources, or availability of labor, which gives a country an advantage in producing some product.

Need hierarchy: *See* Hierarchy of needs.

Neomercantilism: The approach of countries that apparently try to run favorable balances of trade in an attempt to achieve some social or political objective.

Net capital flow: Capital inflow minus capital outflow, for other than import and export payment.

Net export effect: Export stimulus minus export reduction.

Net import change: Import displacement minus import stimulus.

Net present value: The sum of the present values of the annual cash flows minus the initial investment.

Netting: The transfer of funds from subsidiaries in a net payable position to a central clearing account and from there to the accounts of the net receiver subsidiaries.

Network alliance: Interdependence of companies; each company is a customer of and a supplier to other companies.

Network organization: A situation in which a group of companies is interrelated and in which the management of the interrelation is shared among so-called equals.

Newly industrializing country (NIC): A developing country in which the cultural and economic climate has led to a rapid rate of industrialization and growth since the 1960s.

Nonmarket economy: *See* Command economy.

Nonmarket environment: Public institutions (such as government, government agencies, and government-owned businesses) and nonpublic institutions (such as environmental and other special-interest groups).

Nonpublic institutions: Special-interest groups, such as environmentalists.

Nonresident convertibility: The ability of a nonresident of a country to convert deposits in a bank to the currency of any other country; also known as external convertibility.

Nontariff barriers: Barriers to imports that are not tariffs; examples include administrative controls, "Buy America" policies, and so forth.

Nontradable goods: Products and services that are seldom practical to export, primarily because of high transportation costs.

Normal trade relations: A privilege that replaced the most-favored-nation clause and is granted to official members of the WTO.

Normal quote: Synonym for direct quote.

Normativism: A theory stating that universal standards of behavior (based on people's own values) exist that all cultures should follow, making nonintervention unethical.

North American Free Trade Agreement (NAFTA): A free-trade agreement involving the United States, Canada, and Mexico that went into effect on January 1, 1994, and will be phased in over a period of 15 years.

OAU: *See* Organization of African Unity.

Objectives: Specific performance targets to fulfill a company's mission.

Obsolescing bargain (theory of): The premise that a company's bargaining strength with a host government diminishes after the company transfers assets to the host country.

OECD: *See* Organization for Economic Cooperation and Development.

OEEC: *See* Organization for European Economic Cooperation.

Offer rate: The amount for which a foreign-exchange trader is willing to sell a currency.

Official reserves: A country's holdings of monetary gold, Special Drawing Rights, and internationally acceptable currencies.

Offset: A form of barter transaction in which an export is paid for with other merchandise.

Offset trade: A form of countertrade in which an exporter sells goods for cash but then helps businesses in the importing country to find opportunities to earn hard currency.

Offshore financial centers: Cities or countries that provide large amounts of funds in currencies other than their own and are used as locations in which to raise and accumulate cash.

Offshore financing: The provision of financial services by banks and other agents to nonresidents.

Offshoring: The process of shifting production to a foreign country.

Oligopolistic reaction: The process in oligopoly industries for competitors to emulate each other, such as going to the same locations.

Oligopoly: An industry in which there are few producers or sellers.

OPEC: *See* Organization of Petroleum Exporting Countries.

Open account: Conditions of sale under which the exporter extends credit directly to the importer.

Operational centers: Offshore financial centers that perform specific functions, such as the sale and servicing of goods.

OPIC: *See* Overseas Private Investment Corporation.

Opinion leader: One whose acceptance of some concept is apt to be emulated by others.

Optimism: A characteristic of an accounting system that implies that companies are more liberal in recognition of income.

Optimum-tariff theory: The argument that a foreign producer will lower its prices if an import tax is placed on its products.

Option: A foreign-exchange instrument that gives the purchaser the right, but not the obligation, to buy or sell a certain amount of foreign currency at a set exchange rate within a specified amount of time.

Organization of African Unity (OAU): An organization of African nations that is more concerned with political than economic objectives.

Organization culture: The values, beliefs, business principles, traditions, ways of doing things, and nature of internal work environment within a company.

Organization for Economic Cooperation and Development (OECD): A multilateral organization of industrialized and semi-industrialized countries that helps to formulate social and economic policies.

Organization for European Economic Cooperation (OEEC): A 16-nation organization established in 1948 to facilitate the utilization of aid from the Marshall Plan; it evolved into the EU and EFTA.

Organization of Petroleum Exporting Countries (OPEC): A producers' alliance among 12 petroleum-exporting countries that attempt to agree on oil production and pricing policies.

Organization structure: The formal arrangement of roles, responsibilities, and relationships within an organization.

Outright forward: A forward contract that is not connected to a spot transaction.

Outsourcing: The use by a domestic company of foreign suppliers for components or finished products.

Overseas Private Investment Corporation (OPIC): A U.S. government agency that provides insurance for companies involved in international business.

Over-the-counter (OTC) market: Trading in stocks, usually of smaller companies, that are not listed on one of the stock exchanges; also refers to how government and corporate bonds are traded, through dealers who quote bids and offers to buy and to sell "over the counter."

Par value: The benchmark value of a currency, originally quoted in terms of gold or the U.S. dollar and now quoted in terms of Special Drawing Rights.

Parliamentary system: A form of government that involves the election of representatives to form the executive branch.

Passive income: Income from investments in tax-haven countries or sales and services income that involves buyers and sellers in other than the tax-haven country, where either the buyer or the seller must be part of the same organizational structure as the corporation that earns the income; also known as Subpart F income.

Patent: A right granted by a sovereign power or state for the protection of an invention or discovery against infringement.

Patent Cooperation Treaty (PCT): A multilateral agreement to protect patents.

Payback: The number of years required to recover the initial investment made.

PCT: *See* Patent Cooperation Treaty.

Peg: To fix a currency's exchange rate to some benchmark, such as another currency.

Penetration strategy: A strategy of introducing a product at a low price to induce a maximum number of consumers to try it.

Philadelphia Stock Exchange (PHLX): The only exchange in the United States that trades foreign-currency options.

Piggyback exporting: Use by an exporter of another exporter as an intermediary.

Piracy: The unauthorized use of property rights that are protected by patents, trademarks, or copyrights.

Planning: The meshing of objectives with internal and external constraints in order to set means to implement, monitor, and correct operations.

Plant layout: Decisions about the physical arrangement of economic activity centers within a manufacturing facility.

PLC: *See* Product life cycle theory.

Pluralistic societies: Societies in which different ideologies are held by various segments rather than one ideology being adhered to by all.

Political freedom: The right to participate freely in the political process.

Political ideology: The body of constructs (complex ideas), theories, and aims that constitute a sociopolitical program.

Political risk: Potential changes in political conditions that may cause a company's operating positions to deteriorate.

Political science: A discipline that helps explain the patterns of governments and their actions.

Political system: The system designed to integrate a society into a viable, functioning unit.

Polycentrism: Characteristic of an individual or organization that feels that differences in a foreign country, real and imaginary, great and small, need to be accounted for in management decisions.

Polychronic culture: A culture in which most people are more comfortable dealing simultaneously with all the situations facing them.

Porter diamond: A diagram showing four conditions—demand (conditions); factor endowments (conditions); related and supporting industries; and firm strategy, structure, and rivalry—that usually must all be favorable for an industry in a country to develop and sustain a global competitive advantage.

Portfolio investment: An investment in the form of either debt or equity that does not give the investor a controlling interest.

Positive-sum gain: A situation in which the sums of gains and losses, if added together among participants, is positive, especially if all parties gain from a relationship.

Power distance: A measurement of preference for consultative or autocratic styles of management.

PPP: *See* Purchasing-power parity.

Pragmatism: Settling small issues before deciding on principles.

Premium (in foreign exchange): The difference between the spot and forward exchange rates in the forward market; a foreign currency sells at a premium when the forward rate exceeds the spot rate and when the domestic currency is quoted on a direct basis.

Pressure group: A group that tries to influence legislation or practices to foster its objectives.

Price escalation: The process by which the lengthening of distribution channels increases a product's price by more than the direct added costs, such as transportation, insurance, and tariffs.

Principles-based accounting: A system of accounting that identifies key principles in a conceptual framework and establishes simple rules that conform to the key principles.

Prior informed consent (PIC): The concept of requiring each exporter of a banned or restricted chemical to obtain, through the home-country government, the expressed consent of the importing country to receive the banned or restricted substance.

Privatization: Selling of government-owned assets to private individuals or companies.

Product division: An organizational structure in which different foreign operations report to different product groups at headquarters.

Product life cycle (PLC) theory: The theory that certain kinds of products go through a cycle consisting of four stages (introduction, growth, maturity, and decline) and that the location of production will shift internationally depending on the stage of the cycle.

Production switching: The movement of production from one country to another in response to changes in cost.

Pro forma invoice: The first draft of an exporter's bill to an importer that specifies the goods to be delivered, their quality, quantity, and price.

Promotion: The process of presenting messages intended to help sell a product or service.

Protectionism: Government restrictions on imports and occasionally on exports that frequently give direct or indirect subsidies to industries to enable them to compete with foreign production either at home or abroad.

Protestant ethic: A theory that there is more economic growth when work is viewed as a means of salvation and when people prefer to transform productivity gains into additional output rather than into additional leisure.

PTX: An online collaboration model that brings manufacturers, distributors, value-added resellers, and customers together to execute trading transactions and to share information about demand, production, availability, and more.

Pull: A promotion strategy that sells consumers before they reach the point of purchase, usually by relying on mass media.

Purchasing power: What a sum of money actually can buy.

Purchasing-power parity (PPP): A theory that explains exchange-rate changes as being based on differences in price levels in different countries. Also, the number of units of a country's currency to buy the same products or services in the domestic market that $1 U.S. would buy in the United States.

Push: A promotion strategy that involves direct selling techniques.

Quality: Meeting or exceeding the expectations of a customer.

Quantity controls: Government limitations on the amount of foreign currency that can be used for specific purposes.

Quota: A limit on the quantitative amount of a product allowed to be imported into or exported out of a country in a year.

Quota system: A commodity agreement whereby producing and/or consuming countries divide total output and sales in order to stabilize the price of a particular product.

Quoted currency: The currency whose value is not 1 when an exchange rate is quoted for two currencies.

Rationalization: *See* Rationalized production.

Rationalized production: The specialization of production by product or process in different parts of the world to take advantage of varying costs of labor, capital, and raw materials.

Reciprocal quote: The reciprocal of the direct quote. Also known as the indirect quote.

Regional integration: A form of integration in which a group of countries located in the same geographic proximity decide to cooperate.

Regression: A statistical method showing relationships among variables.

Reinvestment: The use of retained earnings to replace depreciated assets or to add to the existing stock of capital.

Relationship enterprises: Networks of strategic alliances among big companies, spanning different industries and countries.

Relativism: A theory stating that ethical truths depend on the groups holding them, making intervention by outsiders unethical.

Renegotiation: A process by which international companies and governments decide on a change in terms for operations.

Repatriation: An expatriate's return to his or her home country.

Representative democracy: A type of government in which individual citizens elect representatives to make decisions governing the society.

Resource-based view of the firm: A perspective that holds that each company has a unique combination of competencies.

Return on investment (ROI): The amount of profit, sometimes measured before and sometimes after the payment of taxes, divided by the amount of investment.

Revaluation: A formal change in an exchange rate by which the foreign-currency value of the reference currency rises, resulting in a strengthening of the reference currency.

Reverse culture shock: The experience of culture shock when returning to one's own country that is caused by having accepted what was experienced abroad.

Revocable letter of credit: A letter of credit that can be changed by any of the parties involved.

Rio Declaration: The result of the Rio Earth Summit, which sets out fundamental principles of environmentally responsive behavior.

Rio Earth Summit: A meeting held in Rio de Janeiro in June 1992 that brought together people from around the world to discuss major environmental issues.

ROI: *See* Return on investment.

Rounds: Conferences held by GATT to establish multilateral agreements to liberalize trade.

Royalties: Payments for the use of intangible assets abroad.

Rules-based accounting: A legalistic accounting system filled with specific details in an attempt to address as many potential contingencies as possible.

SADC: *See* Southern African Development Community.

SADCC: *See* Southern African Development Co-ordination Conference.

Sales representative (foreign): A representative that usually operates either exclusively or nonexclusively within an assigned market and on a commission basis, without assuming risk or responsibility.

Sales response function: The amount of sales created at different levels of marketing expenditures.

SDR: *See* Special Drawing Right.

Second-tier subsidiaries: Subsidiaries that report to a tax-haven subsidiary.

Secondary boycott: The boycotting of a company that does business with a company being boycotted.

Secrecy: A characteristic of an accounting system that implies that companies do not disclose much information about accounting practices; more common in Germanic countries.

Secular totalitarianism: A dictatorship not affiliated with any religious group or system of beliefs.

Securities and Exchange Commission (SEC): A U.S. government agency that regulates securities brokers, dealers, and markets.

Separate entity approach: A system for taxation of corporate income in which each unit is taxed when it receives income, with the result being double taxation.

Service exports: International received earnings other than those derived from the exporting of tangible goods.

Service imports: International paid earnings other than those derived from the importing of tangible goods.

Services: International earnings other than those on goods sent to another country. Also referred to as invisibles.

Services account: The part of a country's current account that measures travel and transportation, tourism, and fees and royalties.

Settlement: The actual payment of currency in a foreign-exchange transaction.

Shipper's export declaration: A shipping document that controls exports and is used to compile trade statistics.

Sight draft: A commercial bill of exchange that requires payment to be made as soon as it is presented to the party obligated to pay.

Silent language: The wide variety of cues other than formal language by which messages can be sent.

Single European Act: A 1987 act of the EU (then the EC) allowing all proposals except those relating to taxation, workers' rights, and immigration to be adopted by a weighted majority of member countries.

Six Sigma: A highly focused system of quality control that uses data and rigorous statistical analysis to identify "defects" in a process or product, reduce variability, and achieve as close to zero defects as possible.

Skimming strategy: The strategy of charging a high price for a new product by aiming first at consumers willing to pay the price and then progressively lower the price.

Smithsonian Agreement: A 1971 agreement among countries that resulted in the devaluation of the U.S. dollar, revaluation of other world currencies, a widening of exchange-rate flexibility, and a commitment on the part of all participating countries to reduce trade restrictions; superseded by the Jamaica Agreement of 1976.

Society: A broad grouping of people having common traditions, institutions, and collective activities and interests; the term nation-state is often used in international business to denote a society.

Soft budget: A financial condition in which an enterprise's excess of expenditures over earnings is compensated for by some other institution, typically a government or a state-controlled financial institution.

Soft currency: *See* Weak currency.

Sogo shosha: Japanese trading companies that import and export merchandise.

Sourcing strategy: The strategy that a company pursues in purchasing materials, components, and final products; sourcing can be from domestic and foreign locations and from inside and outside the company.

Southern African Development Community (SADC): An organization endeavoring to counter the economic influence of South Africa in the region by focusing on economic objectives, such as regional cooperation in attracting investment.

Sovereignty: Freedom from external control, especially when applied to a body politic.

Special Drawing Right (SDR): A unit of account issued to countries by the International Monetary Fund to expand their official reserves bases.

Specific duty: A duty (tariff) assessed on a per-unit basis.

Speculation: The buying or selling of foreign currency with the prospect of great risk and high return.

Speculator: A person who takes positions in foreign exchange with the objective of earning a profit.

Spillover effects: Situations in which the marketing program in one country results in awareness of the product in other countries.

Spin-off organization: A company now operating almost independently of the parent because its activities do not fit easily with the parent's existing competencies.

Spot market: The market in which an asset is traded for immediate delivery, as opposed to a market for forward or future deliveries.

Spot rate: An exchange rate quoted for immediate delivery of foreign currency, usually within two business days.

Spot transactions: Foreign exchange transactions involving the exchange of currency the second day after the date on which the two foreign-exchange traders agree to the transaction.

Spread: In the forward market, the difference between the spot rate and the forward rate; in the spot market, the difference between the bid (buy) and offer (sell) rates quoted by a foreign-exchange trader.

Stakeholders: The collection of groups, including stockholders, employees, customers, and society at large, that a company must satisfy to survive.

State capitalism: A condition in which some developed countries, such as Japan and Korea, have intervened in the economy to direct the allocation and control of resources.

Static effects of integration: The shifting of resources from inefficient to efficient companies as trade barriers fall.

Stereotype: A standardized and oversimplified mental picture of a group.

Strategic alliance: An agreement between companies that is of strategic importance to one or both companies' competitive viability.

Strategic intent: An objective that gives an organization cohesion over the long term while it builds global competitive viability.

Strategic plan: A long-term plan involving major commitments.

Strategic trade policy: The identification and development of target industries to be competitive internationally.

Strategy: The means companies select to achieve their objectives.

Subpart F income: Income of a CFC that comes from sources other than those connected with the active conduct of a trade or business, such as holding company income.

Subsidiarity: A principle that implies that EU interference should take place only in areas of common concern and that most policies should be set at the national level.

Subsidiary: A foreign operation that is legally separate from the parent company, even if wholly owned by it.

Subsidies: Direct assistance from governments to companies, making them more competitive.

Substitution drawbacks: A provision allowing domestic merchandise to be substituted for merchandise that is imported for eventual export, thus allowing the U.S. firm to exclude the duty paid on the merchandise in costs and in sales prices.

Supply chain: The coordination of materials, information, and funds from the initial raw material supplier to the ultimate customer.

Swap: A simultaneous spot and forward foreign-exchange transaction.

Syndication: Cooperation by a lead bank and several other banks to make a large loan to a public or private organization.

Tariff: A government tax levied on goods, usually imports, shipped internationally; the most common type of trade control.

Tax credit: A dollar-for-dollar reduction of tax liability that must coincide with the recognition of income.

Tax deferral: Income is not taxed until it is remitted to the parent company as a dividend.

Tax-haven countries: Countries with low income taxes or no taxes on foreign-source income.

Tax-haven subsidiary: A subsidiary of a company established in a tax-haven country for the purpose of minimizing income tax.

Tax treaty: A treaty between two countries that generally results in the reciprocal reduction on dividend withholding taxes and the exemption of taxes or royalties and sometimes interest payments.

Technical forecasting: A forecasting tool that uses past trends in exchange rates themselves to spot future trends in rates.

Technology: The means employed to produce goods or services.

Technology absorbing capacity: The ability of the recipient to work effectively with technology, particularly in relation to the need for training and equity in the recipient in order to effect a transfer.

Temporal method: A method of translating foreign-currency financial statements used when the functional currency is that of the parent company.

Terms currency: Exchange rates are quoted as the number of units of the terms currency per base currency.

Terms of trade: The quantity of imports that can be bought by a given quantity of a country's exports.

Theocratic law system: A legal system based on religious precepts.

Theocratic totalitarianism: A dictatorship led by a religious group.

Theory of country size: The theory which holds that countries with large land areas are more apt to have varied climates and natural resources, and, therefore, generally are more nearly self-sufficient than smaller countries.

Theory of obsolescing bargain: The erosion of bargaining strength from a group as countries gain assets from them.

Third-country nationals: Expatriate employees who are neither citizens of the country in which they are working nor citizens of the country where the company is headquartered.

Tie-in provisions: Stipulations in licensing that require the license*see* to purchase or sell products from/to the licensor.

Time draft: A commercial bill of exchange calling for payment to be made at some time after delivery.

Time series: A statistical method of illustrating a pattern over time, such as in demand for a particular product.

TNC: *See* Transnational company.

Tort: A civil wrong independent of a contract.

Total quality management (TQM): The process that a company uses to achieve quality, where the goal is elimination of all defects.

Totalitarianism: A political system characterized by the absence of widespread participation in decision making.

TQM: *See* Total quality management.

Trade creation: Production shifts to more efficient producers for reasons of comparative advantage, allowing consumers access to more goods at a lower price than would have been possible without integration.

Trade diversion: A situation in which exports shift to a less efficient producing country because of preferential trade barriers.

Trade Related Aspects of Intellectual Property Rights (TRIPS): A provision from the Uruguay round of trade negotiations requiring countries to agree to enforce procedures under their national laws to protect intellectual property rights.

Trademark: A name or logo distinguishing a company or product.

Transaction exposure: Foreign-exchange risk arising because a company has outstanding accounts receivable or accounts payable that are denominated in a foreign currency.

Transfer price: A price charged for goods or services between entities that are related to each other through stock ownership, such as between a parent and its subsidiaries or between subsidiaries owned by the same parent.

Transit tariff: A tax placed on goods passing through a country.

Translation: The restatement of foreign-currency financial statements into U.S. dollars.

Translation exposure: Foreign-exchange risk that occurs because the parent company must translate foreign-currency financial statements into the reporting currency of the parent company.

Transnational: (1) An organization in which different capabilities and contributions among different country-operations are shared and integrated; (2) multinational enterprise; (3) company owned and managed by nationals from different countries.

Transnational company (TNC): A company owned and managed by nationals in different countries; also may be synonymous with multinational enterprise.

Transparency: A characteristic of an accounting system that implies that companies disclose a great deal of information about accounting practices; more common in Anglo-Saxon countries (United States, United Kingdom).

Triad strategy: A strategy proposing that an MNE should have a presence in Europe, the United States, and Asia (especially Japan).

TRIPS: *See* Trade Related Aspects of Intellectual Property Rights.

Turnkey operation: An operating facility that is constructed under contract and transferred to the owner when the facility is ready to begin operations.

Type of ownership: The form of a company's involvement in a foreign venture.

Underemployed: Those people who are working at less than their capacity.

Unfavorable balance of trade: An indication of a trade deficit—that is, imports are greater than exports. Also called deficit.

Unilateral transfer: A transfer of currency from one country to another for which no goods or services are received; an example is foreign aid to a country devastated by earthquake or flood.

Unit of account: A benchmark on which to base the value of payments.

United Nations (UN): An international organization of countries formed in 1945 to promote world peace and security.

United Nations Conference on Trade and Development (UNCTAD): A UN body that has been especially active in dealing with the relationships between developing and industrialized countries with respect to trade.

Universal Copyright Convention (UCC): A multilateral agreement to protect copyrights.

Unrequited transfer: *See* Unilateral transfer.

U.S.-Canada Free Trade Agreement: *See* Canada-U.S. Free Trade Agreement.

U.S. shareholder: For U.S. tax purposes, a person or company owning at least 10 percent of the voting stock of a foreign subsidiary.

U.S. terms: The practice of using the direct quote for exchange rates.

Value: the measure of a firm's capability to sell what it makes for more than the costs incurred to make it

Value-added tax (VAT): A tax that is a percentage of the value added to a product at each stage of the business process.

Value chain: The collective activities that occur as a product moves from raw materials through production to final distribution.

Variable price: A method of pricing in which buyers and sellers negotiate the price.

VAT: *See* Value-added tax.

VER: *See* Voluntary export restrictions.

Vertical differentiation: The matter of where in the hierarchy is the authority to make what decisions.

Vertical integration: The control of the different stages as a product moves from raw materials through production to final distribution.

Virtual manufacturing: Subcontracting the manufacturing process to another firm.

Virtual organization: A form of company that acquires strategic capabilities by creating a temporary network of independent companies, suppliers, customers, and even rivals.

Visible exports: *See* Merchandise exports.

Visible imports: *See* Merchandise imports.

Voluntary export restraint (VER): A negotiated limitation of exports between an importing and an exporting country.

Weak currency: A currency that is not fully convertible.

West African Economic Community: A regional economic group involving Benin, Burkina Faso, Ivory Coast, Mali, Mauritania, Niger, and Senegal.

Western Hemisphere: Literally the earth's area between the zero and 180th meridian, but it usually indicates the continents of the Americas and adjacent islands, excluding Greenland.

WIPO: *See* World Intellectual Property Organization.

World Bank: A multilateral lending institution that provides investment capital to countries.

World Intellectual Property Organization (WIPO): A multilateral agreement to protect patents.

World Trade Organization (WTO): A voluntary organization through which groups of countries negotiate trading agreements and which has authority to over*see* trade disputes among countries.

WTO: *See* World Trade Organization.

Zaibatsu: Large, family-owned Japanese businesses that existed before World War II and consisted of a series of financial and manufacturing companies usually held together by a large holding company.

Zero defects: The elimination of defects, which results in the reduction of manufacturing costs and an increase in consumer satisfaction.

Zero-sum game: A situation in which one party's gain equals another party's loss.

PHOTO CREDITS

COMPANY INDEX AND TRADEMARKS

NAME INDEX

SUBJECT INDEX

price negotiations, for imports and
   exports, 576
pricing, 419, 564, 572–577. *See also* transfer pricing
primary activities, 382
private insurance, for political risk, 101
private technology exchange (PTX), 608
privatization, 148, 150, 158
procedural political risks, 100, 102
producers' alliances, 294–296
product adaptation, 440
product alterations
   exporting and, 487–488
   reasons for, 567–568, 570–571
product division structure, 530
product flows, 731
product images, country-of-origin, 581
production
   absolute advantage and, 209
   Zara, 373
   See also global manufacturing
      strategies
production costs, exporting and, 486–487
production decisions, exchange-rate
   changes and, 362
production factors
   factor mobility and, 225–226, 228
   factor-proportions theory and, 215
production locations, efficiencies of, 229
production methods, flexible and small-
   scale, 229
production orientation, 564
production runs, 216
production strategy, 611
production technology, 216
product leapfrogging, 419
product life cycle (PLC) theory, 205,
   219–221, 571–572
product line, extent and mix of, 571
product line gap, 588, 589
product origin, 108
product policy, 567–572
products
   concentration versus diversification
      and, 439
   industrialization argument and, 247
   trade patterns and, 215–216
product safety and liability, 108
product technology, 216
professional sports case, 3–6
pro forma invoice, 470
program control requirements, 440
project structure, 535
promotion, 577–579
propaganda, 496
property rights, 149
proprietary name, 582
protectionism, 229, 241, 244. *See also*
   government intervention
publicity, 189

pull, 577
punctuality, perception of, 68–69
purchasing function, 617–618
purchasing power parity (PPP), 128–129,
   130–131, 355–357
push, 577
push-pull mix, 577

QS9000, 625
quality, 604, 605, 608–611
quality standards, 610–611
quantity controls, 256–259, 318
quotas, 58–59, 256–257
quota system, 295

racial quotas, 58–59
rate of change, 128
real interest rate, 357, 358
real value chains, 391–392
receivables, 639, 650
reciprocal requirements, 258
reciprocity, 536
recording, foreign currency transactions,
   649–650
red tape, 422–423
regional banks, 321
regional content rules, 284
regional economic integration, 257,
   272–274, 297
   Africa, 293–294
   Asia, 291–293
   Central and South America, 287–291
   European Union, 274–282
   NAFTA, 283–287
regionalism, 297
regionalization, 25
regional trade agreements (RTAs), 272
regulations. *See* government intervention; government regulations
reinvestment, 437
related and supporting industries, 221–222
relationship preferences, 63–64
relativism, 172
religion
   as cultural stabilizer, 55, 56–57
   ethical behavior and, 172
   product alterations and, 570
   theocratic law systems, 103
   theocratic totalitarianism and, 96
reorganization. *See* organizational
   change; organization structure
repairs, 585
repatriation, 727–729
reports/reporting
   as control mechanisms, 540–541, 554
   environmental, 653–654
   foreign-exchange exposure, 687–688
   individualized, 432
representative democracy, 94
reputation, 536

research, specialized, 432
research results, problems with, 430–431
resource acquisition, 18
resource allocation, 437–440
resource-based view, 492
resource constraints, 440
resource efficiency example, 208–209
resource flows, 731
resource mobility, 213
resource movements, liberalization of, 10
resources
   in China, 88
   MNEs and, 170
responsibility. *See* social responsibility
restitution, 158
restructuring. *See* organizational change;
   organization structure
retail transactions, 312
retaliation, 243, 249
return on investment (ROI), 423, 424
reverse culture shock, 72
revocable letter of credit, 684
reward, expectation of, 61
reward sharing, 76
rights, political, 94, 95
risk
   collaborative arrangements and, 494
   environmental climate, 423–429
   political, 99–102, 427–429, 681
risk management, foreign-exchange,
   685–690
risk minimization, 18
risk-taking behavior, 64–65
rivalry, 222
royalties, 20
rules of origin, 284
Russia economic environment case,
   119–122

salary, for expatriates, 723
sales expansion, through international
   business, 16, 18
sales income, 692
sales orientation, 565
sales representatives, 469
sales stability, concentration versus
   diversification based on, 439
sales tax, 690
sales
   commodity, 564
   passive, 564
   pharmaceutical, 183–185
Samsonite case, 599–601, 602
Sarbanes-Oxley Act, 176, 329
Saudi Arabian culture case, 45–48
scale alliances, 491
scanning, 416–418
secrecy, 641
secular totalitarianism, 95
securities exchanges, 307